C000090430

Collins

Collins
Polish
Dictionary

HarperCollins Publishers
Westerhill Road
Bishopbriggs
Glasgow
G64 2QT
Great Britain

First Edition/Pierwsze wydanie 2007

Reprint 10 9 8 7 6 5 4 3 2 1 0

© HarperCollins Publishers 2007

ISBN 978-0-00-725998-4

Collins® and Bank of English® are
registered trademarks of
HarperCollins Publishers Limited

www.collins.co.uk

A catalogue record for this book is
available from the British Library

Typeset by/Przygotowanie do druku
Wordcraft, Glasgow

Printed in Italy by/
Wydrukowano we Włoszech w
Legoprint S.p.A.

Acknowledgements
We would like to thank those authors
and publishers who kindly gave
permission for copyright material to
be used in the Collins Word Web. We
would also like to thank Times
Newspapers Ltd for providing
valuable data.

MANAGING EDITOR/
REDAKTORKA PROWADZĄCA
Maree Airlie

EDITORIAL COORDINATION/
KOORDYNACJA WYDAWNICZA
Lisa Sutherland

CONTRIBUTORS/WSPÓŁPRACA
Magdalena Herok
Dorota Hołowiak
Meg Hunter
Horst Kopleck
Jacek Kowzan
Sabina Siebert
Valerie McNulty
Elizabeth Simpson
Gavin Simpson
Piotr Stasiak
Franek Strzeszewski
Paul Vickers
Karolina Zioło

SERIES EDITOR/WYDAWCA SERII
Robert Scriven

SPIS TREŚCI

CONTENTS

William Collins' dream of knowledge for all began with the publication of his first book in 1819. A self-educated mill worker, he not only enriched millions of lives, but also founded a flourising publishing house. Today, staying true to this spirit, Collins books are packed with inspiration, innovation, and practical expertise. They place you at the centre of a world of possibility and give you exactly what you need to explore it.

Language is the key to this exploration, and at the heart of Collins Dictionaries is language as it is really used. New words, phrases, and meanings spring up every day, and all of them are captured and analysed by the Collins Word Web. Constantly updated, and with over 2.5 billion entries, this living language resource is unique to our dictionaries.

Words are tools for life. And a Collins Dictionary makes them work for you.

Collins. Do more.

WPROWADZENIE

Cieszymy się, że wybraliście Państwo nasz słownik Collins Polish Dictionary i mamy nadzieję, że z przyjemnością będziecie z niego korzystać w domu, w podróży i w pracy.

W niniejszym wprowadzeniu podajemy kilka wskazówek jak najlepiej korzystać ze słownika – nie tylko z samych jego haseł, lecz również z informacji znajdujących się przy każdym z nich. Pomoże to Państwu nie tylko lepiej czytać i rozumieć współczesny język angielski, ale również skutecznie w nim się porozumiewać.

JAK KORZYSTAĆ ZE SŁOWNIKA
Wiele informacji jest przekazanych w słowniku za pomocą różnego rodzaju czcionek, skrótów oraz nawiasów. Użyte oznaczenia i symbole wyjaśnione są w poniższych poniżej.

WYRAZY HASŁOWE
Wyrazy hasłowe, czyli słowa, których szukacie Państwo w słowniku są ułożone alfabetycznie. W celu szybkiej identyfikacji wydrukowane zostały one w kolorze. U góry każdej strony znaleźć można pierwszy (na stronie lewej) i ostatni wyraz hasłowy (na stronie prawej) pojawiający się na danej stronie.

Popularne zwroty w których użyty jest wyraz hasłowy zapisane są wytłuszczonym drukiem, na przykład:

da|ta (**-ty**, **-ty**; *dat & loc sg* **-cie**) *f*
(*termin*) date; **~ urodzenia** date
of birth

ZNACZENIA
Znaczenia wyrazów hasłowych podane są zwykłą czcionką. Często napotkacie Państwo również słowa pisane *kursywą* w nawiasach przed tłumaczeniami – są one po to aby podawać synonimy, sugerowane konteksty albo pola znaczeniowe, w których słowo hasłowe może wystąpić, na przykład:

drama|t (**-tu**, **-ty**; *loc sg* **-cie**)
m **1** (*Lit*) drama **2** (*nieszczęście*)
tragedy

SŁOWA KLUCZOWE
Specjalną rangę otrzymały niektóre polskie bądź angielskie słowa, które potraktowane zostały jako „słowa kluczowe". Mogą one na przykład często występować w danym języku albo też mieć wiele

różnych zastosowań (na przykład **mieć, get, have**). Układ graficzny hasła ma za zadanie pomóc Państwu w odpowiednim rozpoznaniu części mowy i znaczeń. Dalszej pomocy udzielić mogą informacje zawarte w nawiasach bądź pisane *kursywą*.

INFORMACJE GRAMATYCZNE

Części mowy oznaczone są za pomocą skrótów (na przykład: *adj, conj*). Znaleźć je można po informacji o końcówkach fleksyjnych wyrazu hasłowego (w części polsko-angielskiej) lub po transkrypcji fonetycznej (w części angielsko-polskiej). Rodzaje polskich rzeczowników oznaczone są następująco: *m* dla rzeczowników rodzaju męskiego, *f* dla rodzaju żeńskiego, a *nt* dla rodzaju nijakiego.

Liczba mnoga jest oznaczona skrótem *pl*.
Informacja odnośnie odmiany wyrazów hasłowych (koniugacje czasowników, przypadki, nieregularne formy liczby mnogiej, itp.) podana jest w nawiasach zaraz po wyrazie hasłowym.

lie¹ [laɪ] (*pt* **lay**, *pp* **lain**) *vi* leżeć

Końcówki dopełniacza oraz liczby mnogiej podane zostały dla wszystkich rzeczowników zamieszczonych w słowniku, końcówki pozostałych przypadków tylko gdy są one nieregularne.

Formy koniugacji czasowników zostały podane tylko w przypadku nieregularnej ich odmiany. Jeśli chodzi o polskie tłumaczenia przymiotników to podane one są w rodzaju męskim, zaś tłumaczenia

zwrotów domyślnie używają pierwszej osoby liczby pojedynczej. W przypadku czasowników, oba aspekty (niedokonany/dokonany) podane są tam, gdzie występują obie formy. Tam gdzie nie ma żadnej informacji o aspekcie czasownika należy przyjąć, iż posiada on tylko formę niedokonaną.

Aby uzyskać więcej informacji na temat koniugacji angielskich czasowników, patrz strony xvi – xvii.

INTRODUCTION

We are delighted that you have decided to use the Collins Polish Dictionary and hope that you will enjoy using it at home, on holiday or at work.

This introduction gives you a few tips on how to get the most out of your dictionary, not simply from its comprehensive wordlist, but also from the information provided in each entry. This will help you to read and understand modern Polish, as well as communicate and express yourself in the language.

USING THE DICTIONARY

A wealth of information is presented in the dictionary, using various typefaces, sizes of type, symbols, abbreviations and brackets. The various conventions and symbols used are explained in the following sections.

HEADWORDS

The words you look up in a dictionary – 'headwords' – are listed alphabetically. They are printed in colour for rapid identification. The headwords appearing at the top of each page indicate the first word (if it appears on a left-hand page) and last word (if it appears on a right-hand page) dealt with on the page in question.

Common expressions in which the headword is used are shown in bold roman type, for example:

jealous ['dʒɛləs] *adj* zazdrosny;
   to be ~ of sb/sth być zazdrosnym
   o kogoś/coś

TRANSLATIONS

Headword translations are given in ordinary type. You will often find other words in *italics* in brackets before the translations – these offer synonyms or suggested contexts or subject fields in which the headword might appear, for example:

landing ['lændɪŋ] *n* **1** (*on stairs*)
   podest **2** (*Aviat*) lądowanie

KEY WORDS

Special status is given to certain Polish and English words which are considered 'key' words in each language. They may, for example, occur very frequently or have several types of usage (eg get, have, mieć). The layout of the entry helps you to distinguish different parts of speech and meanings. Further helpful information is provided in brackets and *italics*.

GRAMMATICAL INFORMATION

Parts of speech are given in abbreviated form after the inflected forms of the headword on the Polish-English side, and after the phonetic spellings on the English-Polish side of the dictionary. Genders of Polish nouns are indicated as follows: *m* for masculine nouns, *f* for feminine nouns and *nt* for neuter nouns. Plural is shown with the abbreviation *pl*.

Information about the inflected forms of headwords (verb conjugations, cases, irregular plurals and so on) is given in brackets immediately after the headword on the Polish-English side of the dictionary. The first letter of the inflection corresponds to the point where the ending adds onto the main form, for example:

fot|ka (**-ki**, **-ki**; *dat sg* **-ce**; *gen pl*
-ek) *f* (*fotografia*) snap

We have shown genitive and plural information for all nouns, and other cases only where they are irregular. Verb conjugations have also been shown for all verbs. Polish translations of adjectives have been given in the masculine as the default, as have translations of phrases which use the first person singular.

The second person singular has been translated into Polish using the formal *pan/pani* construction, unless otherwise indicated.

We have shown which cases follow particular parts of speech. Where there is no information about case, it can be assumed that the accusative case is used.

Finally, the perfective aspect of each verb has been shown at the imperfective headword, where it exists. In phrases, verbs have been shown with both aspects where they both work in the context. Where there is no information about the aspect of a verb, it can be assumed that it only works in that context in the imperfective, and therefore does not need to be marked.

For more information on Polish irregular forms, see pages xviii–xxxiii.

skrót	*abbr*	abbreviation
biernik	*acc*	accusative
przymiotnik	*adj*	adjective
administracja	*Admin*	administration
przysłówek	*adv*	adverb
rolnictwo	*Agr*	agriculture
anatomia	*Anat*	anatomy
architektura	*Archit*	architecture
astrologia	*Astrol*	astrology
astronomia	*Astron*	astonomy
motoryzacja	*Aut*	automobiles
czasownik posiłkowy	*aux verb*	auxiliary verb
lotnictwo	*Aviat*	aviation
biologia	*Bio*	biology
botanika	*Bot*	botany
język angielski brytyjski	*Brit*	British English
budownictwo	*Bud*	construction
chemia	*Chem*	chemistry
kino	*Cine*	cinema
handel i biznes	*Comm*	business
stopień wyższy	*compar*	comparative
komputery	*Comput*	computing
spójnik	*conj*	conjunction
budownictwo	*Constr*	construction
kulinaria	*Culin*	cookery
celownik	*dat*	dative
przedimek określony	*def art*	definite article
dosłowny	*dosl*	literal
drukarstwo	*Druk*	printing
ekonomia	*Econ, Ekon*	economics
elektronika	*Elec, Elektr*	electronics
szczególnie	*esp*	especially
i temu podobne	*etc*	et cetera
wykrzyknienie	*excl*	exclamation
rodzaj żeński	*f*	feminine
w przenośnym znaczeniu	*fig*	figurative
finanse	*Fin*	finance
fizyka	*Fiz*	physics
fotografia	*Fot*	photography
ogólnie rzecz biorąc	*gen*	generally
dopełniacz	*gen*	genitive
geografia	*Geo*	geography
geologia	*Geol*	geology
geometria	*Geom*	geometry
historia	*Hist*	history

aspekt niedokonany	*impf*	imperfective
wyraz nieodmienny	*ind*	indeclinable
przedimek nieokreślony	*indef art*	indefinite article
nieformalny	*inf*	informal
obraźliwy	*inf!*	offensive
bezokolicznik	*infin*	infinitive
narzędnik	*inst*	instrumental
niezmienny	*inv*	invariable
nieregularny	*irreg*	irregular
językoznawstwo	*Jęz*	lingusitics
prawniczy	*Jur*	law
informatyka, komputery	*Komput*	computing
kulinaria	*Kulin*	cookery
język	*Ling*	language
literatura	*Lit*	literature
dosłowny	*lit*	literal
miejscownik	*loc*	locative
lotnictwo	*Lot*	aviation
rodzaj męski	*m*	masculine
matematyka	*Mat, Math*	mathematics
medycyna	*Med*	medicine
meteorologia	*Meteo, Meteor*	meteorology
rodzaj męski/rodzaj żeński	*m/f*	masculine/feminine
wojskowy	*Mil*	military
motoryzacja	*Mot*	motoring
muzyka	*Mus, Muz*	music
mitologia	*Myth*	mythology
rzeczownik	*n*	noun
żeglarstwo	*Naut*	sailing
mianownik	*nom*	nominative
rodzaj męski nieosobowy	*non-vir*	non-virile
rodzaj nijaki	*nt*	neuter
liczba	*num*	number
staromodny	*o.f.*	old-fashioned
siebie, się, sobie, sobą,	*o.s.*	oneself
parlament	*Parl*	parliament
aspekt dokonany	*pf*	perfective
fotografia	*Phot*	photography
fizyka	*Phys*	physics
fizjologia	*Physiol*	physiology
pejoratywny	*pej*	pejorative
liczba mnoga	*pl*	plural
polityka	*Pol*	politics
potoczny	*pot*	informal
obraźliwy	*pot!*	offensive
imiesłów przeszły	*pp*	past participle

przyimek	prep	preposition
zaimek	pron	pronoun
przenośny	przen	figurative
psychologia	Psych	psychology
czas przeszły	pt	past tense
radio	Rad	radio
koleje	Rail	railways
religia	Rel	religion
rolnictwo	Rol	agriculture
ktoś	sb	somebody
nauka	Sci	science
szkolnictwo	Scol, Szkol	schooling
liczba pojedyncza	sg	singular
socjologia	Sociol	sociology
coś	sth	something
stopień najwyższy	superl	superlative
technologia	Tech	technology
telekomunikacja	Tel	telecommunications
teatr	Teatr, Theat	theatre
telewizja	TV	television
typografia	Typ	typography
uniwersytet	Univ, Uniw	university
język angielski amerykański	US	American English
zazwyczaj	usu	usually
czasownik	vb	verb
czasownik nieprzechodni	vi	intransitive verb
rodzaj męskoosobowy	vir	virile
wołacz	voc	vocative
czasownik przechodni	vt	transitive verb
czasownik złożony (nierozdzielny)	vt fus	phrasal verb (where the particle is inseparable)
wojskowość	Wojsk	military
zoologia	Zool	zoology
żegluga	Zegl	nautical
znak towarowy zastrzeżony	®	registered trademark
poprzedza ekwiwalent kulturowy	≈	introduces a cultural equivalent

POLISH PRONUNCIATION

Generally, every letter in Polish corresponds to one sound and, apart from ch, cz, sz, dz, dź, dż, rz, every letter is pronounced separately.

VOWELS

The pronunciation of Polish vowels resembles that of Spanish or Italian. Every vowel is pronounced and there is no variation in their sound as in English.

h<u>a</u>t	a	m<u>a</u>tka
b<u>e</u>st	e	g<u>e</u>st, t<u>e</u>kst
s<u>ee</u>k	i	bl<u>i</u>sko
sl<u>o</u>t	o	P<u>o</u>lska, m<u>o</u>st
g<u>oo</u>se, l<u>oo</u>	u = ó	st<u>u</u>dent, b<u>ó</u>l
gr<u>i</u>m	y	s<u>y</u>n, p<u>y</u>tam

NASAL VOWELS

so<u>ng</u>	ą	m<u>ą</u>dry, ksi<u>ą</u>żka
<u>Tom</u>	<u>ą</u>b, <u>ą</u>p	zi<u>ą</u>b, g<u>ą</u>bka
t<u>en</u>, B<u>en</u>gali	ę	cz<u>ę</u>sto, wi<u>ę</u>cej
th<u>em</u>	<u>ę</u>b, <u>ę</u>p	g<u>ę</u>ba, s<u>ę</u>p
n<u>et</u>	final ę	ucz<u>ę</u> si<u>ę</u>

CONSONANTS

Most Polish consonants are pronounced just as in English. A few are pronounced differently:

g<u>uts</u>, lo<u>ts</u>	c	<u>c</u>o, ni<u>c</u>
<u>h</u>ill, <u>h</u>orse	ch = h	<u>ch</u>yba, <u>h</u>otel
mu<u>ch</u>, <u>church</u>	cz	wie<u>cz</u>ór, cze<u>ść</u>
<u>ch</u>eese	ć = ci	rozumie<u>ć</u>, <u>ci</u>ę
good<u>s</u>	dz	bar<u>dz</u>o, <u>dz</u>won
<u>J</u>immy, <u>j</u>eans	dź = dzi	<u>dź</u>więk, <u>dzi</u>ś
<u>j</u>ungle, <u>g</u>entlemen	dż	<u>dż</u>ungla, <u>dż</u>entelmen
<u>y</u>ellow	j	<u>j</u>eden, ma<u>j</u>
<u>w</u>indow, <u>wow</u>	ł	<u>ł</u>adny, mi<u>ł</u>o
oni<u>on</u>	ń = ni	Gdań<u>sk</u>, <u>do</u> widze<u>ni</u>a
"rolling r"	r	p<u>r</u>oszę, dob<u>r</u>a
<u>s</u>ure	ś, si	dzi<u>ś</u>, dzi<u>si</u>aj
<u>m</u>a<u>sh</u>, <u>sh</u>ow	sz	pa<u>sz</u>port, ma<u>sz</u>
Vi<u>c</u>toria	w	<u>W</u>iktoria, pi<u>w</u>o
ga<u>r</u>age, plea<u>s</u>ure	ż = rz	ga<u>raż</u>, dob<u>rz</u>e
Rho<u>de</u>sia	ź = zi	<u>ź</u>le, <u>zi</u>elony

VOICED AND UNVOICED CONSONANTS

Some consonants become unvoiced in certain positions in a word,
i.e. at the end of a word and before or after a voiceless consonant:

chle*b*	pronounced	[chle*p*]
ja*bł*ko	pronounced	[ya*p*ko]
wó*d*ka	pronounced	[voo*t*ka]
ogró*d*	pronounced	[ogru*t*]
ró*g*	pronounced	[ru*k*]
le*w*	pronounced	[le*f*]
*w*szystko	pronounced	[*f*shystko]
wyra*z*	pronounced	[wyra*s*]
we*ź*	pronounced	[ve*sh*]
wó*dz*	pronounced	[voo*ts*]
Łó*dź*	pronounced	[Woo*tch*]
te*ż*	pronounced	[te*sh*]
bry*dż*	pronounced	[bry*ch*]

WYMOWA ANGIELSKA   ENGLISH PRONUNCIATION

SPÓŁGŁOSKI   CONSONANTS

Polska	[p]	puppy
bilet	[b]	baby
tutaj, tenis	[t]	tent
dom	[d]	daddy
korek, kawa	[k]	cork kiss chord
gag, gazeta	[g]	gag guess
sklep, masło	[s]	so rice kiss
kuzyn, zero	[z]	cousin buzz
szok, szelest	[ʃ]	sheep sugar
ważny, beż	[ʒ]	pleasure beige
czerwony, czas	[tʃ]	church
dżem, dżungla	[dʒ]	judge general
farma, fotel	[f]	farm raffle
Warszawa, woda	[v]	very rev
wymawia się jak "s" z	[θ]	thin maths
językiem między zębami		
wymawia się jak "z" z	[ð]	that other
językiem między zębami		
list, lato	[l]	little ball
brak polskiego	[R]	
odpowiednika, wymawiać		
jak polskie 'r'		
retrofleksyjne "r"	[r]	rat rare
mama, minuta	[m]	mummy comb
noga, mina	[n]	no ran
Bank (wymowa z	[ŋ]	singing bank
niemym "k")		
hotel, wiecha	[h]	hat reheat
jeden, Maja	[j]	yet
łaska, łoskot	[w]	wall bewail
loch	[x]	loch

NB. Zestawienie niektórych par angielskich samogłosek i ich polskich odpowiedników odzwierciedla tylko ich częściowe podobieństwo brzmieniowe.

NB. The pairing of some vowel sounds only indicates approximate equivalence.

SAMOGŁOSKI / VOWELS

Polski	IPA	English
list	iː	heel bead
syn.	ɪ	hit pity
tekst, prezent	ɛ	set tent
otwarte "e"	æ	bat apple
Ala, mały, kasa	ɑː	after car calm
fanfary	ʌ	fun cousin
samogłoska centralna nieakcentowana	ə	over above
długa samogłoska centralna	əː	fern work
potok, grosz	ɔ	wash pot
korek, lotnisko	ɔː	born cork
gust, bufet	u	full soot
długie "u" z zakrąglonymi wargami	uː	boot crew
myśl	ɪ	lynch

DYFTONGI / DIPHTHONGS

Polski	IPA	English
połączenie	ɪə	beer pier
połączenie	ɛə	tear fair
lejce,	eɪ	date place day
maj, kraj	aɪ	life buy cry
mały	au	owl foul now
ołtarz	əu	low no
moje	ɔɪ	boil boy oil
połączenie	uə	poor tour

Poprawną wymowę wyrazu hasłowego podajemy w nawiasach kwadratowych, umieszczonych po danym słowie. W części angielsko-polskiej jednakże, tam gdzie wyraz hasłowy składa się z dwóch lub więcej wyrazów składowych, które niezależnie posiadają w słowniku swoje własne hasła, tam właśnie podana też będzie ich wymowa.

ANGIELSKIE CZASOWNIKI NIEREGULARNE

present	pt	pp	present	pt	pp
arise	arose	arisen	fight	fought	fought
awake	awoke	awoken	find	found	found
be (am, is,	was,were	been	fling	flung	flung
are; being)			fly	flew	flown
bear	bore	born(e)	forbid	forbad(e)	forbidden
beat	beat	beaten	forecast	forecast	forecast
begin	began	begun	forget	forgot	forgotten
bend	bent	bent	forgive	forgave	forgiven
bet	bet,	bet,	freeze	froze	frozen
	betted	betted	get	got	got,
bid (at auction)	bid	bid			(US) gotten
bind	bound	bound	give	gave	given
bite	bit	bitten	go (goes)	went	gone
bleed	bled	bled	grind	ground	ground
blow	blew	blown	grow	grew	grown
break	broke	broken	hang	hung	hung
breed	bred	bred	hang (execute)	hanged	hanged
bring	brought	brought	have	had	had
build	built	built	hear	heard	heard
burn	burnt,	burnt,	hide	hid	hidden
	burned	burned	hit	hit	hit
burst	burst	burst	hold	held	held
buy	bought	bought	hurt	hurt	hurt
can	could	(been able)	keep	kept	kept
cast	cast	cast	kneel	knelt,	knelt,
catch	caught	caught		kneeled	kneeled
choose	chose	chosen	know	knew	known
cling	clung	clung	lay	laid	laid
come	came	come	lead	led	led
cost	cost	cost	lean	leant,	leant,
creep	crept	crept		leaned	leaned
cut	cut	cut	leap	leapt,	leapt,
deal	dealt	dealt		leaped	leaped
dig	dug	dug	learn	learnt,	learnt,
do (does)	did	done		learned	learned
draw	drew	drawn	leave	left	left
dream	dreamed,	dreamed,	lend	lent	lent
	dreamt	dreamt	let	let	let
drink	drank	drunk	lie (lying)	lay	lain
drive	drove	driven	light	lit,	lit,
eat	ate	eaten		lighted	lighted
fall	fell	fallen	lose	lost	lost
feed	fed	fed	make	made	made
feel	felt	felt	may	might	–

present	pt	pp	present	pt	pp
mean	meant	meant	speed	sped, speeded	sped, speeded
meet	met	met	spell	spelt, spelled	spelt, spelled
mistake	mistook	mistaken	spend	spent	spent
mow	mowed	mown, mowed	spill	spilt, spilled	spilt, spilled
must	(had to)	(had to)	spin	spun	spun
pay	paid	paid	spit	spat	spat
put	put	put	spoil	spoiled, spoilt	spoiled, spoilt
quit	quit, quitted	quit, quitted	spread	spread	spread
read	read	read	spring	sprang	sprung
rid	rid	rid	stand	stood	stood
ride	rode	ridden	steal	stole	stolen
ring	rang	rung	stick	stuck	stuck
rise	rose	risen	sting	stung	stung
run	ran	run	stink	stank	stunk
saw	sawed	sawed, sawn	stride	strode	stridden
say	said	said	strike	struck	struck
see	saw	seen	swear	swore	sworn
sell	sold	sold	sweep	swept	swept
send	sent	sent	swell	swelled	swollen, swelled
set	set	set			
sew	sewed	sewn	swim	swam	swum
shake	shook	shaken	swing	swung	swung
shear	sheared	shorn, sheared	take	took	taken
shed	shed	shed	teach	taught	taught
shine	shone	shone	tear	tore	torn
shoot	shot	shot	tell	told	told
show	showed	shown	think	thought	thought
shrink	shrank	shrunk	throw	threw	thrown
shut	shut	shut	thrust	thrust	thrust
sing	sang	sung	tread	trod	trodden
sink	sank	sunk	wake	woke, waked	woken, waked
sit	sat	sat			
sleep	slept	slept	wear	wore	worn
slide	slid	slid	weave	wove	woven
sling	slung	slung	weep	wept	wept
slit	slit	slit	win	won	won
smell	smelt, smelled	smelt, smelled	wind	wound	wound
			wring	wrung	wrung
sow	sowed	sown, sowed	write	wrote	written
speak	spoke	spoken			

TABLES OF POLISH IRREGULAR FORMS

CARDINAL NUMERALS

The number 1 has three forms: **jeden** (*m*); **jedna** (*f*); **jedno** (*nt*) and declines like an adjective.

	m	*f*	*nt*
nom	jeden	jedna	jedno
gen	jednego	jednej	jednego
dat	jednemu	jednej	jednemu
acc	jeden, jednego	jedną	jedno
inst	jednym	jedną	jednym
loc	jednym	jednej	jednym

2 (**dwa**) declines as follows:

	vir	*non-vir* *nt*	*f*
nom	dwaj	dwa	dwie
gen	dwóch, dwu	dwóch, dwu	dwóch, dwu
dat	dwóm, dwu, dwom	dwóm, dwu, dwom	dwóm, dwu, dwom
acc	dwóch	dwa	dwie
inst	dwoma	dwoma	dwoma, dwiema
loc	dwóch, dwu	dwóch, dwu	dwóch, dwu

3 and 4 follow the same pattern:

	vir	*non-vir*
nom	czterej	cztery
gen	czterech	czterech
dat	czterem	czterem
acc	czterech	cztery
inst	czterema	czterema
loc	czterech	czterech

5, 6, 7, 8, 9 and 10 follow this pattern:

	vir	*non-vir*
nom	pięciu	pięć
gen	pięciu	pięciu
dat	pięciu	pięciu
acc	pięciu	pięć
inst	pięciu, pięcioma	pięciu, pięcioma
loc	pięciu	pięciu

11, 13, 14, 15, 16, 17, 18 and 19 follow this pattern:

	vir	*non-vir*
nom	jedenastu	jedenaście
gen	jedenastu	jedenastu
dat	jedenastu	jedenastu
acc	jedenastu	jedenaście
inst	jedenastu, jedenastoma	jedenastu, jedenastoma
loc	jedenastu	jedenastu

The stem 'dwa' declines in numbers 12 and 20.

	vir	*non-vir*
nom	dwunastu	dwanaście
gen	dwunastu	dwunastu
dat	dwunastu	dwunastu
acc	dwunastu	dwanaście
inst	dwunastu, dwunastoma	dwunastu, dwunastoma
loc	dwunastu	dwunastu

20 declines as follows. 30 and 40 decline in the same way as 20.

	vir	*non-vir*
nom	dwudziestu	dwadzieścia
gen	dwudziestu	dwudziestu
dat	dwudziestu	dwudziestu
acc	dwudziestu	dwadzieścia
inst	dwudziestu, dwudziestoma	dwudziestu, dwudziestoma
loc	dwudziestu	dwudziestu

50, 60, 70, 80 and 90 follow this pattern:

	vir	*non-vir*
nom	pięćdziesięciu	pięćdziesiąt
gen	pięćdziesięciu	pięćdziesiąt
dat	pięćdziesięciu	pięćdziesięciu
acc	pięćdziesięciu	pięćdziesiąt
inst	pięćdziesięciu, pięćdziesięcioma	pięćdziesięciu, pięćdziesięcioma
loc	pięćdziesięciu	pięćdziesięciu

100 and 200 decline as follows:

	vir	*non-vir*
nom, acc	stu	sto
gen, dat, loc	stu	stu
inst	stoma	stoma

	vir	*non-vir*
nom, acc	dwustu	dwieście
gen, dat, loc	dwustu	dwustu
inst	dwustoma	dwustoma

300 and 400 decline as follows:

	vir	*non-vir*
nom, acc	trzystu	trzysta
gen, dat, loc	trzystu	trzystu
inst	trzystoma	trzystoma

500, 600, 700, 800 and 900 follow this pattern:

	vir	*non-vir*
nom, acc	pięciuset	pięćset
gen, dat, loc, inst	pięciuset	pięciuset

1000 declines as follows:

	sg	*pl*
nom	tysiąc	tysiące
gen	tysiąca	tysięcy
dat	tysiącowi	tysiącom
acc	tysiąc	tysiące
inst	tysiącem	tysiącami
loc	tysiącu	tysiącach

COLLECTIVE NUMERALS

Collective numerals refer to mixed gender groups.

The numbers **dwoje** (2), **troje** (3), **czworo** (4), **pięcioro** (5), **sześcioro** (6), **siedmioro** (7), **ośmioro** (8), **dziewięcioro** (9), **dziesięcioro** (10), **jedenaścioro** (11), **dwanaścioro** (12) decline as follows. Each numeral takes the case shown in the table.

nom	dwoje	czworo	pięcioro	+gen
gen	dwojga	czworga	pięciorga	+gen
dat	dwojgu	czworgu	pięciorgu	+dat
acc	dwoje	czworo	pięcioro	+gen
inst	dwojgiem	czworgiem	pięciorgiem	+gen
loc	dwojgu	czworgu	pięciorgu	+loc

PERSONAL PRONOUNS

Singular

nom	ja	ty	on (m)	ona (f)	ono (nt)
gen	mnie	ciebie, cię	jego, niego go	jej, niej	jego, niego, go
dat	mnie, mi	tobie, ci	jemu, niemu, mu	jej, niej	jemu, niemu, mu
acc	mnie	ciebie, cię	jego, niego go	ją, nią	je, nie
inst	mną	tobą	nim	nią	nim
loc	mnie	tobie	nim	niej	nim

Plural

nom	my	wy	oni (vir)	one (non-vir)
gen	nas	was	ich, nich	ich, nich
dat	nam	wam	im, nim	im, nim
acc	nas	was	ich, nich	je, nie
inst	nami	wami	nimi	nimi
loc	nas	was	nich	nich

pan/pani

	m sg	*f sg*	*m pl*	*f pl*	*m & f pl*
nom	pan	pani	panowie	panie	państwo
gen	pana	pani	panów	pań	państwa
dat	panu	pani	panom	paniom	państwu
acc	pana	panią	panów	panie	państwa
inst	panem	panią	panami	paniami	państwem
loc	panu	pani	panach	paniach	państwie
voc	pan	pani	panowie	panie	państwo

REFLEXIVE PRONOUNS

nom	—
gen, acc	siebie, się
dat, loc	sobie
inst	sobą

POSSESSIVE PRONOUNS

mój, **swój** and **twój** decline as follows:

Singular

	m	*f*	*nt*	*vir pl*	*non-vir pl*
nom	mój	moja	moje	moi	moje
gen	mojego	mojej	mojego	moich	moich
dat	mojemu	mojej	mojemu	moim	moim
acc	mój, mojego	moją	moje	moich	moje
inst	moim	moją	moim	moimi	moimi
loc	moim	mojej	moim	moich	moich

wasz follows the same pattern as **nasz**:

Singular

	m	*f*	*nt*	*vir pl*	*non-vir pl*
nom	nasz	nasza	nasze	nasi	nasze
gen	naszego	naszej	naszego	naszych	naszych
dat	naszemu	naszej	naszemu	naszym	naszym
acc	nasz, naszego	naszą	nasz, naszego	naszych	nasze
inst	naszym	naszą	naszym	naszymi	naszymi
loc	naszym	naszej	naszym	naszymi	naszych

The following do not decline:

its, his	jego
her, hers	jej
their, theirs	ich
your, yours (*polite m sg*)	pana
your, yours (*polite f sg*)	pani

INTERROGATIVE PRONOUNS

kto/co

nom	kto	co
gen	kogo	czego
dat	komu	czemu
acc	kogo	co
inst	kim	czym
loc	kim	czym

RELATIVE PRONOUNS

czyj

	m	f	nt	vir pl	non-vir pl
nom	czyj	czyja	czyje	czyi	czyje
gen	czyjego	czyjej	czyjego	czyich	czyich
dat	czyjemu	czyjej	czyjemu	czyim	czyim
acc	czyj, czyjego	czyją	czyje	czyich	czyje
inst	czyim	czyją	czyim	czyimi	czyimi
loc	czyim	czyjej	czyim	czyich	czyich

jaki follows the same pattern as **który**:

	m	f	nt	vir pl	non-vir pl
nom	który	która	które	którzy	które
gen	którego	której	którego	których	których
dat	któremu	której	któremu	którym	którym
acc	który, którego	którą	które	których	które
inst	którym	którą	którym	którymi	którymi
loc	którym	której	którym	których	których

DEMONSTRATIVE PRONOUNS

	m	f	nt	vir pl	non-vir pl
nom	ten	ta	to	ci	te
gen	tego	tej	tego	tych	tych
dat	temu	tej	temu	tym	tym
acc	ten, tego	tę	to	tych	te
inst	tym	tą	tym	tymi	tymi
loc	tym	tej	tym	tych	tych

NOUNS

Masculine

	animate			
	singular	*plural (irreg)*	*singular*	*plural (irreg)*
nom	mąż	mężowie	człowiek	ludzie
gen	męża	mężów	człowieka	ludzi
dat	mężowi	mężom	człowiekowi	ludziom
acc	męża	mężów	człowieka	ludzi
inst	mężem	mężami	człowiekiem	ludzmi
loc	mężu	mężach	człowieku	ludziach
voc	mężu	mężowie	człowieku	ludzie

	inanimate			
	singular	*plural*	*singular*	*plural*
nom	sklep	sklepy	stół	stoły
gen	sklepu	sklepów	stół	stołów
dat	sklepowi	skleom	stołowi	stołom
acc	sklep	sklepy	stół	stoły
inst	sklepem	sklepami	stołem	stołami
loc	sklepie	sklepach	stole	stołach
voc	sklep	sklepy	stole	stoły

Feminine

	singular	*plural*	*singular*	*plural*
nom	kobieta	kobiety	noga	nogi
gen	kobiety	kobiet	nogi	nóg
dat	kobiecie	kobietom	nodze	nogom
acc	kobietę	kobiety	nogę	nogi
inst	kobietą	kobietami	nogą	nogami
loc	kobiecie	kobietach	nodze	nogach
voc	kobieto	kobiety	nogo	nogi

Neuter

	singular	plural	singular	plural
nom	miasto	miasta	dziecko	dzieci
gen	miasta	miast	dziecka	dzieci
dat	miastu	miastom	dziecku	dzieciom
acc	miasto	miasta	dziecko	dzieci
inst	miastem	miastami	dzieckiem	dziećmi
loc	mieście	miastach	dziecku	dzieciach
voc	miasto	miasta	dziecko	dzieci

	singular	plural
nom	imię	imiona
gen	imienia	imion
dat	imieniu	imionom
acc	imię	imiona
inst	imieniem	imionami
loc	imieniu	imionach
voc	imię	imiona

ADJECTIVES

	m	f	nt	vir pl	non-vir pl
nom	dobry	dobra	dobre	dobrzy	dobre
gen	dobrego	dobrej	dobrego	dobrych	dobrych
dat	dobremu	dobrej	dobremu	dobrym	dobrym
acc	dobry, dobrego	dobrą	dobre	dobrych	dobre
inst	dobrym	dobrą	dobrym	dobrymi	dobrymi
loc	dobrym	dobrej	dobrym	dobrych	dobrych
voc	dobry	dobra	dobre	dobrzy	dobre

VERB CONJUGATIONS

First Conjugation

pisać to write

PRESENT

(ja)	piszę
(ty)	piszesz
(on)	pisze
(ona)	pisze
(ono)	pisze
(my)	piszemy
(wy)	piszecie
(oni)	piszą
(one)	piszą

PAST

(ja)	pisałem/pisałam
(ty)	pisałeś/pisałaś
(on)	pisał
(ona)	pisała
(ono)	pisało
(my)	pisaliśmy/pisałyśmy
(wy)	pisaliście/pisałyście
(oni)	pisali
(one)	pisały

IMPERATIVE

(ja)	—
(ty)	pisz
(on, ona, ono)	niech pisze
(my)	piszmy
(wy)	piszcie
(oni, one)	niech piszą

FUTURE

The way the future tense is formed depends on whether you are using an imperfective or a perfective verb.

Perfective: Conjugate the verb as if it were the present tense.

powiedzieć (*to say*)
powiem ci później – I will tell you later

Imperfective: Use the verb **być** (*to be*) in its future form, followed either by the infinitive or the third person past form of the verb.

być (future form) + infinitive
or
być (future form) + past form

będę pisać – I will write
będzie czytał – he will read
będą zaczynali – they will begin

Second Conjugation

płacić to pay

PRESENT

(ja)	płacę
(ty)	płacisz
(on)	płaci
(ona)	płaci
(ono)	płaci
(my)	płacimy
(wy)	płacicie
(oni)	płacą
(one)	płacą

PAST

(ja)	płaciłem/płaciłam
(ty)	płaciłeś/płaciłeś
(on)	płacił
(ona)	płaciła
(ono)	płaciło
(my)	płaciliśmy/płaciłyśmy
(wy)	płaciliście/płaciłyście
(oni)	płacili
(one)	płaciły

IMPERATIVE

(ja)	—
(ty)	płać
(on, ona, ono)	niech płaci
(my)	płaćmy
(wy)	płaćcie
(oni, one)	niech płacą

FUTURE

See page xxviii

Third Conjugation

czytać to read

PRESENT

(ja) czytam
(ty) czytasz
(on) czyta
(ona) czyta
(ono) czyta
(my) czytamy
(wy) czytacie
(oni) czytają
(one) czytają

PAST

(ja) czytałem/czytałam
(ty) czytałeś/czytałaś
(on) czytał
(ona) czytała
(ono) czytało
(my) czytaliśmy/czytałyśmy
(wy) czytaliście/czytałyście
(oni) czytali
(one) czytały

IMPERATIVE

(ja) —
(ty) czytaj
(on, ona, ono) niech czyta
(my) czytajmy
(wy) czytajcie
(oni, one) niech czytają

FUTURE

See page xxviii

Fourth Conjugation

wiedzieć to know

PRESENT

(ja)	wiem
(ty)	wiesz
(on)	wie
(ona)	wie
(ono)	wie
(my)	wiemy
(wy)	wiecie
(oni)	wiedzą
(one)	wiedzą

PAST

(ja)	wiedziałem/wiedziałam
(ty)	wiedziałeś/wiedziałaś
(on)	wiedział
(ona)	wiedziała
(ono)	wiedziało
(my)	wiedzieliśmy/wiedziałyśmy
(wy)	wiedzieliście/wiedziałyście
(oni)	wiedzieli
(one)	wiedziały

IMPERATIVE

(ja)	—
(ty)	wiedz
(on, ona, ono)	niech wie
(my)	wiedzmy
(wy)	wiedzcie
(oni, one)	niech wiedzą

FUTURE

See page xxviii

IRREGULAR VERBS

być to be

PRESENT	PAST
(ja) jestem	(ja) byłem/byłam
(ty) jesteś	(ty) byłeś/byłaś
(on) jest	(on) był
(ona) jest	(ona) była
(ono) jest	(ono) było
(my) jesteśmy	(my) byliśmy/byłyśmy
(wy) jesteście	(wy) byliście/byłyście
(oni) są	(oni) byli
(one) są	(one) były

IMPERATIVE	FUTURE
(ja) —	(ja) będę
(ty) bądź	(ty) będziesz
(on, ona, ono) niech będzie	(on, ona, ono) będzie
(my) bądźmy	(my) będziemy
(wy) bądźcie	(wy) będziecie
(oni, one) niech będą	(oni, one) będą

---

iść to go

PRESENT	PAST
(ja) idę	(ja) szedłem/szłam
(ty) idziesz	(ty) szedłeś/szłaś
(on) idzie	(on) szedł
(ona) idzie	(ona) szła
(ono) idzie	(ono) szło
(my) idziemy	(my) szliśmy/szłyśmy
(wy) idziecie	(wy) szliście/szłyście
(oni) idą	(oni) szli
(one) idą	(one) szły

IMPERATIVE	FUTURE
(ja) —	See page xxviii
(ty) idź	
(on, ona, ono) niech idzie	
(my) idźmy	
(wy) idźcie	
(oni, one) niech idą	

mieć to have

PRESENT

      (ja) mam
      (ty) masz
     (on) ma
   (ona) ma
   (ono) ma
    (my) mamy
    (wy) macie
   (oni) mają
   (one) mają

IMPERATIVE

       (ja) —
       (ty) miej
(on, ona, ono) niech ma
     (my) miejmy
    (wy) miejcie
 (oni, one) niech mają

PAST

    (ja) miałem/miałam
    (ty) miałeś/miałaś
   (on) miał
 (ona) miała
 (ono) miało
   (my) mieliśmy/miałyśmy
  (wy) mieliście/miałyście
 (oni) mieli
 (one) miały

FUTURE

See page xxviii

---

móc to be able to

PRESENT

      (ja) mogę
      (ty) możesz
     (on) może
   (ona) może
   (ono) może
    (my) możemy
    (wy) możecie
   (oni) mogą
   (one) mogą

IMPERATIVE

not used

PAST

    (ja) mogłem/mogłam
    (ty) mogłeś/mogłaś
   (on) mógł
 (ona) mogła
 (ono) mogło
   (my) moglismy/mogłyśmy
  (wy) mogliście/mogłyście
 (oni) mogli
 (one) mogły

FUTURE

See page xxviii

English-Polish

Angielsko-Polski

a

ABC *nt inv* ABC
abecad|ło (-ła, -ła; *loc sg*
-le; *gen pl* **-eł**) *nt* 1 alphabet
2 (*przen: podwaliny*) the basics *pl*
abonamen|t (-tu, -ty; *loc sg* **-cie**)
m 1 (*dla telewizji*) subscription
2 (*w telekomunikacji*) standing
charges *pl*
abonen|t (-ta, -ci; *loc sg* **-cie**) *m*
subscriber
abonent|ka (-ki, -ki; *dat sg & loc sg*
-ce; *gen pl* **-ek**) *f* subscriber
aborcj|a (-i, -e; *gen pl* **-i**) *f*
abortion; **dokonywać (dokonać**
pf) **aborcji** to have an abortion
absencj|a (-i, -e; *gen pl* **-i**) *f*
1 (*nieobecność: w szkole, w pracy*)
absence 2 (*stała*) absenteeism;
usprawiedliwiona/
nieusprawiedliwiona ~

excused/unexcused absence
absolutnie *adv* absolutely
absolwen|t (-ta, -ci; *loc sg* **-cie**)
m graduate; **zjazd ~ów** class
reunion
absolwent|ka (-ki, -ki; *dat sg & loc
sg* **-ce**; *gen pl* **-ek**) *f* graduate
abstynen|t (-ta, -ci; *loc sg* **-cie**) *m*
teetotaller (*Brit*), teetotaler (*US*)
abstynent|ka (-ki, -ki; *dat sg &
loc sg* **-ce**; *-ek* **gen pl**) *f* teetotaller
(*Brit*), teetotaler (*US*)
absurdalny *adj* (*pomysł*) absurd
aby *conj* (so as) to; **pojechał
do Francji, ~ nauczyć się
francuskiego** he went to
France to learn French; **~ nie
przestraszyć psa** so as not to
frighten the dog
ach *excl* oh
adidas|y (-ów) *pl* trainers (*Brit*),
sneakers (*US*)
administracj|a (-i, -e; *gen pl* **-i**) *f*
1 (*w zarządzaniu*) administration
2 (*funkcja kierownicza*)
management 3 (*organ władzy*)
administration; **~ rządowa/
lokalna** central government/
local government
administracyjny *adj* 1 (*podział*)
administrative 2 (*zarządzający*)
managing 3 (*Prawo*): **sąd ~** court
*with special jurisdiction in the area of
administrative law*
administrato|r (-ra, -rzy; *loc sg*
-rze) *m* 1 (*zarządca*) administrator
2 (*w zarządzaniu*) manager; **~
budynku** property manager
adopcj|a (-i, -e; *gen pl* **-i**) *f*
adoption
adopt|ować (-uję, -ujesz; *pf* **za-**)
vt to adopt; **~ dziecko** to adopt

a child

ador|ować (**-uję, -ujesz**) *vt*
(*dziewczynę*) to adore

adre|s (**-su, -sy**; *loc sg* **-sie**) *m*
address; **~ odbiorcy/nadawcy**
recipient's/sender's address;
podawać (**podać** *pf*) **~**
korespondencyjny to give a
contact address

adresa|t (**-ta, -ci**; *loc sg* **-cie**) *m*
addressee; **~ nieznany** addressee
unknown

adres|ować (**-uję, -ujesz**; *pf* **za-**)
vt (*list*) to address

adwen|t (**-tu, -ty**; *loc sg* **-cie**) *m*
Advent

adwoka|t (**-ta, -ci**; *loc sg* **-cie**) *m*
barrister (*Brit*), attorney (*US*)

aerobi|k (**-ku**; *inst sg* **-kiem**) *m*
aerobics; **uprawiać ~** to do
aerobics

aerozo|l (**-lu, -le**; *gen pl* **-li**) *m*
aerosol; **w ~u** in aerosol form

afe|ra (**-ry, -ry**; *dat sg & loc sg*
-rze) *f* scandal; **~ gospodarcza**
swindle

Afry|ka (**-ki**; *dat sg* **-ce**) *f* Africa

afrykański *adj* African

agencj|a (**-i, -e**; *gen pl* **-i**) *f* (*biuro*)
agency; **~ turystyczna** travel
agency; **~ towarzyska** escort
agency

agen|t (**-ta, -ci**; *loc sg* **-cie**) *m*
1 (*szpieg*) agent 2 (*przedstawiciel*)
rep; **~ ubezpieczeniowy**
insurance agent

agent|ka (**-ki, -ki**; *dat sg & loc sg*
-ce; *gen pl* **-ek**) *f* 1 agent 2 rep

agraf|ka (**-ki, -ki**; *dat sg & loc sg* **-ce**;
gen pl **-ek**) *f* safety pin

agresj|a (**-i, -e**; *gen pl* **-i**) *f*
aggression; **~ wobec** +*gen*

hostility to

agre|st (**-stu, -sty**; *loc sg* **-ście**) *m*
gooseberry

agresywny *adj* (*człowiek,
zachowanie*) aggressive

aha *excl* 1 (*zgadzanie*) uh-huh
2 (*przypomnienie sobie*) oh
3 (*rozumienie*) ah

AIDS *abbr* AIDS (= *acquired immune
deficiency syndrome*); **chory na ~**
suffering with AIDS

akademi|a (**-i, -e**; *gen pl* **-i**) *f*
1 (*uczelnia*) academy 2 (*spotkanie*)
ceremony; **~ dla uczczenia
rocznicy** anniversary celebration
ceremony; **polska A~ Nauk**
Polish Academy of Sciences; **A~
Teatrealna** Theatre Academy

akademicki *adj* (*dyskusja*)
academic; **dom ~** hall(s *pl*) of
residence (*Brit*), dormitory (*US*);
rok ~ the academic year

akademi|k (**-ka, -ki**; *inst sg* **-kiem**)
m (*pot: na uniwersytecie*) hall (*Brit*),
dorm (*US*)

akapi|t (**-tu, -ty**; *loc sg* **-cie**) *m*
paragraph; **zaczynać** (**zacząć** *pf*)
od nowego ~u to begin with a
new paragraph

akcen|t (**-tu, -ty**; *loc sg* **-cie**) *m* 1 (*w
językoznawstwie*) stress 2 (*sposób
wymiawiania*) accent 3 (*symbol*)
accent (mark) 4 (*podkreślenie*)
emphasis 5 (*w muzyce*) emphasis

akcent|ować (**-uję, -ujesz**; *pf* **za-**)
vt 1 (*w językoznawstwie*) to stress
2 (*przen*) to emphasize

akceptacj|a (**-i, -e**; *gen pl*
-i) *f* 1 (*prezentu*) acceptance
2 (*propozycji*) approval

akcept|ować (**-uję, -ujesz**; *pf* **za-**)
vt 1 (*prezent*) to accept 2 (*decyzję*)

to approve of
akcj|a (**-i**, **-e**; *gen pl* **-i**) *f* **1** (*wojskowa*)
campaign **2** (*działanie*) action
3 (*w powieści*) plot **4** (*Fin*) share;
**spadek/wzrost cen akcji na
giełdzie** a fall/rise in the share's
market price; **~ zbrojna** military
action
akcyz|a (**-y**, **-y**; *dat sg* **-ie**) *f* excise
ak|t (**-tu**, **-ty**; *loc sg* **-cie**) *m* **1** act
2 (*uroczystość*) ceremony **3** (*w
sztuce*) nude **4** (*nom pl* **-ta** *lub*
-ty) (*zaświadczenie*) certificate;
akta (*gen pl* **akt**) *pl* **1** (*dokumenty*)
files **2** (*zbiór dokumentów na jakiś
temat*) dossier; **~ urodzenia** birth
certificate
akto|r (**-ra**, **-rzy**; *loc sg* **-rze**) *m*
actor
aktor|ka (**-ki**, **-ki**; *dat sg & loc sg*
-ce; *gen pl* **-ek**) *f* actress
aktów|ka (**-ki**, **-ki**; *dat sg & loc sg*
-ce; *gen pl* **-ek**) *f* briefcase
aktualiz|ować (**-uję**, **-ujesz**; *pf*
z-) *vt* (*dane*) to update
aktualnie *adv* (*obecnie*) currently
aktualny *adj* current; **aktualne
zagadnienia** current affairs
aktywi|sta (**-sty**, **-ści**; *dat sg & loc
sg* **-ście**) *m decl like f in sg* activist;
~ organizacji ekologicznej green
activist
aktywist|ka (**-ki**, **-ki**; *dat sg & loc sg*
-ce; *gen pl* **-ek**) *f* activist
aktywnoś|ć (**-ci**) *f* activity; **~
fizyczna** physical activity
aktywny *adj* (*działacz*) active
akumulato|r (**-ra**, **-ry**; *loc sg* **-rze**)
m (*w motoryzacji*) battery
akurat *adv* **1** (*dokładnie*) exactly
2 (*właśnie w tym momencie*) at this
lub that very moment; **~ kiedy**

wychodził zadzwonił telefon
the very moment he left the
phone rang
akwari|um (**-um**, **-a**; *gen pl* **-ów**)
nt aquarium
alar|m (**-mu**, **-my**; *loc sg* **-mie**) *m*
1 alarm **2** (*stan gotowości*) alert
3 (*pot: urządzenie*) alarm system
4 (*w muzeum*) anti-theft system; **~
pożarowy** fire alarm; **fałszywy ~**
a false alarm
alarm|ować (**-uję**, **-ujesz**; *pf* **za-**)
vt **1** (*informować o zagrożeniu*) to
alert **2** (*przestraszyć*) to alarm
alarmowy *adj* (*sygnał*) alarm
albo *conj* or; **~...~...** either... or...
ale *conj* but ▷ *part*: **~ deszcz!**
that's some rain!; **~ jaja!** (*pot!*)
well, I never!
ale|ja (**-i**, **-je**; *gen pl* **-i**) *f* **1** (*droga*)
alley **2** (*ulica*) avenue
alergi|a (**-i**, **-e**; *gen pl* **-i**) *f* allergy;
mieć alergię na coś to be allergic
to sth
alergiczny *adj* (*Med*) allergic
alfabe|t (**-tu**, **-ty**; *loc sg* **-cie**) *m*
alphabet
alfabetyczny *adj* alphabetical;
ułożyć (**układać** *pf*) **coś w
porządku ~m** to arrange sth in
alphabetical order
alkohol (**-u**, **-e**; *gen pl* **-i** *lub* **-ów**)
m **1** (*napój alkoholowy*) alcohol
2 (*Chem*): **~ przemysłowy**
industrial alcohol
alkoholi|k (**-ka**, **-cy**; *inst sg* **-kiem**)
m alcoholic
alkoholicz|ka (**-ki**, **-ki**; *dat sg & loc
sg* **-ce**; *gen pl* **-ek**) *f* alcoholic
alkoholiz|m (**-mu**; *loc sg* **-mie**) *m*
alcoholism
alpini|sta (**-sty**, **-ści**; *dat sg &*

loc sg **-ście**) *m decl like f in sg* mountaineer

alpinist|ka (**-ki, -ki**; *dat sg & loc sg* **-ce**; *gen pl* **-ek**) *f* mountaineer

alpiniz|m (**-mu**; *loc sg* **-mie**) *m* mountaineering

Alp|y (**-**) *pl* the Alps

alternaty|wa (**-wy, -wy**; *dat sg & loc sg* **-wie**) *f* alternative

alternatywny *adj* (*styl życia, metoda, plan*) alternative

aluminium *nt inv* aluminium (*Brit*), aluminum (*US*)

amato|r (**-ra, -rzy**; *loc sg* **-rze**) *m* **1** (*niezawodowiec*) amateur **2** (*zwolennik*) enthusiast **3** (*Sport*) amateur; **~ dobrego jedzenia** gourmet

amator|ka (**-ki, -ki**; *dat sg & loc sg* **-ce**; *gen pl* **-ek**) *f* amateur

amatorski *adj* **1** (*niezawodowy: pej*) amateurish **2** (*nieprofesjonalny*) amateur; **teatr ~** amateur dramatics

ambasa|da (**-dy, -dy**; *dat sg & loc sg* **-dzie**) *f* embassy

ambasado|r (**-ra, -rzy** *lub* **-rowie**; *loc sg* **-rze**) *m* ambassador; **~ dobrej woli** good will ambassador

ambicj|a (**-i, -e**; *gen pl* **-i**) *f* **1** (*dążenie*) ambition **2** (*pycha*) self-respect

ambitny *adj* ambitious

ambulatori|um (**-um, -a**; *gen pl* **-ów**) *nt* out-patient clinic

ambulatoryjny *adj*: **leczenie ambulatoryjne** out-patient treatment

Amery|ka (**-ki, -ki**; *dat sg* **-ce**) *f* America; **~ Łacińska** Latin America

Ameryka|nin (**-nina, -nie**; *loc sg* **-ninie**; *gen pl* **-nów**) *m* American

Amerykan|ka (**-ki, -ki**; *dat sg* **-ce**; *gen pl* **-ek**) *f* American

amerykański *adj* American

amfiteat|r (**-ru, -ry**; *loc sg* **-rze**) *m* amphitheatre (*Brit*), amphitheater (*US*)

amputacj|a (**-i, -e**; *gen pl* **-i**) *f* amputation

amput|ować (**-uję, -ujesz**) *vt impf/pf* to amputate

analfabe|ta (**-ty, -ci**; *dat sg & loc sg* **-cie**) *m decl like f in sg* illiterate person

analfabet|ka (**-ki, -ki**; *dat sg & loc sg* **-ce**; *gen pl* **-ek**) *f* illiterate person

anali|za (**-zy, -zy**; *dat sg & loc sg* **-zie**) *f* **1** (*Med*) test **2** (*Chem*) analysis

analiz|ować (**-uję, -ujesz**; *pf* **z-**) *vt* to analyse (*Brit*), to analyze (*US*)

anana|s (**-sa, -sy**; *loc sg* **-sie**) *m* pineapple

andrzej|ki (**-ek**) *pl* St Andrew's Day

● **ANDRZEJKI**
●
● St Andrew's Day (30
● November) is celebrated in
● the evening of 29 November,
● and is referred to as **andrzejki**.
● Games are organized for
● young people and some tell
● fortunes by, for example,
● pouring hot wax into water.
● The congealed wax forms
※ various shapes, which
● supposedly tell the fortune
● of the person who poured
● the wax.

anegdo|ta (**-ty**, **-ty**; *loc sg* **-cie**) *f* anecdote

anemi|a (**-i**) *f* anaemia (*Brit*), anemia (*US*)

Angiel|ka (**-ki**, **-ki**; *dat sg* **-ce**; *gen pl* **-ek**) *f* Englishwoman

angielski *adj* English ▷ *m decl like adj* English; **mówić po angielsku** to speak English

angi|na (**-ny**; *loc sg* **-nie**) *f* tonsillitis

Angli|a (**-i**) *f* England

Angli|k (**-ka**, **-cy**; *inst sg* **-kiem**) *m* Englishman

anglikański *adj* Anglican; **Kościół A~** the Church of England

ani *conj*: **~... ~...** neither... nor...; (*z innym wyrazem przeczącym*) either... or... ▷ *part* **1** not a (single) **2** (*z innym wyrazem przeczącym*) a (single); **~ be ~ me** not a single word; **~ jeden** not a single one; **~ trochę** not even a little bit; **~ jeden** not a single one, none

animowany *adj*: **film ~** (*TV*) cartoon

ani|oł (**-oła**, **-ołowie** *lub* **-oły**; *loc sg* **-ele**) *m* angel

ankie|ta (**-ty**, **-ty**; *dat sg* & *loc sg* **-cie**) *f* **1** (*badanie opinii*) survey **2** (*formularz*) questionnaire; **wypełniać** (**wypełnić** *pf*) **ankietę** to fill out a questionnaire

anonimowy *adj* (*list, utwór*) anonymous

Antarkty|ka (**-ki**; *dat sg* **-ce**) *f* the Antarctic

ante|na (**-ny**, **-ny**; *dat sg* & *loc sg* **-nie**) *f* aerial (*Brit*), antenna (*US*); **zakładać** (**założyć** *pf*) **antenę satelitarną** to install a satellite dish

antropologi|a (**-i**) *f* anthropology

antybioty|k (**-ku**, **-ki**; *inst sg* **-kiem**) *m* antibiotic; **brać** (**wziąć** *pf*) **~** to take an antibiotic

antykoncepcj|a (**-i**) *f* contraception

antykoncepcyjny *adj*: **środek ~** contraceptive

antysemi|ta (**-ty**, **-ci**; *dat sg* & *loc sg* **-cie**) *m decl like f in sg* anti-Semite

antysemit|ka (**-ki**, **-ki**; *dat sg* & *loc sg* **-ce**; *gen pl* **-ek**) *f* anti-Semite

antysemityz|m (**-mu**; *loc sg* **-mie**) *m* anti-Semitism

anul|ować (**-uję**, **-ujesz**) *vt impf/pf* **1** (*rezerwację*) to cancel **2** (*małżeństwo*) to annul

apara|t (**-tu**, **-ty**; *loc sg* **-cie**) *m* (*naukowy*) apparatus; **~ fotograficzny** camera; **~ telefoniczny** telephone

apartamen|t (**-tu**, **-ty**; *loc sg* **-cie**) *m* **1** (*mieszkanie w luksusowym bloku*) apartment **2** (*w hotelu*) suite

apel (**-u**, **-e**; *gen pl* **-i** *lub* **-ów**) *m* **1** (*wezwanie*) appeal **2** (*Wojsk*) assembly; **~ poranny** morning assembly

apetyczny *adj* appetizing

apety|t (**-tu**, **-ty**; *loc sg* **-cie**) *m* appetite

aplik|ować (**-uję**, **-ujesz**; *pf* **za-**) *vt* +*dat* **1** (*lek*) to administer **2** (*makijaż, kosmetyk*) to apply

aproba|ta (**-ty**; *dat sg* & *loc sg* **-cie**) *f* approval; **okazywać** (**okazać** *pf*) **aprobatę** to show one's approval

aprob|ować (**-uję**, **-ujesz**; *pf* **za-**)

vt (pomysł) to approve of

aptecz|ka (**-ki, -ki**; *dat sg & loc sg* **-ce**; *gen pl* **-ek**) *f* medicine cabinet; **~ samochodowa** first-aid kit

apte|ka (**-ki, -ki**; *dat sg & loc sg* **-ce**) *f* pharmacy

aptekar|ka (**-ki, -ki**; *dat sg & loc sg* **-ce**; *gen pl* **-ek**) *f* pharmacist

apteka|rz (**-rza, -rze**; *gen pl* **-rzy**) *m* pharmacist

arbu|z (**-za, -zy**; *loc sg* **-zie**) *m* watermelon

archeolo|g (**-ga, -dzy** *lub* **-gowie**; *inst sg* **-giem**) *m* archaeologist (Brit), archeologist (US)

archeologi|a (**-i**) *f* archaeology (Brit), archeology (US); **~ śródziemnomorska** Mediterranean archaeology

archeologiczny *adj* archaeological (Brit), archeological (US); **wykopaliska archeologiczne** archaeological excavations

architek|t (**-ta, -ci**; *loc sg* **-cie**) *m* architect

architektu|ra (**-ry**; *dat sg & loc sg* **-rze**) *f* architecture

archiwalny *adj* archival

archiw|um (**-um, -a**; *gen pl* **-ów**) *nt inv in sg* archive

arcydzie|ło (**-ła, -ła**; *loc sg* **-le**) *nt* masterpiece

aresz|t (**-tu, -ty**; *loc sg* **-cie**) *m* 1 *(pozbawienie wolności osobistej)* arrest 2 *(pomieszczenie)* jail; **zatrzymać** (**zatrzymać** *pf*) **kogoś w areszcie** to keep sb in custody

areszt|ować (**-uję, -ujesz**; *pf also* **za-**) *vt impf/pf* to arrest; **jest pan**

aresztowany you're under arrest

Argenty|na (**-ny**; *dat sg* **-nie**) *f* Argentina

argumen|t (**-tu, -ty**; *loc sg* **-cie**) *m* argument

arkusz (**-a, -e**; *gen pl* **-y**) *m* sheet; **~ kalkulacyjny** spreadsheet

armi|a (**-i, -e**; *gen pl* **-i**) *f* army; **powoływać** (**powołać** *pf*) **do armii** to call up for military service

arogancki *adj* arrogant

artyku|ł (**-łu, -ły**; *loc sg* **-le**) *m* article; **~y spożywcze** groceries

arty|sta (**-sty, -ści**; *dat sg & loc sg* **-ście**) *m decl like f in sg* 1 artist 2 *(pot: Teatr)* actor; **~ malarz** painter

artyst|ka (**-ki, -ki**; *dat sg & loc sg* **-ce**; *gen pl* **-ek**) *f* 1 artist 2 *(pot: Teatr)* actress

artystyczny *adj* artistic

arystokracj|a (**-i**) *f* aristocracy

arystokra|ta (**-ty, -ci**; *loc sg* **-cie**) *m decl like f in sg* aristocrat

arystokrat|ka *f* (**-ki, -ki**; *dat sg & loc sg* **-ce**; *gen pl* **-ek**) *f* aristocrat

as (**asa, asy**; *loc sg* **asie**) *m* ace; **as kier/karo/pik/trefl** ace of hearts/diamonds/spades/clubs; **mieć asa w rękawie** to have an ace up one's sleeve

aspiry|na (**-ny, -ny**; *loc sg* **-nie**) *f* aspirin

asysten|t (**-ta, -ci**; *loc sg* **-cie**) *m* assistant

asystent|ka (**-ki, -ki**; *dat sg & loc sg* **-ce**; *gen pl* **-ek**) *f* assistant

asyst|ować (**-uję, -ujesz**) *vi:* **~ komuś** *(towarzyszyć)* to accompany sb; *(współdziałać)* to assist sb

ata|k (**-ku, -ki**; *inst sg* **-kiem**) *m*
attack; **dostawać** (**dostać** *pf*)
~u nerwowego to get an attack
of nerves

atak|ować (**-uję, -ujesz**; *pf* **za-**)
vt to attack

atlantycki *adj* Atlantic; **Ocean
A~** the Atlantic (Ocean)

Atlantyk (**-ku**; *inst sg* **-kiem**) *m*
the Atlantic

atla|s (**-su, -sy**; *loc sg* **-sie**) *m* atlas;
~ samochodowy road atlas

atmosfe|ra (**-ry, -ry**; *loc sg* **-rze**)
f (*przen*) atmosphere; **stwarzać**
(**stworzyć** *pf*) **przyjazną
atmosferę** to create a welcoming
atmosphere

atrakcyjny *adj* (*wygląd*)
attractive

atramen|t (**-tu, -ty**; *loc sg* **-cie**) *m*
ink; **~ sympatyczny** invisible ink

atu|t (**-tu, -ty**; *loc sg* **-cie**) *m* trump
(card); **mieć niezaprzeczalne ~y**
to be in an unassailable position

audycj|a (**-i, -e**; *gen pl* **-i**) *f* (radio)
programme

Australi|a (**-i**) *m* Australia

Australijczy|k (**-ka, -cy**; *inst sg*
-kiem) *m* Australian

Australij|ka (**-ki, -ki**; *dat sg & loc sg*
-ce; *gen pl* **-ek**) *f* Australian

australijski *adj* Australian

Austri|a (**-i**) *f* Austria

austriacki *adj* Austrian

autentyczny *adj* (*document*)
authentic

au|to (**-ta, -ta**; *loc sg* **-cie**) *nt* car

autobiografi|a (**-i, -e**; *gen pl* **-i**) *f*
autobiography

autobu|s (**-su, -sy**; *loc sg* **-sie**) *m*
(*w mieście*) bus

autobusowy *adj* bus;

przystanek ~ bus stop; **dworzec
~** bus station

autoka|r (**-ru, -ry**; *loc sg* **-rze**) *m*
coach

automa|t (**-tu, -ty**; *loc sg* **-cie**) *m*
(*telefoniczny*) public telephone

automatyczny *adj* automatic;
sekretarka automatyczna
answering machine

auto|r (**-ra, -rzy**; *loc sg* **-rze**) *m*
author

autor|ka (**-ki, -ki**; *dat sg & loc sg*
-ce; *gen pl* **-ek**) *f* author

autorski *adj* author's; **prawa ~e**
author's rights; **wieczór ~** meet-
the-author event

autoryte|t (**-tu, -ty**; *loc sg* **-cie**) *m*
1 authority **2** (*uznanie*) prestige;
mieć ~ to enjoy respect

autosto|p (**-pu**; *loc sg* **-pie**) *m*
hitch-hiking; **jechać** (**pojechać**
pf) **~em** to hitch-hike

autostopowicz (**-a, -e**) *m*
hitch-hiker

autostopowicz|ka (**-ki, -ki**;
dat sg & loc sg **-ce**; *gen pl* **-ek**) *f*
hitch-hiker

autostra|da (**-dy, -dy**; *dat sg &
loc sg* **-dzie**) *f* motorway (*Brit*),
freeway (*US*)

awan|s (**-su, -se** *lub* **-sy**; *loc sg*
-sie) *m* promotion; **otrzymywać**
(**otrzymać** *pf*) **~** to get promoted

awans|ować (**-uję, -ujesz**) *vt*
impf/pf to promote ▷ *vi* to be
promoted

awantu|ra (**-ry, -ry**; *dat sg & loc sg*
-rze) *f* disturbance; **wszczynać**
(**wszcząć** *pf*) **awanturę** to start
a fight

awantur|ować się (**-uję, -ujesz**)
vr to cause a disturbance

awari|a (**-i**, **-e**; *gen pl* **-i**) *f*
breakdown; **~ sieci elektrycznej**
power failure

awi|zo (**-za**, **-za**; *loc sg* **-zie**; *gen pl*
-zów) *nt* advice note

Azj|a (**-i**) *m* Asia

azyatycki *adj* Asian

azyl (**-u**, **-e**) *m* (*Pol*) (political)
asylum; **udzielać (udzielić)**
komuś ~u to grant sb asylum

ba|ba (**-by**, **-by**; *dat sg & loc sg* **-bie**)
f (*pot: pej: starsza pani*) biddy: **~**
Wielkanocna Easter cake

bab|cia (**-ci**, **-cie**; *gen pl* **-ci** *lub* **-ć**) *f*
1 grandma **2** (*pot: starsza kobieta*)
old woman

bać się (**boję się**, **boisz się**; *impf*
bój się) *vr* to be afraid; **~ kogoś/**
czegoś to be afraid of sb/sth; **~ o**
przyszłość to be worried about
the future; **nie bój się, na pewno**
jej się uda don't worry, she's
bound to succeed

bad|acz (**-a**, **-e**; *gen pl* **-y**)
m **1** (*uczony*) researcher
2 (*poszukiwacz*) explorer

badacz|ka (**-ki**, **-ki**; *dat & loc sg* **-ce**;
gen pl **-ek**) *f* researcher

bad|ać (**-am**, **-asz**; *pf* **z-**) *vt*
1 (*przedmiot*) to study **2** (*stan*

zdrowia) to test **3** (*u lekarza*) to examine

bada|nie (**-nia, -nia**; *gen pl* **-ń**) *nt* **1** test **2** (*Med*) examination; **badania** *pl* research; **~ moczu** urine test

badawczy *adj* **1** (*praca*) research **2** (*przenikliwy*) scrutinizing

bagaż (**-u, -e**; *gen pl* **-y**) *m* luggage (*Brit*), baggage (*US*); **~ podręczny** hand baggage

bagażni|k (**-ka, -ki**; *inst sg* **-kiem**) *m* **1** (*Mot*) boot (*Brit*), trunk (*US*) **2** (*na dachu samochodu*) roof rack **3** (*na rowerze*) carrier

baje|r (**-ru, -ry**; *dat sg & loc sg* **-rze**) *m*: **wstawiać** (**wstawić** *pf*) **komuś ~** to tell sb a cock and bull story; **bez żadnych ~ów** with no frills

baj|ka (**-ki, -ki**; *dat sg & loc sg* **-ce**; *gen pl* **-ek**) *f* **1** fairy tale **2** (*Lit*) fable; **opowiadać o czymś bajki** (*przen*) to tell tales about sth

bajkowy *adj* (*niezwykłej urody*) fabulous

ba|k (**-ku, -ki**; *inst sg* **-kiem**) *m* (fuel) tank; **napełniać** (**napełnić** *pf*) **~** to fill up (a fuel tank)

bakali|e (**-i**) *pl* (*Kulin*) dried fruit and nuts; **ciasto z bakaliami** rich fruit cake

bakłaża|n (**-na** *lub* **-nu, -ny**; *loc sg* **-nie**) *m* aubergine (*Brit*), eggplant (*US*)

bakteri|a (**-i, -e**; *gen pl* **-i**) *f* germ; **bakterie** *pl* bacteria *pl*

bakteriobójczy *adj* antiseptic; **środek ~** antiseptic

bal (**-u, -e**; *gen pl* **-ów**) *m* (*zabawa taneczna*) ball; **~ maskowy** masked (*Brit*) *lub* costume (*US*) ball

balero|n (**-nu, -ny**; *loc sg* **-nie**) *m* smoked ham

bale|t (**-tu, -ty**; *loc sg* **-cie**) *m* ballet

balko|n (**-nu, -ny**; *loc sg* **-nie**) *m* balcony

balo|n (**-nu, -ny**; *loc sg* **-nie**) *m* balloon; **robił z niego ~a** he took him for a ride (*pot*)

balsa|m (**-mu, -my**; *loc sg* **-mie**) *m* balm; **twoje słowa są dla mnie jak ~** your words are music to my ears

bałaga|n (**-nu**; *loc sg* **-nie**) *m* mess

bałaga|nić (**-nię, -nisz**; *impf* **-ń**; *pf* **na-**) *vi* to make a mess

Bałkan|y (**-ów**) *m pl* the Balkans

bałtycki *adj* (*państwo, region*) Baltic; **Morze B~e** the Baltic (Sea)

Bałty|k (**-ku**; *inst sg* **-kiem**) *m* the Baltic (Sea)

bałwa|n (**-na, -ny**; *loc sg* **-nie**) *m* **1** (*śniegowy*) snowman **2** (*morski*) breaker; **robić** (**zrobić** *pf*) **z kogoś ~a** (*pot*) to make a fool of sb

bana|n (**-na, -ny**; *loc sg* **-nie**) *m* banana

ban|da (**-dy, -dy**; *dat sg & loc sg* **-dzie**) *f* gang

bandaż (**-a, -e**; *gen pl* **-y**) *m* (*elastyczny*) bandage

bandaż|ować (**-uję, -ujesz**; *pf* **o-** *lub* **za-**) *vt* to bandage

bandy|ta (**-ty, -ci**; *dat sg & loc sg* **-cie**) *m decl like f in sg* bandit

ban|k (**-ku, -ki**; *inst sg* **-kiem**) *m* bank; **~ krwi/szpiku** blood/marrow bank; **masz to u mnie jak w ~u!** (*pot*) it's in the bag!

bankno|t (**-tu, -ty**; *loc sg* **-cie**) *m* (bank)note (*Brit*), bill (*US*); **~ dziesięciozłotowy** a 10-zloty note

bankoma|t (-tu, -ty; loc sg -cie) m
cash machine, ATM

ba|r (-ru, -ry; loc sg -rze)
m 1 (kawowy, mleczny) café
2 (stołówka) cafeteria; ~
samoobsługowy self-service
restaurant

bara|n (-na, -ny; loc sg -nie)
m 1 ram 2 (dureń) idiot
3 (Astrologia): **B~** Aries; **jak stado
~ów** (przen) like a flock of sheep

barani|na (-ny; dat sg & loc sg -nie)
f mutton

bardziej adv comp od **bardzo**
more; ~ **sprawny** more effective;
**im więcej pracował tym ~ miał
dość** the more he worked, the
more fed up he was; **coraz ~**
more and more

bardzo adv 1 (szczególnie) very
2 (mocno) very much; ~ **coś lubić**
to love sth very much; ~ **dobry**
very good; (Szkol) ≈ A; **tak ~ mi
go brak** I miss him so much; **za
~ się męczy** he is working too
hard; ~ **dziękuję** thank you very
much; ~ **przepraszam za jej
zachowanie** I'm very sorry about
her behaviour (Brit) lub behavior
(US)

bar|k (-ku, -ki; inst sg -kiem) m
shoulder; **jest szeroki w ~ach** he
is broad-shouldered

barma|n (-na, -ni; loc sg -nie) m
barman (Brit), bartender (US)

barman|ka (-ki, -ki; dat sg & loc sg
-ce; gen pl -ek) f barmaid

● **BAR MLECZNY**
●

● **Bar mleczny** is a Polish type
● of a fast-food restaurant.
● Its name comes from the
● large number of dairy and
● vegetarian dishes on the
● menu and relative lack of
● meat dishes. **Bary mleczne**
● were first set up during the
● **PRL** and are characterised by
● low prices.

barszcz (-u, -e; gen pl -y) m
beetroot soup

● **BARSZCZ**
●
●

● **Barszcz** is a soup made
● from beetroot, one of the
● specialities of Central
● European cuisine. **Barszcz**
● **biały**, otherwise known as
● **żur**, is also popular in Poland.
● This is made with flour,
● sausage, milk and vinegar.

bar|wa (-wy, -wy; dat sg & loc sg
-wie) f (kolor) colour (Brit), color
(US); **feria barw** a riot of colour

barwny adj 1 (różnobarwny)
colourful (Brit), colorful (US)
2 (kolorowy) colour (Brit), color
(US) 3 (zajmujący) vivid

base|n (-nu, -ny; loc sg -nie)
m 1 (zbiornik na wodę) basin
2 (pływalnia) (swimming) pool; ~
kryty/otwarty covered/open-
air swimming pool

bateri|a (-i, -e; gen pl -i) f battery

bato|n (-nu, -ny; loc sg -nie) m
(czekoladowy) bar (of chocolate)

bawełn|a (-ny; dat sg & loc sg -nie)
f cotton

bawełniany adj cotton

ba|wić (-wię, -wisz; pf u-) vt to

entertain; **~ się** vr 1 (grać) to play 2 (uprzyjemniać sobie czas) to have a good time; **~ się z kimś w kotka i myszkę** to play cat and mouse with sb; **baw się dobrze!** have a good time!

baza|r (-ru, -ry; loc sg **-rze)** m bazaar

bąbe|l (-la, -le; gen pl **-li)** m 1 (odcisk) blister 2 (pęcherzyk na wodzie) bubble

becz|ka (-ki, -ki; dat sg & loc sg **-ce;** gen pl **-ek)** f barrel; **jeść (zjeść** pf**) z kimś beczkę soli** to go back a long way with sb

bek|ać (-am, -asz; pf **-nąć)** vi (pot) to burp

beko|n (-nu, -ny; loc sg **-nie)** m bacon

Belgi|a (-i) f Belgium

belgijski adj Belgian

benzy|na (-ny; dat sg & loc sg **-nie)** f petrol (Brit), gas(oline) (US); **~ bezołowiowa** lead-free petrol

benzynowy adj (stacja, zapalniczka) petrol (Brit) lub gas (US) station

bere|t (-tu, -ty; loc sg **-cie)** m beret

besti|a (-i, -e; gen pl **-i)** f beast

bestialski adj bestial; **bestialska zbrodnia** brutal crime

beto|n (-nu, -ny; loc sg **-nie)** m concrete; **~ partyjny** (pot) party hardliners

betoniar|ka (-ki, -ki; dat sg & loc sg **-ce;** gen pl **-ek)** f concrete mixer

beton|ować (-uję, -ujesz) vt to concrete

bez prep +gen without; **~ celu** aimless; **~ sensu** pointless; **mówił ~ ładu i składu** he

rambled on

bezalkoholowy adj 1 (napój) non-alcoholic 2 (płyn kosmetyczny) alcohol-free; **napoje bezalkoholowe** soft drinks

bezbarwny adj colourless (Brit), colorless (US)

bezbolesny adj painless

bezbronny adj 1 (bezsilny) helpless 2 (nie stawiający oporu) defenceless (Brit), defenseless (US)

bezcenny adj 1 (nieoceniony) invaluable 2 (skarb) priceless

bezcłowy adj duty-free; **strefa bezcłowa** duty-free zone

bezczelny adj insolent

bezdomny adj homeless; **bezdomni** pl the homeless

bezkofeinowy adj decaffeinated

beznadziejny adj (sprawa, sytuacja) hopeless

bezokoliczni|k (-ka, -ki; inst sg **-kiem)** m infinitive

bezpieczeńst|wo (-wa; loc sg **-wie)** nt security; **~ i higiena pracy** (bhp) health and safety at work

bezpieczni|k (-ka, -ki; inst sg **-kiem)** m (urządzenie elektryczne) fuse (Brit), fuse (US)

bezpieczny adj 1 (pewny) secure 2 (nie stwarzający zagrożenia) safe

bezpłatnie adv free of charge

bezpłatny adj 1 (darmowy) free 2 (bez wynagrodzenia) unpaid

bezpłodnoś|ć (-ci) f infertility

bezpłodny adj 1 infertile 2 (przen) sterile

bezpośredni adj (pociąg, trasa, odpowiedź) direct

bezroboci|e (-a) nt unemployment

bezrobotny *adj* unemployed ▷ *m
decl like adj* unemployed person;
  bezrobotni *pl* the unemployed
bezsennoś|ć (-ci) *f* insomnia
beztłuszczowy *adj* fat-free
beżowy *adj* beige
będę, będzie *itd. vb zob.* **być**
białacz|ka (-ki, -ki; *dat sg & loc sg*
  -ce) *f* leukaemia (Brit), leukemia
  (US)
biał|ko (-ka, -ka; *inst sg* **-kiem;**
  gen pl **-ek)** *nt* 1 *(Kulin)* (egg)white
  2 *(Bio)* protein 3 *(oka)* white
Białoru|ś (-si) *f* Belarus
biały *adj* white ▷ *m decl like adj*
  white person; **biali** *pl* the whites
  pl; **w ~ dzień** in broad daylight;
  białe mięso white meat; **biała
  kawa** white coffee
Bibli|a (-i, -e; *gen pl* **-i)** *f* the Bible
bibliote|ka (-ki, -ki; *dat sg & loc sg*
  -ce) *f* 1 library 2 *(półka na książki)*
  bookcase
bibliotekar|ka (-ki, -ki; *dat sg & loc
  sg* **-ce;** *gen pl* **-ek)** *f* librarian
bibliotekarz (-a, -e; *gen pl* **-y)** *m*
  librarian
bi|ć (-ję, -jesz) *vt* 1 *(osobę)* to
  hit 2 *(pf* **u-)** *(zabijać: w rzeźni)* to
  slaughter ▷ *vi (serce)* to beat; **~ się**
  vr to fight; **~ na alarm** to raise
  the alarm; **bije go na głowę w
  matematyce** he beats him hands
  down in maths
bie|c (-gnę, -gniesz; *impf* **-gnij;**
  pt **-gł)** *vi* to run; **czas biegnie
  bardzo szybko** time passes very
  quickly
bie|da (-dy; *dat sg & loc sg* **-dzie)**
  f 1 *(brak pieniędzy)* poverty
  2 *(problem: przen)* trouble; **~ aż
  piszczy** dire poverty

biedny *adj* poor; **~ jak mysz
  kościelna** as poor as a church
  mouse
bie|g (-gu, -gi; *inst sg* **-giem)** *m*
  1 run 2 *(ciąg wydarzeń)* course 3 *(w
  samochodzie)* gear; **skrzynia ~ów**
  gearbox
biega|ć (-am, -asz) *vi* 1 to run
  2 *(amatorsko)* to jog
biegle *adv (mówić, pisać)* fluently;
  mówić ~ po francusku to speak
  fluent French
bieg|nąć (-nę, -niesz; *pt* **-ł)** *vb*
  = **biec**
biegun|ka (-ki, -ki; *dat sg & loc sg*
  -ce; *gen pl* **-ek)** *f* diarrhoea (Brit),
  diarrhea (US)
bieli|zna (-zny; *dat sg & loc sg*
  -źnie) *f* 1 *(poszwa)* (bed) linen
  2 *(majtki, stanik)* underwear
biernie *adv* passively
bierni|k (-ka, -ki; *inst sg* **-kiem)** *m*
  accusative
bieżący *adj* 1 *(rachunek w banku)*
  current 2 *(okres)* current 3 *(woda)*
  running
bigo|s (-su, -sy; *loc sg* **-sie)** *m*
  typical Polish dish consisting of
  sauerkraut and sausage

○ **BIGOS**
○
○ **Bigos** is a traditional Polish
○ dish, made from sauerkraut
○ and meat as well as various
○ other ingredients, including
○ mushrooms, prunes, and
○ onion.

bilar|d (-du, -dy; *loc sg* **-dzie)** *m*
  billiards *sg*
bile|t (-tu, -ty; *loc sg* **-cie)** *m* ticket

biletowy *adj*: **kasa biletowa**
(*kasa na dworcu*) ticket office;
(*kasa w teatrze*) box office

bilio|n (**-na, -ny**; *loc sg* **-nie**) *m*
trillion

bilo|n (**-nu**; *loc sg* **-nie**) *m* (loose)
change

bimbe|r (**-ru**; *loc sg* **-rze**) *m* (*pot*)
bootleg vodka, ≈ moonshine (*US*);
pędzić ~ to brew moonshine

biod|ro (**-ra, -ra**; *loc sg* **-rze**; *gen
pl* **-er**) *nt* hip; **ona ma smukłe
biodra** she has slender hips

biologi|a (**-i**) *f* biology

bisku|p (**-pa, -pi**; *loc sg* **-pie**) *m*
bishop

biszkop|t (**-tu, -ty**; *loc sg* **-cie**)
m **1** (*lekkie ciasto*) sponge cake
2 (*ciastko*) biscuit (*Brit*), cookie
(*US*)

bit|wa (**-wy, -wy**; *dat sg* & *loc sg*
-wie) *f* (*bój*) battle

biur|ko (**-ka, -ka**; *inst sg* **-kiem**; *gen
pl* **-ek**) *nt* desk

biu|ro (**-ra, -ra**; *loc sg* **-rze**) *nt*
1 (*miejsce pracy*) office **2** (*urząd*)
office, bureau; **~ rzeczy
znalezionych** lost property
(office) (*Brit*), lost-and-found
(office) (*US*)

biuro|wiec (**-wca, -wce**) *m* office
building

biu|st (**-stu, -sty**; *loc sg* **-ście**) *m*
1 (*kobiecy*) breasts *pl*, bosom
2 (*o.f.: popiersie*) bust

biustonosz (**-a, -e**; *gen pl* **-y**)
m bra

biwa|k (**-ku, -ki**; *inst sg* **-kiem**) *m*
bivouac

bizne|s (**-su, -sy**; *loc sg* **-sie**) *m*
(*interes*) business

biznesme|n (**-na, -ni**; *loc sg* **-nie**)

m businessman

biżuteri|a (**-i**; *gen pl* **-i**) *f* jewellery
(*Brit*), jewelry (*US*); **nosić
biżuterię** to wear jewellery

blady *adj* pale; **~ świt** early hours

blas|k (**-ku, -ki**; *inst sg* **-kiem**) *m*
1 (*złota*) glitter **2** (*promieni słońca*)
glare **3** (*poświata*) glow

bled|nąć (**-nę, -niesz**; *impf* **-nij**;
pf **z-**) *vi* to go pale; **zbladł ze
strachu** he went white with fear

bliski *adj* **1** (*niedaleki*) near
2 (*znajomy*) close **3** (*krewny*) close
4 (*relacja*) close **5** (*przyszłość*) near
▷ *m decl like adj* relative; **bliscy**
pl relatives *pl*; **~ rozpaczy** close
to despair; **być ~m prawdy** to
be close to the truth; **z bliska**
at close range; **B~ Wschód** the
Middle East

blisko *adv* **1** (*niedaleko*) close
2 (*niedługo*) near **3** (*prawie*) almost
▷ *prep* +*gen* close to, near (to)

bli|zna (**-zny, -zny**; *dat sg* & *loc sg*
-źnie) *f* scar

bliźniacz|ka (**-ki, -ki**; *dat sg* & *loc sg*
-ce; *gen pl* **-ek**) *f* twin (sister)

bliźnia|k (**-ka, -ki**; *inst sg* **-kiem**) *m*
1 (*bliźnię*) twin **2** (*szeregowiec: pot*)
semidetached house

Bliźnięta *pl* (*Astrol*) Gemini

bliżej *adv comp od* **blisko**

bliższy *adj comp od* **bliski**;
(*sprecyzowany*) specific

blo|k (**-ku, -ki**; *inst sg* **-kiem**)
m **1** (*kształt*) block **2** (*budynek
mieszkalny*) block of flats (*Brit*),
apartment house (*US*) **3** (*notatnik*)
writing pad **4** (*partyjny*) bloc
5 (*startowy*) (starting) block

blond *adj*: **włosy ~** blonde hair

blondy|n (**-na, -ni**; *loc sg* **-nie**) *m*

blond, blonde (*esp Brit*)

blondyn|ka (**-ki**, **-ki**; *dat sg & loc sg* **-ce**; *dat pl* **-ek**) *f* blonde

blu|za (**-zy**, **-zy**; *dat sg & loc sg* **-zie**) *f* (*dresowa*) sweatshirt

bluz|ka (**-ki**, **-ki**; *dat sg & loc sg* **-ce**; *gen pl* **-ek**) *f* blouse

błą|d (**-ędu**, **-ędy**; *loc sg* **-ędzie**) *m* **1** (*omyłka*) mistake **2** (*usterka*) fault; **robić** (**zrobić** *pf*) **~ ortograficzny** to make a spelling mistake; **jesteś w błędzie** you are wrong; **nie popełniaj błędów** don't make any mistakes

błą|dzić (**-dzę**, **-dzisz**; *impf* **-dź**) *vi* **1** (*szukać celu*) to wander round in circles **2** (*wykonywać niewłaściwie*) to make a mistake

błękitny *adj* blue

bło|na (**-ny**, **-ny**; *dat sg & loc sg* **-nie**) *f* membrane; **~ śluzowa** mucous membrane; **~ dziewicza** hymen

bło|to (**-ta**, **-ta**; *loc sg* **-cie**) *nt* mud

błyskawic|a (**-y**, **-e**) *f* lightning; **informacje rozeszły się lotem błyskawicy** the news spread like wildfire

błyskawicznie *adv* **1** (*bardzo szybko*) in a flash **2** (*natychmiastowo*) instantly

bm. *abbr* (= **bieżącego miesiąca**) (of) the current month

bo *conj* **1** (*ponieważ*) because **2** (*w przeciwnym razie*) or (else); **pospiesz się, bo nie zdążysz** hurry up, or you'll be late

bochen|ek (**-ka**, **-ki**; *inst sg* **-kiem**) *m* loaf

bocian (**-na**, **-ny**; *loc sg* **-nie**) *m* stork; **on nadal wierzy w ~y** he still believes that the stork brings babies

- **BOCIANY**
-
- **Bocian biały** (the White Stork) is an integral part of the Polish landscape, particularly in the north-eastern part of the country. Every year Poland hosts approximately one quarter of the world's stork population. Numerous beliefs, traditions and proverbs are connected with the stork.

bocz|ek (**-ku**, **-ki**; *inst sg* **-kiem**) *m* bacon

boczny *adj* (*wejście*) side

bogaty *adj* **1** rich **2** (*majętny*) wealthy; **bogaci** *pl* the wealthy; **jego życie było bogate w wydarzenia** he led an eventful life

bohate|r (**-ra**, **-rowie** *lub* **-rzy**; *loc sg* **-rze**) *m* (*narodowy, powieści*) hero

bohater|ka (**-ki**, **-ki**; *dat sg & loc sg* **-ce**; *gen pl* **-ek**) *f* (*filmu*) heroine

bohaterski *adj* (*czyn*) heroic

bohaterst|wo (**-wa**; *loc sg* **-wie**) *nt* (*odwaga*) heroism

bois|ko (**-ka**, **-ka**; *inst sg* **-kiem**) *nt* sports field

bo|k (**-ku**, **-ki**; *inst sg* **-kiem**) *m* side; **sklep jest pod ~iem** the shop is nearby; **omijać ~iem** to sidestep; **odsunął się na ~** he moved aside; **cały wieczór zrywał ~i ze śmiechu** he split his sides laughing all evening; **przez całą noc przewracał się z ~u na**

~ he tossed and turned all night
bok|s (**-su**; *loc sg* **-sie**) *m*
(*pięściarstwo*) boxing
bokse|r (**-ra**; *loc sg* **-rze**) *m* **1** (*nom
pl* **-rzy**) (*pięściarz*) boxer **2** (*nom pl*
-ry) (*rasa psa*) boxer
bol|ec (**-ca**, **-ce**) *m* **1** (*Tech*) pin **2** (*z
gwintem*) bolt
bol|eć (**-i**) *vi* to hurt; **boli mnie
głowa** I've got a headache; **boli
mnie, że tak o nim myślisz** it
hurts me that you think of him
this way
bolesny *adj* **1** painful
2 (*uszkodzenie nogi, ręki*) sore
bom|ba (**-by**, **-by**; *dat sg & loc sg*
-bie) *f* (*ładunek wybuchowy*) bomb;
ale ~! (*pot*) sensational!
bombka (**-ki**, **-ki**; *dat sg & loc sg* **-ce**;
gen pl **-ek**) *f* (*na choince*) bauble
bombonier|ka (**-ki**, **-ki**; *dat sg & loc
sg* **-ce**; *gen pl* **-ek**) *f* chocolate box
bój *vb zob.* **bać się**
ból (**-u**, **-e**; *dat sg* **-owi**) *m* **1** (*nogi,
ręki, pleców*) pain **2** (*przen: kłopot*)
distress; **odczuwać ~ głowy** to
have a headache; **cierpieć na ~
zęba** to have toothache; **mieć
~ gardła** to have a sore throat;
skarżyć się na ~ brzucha to
complain of stomach ache
Bośni|a (**-i**) *f* Bosnia
br. *abbr* (= *bieżącego roku*) (of) the
current year
brać (**biorę**, **bierzesz**; *pf* **wziąć**)
vt **1** to take **2** (*pieniądze*) to get
3 (*prysznic*) to take **4** (*przykład*) to
follow; **~ (za~** *pf*) **się do czegoś**
to set about doing sth; **skąd się
bierze twój upór?** where does
your stubbornness come from?
bra|k¹ (**-ku**; *inst sg* **-kiem**) *m*

lack: **braki** *pl* (*usterki*) defects
brak² *inv*: **~ mi 300 złotych** I'm
short of 300 zloty; **ciągle ~ mi
mojej matki** I miss my mother; **~
mi słów** I'm lost for words
brak|ować (**-uje**) *vi* to lack; **Ewie
brakuje Adama** Ewa misses
Adam; **kogo dziś brakuje na
lekcji?** who is missing from
the class today?; **tylko tego
brakowało!** that's all we needed!
bra|ma (**-my**, **-my**; *dat sg & loc sg*
-mie) *f* gate(way)
bram|ka (**-ki**, **-ki**; *dat sg & loc sg*
-ce; *gen pl* **-ek**) *f* **1** (*drzwiczki*) gate
2 (*gol*) goal
bramkarz (**-a**, **-e**; *gen pl* **-y**) *m*
1 (*w piłkę nożną*) goalkeeper **2** (*w
nocnym lokalu*) bouncer
bra|t (**-ta**, **-cia**; *dat sg* **-tu**; *loc
sg* **-cie**; *gen pl* **-ci**; *dat pl* **-ciom**;
inst pl **-ćmi**; *loc pl* **-ciach**) *m*
1 brother **2** (*Rel*) friar; **~ przyrodni**
stepbrother, half-brother; **~ łata**
a very open and friendly person
bratane|k (**-ka**, **-kowie**; *inst sg*
-kiem) *m* nephew (*brother's son*)
bratanic|a (**-y**, **-e**) *f* niece
(*brother's daughter*)
bratow|a (**-ej**, **-e**) *f decl like adj*
sister-in-law
Brazyli|a (**-i**) *f* Brazil
brą|z (**-zu**, **-zy**; *loc sg* **-zie**) *m*
1 (*kolor*) brown **2** (*metal*) bronze
brązowy *adj* **1** brown **2** (*wykonany
z brązu*) bronze
br|ew (**-wi**, **-wi**; *gen pl* **-wi**)
f eyebrow; **marszczyć
(zmarszczyć** *pf*) **brwi** to
frown; **spoglądać (spojrzeć** *pf*)
spod brwi (na kogoś) to look
disapprovingly (at sb)

br|oda (-ody, -ody; *dat sg & loc sg* -odzie; *gen pl* -ód) *f* 1 (*dolna część twarzy*) chin 2 (*zarost na twarzy*) beard; **pluć sobie w brodę** to kick o.s.

brokuł|y (-ów) *pl* broccoli

bro|nić (-nię, -nisz; *imp* -ń; *pf* o-) *vt* +*gen* 1 to defend 2 (*ochraniać*) to guard 3 (*pf* za-) (*zakazywać*) to forbid; ~ się *vr* (*przed kimś, zarzutami*) to defend o.s.

bru|d (-du, -dy; *loc sg* -dzie) *m* dirt; **brudy** *pl* (*brudna bielizna*) dirty laundry

● **BRUDERSZAFT**
●
● **Bruderszaft**, also colloquially
● referred to as **brudzio**, is a
● kind of ceremonial move to
● first-name terms. Two people
● simultaneously raise their
● glasses in a toast, link arms
● and empty their glasses in
● one gulp. They then kiss each
● other on the cheeks and say
● their first names. From this
● moment on they can be on
● first name terms with each
● another.

brudno *adv*: **jest tu bardzo ~** it's very dirty here; **najpierw napisz to na ~** first write a rough version

brudny *adj* dirty, filthy

brunatny *adj* dark brown

brune|t (-ta, -ci; *loc sg* -cie) *m* dark-haired man

brunet|ka (-ki, -ki; *dat sg & loc sg* -ce; *gen pl* -ek) *f* brunette

Brytyjczy|k (-ka, -cy; *loc sg* -kiem) *m* Briton; **Brytyjczycy** *pl* the British

Brytyj|ka (-ki, -ki; *dat sg* -ce; *gen pl* -ek) *f* Briton

brytyjski *adj* British

brze|g (-gu, -gi; *inst sg* -giem) *m* 1 (*o rzece*) bank 2 (*o jeziorze*) shore 3 (*o morzu*) shore 4 (*krawędź*) brink 5 (*piaszczysty*) beach 6 (*szklanki*) brim 7 (*kant*) edge

brzoskwi|nia (-ni, -nie; *gen pl* -ń) *f* peach

brzuch (-a, -y) *m* stomach, belly (*pot*); **wiercić komuś dziurę w ~u** (*przen*) to pester sb

brzydki *adj* 1 (*nieestetyczny*) ugly 2 (*działanie*) dirty

brzydko *adv* 1 (*nieładnie*) ugly 2 (*rysować*) terribly 3 (*czynić*) meanly

budo|wa (-wy, -wy; *dat sg & loc sg* -wie) *f* 1 (*budowanie: kościół*) building 2 (*konstrukcja*) construction 3 (*kształt*) structure 4 (*fizjonomia*) build

bud|ować (-uję, -ujesz; *pf* z- *lub* wy-) *vt* 1 (*blok*) to build 2 (*maszynę*) to construct; **w przyszłym roku będziemy się ~** we will build next year

budowl|a (-i, -e; *gen pl* -i) *f* 1 (*dom, wieżowiec*) building 2 (*konstrukcja*) structure

budownict|wo (-wa; *loc sg* -wie) *nt* construction industry

budyn|ek (-ku, -ki; *inst sg* -kiem) *m* building

bud|zić (-dzę, -dzisz; *impf* -dź) *vt* (*pf* z- *lub* o-) 1 (*osobę*) to wake (up) 2 (*pf* wz-) (*strach*) to arouse; ~ się (*pf* o-) *vr* to wake (up); **efekty badań budzą nadzieję** the test results give reason to hope

budzi|k (**-ka, -ki**; *inst sg* **-kiem**) *m* alarm clock; **nastawiać** (**nastawić** *pf*) **~** to set an alarm clock

bufe|t (**-tu, -ty**; *loc sg* **-cie**) *m* buffet; **zimny ~** cold buffet

bukie|t (**-tu, -ty**; *loc sg* **-cie**) *m* bouquet

bulio|n (**-nu, -ny**; *loc sg* **-nie**) *m* consommé

Bułgari|a (**-i**) *f* Bulgaria

buł|ka (**-ki, -ki**; *dat sg & loc sg* **-ce**; *gen pl* **-ek**) *f* **1** roll **2** (*drożdżówka*) bun

bura|k (**-ka, -ki**; *inst sg* **-kiem**) *m* beet; **ale z niego ~!** (*przen: pej*) what a bumpkin!

burz|a (**-y, -e**) *f* (*Meteo*) (thunder)storm

burz|yć (**-ę, -ysz**; *pf* **z-**) *vt* **1** (*dom*) to demolish **2** (*spokój*) to destroy

bu|t (**-ta, -ty**; *loc sg* **-cie**) *m* **1** shoe **2** (*z cholewami*) boot; **no to umarł w ~ach!** (*pot*) it's too late; there's nothing more we can do

butel|ka (**-ki, -ki**; *dat sg & loc sg* **-ce**; *gen pl* **-ek**) *f* bottle

buti|k (**-ku, -ki**; *inst sg* **-kiem**) *m* boutique

bu|zia (**-zi, -zie**; *gen pl* **-zi** *lub* **-ź**) (*pot*) *f* **1** (*usta*) mouth **2** (*twarz*) face; **wycierać sobie kimś buzię** to mouth off about sb

być (**jestem, jesteś**; 1 *pl* **jesteśmy**; 2 *pl* **jesteście**; 3 *pl* **są**; *impf* **bądź**; *pt* **był, była, byli**; 1 *sg fut* **będę**; 2 *sg fut* **będziesz**) *vi* to be; **jestem!** here!; **jestem autobusem** I've come by bus; **jest chłodno** it's cold; **jest mi niedobrze** I feel sick; **będę krzyczeć** I'll scream; **ta książka była napisana w 1967** roku this book was written in 1967; **~ może** maybe

by|k (**-ka, -ki**; *inst sg* **-kiem**) *m* **1** bull **2** (*Astrologia*): **B~** Taurus; **tylko nie narób ~ów** (*pot: przen*) just don't make mistakes

były *adj* (*mąż,ambasador*) former

by|t (**-tu, -ty**; *loc sg* **-cie**) *m* **1** (*życie*) existence **2** (*istnienie*) being

bzdu|ra (**-ry, -ry**; *dat sg & loc sg* **-rze**) *f* nonsense; **pleść bzdury** to talk nonsense

C

ca|l (**-la**, **-le**; *gen pl* **-li**) *m* inch
całkiem *adv* **1** (*zupełnie*) entirely
2 (*dość*) quite; **jest ~ szalony**
he is completely crazy; **ciasto
jest ~ smaczne** the cake tastes
pretty good
całkowicie *adv* completely
całkowity *adj* **1** (*ciemność*)
total **2** (*wartość*) total **3** (*w
matematyce: liczba*) integer
całodobowy *adj* twenty-four-
hour; **sklep ~** twenty-four-hour
store
całodzienny *adj* all-day;
całodzienne wyżywienie full
board
całonocny *adj* all-night
cał|ować (**-uję**, **-ujesz**; *pf* **po-**) *vt*
to kiss: **~ się** *vr* to kiss
cały *adj* whole; **~ czas** all the

time; **~ tydzień** all week (long);
cała okolica the whole district;
cała nuta (*Muz*) semibreve (*Brit*),
whole note (*US*) **~mi godzinami**
for hours on end; **całą parą** full
steam ahead
cdn. *abbr* (= *ciąg dalszy nastąpi*) to
be continued
CD-ROM (**-u**, **-y**; *dat sg & loc sg* **-ie**)
m CD-ROM
cebu|la (**-li**, **-le**) *f* onion; **ubierać
(ubrać** *pf*) **się na cebulę** (*przen*)
to wear plenty of layers
ce|cha (**-chy**, **-chy**; *dat sg & loc
sg* **-sze**) *f* feature; **~ ujemna/
dodatnia** negative/positive
characteristic; **~ dziedziczna**
inherited characteristic
ce|gła (**-gły**, **-gły**; *dat sg & loc sg*
-gle; *gen pl* **-gieł**) *f* brick
cel (**-u**, **-e**) *m* **1** (*działania*) purpose
2 (*wyprawy*) destination **3** (*punkt
w środku tarczy*) target; **chybiać
(chybić** *pf*) **~u** to miss the
target; **osiągać (osiągnąć** *pf*)
~ to achieve one's objective; **~
uświęca środki** the end justifies
the means
ce|la (**-li**, **-le**) *f* cell
celni|k (**-ka**, **-cy**; *inst sg* **-kiem**) *m*
customs officer
celny *adj* **1** (*rzut*) accurate
2 (*udany, zręczny*) relevant **3** (*urząd
celny*) customs
cel|ować (**-uję**, **-ujesz**; *pf* **wy-**)
vi to take aim; **~ do kogoś z
pistoletu** to aim a pistol at sb
celowo *adv* (*umyślnie*) deliberately
ce|na (**-ny**, **-ny**; *dat sg & loc sg*
-nie) *f* (*hurtowa/detaliczna*)
price; **~ okazyjna/fabryczna/
sugerowana** bargain/factory/

recommended price

ce|nić (**-nię, -nisz**; *imp* **-ń**) *vt* (*poważać*) to value; **~ kogoś/coś** to appreciate sb/sth; **on się wysoko ceni** he thinks highly of himself

cenni|k (**-ka, -ki**; *inst sg* **-kiem**) *m* price list

cenny *adj* (*wartościowy*) valuable

centra|la (**-li, -le**; *gen pl* **-li** *lub* **-l**) *f* **1** (*telefoniczna*) (telephone) exchange **2** (*banku, firmy*) head office

centralny *adj* (*położony w środku*) central; **centralne ogrzewanie** central heating

centr|um (**-um, -a**; *gen pl* **-ów**) *nt inv in sg* (*środek*) centre (*Brit*), center (*US*); **~ miasta** town *lub* city centre (*Brit*), downtown (*US*); **~ handlowe** shopping centre (*Brit*), mall (*US*); **znajdować** (**znaleźć** *pf*) **się w ~ uwagi** to find o.s. the centre of attention

centymet|r (**-ra, -ry**; *loc sg* **-rze**) *m* **1** centimetre (*Brit*), centimeter (*US*) **2** (*centymetr: do mierzenia*) tape measure

cenzu|ra (**-ry**; *dat sg & loc sg* **-rze**) *f* censorship; **~ represyjna** repressive censorship

cer|kiew (**-kwi, -kwie**; *gen pl* **-kwi**) *f* Orthodox church

certyfika|t (**-tu, -ty**; *loc sg* **-cie**) *m* (*jakości, bezpieczeństwa*) certificate

cesarst|wo (**-wa, -wa**; *loc sg* **-wie**) *nt* empire

cesarz (**-a, -e**; *gen pl* **-y**) *m* emperor

cha|m (**-ma, -my**; *loc sg* **-mie**) *m* (*pot!*) lout; **robić** (**zrobić** *pf*) **coś na ~a** (*pot!*) to do sth in a

slapdash way

chamski *adj* (*pej: niekulturalny*) boorish

chaotyczny *adj* (*rozmowa, działanie*) chaotic

charakte|r (**-ru, -ry**; *loc sg* **-rze**) *m* **1** (*osoby*) character **2** (*rzeczy, zjawiska*) nature; **w ~ze** +*gen* in the capacity of; **człowiek z ~em/ bez ~u** a person of character/ of no character; **~ pisma** handwriting

charakterystyczny *adj*: **~** (**dla** +*gen*) typical (of)

charakterysty|ka (**-ki, -ki**; *dat sg & loc sg* **-ce**) *f* (*osoby, dzieła*) profile

chcieć (**chcę, chcesz**) *vt* to want

chciwy *adj* greedy

chemi|a (**-i**) *f* chemistry

chemiczny *adj* (*skład, analiza*) chemical

chemi|k (**-ka, -cy**; *inst sg* **-kiem**) *m* **1** (*specjalista*) chemist **2** (*Szkol*) chemistry teacher

chę|ć (**-ci, -ci**) *f* desire; **~ do działania** a desire to be active; **zrobię to z miłą chęcią** I'll be glad to do that

chętnie *adv* eagerly

chętny *adj* eager

Chile *nt inv* Chile

Chi|ny (**-n**) *pl* China

chiński *adj* Chinese; **Chińska Republika Ludowa** the People's Republic of China

chips|y (**-ów**) *pl* crisps (*Brit*), chips (*US*)

chirur|g (**-ga, -dzy**; *inst sg* **-giem**) *m* surgeon

chirurgi|a (**-i**) *f* surgery

chle|b (**-ba, -by**; *loc sg* **-bie**) *m* bread; **przeciętny zjadacz ~a**

(*przen*) the average person
chłodno *adv* (*traktować kogoś*)
coolly; **dziś było ~** it was chilly
today; **nagle zrobiło się ~** it got
cold all of a sudden
chłodny *adj* cool
chłopa|k (**-ka, -cy**; *inst sg* **-kiem**)
m **1** boy **2** (*sympatia*) boyfriend
chło|piec (**-pca, -pcy**; *dat sg & loc
sg* **-pcu**) *m* **1** boy **2** (*narzeczony*)
boyfriend; **~ do bicia** (*przen*)
whipping boy
chmu|ra (**-ry, -ry**; *dat sg & loc sg*
-rze) *f* cloud; **drapacz chmur**
skyscraper
chmurz|yć się (**-ę, -ysz**; *pf* **za-**)
vr **1** (*marszczyć czoło*) to frown **2** to
cloud over
choć *conj* = **chociaż**
chociaż *conj* though, although
cho|dzić (*imp* **-dź**) *vi*
1 (*spacerować*) to walk
2 (*uczęszczać*) to go **3** (*działać*)
to work; **chodzić z kimś** (*pot*)
to go out with sb; **chodźmy do
kina** let's go to the cinema; **o co
chodzi?** what's the problem?;
chodzi o to, że... the thing is...

- **CHODZIĆ/IŚĆ/PÓJŚĆ**
-
- **Chodzić, iść** and **pójść** are
- all verbs of motion meaning
- to go (on foot), but they have
- different implications. With
- the perfective verb – **pójść**
- – the emphasis is on the act
- of going to and arriving at
- the destination, whereas
- with the imperfective verbs
- – **chodzić** and **iść** – the focus
- is more on the act of going

- itself and it is not made
- clear whether the subject
- arrives at the destination or
- not. **Chodzić** is also used to
- describe habitual activities
- and **iść** is used to describe
- going to or from a particular
- point on one occasion.

choin|ka (**-ki, -ki**; *dat sg & loc
sg* **-ce**; *gen pl* **-ek**) *f* **1** (*drzewo w
lesie*) spruce **2** (*drzewo iglaste z
bombkami*) Christmas tree
chole|ra (**-ry**; *dat sg & loc sg*
-rze) *f* **1** (*choroba*) cholera
2 (*wulgaryzm*): **~!** shit! (*pot!*); **do
jasnej cholery!** (*pot!*) for Christ's
sake! (*pot!*)
chomi|k (**-ka, -ki**; *inst sg* **-kiem**)
m hamster
chor|oba (**-oby, -oby**; *dat sg &
loc sg* **-obie**; *gen pl* **-ób**) *f* disease
(*słabość*) illness; **zamknięte z
powodu choroby** closed because
of illness
chor|ować (**-uję, -ujesz**) *vi* to
be ill, to be sick (*esp US*); **~ (za~
pf) obłożnie** to be confined to
bed; **~ (za~ pf) na anginę** to have
a throat infection; **~ (za~ pf) z
przepracowania** to make o.s. ill
from overwork
Chorwacj|a (**-i**) *f* Croatia
chory *adj* **1** (*osoba*) sick **2** (*obolały*)
sore **3** (*oko*) bad **4** (*zwierzę*) sick
▷ *m decl like adj* **1** (*człowiek który
się choruje*) sick person **2** (*pacjent*)
patient; **śmiertelnie/ciężko ~**
terminally/seriously ill
chow|ać (**-am, -asz**) *vt* **1** (*pf* **s-**)
(*kłaść*) to put (*somewhere*) **2** (*pf* **s-**)
(*odłożyć*) to put away **3** (*pf* **s-**) (*w

ukryciu) to hide **4** (*mieć: tajemnicę, sekret*) to keep **5** (*pf* **po-**) (*grzebać*) to bury; **~ się** (*pf* **s-**) *vr* (*ukryć się*) to hide

Chrystu|s (-sa; *loc sg* **-sie**) *m* Christ; **Jezus ~** Jesus Christ

chrz|est (-tu, -ty; *loc sg* **-cie**) *m* **1** (*nadanie imienia w kościele*) christening **2** (*statku*) naming ceremony

chrześcija|nin (-nina, -nie; *loc sg* **-ninie**) *m* Christian

chrześcijański *adj* Christian

chrześcijańst|wo (-wa; *loc sg* **-wie**) *nt* Christianity

chud|nąć (-nę, -niesz; *imp* **-nij**; *pf* **s-**) *vi* to slim down

chudy *adj* **1** (*o osobie*) thin **2** (*o mięsie*) lean; **~ jak patyk** as thin as a rake

chuliga|n (-na, -ni; *loc sg* **-nie**) *m* (*łobuz: pej*) yob

chustecz|ka (-ki, -ki; *dat sg & loc sg* **-ce**; *gen pl* **-ek**) *f* (*do nosa*) handkerchief; **~ higieniczna** tissue

chwa|lić (-lę, -lisz; *pf* **po-**) *vt* (*mówić z aprobatą o kimś*) to praise; **~ się** *vr*: **~ (po~ pf) się** (+*loc*) to brag (about); **nie chwaląc się jestem najlepszy** with all due modesty, I'm the best

chwi|la (-li, -le) *f* moment, instant; **poczekaj na mnie chwilę!** wait a moment!; **~mi pada** from time to time it rains; **co ~ budzi się** every now and then he wakes up; **lada ~ może przyjść** he could be here any moment; **za chwilę pójdę** I'll go in a minute

chwy|cić (-cę, -cisz; *imp* **-ć**) *vb pf*

od **chwytać**

chwyt|ać (-am, -asz) *vb* to catch, to capture

chyba *part* probably ▷ *conj*: **~ że** unless; **~ tak/~ nie** I think so/I don't think so

ci|ało (-ała, -ała; *loc sg* **-ele**) *nt* body; **przybierać (przybrać** *pf*) **na ciele** to put on weight

cia|sny *adj* **1** tight **2** (*pomieszczenie*) cramped

ciast|ko (-ka, -ka; *inst sg* **-kiem**; *gen pl* **-ek**) *nt* cake

ci|asto (-asta, -asta; *loc sg* **-eście**) *nt* **1** (*masa*) dough **2** (*wypiek z ciasta*) cake

ciąć (tnę, tniesz; *imp* **tnij**) *vt* (*narzędziem z ostrzem*) to cut

ciągle *adv* **1** (*wciąż, nadal*) still **2** (*nieprzerwanie*) all the time; **on ~ jeszcze choruje** he is still a sick man

ciąg|nąć (-nę, -niesz; *imp* **-nij**; *pf* **po-**) *vt* (*wlec*) **1** to pull **2** (*w loterii*) to draw ▷ *vi* (*kontynuować wypowiedź*) to continue; **~ się** *vr* **1** (*o brzegu, trasie*) to extend, to stretch **2** (*o rozmowie*) to drag on

cicho *adv* **1** quietly **2** (*bez głosu*) silently; **mówić ~** to speak quietly; **~ !** quiet!

cichy *adj* **1** (*ulica*) quiet **2** (*dźwięk*) low; **wszedł po cichu** he came in quietly

ciecz (-y, -e; *gen pl* **-y**) *f* liquid

ciekawost|ka (-ki, -ki; *dat sg & loc sg* **-ce**; *gen pl* **-ek**) *f* **1** (*osobliwość*) curiosity **2** (*przyrodnicza, historyczna*) interesting fact

ciekawoś|ć (-ci) *f* curiosity; **~ to pierwszy stopień do piekła** curiosity killed the cat

ciekawy adj 1 (zajmujący)
interesting 2 (wykazujący
zainteresowanie) curious
cielęci|na (-ny; dat sg & loc sg
-nie) f veal
ciem|no (-na; loc sg -nie) nt dark
▷ adv dark; **w ~** on spec; **iść**
(**pójść** pf) **na randkę w ~** to go
on a blind date; **robi się ~** it's
getting dark
ciemnoś|ć (-ci, -ci; dat sg & loc
sg -ci) f darkness; **egipskie
ciemności** pitch darkness
ciemny adj 1 (kolor) dark
2 (pomieszczenie) dark 3 (pieczywo)
brown 4 (nierozgarnięty) dim
cie|nki adj thin
cie|ń (-nia, -nie; gen pl -ni) m
1 (człowieka, domu) shadow
2 (miejsce osłonięte od słońca)
shade; **pozostawać** (**pozostać**
pf) **w cieniu** to remain in the
background; **~ do powiek**
eyeshadow
ciep|ło (-ła; loc sg -le) nt 1 warmth
2 (Fiz) heat ▷ adv: **było ~** it was
warm; **jest mi ~** I'm warm
ciepły adj warm; **ciepłe kluchy**
(pot) wimp
ciesz|yć (-ę, -ysz; pf u-) vt to
delight; **~ się** vr: **~ się** (**z** +gen)
to be pleased (with); **cieszę się
na twój widok** I look forward to
seeing you; **~ się powodzeniem**
to be popular
cię pron gen, acc sg od **ty**
cio|cia (-ci, -cie; gen pl -ć) f (pot)
auntie
ciota (pot!: pej) poofter (pot!)
ciot|ka (-ki, -ki; dat sg & loc sg -ce;
gen pl -ek) f aunt
cisz|a (-y) f silence; **~ przed**

burzą the calm before the storm
ciszej adv comp od **cicho**
ciśnie|nie (-nia, -nia; gen pl -ń) nt
pressure; **mierzyć** (**zmierzyć** pf)
komuś ~ krwi to take sb's blood
pressure
cm abbr (= centymetr) cm
cmentarz (-a, -e; gen pl -y) m
1 (komunalny, wojskowy) cemetery
2 (przykościelny) graveyard
c.o. abbr (= centralne ogrzewanie)
central heating

○ KEYWORD

co pron 1 (w pytaniu) what; **co to
jest?** what is that?; **co to za film?**
what film is this?
2 (w zdaniach względnych): **ten
samochód, co stoi przed
domem** the car that is parked in
front of the house; **mówił o tych,
co odeszli** he talked about those
who had left; **udało mu się, co
nas zaskoczyło** he managed it,
which surprised us
3 (w równoważnikach zdań): **rób,
co chcesz** do what you want; **nie
ma co narzekać** there's no use
complaining
4 (w zdaniach wykrzyknikowych): **co
za pomysł!** what a thought!
▷ part 1 (wzmacniająco): **co
najmniej** at least; **co najwyżej** at
the most; **co gorsza** what's worse;
co prawda as a matter of fact
2: **co drugi/trzeci raz** every
second/third; **nie ma za co**
you're welcome, don't mention it
3 (odnośnie do): **co do** +gen as for;
wszyscy co do jednego wyszli
to a man, they went out

codziennie *adv* every day

codzienny *adj* 1 (*spacer*) daily, everyday 2 (*gazeta*) daily 3 (*zajęcia*) everyday

cof|ać (**-am, -asz**; *pf* **-nąć**) *vt* 1: **~ swoje słowa** to take back one's words 2 (*pojazd*) to reverse 3 (*zegar*) to put back 4 (*wojska*) to withdraw; **~ się** *vr* 1 (*usuwać się w tył*) to draw back 2 (*ustępować*) to retreat, to pull back

coraz *adv*: **~ lepiej** better and better

coś *pron* 1 (*w zdaniach twierdzących*) something 2 (*w zdaniach pytajnych*) anything; **robić (zrobić** *pf*) **~ innego** to do something else; **~ ciekawego** something interesting; **~ do czytania** something to read

cór|ka (**-ki, -ki**; *dat sg & loc sg* **-ce**; *gen pl* **-ek**) *f* daughter

cuch|nąć (**-nę, -niesz**; *imp* **-nij**) *vi* to stink

cudowny *adj* 1 (*siła*) miraculous 2 (*pomysł, obraz*) wonderful

cudzozie|miec (**-mca, -mcy**) *m* (*obcokrajowiec*) foreigner

cudzoziem|ka (**-ki, -ki**; *dat sg & loc sg* **-ce**; *gen pl* **-ek**) *f* foreigner

cudzoziemski *adj* foreign; **~ akcent** a foreign accent

cudzy *adj* somebody else's

cu|kier (**-kru**; *loc sg* **-krze**) *m* (*puder, w kostkach*) sugar

cukier|ek (**-ka, -ki**; *inst sg* **-kiem**) *m* (*orzechowy, owocowy*) sweet (*Brit*), candy (*US*)

cukier|nia (**-ni, -nie**; *gen pl* **-ni** *lub* **-ń**) *f* pastry shop

cukrzyc|a (**-y**) *f* (*choroba*) diabetes

cyf|ra (**-ry, -ry**; *dat sg & loc sg* **-rze**) *f* figure; **cyfry arabskie/ rzymskie** Arabic/Roman numerals

Cyga|n (**-na, -nie**; *loc sg* **-nie**) *m* gypsy

Cygan|ka (**-ki, -ki**; *dat sg & loc sg* **-ce**; *gen pl* **-ek**) *f* gypsy

Cyp|r (**-ru**; *loc sg* **-rze**) *m* (*Geo*) Cyprus

cyr|k (**-ku, -ki**; *inst sg* **-kiem**) *m* circus; **urządzać (urządzić** *pf*) **~** (*pot*) to make a fuss

cytry|na (**-ny, -ny**; *dat sg & loc sg* **-nie**) *f* lemon; **herbatę z cytryną** tea with lemon

cywilizacj|a (**-i, -e**; *gen pl* **-i**) *f* civilization

cywilny *adj* 1 (*nie odnoszący się do wojska*) civil 2 (*strój niewojskowy*) ordinary; **stan ~** marital status; **ślub ~** civil marriage ceremony

czadowy *adj* (*pot*) funky

czajni|k (**-ka, -ki**; *inst sg* **-kiem**) *m* kettle

czap|ka (**-ki, -ki**; *dat sg & loc sg* **-ce**; *gen pl* **-ek**) *f* 1 hat 2 (*nakrycie głowy z daszkiem*) cap; **czapki z głów!** hats off!

czap|la (**-li, -le**; *gen pl* **-li**) *f* heron

czarny *adj* 1 (*barwa*) black 2 (*smutny: obraz, pogląd*) black; **czarna lista** blacklist; **podawać (podać** *pf*) **czarną polewkę** (*przen*) to discourage someone's advances; **~ rynek** black market; **czarna porzeczka** blackcurrant; **czarno na białym** (*przen*) in black and white

czarterowy *adj* (*lot, samolot*) charter

cza|s (**-su**; *loc sg* **-sie**) *m* 1 time

2 (nom pl **-sy**) (odcinek czasu) period **3** (nom pl **-sy**) (w językoznawstwie) tense; **dawne/dobre/złe ~y** old/good/bad/times; **zabijać** (**zabić** pf) **~** (przen) to kill time; **to tylko kwestia ~u** it's only a matter of time; **najwyższy ~** it is high time; **na ~** on time; **od ~u do ~u** from time to time

czasami adv sometimes

czasem adv (czasami) sometimes

czasopi|smo (**-sma, -sma**; loc sg **-śmie**) nt (dla dzieci, kobiet) periodical

czasowni|k (**-ka, -ki**; inst sg **-kiem**) m (w językoznawstwie) verb; **~ dokonany/niedokonany** perfective/imperfective verb; **~ przechodni/nieprzechodni** transitive/intransitive verb

czasowy adj **1** (tymczasowy) temporary **2** (odnoszący się do czasu) temporal

czasz|ka (**-ki, -ki**; dat sg & loc sg **-ce**; gen pl **-ek**) f skull

cza|t (**-tu**; dat sg & loc sg **-cie**) m (Komput) chat

czcion|ka (**-ki, -ki**; dat sg & loc sg **-ce**; gen pl **-ek**) f **1** (w drukarstwie) type **2** (w komputerze) font

Czech|y (**-**) pl the Czech Republic

czego pron gen od **co**

czegoś pron gen od **coś**

cze|k (**-ku, -ki**; inst sg **-kiem**) m cheque (Brit), check (US); **wypisywać** (**wypisać** pf) **~ na sumę 100 złotych** to write a cheque for 100 złotys; **płacić** (**zapłacić** pf) **~iem** to pay by cheque

czek|ać (**-am, -asz**) vi: **~ na** to wait for

czekola|da (**-dy, -dy**; dat sg & loc sg **-dzie**) f chocolate; **tabliczka czekolady** a bar of chocolate

czekolad|ka (**-ki, -ki**; dat sg & loc sg **-ce**; gen pl **-ek**) f (a)chocolate; **pudełko czekoladek** a box of chocolates

czekoladowy adj (cukierek, batonik) chocolate

czemu pron dat od **co**; **~?** (pot) how come?

czereś|nia (**-ni, -nie**; gen pl **-ni**) f **1** (owoc z drzewa) cherry **2** (drzewo) cherry tree

czerwiec (**-wca, -wce**) m June

czer|wony adj (barwa) red ▷ m decl like adj (pot, pej: komunista) Red; **~ jak burak** (przen) red as a beetroot; **~ Krzyż** Red Cross

cze|sać (**-szę, -szesz**; pf **u-**) vt **1** (siebie) to brush **2** (układać fryzurę) to style; **~ się** vr **1** (grzebieniem) to comb one's hair **2** (szczotką) to brush one's hair

czeski adj Czech; **Republika Czeska** the Czech Republic

czesn|e (**-ego**) nt decl like adj (Szkol, Uniw) tuition (fee)

cześć (**czci**) f (uznanie: książk) reverence ▷ inter: **~!** (pot: witaj!) hi!; (pot: do zobaczenia!) see you!; **człowiek bez czci i wiary** a total scoundrel; **przyjęcie na ~ kogoś/czegoś** a reception in honour (Brit) lub honor (US) of sb/sth

częś|ć (**-ci**) f (domu, urządzenia, ciała) part

czę|sto adv often, frequently

częsty adj common, frequent

człon|ek (**-ka**; *inst sg* **-kiem**)
m **1** (*nom pl* **-kowie**) (*partii,
stowarzyszenia*) member **2** (*nom
pl* **-ki**) (*ręka, noga*) limb **3** (*też:* **~
męski**) penis
człowie|k (**-ka, ludzie**; *inst sg*
-kiem; *gen pl* **ludzi**; *dat pl* **ludziom**;
inst pl **ludźmi**; *loc pl* **ludziach**)
m **1** human being **2** (*osoba płci
męskiej*) man **3** (*bezosobowo*): **~ nie
wie, co powiedzieć** one doesn't
know what to say; *zob. też* **ludzie**
cz|oło (**-oła, -oła**; *dat sg & loc sg*
-ołu; *loc sg* **-ole**; *gen pl* **-ół**) *nt*
1 forehead **2** (*loc sg* **-ele**) (*część
z przodu*) front; **puknij się w ~!**
(*pot: przen*) you're crazy!
czosn|ek (**-ku, -ki**; *inst sg* **-kiem**)
m garlic
czterdziest|ka (**-ki, -ki**; *dat sg &
loc sg* **-ce**; *gen pl* **-ek**) *f* forty; **ona
jest po czterdziestce** she is in
her forties
czterdziesty *num* fortieth; **~
pierwszy** forty-first
czterdzieści *num* forty
czternasty *num* fourteenth
czternaście *num* fourteen
cztery *num* four
czterysta *num* four hundred
czu|ć (**-ję, -jesz**; *pf* **po-**) *vt* **1** to feel
2 (*woń*) to smell; **~ się** *vr*: **~ się
dobrze/źle** to feel well/unwell;
czułem, że… I felt that…; **czuję,
jak…** I feel like…; **jak się dziś
czujesz?** how are you feeling
today?
czule *adv* (*witać, przytulać*)
affectionately
czu|ły *adj* **1** (*serdeczny*)
affectionate **2** (*wyczulony*): **~ (na)**
sensitive (to) **3** (*punkt, miejsce*)

sensitive; **to jego ~ punkt** that's
a sore point with him
czwartek (**-ku, -ki**; *inst sg* **-kiem**)
m Thursday; **Wielki C~** (*Rel*)
Maundy Thursday; **tłusty ~** the
last Thursday before Lent
czwarty *num* fourth; **spotkajmy
się o czwartej** let's meet at four;
jedna czwarta a quarter

○ **KEYWORD**

czy *part* **1** (*w pytaniach*): **czy znasz
tę dziewczynę?** do you know this
girl?; **czy byłeś kiedyś w Polsce?**
have you ever been to Poland?;
czy mogę wyjść? can I go?; **czy ja
wiem?** (*pot*) how would I know?
2 (*w zdaniach podrzędnych*) if,
whether; **nie wiem, czy to ma
sens** I don't know if this makes
sense; **zapytaj ją, czy go lubi** ask
her if she loves him
▷ *conj* or; **wódka czy piwo?**
vodka or beer?

czyj *pron* whose; **~ to dom?**
whose house is this?
czyli *part* (*zatem*) in other words;
**~ nie będziesz mógł dzisiaj
przyjść?** in other words you won't
be able to come today?
czynnoś|ć (**-ci, -ci**) *f* (*działalność*)
activity; **czynności** *pl* (*działanie w
urzędzie*) measures
czynny *adj* **1** active **2** (*urząd*) open
3 (*winda, toaleta*) working; **strona
czynna** the active (voice)
czynsz (**-u, -e**; *gen pl* **-ów**) *m* (*stała
opłata mieszkaniowa*) rent
czy|sto *adv* **1** (*bez brudu*) clean(ly)
2 (*wyraźnie*) clear(ly) **3** (*grać*) in

tune **4** (*wyłącznie*) purely; **sprawa ~ osobista** a purely personal matter

czysty *adj* **1** (*nie brudny*) clean **2** (*bez dodatków*) pure **3** (*pot: wariactwo*) sheer **4** (*pot: nie łamiący prawa*) clean; **mieć czyste sumienie** to have a clear conscience

czy|ścić (**-szczę, -ścisz**; *impf* **-ść**; *pf* **wy-**) *vt* to clean; **czyści mnie** (*pot: przen*) I've got diarrhoea (*Brit*) *lub* diarrhea (*US*)

czyt|ać (**-am, -asz**; *pf* **prze-**) *vt/vi* to read; **zawsze czyta od deski do deski** he reads everything from cover to cover

czytel|nia (**-ni, -nie**; *gen pl* **-ni**) *f* reading room

czytelni|k (**-ka, -cy**; *inst sg* **-kiem**) *m* reader

czytelny *adj* legible; **~ podpis** a legible signature

ćwicze|nie (**-nia, -nia**; *gen pl* **-ń**) *nt* **1** (*trening*) practice **2** (*w szkole, fizyczne*) exercise; **ćwiczenia** *pl* (*na uniwersytecie*) classes *pl*

ćwicz|yć (**-ę, -ysz**) *vt* **1** (*trenować*) to practise (*Brit*), to practice (*US*) **2** (*pf* **wy-**) (*kształcić: człowieka*) to train **3** (*pamięć, umysł*) to train **4** (*pf* **wy-**) to exercise ▷ *vi* **1** to practise (*Brit*), to practice (*US*) **2** (*wykonywać ćwiczenia fizyczne*) to exercise

d

dach (**-u, -y**) *m* (*budynku, samochodu*) roof

dać (**dam, dasz**; *3 pl* **dadzą**) *vt pf* *od* **dawać**

dalej *adv comp od* **daleko 1** (*w odległym miejscu*) farther **2** (*w przyszłości*) further; **i tak ~** and so forth

daleko *adv* far; **jak ~ jest stąd do kina?** how far is it from here to the cinema?

dalszy *adj comp od* **daleki 1** (*w odległym miejscu, w następnej kolejności*) farther **2** (*w przyszłości*) further; **dopełnienie dalsze** (*Jez*) indirect object; **ciąg ~ nastąpi** to be continued

da|ma (**-my, -my**; *dat & loc sg* **-mie**) *f* **1** (*kobieta*) lady **2** (*w grze w karty, w szachach*) queen

damski adj 1 (fryzjer) ladies';
(odzież) women's 2 (składający się z
kobiet) female
dan|e (-ych) pl (informacje) data
Dani|a (-i) f Denmark
da|nie (-nia, -nia; gen pl **-ń)** nt
1 (mięsne, jarskie) dish 2 (część
obiadu) course; **drugie ~** main
course
da|r (-ru, -ry; loc sg **-rze)** m
(prezent, zdolność) gift
darmowy adj (bezpłatny) free
da|ta (-ty, -ty; dat & loc sg **-cie)** f
(termin) date; **~ urodzenia** date
of birth
da|wać (-ję, -jesz; pf **dać)** vt
(prezent, pozwolenie, pracę) to
give; **~ (dać** pf) **komuś coś** to
give sb sth; **daj mi spokój** leave
me alone; **daj mi znać** let me
know; **to się da zrobić** it can
be done
dawk|ować (-uję, -ujesz) vt
to dose
dawno adv 1 (w odległych
czasach): **~ (temu)** long ago 2 (od
długiego czasu) for a long time; **już
~ jej nie widziałam** it's been a
long time since I saw her
dawny adj 1 (były, poprzedni)
former 2 (stary, zabytkowy)
ancient 3 (czasy, znajomy) old; **od
dawna** for a long time
db|ać (-am, -asz; pf **za~**)
pf) **o kogoś/coś** to look after
sb/sth; **nie ~ (impf) o coś** to be
unconcerned about sth
debiu|t (-tu, -ty; loc sg **-cie)** m
(aktorski, literacki) debut
decyd|ować (-uję, -ujesz) vi: **~
(o czymś)** (pf **z-**) (postanawiać
coś) to decide (on sth); (pf **za-**)

(mieć wpływ na coś) to determine
(sth); **~ się** (pf **z-**) vr 1 (dokonywać
wyboru) to make up one's mind
2 (rozstrzygać czyjś los) to be
determined; **~ (z~** pf) **się na coś**
to opt for sth
decyzj|a (-i, -e; gen pl, dat & loc
sg **-i)** f (postanowienie) decision;
podejmować (podjąć pf)
decyzję to make a decision
definicj|a (-i, -e; gen pl, dat & loc
sg **-i)** f (wyrażenia, znaczenia)
definition
deklar|ować (-uję, -ujesz; pf
za-) vt 1 (obwieszczać) to declare
2 (zobowiązywać się) to pledge;
~ się (pf **z-**) vr: **~ (z~** pf) **się za
czymś** to declare o.s. in favour
(Brit) lub favor (US) of sth; **~ (z~** pf)
się przeciw czemuś to declare
o.s. against sth
deklinacj|a (-i, -e; gen pl, dat & loc
sg **-i)** f (Jęz) declension
dekol|t (-tu, -ty; loc sg **-cie)** m 1 (w
bluzce) neckline 2 (niezasłonięte
piersi) cleavage; **koszulka z ~em**
low-cut top
dekoracj|a (-i, -e; gen pl, dat & loc
sg **-i)** f 1 (ozdoba) decoration 2 (w
teatrze lub filmie) scenery
delfi|n (-na, -ny; loc sg **-nie)** m
(Zool) dolphin
delikates|y (-ów) pl 1 (sklep
z jedzeniem) delicatessen sg
2 (wykwintne jedzenie) delicacies
delikatnie adv 1 (wrażliwie, z
taktem) gently 2 (nieintensywnie)
delicately
delikatny adj 1 (wrażliwy,
taktowny) gentle 2 (o drobnej
budowie) delicate 3 (nieintensywny,
przyjemny) soft 4 (o zapachu) mild

5 (*zdrowie*) delicate **6** (*drażliwy, wymagający ostrożności*) sensitive
demokracj|a (*-i, -e*; *gen pl, dat & loc sg* **-i**) *f* (*sposób rządzenia*) democracy
demon (*-a, -y*) *m* demon
demonstr|ować (*-uję, -ujesz*; *pf* **za-**) *vt* (*nowe produkty*) to demonstrate ▷ *vi* (*protestować*) to demonstrate
denerw|ować (*-uję, -ujesz*; *pf* **z-**) *vt* (*działać na nerwy*) to irritate, to annoy; **~ się** (*pf* **z-**) *vr* **1** (*być stale niespokojnym*) to be nervous **2** (*być rozdrażnionym w danej chwili*) to be irritated **3** (*martwić się*) to be anxious; **~ się czymś** to be nervous about sth; **on mnie denerwuje** he gets on my nerves
denerwujący *adj* (*irytujący*) irritating, annoying
denty|sta (*-sty, -ści*; *dat & loc sg* **-ście**) *m decl like f in sg* (*Med*) dentist
dentystyczny *adj* **1** (*o gabinecie, fotelu*) dentist's **2** (*o zabiegu*) dental
departamen|t (*-tu, -ty*; *loc sg* **-cie**) *m* (*w ministerstwie*) department
depozy|t (*-tu, -ty*; *loc sg* **-cie**) *m* (*w banku*) deposit
dep|tać (*-czę, -czesz*; *pf* **po-**) *vt* (*przygniatać, łamać*) to trample (on); **"nie ~ trawnika"** "keep off the grass"
dese|r (*-ru, -ry*; *loc sg* **-rze**) *m* (*Kulin*) dessert; **na ~ są lody** for dessert there is ice cream
des|ka (*-ki, -ki*; *dat & loc sg* **-ce**; *gen pl* **-ek**) *f* **1** (*gruba, do krojenia*) board **2** (*wąska, płaska*) plank

3 (*snowboardowa*) snowboard; **deski** *pl* (*pot: narty*) skis; **~ do prasowania** ironing board
deszcz (*-u, -e*) *m* **1** (*opady*) rain **2** (*duża ilość czegoś*) floods *pl*; **pada ulewny ~** it is pouring; **~ obelg** a torrent of abuse
deszczowy *adj* (*dzień, pogoda*) rainy
dezodoran|t (*-tu, -ty*; *loc sg* **-cie**) *m* (*higiena osobista*) deodorant; **~ w kulce** roll-on deodorant
diab|eł (*-ła, -ły* lub **-li**; *dat sg* **-łu**; *loc sg* **-le**) *m* (*szatan*) devil; **idź do diabła!** go to hell!
dialo|g (*-gu, -gi*; *inst sg* **-giem**) *m* (*konwersacja*) dialogue (*Brit*), dialog (*US*)
die|ta (*-ty, -ty*; *dat & loc sg* **-cie**) *f* (*styl odżywiania*) diet; **diety** *pl* (*pokrycie kosztów podróży służbowej*) expenses; **być na diecie** to be on a diet
dietetyczny *adj* **1** (*np. reżim*) dietary **2** (*potrawa*) diet **3** (*niskokaloryczny*) diet
disco *nt inv* (*muzyka*) disco
dla *prep* +*gen* **1** (*przeznaczenie, cel*) for **2** (*względem*) to; **ta wiadomość jest ~ ciebie** this message is for you; **była to ~ niego wielka niespodzianka** it was a big surprise for him; **przyjazny ~ środowiska** environmentally friendly; **~ przyjemności** for pleasure
dlaczego *adv, conj* why; **~ to zrobiłeś?** why did you do that?
dlatego *conj* **1** (*więc*) so, therefore **2** (*z tej przyczyny*) that's why; **było jej zimno, ~ założyła sweter** she was cold, so she put on a jumper;

pojechał taksówką, ~ że nie chciał się spóźnić he took a taxi because he didn't want to be late

dłu|g (**-gu**, **-gi**; *inst sg* **-giem**) *m* debt

dłu|gi *adj* (*film, lekcja, podróż*) long

dłu|go *adv* **1** (*trwać, rozmawiać*) long **2** (*iść, podróżować*) far; **jak ~ czekałeś?** how long did you wait?; **na jak ~ przyjechałeś do Anglii?** how long are you in Britain for?

długopi|s (**-su**, **-sy**; *loc sg* **-sie**) *m* ballpoint (pen)

długoś|ć (**-ci**, **-ci**; *gen pl, dat & loc sg* **-ci**) *f* (*odległość, czas trwania*) length; **~ geograficzna** longitude; **szlak spacerowy o długości sześciu kilometrów** a 6km route for walkers

dłużej *adv comp od* **długo**

dmuch|ać (**-am**, **-asz**; *pf* **-nąć**) *vi* (*na gorącą zupę*) to blow

dno (**dna**, **dna**; *loc sg* **dnie**; *gen pl* **den**) *nt* **1** (*butelki*) bottom **2** (*rzeki*) bed **3** (*przen: beznadziejnej jakości*) depths

○ KEYWORD

do *prep* +*gen* **1** (*w stronę*) to; **jadę do Polski** I'm going to Poland; **idę do teatru/pubu** I'm going to the theatre/the pub; **jadę do dziadka** I'm going to my granddad's (place); **chodźmy do domu** let's go home **2** (*do środka*) into; **do torby/ kieszeni/portfela** into a bag/ pocket/wallet; **wejść do biura** to walk into the office **3** (*do jakiegoś punktu, miejsca*) to;

odprowadź ją do samochodu see her to the car; **podejdź do okna** come up to the window **4** (*dopóki*) till, until; **zostanę do soboty** I'll stay until Saturday; **zrobię to do poniedziałku** I'll do it by Monday; **(w)pół do czwartej** half past three; **do jutra!** see you tomorrow!; **do widzenia/zobaczenia!** see you! **5** (*o górnej granicy czegoś*) up to; **czas oczekiwania wynosi do 2 tygodni** the waiting time is up to 2 weeks **6** (*dla wyrażenia przeznaczenia*): **do czego to jest?** what is it for?; **płyn do mycia naczyń** washing-up liquid; **pasta do zębów** toothpaste; **coś do czytania** something to read

doba (**doby**, **doby**; *dat & loc sg* **dobie**; *gen pl* **dób**) *f* **1** (*24 godziny*) day (and night) **2** (*przen: okres, era*) age; **(przez) całą dobę** day and night

dobranoc *inv*: **~!** good night!

dob|ro (**-ra**, **-ra**; *loc sg* **-ru**; *gen pl* **dóbr**) *nt* (*wartość, pożytek*) good; **dobra** *pl* **1** (*o towarach*) goods *pl* **2** (*o majątku*) property *sg*

dobroczynnoś|ć (**-ci**) *f* (*niesienie pomocy*) charity

dobry *adj* **1** (*prawidłowy, moralny, smaczny, grzeczny*) good **2** (*życzliwy*) kind ▷ *m decl like adj* **1** (*w szkole: ocena*) ≈ B **2** (*w uniwersytecie*) ≈ 2:1; **on jest ~ z fizyki** he's good at physics; **~ wieczór!** good evening!; **dobra!** (*pot*) OK!

dobrze *adv* well; **~ się bawić**

to have a good time; **~!** OK!; **~
znany** well-known
dobyt|ek (-ku; *inst sg* **-kiem**) *m*
(*człowieka*) belongings *pl*
dochodze|nie (-nia, -nia; *gen pl*
-ń) *nt* (*policyjny*) investigation
doch|ód (-odu, -ody; *loc sg* **-odzie**)
m **1** (*pensja*) income **2** (*państwa z
podatków*) revenue
dod|ać (-am, -asz; *imp* **-aj**) *vb pf
od* **dodawać**
dodat|ek (-ku, -ki; *inst sg* **-kiem**)
m **1** (*w gazecie*) supplement **2** (*do
pensji*) bonus **3** (*Kulin*) additive;
na ~ *lub* **w dodatku** as well
dodatkowy *adj* **1** (*informacja,
praca, połączenie*) additional
2 (*opłata*) extra
dodawać (-ję, -jesz; *pf* **dodać**) *vt*
(*nadziei*) to add
doj|azd (-azdu, -azdy; *loc sg*
-eździe) *m* **1** (*droga prowadząca
do garażu itp.*) access **2** (*podróż do
pracy*) commute
dojrza|ły *adj* **1** (*o osobie, alkoholu,
decyzji*) mature **2** (*o zbożu, owocu*)
ripe **3** (*o serze*) mature
dojrz|eć (-eję, -ejesz) *vb pf od*
dojrzewać
dojrzew|ać (-am, -asz; *pf*
dojrzeć) *vi* **1** (*o osobie, alkoholu,
zamierzeniach, uczuciach*) to
mature **2** (*do zbiorów*) to ripen
3 (*Kulin*) to mature
dojrzewani|e (-a) *nt* (*stawanie się
dorosłym*) adolescence; **~ płciowe**
puberty
dokąd *pron* where (to); **nie
wiem, ~ poszedł** I don't know
where he went; **nie miał ~
pojechać** he had nowhere to go
dokład|ka (-ki, -ki; *dat & loc sg* **-ce;**

gen pl **-ek**) *f* (*pot: obiadu, deseru*)
seconds *pl*
dokładnie *adv* (*precyzyjnie*)
precisely
dokładny *adj* **1** accurate **2** (*o
czasie*) exact **3** (*osoba*) meticulous
dokoła *adv* (*ze wszystkich stron*)
(all) (a)round ▷ *prep* +*gen* (*wokół*)
(a)round
dokon|ać (-am, -asz) *vb pf od*
dokonywać
dokon|ywać (-uję, -ujesz; *pf* **-ać**)
vt +*gen* **1** (*zrobić*) to accomplish
2 (*zbrodni*) to commit; **~ się** *vr*
(*mieć miejsce*) to take place; **~
(dokonać** *pf*) **cudów** to work
wonders
dokto|r (-ra, -rzy; *loc sg* **-rze**) *m*
(*lekarz*) doctor
doktora|t (-tu, -ty; *loc sg* **-cie**) *m*
1 (*stopień naukowy*) doctorate, PhD
2 (*dysertacja*) doctoral thesis
doktorski *adj*: **praca doktorska**
doctoral thesis
dokumen|t (-tu, -ty; *loc sg*
-cie) *m* (*urzędowy, komputerowy*)
document; **dokumenty** *pl*
(*dowód potwierdzający tożsamość*)
means *sg* of identification
dola|r (-ra, -ry; *loc sg* **-rze**) *m*
(*waluta*) dollar
doli|na (-ny, -ny; *dat & loc sg* **-nie**)
f (*Geo*) valley
dolny *adj* **1** (*część ciała*) lower
2 (*szuflada, półka*) bottom
3 (*granica wieku*) minimum
dom (-u, -y) *m* **1** (*o budynku*) house
2 (*o mieszkaniu, rodzinie*) home
3 (*o gospodarstwie domowym*)
household; **~ studencki** hall of
residence (*Brit*), dormitory (*US*);
w ~u at home; **iść (pójść** *pf*) **do**

~u to go home

dom|ek (-ku, -ki; *inst sg* **-kiem**) *m zob.* **dom**

domofo|n (-nu, -ny; *loc sg* **-nie**) *m* (*urządzenie przy drzwiach wejściowych*) intercom

domowy *adj* 1 (*dotyczący domu*) home 2 (*zrobiony w domu*) homemade 3 (*o zwierzętach*) domestic; **praca domowa** homework

domyśl|ać się (-am, -asz; *pf* **-ić**) *vr* +*gen* to guess

donicz|ka (-ki, -ki; *dat & loc sg* **-ce**; *gen pl* **-ek**) *f* (*do kwiatów*) flowerpot

dookoła *adv, prep* = **dokoła**

dopełniacz (-a, -e; *gen pl* **-y**) *m* (*przypadek gramatyczny*) genitive

dopełnie|nie (-nia, -nia; *gen pl* **-ń**) *nt* (*część zdania*) object; **~ dalsze/bliższe** indirect/direct object

dorosły *adj* 1 (*osoba, zwierzę*) adult ▷ *m decl like adj* (*dorosła osoba*) adult; **dorośli** *pl* adults *pl*

dorsz (-a, -e; *gen pl* **-y**) *m* (*ryba*) cod

doskonale *adv* (*wspaniale*) perfectly; **~!** (*pot*) outstanding!

doskonal|ić (-ę, -isz; *pf* **u-**) *vt* (*umiejętności, technikę*) to improve; **~ się** (*pf* **u-**) *vr*: **~ (u~** *pf*) **się (w czymś**) (*śpiewie, sporcie, nauce*) to improve (in sth)

doskonały *adj* 1 (*perfekcyjny*) perfect 2 (*wspaniały*) splendid 3 (*zupełny*) absolute

dosłownie *adv* 1 (*w dosłownym znaczeniu*) literally 2 (*przetłumaczyć, zacytować*) word for word

dosłowny *adj* (*znaczenie, cytat*) literal

dosta|ć (-nę, -niesz; *imp* **-ń**) *vb pf*

od dostawać

dostarcz|ać (-am, -asz; *pf* **-yć**) *vt* (*przynosić, przywozić*) to deliver; **~ komuś czegoś** to provide sb with sth; **~ (dostarczyć** *pf*) **coś komuś** to deliver sth to sb

dosta|wa (-wy, -wy; *dat & loc sg* **-wie**) *f* 1 (*towaru, listu*) delivery 2 (*prądu, gazu*) supply 3 (*dostarczone towary*) supplies *pl*

dost|awać (-aję, -ajesz; *imp* **-awaj**; *pf* **-ać**) *vt* 1 (*list, nagrodę, awans*) to get 2 (*zawału*) to have ▷ *vi* (*być bitym*) to get beaten up; **~ się** *vr*: **~ (dostać** *pf*) **się do niewoli** to be taken prisoner; **~ (dostać** *pf*) **się na studia** to be accepted for university; **dostać** (*pf*) **się w czyjeś ręce** to fall into sb's hands

dostosow|ywać (-uję, -ujesz; *pf* **-ać**) *vt*: **~ coś do czegoś** to adjust sth to sth; **~ się** *vr*: **~ się do** +*gen* (*do potrzeb, sytuacji*) to adjust to; (*do reguł, zasad*) to conform to

dosyć, dość *adv* 1 (*dostatecznie dużo*) enough 2 (*całkiem*) fairly 3 (*raczej*) rather; **mam tego ~!** I've had enough!; **~ długi** long enough; **mieć ~ czegoś** to be fed up with sth

doświadczony *adj* (*alpinista*) experienced

dotąd *adv* 1 (*do danego miejsca: niedaleko*) this far 2 (*do dalszego miejsca*) that far 3 (*do tej pory, dotychczas*) so far

dotk|nąć (-nę, -niesz; *imp* **-nij**) *vb pf od* **dotykać**

dotyk|ać (-am, -asz; *pf* **dotknąć**) *vt* +*gen* 1 (*mieć punkt styczny*) to touch 2 (*palcem, ręką*) to feel

3 (*dosięgać: nogami pedałów*) to reach **4** (*kwestii*) to touch on **5** (*o pechu, dolegliwości*) to afflict

dowci|p (-**pu**, -**py**; *loc sg* -**pie**) *m* **1** (*śmieszna historia*) joke **2** (*bystrość umysłu*) wit

dow|odzić (-**odzę**, -**odzisz**; *imp* -**ódź**; *pf* **dowieść**) *vt* +*gen* **1** (*podawać dowody*) to establish **2** (*wykazywać np. prawdziwość czegoś*) to establish **3** (*stanowić dowód czegoś*) to prove ▷ *vi* (*argumentować*) to argue

dowolny *adj* **1** (*którykolwiek*) any **2** (*fakultatywny*) discretionary **3** (*tłumaczenie, styl sportowy*) free

dow|ód (-**odu**, -**ody**; *loc sg* -**odzie**) *m* **1** (*okoliczność lub rzecz potwierdzająca coś*) evidence **2** (*wdzięczności, szacunku, przyjaźni*) token **3** (*Mat*) proof **4** (*wpłaty, odbioru*) receipt; **~ osobisty** form of identification

⊙ DOWÓD OSOBISTY

⊙
⊙ **Dowód osobisty** is a
⊙ mandatory identity card.
⊙ It contains basic personal
⊙ details, including your
⊙ permanent address. It is
⊙ a plastic card the size of a
⊙ business card.

dowódc|a (-**y**, -**y**) *m decl like f in sg* (*Wojsk*) commander

dozorc|a (-**y**, -**y**) *m decl like f in sg* **1** (*osoba utrzymująca porządek w budynku*) caretaker (*Brit*), janitor **2** (*osoba pilnująca kogoś lub czegoś*) guard

dół (**dołu**, **doły**; *loc sg* **dole**) *m*

1 (*zagłębienie w ziemi*) pit **2** (*dolna część*) bottom **3** (*w budynku, domu*) downstairs; **iść** (**zejść** *pf*) **na ~** to go downstairs; **na dole** at the bottom

dr *abbr* = **doktor**

drabi|na (-**ny**, -**ny**; *dat & loc sg* -**nie**) *f* **1** (*duża, ze szczeblami*) ladder **2** (*mała, ze stopniami*) stepladder

drama|t (-**tu**, -**ty**; *loc sg* -**cie**) *m* **1** (*Lit*) drama **2** (*nieszczęście*) tragedy

dra|pać (-**pię**, -**piesz**) *vt* (*pf* **po-**) (*paznokciami, narzędziami*) to scratch ▷ *vi* **1** (*o kurzu*) to be an irritant **2** (*o swetrze itp.*) to be itchy; **~ się** (*pf* **po-**) *vr* (*skrobać się*) to scratch (o.s.)

draż|nić (-**nię**, -**nisz**; *imp* -**nij**) *vt* **1** (*o kurzu, dymie*) to irritate **2** (*wywoływać negatywne emocje*) to annoy; **~ się** *vr*: **~ się z kimś** to tease sb

dre|s (-**su**, -**sy**; *loc sg* -**sie**) *m* (*strój sportowy*) tracksuit

dreszcz (-**u**, -**e**; *gen pl* -**y**) *m* (*z zimna, ze strachu*) shiver; **mieć ~e** to be shivering

drewniany *adj* wooden; **instrumenty drewniane** (*Muz*) woodwind instruments

dre|wno (-**wna**, -**wna**; *loc sg* -**wnie**; *gen pl* -**wien**) *nt* **1** (*surowiec*) wood **2** (*polano*) piece of wood

dręcz|yć (-**ę**, -**ysz**) *vt* (*o wyrzutach sumienia, pytaniu*) to torment

drin|k (-**ka**, -**ki**; *inst sg* -**kiem**) *m* (*pot: napój alkoholowy*) drink

drobiaz|g (-**gu**, -**gi**; *inst sg* -**giem**) *m* **1** (*mały przedmiot*) knick-knack **2** (*nieistotna sprawa*) trifle

drobiazgowy *adj* (*analiza, osoba*)

meticulous

drobny adj 1 (*o małych rozmiarach*) small 2 (*mało ważny*) petty 3 (*delikatny*) slight 4 (*piasek, sól*) fine

dr|oga (**-ogi, -ogi**; *dat & loc sg* **-odze**; *gen pl* **-óg**) f 1 (*ulica*) road 2 (*szlak komunikacyjny*) route 3 (*kierunek podróży*) way 4 (*podróż, wędrówka*) journey 5 (*długość trasy między dwoma punktami*) distance 6 (*metoda działania*) way; **drogą lądową/morską** by land/sea; **swoją drogą...** still,...; **po drodze** on the way

drogeri|a (**-i, -e**; *gen pl, dat & loc sg* **-i**) f (*sklep*) ≈ chemist's (*Brit*), ≈ drugstore (*US*)

dro|gi adj 1 (*o wysokiej cenie*) expensive 2 (*bliski uczuciowo*) dear

dro|go adv 1 (*sprzedawać*) at a high price 2 (*płacić za coś*) a lot

drogocenny adj valuable

drogowy adj (*prace, znaki*) road; **kodeks ~** ≈ Highway Code (*Brit*); **wypadek ~** traffic accident

drożdżów|ka (**-ki, -ki**; *dat & loc sg* **-ce**; *gen pl* **-ek**) f (*słodka bułka*) sweet bun

dr|ób (**-obiu**) m (*Kulin*) poultry

drugi num *decl like adj* 1 (*po pierwszym*) second 2 (*strona, koniec itp.*) the other; **z ~ej strony...** on the other hand...; **druga klasa** (*kolejowa*) second class; (*Szkol*) second year of primary school (*Brit*), second grade (*US*); **~ maja** the second of May; **po ~e,...** second(ly),...; **druga wojna światowa** the Second World War; **~e śniadanie** (*o posiłku*) midmorning snack; (*kanapki*) packed lunch (*Brit*), box *lub* bag

lunch (*US*); **~ od góry** second from the top; **co ~ dzień** every other day; **jest godzina druga** it's two (o'clock)

dru|k (**-ku**; *inst sg* **-kiem**) m 1 (*proces*) printing 2 (*czcionka*) type 3 (*odbitka*) print 4 (*formularz*) form; **druki** pl (*materiały drukowane*) printed matter *sg*

drukar|ka (**-ki, -ki**; *dat & loc sg* **-ce**; *gen pl* **-ek**) f (*Tech: Komput*) printer

druk|ować (**-uję, -ujesz**; *pf* **wy-**) vt 1 (*document z komputera*) to print 2 (*gazety, książki*) to publish

drukowany adj (*tekst, informator*) printed; **pisać ~mi literami** to print

dru|t (**-tu, -ty**; *loc sg* **-cie**) m 1 (*pręt, przewód*) wire 2 (*do robienia swetrów*) knitting needle; **robić szalik na ~ach** to knit a scarf

druży|na (**-ny, -ny**; *dat & loc sg* **-nie**) f 1 (*sportowa*) team 2 (*w wojsku*) squad; **~ harcerska** scout troop

dr|wić (**-wię, -wisz**; *imp* **-wij**; *pf* **za-**) vi: **~ (z** +*gen*) (*śmiać się z kogoś*) to sneer (at)

drzem|ka (**-ki, -ki**; *dat & loc sg* **-ce**; *gen pl* **-ek**) f (*krótki sen*) nap

drze|wo (**-wa, -wa**; *loc sg* **-wie**) nt 1 (*Bot*) tree 2 (*materiał budowlany*) wood 3 (*na opał*) firewood

drzwi (**-**) pl (*wejściowe, do pokoju*) door

duch (**-a, -y**) m 1 (*nastrój, usposobienie, odwaga*) spirit 2 (*bezcielesna istota*) ghost; **w ~u** inwardly

du|ma (**-my**; *dat & loc sg* **-mie**) f (*poczucie zadowolenia, godności*) pride

dumny adj: ~ **(z** +gen) (zadowolony,
z poczuciem godności) proud (of)
du|pa (-py, -py; dat & loc sg **-pie)**
f **1** (pot!: pośladki: pośladki) arse
(Brit), ass (US) **2** (pot!: niezaradna
osoba) arsehole (Brit), asshole (US)
3 (pot!: atrakcyjna młoda kobieta) a
nice piece of stuff
duszność|ć (-ci, -ci) f (brak
powietrza) shortness of breath;
mieć duszności to be short of
breath
duszny adj (bez powietrza)
oppressive
dużo pron (osób, książek) a lot ▷ adv
(coś robić) a lot; ~ +gen a lot of
duży adj **1** (dom, samochód, zysk)
big **2** (niezwykły, poważny) great
3 (dorosła osoba) grown-up
4 (szansa) good; **duże litery**
capital letters; ~ **palec** (u ręki)
thumb; (u nogi) big toe
DVD nt inv DVD; **odtwarzacz** ~
DVD player
dwa m/nt num two; ~ **kwiaty/
lewy/krzesła** two flowers/lions/
chairs; **co** ~ **dni/miesiące/lata**
every other day/month/year; ~
razy twice
dwadzieścia num decl like adj
twenty
dwaj num zob. **dwa**
dwanaście num decl like adj
twelve
dwie f num decl like adj two; ~
dziewczyny/butelki/gazety
two girls/bottles/newspapers
dwieście num decl like adj two
hundred
dwo|rzec (-rca, -rce) m
(miejsce przyjazdu i odjazdu
środków transportu) station; ~

autobusowy bus station; ~
kolejowy railway (Brit) lub
railroad (US) station; ~ **centralny**
central station
dwóch num zob. **dwa**
dw|ór (-oru, -ory; loc sg **-orze)** m
1 (przy zamku królewskim) court
2 (duży dom, majątek ziemski)
manor **3** (teren na zewnątrz domu)
outside; **wyjść na** ~ to go outside
dwudziest|ka (-ki, -ki; dat & loc sg
-ce; gen pl **-ek)** f twenty
dwudziestoletni adj **1** (plan,
wojna) twenty-year **2** (chłopak,
dziewczyna) twenty-year-old
dwudziesty num decl like adj
twentieth
dwujęzyczny adj (słownik, osoba)
bilingual
dwunast|ka (-ki, -ki; dat & loc sg
-ce; gen pl **-ek)** f twelve
dwunasty num decl like adj
twelfth; **o dwunastej** (godzinie)
at twelve (o'clock); **jest
dwunasta** (godzina) it's twelve
(o'clock)
dwuosobowy adj **1** (dla dwóch
osób) double **2** (składający się z
dwóch osób) two-person
dwupokojowy adj (mieszkanie)
two-room
dwuznaczny adj **1** (mający
dwa możliwe wytłumaczenia)
ambiguous **2** (z ukrytą aluzją)
suggestive
dy|cha (-chy, -chy; dat & loc sg
-sze) f (banknot: pot) tenner
dykt|ować (-uję, -ujesz; pf **po-)**
vt to dictate
dy|m (-mu, -my; loc sg **-mie)** m (z
papierosa) smoke
dynamiczny adj (żywiołowy,

prężny) dynamic

dynasti|a (-i, -e; *gen pl, dat & loc sg* **-i)** *f (ród)* dynasty

dyplo|m (-mu, -my; *loc sg* **-mie)** *m (dokument)* diploma

dyr. *abbr (=dyrektor)* Mgr *(=manager)*

dyrekcj|a (-i, -e; *gen pl* **-i)** *f (zarządzenia)* management

dyrekto|r (-ra, -rzy *lub* **-rowie**; *loc sg* **-rze)** *m* **1** *(zakładu pracy)* manager **2** *(Szkol)* head teacher *(Brit)*, principal *(US)*

dyskiet|ka (-ki, -ki; *dat & loc sg* **-ce**; *gen pl* **-ek)** *f (Komput)* (floppy) disk

dyskot|eka (-eki, -eki; *dat & loc sg* **-ece**; *gen pl* **-ek)** *f (zabawa)* disco(theque)

dyskusj|a (-i, -e; *gen pl, dat & loc sg* **-i)** *f*: **~ o** +*loc (omówienie, rozmowa)* discussion about

dyskut|ować (-uję, -ujesz; *pf* **prze-)** *vt*: **~ nad** *lub* **o czymś** *(omawiać, rozmawiać)* to discuss sth ▷ *vi (prowadzić debatę)* to debate

dyskwalifik|ować (-uję, -ujesz; *pf* **z-)** *vt (zawodnika)* to disqualify

dyspon|ować (-uję, -ujesz; *imp* **-uj**; *pf* **za-)** *vt*: **~ czasem** to have time on one's hands; **~ gotówką** to have spare cash

dywa|n (-nu, -ny; *loc sg* **-nie)** *m (tkanina na podłodze)* carpet

dyżu|r (-ru, -ry; *loc sg* **-rze)** *m (lekarza)* surgery hours *pl*; **być na ~ze** *(strażak)* to be on call

dyżurny *adj* **1** *(pracownik pełniący dyżur)* on duty **2** *(często używany np. argument)* tried-and-tested

dzban|ek (-ka, -ki; *inst sg* **-kiem)** *m (naczynie)* jug *(Brit)*, pitcher

(US); **~ do kawy** coffee pot; **~ do herbaty** teapot; **~ do wody** water jug

dziać się (dzieje) *vr (wydarzać się)* to happen; **co tam się dzieje?** what's going on there?; **co się z nim dzieje?** what's the matter with him?

dziad|ek (-ka, -kowie; *inst sg* **-kiem)** *m* **1** *(krewny)* grandfather **2** *(starszy mężczyzna)* old man **3** *(brakujący gracz do brydża itp.)* dummy; **dziadkowie** *pl* grandparents *pl*; **~ do orzechów** nutcracker

dział|ać (-am, -asz) *vt (robić coś)* to bring about ▷ *vi* **1** *(w czyimś imieniu, w jakiejś sprawie)* to act **2** *(o lekach)* to have an effect **3** *(o prawie, regułach)* to operate **4** *(o urządzeniach)* to work; **~ cuda** to work wonders

działalnoś|ć (-ci) *f (działanie, zajęcie)* activity

działa|nie (-nia, -nia; *gen pl* **-ń)** *nt* **1** *(podjęte kroki)* action **2** *(urządzeń, maszyn itp.)* operation **3** *(leków itp.)* effect **4** *(zadanie matematyczne)* operation

dział|ka (-ki, -ki; *dat sg* **-ce**; *gen pl* **-ek)** *f* **1** *(parcela pod ogródek)* plot **2** *(ogródek warzywny)* allotment **3** *(dom)* holiday cottage *(in the country)* **4** *(pot: zakres obowiązków)* department **5** *(pot: porcja narkotyków)* fix **6** *(pot: udział w zysku)* cut

dzieci *n pl* = **dziecko**

dziecięcy *adj* **1** *(przeznaczony dla dzieci)* children's **2** *(śmiech)* child's **3** *(zachowujący się jak dziecko)* childish

dziecinny adj 1 (przeznaczony dla dziecka) child's 2 (zachowujący się jak dziecko) childish; **pokój ~** nursery; **wózek ~** pram (Brit), baby carriage (US)

dzieciństwo (**-wa**; loc sg **-wie**) nt (wczesny okres życia) childhood

dziecko (**-cka**, **-ci**; inst sg **-ckiem**; gen pl **-ci**) child; **mieć ~** to have a baby

dziedzic (**-a**, **-e**) m heir

dziedziczny adj (choroba, tytuł, posiadłość) hereditary

dziedziczyć (**-ę**, **-ysz**; pf **od-**) vt (majątek, bogactwo) to inherit

dziekan (**-na**, **-ni**; loc sg **-nie**) m (Uniw) dean

dziekanat (**-tu**, **-ty**; loc sg **-cie**) m (Uniw) faculty office

dzielenie (**-a**) nt (w matematyce) division

dzielić (**-ę**, **-isz**; pf **po-**) vt 1 (Mat) to divide 2 (pf **roz-**) (dawać coś innym) to share out 3 (stanowić granicę, podział) to separate 4 (wspólnie korzystać z mieszkania, kuchni) to share; **~ się** vr to divide; **cztery dzieli się przez dwa** four is divisible by two; **~ (po~ pf) się czymś z kimś** to share sth with sb

dzielnica (**-y**, **-e**) f 1 (w mieście) district, quarter 2 (w kraju) region

dzielny adj 1 (odważny) brave 2 (umiejący sobie radzić) resourceful

dziennie adv (co dzień) daily; **osiem godzin ~** eight hours a day

dziennikarka (**-ki**, **-ki**; dat & loc sg **-ce**; gen pl **-ek**) f (radiowa, telewizyjna) journalist

dziennikarstwo (**-wa**; loc sg **-wie**) nt (śledcze, sportowe, ekonomiczne) journalism

dziennikarz (**-a**, **-e**; gen pl **-y**) m (radiowy, telewizyjny) journalist

dzienny adj 1 (edukacja, telewizja) daytime 2 (o zwierzętach) diurnal 3 (zysk, wydanie gazety) daily

dzień (**dnia**, **dni** lub **dnie**) m 1 (nie noc) day 2 (cała doba) day (including night) 3 (wyznaczony termin) date; **~ dobry!** (rano) good morning!; (po południu) good afternoon!

dziesiątka (**-ki**, **-ki**; dat & loc sg **-ce**; gen pl **-ek**) f ten

dziesiąty num decl like adj tenth

dziesięć num ten

dziewczyna (**-ny**, **-ny**; dat & loc sg **-nie**) f 1 (o młodej kobiecie) girl 2 (o sympatii) girlfriend

dziewczynka (**-ki**, **-ki**; dat & loc sg **-ce**; gen pl **-ek**) f (mała dziewczyna) girl

dziewiątka (**-ki**, **-ki**; dat & loc sg **-ce**; gen pl **-ek**) f nine

dziewiąty num decl like adj ninth

dziewięć num nine

dziewięćdziesiąt num ninety

dziewięćdziesiąty num decl like adj ninetieth

dziewięćset num nine hundred

dziewiętnasty num decl like adj nineteenth

dziewiętnaście num nineteen

dziękować (**-uję**, **-ujesz**; pf **po-**) vi: **dziękuję (bardzo)!** thank you (very much)!; **~ komuś (za coś)** to thank sb (for sth)

dziki adj 1 (nieoswojony, pierwotny, niedostępny, niepohamowany) wild 2 (niecywilizowany) savage 3 (agresywny) fierce 4 (nieśmiały) unsociable 5 (nielegalny) illegal

dzisiaj, **dziś** adv 1 (w dniu

bieżącym) today **2** (*w bieżącym okresie*) nowadays; **którego ~ mamy?** what date is it today?; **~ rano/wieczorem** this morning/evening; **~ w nocy** tonight; **od ~** starting today

dzisiejszy *adj* **1** (*dotyczący bieżącego dnia*) today's **2** (*dotyczący bieżącego okresu*) present-day

dziś *adv* = **dzisiaj**; **od ~** from now on

dziwny *adj* (*dziwaczny*) strange; **nic dziwnego, że...** (it's) no wonder that...

dzwo|n (**-nu**, **-ny**; *loc sg* **-nie**) *m* (*kościelny*) bell; **dzwony** *pl* (*o spodniach*) flares

dzwon|ek (**-ka**, **-ki**; *inst sg* **-kiem**) *m* **1** (*mechanizm*) bell **2** (*do drzwi*) doorbell **3** (*dźwięk*) ring **4** (*roślina*) bluebell

dzwo|nić (**-nię**, **-nisz**; *imp* **-ń**; *pf* **za-**) *vi* +*inst* **1** (*dzwonkiem*) to ring **2** (*czymś metalowym*) to make a clattering noise with **3** (*czymś szklanym*) to clink **4** (*pot: zatelefonować*): **~ (za~** *pf*) **do kogoś** to give sb a ring (*Brit*), to give sb a call (*US*)

dźwię|k (**-ku**, **-ki**; *inst sg* **-kiem**) *m* **1** (*brzmienie*) sound **2** (*w muzyce*) tone

dźwig|ać (**-am**, **-asz**; *pf* **-nąć**) *vt* **1** (*podnieść*) to lift **2** (*nosić*) to carry

dże|m (**-mu**, **-my**; *loc sg* **-mie**) *m* (*Kulin*) jam

dżentelme|n (**-na**, **-ni**; *loc sg* **-nie**) *m* gentleman

dżin|s (**-su**; *loc sg* **-sie**) *m* (*tkanina*) denim; **dżinsy** *pl* **1** denims **2** (*spodnie*) jeans

dżinsowy *adj* denim

e

edukacj|a (**-i**) *f* (*dobra, wyższa, solidna*) education

efek|t (**-tu**, **-ty**; *loc sg* **-cie**) *m* **1** (*rezultat: doskonały, marny*) effect **2** (*wrażenie: dobre, doskonałe, świetne*) impression; **~ cieplarniany** greenhouse effect; **~y specjalne** special effects; **nasze wysiłki dały dobry ~** our efforts have been successful

efektowny *adj* **1** (*wygląd, makijaż, fryzura*) striking **2** (*aktorka*) glamorous

efektywny *adj* (*praca, pracownik, czas pracy*) effective

Egip|t (**-tu**; *loc sg* **-cie**) *m* Egypt

egoi|sta (**-sty**, **-ści**; *dat sg & loc sg* **-ście**) *m decl like f in sg* (*nieznośny, prawdziwy, okropny*) egotist

egoiz|m (**-mu**; *loc sg* **-mie**) *m*

selfishness

egz. *abbr* (= *egzemplarz*) copy

egzami|n (**-nu, -ny**; *loc sg* **-nie**) *m* (*trudny, ciężki, ważny*) exam(ination); **~ poszedł mu jak z płatka** he sailed through the exam; **~ dojrzałości** school-leaving exam, ≈ A-levels *pl* (*Brit*); **~ na prawo jazdy** driving test; **zdawać** (*impf*) **~** to take an examination; **zdać** (*pf*) **~** to pass an examination; **nie zdać** (*pf*) **~u** to fail an examination

egzamin|ować (**-uję, -ujesz**; *pf* **prze-**) *vt*: **~ kogoś (z czegoś)** to examine sb (in sth)

egzemplarz (**-a, -e**; *gen pl* **-y**) *m* **1** (*książki, listu, gazety*: *rzadki*) copy **2** (*o zwierzęciu*) specimen; **niezły z niego ~!** (*pot*: *pej*) he's quite a character!

egzotyczny *adj* (*kraj, roślina, danie*) exotic

ekonomi|a (**-i**) *f* **1** (*Uniw*) economics **2** (*gospodarka*: *chwiejna, silna*) economy; **~ od paru lat znów nabiera tempa** for a year or two the economy has been growing more rapidly again

ekonomiczny *adj* **1** (*klimat*) economic **2** (*oszczędny*) economical

ekonomi|sta (**-sty, -ści**; *dat sg* & *loc sg* **-ście**) *m decl like f in sg* (*znany, poważany, szanowany*) economist

ekra|n (**-nu, -ny**; *loc sg* **-nie**) *m* screen; **gwiazda ~u** film star

eksmit|ować (**-uję, -ujesz**; *pf* **wy-**) *vt* to evict; **nakaz eksmisji** eviction notice

ekspedien|t (**-ta, -ci**; *loc sg* **-cie**) *m*

(*uprzejmy, uśmiechnięty, pomocny*) shop assistant

ekspedient|ka (**-ki, -ki**; *dat sg* & *loc sg* **-ce**; *gen pl* **-ek**) *f* shop assistant

eksper|t (**-ta, -ci**; *loc sg* **-cie**) *m* (*słynny, znany*) expert; **światowej sławy ~** world authority

eksperymen|t (**-tu, -ty**; *loc sg* **-cie**) *m* (*chemiczny, naukowy, genetyczny*) experiment

eksperyment|ować (**-uję, -ujesz**) *vi*: **~ (na** +*inst*) to experiment (on)

ekspon|ować (**-uję, -ujesz**; *pf* **wy-**) *vt* **1** (*wystawiać sztukę*) to display **2** (*wysuwać na miejsce opowiadzialne*) to emphasize; **ta fryzura ładnie eksponuje kształt jej twarzy** this hairstyle nicely complements the shape of her face; **wystawa eksponuje osiągnięcia uczniów naszej szkoły** the exhibition showcases what our school's pupils have achieved

ekspor|t (**-tu**; *loc sg* **-cie**) *m* export; **nadwyżka ~u** export surplus

ekspre|s (**-su, -sy**; *loc sg* **-sie**) *m* **1** (*pociąg pośpieszna*) express (train) **2** (*maszyna do kawy*) espresso machine; **kawa z ~u** espresso

elastyczny *adj* **1** (*sprężysty*: *materiał*) elastic **2** (*przen*: *człowiek, natura, czas pracy*) flexible

elegancj|a (**-i**) *f* elegance

elegancki *adj* (*człowiek, zachowanie, ubiór*) elegant

elektroniczny *adj* **1** electronic **2** (*zegarek*) quartz-crystal

elektroni|ka (**-ki**; *dat sg* & *loc sg*

-ce) f (Uniw) electronics
elektryczność (**-ci**) f electricity
elektryczny adj **1** (prąd, światło)
electric **2** (usterka, urządzenie)
electrical; **krzesło elektryczne**
electric chair
elektry|k (**-ka, -cy**; inst sg **-kiem**)
m (znajomy, solidny) electrician
elemen|t (**-tu, -ty**; loc sg **-cie**)
m **1** (część) component **2** (grupa
ludzi: podejrzany, społeczny)
element (pej); **elementy** pl
(podstawy) basics; **tej okolicy
trzeba unikać; tu spotyka się
lokalny ~** this is an area to be
avoided; it is a hang-out for local
criminals
elimin|ować (**-uję, -ujesz**; pf
wy-) vt (ekipę, drużynę, kandydata)
to eliminate; **jego zgłoszenie
zostało wyeliminowane po
egzaminie wstępnym** he didn't
get beyond the entrance exam
emancypacj|a (**-i**) f (wyzwolenie)
emancipation; **~ kobiet** the
emancipation of women
emery|t (**-ta, -ci**; loc sg **-cie**) m
(rencista) (old-age) pensioner
emeryt|ka (**-ki, -ki**; dat sg & loc sg
-ce; gen pl **-ek**) f (rencistka) (old-
age) pensioner
emerytu|ra (**-ry, -ry**; dat sg & loc
sg **-rze**) f **1** (zasłużona, wysoka,
skromna) (old-age) pension
2 (okres) retirement
emigracj|a (**-i, -e**; gen pl **-i**) f
(zarobkowa, polityczna, powojenna) f
emigration; **fala emigracji** wave
of emigration
emigracyjny adj emigration;
rząd ~ government in exile;
przepisy emigracyjne

emigration regulations; **urząd ~**
emigration office
emigran|t (**-ta, -ci**; loc sg **-cie**) m
1 emigrant **2** (Pol) émigré
emigr|ować (**-uję, -ujesz**; pf **wy-**)
vi to emigrate; **~ za chlebem** to
go and work abroad
emocjonalny adj (ból, przeżycie,
chwila) emotional
encyklopedi|a (**-i, -e**; gen pl
-i) f (wiedzy, roślin, dla dzieci)
encyclop(a)edia
energetyczny adj energy;
przemysł ~ energy industry;
sektor ~ the energy sector;
surowiec ~ source of energy
energi|a (**-i**) f energy; **~
słoneczna/atomowa** solar/
atomic power
entuzjastyczny adj (odbiór,
ocena, recenzja) enthusiastic
epidemi|a (**-i, -e**; gen pl **-i**) f
epidemic
epilepsj|a (**-i**) f (padaczka)
epilepsy; **cierpieć na epilepsję** to
suffer from epilepsy
epo|ka (**-ki, -ki**; dat sg & loc sg **-ce**) f
1 epoch **2** (kamienia) age
era (**ery, ery**; dat sg & loc sg **erze**) f
era; **przed naszą erą** BC; **naszej
ery** AD
erotyczny adj (taniec, film) erotic
esej (**-u, -e**) m (filozoficzny, literacki)
essay
Estoni|a (**-i**) f Estonia
eta|p (**-pu, -py**; loc sg **-pie**) m
(faza: ważny, decydujący) stage
eta|t (**-tu, -ty**; loc sg **-cie**) m
(stanowisko) job; **wolny ~**
vacancy; **na pół ~u** part-time; **na
pełen ~** full-time
ety|ka (**-ki**; dat sg & loc sg **-ce**) f

1 (*pracy, postępowania*) ethics *pl*
2 (*filozofia moralności*) ethics *sg*
euro *nt inv* euro
Euro|pa (**-py**; *dat sg* **-pie**) *f* Europe
europejski *adj* European
ewentualnie *adv* ▷ *conj* **1** (*albo*)
  alternatively **2** (*w razie czego*)
  perhaps

fabry|ka (**-ki, -ki**; *dat & loc sg* **-ce**) *f*
  (*zakład pracy*) factory
face|t (**-ta, -ci**; *loc sg* **-cie**) *m*
  (*mężczyzna: pot*) bloke (Brit), guy
fachowy *adj* **1** (*specjalistyczny*)
  specialist **2** (*rada*) professional
  3 (*z kwalifikacjami*) skilled
fajerwer|ki (**-ków**) *pl* (*sztuczne
  ognie*) fireworks
faj|ka (**-ki, -ki**; *dat & loc sg* **-ce**; *gen pl*
  -ek) *f* (*do palenia tytoniu*) pipe
fajnie *adv* (*pot: świetnie, super*)
  great
fajny *adj* (*pot: świetny, super*) great
fak|s (**-su, -sy**; *loc sg* **-sie**) *m* fax
fak|t (**-tu, -ty**; *loc sg* **-cie**) *m*
  (*niezbity, suchy*) fact; **literatura
  ~u** non-fiction; **suche ~y** plain
  facts
faktu|ra (**-ry, -ry**; *dat & loc sg* **-rze**)

f 1 (*rachunek*) invoice **2** (*materiału*) texture

faktycznie *adv* **1** actually **2** (*rzeczywiście, istotnie*) in fact

fa|la (**-li, -le**; *dat & loc sg* **-li**) *f* (*morska, włosów*) wave

falisty *adj* (*włosy, linia*) wavy

falsyfika|t (**-tu, -ty**; *loc sg* **-cie**) *m* forgery

fałsz (**-u, -e**) *m* (*kłamstwo*) falsehood

fałszerst|wo (**-wa, -wa**; *loc sg* **-wie**) *nt* forgery

fałsz|ować (**-uję, -ujesz**; *pf* **s-**) *vt* **1** to forge **2** (*przen: przedstawiać nieprawdę*) to falsify ▷ *vi* (*Muz*) to be out of tune

fałszywie *adv* **1** (*kłamliwie*) falsely **2** (*nieszczerze*) insincerely **3** (*Muz*) out of tune

fałszywy *adj* **1** (*banknot, dzieło sztuki*) counterfeit **2** (*dokument*) forged **3** (*dowód, wniosek*) false **4** (*uśmiech, skromność*) insincere **5** (*Muz*) out of tune

fa|n (**-na, -ni**; *loc sg* **-nie**) *m* (*wielbiciel, sympatyk: pot*) fan

fantastyczny *adj* (*wspaniały, baśniowy*) fantastic; **film ~** science-fiction film

fantazjować (**-uję, -ujesz**) *vi* to fantasize

far|ba (**-by, -by**; *dat & loc sg* **-bie**) *f* **1** (*malarska*) paint **2** (*do drukarki*) ink **3** (*do farbowania*) dye

farb|ować (**-uję, -ujesz**) *vt* (*pf* **u-** *lub* **po-**) (*ubranie, włosy*) to dye ▷ *vi* (*o tkaninie: puścić kolor*) to run

fartuch (**-a, -y**) *m* **1** (*kucharza*) apron **2** (*lekarza*) gown

fascynujący *adj* (*urzekający*) fascinating

faso|la (**-li, -le**; *gen pl & loc sg* **-li**) *f* (*Kulin*) bean(s *pl*)

faszyz|m (**-mu**; *loc sg* **-mie**) *m* (*Pol*) fascism

faul|ować (**-uję, -ujesz**; *pf* **s-**) *vt* (*w piłce nożną*) to foul

faworki *pl* crispy ribbons of pastry, deep-fried and sprinkled with powdered sugar, traditionally eaten on the last Thursday before Lent

feri|e (**-i**) *pl* **1** (*zimowe*) break **2** (*letnie*) holiday(s *pl*) (*Brit*), vacation *sg* (*US*)

festiwa|l (**-lu, -le**; *gen pl* **-li** *lub* **-lów**) *m* (*filmowy, muzyczny*) festival

festy|n (**-nu, -ny**; *loc sg* **-nie**) *m* (*pierwszomajowy, odpustowy*) gala

figu|ra (**-ry, -ry**; *dat & loc sg* **-rze**) *f* **1** (*sylwetka*) figure **2** (*w szachach*) piece **3** (*w kartach*) face card

fikcj|a (**-i, -e**; *gen pl & loc sg* **-i**) *f* (*Lit: coś wymyślonego*) fiction

fikcyjny *adj* **1** (*Lit*) fictional **2** (*adres, małżeństwo*) fictitious

Filipin|y (**-**) *pl* the Philippines

filiżan|ka (**-ki, -ki**; *dat & loc sg* **-ce**; *gen pl* **-ek**) *f* **1** (*o naczyniu*) cup **2** (*o zawartości*) cupful; **~ herbaty/kawy** a cup of tea/coffee

fil|m (**-mu, -my**; *loc sg* **-mie**) *m* **1** (*utwór*) film (*Brit*), movie (*US*) **2** (*fotograficzny*) film; **~ fabularny** (*feature*) film; **~ dokumentalny** documentary (film); **kręcić** (**nakręcić** *pf*) **~** to make a film; **przemysł ~owy** film (*Brit*) *lub* movie (*US*) industry

film|ować (**-uję, -ujesz**; *pf* **s-**) *vt* **1** (*robić zdjęcia*) to film **2** (*ekranizować*) to make into a film

filmowy *adj* (*reżyser, festiwal,*

magazyn) film *(Brit)*, movie *(US)*
filologi|a (**-i, -e**; *gen pl & loc sg*
-i) *f (nauka)* philology; **student
filologii francuskiej** a student of
French (studies)
filozo|f (**-fa, -fowie**; *loc sg* **-fie**) *m*
(uczony) philosopher
filozofi|a (**-i, -e**; *gen pl & loc sg* **-i**) *f*
(nauka, zasada, idea) philosophy
filt|r (**-ru** *lub* **-ra, -ry**; *loc sg*
-rze) *m (urządzenie)* filter; **~ do
wody** water filter; **krem z ~em
przeciwsłonecznym** sunscreen
fina|ł (**-łu, -ły**; *loc sg* **-le**) *m*
1 *(filmu itp.)* ending **2** *(zawodów
sportowych)* final **3** *(Muz)* finale
finałowy *adj* **1** *(zawodów
sportowych)* final **2** *(Muz)*: **scena
finałowa** finale
finansowy *adj (rok, rozliczenie)*
financial
finisz|ować (**-uję, -ujesz**) *vi*
(peleton, bieg) to put on a spurt
(in a race)
Finlandi|a (**-i**) *f* Finland
fioletowy *adj (kolor)* purple
firan|ka (**-ki, -ki**; *dat & loc sg* **-ce**;
gen pl **-ek**) *f (przejrzysta zasłona na
okno)* net curtain
fir|ma (**-my, -my**; *dat & loc sg* **-mie**)
f **1** *(mała)* firm, business **2** *(duża)*
company
fizy|k (**-ka, -cy**; *inst sg* **-kiem**) *m*
1 *(naukowiec)* physicist **2** *(Szkol)*
physics teacher
fizy|ka (**-ki**; *dat & loc sg* **-ce**) *f*
(nauka) physics
fla|ga (**-gi, -gi**; *dat & loc sg* **-dze**) *f*
(państwowa) flag
fle|t (**-tu, -ty**; *loc sg* **-cie**) *m (Muz)*
flute; **~ prosty** recorder
flirt|ować (**-uję, -ujesz**) *vi*: **~ (z**

+inst) to flirt (with)
fontan|na (**-ny, -ny**; *dat & loc sg*
-nie) *f (budowla; tryskająca woda)*
fountain
for|ma (**-my, -my**; *dat & loc sg*
-mie) *f* **1** *(kształt)* form **2** *(do
wypieków)* baking tin **3** *(matryca,
odlew)* mould *(Brit)*, mold *(US)*;
być w złej/dobrej formie to be in
bad/good shape
formalnoś|ć (**-ci, -ci**; *gen pl & dat,
loc sg* **-ci**) *f (urzędowa, prawna)*
formality
formalny *adj (język, list)* formal
formularz (**-a, -e**; *gen pl* **-y**) *m*
form; **wypełniać** (**wypełnić** *pf*) **~**
to fill in *(Brit) lub* out *(US)* a form
for|sa (**-sy**; *dat & loc sg* **-sie**) *f*
(pieniądze: pot) dough, dosh
fortepia|n (**-nu, -ny**; *loc sg* **-nie**) *m*
(Muz) (grand) piano
fotel (**-a** *lub* **-u, -e**; *gen pl* **-i**)
m (mebel) armchair; **~ na
biegunach** rocking chair
fot|ka (**-ki, -ki**; *dat sg* **-ce**; *gen pl*
-ek) *f (fotografia)* snap
fotogra|f (**-fa, -fowie**; *loc sg* **-fie**)
m (osoba) photographer
fotografi|a (**-i**) *f* **1** *(sztuka,
technika)* photography **2** *(nom pl*
-e; *gen pl, dat & loc sg* **-i**) *(zdjęcie)*
photo(graph)
fotograf|ować (**-uję, -ujesz**; *pf*
s-) *vt (robić zdjęcia)* to photograph
fragmen|t (**-tu, -ty**; *loc sg* **-cie**) *m*
(kawałek) fragment
Francj|a (**-i**) *f* France
francuski *adj* French
fruw|ać (**-am, -asz**) *vi (latać)* to fly
fryt|ki (**-ek**) *pl (Kulin)* chips *pl*
(Brit), (French) fries *pl (US)*
fryzje|r (**-ra, -rzy**; *loc sg* **-rze**)

m **1** (*damski*) hairdresser **2** (*dla mężczyzn*) barber

fryzjer|ka (*-ki, -ki*; *dat & loc sg* **-ce**; *gen pl* **-ek**) *f* (*osoba*) hairdresser

fryzu|ra (*-ry, -ry*; *dat & loc sg* **-rze**) *f* (*uczesanie*) haircut, hairstyle

fund|ować (*-uję, -ujesz*) *vt* **1** (*pf* **za-**) (*stawiać*): **~** (**za~** *pf*) **komuś coś** to treat sb to sth **2** (*pf* **u-**) to found, to establish

funkcj|a (*-i, -e*; *gen pl, dat & loc sg* **-i**) *f* function

fun|t (*-ta, -ty*; *loc sg* **-cie**) *m* (*pieniądz, jednostka wagi*) pound; **~ szterling** (pound) sterling

futbol (*-u*) *m* (*piłka nożna*) football (*Brit*), soccer (*US*); **~ amerykański** American football (*Brit*), football (*US*)

fut|ro (*-ra, -ra*; *loc sg* **-rze**; *gen pl* **-er**) *nt* **1** (*na zwierzęciu*) fur **2** (*ubranie*) fur coat

g

gabine|t (*-tu, -ty*; *loc sg* **-cie**) *m* **1** (*w mieszkaniu*) study **2** (*w miejscu pracy*) office **3** (*w przychodni*) surgery (*Brit*), office (*US*) **4** (*Rada Ministrów*) Cabinet

ga|d (*-da, -dy*; *loc sg* **-dzie**) *m* (*w zoologii*) reptile

gad|ać (*-am, -asz*) *vi* (*pot: mówić*) to chatter; **~ co ślina na język przyniesie** to talk a load of rubbish

gadu|ła (*-ły, -ły*; *dat sg & loc sg* **-le**) *m/f decl like f* (*pot: osoba dużo mówiąca*) chatterbox

ga|j (*-ju, -je*; *gen pl* **-i**) *m* grove

gajo|wy (*-wego, -wi*) *m decl like adj* (*leśniczy*) forester

galaret|ka (*-ki, -ki*; *dat sg & loc sg* **-ce**; *gen pl* **-ek**) *f* jelly

galeri|a (*-i, -e*; *gen pl* **-i**) *f* gallery;

~ sztuki współczesnej gallery of modern art

gał|ąź (**-ęzi, -ęzie**; *gen pl* **-ęzi**; *inst pl* **-ęziami** *lub* **-ęźmi**) *f* branch; **~ przemysłu** branch of industry

gangste|r (**-ra, -rzy**; *loc sg* **-rze**) *m* gangster

garbaty *adj* **1** (*o człowieku*) hunchbacked **2** (*o nosie*) hooked

gar|bić się (**-bię, -bisz**; *pf* **z-**) *vr* (*pochylać się*) to stoop

gar|dzić (**-dzę, -dzisz**; *impf* **-dź**; *pf* **wz-**) *vt*: **~** *+inst* to despise

garn|ek (**-ka, -ki**; *inst sg* **-kiem**) *m* (*Kulin*) pot

garnitu|r (**-ru, -ry**; *loc sg* **-rze**) *m* (*marynarka i spodnie*) suit

garson|ka (**-ki, -ki**; *dat sg & loc sg* **-ce**; *gen pl* **-ek**) *f* (*garnitur dla kobiet*) suit

ga|sić (**-szę, -sisz**; *imp* **-ś**; *pf* **z-**) *vt* **1** (*pożar*) to put out **2** (*niedopałek*) to put out **3** (*urządzenie elektryczne*) to switch off **4** (*nadzieję*) to kill **5** (*pf* **u-**) (*zaspokajać pragnienie*) to quench

ga|snąć (**-snę, -śniesz**; *impf* **-śnij**; *pf* **z-**) *vi* **1** (*o płomieniu*) to go out **2** (*o motorze*) to stall **3** (*o uczuciach*) to fade; **jej gwiazda zgasła już dawno** her star went out years ago

gastronomi|a (**-i**) *f* **1** (*sztuka gotowania*) gastronomy **2** (*prowadzenie restauracji*) catering industry

gaśnic|a (**-y, -e**) *f* fire extinguisher

gatun|ek (**-ku, -ki**; *inst sg* **-kiem**) *m* **1** (*odmiana*) kind **2** (*w biologii*) species **3** (*wartość*) quality; **być w pierwszym gatunku** to be top

quality; **romans to ~ literacki** romanticism is a literary genre

ga|z (**-zu, -zy**; *loc sg* **-zie**) *m* **1** (*w naukach przyrodniczych*) gas **2** (*w motoryzacji*) accelerator (*Brit*), gas pedal (*US*) **3** (*pot: instalacja gazowa*) gas fittings *pl*; **gazy** *n pl* (*wiatry*) wind *sg*; **on ciągle jest na ~ie** (*pot: podpity*) he's always drunk

gaze|ta (**-ty, -ty**; *dat sg & loc sg* **-cie**) *f* (*codzienna, brukowa*) newspaper

gazomierz (**-a, -e**; *gen pl* **-y**) *m* gas meter

gazowy *adj* **1** (*butla, licznik*) gas **2** (*rodzaj opatrunku*) gauze

gąb|ka (**-ki, -ki**; *dat sg & loc sg* **-ce**; *gen pl* **-ek**) *f* sponge; **on ma umysł chłonny jak ~** he has a brain like a sponge

gąsienic|a (**-y, -e**) *f* **1** caterpillar **2** (*w traktorze*) caterpillar tread

○ **KEYWORD**

gdy *conj* **1** (*kiedy*) when, as; **ściemniało się, gdy nagle zatrzymał sie i krzyknął do nas** it was getting dark when he suddenly stopped and shouted to us; **podczas gdy** ((*wtedy*) *kiedy*) while

2 (*natomiast*) whereas; **gdy tylko zrozumiał, odszedł** he left as soon as he understood **3** (*jeżeli*) when; **gdy będziesz chciał wyjść, zamknij drzwi** when you want to leave, close the door

gdyby *conj* if; **~ś to zrozumiał,**

zdałbyś egzamin if you'd understood that, you'd have passed the exam

○ KEYWORD

gdzie *pron* **1** (*w pytaniach*) where; **gdzie on teraz jest?** where is he now?
2 (*w zdaniach podrzędnych*) where; **nie wiem, gdzie ona poszła** i don't know where she went
3 (*w zdaniach względnych*) where; **wszedł do pokoju, gdzie było ciemno** he went into the room where it was dark
4: nie miał gdzie usiąść he had nowhere to sit; **byle gdzie** anywhere

gdziekolwiek *pron* anywhere
gdzieniegdzie *adv* here and there
gdzieś *adv* somewhere
gej (**-a, -e**) *m* (*osoba homoseksualna*) gay
gejowy *adj* (*homoseksualny*) gay
generacj|a (**-i, -e**; *gen pl* **-i**) *f* (*młodsza, starsza*) generation
generalny *adj* **1** (*porządki, przegląd*) general **2: Sekretarz G~** Secretary General **3** (*w teatrze*): **próba generalna** dress rehearsal
genera|ł (**-ła, -łowie**; *loc sg* **-le**) *m* (*Wojsko*) general
gen|za (**-zy**; *dat sg & loc sg* **-zie**) *f* (*pochodzenie*) origin
genialny *adj* (*bardzo zdolny*) brilliant
genitali|a (**-ów**) *pl* genitals
geografi|a (**-i**) *f* (*fizyczna,*

historyczna) geography
geograficzny *adj* (*atlas, odkrycie*) geographic(al)
geologi|a (**-i**) *f* geology
geometri|a (**-i**) *f* geometry
germanisty|ka (**-ki**; *dat sg & loc sg* **-ce**) *f* (*nauka o kulturze i niemieckiej*) German studies
ge|st (**-stu, -sty**; *loc sg* **-ście**) *m* (*pusty, teatralny*) gesture
gestykul|ować (**-uję, -ujesz**) *vi* to gesticulate
get|to (**-ta, -ta**; *loc sg* **-cie**) *nt* ghetto
gę|ś (**-si, -si**) *f* goose; **a niech cię ~ kopnie** (*przen*) stuff you then
gieł|da (**-dy, -dy**; *dat sg & loc sg* **-dzie**) *f* (*papierów wartościowych, pracy*) exchange
gigantyczny *adj* (*ogromny*) gigantic

● GIMNAZJUM
●
● **Gimnazjum** is a compulsory
● three-year secondary school,
● for students aged 13 to 16.

gimnasty|ka (**-ki**; *dat sg & loc sg* **-ce**) *f* (*poranna, artystyczna*) gymnastics
gimnastyk|ować (**-uję, -ujesz**) *vt* to exercise; **~ się** *vr* **1** to exercise **2** (*starać się*) to exert o.s.; **gimnastykuje się, aby mu starczyło pieniędzy** he struggles to make ends meet
ginekolo|g (**-ga, -dzy** *lub* **-gowie**; *inst sg* **-giem**) *m* gynaecologist (Brit), gynecologist (US)
gip|s (**-su**; *loc sg* **-sie**) *m* (*murarski*) plaster; **mieć rękę w ~ie** to have

one's arm in plaster

gita|ra (**-ry**, **-ry**; *dat sg & loc sg* **-rze**) *f* (*elektryczna, klasyczna*) guitar

gitarzy|sta (**-sty**, **-ści**; *dat sg & loc sg* **-ście**) *m decl like f in sg* guitarist

gitarzystka (**-ki**, **-ki**; *dat sg & loc sg* **-tce**) *f* guitarist

gli|na (**-ny**, **-ny**; *dat sg & loc sg* **-nie**) *f* (*skała*) clay ▷ *m decl like adj* (*pot: policjant*) cop; **z innej gliny** (*przen*) from a different mould (*Brit*) *lub* mold (*US*)

gliniarz (**-a**, **-e**; *gen pl* **-y**) *m* (*pot: policjant*) cop

gluko|za (**-zy**; *dat sg & loc sg* **-zie**) *f* glucose

gładki *adj* 1 (*cera, materiał*) smooth 2 (*trasa*) smooth 3 (*sierść*) sleek 4 (*bez wzoru*) plain

gładko *adv* (*równo*) smoothly; **~ ogolony** clean-shaven; **~ mu poszedł egzamin** his exam went smoothly

gła|dzić (**-uję**, **-ujesz**; *pf* **po-**) *vt* to stroke

głębia *f* depth

głęboki *adj* 1 deep 2 (*pochylenie się*) low 3 (*dekolt*) low-cut 4 (*doniosły*) profound 5 (*uczucia*) strong; **zapadł w ~ sen** he fell into a deep sleep

głęboko *adv* 1 (*zanurzyć się*) deep 2 (*zadać ranę*) deeply

głodny *adj* hungry; **opowiadać głodne kawałki** to talk nonsense

gło|s (**-su**, **-sy**; *loc sg* **-sie**) *m* 1 voice 2 (*prawo wypowiedzi*) say 3 (*podczas wyborów*) vote; **podnosić** (**podnieść** *pf*) **~ na kogoś** to vote for sb; **mówić na ~** to speak out loud; **krzyczeć** (**krzyknąć** *pf*) **na cały ~** to shout at the top of one's voice; **oddawać** (**oddać** *pf*) **~ na partię** to vote for the party

głos|ka (**-ki**, **-ki**; *dat sg & loc sg* **-ce**; *gen pl* **-ek**) *f* (*w językoznawstwie*) sound

głos|ować (**-uję**, **-ujesz**; *pf* **za-**) *vi* (*na partię, za zmianami*) to vote

głosowa|nie (**-nia**, **-nia**; *gen pl* **-ń**) *nt* (*tajne, jawne*) vote

głośno *adv* loudly; **myśleć ~** to think out loud

głośny *adj* 1 (*donośny*) loud 2 (*hałas*) noisy 3 (*znany*) famous

gł|owa (**-owy**, **-owy**; *dat sg & loc sg* **-owie**; *gen pl* **-ów**) *f* 1 head 2 (*pot: mózg*) brain; **dochód na głowę** income per capita; **mieć dach nad głową** to have a roof over one's head; **od stóp do głów** from top to toe; **mieć głowę nie od parady** to have one's head screwed on; **tracić** (**stracić** *pf*) **głowę** to lose one's head; **przyszło mi dziś do głowy, że...** it occurred to me today that...

głównie *adv* mainly

główny *adj* 1 (*problem, ulica*) main 2 (*księgowy*) head 3 (*aktor, aktorka*) lead; **główna wygrana** star prize; **Kraków G~** Cracow Central

głuchy *adj* 1 (*niesłyszący*) deaf 2 (*bez dźwięku*) hollow

głupi *adj* (*pot*) 1 (*ograniczony*) foolish 2 (*nieistotny*) silly 3 (*niezdarny*) awkward

głupo|ta (**-ty**; *dat sg & loc sg* **-cie**) *f* (*brak rozumu*) foolishness

głupst|wo (**-wa**, **-wa**; *loc sg* **-wie**) *nt* 1 foolish thing 2 (*brednia*) nonsense 3 (*drobnostka*) trifle

gmach (**-u**, **-y**) *m* (*ogromny*

budynek) edifice

gmi|na (**-ny, -ny**; *dat sg & loc sg* **-nie**) *f* commune; **izba Gmin** House of Commons; **urząd gminny** *local government office*

gniazdko (**-ka, -ka**; *inst sg* **-kiem**; *gen pl* **-dek**) *nt* (*Elec*) socket, outlet (*US*)

gni|azdo (**-azda, -azda**; *loc sg* **-eździe**) *nt* nest; **~ rodzinne** the family nest

gnić (**gniję, gnijesz**; *impf* **gnij**; *pf* **z-**) *vi* to rot; **~ w łóżku** (*pot: przen*) to lay in one's pit

gnie|w (**-wu**; *loc sg* **-wie**) *m* anger; **wpadać** (**wpaść** *pf*) **w ~** to fly into a rage; **powściągać** (**powściągnąć** *pf*) **~** to keep one's temper

gniew|ać (**-am, -asz**; *pf* **roz-**) *vt* to anger; **~ się** *vr* to be angry; **~ się na** to be angry at; **od dawna gniewa się z ciocią** he has been angry with his aunt for a long time

godz. *abbr* (= *godzina*) hr.

godzi|na (**-ny, -ny**; *dat sg & loc sg* **-nie**) *f* hour; **jest (~) ósma** it's eight o'clock; **półtora godziny** an hour and a half; **czekał (całymi) ~mi** he waited for hours (on end); **która (jest) ~?** what time is it?

go|ić (**-ję, -isz**) *vi* to heal; **rana szybko się goi** the wound is healing quickly

go|l (**-la, -le**; *gen pl* **-li**) *m* goal; **Adam strzelił ~a** Adam scored a goal

gol|f (*loc sg* **-fie**) *m* (*gen sg* **-fa**) **1** (*gra*) golf **2** (*gen sg* **-fu**; *nom pl* **-fy**) (*sweter z wysokim kołnierzem*) polo-necked sweater **3** (*sweter z przylegającym wysokim kołnierzem*) turtle-necked sweater

golić (**-golę, -golisz**; *impf* **gol**; *pf* **o-**) *vt* to shave; **~ się** *vr* to shave

goł|ąb (**-ębia, -ębie**; *gen pl* **-ębi**) *m* (*pocztowy, pokoju*) pigeon

goły *adj* **1** (*bez ubrania*) naked **2** (*bez zawartości*) bare **3** (*pot: bez grosza*) broke; **widzieć ~m okiem** to see with the naked eye; **spać pod ~m niebem** to sleep in the open air

gor|ąco (**-ąca**) *nt* (*skwar*) heat ▷ *adv* **1** (*ciepło*) hot **2** (*przen: przywitać, pożegnać*) warmly; **jest mi ~** I'm hot; **danie na ~** hot meal

gor|ący *adj* **1** (*klimat, kraj*) hot **2** (*list*) urgent **3** (*zwolennik, fan*) fervent; **~ czas/okres** hectic time/period; **łapać (złapać** *pf*) **kogoś na ~m uczynku** to catch sb red-handed

gorącz|ka (**-ki, -ki**; *dat sg & loc sg* **-ce**) *f* (*wysoka temperatura*) fever

gorszy *adj comp od* **zły** worse

gorzej *adv comp od* **źle** worse

gorzki *adj* **1** (*smak*) bitter **2** (*napój*) unsweetened

gospodarczy *adj* (*rozwój, polityka*) economic

gospodar|ka (**-ki, -ki**; *dat sg & loc sg* **-ce**; *gen pl* **-ek**) *f* (*rynkowa, komunalna*) economy

gospodarz (**-a, -e**; *gen pl* **-y**) *m* **1** (*na wsi*) farmer **2** (*w domu*) host **3** (*właściciel domu*) landlord

gospody|ni (**-ni, -nie**; *gen pl* **-ń**) *f* **1** (*w domu*) hostess **2** (*właścicielka mieszkania*) landlady **3** (*na wsi*) farmer's wife

go|ścić (**-szczę, -ścisz**; *impf* **-ść**) *vt*

(*częstować*) (*pf* **u-**) **1** to entertain **2** (*w hotelu*) to accommodate ▷ *vi*: **~ (u kogoś)** to stay (at sb's place); **ciocia gości u nas od czwartku** auntie has been staying with us since Thursday
gościnność|ć (-ci) f (*serdeczność wobec gości*) hospitality
gościnny *adj* **1** (*o człowieku*) hospitable **2** (*dla przyjezdnych*) guest
gość (-cia, -cie; *gen pl* **-ci**; *inst pl* **-ćmi**) *m* **1** (*przyjezdny*) guest **2** (*wczasowicz*) guest **3** (*pot: mężczyzna*) guy, bloke (*Brit*)
got|ować (-uję, -ujesz) *vt* **1** (*pf* **u-**) (*obiad*) to cook **2** (*pf* **u-**) (*warzywa*) to boil **3** (*pf* **za-**) (*płyn*) to boil; **~ się** *vr* **1** (*pf* **u-**) (*o obiedzie*) to cook **2** (*pf* **u-**) (*o warzywach*) to boil **3** (*pf* **za-**) (*o płynie*) to boil
gotowany *adj* boiled
gotowy *adj* **1** (*ukończony*) finished **2** (*obiad*) ready **3** (*zrobiony fabrycznie*) ready-made **4** (*ubranie seryjne w sklepie*) ready-to-wear
gotów|ka (-ki; *dat sg & loc sg* **-ce**) f cash; **kupować** (**kupić** *pf*) **coś za gotówkę** to buy sth for cash; **płacić** (**zapłacić** *pf*) **gotówką** to pay in cash
gó|ra (-ry, -ry; *dat sg & loc sg* **-rze**) f **1** (*lodowa*) mountain **2** (*bluzka*) top **3** (*piętro w domu*) upstairs **4** (*śmieci*) heap; **w ~ch** in the mountains; **obiecywać** (**obiecać** *pf*) **złote góry** to promise the earth; **ona mieszka na górze** she lives upstairs; **on chodzi do szkoły pod górę** he walks uphill to school; **do góry nogami** upside down; **ceny poszły w**

górę the prices have gone up; **płacić/dziękować z góry** to pay/thank in advance
górni|k (-ka, -cy; *inst sg* **-kiem**) *m* miner
górzysty *adj* (*teren, okolica*) hilly
gó|wno (-wna, -wna; *loc sg* **-wnie**; *gen pl* **-wien**) *nt* (*pot!*) shit; **~ mnie to obchodzi** (*pot!*) I don't give a shit about this (*pot!*)
gra (gry, gry; *dat sg & loc sg* **grze**; *gen pl* **gier**) f **1** game **2** (*na scenie*) acting **3** (*przen: pozorowanie*) act
gracz (-a, -e; *gen pl* **-y**) *m* (*zręczny, nałogowy*) player
gr|ać (-am, -asz; *pf* **za-**) *vt, vi* to play; **~ na pianinie** to play the piano; **~ w szachy** to play chess; **wiesz, że grasz mi na nerwach?** you know you're getting on my nerves?; **coś grają w kinie w środę?** is there anything on at the cinema on Wednesday?
gra|m (-ma, -my; *loc sg* **-mie**) *m* gram(me)
gramaty|ka (-ki, -ki; *dat sg & loc sg* **-ce**) f **1** (*reguły języka*) grammar **2** (*książka do nauki*) grammar (book)
granic|a (-y, -e) f **1** (*międzypaństwowa*) border **2** (*między miastami*) boundary, limit(*s pl*) (*US*) **3** (*limit*) limit; **mieszkać za granicą** to live abroad; **jechać** (**pojechać** *pf*) **za granicę** to go abroad
graniczy|ć (-ę, -ysz) *vi*: **~ z** +*inst* (*dzielić granicę*) to border on
grani|t (-tu, -ty; *loc sg* **-cie**) *m* (*skała, złoża*) granite
gratis *adv inv* (*obiad, usługa*) free (of charge)
gratulować (-uję, -ujesz; *pf*

po-) *vi*: **~ (komuś czegoś)**
to congratulate (sb on sth);
gratulował nam zwycięstwa he
congratulated us on our victory
Grecj|a (-i) *f* Greece
grecki *adj* **1** Greek **2** *(sztuka)* Grecian
grill (-a, -e; *gen pl* **-ów)** *m*
barbecue; **mięso pieczone na ~u**
meat cooked on the barbecue
groch (-u) *m* **1** *(roślina)* pea
2 *(zbiór)* peas *pl*; **grochy** *pl* *(wzór)*
polka dots
grochów|ka (-ki, -ki; *dat sg & loc sg*
-ce; *gen pl* **-ek)** *f* pea soup
groma|dzić (-dzę, -dzisz; *imp* **-dź**;
pf **z-)** *vt* to accumulate; **~ się** *vr* *(o
osobach, o rzeczach)* to gather
grosz (-a, -e; *gen pl* **-y)** *m* grosz
*(Polish monetary unit equal to
1/100 złoty)*; **kupować (kupić**
pf) **za ~e** to buy dirt-cheap; **nie
śmierdzieć ~em** to be skint
gr|ozić (-ożę, -ozisz; *impf* **-oź)**
vi **1** *(zastraszać)* to threaten
2 *(stwarzać zagrożenie)* to be
imminent
gr|oźba (-oźby, -oźby; *dat sg & loc
sg* **-oźbie**; *gen pl* **-óźb)** *f* threat
groźny *adj* **1** *(zachowanie, zjawisko)*
dangerous **2** *(gest)* threatening
gruba|s (-sa, -sy; *loc sg* **-sie)** *m*
(pot) fatty
gruby *adj* **1** *(książka)* thick
2 *(osoba)* fat; **to była gruba
przesada!** *(pot)* that was a gross
exaggeration!
gru|pa (-py, -py; *dat sg & loc sg*
-pie) *f* **1** group **2** *(kiść, kępka)*
cluster; **ma grupę krwi ABRH +**
he is blood group ABRH +
grusz|ka (-ki, -ki; *dat sg & loc sg*
-ce; *gen pl* **-ek)** *f* **1** *(drzewo)* pear

tree **2** *(owoc)* pear; **obiecywać
(obiecać** *pf)* **gruszki na wierzbie**
to promise the moon on a stick
gruziński *adj* Georgian
Gruzj|a (-i) *f* Georgia
gruźlic|a (-y) *f* *(w medycynie)* TB
gry|pa (-py; *dat sg & loc sg* **-pie)** *f*
influenza, flu *(pot)*
gry|źć (-zę, -ziesz; *imp* **-ź**; *pt* **-zł,
-zła, -źli)** *vt* **1** to bite **2** *(gnat)*
to gnaw ▷ *vi* **1** *(dym)* to sting
2 *(wełna)* to itch; **~ się** *vr* **1** *(o
zwierzętach)* to fight **2** *(o barwach,
wzorach)* to clash
grz|ać (-eję, -ejesz) *vt* **1** *(pf* **za-)**
(zupę) to heat **2** *(pf* **o-)** *(dłonie)*
to warm ▷ *vi* **1** *(słońce)* to beat
down **2** *(grzejnik)* to be hot; **~ się**
vr **1** *(w promieniach słońca)* to bask
2 *(przy kaloryferze)* to warm o.s.
3 *(podnosić temperaturę)* to heat up
grzeb|ać (-ię, -iesz) to bury; **~
się** *vr* *(pot)* to take a long time
getting ready; **~ zmarłych** to
bury the deceased
grzebie|ń (-nia, -nie; *gen pl* **-ni)** *m*
1 comb **2** *(u koguta)* crest
grzech (-u, -y) *m* sin; **popełniać
(popełnić** *pf)* **~** to sin
grzeczny *adj* **1** *(człowiek)* polite
2 *(dobrze wychowany)* good
grzejni|k (-ka, -ki; *inst sg* **-kiem)** *m*
radiator; **~ elektryczny** electric
heater
grzesz|yć (-ę, -ysz; *pf* **z-)** *vi* to sin;
nie ~ mądrością to be a bit soft
in the head
grzy|wna (-wny, -wny; *dat sg &
loc sg* **-wnie**; *gen pl* **-wien)** *f* fine;
płacić (zapłacić *pf)* **grzywnę za**
to pay a fine for
gu|bić (-bię, -bisz; *pf* **z-)** *vt* to lose;

~ się vr 1 (w drodze) to lose one's way 2 (o rzeczach) to get lost

gu|ma (**-my, -my**; dat sg & loc sg **-mie**) f (wyrób kauczukowy) rubber; **~ do żucia** chewing gum; **złapał gumę na drodze** (pot) he got a flat tyre (Brit) lub tire (US) on the way

gum|ować (**-uję, -ujesz**) vt to erase

gustowny adj tasteful

gu|z (**-za, -zy**; loc sg **-zie**) m 1 (obrzmiałe stłuczenie) bump 2 (w medycynie) tumour (Brit), tumor (US); **nabijać** (**nabić** pf) **sobie ~a** to bump one's head

gwał|cić (**-cę, -cisz**; impf **-ć**) vt 1 (pf **z-**) (zmuszać do stosunku seksualnego) to rape 2 (pf **po-**) (łamać prawo) to violate

gwał|t (**-tu, -ty**; dat sg & loc sg **-cie**) m 1 (akt przemocy) violence 2 (na osobie) rape

gwarancj|a (**-i, -e**; gen pl **-i**) f guarantee; **na gwarancji** under guarantee

gwarant|ować (**-uję, -ujesz**; pf **za-**) vt (bezpieczeństwo, zysk) to guarantee

gwi|azda (**-azdy, -azdy**; dat sg & loc sg **-eździe**) f 1 star 2 (przen: osobistość) celebrity; **~ filmowa** film (Brit) lub movie (US) star

gwiazdo|r (**-ra, -rzy**; loc sg **-rze**) m (filmowy) film (Brit) lub movie (US) star

gwi|zdać (**-żdżę, -żdżesz**; pf **-zdnąć**) vi 1 to whistle 2 (o syrenie) to whine 3 (podczas występu) to boo; **gwiżdżę na to** (pot) I couldn't care less about that

h

ha|k (**-ka, -ki**; inst sg **-kiem**) m (przyrząd) hook

halo excl (i przez telefon) hello

hała|s (**-su, -sy**; loc sg **-sie**) m 1 (głośny dźwięk) noise 2 (rozgłos) noise; **narobić** (pf) **~u** (przen) to make a fuss

hałas|ować (**-uję, -ujesz**) vi (głośno się zachowywać) to make a noise

hałaśliwy adj (sąsiad, uczeń) noisy

hamburge|r (**-ra, -ry**; dat sg **-rze**) m (Kulin) hamburger

ham|ować (**-uję, -ujesz**) vt 1 (pf **po-**; pf **za-**) (powstrzymywać, utrudniać) to slow down 2 (pf **po-**) (śmiech, łzy) to hold back ▷ vi (pf **za-**) (zmniejszać prędkość) to brake; **~ się** (pf **po-**) vr to hold o.s. back; zob. też **zahamować**

hamul|ec (-ca, -ce) m
(*urządzenie*) brake; **~ ręczny**
handbrake (*Brit*), parking
brake (*US*); **~ bezpieczeństwa**
communication cord (*Brit*),
emergency brake (*US*)
hand|el (-lu) m (*Ekon*) trade,
commerce
handl|ować (-uję, -ujesz) vi +inst
1 (*kupno i sprzedaż produktów*) to
trade in **2** (*narkotykami*) to deal in
handlo|wiec (-wca, -wcy) m
salesman
handlowy adj (*umowa,
działalność, izba*) trade; **szkoła
handlowa** business school;
centrum handlowe shopping
centre (*Brit*), mall (*US*)
hań|ba (-by; dat & loc sg **-bie)** f
(*wstyd, ujma*) dishonour (*Brit*),
dishonor (*US*)
harcerz (-a, -e; gen pl **-y)** m
(*członek organizacji młodzieżowej*)
scout
harmoni|a (-i) f (*zgoda*) harmony
ha|sło (-sła, -sła; loc sg **-śle;** gen pl
-seł) nt **1** (*Pol*) watchword **2** (*do
działania*) signal **3** (*w komputerze*)
password **4** (*w encyklopedii*) entry

● **HEJNAŁ MARIACKI**
●
● **Hejnał Mariacki** is the bugle
● call played every hour from the
● tower of the Mariacki Church
● in Kraków. Legend has it that
● its melody is characteristically
● interrupted to commemorate
● an event from the Tartar raids
● in XIII century, when the
● bugle call was played to alert
● the city to an attack . One of

● the arrows shot by the Tatars
● pierced the bugle player's
● neck before he finished the
● call. Every day the bugle call is
● broadcast throughout Poland
● on Polish radio.

helikopte|r (-ra, -ry; loc sg **-rze)** m
(*Lot*) helicopter
herba|ta (-ty, -ty; dat & loc sg **-cie)**
f (*Kulin*) tea
herbatni|k (-ka, -ki; inst sg **-kiem)**
m (*ciastko*) biscuit
heroi|na (-ny; dat sg **-nie)** f heroin
Himalaj|e (-ów) pl (*Geo*) the
Himalayas
hinduski adj Hindu
hipermarke|t (-tu, -ty; dat & loc sg
-cie) m hypermarket
hipote|ka (-ki, -ki; dat & loc sg
-ce) f **1** (*Fin*) collateral **2** (*księga
wieczysta*) mortgage deed;
brać (wziąć pf**) pożyczkę pod
hipotekę** to take out a secured
loan
hipotetyczny adj
(*prawdopodobny*) hypothetical
histori|a (-i, -e; gen pl & dat,
loc sg **-i)** f **1** (*dzieje*) history
2 (*opowiadanie*) story
historyczny adj **1** (*dotyczący
przeszłości*) historical **2** (*istotny*)
historic **3** (*zabytki, budynki*)
historic
history|k (-ka, -cy; inst sg **-kiem)**
m **1** (*naukowiec*) historian **2** (*Szkol*)
history teacher
Hiszpani|a (-i) f Spain
hiszpański adj Spanish
HIV abbr HIV
hobby nt inv (*zainteresowanie*)
hobby

hokej (**-a**) *m* (*sport*): **~ na trawie**
hockey (*Brit*), field hockey (*US*); **~
na lodzie** ice hockey

Holandi|a (**-i**) *f* the Netherlands

holenderski *adj* Dutch

homoseksuali|sta (**-sty**, **-ści**;
dat & loc sg **-ście**) *m decl like f in sg*
(*osoba*) gay

hono|r (**-ru**; *loc sg* **-rze**) *m* (*godność,
zaszczyt*) honour (*Brit*), honor
(*US*); **honory** *pl* (*hołd*): **oddawać
(oddać** *pf*) **~y** to salute; **słowo ~u**
word of hono(u)r

hormo|n (**-nu**, **-ny**; *loc sg* **-nie**) *m*
(*Bio*) hormone

horosko|p (**-pu**, **-py**; *loc sg* **-pie**) *m*
horoscope

horro|r (**-ru**, **-ry**; *loc sg* **-rze**) *m*
1 (*gatunek filmu*) horror (movie)
2 (*pot: groźna sytuacja*) horror

hot-do|g (**-ga**, **-gi**; *inst sg* **-giem**)
m (*Kulin*) hot dog

hotel (**-u**, **-e**; *gen pl* **-i**) *m*
(*luksusowy, tani*) hotel;
zatrzymać się w ~u to stay in
a hotel

hu|k (**-ku**, **-ki**; *inst sg* **-kiem**) *m*
1 (*wybuchu*) bang **2** (*wody*) rumble
3 (*w czasie burzy*) roll **4** (*duża
ilość*): **~ +***gen* loads of; **z ~iem**
(*zamknąć się*) with a bang

humo|r (**-ru**; *loc sg* **-rze**) *m*
1 (*komiczna scena, sytuacja*)
humour (*Brit*), humor (*US*) **2** (*stan
usposobienia*) mood; **poczucie ~u**
sense of humo(u)r

hura!, hurra! *excl* hurrah!

huraga|n (**-nu**, **-ny**; *loc sg* **-nie**) *m*
(*porywisty wiatr*) hurricane

hurtow|nia (**-ni**, **-nie**; *gen pl & dat,
loc sg* **-ni**) *f* **1** (*o przedsiębiorstwie*)
wholesalers *pl* **2** (*o magazynie*)
(wholesale) warehouse

hutni|k (**-ka**, **-cy**; *inst sg* **-kiem**) *m*
(*stali, żelaza*) steelworker

hydrauli|k (**-ka**, **-cy**; *inst sg* **-kiem**)
m (*robotnik wykonujący prace
wodnokanalizacyjne*) plumber

~ się *vr:* **~ się z kimś/czymś**
(*utożsamiać się*) to identify with
sb/sth
ideologi|a (**-i**, **-e**; *gen pl & dat, loc sg*
-i) *f* (*system poglądów*) ideology
idio|ta (**-ty**, **-ci**; *dat & loc sg* **-cie**) *m*
decl like f in sg (*pot: głupek*) idiot
idiot|ka (**-ki**, **-ki**; *dat & loc sg* **-ce**;
gen pl **-ek**) *f* (*pot: głupek*) idiot
idol (**-a**, **-e**; *gen pl* **-i**) *m* (*bożyszcz*)
idol
idziesz *itd. vb zob.* **iść**
igła (**igły**, **igły**; *dat & loc sg* **igle**; *gen
pl* **igieł**) *f* (*narzędzie: Bot*) needle
ignor|ować (**-uję**, **-ujesz**; *pf* **z-**) *vt*
(*lekceważyć*) to ignore
ikonka (**-ki**, **-ki**; *dat sg* **-ce**) *f*
(*komputerowy*) icon

○ **KEYWORD**

ich *pron gen pl od* **oni, one**
▷ *possessive pron* **1** (*z rzeczownikiem*)
their **2** (*bez rzeczownika*) theirs;
nie ma ~ they are not here;
zadzwoniłem do n~ I phoned
them; **to jest ~ dom** this is their
house; **~ znajomy** a friend of
theirs; **ten dom jest ~** this house
is theirs
ide|a (**-i**, **-e**; *gen pl & dat, loc sg* **-i**) *f*
(*pomysł, koncepcja*) idea
idealny *adj* **1** (*perfekcyjny*) perfect
2 (*nierzeczywisty*) ideal
ideal|t (**-łu**, **-ły**; *loc sg* **-le**) *m* (*wzór
doskonałości*) ideal; **~ studenta**
the ideal student
identyczny *adj* (*taki sam*)
identical
identyfik|ować (**-uję**, **-ujesz**; *pf*
z-) *vt* (*rozpoznawać*) to identify;

ile *pron +gen* **1** (*z rzeczownikami
policzalnymi*) how many; **ile
kobiet/sióstr?** how many
women/sisters?; **ilu chłopców/
braci?** how many boys/brothers?;
ile on ma lat? how old is he?; **ile
razy?** how many times?
2 (*w zdaniach względnych: z
rzeczownikami policzalnymi*)
as many; (*z rzeczownikami
niepoliczalnymi*) as much; **jedz, ile
chcesz** eat as much as you want
3 (*z rzeczownikami niepoliczalnymi*)
how much; **ile soku/ryżu/
kawy?** how much juice/rice/
coffee?; **ile czasu?** how long?; **ile
kosztuje ta bluzka?** how much is
this blouse?
4: **ile jedzenia!** what a lot of food!

ileś *pron +gen* (*non-vir*) some, a

number of
iloś|ć (**-ci**, **-ci**; gen pl & dat, loc sg
-ci) f (liczba, wielkość) amount,
quantity
ilustracj|a (**-i**, **-e**; gen pl & dat, loc sg
-i) f (przykład, rysunek) illustration
iluś pron +gen (vir) some, a
number of
ił (**iłu**, **iły**; loc sg **ile**) m (Geol) loam
im pron dat pl od **oni, one** (to)
them ▷ adv: **im prędzej, tym
lepiej** the sooner the better; **nie
ufam im** I don't trust them; **daj
im tę książkę** give them the
book
im. abbr (= imienia): **uniwersytet
~ Adama Mickiewicza** Adam
Mickiewicz University
imienin|y (**-**) pl (uroczystość) name
day sg

> **IMIENINY**
>
> **Imieniny** is the popular Polish
> custom of celebrating the
> name day of one's patron
> saint. **Imieniny** are celebrated
> like birthdays – the person
> celebrating is given presents
> and good wishes.

imi|ę (**-enia**, **-ona**) nt 1 (nazwa)
name 2 (pierwsze imię) first name
3 (honor) reputation; **szkoła
imienia Tadeusza Kościuszki**
Tadeusz Kosciuszko School; **jak
masz na ~?** (pot) what's your
name?; **w czyimś imieniu** on
(Brit) lub in (US) behalf of sb; **w ~
Ojca, i Syna i Ducha Świętego**
in the name of the Father, the Son
and the Holy Spirit

imigracj|a (**-i**, **-e**; gen pl & dat, loc sg
-i) f (proces, ludzie) immigration
imigran|t (**-ta**, **-ci**; loc sg **-cie**) m
(osoba) immigrant
imigrować (**-uję**, **-ujesz**) vi to
immigrate
imit|ować (**-uję**, **-ujesz**) vt
(naśladować) to imitate
impon|ować (**-uję**, **-ujesz**; pf **za-**)
vi (wzbudzać podziw): **~ komuś
(czymś)** to impress sb (with sth)
impor|t (**-tu**; loc sg **-cie**) m (Ekon)
import
import|ować (**-uję**, **-ujesz**) vt
(towary, surowce) to import
impre|za (**-zy**, **-zy**; dat & loc
sg **-zie**) f 1 (kulturalna) event
2 (pot: towarzyska) party
imprez|ować (**-uję**, **-ujesz**) vi
to party
impulsywny adj (popędliwy)
impulsive
inaczej adv 1 (odmiennie)
differently 2 (w konsekwencji)
otherwise, or (else); **tak czy ~**
one way or another
indek|s (**-su**, **-sy**; loc sg **-sie**) m
1 (skorowidz) index 2 (studenta)
student record book
Indi|e (**-i**) pl India
indyjski adj (Geo) Indian; **Ocean
I~** the Indian Ocean
indy|k (**-ka**, **-ki**; inst sg **-kiem**) m
(drób) turkey
indywidualny adj individual
infekcj|a (**-i**, **-e**; gen pl & dat, loc sg
-i) f (zakażenie) infection
informacj|a (**-i**, **-e**; gen pl &
dat, loc sg **-i**) f 1 (o wiadomości)
piece of information 2 (o
danych) information 3 (o biurze)
information office (Brit) lub

bureau (US); **~ turystyczna** tourist information centre (Brit) lub center (US)

informatycz|ka (**-ki**, **-ki**; dat & loc sg **-ce**; gen pl **-ek**) f computer scientist

informaty|k (**-ka**, **-cy**; inst sg **-kiem**) m (specjalista komputerowy) computer scientist

informaty|ka (**-ki**; dat sg **-ce**) f (technologia, nauka) computer science

inform|ować (**-uję**, **-ujesz**; pf **po-**) vt: **~ kogoś (o czymś)** (powiadamiać) to inform sb (of sth); **~ się** vr (zasięgać informacji): **~ się o czymś** to inquire about sth

inhalacj|a (**-i**, **-e**; gen pl & dat, loc sg **-i**) f (zabieg leczniczy) inhalation

inicja|ł (**-łu**, **-ły**; loc sg **-le**) m (początkowa litera) initial

inny pron **1** (nie ten, nie taki) another **2** (różny) other, different ▷ m decl like adj: pot: człowiek) another man: **inni** pl (the) others pl; **coś innego** something else

inspekto|r (**-ra**, **-rzy** lub **-rowie**; loc sg **-rze**) m (kontroler) inspector

inspektor|ka (**-ki**, **-ki**; dat & loc sg **-ce**; gen pl **-ek**) f inspector

inspir|ować (**-uję**, **-ujesz**; pf **za-**) vt (artystę, dziecko) to inspire

instrukcj|a (**-i**, **-e**; gen pl & dat, loc sg **-i**) f (wskazówka) instruction; **~ obsługi** instructions pl (for use)

instrumen|t (**-tu**, **-ty**; loc sg **-cie**) m (przyrząd, narzędzie) instrument

instynk|t (**-tu**, **-ty**; loc sg **-cie**) m (przetrwania) instinct

insuli|na (**-ny**; dat & loc sg **-nie**) f (Med) insulin

intelektuali|sta (**-sty**, **-ści**; dat & loc sg **-ście**) m decl like f in sg (wykształcona osoba) intellectual

intelektualist|ka (**-ki**, **-ki**; dat & loc sg **-ce**; gen pl **-ek**) f intellectual

inteligencj|a (**-i**) f **1** (umysł) intelligence **2** (grupa społeczna) intelligentsia

inteligentny adj (pomysł, odpowiedź) intelligent

intensywny adj **1** (uczenie się, szukanie) intensive **2** (kolor) intense

intere|s (**-su**, **-sy**; loc sg **-sie**) m **1** (pożytek, zysk) interest **2** (sprawa, przedsiębiorstwo) business **3** (przedsięwzięcie) deal

interes|ować (**-uję**, **-ujesz**; pf **za-**) vt (wzbudzać chęć poznania) to interest; **~ się** vr: **~ się** +inst (być zaciekawionym) to be interested in

interesujący adj (zajmujący, absorbujący) interesting

interna|t (**-tu**, **-ty**; loc sg **-cie**) m (miejsce zamieszkania uczniów) (school) dormitory; **szkoła z ~em** boarding school

internet (**-tu**, **-cie**) m internet

interni|sta (**-sty**, **-ści**; dat & loc sg **-ście**) m decl like f in sg (lekarz) internist

internist|ka (**-ki**, **-ki**; dat & loc sg **-ce**; gen pl **-ek**) f internist

interpretacj|a (**-i**, **-e**; gen pl & dat, loc sg **-i**) f (wyjaśnienie) interpretation

interpunkcj|a (**-i**; dat & loc sg **-i**) f (zasady pisowni) punctuation

interweni|ować (**-uję**, **-ujesz**) vi (w jakiejś sprawie) to intervene

intymny adj (prywatny, osobisty) intimate

inwali|da (**-dy**, **-dzi**; *dat & loc sg* **-dzie**) *m decl like f in sg* (*osoba niepełnosprawna*) disabled person

inwalid|ka (**-ki**, **-ki**; *dat & loc sg* **-ce**; *gen pl* **-ek**) *f* disabled person

inwest|ować (**-uję**, **-ujesz**; *pf* **za-**) *vt* to invest ▷ *vi*: **~ w** (*pieniądze, czas, energię*) to invest in

inwestycj|a (**-i**, **-e**; *gen pl & dat, loc sg* **-i**) *f* investment

inż. *abbr* (=*inżynier*) engineer

inżynie|r (**-ra**, **-rowie**; *loc sg* **-rze**) *m* (*osoba*) engineer

inżynier|ka (**-ki**, **-ki**; *dat & loc sg* **-ce**; *pl* **-ek**) *f* engineer

Ira|k (**-ku**; *inst sg* **-kiem**) *m* Iraq

Ira|n (**-nu**; *loc sg* **-nie**) *m* Iran

Irlandczy|k (**-ka**, **-cy**; *inst sg* **-kiem**) *m* Irishman

Irlandi|a (**-i**) *f* Ireland; **~ Północna** Northern Ireland

Irland|ka (**-ki**, **-ki**; *dat sg* **-ce**; *gen pl* **-ek**) *f* Irishwoman

irlandzki *adj* Irish

ironi|a (**-i**; *dat & loc sg* **-i**) *f* (*losu, sytuacji, komentarza*) irony

ironiczny *adj* (*sarkastyczny, kąśliwy*) ironic

iryt|ować (**-uję**, **-ujesz**; *pf* **z-**) *vt* (*drażnić, denerwować*) to irritate; **~ się** *vr*: **~ się czymś** (*denerwować się*) to get annoyed at sth

isla|m (**-mu**; *loc sg* **-mie**) *m* (*Rel*) Islam

islamski *adj* (*kraj*) Islamic

Islandi|a (**-i**) *f* Iceland

ist|nieć (**-nieję**, **-niejesz**) *vi* (*egzystować*) to exist; **~ od** +*gen*... to have existed since...

isto|ta (**-ty**, **-ty**; *dat & loc sg* **-cie**) *f* **1** (*sens*) essence **2** (*Bio*) creature; **~ ludzka** human being; **w istocie**

in fact

istotnie *adv* **1** (*prawdziwie*) indeed **2** (*całkowicie*) essentially, fundamentally **3** (*w ważny sposób*) significantly

istotny *adj* **1** (*prawdziwy*) real **2** (*całkowity*) essential **3** (*ważny*) significant

iść (**idę, idziesz**) *vi* to go; **~ piechotą** to go on foot

○ CHODZIĆ/IŚĆ/PÓJŚĆ
○
○ **Chodzić, iść** and **pójść** are
○ all verbs of motion meaning
○ to go (on foot), but they have
○ different implications. With
○ the perfective verb – **pójść**
○ – the emphasis is on the act
○ of going to and arriving at
○ the destination, whereas
○ with the imperfective verbs
○ – **chodzić** and **iść** – the focus
○ is more on the act of going
○ itself and it is not made clear
○ whether the subject arrives at
○ the destination or not.

itd. *abbr* (=*i tak dalej*) etc.

itp. *abbr* (=*i tym podobne lub podobnie*) etc.

izolat|ka (**-ki**, **-ki**; *dat & loc sg* **-ce**; *gen pl* **-ek**) *f* (*oddział w szpitalu*) isolation ward

izol|ować (**-uję**, **-ujesz**) *vt* **1** (*pf* **od-**) (*ludzi*) to isolate **2** (*pf* **za-**) (*okno*) to insulate

iż *conj* (*książk*) *od* **że** that

Izrael (**-a**) *m* Israel

j

ja pron I ▷ nt inv **1** (*jako podmiot zdania*) I **2** (*jako podmiot lub dopełnienie w zdaniu*) I **3** (*osobiście*) self; **ja też lubię lody** I like ice cream too; **mój brat i ja** my brother and I; **niższy niż ja** shorter than me; **ja sam to zrobię** I'll do it myself

jabł|ko (-**ka**, -**ka**; *inst sg* -**kiem**; *gen pl* -**ek**) *nt* (*owoc*) apple

jadal|nia (-**ni**, -**nie**; *gen pl & dat, loc sg* -**ni**) *f* dining room

jadalny *adj* (*rośliny*) edible ▷ *m decl like adj* (*miejsce*) dining room

jadę *itd. vb zob.* **jechać**

jadł *itd. vb zob.* **jeść**

jadłospi|s (-**su**, -**sy**; *loc sg* -**sie**) *m* (*spis dań*) menu

jaj|ko (-**ka**, -**ka**; *inst sg* -**kiem**; *gen pl* -**ek**) *nt* (*Kulin*) egg; **~ sadzone** fried egg

jaj|o (-**a**, -**a**) *nt* **1** egg **2** (*rozmnażanie*) egg **3** (*jądro męskie*) ball

○ **KEYWORD**

jak *pron* **1** (*zaimek pytajny*) how; **jak daleko?** how far?; **jak się masz?** (*familiar sg*) how are you?; **jak smakuje?** how does it taste?; **jak wygląda?** what does he look like? **2** (*zaimek względny*) as, like; **zrobił, jak chciałem** he did as I wanted; **wiesz, jak to napisać?** do you know how to write that?; **nie wiemy, jak wygląda nowe mieszkanie** we don't know what the new flat looks like **3** (*opisując nasilenie*): **jak wspaniale!** how wonderful! ▷ *conj* **1** (*porównując*) as; **tak przystojny jak ja** as handsome as me; **za młody jak na dyrektora** too young to be a director; **tak jak...** just like... **2** (*kiedy*) when; **jak skończysz, idź do domu** go home when you finish; **widziałem go, jak przechodził przez ulicę** I saw him crossing the street **3** (*jeżeli*) if; **jak chcesz, możemy pójść na spacer** we can go for a walk if you like; **jak nie ten, to tamten** if not this one, then that one ▷ *part*: **jak najszybciej** as soon as possible; **jak gdyby** as if

○ **KEYWORD**

jaki *pron decl like adj* **1** (*wprowadzając pytanie ogólne*)

what; **jakie lody lubisz?** what ice cream do you like?; **jaki to język?** what language is that?
2 (*dokonując wyboru z podanych opcji*) which; **jakie chcesz piwo: małe czy duże?** which would you prefer, a pint or a half?
3 (*przed przymiotnikiem*) how; **jaka ona jest piękna!** how beautiful she is!
4 (*przed rzeczownikiem*) what; **jaki piękny dom!** what a beautiful house!
jakiś (*f* **jakaś**; *nt* **jakieś**) *pron* **1** some **2** (*nieco, trochę*) a little bit; **~ student pytał o ciebie** some student was asking about you; **wróci za jakąś godzinę** he'll be back in an hour or so; **był ~ markotny** he was a little bit glum
jako *conj* (*w charakterze kogoś/czegoś*) as; **ja ~ były prezydent...** as a former chairman,...; **~ tako** (*nieźle*) so-so
jakoś|ć (**-ci**; *dat & loc sg* **-ci**) *f* (*towaru, życia*) quality
Japoni|a (**-i**) *f* Japan
japoński *adj* Japanese

jarski *adj* (*bezmięsny*) vegetarian
ja|sno *adv* **1** (*wyjaśniać, pisać*) clearly **2** (*błyszczeć, ubierać się*) brightly
ja|sny *adj* **1** (*pokój, spojrzenie, żarówka*) bright **2** (*włosy*) blonde **3** (*o kolorze*) light **4** (*skóra*) pale **5** (*zrozumiały*) clear; **czy to jest jasne?** is that clear?
jawny *adj* **1** (*spotkanie, proces*) public **2** (*podziw, żal, niechęć*) open **3** (*kłamstwo*) blatant
jaz|da (**-dy, -dy**; *dat & loc sg* **jeździe**) *f* **1** (*samochodem*) drive; (*autobusem*) journey; (*motocyklem, rowerem*) ride **2** (*ruch samochodu*) driving; (*ruch motocykla, roweru*) riding; **~ konna** horse riding; **~ na nartach** skiing; **prawo jazdy** driving licence (*Brit*), driver's license (*US*); **rozkład jazdy** timetable (*Brit*), schedule (*US*)
ją *pron acc od* **ona**
je *pron* **1** *acc sg od* **ono 2** *acc pl od* **one**
jechać (**jadę, jedziesz**; *imp* **jedź**; *pf* **po-**) *vi* **1** (*na wakacje, do innych krajów, do pracy*) to go **2** (*na motocyklu, koniu*) to ride **3** (*prowadzić samochód*) to drive **4** (*o środkach lokomocji: kursować*) to run; **~ na nartach** to ski; **~ (po~ pf) za granicę** to go abroad
jeden *decl like adj num* (*cyfra*) one ▷ *adj* **1** (*los, charakter*) one **2** (*jakiś*) a; **jedna druga** one half; **jeszcze ~** one more; **z jednej strony... z drugiej strony...** on the one

hand... on the other hand...; **ani ~** not a single one

jedenasty num decl like adj eleventh

jedenaście num decl like adj eleven

jednak conj (ale) but, yet

jednakowy adj **1** (równy) equal **2** (taki sam, identyczny) identical

jedno pron **1** one thing **2** (jedność, wszystko) one **3** (ta sama rzecz) one and the same; **~ jest pewne** one thing is for certain

jednocześnie adv (w tym samym czasie) simultaneously

jednodniowy adj **1** (seminarium, wyjazd) one-day **2** (zarost, pisklę) one-day-old

jednoosobowy adj **1** (firma) one-man **2** (pokój, łóżko) single

jednost|ka (**-ki**, **-ki**; dat & loc sg **-ce**; gen pl **-ek**) f **1** (pojedyncza osoba) individual **2** (przy pomiarach) unit

jednoś|ć (**-ci**; dat & loc sg **-ci**) f **1** (spójność, zgoda) unity **2** (bycie całością) whole

jedyna|k (**-ka**, **-cy**; inst sg **-kiem**) m only child

jedynie adv **1** (wyłącznie) only **2** (zaledwie) merely

jedyn|ka (**-ki**, **-ki**; dat sg **-ce**; gen pl **-ek**) f **1** (cyfra) one **2** (nr autobusu/ domu, stacja radiowa) one **3** (ocena w szkole) ≈ F

jedyny adj **1** (kraj, gatunek) only **2** (umiłowany) dearest; **~ w swoim rodzaju** unique

jedzeni|e (**-a**) nt **1** (pokarm) food **2** (konsumowanie) eating

jego pron gen od **on, ono**

jej pron gen od **ona**

jemu pron dat od **on, ono**

jesie|ń (**-ni**, **-nie**; gen pl & dat, loc sg **-ni**) f (o porze roku) autumn (Brit), fall (US)

jest itd. vb zob. **być**

jeszcze part **1** (nadal) still **2** (już) still **3** (w przeczeniu) yet **4** (nawet; w porównaniu) even **5** (ponadto, więcej) more; **mamy ~ godzinę** we still have an hour; **~ przed miesiącem się nie znaliśmy** only a month ago we had not even met; **spotkali się ~ na studiach** they met whilst they were still students; **~ nie zadzwonił** he hasn't called yet; **~ droższy** even more expensive; **dziś jest ~ cieplej niż wczoraj** it's even warmer today than it was yesterday; **coś ~?** anything else?; **~ raz** one more time; **poczekaj ~ parę minut** wait another few minutes; **~ jeden przykład** one more example

jeść (**jem, jesz**; 3 pl **jedzą**; imp **jedz**; pt **jadł, jedli**; pf **z-**) vt (spożywać) to eat; **~ (z~ pf) śniadanie/ kanapkę** to have breakfast/a sandwich; **chce mi się ~** I'm hungry

jeśli conj (jeżeli, pod warunkiem) if; **~ chcesz, pójdziemy do kina** we can go to the cinema if you want; **~ nie teraz, to kiedy?** if not now, then when?; **~ nie przestanie padać, zostaniemy w domu** if it doesn't stop raining we'll stay at home

jezio|ro (**-ra**, **-ra**; loc sg **-rze**) nt (Geo) lake

je|ździć (**-żdżę, -ździsz**; imp **-źdź**) vi **1** (na wakacje, do innych krajów, *do pracy)* to go **2** *(na motocyklu, rowerze)* to ride **3** *(prowadzić samochód)* to drive **4** *(być pasażerem w samochodzie)* to ride **5** *(o środkach lokomocji: kursować)* to run; **czym jeździsz do pracy?** *(familiar sg)* how do you get to work?; **~ na nartach** to ski

jeżeli *conj* if; *zob. też* **jeśli**

język|k (**-ka**, **-ki**; *inst sg* **-kiem**) *m* **1** *(obcy, literacki, ciała, programowania)* language **2** *(organ mowy)* tongue; **~ ojczysty** mother tongue

jogur|t (**-tu**, **-ty**; *loc sg* **-cie**) *m* *(Kulin)* yoghurt

jubile|r (**-ra**, **-rzy**; *loc sg* **-rze**) *m* **1** *(osoba)* jeweller *(Brit)*, jeweler *(US)* **2** *(sklep)* jeweller's *(Brit)*, jeweler's *(US)*

Jugosławi|a (**-i**) *f*: **Republiki byłej Jugosławii** the former Yugoslavia

jury *nt inv* *(komisja sędziowska)* jury

jut|ro (**-ra**; *loc sg* **-rze**) *nt* *(następny dzień)* tomorrow ▷ *adv* *(następnego dnia)* tomorrow; **do jutra!** see you tomorrow!; **~ rano** tomorrow morning

jutrzejszy *adj* *(lekcja, gazeta, spotkanie)* tomorrow's

już *adv* **1** *(twierdząco)* already **2** *(pytająco)* yet **3** *(w przeczeniach)* any more; **~ to zrobiliśmy** we've already done it; **czy skończyła ~ czytać tę gazetę?** has she finished reading that newspaper yet?; **ona ~ tutaj nie mieszka** she no longer lives here

● **JUWENALIA**
●
● **Juwenalia** is a student event
● that takes place every year
● in May or June in university
● cities. **Juwenalia** lasts up
● to around ten days, during
● which a wide range of
● sporting events are organized
● by students for students.

k

kabe|l (**-la**, **-le**; *gen pl* **-li**) *m* (*telefoniczny, elektryczny*) cable

kab|ina (**-ny**, **-ny**; *dat sg & loc sg* **-nie**) *f* 1 (*w pojeździe mechanicznym*) cabin 2 (*w łazience*) cubicle 3 (*telefoniczna*) booth

kac (**-a**) *m* hangover

kacz|ka (**-ki**, **-ki**; *dat sg & loc sg* **-ce**; *gen pl* **-ek**) *f* duck

kaja|k (**-ku**, **-ki**) *m* canoe

kakao *nt inv* (*nasiona, napój*) cocoa

kalafio|r (**-ra**, **-ry**; *loc sg* **-rze**) *m* cauliflower

kaleczyć (**-ę**, **-ysz**; *pf* **s-**) *vt* 1 to cut 2 (*przen: mowę: robiąc błędy w języku*) to murder; **~ się** *vr* to cut o.s.; **~ (s~ *pf*) się w nogę** to cut one's leg

kale|ka (**-ki**, **-ki**; *dat sg & loc sg* **-ce**) *m/f decl like f* cripple; **~ życiowy** lame duck

kalendarz (**-a**, **-e**; *gen pl* **-y**) *m* (*ścienny, juliański*) calendar

kalkulato|r (**-ra**, **-ry**; *loc sg* **-rze**) *m* calculator

kaloryfe|r (**-ra**, **-ry**; *loc sg* **-rze**) *m* radiator

kame|ra (**-ry**, **-ry**; *loc sg* **-rze**) *f* camera; **~ wideo** video camera

kamienic|a (**-y**, **-e**) *f* (*czynszowa, ośmiopiętrowa*) tenement (house)

kamienny *adj* 1 (*mur*) stone 2 (*wyraz twarzy*) stony 3 (*sen*) deep; **wydobywać** (**wydobyć** *pf*) **węgiel ~** to mine coal

kamie|ń (**-nia**, **-nie**; *gen pl* **-ni**) *m* 1 stone 2 (*Tech: panewka, w zegarku*) jewel 3 (*w zapalniczce*) flint; **~ szlachetny** gem(stone); **~ żółciowy** gallstone; **~ nazębny** tartar; **śpi jak ~** he is sleeping like a log; **~ spadł mu z serca** (*przen*) it was a load off his mind

kamizel|ka (**-ki**, **-ki**; *dat sg & loc sg* **-ce**; *gen pl* **-ek**) *f* waistcoat (Brit), vest (US); **policjant ma kamizelkę kuloodporną** the policeman has a bullet-proof vest; **mieć na sobie kamizelkę ratunkową** to wear a life jacket

kamy|k (**-ka**, **-ki**; *inst sg* **-kiem**) *m* pebble; **wrzucać** (**wrzucić** *pf*) **~ do czyjegoś ogródka** (*przen*) to provoke sb

Kana|da (**-dy**; *loc sg* **-dzie**) *f* Canada

kanadyjski *adj* Canadian

Kanadyjczy|k (**-ka**, **-cy**; *inst sg* **-kiem**) *m* Canadian

Kanadyj|ka (**-ki**, **-ki**; *dat sg* **-ce**; *gen pl* **-ek**) *f* Canadian

kana|ł (**-łu**, **-ły**; *loc sg* **-le**)

m **1** (*wodny*) ditch **2** (*rów odprowadzający nieczystości*) sewer **3** (*w telewizji, na morzu*) channel **4** (*droga łącząca dwa morza*) canal

kana|pa (**-py, -py**; *dat sg & loc sg* **-pie**) *f* (*mebel do spania, do siedzenia*) sofa

kanap|ka (**-ki, -ki**; *dat sg & loc sg* **-ce**; *gen pl* **-ek**) *f* (*z serem, z masłem*) sandwich

kancelari|a (**-i, -e**; *gen pl* **-i**) *f* office; **~ adwokacka** chambers *pl* (*Brit*); **K~ Prezesa Rady Ministrów** Prime Minister's Office

kandyda|t (**-ta, -ci**; *loc sg* **-cie**) *m* candidate; **jest dobrym ~em na męża** he is good husband material

kandyd|ować (**-uję, -ujesz**) *vi:* **~ (do parlamentu)** to stand (for Parliament) (*Brit*), to run (for Congress) (*US*)

kangu|r (**-ra, -ry**; *loc sg* **-rze**) *m* kangaroo

kanto|r (**-ra, -ry**; *loc sg* **-rze**) *m* (*wymiany walut*) bureau de change

kapelusz (**-a, -e**; *gen pl* **-y**) *m* **1** (*góralski, męski*) hat **2** (*u grzyba*) cap

kapitalistyczny *adj* (*ustrój, kraj*) capitalist

kapitaliz|m (**-mu**; *loc sg* **-mie**) *m* capitalism; **~ z ludzką twarzą** capitalism with a human face

kaplic|a (**-y, -e**) *f* chapel

kapła|n (**-na, -ni**; *loc sg* **-nie**) *m* (*w kościele*) priest

kapu|sta (**-sty**; *dat sg & loc sg* **-ście**) *f* **1** cabbage **2** (*kiszona lub kwaszona*) sauerkraut **3** (*włoska*)

savoy (cabbage); **groch z kapustą** (*przen*) hodgepodge

kapuśnia|k¹ (**-ku, -ki**) *m* cabbage soup

kapuśnia|k² (**-ka, -ki**; *inst sg* **-kiem**) *m* (*drobny deszcz*) drizzle

ka|ra (**-ry, -ry**; *dat sg & loc sg* **-rze**) *f* **1** (*cielesna, dotkliwa*) punishment **2** (*urzędowa, pieniężna*) fine; **~ śmierci** capital punishment

karabi|n (**-nu, -ny**; *loc sg* **-nie**) *m* rifle; **strzelać** (**strzelić** *pf*) **z ~u maszynowego** to fire a machine gun

ka|rać (**-rzę, -rzesz**; *pf* **u-**) *vt* **1** to punish **2** (*urzędowo*) to penalize

kardiolo|g (**-ga, -dzy** *lub* **-gowie**; *inst sg* **-giem**) *m* (*lekarz specjalista*) cardiologist

karet|ka (**-ki, -ki**; *dat sg & loc sg* **-ce**; *gen pl* **-ek**) *f* (*pogotowia, szpitalna*) ambulance

karie|ra (**-ry, -ry**; *dat sg & loc sg* **-rze**) *f* (*praca zawodowa*) career

kar|k (**-ku, -ki**; *inst sg* **-kiem**) *m* nape of the neck; **ona ma głowę na ~u** she has her head screwed on; **nadstawiać** (**nadstawić** *pf*) **~u** to stick one's neck out

kar|mić (**-mię, -misz**) *vt* (*żywić*) (*pf* **na-**) **1** to feed **2** (*niemowlę piersią*) to breast-feed **3** (*niemowlę butelką*) to bottle-feed; **~ się** *vr* (*o zwierzętach*): **~ się (czymś)** to feed (on sth)

karnawa|ł (**-łu, -ły**; *loc sg* **-le**) *m* carnival

karne|t (**-tu, -ty**; *loc sg* **-cie**) *m* **1** (*na występy artystyczne*) subscription card **2** (*na komunikację*) book of tickets

kar|p (**-pia, -pie**; *gen pl* **-pi**) *m* (*Zool,*

Culin: smażony, w galarecie) carp

Karpat|y (-) *pl* the Carpathian Mountains

kar|ta (-ty, -ty; *dat sg & loc sg* **-cie)** *f* **1** (*w zeszycie*) sheet **2** (*w książce*) page **3** (*walet, król*) (playing) card **4** (*jadłospis*) menu; **~ kredytowa** credit card; **~ płatnicza** cash card; **~ gwarancyjna** guarantee slip; **~ do biblioteki** library card; **~ telefoniczna** phonecard; **~ pocztowa** postcard; **domek z kart** (*przen*) house of cards

kart|ka (-ki, -ki; *dat sg & loc sg* **-ce**; *gen pl* **-ek)** *f* **1** (*w zeszycie*) sheet **2** (*w książce*) page **3** (*żywieniowa*) ration card; **~ widokówka** postcard

kartofe|l (-la, -le; *gen pl* **-li)** *m* (*gotowany, w mundurku*) potato

kartot|eka (-eki, -eki; *dat sg & loc sg* **-ece**; *gen pl* **-ek)** *f* **1** (*katalog kartkowy*) card index **2** (*karty z danymi*) files *pl*

ka|sa (-sy, -sy; *dat sg & loc sg* **-sie)** *f* **1** (*sklepowa*) cash desk **2** (*w supermarkecie*) checkout **3** (*w centrum handlowym*) till **4** (*w kinie, teatrze*) box office **5** (*okienko na dworcu*) ticket office **6** (*pieniądze państwa*) treasury **7** (*sejf*) safe

kase|ta (-ty, -ty; *dat sg & loc sg* **-cie)** *f* **1** (*taśma z nagraniem*) cassette **2** (*w fotografii*) cartridge

kasje|r (-ra, -rzy; *loc sg* **-rze)** *m* **1** (*sklep*) cashier **2** (*kino, teatr*) box-office clerk **3** (*bank*) teller **4** (*dworzec*) ticket clerk

kasjer|ka (-ki, -ki; *dat sg & loc sg* **-ce**; *gen pl* **-ek)** *f* **1** (*sklep*) cashier **2** (*kino, teatr*) box-office clerk **3** (*bank*) teller **4** (*dworzec*) ticket clerk

kasz|a (-y, -e) *f* **1** (*produkt spożywczy*) groats *pl* **2** (*potrawa*) porridge; **~ gryczana/jęczmienna** buckwheat/barley; **jeść (zjeść** *pf*) **kogoś w kaszy** to walk all over sb

kaszan|ka (-ki, -ki; *dat sg & loc sg* **-ce**; *gen pl* **-ek)** *f* black pudding (*Brit*), blood sausage (*US*)

kasze|l (-lu) *m* (*suchy, mokry*) cough; **dostawać (dostać** *pf*) **atak kaszlu** to have a coughing fit

kaszl|eć (-ę, -esz; *pf* **-nąć)** *vi* to cough

katakliz|m (-mu, -my; *loc sg* **-mie)** *m* (*powódź, trzęsienie ziemi*) disaster

katalo|g (-gu, -gi; *inst sg* **-giem)** *m* catalogue (*Brit*), catalog (*US*); **~ alfabetyczny/rzeczowy** catalogue arranged alphabetically/by subject

kata|r (-ru, -ry; *loc sg* **-rze)** *m* catarrh; **on ma ~** he has a runny nose; **~ sienny** hay fever

katastro|fa (-fy, -fy; *dat sg & loc sg* **-fie)** *f* **1** (*motoryzacyjna*) accident **2** (*powietrzna*) (plane) crash **3** (*tragedia*) catastrophe

kated|ra (-ry, -ry; *dat sg & loc sg* **-rze)** *f* **1** (*główny kościół*) cathedral **2** (*pulpit wykładowcy*) teacher's desk **3** (*na uniwersytecie: jednostka administracyjna*) department **4** (*stanowisko profesora*) chair

kategori|a (-i, -e; *gen pl* **-i)** *f* (*klasa*) category

katolicki *adj* (*kościół, wiara*) (Roman) Catholic

katolicyz|m (-mu; *loc sg* **-mie)** *m*

(Roman) Catholicism

katolicz|ka (**-ki, -ki**; *loc sg* **-ce**; *gen pl* **-ek**) *f* (Roman) Catholic

katoli|k (**-ka, -cy**; *inst sg* **-kiem**) *m* (Roman) Catholic

ka|wa (**-wy**; *dat sg & loc sg* **-wie**) *f* **1** (*drzewo*) coffee plant **2** (*ziarna*) coffee (beans *pl*) **3** (*czarna, z mlekiem*) coffee **4** (*nom pl* **-wy**) (*porcja napoju*) a (cup of) coffee

kawale|r (**-ra, -rowie** *lub* **-rzy**; *loc sg* **-rze**) *m* **1** (*mężczyzna bez żony*) bachelor **2** (*młody mężczyzna*) youth; **stary ~** confirmed bachelor

kawaler|ka (**-ki, -ki**; *dat sg & loc sg* **-ce**; *gen pl* **-ek**) *f* (*mieszkanie jednopokojowe*) one-room flat (*Brit*) *lub* apartment (*US*)

kawa|ł (**-łu, -ły**; *loc sg* **-le**) *m* **1** (*znaczna część*) chunk **2** (*żart*) joke **3** (*figiel*) trick; **powiedzieć** (**opowiedzieć** *pf*) **pieprzny ~** to tell a dirty joke

kawa|łek (**-ka, -ki**; *inst sg* **-kiem**) *m* (*fragment całości*) piece; **grać** (**zagrać** *pf*) **~** to play a piece; **ciężki ~ chleba** a hard-earned crust

kawiar|nia (**-ni, -nie**; *gen pl* **-ni**) *f* café

ka|zać (**-żę, -żesz**) *vi impf/pf*: **~ komuś coś zrobić** to tell sb to do sth; **kazał mi odpowiedzieć na pytanie** he told me to answer the question

każdy *pron decl like adj* **1** every **2** (*każdy człowiek*) everybody **3** (*z wymienionych przedmiotów*) each; **każdego dnia/roku** every day/year; **o każdej porze dnia** any time of the day; **ma rację**

za ~m razem he is right every time; **w ~m razie trzeba tam pójść** in any case one should go; **~ z nas umie pływać** each one of us knows how to swim; **mamy prezent dla każdego z was** we have a present for each of you

k|ąpać (**-pię, -piesz**; *pf* **wy-**) *vt* to bath (*Brit*), to bathe (*US*); **~ się** *vr* **1** (*w wannie*) to have a bath, to bathe (*US*) **2** (*w basenie*) to swim; **~ się w promieniach słońca** to sunbathe

kąpiel (**-i, -e**; *gen pl* **-i**) *f* **1** (*w wannie*) bath **2** (*w basenie*) swim; **brać** (**wziąć** *pf*) **~** to have a bath

kąpielówk|i (**-ek**) *pl* swimming trunks

ką|t (**-ta, -ty**; *loc sg* **-cie**) *m* **1** (*Mat*) angle **2** (*róg*) corner **3** (*pot*: *lokum*) pad

kciu|k (**-ka, -ki**; *inst sg* **-kiem**) *m* thumb; **trzymam za ciebie ~i** (*przen*) I'm keeping my fingers crossed for you

keczu|p (**-pu**; *loc sg* **-pie**) *m* (*sos pomidorowy*) ketchup

kefi|r (**-ru**; *loc sg* **-rze**) *m* fermented milk drink popular in Eastern European countries

kelne|r (**-ra, -rzy**; *loc sg* **-rze**) *m* waiter

kelner|ka (**-ki, -ki**; *dat sg & loc sg* **-ce**; *gen pl* **-ek**) *f* waitress

kempin|g (**-gu, -gi**; *inst sg* **-giem**) *m* campsite (*Brit*), camping ground (*US*)

kg *abbr* (= kilogram) kg

kibi|c (**-a, -e**) *m* **1** (*widz sportowy*) supporter **2** (*fan sportu: Sport*) fan

kibic|ować (**-uję, -ujesz**) *vi* to look on; **kibicuje naszej**

drużynie od lat he has supported our team for years

kich|ać (-am, -asz; *pf* **-nąć)** *vi* to sneeze; **kicham na problemy** (*przen*) I couldn't care less about the problems

kiedy *pron* when ▷ *conj* **1** when **2** (*podczas gdy*) while; **~ przyjdziesz?** when will you arrive?; **od ~ pracujesz?** since when have you been working?; **pójdziemy ~ bądź** we can go at any time; **zrobimy to ~ indziej** we'll do it some other time; **~ tylko będę miał okazję** whenever I have a chance; **~ tylko wstałem, on wyszedł** as soon as I got up, he went out

kiedykolwiek *adv* **1** (*nieważne kiedy*) whenever **2** (*w pytaniach*) ever; **czy byłaś ~ w Londynie?** have you ever been to London?

kielisz|ek (-ka, -ki; *inst sg* **-kiem)** *m* **1** (*do alkoholu*) glass **2** (*do jajek*) (egg) cup; **stuknijmy się kieliszkami!** let's clink glasses!

kiełbas|a (-sy, -sy; *loc sg* **-sie)** *f* sausage

kier|ować (-uję, -ujesz) *vt* **1** (*pf* **s-**) (*wysłać*) to refer **2** (*słowa*) to direct **3** (*reflektor, lunetę*) to aim **4** (*wzrok*) to direct **5** (*donos*) to file ▷ *vi* +*inst* **1** (*pojazdem mechanicznym*) to drive **2** (*sterować*) to steer **3** (*zarządzać*) to manage; **~ się** (*pf* **s-**) *vr*: **~ się do** +*gen* to head towards; **~ się sercem** to be governed by one's emotions

kierowc|a (-y, -y) *m decl like f in sg* **1** driver **2** (*limuzyny*) chauffeur

kierownic|a (-y, -e) *f* **1** (*w samochodzie*) (steering) wheel **2** (*w rowerze*) handlebars *pl*

kierowni|k (-ka, -cy; *inst sg* **-kiem)** *m* (*biura, firmy*) manager

kierun|ek (-ku, -ki) *m* **1** (*trasy*) direction **2** (*w literaturze*) trend **3** (*na wyższej uczelni*) subject (*Brit*), major (*US*); **w kierunku Warszawy** towards Warsaw; **w tym samym kierunku** in the same direction

ki|j (-ja, -je; *gen pl* **-jów)** *m* stick; **~ bilardowy** cue; **~ golfowy** (golf) club; **bez ~a nie przystąp** stay well away from him/her/them

kilka *num* several

kilo *nt inv* kilo

kilogra|m (-ma, -my; *loc sg* **-mie)** *m* kilogram(me), kilo; **29 złotych za ~** 29 zloty a *lub* per kilo

kilomet|r (-ra, -ry; *loc sg* **-rze)** *m* kilometre (*Brit*), kilometer (*US*); **90 ~ów na godzinę** 90 kilometres an hour; **w odległości pięciu ~ów** five kilometres away

kim *pron inst, loc od* **kto; z ~ się spotkałeś?** who did you meet?

kimś *pron inst, loc od* **ktoś**

ki|no (-na, -na; *loc sg* **-nie)** *nt* **1** (*obiekt*) cinema (*Brit*), (movie) theater (*US*) **2** (*rodzaj sztuki*) the cinema (*Brit*), the movies *pl* (*US*); **iść (pójść** *pf*) **do kina** to go to the cinema; **co grają dziś w kinie?** what's on at the cinema today?

kios|k (-ku, -ki; *inst sg* **-kiem)** *m* (*z gazetami, z biletami*) kiosk

kiszony *adj* (*ogórek*) pickled; **kiszona kapusta** sauerkraut

klap|ki (-ek) *pl* (*buty*) flip-flops *pl*

kla|sa (-sy, -sy; *dat sg & loc sg* **-sie)** *f* **1** class **2** (*w szkole*) class **3** (*pomieszczenie w szkole*) classroom **4** (*rocznik uczniów*) form (*Brit*), grade (*US*); **miejsca w pierwszej/drugiej klasie** seats in first/second class

klasów|ka (**-ki, -ki**; *dat sg & loc sg* **-ce**; *gen pl* **-ek**) *f* test; **dostawać** (**dostać** *pf*) **piątkę z klasówki** to get top marks in the class test

klasyfik|ować (**-uję, -ujesz**; *pf* **s-**) *vt* to classify

klaszto|r (**-ru, -ry**; *loc sg* **-rze**) *m* **1** (*dla zakonników*) monastery **2** (*dla zakonnic*) convent; **wstępować** (**wstąpić** *pf*) **do ~u** to enter a monastery/convent

klawiatu|ra (**-ry, -ry**; *dat sg & loc sg* **-rze**) *f* (*komputera, fortepianu*) keyboard

klej (**-u, -e**) *m* (*roślinny, stolarski*) glue

klien|t (**-ta, -ci**; *loc sg* **-cie**) *m* **1** (*kupujący*) customer **2** (*interesant*) client

klient|ka (**-ki, -ki**; *dat sg & loc sg* **-ce**; *gen pl* **-ek**) *f* **1** (*kupująca*) customer **2** (*interesantka*) client

klima|t (**-tu**; *loc sg* **-cie**) *m* (*nom pl* **-ty**) (*zwrotnikowy, łagodny*) climate

klimatyzacj|a (**-i**) *f* air conditioning

klimatyzowany *adj* (*samochód, pomieszczenie*) air-conditioned

klini|ka (**-ki, -ki**; *dat sg & loc sg* **-ce**) *f* clinic

klisz|a (**-y, -e**) *f* (*w fotografii*) film

klu|b (**-bu, -by**; *loc sg* **-bie**) *m* (*nocny, sportowy*) club; **~ studencki** students' union

klucz (**-a, -e**; *gen pl* **-y**) *m* **1** (*do zamykania i otwierania zamka*) key **2** (*w muzyce*) clef **3** (*w technice*)

spanner (*Brit*), wrench (*US*); **dobra dieta to ~ do zdrowia** a good diet is the key to good health; **zamykać** (**zamknąć** *pf*) **coś na ~** to lock sth

klus|ka (**-ki, -ki**; *dat sg & loc sg* **-ce**; *gen pl* **-ek**) *f* dumpling; **mieć kluski w gębie** (*przen*) to mumble

kłamać (**-ię, -iesz**; *pf* **s-**) *vi* to lie; **on zawsze kłamie jak najęty** he always tells bare-faced lies

kłamc|a (**-y, -y**) *m decl like f in sg* liar

kłamst|wo (**-wa, -wa**; *loc sg* **-wie**) *nt* lie

kłaniać się (**-am, -asz**; *pf* **ukłonić**) *vr* **1** (*schylać się*) to bow **2** (*kiwnąć głową*) to nod **3** (*przen*) to say hello

kła|ść (**-dę, -dziesz**; *imp* **-dź**; *pt* **-dł**; *pf* **położyć**) *vt* **1** (*na półce, na półkę*) to put **2** (*do kieszeni*) to put **3** (*układać*) to lay; **~ się** *vr* **1** (*na wersalce*) to lie down **2** (*iść spać*) to go to bed; **~ coś do głowy komuś** to put something in sb's head

kłopot (**-tu, -ty**; *loc sg* **-cie**) *m* (*domowy, finansowy*) problem; **kłopoty** *pl* trouble; **w szkole ma ciągle ~y** he's always having problems at school; **on znów wpadł w ~y** he's in trouble again

kłopotliwy *adj* **1** (*przysparzający kłopot*) inconvenient **2** (*cisza, pytanie*) embarrassing

kłócić się (**-cę, -cisz**; *imp* **-ć**; *pf* **po-**) *vr* (*spierać się*) to quarrel

kłót|nia (**-ni, -nie**; *gen pl* **-ni**) *f* (*spór*) quarrel

kobiecy *adj* **1** (*urok*) feminine **2** (*narządy*) female **3** (*powieść, dolegliwość*) women's

kobie|ta (**-ty, -ty**; *dat sg & loc*

sg **-cie**) *f* woman; **~ lekkich obyczajów** loose woman

koch|ać (**-am, -asz**) *vt* (*z całego serca, namiętnie*) to love; **~ się** *vr* to love each other; **kochają się dwa razy dziennie** they make love twice a day; **kocha się w niej od lat** he has been in love with her for years

kochany *adj* dear

ko|d (**-du, -dy**; *loc sg* **-dzie**) *m* code; **podaj mi swój ~ pocztowy** give me your postcode (*Brit*) *lub* zip code (*US*)

kodek|s (**-su, -sy**; *loc sg* **-sie**) *m* (*cywilny, handlowy*) code; **~ drogowy** rules of the road, ≈ Highway Code (*Brit*)

kogo *pron gen, acc od* **kto**; **~ brakuje?** who's absent?; **~ widziałeś?** who(m) did you meet?; **ktoś, ~ znam** someone I know

kogoś *pron gen, acc od* **ktoś**

koko|s (**-su** *lub* **-sa, -sy**; *loc sg* **-sie**) *m* coconut

kolacj|a (**-i, -e**; *gen pl* **-i**) *f* 1 supper 2 (*wystawna, uroczysta*) dinner

kola|no (**-na, -na**; *loc sg* **-nie**) *nt* knee; **przeprosił na kolanach** he asked pardon on bended knees; **dziecko siedzi na kolanach u mamy** the child sits on his mother's lap; **stał w wodzie po kolana** he was standing knee-deep in water

kolarst|wo (**-wa**; *loc sg* **-wie**) *nt* cycling

kolczy|k (**-ka, -ki**; *inst sg* **-kiem**) *m* earring

kole|ga (**-gi, -dzy**; *dat sg & loc sg* **-dze**) *m decl like f in sg* 1 friend 2 (*w szkole*) school friend 3 (*w pracy*) colleague

kolej|j (**-i, -je**; *gen pl* **-i**) *f* 1 (*pociągi*) railway (*Brit*), railroad (*US*) 2 (*środek transportu*) rail 3 (*jeden po drugim*) turn; **jechał ~ą do Warszawy** he took the train to Warsaw; **jego ~** *lub* **~ na niego** (it's) his turn; **po kolei** in turn

kolej|ka (**-ki, -ki**; *dat sg & loc sg* **-ce**; *gen pl* **-ek**) *f* 1 (*podmiejska, na krótkich trasach*) local train 2 (*zabawka elektryczna*) model railway (*Brit*) *lub* railroad (*US*) 3 (*wyznaczone miesce, w szeregu*) turn 4 (*ogonek*) queue (*Brit*), line (*US*)

kolejno *adv* in turn

kolejny *adj* 1 (*jeden po drugim*) next 2 (*sąsiadujący*) consecutive 3 (*jeszcze jeden*) another

kolekcj|a (**-i, -e**; *gen pl* **-i**) *f* (*monet, obrazów*) collection

koleżan|ka (**-ki, -ki**; *dat sg & loc sg* **-ce**; *gen pl* **-ek**) *f* 1 friend 2 (*w szkole*) school friend 3 (*w pracy*) colleague

koleżeński *adj* (*relacja, osoba*) friendly

kolę|da (**-dy, -dy**; *dat sg & loc sg* **-dzie**) *f* (Christmas) carol

kolo|r (**-ru, -ry**; *loc sg* **-rze**) *m* 1 (*barwa: jasny, intensywny*) colour (*Brit*), color (*US*) 2 (*karo, pik*) suit; **jaki ~ mają te spodnie?** what colour are these trousers?; **jakiego ~u jest ta bluzka?** what colour is this blouse?

kolorowy *adj* 1 (*barwny*) colour (*Brit*), color (*US*) 2 (*różnorodny*) colourful (*Brit*), colorful (*US*) 3 (*o rasie*) coloured (*Brit*), colored (*US*)

kołd|ra (**-ry**, **-ry**; *dat sg & loc sg* **-rze**; *gen pl* **-er**) *f* quilt

ko|ło (**-ła**, **-ła**; *loc sg* **-le**; *gen pl* **kół**) *nt* **1** (*okrąg*) circle **2** (*w matematyce*) circle **3** (*w samochodzie*) wheel ▷ *prep +gen* (*niedaleko*) by, next to; **jeździć w ~** to go round in circles

kołysan|ka (**-ki**, **-ki**; *dat sg & loc sg* **-ce**; *gen pl* **-ek**) *f* lullaby

kołys|ka (**-ki**, **-ki**; *dat sg & loc sg* **-ce**; *gen pl* **-ek**) *f* cradle; **taki był od kołyski** he's been like that since he was a baby

komedi|a (**-i**, **-e**; *gen pl* **-i**) *f* **1** (*gatunek w sztuce*) comedy **2** (*przen: obłuda*) game

komen|da (**-dy**, **-dy**; *dat sg & loc sg* **-dzie**) *f* command; **~ policji** headquarters

komentarz (**-a**, **-e**; *gen pl* **-y**) *m* **1** commentary **2** (*uwaga*) comment; **odmawiać** (**odmówić** *pf*) **~a** to make no comment

komentato|r (**-ra**, **-rzy**; *loc sg* **-rze**) *m* commentator

koment|ować (**-uję**, **-ujesz**; *pf* **s-**) *vt* **1** (*robić uwagi*) to comment on **2** (*relacjonować: w sporcie*) to commentate on

komercyjny *adj* (*sukces, film*) commercial

komfortowy *adj* **1** (*łóżko, sytuacja*) comfortable **2** (*apartament*) luxury

komi|k (**-ka**, **-cy**; *inst sg* **-kiem**) *m* **1** (*artysta sceniczny*) comic actor **2** (*satyryk*) comedian

komik|s (**-su**, **-sy**; *loc sg* **-sie**) *m* **1** (*w gazecie*) strip cartoon **2** (*książka*) comic

komi|n (**-na**, **-ny**; *loc sg* **-nie**) *m* **1** chimney **2** (*w fabryce*) chimney **3** (*lokomotywy*) funnel

komin|ek (**-ka**, **-ki**; *inst sg* **-kiem**) *m* fireplace

komisaria|t (**-tu**, **-ty**; *loc sg* **-cie**) *m* (*też*: **~ policji**) police station

komisj|a (**-i**, **-e**; *gen pl* **-i**) *f* **1** (*śledcza, dyscyplinarna*) committee **2** (*rewizyjna*) board

komite|t (**-tu**, **-ty**; *loc sg* **-cie**) *m* (*organizacyjny, powitalny*) committee; **~ rodzicielski** ≈ parent-teacher association, ≈ PTA

komo|da (**-dy**, **-dy**; *dat sg & loc sg* **-dzie**) *f* chest of drawers

komór|ka (**-ki**, **-ki**; *dat sg & loc sg* **-ce**; *gen pl* **-ek**) *f* **1** (*w biologii*) cell **2** (*pot: telefon*) mobile (*Brit*), cellphone (*US*)

komórkowy *adj* cellular

komplek|s (**-su**, **-sy**; *loc sg* **-sie**) *m* (*budynków, niższości*) complex

komplemen|t (**-tu**, **-ty**; *loc sg* **-cie**) *m* compliment

komple|t (**-tu**, **-ty**; *loc sg* **-cie**) *m* **1** (*zestaw*) set **2** (*ubrań*) suit **3** (*na widowni*) full house **4** (*w samolocie*) full complement of passengers

kompletny *adj* **1** (*zbiór*) complete **2** (*absurd, pomyłka*) total

komplik|ować (**-uję**, **-ujesz**; *pf* **s-**) *vt* to complicate; **~ się** *vr* to become more complicated

kompo|t (**-tu**, **-ty**; *loc sg* **-cie**) *m* (*napój z owoców*) stewed fruit

kompromi|s (**-su**, **-sy**; *loc sg* **-sie**) *m* compromise

kompute|r (**-ra**, **-ry**; *loc sg* **-rze**) *m* (*osobisty, stacjonarny*) computer

komputerowy *adj* computer

komu *pron dat od* **kto**; **~ to zabrałeś?** who did you take that from?

komuni|a (**-i**, **-e**; *gen pl* **-i**) *f*

communion; **przystępować**
(**przystąpić** pf) **do Pierwszej
Komunii** (**Świętej**) ≈ to receive
one's first (Holy) Communion
komunikacj|a (-i) f
1 (miejska, morska) transport
(Brit), transportation (US)
2 (międzyludzka) communication
komunika|t (-tu, -ty; loc sg **-cie)**
m 1 (wiadomość) communiqué
2 (ogłoszenie) announcement
**komunik|ować się (-uję,
-ujesz)** vr 1 (między ludźmi) to
communicate 2 (kontaktować
się) to keep in touch (with one
another)
komuni|sta (-sty, -ści; dat sg
& loc sg **-ście)** m decl like f in sg
communist
komunistyczny adj (ustrój, kraj)
communist
komuniz|m (-mu; loc sg **-mie)** m
communism
komuś pron dat sg od **ktoś**
koncentr|ować (-uję, -ujesz; pf
s-) vt (gromadzić) to concentrate
koncepcj|a (-i, -e; gen pl **-i)** f
(projekt) conception
koncer|t (-tu, -ty; loc sg **-cie)** m
1 (symfoniczny, kameralny) concert
2 (utwór instrumentalny) concerto
kondycj|a (-i) f (forma) fitness
konfitur|y (-) pl conserve sg
konflik|t (-tu, -ty; loc sg **-cie)** m
(spór) conflict
kongre|s (-su, -sy; loc sg **-sie)** m
(zjazd partii, organizacji) congress;
K~ Stanów Zjednoczonych the
U.S. Congress
ko|niec (-ńca, -ńce) m 1 end
2 (w ołówku) point; **do samego
końca** to the bitter end; **liczyć**

(**policzyć** pf) **od końca** to count
(off) in reverse order; **na końcu
języka miałem pytanie** the
question was on the tip of my
tongue; **w końcu się nam udało**
we succeeded in the end; **potrafi
związać ~ z końcem** (przen) he
can make ends meet
koniecznie adv absolutely
koniecznoś|ć (-ci) f (potrzeba)
necessity
konieczny adj (niezbędny)
necessary
konkretny adj 1 (wypowiedź)
accurate 2 (pytanie, sytuacja)
specific 3 (osoba) matter-of-fact
konkurencj|a (-i) f 1 (rywalizacja)
competition 2 (nom pl **-e**; gen pl **-i)**
(rozgrywka sportowa) event
konkuren|t (-ta, -ci; loc sg **-cie)**
m rival
konkur|ować (-uję, -ujesz) vi: **~
z** +inst to compete with
konkur|s (-su, -sy; loc sg **-sie)** m
(piękności, poetycki) contest
konsekwentny adj consistent
konserwacj|a (-i) f 1 (dzieł
sztuki) conservation 2 (urządzeń
mechanicznych) maintenance
konserwatywny adj (pogląd,
partia) conservative
konserwatyz|m (-mu; loc sg
-mie) m conservatism
konserwowy adj 1 (Culin: mięso)
tinned (Brit), canned (US)
2 (ogórek) pickled
konsula|t (-tu, -ty; loc sg **-cie)** m
consulate
konsumen|t (-ta, -ci; loc sg **-cie)**
m consumer
konsum|ować (-uję, -ujesz; pf **s-)**
vt (jeść, używać) to consume

konsumpcj|a (**-i**) f (*jedzenie, używanie*) consumption

kontak|t (**-tu, -ty**; *loc sg* **-cie**) m **1** (*relacja osobista*) contact **2** (*gniazdko elektryczne*) socket (*Brit*), outlet (*US*) **3** (*w instalacji elektrycznej: pot*) switch

kontakt|ować (**-uję, -ujesz**; *pf* **s-**) *vt*: **~ kogoś z kimś** to put sb in touch with sb; **~ się** *vr*: **~ się (z kimś)** to be in touch (with sb); **często kontaktuje się z rodzicami** he is in regular contact with his parents

kontek|st (**-stu, -sty**; *loc sg* **-ście**) m (*sytuacji, wydarzenia*) context

kon|to (**-ta, -ta**; *loc sg* **-cie**) nt (*bankowe, osobiste*) account; **zakładać** (**założyć** *pf*) **~ w banku** to open a bank account

kontrak|t (**-tu, -ty**; *loc sg* **-cie**) m (*umowa*) contract

kontra|st (**-stu, -sty**; *loc sg* **-ście**) m (*przeciwieństwo*) contrast

kontrol|a (**-i**) f **1** (*sprawowanie nadzoru*) control **2** (*nom pl* **-e**; *gen pl* **-i**) (*zbadanie*) check **3** (*badanie okresowe*) check-up

kontrole|r (**-ra, -rzy**; *loc sg* **-rze**) m ticket inspector

kontrol|ować (**-uję, -ujesz**; *pf* **s-**) *vt* (*sprawdzać*) to control; **~ się** *vr* **1** (*panować nad sobą*) to control o.s. **2** (*sprawdzać się wzajemnie*) to check one another

kontuzj|a (**-i, -e**; *gen pl* **-i**) f (*sportowa, nogi*) (minor) injury

kontynen|t (**-tu, -ty**; *loc sg* **-cie**) m (*europejski, amerykański*) continent

kontyn|uować (**-uję, -ujesz**) *vt* to continue

konwencj|a (**-i, -e**; *gen pl* **-i**) f (*sposób, styl*) convention

konwencjonalny *adj* **1** (*sposób, transport*) conventional **2** (*gest, rozmowa*) polite

ko|ń (**-nia, -nie**; *gen pl* **-ni**; *inst pl* **-ńmi**) m horse; **policjant na koniu** mounted policeman; **silnik o mocy 75 koni mechanicznych** a 75-horsepower engine; **znamy się jak łyse konie** we know each other inside out

końcowy *adj* (*przystanek, rezultat*) final

końców|ka (**-ki, -ki**; *dat sg & loc sg* **-ce**; *gen pl* **-ek**) f ending

kończ|yć (**-ę, -ysz**) *vt* **1** (*pf* **s-**) (*rozmowę*) to end **2** (*pf* **s-**) (*obiad, zadanie*) to finish **3** (*pf* **u-**) (*szkołę wyższą*) to graduate from **4** (*pf* **u-** *lub* **s-**) (*szkolenie*) to finish ▷ *vi* to finish; **~ się** *vr* (*pf* **s-**) (*o wycinku czasu*) to end; **kończy nam się chleb** we are running out of bread; **~ nad czymś pracować** to finish working on sth

kooperacj|a (**-i, -e**; *gen pl* **-i**) f (*współpraca*) co-operation

koordyn|ować (**-uję, -ujesz**; *pf* **s-**) *vt* (*zamierzenia, działania*) to co-ordinate

ko|pać (**-pię, -piesz**) *vt* **1** (*pf* **-pnąć**) (*piłkę, przeciwnika*) to kick **2** (*pf* **wy-**) (*w ziemi*) to dig ▷ *vi* (*uderzać nogą*) to kick

kopal|nia (**-ni, -nie**; *gen pl* **-ni**) f (*soli, węgla*) mine

koper|ta (**-ty, -ty**; *dat sg & loc sg* **-cie**) f (*na korespondencję*) envelope

kopi|a (**-i, -e**; *gen pl* **-i**) f **1** (*nie oryginał*) reproduction **2** (*odbitka*) copy

kopi|ować (**-uję, -ujesz**) vt 1 (pf **s-**) (*dokumenty, obrazy*) to copy 2 (pf **prze-**) (*w informatyce*) to copy

kop|nąć (**-nę, -niesz**; imp **-nij**) vb pf od **kopać**

Kora|n (**-nu**; loc sg **-nie**) m (*święta księga islamu*) the Koran

kore|k (**-ka, -ki**; inst sg **-kiem**) m 1 (*do butelki*) cork 2 (*nom pl* **-ki**) (*do zlewu*) plug 3 (pot: *w instalacji elektrycznej: bezpiecznik*) fuse (*Brit*), fuze (*US*) 4 (*na drodze*) traffic jam

korepetycj|e (**-i**) pl (*z matematyki*) private lessons

korespondencj|a (**-i**) f 1 (*wysyłanie i otrzymywanie listów*) correspondence 2 (*listy, pocztówki*) post (*Brit*), mail (*US*) 3 (*nom pl* **-e**; gen pl **-i**) (*artykuł*) report

korespond|ować (**-uję, -ujesz**) vi: **~ z** +inst to correspond with

korkociąg (**-gu, -gi**; inst sg **-giem**) m 1 (*do otwierania butelek*) corkscrew 2 (*w lotnictwie*) spin

koro|na (**-ny, -ny**; loc sg **-nie**) f crown; **zrób to, a ~ ci z głowy nie spadnie** it wouldn't hurt you to do it

korupcj|a (**-i**) f (*branie, dawanie łapówek*) corruption

koryg|ować (**-uję, -ujesz**; pf **s-**) vt (*naprawiać*) to correct

korytarz (**-a, -e**; gen pl **-y**) m (*w budynku*) corridor

korze|ń (**-nia, -nie**; gen pl **-ni**) m root; **korzenie** pl 1 (*genealogia, początki*) roots 2 (*przyprawy*) spice(s pl)

korzyst|ać (**-am, -asz**; pf **s-**) vi: **~ z czegoś** (*z urządzenia, pomieszczenia*) to use sth; (*z*

przysługujących praw) to exercise sth; **~ z okoliczności** to take advantage of the circumstances

korzystny adj 1 (*przynoszący zyski*) profitable 2 (*wpływ, okoliczności*) auspicious

korzyś|ć (**-ci, -ci**; gen pl **-ci**) f 1 (*osobista*) advantage 2 (*finansowa*) benefit

kosmetyczny adj (*zabieg, preparat*) cosmetic; **gabinet ~** beauty salon lub parlor (*US*)

kosmety|k (**-ku, -ki**; inst sg **-kiem**) m (*upiększający, naturalny*) cosmetic

kosmonau|ta (**-ty, -ci**; loc sg **-cie**) m decl like f in sg 1 astronaut 2 (*rosyjski*) cosmonaut

kosmopoli|ta (**-ty, -ci**; dat sg & loc sg **-cie**) m decl like f in sg (*osoba*) cosmopolitan

kosmo|s (**-su**; loc sg **-sie**) m 1 (*przestrzeń pozaziemska*) (outer) space 2 (*wszechświat*) cosmos

kostiu|m (**-mu, -my**; loc sg **-mie**) m 1 (*żakiet i spódnica*) suit 2 (*dla aktora*) costume; **~ kąpielowy** bathing costume

kosz (**-a, -e**; gen pl **-y** lub **-ów**) m (*wiklinowy, z kwiatami*) basket; **mecz ~a** (pot) basketball game; **~ na śmieci** dustbin (*Brit*), garbage can (*US*)

koszma|r (**-ru, -ry**; loc sg **-rze**) m (*zły sen, tragedia*) nightmare

koszmarny adj (*sen, sytuacja*) nightmarish

kosz|t (**-tu, -ty**; loc sg **-cie**) m (*w gospodarce*) cost; **koszty** pl 1 (*społeczne, zdrowotne*) costs 2 (*wydana suma pieniędzy*) expenses; **robić** (**zrobić** pf) **coś**

~em czegoś/kogoś (*przen*) to do something at the cost of sth/at sb's expense

kosztory|s (**-su, -sy**; *loc sg* **-sie**) *m* (*plan wydatków*) estimate (of costs)

koszt|ować (**-uję, -ujesz**) *vt* 1 (*o produkcie*) to cost 2 (*pf* **s-**) (*o jedzeniu, napojach*) to try

kosztowny *adj* (*prezent, zabawa*) expensive

koszul|a (**-i, -e**) *f* (*z krótkimi, długimi rękawami*) shirt; **~ nocna** nightdress

koszul|ka (**-ki, -ki**; *dat sg & loc sg* **-ce**; *gen pl* **-ek**) *f* (*bawełniana, sportowa*) T-shirt

koszy|k (**-ka, -ki**; *inst sg* **-kiem**) *m dimin od* **kosz**

koszyków|ka (**-ki**; *dat sg & loc sg* **-ce**) *f* basketball

koś|ciół (**-cioła, -cioły**; *loc sg* **-ciele**) *m* 1 (*budowla*) church 2 (*instytucja*) Church; **Głowa Kościoła** Head of the Church

koś|ć (**-ci, -ci**; *gen pl* **-ci**) *f* 1 (*człowieka, zwierzęcia*) bone 2 (*w komputerze*) chip; **kości** *pl* (*gra*) dice; **wieża z kości słoniowej** ivory tower; **spadek był kością niezgody między nimi** the inheritance was a bone of contention between them

ko|t (**-ta, -ty**; *loc sg* **-cie**) *m* cat; **oni ciągle drą ze sobą ~y** (*przen*) they are still at loggerheads

kotle|t (**-ta, -ty**; *loc sg* **-cie**) *m* (*schabowy, smażony*) chop

ko|za (**-zy, -zy**; *dat sg & loc sg* **-zie**; *gen pl* **kóz**) *f* goat

ko|zioł (**-zła, -zły**; *loc sg* **-źle**) *m* billy-goat

Kozioroż|ec (**-ca, -ce**) *m* (*Astrol*) Capricorn; **Zwrotnik Koziorożca** Tropic of Capricorn

kożuch (**-a, -y**) *m* 1 (*skóra owcy*) sheepskin 2 (*ciepłe ubranie*) sheepskin coat 3 (*gęsta warstwa na mleku*) skin

kół|ko (**-ka, -ka**; *inst sg* **-kiem**) *nt dimin od* **koło** 1 (*rzecz*) ring 2 (*zakreślenie*) circle 3 (*organizacja*) circle; **w ~** (*chodzić*) round in circles; (*mówić*) endlessly

kradzież (**-y, -e**; *gen pl* **-y**) *f* theft; **popełniać** (**popełnić** *pf*) **~** to steal

kraj (**-u, -e**) *m* (*państwo, ojczyzna*) country; **w ~u** at home; **odwiedzać** (**odwiedzić** *pf*) **ciepłe ~e** to travel to warmer climes; **wiadomości z ~u i ze świata** domestic and international news

krajobra|z (**-zu, -zy**; *loc sg* **-zie**) *m* (*nizinny, górski*) scenery

kraker|s (**-sa, -sy**; *loc sg* **-sie**) *m* cracker

Krak|ów (**-owa**; *loc sg* **-owie**) *m* Cracow

kra|n (**-nu, -ny**; *loc sg* **-nie**) *m* (*z wodą*) tap, faucet (*US*)

kra|ść (**-dnę, -dniesz**; *imp* **-dnij**; *pf* **u-**) *vt* to steal; **ukradł mi portfel** he stole my wallet

kra|ta (**-ty, -ty**; *dat sg & loc sg* **-cie**) *f* 1 (*zabezpieczenie*) grating 2 (*na materiale*) check 3 (*w więzieniu*) bars *pl*; **za kradzież dostał się za kraty** he went to prison for theft

krat|ka (**-ki, -ki**; *dat sg & loc sg* **-ce**; *gen pl* **-ek**) *f dimin od* **krata**; (*puste miejsce w formularzu*) blank; **w kratkę** (*materiał*) checked; **chodzi do szkoły w kratkę** (*pot*) he goes to school on and off

kraul (-a) m (*styl pływacki*) crawl

krawa|t (-ta lub **-tu, -ty**; *loc sg* **-cie)** m tie

krawco|wa (-wej, -we) f *decl like adj* dressmaker

krawę|dź (-dzi, -dzie; *gen pl* **-dzi)** f (*skraj*) edge

krawężni|k (-ka, -ki; *inst sg* **-kiem)** m kerb (*Brit*), curb (*US*)

kra|wiec (-wca, -wcy) m **1** (*dla mężczyzn*) tailor **2** (*dla kobiet*) dressmaker

krawiect|wo (-wa; *loc sg* **-wie)** nt **1** (*dla kobiet*) dressmaking **2** (*dla mężczyzn*) tailoring

kr|ąg (-ęgu, -ęgi; *inst sg* **-ęgiem)** m **1** (*figur geometryczna*) circle **2** (*przen: przyjaciół*) circle **3** (*przen: badań*) area

krąże|nie (-nia) nt (*obieg*) circulation

krąż|yć (-ę, -ysz) vi **1** (*o ptaku*) to circle **2** (*o krwi*) to circulate **3** (*o rzeczy*) to be passed around **4** (*po obicie*) to rotate

kreacj|a (-i, -e; *gen pl* **-i)** f (*elegancki strój*) outfit

kre|da (-dy (*nom pl* **-dy**) (*dat sg & loc sg* **-dy**) f (*do tablicy*) chalk

kred|ka (-ki, -ki; *dat sg & loc sg* **-ce**; *gen pl* **-ek)** f **1** crayon **2** (*do rysowania*) coloured (*Brit*) lub colored (*US*) pencil; **~ do ust** lipstick

kredy|t (-tu, -ty; *loc sg* **-cie)** m (*hipoteczny, inwestycyjny*) credit; **tracić** (**stracić** *pf*) **u kogoś ~** (*przen*) to lose favour (*Brit*) lub favor (*US*) with sb

kre|m (-mu, -my; *loc sg* **-mie)** m (*czekoladowy, waniliowy*) cream; **~ do rąk/stóp** hand/foot cream

kremowy adj cream

kres|ka (-ki, -ki; *dat sg & loc sg* **-ce**; *gen pl* **-ek)** f **1** (*prosta linia*) line **2** (*myślnik*) dash **3** (*łącznik*) hyphen **4** (*nad, pod wyrazem*) diacritical mark **5** (*pozioma linia na termometrze*) mark

kresków|ka (-ki, -ki; *dat sg & loc sg* **-ce**; *gen pl* **-ek)** f (*gatunek filmowy*) cartoon

kreś|lić (-ę, -isz) vt **1** (*szkicować*) to draw **2** (*słowa*) to cross out

kre|w (-wi) f blood; **grupa krwi** blood group; **to bohater z krwi i kości** he's every inch a hero; **~ odpłynęła z twarzy** the blood drained from his face; **zbrodnia z zimną krwią** a crime committed in cold blood

krewet|ka (-ki, -ki; *dat sg & loc sg* **-ce**; *gen pl* **-ek)** f prawn

krewn|a (-ej) f *decl like adj* relative

krew|ny (-nego, -ni) m *decl like adj* relative

krę|cić (-cę, -cisz; *imp* **-ć)** vt **1** (*włosy w loki*) to curl **2** (*o wąsach*) to twirl **3** (*mieszać składniki*) to mix; **~ się** vr **1** (*wirować*) to spin **2** (*na siedzeniu*) to squirm; **~ (po~ pf) głową z niedowierzaniem** to shake one's head in disbelief; **~ film w Polsce** to shoot a film (*Brit*) lub movie (*US*) in Poland; **łza kręci mi się w oku** it brings a tear to my eye; **kręci mu się w głowie** his head is spinning

kręgosłu|p (-pa, -py; *loc sg* **-pie)** m spine; **~ moralny** (*przen*) moral backbone; **to człowiek bez ~a** (*przen*) he's a spineless individual

krępy adj stocky

kr|oić (**-oję, -oisz;** *imp* **-ój**) *vt*
1 (*pf* **u-**) (*na kawałki*) to cut 2 (*pf*
s-) (*ubranie*) to tailor; **~ (po~** *pf*)
coś w kostkę/w paski to dice
sth/cut sth in strips; **kroi mi się
podwyżka** (*przen*) I'm due a (pay)
rise (*Brit*) *lub* raise (*US*)

kro|k (**-ku, -ki;** *inst sg* **-kiem**) *m*
1 (*do przodu, do tyłu*) step 2 (*przen:
przedsięwzięcie*) measure 3 (*krocze*)
crotch; **co ~ ich spotykam** I meet
them at every turn; **robić coś ~
po~u** to do sth step by step; **o ~
stąd jest nasz dom** our house
is (just) a step away; **spotykam
go na każdym ~u** I meet him at
every turn; **muszę podjąć ~i w
celu zmiany pracy** I must make
an effort to get a new job

krokodyl (**-a, -e;** *gen pl* **-i**) *m*
crocodile

krom|ka (**-ki, -ki;** *dat sg & loc sg* **-ce;**
gen pl **-ek**) *f* (*chleba*) slice

krop|ka (**-ki, -ki;** *dat sg & loc sg* **-ce;**
gen pl **-ek**) *f* 1 (*punkt*) dot 2 (*znak
na końcu zdania*) full stop (*Brit*),
period (*US*); **czas postawić
kropkę nad i** (*przen*) it's time to
spell it out; **znów znalazł się w
kropce** he found himself once
again put on the spot

kropl|a (**-i, -e;** *gen pl* **-i**) *f* drop;
krople *pl* (*żołądkowe, do oczu*)
drops; **~ w morzu potrzeb**
(*przen*) a drop in the ocean

kroplów|ka (**-ki, -ki;** *dat sg & loc
sg* **-ce;** *gen pl* **-ek**) *f* (*w medycynie*)
drip; **dwa dni leżał pod
kroplówką** he was on a drip for
two days

kro|sta (**-sty, -sty;** *loc sg* **-ście**)
f pimple

kr|owa (**-owy, -owy;** *dat sg & loc sg*
-owie; *gen pl* **-ów**) *f* cow

król (**-a**) *m* 1 (*nom pl* **-owie**)
(*dziedziczny, elekcyjny*) king
2 (*nom pl* **-e**) (*figura w szachach,
kartach*) king; **Święto Trzech K~i**
(*uroczystość religijna*) Epiphany

królest|wo (**-wa, -wa;** *loc sg* **-wie**)
nt kingdom

królewicz (**-a, -e**) *m* (*syn króla*)
prince

króle|wna (**-wny, -wny;** *dat sg &
loc sg* **-wnie;** *gen pl* **-wien**) *f* (*córka
króla*) princess

królewski *adj* (*zamek, dwór*) royal

króli|k (**-ka, -ki;** *inst sg* **-kiem**)
m rabbit; **nie jestem ~iem
doświadczalnym** I'm not a
guinea pig

królo|wa (**-wej, -we**) *f decl like
adj* queen

król|ować (**-uję, -ujesz**) *vi*
(*rządzić*) to reign

krótki *adj* 1 (*fryzura, ubranie*) short
2 (*zdawkowy*) brief; **~e spodnie**
lub **spodenki** shorts; **to się uda
tylko na krótką metę** (*przen*)
that will only be successful in the
short term

krótko *adv* 1 (*o włosach*) short 2 (*o
wypowiedzi*) briefly; **~ mówiąc, on
ma rację** in short, he's right

krótkometrażowy *adj* (*o filmie*)
short

krótkowidz (**-a, -e**) *m*: **być ~em**
to be near-sighted *lub* short-
sighted

kruchy *adj* 1 (*delikatny*) fragile
2 (*bułka*) crisp 3 (*cielęcina*) tender
4 (*przen*) fragile

kru|k (**-ka, -ki;** *inst sg* **-kiem**) *m*
(*ptak*) raven

krupni|k (**-ku, -ki**; *inst sg* **-kiem**) *m* barley soup

krwi *itd. n zob.* **krew**

krwoto|k (**-ku, -ki**; *inst sg* **-kiem**) *m* (*wewnętrzny, z nosa*) bleeding

krykie|t (**-ta**; *loc sg* **-cie**) *m* (*gra*) cricket

Kry|m (**-mu**; *loc sg* **-mie**) *m* the Crimea

kryminali|sta (**-sty, -ści**; *dat sg & loc sg* **-ście**) *m decl like f in sg* (*przestępca*) criminal

kryminalny *adj* (*więzień, policja*) criminal; **film ~** detective film (*Brit*) *lub* movie (*US*)

krymina|ł (**-łu, -ły**; *loc sg* **-le**) *m* **1** (*powieść*) detective novel **2** (*film*) detective film (*Brit*) *lub* movie (*US*)

kryszta|ł (**-łu, -ły**; *loc sg* **-le**) *m* **1** (*skała*) crystal **2** (*szkło*) crystal (*glass*) **3** (*produkt*) crystal vase

kryształowy *adj* crystal; **to ~ człowiek** he's an honest man

kryty|k (**-ka, -cy**; *inst sg* **-kiem**) *m* (*filmowy, teatralny*) critic

kryty|ka (**-ki**; *dat sg & loc sg* **-ce**; *nom pl* **-ki**) *f* **1** (*wypowiedź oceniająca*) criticism **2** (*filmowa, teatralna*) review

krytyk|ować (**-uję, -ujesz**; *pf* **s-**) *vt* (*oceniać negatywnie*) to criticize

kryzy|s (**-su, -sy**; *loc sg* **-sie**) *m* crisis

kryzysowy *adj* crisis

krza|k (**-ka** *lub* **-ku, -ki**; *inst sg* **-kiem**) *m* bush; **krzaki** *pl* shrubbery *sg*

krze|sło (**-sła, -sła**; *loc sg* **-śle**; *gen pl* **-seł**) *nt* (*drewniane, elektryczne*) chair

krztu|sić się (**-szę, -sisz**; *imp* **-ś**) *vr* to choke

krzy|czeć (**-czę, -czysz**; *pf* **-knąć**) *vi* to shout; **nie krzycz na nią** don't shout at her

krzy|k (**-ku, -ki**; *inst sg* **-kiem**) *m* shout; **i już po ~u** (*przen*) all done

krzyk|nąć (**-nę, -niesz**; *imp* **-nij**) *vb pf od* **krzyczeć**

krzyw|da (**-dy, -dy**; *dat sg & loc sg* **-dzie**) *f* (*fizyczna, moralna*) harm; **wyrządził jej krzywdę** he hurt her

krzyw|dzić (**-dzę, -dzisz**; *imp* **-dź**; *pf* **s-**) *vt* to harm

krzywy *adj* **1** (*nie prosty*) crooked **2** (*o nogach*) knock-kneed **3** (*o powierzchni*) uneven; **patrzy na niego ~m okiem** (*przen*) she is frowning at him

krzyż (**-a, -e**; *gen pl* **-y**) *m* **1** (*rzecz*) cross **2** (*Anat: w okolicach miednicy*) lower back; **Czerwony K~** Red Cross; **przyszło parę osób na ~** (*pot*) only a handful of people turned up

krzyżów|ka (**-ki, -ki**; *dat sg & loc sg* **-ce**; *gen pl* **-ek**) *f* **1** (*zagadka*) crossword (*puzzle*) **2** (*Bio*) hybrid

krzyży|k (**-ka, -ki**; *inst sg* **-kiem**) *m dimin od* **krzyż**; (*w muzyce*) sharp; **ma piąty ~ na karku** he's in his fifties

ksero *nt inv* **1** (*pot: maszyna robiąca kopie*) photocopier **2** (*pot: kopia*) photocopy

kserokopia (**-i, -e**; *gen pl* **-i**) *f* photocopy

kser|ować (**-uję, -ujesz**; *pf* **s-**) *vt* (*robić kopie*) to photocopy

ksiądz (**księdza, księża**; *voc sg* **księże**; *gen pl* **księży**; *inst pl* **księżmi**) *m* priest

książę (**księcia**, **książęta**; *gen pl*
książąt) *m* **1** (*tytuł szlachecki*) duke
2 (*syn króla, królowej*) prince
książ|ka (**-ki**, **-ki**; *dat sg & loc sg* **-ce**;
gen pl **-ek**) *f* (*dla dzieci, z obrazkami*)
book; **~ dla dzieci** a children's
book; **~ telefoniczna** phone book
książkowy *adj* **1** (*publikacja*) in
book form **2** (*styl*) bookish
księgar|nia (**-ni**, **-nie**; *gen pl* **-ń**) *f*
bookshop (*Brit*), bookstore (*US*)
księgo|wa (**-wej**, **-we**) *f decl like
adj* accountant
księgowoś|ć (**-ci**) *f*
1 (*rachunkowość*) accounting
2 (*dział firmy*) accounts
department
księgo|wy (**-wego**, **-wi**) *m decl like
adj* accountant
księżnicz|ka (**-ki**, **-ki**; *dat sg & loc sg*
-ce; *gen pl* **-ek**) *f* princess
księżyc (**-a**, **-e**) *m* moon
kształ|cić (**-cę**, **-cisz**; *imp* **-ć**; *pf*
wy-) *vt* **1** (*w szkole*) to educate
2 (*charakter*) to form; **~ się** *vr*: **~
się (na inżyniera)** to train (to be
an engineer); **podróże kształcą**
travel broadens the mind
kształ|t (**-tu**, **-ty**; *loc sg* **-cie**) *m*
shape; **ma bujne, kobiece ~y**
she has voluptuous, feminine
curves; **w kształcie piłki** shaped
like a ball
kształt|ować (**-uję**, **-ujesz**; *pf* **u-**)
vt to shape; **~ się** *vr* to develop

○ **KEYWORD**

kto *pron* **1** (*w zdaniach pytajnych*)
who; **kto to (jest)?** who is it?;
kto przyjdzie? who's there?
2 (*w zdaniach podrzędnych*) who;

sprawdź, kto wyszedł see who
has left; **ten, kto go spotka**
whoever meets him
3: nieważne kto przyjedzie it
doesn't matter who comes

ktokolwiek *pron* **1** (*nieważne kto*)
anyone **2** (*ten, kto*) whoever; **~
z nas** any one of us; **~ widział...**
whoever saw...
ktoś 1 *pron* (*w zdaniach
orzekających*) someone **2** (*w
zdaniach pytających*) anyone; **czy
widziałeś kogoś?** did you see
anybody *lub* anyone?; **ona myśli,
że jest naprawdę kimś** she
thinks she's really somebody; **~
inny przyjdzie** someone else is
coming; **~, kogo nie widziałem**
someone I didn't see
którędy *pron* which way

○ **KEYWORD**

który *pron decl like adj* **1** (*w zdaniach
pytajnych*) which; **którą gazetę
chcesz?** which paper do you
want?; **którego dzisiaj?** what's
the date today?; **która jest
godzina?** what time is it?, what's
the time?; **który z was to zna?**
which one of you knows?
2 (*w zdaniach podrzędnych*):
człowiek, którego znasz...
the man (that) you know...; **nie
wiem, którą z nich wybrać** I
don't know which to choose;
ludzie, z którymi mieszkam
the people (that) I live with;
**dziewczyna, z której mamą
rozmawiałem** the girl whose
mother I was talking to

kub|ek (-ka, -ki; *inst sg* **-kiem)**
m mug

kub|eł (-ła, -ły; *loc sg* **-le)** *m*
1 (*plastikowy, aluminiowy*) bucket
2 (*kosz na śmieci*) bin (*Brit*), trash
can (*US*)

kuchar|ka (-ki, -ki; *dat sg & loc sg*
-ce; *gen pl* **-ek)** *f* cook

kucharski *adj*: **książka**
kucharska cookbook

kucharz (-a, -e; *gen pl* **-y)** *m* cook,
chef

kuchen|ka (-ki, -ki; *dat sg & loc*
sg **-ce**; *gen pl* **-ek)** *f* **1** (*gazowa,*
elektryczna) cooker **2** (*też:* **~**
turystyczna) camping stove; **~**
mikrofalowa microwave (oven)

kuchenny *adj* (*zestaw, mebel*)
kitchen

kuch|nia (-ni, -nie; *gen pl* **-ni)**
f **1** (*miejsce w domu*) kitchen
2 (*sztuka kulinarna*) cuisine
3 (*przyrządzanie potraw*) cooking

kufe|l (-la, -le; *gen pl* **-li)** *m* **1** (*do*
piwa) (beer) mug **2** (*ilość płynu*)
≈ pint (of beer)

kul|a (-i, -e) *f* **1** (*rzecz*) ball **2** (*w*
geometrii: bryła) sphere **3** (*nabój*)
bullet; **kule** *pl*: **chodzić o**
kuli/~ch to walk on crutches; **~**
ziemska the globe

kulisty *adj* (*kształt*) spherical

kultu|ra (-ry, -ry; *dat sg & loc sg*
-rze) *f* (*narodowa, starożytna*)
culture; **dom kultury** ≈
community centre (*Brit*) *lub*
center (*US*)

kulturalny *adj* **1** (*dorobek,*
wydarzenie) cultural **2** (*osoba*) well-
mannered, cultured

kulturowy *adj* (*krąg*) cultural

kumpe|l (-la, -le; *gen pl* **-li)** *m*

(*pot*) mate

ku|pić (-pię, -pisz) *vb pf od*
kupować

kupny *adj* (shop-) bought (*Brit*),
store-bought (*US*)

ku|pować (-puję, -pujesz; *pf* **-pić)**
vt to buy

kupując|y (-ego, -y) *m decl like*
adj buyer

ku|ra (-ry, -ry; *loc sg* **-rze)** *f* hen;
ale z niej ~ domowa (*pej*) she's
such a homebody; **ten interes**
to ~ znosząca złote jaja this
business is a sure-fire winner

kuracj|a (-i, -e; *gen pl* **-i)** *f*
(*odchudzająca, zdrowotna*)
treatment

kurczak (-ka, -ki; *inst sg* **-kiem)**
m chicken

kur|s (-su, -sy; *loc sg* **-sie)** *m*
1 (*autobusem, taksówką*) journey
2 (*Kierunek*) course **3** (*wymiany*
walut) (exchange) rate **4** (*cena*
na giełdzie) price **5** (*w szkole, na*
uniwersytecie) course

kurt|ka (-ki, -ki; *dat sg & loc sg* **-ce**;
gen pl **-ek)** *f* jacket

kur|wa (-wy, -wy; *dat sg*
& loc sg **-wie**; *gen pl* **-ew)** *f*
(*pot!: prostytutka*) whore (*pot!*)

kuzy|n (-na, -ni; *loc sg* **-nie)** *m*
cousin

kuzyn|ka (-ki, -ki; *dat sg & loc sg*
-ce; *gen pl* **-ek)** *f* cousin

kwadran|s (-sa, -se; *loc sg* **-sie)**
m quarter (*of an hour*); **~ po**
czwartej a quarter past (*Brit*)
lub after (*US*) four; **za ~ ósma** a
quarter to eight; **~ akademicki**
15 minute period at the start of each
lecture during which the lecture
must begin

kwadra|t (**-tu**, **-ty**; *loc sg* **-cie**) *m*
1 (*figura geometryczna*) square
2 (*potęga*): **sześć do ~u** six
squared; **dureń do ~u** (*pot: pej*) a
complete idiot
kwadratowy *adj* square
kwarantan|na (**-ny**, **-ny**; *dat sg &*
loc sg **-nie**) *f* quarantine
kwa|s (**-su**, **-sy**; *loc sg* **-sie**) *m* acid
kwaśny *adj* sour; **mleko jest już**
kwaśne the milk's gone off; **~**
deszcz acid rain
kwiaciar|nia (**-ni**, **-nie**; *gen pl* **-ni**)
f florist('s)
kwia|t (**-tu**, **-ty**; *loc sg* **kwiecie**) *m*
1 (*ogrodowy*) flower **2** (*na drzewie*)
blossom **3** (*doniczkowy*) plant
kwie|cień (**-tnia**, **-tnie**; *gen pl* **-tni**)
m April
kwit|nąć (**-nie**) *vi* **1** (*kwiaty*) to
bloom **2** (*drzewa*) to blossom;
jego życie towarzyskie kwitnie
od lat he has had a busy social
life for years
kwo|ta (**-ty**, **-ty**; *dat sg & loc sg*
-cie) *f* (*suma pieniędzy*) sum; **~ 200**
złotych the sum of 200 zloty

laborator|ium (**-um**, **-a**; *gen*
pl **-ów**) *nt inv in sg* (*językowe,*
chemiczne) lab
lać (**leję, lejesz**) *vt* **1** (*wodę*) to pour
2 (*pf* **z-**) (*pot: bić człowieka*) to belt
▷ *vi* **1** (*o ulewnym deszczu*) to pour
2 (*pot!: sikać*) to piss (*pot!*); **leję na**
to! (*pot!*) I don't give a damn!; **~**
się *vr* **1** (*o płynie*) to flow **2** (*pot: w*
bijatyce) to fight
lakie|r (**-ru**, **-ry**; *loc sg* **-rze**) *m* (*do*
malowania powierzchni) varnish;
malować (**pomalować** *pf*)
paznokcie ~em do paznokci to
varnish one's nails; **niestety nie**
ma ~u do włosów sorry, we don't
have any hair spray
lakier|ować (**-uję, -ujesz**; *pf*
po-) *vt* **1** (*paznokcie*) to varnish
2 (*drewno*) to varnish **3** (*karoserię*)

to paint

lal|ka (**-ki, -ki**; *dat sg & loc sg* **-ce**; *gen pl* **-ek**) *f* **1** (*dla dzieci*) doll **2** (*w teatrze*) puppet

lament|ować (**-uję, -ujesz**) *vi* (*użalać się*) to lament

lam|pa (**-py, -py**; *dat sg & loc sg* **-pie**) *f* **1** (*wisząca, naftowa*) lamp **2** (*w elektronice*) valve (*Brit*), (vacuum) tube (*US*); **~ błyskowa** (*Fot*) flash; **~ jarzeniowa** fluorescent light

lapto|p (**-pa, -py**; *loc sg* **-pie**) *m* (*komputer przenośny*) laptop (computer)

laryngolo|g (**-ga, -gowie** *lub* **-dzy**; *inst sg* **-giem**) *m* ear, nose and throat specialist

la|s (**-su, -sy**; *loc sg* **lesie**) *m* **1** (*rozległy*) forest **2** (*niewielki*) wood **3** (*przen: chorągwi, rąk*) forest; **jestem całkiem w lesie z robotą** (*pot: przen*) I am well behind schedule with work

las|ka (**-ki, -ki**; *dat sg & loc sg* **-ce**; *gen pl* **-ek**) *f* **1** walking stick **2** (*pot: atrakcyjna dziewczyna*) chick; **kuleje i musi chodzić o lasce** he has a limp and needs to walk with a stick

lat|a (**-**) *pl* **1** years *pl* **2** (*określenie wieku*) age; **~ pięćdziesiąte/ sześćdziesiąte** the fifties/the sixties; **pracuje już od wielu lat** he has been working for many years; **miało to miejsce przed laty** it happened years ago; **ile masz lat?** (*familiar sg*) how old are you?; **mam 20 lat** I'm 20 years old; **sto lat!** many happy returns!; *zob. też* **rok**

lat|ać (**-am, -asz**) *vi +inst*

1 (*samolotem*) to fly **2** (*pot: być zabieganym*) to run; **od tygodnia latam z wywieszonym jęzorem** I've been run ragged for weeks

latar|ka (**-ki, -ki**; *dat sg & loc sg* **-ce**; *gen pl* **-ek**) *f* torch (*Brit*), flashlight (*US*)

latar|nia (**-ni, -nie**; *gen pl* **-ni**) *f* (*na ulicy*) street lamp; **~ morska** (*Żegl*) lighthouse; **latarnie lotniskowe** (*Aviat*) landing lights

la|to (**-ta, -ta**; *loc sg* **lecie**) *nt* summer; **wakacje są latem** *lub* **w lecie** the holidays are in the summer

laurea|t (**-ta, -ci**; *loc sg* **-cie**) *m* (*zdobywca nagrody*) laureate

laureat|ka (**-ki, -ki**; *dat sg & loc sg* **-ce**; *gen pl* **-ek**) *f* (*zdobywczyni nagrody*) laureate

lą|d (**-du, -dy**; *loc sg* **-dzie**) *m* land; **stały ~** mainland, dry land

ląd|ować (**-uję, -ujesz**; *pf* **wy-**) *vi* (*znaleźć się na ziemi*) to land

lądowa|nie (**-nia, -nia**; *gen pl* **-ń**) *nt* (*samolotu*) landing

lądowy *adj* **1** (*formacja wojskowa*) ground **2** (*zwierzęta, rośliny*) terrestrial **3** (*granica państwa*) land **4** (*Geo: klimat*) continental **5** (*komunikacja*) overland; **inżynieria lądowa** civil engineering

lecie *n zob.* **lato**

le|cieć (**-cę, -cisz**; *impf* **-ć**) *vi* **1** (*pf* **po-**) (*owad, samolot*) to fly **2** (*pf* **po-**) (*o cieczy*) to flow **3** (*pf* **z-**) (*spadać*) to fall (down) **4** (*pf* **po-**) (*pot: szybko biec*) to fly **5** (*pot: program w radiu, telewizji*) to be on

lecz *conj* but

leczeni|e (**-a**) *nt* (*kuracja*) treatment

lecznic|a (**-y**, **-e**) *f* (*weterynaryjna, dla ludzi*) clinic

lecz|yć (**-ę**, **-ysz**; *pf* **wy-**) *vt* 1 (*pacjenta*) to treat 2 (*przy pomocy lekarstwa*) to cure; **~ się** *vr* to get treatment

legalnie *adv* legally

legalny *adj* legal

legen|da (**-dy**, **-dy**; *dat sg & loc sg* **-dzie**) *f* legend; **jego czyn przejdzie do legendy** his deed will become legendary

legitymacj|a (**-i**, **-e**; *gen pl* **-i**) *f* 1 (*do identyfikacji*) ID 2 (*dowód członkostwa*) membership card

le|k (**-ku**, **-ki**; *inst sg* **-kiem**) *m* medicine

lekar|ka (**-ki**, **-ki**; *dat sg & loc sg* **-ce**; *gen pl* **-ek**) *f* doctor

lekarski *adj* 1 (*wizyta, przychodnia*) doctor's 2 (*recepta, zalecenie*) doctor's 3 (*badanie*) medical; **dostał zwolnienie ~e na 2 dni** he got 2 days' sick leave

lekarst|wo (**-wa**, **-wa**; *loc sg* **-wie**) *nt* 1 medicine 2 (*przen: środek przeciw problemom duchowym*) remedy; **nie było jedzenia ani na ~** there was absolutely no food

lekarz (**-a**, **-e**; *gen pl* **-y**) *m* doctor

lekcj|a (**-i**, **-e**; *gen pl* **-i**) *f* lesson; **lekcje** *pl* (*praca domowa*): **odrabiać** (**odrobić** *pf*) **lekcje** to do (one's) homework; **~ fizyki/ polskiego** physics/Polish class

lekki *adj* 1 (*mało ważący*) light 2 (*nieznaczny*) slight 3 (*mało wyczuwalny*) faint

lekko *adv* 1 lightly; 2 (*nieznacznie: unosić się, posuwać*) slightly; **~**

licząc wydał 200 złotych he spent at least 200 zlotys

lekkomyślnie *adv* recklessly

lekkomyślny *adj* reckless

le|nić się (**-nię**, **-nisz**; *imp* **-ń**) *vr* to sit around idle

lenist|wo (**-wa**; *loc sg* **-wie**) *nt* laziness; **oddawać** (**oddać** *pf*) **się słodkiemu lenistwu** to laze about

le|ń (**-nia**, **-nie**; *gen pl* **-ni** *lub* **-niów**) *m* layabout; **ale z niego śmierdzący ~!** (*pot*) what a shirker!

lepiej *adv comp od* **dobrze** better; **coraz ~ pracował** he worked better and better; **im prędzej to zrobisz tym ~** the sooner you do it, the better; **~ już wyjdę** I'd better go now

lepszy *adj comp od* **dobry** better; **wziął z sobą pierwszy ~ parasol** (*pot*) he took any old umbrella

lesbij|ka (**-ki**, **-ki**; *dat sg & loc sg* **-ce**; *gen pl* **-ek**) *f* lesbian

lesie *n zob.* **las**

letni *adj* 1 (*wypoczynek, strój*) summer 2 (*o napojach: nie gorący*) lukewarm; **przestawiać** (**przestawić** *pf*) **zegarek na czas ~** to put the clocks forward

letniskowy *adj* (*domek, kurort*) holiday

lew (**lwa**, **lwy**; *loc sg* **lwie**) *m* 1 (*zwierzę*) lion 2 (*znak zodiaku*): **L~** Leo

lewicowy *adj* (*polityk, poglądy*) left-wing

lewo *adv*: **w** *lub* **na ~** (to the) left; **na prawo i ~** all over the place; **na ~** (*pot: prowadzić interesy*) on the quiet

lewy adj 1 (noga, strona) left 2 (spodnia strona tkaniny) reverse 3 (pot: o dokumentach: nieprawdziwy) dodgy; **~ pas** (na drodze) outside lub fast lane

leże|ć (-ę, -ysz; pt -ał) vi 1 to lie 2 (o stroju: pasować) to fit; **jest chory i musi ~ w łóżku** he is ill and must stay in bed; **całe dnie leży do góry brzuchem** (pot) he lies around all day

lę|k (-ku, -ki; inst sg -kiem) m (strach) anxiety; **cierpieć na ~ przestrzeni/wysokości** to be afraid of open spaces/heights

lęk|ać się (-am, -asz) vr +gen (bać się) to fear

lice|um (-um, -a; gen pl -ów) nt inv in sg secondary school (Brit), high school (US); **~ zawodowe** vocational school; **~ ogólnokształcące** ≈ grammar school (Brit), ≈ high school (US)

○ **LICEUM**
○
○ **Liceum** is a type of secondary
○ school. At present there
○ are some **licea** which
○ teach a general curriculum
○ (humanities, mathematics
○ and science) as well as
○ those **licea** which are more
○ focused on providing training
○ for specific professions.
○ Graduates of both **licea** can
○ take the **matura**.

licyt|ować (-uję, -ujesz) vt 1 (pf z-) (przedmioty na aukcji) to auction 2 (pf za-) (podczas gry w karty) to bid

licz|ba (-by, -by; dat sg & loc sg -bie) f 1 number 2 (w językoznawstwie): **~ pojedyncza/mnoga** singular/plural

liczebni|k (-ka, -ki; inst sg -kiem) m (główny, porządkowy) number

licznie adv (pojawić się, przyjść) in large numbers

liczni|k (-ka, -ki; inst sg -kiem) m (urządzenie do mierzenia) meter

liczny adj (rodzina, obowiązek) numerous

licz|yć (-ę, -ysz) vt (pf po-) to count ▷ vi (pf po-) 1 (wykonywać działania matematyczne) to calculate 2 (dawać wynik): **klasa liczy 15 osób** there are 15 in the class 3 (o oczekiwaniach): **~ na** to count on; **liczę na was** I am counting on you

lide|r (-ra, -rzy; loc sg -rze) m (przywódca) leader

liftin|g (-gu, -gi; inst sg -giem) m facelift

likwid|ować (-uję, -ujesz; pf z-) vt 1 (biedę, dolegliwość) to eliminate 2 (przedsiębiorstwo: zam ykać) to liquidate

limi|t (-tu, -ty; loc sg -cie) m limit

li|na (-ny, -ny; dat sg & loc sg -nie) f rope

lin|ka (-ki, -ki; dat sg & loc sg -ce; gen pl -ek) f line; **~ holownicza** (Żegl, Aut) towrope

li|piec (-pca, -pce) m July

li|s (-sa, -sy; loc sg -sie) m fox; **on jest chytry jak ~** he is as sly as a fox; **uważaj, to farbowany ~** (przen) look out, it's a con

li|st (-stu, -sty; loc sg -ście) m (miłosny, oficjalny) letter; **~ zwykły** surface-mail letter; **~ lotniczy**

airmail letter; **mamy ~ polecony dla pana** we have a recorded-delivery letter for you; **poprosił o ~ polecający** he asked for a letter of recommendation

li|sta (**-sty, -sty**; *dat sg & loc sg* **-ście**) *f* (*spis przedmiotów, osób*) list; **~ przebojów** (*spis utworów*) the charts *pl*; **sprawdzać** (**sprawdzić** *pf*) **listę obecności** to take the register

listonosz (**-a, -e**; *gen pl* **-y**) *m* postman (*Brit*), mailman (*US*)

listopa|d (**-da, -dy**; *loc sg* **-dzie**) *m* November

liś|ć (**-cia, -cie**; *gen pl* **-ci**; *inst pl* **-ćmi**) *m* leaf

lite|ra (**-ry, -ry**; *loc sg* **-rze**) *f* letter; **pisać** (**napisać** *pf*) **wielką** *lub* **dużą/małą literą** to write in upper case/lower case letters; **litery drukowane** printed characters

literatu|ra (**-ry, -ry**; *dat sg & loc sg* **-rze**) *f* (*fachowa, historyczna*) literature; **~ piękna** belles-lettres

lit|r (**-ra, -ry**; *loc sg* **-rze**) *m* litre (*Brit*), liter (*US*)

Lit|wa (**-wy**; *loc sg* **-wie**) *f* Lithuania

li|zać (**-żę, -żesz**; *pf* **-znąć**) *vt* to lick

liza|k (**-ka, -ki**; *inst sg* **-kiem**) *m* lollipop

lodowis|ko (**-ka, -ka**; *inst sg* **-kiem**) *nt* skating *lub* ice rink

lodów|ka (**-ki, -ki**; *dat sg & loc sg* **-ce**; *gen pl* **-ek**) *f* fridge (*Brit*), refrigerator

lod|y (**-ów**) *pl* (*owocowe, czekoladowe*) ice cream *sg*

logiczny *adj* (*błąd, argument*)

logical

lokal (**-u, -e**; *gen pl* **-i** *lub* **-ów**) *m* **1** (*pomieszczenie*) premises *pl* **2** (*gastronomiczny*) restaurant; **bawili się w nocnych ~ach** they went clubbing

lokato|r (**-ra, -rzy**; *loc sg* **-rze**) *m* (*mieszkaniec*) occupant; **dziki ~** squatter

Londy|n (**-nu**; *loc sg* **-nie**) *m* London

lo|s (**-su, -sy**; *loc sg* **-sie**) *m* **1** (*droga życiowa*) lot **2** (*przeznaczenie*) fate **3** (*kupon na loterii*) (lottery) ticket; **zrządzenie ~u** bad fortune; **to prawdziwa ironia ~u!** (*przen*) an ironic twist of fate!

lo|t (**-tu, -ty**; *loc sg* **-cie**) *m* (*ptaka, samolotu*) flight

lotnict|wo (**-wa**; *loc sg* **-wie**) *nt* **1** (*pasażerskie*) aviation **2** (*formacja wojskowa*) air force

lotniczy *adj* (*transport, terminal*) air; **linia lotnicza** airline

lotnis|ko (**-ka, -ka**; *inst sg* **-kiem**) *nt* **1** (*dla pasażerów*) airport **2** (*miejsce do lądowania*) airfield

ló|d (**lodu, lody**; *loc sg* **lodzie**) *m* ice; **jesteś zimny jak ~** you're as cold as ice; **ma pieniędzy jak lodu** (*pot*) he is rolling in money; *zob. też* **lody**

lś|nić (**-nię, -nisz**; *imp* **-nij**) *vi* to glisten

lub *conj* or; **~ też** or else

lubiany *adj* popular

lu|bić (**-bię, -bisz**) *vt* to like; **~ coś robić** to like doing sth *lub* to do sth; **lubi biegać** he likes running; **~ się** *vr* to like one another; **lubią się od dziecka** they've been friends since childhood

ludnoś|ć (-ci) f (miasta, kraju) population

ludowy adj 1 (sztuka, ubiór) folk 2 (Pol: ustrój państwa) people's

lu|dzie (-dzi; inst pl **-dźmi)** pl people; zob. też **człowiek**

ludzki adj 1 (charakter, stworzenie) human 2 (stosunek do innych) humane; **musisz traktować go po ludzku** you've got to treat him humanely

ludzkoś|ć (-ci) f humanity

luksusowy adj (dom, strój) luxury

luster|ko (-ka, -ka; inst sg **-kiem**; gen pl **-ek)** nt 1 mirror 2 (wsteczne w samochodzie) rear-view mirror 3 (boczne w samochodzie) wing (Brit) lub outside (US) mirror

lust|ro (-ra, -ra; loc sg **-rze**; gen pl **-er)** nt mirror; **co wieczór pije do lustra** he drinks alone every night

lut|y (-ego, -e) m decl like adj February

luźny adj 1 (marynarka, spódnica) loose(-fitting) 2 (w książce: kartka) loose 3 (przen: niepoważny: opinia) casual 4 (niezobowiązujący: relacja) casual 5 (pot: poufały: rozmowa) casual

lżej adv comp od **lekko**

lżejszy adj comp od **lekki**

łaci|na (-ny; dat sg & loc sg **-nie)** f Latin; **~ kuchenna** (pot: przen) swear words

łaciński adj (alfabet, język) Latin

ładnie adv (wyglądać, zachowywać się) nicely; **to ciasto ~ pachnie** that cake smells nice

ładny adj 1 (kobieta) pretty 2 (widok) nice

ład|ować (-uję, -ujesz) vt 1 (pf **za-**) (towar) to load 2 (pf **na-**) (baterię) to charge

ładun|ek (-ku, -ki; inst sg **-kiem)** m 1 load 2 (towary na statku, w samolocie) cargo 3 (wybuchowy) charge 4 (elektryczny) charge

łagodnie adv 1 (z sympatią) softly 2 (delikatnie) gently

łagodny adj 1 (spokojny) gentle 2 (delikatny) mild 3 (efekt działania) mild

łag|odzić (-odzę, -odzisz; imp **-odź** lub **-ódź;** pf **z-** lub **za-)** vt **1** (smutek, rozpacz) to soothe **2** (mękę) to alleviate **3** (kłótnię) to moderate

ła|mać (-mię, -miesz; pf **z-)** vt **1** (nogę, przepisy) to break **2** (pokonywać: opór, przeszkody) to overcome; **~ się** vr (o gałęzi) to break; **powiedział to łamiącym się głosem** he said it in a faltering voice; **przed deszczem zawsze łamie mnie w kościach** my bones always ache before it rains

łańcuch (-a, -y) m chain; **~ górski** (Geo) mountain range

łańcusz|ek (-ka, -ki; inst sg **-kiem)** m **1** dimin od **łańcuch 2** (fragment biżuterii) chain

ła|pać (-pię, -piesz; pf **z-)** vt to catch; **proszę nie ~ mnie za słowa** please stop interrupting me

łapów|ka (-ki, -ki; dat sg & loc sg **-ce;** gen pl **-ek)** f bribe

łapu-capu adv: **na ~** in a mad rush; **robić coś na ~** to do sth quickly and carelessly

łaskawy adj (przychylny) favourable (Brit), favorable (US)

łat|ać (-am, -asz; pf **za-)** vt (dziurę, spodnie) to patch

łatwo adv easily; **ta uwaga była ~ zrozumiała** that point of view was easy to understand

łatwopalny adj (materiał, płyn) flammable

łatwowierny adj (człowiek) gullible

łatwy adj (nieskomplikowany, jasny) easy

ła|wa (-wy, -wy; dat sg & loc sg **-wie)** f **1** (miejsce do siedzenia) bench **2** (niski stół) coffee table; **3** (ława przysięgłych: w sądzie) jury box; **zasiąść na ławie oskarżonych** to be in the dock; **powiedział wszystko kawa na ławę** he put all his cards on the table

ław|ka (-ki, -ki; dat sg & loc sg **-ce;** gen pl **-ek)** f **1** (na zewnątrz) bench **2** (w klasie) desk; **~ kościelna** a pew

łazien|ka (-ki, -ki; dat sg & loc sg **-ce;** gen pl **-ek)** f bathroom

łącznie adv (wraz z): **~ z** +inst including; **to należy pisać ~** that should be written as one word

łącz|yć (-ę, -ysz; pf **po-)** vt **1** (składniki, części, kolory, funkcje) to combine **2** (poprzez komunikację) to connect; **~ się** vr **1** (stykać się: o częściach) to be joined **2** (o dłoniach, gałęziach) to meet **3** (o trasach) to merge; **proszę czekać, już łączę!** hold on, I'm putting you through!

łą|ka (-ki, -ki; dat sg & loc sg **-ce)** f meadow

łobu|z (-za, -zy; loc sg **-zie)** m **1** (niegrzeczny chłopiec) yob (Brit), punk (US) **2** (osoba podła) rat

ło|kieć (-kci, -kcie; gen pl **-kci)** m elbow; **rozpychać się łokciami** to elbow one's way

łopa|ta (-ty, -ty; dat sg & loc sg **-cie)** f shovel

łoso|ś (-sia, -sie; gen pl **-si)** m salmon

Łot|wa (-wy; dat sg **-wie)** f Latvia

ło|wić (-wię, -wisz; imp **łów;** pf **z-)**

vt 1 (*polować*) to hunt **2** (*łapać ryby, zwierzynę*) to catch; **~ ryby** to fish

łódź (**łodzi, łodzie**; *gen pl* **łodzi**) *f* boat; **~ podwodna** submarine; **~ ratownicza** lifeboat

łóż|ko (**-ka, -ka**; *inst sg* **-kiem**; *gen pl* **-ek**) *nt* bed

łupież (**-u**) *m* dandruff

łyd|ka (**-ki, -ki**; *dat sg & loc sg* **-ce**; *gen pl* **-ek**) *f* calf

ły|k (**-ku, -ki**; *inst sg* **-kiem**) *m* (*wody, powietrza*) gulp

łyk|ać (**-am, -asz**; *pf* **-nąć**) *vt* (*kęs jedzenia, napój*) to swallow

łyk|nąć (**-nę, -niesz**; *imp* **-nij**) *vb pf od* **łykać**

łysi|eć (**-eję, -ejesz**; *pf* **wy-**) *vi* to go bald

łysi|na (**-ny, -ny**; *loc sg* **-nie**) *f* **1** (*miejsce bez włosów*) bald patch **2** (*na głowie*) baldness

łysy *adj* (*o człowieku, o terenie*) bald

łyżecz|ka (**-ki, -ki**; *dat sg & loc sg* **-ce**; *gen pl* **-ek**) *f* **1** teaspoon **2** (*pojemność*) teaspoonful

łyż|ka (**-ki, -ki**; *dat sg & loc sg* **-ce**; *gen pl* **-ek**) *f* **1** spoon **2** (*pojemność*) spoonful; **~ wazowa** ladle; **~ stołowa cukru** a tablespoon of sugar; **~ do butów** shoehorn

łyż|wa (**-wy, -wy**; *dat sg & loc sg* **-wie**; *gen pl* **-ew**) *f* skate; **pójść na łyżwy** to go skating

łza (**łzy, łzy**; *dat sg & loc sg* **łzie**; *gen pl* **łez**) *f* tear; **on jest czysty jak ~** he's as pure as the driven snow

Macedoni|a (**-i**) *f* Macedonia

mach|ać (**-am, -asz**; *pf* **-nąć**) *vi* **1** (*chorągiewką*) to wave **2** (*o psie*) to wag **3** (*o ptaku*) to flap **4** (*wywijać szablą*) to brandish

macierzyński *adj* **1** (*instynkt*) maternal **2** (*uczucie*) motherly; **brać** (**wziąć** *pf*) **urlop ~** to be on maternity leave

macierzyńst|wo (**-wa**; *loc sg* **-wie**) *nt* motherhood

maco|cha (**-chy, -chy**; *dat sg & loc sg* **-sze**) *f* stepmother

magazy|n (**-nu, -ny**; *loc sg* **-nie**) *m* **1** (*budowla*) warehouse **2** (*miejsce do przechowywania rzeczy*) storeroom **3** (*miesięcznik, tygodnik*) magazine

magi|a (**-i, -e**; *gen pl* **-i**) *f* magic; **to jest dla mnie czarną magią** it's all Greek to me

magiczny adj **1** (przyrząd, zaklęcie) magic **2** (moc) magical

magist|er (-ra, -rzy lub -rowie; loc sg -rze) m **1** (matematyki, biologii) Master of Science **2** (historii, filozofii) Master of Arts

magisterski adj master's (degree); **egzamin ~** finals

magne|s (-su; loc sg -sie) m magnet

magnetofo|n (-nu, -ny; loc sg -nie) m tape recorder; **odtwarzać** (**odtworzyć** pf) **muzykę z ~u** to play music from a tape

magnetowi|d (-du, -dy; loc sg -dzie) m (wideo) VCR

maho|ń (-niu, -nie; gen pl -ni lub -niów) m (drzewo, kolor) mahogany; **meble z mahoniu** mahogany furniture

maj (-a, -e) m May; **Święto Pierwszego M~a** May Day; **Święto Trzeciego M~a** Third of May Holiday (Polish national holiday)

mają vb zob. **mieć**

mają|tek (-ku; inst sg -kiem) m **1** (dobytek) property **2** (wielki dorobek pieniężny) fortune **3** (posiadłość) estate; **~ ruchomy/ nieruchomy** personal property/ real estate

majone|z (-zu, -zy; loc sg -zie) m mayonnaise

majo|r (-ra, -rowie lub -rzy; loc sg -rze) m (Wojsk) major

majów|ka (-ki, -ki; dat sg & loc sg -ce; gen pl -ek) f (wycieczka za miasto) picnic

majst|er (-ra, -rowie lub -rzy; loc

sg **-rze**) m **1** (nadzorca na budowie, w fabryce) foreman **2** (szewc, zegarmistrz) master

majstr|ować (-uję, -ujesz) vi: **~ przy czymś** (pot) to interfere with sth; **nie majstruj przy radiu** stop fiddling about with the radio

majt|ki (-ek) pl **1** (dla kobiet) panties **2** (dla mężczyzn) briefs

makaro|n (-nu, -ny; loc sg -nie) m (nitki, rurki) pasta

makijaż (-u, -e; gen pl -y lub -ów) m make-up; **robić** (**zrobić** pf) **sobie ~** to make o.s. up; **zrobiła sobie wyzywający ~** her make- up was outrageous

maksymalny adj maximum

malar|ka (-ki, -ki; dat sg & loc sg -ce; gen pl -ek) f painter

malarst|wo (-wa; loc sg -wie) nt **1** (rodzaj sztuki) painting **2** (zbiór obrazów) paintings pl

malarz (-a, -e; gen pl -y) m (artysta) painter

mal|eć (-eję, -ejesz; pf z-) vi **1** (popularność) to diminish; **2** (temperatura) to decrease

mali|na (-ny, -ny; dat sg & loc sg -nie) f raspberry; **nie daj się wpuścić w maliny!** (pot) don't let yourself get taken in!

mal|ować (-uję, -ujesz) vt **1** (pf po-) (powierzchnię farbą) to paint **2** (pf wy-) (pokój) to decorate, to paint **3** (pf na-) (dzieło sztuki) to paint; **~ się** vr (robić makijaż) to apply one's make-up; **"świeżo malowane"** "wet paint"

maltret|ować (-uję, -ujesz; pf z-) vt (dręczyć) to abuse; **~ fizycznie/psychicznie** to abuse physically/psychologically

małoduszny adj (podły) mean

Małopols|ka (**-ki**; dat sg & loc sg **-ce**) f a province in southern Poland whose capital is Cracow

małostkowy adj (przejmujący się drobnostkami) petty

mał|pa (**-py, -py**; dat sg & loc sg **-pie**) f **1** (zwierzę) monkey **2** (człekokształtna) ape **3** (Komput) @ sign; **ale z ciebie ~!** (pot) you're a right monkey!

mały adj **1** (niewielkiego rozmiaru) small **2** (dom, przestrzeń) little **3** (o dziecku) small **4** (o literze) lower-case

małżeński adj **1** (o pożyciu) married **2** (kryzys, obowiązek) marital; **zawierać** (**zawrzeć** pf) **związek ~** to enter the state of matrimony

małżeńst|wo (**-wa, -wa**; loc sg **-wie**) nt **1** (związek formalny) marriage **2** (mąż i żona) (married) couple **3** (sakrament) matrimony; **~ mieszane** mixed marriage

małżon|ek (**-ka, -kowie**; inst sg **-kiem**) m (mąż) husband; **małżonkowie** pl (mąż i żona) husband and wife

małżon|ka (**-ki, -ki**; dat sg & loc sg **-ce**; gen pl **-ek**) f (żona) wife

mam vb zob. **mieć**

ma|ma (**-my, -my**; dat sg & loc sg **-mie**) f (pot: matka) mum

maminsyn|ek (**-ka, -kowie** lub **-ki**; inst sg **-kiem**) m (pej) mummy's boy

mamy vb zob. **mieć**

manifestacj|a (**-i, -e**; gen pl **-i**) f **1** (wyraz) expression **2** (protest społeczny) demonstration

manifest|ować (**-uję, -ujesz**; pf **za-**) vi (brać udział w demonstracji) to demonstrate

manipul|ować (**-uję, -ujesz**) vi +inst (uczuciami, faktami) to manipulate

mańku|t (**-ta, -ci**; loc sg **-cie**) m left-hander; **on jest ~em** (pej) he's left-handed

ma|pa (**-py, -py**; loc sg **-pie**) f map; **~ samochodowa Europy** road map of Europe

march|ew (**-wi, -wie**; gen pl **-wi**) f carrot

margary|na (**-ny, -ny**; dat sg & loc sg **-nie**) f margarine

marmola|da (**-dy, -dy**; dat sg & loc sg **-dzie**) f preserve

marmu|r (**-ru, -ry**; loc sg **-rze**) m marble

marn|ować (**-uję, -ujesz**; pf **z-**) vt (czas, pieniądze) to waste; **~ się** vr to be wasted

marny adj **1** (nieznaczny) paltry **2** (kiepski, słaby) poor; **wysiłki poszły na marne** the efforts went to waste

marsz (**-u, -e**) m march; **~ do szkoły!** (pot) off to school with you!

marszcz|yć (**-ę, -ysz**; pf **z-**) vt **1** (twarz) to wrinkle **2** (ubranie) to gather; **~ się** vr **1** (na twarzy) to wrinkle **2** (o tkaninie) to crease

mart|wić (**-wię, -wisz**; pf **z-**) vt to upset; **~ się** vr to worry; **martwię się twoim zdrowiem** I'm worried about your health; **martwię się o ciebie** I'm concerned about you; **nie martw się już tym!** don't worry about it any more!

martwy adj dead; **ten obraz to**

martwa natura this painting is a still life

maru|dzić (**-dzę, -dzisz**; *imp* **-dź**) *vi* (*narzekać*) to whine

marynar|ka (**-ki**; *dat sg & loc sg* **-ce**; *nom pl* **-ki**; *gen pl* **-ek**) *f* **1** (*strój*) jacket **2** (*formacja wojskowa*) navy; **~ dwurzędowa/jednorzędowa** a double-/single-breasted jacket

marynarz (**-a, -e**; *gen pl* **-y**) *m* **1** (*członek załogi na statku*) seaman **2** (*Wojsk*) sailor

ma|rzec (**-rca, -rce**) *m* March

marze|nie (**-nia, -nia**; *gen pl* **-ń**) *nt* dream; **~ senne** dream

marz|nąć (**-nę, -niesz**; *imp* **-nij**) *vi* **1** (*pf* **z-**) (*o osobie*) to freeze **2** (*pf* **za-**) (*o pogodzie*) to freeze

marz|yć (**-ę, -ysz**) *vi* to (day)dream; **~ o** +*loc* to dream of; **~ o niebieskich migdałach** to daydream

ma|sa (**-sy, -sy**; *dat sg & loc sg* **-sie**) *f* mass; **ale z ciebie ciemna ~** (*pot: pej*) you really are an idiot; **masy** *pl* (*zwykłe ludzie*) the masses

mas|ka (**-ki, -ki**; *dat sg & loc sg* **-ce**; *gen pl* **-ek**) *f* **1** mask **2** (*w samochodzie*) bonnet (*Brit*), hood (*US*)

mask|ować (**-uję, -ujesz**; *pf* **za-**) *vt* **1** (*ukrywać*) to camouflage **2** (*uczucia: przen*) to mask; **~ się** *vr* to put on a facade

ma|sło (**-sła**; *loc sg* **-śle**) *nt* (*orzechowe, kakaowe*) butter; **wszystko idzie jak po maśle** everything is going swimmingly

mas|ować (**-uję, -ujesz**; *pf* **po-**) *vt* to massage

mass-medi|a (**-ów**) *pl* the (mass) media

masz *vb zob.* **mieć**

maszy|na (**-ny, -ny**; *dat sg & loc sg* **-nie**) *f* (*urządzenie*) machine; **~ do szycia** sewing machine; **mam w domu starą maszynę do pisania** I have an old typewriter at home

maszynopi|s (**-su, -sy**; *loc sg* **-sie**) *m* typescript

maszynowy *adj* **1** (*odnoszący się do maszyny*) machine **2** (*zrobiony maszyną*) machine-made; **broń maszynowa** machine gun

maś|ć (**-ci, -ci**; *gen pl* **-ci**) *f* **1** (*lekarstwo*) ointment **2** (*ubarwienie konia*) colour (*Brit*), color (*US*); **aktywiści wszelkiej maści** activists of every description

matematyczny *adj* (*działanie*) mathematical

matematy|ka (**-ki**; *dat sg & loc sg* **-ce**) *f* **1** mathematics **2** (*w szkole*) maths (*Brit*), math (*US*)

matera|c (**-ca, -ce**; *gen pl* **-cy** lub **-ców**) *m* (*sprężynowy, dmuchany*) mattress

materialny *adj* **1** (*dobra kultury*) material **2** (*trudności, położenie*) financial

materia|ł (**-łu, -ły**; *loc sg* **-le**) *m* **1** (*tworzywo sztuczne*) material **2** (*jedwab, bawełna*) fabric; **~ wybuchowy** explosives *pl*

mat|ka (**-ki, -ki**; *dat sg & loc sg* **-ce**; *gen pl* **-ek**) *f* **1** (*rodzona*) mother **2**: **~ chrzestna** (*Rel*) godmother; **M~ Boska** the Virgin Mary

matowy *adj* **1** (*nieprzezroczysty*) frosted **2** (*barwa głosu*) dull **3** (*zdjęcie*) mat(t)

matrymonialny *adj*
matrimonial; **biuro**
matrymonialne marriage
bureau; **ogłoszenie**
matrymonialne lonely-hearts
ad; **oszust ~** adulterer
matu|ra (-ry, -ry; *dat sg & loc*
sg **-rze**) *f (egzamin dojrzałości)* ≈
A-levels *(Brit)*, ≈ high school finals
(US); **zdać** *(pf)* **maturę**
≈ to pass one's A-Levels *(Brit)*,
≈ to graduate *(US)*

⊙ **MATURA**

Matura is the exam taken at
the end of secondary school
and is compulsory for those
students who wish to study at
university. It is also referred
to as 'the maturity exam' as it
is usually taken at the age of
seventeen or eighteen. See
also **liceum**.

Mazur|y (-) *pl a region in north-*
eastern Poland, famous for its great
lakes
mądroś|ć (-ci, -ci; *gen pl* **-ci**) *f*
wisdom; **cechuje go ~ życiowa**
he has a lot of common sense
mąd|ry *adj* wise
mądrz|eć (-eję, -ejesz; *pf* **z-**) *vi* to
grow wise
mądrz|yć się (-ę, -ysz) *vr (pot)* to
talk pretentious rubbish
mą|ka (-ki, -ki; *dat sg & loc sg*
-ce) *f* flour; **z tej mąki chleba**
nie będzie *(przen)* it's a waste
of effort
mąż (męża, mężowie) *m*
husband; **wychodzić (wyjść**

pf) **za ~** to get married *(about a*
woman); **to prawdziwy ~ stanu**
he is a true statesman
mdl|eć (-eję, -ejesz; *pf* **ze-**) *vi*
to faint
mdły *adj* **1** *(bez wyrazu)* bland
2 *(powodujący mdłości)* nauseating
meb|el (-la, -le) *m* piece of
furniture; **meble** *(gen pl* **-li)** *pl*
(kuchenne, do salonu) furniture
mebl|ować (-uję, -ujesz; *pf* **u-**) *vt*
(pokój, mieszkanie) to furnish
mecena|s (-sa, -si *lub* **-sowie**; *loc*
sg **-sie)** *m (sztuki)* patron
mechaniczny *adj* **1** mechanical
2 *(pojazd)* motor
mechani|k (-ka, -cy) *m* mechanic
mechaniz|m (-mu, -my;
loc sg **-mie)** *m* **1** *(w maszynie)*
mechanism **2** *(społeczny, historii)*
mechanics
mecz (-u, -e) *m (piłkarski, tenisowy)*
match
medal (-u, -e; *gen pl* **-i)** *m* medal;
zdałeś egzamin na ~ you have
passed the exam with flying
colours
medi|a (-ów) *pl* **1** *(elektroniczne,*
drukowane) media **2** *(woda, prąd)*
utilities
medycy|na (-ny; *dat sg & loc sg*
-nie) *f (nauka)* medicine
medyczny *adj (personel, wydział)*
medical; **studia medyczne**
medicine
medytacj|a (-i, -e; *gen pl* **-i)** *f*
meditation
Meksy|k (-ku; *inst sg* **-kiem)** *m*
Mexico
melancholi|a (-i) *f* melancholy;
wpadać (wpaść *pf)* **w**
melancholię to get depressed

melancholijny adj (charakter,
nastrój) melancholy
meld|ować (-uję, -ujesz; pf **za-)**
vt **1** to report **2** (na komisariacie:
mieszkańca) to register; **~ się** vr
1 (Wojsk: na stanowisku) to report
2 (jako mieszkaniec) to register; **~ o**
+loc to report
melodi|a (-i, -e; gen pl **-i)** f melody
melo|n (-na, -ny; loc sg **-nie)** m
melon
menedże|r (-ra, -rowie; loc sg
-rze) m (kierownik) manager
menstruacj|a (-i, -e; gen pl **-i)** f
(miesiączka) menstruation
menu nt inv (karta dań) menu
merytoryczny adj substantive;
**książka zawiera wiele błędów
~ch** the book contains many
factual errors
me|ta (-ty, -ty; dat sg & loc sg
-cie) f finishing line; **to się nie
uda na dłuższą/krótszą metę**
this is unlikely to succeed in the
long/short term
metaboliz|m (-mu; loc sg **-mie)** m
metabolism
metafo|ra (-ry, -ry; dat sg & loc sg
-rze) f (przenośnia) metaphor
metal (-u, -e; gen pl **-i)** m (kolorowy,
szlachetny) metal
metalowy adj (przedmiot) metal
met|ka (-ki, -ki; dat sg & loc sg
-ce; gen pl **-ek)** f **1** (naklejana na
produkcie) label **2** (przywieszana na
bagażu) tag
meto|da (-dy, -dy; dat sg & loc sg
-dzie) f (badawcza, poznawcza)
method
metodyczny adj **1** (planowy)
methodical **2** (związany z metodą)
methodological

met|r (-ra, -ry; loc sg **-rze)** m
metre (Brit), meter (US); **pokój
ma 20 ~ów kwadratowych** the
room is 20 square metres
met|ro (-ra; loc sg **-rze)** nt (Rail)
underground (Brit), subway (US)
metryczny adj (system) metric
me|wa (-wy, -wy; dat sg & loc sg
-wie) f seagull
męcz|yć (-ę, -ysz) vt **1** (pf **z-)**
(powodować wyczerpanie) to tire
out **2** (maltretować) to harass
3 (dokuczać) to bother; **~ się** vr
1 (pf **z-)** (odczuwać wyczerpanie)
to tire **2** (odczuwać cierpienie) to
suffer; **on męczy się nad pracą
domową** he is toiling over his
homework
mę|ka (-ki, -ki; dat sg & loc sg **-ce**;
gen pl **mąk)** f **1** (tortura fizyczna)
torture **2** (cierpienie psychiczne)
torment
męski adj **1** (ubranie) men's;
2 (zachowanie) manly; **rodzaj ~**
masculine (gender)
męskoosobowy adj: **rodzaj ~** (w
językoznawstwie) virile gender
męskoś|ć (-ci) f (zbiór cech
męskich) masculinity
mężat|ka (-ki, -ki; dat sg & loc sg
-ce; gen pl **-ek)** f (żona) married
woman
mężczy|zna (-zny, -źni; dat sg &
loc sg **-źnie**; gen pl **-zn)** m decl like
f in sg man
mglisty adj **1** (pogoda) foggy
2 (niewyraźny) hazy **3** (niekonkretny)
indistinct
mg|ła (-ły, -ły; dat sg & loc sg **-le**;
gen pl **mgieł)** f **1** (zawiesista) fog
2 (przeciętna) mist **3** (delikatna)
haze

mgr *abbr* **1** (= *magister*) (*historii, filozofii*) ≈ MA (= *Master of Arts*) **2** (*biologii, matematyki*) ≈ MSc (= *Master of Science*)

mianowni|k (**-ka, -ki**; *inst sg* **-kiem**) *m* **1** (*w językoznawstwie*) nominative **2** (*w matematyce*) denominator

mia|ra (**-ry, -ry**; *dat sg & loc sg* **mierze**) *f* **1** (*wielkość*) measure **2** (*ubrania*) size **3** (*umiar*) moderation; **w dużej mierze zależy to od ciebie** it depends on you to a great extent

miastecz|ko (**-ka, -ka**; *gen pl* **-ek**; *inst sg* **-kiem**) *nt* (small) town; **~ uniwersyteckie** university campus; **wesołe ~** funfair (*Brit*), amusement park (*US*)

miast|o (**-a, -a**; *loc sg* **mieście**) *nt* **1** (*średniej wielkości*) town **2** (*wielkie*) city; **iść** (**pójść** *pf*) **do centrum miasta** to go (in)to town (*Brit*), to go downtown (*US*)

miażdż|yć (**-ę, -ysz**; *pf* **z-**) *vt* (*zgniatać*) to crush

miąższ (**-u**) *m* (*owocowy*) pulp, flesh

○ KEYWORD

mieć (**mam, masz**; *imp* **miej**; *pt* **miał, mieli**) *vt* **1** (*posiadać własność*) to have; **mieć na sobie spodnie** to be wearing trousers (*Brit*) *lub* pants (*US*)
2 (*katar, kłopoty*) to have; **mieć coś do kogoś** to have sth against sb **3** (*z różnymi dopełnieniami*) to have; **przedstawienie będzie mieć miejsce w czwartek** the performance will take place on

Thursday; **masz (jeszcze) dużo czasu!** take your time!; **mam ochotę na ciastko** I feel like a cake
4 (*dla wyrażenia powinności*) to be supposed to; **masz się uczyć** you're supposed to be studying **5** (*dla wyrażenia zamiaru*) to be going to; **ona ma przyjść we wtorek** she's going to come on Tuesday
6 (*forma zaprzeczona czasownika być*): **nie ma** (*liczba pojedyncza*) there is none
7 (*liczba mnoga*) there are no; **nie ma pieniędzy** there's no money; **nie ma chleba** there is no bread; **nie ma co o tym myśleć** there's no use thinking about it; **nie ma się czemu więcej dziwić** (there's) no wonder; **nie ma za co!** don't mention it!; **cudów nie ma** (*pot*) that's the way the cookie crumbles!

mieć się *vr*: **jak się masz?** how are you?; **mieć się za** to take o.s. to be; **ma się za niezłą aktorkę** she considers herself to be a decent actress

mie|dź (**-dzi**) *f* (*metal*) copper
miejsc|e (**-a, -a**) *nt* **1** (*przestrzeń*) space **2** (*fragment przestrzeni*) place **3** (*usytuowanie*) position **4** (*miejscowość*) place **5** (*w pensjonacie*) vacancy **6** (*w pociągu*) seat **7** (*paragraf w tekście*) passage **8** (*w hierarchii*) position; **musimy dojechać do ~ przeznaczenia** we must reach our destination; **proszę podać ~ zamieszkania** please give your place of

residence; **na miejscu czeka na nas obiad** dinner will be waiting for us when we arrive; **spotkanie ma ~ w sali numer...** the meeting is taking place in room number...; **na twoim miejscu obraziłabym się** if I were you, I would be offended; **miejscami masz rację** you are partially right; **z miejsca odrzucam twoją propozycję** I am rejecting your proposal out of hand

miejscowni|k (**-ka, -ki**; *inst sg* **-kiem**) *m* (*w językoznawstwie*) locative

miejscowoś|ć (**-ci, -ci**; *gen pl* **-ci**) *f* place; **~ turystyczna** tourist destination

miejscowy *adj* (*gazeta, zwyczaj*) local

miejscłów|ka (**-ki, -ki**; *dat sg & loc sg* **-ce**; *gen pl* **-ek**) *f* (*w pociągu*) seat reservation

miejski *adj* (*transport*) urban

mielone (**-go**) *nt decl like adj* (*mięso*) mince (*Brit*), ground beef (*US*)

mielony *adj* **1** (*kawa, mąka*) ground **2** (*mięso*) minced ▷ *m decl like adj*: **kotlet ~** ≈ meat patty, hamburger

mieni|e (**-a**) *nt* (*prywatne, państwowe*) property

mierz|yć (**-ę, -ysz**; *pf* **z-**) *vt* (*robić pomiar*) to measure ▷ *vi*: **~** (*pf* **wy-**) **(do kogoś/czegoś)** to aim (at sb/sth); **~ w tarczę** to aim at a target; **on mierzy wszystkich własną miarą** he judges everyone by his own standards

miesi|ąc (**-ąca, -ące**; *gen pl* **-ęcy**) *m* (*część roku*) month; **miodowy ~**

honeymoon

miesiącz|ka (**-ki, -ki**; *dat sg & loc sg* **-ce**; *gen pl* **-ek**) *f* (*menstruacja*) period

miesięczni|k (**-ka, -ki**; *inst sg* **-kiem**) *m* (*gazeta*) monthly

miesięczny *adj* (*dochód, rozliczenie*) monthly

miesz|ać (**-am, -asz**) *vt* **1** (*pf* **wy-** *lub* **za-**) (*rozrabiać składniki*) to stir **2** (*pf* **z-**) (*łączyć składniki*) to mix **3** (*pf* **w-**) (*wplątywać w sprawę*) to involve **4** (*pf* **po-**) (*mylić fakty, osoby*) to confuse; **~ się 1** *vr* (*łączyć się*) to mix **2** (*ingerować*) to meddle; **nie mieszaj się w ich sprawy** don't stick your nose into their business; **ostatnio wszystko mi się miesza** recently I have been getting things all mixed up

mieszani|na (**-ny, -ny**; *dat sg & loc sg* **-nie**) *f* (*substancja*) mixture

mieszan|ka (**-ki, -ki**; *dat sg & loc sg* **-ce**; *gen pl* **-ek**) *f* (*substancja*) mixture

mieszany *adj* (*małżeństwo, emocje*) mixed

mieszk|ać (**-am, -asz**) *vi* **1** (*być zameldowanym*) to live **2** (*przebywać chwilowo*) to stay

mieszkalny *adj* (*część miasta*) residential

mieszka|nie (**-nia, -nia**; *gen pl* **-ń**) *nt* (*jednopokojowe, dwupokojowe*) flat (*Brit*), apartment (*US*)

mieszka|niec (**-ńca, -ńcy**) *m* **1** (*w domu*) occupant **2** (*w mieście*) inhabitant **3** (*w państwie*) resident

między *prep* +*loc* **1** (*pomiędzy dwoma obiektami, osobami*) between **2** (*wśród ludzi,* *przedmiotów*) among **3** (*dla określenia przedziału czasu*) between ▷ *prep* +*inst* between; **~ (godziną) ósmą a dziewiątą** between eight and nine o'clock; **~ nami mówiąc, masz rację** just between you and me, I think you are right; **załatwcie to ~ sobą** sort it out between yourselves; **~ innymi czyta książki** among other things he reads books

międzymiastowy *adj* **1** (*komunikacja*) intercity **2** (*rozmowa telefoniczna*) long-distance

międzynarodowy *adj* (*umowa, festiwal*) international

miękki *adj* soft; **masz ~e serce** you are too soft with people

miękko *adv* (*chodzić, mówić*) softly; **jajko na ~** soft-boiled egg

mię|sień (**-śnia, -śnie**; *gen pl* **-śni**) *m* muscle

mięsny *adj* meat; **sklep ~** butcher's (shop)

mię|so (**-sa, -sa**; *loc sg* **-sie**) *nt* meat; **~ wieprzowe/wołowe/drobiowe** pork/beef/poultry

miętowy *adj* (*cukierek, smak*) mint

mig|ać (**-am, -asz**; *pf* **-nąć**) *vi* +*inst* (*światłami*) to flash

migre|na (**-ny**; *dat sg & loc sg* **-nie**) *f* migraine; **cierpieć na migrenę** to suffer from migraine

mij|ać (**-am, -asz**; *pf* **minąć**) *vt* to pass ▷ *vi* to pass; **~ się** *vr* **1** (*wymijać się: w przeciwnych kierunkach*) to pass (each other) **2** (*nie rozumieć się*) to differ (in opinion)

Mikołaj (**-a, -e**) *m* (*też:* **Święty ~**) Father Christmas (*Brit*), Santa

(Claus); **mikołajki** St Nicholas's Day

mikrofalów|ka (**-ki, -ki**; *dat sg & loc sg* **-ce**; *gen pl* **-ek**) *f* (*pot: kuchenka mikrofalowa*) microwave

mil|a (**-i, -e**) *f* mile

milczący *adj* (*człowiek*) silent

milcz|eć (**-ę, -ysz**) *vi* to remain silent; **milczał jak zaklęty** he was as quiet as a mouse

milczeni|e (**-a**) *nt* silence; **~m pominął zdradę** he kept silent about his betrayal

miliar|d (**-da, -dy**; *loc sg* **-dzie**) *m* billion

milimet|r (**-ra, -ry**; *loc sg* **-rze**) *m* millimetre (*Brit*), millimeter (*US*)

milio|n (**-na, -ny**; *loc sg* **-nie**) *m* million

milione|r (**-ra, -rzy**; *loc sg* **-rze**) *m* millionaire

militarny *adj* (*akcja*) military

miło *adv* **1** (*spędzać czas, rozmawiać*) pleasantly **2** (*życzliwie*) kindly; **~ mi (pana/panią) poznać** pleased to meet you; **to bardzo ~ z państwa strony/pani strony** that's very kind of you

miłosny *adj* (*zawód, podbój*) amorous

miłoś|ć (**-ci, -ci**; *gen pl* **-ci**) *f* (*odwzajemniona, bez wzajemności*) love; **na ~ boską!** (*pot*) for God's sake!

miłośni|k (**-ka, -cy**; *inst sg* **-kiem**) *m* (*amator*) enthusiast

miły *adj* nice; **bądź tak ~ i przyjdź tu** be so kind and come over here

mimo *prep* +*gen* in spite of; **~ wszystko udało się** in spite of everything, it worked out; **~ woli opuścił pokój** he left the room against his will; **~ że** *lub* **iż padało, wyszliśmy** even though it was raining, we headed out

m.in. *abbr* (= *między innymi*) among other things

mi|na (-**ny**, -**ny**; *dat sg & loc sg* -**nie**) *f* 1 (*na twarzy*) facial expression 2 (*przeciwpiechotna, lądowa*) mine

mi|nąć (-**nę**, -**niesz**; *imp* -**ń**) *vb pf od* **mijać**

minimalnie *adv* 1 (*nieznacznie*) minimally 2 (*ledwo*) narrowly

minimalny *adj* minimal

minim|um (-**um**, -**a**; *gen pl* -**ów**) *nt inv in sg* minimum ▷ *adv* (*co najmniej*) at least

miniony *adj* 1 (*epoka*) past 2 (*rok, tydzień*) last

minist|er (-**ra**, -**rowie**; *loc sg* -**rze** *m* (*sekretarz stanu*) government minister (*Brit*), Secretary (*US*); **M~ Spraw Zagranicznych** foreign minister, ≈ Foreign Secretary (*Brit*), ≈ Secretary of State (*US*); **M~ Spraw Wewnętrznych** minister of the interior, ≈ Home Secretary (*Brit*), ≈ Secretary of the Interior (*US*); **~ bez teki** (*członek rządu, nie kierujący ministerstwem*) minister without portfolio; **posiedzenie rady ministrów** cabinet meeting

ministerst|wo (-**wa**, -**wa**; *loc sg* -**wie**) *nt* department of state

minu|s (-**sa**, -**sy**; *loc sg* -**sie**) *m* minus; **plus ~** more or less; **jestem na ~ie** I'm in debt

minusowy *adj* 1 (*temperatura poniżej zera*) subzero 2 (*wynik, bilans*) negative

minu|ta (-**ty**, -**ty**; *dat sg & loc sg* -**cie**) *f* minute; **za parę minut** in a couple of minutes

miot|ła (-**ły**, -**ły**; *dat sg & loc sg* -**le**; *gen pl* -**eł**) *f* (*do sprzątania*) broom

miód (**miodu**; *loc sg* **miodzie**) *m* 1 honey 2 (*pitny*) mead

mis|ka (-**ki**, -**ki**; *dat sg & loc sg* -**ce**; *gen pl* -**ek**) *f* bowl

mistrz (-**a**, -**owie**) *m* 1 (*radzący sobie doskonale w czymś*) master 2 (*sportowy*) champion

mistrzost|wo (-**wa**, -**wa**; *loc sg* -**wie**) *nt* 1 (*biegłość*) mastery 2 (*sportowe*) championship; **mistrzostwa świata** world championships

mistrzowski *adj* 1 (*osiągnięcie*) brilliant 2 (*drużyna*) title-holding

mistrzy|ni (-**ni**, -**nie**; *dat sg & loc sg* -**ni**; *gen pl* -**ń**) *f* champion

mistyczny *adj* (*poezja, rytuał*) mystic(al)

mistyfikacj|a (-**i**, -**e**; *gen pl* -**i**) *f* mystification

mi|ś (-**sia**, -**sie**) *m* (*pot*) 1 (*niedźwiedź*) (little) bear 2 (*pluszowy*) teddy (bear)

mi|t (-**tu**, -**ty**; *loc sg* -**cie**) *m* myth

mitologi|a (-**i**, -**e**; *gen pl* -**i**) *f* (*grecka, słowiańska*) mythology

mityczny *adj* (*postać, opowieść*) mythical

mizeri|a (-**i**, -**e**; *gen pl* -**i**) *f* (*potrawa*) cucumber salad

mizerny *adj* 1 (*źle wyglądający*) sickly 2 (*kiepski*) miserable

mleczar|nia (-**ni**, -**nie**; *gen pl* -**ni** *lub* -**ń**) *f* dairy

mleczny *adj* 1 (*napój, zupa*) milky 2 (*gruczoł*) mammary

3 (*nieprzezroczysty*) frosted; **Droga Mleczna** the Milky Way

mle|ko (-ka) *nt* milk; **~ zsiadłe** (*Culin*) sour milk; **~ w proszku** (*Culin*) powdered milk

młod|e (-ych) *pl decl like adj* (*Zool*) young *pl*

młodociany *adj* (*przestępca*) juvenile ▷ *m decl like adj* juvenile

młodoś|ć (-ci) *f* youth; **przeżywać (przeżyć** *pf*) **drugą ~** to experience a second youth

młodszy *adj comp od* **młody**

młody *adj* **1** young **2** (*o ziemniakach*) new; **pan ~** (bride)groom; **panna młoda** bride; **młoda para** *lub* **młodzi** (*przed przysięgą*) bride and groom; (*po przysiędze*) newlyweds

młodzie|niec (-ńca, -ńcy) *m* (*młody mężczyzna*) youth

młodzież (-y) *f* youth

młodzieżowy *adj* (*zespół, obóz*) youth

młot|ek (-ka, -ki; *inst sg* **-kiem)** *m* **1** hammer **2** (*z drewna*) mallet

mły|n (-na, -ny; *loc sg* **-nie)** *m* mill; **ale dziś był ~ w pracy** (*pot: przen*) it's been nose to the grindstone today at work

mną *pron inst od* **ja** me; **chodź ze ~** come with me

mni|ch (-cha, -si) *m* monk

mnie *pron gen, dat, acc, loc od* **ja** me; **myśl o ~** think about me

mniej *adv comp od* **mało 1** (*o przedmiotach*) fewer **2** (*o czasie*) less; **ten film jest ~ interesujący** this film is less interesting; **~ więcej to mam na myśli** that is more or less what I have in mind

mniejszoś|ć (-ci, -ci; *gen pl* **-ci)** *f*

(*seksualna, etniczna*) minority

mniejszy *adj comp od* **mały**; **mniejsza o to** *lub* **mniejsza z tym, kto wydał rozkaz** never mind who gave the order

mnoże|nie (-nia, -nia; *gen pl* **-ń)** *nt* (*działanie matematyczne*) multiplication; **tabliczka/znak mnożenia** multiplication table/sign

mnoż|yć (-ę, -ysz; *imp* **mnóż;** *pf* **po-)** *vt* (*w matematyce*) to multiply; **~ się** *vr* (*zwiększać ilość*) to increase

moc (-y, -e; *gen pl* **-y)** *f* power

mocarst|wo (-wa, -wa; *loc sg* **-wie)** *nt* (*Pol*) superpower

mocno *adv* **1** (*przyciskać*) firmly **2** (*bić*) hard **3** (*przykręcać*) tightly **4** (*pragnąć*) very much **5** (*pachnieć*) strongly; (*zaskoczony*) very; **wczoraj ~ wiało** it was very windy yesterday; **~ spała** she was deeply asleep

mocny *adj* **1** strong **2** (*solidny*) firm, tight; (*mechanizm*) powerful

mocz (-u) *m* urine

mocz|yć (-ę, -ysz) (*imp; pf* **z-)** *vt* to moisten; **~ się** *vr* to wet o.s.

mo|da (-dy, -dy; *loc sg* **-dzie;** *gen pl* **mód)** *f* fashion; **szary jest w modzie** grey (*Brit*) *lub* gray (*US*) is in fashion; **mini wyszło z mody** mini skirts have gone out of fashion

model (*nom pl* **-e)** *m* **1** (*gen sg* **-u;** *gen pl* **-i**) (*samolotu, silnika*) model **2** (*gen sg* **-a;** *gen pl* **-i**) (*na wybiegu*) model

model|ka (-ki, -ki; *dat sg & loc sg* **-ce;** *gen pl* **-ek**) *f* (*kobieta na wybiegu*) model

modl|ić się (-ę, -isz; *imp* **módl)**
vr to pray

modlit|wa (-wy, -wy; *dat sg &*
loc sg **-wie)** *f* prayer; **odmawiać**
(odmówić *pf*) **modlitwę** to say
one's prayers

modny *adj* fashionable

mogę *itd. vb zob.* **móc**

moi *itd. pron zob.* **mój**

moja, moje *itd. pron zob.* **mój**

mok|nąć (-nę, -niesz; *imp* **-nij;** *pt*
mókł; *pf* **z-)** *vi* (*na deszczu*) to get
wet (*in the rain*)

mokro *adv*: **jest dziś bardzo ~** it
is very wet today

mokry *adj* wet

molest|ować (-uję, -ujesz)
vt **1** to harass **2** (*wykorzystać*
seksualnie) to molest

momen|t (-tu, -ty; *loc sg* **-cie)**
m (*chwila*) moment; **czeka**
na ~! wait a minute!; **w tym**
momencie nie mogłem skłamać
at that moment I couldn't lie; **w**
pewnym momencie at one point

momentalny *adj*
(*natychmiastowy*) instant

MON *abbr* (= *Ministerstwo Obrony*
Narodowej) ≈ MoD (*Brit*), ≈ DOD
(*US*)

monarchi|a (-i, -e; *gen pl* **-i)**
f (*konstytucyjna, dziedziczna*)
monarchy

mone|ta (-ty, -ty; *dat sg & loc sg*
-cie) *f* coin

monito|r (-ra, -ry; *loc sg* **-rze)** *m*
(*komputera, telewizora*) monitor

mont|ować (-uję, -ujesz) *vt* **1** (*pf*
z-) (*meble*) to assemble **2** (*pf* **za-**)
(*urządzenie elektryczne*) to install
3 (*pf* **z-**) (*pot: Pol: grupę*) to put
together **4** (*pf* **z-**) (*Cine, TV*) to edit

moralnoś|ć (-ci) *f* morality;
podwójna ~ double standards *pl*

moralny *adj* (*czyn, człowiek*) moral

morderc|a (-y, -y) *m decl like f in*
sg murderer

morderczy *adj* (*instynkt*)
murderous

morderst|wo (-wa; *loc sg* **-wie)**
nt murder

mord|ować (-uję, -ujesz; *pf* **za-)**
vt (*odbierać komuś życie*) to murder

morel|a (-i, -e; *gen pl* **-i)**
f **1** (*Culin: owoc*) apricot
2 (*Bot: drzewo*) apricot (tree)

morski *adj* **1** (*transport*) sea
2 (*przemysł*) maritime **3** (*akademia*)
naval; **Gdańsk to stary port ~**
Gdańsk is an ancient seaport;
choroba morska seasickness;
katastrofa morska disaster
at sea; **świnka morska** guinea
pig

morz|e (-a, -a; *gen pl* **mórz)** *nt*
(*Bałtyckie, Śródziemne*) sea; **nad**
~m (*niedaleko morza*) by the sea;
(*spędzać wakacje*) at the
seaside; **wysokość nad**
poziomem morza height above
sea level; **poniżej poziomu**
morza below sea level; **jechać**
(**pojechać** *pf*) **nad ~** to go to the
seaside

mo|st (-stu, -sty; *loc sg* **-ście)** *m*
bridge; **powiem ci to prosto z ~u**
I'll tell it to you like it is

motel (-u, -e; *gen pl* **-i)** *m* motel

motocykl (-a, -e; *gen pl* **-i)** *m*
motorcycle

motyl (-a, -e; *gen pl* **-i)** *m* butterfly

motywacj|a (-i, -e; *gen pl* **-i)**
f (*uzasadnienie postępowania*)
motivation

motyw|ować (**-uję, -ujesz**; *pf* **u-**) *vt* **1** (*wspierać*) to motivate **2** (*tłumaczyć*) to justify

mo|wa (**-wy**; *dat sg & loc sg* **-wie**) *f* **1** (*obca, rodzima*) language **2** (*umiejętność mówienia*) speech **3** (*nom pl* **-wy**; *gen pl* **mów**) (*powitalna, na konferencji*) speech; **nie ma mowy o tym!** (*pot*) that's out of the question!; **część mowy** (*w językoznawstwie*) part of speech; **~ zależna/niezależna** (*w językoznawstwie*) reported/ direct speech

może *inv* perhaps; **być ~** maybe; **~ coś zjemy?** perhaps we'll get a bite to eat?; **~ byśmy poszli do kina?** how about we go to the cinema?

możesz *itd. vb zob.* **móc**

możliwoś|ć (**-ci, -ci**; *gen pl* **-ci**) *f* **1** possibility **2** (*okazja*) opportunity; **możliwości** *pl* capabilities; **zrobimy to w miarę możliwości** we'll do it as well as possible

możliwy *adj* **1** (*wyobrażalny*) conceivable **2** (*realny*) feasible **3** (*pot: wystarczająco dobry*) passable; **możliwe, że przyjdzie jutro** it is likely that he will come tomorrow; **zrobię to o ile to możliwe** I'll do it as far as it's possible; **~ do uniknięcia/ rozpoznania** avoidable/ recognizable

można *inv*: **~ stwierdzić, że masz rację** one *lub* you might say that you are indeed right; **~ już jeść** you may eat now; **nie ~ tego oddać** this cannot be returned; **nie ~ tak robić** you must not

do that; **czy ~ siadać?** can I sit down?

○ **KEYWORD**

móc (**mogę, możesz**; *pt* **mógł, mogła, mogli**) *vi* **1** (*być w stanie*) to be able; **czy możesz to przeczytać?** can *lub* could you read this?; **nie będę mógł wam pomóc** I shall not be able to help you; **szkoda, że nie możesz z nami pójść** it is a pity that you can't come with us; **gdybym tylko mógł, to bym poszedł** if only I could, then I would go **2** (*mieć zgodę*): **móc coś zrobić** to be allowed to do sth; **czy mogę przyjść później?** may I come later?; **czy mógłbym rozmawiać z Kasią?** could I speak to Kasia, please? **3** (*wyrażenie prawdopodobieństwa*): **on może nie przyjść** he might not come; **gdzie może być życie pozaziemskie?** where can there be extraterrestrial life?; **mogła o tym zapomnieć** she may have forgotten; **mógli nas zabić!** they could have killed us! **4** (*w prośbach*): **czy mógłbyś zamknąć drzwi?** could you close the door? **5** (*dla wyrażenia niezadowolenia*): **mogłeś mnie uprzedzić** you might have warned me

mój *possessive pron* **1** (*z rzeczownikiem*) my **2** (*bez rzeczownika*) mine; **to są moje rzeczy** these are my things; **te rzeczy są moje** these things are mine

mó|wić (**-wię, -wisz**) *vt* **1** (*coś*)
to say **2** (*opowiadać*) to tell ▷ *vi*
1 (*wygłosić przemówienie*) to speak
2 (*prowadzić rozmowę*) to talk; **on
mówi, że masz rację** he says
that you're right; **mówił mi,
że się uda** he told me that it
would work out; **~ po włosku/
hiszpańsku** to speak Italian/
Spanish; **nie mówiąc (już) o** +*loc*
not to mention; **prawdę mówiąc
nie interesuje mnie to** to tell the
truth, it doesn't interest me

mózg (**-u, -i**) *m* **1** brain **2** (*osoba
bardzo inteligentna: przen*)
mastermind

mroczny *adj* (*sekret, nastrój*) dark

mro|k (**-ku, -ki**; *inst sg* **-kiem**) *m*
(*ciemność*) darkness

mro|zić (**-żę, -zisz**; *imp* **-ź**) *vt*
1 (*oziębiać*) to chill **2** (*o zamrażarce*)
to freeze

mroźny *adj* (*dzień, pogoda*) frosty

mrożon|ki (**-ek**) *pl* frozen foods

mrożony *adj* (*mięso, produkty*)
frozen; **kawa mrożona** iced
coffee

mrów|ka (**-ki, -ki**; *dat sg & loc sg*
-ce; *gen pl* **-ek**) *f* ant

mr|óz (**-ozu, -ozy**; *loc sg* **-ozie**) *m*
frost; **7 stopni mrozu** 7 degrees
below (zero)

MSW *abbr* = **Ministerstwo Spraw
Wewnętrznych**

MSZ *abbr* = **Ministerstwo Spraw
Zagranicznych**

msz|a (**-y, -e**; *gen pl* **-y**) *f* (*Rel: w
intencji, poranna*) mass

mścić się (**mszczę, mścisz**; *imp*
mścij; *pf* **ze-**) *vr*: **~ się (na kimś)**
to take revenge (on sb); **~ się za**

krzywdę to revenge o.s. for a
wrong suffered

mu *pron dat od* **on, ono**

mu|cha (**-chy, -chy**; *dat sg & loc
sg* **-sze**) *f* **1** (*owad*) fly **2** (*element
męskiego stroju*) bow tie

multimedi|a (**-ów**) *pl*
multimedia

multimedialny *adj* multimedia

mundu|r (**-ru, -ry**; *loc sg* **-rze**) *m*
(*służbowy, wojskowy*) uniform

mu|r (**-ru, -ry**; *loc sg* **-rze**) *m* wall;
~em stanęła za nim she stood
firmly behind him; **na ~ beton**
(*pot*) for sure

muro|wać (**-uję, -ujesz**; *pf* **wy-**)
vt to build ▷ *vi* to lay bricks

murowany *adj* **1** (*ściana: z cegieł*)
brick **2** (*z kamienia*) stone; **~
sukces** a dead cert (*pot*)

Murzy|n (**-na, -ni**; *loc sg* **-nie**) *m*
black (man); **Murzyni** *pl* black
people

Murzyn|ka (**-ki, -ki**; *dat sg & loc sg*
-ce; *gen pl* **-ek**) *f* black (woman)

murzyński *adj* (*kultura, getto*)
black

○ **KEYWORD**

mu|sieć (**-szę, -sisz**) *vi* **1** (*wyrażenie
konieczności*): **czy muszę złożyć
depozyt pieniężny, aby grać?**
do I have to pay a deposit to be
allowed to play?; **nie musisz nas
pytać** you don't need to ask us
2 (*wyrażenie zobowiązania*):
**musimy zapewnić ochronę
środowiska naturalnego** we
have to ensure the protection of
the natural environment; **czy
musisz tam jechać?** do you have

to go there?; **nie musiałeś tego robić** you need not have done it; **musiała mu to wyznać** she must have told him

muszę *itd. vb zob.* **musieć**
musztar|da (**-dy**; *dat sg & loc sg* **-dzie**) *f* mustard
muze|um (**-um, -a**; *gen pl* **-ów**) *nt inv in sg* (*zbiór eksponatów*) museum
muzułma|nin (**-nina, -nie**; *loc sg* **-ninie**; *gen pl* **-nów**) *m* Muslim
muzułmański *adj* (*państwo, tradycja*) Muslim
muzyczny *adj* musical
muzy|k (**-ka, -cy**; *inst sg* **-kiem**) *m* musician
muzy|ka (**-ki**; *dat sg & loc sg* **-ce**) *f* music
my *pron* we; **halo, to my** hello, it's us
myci|e (**-a**) *nt* 1 (*czynność*) washing 2 (*naczyń*) washing-up
my|ć (**-ję, -jesz**; *pf* **u-**) *vt* 1 (*ciało, samochód*) to wash 2 (*wannę*) to clean 3 (*zęby*) to brush; **~ się** *vr* to wash (o.s.); **ręka rękę myje** you scratch my back and I'll scratch yours
myd|ło (**-ła, -ła**; *loc sg* **-le**; *gen pl* **-eł**) *nt* soap
myj|nia (**-ni, -nie**; *gen pl* **-ni**) *f*: **~ (samochodowa)** car wash
myl|ić (**-ę, -isz**) *vt* 1 (*pf* **po-**) (*osoby, fakty*) to confuse 2 (*pf* **z-**) (*wprowadzać w błąd*) to mislead; **~ się** *vr* (*robić błędy*) to make mistakes; **jesteś w błędzie** you are mistaken
mysz (**-y, -y**; *gen pl* **-y**) *f* 1 mouse 2 (*komputerowa*) mouse (*for computer*); **myszy** *pl* mice
myśl (**-i, -i**; *gen pl* **-i**) *f* thought; **mam coś innego na ~i** I have something else in mind; **tego nie miałem na ~i** I didn't mean that; **złota ~** words of wisdom
myślący *adj* intelligent
myśl|eć (**-ę, -isz**; *pt* **-ał, -eli**) *vi* to think; **~ o czymś** (*zastanawiać się nad czymś*) to think about sth; **~ o kimś** (*troszczyć się*) to think of sb; **myślę, że tak/ nie** I think so/I don't think so
myśleni|e (**-a**) *nt* (*proces intelektualny*) thinking
myśliwski *adj* (*pies, strój*) hunting; **samolot ~** fighter (plane)
myśli|wy (**-wego, -wi**) *m decl like adj* hunter
mż|yć (**-y**) *vi*: **mży** (*o deszczu*) it's drizzling

n

na *prep* +*loc* (*miejsce*) on; **na stole/drzwiach/ścianie** on the table/door/wall; **na Słowacji/ Śląsku** in Slovakia/Silesia; **wakacje na wsi** holidays in the country; **firma szuka ludzi na Wschodzie** the firm is looking for people in the East; **na Kubie** in Cuba; **na morzu** at sea; **na niebie** in the sky; **na naszej ulicy** in (*Brit*) *lub* on (*US*) our street; **na uniwersytecie/zajęciach** at the university/in class
▷ *prep* +*acc* **1** (*wskazywanie kierunku*) to; **na salę operacyjną** to the operating theatre; **na Słowację/Majorkę** to Slovakia/

Majorca; **na wschód/północ** east/north; **wpadałam na niego przypadkowo** I bumped into him by accident
2 (*odcinek czasu*): **na cztery dni** for four days; **na dziesięć minut przed** +*loc* ten minutes before
3 (*wyznaczanie terminu*): **na środę** for Wednesday; **na szóstą** (*wykonać coś*) by six o'clock; (*przybyć*) at six o'clock
4 (*wydarzenie*): **na obiad** for lunch; **na jesień** for autumn (*Brit*) *lub* fall (*US*)
5 (*sposób*): **na kilogramy/litry** by the kilogram/the litre (*Brit*) *lub* liter (*US*); **na czyjś koszt** at sb's expense; **na raty** on hire purchase (*Brit*) *lub* instalment plan (*US*); **jajko na miękko** soft-boiled egg
6 (*z jakiejś przyczyny*): **na czyjeś zaproszenie** at sb's invitation; **chory na gruźlicę** ill *lub* sick (*US*) with TB
7 (*tempo*): **tysiąc litrów na godzinę** a thousand litres (*Brit*) *lub* liters (*US*) per hour; **dwa razy na dzień** twice a day
8 (*rezultat*): **kroić (pokroić** *pf*) **coś na plasterki** to cut sth into slices; **malować (pomalować** *pf*) **coś na żółto** to paint sth yellow
9 (*przeznaczenie*): **szafka na buty** shoe cupboard; **kosz na śmieci** dustbin (*Brit*), garbage can (*US*); **przerwa na herbatę** tea break
10 (*cel*): **wyjść (*pf*) na spacer** to go for a walk; **jechać na wakacje** to go on holiday (*Brit*) *lub* vacation (*US*); **iść na lekcję/koncert** to go to class/to a concert

nabia|ł (**-łu**; *loc sg* **-le**) *m* (*mleko, ser, jajka*) dairy products *pl*

nabier|ać (**-am, -asz**; *pf* **nabrać**) *vt*: ~ +*gen* **1** (*pożywienie*) to take in **2** (*prędkości*) to gather **3** (*masy*) to gain; ~ **biegłości w czymś** to acquire facility with sth; ~ **kogoś** (*pot: robić żarty*) to pull sb's leg; (*pot: okłamywać*) to deceive sb

na|być (**-będę, -będziesz**; *imp* **-bądź**) *vb pf od* **nabywać**

na|bywać (**-będę, -będziesz**; *imp* **-bądź**) *vt* to purchase

nachalny *adj* (*pej: natarczywy*) pushy

nachyl|ać się (**-am, -asz**) *vr* **1** (*pf* **-ić**) (*o osobie*) to bend down **2** (*o krzywiźnie terenu*) to slope

naciąg|ać (**-am, -asz**; *pf* **-nąć**) *vt* **1** (*naprężać*) to tighten **2** (*cięciwę łuku*) to draw **3** (*ubierać*) to pull on **4** (*nadwerężyć mięśni*) to pull

nacinać (**-am, -asz**; *pf* **naciąć**) *vt*: ~ **coś** (*skórę, powierzchnię przedmiotu*) to make an incision into sth

nacis|kać (**-kam, -kasz**; *pf* **-nąć**) *vt* to press; **naciskał mnie, żebym przyszła** he was pressuring me into coming

naci|snąć (**-snę, -śniesz**; *imp* **-śnij**) *vb pf od* **naciskać**

nacjonali|sta (**-sty, -ści**; *dat sg* **-ście**) *m decl like f in sg* (*Pol*) nationalist

nacjonalistyczny *adj* (*partia, poglądy: Pol*) nationalist

nacjonaliz|m (**-mu**; *loc sg* **-mie**) *m* (*Pol*) nationalism

naczelni|k (**-ka, -cy**; *inst sg* **-kiem**) *m* **1** (*dowódca*) chief **2** (*w więzieniu*)

governor **3** (*oddziału*) head

naczy|nie (**-nia, -nia**; *gen pl* **-ń**) *nt* **1** (*talerz, miska*) dish **2** (*drewniany, gliniany*) vessel; **naczynia** *pl* dishes *pl*; ~ **krwionośne** (*Anat*) blood vessel; **zmywać** (**pozmywać** *pf*) **naczynia** to do the washing-up

○ **KEYWORD**

nad *prep* +*inst* **1** (*powyżej*) above; **nad stołem/górami** over the table/mountains **2** (*mieć przewagę, władzę*) over **3** (*niedaleko*): **nad Tamizą** by the Thames; **nad Morzem Północnym** by the North Sea; **nad ranem** at dawn **4** (*na jakiś temat*): **dyskusja nad polityką** a discussion on politics; **nad czym pracujesz?** what are you working on? ▷ *prep* +*acc* (*wyznaczający kierunek*): **nad jezioro** to the lake

nadajni|k (**-ka, -ki**; *inst sg* **-kiem**) *m* (*Tel*) transmitter

nad|awać (**-aję, -ajesz**; *pf* **-ać**) *vt* **1** (*w radiu, telewizji*) to broadcast **2** (*sygnał dźwiękowy*) to transmit **3** (*przesyłkę na poczcie*) to send, to mail (*US*); ~ **się** *vr*: ~ **się (do czegoś)** to be suitable (for sth); **to nie nadaje się do spania** this isn't fit for sleeping in/on

nadawc|a (**-y, -y**) *m decl like f in sg* (*listu, wiadomości*) sender

nadąż|ać (**-am, -asz**; *pf* **-yć**) *vi*: **nie ~ (z czymś)** to be unable to keep up (with sth); **nie nadążam z pracą** I can't keep up with the workload; **nie nadążałem za nimi** I could not keep up with them

nadbagaż (-u, -e; *gen pl* -y) *m* (*Aviat*) excess baggage

nadcho|dzić (-dzę, -dzisz; *imp* -dź; *pf* **nadejść**) *vi* 1 (*o osobie, o wydarzeniu*) to come 2 (*o informacji, przesyłce*) to arrive

nadciąg|ać (-am, -asz; *pf* -nąć) *vi* (*o burzy, wydarzeniu*) to approach

nadciśnie|nie (-nia) *nt* (*choroba*) hypertension

nadej|ść (-dę, -dziesz; *imp* -dź) *vb pf od* **nadchodzić**

nades|łać (-ślę, -ślesz; *imp* -ślij) *vb pf od* **nadsyłać**

nadgarst|ek (-ka, -ki; *inst sg* -kiem) *m* (*Anat*) wrist

nadgodzin|y (-) *pl* overtime

nadgorliwy *adj* (*urzędnik*) officious

nadjeżdż|ać (-am, -asz; *pf* **nadjechać**) *vi* (*o osobie, o pojeździe*) to arrive

nadmia|r (-ru; *loc sg* -rze) *m* excess; **alkohol w ~ze szkodzi** excessive alcohol consumption is harmful

nadobowiązkowy *adj* (*zajęcia*) optional

nadpła|ta (-ty, -ty; *dat sg* -cie) *f* overpayment; **~ wynosi dziesięć złotych** the overpayment amounts to 10 zlotys

nadprzyrodzony *adj* (*siła, zjawisko*) supernatural

nadrabi|ać (-am, -asz; *pf* **nadrobić**) *vt* to make good; **~ straty** to recoup one's losses

nadro|bić (-bię, -bisz; *imp* **nadrób**) *vb pf od* **nadrabiać**

nadsył|ać (-am, -asz; *pf* **nadesłać**) *vt* to send

naduży|cie (-cia, -cia; *gen pl* -ć) *nt* misuse

nadużyw|ać (-am, -asz; *pf* **nadużyć**) *vt* +*gen* to abuse

nadwa|ga (-gi; *dat sg* -dze) *f* excess weight; **mam lekką nadwagę** I'm a little overweight

nadziej|a (-i, -je; *gen pl* -i) *f* hope; **mam nadzieję, że przyjdziesz** I hope that you will come; **mam nadzieję, że zwyciężymy** I hope that we win

nadzie|nie (-nia, -nia; *gen pl* -ń) *nt* 1 (*w wypiekach, słodyczach*) filling 2 (*w kurczaku, indyku*) stuffing

nadz|ór (-oru; *loc sg* -orze) *m* (*nad pracą, osobą*) supervision

naf|ta (-ty; *dat sg* -cie) *f* 1 (*Aviat*) kerosene 2 (*pot: ropa naftowa*) oil

naftowy *adj* 1 (*wydobycie*) oil 2 (*lampa, ogrzewanie*) paraffin; **ropa naftowa** petroleum, oil

nagi *adj* 1 (*osoba bez ubrania*) naked, nude 2 (*bez dodatków*) plain

nagin|ać (-am, -asz; *pf* **nagiąć**) *vt* to bend

naglący *adj* urgent

nagle *adv* 1 (*raptem*) suddenly 2 (*bez uprzedzenia*) unexpectedly

nagłów|ek (-ka, -ki; *inst sg* -kiem) *m* 1 (*w artykule*) heading 2 (*w gazecie*) headline 3 (*na papeterii*) letterhead

nagły *adj* 1 (*przyjazd, spotkanie*) sudden 2 (*wymagający szybkiej reakcji*) urgent; **w ~m wypadku należy zadzwonić na numer 112** in case of emergency, ring 112

nago *adv* in the nude

nagoś|ć (-ci) f nudity
nagradz|ać (-am, -asz; pf
  nagrodzić) vt (za zwycięstwo,
  medalem) to reward
nagra|nie (-nia, -nia; gen pl **-ń)** nt
  (muzyczne, filmowe) recording
nagro|da (-dy, -dy; loc sg **-dzie**;
  gen pl **nagród)** f **1** (w konkursie)
  prize **2** (za osiągnięcia) reward
  3 (dawana przez stowarzyszenie)
  award; **~ Nobla** the Nobel prize
nagr|odzić (-odzę, -odzisz; imp
  -odź lub **-ódź)** vb pf od **nagradzać**
nagryw|ać (-am, -asz; pf **nagrać)**
  vt to record
naiwny adj naive; **pierwsza
  naiwna** ingénue
najbardziej adv superl od **bardzo**;
  jak ~! by all means!
najbliższy adj superl od **bliski**;
  przyjdę w ~m czasie I will come
  very soon
najdalej adv superl od **daleko**
najeść się (-em, -esz; 3 pl **-edzą**;
  imp **-edz**; pt **-adł, -adła, -edli)** vr
  pf to eat one's fill; **najadł się do
  syta** he had had enough to eat
najgorszy adj superl od **zły**; **w ~m
  wypadku** lub **razie przyjdziemy
  jutro** if the worst comes to the
  worst, we'll come tomorrow
najgorzej adv superl od **źle**; **nie
  jest z nami ~** we're not doing
  too badly
najlepiej adv superl od **dobrze**
najlepszy adj superl od **dobry**;
  **w ~m wypadku pójedziemy
  razem** the best-case scenario
  is that we would go together;
  **najlepsze, co możesz zrobić,
  to...** the best thing you can do is...
najmniej adv superl od **mało**; **~**

problemów the least problems;
  ~ osób/ towarów the fewest
  people/goods; **co ~ 5 osób
  zostało rannych** at least five
  people were injured
najmniejszy adj superl od
  **mały; on zawsze idzie po linii
  najmniejszego oporu** he always
  takes the line of least resistance
najnowszy adj superl od **nowy**
najpierw adv to begin with
najpóźniej adv superl od **późno**;
  ~ w niedzielę on Sunday at the
  (very) latest
najstarszy adj superl od **stary**
najwięcej adv superl od **dużo,
  wiele**
najwyżej adv superl od **wysoko**; **~
  cztery** four at the (very) most
najwyższy adj superl od **wysoki**;
  ~ czas, żeby przeprosił it's high
  time he apologized; **sąd N~** ≈ the
  High Court (Brit), ≈ the Supreme
  Court (US); **najwyższe piętro** the
  top floor
nakar|mić (-mię, -misz) vb pf
  od **karmić**
naka|z (-zu, -zy; loc sg **-zie)** m
  1 order **2** (w prawie: eksmisji,
  konfiskaty) warrant
nakaz|ywać (-uję, -ujesz; pf **-ać)**
  vt to order; **nakazuję ci przestać
  mówić** I order you to stop
  talking!; **lekarz nakazał mi dietę**
  the doctor put me on a diet
nakle|jać (-jam, -jasz; pf **-ić)** vt
  (naklejki, plakaty) to stick
naklej|ka (-ki, -ki; dat sg **-ce**; gen
  pl **-ek)** f **1** (na produkcie) label **2** (z
  nazwiskiem, obrazkiem) sticker
nakła|d (-du, -dy; loc sg **-dzie)** m
  (publikacji) edition; **nakłady** pl

(*Fin*) expenditure *sg*; **~ książki jest wyczerpany** the book is out of print; **ponosić (ponieść** *pf*) **znaczne ~y finansowe** to incur considerable costs

nakry|cie (-cia, -cia; *gen pl* **-ć)** *nt* 1 covering 2 (*sztućce, naczynia*) place setting; **~ głowy** headgear; **podaj na trzy osoby** set the table for three

nakryć (-ję, -jesz) *vt pf od* **nakrywać**; (*pot: przestępcę*) to nail; **nakryli go na gorącym uczynku** they caught him red-handed

nakryw|ać (-am, -asz; *pf* **nakryć)** *vt* to cover; **nakrywała dziecko kocem** she covered the child with a blanket

nal|ać (-eję, -ejesz) *vb pf od* **nalewać**

naleg|ać (-am, -asz) *vi*: **~ na coś** to insist on sth; **nalegam, abyś to przeczytał** I insist that you read this

naleśni|k (-ka, -ki; *inst sg* **-kiem)** *m* (*Kulin*) pancake (*Brit*), crepe (*US*)

nalew|ać (-am, -asz; *pf* **nalać)** *vt* (*napełniać płynem naczynie*) to pour (out)

należ|eć (-ę, -ysz) *vi*: **~ do** +*gen* to belong to; **~ się** *vr*: **ile się należy?** what do I owe you?; **należy to oddać** it's necessary to return it; **należy mi się pięć złotych** I am owed 5 zlotys; **to mi się od nich należy** I am entitled to this from them

należnoś|ć (-ci, -ci; *gen pl* **-ci)** *f* amount payable; **musimy uiścić ~ za te usługi** we have to settle the bill for these services

nałogo|wiec (-wca, -wcy) *m* (*osoba uzależniona*) addict

nałogowy *adj* 1 (*alkoholik*) confirmed 2 (*hazardzista*) problem

nał|óg (-ogu, -ogi; *inst pl* **-ogiem)** *m* 1 (*szkodliwy nawyk*) habit 2 (*zależność od substancji*) addiction

nam *pron dat od* **my**

nami *pron inst od* **my**; **chodź z ~** come with us

namiętnoś|ć (-ci, -ci; *gen pl* **-ci)** *f* passion

namiętny *adj* 1 (*kochanek*) passionate 2 (*kinoman*) avid

namio|t (-tu, -ty; *loc sg* **-cie)** *m* tent

namó|wić (-wię, -wisz) *vt pf*: **namówił mnie na kupno samochodu** he talked me into buying a car

naokoło *prep* +*gen* round ▷ *adv* (all) around

napa|d (-du, -dy; *loc sg* **-dzie)** *m* 1 (*akt agresji*) assault 2 (*bólu, płaczu*) fit

napa|dać (-dnę, -dniesz; *pf* **napaść)** *vt* to attack

napastni|k (-ka, -cy; *inst sg* **-kiem)** *m* 1 (*osoba atakująca*) assailant 2 (*piłkarz*) striker

napaś|ć¹ (-ci, -ci; *gen pl* **-ci)** *f* (*akt fizycznej agresji*) assault

napa|ść² (-dnę, -dniesz; *imp* **-dnij)** *vb pf od* **napadać**

napeł|niać (-niam, -niasz; *pf* **-nić)** *vt* (*naczynie, pojemnik*) to fill

napeł|nić (-nię, -nisz; *imp* **-nij)** *vb pf od* **napełniać**

napi|ć się (-ję, -jesz) *vr pf* (*wody, alkoholu*) to have a drink

napię|cie (-cia, -cia; *gen pl* **-ć)** *nt*

1 (*elektryczne*) voltage **2** (*mięśni*) tension **3** (*emocjonalne*) tension
napięty *adj* **1** (*plan dnia*) full **2** (*sytuacja, emocje*) tense
napi|s (**-su, -sy**; *loc sg* **-sie**) *m* notice; **napisy** *pl* (*Cine*) **1** (*czołówka*) the credits **2** (*dialogowe*) subtitles
napi|sać (**-szę, -szesz**; *imp* **-sz**) *vb pf od* **pisać**
napiw|ek (**-ku, -ki**; *inst sg* **-kiem**) *m* (*w restauracji, w hotelu*) tip
nap|ój (**-oju, -oje**; *gen pl* **-ojów**) *m* drink
napra|wa (**-wy, -wy**; *dat sg* **-wie**) *f* repair; **samochód jest w naprawie** the car is being repaired
naprawdę *adv* really; **~ to powiedział?** did he really say that?
napra|wiać (**-wiam, -wiasz**; *pf* **-wić**) *vt* **1** (*likwidować wady*) to repair **2** (*przen: likwidować negatywne skutki*) to put right **3** (*brak*) to compensate for
naprzód *adv* forward
naraz *adv* **1** (*raptem*) all of a sudden **2** (*w tym samym czasie*) at the same time; **nie (mówcie) wszyscy ~!** don't all talk at the same time!
narciarst|wo (**-wa**; *loc sg* **-wie**) *nt* skiing
narciarz (**-a, -e**; *gen pl* **-y**) *m* skier
nareszcie *adv* at (long) last
narkoma|n (**-na, -ni**; *loc sg* **-nie**) *m* drug addict
narkomani|a (**-i**) *f* drug addiction
narkoty|k (**-ku, -ki**; *inst sg* **-kiem**) *m* (*substancja odurzająca*) drug

narko|za (**-zy, -zy**; *dat sg* **-zie**) *f* (*w medycynie*) anaesthesia (*Brit*), anesthesia (*US*); **być pod narkozą** to be under anaesthetic (*Brit*) *lub* anesthetic (*US*)
narodowoś|ć (**-ci, -ci**; *gen pl* **-ci**) *f* (*polska, francuska*) nationality
narodowy *adj* national
narodze|nie (**-nia, -nia**; *gen pl* **-ń**) *nt* birth; **Boże N~** Christmas
nar|odzić się (**-odzę, -odzisz**; *imp* **-ódź**) *vr* to come into being
nar|ód (**-odu, -ody**; *loc sg* **-odzie**) *m* **1** (*społeczność*) nation **2** (*mieszkańcy kraju*) people; **Organizacja Narodów Zjednoczonych** the United Nations
narys|ować (**-uję, -ujesz**) *vb pf od* **rysować**
narzą|d (**-du, -dy**; *loc sg* **-dzie**) *m* (*wewnętrzny, władzy*) organ
narzeczon|a (**-ej, -e**) *f decl like adj* fiancée
narzecz|ony (**-onego, -eni**) *m decl like adj* fiancé; **narzeczeni** *pl* the engaged couple
narzek|ać (**-am, -asz**) *vi*: **nigdy nie narzekał na brak pieniędzy** he never complained about being short of money
narzę|dzie (**-dzia, -dzia**; *gen pl* **-dzi**) *nt* **1** (*instalatorski, stolarski*) tool **2** (*elektrotechniczny*) instrument
nas *pron gen, acc, loc od* **my**; **nie ma ~ w pracy** we're out (at the moment); **mówią o ~** they're talking about us; **idą bez ~** they're going without us
nasenny *adj*: **lek ~** sleeping pill
nasi *pron zob.* **nasz**

nasil|ać się (**-a**; *pf* **-ić**) *vr*
(*zwiększać prędkość, intensywność*)
to intensify

nastawie|nie (**-nia**) *nt* attitude;
~ do życia attitude to life;
przyjechał z ~m, że wygra he
came with the expectation of
winning

nastą|pić (**-pię, -pisz**; *impf*
następować) *vi*: **nastąpił psu na
ogon** he stepped on the dog's tail

następc|a (**-y, -y**) *m decl like f in sg*
successor

następnie *adv* next

następny *adj* next; **następnego
dnia** the next *lub* following day; **~
proszę!** next, please!; **~m razem,
uważaj co mówisz!** next time,
mind what you say!

nastę|pować (**-puję, -pujesz**)
to follow

nastolat|ek (**-ka, -ki**; *inst sg*
-kiem) *m* teenager

nastr|ój (**-oju, -oje**) *m*
1 (*samopoczucie psychiczne*) mood
2 (*atmosfera*) atmosphere; **jestem
dziś w dobrym/złym nastroju**
I'm in a good/bad mood today

nasu|nąć (**-nę, -niesz**; *imp* **-ń**) *vb*
pf od **nasuwać**

nasuw|ać (**-am, -asz**; *pf*
nasunąć) *vt*: **nasunął kaptur na
głowę** he pulled his hood over his
head; **~ się** *vr* (*o pomyśle*) to come
to mind; **nasunęło mi się to na
myśl** it crossed my mind

nasz *possessive pron* 1 (*przed
rzeczownikiem*) our 2 (*bez
rzeczownika*) ours; **to jest ~ dom**
this is our house; **ten dom jest ~**
this house is ours

naszyjni|k (**-ka, -ki**; *inst sg* **-kiem**)
m necklace

naślad|ować (**-uję, -ujesz**) *vt*
1 (*kopiować*) to copy 2 (*imitować*)
to imitate

naśladowc|a (**-y, -y**) *m decl like f
in sg* imitator

naśmiew|ać się (**-am, -asz**) *vr* to
ridicule; **inne dzieci ciągle się
z niego naśmiewali** the other
children always made fun of him

natchnie|nie (**-nia, -nia**; *gen pl* **-ń**)
nt (*inspiracja*) inspiration

natk|nąć się (**-nę, -niesz**; *imp*
-nij) *vb pf od* **natykać się**

natomiast *adv* however

natrętny *adj* obtrusive;
prześladują go natrętne myśli
he is tormented by obsessional
ideas

natrys|k (**-ku, -ki**; *inst sg* **-kiem**) *m*
(*prysznic*) shower

natu|ra (**-ry**; *loc sg* **-rze**) *f* nature;
ten obraz to martwa ~ this
picture is a still life

naturalnie *adv* naturally

naturalny *adj* natural; **jest
naturalną brunetką** she's a
natural brunette

natychmiast *adv* immediately,
instantly

natychmiastowy *adj*
immediate, instant

natyk|ać się (**-am, -asz**; *pf*
natknąć się) *vr*: **natykać się na
kogoś/coś** to bump into sb/sth

naucz|ać (**-am, -asz**) *vt*: **~
dzieci języków obcych** to teach
children foreign languages,
to teach foreign languages
to children; **poświęca się
nauczaniu młodzieży** he is
dedicated to teaching young

people

nauczyciel (-a, -e; gen pl **-i)** m
teacher; **~ polskiego/chemii**
Polish/chemistry teacher

nauczyciel|ka (-ki, -ki; dat sg **-ce**;
gen pl **-ek)** f teacher

naucz|yć (-ę, -ysz) vb pf od **uczyć**

nau|ka (-ki, -ki; dat sg **-ce)** f
1 (dziedzina wiedzy) science
2 (edukacja) study **3** (morał) lesson;
~ jazdy (kurs) driving lessons pl

nauko|wiec (-wca, -wcy) m
1 scholar **2** (w fizyki, biologii)
scientist

naukowy adj **1** (eksperyment)
scientific **2** (dyskusja, referat)
scholarly; **przeprowadzać**
(**przeprowadzić** pf) **badania**
naukowe to (carry out)
research; **pracownik ~** (na
uniwersytecie) research worker;
pomoce naukowe (w szkole, na
uniwersytecie) teaching aids

naumyślnie adv deliberately

na|wa (-wy, -wy; loc sg **-wie)** f: **~**
główna (w koście) nave; **~ boczna**
(w kościele) aisle

nawet adv even

nawia|s (-su, -sy; loc sg **-sie)** m
bracket; **w ~ach kwadratowych**
in square brackets; **w ~ach**
okrągłych in round brackets;
w ~ach klamrowych in curly
brackets; **to słowo jest w ~ie** this
word is in parentheses

nawierzch|nia (-ni, -nie; gen pl
-ni) (drogi) surface

nawilż|ać (-am, -asz; pf **-yć)** vt
1 (ubranie) dampen **2** (twarz, ciało)
to moisturize

nawy|k (-ku, -ki; inst sg **-kiem)**
m habit

nawzajem adv each other; **oni**
lubią się ~ they like each other;
Wesołych Świąt! N~! Merry
Christmas! Same to you!

nazajutrz adv (książk) (on) the
next lub following day

naz|wa (-wy, -wy; dat sg **-wie)** f
name; **to jest restauracja tylko**
z nazwy this is a restaurant in
name only

naz|wać (-wę, -wiesz; imp **-wij)**
vb pf od **nazywać**

nazwis|ko (-ka, -ka; inst sg **-kiem)**
nt surname (Brit), last name (US);
~ panieńskie maiden name;
wypisywać (**wypisać** pf) **czek na**
czyjeś ~ to write (out) a cheque
(Brit) lub check (US) in sb's name;
wyrobił sobie ~ w świecie sztuki
he made a name for himself in the
art world

nazyw|ać (-am, -asz; pf **nazwać)**
vt to call; **~ się** vr to be called;
musimy ~ rzeczy po imieniu we
need to call a spade a spade; **jak**
się pan/pani nazywa? what's
your name, please?; **to nazywa**
się marketing bezpośredni this
is known as direct marketing

n.e. abbr (= naszej ery) AD

negatywny adj negative

negocjacj|e (-i) pl (pokojowe,
biznesowe) negotiations

negocj|ować (-uję, -ujesz) to
negotiate

nekrolo|g (-gu, -gi; inst sg **-giem)**
m obituary

ner|ka (-ki, -ki; dat sg **-ce**; gen pl
-ek) f kidney

nerwic|a (-y, -e) f (Med, Psych)
neurosis

nerwowy adj (załamanie,

zachowanie) nervous; **tik ~a**
nervous tic

neurolo|g (-ga, -dzy *lub* **-gowie)**
m neurologist

neutralny *adj* **1** neutral **2** *(polityk)*
independent; *(kraj)* neutral

nędz|a (-y, -e) *f* misery

nędzarz (-a, -e; *gen pl* **-y)** *m*
destitute person

nędzny *adj (ubogi, marny)*
miserable

nia|nia (-ni, -nie; *gen pl* **-ń)** *f*
nanny

nią *pron inst od* **ona**

nic *pron* **1** nothing **2** *(z innym*
wyrazem przeczącym) anything; **~**
dziwnego, że wygrał no wonder
he won; **~ z tego nie będzie**
it's no use!; **to ~** *(nie ma sprawy)*
never mind; **~ nie wie** he knows
nothing

nicpo|ń (-nia, -nie; *gen pl* **-ni** *lub*
-niów) *m* good-for-nothing

niczyj *adj* nobody's; **ziemia ~a**
no-man's-land

ni|ć (-ci, -ci; *inst pl* **-ćmi)** *f* thread;
z interesu wyszły nici the
business came to nothing

nie *part* **1** no **2** *(z czasownikiem)*
not; **~ ma jej tam** she's not there;
o ~! oh no!; **~ ma na co czekać** it's
no use waiting; **~ przejmuj się!**
don't worry!

nieaktualny *adj* **1** *(wejściówka)*
invalid **2** *(oferta handlowa)*
unavailable **3** *(wiadomość)* out-
of-date

niebezpieczeńst|wo (-wa,
-wa; *loc sg* **-wie)** *nt* **1** *(zagrożenie)*
danger **2** *(ryzyko)* risk

niebezpieczny *adj* **1** *(przestępca,*
miejsce) dangerous **2** *(ruch)* risky

3 *(praca, wyprawa)* hazardous

niebieski *adj* **1** *(barwa)* blue
2 *(Astron)* celestial; **ciała**
~e *(Astron)* heavenly bodies;
królestwo ~e *(Rel)* the kingdom
of heaven; **~ ptak** free-loader

nie|bo (-ba, -ba; *loc sg* **-bie;** *gen*
pl **-bios;** *dat pl* **-biosom;** *inst pl*
-biosami; *loc pl* **-biosach)** *nt* **1** sky
2 *(królestwo boże lub niebieskie)*
heaven; **gwiazdy na niebie**
stars in the sky; **nie każdy anioł**
mieszka w niebie not all angels
dwell in heaven; **na wakacjach**
śpi pod gołym niebem during
the holidays *(Brit) lub* vacation
(US) he sleeps outdoors; **ta**
potrawa to ~ w gębie! *(pot)*
this dish is divine!; **on jest o ~**
lepszym uczniem he is streets
ahead of the other pupils

nieboszczy|k (-ka, -cy *lub* **-ki;** *inst*
sg **-kiem)** *m* the deceased

niech *part:* **~ przyjdą** let them
come; **~ się zastanowię** let me
think *lub* see; **~ ci będzie** have it
your way

niechcący *adv (nieumyślnie)*
accidentally

niechę|ć (-ci, -ci) *f* dislike; **żywi ~**
do niej od dawna he has disliked
her for a long time; **czuł ~ do**
swojej nudnej pracy he had
an aversion to his boring job; **z**
niechęcią pomyślała o nim she
thought of him with distaste

niechętnie *adv* reluctantly

niechlujny *adj (zaniedbany)*
slovenly

nieciekawy *adj* **1** boring
2 *(dzielnica)* unpleasant

niecierpliwy *adj* impatient

nieco adv somewhat; **~ mniejszy** somewhat smaller; **wiedział co ~ o niej** he knew a little bit about her

nieczynny adj 1 (*firma*) defunct 2 (*mechanizm*) non-functioning 3 (*wulkan*) extinct

nieczytelny adj 1 (*charakter pisma*) illegible 2 (*wiadomość*) unintelligible

niedaleko adv 1 (*w przestrzeni*) near (by) 2 (*w czasie*) soon

niedawno adv recently

niedawny adj recent; **studiował tu do niedawna** he studied here until recently; **studiuje tu od niedawna** he began studying here recently

niedługo adv 1 (*zaraz*) soon, before long 2 (*przez krótki czas*) briefly

niedobrany adj mismatched

niedobry adj 1 (*osoba*) bad 2 (*informacja*) bad 3 (*niesmaczny*) disgusting

niedobrze adv 1 (*czuć się, wyglądać*) unwell 2 (*w sposób niepożądany*) badly 3 (*z trudem*) not well; **~ mi** I feel sick; **zrobiło mi się ~** I started to feel sick; **z babcią bardzo ~, trzeba wezwać lekarza** grandma's really not doing well, we'll need to call the doctor; **żylaste mięso ~ się kroi** stringy meat doesn't cut well

niedojrzałoś|ć (-ci) f (*psychiczna, fizyczna*) immaturity

niedojrzały adj 1 (*osoba*) immature 2 (*warzywo, owoc*) unripe 3 (*wino, ser*) immature

niedokładny adj 1 (*osoba, praca*) careless 2 (*pomiar, dane*) imprecise

niedokonany adj (*w językoznawstwie*) imperfective

niedokończony adj (*praca, zdanie*) incomplete

niedopuszczalny adj (*zachowanie*) unacceptable

niedorozwinięty adj: **dzieci niedorozwinięte** children with learning difficulties

niedostępny adj inaccessible

niedrogi adj inexpensive

niedwuznaczny adj (*oczywisty*) unambiguous

niedziel|a (-i, -e) f Sunday; **~ Palmowa/Wielkanocna** Palm/Easter Sunday

niedźwie|dź (-dzia, -dzie; *gen pl* **-dzi**) m bear

nieefektowny adj (*styl, wygląd*) unremarkable

nieformalny adj irregular

niefortunny adj (*wypowiedź, wydarzenie*) unfortunate

niefrasobliwy adj (*człowiek, rozrywka*) light-hearted

niegazowany adj (*płyn*) still

niegrzeczny adj 1 (*niekulturalny*) impolite 2 (*źle wychowany: o dzieckach*) naughty

nieistotny adj 1 (*bez znaczenia*) unimportant 2 (*bez związku*) irrelevant

niej pron gen, dat, loc od **ona**

niejadalny adj inedible

niejaki adj (*pewien*) a (certain); **~ pan Smith** a (certain) Mr Smith

niejednoznaczny adj ambiguous

niekiedy adv sometimes

niekoleżeński adj (*relacja, osoba*)

unfriendly

niekompetentny adj **1** (bez odpowiednich kwalifikacji) incompetent **2** (bez uprawnień) unauthorized

niekompletny adj incomplete

niektórzy (f, nt **niektóre**) pron some; **~ sądzą, że masz rację** some (people) say that you're right

nielegalny adj (substancja, emigrant) illegal

nieletni adj (Jur: przestępca) juvenile ▷ m decl like adj (Jur) minor; **sąd dla ~ch** juvenile court

nieła|d (**-du**; loc sg **-dzie**) m (brak porządku) disarray

niemal adv almost; **jestem ~ pewien, że wyszedł** I am almost certain that he has left; **~ mu się udało** he was very nearly successful

niemiecki adj German

Niemcy pl Germany

niemniej adv however; **tym ~** even so; **nie jest to krokodyl, ~ jednak jest niebezpieczny** it isn't a crocodile, but it is dangerous all the same

niemodny adj unfashionable

niemoralny adj immoral

niem|owa (**-owy, -owy**; dat sg **-owie**; gen pl **-ów**) m/f decl like f in sg (osoba niema) mute

niemowl|ę (**-ęcia, -ęta**; gen pl **-ąt**) nt infant

niemożliwy adj impossible; **~ do osiągnięcia** unachievable

niemy adj **1** (o osobie) without speech **2** (kino, zgoda) silent

nienaturalny adj unnatural

nienawi|dzić (**-dzę, -dzisz**; imp **-dź**) vt +gen to hate

nienawiś|ć (**-ci**) f hatred, hate

nieobecny adj (w szkole, pracy) absent; **był obecny ciałem, ale ~ duchem** (przen) he was physically present but his mind was elsewhere

nieoczekiwany adj (efekt, wydarzenie) unexpected

nieodpłatnie adv free of charge

nieodpłatny adj (gratis) free

nieodpowiedni adj (strój, zachowanie) inappropriate

nieodpowiedzialny adj irresponsible

nieoficjalny adj unofficial

nieograniczony adj unlimited

nieosiągalny adj (cel, wynik) unattainable

niepalący adj non-smoking ▷ m decl like adj non-smoker; **sala dla ~ch** non-smoking room

nieparzysty adj (liczba, cyfra) odd

niepełnoletni adj under-age

niepełnosprawny adj disabled

niepewny adj **1** (przyszłość) uncertain **2** (nie godny zaufania) unreliable **3** (wahający się) faltering

niepodległoś|ć (**-ci**) f independence

niepodległy adj independent

niepok|oić (**-oję, -oisz**; imp **-ój**; pf **za-**) vt **1** (powodować zmartwienie) to worry **2** (nachodzić) to bother; **~ się** vr to worry; **niepokoił się o swoją pracę** he was worried about his job

niepokojący adj disturbing

niepokonany adj invincible

nieporęczny adj (pakunek, bagaż) cumbersome

nieposłuszeńst|wo (-wa; *loc sg*
-wie) *nt* disobedience
niepotrzebny *adj* **1** (*gest,*
wysiłek: niekonieczny) unnecessary
2 (*niepożądany*) superfluous
nieprawdopodobny *adj*
improbable, unlikely
nieprawdziwy *adj* **1** (*zmyślony,*
nierzeczywisty) false **2** (*fałszywy*)
artificial
nieprawidłowy *adj* **1** (*niepoprawny,*
nie odpowiadający normom)
wrong
nieprzychylny *adj* **1** (*wrogo*
nastawiony) disapproving
2 (*niepomyślny: wiatr*)
unfavourable (*Brit*), unfavorable
(*US*)
nieprzydatny *adj* (*bezużyteczny*)
useless
nieprzyja|ciel (-ciela, -ciele;
gen pl **-ciół**; *dat pl* **-ciołom**; *inst pl*
-ciółmi; *loc pl* **-ciołach**) *m* (*wróg*)
enemy
nieprzyjacielski *adj* enemy
nieprzyjazny *adj* hostile
nieprzyjemny *adj* unpleasant
nieprzytomny *adj* **1** (*bez*
świadomości) unconscious
2 (*nieobecny: wzrok*) vacant **3** (*z*
nienawiści) mad; (*ze strachu*)
paralysed
nieprzyzwoity *adj* (*zachowanie,*
obraz) indecent
niepunktualny *adj* unpunctual
nierealny *adj* **1** (*wymyślony*)
unreal **2** (*nie możliwy do wykonania*)
unrealistic
nieregularny *adj* irregular
nierentowny *adj* unprofitable
nierówny *adj* **1** (*podłoga, blat*)
uneven, rough **2** (*ulica*) bumpy

3 (*tempo, oddech*) uneven
4 (*podzielony nie równo*) unequal
5 (*zmienny*) erratic
niesamowity *adj* **1** (*straszny*)
uncanny **2** (*zachwycający*)
extraordinary
niesiesz *itd. vb zob.* **nieść**
nieskomplikowany *adj*
straightforward
niesmaczny *adj* tasteless
niespodzian|ka (-ki, -ki; *dat sg*
-ce; *gen pl* **-ek**) *f* surprise; **zrobił**
mi niespodziankę z okazji
urodzin he gave me a surprise for
my birthday
niespokojny *adj* **1** restless
2 (*morze*) rough
niesprawiedliwoś|ć (-ci, -ci; *gen*
pl **-ci**) *f* injustice
niesprawiedliwy *adj*
(*krzywdzący*) unfair, unjust
niestety *adv* unfortunately
niestrawnoś|ć (-ci) *f* indigestion
niestrawny *adj* indigestible
niesumienny *adj* unreliable
nieszczeroś|ć (-ci) *f* insincerity
nieszczery *adj* insincere; **ma**
~ uśmiech she has an insincere
smile
nieszczęś|cie (-cia, -cia; *gen pl* **-ć**)
nt **1** (*pech*) misfortune **2** (*tragedia*)
disaster; **nieszczęścia chodzą**
parami misfortunes never come
singly
nieszczęśliwy *adj* **1** unhappy
2 (*żałosny*) miserable **3** (*przypadek*)
unfortunate
nieszkodliwy *adj* **1** (*niegroźny*)
harmless **2** (*niewinny*) innocent
nieść (niosę, niesiesz; *imp* **nieś**;
pt **niósł, niosła, nieśli**) *vt* **1** to
carry **2** (*pf* **przy-**) (*unosić*) to

bring **3** (pf **z-**) (składać: jaja) to
lay; **~ radość/smutek** to bring
joy/sorrow; **wieść niesie, że był
dobrym szefem** it is said that he
was a good boss
nieślubny adj: **nieślubne
dziecko** child born out of
wedlock; **żyć w ~m związku** to
co-habit
nieśmiały adj shy, timid
nieświadomy adj unaware;
on jest ~ konsekwencji he is
unaware of the consequences
nieświeży adj **1** (czerstwy) stale
2 (zapach, potrawa) bad, off
3 (ubranie) dirty; **czuję się jakaś
nieświeża** I feel a bit worn out
nietolerancja (**-i**) f intolerance
nietolerancyjny adj intolerant
nietoperz (**-a**, **-e**; gen pl **-y**) m bat
nietrzeźwy adj drunk; **kierowca
znajdował się w stanie ~m**
the driver was in a state of
intoxication
nietypowy adj **1** (nie zwyczajny)
uncharacteristic **2** (wielkość)
non-standard
nieuczciwoś|ć (**-ci**, **-ci**; gen pl **-ci**)
f dishonesty
nieuczciwy adj dishonest
nieudany adj (eksperyment,
przedsięwzięcie) unsuccessful
nieudolny adj **1** (niezdarny)
clumsy **2** (nieudany) ineffectual
nieufnoś|ć (**-ci**) f distrust
nieuleczalnie adv: **~ chory**
incurably ill
nieuleczalny adj (choroba, ból)
incurable
nieustannie adv (nieprzerwanie,
trwale) unceasingly, continuously
nieuważny adj **1** (słuchacz)

inattentive **2** (zachowanie)
careless
nieważny adj **1** (fakt, osoba)
insignificant **2** (bilet, dokument)
invalid
niewątpliwie adv undoubtedly
niewdzięcznoś|ć (**-ci**) f
ingratitude
niewdzięczny adj **1** (o
osobie) ungrateful **2** (zadanie)
unrewarding
niewiarygodny adj **1** (nie godny
zaufania) unreliable **2** (nie do wiary)
incredible
niewidoczny adj invisible
niewidomy adj blind;
niewidomi pl decl like adj the
blind
niewiele pron **1** (czasu) not much
2 (przedmiotów) not many ▷ adv
(trochę) little
niewielki adj little
niewielu pron: **~ ludzi** few people
zob. **niewiele**
niewiernoś|ć (**-ci**, **-ci**; gen pl **-ci**)
f infidelity
niewierny adj (partner) unfaithful
niewierzący adj unbelieving
▷ m decl like adj non-believer
niewinny adj innocent; **sąd
uznał go za niewinnego** the
court found him innocent
niewola (**-i**) f imprisonment; **jest
w niewoli pieniądza** he is a slave
to money
niewolnict|wo (**-wa**; loc sg **-wie**)
nt slavery
niewolni|k (**-ka**, **-cy**; inst sg **-kiem**)
m slave
niewrażliwy adj insensitive;
jest całkiem ~ na ludzką biedę
he is absolutely insensitive to

poverty
niewybaczalny adj (błąd, czyn)
unforgivable
niewygodny adj **1** (fotel, ubranie)
uncomfortable **2** (sytuacja)
inconvenient
niewyraźny adj **1** (trudny do
usłyszenia, do zobaczenia) indistinct
2 (trudny do zrozumienia) obscure
3 (nieswój) out of sorts **4** (niegodny
zaufania: postać, działanie)
suspicious
niezadowolony adj dissatisfied;
**ona jest ciągle niezadowolona
ze swojego wyglądu** she
is always unhappy with her
appearance
niezależnoś|ć (-ci) f
independence
niezależny adj (ocena, fachowiec)
independent; **mowa niezależna**
(w językoznawstwie) direct speech;
on od lat jest ~ materialnie he
has been financially independent
for years
niezamężna adj: **~ kobieta**
(panna) single woman
niezaprzeczalny adj (fakt)
incontrovertible
niezaradny adj useless
niezbędny adj indispensable
niezbyt adv not very; **~ wysoki**
not very tall
niezgrabny adj **1** (człowiek, nogi)
unshapely **2** (ruch) awkward
niezły adj pretty good
nieznajomoś|ć (-ci) f: **~ języka
polskiego** ignorance of Polish;
zgubiła go ~ przepisów he was
undone by his ignorance of the
rules
nieznajomy adj unknown,

unfamiliar ▷ m decl like adj
stranger
nieznany adj unknown
niezręczny adj awkward
niezwykły adj unusual
nieźle adv not bad
nieżonaty adj (kawaler)
unmarried, single
nieżywy adj dead
nigdy adv **1** never **2** (w pytaniach,
po przeczeniu) ever; **nie rób tego
~ więcej** don't ever do that again;
już ~ (więcej) tego nie powiem
I will never (ever) say that again;
~ nie wiadomo kiedy przyjdzie
you never know when he'll come
nigdzie adv **1** nowhere **2** (w
pytaniach, po przeczeniu)
anywhere; **~ indziej nie czułem
się lepiej** I never felt better
anywhere else
nijaki adj (osoba, propozycja)
unremarkable; **rodzaj ~** (w
językoznawstwie) neuter
nikoty|na (-ny; dat sg **-nie)** f
nicotine
nikt pron **1** nobody **2** (w pytaniach,
po przeczeniu) anyone, anybody;
~ z nas go nie zna none of us
knows him
nim pron loc, inst od **on, ono**
nimi pron inst od **oni, one**
niosę itd. vb zob. **nieść**
niski adj **1** (stół, budynek) low
2 (osoba) short
nisko adv low
niszcze|ć (-eję, -ejesz) vi to
deteriorate
niszcz|yć (-ę, -ysz; pf **z-)** vt to
destroy
nit|ka (-ki, -ki; dat sg **-ce**; gen pl **-ek)**
f thread; **nitki** pl (Kulin: makaron)

vermicelli; **krytycy nie zostawili na filmie suchej nitki** the critics tore the film to pieces; **~ dentystyczna** dental floss

nizi|na (**-ny, -ny**; *dat sg* **-nie**) *f* lowland

nizinny *adj* **1** (*teren*) lowland **2** (*region*) low-lying

niż¹ (**-u, -e**) *m* **1** (*niskie ciśnienie atmosferyczne*) low **2** (*w geografii*) lowland

niż² *conj* than

niżej *adv comp od* **nisko**; **wykonawca musi umieścić w ofercie ~ wymieniony document** the contractor must submit the document mentioned below; **ja, ~ podpisany, oświadczam...** I, the undersigned, declare...

niższy *adj comp od* **niski 1** (*stół, dom*) lower **2** (*o osobie*) shorter **3** (*standard*) inferior **4** (*w hierarchii*) subordinate

no *part* **1: no, no!** (*wyrażający podziw, zdziwienie*) well, well!; (*uspokajający*) there, now! **2** (*twierdzący: pot*) yeah; **no to idź już stąd!** so go!; **no to co, że wyszedł?** so what, he left?

noc (**-y, -e**; *gen pl* **-y**) *f* night; **w ~y** at night; **śni o tym co ~** he dreams about this every night

nocle|g (**-gu, -gi**; *inst sg* **-giem**) *m* (*w hotelu*) accommodation, accommodations *pl* (*US*)

nocni|k (**-ka, -ki**; *inst sg* **-kiem**) *m* (*dla małych dzieci*) potty; **obudzić się z ręką w ~u** (*pot: przen*) to have been caught napping

nocny *adj* (*lot, autobus*) night

noc|ować (**-uję, -ujesz**; *pf* **prze-**)

vi to stay overnight *lub* for the night

no|ga (**-gi, -gi**; *dat sg* **-dze**; *gen pl* **nóg**) *f* **1** (*Anat: kończyna*) leg **2** (*stopa*) foot **3** (*krzesła*) leg; **od rana jest na ~ch** he's been on his feet since the morning; **wywrócił wszystko do góry ~mi** he turned everything upside down

nominacj|a (**-i, -e**; *gen pl* **-i**) *f* **1** (*w pracy*) appointment **2** (*do odznaczenia*) nomination

nomin|ować (**-uję, -ujesz**) *vt* (*im*)*pf* **1** (*w pracy*) to appoint **2** (*do odznaczenia*) to nominate

nonsens (**-u, -y**) *m* nonsense

nor|ma (**-my, -my**; *dat sg* **-mie**) *f* norm

normalnie *adv* normally

normalny *adj* **1** normal **2** (*bilet*) full-fare

Norwegi|a (**-i**) *f* Norway

norweski *adj* Norwegian

no|s (**-sa, -sy**; *loc sg* **-sie**) *m* nose; **nie wtykaj ~a w nie swoje sprawy** (*przen*) don't stick your nose into other people's affairs; **on ma ~a do interesów** he's got a flair for business

nosi|ć (**-szę, -sisz**; *imp* **noś**) *vt* **1** (*przedmiot*) to carry **2** (*ubranie, krawat, brodę, perukę*) to wear **3** (*imię, tytuł*) to bear **4** (*nazwisko*) to use

nosoroże|c (**-ca, -ce**) *m* rhinoceros

nostalgi|a (**-i**) *f* nostalgia

nostalgiczny *adj* (*atmosfera, utwór*) nostalgic

nosz|e (**-y**) *pl* stretcher *sg*

notariusz (**-a, -e**; *gen pl* **-y**) *m* notary (public)

notatk|a (-i) f note
notatni|k (-ka, -ki; *inst sg* **-kiem)**
  m notebook
noteboo|k (-ka, -ki; *inst sg* **-kiem)**
  m notebook (computer)
note|s (-su, -sy; *loc sg* **-sie)** m
  notebook
not|ować (-uję, -ujesz; *pf* **za-)**
  vt to note
nowatorski adj (*pomysł,
  rozwiązanie*) innovative
**Nowa Zelandia (Nowej
  Zelandii)** f New Zealand
nowel|a (-i, -e) f short story
nowicjusz (-a, -e; *gen pl* **-y)** m
  novice
nowi|na (-ny, -ny; *dat sg* **-nie)** f
  (*wiadomość*) news
nowoczesnoś|ć (-ci) f modernity
nowoczesny adj (*sztuka,
  technologia*) modern
noworod|ek (-ka, -ki; *inst sg*
  -kiem) m newborn baby
nowoś|ć (-ci, -ci; *gen pl* **-ci)** f
  1 (*wprowadzenie czegoś nowego*)
  novelty 2 (*wydawnicza*) new
  release
nowotw|ór (-oru, -ory; *loc sg*
  -orze) m (*w medycynie*) tumour
  (Brit), tumor (US)
nowy adj new; **samochód
  fabrycznie ~ a** (brand) new car;
  stół jak ~ the table is as good as
  new; **~ Rok** New Year
nożycz|ki (-ek) pl scissors; **~ do
  paznokci** nail scissors
nóż (noża, noże; *gen pl* **noży)** m
  knife; **jest zadłużony i ma ~ na
  gardle** he is in debt and in an
  impossible situation
np. abbr (= *na przykład*) e.g.
nr abbr (= *numer*) no.

nu|da (-dy, -dy; *dat sg* **-dzie**; *gen pl*
  -dów) f boredom
nudny adj (*nieciekawy*) boring
nudziarz (-a, -e; *gen pl* **-y)** m bore
nudz|ić (-ę, -isz; *pf* **za-)** to bore: **~
  się** vr to be bored; **za~ kogoś na
  śmierć** to bore sb to death
nume|r (-ru, -ry; *loc sg* **-rze)**
  m 1 (*telefonu, pokoju*) number
  2 (*ubrania*) size 3 (*w teatrze,
  kabarecie*) act 4 (*czasopisma*)
  issue; **sprzedują stary ~y
  „National Geographic"** they are
  selling old issues of the National
  Geographic; **~ rejestracyjny
  samochodu** registration number
nur|ek (-ka; *inst sg* **-kiem)** m
  1 (*nom pl* **-kowie)** (*osoba*) diver
  2 (*nom pl* **-ki)** (*skok do wody*) dive
nurk|ować (-uję, -ujesz; *pf* **za-)** vi
  1 (*o osobie*) to dive 2 (*o samolocie*)
  to nosedive
nu|ta (-ty, -ty; *dat sg* **-cie)** f note;
  nuty pl score; **kłamie cały czas
  jak z nut** he lies through his teeth
  the whole time
nużący adj tiresome
nuż|yć (-ę, -ysz; *pf* **z-)** to tire: **~ się**
  vr to tire

2 (*z czasownikiem*): **martwić się o kogoś/coś** to worry about sb/sth; **prosić/pytać o coś** to ask about *lub* for sth; **kłócić się o coś** to argue about sth
3: **opiera się o ścianę** he is leaning against the wall
▷ *excl* oh

oa|za (**-zy**, **-zy**; *loc sg* **-zie**) *f* oasis; **~ spokoju** an oasis of calm
oba *num* both; **~ psy/przepisy** both dogs/recipes
obaj *num* both; **~ chłopcy** both boys
obal|ać (**-am**, **-asz**; *pf* **-ić**) *vt* **1** (*na ringu*) to knock down **2** (*płot*) to fell **3** (*rząd*) to overthrow **4** (*hipotezę*) to refute
oba|wa (**-wy**, **-wy**; *dat sg & loc sg* **-wie**) *f*: **~ (o kogoś/coś)** concern (for sb/sth); **wyraził obawę przed nią** he expressed his fear of her
obawi|ać się (**-am**, **-asz**) *vr*: **~ się kogoś/czego** to fear sb/sth; **obawiam się, że nie masz racji** I am afraid (that) you're wrong
obca|s (**-sa**, **-sy**; *loc sg* **-sie**) *m* (*na butach*) heel
obci|ąć (**-etnę**, **-etniesz**; *imp* **-etnij**) *vb pf od* **obcinać**
obciąż|ać (**-am**, **-asz**; *pf* **-yć**) *vt* **1** (*pakunkami, towarem*) to weigh down **2** (*w balonach*) to ballast **3** (*pracą*) to burden, to saddle **4** (*umysł*) to burden; **~ kogoś winą za coś** to blame sb for sth
obcier|ać (**-am**, **-asz**; *pf* **obetrzeć**) *vt* **1** (*chusteczką*) to wipe **2** (*kaleczyć skórę*) to graze, to scrape **3** (*o butach*) to rub

O

o *prep* +*loc* **1** (*na temat*) about, on; **książka o historii** a book about *lub* on history; **rozmawiać/ myśleć/wiedzieć o czymś** to talk/think/know about sth
2 (*za pomocą*): **o własnych siłach** unaided; **o kulach** on crutches
3 (*czas*) at; **o (godzinie) ósmej** at eight (o'clock); **o świcie/ zmierzchu/północy** at dawn/ dusk/midnight
4 (*do opisania*) with; **dziewczyna o niebieskich oczach** a girl with blue eyes
▷ *prep* +*acc* **1** (*do porównania*) by; **o połowę niższy** (*o człowieku*) half the size; **starszy o dwa lata** two years older

obcin|ać (**-am, -asz**; pf **obciąć**) vt
1 (włosy) to cut 2 (krzew) to cut off
3 (zmniejszyć) to cut down on
obcisły adj (o ubraniu) tight
obco adv: **okolica wyglądała
~ i nieprzyjaźnie** the
neighbourhood (Brit) lub
neighborhood (US) looked
strange and unfriendly
obcokrajo|wiec (**-wca, -wcy**; voc
sg **-wce** lub **-wcu**) m foreigner
obcy adj 1 (należący do kogoś innego)
someone else's 2 (nie stąd) alien
3 (zagraniczny) foreign ▷ m decl
like adj (osoba nie stąd) stranger;
(w biurze, sklepie) "private"; (w
budynku strzeżonym) "authorized
personnel only"; „**~m wstęp
wzbroniony**" (w terenie) "no
trespassing"
obecnie adv at present, currently
obecnoś|ć (**-ci**) f 1 (istnienie)
existence 2 (w szkole, pracy)
attendance; **spotkanie odbyło
się w obecności prezesa** the
meeting took place in the
chairman's presence
obecny adj present; **obecni**
pl those present; **jest ~ na
zajęciach** he attends lessons; **w
chwili obecnej** at present; **~/
obecna!** (w szkole) here!, present!
obejm|ować (**-uję, -ujesz**;
pf **objąć**) vt 1 (rękoma) to hug
2 (zawierać) to include, to
encompass; **~ się** vr to hug each
other
obejrz|eć (**-ę, -ysz**; imp **-yj**) vb pf
od **oglądać**
obel|ga (**-gi, -gi**; dat sg & loc sg
-dze) f (obraza) insult
obfitoś|ć (**-ci**) f (towarów)

abundance
obfity adj abundant; **mleko
jest obfite w wapń** milk is
rich in calcium; **kobieta o ~ch
kształtach** a corpulent woman
obgad|ywać (**-uję, -ujesz**; pf **-ać**)
(pot) vt 1 (dyskutować) to talk over
lub about 2 (oczerniać) to backbite
obi|ad (**-adu, -ady**; loc sg **-edzie**) m
1 (w południe) lunch 2 (wieczorem)
dinner; **jeść** (**zjeść** pf) **~** to have
lunch/dinner; **~ proszony** dinner
(party)
obiadowy adj (zestaw, danie)
lunch, dinner
obie num both; **~ dziewczyny**
both girls
obiec|ywać (**-uję, -ujesz**; pf **-ać**)
vi to promise ▷ vt: **~ (komuś) coś**
to promise (sb) sth; **~ gruszki
na wierzbie** to make empty
promises
obie|g (**-gu**; inst **-giem**) m (krwi,
informacji) circulation
obiek|t (**-tu, -ty**; loc sg **-cie**)
m 1 (rzecz) object 2 (budowla)
structure, building; **była ~em
ciągłej krytyki** she was the
target of constant criticism
obiektywnie adv objectively
obiektywny adj objective
objaś|niać (**-niam, -niasz**; pf **-nić**)
vt 1 (zadanie, problem) to explain
2 (interpretować) to interpret
objaśnie|nie (**-nia, -nia**; gen pl **-ń**)
nt explanation
obja|w (**-wu, -wy**; loc sg **-wie**) m
(choroby, niechęci) symptom
obj|azd (**-azdu, -azdy**; loc sg
-eździe) m 1 (droga dookoła) tour
2 (obwodnica: na stałe) by-pass
3 (droga alternatywna) (traffic)

diversion (*Brit*), detour (*US*)
ob|jąć (-ejmę, -ejmiesz; *imp*
-ejmij) *vb pf od* **obejmować**
objętoś|ć (-ci) *f* **1** (*słoja*) capacity
2 (*część*) part, measure **3** (*książki*)
length **4** (*Mat*) (cubic) volume
oblew|ać (-am, -asz; *pf* **oblać)**
vt **1** (*polewać: płynem*) to pour
2 (*pokryć warstwą czegoś*) to coat
3 (*pot: egzamin*) to fail (*Brit*),
to flunk (*US*) **4** (*chrzciny*) to
celebrate; **~ (oblać** *pf*) **coś czymś**
to spill sth on sth
oblicz|ać (-am, -asz; *pf* **-yć)** *vt*
1 (*finanse*) to count **2** (*wynik,*
szybkość) to calculate **3** (*oceniać*)
to estimate
oblicz|e (-a, -a; *gen pl* **-y)**
nt **1** (*twarz*) face **2** (*cechy*
charakterystyczne) facet; **w obliczu**
problemów/śmierci in the face
of troubles/death; **w obliczu**
prawa in the eyes of the law
oblodzony *adj* (*stok, ulica*) icy
obłę|d (-du, -dy; *loc sg* **-dzie)** *m*
1 (*pomieszanie zmysłów*) insanity
2 (*nieporządek*) bedlam
obłędny *adj* (*pot: zachwycający*)
wicked (*Brit*), bad (*US*)
obmac|ywać (-uję, -ujesz; *pf*
-ać) *vt* **1** to finger **2** (*napastować*
kobietę: pej) to fondle, to grope
obmyśl|ać (-am, -asz; *pf* **-ić)** *vt*
(*plan*) to devise
obnaż|ać (-am, -asz; *pf* **-yć)** *vt*
(*błędy, przewinienia*) to expose, to
bare; **~ się** *vr* to expose o.s.
obniż|ać (-am, -asz; *pf* **-yć)** *vt* to
lower; **~ się** *vr* to fall
obniż|ka (-ki, -ki; *dat sg & loc sg*
-ce) *f* (*cen, kosztów*) cut
obojczy|k (-ka, -ki; *inst* **-kiem)** *m*

(*w anatomii*) collarbone
oboje *num* both
obojętnie *adv* (*bez*
zainteresowania) indifferently;
~ kto przyjdzie, będziemy
zadowoleni (*nieważne kto*) no
matter who comes, we'll be
satisfied; **~ kto wie, niech się**
przyzna (*ktokolwiek wie, niech*
się przyzna) whoever knows,
(please) own up; **~ kiedy będzie**
spotkanie, to przyjedziemy
whatever the time of the
meeting, we'll be there
obojętnoś|ć (-ci) *f* indifference
obojętny *adj* (*nieczuły*) indifferent
obok *prep* +*gen* **1** (*niedaleko*) by,
near, close to **2** (*poza*) beside
▷ *adv:* **(tuż) ~** nearby, (very)
close; **przeszła ~ niego i nic nie**
powiedziała she walked past
him without saying a word;
usiedli ~ siebie they sat down
next to each other
obowiąz|ek (-ku, -ki; *inst* **-kiem)**
m duty, obligation; **obowiązki**
pl duties *pl*; **pełniący obowiązki**
dyrektora acting chairman
obowiązkowo *adv* **1** (*pod*
przymusem) obligatorily
2 (*pot: koniecznie*) whatever
happens; **pasażerowie ~ muszą**
zapiąć (*pf*) **pasy** passengers
are required to wear seat belts;
musisz ~ ten spektakl obejrzeć
you just have to see this play
obowiązkowy *adj* **1** (*lekcje,*
zadania) obligatory **2** (*uczeń*)
conscientious
obowiązujący *adj* **1** (*rozkład*
jazdy) (currently) valid, current
2 (*przepis*) (currently) in force,

(legally) binding

obowiąz|ywać (-uje) vi to be in force; **na przyjęciu obowiązuje strój wieczorowy** it is a black tie event

ob|ój (-oju, -oje) m oboe

ob|óz (-ozu, -ozy; loc sg **-ozie)** m (harcerski) camp; **~ dla uchodźców** refugee camp; **~ koncentracyjny** concentration camp

obrab|ować (-uję, -ujesz) vt pf to rob

obrac|ać (-am, -asz) vt (przekręcić) to turn; **~ się** vr to whirl, to rotate; **obrócić wzrok na kogoś** to look at sb; **obrócić coś w żart** to turn sth into a joke; **Ziemia obraca się wokół Słońca** the Earth revolves around the Sun; **~ się wśró--d** (przen) to socialize with; **obrócić się przeciwko komuś** to turn against sb

obra|z (-zu, -zy; loc sg **-zie)** m **1** (dzieło sztuki) painting, picture **2** (sceneria) sight, scenery **3** (rys: wydarzeń, historyczny) picture **4** (telewizyjny) image, picture **5** (film) film **6** (w fizyce, fotografii) image

obraz|ek (-ka, -ki; inst sg **-kiem)** m picture

obraźliwy adj **1** (uwaga, zachowanie) offensive **2** (łatwo obrażający się) touchy

obraż|ać (-am, -asz; pf **obrazić)** vt to offend; **~ się** vr: **~ się na kogoś** to be offended by sb; **obraził się za jego słowa** he took offence (Brit) lub offense (US) at his words; **nie obrażaj się** don't

be offended

obrażony adj offended; **być ~m na** to be offended by

obrącz|ka (-ki, -ki; dat sg & loc sg **-ce)** f **1** (ślubna) wedding ring **2** (dla zwierząt) ring

obro|na (-ny; dat sg & loc sg **-nie)** f **1** (reakcja na atak) defence (Brit), defense (US) **2** (zabezpieczenie) protection; **zrobił to w obronie własnej** he did it in self-defence (Brit) lub self-defense (US)

● ● **OBRONA CZĘSTOCHOWY**

● ●

● **Obrona Częstochowy** is one

● of Poland's patriotic myths.

● The siege of the monastery of

● Jasna Góra in Częstochowa

● took place in the 17th century

● during the Polish-Swedish

● war. Over time this event

● became steeped in legend

● and became a symbol of the

● "nation's victorious spirit"

● and the "defence of the faith",

● with the phrase **Obrona**

● **Częstochowy** becoming part

● of everyday language.

obro|nić (-nię, -nisz; imp **-ń)** vb pf od **bronić**

obronny adj **1** (działanie) defensive **2** (budowla) fortified; **mury obronne** fortifications

obrońc|a (-y, -y) m decl like f in sg **1** (kraju, poglądów) defender **2** (sprawy) advocate **3** (w prawie) defence counsel (Brit), defense attorney (US)

obrotny adj resourceful; **on jest ~ w gębie** (pot!) he has the gift of the gab

obroż|a (**-y, -e**; gen pl **-y**) f collar

obró|cić (**-cę, -cisz**; imp **-ć**) vb pf od **obracać**

obru|s (**-sa** lub **-su, -sy**; loc sg **-sie**) m tablecloth

obrzę|k (**-ku, -ki**; inst **-kiem**) m (gardła, nogi) swelling

obrzu|cać (**-cam, -casz**; pf **-cić**) vt: **~ kogoś/coś czymś** to throw sth at sb/sth; **obrzucali go bezustanie błotem** they were constantly showering him with abuse

obrzydliwy adj (człowiek, zapach) disgusting

obserwacj|a (**-i, -e**; gen pl **-i**) f observation

obserwacyjny adj (sprzęt) observational; **punkt ~** vantage point

obserw|ować (**-uję, -ujesz**) vt (uważnie przyglądać się) to observe

obsesj|a (**-i, -e**; gen pl **-i**) f (uporczywa myśl) obsession

obsłu|ga (**-gi**; dat sg & loc sg **-dze**) f 1 (urządzenia) maintenance 2 (klientów) service 3 (pracownicy usług) staff; **instrukcja obsługi** instruction manual

obsłu|giwać (**-guję, -gujesz**; pf **-żyć**) vt 1 (w restauracji) to serve 2 (urządzenie) to operate ▷ vi (obsługiwać do stołu) to wait at table; **~ się** vr: **w tym domu, obsługuje się sam** you help yourself in this house

obsza|r (**-ru, -ry**; loc sg **-rze**) m 1 (powierzchnia terenu) area 2 (wodny) territory; **na ~ze całego kraju** all over the country/ nationwide; **~ leśny/górzysty** forest/mountainous area

obszerny adj (room) spacious; **obszerne sprawozdanie** extensive report

obud|owa (**-owy, -owy**; gen pl **-ów**) f (osłona) casing

obu|dzić (**-dzę, -dzisz**; imp **-dź**) vb pf od **budzić**; **~ się** vr to wake up

oburz|ać (**-am, -asz**; pf **-yć**) vt (denerwować) to outrage; **~ się** vr: **~ się (na kogoś/coś)** to be outraged (at sb/sth)

oburzający adj (uwaga, zachowanie) outrageous

oburzeni|e (**-a**) nt indignation

oburzony adj: **~ (na kogoś/coś)** outraged (at sb/sth)

obustronny adj mutual

obuwi|e (**-a**) nt (buty) footwear

obwieszcze|nie (**-nia, -nia**; gen pl **-ń**) nt (ogłoszenie) announcement

obwi|niać (**-niam, -niasz**; pf **-nić**) vt: **~ kogoś (o coś)** to accuse sb (of sth)

obwodnic|a (**-y, -e**) f (trasa okrążająca miasto) bypass

obw|ód (**-odu, -ody**; loc sg **-odzie**) m 1 (w geometrii: okręgu) circumference 2 (wielokąta) perimeter 3 (w elektronice) circuit 4 (jednostka podziału administracyjnego) district

obyczaj (**-u, -e**) m 1 (tradycja) custom 2 (codzienna czynność) habit; **obyczaje** pl 1 (zachowanie się) manners 2 (zasady moralne) morals

obyczajowy adj (skandal) moral; **swoboda obyczajowa** moral freedom; **powieść obyczajowa** a novel of manners; **film ~** (film) drama

obydwa *num* both; *zob. też* **oba**

obydwaj *num* both; *zob. też* **obaj**

obydwie *num* both; *zob. też* **obie**

obydwoje *num* both; *zob. też*
   oboje

obywatel (**-a**, **-e**; *gen pl* **-i**) *m*
   (*mieszkaniec kraju*) citizen; **szary ~**
   the man in the street

obywatelst|wo (**-wa**; *loc sg*
   -wie) *nt* (*honorowe, podwójne*)
   citizenship

ocea|n (**-nu**, **-ny**; *loc sg* **-nie**)
   m ocean; **~ smutków** ocean
   of sorrows; **~ Atlantycki** the
   Atlantic (Ocean); **~ Indyjski** the
   Indian Ocean; **~ Spokojny** the
   Pacific (Ocean)

oce|na (**-ny**, **-ny**; *dat sg & loc sg*
   -nie) *f* 1 (*opinia*) assessment 2 (*w*
   szkole: stopień) mark (*Brit*), grade
   (*US*) 3 (*wycena*) estimation,
   evaluation

oce|niać (**-niam**, **-niasz**; *pf*
   -nić) *vt* 1 (*wydać sąd*) to judge
   2 (*wyceniać*) to evaluate

oce|t (**-tu**, **-ty**; *loc sg* **-cie**) *m* (*w*
   gotowaniu) vinegar

ochładz|ać (**-am**, **-asz**; *pf*
   ochłodzić) *vt* 1 (*herbatę, płyn*) to
   cool 2 (*piwo*) to chill 3 (*odświeżać*
   się) to refresh; **~ się** *vr* 1 (*być*
   chłodnym) to cool 2 (*stawać*
   się zimnym) to cool (down)
   3 (*orzeźwiać się*) to cool off 4 (*o*
   relacjach międzyludzkich) to chill;
   wczoraj ochłodziło się it got
   cooler yesterday

ochot|a (**-ty**; *dat sg & loc sg* **-cie**)
   f (*chęć*) willingness; **przyjdę z**
   ochotą I'll gladly come; **mam**
   ochotę na coś do jedzenia I

feel like something to eat; **mam**
ochotę pojechać w góry I feel
like going to the mountains; **czy**
masz ochotę na lody? do you
fancy some ice cream?

ochotnicz|ka (**-ki**, **-ki**; *dat sg* **-ce**;
   gen pl **-ek**) *f* volunteer

ochotni|k (**-ka**, **-cy**; *inst sg* **-kiem**)
   m volunteer

ochrani|ać (**-am**, **-asz**; *pf*
   ochronić) *vt*: **~ kogoś/coś (od**
   czegoś *lub* **przed czymś**) to
   protect sb/sth (from sth); **~ się**
   vr: **~ się przed czymś** to protect
   o.s. from sth; **ochraniał go przed**
   deszczem he protected him from
   the rain

ochron|a (**-ny**; *dat sg & loc sg* **-nie**)
   f 1 (*przed chorobą, nieszczęściem*)
   protection 2 (*w klubie, rządu*)
   security; **~ środowiska**
   naturalnego environment(al)
   protection; **~ osobista**
   bodyguard

ochroniarz (**-a**, **-e**; *gen pl* **-y**) *m*
   (*pot*) security guard

ochronny *adj* (*ubranie, sprzęt*)
   protective; **szczepienie**
   ochronne vaccination

ociąg|ać się (**-am**, **-asz**) *vr*: **~ się**
   (z czymś) to be reluctant (about
   sth); **nie ociągaj się z tą pracą**
   don't delay doing the work

ocze|kiwać (**-kuję**, **-kujesz**) *vt*: **~**
   kogoś/czegoś to wait for sb/sth;
   (*być przygotowanym na coś*) to
   expect sb/sth

oczy *itd. n zob.* **oko**

oczyszcz|ać (**-am**, **-asz**; *pf*
   oczyścić) *vt* 1 (*skórę*) to clean
   2 (*płyn z zanieczyszczeń*) to purify; **~**
   się *vr* to clean *lub* cleanse o.s.

oczywisty *adj* obvious
oczywiście *adv* obviously; **~ masz rację!** of course you're right!

○ **KEYWORD**

od *prep +gen* **1** (*kierunek*) from; **od domu** from home *lub* from the house; **od wschodu** from the west; **na południe od Polski** south of Poland
2 (*czas trwania*) for; **od dwóch dni** for two days; **od bardzo dawna** for a long time
3 since; **od środy** since Wednesday; **od rana do wieczora** from morning till night; **od wczoraj** since yesterday; **od jutra** as from tomorrow; **od poniedziałku do piątku** Monday to Friday (*Brit*), Monday through Friday (*US*)
4 (*odległość*) (away) from; **sto metrów od brzegu** a hundred metres (*Brit*) *lub* meters (*US*) away from the shore
5 (*dolna granica zakresu*) from; **od dwóch do sześciu razy w tygodniu** (from) two to six times a week
6 (*początkowa granica skali*) (starting) from; **od wierszy po powieści** from poems to novels
7 (*przyczyna*) with, from; **twarz mokra od deszczu** a face wet from the rain; **zamarzł od zimna** he froze from the cold
8 (*pochodzenie*) from; **prezent od mojej siostry** a present from my sister
9 (*przeznaczenie*): **klucze od mieszkania** house keys; **syrop od kaszlu** cough mixture; **pudełko od zapałek** matchbox; **ubezpieczenie od następstw nieszczęśliwych wypadków** accident insurance
10 (*specjalizacja*): **nauczyciel od polskiego** Polish teacher; **fachowiec od pralek** washing machine technician
11 (*przy porównaniach*) than; **ona jest młodsza od siostry** she is younger than her sister; **on jest grubszy od niej** he is fatter than her

odbi|cie (**-cia, -cia**; *gen pl* **-ć**) *nt*
1 (*w lustrze, tafli wody*) reflection **2** (*kopia*) image **3** (*w fizyce*) reflection **4** (*odcisk buta, dłoni*) print **5** (*ataku*) parry
odbier|ać (**-am, -asz**; *pf* **odebrać**) *vt* **1** (*należność*) to take back **2** (*otrzymywać*) to receive **3** (*walizkę, wezwanie*) to collect **4** (*dziecko ze szkoły*) to pick up **5** (*telefon*) to answer **6** (*pozbawiać: ochotę*) to deprive of **7** (*prawo, przywilej*) to withdraw **8** (*zabierać przy użyciu przemocy*) to confiscate **9** (*program radiowy, telewizyjny*) to receive **10** (*doświadczać uczucia*) to experience; **odebrał sobie życie** he took his own life
odbij|ać (**-am, -asz**; *pf* **odbić**) *vt* **1** (*odzwierciedlać*) to reflect **2** (*piłkę*) to return **3** (*o ziemię*) to bounce **4** (*pieczątkę*) to stamp **5** (*zostawiać ślady*) to leave **6** (*z niewoli*) to rescue ▷ *vi* (*odłączać się od grupy*) to break away; **~ się** *vr* **1** to be

reflected 2 (*ślad*) to leave traces 3 (*piłka*) to bounce (off), to deflect; **~ od czegoś** (*odróżniać się*) to stand out against sth; **palenie papierosów odbiło się na jego zdrowiu** smoking affected his health; **odbiło mu się po posiłku** he belched after the meal

odbiorc|a (**-y, -y**) *m decl like f in sg* 1 (*danych, wiadomości*) recipient 2 (*listu*) addressee 3 (*prądu*) consumer; **~ audycji radiowej** listener; **~ programu telewizyjnego** viewer

odbudo|wa (**-wy**; *dat sg & loc sg* **-wie**) *f* (*zamku, miasta*) reconstruction

odby|t (**-tu, -ty**; *loc sg* **-cie**) *m* anus

odbyw|ać (**-am, -asz**; *pf* **odbyć**) *vt* 1 (*zajęcia*) to undergo 2 (*służbę wojskową*) to serve 3 (*nauczycielska*) to do teaching practice; **~ się** *vr* (*o wydarzeniu*) to take place; **odbywał praktykę w fabryce** he served his apprenticeship (in a factory)

odchod|y (**-ów**) *pl* (*ludzkie, zwierzęce*) faeces (Brit), feces (US)

odcho|dzić (**-dzę, -dzisz**; *imp* **-dź**; *pf* **odejść**) *vi* 1 (*opuszczać*) to walk away 2 (*o pociągu, autobusie*) to depart 3 (*umierać*) to pass away 4 (*z pracy*) to leave 5 (*gałęzi*) to spread out 6 (*ulicy*) to diverge 7 (*odpryskiwać*) to peel (off)

odchu|dzać się (**-dzam, -dzasz**; *pf* **-dzić**) *vr* (*tracić na wadze*) to lose weight

odchudzani|e (**-a**) *nt* dieting

odcie|ń (**-nia**) *m* 1 shade 2 (*głosu*) tone

odcin|ać (**-am, -asz**; *pf* **odciąć**) *vt* 1 to cut off 2 (*sznur*) to sever 3 (*amputować*) to amputate 4 (*wyjście*) to seal off; **~ się** *vr* (*ostro reagować na wypowiedź*): **~ się od** +*gen* (*zerwać się z*) to distance o.s. from; (*wyróżniać się*) to stand out against

odcin|ek (**-ka, -ki**; *inst sg* **-kiem**) *m* 1 (*trasy*) section 2 (*czas*) period 3 (*rachunek*) receipt 4 (*w radiu, telewizji*) episode 5 (*w matematyce*) segment 6 (*dziedzina, zakres*) area

odcis|k (**-ku, -ki**; *inst sg* **-kiem**) *m* 1 (*zostawiony ślad*) imprint 2 (*ślad stopy*) footprint 3 (*ślad palca*) fingerprint 4 (*zgrubienia naskórka na ręce, stopie*) corn

odd|ać (**-am, -asz**; *3 pl* **-adzą**) *vb pf od* **oddawać**

oddal|ać (**-am, -asz**; *pf* **-ić**) *vt* (*sprawę sądową*) to dismiss; **~ się** *vr* 1 (*odchodzić*) to walk away 2 (*odjeżdżać: o pojeździe*) to drive away 3 (*o koniu, rowerze*) to ride away 4 (*o samolocie*) to fly away 5 (*odpływać: o łodzi*) to sail away 6 (*o lądzie*) to vanish away

oddalony *adj* (*punkt, cel*) remote

oddany *adj* devoted

odd|awać (**-aję, -ajesz**; *imp* **-awaj**; *pf* **-ać**) *vt* 1 (*rzecz do wypożyczalni*) to return 2 (*wydawać resztę*) to give 3 (*pieniądze*) to pay back 4 (*zostawiać w zakładzie usługowym: buty, spodnie*) to leave 5 (*w przechowalni, sejfie: kosztowności, bagaż*) to deposit 6 (*pod opiekę: chorego, ucznia*) to send 7 (*głos, pierwszeństwo*) to give 8 (*majątek, bogactwo*) to renounce **9** (*odwzajemniać*) to return **10** (*uderzenie*) to hit back **11** (*miłość*) to reciprocate; **~ się** *vr* **1** (*poddawać się*) to surrender **2** (*ulegać*) to give o.s.; **~ komuś przysługę** to do sb a favour (*Brit*) *lub* favor (*US*); **oddaje się nałogowemu pijaństwu** he has surrendered to drink; **~ się czemuś** (*pracy, marzeniom*) to devote o.s. to sth; (*relaksowi*) to indulge in sth

oddech (-**u**, -**y**) *m* (*wdech i wydech*) breath; **wstrzymywać** (**wstrzymać** *pf*) **~** to hold one's breath

oddych|ać (-**am**, -**asz**) *vi* to breathe; **ulżyło mu i odetchnął pełną piersią** he felt relieved and breathed deeply

oddychani|e (-**a**) *nt* breathing; **sztuczne ~** artificial respiration

oddzia|ł (-**łu**, -**ły**; *loc sg* -**le**) *m* **1** (*w wojsku*) unit **2** (*w policji*) squad **3** (*ministerstwa*) department **4** (*banku, agencji*) branch **5** (*w szpitalu*) ward

oddział|ywać (-**uję**, -**ujesz**) *vi*: **~ na** (*o ludzi, zjawiska*) to influence

oddziaływani|e (-**a**) *nt* **1** (*wpływ na ludzi, zjawiska*) influence **2** (*działanie*) effect **3** (*wzajemne*) interaction

oddziel|ać (-**am**, -**asz**; *pf* -**ić**) *vt* to separate

oddzielnie *adv* (*mieszkać, pracować*) separately

oddzielny *adj* (*pomieszczenie*) separate

ode *prep* = **od**; **jest młodszy ~ mnie** he is younger than me

odebrać (**odbiorę, odbierzesz**;

imp **odbierz**) *vb pf od* **odbierać**

odejm|ować (-**uję**, -**ujesz**; *pf* **odjąć**) *vt* **1** (*w matematyce*) to subtract **2** (*nadwyżkę*) to deduct **3** (*odbierać*) to take away

odejmowani|e (-**a**) *nt* (*działanie matematyczne*) subtraction

odejści|e (-**a**) *nt* (*pociągu, człowieka*) departure

odej|ść (-**dę**, -**dziesz**; *imp* -**dź**; *pt* **odszedł, odeszła, odeszli**) *vb pf od* **odchodzić**

oder|wać (-**wę**, -**wiesz**; *imp* -**wij**) *vb pf od* **odrywać**

odgło|s (-**su**, -**sy**; *loc sg* -**sie**) *m* (*dźwięk*) sound

odgraż|ać się (-**am**, -**asz**) *vr* to make threats; **odgrażał się, że go zwolni z pracy** he threatened to sack him

odj|azd (-**azdu**, -**azdy**; *loc sg* -**eździe**) *m* (*pociągu, autobusu*) departure; **~!** all aboard!

odjeżdż|ać (-**am**, -**asz**; *pf* **odjechać**) *vi* **1** (*o człowieku*) to leave **2** (*o pojeździe*) to depart, to leave **3** (*Mot*) to drive off **4** (*na rowerze*) to ride off; **nasz pociąg już odjechał** our train has already departed

odkaż|ać (-**am**, -**asz**; *pf* **odkazić**) *vt* **1** (*ranę*) to disinfect **2** (*o ziemi, wodzie*) to decontaminate

odkąd *pron* since; **~ go znasz?** how long have you known him?; **~ mamy zacząć czytać?** where shall we start reading from?; **~ wyjechała, on tęskni** he has missed her (ever) since she left; **~ pamiętam** for as long as I can remember

odkład|ać (-**am**, -**asz**; *pf*

odłożyć vt 1 (na półkę) to put away 2 (przekładać, opóźniać) to postpone 3 (oszczędzać) to put aside; **~ się** vr to accumulate; **nie odkładaj słuchawki!** don't hang up (the phone)!

odkręc|ać (**-am, -asz**; pf **odkręcić**) vt 1 (śrubokrętem) to unscrew 2 (słoik) to twist off lub open 3 (wodę) to turn on 4 (przen) to undo; **tego błędu nie da się już odkręcić** it is impossible to rectify the mistake now

odkry|cie (**-cia, -cia**; gen pl **-ć**) nt (geograficzne, naukowe) discovery

odkryty adj 1 (bez dachu) open 2 (basen) outdoor 3 (pod gołym niebem: koncert, występ) open-air

odkryw|ać (**-am, -asz**; pf **odkryć**) vt 1 (zdejmować wierzchnie przykrycie) to uncover 2 (otwierać) to open 3 (ląd) to discover 4 (sekret, tajemnicę) to uncover 5 (wyjaśniać) to reveal

odkrywc|a (**-y, -y**) m decl like f in sg 1 (badacz) discoverer 2 (lądów, krajów) explorer

odkurzacz (**-a, -e**; gen pl **-y**) m vacuum cleaner, hoover ® (Brit)

odkurz|ać (**-am, -asz**; pf **-yć**) vt 1 (powierzchnię ścierką) to dust 2 (odkurzaczem) to vacuum, to hoover (Brit)

odległoś|ć (**-ci, -ci**) f distance; **na ~ dwóch metrów** two metres (Brit) lub meters (US) apart; **w niewielkiej odległości od domu** not far away from the house

odludny adj (budynek, teren) deserted

odlu|dzie (**-dzia, -dzia**; gen pl **-dzi**) nt secluded spot; **dom na odludziu** a house in the middle of nowhere

odmawi|ać (**-am, -asz**; pf **odmówić**) vi (odrzucać propozycję, plan) to decline ▷ vt (odwoływać wizytę, spotkanie) to cancel; **~ modlitwę** to say one's prayers; **odmawiał mu pomocy** he refused to help him; **odmawia zjedzenia obiadu** he refuses to eat lunch/dinner; **ojciec odmawia zgody na małżeństwo** father refuses to grant his approval to the marriage

odmia|na (**-ny, -ny**; dat sg & loc sg **-nie**) f 1 (przemiana) change 2 (wariant) variety 3 (gatunek, rodzaj) strain, variety 4 (w językoznawstwie) inflection; **dla odmiany pójdę do kina** for a change I'll go to the cinema (Brit) lub movies (US)

odmie|niać (**-niam, -niasz**; pf **-nić**) vt 1 (osobę) to transform 2 (w językoznawstwie) to inflect; **~ się** vr (o wyrazach) to inflect

odmienny adj 1 (odróżniający się) different 2 (swoisty) distinct 3 (w językoznawstwie) inflected

odmierz|ać (**-am, -asz**; pf **-yć**) vt 1 (ilość, objętość) to measure 2 (wydzielać) to measure out; **~ takt** to beat time

odmo|wa (**-wy, -wy**; dat sg & loc sg **-wie**; gen pl **odmów**) f (zapłaty, wykonania usługi) refusal

odmraż|ać (**-am, -asz**; pf **odmrozić**) vt 1 (mięso) to defrost 2 (samolot) to de-ice; **tej zimy odmroziłem sobie ręce** my hands got frostbitten this winter

odmroże|nie (**-nia**) nt (nom pl
-nia; gen pl **-ń**) **1** (w medycynie)
frostbite **2** (palców rąk lub nóg)
chilblain

odnajd|ować (**-uję, -ujesz**; pf
odnaleźć) vt to find; **~ się** vr
1 (pojawiać się ponownie) to show
up **2** (w nowych okolicznościach
życiowych) to find one's feet

odnawi|ać (**-am, -asz**; pf
odnowić) vt **1** (pokój) to renovate,
to refurbish **2** (zabytek) to restore
3 (znajomość) to renew

odno|sić (**-szę, -sisz**; imp **-ś**;
pf **odnieść**) vt **1** (przynosić z
powrotem) to take (back) **2** (sukces)
to achieve **3** (porażkę) to suffer
4 (rany) to sustain; **~ się** vr: **~
się do kogoś/czegoś** to treat
sb/sth; (ustosunkowywać się) to
feel about sb/sth; (dotyczyć) to
relate to sb/sth; **interwencja
odniosła oczekiwany skutek**
the intervention brought the
expected results

odn|owa (**-owy**) f revival

odosobniony adj **1** (oddalony)
isolated **2** (samotny) secluded
3 (pojedynczy: fakt, przypadek,
zjawisko) isolated

od|ór (**-oru, -ory**; loc sg **-orze**) m
(smród) odour (Brit), odor (US)

odpad|ać (**-am, -asz**; pf
odpaść) vi **1** to come off **2** (nie
wytrzymywać konkurencji) to drop
out **3** (przegrywać w wyborach) to
be defeated

odpad|ki (**-ków**) pl waste

odpad|y (**-ów**) pl (toksyczne,
przemysłowe) waste (material)

odpier|ać (**-am, -asz**; pf
odeprzeć) vt **1** (atak) to fight

off **2** (walczyć z nieprzyjacielem)
to repel, to repulse **3** (ciosy) to
fight off **4** (argumenty w dyskusji)
to refute

odpin|ać (**-am, -asz**; pf **odpiąć**)
vt **1** (suwak) to undo **2** (kurtkę,
bluzkę) to unbutton **3** (sprzączkę)
to unbuckle **4** (broszkę) to unclip;
~ się vr to come undone

odpi|s (**-su, -sy**; loc sg **-sie**) m
1 (duplikat dokumentu) copy **2** (od
podatku) deduction

odpis|ywać (**-uję, -ujesz**; pf
-ać) vt **1** (przepisywać) to copy
2 (w szkole: ściągać) to copy **3** (w
księgowości) to deduct ▷ vi: **~ (na
list)** (odpowiadać) to reply (to a
letter)

odplamiacz (**-a, -e**; gen pl **-y**) m
(do zaplamionych materiałów) stain
remover

odpła|cać (się) (**-cam, -casz**; pf
-cić) vb: **~ komuś za coś
(czymś)** to repay sb for sth (with
sth)

odpłatnie adv (wykonywać usługę)
for a fee

odpłatnoś|ć (**-ci**) f payment,
charge

odpłatny adj paid

odpły|w (**-wu, -wy**; loc sg **-wie**)
m **1** (wody) outflow **2** (ludzi)
emigration **3** (Geo) low tide

odpływ|ać (**-am, -asz**; pf
odpłynąć) vi **1** (statek, łódź) to sail
away **2** (ryba) to swim away **3** (o
rzeczy) to float away **4** (o cieczy) to
flow away

odpoczyn|ek (**-ku**) m (przerwa w
pracy) rest, break

odpoczyw|ać (**-am, -asz**; pf
odpocząć) vi (relaksować się) to

have a rest

odpornoś|ć (-ci) f resistance

odporny adj (chwila, osoba): **~ (na coś)** (nie poddający się) unaffected (by sth); (wytrzymały) resistant (to sth); (w medycynie) immune (to sth)

odpowiad|ać (-am, -asz; pf **odpowiedzieć)** vi **1** to answer, to reply **2** (w szkole: no pf) to answer **3** (na coś) to respond; **nie odpowiadał na jej zaczepki** he did not react to her taunts; **odpowiadał nauczycielowi na pytanie** he replied to the teacher's question; **~ na pukanie w drzwi** to answer the door; **odpowiada za bezpieczeństwo w pracy** (być odpowiedzialnym) he is responsible for safety at work; **w pełni odpowiada za wypadek** he is fully responsible for the accident

odpowiedni adj (chwila, osoba) suitable, right **1** (miejsce) appropriate **2** (adekwatny) right **3** (doświadczenie, wykształcenie) adequate **4** (zachowanie, ubranie) suitable

odpowiedzialnoś|ć (-ci) f responsibility; **spółka z ograniczoną odpowiedzialnością** (Comm) limited (liability) company; **ponosi ~ za straty** he bears responsibility for the losses

odpowiedzialny adj responsible

odpowie|dź (-dzi, -dzi; gen pl **-dzi)** f **1** (na zadane pytanie) answer, reply **2** (na korespondencję) answer **3** (na krytyczną uwagę) response **4** (na prośbę) reply **5** (w szkole) answer; **w odpowiedzi na**

Pański list z 12 stycznia in reply to your letter dated 12th January

Od|ra (-ry; dat sg & loc sg **-rze)** f (nazwa geograficzna) the Oder (river)

odrabi|ać (-am, -asz; pf **odrobić)** vt **1** (zaległą pracę) to catch up on **2** (straty) to make up for; **~ pracę domową** to do homework

odracz|ać (-am, -asz; pf **odroczyć)** vt **1** (odkładać na późniejszy termin) to postpone **2** (karę) to reprieve **3** (Wojsk) to defer

odradz|ać¹ (-am, -asz; pf **odradzić)** vt: **~ komuś coś** to advise sb against sth

odradz|ać² (-am, -asz; pf **odrodzić)** vt **1** (regenerować) to bring back to life **2** (dawne obyczaje) to revive; **~ się** vr (odżywać) to regenerate

odrębnoś|ć (-ci, -ci) f **1** (autonomia) autonomy, independence **2** (cecha wyróżniająca) difference

odrębny adj (niezależny) distinct

odręcznie adv **1** manually **2** (od razu) immediately

odróż|niać (-niam, -niasz; pf **-nić)** vt **1** (widzieć różnicę) to distinguish **2** (wyróżniać) to differentiate; **~ się** vr (być innym) to be distinct, to differ

odruch (-u, -y) m **1** (w medycynie, psychologii) reflex **2** (automatyczna reakcja) impulse

odruchowy adj **1** (reakcja) reflex, spontaneous **2** (automatyczny) involuntary

odryw|ać (-am, -asz; pf **oderwać)** vt (kawałek materiału) to tear off;

~ się vr (odłączyć się) to come off;
nie mogłem się oderwać od pracy I couldn't get away from my work

odstrasz|ać (-am, -asz; pf -yć) vt (ptaki, złodziei) to scare away; **~ kogoś (od czegoś)** (zniechęcać) to deter sb (from sth)

odstraszający adj 1 (środek) deterrent 2 (wygląd) scary; **środek ~ komary** mosquito repellito

odsuw|ać (-am, -asz) vt (pf **odsunąć**) 1 (meble) to move back 2 (zasłonę, firankę) to draw (back) 3 (zasuwkę) to pull back 4 (natrętne myśli) to put aside 5 (zagrożenie) to avert; **~ się** vr 1 (cofać się) to stand back 2 (zostawiać wolne miejsce) to step aside

odszkodowa|nie (-nia, -nia; gen pl -ń) nt 1 (od firmy ubezpieczeniowej) compensation 2 (kara) damages pl, compensation 3 (rekompensata) settlement

odśnież|ać (-am, -asz; pf -yć) vt to clear (of snow)

odtąd adv 1 (od tamtego czasu) since then 2 (od tej chwili) from now on 3 (poczynając od tamtego momentu) from that time on, from then on 4 (od tego miejsca) (starting) from here

odtrą|cać (-cam, -casz; pf -cić) vt 1 (rękę) to push away 2 (miłość, osobę) to reject

odtrut|ka (-ki, -ki; dat sg & loc sg -ce; gen pl -ek) f (antidotum) antidote; **on jest odtrutką na złamane serce** he's the remedy for a broken heart

odtwarzacz (-a, -e; gen pl -y) m 1 (magnetofon) cassette player 2 (magnetowid) video (cassette) player 3 (kompaktowy) CD player

odwa|ga (-gi; dat sg & loc sg -dze) f courage; **miał odwagę się sprzeciwić** he had the courage to object; **dodawał jej odwagi przed egzaminem** he bolstered her courage before the exam; **zdobył się na odwagę i powiedział prawdę** he mustered up his courage and told the truth

odważny adj brave

odwie|dzać (-dzam, -dzasz; pf -dzić) vt to visit; **odwiedź mnie dzisiaj wieczorem** come and see me tonight

odwodnieni|e (-a) nt dehydration

odwoł|ywać (-uję, -ujesz; pf -ać) vt 1 (pozbawiać stanowiska) to dismiss 2 (dyplomatę) to recall 3 (lekcję, samolot) to cancel 4 (obietnicę) to retract, to withdraw; **~ się** vr (w sądzie) to appeal; **odwołał się od decyzji sądu** he appealed against the court's decision

odwrac|ać (-am, -asz; pf **odwrócić**) vt 1 (wzrok) to avert 2 (głowę) to turn away 3 (zmieniać bieg rzeki) to reverse; **~ się** vr to turn away

odwrotnie adv 1 (przeciwnie) conversely 2 (na odwrót) inversely, the other way around 3 (do góry nogami) upside down 4 (na lewą stronę) inside out; **~ niż sądził** contrary to his judgement

odwrotny adj (przeciwny) opposite

odwzajem|niać (**-niam, -niasz**; *pf* **-nić**) *vt* to return; **~ się** *vr* to return

odziedzicz|yć (**-ę, -ysz**) *vt pf od* **dziedziczyć**; (*majątek, dom*) to inherit

odzież (**-y**) *f* (*ubrania*) clothing; **~ ochronna** protective clothing

odzna|ka (**-ki, -ki**; *dat sg & loc sg* **-ce**) *f* **1** (*medal*) distinction, award **2** (*symbol przynależności*) badge

odzwierciedl|ać (**-am, -asz**; *pf* **-ić**) *vt* (*poglądy*) to mirror; **~ się** *vr* to be reflected

odżywczy *adj* **1** (*napój, posiłek*) nutritious **2** (*element*) nutritious **3** (*wartość*) nutritional **4** (*balsam*) nourishing

odży|wiać (**-wiam, -wiasz**; *pf* **-wić**) *vt* (*podawać jedzenie*) to nourish; **~ się** *vr* **1** (*o osobie*) to feed o.s. **2** (*o kocie, psie*) to feed

odżywiani|e (**-a**) *nt* nutrition

odżyw|ka (**-ki, -ki**; *dat sg & loc sg* **-ce**; *gen pl* **-ek**) *f* **1** (*jedzenie*) nutrient **2** (*dla niemowląt*) formula **3** (*do włosów*) conditioner

ofer|ma (**-my, -my**; *dat sg & loc sg* **-mie**) *f* (*pot*) wimp

ofer|ować (**-uję, -ujesz**; *pf* **za-**) *vt* (*proponować*) to offer

ofer|ta (**-ty, -ty**; *dat sg & loc sg* **-cie**) *f* (*handlowa*) offer; **~ matrymonialna** marriage proposal

ofi|ara (**-ary, -ary**; *dat sg & loc sg* **-erze**) *f* **1** (*datek*) gift, donation **2** (*pieniężny*) donation **3** (*w religii*) offering **4** (*poświęcenie*) sacrifice **5** (*wypadku, przestępstwa*) victim **6** (*pot: pechowiec*) sucker

ofice|r (**-ra, -rowie**; *loc sg* **-rze**) *m* officer

oficjalny *adj* formal

ogień (**ognia, ognie**; *gen pl* **ogni**) *m* **1** (*płomień*) fire **2** (*zapalniczka*) light **3** (*przen: zapał*) fervour (*Brit*), fervor (*US*) **4** (*gwałtowna uczucie*) passion; **zimne ognie** sparklers; **sztuczne ognie** fireworks

oglą|dać (**-am, -asz**; *pf* **obejrzeć**) *vt* **1** (*ilustrację*) to look at **2** (*telewizję*) to watch **3** (*wystawę, zabytki*) to see; **~ się** *vr* **1** (*patrzeć na swoje odbicie*) to look at o.s. **2** (*spoglądać w tył*) to look back **3** (*rozglądać się*) to look around

ogłasz|ać (**-am, -asz**; *pf* **ogłosić**) *vt* **1** (*w gazecie*) to announce **2** (*program polityczny*) to issue **3** (*niepodległość*) to declare **4** (*konkurs*) to announce **5** (*w sądzie*) to publish **6** (*stan wyjątkowy*) to proclaim; **~ się** *vr* (*w gazecie*) to advertise

ogłosze|nie (**-nia, -nia**; *gen pl* **-ń**) *nt* **1** announcement **2** (*w prasie*) notice **3** (*informacja w gazecie*) announcement **4** (*reklama*) ad, advertisement

ognis|ko (**-ka, -ka**; *inst sg* **-kiem**) *nt* **1** (*ogień*) bonfire **2** (*impreza na powietrzu*) (camp)fire **3** (*centrum*) centre (*Brit*), center (*US*) **4** (*kółko hobbystyczne*) group **5** (*w fizyce, fotografii, medycynie*) focus

ogol|ić (**-ę, -isz**; *imp* **ogol** *lub* **ogól**) *vb pf od* **golić**

ogo|n (**-na, -ny**; *loc sg* **-nie**) *m* tail; **diabeł to ~em nakrył** it vanished into thin air

ogólnie *adv* generally; **~ biorąc należy się temu raz jeszcze przyjrzeć** it is necessary, on the whole, to have another look at this; **~ mówiąc wszystko się powiodło** generally speaking everything was successful

ogólnokrajowy adj nationwide

ogólnokształcący adj (liceum) secondary education

ogólnopolski adj all-Poland

ogólny adj 1 (opinia) general 2 (powszechny) common 3 (bez szczegółów) general 4 (suma) total

ogór|ek (-ka, -ki; inst sg -kiem) m cucumber

ogranicz|ać (-am, -asz; pf -yć) vt 1 (teren) to delimit 2 (zakres działań) to limit 3 (swobodę) to restrict 4 (koszty) to reduce 5 (szybkość) to limit; **~ się** vr to limit o.s.; **~ wydatki** to cut down on spending; **~ się do** +gen (jednej kanapki) to limit o.s. to; (jednej sprawy) to be restricted to; (sprowadzać się do) to boil down to

ogranicze|nie (-nia, -nia; gen pl -ń) nt 1 (przepis) restriction 2 (głupota) limitations pl; **~ prędkości do 50 km/h** 50 km/h speed limit

ogrodnict|wo (-wa; loc sg -wie) nt gardening

ogrodni|k (-ka, -cy; inst sg -kiem) m (zawodowy, amator) gardener

ogrodze|nie (-nia, -nia; gen pl -ń) nt fence; **~ murowane** wall; **~ z żywopłotu** hedge

ogromny adj 1 (budynek) huge 2 (rozległy) vast 3 (uczucie) immense

ogr|ód (-odu, -ody; loc sg -odzie) m garden; **~ zoologiczny** zoo, zoological garden(s pl); **~ botaniczny** botanical garden(s

pl); **warzywa prosto z ogrodu** garden-fresh vegetables

ogród|ek (-ka, -ki; inst sg -kiem) m 1 (niewielki ogród) garden 2 (przy restauracji) open-air café; **~ działkowy** allotment

ogródek inv: **mówić (powiedzieć** pf) **coś bez ~** to say sth bluntly

ogrzew|ać (-am, -asz; pf ogrzać) vt 1 (mieszkanie) to heat 2 (dłonie) to warm up; **~ się** vr to warm up; **pokój szybko się ogrzał** the room got warm quickly

ogrzewani|e (-a) nt heating; **centralne ~** central heating

ogumieni|e (-a) nt (opony samochodowe) tyres pl (Brit), tires pl (US)

ohydny adj (obrzydliwy) hideous

oj|ciec (-ca, -cowie; dat sg & loc sg -cu; voc sg -cze) m 1 father 2 (założyciel instytucji) (founding) father; **ojcowie** pl (przodkowie) forefathers, ancestors; **~ chrzestny** godfather; **~ Święty** (papież) holy Father, the Pope

ojczy|m (-ma, -mowie lub -mi; loc sg -mie) m stepfather

ojczysty adj (język, kraj) native; **język ~** mother tongue

ojczy|zna (-zny, -zny; dat sg & loc sg -źnie) f 1 (kraj rodzinny) homeland 2 (przen: kolebka) cradle

ok. abbr (= około) about, ca.

okazj|a (-i, -e; gen pl -i) f 1 (szansa) opportunity 2 (korzystnego zakupu) bargain 3 (sprzyjająca okoliczność) occasion; **a przy okazji, wpadnij do nas jutro** if you get the chance, pay us a visit tomorrow; **wszystkiego najlepszego z okazji urodzin**

happy birthday

okaz|ywać (**-uję, -ujesz**; *pf* **-ać**) *vt* **1** (*pokazywać*) to show **2** (*wyrażać uczucia*) to demonstrate **3** (*odwagę, zainteresowanie*) to demonstrate; **~ się** *vr* to turn out (to be); **okazało się, że wyszedł wcześniej** it turned out that he left earlier

okien|ko (**-ka, -ka**; *inst sg* **-kiem**; *gen pl* **-ek**) *nt* **1** *dimin od* **okno 2** (*stanowisko w sklepie, urzędzie*) counter **3** (*w kopercie*) window **4** (*w szkole: wolna godzina*) free period

oklas|ki (**-ków**) *pl* applause *sg*

oklas|kiwać (**-kuję, -kujesz**) *vt* to applaud; **gorąco oklaskiwano jej występ** she received rapturous applause for her performance

okłam|ywać (**-uję, -ujesz**; *pf* **-ać**) *vt* to deceive; **nie okłamuj się** don't deceive yourself

okno (**okna, okna**; *loc sg* **oknie**; *gen pl* **okien**) *nt* window; **~ wystawowe** shop window

oko¹ (**oka, oczy**; *gen pl* **oczu**; *dat pl & loc sg* **oczom**; *inst pl* **oczami** *lub* **oczyma**) *nt* **1** (*Anat*) eye **2** (*zmysł*) (eye)sight; **na ~ sto metrów** roughly one hundred metres (*Brit*) *lub* meters (*US*); **na pierwszy rzut oka wygląda nieźle** at first glance it doesn't look too bad; **rozmawiali w cztery oczy** they spoke face to face; **od dawna ma ją na oku** he's had his eye on her for a long time; **ona nie spuszcza go z oczu** she never lets him out of her sight; **przymykała oczy na jego wady** she turned a blind

eye to his faults; **ten wzór rzucał się w oczy** the design *lub* pattern stood out

oko² (**oka, oka**) *nt* **1** (*cyklonu*) eye **2** (*w sieci*) mesh **3** (*w rosole*) drops of fat in a broth

okolic|a (**-y, -e**) *f* **1** (*bliskie otoczenie*) neighbourhood (*Brit*), neighborhood (*US*) **2** (*region*) district

okoliczność (**-ci, -ci**) *f* **1** (*sposobność*) occasion **2** (*sytuacja*) circumstance; **okoliczności** *pl* circumstances

około *prep* +*gen* about

okrad|ać (**-am, -asz**; *pf* **okraść**) *vt*: **~ kogoś (z czegoś)** to rob sb (of sth)

okr|ąg (**-ęgu, -ęgi**; *inst sg* **-ęgiem**) *m* (*figura geometryczna*) circle

okrągły *adj* round

okre|s (**-su, -sy**; *loc sg* **-sie**) *m* **1** (*w życie*) period **2** (*czas*) time **3** (*faza*) stage **4** (*romantyzmu*) era **5** (*Szkol*) term, semester **6** (*menstruacja*) period **7** (*w astronomii, fizyce*) period

określe|nie (**-nie, -nia**; *gen pl* **-ń**) *nt* **1** (*epitet*) epithet, name **2** (*w językoznawstwie*) modifier **3** (*termin*) terminology

określony *adj* (*konkretny*) specific, definite

okręc|ać (**-am, -asz**; *pf* **okręcić**) *vt* **1** (*owijać wokół*) to wrap **2** (*w tańcu*) to spin; **~ się** *vr* **1** (*wokół palca*) to twist around **2** (*kręcić się wkoło*) to turn (round *lub* around), to spin (round *lub* around)

okrę|t (**-tu, -ty**; *loc sg* **-cie**) *m* **1** (*wojenny*) warship **2** (*pot: duży statek*) ship **3** (*podwodny*) submarine

okropny adj **1** (widok, charakter) horrible **2** (osoba nie do zniesienia) terrible **3** (aura) awful

okrucieńst|wo (**-wa**; loc sg **-wie**) nt cruelty; **okrucieństwa** pl atrocities

okrutny adj (czyn, człowiek) cruel

okryw|ać (**-am, -asz**; pf **okryć**) vt (przykrywać) to cover

okrzy|k (**-ku, -ki**; inst sg **-kiem**) m (radości, bólu) shout, cry

okular|y (**-ów**) pl **1** (korekcyjne) glasses, spectacles **2** ((przeciw)słoneczne) sunglasses **3** (ochronne) (safety) goggles; **patrzy na sytuację przez różowe ~** to see things through rose-tinted spectacles

okuli|sta (**-sty, -ści**; dat sg & loc sg **-ście**) m decl like f in sg optician (Brit), optometrist (US)

oku|p (**-pu**; loc sg **-pie**) m ransom

okupacj|a (**-i, -e**; gen pl **-i**) f **1** (wojskowa) occupation **2** (w prawie) occupancy

okup|ować (**-uję, -ujesz**) vt (zajmować) to occupy

olbrzymi adj enormous

ole|j (**-ju, -je**; gen pl **-i** lub **-jów**) m oil; **obraz ~ny** oil painting; **~ słonecznikowy/rzepakowy** sunflower/rape-seed oil; **~ napędowy** diesel oil

olimpia|da (**-dy, -dy**; dat sg & loc sg **-dzie**) f **1** (Sport) the Olympics pl, the Olympic Games pl **2** (zawody) contest

olimpijski adj **1** (związany z Olimpiadą) Olympic **2** (postawa) Olympian

oli|wa (**-wy**; dat sg & loc sg **-wie**) f **1** (z oliwek) olive oil **2** (Kulin) (salad lub cooking) oil **3** (mineralny) oil (lubricant)

oliw|ka (**-ki, -ki**; dat sg & loc sg **-ce**; gen pl **-ek**) f **1** (owoc) olive **2** (drzewo) olive (tree)

oł|ów (**-owiu**) m lead; **benzyna bezołowiowa** unleaded fuel

ołów|ek (**-ka, -ki**; inst sg **-kiem**) m **1** pencil **2** (automatyczny) propelling lub mechanical pencil **3** (do brwi) eyebrow pencil

ołtarz (**-a, -e**; gen pl **-y**) m altar

omawi|ać (**-am, -asz**; pf **omówić**) vt (problem, zagadnienie) to discuss, to talk over

omij|ać (**-am, -asz**; pf **ominąć**) vt **1** (wybierać okrężną drogę) to go (a)round **2** (unikać: problemów) to avoid **3** (łamać zakaz, prawo) to dodge

omle|t (**-tu** lub **-ta, -ty**; loc sg **-cie**) m omelette (Brit), omelet (US)

on pron **1** (o osobie: w pozycji podmiotu) he **2** (w innych pozycjach) him **3** (o zwierzęciu, rzeczy, pojęciu) it; **to on!** that's him!

ona pron **1** (o osobie: w pozycji podmiotu) she **2** (w innych pozycjach) her **3** (o zwierzęciu, rzeczy, pojęciu) it; **to ~!** that's her!

onaniz|ować się (**-uję, -ujesz**) vr to masturbate

one pron **1** (w pozycji podmiotu) they **2** (w innych pozycjach) them

oni pron **1** (w pozycji podmiotu) they **2** (w innych pozycjach) them

onieśmiel|ać (**-am, -asz**; pf **-ić**) vt (zawstydzać) to intimidate

onieśmielony adj (zawstydzony) intimidated

onkologi|a (**-i**) f oncology

ono *pron* it

ONZ (**ONZ-etu**; *loc sg* **ONZ-ecie**) *m abbr* (= *Organizacja Narodów Zjednoczonych*) UN

opad|ać (**-am, -asz**; *pf* **opaść**) *vi* **1** (*liści*) to fall **2** (*mgła*) to descend **3** (*o zawiesinie*) to settle **4** (*o roślinach*) to die **5** (*o ciśnieniu*) to fall **6** (*obniżać się*) to descend, to subside **7** (*ustępować*) to subside

opak: na ~ the wrong way round

opakowa|nie (**-nia, -nia**; *gen pl* **-ń**) *nt* **1** (*szklane, plastikowe*) packaging **2** (*z zawartością*) package

opal|ać (**-am, -asz**; *pf* **-ić**) *vt* (*dom*) to heat; **~ się** *vr*: **~ się na słońcu** to sunbathe

opalony *adj* (sun)tanned

oparze|nie (**-nia, -nia**; *gen pl* **-ń**) *nt* (*słoneczne, chemiczne*) burn

oparz|yć (**-ę, -ysz**) *vt pf* **1** (*płomieniem, gorącym metalem*) to burn **2** (*gorącą wodą*) to scald **3** (*chemiczne*) to burn; **~ się** *vr pf* to get burned; **~ się w rękę** to burn one's hand

opatrun|ek (**-ku, -ki**; *inst sg* **-kiem**) *m* (*plaster, bandaż*) dressing

opcj|a (**-i, -e**; *gen pl* **-i**) *f* (*możliwość*) option

ope|ra (**-ry, -ry**; *dat sg & loc sg* **-rze**) *f* **1** (*przedstawienie*) opera **2** (*budynek*) opera house

operacj|a (**-i, -e**; *gen pl* **-i**) *f* **1** (*zabieg chirurgiczny*) operation, surgery **2** (*finansowa*) transaction **3** (*wojskowa*) operation; **~ plastyczna** (*w medycynie*) cosmetic surgery

oper|ować (**-uję, -ujesz**) *vi*

to operate ▷ *vt* (*pf* **z-**) (*zabieg chirurgiczny*) to operate on; **doskonale operował głosem** he used his voice brilliantly

opie|ka (**-ki**; *dat sg & loc sg* **-ce**) *f* **1** (*troska*) care, protection **2** (*dozór*) care, charge **3** (*pomoc: medyczna*) care, assistance **4** (*Jur*) protection **5** (*przyznawana przez sąd*) custody, guardianship; **~ społeczna** social welfare

opiek|ować się (**-uję, -ujesz**; *pf* **za-**) *vr*: **~ się kimś/czymś** (*troszczyć się*) to look after sb/sth; (*zajmować się*) to take care of sb/sth

opieku|n (**-na, -nowie**; *loc sg* **-nie**) *m* **1** (*osób starszych*) carer **2** (*przyznawany przez sąd*) guardian; **~ społeczny** social worker

opiekun|ka (**-ki, -ki**; *dat sg & loc sg* **-ce**; *gen pl* **-ek**) *f* carer; **~ do dziecka** (*niania*) child-minder, baby-sitter

opier|ać (**-am, -asz**; *pf* **oprzeć**) *vt*: **~ coś o** to prop *lub* lean sth against; **~ coś na** +*loc* to rest sth against, to put sth on; (*przen*) to base sth on; **~ się** *vr*: **~ się komuś/czemuś** to resist sb/sth; **~ się o** to lean against; **~ się na** +*loc* (*o poglądach, opiniach*) to be based on; (*polegać na: bliskich, znajomych*) to rely on; **~ się na lasce** to lean on a walking stick

opini|a (**-i, -e**; *gen pl* **-i**) *f* **1** (*pogląd*) view, opinion **2** (*renoma*) opinion, reputation **3** (*ocena*) judgement; **badanie opinii publicznej** (public) opinion poll

opi|s (**-su, -sy**; *loc sg* **-sie**) *m* **1** description **2** (*relacja wydarzenia*)

account
opis|ywać (-uję, -ujesz; pf **-ać**) vt
to describe
opłac|ać (-am, -asz; pf **opłacić**) vt
1 (czesne) to pay 2 (dawać łapówkę)
to bribe; **~ się** vr to pay; **nie
opłaca się tego robić** it's not
worth doing; **ta transakcja się
nie opłaca** this deal isn't worth
the trouble; **w końcu opłaciło
się!** finally, it was worth my
while!
opłacalny adj (interes) profitable
opła|ta (-ty, -ty; dat sg & loc sg **-cie**)
f 1 (za usługę) payment 2 (za naukę)
fee 3 (za bilet) fare 4 (urzędowa)
payment
opodatkowani|e (-a) nt
taxation
opo|na (-ny, -ny; dat sg & loc sg
-nie) f (ogumienie) tyre (Brit), tire
(US); **opony** pl: **zapalenie opon
mózgowych** meningitis
opowiad|ać (-am, -asz; pf
opowiedzieć) vi: **~ (o** +loc) (bajkę,
wydarzenie) to talk (about) ▷ vt
to tell; **~ się** vr: **~ się za** +inst
(popierać) to be in favour (Brit) lub
favor (US) of
opowiada|nie (-nia, -nia; gen pl
-ń) nt 1 (historia) story 2 (krótki
utwór literacki) short story
opowieś|ć (-ci, -ci; gen pl **-ci**) f
tale, story
opozycj|a (-i, -e; gen pl **-i**) f
(parlamentarna, polityczna)
opposition
opozycyjny adj 1 (partia,
stowarzyszenie) opposition
2 (postępowanie) oppositional
op|ór (-oru; loc sg **-orze**) m
(sprzeciw) resistance; **ruch oporu**

resistance movement
opóźnie|nie (-nia, -nia; gen pl **-ń**)
nt delay
opóźniony adj 1 (samolot) delayed
2 (intelektualnie) retarded (pej)
oprocentowa|nie (-nia, -nia; gen
pl **-ń**) nt interest (rate)
oprogramowa|nie (-nia, -nia;
gen pl **-ń**) nt software
oprócz prep +gen 1 (poza czymś)
apart from 2 (z wyjątkiem) except;
~ tego jest lekarzem apart from
that he is also a doctor
optyczny adj (urządzenie,
złudzenie) optical
opty|k (-ka, -cy; inst sg **-kiem**) m
optician
optymalny adj optimal
optymi|sta (-sty, -ści; loc sg **-ście**)
m decl like f in sg optimist
optymist|ka (-ki, -ki; dat sg & loc
sg **-ce**) f optimist
optymistyczny adj (wiadomość,
stosunek) optimistic
optymiz|m (-mu; loc sg **-mie**) m
optimism
opuchli|zna (-zny; dat sg & loc sg
-źnie) f (narządów wewnętrznych,
zewnętrznych) swelling
opuchnięty adj (człowiek, noga)
swollen
opuszcz|ać (-am, -asz; pf
opuścić) vt 1 (obniżać) to lower
2 (Mot: szybę) to wind down
3 (porzucać rodzinę) to abandon
4 (dom, firmę) to leave 5 (lekcje,
zajęcia) to miss 6 (pomijać) to
leave out; **~ się** vr 1 (obniżać się)
to lower 2 (na linie) to let o.s. down;
nie opuściła go mimo kłopotów
in spite of the problems she stuck
by him

oranguta|n (**-na**, **-ny**; *loc sg* **-nie**) *m* orang-utan(g)

oranża|da (**-dy**, **-dy**; *dat sg & loc sg* **-dzie**) *f* (*gazowany napój owocowy*) orangeade

oraz *conj* as well as

orga|n (**-nu**, **-ny**; *loc sg* **-nie**) *m* (*wewnętrzny w ciele, władzy*) organ; **organy** *pl* (*instrument muzyczny*) organ *sg*

organizacj|a (**-i**, **-e**; *gen pl* **-i**) *f* organization

organizato|r (**-ra**, **-rzy**; *loc sg* **-rze**) *m* organizer

organiz|m (**-mu**, **-my**; *loc sg* **-mie**) *m* organism; **~ człowieka** the human body

organiz|ować (**-uję**, **-ujesz**; *pf* **z-**) *vt* **1** (*wyjazd, zawody*) to organize **2** (*imprezę*) to arrange **3** (*stowarzyszenie*) to set up **4** (*pot: samochód*) to sort out; **~ się** *vr* to organize

orgaz|m (**-mu**, **-my**; *loc sg* **-mie**) *m* orgasm

orientalny *adj* (*kuchnia, styl*) oriental

orkiest|ra (**-ry**, **-ry**; *dat sg & loc sg* **-rze**) *f* **1** orchestra **2** (*na weselu*) band

ortografi|a (**-i**, **-e**; *gen pl* **-i**) *f* **1** (*zasady pisowni*) orthography **2** (*pisownia*) spelling

ortograficzny *adj*: **słownik/ błąd ~** dictionary/spelling mistake

oryginalny *adj* **1** (*niepowtarzalny*) original **2** (*prawdziwy*) genuine **3** (*unikatowy*) unique

orygina|ł (**-łu**, **-ły**; *loc sg* **-le**) *m* **1** (*pisma, dzieła sztuki*) original **2** (*o osobie*) eccentric

orzech (**-a**, **-y**) *m* (*owoc*) nut; **~ ziemny** peanut; **~ laskowy** hazelnut; **~ włoski** walnut; **czekolada z ~ami** chocolate with nuts; **dziadek do ~ów** nutcracker

orzechowy *adj* (*barwa*) nut-brown; **masło orzechowe** peanut butter

orze|ł (**orła**, **orły**; *loc sg* **orle**) *m* **1** eagle **2** (*przen: osoba pozytywnie wyróżniająca się*) high-flier; **~ czy reszka?** heads or tails?

orzeź|wiać (**-wiam**, **-wiasz**; *pf* **-wić**) *vt* to refresh; **~ się** *vr* (*odświeżać się*) to refresh o.s.

osa (**osy**, **osy**; *dat sg & loc sg* **osie**) *f* wasp

osiąg|ać (**-am**, **-asz**; *pf* **-nąć**) *vt* **1** (*efekt, cel*) to achieve, to accomplish **2** (*szczyt*) to reach

osiągalny *adj* (*możliwy do zrealizowania*) attainable

osiągnię|cie (**-cia**, **-cia**; *gen pl* **-ć**) *nt* achievement

osiedl|e (**-a**, **-a**; *gen pl* **-i**) *nt* **1** (*też:* **~ mieszkaniowe**) (housing) estate (*Brit*), housing development (*US*) **2** (*Hist*) settlement

○ **OSIEDLE MIESZKANIOWE**
○
○ **Osiedle mieszkaniowe** is
○ a common feature in Polish
○ cities. This is a small area
○ where there are a large
○ number of huge blocks of flats
○ with thousands of residents.
○ Residential areas such as
○ these were built on a large
○ scale in the 1970s and 1980s.

osiem *num* eight
osiemdziesiąt *num* eighty
osiemnasty *adj* eighteenth
osiemnaście *num* eighteen
osiemset *num* eight hundred
oskarż|ać (**-am, -asz**; *pf* **-yć**)
vt: **~ kogoś (o coś)** to accuse sb
(of sth); (*w sądzie*) to charge sb
(with sth)
oskarże|nie (**-nia, -nia**; *gen*
pl **-ń**) *nt* **1** (*zarzut*) accusation
2 (*w sądzie: strona oskarżająca*)
prosecution; **akt oskarżenia**
indictment
oskarżon|a (**-ej, -e**) *f decl like*
adj (*w sądzie*) the accused, the
defendant
oskarż|ony (**-onego, -eni**) *m decl*
like adj (*w sądzie*) the accused, the
defendant
oskarżyciel (**-a, -e**) *m* (*prokurator*)
prosecutor
osłabiony *adj* (*psychicznie,*
fizycznie) weak
os|oba (**-oby, -oby**; *dat sg & loc*
sg **-obie**; *gen pl* **-ób**) *f* **1** (*człowiek*)
person **2** (*w językoznawstwie*)
person **3** (*w filmie*) character,
protagonist; **namiot**
mieszczący cztery osoby four-
man tent; **~ fizyczna** private
individual; **~ prawna** legal entity
lub person; **~ trzecia** third party
osobistoś|ć (**-ci, -ci**; *gen pl* **-ci**)
f **1** (*ważna osoba*) personage
2 (*sławna osoba*) celebrity,
personality
osobisty *adj* (*bielizna, sukces*)
personal; **dowód ~** ≈ identity
card; **komputer ~** personal
computer
osobiście *adv* (*we własnej osobie*)

personally, in person
osobno *adv* (*oddzielnie*) separately
osobny *adj* (*pokój*) separate;
każdy z osobna separately,
individually
osobowoś|ć (**-ci, -ci**; *gen pl* **-ci**) *f*
(*charakter*) personality
osobowy *adj* **1** (*dla pasażerów*)
passenger **2** (*w językoznawstwie*)
personal; **pociąg ~** slow *lub*
local train
ostatecznie *adv* **1** (*zdecydować,*
zakończyć) finally, ultimately
2 (*ewentualnie*) after all
ostateczny *adj* (*definitywny*) final
ostatni *adj* **1** (*końcowy*) last
2 (*najnowszy*) latest **3** (*finałowy*)
final **4** (*pośród wymienionych*)
(the) latter
ostatnio *adv* (*niedawno*) recently,
lately
ostro *adv* sharply, harshly
ostrożnie *adv* carefully; **~!** watch
out!; **„~"** (*poczta*) "(handle) with
care"
ostry *adj* **1** sharp **2** (*mróz*) severe,
hard **3** (*przyprawa*) spicy **4** (*Mat*)
acute **5** (*ból*) acute
ostrz|e (**-a, -a**; *gen pl* **-y**) *nt* **1** (*noża*)
blade, edge **2** (*ostre zakończenie*)
point
ostrzeg|ać (**-am, -asz**; *pf* **ostrzec**)
vt: **~ kogoś (o czymś)** to warn
sb (of sth); **ostrzegł go przed**
niebezpieczeństwem he warned
him of the danger
ostrzegawczy *adj* (*sygnał, strzał*)
warning
ostrzeże|nie (**-nia, -nia**; *gen pl* **-ń**)
nt warning
ostrz|yć (**-ę, -ysz**; *pf* **na-**) *vt* (*nóż*)
to sharpen

osusz|ać (**-am, -asz**; pf **-yć**) vt
1 (wycierać z potu, łez) to wipe, to
dry 2 (teren) to drain

oszac|ować (**-uję, -ujesz**) vb pf
od **szacować**

oszale|ć (**-ję, -jesz**) vi pf
(zwariować) to go mad

oszczędnoś|ć (**-ci**) f 1 (sposób
postępowania) thrift 2 (wody,
prądu) economy; **oszczędności**
pl savings

oszczędny adj 1 (osoba) thrifty
2 (sposób działania) economical
3 (maszyna) energy-efficient

oszczędz|ać (**-am, -asz**) vt
1 (pieniądze) to save 2 (czas) to
save 3 (prąd) to conserve, to
save 4 (siły, osobę) to spare ▷ vi
1 (żyć oszczędnie) to economize
2 (oszczędzać pieniądze) to save (up)

oszczę|dzić (**-dzę, -dzisz**; imp
-dź) vt pf: **~ kogoś** (chronić
kogoś) to spare sb; **tragedia
nie oszczędziła nikogo** the
catastrophe spared nobody;
chciał ~ sobie kłopotów he
wanted to spare himself the
trouble

oszu|kiwać (**-kuję, -kujesz**; pf
-kać) vi (na egzaminie) to cheat
▷ vt (zdradzać) to deceive

oszu|st (**-sta, -ści**; loc sg **-ście**)
m cheat

oszust|ka (**-ki, -ki**; dat sg & loc sg
-ce; gen pl **-ek**) f cheat

oszust|wo (**-wa, -wa**; loc sg **-wie**)
nt (finansowe, podatkowe) fraud

ośmiel|ać (**-am, -asz**; pf **-ić**) vt
(dodawać odwagi) to encourage;
~ się vr 1 (stać się śmiałym) to gain
confidence 2 (mieć odwagę) to
dare 3 (mieć czelność) to dare

ośmiesz|ać (**-am, -asz**; pf **-yć**) vt
(wyśmiewać się) to ridicule; **~ się** vr
(poniżać się) to make a fool of o.s.

ośmioro num eight

ośrod|ek (**-ka, -ki**; inst sg **-kiem**) m
(centrum, instytucja) centre (Brit),
center (US); **~ zdrowia** health
centre; **~ wypoczynkowy** resort,
holiday camp

oświadcz|ać (**-am, -asz**; pf **-yć**)
vt (stwierdzać) to declare; **~ się**
vr: **~ się komuś** (proponować
małżeństwo) to propose to sb

oświadcze|nie (**-nia, -nia**; gen pl
-ń) nt (deklaracja) statement; **~
podatkowe** tax return

oświadczyn|y (**-**) pl marriage
proposal

oświa|ta (**-ty**; dat sg & loc sg **-cie**) f
(nauka, edukacja) education

oświetl|ać (**-am, -asz**; pf **-ić**) vt to
illuminate

oświetleni|e (**-a**) nt lighting

Oświęci|m (**-mia**; loc sg **-miu**) m
Auschwitz

otacz|ać (**-am, -asz**; pf **otoczyć**)
vt 1 (okrążać) to surround 2 (o
ogrodzeniu) to enclose; **~ się** vr: **~
się kimś/czymś** to surround o.s.
with sb/sth

oto part: **~ nasz kot** that's our cat;
~ wszystko, co wiem that's all I
know; **~ jestem** here I am

otoczeni|e (**-a**) nt 1 (okolica)
surroundings pl 2 (środowisko
naturalne) environment

otru|ć (**-ję, -jesz**) vt pf (podać
truciznę) to poison; **~ się** vr pf to
poison o.s.

otrzym|ywać (**-uję, -ujesz**; pf
-ać) vt (list, wynagrodzenie) to
receive

otwarcie¹ adv (szczerze) openly

otwar|cie² (**-cia, -cia**; gen pl **-ć**) nt
(sklepu, firmy) opening; **godziny
otwarcia od 8.00 do 16.00**
opening hours: 8 am to 4 pm

otwarty adj (sklep, człowiek) open;
list ~ open letter; **grał z nimi w
otwarte karty** (przen) to lay one's
cards on the table; **posiedzenie
obyło się przy drzwiach ~ch** it
was an open meeting (attended
by the media); **u otwarte** (w
językoznawstwie) the letter u

otwieracz (**-a, -e**; gen pl **-y**) m
opener; **~ do puszek** lub **konserw**
tin-opener (Brit), can-opener
(US); **~ do butelek** bottle-opener

otwier|ać (**-am, -asz**; pf
otworzyć) vt 1 to open 2 (zamek
w drzwiach) to unlock 3 (odkręcać
wodę, gaz) to turn on; **~ się** vr
1 to open 2 (widok) to open
up; **otworzył się przed nią** he
opened up to her

otyłoś|ć (**-ci**) f obesity

otyły adj obese

owa|d (**-da, -dy**; loc sg **-dzie**) m
insect

owadobójczy adj: **rodek ~**
insecticide

owca (**owcy, owce**; gen pl **owiec**)
f sheep; **był czarną owcą w
rodzinie** (przen) he was the black
sheep of the family

owij|ać (**-am, -asz**; pf **owinąć**)
vt 1 (bandażem) to wrap (around)
2 (papierem, folią) to wrap up
3 (kołdrą, kocem) to wrap (up); **był
szczery i nie owijał w bawełnę**
he was honest and didn't beat
about the bush

owłosiony adj (nogi) hairy

owoc (**-u, -e**) m fruit; **owoce**
pl fruit

owocowy adj (napój, sad) fruit

owsian|ka (**-ki, -ki**; dat sg & loc sg
-ce) f porridge

ozdabi|ać (**-am, -asz**; pf **ozdobić**)
vt (pokój) to decorate

ozdobny adj (wazon, mebel)
decorative

oznacz|ać (**-am, -asz**)
vt 1 (znaczyć) to mean
2 (przedstawiać) to represent, to
signify 3 (o wyrazie) to stand for,
to mean 4 (pf **-yć**) (postawić znak)
to mark; **co to oznacza?** what
does this mean?; **oznacza to, że
wygrał** this means that he won

ozo|n (**-nu**; loc sg **-nie**) m (gaz)
ozone

ó p

ósem|ka (**-ki**, **-ki**; *dat sg & loc sg*
-ce) *f* **1** eight **2** (*kształt*) figure
of eight (*Brit*), figure eight (*US*)
3 (*w muzyce*) quaver (*Brit*), eighth
note (*US*)

ósmy *adj* eighth; **jedna ósma**
one eighth; **jest (godzina) ósma**
it's eight o'clock

ówczesny *adj*: **~ premier** the
then Prime Minister

p. *abbr* **1** (= *pan*) Mr **2** (= *pani*) Mrs
pa|cha (**-chy**, **-chy**; *dat sg & loc sg*
-sze) *f* armpit
pach|nieć (**-nę, -niesz**; *imp* **-nij**) *vi*
to smell; **~ czymś** to smell of sth
pacjen|t (**-ta, -ci**; *loc sg* **-cie**) *m*
(*nowy, regularny, stały*) patient
pacjent|ka (**-ki, -ki**; *dat sg & loc
sg* **-ce**; *gen pl* **-ek**) *f* (*szpitala,
przychodni*) patient
Pacyfi|k (**-ku**; *inst sg* **-kiem**) *m*
(*Ocean Spokojny*) the Pacific
pacyfi|sta (**-sty, -ści**; *dat sg & loc sg*
-ście) *m decl like f in sg* (*zagorzały*)
pacifist
pacz|ka (**-ki, -ki**; *dat sg* **-ce**; *gen
pl* **-ek**) *f* **1** (*mała paka*) package
2 (*Poczta*) parcel **3** (*papierosów*)
packet (*Brit*), pack(age) (*US*)
padacz|ka (**-ki**; *dat sg & loc sg* **-ce**)

(*epilepsja*) f epilepsy; **cierpieć na padaczkę** to suffer from epilepsy; **atak padaczki** epileptic fit

pad|ać (**-am, -asz**; *pf* **paść**) *vi* to fall; **pada (deszcz)** it's raining; **pada śnieg/grad** it's snowing/hailing

pagór|ek (**-ka, -ki**; *inst sg* **-kiem**) *m* hillock

pają|k (**-ka, -ki**; *inst sg* **-kiem**) *m* spider

pak|ować (**-uję, -ujesz**) *vt* 1 (*pf* **s-** *lub* **za-**) (*walizkę*) to pack 2 (*pf* **o-**) (*prezent*) to wrap (up); **~ się** *vr* 1 (*pf* **s-** *lub* **za-**) to pack (up) 2 (*pf* **w-**) (*pot: pychać się*) to barge in

palący *adj* 1 (*słońce, ból*) blazing 2 (*przen: pytanie*) urgent ▷ *m decl like adj* (*ten który pali*) smoker; **przedział/wagon dla ~ch** smoking compartment/carriage

pal|ec (**-ca, -ce**) *m* 1 (*u nogi*) toe 2 (*u ręki*) finger; **ten starszy człowiek jest sam jak ~** that elderly person is all alone; **maczać w czymś palce** (*przen*) to have a hand in sth; **mieć coś w małym palcu** (*przen*) to know sth inside out; **chodzić na palcach** to tiptoe

paleni|e (**-a**) *nt* 1 (*tytoniu, fajki, papierosów*) smoking 2 (*śmieci*) incineration; **~ wzbronione** no smoking; **~ szkodzi zdrowiu** smoking is bad for your health

Palesty|na (**-ny**; *dat sg* **-nie**) f Palestine

pal|ić (**-ę, -isz**) *vt* 1 (*świecy*) to burn 2 (*światła*) to keep on 3 (*papierosy*) to smoke 4 (*pf* **s-**) (*niszczyć ogniem*) to burn (down) ▷ *vi* (*palić papierosy*) to smoke; **~**

się *vr* 1 (*płonąć*) to burn 2 (*o domu*) to be on fire 3 (*o świetle*) to be on; **pali się!** fire!

palny *adj* (*materiał, substancja, produkt*) flammable; **łatwo ~** (highly) flammable; **broń palna** firearms *pl*

pałac (**-u, -e**) *m* (*królewski, książęcy, wspaniały*) palace

pamiąt|ka (**-ki, -ki**; *dat sg & loc sg* **-ce**; *gen pl* **-ek**) f 1 (*z wakacji*) souvenir 2 (*symbol*) token; **sklep z ~mi** souvenir shop; **na pamiątkę (czegoś)** in memory (of sth); **nasze miejscowe muzeum gromadzi pamiątki z przeszłości miasta** our local museum collects mementos of the town's history

pamię|ć (**-ci**) f memory; **z pamięci** from memory; **uczyć (nauczyć** *pf*) **się czegoś na ~** to learn sth by heart

pamięt|ać (**-am, -asz**; *pf* **za-**) *vt* to remember ▷ *vi*: **~ o kimś/ czymś** to keep sb/sth in mind; **~ coś zrobić** to remember to do sth

pamiętni|k (**-ka, -ki**; *inst sg* **-kiem**) *m* (*nastolatki: dziecięcy, sekretny*) diary; **pamiętniki** *pl* (*Lit: opasłe, wieloletnie*) memoirs *pl*

○ **PAN/PANI**
○
○ The polite form of address
○ in Polish is expressed using
○ **Pan** (gentleman) or **Pani**
○ (lady) in the singular and
○ **Panowie** (gentlemen), **Panie**
○ (ladies) or **Państwo** (ladies
○ and gentlemen) in the plural
○ plus the verb in the third

person. The polite form is very common and should be used when addressing someone you do not know well, or someone who is older or more senior than yourself. Unlike English, which commonly includes the surname in polite forms of address, e.g. Mr Brown, it is more common in Polish to address someone simply as **Pan** or **Pani**.

pa|n (**-na, -nowie**; *dat sg & loc sg* **-nu**; *voc sg* **-nie**) *m* **1** (*mężczyzna*) gentleman **2** (*zaimek*) you **3** (*Bóg*) Lord **4** (*arystokrata*) lord **5** (*właściciel psa*) master **6** (*pot: nauczyciel*) teacher; **P~ Kowalski** Mr Kowalski; **proszę P~a!** excuse me, sir!; **P~ Bóg** Lord God; **~ młody** (bride)groom

pa|ni (**-ni, -nie**; *acc sg* **-nią**; *gen pl* **-ń**) *f* **1** (*kobieta*) lady **2** (*przy zwracaniu się*) you **3** (*pot: nauczycielka*) teacher; **P~ Kowalska** Mrs Kowalski; **proszę P~!** excuse me, madam!

panieński *adj:* **nazwisko ~e** maiden name; **stan ~** unmarried

pani|ka (**-ki**; *dat sg & loc sg* **-ce**) *f* panic; **gdy wyłączono prąd, miasto ogarnęła ~** the town was in a state of panic when the power was cut

panik|ować (**-uję, -ujesz**; *pf* **s-**) *vi* (*pot*) to panic; **nie panikuj! wszystko będzie dobrze** don't panic, everything will be fine

pa|nna (**-nny, -nny**; *dat sg & loc sg* **-nnie**; *gen pl* **-nien**) *f* **1** (*young*) girl **2** (*stan cywilny*) unmarried

woman **3** (*Astrol*): **P~** Virgo; **P~ Kowalska** Miss Kowalski; **~ młoda** bride; **stara ~** (*pej*) old maid

panora|ma (**-my, -my**; *dat sg & loc sg* **-mie**) *f* (*rozległy widok*) panorama

pan|ować (**-uję, -ujesz**) *vi* **1** (*długo, mądrze, sprawiedliwie*) to rule **2** (*pf* **za-**) (*hałas*) to reign **3** (*poglądy*) to prevail; **~ nad kimś/czymś** to be master of sb/sth; **~ nad sobą** to be in control of o.s.

państ|wo (**-wa**; *loc sg & dat sg* **-wie**) *nt* **1** (*pl* **-wa**) (*kraj: bogate, zasobne*) state **2** (*forma grzecznościowa*) you; **P~ Kowalscy** the Kowalskis; **proszę Państwa!** Ladies and Gentlemen!; **~ młodzi** the bride and bridegroom

państwowy *adj* **1** (*hymn, święto, obchody*) national **2** (*szkoła*) state-owned

papie|r (**-ru, -ry**; *loc sg* **-rze**) *m* (*elegancki, delikatny, do kaligrafii*) paper; **papiery** *pl* (*dokumenty*) papers *pl*; **arkusz ~u** a sheet of paper; **~ firmowy** letterhead; **ściana jest cienka jak z ~u, wszystko przez nią słychać** the wall is paper thin, you can hear everything through it; **~ toaletowy** toilet paper; **~y wartościowe** (*Fin*) securities *pl*; **komisja P~ów Wartościowych** (*Ekon*) state organization set up to supervise trading in securities and give reliable information on stocks and shares

papiero|s (**-sa, -sy**; *loc sg* **-sie**) *m* cigarette; **palić ~y** to smoke cigarettes; **zaciągać się ~em** to smoke a cigarette

papierowy adj (opakowanie, osłona, kubek) paper

papież (**-a, -e**; gen pl **-y**) m the Pope

papry|ka (**-ki, -ki**; dat sg & loc sg **-ce**) f (suszona) paprika; **~ zielona/czerwona** green/red pepper; **piekielnie ostra ~** devilishly hot pepper

pa|ra (**-ry**; dat sg & loc sg **-rze**) f 1 (nom pl **-ry**) (rękawiczek) pair 2 (nom pl **-ry**) (dwoje ludzi) couple 3 (Fiz) vapour (Brit), vapor (US); **nie puszczać** (**puścić** pf) **pary z ust** (przen) not to breathe a word; **młoda ~** (w czasie ślubu) the bride and groom; (po ślubie) the newly-weds; **~mi** (siedzieć) in pairs; **iść w parze z czymś** (przen) to go hand in hand with sth

paradok|s (**-su, -sy**; loc sg **-sie**) m paradox

paradoksalny adj (przypadek, sytuacja, położenie) paradoxical

parafi|a (**-i, -e**; gen pl **-i**) f parish

parago|n (**-nu, -ny**; loc sg **-nie**) m (zakupu, nabycia towaru, VAT) receipt

paragra|f (**-fu, -fy**; loc sg **-fie**) m 1 (Jur) article 2 (akapit) paragraph

paraliż|ować (**-uję, -ujesz**; pf **s-**) vt to paralyse (Brit), to paralyze (US); **~ ruch uliczny** (przen) to stop traffic

parapetów|ka (**-ki, -ki**; dat sg **-ce**; gen pl **-ek**) f housewarming

parasol (**-a, -e**; gen pl **-i**) m 1 (od słońca) parasol 2 (od deszczu) umbrella

parasol|ka (**-ki, -ki**; dat sg & loc sg **-ce**; gen pl **-ek**) f umbrella

parę num a few; **~ lat temu** a few years ago; **~ minut/godzin/dni** a few minutes/hours/days; **od paru minut/godzin/dni** for a few minutes/hours/days; **za ~ lat** in a few years

par|k (**-ku, -ki**; inst sg **-kiem**) m (krajobrazowy, miejski) park; **~ narodowy** national park

parkin|g (**-gu, -gi**; inst sg **-giem**) m (wielopoziomowy, podziemny) car park (Brit), parking lot (US); **~ strzeżony/nie strzeżony** attended/unattended car park; **~ płatny/bezpłatny** paid/free parking

parkomet|r (**-ru, -ry**; loc sg **-rze**) m parking meter

park|ować (**-uję, -ujesz**; pf **za-**) vt, vi to park; **~ nielegalnie** to park illegally

parkowani|e (**-a**) nt parking

parlamen|t (**-tu, -ty**; loc sg **-cie**) m parliament; **posiedzenie ~u** sitting of parliament

parlamentarny adj (sesja parlamentarna) parliamentary

parte|r (**-ru, -ry**; loc sg **-rze**) m (najniższe piętro) ground floor (Brit), first floor (US)

parterowy adj: **dom ~** (budynek) bungalow

parti|a (**-i, -e**; gen pl **-i**) f 1 (Pol) party 2 (pewna ilość towaru) batch 3 (szachów) game 4 (Teatr) part

partne|r (**-ra, -rzy**; loc sg **-rze**) m (życiowy, lojalny) (male) partner

partner|ka (**-ki, -ki**; dat sg & loc sg **-ce**; gen pl **-ek**) f (female) partner

partnerski adj (układ, związek) based on partnership

partnerst|wo (**-wa**; loc sg & dat sg

-wie) *nt* partnership
party *nt inv* (*urodzinowe*) party
partyjny *adj* (*działacz, aktywista*)
party
paryski *adj*: **bułka paryska**
French bread
pas (**-a**) *m* belt; **~ zieleni** green
belt; **~ jezdni** (*motorway*) lane
pasaż (**-u, -e**; *gen pl* **-y**) *m* passage
pasaże|r (**-ra, -rowie**; *loc sg* **-rze**)
m passenger
pasażer|ka (**-ki, -ki**; *loc sg & dat
sg* **-ce**; *gen pl* **-ek**) *f* (female)
passenger
pasażerski *adj* (*statek, rejs*)
passenger
pas|ek (**-ka, -ki**; *inst sg* **-kiem**) *m*
dimin od **pas**; (*skórzany, damski,
męski*) belt; **~ do zegarka** watch
strap; **~ klinowy** (*Aut*) fan belt; **w
paski** (*wzór*) striped
pasier|b (**-ba, -bowie**; *loc sg* **-bie**)
m stepson
pasierbic|a (**-y, -e**) *f*
stepdaughter
pasjon|ować (**-uję, -ujesz**) *vt* to
fascinate; **~ się** *vr*: **~ się czymś**
(*sztuką*) to be very keen on sth
pasjonujący *adj* (*książka, film,
wykład*) fascinating
paskudny *adj* (*pogoda, nastrój,
humor*) nasty
pa|sta (**-sty, -sty**; *dat sg & loc sg*
-ście) *f*: **~ do zębów** toothpaste;
~ mięsna/pomidorowa meat/
tomato spread; **~ do butów** shoe
polish
pastyl|ka (**-ki, -ki**; *dat sg & loc
sg* **-ce**; *gen pl* **-ek**) *f* **1** (*Med*) pill
2 (*cukierek*) pastille
pasywny *adj* (*zachowanie*) passive
paszpor|t (**-tu, -ty**; *loc sg* **-cie**) *m*

passport
paszportowy *adj* (*urząd,
formularz*) passport; **kontrola
paszportowa** passport control
paszte|t (**-tu, -ty**; *loc sg* **-cie**) *m*
(*drobiowy, cielęcy*) pâté
pa|ść¹ (**-dnę, -dniesz**; *imp* **-dnij**; *pt*
-dł) *vb pf od* **padać**; **~ trupem** to
drop dead
pa|ść² (**-sę, -siesz**; *imp* **-ś**; *pt* **-sł,
-śli**) *vt* **1** (*krowy, owce*) to graze
2 (*karmić*) to fatten; **~ się** *vr* to
graze
patel|nia (**-ni, -nie**; *gen pl* **-ni**) *f*
(*teflonowa*) frying pan
patrio|ta (**-ty, -ci**; *dat sg & loc sg*
-cie) *m decl like f in sg* (*zagorzały,
prawdziwy, wielki*) patriot
patriotyczny *adj* (*pieśń, wiersz,
przemowa*) patriotic
patriotyz|m (**-mu**; *loc sg & dat sg*
-mie) *m* (*głęboki*) patriotism
patrol (**-u, -e**; *gen pl* **-i**) *m* (*policyjny,
wojskowy, harcerski*) patrol
patrol|ować (**-uję, -ujesz**) *vt*
to patrol
patro|n (**-na, -nowie** *lub* **-ni**;
loc sg **-nie**) *m* **1** (*szkoły, kościoła,
parafii: opiekun*) patron **2** (*Rel*)
patron saint
patrz|eć (**-ę, -ysz**) *vi* to look; **~ na
coś trzeźwo/optymistycznie**
to look at sth objectively/
optimistically; **~ na coś przez
palce** (*przen*) to turn a blind eye to
sth; **~ na kogoś z góry** (*przen*) to
look down on sb
patrz|yć (**-ę, -ysz**) *vi* = **patrzeć**
pau|za (**-zy, -zy**; *dat sg & loc sg* **-zie**)
f **1** (*przerwa*) pause **2** (*Szkol*) break
pa|w (**-wia, -wie**; *gen pl* **-wi**) *m*
peacock; **dumny jak ~** (as) proud

as a peacock

pazno|kieć (**-kcia, -kcie**; *gen pl* **-kci**) *m* **1** (*u nogi*) toenail **2** (*u ręki*) fingernail

październi|k (**-ka, -ki**; *inst sg* **-kiem**) *m* October

pącz|ek (**-ka, -ki**; *inst sg* **-kiem**) *m* **1** (*Bot*) bud **2** (*Kul*) doughnut, donut (*US*); **żyć wygodnie jak ~ w maśle** to live in the lap of luxury

pch|ać (**-am, -asz**; *pf* **-nąć**) *vt* **1** (*gwałtownie, brutalnie*) to push **2** (*wpychać*) to thrust; **~ się** *vr* (*przez tłum*) to force one's way; **~ push**

pch|ła (**-ły, -ły**; *dat sg & loc sg* **-le**; *gen pl* **-eł**) *f* flea

pch|nąć (**-nę, -niesz**; *imp* **-nij**) *vt pf od* **pchać**; (*nożem*) to stab

pchnię|cie (**-cia, -cia**; *gen pl* **-ć**) *nt* (*nożem*) stab

pech (**-a**) *m* bad luck; **mieć ~a** to be unlucky

pecho|wiec (**-wca, -wcy**) *m* unlucky person

pechowy *adj* (*dzień, okres*) unlucky

pedago|g (**-ga, -gowie** *lub* **-dzy**; *inst sg* **-giem**) *m* (*lubiany, szanowany, szacowny*) educator

pedagogi|ka (**-ki**; *dat sg & loc sg* **-ce**) *f* pedagogy; **Wydział Pedagogiki** (*Uniw*) Department of Pedagogy

pediat|ra (**-ry, -rzy**; *dat sg & loc sg* **-rze**) *m decl like f in sg* paediatrician (*Brit*), pediatrician (*US*)

pełen *adj* = **pełny**

pełno *adv* (*wiele*) a lot of; **w autobusie było ~ ludzi** the bus

was full; **w butelce jest ~ wody** the bottle is full of water

pełnoletni *adj* (*widz, pasażer, czytelnik*) of age

pełnomocnict|wo (**-wa, -wa**; *loc sg & dat sg* **-wie**) *nt* power of attorney

pełnomocni|k (**-ka, -cy**; *inst sg* **-kiem**) *m* proxy, plenipotentiary (*in foreign diplomacy*)

pełnopłatny *adj* (*bilet, wstęp, przejazd*) full-price

pełnotłusty *adj* (*mleko, śmietana, masło*) full-fat

pełnoziarnisty *adj* (*chleb, makaron*) wholemeal (*Brit*), wholewheat (*US*)

pełny *adj* (*kubek, worek, sala*) full; (*szczęście*) complete; **pełen entuzjazmu** full of enthusiasm; **pełen nadziei** hopeful; **pełne mleko** full-cream milk; **pełne morze** open sea; **do pełna proszę!** fill her up, please!

penicyli|na (**-ny**; *dat sg & loc sg* **-nie**) *f* penicillin

peni|s (**-sa, -sy**; *loc sg* **-sie**) *m* penis

pen|s (**-sa, -sy**; *loc sg* **-sie**) *m* penny; **dziesięć ~ów** 10 pence

pensj|a (**-i, -e**; *gen pl* **-i**) *f* (*płaca: tygodniowa, miesięczna, stała*) salary

pensjona|t (**-tu, -ty**; *loc sg* **-cie**) *m* (*górski, nadmorski, rodzinny*) guesthouse

perfekcjoni|sta (**-sty, -ści**; *dat sg & loc sg* **-ście**) *m decl like f in sg* perfectionist; **on jest perfekcjonistą w każdym calu** he is a perfectionist about everything

perfekcyjny *adj* (*wykonanie,*

występ) perfect

perfum|y (-) pl (*ekskluzywne, najnowsze, eleganckie*) perfume

periody|k (-ku, -ki; *inst sg* **-kiem)** m periodical

perkusj|a (-i, -e; *gen pl* **-i)** f drums pl; **grać na perkusji** to play the drums

per|ła (-ły, -ły; *dat sg & loc sg* **-le**; *gen pl* **-eł)** f (*rzadka, olbrzymia, bezcenna*) pearl

perłowy adj (*naszyjnik, bransoleta, kolczyki*) pearl; **masa perłowa** mother-of-pearl; **macica perłowa** mother-of-pearl

pero|n (-nu, -ny; *loc sg* **-nie)** m platform

perski adj: **Zatoka Perska** the (Persian) Gulf

personalny adj 1 (*dane, akta, dokumenty*) personal 2 (*dział*) personnel

personel (-u) m (*sklepu, firmy: uprzejmy*) personnel

pertrakt|ować (-uję, -ujesz) vi to negotiate; **~ z kimś** to negotiate with sb

peru|ka (-ki, -ki; *dat sg & loc sg* **-ce)** f wig; **nosić perukę** to wear a wig

peryferi|e (-i) pl 1 (*krańce miasta*) outskirts pl 2 (*zewnętrzne części*) periphery sg

pest|ka (-ki, -ki; *dat sg & loc sg* **-ce**; *gen pl* **-ek)** f 1 (*wiśni*) stone 2 (*pomarańczy*) pip 3 (*słonecznika*) seed; **to (dla mnie) ~** (*pot*) it's a piece of cake (for me)

pesymi|sta (-sty, -ści; *dat sg & loc sg* **-ście)** m decl like f in sg (*urodzony, zgorzkniały*) pessimist

pesymistyczny adj (*prognoza,*

przepowiednia, wróżba) pessimistic

pesymiz|m (-mu; *loc sg* **-mie)** m pessimism

peten|t (-ta, -ci; *loc sg* **-cie)** m (*urzędu, administracji*) inquirer

petycj|a (-i, -e; *gen pl* **-i)** f petition; **podpisywać petycję** to sign a petition; **zbierać podpisy pod petycją** to collect signatures for a petition

pewien (*f* **pewna**; *nt* **pewne**) adj 1 (*jakiś*) a certain 2 (*pewny*) certain; **~ pan** a certain gentleman; **pewnego dnia** one day; **pewnego razu** once (upon a time); **przez ~ czas** for some time; **w pewnym stopniu** to some extent; **w pewnym sensie** in a sense

pewnie adv 1 (*zdecydowanie*) firmly 2 (*sprawnie*) confidently 3 (*niezawodnie*) reliably 4 (*prawdopodobnie*) probably; **(no) ~!** (*pot*) you bet!

pewnoś|ć (-ci) f 1 (*przekonanie: niezachwiana, absolutna*) certainty 2 (*zdecydowanie*) firmness 3 (*sprawność*) confidence 4 (*niezawodność*) reliability; **dla pewności** to be on the safe side; **~ siebie** self-confidence; **z pewnością** surely; **mieć ~** to be sure

pewny adj 1 (*śmierć*) certain 2 (*wniosek*) unquestionable 3 (*krok*) firm 4 (*oko*) steady 5 (*człowiek*) reliable 6 (*bezpieczny*) secure; **być ~m czegoś** to be sure of sth; **~ siebie** self-confident; **on jest ~ lub pewien, że...** he's sure (that)...

pęcherzy|k (**-ka, -ki**; *inst sg* **-kiem**) *m* **1** (*na skórze*) blister **2** (*mydło*) bubble; **~ żółciowy** gall bladder

pędz|el (**-la, -le**; *gen pl* **-li**) *m* **1** (*do golenia*) (shaving) brush **2** (*do malowania*) (paint)brush; **wystawa obrazów pędzla Rembrandta** exhibition of paintings by Rembrandt

pę|dzić (**-dzę, -dzisz**; *imp* **-dź**) *vt* (*bydło*) to drive ▷ *vi* (*pf* **po-**) to speed along; **~ na złamanie karku** to go at breakneck speed

pęk|ać (**-am, -asz**; *pf* **-nąć**) *vi* **1** (*szyba*) to crack **2** (*sznurek*) to burst **3** (*koszula*) to rip; **głowa mi pęka** (*przen*) my head is splitting; **nie pękaj, wytrzymaj jeszcze trochę** (*pot*) don't give up, hold on a bit longer; **~ ze śmiechu** (*przen*) to laugh one's head off

pęknię|cie (**-cia, -cia**; *gen pl* **-ć**) *nt* **1** (*kości, czaszki*) fracture **2** (*rysa: szyby*) crack

pęp|ek (**-ka, -ki**; *inst sg* **-kiem**) *m* navel, belly button (*pot*)

pępowi|na (**-ny, -ny**; *dat sg & loc sg* **-nie**) *f* umbilical cord

pia|na (**-ny**; *dat sg & loc sg* **-nie**) *f* **1** (*aromatyczna, obfita*) foam **2** (*szampon*) lather **3** (*na powierzchni piwa*) head

piani|no (**-na, -na**; *loc sg* **-nie**) *nt* piano

piani|sta (**-sty, -ści**; *dat sg & loc sg* **-ście**) *m decl like f in sg* pianist

pianist|ka (**-ki, -ki**; *dat sg & loc sg* **-ce**; *gen pl* **-ek**) *f* pianist

pian|ka (**-ki**; *dat sg & loc sg* **-ce**) *f dimin od* **piana**; **~ do włosów** styling mousse; **~ do golenia** shaving foam

pias|ek (**-ku, -ki**; *inst sg* **-kiem**) *m* (*miękki, złoty*) sand

piaskownic|a (**-y, -e**) *f* sandpit (*Brit*), sandbox (*US*)

piąć się (**pnę, pniesz**; *imp* **pnij**) *vr* to climb (up)

piąt|ek (**-ku, -ki**; *inst sg* **-kiem**) *m* Friday; **Wielki P~** Good Friday; **~ zły początek** (*przysł*) popular Polish phrase meaning that it is not wise to start doing something new on a Friday

piąt|ka (**-ki, -ki**; *dat sg & loc sg* **-ce**; *gen pl* **-ek**) *f* **1** five **2** (*Szkol*) ≈ A

piąty *num decl like adj* fifth

pi|cie (**-cia**) *nt* **1** (*czynność*) drinking **2** (*pot: napój*) drink; **ta woda jest do picia** this water is drinkable

pi|ć (**-ję, -jesz**) *vt* (*pf* **wy-**) (*łapczywie*) to drink ▷ *vi* to drink; **chce mi się ~** I'm thirsty

piec¹ (**-a, -e**) *m* **1** (*kuchenny*) stove **2** (*piekarniczy*) oven **3** (*hutniczy*) furnace

pie|c² (**-kę, -czesz**; *imp* **-cz**) *vt* **1** (*pf* **u-**) (*chleb*) to bake **2** (*pf* **u-**) (*wołowinę*) to roast ▷ *vi* (*o słońcu*) to beat down; **~ się** (*pf* **u-**) *vr* **1** (*o chlebie*) to bake **2** (*o wołowinie*) to roast

piecho|ta (**-ty**; *dat sg* **-cie**) *f* (*Wojsk*) infantry; **~ morska** Royal Marines *pl* (*Brit*), Marine Corps (*US*), Marines *pl* (*US*); **iść piechotą** *lub* **na piechotę** to walk

pieczar|ka (**-ki, -ki**; *dat sg & loc sg* **-ce**; *gen pl* **-ek**) *f* (field) mushroom

pieczą|tka (**-ki, -ki**; *dat sg & loc sg* **-ce**; *gen pl* **-ek**) *f* stamp

piecze|ń (**-ni, -nie**; *gen pl* **-ni**) *f* (*smakowita, aromatyczna,*

chrupiąca) roast; **~ wołowa**
roast beef
piecz|ę|ć (**-ci, -cie**; *gen pl* **-ci**) *f*
1 (*urzędowa, oficjalna*) stamp
2 (*lakowa*) seal
pieczy|wo (**-wa**; *loc sg & dat sg*
-wie) *nt* (*świeże, czerstwe*) bread
piegowaty *adj* (*twarz, nos, cera*)
freckled
piekar|nia (**-ni, -nie**; *gen pl* **-ni**) *f*
(*pomieszczenie*) bakery
piekarni|k (**-ka, -ki**; *inst sg* **-kiem**)
m oven
piekarz (**-a, -e**; *gen pl* **-y**) *m* baker;
u ~a at the baker's
piek|ło (**-ła**; *loc sg & dat sg* **-le**)
nt hell
pielęgniar|ka (**-ki, -ki**; *dat sg &
loc sg* **-ce**; *gen pl* **-ek**) *f* (*rejonowa,
oddziałowa*) (female) nurse
pielęgniarz (**-a, -e**; *gen pl* **-y**) *m*
(*male*) nurse
pielęgn|ować (**-uję, -ujesz**) *vt*
1 (*osobę*) to nurse **2** (*zwierzę*) to
take care of **3** (*ogródek*) to tend
4 (*skóra*) to take care of **5** (*tradycje*)
to foster
pielgrzy|m (**-ma, -mi**; *loc sg* **-mie**)
m pilgrim
pielgrzym|ka (**-ki, -ki**; *dat sg & loc
sg* **-ce**; *gen pl* **-ek**) *f* pilgrimage
pielu|cha (**-chy, -chy**; *dat sg & loc
sg* **-sze**) *f* (*tetrowa, jednorazowa*)
nappy (*Brit*), diaper (*US*)
pieni|ądz (**-ądza, -ądze**; *gen pl*
-ędzy) *m* money; **pieniądze** *pl*
money *sg*
pieprz (**-u**) *m* pepper
pierni|k (**-ka, -ki**; *inst sg* **-kiem**) *m*
gingerbread
piero|gi (**-gów**) *pl* (*ruskie,
nadziewane, z farszem*) boiled dough

*pockets filled with meat, cheese
or fruit*

● **PIEROGI**
●
● **Pierogi** is a popular dish in
● Central and Eastern European
● cuisine. **Pierogi** are small
● dumplings, made from dough
● which has been boiled or
● fried in fat and stuffed with
● various fillings, such as meat,
● cabbage with mushrooms
● or potato and onion. **Pierogi**
● can also be served sweet with
● cottage cheese or fruit, and
● covered in thick cream.

pier|ś (**-si, -si**; *gen pl* **-si**) *f* **1** (*Anat*)
chest **2** (*u kobiety*) breast; **karmić
dziecko piersią** to breast-feed
a child
pierścion|ek (**-ka, -ki**; *inst sg*
-kiem) *m* ring
pierwszeńst|wo (**-wa**; *loc sg &
dat sg* **-wie**) *nt* **1** (*prawo, przywilej*)
precedence **2** (*Mot*): **~ przejazdu**
right of way; **ustąpić** (*pf*)
pierwszeństwa to give way
pierwszy *num decl like adj* first; **~
maja** the first of May; **pierwsze
piętro** first floor (*Brit*), second
floor (*US*); **pierwsza pomoc** first
aid; **pierwsze danie** first course;
pierwsza litera initial; **pierwsza
wojna światowa** World War
One; **pierwsza w prawo/lewo**
the next on the right/left; **po
pierwsze** firstly; **~ raz** *lub* **po raz
~** (for) the first time
pies (**psa, psy**; *loc sg & dat sg*
psie) *m* dog; **pogoda pod**

psem dreadful weather; **~ z rodowodem** pedigree dog

pieszo adv on foot; **iść (pójść** pf) **~** to go on foot

pieszy adj **1** (żołnierz) foot **2** (oddział) infantry ▷ m decl like adj pedestrian; **piesza wycieczka** hike; **~ turysta** hiker; **przejście dla ~ch** (pedestrian) crossing

pieś|ń (**-ni, -ni**; gen pl **-ni**) f (religijna, wzniosła, uroczysta) song

pietrusz|ka (**-ki, -ki**; dat sg & loc sg **-ce**; gen pl **-ek**) f **1** (korzeń) parsleyroot **2** (roślina) parsley

pięć num five

pięćdziesiąt num fifty

pięćset num five hundred

pięknie adv beautifully; **~ wyglądać** to look beautiful; **no ~!** (pej) oh great!

pięk|no (**-na**; loc sg & dat sg **-nie**) nt (wewnętrzne) beauty

piękny adj beautiful; **literatura piękna** belles-lettres; **sztuki piękne** fine arts; **płeć piękna** the fair sex

pięś|ć (**-ci, -ci**; gen pl **-ci**) f (żelazna) fist

pię|ta (**-ty, -ty**; dat sg & loc sg **-cie**) f heel; **~ Achillesa** lub **achillesowa** Achilles' heel

piętnasty num decl like adj fifteenth

piętnaście num fifteen; **za ~ czwarta** quarter to four

pię|tro (**-ra, -ra**; loc sg **-rze**; gen pl **-er**) nt (w budynku) floor; **mieszkać na drugim piętrze** to live on the second (Brit) lub third (US) floor; **na piętrze** upstairs; **iść na ~** to go upstairs

piętrowy adj: **dom ~, budynek** house (with more than one storey); **łóżko piętrowe** bunk beds pl; **autobus ~** double-decker bus

piguł|ka (**-ki, -ki**; dat sg & loc sg **-ce**; gen pl **-ek**) f pill; **~ nasenna** sleeping pill; **~ antykoncepcyjna** the pill

pija|k (**-ka, -cy** lub **-ki**; inst sg **-kiem**) m drunk

pijany adj drunk(en) ▷ m decl like adj drunk; **on jest ~ w sztok** he is steaming (drunk); **jazda po pijanemu** drink driving (Brit), drunk driving (US)

pikantny adj **1** (smak) piquant **2** (ostry) hot **3** (przen: historia) juicy **4** (anegdota) bawdy

pikni|k (**-ku, -ki**; inst sg **-kiem**) m picnic

piln|ować (**-uję, -ujesz**) vt +gen **1** (dziecka) to look after **2** (interesów) to look after **3** (pf **przy-**) (robotników) to supervise **4** (porządku) to maintain; **~ się** vr to look after o.s.

pilny adj **1** (student) diligent **2** (sprawa) urgent

pilo|t (**-ta**; loc sg **-cie**) m **1** (nom pl **-ci**) (samolot) pilot **2** (nom pl **-ty**) (do telewizora) remote control **3** (nom pl **-ci**) (wycieczek) guide

pił|ka (**-ki, -ki**; dat sg & loc sg **-ce**; gen pl **-ek**) f **1** (do zabaw) ball **2** (mała piła) handsaw; **grać w piłkę** to play ball; **~ nożna** football (Brit), soccer (US); **~ ręczna** (Sport) handball

piłkarz (**-a, -e**; gen pl **-y**) m footballer (Brit), soccer player (US)

pingwi|n (**-na, -ny**; loc sg **-nie**) m penguin

pionie|r (**-ra, -rzy**; *loc sg* **-rze**) *m* pioneer

pionowo *adv* **1** vertically **2** (*w krzyżówce*) down

pionowy *adj* **1** vertical **2** (*w pozycji pionowej*) upright

pioru|n (**-na, -ny**; *loc sg* **-nie**) *m* thunder and lightning; **burza z ~ami** thunderstorm

piosen|ka (**-ki, -ki**; *dat sg & loc sg* **-ce**; *gen pl* **-ek**) *f* (*popularna, skoczna*) song

piosenkar|ka (**-ki, -ki**; *dat sg & loc sg* **-ce**; *gen pl* **-ek**) *f* singer

piosenkarz (**-a, -e**; *gen pl* **-y**) *m* singer

piórni|k (**-ka, -ki**; *inst sg* **-kiem**) *m* pencil case

pió|ro (**-ra, -ra**; *loc sg & dat sg* **-rze**) *nt* **1** (*ptaka*) feather **2** (*też:* **wieczne pióro**) fountain pen **3** (*wycieraczki*) blade; **powieść pióra Prousta** a novel penned by Proust

Pirenej|e (**-ów**) *pl* the Pyrenees

pi|sać (**-szę, -szesz**; *pf* **na-**) *vi* to write ▷ *vi* to write; **~ się** *vr*: **jak to się pisze?** how do you spell it?; **~ na maszynie** to type

pisan|ka (**-ki, -ki**; *dat sg & loc sg* **-ce**; *gen pl* **-ek**) *f* Easter egg

pisar|ka (**-ki, -ki**; *dat sg & loc sg* **-ce**; *gen pl* **-ek**) *f* writer

pisarz (**-a, -e**; *gen pl* **-y**) *m* writer

pisemnie *adv* in writing

pisemny *adj* (*wniosek, egzamin, test*) written

pi|smo (**-sma**; *loc sg & dat sg* **-śmie**) *nt* **1** writing **2** (*litery*) alphabet **3** (*kreślenie liter*) hand(writing) **4** (*nom pl* **-sma**) (*czasopismo*) magazine **5** (*nom pl* **-sma**) (*dokument*) letter; **na piśmie**

in writing; **~ Święte** the (Holy) Scriptures; **~ pochyłe** italics

pisow|nia (**-ni, -nie**; *gen pl* **-ni**) *f* spelling

pistole|t (**-tu, -ty**; *loc sg* **-cie**) *m* gun; **~ maszynowy** submachine gun

PIT *nt* tax return

pitny *adj* (*woda*) drinking; **miód ~** mead

piwnic|a (**-y, -e**) *f* (*winna, zatęchła*) cellar

pi|wo (**-wa, -wa**; *dat sg* **-wu**; *loc sg* **-wie**) *nt* **1** (*napój*) beer **2** (*porcja*) pint

pizz|a (**-y, -e**) *f* pizza

piża|ma (**-my, -my**; *dat sg & loc sg* **-mie**) *f* (*flanelowa, ciepła, dziecięca*) pyjamas *pl* (Brit), pajamas *pl* (US)

PKP *abbr* (= *Polskie Koleje Państwowe*) Polish State Railways

PKS *abbr* (= *Państwowa Komunikacja Samochodowa*) National Transport Company

pkt *abbr* (= *punkt*) pt.

pl. *abbr* (= *plac*) sq.

plac (**-u, -e**) *m* square; **~ budowy** building site; **~ zabaw** playground

plac|ek (**-ka, -ki**; *inst sg* **-kiem**) *m* (*słodki*) cake; **placki kartoflane** potato pancakes; **~ drożdżowy** yeast cake; **masz babo ~!** damn and blast! (*pot*)

plaka|t (**-tu, -ty**; *loc sg* **-cie**) *m* (*filmowy, teatralny*) poster

pla|ma (**-my, -my**; *dat sg & loc sg* **-mie**) *f* stain; **tłusta ~** greasy spot

pla|mić (**-mię, -misz**) *vt* (*pf* **po-**) **1** (*robić plamy*) to stain **2** (*pf* **s-**) (*zniesławiać*) to tarnish; **~ się** *vr*

1 (*pf* **po-**) (*brudzić się*) to get dirty **2** (*pf* **s-**) (*przen*) to tarnish one's reputation

pla|n (**-nu, -ny**; *loc sg* **-nie**) *m* **1** (*zamierzenie*) plan **2** (*program*) schedule **3** (*inwestycyjny*) scheme **4** (*miasta*) street map **5** (*Teatr*) set; **mieć coś w ~ie** to plan sth; **~ zajęć** (*Szkol*) timetable; **według ~u** *lub* **zgodnie z ~em** according to plan

plane|ta (**-ty, -ty**; *dat sg & loc sg* **-cie**) *f* planet

plan|ować (**-uję, -ujesz**; *pf* **za-**) *vt* **1** (*wakację*) to plan **2** (*zebranie*) to schedule

plast|er (**-ra, -ry**; *loc sg* **-rze**) *m* **1** (*Med*) (sticking) plaster (*Brit*), Bandaid ® (*US*) **2** (*sera*) slice

plaster|ek (**-ka, -ki**; *inst sg* **-kiem**) *m dimin od* **plaster**

plastyczny *adj* **1** (*materiał*) plastic **2** (*sztuka*) artistic **3** (*opis*) vivid; **operacja plastyczna** (*zabieg chirurgiczny*) plastic surgery

plasty|k (**-ka, -cy**; *inst sg* **-kiem**) *m* artist

plaż|a (**-y, -e**) *f* beach; **~ dla nudystów** nudist beach

pleca|k (**-ka, -ki**; *inst sg* **-kiem**) *m* (*wodoodporny, górski*) rucksack, backpack (*US*)

plec|y (**-ów**) *pl* back

pl|eść (**-otę, -eciesz**; *imp* **-eć**; *pt* **plótł, plotła, pletli**) *vt* **1** (*pf* **s-** *lub* **za-**) (*wyplatać*) to plait **2** (*pf* **na-**) (*pot: bzdury*) to blabber; **~ trzy po trzy** to talk rubbish

pleś|ń (**-ni**) *f* mould (*Brit*), mold (*US*)

pli|k (**-ku, -ki**; *inst sg* **-kiem**) *m* **1** (*dokumentów, gazet, papierów*) bundle **2** (*Komput*) file

plom|ba (**-by, -by**; *dat sg & loc sg* **-bie**) *f* **1** (*przy drzwiach*) seal **2** (*u dentysty*) filling

plot|ka (**-ki, -ki**; *dat sg & loc sg* **-ce**; *gen pl* **-ek**) *f* rumour (*Brit*), rumor (*US*); **plotki** *pl* gossip *sg*; **wylęgarnia plotek** hotbed of gossip

plotk|ować (**-uję, -ujesz**) *vi* to gossip

plu|s (**-sa, -sy**; *loc sg* **-sie**) *m* **1** (*w matematyce*) plus **2** (*coś pozytywnego*) advantage; **~y i minusy** pros and cons; **~ minus** more or less

płac|a (**-y, -e**) *f* **1** (*ogólnie: tygodniowa, miesięczna, stała*) pay **2** (*dzienna, tygodniowa*) wages *pl*; (*roczna*) salary

pła|cić (**-cę, -cisz**; *imp* **-ć**; *pf* **za-**) *vt, vi* to pay; **~ za coś** to pay for sth; **on drogo za to zapłaci** (*przen*) he'll pay dearly for that

płacz (**-u, -e**) *m* (*rozpaczliwy*) crying

płaczliwy *adj* **1** (*człowiek*) tearful **2** (*smutny*) tearful **3** (*piosenka*) moving

pła|kać (**-czę, -czesz**) *vi* to cry

płaski *adj* flat; **~ talerz** dinner plate

płaszcz (**-a, -e**; *gen pl* **-y**) *m* (*okrycie: wełniany, ciepły*) (over)coat

płatni|k (**-ka, -cy**; *inst sg* **-kiem**) *m* payer

płatnoś|ć (**-ci, -ci**; *gen pl* **-ci**) *f* (*gotówką, kartą, przelewem*) payment

płatny *adj* paid; **dobrze/nisko ~** well-/low-paid; **parking ~** paid parking

płd. *abbr* (= *południowy*) S.

pł|eć (**-ci**, **-ci**; *gen pl* **-ci**) *f* sex

płn. *abbr* (= *północny*) N.

płodny *adj* **1** fertile **2** (*pisarz, rok, twórca*) prolific

płomie|ń (**-nia**, **-nie**; *gen pl* **-ni**) *m* **1** (*blask*) blaze **2** (*ogień*) flame **3** (*pasja*) flame

pło|nąć (**-nę, -niesz**; *imp* **-ń**) *vi* to burn

pło|t (**-tu, -ty**; *loc sg* **-cie**) *m* (*drewniany, druciany, stalowy*) fence

pł|ód (**-odu, -ody**; *loc sg* **-odzie**) *m* foetus (*Brit*), fetus (*US*); **płody** *pl* (*leśne*) produce *sg*

płuc|o (**-a, -a**) *nt* lung; **zapalenie płuc** pneumonia; **ten park to prawdziwe płuca miasta** (*przen*) the park is at the heart of the city

płu|kać (**-czę, -czesz**) *vt* (*pf* **wy-**) **1** (*tkaninę*) to rinse **2** (*pf* **o-** *lub* **wy-**) (*sałatę*) to rinse **3** (*pf* **wy-** *lub* **prze-**) (*usta*) to rinse; **~ gardło** to gargle

Płw. *abbr* (= *półwysep*) Pen.

pły|n (**-nu, -ny**; *loc sg* **-nie**) *m* liquid; **~ po goleniu** aftershave (lotion); **~ do mycia naczyń** washing-up liquid

pły|nąć (**-nę, -niesz**; *imp* **-ń**) *vi* **1** to flow **2** (*człowiek*) to swim **3** (*statkiem*) to sail

płynnie *adv* **1** (*mówić, czytać, recytować*) fluently **2** (*chodzić*) smoothly

płynny *adj* **1** (*miód*) liquid **2** (*ruch*) smooth **3** (*wymowa*) fluent

pły|ta (**-ty, -ty**; *dat sg & loc sg* **-cie**) *f* **1** (*z kamienia, metalu*) plate **2** (*Muz*) record; **~ kompaktowa** compact disc

pływacz|ka (**-ki, -ki**; *dat sg & loc sg* **-ce**; *gen pl* **-ek**) *f* swimmer

pływ|ać (**-am, -asz**) *vi* **1** (*człowiek*) to swim **2** (*statek*) to sail **3** (*korek*) to float

pływa|k (**-ka**; *inst sg* **-kiem**) *m* **1** (*nom pl* **-cy**) (*człowiek*) swimmer **2** (*nom pl* **-ki**) (*przyrząd*) float

pływal|nia (**-ni, -nie**; *gen pl* **-ni**) *f* (*publiczna, szkolna, kryta*) swimming pool

pływani|e (**-a**) *nt* swimming

p.n.e. *abbr* (= *przed naszą erą*) BC

○ KEYWORD

po *prep* +*loc* **1** (*czas*) after; **po kolacji** after dinner; **po chwili** after a while; **pięć po drugiej** five past *lub* after (*US*) two **2** (*kolejność*) after; **jeden po drugim** one after another; **butelka po piwie** beer bottle **3** (*na podstawie*) by; **rozpoznać kogoś po głosie** to recognize sb by his voice

4 (*dziedziczenie*) from; **ma urodę po babce** she gets her beauty from her grandmother; **spadek po ojcu** inheritance from one's father

5 (*hierarchia*) after; **po kapitanie** second to the captin; **pierwszy po Bogu** next to God

6: **chodzić po parku/górach** to walk in the park/mountains; **po niebie** in the sky; **chodzić po piasku/trawie** to walk on sand/grass; **jeździć po mieście/ kraju** to travel around the town/country; **po szynach** on rails; **spacerować po korytarzu**

to walk along the corridor; **po całym globie** all over the globe; **po lewej stronie** on the left side; **schodzić po drabinie/schodach** to go down the ladder/stairs; **głaskać kogoś po włosach** to stroke sb's hair

7: **po kawałku** piece by piece ▷ *prep +acc* **1** (*kres*) to; **wody było po kostki** the water was ankle-deep; **po brzegi** to the rim **2** (*cel*) for; **przychodzić** (**przyjść** *pf*) **po mleko** to come to get milk; **posłać** (**posyłać** *pf*) **po lekarza** to send for a doctor; **po co?** what for?; **po trzydzieści sztuk w paczce** thirty items per pack; **po cztery złote za sztukę** (at) four zloty a piece

▷ *prep +dat*: **po cichu** (*bezgłośnie*) quietly; (*potajemnie*) on the quiet; **po trochu** bit by bit; **po polsku/angielsku** in Polish/English; **mówić po polsku/angielsku** to speak Polish/English

po|bić (**-biję, -bijesz**) *vt* **1** (*w walce*) to defeat **2** (*kogoś*) to beat up; **~ się** *vr pf* to have a fight; **~** (*pf*) **kogoś na kwaśne jabłko** (*pot*) to beat sb to a pulp

pobud|ka (**-ki, -ki**; *dat sg & loc sg* **-ce**; *gen pl* **-ek**) *f* (*sygnał*) alarm; **pobudki** *pl* (*powody: niskie, szlachetne*) motives

poby|t (**-tu, -ty**; *loc sg* **-cie**) *m* stay

pocał|ować (**-uję, -ujesz**) *vb pf od* **całować**

pocałun|ek (**-ku, -ki**; *inst sg* **-kiem**) *m* (*delikatny, płomienny*) kiss; **~ śmierci** (*przen*) kiss of death

pochmurno *adv*: **jest ~** it's cloudy

pochmurny *adj* **1** (*pogoda*) cloudy **2** (*twarz, wzrok, nastrój*) gloomy

pochodzeni|e (**-a**) *nt* origin; **on jest Szkotem z pochodzenia** he is of Scottish descent

pocho|dzić (**-dzę, -dzisz**) *vi*: **pochodzę z Anglii/biednej rodziny** I come from England/a poor family

poch|wa (**-wy, -wy**; *dat sg & loc sg* **-wie**; *gen pl* **-ew**) *f* **1** (*Anat*) vagina **2** (*futerał*) sheath

pochwal|ać (**-am, -asz**) *vt* (*zachowanie*) to approve of; **nie ~ czegoś** to disapprove of sth

pochwal|ić (**-ę, -isz**) *vb pf od* **chwalić**

pochwa|ła (**-ły, -ły**; *dat sg & loc sg* **-le**) *f* **1** (*wyraz uznania: pisemna, ustna*) praise **2** (*pisana*) citation

po|ciąć (**-tnę, -tniesz**; *imp* **-tnij**) *vt pf* to cut up; **~** (*pf*) **na kawałki** to cut into pieces

pocią|g (**-gu, -gi**; *inst sg* **-giem**) *m* **1** (*transport*) train **2** (*do ciastka*) attraction; **jechać ~iem** to go by train; **~ towarowy** goods (*Brit*) *lub* freight (*US*) train; **~ ekspresowy** express (train)

pociąg|ać (**-am, -asz**) *vt* to attract ▷ *vi*: **~** (**pociągnąć** *pf*) **za coś** to pull (at) sth; **~** (**pociągnąć** *pf*) **za sobą** to entail; **~** (**pociągnąć** *pf*) **nosem** to sniff

pociąg|nąć (**-nę, -niesz**; *imp* **-nij**) *vb pf od* **pociągać, ciągnąć**

po|cić się (**-cę, -cisz**; *imp* **-ć**) *vr* **1** (*pf* **s-**) (*stopy*) to sweat **2** (*pf* **za-**) (*okulary*) to steam up; **pocić się ze strachu** to sweat with fear

pociesz|ać (**-am, -asz**; *pf* **-yć**) *vt*

to comfort; **~ się** vr to console o.s.

począt|ek (**-ku**, **-ki**; inst sg **-kiem**) m (udany, dobry, obiecujący) beginning; **na ~** for a start; **na początku** at the beginning; **od początku** from the beginning; **z początku** at first

początkowo adv initially

początkowy adj (etap, plan, zamysł) initial

początkujący adj (pisarz) novice ▷ m decl like adj beginner

poczekal|nia (**-ni**, **-nie**; gen pl **-ni**) f waiting room; **~ u lekarza** doctor's waiting room

pocz|ta (**-ty**, **-ty**; dat sg & loc sg **-cie**) f 1 (urząd pocztowy: miejscowa, wiejska, główna) post office 2 (korespondencja) post (Brit), mail (US); **pocztą lotniczą** (by) airmail; **~ elektroniczna** email

pocztowy adj postal; **kod ~** postcode (Brit), zip code (US); **urząd ~** post office; **znaczek ~** postage stamp; **skrzynka pocztowa** lub **na listy** letterbox (Brit), mailbox (US); **skrzynka pocztowa** (na ulicy) postbox (Brit), mailbox (US)

pocztów|ka (**-ki**, **-ki**; dat sg & loc sg **-ce**; gen pl **-ek**) f postcard

pocz|uć (**-uję**, **-ujesz**) vb pf od **czuć**

pod prep +inst 1 (poniżej) under; **pod krzesłem** under the chair; **pod ziemią/wodą** underground/underwater; **pod spodem** underneath

2 (obok) by; **pod domem** by the house; **pod drzwiami** at the door 3 (w pobliżu) near; **wieś pod miastem** a village near the town; **bitwa pod Grunwaldem** the Battle of Grunwald 4 (dla wyrażenia przyczyny) under; **pod przymusem/wpływem** under pressure/the influence ▷ prep +acc 1 (kierunek) under; **mysz wszedł pod łóżko** the mouse went under the bed; **pod prąd/wiatr** against the current/wind; **iść pod górę** to walk uphill; **wpaść** (pf) **pod autobus** to get run over by a bus 2 (dla wyrażenia czasu): **pod koniec/wieczór** towards the end/evening; **pod czyjąś nieobecność** in sb's absence 3: **pod kierunkiem matki** under mother's supervision; **pod czyjąś opieką** in sb's care; **pod nazwiskiem Kowalski** under the name of Kowalski; **pod warunkiem, że...** on condition (that)...; **książka pod tytułem...** a book entitled...

pod|ać (**-am**, **-asz**) vb pf od **podawać**

poda|nie (**-nia**, **-nia**; gen pl **-ń**) nt 1 (wniosek: oficjalne, pisemne) application 2 (w piłce nożnej) pass

podarty adj (materiał, papier) tattered

podat|ek (**-ku**, **-ki**; inst sg **-kiem**) m tax; **~ dochodowy** income tax; **~ od wartości dodanej** value added tax, VAT

podatkowy adj (system) tax

podatni|k (**-ka**, **-cy**; inst sg **-kiem**)

m taxpayer

pod|awać (**-aję, -ajesz**; *pf* **-ać**) *vt* **1** (*masło*) to pass **2** (*przykład*) to give **3** (*wiadomość*) to announce **4** (*lekarstwo*) to administer **5** (*w tenisie*) to serve **6** (*w piłce nożnej*) to pass; **~ się** *vr*: **~ się za kogoś** to pose as sb; **~ (podać** *pf*) **komuś coś** to pass sb sth *lub* sth to sb; **~ (podać** *pf*) **do stołu** to wait at table; **podać się do dymisji** to hand in one's resignation

podczas *prep* +*gen* during; **~ gdy** (*kiedy*) while; (*natomiast*) whereas

poddasz|e (**-a, -a**; *gen pl* **-y**) *nt* loft; **pokój na poddaszu** attic

podejm|ować (**-uję, -ujesz**; *pf* **podjąć**) *vt* **1** (*ryzyko*) to take **2** (*obowiązki*) to take up **3** (*walkę*) to put up **4** (*dyskusję*) to take up **5** (*gościć*) to receive **6** (*pieniądze*) to withdraw; **~ się** *vr*: **~ się czegoś/ coś zrobić** to undertake sth/to do sth; **~ (podjąć** *pf*) **decyzję** to make a decision

podejrzany *adj* (*zachowanie, typ, transakcja*) suspicious ▷ *m decl like adj* suspect

podejrzew|ać (**-am, -asz**) *vt* to suspect; **~ kogoś o coś** to suspect sb of sth

podejrzliwy *adj* suspicious

podeszły *adj*: **w ~m wieku** advanced in years; **osoby w ~m wieku** the aged

pod|jąć (**-ejmę, -ejmiesz**; *imp* **-ejmij**) *vb pf od* **podejmować**

podkoszul|ek (**-ka, -ki**; *inst sg* **-kiem**) *m* (*męski, bawełniany, ciepły*) vest (*Brit*), undershirt (*US*)

podleg|ać (**-am, -asz**) *vi*: **~ komuś/czemuś** (*kierownictwu*) to be subordinate to sb/sth; **~ czemuś** (*obowiązkowi*) to be subject to sth

podliz|ywać się (**-uję, -ujesz**; *pf* **-ać**) *vr*: **~ (podlizać** *pf*) **się komuś** (*pot*) to suck up to sb

podłącz|ać (**-am, -asz**; *pf* **-yć**) *vt* (*kable, sieć, urządzenie*) to connect

podł|oga (**-ogi, -ogi**; *dat sg & loc sg* **-odze**; *gen pl* **-óg**) *f* floor

podły *adj* mean

podniecający *adj* (*perspektywa, pomysł, doznanie*) exciting

podniece|nie (**-nia**) *nt* **1** excitement **2** (*seksualne*) arousal

podniecony *adj* **1** (*ożywiony*) excited **2** (*pobudzony seksualnie*) aroused

pod|nieść (**-niosę, -niesiesz**; *imp* **-nieś**; *pt* **-niósł, -niosła, -nieśli**) *vb pf od* **podnosić**

podno|sić (**-szę, -sisz**; *imp* **-ś**; *pf* **podnieść**) *vt* **1** (*ręcy*) to raise **2** (*kieliszek*) to lift **3** (*zbierać*) to pick up **4** (*pomagać wstać*) to lift **5** (*alarm*) to raise **6** (*kwestię*) to raise; **~ się** *vr* **1** (*z krzesła*) to lift o.s. **2** (*ceny*) to rise; **~ głos** to raise one's voice

podob|ać się (**-am, -asz**) *vr*: **ona mi się podoba** I like her; **to mi się nie podoba** I don't like it

podobieńst|wo (**-wa, -wa**; *dat sg* **-wu**; *loc sg* **-wie**) *nt* **1** similarity **2** (*jednakowy wygląd*) likeness; **rzeźba na ~ sławnego pisarza** a sculpture of a famous writer

podobnie *adv* **1** (*w podobny sposób*) similarly **2** (*równie*) as; **~ jak** like

podobno *adv* supposedly

podobny *adj* similar; **być ~m do kogoś/czegoś** to be similar to sb/sth; **i tym podobne** and the like

podpal|ać (-am, -asz; pf **-ić)** vt: **~ (podpalić** pf) **coś** to set fire to sth

podpas|ka (-ki, -ki; dat sg & loc sg **-ce**; gen pl **-ek)** f (też: **~ higieniczna)** sanitary towel (Brit) lub napkin (US)

podpi|s (-su, -sy; loc sg **-sie)** m 1 (czyjś: zamaszysty, nieczytelny, wyraźny) signature 2 (pod obrazem) caption

podpis|ywać (-uję, -ujesz; pf **-ać)** vt (dokument, traktat, książkę) to sign; **~ się** vr to sign one's name

podręczni|k (-ka, -ki; inst sg **-kiem)** m (szkolny, do matematyki, opasły) textbook

podrób|ka (-ki, -ki; dat sg **-ce**; gen pl **-ek)** f fake

podróż (-y, -e; gen pl **-y)** f 1 (wycieczka) trip 2 (długa) journey; **podróże** pl travels; **biuro ~y** travel agency; **szczęśliwej ~y!** have a safe trip!

podróżni|k (-ka, -cy; inst sg **-kiem)** m traveller (Brit), traveler (US)

podróżny adj: **torba podróżna** travelling (Brit) lub traveling (US) bag ▷ m decl like adj passenger; **czek ~** traveller's cheque (Brit), traveler's check (US)

podróż|ować (-uję, -ujesz) vi to travel

podryw|ać (-am, -asz; pf **poderwać)** vt (pot) to pick up; **~ chłopców** to pick up boys

podstawowy adj (kurs, zasada, wiedza) basic; **szkoła podstawowa** primary (Brit) lub elementary (US) school

podusz|ka (-ki, -ki; dat sg & loc sg **-ce**; gen pl **-ek)** f (puchowa, miękka, niewygodna) pillow; **~ powietrzna** airbag

podwieczor|ek (-ku, -ki; inst sg **-kiem)** m tea (meal)

podwójnie adv doubly; **płacić/ kosztować ~** to pay/cost double

podwójny adj (korzyść) double

podwór|ko (-ka, -ka; inst sg **-kiem**; gen pl **-ek)** nt 1 yard 2 (za domem) backyard

podwyż|ka (-ki, -ki; dat sg & loc sg **-ce**; gen pl **-ek)** f 1 (pensji, płac, emerytur) rise (Brit), raise (US) 2 (cen) rise

podzia|ł (-łu, -ły; loc sg **-le)** m 1 division 2 (Sci) fission; **~ majątku** division of estate

podziel|ić (-ę, -isz) vb pf od **dzielić**

podziemny adj underground; **przejście podziemne** subway (Brit), underpass (US); **kolejka podziemna** underground (train)

podzięk|ować (-uję, -ujesz) vb pf od **dziękować**

podziękowa|nie (-nia, -nia; gen pl **-ń)** nt (serdeczne, szczere, wylewne) thanks pl

podziwi|ać (-am, -asz) vt to admire

poe|ta (-ty, -ci; dat sg & loc sg **-cie)** m decl like f in sg (romantyczny, współczesny) poet

poezj|a (-i, -e; gen pl **-i)** f poetry

pogański adj (zwyczaj, wierzenie, bóstwo) pagan

pogar|dzać (-dzam, -dzasz; pf **-dzić)** vi: **~ kimś/czymś** (odnosić się z pogardą) to hold sb/sth in contempt; (brak szacunku) to disdain sb/sth

poglą|d (**-du, -dy**; *loc sg* **-dzie**) *m* view

pogo|da (**-dy**; *dat sg & loc sg* **-dzie**) *f* 1 weather 2 (*ciepła pora*) sunny weather; **~ ducha** cheerfulness

pogodny *adj* 1 bright 2 (*niebo, dzień*) clear 3 (*humor, nastrój*) bright

pogotowi|e (**-a**) *nt* 1 (*stan*) alert 2 (*górskie*) emergency service 3 (*ambulans*) ambulance; **być w pogotowiu** to be on stand-by; **~ ratunkowe** ambulance service

pogrze|b (**-bu, -by**; *loc sg* **-bie**) *m* funeral

pogrzebać (**-ię, -iesz**) *vb pf od* **grzebać**

poja|wiać się (**-wiam, -wiasz**; *pf* **-wić**) *vr* (*znienacka, regularnie*) to appear

poj|azd (**-azdu, -azdy**; *loc sg* **-eździe**) *m* vehicle

pojedynkę *inv*: **w ~** by oneself

pojemni|k (**-ka, -ki**; *inst sg* **-kiem**) *m* (*plastikowy, nierdzewny*) container; **~ na śmieci** rubbish bin (*Brit*), trash *lub* garbage can (*US*)

pojemnoś|ć (**-ci**) *f* capacity; **~ pamięci** (*Komput*) memory

pojemny *adj* spacious

poję|cie (**-cia, -cia**; *gen pl* **-ć**) *nt* 1 concept 2 (*pot*) idea; **nie mieć (zielonego** *lub* **najmniejszego) pojęcia o czymś** not to have a clue about sth

pojutrze *adv* the day after tomorrow

pokar|m (**-mu, -my**; *loc sg* **-mie**) *m* 1 (*jedzenie*) food 2 (*mleko matki*) breast milk

poka|z (**-zu, -zy**; *loc sg* **-zie**) *m* demonstration

poka|zać (**-żę, -żesz**) *vb pf od* **pokazywać**

pokaz|ywać (**-uję, -ujesz**; *pf* **-ać**) *vt* to show; **~ się** *vr* (*pojawiać się*) to turn up

pokłó|cić (**-cę, -cisz**; *imp* **-ć**) *vt pf*: **~ kogoś z kimś** to turn sb against sb; **~ się** *vr pf*: **~ się z kimś** to have a row with sb

pokoch|ać (**-am, -asz**) *vt pf* to fall in love with

pokojowy *adj* 1 (*rozmowa*) peaceful 2 (*traktat*) peace 3 (*o pokoju*) room

pokojów|ka (**-ki, -ki**; *dat sg & loc sg* **-ce**; *gen pl* **-ek**) *f* (chamber)maid

pokole|nie (**-nia, -nia**; *gen pl* **-ń**) *nt* (*młode, naszych rodziców*) generation

pok|ój (**-oju, -oje**; *gen pl* **-oi** *lub* **-ojów**) *m* 1 (*część mieszkania*) room 2 (*Pol*) peace; **~ gościnny** living room; **~ jadalny** dining room; **~ jednoosobowy/ dwuosobowy** single/double room

pokrewieńst|wo (**-wa**; *loc sg & dat sg* **-wie**) *nt* 1 (*rodzina*) kinship 2 (*przen*) affinity 3 (*Bio*) affinity

Pola|k (**-ka, -cy**; *inst sg* **-kiem**) *m* Pole

pol|e (**-a, -a**; *gen pl* **pól**) *nt* 1 field 2 (*w matematyce*) area; **~ namiotowe** campsite (*Brit*), campground (*US*)

pole|cać (**-cam, -casz**; *pf* **-cić**) *vt* 1 (*film*) to recommend 2 (*powierzać*) to entrust 3 (*kazać*) to command

polepsz|ać (**-am, -asz**; *pf* **-yć**) *vt*
to improve; **~ się** *vr* to improve
policj|a (**-i**) *f* police
policjan|t (**-ta, -ci**; *loc sg* **-cie**) *m*
policeman, (police) officer
policjant|ka (**-ki, -ki**; *dat sg & loc
sg* **-ce**; *gen pl* **-ek**) *f* policewoman,
(police) officer
policyjny *adj* (*mundur, samochód,
patrol*) police; **godzina policyjna**
curfew
policz|ek (**-ka, -ki**; *inst sg* **-kiem**) *m*
(*rumiany, pulchny, różowy*) cheek
politechni|ka (**-ki, -ki**; *dat sg & loc
sg* **-ce**) *f* polytechnic
polity|k (**-ka, -cy**; *inst sg* **-kiem**) *m*
politician
polity|ka (**-ka**; *dat sg & loc sg* **-ce**) *f*
1 politics **2** (*zagraniczna*) policy; **~
biurowa** office politics
Pol|ka (**-ki, -ki**; *dat sg & loc sg*
-ce; *gen pl* **-ek**) *f* (*rodowita, z
pochodzenia*) Polish woman
pol|ka (**-ki, -ki**; *dat sg & loc sg* **-ce**;
gen pl **-ek**) *f* (*skoczna*) polka

POLONEZ

The **polonez** is a Polish
national dance. It is a slow
and dignified dance, often
performed at the opening
of grand balls. See also
studniówki.

Poloni|a (**-i**) *f*: **~ Amerykańska**
Polish Americans *pl*
polonisty|ka (**-ka, -ki**; *dat sg & loc
sg* **-ce**) *f* **1** (*nauka*) Polish language
and literature **2** (*Uniw*) Polish
Department *lub* Faculty
polować (**-uję, -ujesz**) *vi* to hunt

polowanie (**-nia** (*dat sg & loc sg*))
nt hunt
Pols|ka (**-ki**; *dat sg* **-ce**) *f* Poland

POLSKA WÓDKA

Polska wódka (Polish vodka)
is usually drunk straight
out of small shot glasses.
Polska wódka has been
made since the medieval
times and holds an important
place in Polish culture and
customs. There are also many
flavoured vodkas in Poland,
the most famous of which
are **Zubrówka**, **Krupnik**
and **Śliwowica**. See also
bruderszaft.

polski *adj* Polish;
Rzeczpospolita Polska the
Republic of Poland
polu|bić (**-bię, -bisz**) *vt pf* to take
(a liking) to; **~ się** *vr pf* to grow to
like each other
połącze|nie (**-nia, -nia**; *gen pl* **-ń**)
nt (*telefoniczne*) connection
połącz|yć (**-ę, -ysz**) *vt pf*: **~ kogoś
z kimś** (*telefon*) to put sb through
to sb; **~ się** *vr pf*: **~ się z kimś**
(*telefon*) to get through to sb
połk|nąć (**-nę, -niesz**; *imp* **-nij**) *vb*
pf od **połykać**
poło|wa (**-wy, -wy**; *dat sg & loc sg*
-wie) *f* **1** (*rodzaju*) half **2** (*w połowie
drogi*) middle; **na połowę** in half;
o połowę więcej half as much
again; **o połowę mniej** half as
much; **do połowy pusty** half
empty; **po połowie** fifty-fifty;
w połowie drogi halfway; **w**

połowie czerwca in mid-June;
za połowę ceny half-price
położe|nie (-nia) nt 1 (miejsce:
dramatyczne, wygodne) location
2 (wygodne) situation
położn|a (-ej, -e) f decl like adj
midwife
położony adj: **wieś położona
jest nad rzeką** the village is
situated on the river
poł|ożyć (-ożę, -ożysz; imp **-óż)** vb
pf od **kłaść**
połów|ka (-ki, -ki; dat sg & loc
sg **-ce;** gen pl **-ek)** f (jabłka,
pomarańczy) half
południ|e (-a) nt 1 (godzina
dwunasta) midday 2 (strona
świata) south 3 (kraje południowe)
the South; **przed ~m** in the
morning; **po południu** in the
afternoon; **w ~** at midday; **na ~
od** +gen south of
połyk|ać (-am, -asz; pf **połknąć)**
vt 1 to swallow 2 (pot: książkę)
to devour
pomag|ać (-am, -asz; pf **pomóc)**
vi to help; **~ komuś w czymś** to
help sb with sth; **w czym mogę
pomóc?** how can I help you?;
krzyk/płacz nic nie pomoże
shouting/crying won't help (you)
pomału adv slowly; **~!** slow
down!
pomarańcz|a (-y, -e; gen pl **-y)** f
(soczysta) orange
pomarańczowy adj orange
pomarszczony adj (twarz, papier,
bibuła) wrinkled
pomido|r (-ra, -ry; loc sg **-rze)** m
(dojrzały, jędrny) tomato
pomidorowy adj (zupa, sok,
przecier) tomato

pomiędzy prep +inst = **między**
pomimo prep +gen in spite
of; **~ że** even though; **~ to** lub
wszystko nevertheless; zob. też
mimo
pomni|k (-ka, -ki; inst sg **-kiem)** m
monument
pomoc (-y) f 1 help 2 (wsparcie)
aid; **na ~!** help!; **przy ~y** +gen
with the help of; **za ~ą** +gen by
means of; **~ drogowa** emergency
road service; **~ domowa** home
help; **pierwsza ~** first aid
Pomorz|e (-a) nt Pomerania
(region in north-western Poland)
pom|óc (-ogę, -ożesz; imp **-óż)** vb
pf od **pomagać**
pom|pa (-py; dat sg & loc sg **-pie)**
f 1 (nom pl **-py**) (urządzenie)
pump 2 (wystawność) pomp; **~
paliwowa** fuel pump
pomył|ka (-ki, -ki; loc sg & dat
sg **-ce;** gen pl **-ek)** f 1 (życiowa,
drobna) mistake 2 (telefon) wrong
number; **przez pomyłkę** by
mistake
pomy|sł (-słu, -sły; loc sg **-śle)**
m idea
pomysłowy adj ingenious
pomyśl|eć (-ę, -isz) vi pf: **~ o**
+loc (problemach) to think about;
(rodzinie) to think of
ponad prep +inst (dla oznaczenia
miejsca) above, over ▷ prep +acc
1 (dla oznaczenia kierunku) over
2 (więcej niż) above, over 3 (dłużej
niż) over
ponadto adv (książk)
further(more)
ponawi|ać (-am, -asz; pf
ponowić) vt to renew; **~
(ponowić** pf) **prenumeratę** to

renew a subscription

poniedział|ek (-ku, -ki; inst sg -kiem) m Monday

ponieważ conj because

poniż|ać (-am, -asz; pf -yć) vt to demean; ~ **się** vr to demean o.s.

poniżej prep +gen below ▷ adv (w tekście) below; **osiem stopni ~ zera** eight degrees below zero

poniższy adj: **poniższe uwagi** the following remarks

ponownie adv again

ponury adj 1 (wiadomość) gloomy 2 (widok) bleak 3 (pokój) bleak 4 (myśli, nastrój) dismal

pończo|cha (-chy, -chy; dat sg & loc sg -sze) f stocking

poparze|nie (-nia, -nia; gen pl -ń) nt burn; ~ **pierwszego stopnia** first degree burn

poparz|yć (-ę, -ysz) vt pf to burn; ~ **się** vr pf to burn o.s.

popeł|niać (-niam, -niasz; pf -nić) vt 1 (przestępstwo) to commit 2 (błąd, nietakt, gafę) to make; **popełnić** (pf) **samobójstwo** to commit suicide

popielaty adj grey (Brit), gray (US)

Popiel|ec (-ca) m Ash Wednesday

popielnicz|ka (-ki, -ki; dat sg & loc sg -ce; gen pl -ek) f ashtray

popier|ać (-am, -asz; pf **poprzeć**) vt 1 to support 2 (plan) to second 3 (ustnie) to back 4 (uzasadnić) to support

popi|ół (-ołu, -oły; loc sg -ele) m (z papierosa, z ogniska) ash

popołudni|e (-a, -a) nt (spokojne, upalne) afternoon

popra|wiać (-wiam, -wiasz; pf

-wić) vt 1 (krawat) to straighten 2 (wynik) to better 3 (test) to correct; ~ **się** vr 1 (wyrażać się inaczej) to correct o.s. 2 (polepszać się) to improve

poprawnie adv correctly

poprawny adj 1 (odpowiedź, wymowa) correct 2 (zachowanie) proper

popro|sić (-szę, -sisz; imp -ś) vb pf od **prosić**

poprzedni adj 1 (małżeństwo) previous 2 (miesiąc) preceding

poprzednio adv previously

poprze|dzać (-dzam, -dzasz; pf -dzić) vt to precede

popularnoś|ć (-ci) f popularity

popularny adj popular

po|ra (-ry, -ry; dat sg & loc sg -rze; gen pl **pór**) f (okres) time; **od tej pory** from now on; **do tej pory** so far; ~ **roku** season; **w (samą) porę** (just) in time; **uwaga/ wizyta nie w porę** ill-timed remark/visit

porabi|ać (-am, -asz) vi: **co porabiasz?** what are you up to (these days)?

poradni|k (-ka, -ki; inst sg -kiem) m (ogrodniczy, domowy, kucharski) handbook

pora|dzić (-dzę, -dzisz; imp -dź) vi pf: ~ **sobie z czymś** to manage sth; **nic na to nie poradzę** I can't help it

poran|ek (-ka, -ki; inst sg -kiem) m morning

poranny adj (rytuał, gazeta, kawa) morning

poraż|ka (-ki, -ki; dat sg & loc sg -ce; gen pl -ek) f 1 (dotkliwa, nieoczekiwana) defeat 2 (brak *powodzenia*) failure

porcela|na (-ny; *dat sg & loc sg* **-nie**) *f* (*delikatna, cienka, przezroczysta*) porcelain

porcj|a (-i, -e; *gen pl* **-i**) *f* portion

pornografi|a (-i) *f* pornography

pornograficzny *adj* (*film, magazyn*) pornographic

porodowy *adj*: **bóle porodowe** labour (*Brit*) *lub* labor (*US*) pains

poro|nić (-nię, -nisz; *imp* **-ń**) *vi pf* to miscarry

poronie|nie (-nia, -nia; *gen pl* **-ń**) *nt* **1** miscarriage **2** (*Med*) abortion

porozmawia|ć (-am, -asz; *imp* **-aj**) *vi pf*: **~ (z kimś o czymś)** to talk (to sb about sth)

porozumie|nie (-nia, -nia; *gen pl* **-ń**) *nt* agreement; **w porozumieniu z kimś** in consultation with sb

porozumiew|ać się (-am, -asz; *pf* **porozumieć**) *vr* **1** (*komunikować się*) to communicate **2** (*dogadywać się*) to reach an agreement

por|ód (-odu, -ody; *loc sg* **-odzie**) *m* (*naturalny, domowy*) (child)birth

porówna|nie (-nia, -nia; *gen pl* **-ń**) *nt* comparison; **w porównaniu z** +*inst* compared to

porówn|ywać (-uję, -ujesz; *pf* **-ać**) *vt* to compare; **~ kogoś/coś z** +*inst* to compare sb/sth to

por|t (-tu, -ty; *loc sg* **-cie**) *m* port, harbour (*Brit*), harbor (*US*); **~ lotniczy** airport; **zawijać (zawinąć** *pf*) **do ~u** to call at a port

portal (-u, -e; *gen pl* **-i**) *m* (*architektura*) portal

portfel (-a, -e; *gen pl* **-i**) *m* **1** wallet, billfold (*US*) **2** (*ekonomia*) portfolio

portie|r (-ra, -rzy; *loc sg* **-rze**) *m* **1** (*recepcjonista*) receptionist **2** (*przy wejściu*) porter

portre|t (-tu, -ty; *loc sg* **-cie**) *m* portrait

porwa|nie (-nia, -nia; *gen pl* **-ń**) *nt* **1** (*dziecko*) abduction **2** (*autobus*) hijacking

poryw|ać (-am, -asz; *pf* **porwać**) *vt* **1** (*dziecko*) to abduct **2** (*autobus*) to hijack **3** (*liści*) to sweep away **4** (*przen*) to carry away; **~ się** *vr*: **~ się na kogoś** to make an attempt on sb's life

porząd|ek (-ku, -ki; *inst sg* **-kiem**) *m* order; **porządki** *pl* (*sprzątanie*) cleaning *sg*; **w porządku!** all right!; **doprowadzać (doprowadzić** *pf*) **coś do porządku** to put sth in order; **~ dzienny/obrad** the agenda; **być na porządku dziennym** to be on the agenda

porządk|ować (-uję, -ujesz; *pf* **u-**) *vt* **1** (*układać*) to put in order **2** (*sprzątać*) to tidy

porządkowy *adj* **1** (*liczebnik*) ordinal **2** (*numer*) serial

porządny *adj* **1** (*w dobrym stanie*) tidy **2** (*solidny*) respectable **3** (*ogromny*) severe **4** (*pot: ulewa*) heavy **5** (*posiłek*) square; **~ z niego facet** he's a sound bloke

porzecz|ka (-ki, -ki; *dat sg & loc sg* **-ce**; *gen pl* **-ek**) *f* currant; **czarna ~** blackcurrant; **czerwona ~** redcurrant

porzu|cać (-cam, -casz; *pf* **-cić**) *vt* **1** (*kraj*) to abandon **2** (*pracę*) to quit; **~ kogoś/coś na pastwę losu** to leave sb/sth to their/its own fate

posa|g (**-gu, -gi**; *inst sg* **-giem**)
m dowry

po|seł (**-sła, -słowie**; *loc sg* **-śle**) *m*
1 (*członek parlamentu*)
≈ Member of Parliament (*Brit*),
≈ Representative (*US*),
2 (*wysłannik*) envoy

posiadacz (**-a, -e**; *gen pl* **-y**) *m*
(*karty kredytowej, konta bankowego*)
owner

posiad|ać (**-am, -asz**)
vt **1** (*mieszkanie*) to own
2 (*umiejętności*) to possess

posiadłoś|ć (**-ci, -ci**; *gen pl* **-ci**) *f*
property

posił|ek (**-ku, -ki**; *inst sg* **-kiem**) *m*
(*wspólny, wieczorny, obfity*) meal;
posiłki *pl* reinforcements

posła|niec (**-ńca, -ńcy**) *m*
(*pocztowy*) messenger

posłu|giwać się (**-guję, -gujesz**;
pf **posłużyć**) *vr:* ~ **się czymś/kimś**
to use sth/sb

posmutni|eć (**-eję, -ejesz**) *vi pf*
to become sad

pospieszny *itd. zob.* **pośpieszny**
itd.

poszedł *itd. vb zob.* **pójść**

pospolity *adj* (*wygląd, pogląd*)
common; **rzeczownik** ~
common noun

posta|ć (**-ci, -cie** *lub* **-ci**; *gen pl*
-ci) *m* **1** (*kształt*) form **2** (*sylwetka*)
figure **3** (*literacki*) character

postanawi|ać (**-am, -asz**; *pf*
postanowić) *vt* to decide on
▷ *vi* to decide; **postanowić**
coś zrobić to decide to do sth;
postanowić czegoś nie robić
to decide against doing sth;
postanowić, że... to decide
that...; (*Prawo*) to rule that...

postar|ać się (**-am, -asz**) *vb pf*

od **starać się** ▷ *vr pf:* ~ **się o coś**
(*zdobyć*) to obtain sth

posterun|ek (**-ku, -ki**; *inst*
sg **-kiem**) *m* post; **straży**
pożarnej/~ policji fire/police
station; **być na posterunku**
(*przen*) to be on duty

postę|p (**-pu**; *loc sg* **-pie**) *m*
progress; **postępy** *pl* progress *sg*

postęp|ować (**-uję, -ujesz**; *pf*
postąpić) *vi* **1** (*praca*) to proceed
2 (*choroba*) to progress **3** (*dobrze,*
uczciwie) to behave

postępowy *adj* (*umysł*)
progressive

postkomuni|sta (**-sty, -ści**; *dat*
sg **-ście**) *m decl like f in sg* post-
communist

postul|ować (**-uję, -ujesz**) *vt* to
postulate

posuw|ać (**-am, -asz**; *pf*
posunąć) *vt* to move forward;
~ **się** *vr* to move forward; ~ **się**
do desperackich czynów to act
in desperation; ~ **się za daleko**
(*przen*) to go too far

poszedł *itd. vb zob.* **pójść**

poszuk|ać (**-am, -asz**) *vt pf:* ~
kogoś/czegoś to find sb/sth

poszu|kiwać (**-kuję, -kujesz**)
vt: ~ **kogoś/czegoś** to search
for sb/sth

poszukiwany *adj* **1** (*ceniony*)
sought-after **2** (*złodziej*) wanted

pościel (**-i, -e**; *gen pl* **-i**) *f* bedding

poślizg|nąć się (**-nę, -niesz**; *imp*
-nij) *vr pf* to slip

poślu|bić (**-bię, -bisz**) *vt pf* to wed

pośpiech (**-u**) *m* hurry; **bez ~u**
unhurried; **w ~u** hurriedly

pośpieszny *adj* hurried; **pociąg**
~ fast train

pośredni|k (-ka, -cy; *inst sg* **-kiem**) *m* **1** mediator **2** (*Comm*) agent **3** (*też*: **~ handlu nieruchomościami**) (*real*) estate agent

pośród *prep* +*gen* in the midst of

po|t (-tu, -ty; *loc sg* **-cie**) *m* sweat

potem *adv* **1** (*później*) later **2** (*następnie*) then; **na ~** for later

potę|ga (-gi; *dat sg & loc sg* **-dze**) *f* power; **cztery do potęgi trzeciej** four to the power of three

potężny *adj* **1** (*władca*) powerful **2** (*maszyna*) mighty

poto|k (-ku, -ki; *inst sg* **-kiem**) *m* stream

potom|ek (-ka, -kowie; *inst sg* **-kiem**) *m* descendant

potomst|wo (-wa; *loc sg* **-wie**) *nt* offspring

poto|p (-pu; *loc sg* **-pie**) *m* **1** deluge **2** (*Rel*) the Great Flood

potra|fić (-fię, -fisz) *vi*: **on potrafi to zrobić** (*jest zdolny*) he is capable of doing it; (*umie*) he can do it

potra|wa (-wy, -wy; *dat sg & loc sg* **-wie**) *f* (*danie*) dish; **spis potraw** menu

potrą|cać (-cam, -casz; *pf* **-cić**) *vt* **1** (*szturchać*) to jostle **2** (*odliczać*) to deduct

potrw|ać (-a) *vi pf* **1** (*podróż*) to take **2** (*zebrania*) to last; **jak długo to potrwa?** how long is it going to take?; **to nie potrwa długo** it won't take long

potrze|ba¹ (-by, -by; *dat sg* **-bie**) *f* need; **potrzeby** *pl* needs *pl*; **bez potrzeby** unnecessarily; **w razie potrzeby** if necessary; **nie ma potrzeby się spieszyć** there's

no need to hurry; **w potrzebie** in need; **~ matką wynalazków** (*przysł*) necessity is the mother of invention

potrzeba² *inv*: **~ nam pieniędzy/ czasu** we need money/time; **czego ci ~?** what do you need?

potrzebny *adj* necessary; **to mi jest potrzebne** I need that; **jestem ci ~?** do you need me?; **to nie jest potrzebne** this isn't necessary

potrzeb|ować (-uję, -ujesz) *vt pf*: **~ czegoś** *lub* **coś** to need sth; **nie potrzebujesz tego robić** you don't need to do this

potwier|dzać (-dzam, -dzasz; *imp* **-dź**; *pf* **-dzić**) *vt* **1** to confirm **2** (*odbiór przesyłki*) to acknowledge; **~ się** *vr* to be confirmed

potw|ór (-ora, -ory; *loc sg* **-orze**) *m* monster

poważnie *adv* seriously; **wyglądać ~** to look serious; **~?** seriously?; **mówisz ~?** are you serious?

poważny *adj* **1** (*ministrata*) serious **2** (*rola*) substantial **3** (*organizacja*) reputable; **muzyka poważna** classical music

powiadami|ać (-am, -asz; *pf* **powiadomić**) *vt*: **~ kogoś (o czymś)** to notify sb (of sth)

powi|at (-atu, -aty; *loc sg* **-ecie**) *m* Polish administrative unit

powi|edzieć (-em, -esz; *3 pl* **-edzą**; *imp* **-edz**) *vt pf*: **~ coś/, że...** to say sth/that... ▷ *vi pf* to say; **~ komuś coś/o czymś/, że...** to tell sb sth/about sth/ that...; **co chcesz przez to ~?**

what do you mean by that?; **co powiesz na to?** what about that?

powierzch|nia (**-ni, -nie**; *gen pl* **-ni**) *f* **1** (*na zewnątrz*) surface **2** (*teren, Mat*) area

powie|sić (**-szę, -sisz**; *imp* **-ś**) *vt pf* to hang; **~ się** *vr pf* (*samobójstwo*) to hang o.s.

powieś|ć (**-ci, -ci**; *gen pl* **-ci**) *f* (*historyczna, dla dziewcząt*) novel

powietrz|e (**-a**) *nt* air; **na wolnym powietrzu** in the open air

powiększ|ać (**-am, -asz**; *pf* **-yć**) *vt* **1** (*teren*) to expand **2** (*ilość, deficyt*) to increase **3** (*organizację, Fot*) to enlarge; **~ się** *vr* **1** (*terytorium*) to expand **2** (*grupa*) to grow

powiększ|yć (**-ę, -ysz**) *vb pf od* **powiększać**

powinien (*f* **powinna**; *nt* **powinno**) *aux vb*: **powinna tam pójść** she should go there; **~eś mi pokazać** you should show me; **~em był zadzwonić** I should have phoned

powit|ać (**-am, -asz**) *vb pf od* **witać**

powita|nie (**-nia, -nia**; *gen pl* **-ń**) *nt* welcome

powod|ować (**-uję, -ujesz**; *pf* **s-**) *vt* to cause

powodze|nie (**-nia**) *nt* success; **powodzenia!** good luck!

powojenny *adj* postwar

powoli *adv* slowly

powolny *adj* slow

pow|ód (**-odu, -ody**; *loc sg* **-odzie**) *m* **1** (*przyczyna*) cause **2** (*uzasadnienie*) reason; **z powodu** +*gen* because of; **z tego powodu** because of this

pow|ódź (**-odzi, -odzie**; *gen pl* **-odzi**) *f* flood

powrac|ać (**-am, -asz**; *pf* **powrócić**) *vi* to return

powrotny *adj*: **bilet ~** return (*Brit*) *lub* round-trip (*US*) ticket

powr|ót (**-otu, -oty**; *loc sg* **-ocie**) *m* return

powsta|nie (**-nia**) *nt* **1** (*utworzenie*) rise **2** (*nom pl* **-nia**; *gen pl* **-ń**) (*bunt*) uprising

powstrzym|ywać (**-uję, -ujesz**; *pf* **-ać**) *vt* **1** (*zatrzymać*) to restrain **2** (*łzy*) to hold back; **~ kogoś od robienia czegoś** to stop sb from doing sth

powszechny *adj* **1** (*opinia, pogląd*) common **2** (*wybory*) general **3** (*edukacja*) primary (*Brit*), elementary (*US*)

powtarz|ać (**-am, -asz**; *pf* **powtórzyć**) *vt* **1** to repeat **2** (*materiał*) to revise (*Brit*), to review (*US*); **~ się** *vr* **1** (*zdarzać się ponownie*) to recur **2** (*historia*) to repeat itself **3** (*osoba*) to repeat o.s.; **czy mógłby pan to powtórzyć?** could you say that again?

powtór|ka (**-ki, -ki**; *dat sg & loc sg* **-ce**; *gen pl* **-ek**) *f* **1** (*Szkol*) revision (*Brit*), review (*US*) **2** (*TV, Rad*) repeat

powtórnie *adv* again

powtórny *adj* second

powtórze|nie (**-nia, -nia**; *gen pl* **-ń**) *nt* **1** repetition **2** (*materiału*) revision (*Brit*), review (*US*) **3** (*TV, Rad*) repeat

powyżej *prep* +*gen* **1** (*wyżej*) above **2** (*ponad*) over ▷ *adv* above; **mam tego ~ uszu!** that really gets up my nose!

powyższy *adj (cytat)* aforementioned

po|za¹ (-zy, -zy; *dat sg & loc sg* **-zie;** *gen pl* **póz)** *f* pose

poza² *prep +acc* beyond ▷ *prep +inst* **1** *(na zewnątrz)* outside **2** *(z wyjątkiem)* apart from; **~ tym** *(zresztą)* apart from that; *(też)* also

pozdrawi|ać (-am, -asz; *pf* **pozdrowić)** *vt* to greet; **pozdrów ode mnie Mateusza** give my regards to Mateusz

pozio|m (-mu, -my; *loc sg* **-mie)** *m* **1** *(wysokość)* level **2** *(jakość)* standard **3** *(zawartość)* content

poziomo *adv* **1** *(ułożyć, ustawić)* horizontally **2** *(w krzyżówce)* across

poziomy *adj* horizontal

pozn|ać (-am, -asz) *vt pf od* **poznawać;** *(pierwszy raz)* to meet; **~ się** *vr pf (zawrzeć znajomość)* to meet; **~ kogoś z kimś drugim** to introduce sb to sb else; **miło mi pana/panią ~** pleased to meet you; **~ się bliżej** to get to know each other better

pozn|awać (-aję, -ajesz; *pf* **-ać)** *vt* **1** *(miasto)* to get to know **2** *(świat)* to see **3** *(język)* to learn **4** *(rozpoznać)* to recognize **5** *(doświadczać)* to experience **6** *(tajemnice)* to find out; **~ się** *vr* **1** *(rozpoznawać siebie)* to recognize o.s. **2** *(rozpoznawać jeden drugiego)* to recognize each other **3** *(dowiedzieć się o sobie)* to get to know each other

pozostały *adj* **1** remaining **2** *(drugi)* the other

pozost|awać (-aję, -ajesz; *imp* **-awaj;** *pf* **-ać)** *vi* **1** *(przebywać)* to stay **2** *(jeszcze być)* to remain; **~ wiernym** to remain faithful; **~ w tyle** to lag behind

pozosta|wiać (-wiam, -wiasz) *vt (pf* **-wić)** to leave

pozwalać (-alam, -alasz; *pf* **pozwolić)** *vt* to allow

pozwole|nie (-nia, -nia; *gen pl* **-ń)** *nt* **1** *(zgoda)* permission **2** *(dokument)* permit

pozw|olić (-olę, -olisz; *imp* **-ól)** *vb pf od* **pozwalać; on pozwala sobie na zbyt dużo** he takes too many liberties

pozycj|a (-i, -e; *gen pl* **-i)** *f* **1** position **2** *(w kolekcji)* item; **nadużywać (nadużyć** *pf)* **swej pozycji** to abuse one's position

pozytywny *adj* **1** *(reakcja, komentarz)* positive **2** *(rezultaty)* favourable (*Brit*), favorable (*US*)

poża|r (-ru, -ry; *loc sg* **-rze)** *m* fire; **~ doszczętnie strawił budynek** fire completely destroyed the building

pożąd|ać (-am, -asz) *vt +gen* to covet

pożąda|nie (-nia) *nt* desire

pożegn|ać (-am, -asz) *vb pf od* **żegnać; ~ się z kimś** to say goodbye to sb

pożegna|nie (-nia, -nia; *gen pl* **-ń)** *nt* farewell

pożyczać (-am, -asz) *vt (pieniądze, książkę)* to borrow; **~ coś od kogoś** to borrow sth from sb; **~ coś komuś** to lend sth to sb

pożycz|ka (-ki, -ki; *dat sg & loc sg* **-ce;** *gen pl* **-ek)** *f (długoterminowa, nieprocentowana)* loan

pożywie|nie (-nia) *nt* food

pój|ść (**-dę, -dziesz**; *imp* **-dź**; *pt* **poszedł, poszła, poszli**) *vb pf od* **iść**; **~ do diabła** (*przen*) go to hell

- CHODZIĆ/IŚĆ/PÓJŚĆ
-
- **Chodzić, iść** and **pójść** are
- all verbs of motion meaning
- to go (on foot), but they have
- different implications. With
- the perfective verb – **pójść**
- – the emphasis is on the act of
- going to and arriving at the
- destination, whereas with the
- imperfective verbs – **chodzić**
- and **iść** – the focus is more
- on the act of going itself and
- it is not made clear whether
- the subject arrives at the
- destination or not. **Chodzić** is
- also used to describe habitual
- activities and **iść** is used to
- describe going to or from
- a particular point on one
- occasion.

pół *inv* half; **~ szklanki** half a glass; **~ godziny** half an hour; **trzy i ~** three and a half
półfina|ł (**-łu, -ły**; *loc sg* **-le**) *m* the semi-finals *pl*; **~ mistrzostw świata** world championships semi-final
pół|ka (**-ki, -ki**; *dat sg & loc sg* **-ce**; *gen pl* **-ek**) *f* **1** shelf **2** (*książek*) bookshelf **3** (*bagażu*) rack
północ (**-y**) *f* **1** (*godzina*) midnight **2** (*świata*) north; **na ~ od** +*gen* to the north of
północny *adj* **1** (*klimat*) northern **2** (*wiatr*) northerly; **~ zachód** north-west; **Ameryka Północna**

North America; **Irlandia Północna** Northern Ireland
półtora *num* one and a half; **~ kilograma** one and a half kilogrammes; **półtorej godziny** an hour and a half; **on wygląda jak ~ nieszczęścia** (*przen*) he's got a face like a wet weekend
półwys|ep (**-pu, -py**; *loc sg* **-pie**) *m* peninsula
później *adv comp od* **późno** later; **trzy dni ~** three days later
późniejszy *adj comp od* **późny** (*następny: termin*) subsequent; **~ prezydent** the future president
późno *adv* late; **za ~** too late; **lepiej ~ niż wcale** better late than never
późny *adj* late
prac|a (**-y, -e**) *f* work; **~ domowa** homework; **~ magisterska** MA thesis; **być w pracy** to be at work
pracodawc|a (**-y, -y**) *m decl like f in sg* employer
prac|ować (**-uję, -ujesz**) *vi* **1** (*robić pracę*) to work **2** (*mieć stanowisko*) to have a job **3** (*działać*) to work
pracowity *adj* **1** (*człowiek*) hard-working **2** (*dzień*) arduous
pracowni|k (**-ka, -cy**; *inst sg* **-kiem**) *m* (*solidny, lojalny, długoletni*) worker; **~ fizyczny** labourer (*Brit*), laborer (*US*); **~ umysłowy** office worker
prać (**piorę, pierzesz**) *vt* **1** (*pf* **wy-**) to wash **2** (*chemicznie*) to dry-clean **3** (*pf* **s-**) (*pot: bić*) to thrash ▷ *vi* to do the laundry; **~ się** (*pf* **wy-**) *vr* (*być pranym*) to wash; **~ publicznie swoje brudy** (*przen*) to wash one's dirty laundry

in public
pradziad|ek (**-ka, -kowie**; *inst sg* **-kiem**) *m* great-grandfather
praktyczny *adj* practical
pral|ka (**-ki, -ki**; *dat sg & loc sg* **-ce**; *gen pl* **-ek**) *f* (*automatyczna*) washing machine
pral|nia (**-ni, -nie**; *gen pl* **-ni**) *f* **1** (*publiczna, ogólnodostępna*) laundry **2** (*chemiczna*) dry-cleaner's **3** (*samoobsługowa*) Launderette ® (*Brit*), Laundromat ® (*US*)
pra|nie (**-nia**) *nt* **1** (*czynność*) washing **2** (*nom pl* **-nia**; *gen pl* **-ń**) (*ubranie itd*) washing, laundry (*US*)
pra|sa (**-sy**; *dat sg & loc sg* **-sie**) *f* **1** (*kobieca, obcojęzyczna, fachowa*) press **2** (*dziennikarze*) the Press
pras|ować (**-uję, -ujesz**) *vt* (*pf* **wy-**) (*ubranie itd*) to iron
praw|da (**-dy, -dy**; *dat sg & loc sg* **-dzie**) *f* truth; **czy to ~?** is that true?; (**jest**) **zimno, ~?** (it's) cold, isn't it?; **lubisz ją, ~?** you like her, don't you?; **~ w oczy kole** (*przysł*) the truth hurts
prawdopodobnie *adv* (*może*) probably
prawdopodobny *adj* probable
prawdziwy *adj* **1** (*przyjemność*) real **2** (*skóra*) genuine **3** (*historia*) true **4** (*zdarzenie*) authentic
prawicowy *adj* (*partia, aktywista, polityk*) right-wing
prawidłowy *adj* **1** (*poprawny: odpowiedź*) correct **2** (*należyty: ubiór, zachowanie, maniery*) proper **3** (*normalny*) normal
prawie *adv* almost; **~ go nie znam** I hardly know him; **~ nic**

hardly anything; **~ nigdy** hardly ever; **~ nikt** hardly anyone; **~ to zrobiłem** I've almost done it
prawni|k (**-ka, -cy**; *inst sg* **-kiem**) *m* (*znany, ceniony, poważany*) lawyer
pra|wo¹ (**-wa**; *loc sg* **-wie**) *nt* **1** law **2** (*ustawa*) statute **3** (*nom pl* **-wa**) (*uprawnienie*) right **4** (*zasada*) principle; **~ cywilne** civil law; **~ jazdy** (*Mot*) driving licence (*Brit*), driver's license (*US*); **prawa człowieka** human rights; **mieć ~ do czegoś/coś zrobić** to have the right to sth/to do sth; **~ stoi po jego stronie** (*przen*) he has the law on his side
prawo² *adv*: **w ~** (*kręcić*) to the right; **na ~** (*w prawą stronę*) to the right; (*po prawej stronie*) on the right
prawosławny *adj* (*kościół, zwyczaj, pieśń*) Orthodox
prą|cie (**-cia, -cia**; *gen pl* **-ci**) *nt* penis
prą|d (**-du, -dy**; *loc sg* **-dzie**) *m* **1** (*elektryczny*) current **2** (*elektryczność*) electricity **3** (*kierunek*) trend; **iść pod ~** to go against the tide; **iść z ~em** to go with the flow
precyzyjny *adj* **1** (*definicja*) precise **2** (*instumenty*) precision
prekurso|r (**-ra, -rzy**; *loc sg* **-rze**) *m* predecessor
premi|a (**-i, -e**; *gen pl* **-i**) *f* **1** (*dodatek do płacy: roczna, jednorazowa*) bonus **2** (*nagroda*) prize
premie|r (**-ra, -rzy**; *loc sg* **-rze**) *m* prime minister
premie|ra (**-ry, -ry**; *dat sg & loc sg* **-rze**) *f* première

prezen|t (**-tu**, **-ty**; *loc sg* **-cie**) *m*
(*nieoczekiwany, niechciany*)
present

prezentacj|a (**-i**, **-e**; *gen pl* **-i**)
f **1** (*człowieka*) introduction
2 (*pokaz*) presentation

prezent|ować (**-uję**, **-ujesz**;
pf **za-**) *vt* (*ludzi*) to introduce;
~ się *vr*: **dobrze się ~** to look
presentable; **~ (za~** *pf*) **coś
komuś** to show sth to sb

prezerwaty|wa (**-wy**, **-wy**; *dat sg*
-wie) *f* condom

preze|s (**-sa**, **-si**; *loc sg* **-sie**) *m*
chairman (*Brit*), president (*US*); **~
Rady Ministrów** Prime Minister

prezyden|t (**-ta**, **-ci**; *loc sg* **-cie**)
m **1** (*kraju*) president **2** (*miasta*)
mayor

prę|dko *adv* **1** (*szybko*) quickly
2 (*wkrótce*) soon

prędkoś|ć (**-ci**) *f* **1** (*pojazd*) speed
2 (*Fiz*) velocity

prima aprilis *m inv* April Fool's
Day

PRL *abbr* (= *Polska Rzeczpospolita
Ludowa*) (*Hist*) the People's
Republic of Poland

- **PRL**
-
- **PRL** is the abbreviation of
- the **Polska Rzeczpospolita**
- **Ludowa** (the People's
- Republic of Poland). This
- is how the Polish state
- was referred to from the
- post-war era to the collapse
- of communism in 1989.
- Nowadays the word **PRL** is
- often used as a synonym for
- the numerous shortcomings

- of that period: aesthetic
- blandness, shortages and
- queues. See also **sklep**
- **monopolowy, bar mleczny,**
- **osiedle mieszkaniowe**.

proble|m (**-mu**, **-my**; *loc sg* **-mie**)
m problem; **nie ma ~u** (*pot*) no
problem

proc. *abbr* (= *procent*) percent

procen|t (**-tu**, **-ty**; *loc sg* **-cie**) *m*
1 (*setna część*) percent **2** (*odsetki*)
interest; **duży ~** a high
percentage

proce|s (**-su**, **-sy**; *loc sg* **-sie**) *m*
1 process **2** (*Prawo: sądowy, karny*)
(law)suit

produkcj|a (**-i**) *f* production

produk|ować (**-uję**, **-ujesz**; *pf*
wy-) *vt* to produce

produk|t (**-tu**, **-ty**; *loc sg* **-cie**)
m product; **~y spożywcze**
foodstuffs

produktywny *adj* (*pracownik*)
productive

profeso|r (**-ra**, **-rowie**; *loc sg*
-rze) *m* professor; **~ zwyczajny**
professor

progno|za (**-zy**, **-zy**; *dat sg*
-zie) *f* **1** (*przewidywanie: ponura,
obiecująca, gospodarcza*) forecast
2 (*zapowiedź*) prognosis; **~
pogody** weather forecast

progra|m (**-mu**, **-my**; *loc sg*
-mie) *m* **1** programme (*Brit*),
program (*US*) **2** (*Pol*) manifesto
3 (*spotkania*) agenda **4** (*edukacja*)
curriculum **5** (*Komput*) program

projekt|ować (**-uję**, **-ujesz**;
pf **za-**) *vt* (*ubrania, urządzenia,
wnętrza*) to design

prokurato|r (**-ra**, **-rzy**; *loc sg* **-rze**)

m prosecutor

pro|m (-mu, -my; *loc sg* **-mie)**
m ferry

promie|ń (-nia, -nie; *gen pl* **-ni)** *m*
1 (*światła, Roentgena*) ray **2** (*okręgu*)
radius; **~ słońca** sunbeam; **w
promieniu stu metrów od** +*gen*
within 100 metres (*Brit*) *lub*
meters (*US*) of

promocj|a (-i, -e; *gen pl* **-i)** *f*
(*świąteczna*) promotion

prom|ować (-uję, -ujesz)
vt **1** (*pf* **wy-**) to promote
2 (*przen: nagrodzić*) to reward

propag|ować (-uję, -ujesz; *pf*
roz-) *vt* (*ideę, poglądy, zasady*) to
propagate

propon|ować (-uję, -ujesz; *pf*
za-) *vt* to suggest; **~ coś komuś**
to offer sb sth

pro|sić (-szę, -sisz; *imp* **-ś;** *pf* **po-)**
vt: **~ kogoś o coś/żeby coś zrobił**
to ask sb for sth/to do sth; **proszę
państwa** ladies and gentlemen;
proszę bardzo (*odpowiedź na
dziękuję*) you're welcome; (*podając
coś*) here you are; **proszę wejść**
come in

prosto *adv* **1** (*iść*) straight
ahead **2** (*chodzić, stać*)
upright **3** (*tłumaczyć*) clearly
4 (*bezpośrednio*) straight

prostoką|t (-ta, -ty; *loc sg* **-cie)** *m*
rectangle

prostu *inv*: **po ~** (*zwyczajnie*)
basically; (*wprost*) straight

prosty *adj* **1** (*włosy, droga*) straight
2 (*człowiek, maszyna, zdanie*) simple
3 (*wyprostowany*) erect; **kąt ~**
right angle

prostytut|ka (-ki, -ki; *dat sg* & *loc
sg* **-ce;** *gen pl* **-ek)** *f* (*luksusowa*)

prostitute

prosz|ek (-ku, -ki; *inst sg*
-kiem) *m* **1** (*substancja*) powder
2 (*lekarstwo*) pill; **~ do prania**
washing powder; **mleko w
proszku** powdered milk; **~
do pieczenia** baking powder;
zmielić na ~ to grind to a powder

pr|ośba (-ośby, -ośby; *dat sg* & *loc
sg* **-ośbie;** *gen pl* **-óśb)** *f* request;
mam do ciebie prośbę I have a
favour (*Brit*) *lub* favor (*US*) to ask
of you; **chodzić po prośbie** to beg

prote|st (-stu, -sty; *loc sg* **-ście)**
m protest

protestancki *adj* (*kościół,
wyznanie, wiara*) Protestant

protestan|t (-ta, -ci; *loc sg* **-cie)** *m*
Protestant

protestant|ka (-ki, -ki; *loc sg* & *dat
sg* **-ce;** *gen pl* **-ek)** *f* Protestant

prowa|dzić (-dzę, -dzisz; *imp*
-dź) *vt* **1** (*dziecko, życie*) to lead
2 (*samochód*) to drive **3** (*rozmowę*)
to hold **4** (*badania*) to conduct
5 (*śledztwo*) to hold **6** (*zakład*) to
run **7** (*interesy*) to do **8** (*wojnę*) to
wage ▷ *vi* (*Sport*) to lead, to be in
the lead; **~ (do~** *pf*) **do czegoś** to
lead (up) to sth

prowincjonalny *adj* (*pej: szkoła,
pogląd, ubiór*) provincial

prowok|ować (-uję, -ujesz; *pf*
s-) *vt* to provoke; **~ (s-** *pf*) **kogoś
do dyskusji/działania/bójki**
to provoke sb into discussion/
action/a fight

pró|ba (-by, -by; *loc sg* & *dat
sg* **-bie)** *f* **1** (*wytrzymałości itp.*)
test **2** (*w teatrze*) rehearsal; **~
(zrobienia czegoś)** attempt (at
doing sth); **~ generalna** dress

rehearsal

prób|ka (-ki, -ki; dat sg & loc sg **-ce**; gen pl **-ek**) f sample

prób|ować (-uję, -ujesz; pf **s-**) vt 1 (jedzenie) to taste 2 (maszyny) to test; **~ (s~** pf) **coś zrobić** to try to do sth; **~ (s~** pf) **sił w czymś** to try one's hand at sth

prymitywny adj (człowiek, zachowanie, maniery) primitive

prysznic (-u, -e) m shower; **brać (wziąć** pf) **~** to have a shower

prywat|ka (-ki, -ki; dat sg & loc sg **-ce**; gen pl **-ek**) f party

prywatny adj 1 private 2 (szkoła) private, public (Brit) 3 (użytek, sprawa, problem) personal

przebacz|ać (-am, -asz; pf **-yć**) vt: **przebaczyć** (pf) **coś komuś** to forgive sb sth

przebiegły adj cunning; **ależ z niego ~ lis!** well, he's sly fox!

przebieralni|a (-, -e; gen pl **-**) f (damska, koedukacyjna) changing room

przebłys|k (-ku, -ki; inst sg **-kiem**) m 1 (światła) glimmer 2: **~ geniuszu** stroke of genius

przeb|ój (-oju, -oje) m 1 (piosenka) hit 2 (sukces) success; **lista przebojów** the charts pl

przebudow|ywać (-uję, -ujesz; pf **-ać**) vt 1 (budynek) to convert 2 (ulicę) to rebuild

przebu|dzić (-dzę, -dzisz; imp **-dź**) vb pf to awaken; **~ się** vr to awaken

przechadz|ać się (-am, -asz) vr to stroll

przecho|dzić (-dzę, -dzisz; imp **-dź**; pf **przejść**) vt 1 (ulicę) to cross 2 (chorobę) to suffer

3 (doświadczyć) to experience 4 (operację) to undergo ▷ vi 1 (iść) to move on 2 (iść obok) to pass by 3 (ból) to ease 4 (czas) to pass 5 (zostawać zaakceptowanym) to go through 6 (ustawa) to be passed 7 (pomysł) to be accepted

przecho|dzień (-dnia, -dnie) m passer-by

przechow|ywać (-uję, -ujesz; pf **-ać**) vt 1 (żywność, ubrania, rzeczy osobiste) to store 2 (dokumenty) to keep

prze|ciąć (-tnę, -tniesz; imp **-tnij)** vb pf od **ciąć, przecinać**; **~ więzy** to cut ties

przeciek|ać (-a; pf **przeciec)** vi 1 (dachu) to leak 2 (pot: o informacjach) to leak out

przecież adv but; **~ to prawda!** but it's true!; **~ znasz go?** you do know him, don't you?

przecin|ać (-am, -asz; pf **przeciąć)** vt 1 (skórę) to cut 2 (dyskusję) to cut short; **~ się** vr 1 (o dwóch ulicach, liniach, drogach życiowych) to cross 2 (o ulicach, liniach) to criss-cross

przeciw prep +dat against; **argumenty za i ~** pros and cons; **nie mam nic ~ko temu** I've got nothing against it

przeciw... pref anti-, counter-

przeciwbólowy adj (Med): **środek ~** painkiller

przeciwdeszczowy adj: **płaszcz ~** raincoat

przeciwieńst|wo (-wa, -wa; dat sg **-wu**; loc sg **-wie)** nt 1 (sprzeczność) contrast 2 (odwrotny) opposite; **w przeciwieństwie do** +gen unlike

przeciwko *prep* = **przeciw**

przeciwni|k (**-ka**, **-cy**; *inst sg* **-kiem**) *m* **1** (*wróg*) enemy **2** (*rywal*) opponent

przeciwny *adj* **1** (*ściana*) opposite **2** (*poglądy*) contrary; **być ~m czemuś** to oppose sth

przeciwpożarowy *adj* (*schody, wyjście*) fire; **alarm ~** fire alarm

przeciwsłoneczny *adj*: **okulary przeciwsłoneczne** sunglasses

przecz|yć (**-ę**, **-ysz**; *pf* **za-**) *vi*: **~ czemuś** to deny sth

przeczyt|ać (**-am**, **-asz**) *vb pf od* **czytać**; **~ książkę od deski do deski** to read a book from cover to cover

○ **KEYWORD**

przed *prep* +*inst* **1** (*miejsce*) in front of; **przed szkołą** in front of the school
2 (*czas*) before; **przed śniadaniem** before breakfast
3 (*w obronie*): **przed zimnem** against the cold; **chronić się przed czymś** to shelter from sth
4 (*wobec*): **ukrywać coś przed kimś** to hide sth from sb
▷ *prep* +*acc* (*ruch*): **zajechać** (*pf*) **przed szkołę** to pull up in front of the school

przed... *pref* pre...

przedawk|ować (**-uję**, **-ujesz**) *vt pf* (*lekarstwo, narkotyk*) to overdose on

przede *prep* = **przed**; **~ mną** (*w czasie*) before me; (*przestrzeń*) in front of me; **~ wszystkim** (*pierwszy*) first of all

przedłużacz (**-a**, **-e**; *gen pl* **-y**) *m* (*Elektr*) extension lead (*Brit*), extension cord (*US*)

przedłuż|ać (**-am**, **-asz**; *pf* **-yć**) *vt* to extend; **~ się** *vr* to overrun

przedmio|t (**-tu**, **-ty**; *loc sg* **-cie**) *m* **1** object **2** (*dyskusji*) topic **3** (*badań*) subject

przedostatni *adj* last but one (*Brit*), next to last (*US*)

przedpok|ój (**-oju**, **-oje**; *gen pl* **-oi** *lub* **-ojów**) *m* hall

przedpołud|nie (**-nia**, **-nia**; *gen pl* **-ni**) *nt* morning

przedsiębiorc|a (**-y**, **-y**) *m decl like adj in sg* entrepreneur; **~ pogrzebowy** undertaker (*Brit*), funeral director (*US*)

przedsiębiorst|wo (**-wa**, **-wa**; *loc sg & dat sg* **-wie**) *nt* (*usługowe, produkcyjne, zagraniczne*) enterprise

przedstawiciel (**-a**, **-e**; *gen pl* **-i**) *m* **1** representative **2** (*Prawo*) proxy **3** (*handlowy*) agent

przedstawicielst|wo (**-wa**, **-wa**; *gen pl* **-wie**) *nt* **1** (*handlowy*) agency **2** (*Pol*) diplomatic post

przedstawie|nie (**-nia**, **-nia**; *gen pl* **-ń**) *nt* (*widowisko: teatralne, cyrkowe*) show

przedszkol|e (**-a**, **-a**; *gen pl* **-i**) *nt* nursery school (*Brit*), kindergarten (*US*)

przedtem *adv* **1** (*wcześniej*) previously **2** (*dawniej*) formerly

przedwczoraj *adv* the day before yesterday

przedwojenny *adj* (*film, aktor*) pre-war

przedzia|ł (**-łu**, **-ły**; *loc sg* **-le**) *m* **1** (*w pociągu*) compartment

2 (*cenowy*) range

przega|pić (**-pię, -pisz**) *vt pf*
(*pot: okazję*) to overlook

przegląld (**-du, -dy**; *loc sg* **-dzie**) *m*
1 (*kontrolny*) inspection **2** (*filmów*)
review **3** (*wiadomości*) roundup;
dokonać (*pf*) **~u samochodu** to
service a car

przegląd|ać (**-am, -asz**; *pf*
przejrzeć) *vt* to look through; **~**
się *vr*: **~ się w lustrze** to look at
o.s. in the mirror

przeglądar|ka (**-ki, -ki**; *dat sg* **-ce**;
gen pl **-ek**) *f* (*Komput*) browser

przegran|a (**-ej, -e**) *f decl like adj*
1 (*kwota, zakład*) loss **2** (*porażka*)
defeat

przegryw|ać (**-am, -asz**; *pf*
przegrać) *vt* **1** (*mecz, wybory*)
to lose **2** (*CD, DVD*) to copy ▷ *vi*
to lose

przej|azd (**-azdu, -azdy**; *loc sg*
-eździe) *m* **1** (*samochodem*) drive
2 (*pociągiem*) ride **3** (*miejsce*)
crossing; **opłata za ~** fare; **~**
kolejowy level (*Brit*) *lub* grade
(*US*) crossing

przejeżdż|ka (**-ki, -ki**; *dat sg & loc*
sg **-ce**; *gen pl* **-ek**) *f* ride

przejeżdż|ać (**-am, -asz**; *pf*
przejechać) *vt* **1** (*przekraczać*)
to cross **2** (*mijać*) to pass;
przejechać przystanek to miss
one's stop

przejęzycz|ać się (**-am, -asz**; *pf*
-yć) *vr* to slip up

przejm|ować (**-uję, -ujesz**; *pf*
przejąć) *vt* **1** (*majątek, obowiązki*)
to take over **2** (*list, transport*)
to intercept **3** (*tradycje*) to
adopt; **~ się** *vr*: **~ się czymś** to
be concerned about sth; **nie**

przejmuj się don't worry

przejrz|eć (**-ę, -ysz**; *imp* **-yj**) *vb pf*
od **przeglądać** ▷ *vt pf* (*plany*) to
see through

przejrzysty *adj* transparent

przejś|cie (**-cia, -cia**; *gen pl*
-ć) *nt* (*miejsce*) passage; **~ dla**
pieszych (*pedestrian*) crossing;
~ podziemne subway (*Brit*),
underpass (*US*); **~ graniczne**
border checkpoint

przejściowy *adj* **1** (*krótkotrwały*:
etap, sytuacja) transitory
2 (*pośredni*) transitional

przej|ść (**-dę, -dziesz**; *imp* **-dź**) *vb*
pf od **przechodzić**; **~ się** *vr* to go
for a walk

przekleńst|wo (**-wa, -wa**; *loc sg*
-wie) *nt* (*wyraz*) swearword

przeklin|ać (**-am, -asz**; *pf*
przekląć) *vt* to curse ▷ *vi* to
swear

przekła|d (**-du, -dy**; *loc sg* **-dzie**)
m (*wierny, solidny, dosłowny*)
translation

przekon|ać (**-am, -asz**) *vb pf od*
przekonywać; **~ się** *vr pf*: **~ się**
do kogoś/czegoś to grow to
like sb/sth

przekonany *adj*: **być ~m o**
czymś to be convinced of sth

przekonujący *adj* (*argument,*
komentarz) convincing

przekon|ywać (**-uję, -ujesz**; *pf*
-ać) *vt* to convince; **~ się** *vr* to
become convinced; **~ kogoś o**
czymś to convince sb of sth

przekonywający *adj* =
przekonujący

przekracz|ać (**-am, -asz**; *pf*
przekroczyć) *vt* **1** (*granicę*) to
cross **2** (*limit, wiek*) to exceed

przekrawać (**-am, -asz**; pf
przekroić) vt (materiał, ciasto) to
cut through
przekr|oić (**-oję, -oisz**; imp **-ój**) vb
pf od **przekrawać**
przeku|pywać (**-puję, -pujesz**; pf
-pić) vt (urzędnika) to bribe
przele|w (**-wu, -wy**; loc sg **-wie**) m
(Ekon: pieniędzy) transfer
przelicz|ać (**-am, -asz**; pf **-yć**) vt
1 (zamienić) to convert 2 (liczyć)
to count
przelicz|yć (**-ę, -ysz**) vb pf
od **przeliczać**; ~ **się** vr to
miscalculate
przeło|m (**-mu, -my**; loc sg
-mie) m 1 (moment zmiany)
breakthrough 2 (Geol) gorge; ~ **w
sztuce** breakthrough in art; **na
~ie IX wieków** at the turn of the
nineteenth century
przełomowy adj 1 (znaczenie)
crucial 2 (utwór) breakthrough
przeły|k (**-ku, -ki**; inst sg **-kiem**) m
oesophagus (Brit), esophagus (US)
przemarz|ać (**-am, -asz**; pf **-nąć**)
vi to freeze; ~ **na kość/do szpiku
kości** to freeze to the bone
przemarznięty adj frozen
przemawi|ać (**-am, -asz**; pf
przemówić) vi 1 (wygłosić mowę)
to make a speech 2 (mówić) to
speak
przemęczony adj exhausted
przemia|na (**-ny, -ny**; dat sg & loc
sg **-nie**) f transformation
przemoc (**-y**) f violence; **~ą**
forcibly
przemó|wić (**-wię, -wisz**) vb pf
od **przemawiać**
przemówie|nie (**-nia, -nia**; gen
pl **-ń**) nt speech; **wygłaszać**

(**wygłosić** pf) ~ to make a speech
przemy|cać (**-cam, -casz**; pf **-cić**)
vt (papierosy, alkohol, narkotyki) to
smuggle
przemy|sł (**-słu, -sły**; loc sg **-śle**)
m industry
przemysłowy adj (strefa, zakład)
industrial
przemy|t (**-tu**; loc sg **-cie**) m
smuggling
przeno|sić (**-szę, -sisz**; imp **-ś**; pf
przenieść) vt 1 (zakupy, bagaż)
to carry 2 (stolicę) to move
3 (chorobę) to transmit; ~ **się**
vr 1 (przeprowadzić się) to move
2 (ogień, wojnie) to spread
przepadać (**-am, -asz**; pf
przepaść) vi to disappear; **nie
przepadam za wołowiną** I'm not
keen on beef
przepaś|ć¹ (**-ci, -ci**; gen pl **-ci**) f
precipice
przepa|ść² (**-dnę, -dniesz**; imp
-dnij) vb pf od **przepadać**; ~ **bez
wieści/jak kamień w wodę** to
disappear without a trace
przepełniony adj 1 (ludźmi:
autobus, biuro) overcrowded
2 (płynem) overflowing
przepi|s (**-su, -sy**; loc sg **-sie**)
m 1 (Kulin) recipe 2 (Prawo)
regulation
przepis|ywać (**-uję, -ujesz**; pf
-ać) vt 1 (pisać ponownie) to copy
out 2 (na komputerze) to type out
3 (lekarstwo) to prescribe
przeprasz|ać (**-am, -asz**; pf
przeprosić) vt: ~ **kogoś/za
coś** to apologize to sb/for
sth; **przepraszam** excuse
me; **przepraszam, gdzie jest
najbliższy bank?** excuse me,

where's the nearest bank?

przeprosi|ny (-n) pl apology

przeprowa|dzać (-dzam, -dzasz; pf **-dzić)** vt 1 to take 2 (badanie) to carry out; **~ się** vr (do innego miasta itd) to move

przeprowadz|ka (-ki, -ki; dat sg & loc sg **-ce**; gen pl **-ek)** f move

przerażający adj horrifying

prze|rwa (-wy, -wy; dat sg & loc sg **-wie)** f 1 (pauza) break 2 (w szkole) playtime (Brit), recess (US) 3 (w teatrze) interval; (Sport) half-time 4 (szpara) gap; **bez przerwy** without a break; **~ obiadowa** lunch break; **~ na kawę** coffee break

przeryw|ać (-am, -asz; pf **przerwać)** vt 1 (front) to break 2 (rozmowę) to interrupt 3 (produkcję) to discontinue ▷ vi (podczas rozmowy) to pause; **~ się** vr to break; **~ ciążę** to have an abortion

przesa|da (-dy; dat sg & loc sg **-dzie)** f exaggeration

przesadnie adv excessively

przesadny adj (uprzejmość, agresja) exaggerated

przesa|dzać (-dzam, -dzasz; pf **-dzić)** vt 1 (kwiaty) to transplant 2 (widza) to move seats ▷ vi to exaggerate

przesą|d (-du, -dy; loc sg **-dzie)** m 1 superstition 2 (uprzedzenie) prejudice

przesądny adj superstitious

przesiad|ka (-ki, -ki; dat sg & loc sg **-ce**; gen pl **-ek)** f change; **dojechać gdzieś bez przesiadki** to go somewhere direct

prze|słać (-ślę, -ślesz; imp **-ślij)** vb

pf od **przesyłać**

przesłucha|nie (-nia, -nia; gen pl **-ń)** nt 1 (świadka) examination 2 (zatrzymanego) interrogation 3 (aktory) audition

przesłu|chiwać (-chuję, -chujesz; pf **-chać)** vt 1 (świadka) to examine 2 (zatrzymanego) to interrogate 3 (aktorę) to audition

przest|awać (-aję, -ajesz; imp **-awaj**; pf **-ać)** vi: **~ coś robić** to stop doing sth; **przestań!** stop it!

przesta|wiać (-wiam, -wiasz; pf **-wić)** vt 1 (książkę, wazon) to move 2 (meble) to rearrange 3 (zmienić kolejność) to reorder

przestępc|a (-y, -y) m decl like f in sg criminal

przestępst|wo (-wa, -wa; loc sg **-wie)** nt crime; **popełniać (popełnić** pf) **~** to commit a crime

przestraszony adj frightened

przestrasz|yć (-ę, -ysz) vt pf to frighten; **~ się** vr pf to get scared

przestrzeg|ać (-am, -asz) vi +gen 1 (regulaminów) to obey 2 (prawa) to abide by 3 (obyczaju) to observe 4 (pf **przestrzec)** (udzielać przestrogi) to warn; **~ (przestrzec** pf) **kogoś przed czymś** to warn sb about sth

przestrze|ń (-ni, -nie; gen pl **-ni)** f 1 (obszar) space 2 (powierzchnia) expanse; **~ kosmiczna** outer space

przesył|ać (-am, -asz; pf **przesłać)** vt to send; **~ komuś pozdrowienia** to give one's regards to sb

przesył|ka (-ki, -ki; dat sg & loc sg

-ce; *gen pl* **-ek**) *f* (*pocztowa*) (piece of) post; **~ lotnicza** air mail

przeszk|oda (**-ody, -ody**; *dat sg & loc sg* **-odzie**; *gen pl* **-ód**) *f* **1** (*rzecz*) obstruction **2** (*kłopoty*) obstacle

przeszkol|ić (**-ę, -isz**) *vt pf* (*pracownika*) to train

przeszło|ść (**-ci**) *f* the past

przeszły *adj* past

prześcierad|ło (**-ła, -ła**; *loc sg* **-le**; *gen pl* **-eł**) *nt* sheet

prześlad|ować (**-uję, -ujesz**) *vt* **1** (*człowieka*) to persecute **2** (*dręczyć*) to pester **3** (*wspomnienia*) to haunt

przetłumacz|yć (**-ę, -ysz**) *vb pf od* **tłumaczyć**

przetrw|ać (**-am, -asz**) *vt, vi pf* to survive

przetwor|y (**-ów**) *pl* (*Kulin*) preserves

przewa|ga (**-gi**; *dat sg & loc sg* **-dze**) *f* **1** advantage **2** (*stopień*) superiority

przeważnie *adv* mostly

prze|wieźć (**-wiozę, -wieziesz**; *imp* **-wieź**) *vb pf od* **przewozić**

przewlekły *adj* chronic

przewodni|k (**-ka**; *inst sg* **-kiem**) *m* **1** (*nom pl* **-cy**) (*człowiek: górski, miejski*) guide **2** (*nom pl* **-ki**) (*książka*) guidebook; **~ wycieczek** tour guide

prze|wodzić (**-wodzę, -wodzisz**) *vi* +*dat* to lead; **~ zespołowi** to lead a team

prze|wozić (**-wożę, -wozisz**; *imp* **-wieź**) *vt* (*towary, pasażerów*) to transport

przew|ód (**-odu, -ody**; *loc sg* **-odzie**) *m* **1** wire **2** (*gazowy*) pipe

3 (*oddechowy*) canal

○ **KEYWORD**

przez *prep* +*acc* **1** across; **przechodzić** (**przejść** *pf*) **przez ulicę** to cross the street **2** through; **przez ogród** across the garden **3** (*ponad*) over; **przeskakiwać** (**przeskoczyć** *pf*) **przez mur** to jump over a wall **4** (*za pomocą*): **przez telefon** over the phone; **to się pisze przez dwa „t"** it's spelt with double "t"; **co przez to rozumiesz?** what do you mean by that? **5** (*czas*) for; **chorowałem przez miesiąc** I was ill for a month; **robić** (**zrobić** *pf*) **coś przez wakacje** to do something over the holidays **6** (*przyczyna*): **przez niego** because of him; **przez pomyłkę** by mistake **7** (*w konstrukcjach biernych*) by; **skomponowany przez Mozarta** composed by Mozart **8** (*Mat*): **mnożyć/dzielić przez 3** to multiply/divide by 3

przeze *prep* = **przez**

przezię|biać się (**-biam, -biasz**; *pf* **-bić**) *vr* to catch a cold

przeziębie|nie (**-nia, -nia**; *gen pl* **-ń**) *nt* cold

przeziębiony *adj*: **być ~m** to have a cold

przezroczysty *adj* transparent

przezwis|ko (**-ka, -ka**; *inst sg* **-kiem**) *nt* nickname

przeż|yć (**-yję, -yjesz**) *vt pf*

1 (*wojnę*) to survive **2** (*człowieka*) to outlive ▷ *vi* to survive

przeż|ywać (**-ywam, -ywasz**; *pf* **przeżyć**) *vt* to survive; **on bardzo mocno przeżył śmierć ojca** his father's death has affected him very deeply

przod|ek (**-ka, -kowie**; *inst sg* **-kiem**) *m* ancestor

○ KEYWORD

przy *prep* +*loc* **1** (*blisko*): **przy oknie** by the window; **przy stole** at the table; **nie mam przy sobie pieniędzy** I don't have any money on me

2 (*czas*): **przy pracy** at work; **przy kawie** over coffee

3 (*obecność*) in front of; **przy papieżu** in the presence of the Pope

przybieg|ać (**-am, -asz**; *pf* **-nąć** *lub* **przybiec**) *vi* to rush across

przybliżony *adj* (*data, godzina, moment*) approximate

przybrany *adj* **1** (*rodzina*) adoptive **2** (*nazwisko*) assumed

przychod|nia (**-ni, -nie**; *gen pl* **-ni**) *f* (*Med*) out-patients' clinic

przycho|dzić (**-dzę, -dzisz**; *imp* **-dź**; *pf* **przyjść**) *vi* **1** to come **2** (*list*) to arrive; **~ na świat** to be born

przyciąg|ać (**-am, -asz**; *pf* **-nąć**) *vt* to attract

przyczy|na (**-ny, -ny**; *dat sg* & *loc sg* **-nie**) *f* reason; **z tej przyczyny** for that reason

przydatny *adj* useful

przyd|awać się (**-aję, -ajesz**; *pf* **przydać**) *vr*: **~ komuś/czemuś** **(na coś)** to be useful to sb/sth (for sth)

przygląd|ać się (**-am, -asz**; *pf* **przyjrzeć**) *vr*: **~ się komuś/ czemuś** to watch sb/sth

przyg|oda (**-ody, -ody**; *dat sg* & *loc sg* **-odzie**; *gen pl* **-ód**) *f* adventure

przygodowy *adj* (*film, książka, powieść*) adventure

przygotowany *adj*: **~ (na coś/ do czegoś)** prepared (for sth)

przyjaci|el (**-ela, -ele**; *gen pl* **-ół**; *dat pl* **-ołom**; *inst pl* **-ółmi**; *loc pl* **-ołach**) *m* (*długoletni, serdeczny*) friend

przyjacielski *adj* (*uśmiech, gest*) friendly

przyjaciół|ka (**-ki, -ki**; *dat sg* & *loc sg* **-ce**; *gen pl* **-ek**) *f* (girl)friend; **~ od serca** soul mate

przyj|azd (**-azdu, -azdy**; *loc sg* **-eździe**) *m* (*pociągu*) arrival

przyjazny *adj* friendly

przyjaź|nić się (**-nię, -nisz**; *imp* **-nij**) *vr* to be friends

przyjaźnie *adv* **1** (*powitać*) amicably **2** (*usposobiony*) favourably (*Brit*), favorably (*US*)

przyjaź|ń (**-ni, -nie**; *gen pl* **-ni**) *f* friendship

przyj|ąć (**-mę, -miesz**; *imp* **-mij**) *vb pf od* **przyjmować**

przyj|echać (**-adę, -edziesz**; *imp* **-edź**) *vb pf od* **przyjeżdżać**

przyjemnie *adv* pleasantly; **byłoby mu bardzo ~** he would be delighted

przyjemnoś|ć (**-ci, -ci**; *gen pl* **-ci**) *f* pleasure; **z przyjemnością** with pleasure

przyjemny *adj* (*zapach, melodia, głos*) pleasant

przyjeżdż|ać (-am, -asz; *pf*
**przyjechać) **vi* to arrive
przyję|cie (-cia, -cia; *gen pl* **-ć) ***nt*
1 (*impreza*) reception **2** (*prezentu*)
acceptance **3** (*studenta*)
admission
przyjm|ować (-uję, -ujesz; *pf*
**przyjąć) ***vt* (*pacjentów, towar,
gości*) to receive
przyjrz|eć się (-ę, -ysz; *imp* **-yj)** *vb*
pf od **przyglądać się**
przyj|ść (-dę, -dziesz; *imp* **-dź)** *vb*
pf od **przychodzić**
przykła|d (-du, -dy; *loc sg* **-dzie)**
m example; **na ~** for example;
dawać (dać *pf*) **dobry/zły ~** to
set a good/bad example
przykr|ywać (-ywam, -ywasz; *pf*
**przykryć) ***vt* to cover; **~ dziecko
kołdrą** to cover the child with
a quilt; **~ garnek pokrywką** to
cover the pan with a lid
przykryw|ka (-ki, -ki; *dat sg & loc
sg* **-ce**; *gen pl* **-ek) ***f* lid
przylo|t (-tu, -ty; *loc sg* **-cie) ***m*
(*samolotu*) arrival; **~ opóźniony**
delayed arrival
przymierz|ać (-am, -asz; *pf* **-yć)**
vt (*sukienkę, naszyjnik, płaszcz*)
to try on
przymierzal|nia (-ni, -nie; *gen pl*
**-ni) ***f* fitting room
przymiotni|k (-ka, -ki; *inst sg*
**-kiem) ***m* adjective
przymusowy *adj* **1** (*pobyt*)
enforced **2** (*praca*) forced
3 (*bezrobocie*) compulsory
przynajmniej *adv* at least
przyni|eść (-osę, -esiesz; *imp*
-eś; *pt* **-ósł, -osła, -eśli) ***vb pf od*
przynosić
przyno|sić (-szę, -sisz; *imp* **-ś**; *pf*

**przynieść) ***vt* (*zyski, dochód, sławę*)
to bring
przyp|adać (-adam, -adasz;
pf **przypaść) ***vi*: **Wielkanoc
zawsze przypada w niedzielę i
poniedziałek** Easter always falls
on a Sunday and a Monday
przypad|ek (*inst sg* **-kiem**; *nom
pl* **-ki) ***m* **1** (*gen sg* **-ku**) (*traf*)
coincidence **2** (*gen sg* **-ku**) (*Med*)
case **3** (*gen sg* **-ka**) (*Językowy*)
case; **przypadkiem** *lub* **przez ~**
by accident; **w przypadku** +*gen*
in case of
przypadkowo *adv* accidentally
przypadkowy *adj* (*spotkanie*)
accidental
przypomin|ać (-am, -asz; *pf*
przypomnieć) ***vt*: **~ kogoś/coś
to resemble sb/sth; **~ się**
vr: **przypomniało mu się, że...**
he remembered that...; **~ komuś
coś** to make sb think of sth; **~
sobie** to recall; **przypomnieć
komuś o czymś** to remind sb
of sth
przypra|wa (-wy, -wy; *dat sg &
loc sg* **-wie) ***f* (*ostra, egzotyczna,
wonna*) seasoning
**przyprowa|dzać (-dzam,
-dzasz**; *pf* **-dzić) ***vt* to bring
przypuszcz|ać (-am, -asz; *pf*
przypuścić) ***vi* **1 (*snuć domysły*) to
suppose **2** (*zakładać*) to presume;
~ do egzaminu to put o.s.
forward for an examination
przyro|da (-dy; *dat sg & loc sg*
**-dzie) ***f* nature
przyrodni *adj*: **~ brat** half-
brother; **~a siostra** half-sister
przyro|st (-stu, -sty; *loc sg* **-ście)**
m (*dochodów, płac*) increase; **~**

naturalny population growth rate

przysięg|ać (-am, -asz; *pf* **przysiąc) vt, vi** to swear

przy|słać (-ślę, -ślesz; *imp* **-ślij) vb** *pf od* **przysyłać**

przysł|owie (-owia, -owia; *gen pl* **-ów) nt** proverb

przysłów|ek (-ka, -ki; *inst sg* **-kiem) m** adverb

przysłu|ga (-gi, -gi; *dat sg & loc sg* **-dze) f** favour (*Brit*), favor (*US*); **wyświadczać (wyświadczyć** *pf*) **komuś przysługę** to do sb a favour

przysma|k (-ku, -ki; *inst sg* **-kiem) m** delicacy

przyspiesz|ać, przyśpiesz|ać (-am, -asz; *pf* **-yć) vt 1** (*prędkość*) to speed up **2** (*wyjazd*) to advance ▷ *vi* (*zwiększać szybkość*) to speed up

przystan|ek (-ku, -ki; *inst sg* **-kiem) m: ~ autobusowy/ tramwajowy** bus/tram stop

przystojny *adj* handsome

przysył|ać (-am, -asz; *pf* **przysłać) vt 1** (*wiadomość*) to send **2** (*katalog*) to mail **3** (*montera*) to send in

przyszłoś|ć (-ci) f (*przepowiadać*) future

przyszły *adj* **1** (*student*) prospective **2** (*czas*) future **3** (*miesiąc*) next; **w ~m tygodniu/ roku** next week/year; **~ mąż** husband-to-be

przyta|kiwać (-kuję, -kujesz; *pf* **-knąć) vi** to nod

przytomnoś|ć (-ci) f consciousness; **tracić (stracić** *pf*) **~** to lose consciousness

przytomny *adj* **1** (*świadomy*) conscious **2** (*rozsądny*) astute

przytul|ać (-am, -asz; *pf* **-ić) vt** to hug; **~ się vr** to cuddle

przytulny *adj* (*dom, hotel, kąt*) cosy (*Brit*), cozy (*US*)

przywit|ać (-am, -asz) vb *pf od* **witać**

przywódc|a (-y, -y) m *decl like f in sg* leader

przyziemny *adj* (*zmartwienie, sprawy*) mundane

przyzn|awać (-aję, -ajesz; *pf* **-ać) vt: ~ coś komuś** (*kredyt, obywatelstwo*) to grant sb sth; (*nagrodę*) to award sb sth ▷ *vi*: **~, że...** to grant that...; **~ się vr: ~ się do** +*gen* to confess to

przyzwyczaj|ać (-am, -asz; *pf* **przyzwyczaić) vt: ~ kogoś do czegoś** to accustom sb to sth; **~ się vr: ~ się do czegoś** to get used to sth

przyzwyczaje|nie (-nia, -nia; *gen pl* **-ń) nt** habit; **robię to z przyzwyczajenia** I do it out of habit

PS *abbr* (= *postscriptum*) PS

psa *itd. n zob.* **pies**

pstrą|g (-ga, -gi; *inst sg* **-giem) m** trout

psu|ć (-ję, -jesz; *pf* **ze-** *lub* **po-) vt 1** (*maszynę*) to break **2** (*zabawę*) to spoil **3** (*reputację*) to ruin; **~ się vr 1** (*maszyna*) to break down **2** (*żywność*) to go bad **3** (*pogoda*) to deteriorate **4** (*stosunek*) to deteriorate

psycholo|g (-ga, -dzy *lub* **-gowie**; *inst sg* **-giem) m** psychologist

psychologi|a (-i) f psychology; **Wydział Psychologii** (*Uniw*)

Psychology Department

pszcz|oła (-oły, -oły; *dat sg & loc sg* **-ole**; *gen pl* **-ół) f** bee

pta|k (-ka, -ki; *inst sg* **-kiem) m** bird

publiczność (-ci) f audience

publiczny *adj* (*występ, wróg*) public

publikacj|a (-i, -e; *gen pl* **-i) f** (*fachowa*) publication

publik|ować (-uję, -ujesz; *pf* **o-) vt** (*książkę, esej, czasopismo*) to publish

pucha|r (-ru, -ry; *loc sg* **-rze) m** cup; **~ świata** world cup

pudeł|ko (-ka, -ka; *inst sg* **-kiem**; *gen pl* **-ek) nt** box

pudł|ować (-uję, -ujesz; *pf* **s-) vi** (*pot*) to miss

puk|ać (-am, -asz; *pf* **-nąć) vi** to knock; **~ się** *vr*: **puknij się w czoło** *lub* **głowę!** (*pot*) you're nuts!; **~ do drzwi** to knock at the door

pulowe|r (-ru *lub* **-ra, -ry**; *loc sg* **-rze) m** pullover, jumper (*Brit*)

pul|s (-su, -sy; *loc sg* **-sie) m** pulse

pułap|ka (-ki, -ki; *dat sg & loc sg* **-ce**; *gen pl* **-ek) f** trap; **~ na myszy** mousetrap

punk|t¹ (-tu, -ty; *loc sg* **-cie) m 1** point **2** (*sprzedaży*) outlet **3** (*dokumentu*) item; **~ widzenia** point of view; **~ zwrotny** turning point

punkt² adv (*pot*): **~ druga** two o'clock sharp

punktualnie *adv* (*przybyć, nadjechać*) on time; **~ o drugiej** at two o'clock sharp

punktualny *adj* punctual

pu|pa (-py, -py; *dat sg & loc sg* **-pie) f** (*pot*) bum (*Brit*), butt (*US*)

purpurowy *adj* purple

pusto *adv*: **w sklepach jest ~** the shops are empty; **~ brzmiący** hollow

pusty *adj* **1** empty **2** (*przen: człowiek*) hollow; **~ w środku** hollow

pusty|nia (-ni, -nie; *gen pl* **-ń) f** desert

puszcz|ać (-am, -asz; *pf* **puścić) vt 1** (*linę, rękę*) to let go of **2** (*więźnia*) to let go ▷ *vi* **1** (*CD, piosenkę*) to play **2** (*plama*) to come off **3** (*pot: o bluzce*) to bleed; **~ się** *vr* **1** (*nie trzymać*) to let go **2** (*pot: mieć dużo partnerów/partnerek*) to sleep around

py|ł (-łu, -ły; *loc sg* **-le) m** dust

pyt|ać (-am, -asz; *pf* **za-** *lub* **s-) vt, vi** to ask; **~ się** *vr* to ask; **~ kogoś o coś/czy...** to ask sb about sth/if...; **~ kogoś z chemiii** to give sb an oral in chemistry

pyta|nie (-nia, -nia; *gen pl* **-ń) nt** question; **zadawać** (**zadać** *pf*) **~** to ask a question

q r

qui|z (**-zu**, **-zy**; *loc sg* **-zie**) *m*
(*telewizyjny*) quiz show

r. *abbr* y
raba|t (**-tu**, **-ty**; *loc sg* **-cie**) *m*
(*zniżka*) discount; **udzielać**
(**udzielić** *pf*) **~u** to give a discount
rab|ować (**-uję**, **-ujesz**) *vt* **1** (*pf*
z-) (*kraść*) to steal **2** (*pf* **ob-**)
(*człowieka, sklep: okradać*) to rob
rabune|k (**-ku**, **-ki**; *inst sg* **-kiem**)
m robbery
rachune|k (**-ku**, **-ki**; *inst sg* **-kiem**)
m **1** (*obliczenie*) calculation
2 (*bankowy*) account **3** (*spis
naleznóści*) bill (*Brit*), check
(*US*); **robisz to na własny ~**
you are doing this off your
own back; **~ bieżący** current
account (*Brit*), checking account
(*US*); **~ oszczędnościowo-
rozliczeniowy** cheque account,
interest-bearing current account

racj|a (**-i, -e**; *gen pl* **-i**) *f* **1** (*słuszność*) rightness **2** (*przyczyna*) reason **3** (*jedzenia*) ration; **racje** *pl* (*argumenty*) arguments; **mieć rację** to be right; **nie mieć racji** to be wrong; **wiem, że masz rację** I know you are right; **obawiam się, że nie masz racji** I'm afraid you are wrong; **~ stanu** raison d'état; **co ~ to ~** yes, indeed!

raczej *adv* rather; **wolałbym ~ zjeść coś innego** I'd rather have something else to eat

ra|da (**-dy, -dy**; *dat sg & loc sg* **-dzie**) *f* **1** (*w trudności*) tip **2** (*organ*) council; **nie ma rady, trzeba jej pomóc** there's nothing else we can do, we have to help her; **nie ma innej rady, tylko pojechać samochodem** there is no other solution, but to go by car; **~ nadzorcza** supervisory board; **R~ Ministrów** the Cabinet; **~ gminy/miasta** local/municipal council

radi|o (**-a, -a**) *nt* radio; **słuchać radia** to listen to the radio; **w ~** *lub* **radiu** on the radio; **~ taxi** minicab

Radio i Telewizja: **sklep ~** electronics shop (*Brit*) *lub* store (*US*)

radioaktywny *adj* (*odpad, chmura*) radioactive

radiostacj|a (**-i, -e**; *gen pl* **-i**) *f* radio station

radiow|óz (**-ozu, -ozy**; *loc sg* **-ozie**) *m* police car

radosny *adj* (*osoba, atmosfera*) cheerful, happy

radoś|ć (**-ci**) *f* joy

ra|dzić (**-dzę, -dzisz**; *imp* **-dź**) *vt*

(*pf* **po-**): **~ komuś** to advise sb ▷ *vi* (*debatować*) to debate; **nie radzę ci tego jeść** I wouldn't eat that (if I were you); **radzę sobie z tym bardzo dobrze** I'm coping with it very well; **~ się** *vr* to seek advice; **poradził się lekarza** he asked his doctor's advice

radziecki *adj* (*literatura, władza*) Soviet; **Związek R~** the Soviet Union

raj (**-u**) *m* paradise; **czuję się tu jak w ~u** this place feels like heaven to me

rajstop|y (**-**) *pl* tights (*Brit*), pantihose (*US*)

ra|k (**-ka, -ki**; *inst sg* **-kiem**) *m* **1** (*w biologii*) crayfish, crawfish (*US*) **2** (*choroba nowotworowa*) cancer **3**: **Rak** (*Astrol*) Cancer; **Zwrotnik R~a** Tropic of Cancer

rakie|ta (**-ty, -ty**; *dat sg & loc sg* **-cie**) *f* **1** (*kosmiczna, pocisk*) rocket **2** (*do tenisa*) racket

ra|ma (**-my, -my**; *dat sg & loc sg* **-mie**) *f* frame; **ramy** *pl* (*granice*) scope; **zrobił to w ~ch swoich obowiązków** he did it as part of his duties

ramiącz|ko (**-ka, -ka**; *inst sg* **-kiem**) *nt* **1** (*sukienki, bluzki*) (shoulder) strap **2** (*do wieszania*) (coat) hanger

ra|mię (**-mienia, -miona**; *gen pl* **-mion**) *nt* **1** arm **2** (*bark*) shoulder; **wzruszać** (**wzruszyć** *pf*) **ramionami** to shrug (one's shoulders); **wystąpił z ramienia organizacji młodzieżowej** he acted on behalf of the youth organization

ram|ka (**-ki, -ki**; *dat sg & loc sg* **-ce**;

gen pl **-ek**) *f* **1** frame **2** (*Druk: w tekście*) box; **oprawiać** (**oprawić** *pf*) **obraz w ramki** to frame a picture

ra|na (**-ny**, **-ny**; *dat sg & loc sg* **-nie**) *f* (*cięta, kłuta*) wound

rand|ka (**-ki**, **-ki**; *dat sg & loc sg* **-ce**; *gen pl* **-ek**) *f* (*spotkanie towarzyskie*) date; **mam dziś z nim randkę** I'm going on a date with him today; **~ w ciemno** blind date

ra|nić (**-nię**, **-nisz**; *imp* **-ń**; *pf* **z-**) *vt impf* **1** (*kaleczyć*) to wound **2** (*uczucia*) to hurt ▷ *vt pf* = **zranić**

ranny¹ *adj* (*osoba*) wounded ▷ *m decl like adj* casualty

ranny² *adj* (*pociąg, zajęcia*) morning

rano¹ (**-na**; *loc sg* **-nie**) *nt* morning; **co ~ je śniadanie** he eats breakfast every morning; **tańczyli do białego rana** they danced till dawn

rano² *adv* in the morning; **wczoraj/jutro ~** yesterday/ tomorrow morning

rapor|t (**-tu**, **-ty**; *loc sg* **-cie**) *m* report; **on często staje do ~u przed szefem** he is often called to account by the boss

ra|sa (**-sy**, **-sy**; *dat sg & loc sg* **-sie**) *f* **1** (*ludzka*) race **2** (*kota, psa*) breed

rasi|sta (**-sty**, **-ści**; *dat sg & loc sg* **-ście**) *m decl like f in sg* racist

rasist|ka (**-ki**, **-ki**; *dat sg & loc sg* **-ce**; *gen pl* **-ek**) *f* racist

rasistowski *adj* (*pogląd, hasło*) racist

rasiz|m (**-mu**; *loc sg* **-mie**) *m* (*ideologia*) racism

ra|ta (**-ty**, **-ty**; *dat sg & loc sg* **-cie**) *f* instalment (*Brit*), installment

(*US*); **kupił samochód na raty** he bought a car on hire purchase (*Brit*) *lub* on an installment plan (*US*); **zapłacił za to w ~ch** he paid for it in instalments

ratalny *adj*: **sprzedaż ratalna** hire purchase (*Brit*), installment plan (*US*); **spłata ratalna** repayment in instalments

rat|ować (**-uję**, **-ujesz**; *pf* **u-**) *vt* **1** to save **2** (*ofiarę wypadku*) to rescue **3** (*reanimować chorego*) to resuscitate **4** (*dobra materialne*) to salvage; **u~** (*pf*) **komuś życie** to save sb's life

ratowni|k (**-ka**, **-cy**; *inst sg* **-kiem**) *m* **1** (*na basenie*) lifeguard **2** (*w górach*) rescuer

ratun|ek (**-ku**, **-ki**; *inst sg* **-kiem**) *m* **1** (*w stanie zagrożenia*) rescue **2** (*zbawienie*) salvation; **ratunku!** help!; **był dla nas ostatnią deską ratunku** he was our last resort

ratunkowy *adj*: **pogotowie ratunkowe** ambulance service; **akcja ratunkowa** rescue operation; **kamizelka ratunkowa** life jacket; **koło ratunkowe** life belt; **łódź ratunkowa** lifeboat

ratusz (**-a**, **-e**; *gen pl* **-y** *lub* **-ów**) *m* (*siedziba władz miejskich*) town hall

ra|z (**-zu**, **-zy**; *loc sg* **-zie**) *m* (*określając wielokrotność, porównywanie*) time ▷ *num* one; **(jeden) ~ w tygodniu** once a week; **dwa ~y w miesiącu** twice a month; **dwa ~y więcej** (*uczniów, gazet*) twice as many; (*płynu, środków finansowych*) twice as much; **dwa ~y dwa jest cztery** two times two is four; **~ na miesiąc/rok** once a month/year; **ile ~y tu byłeś?** how many times have you been here?; **jeszcze ~ musiał to zrobić** he had to do it (once) again; **na ~ie mu się nie udało** *(do tej pory)* as yet he has not managed to do it; **na ~ie!** *(pot)* see you later!; **od ~u go zobaczyła** she spotted him straight away; **na ~** at a time; **pewnego ~u** *(w bajkach)* once upon a time; **po ~ drugi/szósty** for the second/sixth time; **tym/innym ~em** this/another time; **za każdym ~em ma rację** he's right each *lub* every time; **za jednym ~em** at a *lub* one time; **w ~ie potrzeby proszę dzwonić** should the need arise please call; **ta bluzka jest w sam ~** this top is just right; **na drugi ~ się lepiej przygotuj** next time prepare more thoroughly; **~, dwa, trzy…** one, two, three…

razem *adv* together

razow|iec (-ca, -ce) *m (rodzaj chleba)* wholemeal *(Brit) lub* wholewheat *(US)* bread

rdz|a (-y) *f* rust; **~ zżera karoserię samochodu** rust is eating away at the body of the car

reag|ować (-uję, -ujesz; *pf* **za-)** *vi*: **~ (na)** to respond (to); **czy miedź reaguje z wodą?** *(Chem)* does copper react with water?

reakcj|a (-i, -e; *gen pl* **-i)** *f* **1** response **2** *(w chemii)* reaction

realiz|m (-mu; *loc sg* **-mie)** *m (w sztuce)* realism

realny *adj* **1** *(prawdziwy)* real **2** *(możliwy)* feasible

recenzj|a (-i, -e; *gen pl* **-i)** *f (filmowa, literacka)* review

recepcj|a (-i, -e; *gen pl* **-i)** *f (w hotelu, w biurze)* reception *(Brit)*, front desk *(US)*

recepcjoni|sta (-sty, -ści; *dat sg & loc sg* **-ście)** *m decl like f in sg (pracownik recepcji)* receptionist

recepcjonist|ka (-ki, -ki; *dat sg & loc sg* **-ce;** *gen pl* **-ek)** *f (pracownica recepcji)* receptionist

recep|ta (-ty, -ty; *dat sg & loc sg* **-cie)** *f* **1** *(na leki)* prescription **2** *(kulinarna)* recipe

recyklin|g (-gu; *inst sg* **-giem)** *m* recycling

redag|ować (-uję, -ujesz; *pf* **z-)** *vt (tekst, artykuł)* to edit

redakcj|a (-i, -e; *gen pl* **-i)** *f* **1** *(czynność)* editing **2** *(zespół redakcyjny)* editorial staff **3** *(pomieszczenie redakcyjne)* editorial office

redakcyjny *adj (zespół, spotkanie)* editorial

redakto|r (-ra, -rzy; *loc sg* **-rze)** *m* **1** editor **2** *(w radiu, telewizji)* newscaster **3** *(działu sportowego)* sports editor; **~ naczelny** editor-in-chief

redaktor|ka (-ki, -ki; *dat sg & loc sg* **-ce;** *gen pl* **-ek)** *f* editor

referencj|e (-i) *pl* references

refor|ma (-my, -my; *dat sg & loc sg* **-mie)** *f (zdrowia, rolna)* reform

rega|ł (-łu, -ły; *loc sg* **-le)** *m* bookshelf

regio|n (-nu, -ny; *loc sg* **-nie)** *m (terytorium)* region

regularny *adj (kształt, płatność)* regular

rejestracj|a (-i, -e; *gen pl*

-i) f 1 (*spis*) registration 2 (*u lekarza*) registration 3 (*miejsce*) reception 4 (*nagranie dźwięku, obrazu*) recording 5 (*pot: tablica rejestracyjna pojazdu*) number plate (*Brit*), license plate (*US*)

rejo|n (-nu, -ny; *loc sg* **-nie)** m 1 (*podział administracyjny*) district, region 2 (*obszar*) area

rej|s (-su, -sy; *loc sg* **-sie)** m 1 (*na statku*) voyage 2 (*rekreacyjny*) cruise 3 (*Aviat*) flight

reki|n (-na, -ny) m shark

rekla|ma (-my, -my; *loc sg* **-mie)** f 1 (*produktu*) advertising 2 (*kampania promocyjna*) promotion 3 (*rozgłos*) publicity 4 (*informacja w radiu, telewizji*) commercial 5 (*ogłoszenie drukowane*) advertisement

reklamacj|a (-i, -e; *gen pl* **-i)** f (*wadliwego produktu*) complaint

reklam|ować (-uję, -ujesz; *pf* **za-)** vt 1 (*produkt klientom*) to promote 2 (*wadliwa rzecz*) to complain about

reklamów|ka (-ki, -ki; *dat sg & loc sg* **-ce**; *gen pl* **-ek)** f 1 (*pot: krótki film promocyjny*) commercial 2 (*torba*) carrier bag

rekor|d (-du, -dy; *loc sg* **-dzie)** m (*świata, kraju*) record; **jego płyta bije ~y popularności** his album is beating all sales records

rekordowy *adj* record(-breaking); **osiągnął rekordowe zyski** he achieved record profits

rekordzi|sta (-sty, -ści; *dat sg & loc sg* **-ście)** m *decl like f in sg* record holder

rekordzist|ka (-ki, -ki; *dat sg & loc sg* **-ce**; *gen pl* **-ek)** f record holder

rekto|r (-ra, -rzy; *loc sg* **-rze)** m (*uniwersytetu*) ≈ vice chancellor (*Brit*), ≈ president (*US*)

relak|s (-su; *loc sg* **-sie)** m (*odpoczynek*) relaxation

relaks|ować się (-uję, -ujesz; *pf* **z-)** vr (*odpoczywać*) to relax

religi|a (-i, -e; *gen pl* **-i)** f 1 (*wiara*) religion 2 (*przedmiot w szkole*) religious education

religijny *adj* religious

remi|s (-su, -sy; *loc sg* **-sie)** m (*Sport*) draw

remis|ować (-uję, -ujesz; *pf* **z-)** vi (*Sport*) to draw

remon|t (-tu, -ty; *loc sg* **-cie)** m 1 (*domu, pokoju*) redecoration 2 (*samochodu*) repair

remont|ować (-uję, -ujesz; *pf* **wy-** *lub* **od-)** vt 1 (*dom, pokój*) to redecorate 2 (*samochód*) to repair

renci|sta (-sty, -ści; *dat sg & loc sg* **-ście)** m *decl like f in sg* pensioner

rencist|ka (-ki, -ki; *dat sg & loc sg* **-ce**; *gen pl* **-ek)** f pensioner

ren|ta (-ty, -ty; *dat sg & loc sg* **-cie)** f (*inwalidzka, emerytalna*) pension; **od dwóch lat jest na rencie** he's been drawing his pension for two years

rentgenowski *adj* (*prześwietlenie, promienie*) X-ray

reper|ować (-uję, -ujesz; *pf* **z-)** vt to repair

reportaż (-u, -e; *gen pl* **-y)** m (*w dziennikarstwie*) report

reporte|r (-ra, -rzy; *loc sg* **-rze)** m (*dziennikarz*) reporter

reporter|ka (-ki, -ki; *dat sg & loc sg* **-ce**; *gen pl* **-ek)** f (*dziennikarka*) reporter

reprezentacj|a (-i, -e; *gen pl* **-i)** f

1 (*przedstawiciele*) representation **2** (*w sporcie*): **~ kraju** national team *lub* squad

republi|ka (**-ki, -ki**; *dat sg & loc sg* **-ce**) *f* republic; **R~ Południowej Afryki** the Republic of South Africa

restauracj|a (**-i, -e**; *gen pl* **-i**) *f* **1** (*lokal gastronomiczny*) restaurant **2** (*domu, zamku*) restoration **3** (*okres w historii*) the Restoration

restauracyjny *adj*: **wagon ~** dining *lub* restaurant car

resz|ta (**-ty, -ty**; *dat sg & loc sg* **-cie**) *f* **1** (*jedzenia, pracy*) rest, remainder **2** (*pieniędzy*) change; **dziękuję, reszty nie trzeba!** keep the change!

reszt|ka (**-ki, -ki**; *dat sg & loc sg* **-ce**; *gen pl* **-ek**) *f* (*niewielka pozostałość*) remainder; **resztki jedzenia** *pl* leftovers

retoryczny *adj*: **pytanie retoryczne** rhetorical question

rewelacyjny *adj* (*niesamowity*) sensational

rewolucj|a (**-i, -e**; *gen pl* **-i**) *f* (*przewrót, zmiana*) revolution

rewolucyjny *adj* revolutionary

rezer|wa (**-wy**; *dat sg & loc sg* **-wie**) *f* (*nom pl* **-wy**) reserve; **ona odnosi się do niego z rezerwą** she treats him with reserve

rezerwacj|a (**-i, -e**; *gen pl* **-i**) *f* (*pokoju, podróży*) reservation

rezerw|ować (**-uję, -ujesz**; *pf* **za-**) *vt* **1** (*miejsce w hotelu, restauracji*) to reserve **2** (*pieniądze*) to set aside

rezulta|t (**-tu, -ty**; *loc sg* **-cie**) *m* (*wynik*) result; **w rezultacie spóźniliśmy się** as a result we were late

rezygn|ować (**-uję, -ujesz**; *pf* **z-**) *vi* (*przestać podejmować wysiłki*) to give up; **rezygnuję z tej rezerwacji** I am cancelling this reservation; **rezygnował ze stanowiska w każdej firmie, w której pracował** he resigned from his job at every firm he ever worked for

reżi|m, reży|m (**-mu, -my**; *loc sg* **-mie**) *m* (*wojskowy, w jedzeniu*) regime

reżyse|r (**-ra, -rzy**; *loc sg* **-rze**) *m* (*Kino*) director

reżyseri|a (**-i**) *f*: **„~: Andrzej Wajda"** "directed by Andrzej Wajda"; **w reżyserii Krzysztofa Kieślowskiego** directed by Krzysztof Kieślowski

reżyser|ka (**-ki, -ki**; *dat sg & loc sg* **-ce**; *gen pl* **-ek**) *f* (*Kino*) director

reżyser|ować (**-uję, -ujesz**; *pf* **wy-**) *vt* (*film, sztukę*) to direct

ręczni|k (**-ka, -ki**; *inst sg* **-kiem**) *m* (*kąpielowy, do rąk*) towel

ręczny *adj* hand; **piłka ręczna** (*Sport*) handball; **nie wiem dlaczego nie działa ~ hamulec** I don't know why the handbrake (*Brit*) *lub* emergency brake (*US*) doesn't work; **pudełko ręcznej roboty** handmade box

rę|ka (**-ki, -ce**; *dat sg & loc sg* **-ce**; *gen pl* **rąk**; *inst pl* **-kami** *lub* **-koma**; *loc pl* **-kach**) *f* **1** (*dłoń*) hand **2** (*ramię*) arm; **do rąk własnych adresata** to be opened by addressee only; **załatwimy to od ręki** we'll sort it out while you wait; **zawsze mam to pod ręką** I always have it close at hand; **machała ~mi** she waved her arms about; **informacja z pierwszej ręki** first-hand information; **uzyskać informację z pierwszej ręki** to hear it straight from the horse's mouth; **poszła mu na rękę w pracy** she helped him out at work; **przyszedł do niej z pustymi rękoma** he came to her empty-handed; **nic nie robi i siedzi z założonymi rękoma** he doesn't do anything and just sits on his hands; **ręce do góry!** hands up!; **szła pod rękę z Prezydentem** she walked arm in arm with the President; **prosić kogoś o rękę** (*zaręczyć się*) to propose to sb, to ask for sb's hand in marriage; **ręce przy sobie!** (keep your) hands to yourself!

ręka|w (**-wa**, **-wy**; *loc sg* **-wie**) *m* sleeve; **bluzka bez ~ów** sleeveless blouse *lub* top

rękawicz|ka (**-ki**, **-ki**; *dat sg & loc sg* **-ce**; *gen pl* **-ek**) *f* **1** glove **2** (*z jednym palcem*) mitten; **obchodzą się z nim w białych ~ch** they treat him with kid gloves

rękopi|s (**-su**, **-sy**; *loc sg* **-sie**) *m* manuscript

r.m. *abbr* (= *rodzaj męski*) m (= *masculine*)

r.nij. *abbr* (= *rodzaj nijaki*) nt (= *neuter*)

roba|k (**-ka**, **-ki**; *inst sg* **-kiem**) *m* worm; **robaki** *pl* (*Med: pasożytnicze, inwazyjne*) worms *pl*

ro|bić (**-bię**, **-bisz**; *imp* **rób**; *pf* **z-**) *vt* **1** (*jedzenie, kawę*) to make **2** (*wykonywać*) to do **3** (*powodować*) to cause ▷ *vi* (*pot: wykonywać pracę*) to work; **co tu robisz?**

what are you doing here?; **~ się** *vr* (*stawać się*) to become; **robi się ciemno/ciepło** it's getting dark/ warm; **robi mi się niedobrze po jedzeniu** I'm starting to feel sick after eating

roboczy *adj* **1** (*wersja, strój*) working **2** (*służbowy*) business; **dzień ~** weekday; **rolnik, ubrany po roboczemu** a farm worker, dressed in his work clothes

rob|ota (**-oty**, **-oty**; *dat sg & loc sg* **-ocie**; *gen pl* **-ót**) *f* **1** (*robienie czegoś*) work **2** (*praca fizyczna, umysłowa*) work **3** (*pot: zawód*) job; **roboty** *pl*: **roboty drogowe** road works (*Brit*), roadwork (*US*); **ciasto własnej roboty** home-made cake

robotniczy *adj* (*klasa*) working-class

robotni|k (**-ka**, **-cy**; *inst sg* **-kiem**) *m* (*pracownik fizyczny*) worker; **~ rolny** farm worker

rocznic|a (**-y**, **-e**) *f* anniversary; **~ ślubu** wedding anniversary

roczni|k (**-ka**, **-ki**; *inst sg* **-kiem**) *m* **1** (*ogół urodzonych w tym samym roku*) year-mates group **2** (*w szkole*) class

roczny *adj* **1** (*trwający jeden rok*) year-long **2** (*mający rok*) year-old; **roczna prenumerata** annual subscription fee

rodacz|ka (**-ki**, **-ki**; *dat sg & loc sg* **-ce**; *gen pl* **-ek**) *f* (fellow) countrywoman

roda|k (**-ka**, **-cy**; *inst sg* **-kiem**) *m* (fellow) countryman

rodowó|d (**-odu**, **-ody**; *loc sg* **-odzie**) *m* **1** (*geneza*) origin **2** (*pochodzenie*) lineage

3 (*zwierzęcia*) pedigree

rodza|j (**-ju, -je**; *gen pl* **-jów**) *m* **1** (*gatunek*) kind **2** (*w językoznawstwie*): **~ gramatyczny** gender; **kupiła kozaki lub coś w tym ~u** she bought some knee-high boots or something of the sort

rodzeńst|wo (**-wa, -wa**; *loc sg* **-wie**) *nt* siblings *pl*; **ja też chcę mieć ~!** I want to have brothers and sisters, too!

rodzic|e (**-ów**) *pl* parents

ro|dzić (**-dzę, -dzisz**; *imp* **ródź** *lub* **ródź**; *pf* **u-**) (*wydawać na świat: dziecko*) to give birth to **2** (*płody rolne*) to bear **3** (*pf* **z-**) (*przen: wywoływać*) to give rise to; **~ się** *vr* **1** (*pf* **u-**) (*dosl*) to be born **2** (*pf* **z-**) (*przen: zaczynać istnieć: uczucia*) to arise

rodzi|na (**-ny, -ny**; *dat sg & loc sg* **-nie**) *f* family; **~ wielodzietna/ zastępcza** a large/step-family

rodzinny *adj* **1** (*związany z miejscem urodzenia*) home **2** (*święto*) family

rodzony *adj*: **mój ~ brat** my own brother

rogali|k (**-ka, -ki**; *inst sg* **-kiem**) *m* croissant

ro|k (**-ku, lata**; *inst sg* **-kiem**) *m decl like nt in pl* year; **jeździ na wakacje co ~u** he goes on holiday every year; **w zeszłym/ przyszłym ~u** last/next year; **w tym ~u kupimy samochód** we shall buy a car this year; **kolega z ~u** a class-mate from university; **Nowy R~** New Year

rol|a (**-i, -e**; *gen pl* **ról**) *f* (*w filmie, teatrze*) part; **pieniądze nie gra**

roli money is no object

rolnict|wo (**-wa**; *loc sg* **-wie**) *nt* agriculture

rolniczy *adj* **1** (*uczelnia, ciągnik*) agricultural

rolni|k (**-ka, -cy**; *inst sg* **-kiem**) *m* farmer

roman|s (**-su, -se**; *loc sg* **-sie**) *m* **1** (*gatunek literacki*) love story **2** (*przygoda miłosna*) (love) affair

romantyczny *adj* (*kolacja, wątek*) romantic

ron|do (**-da, -da**; *loc sg* **-dzie**) *nt* (*na ulicy*) roundabout (Brit), traffic circle (US)

ro|pa (**-py**; *dat sg & loc sg* **-pie**) *f* **1** (*w chemii: też*: **~ naftowa**) (crude) oil, petroleum **2** (*w medycynie*) pus

Rosj|a (**-i**) *f* Russia

ro|snąć (**-snę, -śniesz**; *imp* **-śnij**) *vi* **1** (*pf* **u-**) (*o zwierzętach, ludziach, roślinach*) to grow **2** (*pf* **wy-**) (*osiągnąć dojrzałość*) to grow up **3** (*pf* **wz-**) (*o kosztach*) to rise

ros|ół (**-ołu, -oły**; *loc sg* **-ole**) *m* broth

rosyjski *adj* Russian

rośli|na (**-ny, -ny**; *dat sg & loc sg* **-nie**) *f* plant

roślinny *adj* (*pochodzenia roślinnego*) vegetable, plant

rowe|r (**-ru, -ry**; *loc sg* **-rze**) *m* bicycle, bike; **jechać na ~ze** to cycle

rowerzy|sta (**-sty, -ści**; *loc sg* **-ście**) *m* cyclist

rowerzyst|ka (**-ki, -ki**; *dat sg & loc sg* **-ce**; *gen pl* **-ek**) *f* cyclist

rozbier|ać (**-am, -asz**; *pf* **rozebrać**) *vt* **1** (*osobę*) to undress **2** (*rzecz na części*) to take apart **3** (*budowlę*) to pull down; **~ się** *vr*

to undress; **rozbiera mnie grypa**
the flu is making me drowsy
rozbudow|ywać (-uję, -ujesz;
pf **-ać**) *vt* **1** (*osiedle*) to extend
2 (*rozwijać*) to develop
rozchor|ować się (-uję, -ujesz)
vr pf to fall ill
rozczarowa|nie (-nia, -nia;
gen pl **-ń**) *nt* disappointment;
przeżył gorzkie ~ he was bitterly
disappointed
rozczarowany *adj*: **premier
Turcji ~ niemieckim
przewodnictwem w UE** Turkish
premier disappointed with
German EU presidency; **była
rozczarowana, że przegrała** she
was disappointed that she lost
rozd|awać (-aję, -ajesz; *pf* **-ać**)
vt **1** (*foldery, gazety, pieniądze*) to
distribute **2** (*podczas gry w karty*)
to deal
rozdzia|ł (-łu, -ły; *loc sg* **-le**)
m **1** (*fragment książki*) chapter
2 (*podział*) partitioning
3 (*przydzielanie*) apportionment
rozdziel|ać (-am, -asz; *pf* **-ić**)
vt **1** (*rozdawać*) to distribute
2 (*oddzielać*) to separate; **~ się** *vr*
1 (*o osobach*) to split up **2** (*o nurcie
rzeki*) to fork, to branch
rozebrany *adj* undressed
roześmi|ać się (-eję, -ejesz) *vr pf*
to laugh out loud; **roześmiał się
mu prosto w twarz** he laughed
right in his face
rozgląd|ać się (-am, -asz; *pf*
rozejrzeć) *vr* to look around;
rogląda się za lepszą posadą
he is looking around for a better
job
rozgło|s (-su; *loc sg* **-sie**) *m*

publicity
rozgniew|ać (-am, -asz) *vt*
pf: **śmierć matki bardzo
rozgniewała go** his mother's
death greatly angered him; **~ się**
vr to get angry
rozgo|ścić się (-szczę, -ścisz;
imp **-ść**) *vr pf* to make o.s.
comfortable; **każdy może się
wygodnie rozgościć w fotelach**
everybody can relax comfortably
in the armchairs
rozka|z (-zu, -zy; *loc sg* **-zie**) *m*
order; **wydał ~ do odwrotu** he
ordered a retreat; **wykonać** (*pf*) **~**
to obey an order
rozkła|d (-du, -dy; *loc sg* **-dzie**)
m **1** (*jazdy, zajęć*) timetable
2 (*domu*) layout **3** (*w biologii*)
decomposition; **~ jazdy
pociągów/autobusów**
railway/bus timetable (*Brit*) *lub*
schedule (*US*)
rozkład|ać (-am, -asz; *pf*
rozłożyć) *vt* **1** (*obrus na stole*) to
spread **2** (*przedmioty*) to set out
3 (*parasol, wersalkę*) to unfold
4 (*urządzenie*) to dismantle
rozkosz (-y, -e; *gen pl* **-y**)
f **1** (*przyjemność*) pleasure
2 (*szczęście*) delight
rozlew|ać (-am, -asz; *pf* **rozlać**)
vt **1** (*płyn na podłogę*) to spill **2** (*płyn
do butelki*) to pour (out); **~ się** *vr*
to spill
rozmawi|ać (-am, -asz) *vi* to
talk; **rozmawiał ze mną o pracy**
he talked to me about work; **oni
ze sobą nie rozmawiają od
wielu lat** they have not been on
speaking terms for years
rozmia|r (-ru, -ry; *loc sg* **-rze**) *m*

1 (*ubrania, butów*) size **2** (*zasięg*) extent

rozm|owa (**-owy, -owy**; *dat sg & loc sg* **-owie**; *gen pl* **-ów**) *f* **1** conversation **2** (*kwalifikacyjna w pracy*) interview; **rozmowy** *pl* negotiations *pl*; **obyli długą rozmowę telefoniczną** they had a long telephone conversation

rozmowny *adj* talkative

rozmówc|a (**-y, -y**) *m decl like f in sg* interlocutor

rozmówczy|ni (**-ni, -nie**; *gen pl* **-ń**) *f* interlocutor

rozmów|ki (**-ek**) *pl* phrase book *sg*

rozmyśl|ić się (**-ę, -isz**) *vr pf* to change one's mind

rozpacz (**-y**) *f* despair; **to był z jego strony akt ~y** it was an act of desperation on his part

rozpacz|ać (**-am, -asz**) *vi* to despair

rozpad|ać się (**-am, -asz**; *pf* **rozpaść**) *vr* **1** (*o krześle*) to fall apart **2** (*o parze*) to disintegrate, to break up

rozpę|dzać (**-dzam, -dzasz**; *pf* **-dzić**) *vt* **1** (*samochód*) to speed up, to accelerate **2** (*demonstrację*) to disperse; **~ się** *vr* (*zwiększać szybkość*) to speed up

rozpieszczony *adj* (*dziecko, pies*) pampered, spoilt (*Brit*), spoiled (*US*)

rozpin|ać (**-am, -asz**; *pf* **rozpiąć**) *vt* (*bluzkę*) to undo

rozpoczęci|e (**-a**) *nt* (*uroczystości, roku szkolnego*) start

rozpoczyn|ać (**-am, -asz**; *pf* **rozpocząć**) *vt* to begin; **~ się** *vr* to begin

rozrast|ać się (**-am, -asz**; *pf* **rozrosnąć**) *vr* (*powiększać się*) to grow

rozróż|niać (**-niam, -niasz**; *pf* **-nić**) *vt* to distinguish

rozryw|ka (**-ki, -ki**; *dat sg & loc sg* **-ce**; *gen pl* **-ek**) *f* entertainment

rozrywkowy *adj*: **lokal ~** nightclub; **lektura rozrywkowa** light reading; **przemysł ~** entertainment industry

rozrzu|cać (**-cam, -casz**; *pf* **-cić**) *vt* **1** (*rzeczy*) to scatter **2** (*nasiona*) to spread

rozsąd|ek (**-ku**; *inst sg* **-kiem**) *m* good sense; **wykazał się zdrowym rozsądkiem** he demonstrated his common sense

rozsądny *adj* (*człowiek, propozycja*) reasonable

rozsyp|ywać (**-uję, -ujesz**; *pf* **-ać**) *vt* to spill; **~ się** *vr* **1** to spill **2** (*o osobie załamanej nerwowo*) to go to pieces

rozśmiesz|ać (**-am, -asz**; *pf* **-yć**) *vt*: **~ kogoś** to make sb laugh

roztargniony *adj* absent-minded

rozter|ka (**-ki, -ki**; *dat sg & loc sg* **-ce**; *gen pl* **-ek**) *f* dilemma; **przeżywał rozterki moralne** he faced moral dilemmas

roztropny *adj* prudent

rozu|m (**-mu, -my**; *loc sg* **-mie**) *m* reason; **na chłopski** *lub* **zdrowy ~, masz rację** common sense suggests that you're right; **jesteś niespełna ~u!** you're out of your mind!

rozumi|eć (**-em, -esz**; *pf* **z-**) *vt* to understand; **~ się** *vr*: **~ się (ze sobą)** to understand (each other); **rozumiem twój punkt**

widzenia I see your point (of view); **co przez to rozumiesz?** what do you mean by that?; **to rozumiem!** now you're talking!; **~ po rosyjsku** to understand Russian; **rozumiem, że nie jesteś gotów** I understand you're not ready; **do wojska, ma się ~, nie poszliśmy!** naturally, we didn't join the army!

rozumny adj (istota, propozycja) rational

rozwa|ga (-**gi**; dat sg & loc sg -**dze**) f judiciousness; **powinniśmy wziąć to pod rozwagę** we should take that into consideration; **należy to robić z rozwagą** it should be done with deliberation

rozwiąza|nie (-**nia**, -**nia**; gen pl -**ń**) nt 1 (krzyżówki, zagadnienia) solution 2 (parlamentu, małżeństwa) dissolution 3 (urodzenie dziecka) delivery

rozwiąz|ywać (-**uję**, -**ujesz**; pf -**ać**) vt 1 (odplątać: supeł, paczkę, jeńca) to untie 2 (unieważnić: umowę, małżeństwo) to annul 3 (zamknąć: parlament) to dissolve 4 (znaleźć rozwiązanie: problem) to solve

rozwiedziony adj divorced

rozwi|jać (-**jam**, -**jasz**; pf -**nąć**) vt 1 (chodnik, śpiwór) to unroll 2 (rozpakowywać) to unwrap 3 (talent) to develop 4 (firmę) to expand; **~ się** vr 1 (rozprostować się: o drucie) to uncoil 2 (wydarzyć się: o fabule) to unfold 3 (ukształtować się) to grow 4 (osiągnąć wyższy poziom) to develop

rozwodni|k (-**ka**, -**cy**; inst sg -**kiem**) m divorcee (Brit), divorcé (US)

roz|wodzić się (-**wodzę**, -**wodzisz**; imp -**wódź**; pf -**wieść**) vr to get divorced; **rozwodzić się z mężem/żoną** to divorce one's husband/wife; **rozwodzi się nad swoim pechem** he's dwelling on his misfortune

rozwolnie|nie (-**nia**) nt (biegunka) diarrhoea (Brit), diarrhea (US)

rozw|ód (-**odu**, -**ody**; loc sg -**odzie**) m divorce; **brać** (**wziąć** pf) **~** to get a divorce

rozwód|ka (-**ki**, -**ki**; dat sg & loc sg -**ce**; gen pl -**ek**) f divorcee (Brit), divorcée (US)

rozw|ój (-**oju**) m 1 (cywilizacji, człowieka) development 2 (zdarzeń) progress

rób itd. vb zob. **robić**

róg (**rogu**, **rogi**; inst sg **rogiem**) m 1 (u krowy) horn 2 (u jelenia) antler 3 (pokoju) corner 4 (ulicy) corner 5 (instrument muzyczny) horn 6 (w sporcie) corner; **sklep jest na rogu** the shop is on the corner; **za rogiem stoi samochód** the car is parked (a)round the corner; **zapędziła go w kozi ~** she forced him into a corner

rówieśni|k (-**ka**, -**cy**; inst sg -**kiem**) m peer

również adv also, as well; **psy jak ~ koty** dogs and also cats

równo adv 1 (bez wypukłości) evenly 2 (w jednakowej ilości) equally 3 (dokładnie) exactly

równocześnie adv at the same time

równoś|ć (-**ci**) f equality; **znak równości** equals sign

równowa|ga (**-gi**; *dat sg* **-dze**) *f*
1 balance **2** (*psychiczna*) balance,
poise **3** (*w tenisie*) deuce;
zachowywać (**zachować** *pf*)
równowagę to keep one's
balance

równy *adj* **1** (*płaski*) even
2 (*jednakowy*) equal **3** (*jednostajny*)
steady

róż|a (**-y, -e**) *f* rose; **dzika ~** briar
róża|niec (**-ńca, -ńce**) *m* rosary
różnic|a (**-y, -e**) *f* difference; **bez
różnicy** it makes no difference
róż|nić (**-nię, -nisz**; *imp* **-nij**) *vt*: **~
kogoś/coś od** +*gen* to make
sb/sth different from; **~ się** *vr*: **~
się (od kogoś/czegoś)** to be
different (from sb/sth); **różnimy
się w poglądach na tę sprawę**
our opinions differ on this matter

różnorodny *adj* (*rozmaity*)
diverse

różny *adj* different
różowy *adj* **1** (*barwa*) pink
2 (*przen: o przyszłości*) rosy

RP *abbr* = **Rzeczpospolita Polska**
RTV *abbr* = **Radio i Telewizja**
rubry|ka (**-ki, -ki**; *dat sg & loc sg*
-ce) *f* **1** (*do wypełnienia*) blank
space **2** (*tekst w gazecie*) column
ruch (**-u, -y**) *m* **1** (*przesunięcie
w innym kierunku*) movement
2 (*Fiz*) motion **3** (*aktywność
fizyczna*) exercise **4** (*na ulicach*)
traffic **5** (*pionkiem*) move
6 (*ożywienie gospodarcze*) boom
7 (*Hist: w sztuce, polityce, religii*)
movement; **~ oporu** the
Resistance; **zgodnie z ~em
wskazówek zegara** clockwise;
**odwrotnie do ~u wskazówek
zegara** anticlockwise (*Brit*),

counterclockwise (*US*)
ruchomy *adj* **1** (*element*) moving
2 (*majątek*) movable; **ruchome
schody** escalator

rudowłosy *adj* redheaded
rudy *adj* **1** russet **2** (*włosy*) ginger
rugby *nt inv* rugby
rumie|nić (**-nię, -nisz**; *imp* **-ń**)
vt (*pf* **przy-**) (*ciasto, pieczeń*) to
brown; **~ się** (*pf* **za-**) *vr* (*na twarzy*)
to blush

ru|nąć (**-nę, -niesz**; *imp* **-ń**) *vi pf*
1 (*o budowli, osobie*) to collapse
2 (*spaść w dół*) to plummet (down),
to tumble (down) **3** (*przen: o
pomysłach*) to collapse

ru|ra (**-ry, -ry**; *dat sg & loc sg*
-rze) *f* (*kanalizacyjna*) pipe; **~
wydechowa** exhaust (pipe) (*Brit*),
tailpipe (*US*)

ruski *adj* (*pot!*) Russian
rusz|ać (**-am, -asz**; *pf* **-yć**) *vt*: **~
czymś** to move sth ▷ *vi* **1** (*o
pojeździe*) to move **2** (*w podróż*)
to set off **3** (*o fabryce*) to start
working

ry|ba (**-by, -by**; *dat sg & loc sg* **-bie**)
f fish; **jesteś zdrów jak ~** you're
as right as rain; **z niego jest
prawdziwa gruba ~** (*przen*) he's a
real big shot (*pot*); **iść na ryby** to
go fishing; **Ryby** *pl* (*znak zodiaku*)
Pisces

rycerz (**-a, -e**; *gen pl* **-y**) *m* knight
rym (**-u, -y**) *m* rhyme
rynek (**-ku, -ki**; *inst sg* **-kiem**) *m*
1 (*główny plac*) market (square)
2 (*Fin: instytucja*) market; **czarny
~** black market; **wolny ~** free
market

rys (**-u, -y**) *m* feature; **~y twarzy**
facial features

rys|ować (-uję, -ujesz; *pf* **na-)** *vt*
1 to draw **2** (*przen*: *wizję przyszłości*)
to picture **3** (*szkicować*) to sketch;
~ się (*pf* **za-**) *vr* **1** (*uwidaczniać się*)
to appear **2** (*karoserię, blat*) to have
scratches

rysun|ek (-ku, -ki; *inst sg* **-kiem)**
m drawing

rysunkowy *adj* drawing; **film ~**
(*kreskówka*) cartoon

ryt|m (-mu, -my; *loc sg* **-mie)** *m*
rhythm

rytua|ł (-łu, -ły; *loc sg* **-le)** *m* ritual;
**piątkowe spotkania stały się
~em** the Friday meetings have
become a ritual

ryzy|ko (-ka; *inst sg* **-kiem)** *nt*
risk; **robisz to na własne ~** you're
doing this at your own risk

ryż (-u) *m* rice

rzad|ki *adj* **1** (*sos, zupa*) thin
2 (*spotkania*) rare

rzadko *adv* **1** (*nieczęsto*) seldom
2 (*w odstępach*) sparsely; **~ kto
zdaje ten egzamin** hardly
anyone passes this exam; **~
kiedy się spotykają** they hardly
ever meet

rzą|d¹ (rzędu, rzędy; *loc sg* **rzędzie)**
m **1** (*równy szereg*) row **2** (*w biologii*)
order; **musimy to zrobić w
pierwszym rzędzie** this is a
matter of primary concern to us

rzą|d² (-du, -dy; *loc sg* **-dzie)** *m*
(*Rada Ministrów*) government;
rządy *pl* rule; **~y silnej ręki**
strong government

rzą|dzić (-dzę, -dzisz; *imp* **-dź)**
vt: **~ +inst** to govern ▷ *vi* **1** (*mieć
władzę*) to govern **2** (*dowodzić*) to
be in charge; **~ się** *vr* to throw
one's weight about; **młodość**

rządzi się swoimi prawami
youth has its own rules

rzecz (-y, -y; *gen pl* **-y)** *f* thing;
rzeczy *pl* (*przedmioty*) things *pl*;
to nie ma nic do ~y that's beside
the point; **mówi od ~y** he talks
nonsense; **kwesta na ~ szpitala**
a collection in aid of the hospital;
ogólnie ~ biorąc to ma sens
on the whole this makes sense;
w gruncie ~y popełnił błąd
essentially he made a mistake

rzeczowni|k (-ka, -ki; *inst sg*
-kiem) *m* noun

● **RZECZPOSPOLITA**
●
●
● **Rzeczpospolita** means
● 'republic', but in Poland the
● term is used exclusively to
● refer to the Polish state.
● The first **Rzeczpospolita**
● existed in the sixteenth
● and seventeenth centuries
● when Poland formed a union
● with Lithuania. The second
● **Rzeczpospolita** took place
● during the inter-war period,
● and the third **Rzeczpospolita**
● began after the collapse
● of the **PRL** in 1989. In 2005
● the ruling party announced
● the beginning of the fourth
● **Rzeczpospolita**. This,
● however, is seen more as a
● political catchphrase than as
● a real creation.

**Rzeczpospolit|a Polska (-ej
Polskiej, -e Polskie)** *f* Republic
of Poland

rzeczywistoś|ć (-ci) *f* reality;

ten opis nie odpowiada rzeczywistości this description does not match the reality; **w rzeczywistości on wyglądał całkiem inaczej** in reality he looked completely different

rzeczywisty adj (prawdziwy) real

rzeczywiście adv really

rze|ka (-**ki**, -**ki**; dat sg & loc sg -**ce**) f river; **obóz nad rzeką** a camp on the river; **pływać** (**płynąć** pf) **w dół/górę rzeki** to swim down/up (the) river

rzetelny adj (pracownik, sprawozdanie) reliable, honest

rzeź|ba (-**by**, -**by**; dat sg & loc sg -**bie**) f sculpture

rze|źbić (-**źbię**, -**źbisz**; imp -**źb**; pf **wy-**) vt to sculpt

rzę|sa (-**sy**, -**sy**; dat sg & loc sg -**sie**) f (eye)lash

rzęsisty adj **1** (ulewny) torrential **2** (w teatrze: o oklaskach) thunderous

rzodkiew|ka (-**ki**, -**ki**; dat sg & loc sg -**ce**; gen pl -**ek**) f radish

rzu|cać (-**cam**, -**casz**; pf -**cić**) vt **1** (oszczepem, dyskiem) to throw **2** (cień) to cast **3** (męża, żonę) to abandon **4** (pot: chłopaka, dziewczynę) to dump **5** (nałóg) to quit **6** (komentarz) to throw in ▷ vi (o pojeździe) to abandon

Rzymia|nin (-**nina**, -**nie**; loc sg -**ninie**; gen pl -**n**) m Roman

rzymski adj (mitologia, obyczaje) Roman; **pieczeń rzymska** meat loaf

rzymskokatolicki adj Roman Catholic

r.ż. abbr (= rodzaj żeński) f (= feminine)

S

SA, S.A. abbr (= spółka akcyjna: firma) Co.

sa|d (-**du**, -**dy**; loc sg -**dzie**) m (wiśniowy, jabłkowy) orchard

sal|a (-**i**, -**e**; loc & dat sg, gen. pl -**i**) f **1** (większa) hall **2** (mniejsza) room **3** (przen: publika) (the) audience; **~ wykładowa** lecture hall; **~ gimnastyczna** gymnasium; **~ operacyjna** operating theatre (Brit), operating room (US)

salami nt inv (kiełbasa) salami

salceso|n (-**nu**, -**ny**; loc sg -**nie**) m (rodzaj czarnej kiełbasy) black pudding (Brit), blood sausage (US)

salo|n (-**nu**, -**ny**; loc sg -**nie**) m **1** (w mieszkaniu) lounge **2** (zakład usługowy, sklep) salon **3** (literacki, towarzyski) salon

sała|ta (-**ty**, -**ty**; dat & loc sg -**cie**) f

(*warzywo*) lettuce
sałat|ka (**-ki**, **-ki**; *dat & loc sg* **-ce**; *gen pl* **-ek**) *f* (*potrawa*) salad; **~ owocowa** fruit salad

○ **KEYWORD**

sam¹ *pron decl like adj* **1** (*bez niczyjej pomocy*): **sam to zrobił** he did it himself; **okno samo się otworzyło** the window opened by itself
2 (*bez nikogo*): **mieszka sama** she lives alone
3 (*uściślając lub podkreślając*): **na samym dole/początku** at the very bottom/beginning; **w samą porę** just in time
4 (*wyłącznie*): **same problemy** nothing but trouble; **same książki zajęły dużo miejsca w walizce** the books alone took up a lot of room in the suitcase
5 (*wskazując na przyczynę*): **na samą myśl o czymś** at the mere thought of sth
6 (*o ważnej osobie*): **sam król tam był** the king himself was there
7 (*w wyrażeniach z: sobie, siebie, się*): **sam jest sobie winien** he has only himself to blame
8 (*w wyrażeniach z 'ten', 'taki'*): **taki sam** exact same; **taki sam samochód** the exact same car; **ma taką samą spódnicę** she has the exact same skirt

sa|m² (**-mu**, **-my**; *loc sg* **-mie**) *m* (*sklep spożywczy*) self-service shop
samic|a (**-y**, **-e**; *dat & loc sg* **-y**) *f* (*zwierzę*) female
sa|miec (**-mca**, **-mce**) *m* (*zwierzę*)

male
samo *pron decl like adj zob.* **sam** ▷ *pron inv:* **tak ~** (*indentycznie*) in the same way
samobójc|a (**-y**, **-y**; *dat & loc sg* **-y**) *m* (*osoba, która odbiera sobie życie*) suicide (victim)
samobójst|wo (**-wa**, **-wa**; *loc sg* **-wie**) *nt* (*odebranie sobie życia*) suicide; **popełnić** (*pf*) **~** to commit suicide
samoch|ód (**-odu**, **-ody**; *loc sg* **-odzie**) *m* (*auto*) car; **~ ciężarowy** lorry (*Brit*), truck (*US*); **jeździć** (**jechać** *pf*) **samochodem** to go by car; **prowadzić ~** to drive (a car)
samodzielnie *adv* **1** (*samemu, w pojedynkę*) single-handed(ly) **2** (*niezależnie*) independently
samodzielny *adj* **1** (*zaradny*) independent **2** (*pracownik, decyzja*) independent **3** (*odrębny*) self-contained
samolo|t (**-tu**, **-ty**; *loc sg* **-cie**) *m* (*środek transportu*) aeroplane (*Brit*), airplane (*US*); **latać** (**lecieć** *pf*) **~em** to go by plane
samoobro|na (**-ny**; *dat & loc sg* **-nie**) *f* **1** (*pojedynczej osoby*) self-defence (*Brit*), self-defense (*US*) **2** (*kraju*) civil defence (*Brit*) *lub* defense (*US*)
samopoczuci|e (**-a**) *nt* (*fizyczne, psychiczne*) mood
samorzą|d (**-du**, **-dy**; *loc sg* **-dzie**) *m* (*Admin*): **~ miejski** town/city council; **~ terytorialny** local government
samotnoś|ć (**-ci**; *dat & loc sg* **-ci**) *f* **1** (*brak towarzystwa*) loneliness **2** (*bycie na odludziu*) solitude

samotny adj **1** (sam, bez towarzystwa) lonely **2** (odosobniony) solitary **3** (rodzic) single

samoucz|ek (-ka, -ki; inst sg -kiem) m (podręcznik): ~ **języka polskiego** a "Teach Yourself Polish" book

samou|k (-ka, -cy lub -ki; inst sg -kiem) m (osoba): **być ~iem** to be self-taught

sanatori|um (-um, -a; gen pl -ów) nt inv in sg (zakład leczniczy) sanatorium

sandał (-a, -y) m (but) sandal; **sandały** pl sandals

saty|ra (-ry, -ry; dat & loc sg -rze) f: ~ **na** (Lit) satire of

satysfakcj|a (-i; dat & loc sg -i) f (zadowolenie) satisfaction

są vb zob. **być**

są|d (-du, -dy; loc sg -dzie) m **1** (urząd) court of law **2** (proces) trial **3** (książk: zdanie) judgement

są|dzić (-dzę, -dzisz; imp -dź; pf o-) (przestępcę) to try ▷ vi (być zdania, uważać) to think; **co o tym sądzicie?** what do you think of that?

sąsi|ad (-ada, -edzi) m (osoba) neighbour (Brit), neighbor (US)

S.C. abbr = **spółka cywilna**

sce|na (-ny, -ny; dat & loc sg -nie) f **1** (wypadku, wydarzenia: w filmie) scene **2** (podium) stage; ~ **polityczna** political scene

scenariusz (-a, -e; gen pl -y) m **1** (filmu) screenplay **2** (przedstawienia, słuchowiska) script **3** (przen: przebieg wydarzeń) scenario

scenarzy|sta (-sty, -ści; dat & loc sg -ście) m decl like f in sg **1** (filmowy) screenwriter **2** (teatralny) scriptwriter

schabowy adj: **kotlet ~** (Kulin) pork chop

schema|t (-tu, -ty; loc sg -cie) m **1** (zachowania, wydarzeń) pattern **2** (rysunek) diagram

schłodzony adj chilled

sch|nąć (-nę, -niesz; imp -nij) vi to dry; **pranie schnie na słońcu** the laundry is drying in the sun

schod|y (-ów) pl (Bud) stairs pl; **ruchome ~** escalator

scho|dzić (-dzę, -dzisz; imp -dź; pf zejść) vi **1** (po schodach) to go down **2** (zsiadać z konia, roweru) to dismount **3** (wstać z tapczanu) to get off **4** (dać się usunąć/ściągnąć) to come off **5** (o skórze (z nosa), tapecie) to peel; ~ **się** vr **1** (zbierać się) to gather **2** (o ulicach) to join

schow|ać (-am, -asz) vb pf od **chować**

schronis|ko (-ka, -ka; inst sg -kiem) nt **1** (w górach) chalet **2** (hotel dla młodzieży) hostel **3** (dla bezdomnych) shelter

schud|nąć (-nę, -niesz; imp -nij) vb pf od **chudnąć**

schwy|cić (-cę, -cisz; imp -ć) vt pf (ująć) to catch

schwyt|ać (-am, -asz) vb pf od **chwytać**

scyzory|k (-ka, -ki; inst sg -kiem) m (nożyk) penknife

sean|s (-su, -se; loc sg -sie) m (filmowy) show

sede|s (-su, -sy; loc sg -sie) m **1** (o muszli klozetowej) toilet bowl **2** (o desce klozetowej) toilet seat

sej|f (**-fu, -fy**; *loc sg* **-fie**) *m* (*na pieniądze, broń*) safe
sej|m (**-mu, -my**; *loc sg* **-mie**) *m* (*Pol*) the Sejm

● **SEJM**
●
● The Polish parliament
● consists of two houses: **sejm**
● and **senat**. The **sejm** is made
● up of 460 members.

sekre|t (**-tu, -ty**; *loc sg* **-cie**) *m* (*tajemnica*) secret
sekretaria|t (**-tu, -ty**; *loc sg* **-cie**) *m* secretariat
sekretar|ka (**-ki, -ki**; *dat & loc sg* **-ce**; *gen pl* **-ek**) *f* (*osoba*) secretary; **automatyczna ~** answering machine
sekretarz (**-a, -e**; *gen pl* **-y**) *m* (*osoba*) secretary
sek|s (**-su**; *loc s* **-sie**) *m* (*aktywność płciowa*) sex
seksowny *adj* (*pot: głos, taniec, chód*) sexy
sekun|da (**-dy, -dy**; *dat & loc sg* **-dzie**) *f* second; **sekundę!** (*pot*) just a sec!
sele|r (**-ra, -ry**; *loc sg* **-rze**) *m* 1 (*korzeń*) celeriac 2 (*liście*) celery
semest|r (**-ru, -ry**; *loc sg* **-rze**) *m* (*Szkol, Uniw*) semester
sen (**snu, sny**; *loc sg* **śnie**) *m* 1 (*spanie*) sleep 2 (*o marzeniu sennym*) dream; **mieć zły ~** to have a bad dream

● **SENAT**
●
● The Polish parliament
● consists of two houses: **sejm**

● and **senat**. The **senat** is made
● up of one hundred senators,
● who are elected in general
● elections.

senato|r (**-ra, -rowie** *lub* **-rzy**; *loc sg* **-rze**) *m* (*Pol*) senator
senio|r (**-ra, -rzy**; *loc sg* **-rze**) *m* (*osoba najstarsza wiekiem*) senior
senny *adj* 1 (*śpiący, bez energii*) sleepy 2 (*usypiający*) drowsy
sen|s (**-su**; *loc sg* **-sie**) *m* 1 (*cel*) point 2 (*o znaczeniu*) sense; **bez ~u** pointless; **to nie ma ~u** that doesn't make sense
separacj|a (**-i**) *f* (*małżeńska*) separation; **być/żyć w separacji** to be separated
se|r (**-ra, -ry**; *loc sg* **-rze**) *m* (*Kulin*) cheese; **biały ~** cottage cheese; **żółty ~** hard cheese
Serbi|a (**-i**) *f* Serbia
serbski *adj* Serbian
serbsko-chorwacki *adj* Serbo-Croatian
serc|e (**-a, -a**; *nom pl* **-a**) *nt* (*Med*) heart; **jest bez serca** he is heartless; **życzenia płynące z głębi serca** best wishes from the bottom of one's heart
serdecznie *adv* 1 (*powitać, podziękować*) warmly 2 (*bardzo, naprawdę*) heartily; **pozdrawiam ~** (*na zakończenie listu*) kind regards
serdeczny *adj* 1 (*człowiek*) friendly 2 (*o przyjacielu*) bosom 3 (*uśmiech, gest*) warm 4 (*powitanie*) hearty; **~ palec** ring finger; **serdeczne pozdrowienia** heartfelt greetings

ser|ek (**-ka, -ki**; inst sg **-kiem**) m
dimin od **ser** (Kulin) cheese; ~
topiony processed cheese

seri|a (**-i, -e**; gen pl, dat & loc sg **-i**)
f **1** (zdarzeń) series **2** (antybiotyku,
zabiegów) course **3** (kolekcja)
set **4** (negocjacji) round
5 (wyrobów przemysłowych) batch
6 (kosmetyków) line

serial (**-u, -e**; gen pl **-i**) m (TV)
series

serni|k (**-ka, -ki**; inst sg **-kiem**) m
(Kulin) cheesecake

serwe|r (**-ra, -ry**; loc sg **-rze**) m
(Komput) server

sesj|a (**-i, -e**; gen pl **-i**) f **1** (sejmu,
nagraniowa) session **2** (na
uniwersytecie): ~ **egzaminacyjna**
end-of-term examinations pl
3 (na giełdzie) trading session
4 (fotograficzna) shoot

sę|dzia (**-dziego** lub **-dzi,
-dziowie**) m decl like adj lub f in
sg **1** (Prawo) judge **2** (konkursowy)
juror **3** (w piłce nożnej, koszykówce,
boksie) referee **4** (w tenisie,
siatkówce) umpire

sędzi|ować (**-uję, -ujesz**) vi
1 (prowadzić rozprawę) to judge
2 (w meczu piłki nożnej, koszykówki)
to referee **3** (w meczu tenisowym,
siatkówki) to umpire

sfałsz|ować (**-uję, -ujesz**) vb pf
od **fałszować**

sfe|ra (**-ry, -ry**; dat & loc sg **-rze**)
f **1** (szara; podbiegunowa) zone
2 (Astron) sphere **3** (wpływów,
działań, gospodarcza) sphere
4 (klasa społeczna) class

siać (**-eję, -ejesz**) vt to sow

siad|ać (**-am, -asz**; imp **-aj**) vb
impf to sit; **mleko się zsiadło** the

milk has gone off

siat|ka (**-ki, -ki**; dat & loc sg **-ce**; gen
pl **-ek**) f **1** (plecionka) mesh, net
2 (w ogrodzie) wire fence **3** (układ)
network **4** (w tenisie, koszykówce)
net **5** (przestępca) ring; ~ **na
zakupy** string bag

siatków|ka (**-ki**; dat & loc sg **-ce**)
f **1** (nom pl **-ki**; gen pl **-ek**) (oka)
retina **2** (gra sportowa) volleyball

sią|ść (**-dę, -dziesz**; imp **-dź**) vb pf
od **siadać**

siebie pron **1** (dotyczący siebie
samego) oneself **2** (z wzajemnością)
each other; **przed ~** straight
ahead; **być u ~** (w domu) to be
at home; **czuj się jak u ~** make
yourself at home; **oni są o ~
zazdrośni** they are jealous of one
another; **siedzieliśmy obok ~** we
sat next to each other

sie|ć (**-ci, -ci**; gen pl, dat & loc
sg **-ci**) f **1** (do łowienia ryb) net
2 (pajęcza) (cob)web **3** (elektryczna,
internetowa) network **4** (barów,
kin) chain **5** (przen: zasadzka) trap

siedem num seven

siedemdziesiąt num seventy

siedemnasty num decl like adj
seventeenth; **jest siedemnasta**
it's 5 o'clock

siedemnaście num seventeen

siedemset num seven hundred

siedze|nie (**-nia, -nia**; gen pl **-ń**) nt
1 (krzesło, fotel) seat **2** (pot: tyłek)
bum

siedzi|ba (**-by, -by**; dat & loc sg
-bie) f (instytucji) base; **główna ~**
headquarters pl; **firma ma swoją
siedzibę w Poznaniu** the firm is
based in Poznan

sie|dzieć (**-dzę, -dzisz**; imp **-dź**)

vi **1** (*być w pozycji siedzącej*) to sit **2** (*pot: w domu, przed komputerem*) to stay **3** (*pot: odbywać karę więzienia*) to do time **4** (*powtarzać klasę w szkole*) to repeat

sieroci|niec (**-ńca, -ńce**) *m* (*dom dla sierot*) orphanage

siero|ta (**-ty, -ty**; *dat sg* **-cie**) *m/f decl like f* **1** (*dziecko bez rodziców*) orphan **2** (*niezdarna, niezaradna osoba*) waif

sier|pień (**-pnia, -pnie**) *m* August

○ **KEYWORD**

się *pron inv* **1** (*odnoszący się do siebie samego*) oneself; **skompromitował się** he compromised himself **2** (*nawzajem*) each other; **spotykamy się regularnie** we meet up with each other regularly **3** (*przy tworzeniu strony zwrotnej czasownika*): **interesuję się historią** I'm interested in history; **myć** (**umyć** *pf*) **się** to wash oneself; **cieszę się, że tu jesteście** I'm pleased that you are here **4** (*jako odpowiednik strony biernej*): **tę koszulę dobrze się prasuje** this shirt irons well **5** (*bezosobowo*): **robi się późno** it's getting late

sik|ać (**-am, -asz**; *pf* **-nąć**) *vi* **1** (*pot: wytrysnąć strumieniem*) to squirt **2** (*pot: siusiać*) to pee

silnie *adv* **1** (*uderzyć*) hard **2** (*intensywnie*) strongly; **~ przeżyła jego śmierć** she took his death badly

silni|k (**-ka, -ki**; *inst sg* **-kiem**) *m* (*urządzenie*) engine; **~ elektryczny** electric motor

silny *adj* **1** (*mężczyzna, wiatr, organizm*) strong **2** (*stres, ból*) intense **3** (*leki, szkła*) strong **4** (*akcent*) strong

si|ła (**-ły, -ły**; *dat & loc sg* **-le**) *f* **1** (*energia*) strength **2** (*natężenie*) intensity **3** (*w fizyce*) force; **siły** *pl* forces; **siłą** by force; **siły zbrojne** armed forces

siłow|nia (**-ni, -nie**; *gen & loc pl* **-ni**) *f* **1** (*klub sportowy*) body-building gym **2** (*energetyczna, wodna*) power plant

sin|gel, sin|giel (**-gla, -gle**; *gen pl* **-gli**) *m* **1** (*Muz*) single **2** (*w sporcie*) singles *pl*

si|ostra (**-ostry, -ostry**; *dat & loc sg* **-ostrze**; *gen pl* **-óstr**) *f* **1** (*rodzeństwo*) sister **2** (*w szpitalu*) nurse; **~ oddziałowa** charge nurse; **~ zakonna** nun, sister

siostrzenic|a (**-y, -e**) *f* (*krewna*) niece

siostrze|niec (**-ńca, -ńcy**) *m* (*krewny*) nephew

siódmy *num decl like adj* seventh; **jest siódma** it's seven o'clock; **na stronie siódmej** on page seven

siwi|eć (**-eję, -ejesz**; *pf* **o-** *lub* **po-**) *vi* (*o włosach i o osobie*) to go grey (*Brit*) *lub* gray (*US*)

siwy *adj* (*o włosach i o osobie*) grey (*Brit*), gray (*US*)

ska|kać (**-czę, -czesz**; *pf* **skoczyć**) *vi* **1** (*wykonać podskok*) to jump **2** (*na skakance*) to skip **3** (*o wartości, akcjach*) to shoot up

skalecze|nie (**-nia, -nia**; *gen pl* **-ń**)
nt (*mała rana*) cut
skalecz|yć (**-ę, -ysz**) *vt pf* (*zranić,
uszkodzić*) to cut; **~ się** *vr pf* (*zranić
się*) to cut o.s.
ska|ła (**-ły, -ły**; *dat & loc sg* **-le**) *f*
(*Geol*) rock
skandal (**-u, -e**; *gen pl* **-i** *lub* **-ów**)
m (*gorsząca sytuacja/atmosfera*)
scandal
Skandynawi|a (**-i**; *dat & loc sg* **-i**) *f*
(*region*) Scandinavia
skandynawski *adj* (*dotyczący
regionu*) Scandinavian; **półwysep
S~** Scandinavian Peninsula
skanse|n (**-nu, -ny**; *loc sg* **-nie**) *m*
(*muzeum etnograficzne*) heritage
park
skar|b (**-bu, -by**; *loc sg* **-bie**) *m*
(*coś drogocennego*) treasure; **~
państwa** (*Pol*) the treasury
skarbowy *adj* **1** (*przepis, bon,
obligacja*) treasury **2** (*znaczek,
opłata*) duty **3** (*kontrola*) treasury;
urząd ~ ≈ HM Revenue and
Customs (*Brit*), ≈ Internal
Revenue Service (*US*)
skar|ga (**-gi, -gi**; *dat & loc sg* **-dze**) *f*
(*zażalenie*) complaint
skarpet|ka (**-ki, -ki**; *dat & loc sg*
-ce; *gen pl* **-ek**) *f* (*ubranie*) sock
skarż|yć (**-ę, -ysz**) *vt*: **~ kogoś (do
sądu)** (*pozwać do sądu*) to sue sb
▷ *vi*: **~ (na~** *pf*) **na kogoś** (*donosić*)
to tell on sb; **~ się** (*pf* **po~**) *vr*
1 (*utyskiwać, narzekać*) to complain
2 (*mieć problem zdrowotny*): **~ się
na coś** to complain of sth; **~ się
na kogoś/coś** to complain about
sb/sth
skazany *adj* **1** (*w sądzie*) convicted
2 (*przen*): **~ na coś** doomed to

sth ▷ *m decl like adj* (*wyrokiem
sądowym*) convict
skąd *pron* (*z jakiego miejsca/źródła*)
where... from; **~ pan/pani jest?**
where are you from?; **~ wiesz?**
(*familiar sg*) how do you know?
ską|piec (**-pca, -pcy**) *m* (*sknera*)
miser
skąpy *adj* **1** (*sknerowaty*) stingy
2 (*strój, posiłek, blask*) scant
sklej|ać (**-am, -asz**; *pf* **skleić**)
vt (*połączyć klejem*) to glue
together
skle|p (**-pu, -py**; *loc sg* **-pie**) *m*
(*punkt sprzedaży towarów*) shop
(*Brit*), store (*US*); **~ spożywczy**
grocer's; **~ mięsny** butcher's

⊙ **SKLEP MONOPOLOWY**
⊙
⊙ **Sklep monopolowy** is a store
⊙ which sells a wide selection
⊙ of alcohol. Its name comes
⊙ from the fact that during
⊙ the **PRL** the state had a total
⊙ monopoly on the production
⊙ of alcohol.

skła|d (**-du, -dy**; *loc sg* **-dzie**)
m **1** (*opału*) yard **2** (*budynek*)
warehouse **3** (*składniki danego
produktu*) composition **4** (*w
chemii*) composition **5** (*tekstu w
drukarni*) typesetting **6** (*sportowej
grupy*) lineup **7** (*delegacji*) makeup;
wchodzić (**wejść** *pf*) **w ~ czegoś**
to be part of sth
skład|ać (**-am, -asz**; *pf*
złożyć) *vt* **1** (*kartkę, wózek*)
to fold **2** (*parasolkę*) to roll
up **3** (*montować*) to assemble
4 (*przechowywać*) to store

5 (*podanie, wymówienie*) to hand in **6** (*o ofercie, obietnicy*) to make **7** (*o zażaleniu*) to file **8** (*gratulacje, wyrazy szacunku*) to express **9** (*o wizycie*) to pay; **~ się** *vr* **1** (*o meblu, wózeczku*) to fold up **2** (*pot: dawać pieniądze na wspólny cel*) to chip in **3** (*być elementem składowym*): **~ się z czegoś** to consist of sth

składni|k (**-ka, -ki**; *inst sg* **-kiem**) *m* **1** (*część składowa*) ingredient **2** (*w matematyce*) element

skła|mać (**-mię, -miesz**) *vb pf od* **kłamać**

skocz|yć (**-ę, -ysz**) *vb pf od* **skakać**

sko|k (**-ku, -ki**; *inst sg* **-kiem**) *m* **1** (*podskok*) jump **2** (*nagła zmiana: cen*) hike; **~ w dal/wzwyż** long/high jump

skomplikowany *adj* (*trudny*) complicated

skończ|yć (**-ę, -ysz**) *vb pf od* **kończyć**

skoro *conj* (*jeśli*) since, as; **~ tylko** as soon as

skorpio|n (**-na, -ny**; *loc sg* **-nie**) *m* **1** (*zwierzę*) scorpion **2** (*Astrol*): **S~** Scorpio

skowron|ek (**-ka, -ki**; *inst sg* **-kiem**) *m* (*ptak*) lark

skó|ra (**-ry, -ry**; *dat & loc sg* **-rze**) *f* **1** (*Anat*) skin **2** (*na zwierzętach gruboskórnych*) hide **3** (*surowiec na odzież*) leather; **buty ze skóry** leather shoes

skórzany *adj* (*rękawiczki, płaszcz, pasek*) leather

skrę|cać (**-cam, -casz**; *pf* **-cić**) *vt* **1** (*splatać*) to weave **2** (*zwijać np. papierosa*) to roll **3** (*wkrętami, śrubami*) to screw together

4 (*kostkę, nogę*) to cross ▷ *vi* (*o samochodzie, ulicy*) to turn; **~ w prawo/ulicę Prostą** to turn right/into Prosta street; **skręć w trzecią w lewo** take the third turning on the left

skrę|cić (**-cę, -cisz**; *imp* **-ć**) *vb pf od* **skręcać**

skromnoś|ć (**-ci**) *f* (*brak zarozumiałości*) modesty

skromny *adj* (*człowiek, strój, posiłek*) modest

skrytyk|ować (**-uję, -ujesz**) *vb pf od* **krytykować**

skrzyd|ło (**-ła, -ła**; *loc sg* **-le**; *gen pl* **-eł**) *nt* **1** (*ptaka, samolotu*) wing **2** (*Tech*) blade **3** (*u okna*) sash

skrzy|nia (**-ni, -nie**; *dat & loc sg* **-ni**; *gen pl* **-ń**) *f* **1** (*kufer*) chest **2** (*pojemnik bez wieka na jedzenie*) crate **3** (*w tapczanie*) frame; **~ biegów** (*w samochodzie*) gearbox

skrzyn|ka (**-ka, -ki**; *dat sg* **-ce**; *gen pl* **-ek**) *f dimin od* **skrzynia** **1** (*korytko na kwiaty*) window box **2** (*o obudowie*) case; **~ pocztowa** *lub* **na listy** (*w bloku mieszkalnym*) letterbox (Brit), mailbox (US); **~ pocztowa** (*do wysłania listu*) postbox (Brit), mailbox (US); **czarna ~** (*w samolocie*) black box

skrzy|pce (**-piec**) *pl* (*instrument muzyczny*) violin *sg*

skrzyw|dzić (**-dzę, -dzisz**; *imp* **-dź**) *vb pf od* **krzywdzić**

skrzyżowa|nie (**-nia, -nia**; *gen pl* **-ń**) *nt* (*dróg*) crossroads

skuteczny *adj* (*lek, plan, pracownik*) effective

skut|ek (**-ku, -ki**; *inst sg* **-kiem**) *m* (*następstwo*) result; **aż do skutku** to the bitter end; **dojść** (*pf*) **do**

skutku to come into effect; **na ~ czegoś** as a result of sth

slip|y (**-ów**) pl (bielizna) briefs

słab|nąć (**-nę, -niesz**; imp **-nij**; pf **o-**) vi 1 (tracić energię) to weaken 2 (zainteresowanie) to diminish 3 (tracić intensywność) to die down 4 (o problemach, utrapieniach, bólu) to ease off

słabo adv 1 (bez energii, siły) weakly 2 (rozwinięty (kraj), zaludniony) poorly 3 (przygotowany, słyszący) poorly; **~ mi** I feel faint

słaby adj 1 (wątły, bez siły) weak 2 (marny) poor

sła|wa (**-wy**; dat & loc sg **-wie**) f 1 (popularność) fame 2 (opinia) reputation 3 (sławny człowiek) famous person; **światowej sławy aktor** a world-famous actor

sławny adj (znany) famous

słodki adj (uśmiech, smak, człowiek) sweet; **słodka woda** fresh water

słodycz (**-y**) f (smaku, uśmiechu) sweetness; **słodycze** pl (cukierki, czekolada) sweets (Brit), candy sg (US)

sł|odzić (**-odzę, -odzisz**; imp **-ódź** lub **-odź**; pf **o-** lub **po-**) vt (dodawać cukru) to sweeten; **czy pan/pani słodzi?** do you take sugar?

słoi|k (**-ka, -ki**; inst sg **-kiem**) m (dżemu, korniszonów) jar

słom|ka (**-ki, -ki**; dat & loc sg **-ce**; gen pl **-ek**) f (do napojów) straw

słoneczny adj 1 (niebo, mieszkanie) sunny 2 (o energii) solar; **światło słoneczne** sunlight; **okulary słoneczne** sunglasses pl

słony adj 1 (jedzenie) salty 2 (o wodzie) salt 3 (przen: wygórowany) steep

sło|ń (**-nia, -nie**; gen pl **-ni**) m (zwierzę) elephant

słońc|e (**-a, -a**) nt 1 (ciało niebieskie) sun 2 (o świetle słonecznym) sunshine; **w** lub **na słońcu** in the sunshine

Słowacj|a (**-i**) f Slovakia

słowacki adj Slovakian

Słoweni|a (**-i**) f Slovenia

słoweński adj Slovenian

słownict|wo (**-wa**; loc sg **-wie**) nt vocabulary

słownicz|ek (**-ka, -ki**; inst sg **-kiem**) m 1 (lista terminów/ wyrazów) glossary 2 (mały słownik) pocket dictionary

słowni|k (**-ka, -ki**; inst sg **-kiem**) m (jednojęzyczny, dwujęzyczny) dictionary

sł|owo (**-owa, -owa**; loc sg **-owie**; gen pl **-ów**) nt (wyraz) word; **słowa** pl (w tekście piosenki) lyrics pl; **innymi słowy** in other words; **~ w ~** word for word; **dawać** (**dać** pf) **~** to give one's word; **dotrzymywać** (**dotrzymać** pf) **słowa** to keep one's word

słuch (**-u**) m 1 (o zmyśle) hearing 2 (Muz) (an) ear for music; **słuchy** pl (pogłoski): **chodzą ~y, że pogoda będzie ładna** rumour (Brit) lub rumor (US) has it that the weather will be good

słuch|ać (**-am, -asz**) vt +gen (muzyki, radia) to listen to ▷ vi (pf **u-** lub **po-**) (rodziców, nauczycieli) to obey; **słucham?** (halo?) hello?; (nie dosłyszałem) pardon?

słuchaw|ka (**-ki, -ki**; dat & loc sg **-ce**; gen pl **-ek**) f (w telefonie) receiver; **słuchawki** pl

1 (*nakładane na głowę*) headphones **2** (*wkładane do ucha*) earphones

słu|ga (**-gi, -dzy**; *dat & loc sg* **-dze**) *m decl like f* (*książk: służący*) servant

służ|ba (**-by, -by**; *dat sg* **-bie**) *f* **1** (*wojskowa, drogowa, dyplomatyczna, zdrowia*) service **2** (*godziny pracy milicjanta, żołnierza*) duty **3** (*osoby pełniące pracę służącego*) servants *pl*

służbowo *adv* (*odbywać podróż*) on business

służbowy *adj* **1** (*podróż, spotkanie*) business **2** (*obowiązek, funkcja*) official **3** (*samochód, telefon*) company

służ|yć (**-ę, -ysz**) *vi* **1** (*pełnić funkcję, usługiwać*) to serve **2** (*o psie*) to beg **3** (*być użytecznym*) to be useful; **do czego to służy?** what's this for?; **czym mogę ~?** can I help you?

słychać *vi* (*być słyszalnym*): **~ było hałas** there was noise; **~, że...** there's news that...; **nic nie ~** I can't hear a thing; **co ~?** how's it going? (*Brit*), what's up? (*US*)

słynny *adj* (*sławny, znany*) famous

słysz|eć (**-ę, -ysz**; *pf* **u-**) *vt* **1** (*dźwięki*) to hear **2** (*dowiadywać się*) to hear; **słyszysz mnie?** (*familiar sg*) can you hear me?; **nigdy nie słyszałam o tym aktorze** I've never heard of that actor

smaczny *adj* (*posiłek*) tasty; **smacznego!** enjoy your meal!

sma|k (**-ku**; *inst sg* **-kiem**) *m* **1** (*zmysł*) taste **2** (*nom pl* **-ki**) (*dania, napoju*) taste, flavour (*Brit*), flavor (*US*); **bez ~u** tasteless

smak|ować (**-uję, -ujesz**) *vt* (*pf* **po-**) (*kosztować*) to taste ▷ *vi* (*być smacznym*): **~ świetnie** to taste excellent; **jak panu/pani smakuje?** how does it taste to you?

smal|ec (**-cu**) *m* (*Kulin*) lard

smar|ować (**-uję, -ujesz**; *pf* **po-**) *vt* **1** (*kromkę masłem*) to butter **2** (*dżemem, serem*) to spread **3** (*pf* **na-**) (*smarem*) to grease

smażony *adj* (*Kulin*) fried

smaż|yć (**-ę, -ysz**; *pf* **u-**) *vt* (*Kulin*) to fry

smo|k (**-ka, -ki**; *inst sg* **-kiem**) *m* (*z baśni*) dragon

smr|ód (**-odu, -ody**; *loc sg* **-odzie**) *m* (*fetor*) stench

SMS (**SMS-a, SMS-y**; *loc sg* **SMS-ie**) *nt* text message

smukły *adj* (*wysoki i szczupły*) slender

smutno *adv* (*wyglądać, uśmiechać się*) sadly; **~ mi** I feel sad

smutny *adj* (*nieszczęśliwy, niewesoły*) sad

snu *n zob.* **sen**

sobą *pron* **1** (*dotyczący siebie samego*) oneself **2** (*wzajemnie, razem*) each other; **być ~** to be oneself; **chodzili ze ~ przez trzy lata** they were together for three years; **mieszkać ze ~** to live together

sobie *pron* **1** (*dotyczący siebie samego*) oneself **2** (*nawzajem*) each other; **mieć coś na ~** (*ubranie*) to have sth on; **mówić o ~** to talk about oneself; **idź ~!** go away!; **ręce przy ~!** hands off!; **tak ~** (*pot*) so-so

sob|ota (**-oty, -oty**; *dat & loc sg*

-ocie; *gen pl* **-ót**) *f* Saturday
socjalistyczny *adj* (*ruch, związek, partia*) socialist
socjologi|a (**-i**) *f* (*nauka*) sociology
so|fa (**-fy, -fy**; *dat & loc sg* **-fie**) *f* (*kanapa*) sofa
so|k (**-ku, -ki**; *inst sg* **-kiem**) *m* 1 (*Kulin*) juice 2 (*Bot*) sap
solenizan|t (**-ta, -ci**; *loc sg* **-cie**) *m* (*obchodzący urodziny/imieniny*) person celebrating his birthday/nameday
solidarnoś|ć (**-ci**) *f* (*poczucie wspólnoty*) solidarity
solidny *adj* 1 (*spolegliwy*) solid 2 (*budynek*) sturdy 3 (*mocny i trwały*) solid 4 (*gruntowny*) thorough 5 (*dużych rozmiarów*) substantial
solony *adj* (*popcorn, ryba*) salted
SOS *nt inv* (*sygnał wzywania pomocy*) SOS, distress signal
so|s (**-su, -sy**; *loc sg* **-sie**) *m* 1 (*pieczarkowy, czekoladowy*) sauce 2 (*własny z mięsa*) gravy 3 (*sałatkowy*) dressing
so|wa (**-wy, -wy**; *dat & loc sg* **-wie**; *gen pl* **sów**) *f* (*ptak*) owl
sól (**soli**) *f* (*przyprawa*) salt; **sole** *pl* (*mineralne, trzeźwiące*) salts
space|r (**-ru, -ry**; *loc sg* **-rze**) *m* (*przechadzka*) walk; **iść** (**pójść** *pf*) **na ~** to go for a walk
spacer|ować (**-uję, -ujesz**) *vi* (*przechadzać się*) to stroll
spać (**śpię, śpisz**; *imp* **śpij**) *vi* (*być w stanie snu*) to sleep; **on śpi/nie śpi** he's asleep/awake; **iść** (**pójść** *pf*) **~** to go to bed; **chce ci się ~?** are you sleepy?; **~ z kimś** to sleep with sb

spak|ować (**-uję, -ujesz**) *vb pf od* **pakować**
spal|ać (**-am, -asz**; *pf* **-ić**) *vt* 1 (*niszczyć ogniem/słońcem*) to burn 2 (*wysadzać bezpieczniki*) to blow; **~ się** *vr* (*zostać zniszczonym ogniem*) to burn
spal|ić (**-ę, -isz**) *vb pf od* **palić, spalać**
specjali|sta (**-sty, -ści**; *dat sg* **-ście**) *m decl like f in sg* 1 (*fachowiec*) expert 2 (*Med*) specialist
specjaliz|ować się (**-uję, -ujesz**; *pf* **wy-**) *vr* (*być fachowcem w jakiejś dziedzinie*): **~ się w czymś** to specialize in sth
specjalnoś|ć (**-ci, -ci**; *gen pl* **-ci**) *f* (*dziedzina*) speciality (*Brit*), specialty (*US*)
spektakl (**-u, -e**; *gen pl* **-i**) *m* (*przedstawienie*) performance
spinacz (**-a, -e**; *gen pl* **-y**) *m* (*biurowy*) paper clip
spirytu|s (**-su, -sy**; *loc sg* **-sie**) *m* (*mocny alkohol*) spirit
spi|s (**-su, -sy**; *loc sg* **-sie**) *m* (*rejestr*) list; **~ treści** table of contents
spis|ek (**-ku, -ki**; *inst sg* **-kiem**) *m* (*tajny plan*) conspiracy
spisk|ować (**-uję, -ujesz**) *vi* (*zawierać tajne porozumienie*) to conspire
spis|ywać (**-uję, -ujesz**; *pf* **-ać**) *vt* 1 (*sporządzać rejestr*) to make a list of 2 (*dokumenty*) to draw up 3 (*przepisywać skądś, zapisywać*) to copy 4 (*na egzaminie*) to copy; **~ się** *vr* (*działać, postępować*): **dobrze/źle się ~** (*o osobie*) to do well/badly; (*o urządzeniu*) to run well/badly
spleśniały *adj* (*zepsute jedzenie/*

ubranie) mouldy *(Brit)*, moldy *(US)*

spłu|kiwać (-kuję, -kujesz; *pf* **-kać**) *vt (pianę, szampon)* to rinse off

spod *prep +gen (stołu, biurka)* from under; **~ Krakowa** from somewhere around Cracow

spod|nie (-ni) *pl (ubranie)* trousers *(Brit)*, pants *(US)*

spodziew|ać się (-am, -asz) *vr (oczekiwać):* **~ się kogoś/czegoś** to be expecting sb/sth

spogląd|ać (-am, -asz; *pf* **spojrzeć**) *vi (patrzeć)* to look

spojrz|eć (-ę, -ysz; *imp* **spójrz** lub **spojrzyj**) *vb pf od* **spoglądać**

spojrze|nie (-nia, -nia; *gen pl* -ń) *nt (wzrok)* look

spoko *interj* **1** *(w porządku)* no problem! *(pot)* **2** *(nie denerwuj się)* cool it! *(pot)*

spokojnie *adv* **1** *(bez emocji)* calmly **2** *(wolno)* slowly **3** *(cicho)* quietly **4** *(nieśpiesznie)* leisurely **5** *(pewnie)* smoothly

spokojny *adj* **1** *(osoba, wody)* calm **2** *(usposobienie)* placid **3** *(barwa)* sober; **być ~m o kogoś/coś** to be confident about sb/sth

spok|ój (-oju) *m* **1** *(równowaga psychiczna)* peace **2** *(cisza, bezruch)* calm **3** *(bez konfliktów/wojny)* peace; **daj ~!** come off it! *(pot)*; **dać** *(pf)* **komuś ~, zostawić** *(pf)* **kogoś w spokoju** to leave sb in peace; **proszę o ~!** quiet, please!

społeczeńst|wo (-wa, -wa; *loc sg* -wie) *nt (ogół ludzi danego kraju)* society; **~ polskie** *(ogół Polaków)* Polish society

społeczność (-ci, -ci; *gen pl, dat & loc sg* -ci) *f (grupa zawodowa/społeczna)* community

społeczny *adj* **1** *(dotyczący ogółu społeczeństwa)* social **2** *(należący do społeczeństwa)* public **3** *(służący społeczeństwu)* community; **klasa społeczna** social class; **praca społeczna** community service; **ubezpieczenie społeczne** national insurance *(Brit)*, social security *(US)*

spontaniczny *adj (odruchowy)* spontaneous

spor|t (-tu, -ty; *loc sg* -cie) *m (ćwiczenia i gry)* sport(s pl); **uprawiać ~** to do sport

sporto|wiec (-wca, -wcy) *m (osoba uprawiająca sport)* athlete

sportowy *adj* **1** *(o klubie, aucie, sprzęcie)* sports **2** *(o zachowaniu)* sporting **3** *(styl ubierania się)* sporty

spos|ób (-obu, -oby; *loc sg* -obie) *m* **1** *(robienia czegoś)* manner **2** *(komunikacji, działania)* means; **w ten ~** in this way; **~ bycia** manners

spotka|nie (-nia, -nia; *gen pl* -ń) *nt* meeting

spotyk|ać (-am, -asz; *pf* **spotkać**) *vt* **1** *(nowych ludzi)* to meet **2** *(zobaczyć przez przypadek)* to come across **3** *(zdarzyć się)* to happen to; **~ się** *vr (schodzić się)* to meet

spożyw|ać (-am, -asz; *pf* **spożyć**) *vt (książk: jeść)* to consume

spożywczy *adj (dotyczący jedzenia):* **sklep ~** grocer's *(Brit)*, grocery *(US)*; **artykuły spożywcze** groceries

spódnic|a (-y, -e) *f (ubranie)* skirt

spół|ka (**-ki**, **-ki**; *dat sg* **-ce**; *gen pl* **-ek**) *f* (*rodzaj firmy*) company; **~ akcyjna** joint-stock company; **~ z ograniczoną odpowiedzialnością** limited (liability) company; **~ cywilna** civil partnership

spóź|nić się (**-niam**, **-niasz**; *pf* **-nić**) *vr* **1** (*przybyć za późno*) to be late **2** (*o zegarku*) to be slow **3** (*mieć miejsce z opóźnieniem*) to be (running) late; **spóźnić** (*pf*) **się na samolot** to miss one's plane; **spóźnić** (*pf*) **się do pracy** to be late for work

spóźniony *adj* **1** (*o pociągu/autobusie, osobie*) late **2** (*o przesyłce, samolocie*) delayed **3** (*o życzeniach*) belated

spragniony *adj* (*napoju*) thirsty

spra|wa (**-wy**, **-wy**; *dat & loc sg* **-wie**) *f* **1** (*fakt*) matter **2** (*rzecz do załatwienia*) business **3** (*w sądzie*) case; **to nie twoja ~** it's none of your business

sprawc|a (**-y**, **-y**) *m decl like f in sg* (*przestępstwa, wypadku*) perpetrator

spraw|dzać (**-dzam**, **-dzasz**; *pf* **-dzić**) *vt* **1** (*kontrolować*) to check **2** (*pisownię, znaczenie w słowniku*) to look up; **~ się** *vr* **1** (*o przypuszczeniach, przepowiedniach*) to come true **2** (*okazać się użytecznym*) to turn out to be useful

spra|wiać (**-wiam**, **-wiasz**; *pf* **-wić**) *vt* **1** (*zadawać np. ból*) to inflict **2** (*przyjemność*) to give **3** (*problem*) to cause **4** (*być przyczyną czegoś*) to cause; **silny deszcz sprawił, że odwołano**

koncert heavy rain meant that the concert was cancelled

sprawiedliwie *adv* (*oceniać, postępować*) fairly

sprawiedliwoś|ć (**-ci**) *f* **1** (*uczciwość*) fairness **2** (*Prawo*) justice system

sprawiedliwy *adj* (*słuszny*) fair

sprawny *adj* **1** (*fizycznie*) fit **2** (*manualnie*) adroit **3** (*wydajny: pracownik, instytucja, organizacja*) efficient **4** (*o urządzeniu, sprzęcie*) in working order

sprób|ować (**-uję**, **-ujesz**) *vb pf od* **próbować**

sprytny *adj* **1** (*osoba*) shrewd **2** (*pomysł, plan*) clever

sprzątacz|ka (**-ki**, **-ki**; *dat & loc sg* **-ce**; *gen pl* **-ek**) *f* (*kobieta*) cleaning lady

sprząt|ać (**-am**, **-asz**; *pf* **-nąć**) *vt od* **posprzątać 1** (*umyć, odkurzyć: dom, pokój*) to clean **2** (*uporządkować: zabawki, zeszyty*) to clear

sprząt|nąć (**-nę**, **-niesz**; *imp* **-nij**) *vb pf od* **sprzątać**

sprzeci|wiać się (**-wiam**, **-wiasz**; *pf* **-wić**) *vr*: **~ się komuś/czemuś** (*wystąpić przeciwko*) to oppose sb/sth; **~ się czemuś** (*protestować*) to object to sth; (*być sprzecznym z czymś*) to be at odds with sth

sprzed *prep* +*gen* **1** (*miejsca: dworca, bloku*) from in front of **2** (*okresu: lat, wojny*): **budynki ~ rewolucji** pre-revolution buildings; **gazeta ~ miesiąca** a month-old newspaper

sprzed|ać (**-am, -asz**; imp **-aj**) vb
pf od **sprzedawać**

sprzed|awać (**-aję, -ajesz**; imp
-awaj; pf **-ać**) vt (odstępować
za pieniądze) to sell; **~ się** vr 1 (o
produktach) to sell 2 (o osobie) to
sell out

sprzedawc|a (**-y, -y**) m decl like f in
sg 1 (w sklepie lub terenie) salesman
2 (w sklepie) shop assistant (Brit),
salesclerk (US)

sprzedawczy|ni (**-ni, -nie**; gen
pl **-ń**) f 1 (w sklepie lub terenie)
saleswoman 2 (w sklepie) shop
assistant (Brit), salesclerk (US)

sprzedaż (**-y**) f (towaru) sale; **na**
~ for sale

sprzę|t (**-tu**; loc sg **-cie**) m
1 (wyposażenie) equipment 2 (nom
pl **-ty**) (meble) piece of furniture;
~ komputerowy computer
equipment; **~ sportowy** sports
equipment

spuszcz|ać (**-am, -asz**; pf
spuścić) vt 1 (obniżać: cenę,
oczy, głowę) to lower
2 (odprowadzić: ciecz, gaz) to let
out; **~ się** vr (zsunąć się w dół) to
come down; **~ wodę** (w ubikacji)
to flush (the toilet)

spyt|ać (**-am, -asz**) vb pf od **pytać**

srebrny adj (pierścionek, medal)
silver

sreb|ro (**-ra, -ra**; loc sg **-rze**; gen
pl **-er**) nt (metal; kolor, medal
sportowy) silver

ssać (**ssę, ssiesz**; imp **ssij**) vt
(pierś, tabletkę) to suck

ssa|k (**-ka, -ki**; inst sg **-kiem**) m
(zwierzę) mammal

stabilny adj (plan, związek,
budynek) stable

stacj|a (**-i, -e**; gen pl, dat & loc
sg **-i**) f (dworzec) station; **~**
kolejowa/autobusowa railway
(Brit) lub railroad (US)/bus
station; **~ radiowa** radio station;
~ benzynowa petrol (Brit) lub
gas (US) station; **~ dysków** (w
komputerze) disk drive

st|ać (**-oję, -oisz**; pf **-ój**; pf **-anąć**)
vi 1 (o meblach, budynkach) to stand
2 (o urządzeniu, przedsiębiorstwie)
to be at a standstill; **stój!** stop!; **~**
w kolejce to queue (up) (Brit) lub
line up (US)

stadio|n (**-nu, -ny**; loc sg **-nie**) m
(sportowy) stadium

stały adj 1 (nie w formie cieczy
lub gazu) solid 2 (pracownik,
zatrudnienie, zarobki, wystawa)
permanent 3 (o kliencie) regular
4 (o komisji, zaproszeniu) standing
5 (w poglądach, uczuciach,
usposobieniu) constant 6 (koszt,
opłata, temperatura) fixed 7 (o
postępie) steady; **na stałe**
permanently

sta|n (**-nu**; loc sg **-nie**) m
1 (sytuacja, forma, nastrój)
state 2 (nom pl **-ny**) (fizyczny,
gospodarczy: zdrowia) condition
3 (nom pl **-ny**) (jednostka
administracyjna) state 4 (Prawo)
status 5 (umiejętność,
zdolność): **nie jest w ~ie tego**
zrozumieć he is incapable of
understanding this; **w dobrym/**
kiepskim ~ie in good/poor
condition; **~ konta** bank balance;
~ cywilny marital status; **~**
wojenny martial law

sta|nąć (**-nę, -niesz**; imp **-ń**) vb pf
od **stać, stawać**

stani|k (**-ka, -ki**; *inst sg* **-kiem**) *m*
(*bielizna*) bra

stanowczy *adj* (*zdecydowany*)
firm

Stany Zjednoczone Ameryki
(**Stanów Zjednoczonych
Ameryki**) *pl* United States of
America

star|ać się (**-am, -asz**; *pf* **po-**) *vr*
(*usiłować coś zrobić*) to try; **~ się o
coś** (*o pracę, stypendium*) to try for
sth; **staraj się pisać czytelnie** try
to write legibly

staromodny *adj* (*niemodny,
staroświecki*) old-fashioned

staroś|ć (**-ci**) *f* 1 (*ludzi*) old age
2 (*rzeczy*) age

starożytny *adj* (*literatura, sztuka*)
ancient

starszy *adj comp od* **stary**;
starsza siostra older sister

start (**-y, -y**) *m* 1 (*Sport*) start
2 (*Lot*) take off

start|ować (**-uję, -ujesz**; *pf* **wy-**)
vi 1 (*Sport*) to start 2 (*o samolocie*)
to take off

starusz|ek (**-ka, -kowie**; *inst sg*
-kiem) *m* (*mężczyzna*) old man

starusz|ka (**-ki, -ki**; *dat & loc sg* **-ce**;
gen pl **-ek**) *f* (*kobieta*) old lady

stary *adj* 1 (*nienowy, niemłody*) old
2 (*pieczywo*) stale ▷ *m* (*pot decl like
adj*) 1 (*o koledze*) old boy (*pot*) 2 (*o
szefie*) gaffer (*pot*) 3 (*o ojcu*) old
man (*pot*)

starz|eć się (**-eję, -ejesz**; *pf* **ze-**)
vr 1 (*człowiek*) to age 2 (*żywność*) to
go stale 3 (*przen: o dziele, teorii*) to
grow stale

stat|ek (**-ku, -ki**; *inst sg* **-kiem**) *m*
(*w żegludze*) ship; **~ kosmiczny**
spaceship

sta|w (**-wu, -wy**; *loc sg* **-wie**) *m*
1 (*akwen wodny*) pond 2 (*połączenie
kości w ciele*) joint

sta|wać (**-ję, -jesz**; *imp* **-ń**; *pf* **-ć**)
vi impf 1 (*z krzesła*) to stand up
2 (*zatrzymywać się*) to stand ▷ *vi pf*
(*o pomniku, budynku*) to be erected

stawi|ać (**-am, -asz**; *imp* **-aj**;
pf **postawić**) *vt impf* 1 (*kłaść*)
to place 2 (*budynek*) to erect
3 (*oceny*) to make 4 (*kroki*) to make
5 (*pytanie*) to ask 6 (*diagnozę,
wniosek*) to make 7 (*cele, zadanie*)
to set 8 (*fundować*) to provide

stąd *adv* 1 (*o miejscu*) from here
2 (*z tej przyczyny*) hence; **nie
jestem ~** I'm not from round here;
niedaleko ~ not far from here; **to
daleko ~** it's far from here

stewarde|sa (**-sy, -sy**; *dat
& loc sg* **-sie**) *f* 1 (*w samolocie*)
flight attendant 2 (*na statku*)
stewardess

stęsk|nić się (**-nię, -nisz**; *imp*
-nij) *vr pf* (*odczuwać brak*): **~ się za
kimś/czymś** to miss sb/sth

stłuc (**-ukę, -uczesz**) *vt* (*szkło,
talerz, wazon*) to break

stłucz|ka (**-ki, -ki**; *dat & loc sg* **-ce**;
gen pl **-ek**) *f* (*samochodowa*) bump

sto *num* hundred; **~ dwadzieścia**
a hundred and twenty; **~ osób** a
hundred people; **~ lat!** (*życzenia*)
many happy returns; (*pieśń*)
≈ Happy Birthday

stocz|nia (**-ni, -nie**; *gen pl, dat &
loc sg* **-ni**) *f* (*zakład produkcyjny*)
shipyard

stois|ko (**-ka, -ka**; *inst sg* **-kiem**) *nt*
1 (*dział sklepu*) department 2 (*na
kiermaszach, targach*) stall

stoję *vb zob.* **stać**

stokrot|ka (**-ki, -ki**; *dat & loc sg* **-ce**; *gen pl* **-ek**) *f* (*kwiat*) daisy

stolic|a (**-y, -e**) *f* (*główne miasto*) capital

stoli|k (**-ka, -ki**; *inst sg* **-kiem**) *m* **1** (*mały mebel*) (small) table **2** (*w restauracji*) table

stołów|ka (**-ki, -ki**; *dat & loc sg* **-ce**; *gen pl* **-ek**) *f* (*szkolna, zakładowa*) canteen

stomatolo|g (**-ga, -dzy** *lub* **- gowie**; *inst sg* **-giem**) *m* (*dentysta*) dentist

st|opa (**-opy, -opy**; *dat & loc sg* **-opie**; *gen pl* **-óp**) *f* **1** (*część nogi*) foot **2** (*standard, poziom*) level; **~ życiowa** standard of living

sto|pień (**-pnia, -pnie**; *gen pl* **-pni**) *m* **1** (*schody w budynku*) stair **2** (*schody przed budynkiem*) step **3** (*hierarchia*) rank **4** (*Szkol*) mark (*Brit*), grade (*US*) **5** (*o jednostce miary*) degree **6** (*o poziomie, intensywności*) degree; **uwaga ~!** mind the step; **~ naukowy** (university) degree; **10 stopni Celsjusza** 10 degrees centigrade; **do pewnego stopnia** to some degree

stos|ować (**-uję, -ujesz**; *pf* **za-**) *vt* **1** (*zasady, reguły, przemoc*) to apply **2** (*lekarstwa*) to administer; **~ się** *vr:* **~ się do** +*gen* (*być użytecznym*) to apply to; (*przepisów*) to comply with

stosun|ek (**-ku, -ki**; *inst sg* **-kiem**) *m* **1** (*relacja, proporcja, związek*) relation **2** (*nastawienie*) attitude **3** (*Mat*) ratio **4** (*płciowy*) intercourse; **w stosunku do** +*gen* (*porównanie*) in relation to; (*odniesienie*) with reference to

stowarzysze|nie (**-nia, -nia**; *gen pl* **-ń**) *nt* (*związek, organizacja*) association

st|ół (**-ołu, -oły**; *loc sg* **-ole**) *m* (*mebel*) table; **przy stole** at the table; **sprzątać** (**posprzątać** *pf*) **ze stołu** to clear the table

str. *abbr* (= *strona*) p.; (= *strony*) pp.

stra|ch (**-chu**) *m* (*uczucie niepokoju*) fear

stra|cić (**-cę, -cisz**; *imp* **-ć**) *vb pf od* **tracić**

straj|k (**-ku, -ki**; *inst sg* **-kiem**) *m* (*akcja protestacyjna*) strike

strajk|ować (**-uję, -ujesz**; *imp* **-uj**; *pf* **za-**) *vi* (*nie pracować*) to strike

strasznie *adv* **1** (*okropnie*) terribly **2** (*bardzo, niezmiernie*) awfully

straszny *adj* **1** (*budzący przerażenie*) scary **2** (*bardzo zły*) dreadful **3** (*ogromny*) tremendous

strasz|yć (**-ę, -ysz**; *imp* **-**; *pf* **prze-**) *vt* (*wzbudzać strach*) to scare ▷ *vi:* **w tym zamku straszy** this castle is haunted; **~** +*inst* (*grozić*) to threaten

straża|k (**-ka, -cy**; *inst sg* **-kiem**) *m* (*mężczyzna*) firefighter

strażni|k (**-ka, -cy**; *inst sg* **-kiem**) *m* **1** (*w firmie*) (security) guard **2** (*w więzieniu*) warder; **~ leśny** forest ranger

stre|s (**-su, -sy**; *loc sg* **-sie**) *m* (*Psych*) stress; **być w ~ie** to be under stress

stresujący *adj* (*Psych*) stressful

stro|na (**-ny, -ny**; *dat & loc sg* **-nie**) *f* **1** (*bok, część*) side **2** (*książki*) page **3** (*o kierunku*) direction; **strony** *pl* (*rodzinne*) parts *pl*; **po prawej stronie** on the right-hand side; **z jednej strony..., z drugiej**

strony... on the one hand..., on the other hand...; **bilet w jedną stronę/w obie strony** single/return ticket (*Brit*), one-way/round-trip ticket (*US*); **to miło z twojej strony** that's nice of you

str|ój (**-oju, -oje**) *m* (*ubranie*) attire; **~ kąpielowy** swimming costume (*Brit*), swimsuit

strza|ł (**-łu, -ły**; *loc sg* **-le**) *m* (*z broni*) shot

strzał|ka (**-ki, -ki**; *dat & loc sg* **-ce**; *gen pl* **-ek**) *f* **1** (*symbol*) arrow **2** (*wskazówka w urządzeniu*) pointer

strzel|ać (**-am, -asz**; *pf* **-ić**) *vt* (*gola*) to shoot ▷ *vi* **1** (*z pistoletu*) to shoot **2** (*trzaskać palcami*) to snap

Strzelec *n* (*Astrol*) Sagittarius

strzykaw|ka (**-ki, -ki**; *dat & loc sg* **-ce**; *gen pl* **-ek**) *f* (*Med*) syringe

studencki *adj* student; **dom ~** hall of residence (*Brit*), dormitory (*US*)

studen|t (**-ta, -ci**; *loc sg* **-cie**) *m* (*Uniw*) student

student|ka (**-ki, -ki**; *dat & loc sg* **-ce**; *gen pl* **-ek**) *f* (*Uniw*) student

studi|a (**-ów**) *pl* **1** (*licencjackie, magisterskie*) studies **2** (*badania*) research *sg*

studi|ować (**-uję, -ujesz**) *vt* **1** (*Uniw*) to study **2** (*pf* **prze-**) (*plan miasta, książkę*) to study

STUDNIÓWKA

Studniówka is the ceremonial ball held for secondary school students, which takes place about one hundred days before their exams in May. Traditionally the ball opens with a dance called the **Polonez**. See also **matury**.

stule|cie (**-cia, -cia**; *gen pl* **-ci**) *nt* **1** (*sto lat*) century **2** (*rocznica, obchody*) centenary

stuletni *adj* **1** (*o człowieku*) hundred-year-old **2** (*o okresie, budynku*) hundred-year

stwier|dzać (**-dzam, -dzasz**; *pf* **-dzić**) *vt* (*ustalać, uznawać*) to affirm ▷ *vi* (*mówić*) to state

stwierdze|nie (**-nia, -nia**; *gen pl* **-ń**) *nt* **1** (*uznanie, ustalenie*) assertion **2** (*o wypowiedzi*) statement

stycz|eń (**-nia, -nie**) *m* January

styl (**-u, -e**) *m* **1** (*zachowania się, mówienia, malarstwa*) style **2** (*pływacki*) stroke; **~ życia** life style

stypendi|um (**-um, -a**; *gen pl* **-ów**) *nt inv in sg* scholarship

subiektywny *adj* (*osąd, zdanie*) subjective

subtelny *adj* (*wnikliwy, wyszukany*) subtle

suchy *adj* (*niemokry*) dry

Sudet|y (**-ów**) *pl* (*łańcuch górski*) the Sudeten Mountains

sufi|t (**-tu, -ty**; *loc sg* **-cie**) *m* (*w pokoju*) ceiling

su|ka (**-ki, -ki**; *dat & loc sg* **-ce**) *f* (*pies*) bitch (*dog*)

sukce|s (**-su, -sy**; *loc sg* **-sie**) *m* (*powodzenie*) success; **odnieść** (*pf*) **~** to succeed

su|knia (**-kni, -knie**; *gen pl* **-kni** *lub* **-kien**) *f* (*odzież damska*) dress

su|ma (**-my, -my**; *dat & loc sg* **-mie**) *f* **1** (*wynik zadania*) sum

2 (*pieniędzy*) amount; **w sumie** all in all

sumie|nie (**-nia, -nia**; *gen pl* **-ń**) *nt* (*spokojne, czyste*) conscience

supermarke|t (**-tu, -ty**; *loc sg* **-cie**) *m* (*sklep*) supermarket

surowy *adj* **1** (*warzywa, ryba, ciasto*) raw **2** (*materiały budowlane*) unseasoned **3** (*wymagający*) strict **4** (*o krytyce, wyroku*) severe **5** (*bez ozdób, wygód*) austere **6** (*o klimacie, zimie*) harsh **7** (*o warunkach, życiu*) austere

surów|ka (**-ki, -ki**; *dat sg* **-ce**; *gen pl* **-ek**) *f* **1** (*potrawa*) salad **2** (*stop*) pig-iron

suszar|ka (**-ki, -ki**; *dat & loc sg* **-ce**; *gen pl* **-ek**) *f* (*urządzenie, konstrukcja*) dryer; **~ do włosów** hair dryer

susz|yć (**-ę, -ysz**) *vt* **1** (*pf* **wy-**) (*o włosach, praniu*) to dry **2** (*pf* **u-**) (*o kwiatach, grzybach*) to dry; **~ się** *vr* (*schnąć*) to get dry

swet|er (**-ra, -ry**; *loc sg* **-rze**) *m* (*ubranie*) sweater, jumper (*Brit*)

swobodnie *adv* **1** (*decydować, rozwijać się*) freely **2** (*poruszać się, rozmawiać*) freely **3** (*bez trudności, łatwo*) at ease **4** (*ubierać się*) casually

swobodny *adj* **1** (*o wyborze*) free **2** (*o rozwoju, poruszaniu się*) unconstrained **3** (*Jęz*) free **4** (*atmosfera*) informal **5** (*ubiór*) informal **6** (*przekład*) free

swoja *itd. pron zob.* **swój**

swój *od* **mój** *pron* **1** (*własny*) one's **2** (*mój*) my **3** (*twój*) your **4** (*jego*) his **5** (*jej*) her **6** (*nasz*) our **7** (*wasz*) your **8** (*ich*) their **9** (*pot: domowy*) home-made

Syberi|a (**-i**; *dat, loc sg* **-i**) *f* (*Geo*) Siberia

Sycyli|a (**-i**; *dat, loc sg* **-i**) *f* (*Geo*) Sicily

sygna|ł (**-łu, -ły**; *loc sg* **-le**) *m* **1** (*znak*) signal **2** (*w telefonie*) tone **3** (*audycji*) signature tune

sylwest|er (**-ra, -ry**; *loc sg* **-rze**) *m* (*ostatni dzień roku*) New Year's Eve, Hogmanay (*Scottish*)

sylwet|ka (**-ki, -ki**; *dat & loc sg* **-ce**; *gen pl* **-ek**) *f* **1** (*postawa*) figure **2** (*kształt ciała*) silhouette **3** (*pisemna charakterystyka osoby*) profile

symbol (**-u, -e**) *m* (*znak*) symbol

symboliz|ować (**-uje**) *vt* (*oznaczać*) to symbolize

symfoni|a (**-i, -e**; *gen pl, dat & loc sg* **-i**) *f* (*Muz*) symphony

sympatyczny *adj* (*miły, życzliwy*) pleasant

sy|n (**-na, -nowie**; *loc sg* **-nu**) *m* (*dziecko*) son

synow|a (**-ej, -e**) *f decl like adj* (*żona syna*) daughter-in-law

sy|pać (**-pię, -piesz**; *pf* **-pnąć**) *vt* **1** (*proszek, sól*) to sprinkle **2** (*o śniegu*) to fall ▷ *vi* (*pot: donosić*): **~ kogoś/coś** to grass on sb/sth; **~ się** *vr* **1** (*o farbie, ścianie*) to fall off **2** (*o odpryskach*) to fly **3** (*o listkach*) to fall **4** (*o uderzeniach*) to rain down **5** (*pf* **roz-**) (*pot: ulegać zniszczeniu*) to fall apart

sypi|ać (**-am, -asz**) *vi* (*spać*) to sleep

sypial|nia (**-ni, -nie**; *gen pl* **-ni**) *f* (*pokój*) bedroom

syste|m (**-mu, -my**; *loc sg* **-mie**) *m* (*społeczny, operacyjny, planetarny*) system

systematyczny adj 1 (planowy, metodyczny) systematic 2 (student, pracownik) methodical

sytuacj|a (-i, -e; gen pl -i) f (okoliczności, warunki) situation

szach|y (-ów) pl 1 (rodzaj gry) chess 2 (szachownica i komplet figur) chess set

szacun|ek (-ku; inst sg -kiem) m 1 (o poważaniu) respect 2 (określenie wartości) assessment

sza|fa (-fy, -fy; dat & loc sg -fie) f 1 (na odzież) wardrobe 2 (na dokumentację) cabinet

szaf|ka (-ki, -ki; dat & loc sg -ce; gen pl -ek) f cabinet

szale|niec (-ńca, -ńcy) m (wariat) madman

szaleńst|wo (-wa, -wa; loc sg -wie) nt 1 (szalony akt) madness 2 (ogólne zachowanie) frenzy

szali|k (-ka, -ki; inst sg -kiem) m (dodatek do ubrania) scarf

szalony adj 1 (osoba) mad 2 (plan, czyn) crazy 3 (o życiu, tańcu) mad

szampa|n (-na, -ny; loc sg -nie) m (Kulin) champagne

szampo|n (-nu, -ny; loc sg -nie) m (do włosów) shampoo

szan|ować (-uję, -ujesz) vt 1 (ludzi) to respect 2 (ubranie, meble, książki) to take care of; **~ się** vr 1 (mieć godność własną) to have self-respect 2 (poważać się nawzajem) to respect one another

szanowny adj (drogi) honourable (Brit), honorable (US); **~ Panie!/Szanowna Pani!** (list) dear Sir/Madam,; **szanowni Państwo!** Ladies and Gentlemen!

szan|sa (-sy, -se; dat & loc sg -sie) f (okazja) chance

szantaż (-u) m (wymuszenie) blackmail

szantaż|ować (-uję, -ujesz) vt (wymuszać): **~ kogoś czymś** to blackmail sb with sth

szarlot|ka (-ki, -ki; dat & loc sg -ce; gen pl -ek) f (ciasto) apple pie

szary adj 1 (o kolorze) grey (Brit), gray (US) 2 (o dniu, pogodzie) gloomy 3 (o papierze) brown 4 (o życiu) ordinary

szaszły|k (-ka, -ki; inst sg -kiem) m (Kulin) shish kebab

szata|n (-na, -ny lub -ni; loc sg -nie) m 1 (w religii) satan 2 (pot: człowiek zły, niesforny, podstępny) devil 3 (człowiek ruchliwy) ball of fire

szat|nia (-ni, -nie; gen pl -ni) f 1 (na basenie) changing room 2 (w restauracji) cloakroom

szczególnie adv 1 (specjalnie) especially 2 (w dziwaczny sposób) peculiarly

szczegó|ł (-łu, -ły; loc sg -le) m (drobny element) detail; **szczegóły** pl (wszystkie (małe) elementy) details

szczegółowo adv (dokładnie) in detail

szczegółowy adj (dokładny) detailed

szczepion|ka (-ki, -ki; dat & loc sg -ce; gen pl -ek) f (Med) vaccine

szczery adj 1 (osoba, śmiech, serce) sincere 2 (radość, żal) genuine 3 (o prawdzie) plain 4 (o złocie) pure

szczerze adv (prawdziwie) sincerely; **~ mówiąc** frankly speaking

szczęści|e (-a) nt 1 (powodzenie) (good) luck 2 (radość, zadowolenie) happiness; **na ~** luckily; **mieć ~** to be lucky; **nie mieć szczęścia** to be unlucky

szczęśliwy adj **1** (przynoszący powodzenie) lucky **2** (radosny) happy; **szczęśliwego Nowego Roku!** Happy New Year!; **szczęśliwej podróży!** have a good trip!

szczotecz|ka (-ki, -ki; dat & loc sg **-ce**; gen pl **-ek)** f (przedmiot) brush; **~ do zębów** toothbrush

szczot|ka (-ki, -ki; dat sg **-ce**; gen pl **-ek)** f (przedmiot) brush; **~ do włosów** hairbrush; **~ do butów** shoebrush; **~ do zamiatania** broom

szczupły adj **1** (niegruby) slim **2** (nieliczny, wątły) slender

szczy|t (-tu, -ty; loc sg **-cie)** m **1** (górski) summit **2** (u drzewa, schodów) top **3** (szczęścia, powodzenia, choroby, głupoty) peak **4** (Pol) summit **5** (intensywne obciążenie) peak **6** (u stołu) head; **spotkanie na szczycie** summit; **godziny ~u** peak times

szedł itd. vb zob. **iść**

sze|f (-fa, -fowie; loc sg **-fie)** m (zwierzchnik) boss; **~ rządu** prime minister; **~ kuchni** chef

szep|tać (-czę, -czesz; pf **-nąć)** vt (mówić bardzo cicho) to whisper

szermier|ka (-ki; dat & loc sg **-ce)** f (Sport) fencing

szer|oki adj **1** (rzeka, plaża, spódnica) wide **2** (droga, ruch, uśmiech) broad **3** (przen: pytanie, perspektywy, skala) broad **4** (publika, krąg odbiorców) wide; **~ na 2 metry** 2 m wide

sze|roko adv **1** (rozlegle na boki)

widely **2** (rozlegle naokoło) broadly **3** (mówić, opisywać) at length; **otworzyć** (pf) **~ usta** to open one's mouth wide

szerokoś|ć (-ci, -ci; gen pl **-ci)** f **1** (wymiar materiału) width **2** (Geo): **~ geograficzna** latitude; **mieć siedem metrów szerokości** to be 7 m wide

szesnasty num decl like adj sixteenth; **strona szesnasta** page sixteen; **szesnasta** 4 o'clock

szesnaście num sixteen

sześć num six

sześćdziesiąt num sixty

sześćset num six hundred

szewc (-a, -y) m (rzemieślnik) cobbler

szklan|ka (-ki, -ki; dat & loc sg **-ce**; gen pl **-ek)** f **1** (szklane naczynie) glass **2** (mąki, mleka) ≈ cup

szklany adj (ze szkła) glass

sz|kło (-kła; loc sg **-kle)** nt **1** (materiał) glass **2** (nom pl **-kła**; gen pl **-kieł**) (szklane produkty) glass(ware); **szkła** pl (okulary) glasses; **szkła kontaktowe** contact lenses

Szkocj|a (-i) f Scotland

szkocki adj Scottish

szk|oda (-ody, -ody; dat sg **-odzie**; gen pl **-ód)** f (strata materialna) damage ▷ adv (żal, przykro) pity; **~, że...** it's a pity that...; **~!** what a pity!

szkodliwy adj (niszczący) harmful

szko|dzić (-dzę, -dzisz) vi (zdrowiu, reputacji): **~ komuś/ czemuś** to be bad for sb/sth; **palenie szkodzi** smoking is bad for you; **nic nie szkodzi!** never mind!

szk|olić (**-olę, -olisz**; *imp* **-ol** *lub* **-ól**; *pf* **wy-**) *vt* (*kształcić, ćwiczyć*) to train

szkolnict|wo (**-wa**; *loc sg* **-wie**) *nt* (*wyższe, zawodowe*) education

szkolny *adj* (*rok, mundurek, boisko*) school

szk|oła (**-oły, -oły**; *dat & loc sg* **-ole**; *gen pl* **-ół**) *f* (*instytucja*) school; **~ podstawowa** primary (*Brit*) *lub* elementary (*US*) school; **~ średnia** secondary (*Brit*) *lub* high (*US*) school; **chodzić do szkoły** to go to school; **być w szkole** to be at school

Szko|t (**-ta, -ci**; *loc sg* **-cie**) *m* Scotsman

Szkot|ka (**-ki, -ki**; *dat sg* **-ce**; *gen pl* **-ek**) *f* Scotswoman

szlach|ta (**-ty**; *dat & loc sg* **-cie**) *f* (*stan społeczny*) nobility

szlafro|k (**-ka, -ki**; *inst sg* **-kiem**) *m* (*ubranie*) dressing gown (*Brit*), (bath)robe (*US*)

szli *vb zob.* **iść**

szła *itd. vb zob.* **iść**

szmin|ka (**-ki, -ki**; *dat & loc sg* **-ce**; *gen pl* **-ek**) *f* (*pomadka: też:* **~ do ust**) lipstick

sznur|ek (**-ka, -ki**; *inst sg* **-kiem**) *m* (*cienki sznur*) string

szo|k (**-ku**; *inst sg* **-kiem**) *m* (*silny wstrząs emocjonalny*) shock

szokujący *adj* (*wywołujący silny wstrząs*) shocking

szósty *num decl like adj* sixth; **strona szósta** page six

szpie|g (**-ga, -dzy**; *inst sg* **-giem**) *m* (*tajny agent*) spy

szpital (**-a, -e**; *gen pl* **-i**) *m* (*zakład lecznictwa*) hospital; **być** *lub* **leżeć w ~u** to be in (the (*US*)) hospital;

zabrać (*pf*) **kogoś do ~a** to take sb to (the (*US*)) hospital

sztuczny *adj* (*nienaturalny*) artificial; **sztuczne ognie** fireworks

sztuć|ce (**-ów**) *pl* (*przybory do jedzenia*) cutlery

sztu|ka (**-ki, -ki**; *dat & loc sg* **-ce**) *f* **1** (*działalność artystyczna i jej wytwory, talent*) art **2** (*teatralna*) play **3** (*pojedynczy przedmiot*) piece; **~ ludowa** folk art; **sztuki piękne** the fine arts; **po dwa złote ~** *lub* **za sztukę** 2 zloty each

sztywny *adj* **1** (*o kołnierzyku, części ciała, ruchu*) stiff **2** (*o konstrukcji, przepisach*) rigid **3** (*o cenach*) fixed **4** (*o wyglądzie*) prim

szufla|da (**-dy, -dy**; *dat & loc sg* **-dzie**) *f* (*wysuwana część mebla*) drawer

szuk|ać (**-am, -asz**; *pf* **po-**) *vt* +*gen* **1** (*mieszkania, zatrudnienia, przestępcy, możliwości*) to look for **2** (*rozwiązania, pomocy, szczęścia*) to seek **3** (*wyrazu w słowniku*) to look up

szwa|gier (**-gra, -growie**; *loc sg* **-grze**) *m* (*członek rodziny*) brother-in-law

szwagier|ka (**-ki, -ki**; *dat & loc sg* **-ce**; *gen pl* **-ek**) *f* (*członek rodziny*) sister-in-law

Szwajcari|a (**-i**) *f* Switzerland

szwajcarski *adj* Swiss

Szwecj|a (**-i**) *f* Sweden

szwedzki *adj* Swedish

szy|ba (**-by, -by**; *dat & loc sg* **-bie**) *f* **1** (*o szklanej tafli*) (window) pane **2** (*o oknie*) window; **przednia ~** (*w samochodzie*) windscreen (*Brit*), windshield (*US*)

szyb|ki *adj* (*pociąg, samochód*) fast; (*odpowiedź, reakcja*) quick; **bar ~ej obsługi** fast-food restaurant

szyb|ko *adv* **1** (*jeździć, chodzić*) fast **2** (*zareagować, odpowiedzieć*) quickly; **~!** hurry up!

szy|ć (**-ję, -jesz**) *vt* **1** (*pf* **u-**) (*nowe ubranie*) to sew **2** (*pf* **z-**) (*rozprucie*) to stitch **3** (*pf* **z-**) (*ranę*) to suture; **~ na maszynie** to sew (*on a sewing machine*)

szy|ja (**-i, -je**; *dat & loc sg* **-i**) *f* (*Anat*) neck

szyn|ka (**-ki, -ki**; *dat & loc sg* **-ce**; *gen pl* **-ek**) *f* (*wędlina*) ham

ścia|na (**-ny, -ny**; *dat & loc sg* **-nie**) *f* (*część pokoju*) wall

ściąć (**zetnę, zetniesz**; *imp* **zetnij**) *vb pf od* **ścinać**

ścielić (**-ę, -isz**; *imp* **ściel**) *vt:* **~ łóżko** to make one's bed

ścin|ać (**-am, -asz**; *imp* **-aj**) *vt* **1** (*drzewo*) to chop down **2** (*włosy*) to cut; **~ się** *vr* **1** (*o mleku*) to turn **2** (*o krwi*) to curdle **3** (*o sosie*) to curdle

śla|d (**-du, -dy**; *loc sg* **-dzie**) *m* **1** (*stóp*) footprint **2** (*zwierza*) track **3** (*kopyt*) hoofprint; (*zaniepokojenia, radości*) trace

Śląs|k (**-ka**; *inst sg* **-kiem**) *m* (*Geo*) Silesia

śle|dzić (**-dzę, -dzisz**; *imp* **-dź**) *vt* **1** (*obserwować, szpiegować*) to follow **2** (*ruch armii*) to monitor

3 (*radarem*) to track

śledzt|wo (**-wa, -wa**; *loc sg* **-wie**) *nt* (*policyjne*) investigation

śle|dź (**-dzia, -dzie**; *gen pl* **-dzi**) *m* **1** (*ryba*) herring **2** (*przy namiocie*) tent peg

ślepy *adj* (*niewidzący*) blind; **ślepa ulica** dead end

ślę, ślesz *itd. vb zob.* **słać**

ślisko *adv* (*o gładkiej powierzchni*): **na drogach jest ~** the roads are slippery

śliw|ka (**-ki, -ki**; *dat & loc sg* **-ce**; *gen pl* **-ek**) *f* **1** (*o owocu*) plum **2** (*o drzewie*) plum tree; **suszona ~** prune

ślu|b (**-bu, -by**; *loc sg* **-bie**) *m* (*zawarcie małżeństwa*) marriage, wedding; **~ kościelny** church wedding; **~ cywilny** civil marriage ceremony; **brać (wziąć** *pf*) **~** to get married

śmiać się (**śmieję, śmiejesz**; *pf* **za-**) *vr* (*głośno, do rozpuku*) to laugh; **~ się z kogoś/czegoś** to laugh at sb/sth

śmi|ały *adj* (*odważny*) bold

śmieć¹ (**śmiecia, śmieci** *lub* **śmiecie**) *m* (*o odpadku*) piece of litter; **śmieci** *pl* **1** (*do wyrzucenia*) rubbish *sg*, garbage *sg* (US) **2** (*na podwórku, skwerze*) litter *sg*

śmieć² (**śmiem, śmiesz**; *3 pl* **śmią** *lub* **śmieją**; *imp* **śmiej**) *vi* (*mieć czelność; odwagę*) to dare; **jak on śmie!** how dare he!

śmieć³ *vb zob.* **śmiecić**

śmier|ć (**-ci**) *f* (*zgon*) death; **ponieść** (*pf*) **~** to die; **kara śmierci** the death penalty

śmierdzący *adj* (*cuchnący*) stinking

śmier|dzieć (**-dzę, -dzisz**; *imp* **-dź**) *vi* (*cuchnąć*): **~ czymś** to stink of sth

śmiertelny *adj* **1** (*o dawce*) lethal **2** (*o truciźnie, grzybie*) deadly **3** (*bladości, ciszy*) deathly **4** (*o chorobie*) terminal **5** (*stworzenie, cios, wróg*) mortal **6** (*zranienie*) fatal; **wypadek ~** fatal accident; **grzech ~** mortal sin

śmiesznie *adv* (*mówić, opowiadać*) in a comical manner; **~ tani** ridiculously cheap

śmieszny *adj* **1** (*rozweselający*) funny **2** (*żałosny*) ridiculous

śmiesz|yć (**-ę, -ysz**; *pf* **rozśmieszyć**) *vt* (*rozweselać*) to amuse

śmietan|ka (**-ki**; *dat & loc sg* **-ce**; *gen pl* **-ek**) *f* (*Kulin*) cream

śmietni|k (**-ka, -ki**; *inst sg* **-kiem**) *m* **1** (*miejsce z pojemnikami na śmieci*) the bins *pl* **2** (*kosz na śmieci*) skip (*Brit*), dumpster (US)

◉ ŚMIGUS-DYNGUS

Easter Monday, or **Śmigus-dyngus**, is also known as "wet Monday". Traditionally, young bachelors show their interest in girls by throwing water over them. Children often also join in. Some people are content with a symbolic sprinkling while others unscrupulously splash buckets of water over passers-by!

śniada|nie (**-nia, -nia**; *gen pl* **-ń**) *nt* (*posiłek*) breakfast; **jeść ~** to have breakfast; **drugie ~** (o posiłku) midmorning snack; (kanapki) packed lunch (Brit), box lub bag lunch (US)

śnie n zob. **sen**

śnie|g (**-gu, -gi**; inst sg **-giem**) m (opady) snow; **pada ~** it's snowing; **~ z deszczem** sleet

śpiesz|yć, spiesz|yć (**-ę, -ysz**; pf **po-**) vi (być skorym do czegoś): **~ komuś z pomocą** to rush to help sb; **~ się** vr 1 (o osobie) to (be in a) hurry 2 (o zegarku) to be fast; **śpieszy mi się** I'm in a hurry

śpiew|ać (**-am, -asz**; pf **za-**) vt/vi (piosenkę) to sing

śpiw|ór (**-ora, -ory**; loc sg **-orze**) m (turystyczna pościel) sleeping bag

średni adj 1 (zwykły) average 2 (o rozmiarze) medium; **~ego wzrostu** of average height; **w ~m wieku** middle-aged; **szkoła ~a** secondary (Brit) lub high (US) school

średniowiecz|e (**-a**) nt (okres historii) the Middle Ages

średniozaawansowany adj (poziom) intermediate

śr|oda (**-ody, -ody**; dat & loc sg **-odzie**; gen pl **-ód**) f (dzień tygodnia) Wednesday; **~ popielcowa** Ash Wednesday

środ|ek (**-ka, -ki**; inst sg **-kiem**) m 1 (miejsce w centrum) middle 2 (wnętrzna część pomieszczenia) inside 3 (ułatwienie) means 4 (metoda) measure 5 (o preparacie chemicznym) agent 6 (przeciwbólowy, nasenny) medication 7 (zaradczy) remedy; **środki** pl (fundusze) means pl; **w środku** (w centralnym miejscu)

in the middle; **poprosić** (pf) **kogoś do środka** to ask sb in; **~ transportu** means of transport (Brit) lub transportation (US)

środkowoeuropejski adj (Geo) Central European

środkowy adj (centralny) central

śródmieś|cie (**-cia, -cia**; gen pl **-ci**) nt (centrum miasta) city centre (Brit), downtown (US)

śródziemnomorski adj (Geo) Mediterranean

śru|ba (**-by, -by**; dat & loc sg **-bie**) f 1 (do łączenia elementów) screw 2 (wkręt) bolt

św. abbr (= święty, święta) St

świadect|wo (**-wa, -wa**; loc sg **-wie**) nt 1 (urodzenia, zgonu) certificate 2 (udowodnienie) testimony; **~ szkolne** report card; **~ dojrzałości** ≈ GCSE (Brit), ≈ High School Diploma (US)

świad|ek (**-ka, -kowie**; inst sg **-kiem**) m witness; **być świadkiem czegoś** to witness sth

świa|t (**-ta, -ty**; loc sg **świecie**) m (planeta, środowisko) world; **na całym świecie** all over the world

świat|ło (**-ła, -ła**; loc sg **świetle**; gen pl **-eł**) nt (słoneczne, elektryczne) light; **światła** pl (pot: sygnalizacja świetlna) traffic lights

światopoglą|d (**-du, -dy**; loc sg **-dzie**) m (pogląd na świat i życie) outlook

świąteczny adj 1 (uroczysty, podniosły) festive 2 (związany z Bożym Narodzeniem) Christmas 3 (związany z Wielkanocą) Easter

świąty|nia (**-ni, -nie**; dat & loc sg **-ni**; gen pl **-ń**) f (kościół) temple

świec|a (-y, -e; *dat & loc sg* -y) *f*
1 (*z wosku*) candle 2 (*w silniku*): ~
zapłonowa spark plug
świe|cić (-cę, -cisz; *imp* -ć) *vi* 1 (*być
źródłem światła: o żarówce, słońcu*)
to shine 2 (*błyszczeć: o cerze*) to
glow; ~ **się** *vr* 1 (*o żarówce*) to be
on 2 (*błyszczeć*) to shine
świecz|ka (-ki, -ki; *dat & loc sg* -ce;
gen pl -ek) *f* (*z wosku*) candle
świeży *adj* (*owoce, warzywa, śnieg,
pościel*) fresh; **na ~m powietrzu**
in the fresh air
świę|to (-ta, -ta; *loc sg* -cie; *gen pl*
świąt) *nt* (*dzień wolny*) holiday;
~ **państwowe/kościelne**
national/religious holiday;
święta *pl*: **święta Bożego
Narodzenia** Christmas; **Święta
Wielkanocne** Easter; **Wesołych
Świąt!** (*Bożego Narodzenia*) Merry
Christmas!

- **ŚWIĘTO ODZYSKANIA**
- **NIEPODLEGŁOŚCI 11**
- **LISTOPADA**
-
- **Święto Odzyskania**
- **Niepodległości 11 Listopada**
- is the most important
- Polish national holiday. It is
- celebrated on 11 November,
- the date Poland regained
- its independence in 1918,
- following 123 years of
- partitions between Russia,
- Austro-Hungary and Prussia.

święty *adj* 1 (*będący przedmiotem
kultu religijnego*) holy 2 (*w
połączeniu z imieniem*) saint
3 (*bardzo dobry, pokorny, życzliwy*)
saintly 4 (*o prawie*) sacred
▷ *m decl like adj* (*osoba*) saint;
pismo Święte the Holy
Scriptures; **Duch Święty** Holy
Spirit; **Święty Mikołaj** Father
Christmas (*Brit*), Santa (Claus);
świętej pamięci pan Kowalski
the late Mr Kowalski
świ|nia (-ni, -nie; *gen pl* -ń) *f*
1 (*zwierzę*) pig 2 (*pot!: o osobie*)
swine (*pot*)
świ|t (-tu, -ty; *loc sg* -cie) *m*
(*początek dnia*) dawn

t

ta pron fem this od **ten**

tabel|a (**-i**, **-e**; dat sg & loc sg **-i**) f (rubryka) table

tabel|ka (**-ki**, **-ki**; dat sg & loc sg **-ce**; gen pl **-ek**) f dimin od **tabela**

tablet|ka (**-ki**, **-ki**; dat sg & loc sg **-ce**; gen pl **-ek**) f tablet

tablic|a (**-y**, **-e**) f **1** (w szkole) blackboard **2** (plansza) chart; **~ z ogłoszeniami** noticeboard (Brit), bulletin board (US); **tablice rejestracyjne** number plates (Brit), license plates (US)

tabu nt inv taboo

tacy pron decl like adj zob. **taki**

tajemnic|a (**-y**, **-e**) f secret; **~ państwowa** state secret; **~ służbowa** confidential information; **tajemnice natury** mysteries of nature

tajemniczy adj (zagadkowy) mysterious; **zniknął w ~ sposób** he disappeared mysteriously

Tajlandi|a (**-i**) f Thailand

tajny adj **1** (sekretny) secret **2** (ścisłego zarachowania) classified **3** (nielegalny) underground; **ściśle tajne informacje** top secret information

Tajwa|n (**-nu**; loc sg **-nie**) f Taiwan

○ **KEYWORD**

tak pron (twierdzący) yes; **tak jest!** (Wojsk: pot) yes, sir!
▷ adv (w taki sposób): **nie obrażaj się tak** don't take offence (Brit) lub offense (US) like that; **zrobił to tak, jak prosiliśmy** he did it as we requested; **zrobił to tak jak uważał** he did it just as he liked; **i tak dalej** and so on; **tak zwany pomocnik** so-called assistant; **tak czy owak zrobimy to po swojemu** (pot) we'll do it our own way, in any case; (nasilenie): **tak mocno/mocny (, że...)** so hard/strong (that...); **czuję się tak sobie** (pot) so-so

○ **KEYWORD**

taki pron decl like adj **1** (określonego rodzaju) such; **taki sam jak ja** the same as me; **taki jak my** like us; **jest taki jak prosiłeś** it's just what you asked for; **on już taki jest, że lubi pracować całe noce** that's the way he is, he likes to work all through the night; **o takiej a takiej godzinie** (pot) at such-and-such a time; **w takim razie pojedziemy razem** in that case, we'll go together

2 (*w połączeniach zdaniowych*): **była taki deszcz, że zalało piwnice** it was so wet that our basement flooded

3 (*wzmacniająco*): **on jest taki stary** he is so old; **taki szanowany człowiek** such a well-respected man; **taka brzydka pogoda** such rotten weather

taksów|ka (**-ki, -ki;** *dat sg & loc sg* **-ce;** *gen pl* **-ek**) *f* (*osobowa*) taxi; **~ bagażowa** removal van

taksówkarz (**-a, -e;** *gen pl* **-y**) *m* (*kierowca taksówki*) taxi driver

także *adv* as well

talen|t (**-tu, -ty;** *loc sg* **-cie**) *m* talent

talerz (**-a, -e;** *gen pl* **-y**) *m* **1** plate **2** (*głęboki*) soup plate **3** (*płytki*) plate; **latający ~** (*UFO*) flying saucer

tam *adv* there; **tu i ~** here and there

tamci *pron* those

Tami|za (**-zy;** *dat sg & loc sg* **-zie**) *f* the Thames

tampo|n (**-nu, -ny;** *loc sg* **-nie**) *m* (*wata tamująca krew*) tampon

tamta *pron* that

tamte *pron* those

tamten *pron* that

tamtędy *adv* (down) that way; **pójdź ~** go that way

tancerz (**-a, -e;** *gen pl* **-y**) *m* (*zawodowiec, amator*) dancer

tani *adj* (*niedrogi*) cheap

ta|niec (**-ńca, -ńce**) *m* **1** (*czynność*)

dancing **2** (*układ choreograficzny*) dance; **~ towarzyski** ballroom dancing

tanio *adv*: **kupuj ~, sprzedaj drogo** buy cheap, sell dear

tańcz|yć (**-ę, -ysz;** *pf* **za-**) *vt, vi* to dance; **~ twista/rumbę** to do the twist/the rumba

tańszy *itd. adj comp od* **tani**

tar|g (**-gu, -gi;** *inst sg* **-giem**) *m* (*plac handlowy*) market; **targi** *pl* (trade) fair; **dobił z nim ~u** he struck a bargain with him

ta|ta, ta|to (**-ty;** *dat sg & loc sg* **-cie**) *m decl like f* (*ojciec, teść*) dad

tatarski *adj* (*kulinaria*): **sos/ befsztyk ~** tartare sauce/steak tartare

ta|to (**-ty, -towie;** *loc sg* **-cie**) *m* = **tata**

Tatr|y (**-**) *pl* the Tatra Mountains *pl*

tatuaż (**-u, -e;** *gen pl* **-y**) *m* tattoo

tą *pron acc, instr od* **ta**

tchórz (**-a, -e;** *gen pl* **-y**) *m* **1** (*człowiek*) coward **2** (*zwierzę*) polecat; **widać, że ~ go obleciał** (*pot*) he must have got cold feet

te *pron* these; **te okna/koty** these windows/cats

teat|r (**-ru, -ry;** *loc sg* **-rze**) *m* theatre (*Brit*), theater (*US*); **~ lalkowy** puppet theatre

tecz|ka (**-ki, -ki;** *dat sg & loc sg* **-ce;** *gen pl* **-ek**) *f* **1** (*skórzana*) briefcase **2** (*papierowa*) folder

tego *pron gen, acc od* **ten, to**

tegoroczny *adj* (*plan, zima*) this year's

tej *pron gen, dat od* **ta**

tek|st (**-stu, -sty;** *loc sg* **-ście**) *m* (*książki, artykułu*) text; **znam na**

pamięć ~y piosenek I know the lyrics by heart

tel. *abbr* (=*telefon*) tel.

telefo|n (**-nu, -ny**; *loc sg* **-nie**) *m* **1** (*rzecz*) telephone, phone **2** (*numer*) phone number **3** (*rozmowa*) phone call; **dał mi swój ~ domowy** he gave me his home number; **rozmawiał przez ~** he talked on the phone; **rozmawiał z nią przez ~** he talked to her on the phone; **~ komórkowy** mobile phone (*Brit*), cellphone (*US*); **~ zaufania działa już od 5 lat** the telephone helpline has been running for 5 years; **odbierać** (**odebrać** *pf*) **~** to answer the phone; **~ wewnętrzny** extension

telefon|ować (**-uję, -ujesz**; *pf* **za-**) *vi* (*dzwonić*) to call; **telefonował do mnie** he called me

telekomunikacj|a (**-i**) *f* (*gałąź nauki*) telecommunications

telenowel|a (**-i, -e**) *f* soap opera

telewizj|a (**-i, -e**; *gen pl* **-i**) *f* TV; **ogląda telewizję codziennie** he watches TV every day; **~ satelitarna** satellite TV; **~ kablowa** cable TV

telewizo|r (**-ra, -ry**; *loc sg* **-rze**) *m* (*urządzenie*) TV (set)

telewizyjny *adj* TV; (*program, serial*) television

tema|t (**-tu, -ty**; *loc sg* **-cie**) *m* (*myśl przewodnia*) subject

temp. *abbr* (=*temperature*) temp.

temperatu|ra (**-ry, -ry**; *dat sg* & *loc sg* **-rze**) *f* temperature; **~ wrzenia** boiling point; **mam temperaturę** (*w medycynie*) I've got a temperature

temu *pron dat od* **ten, to**

temu *adv*: **trzy lata ~** two years ago; **zdarzyło się to dawno ~** that happened a long time ago; **jak dawno ~ tam byłeś?** how long is it since you were there?; **parę miesięcy ~** a couple of months ago

ten *pron* **1** (*z rzeczownikiem*) this **2** (*bez rzeczownika*) this one **3** (*tamten*) that; **~ sam co wczoraj** the same as yesterday; **~ jest bardzo ładny** this one is very nice; **w ~ piątek** this Friday

teni|s (**-sa**; *loc sg* **-sie**) *m* (*dyscyplina sportu*) tennis

tenisi|sta (**-sty, -ści**; *dat sg* & *loc sg* **-ście**) *m decl like f in sg* tennis player

tenisist|ka (**-ki, -ki**; *dat sg* & *loc sg* **-ce**; *gen pl* **-ek**) *f* tennis player

tenisów|ki (**-ek**) *pl* (*buty sportowe*) tennis shoes

teoretycznie *adv* in theory; **~ masz rację** in theory you are right

teori|a (**-i, -e**; *gen pl* **-i**) *f* theory; **~ względności** relativity theory

teraz *adv* now, nowadays

teraźniejszoś|ć (**-ci**) *f* the present

teraźniejszy *adj* (*obecny*) present, today's; **czas ~** (*w językoznawstwie*) present tense

tere|n (**-nu, -ny**; *loc sg* **-nie**) *m* **1** (*obszar*) terrain **2** (*ziemia*) land

termi|n (**-nu, -ny**; *loc sg* **-nie**) *m* **1** (*czas potrzebny do wykonania czegoś*) deadline **2** (*u lekarza*) appointment **3** (*wyrażenie*) term

terro|r (**-ru**; *loc sg* **-rze**) *m* (*strach, przemoc*) terror

terrory|sta (-sty, -ści; *loc sg* **-ście)** *m decl like f in sg* terrorist

terrorystyczny *adj* (*organizacja, zamach*) terrorist

terroryz|m (-mu; *loc sg* **-mie)** *m* terrorism

terroryz|ować (-uję, -ujesz; *pf* **s-)** *vt* (*zastraszać*) to terrorize

te|st (-stu, -sty; *loc sg* **-ście)** *m* test

testamen|t (-tu, -ty; *loc sg* **-cie)** *m* (*ostatnia wola*) will, testament; **Stary/Nowy T~** the Old/New Testament

teściow|a (-ej, -e) *f decl like adj* (*matka żony, matka męża*) mother-in-law

teś|ć (-cia, -ciowie) *m* (*ojciec żony, ojciec męża*) father-in-law; **teściowie** *pl* in-laws *pl*

też *adv* too; **on ~** him too; **ja ~ nie pójdę** I'm not going either; **to sport niebezpieczny, dlatego ~ nazywają go głupim** it is a dangerous sport, and that is why people call it stupid

tę *pron acc od* **ta**

tęcz|a (-y, -e) *f* rainbow

tędy *adv* this way; **idź ~** go this way

tępy *adj* **1** (*nieostry*) blunt **2** (*osoba*) dense **3** (*wzrok*) vacant **4** (*ból*) dull

tęsk|nić (-nię, -nisz; *impf* **-nij;** *pf* **za-)** *vi*: **~ za** +*inst* to miss; **tęsknię za ojczyzną** (*pragnąć*) I miss my own country

tęskno|ta (-ty, -ty; *dat sg & loc sg* **-cie)** *f* longing; **ogarnęła go ~ za domem** he longed to be home

tj. *abbr* (= *to jest*) i.e.

tkani|na (-ny, -ny; *dat sg & loc sg* **-nie)** *f* (*materiał*) fabric

tle|n (-nu; *loc sg* **-nie)** *m* oxygen

tło|k (*inst sg* **-kiem**) *m* **1** (*gen sg* **-ku**) (*tłum*) crowd **2** (*gen sg* **-ka;** *nom pl* **-ki**) (*w technologii*) piston

tłu|m (-mu, -my; *loc sg* **-mie)** *m* (*dużo ludzi*) crowd

tłumacz (-a, -e; *gen pl* **-y)** *m* **1** (*tekstów pisanych*) translator **2** (*ustny*) interpreter; **~ przysięgły** certified translator

tłumaczenie (-nia) *nt* translation

tłumaczyć (-ę, -ysz) *vt* (*pf* **wy-**) **1** (*wyjaśniać*) to explain **2** (*pf* **prze-**) (*przekładać: tekst*) to translate **3** (*rozmowę*) to interpret; **~ się** (*pf* **wy-**) *vr* (*usprawiedliwiać się*) to explain o.s.

tłusty *adj* **1** (*potrawa*) fatty **2** (*ubranie*) greasy **3** (*człowiek*) fat **4** (*druk, czcionka*) bold; **tłuste mleko** full-cream milk; **~ czwartek** *the last Thursday before Lent*

○ **TŁUSTY CZWARTEK**

Tłusty czwartek is the last Thursday before Lent, when traditionally a large number of doughnuts and **faworki** are consumed.

○ **KEYWORD**

to *pron* **1** (*zaimek wskazujący*) this; **to okno** this window **2** (*w funkcji podmiotu*): **to prawda**

tłuszcz (-u, -e) *m* fat; **tłuszcze dzielimy na ~e roślinne i zwierzęce** we distinguish fats as vegetable and animal fats

it's the truth; **to jest kot** this
lub it is a cat; **co/kto to jest?**
what's/who's this?; **czy to ona?**
is that her?
3 (w funkcji ekspresywnej): **a to
chuligan!** what a lout!
4: jak to? how so?, how come?;
no co z tego? so what of it?;
otóż to! exactly!
▷ conj: **jeśli chcesz, to przyjedź**
come if you want; **nie chcesz, to
nie** if you don't want to, you don't
want to
▷ inv (w funkcji łącznika): **czas to
pieniądz** time is money

toale|ta (-ty, -ty; dat sg & loc sg
-cie) f **1** (ubikacja) toilet, rest room
(US) **2** (eleganckie ubranie damskie)
gown; **~ damska/męska** the
ladies' (room)/gents' (toilet) (Brit)
lub men's room (US)
toaletowy adj (papier, przybory)
toilet
toa|st (-stu, -sty; loc sg -ście) m
toast; **wzniósł ~ za zdrowie
gospodarzy** he drank the
landlord's health
tobie pron zob. **ty**
tolerancj|a (-i) f tolerance
tolerancyjny adj (człowiek,
stosunek) tolerant
toler|ować (-uję, -ujesz) vt
(szanować poglądy) to tolerate
to|pić (-pię, -pisz) vt **1** (pf u-)
(pozbawiać życia) to drown **2** (pf s-)
(roztapiać) to melt; **~ się** vr **1** (pf
u-) (osoba, zwierzę) to drown **2** (pf
s-) (masło) to melt
tor|ba (-by, -by; dat sg & loc sg -bie;
gen pl -eb) f **1** bag **2** (na podróż)
holdall

toreb|ka (-ki, -ki; dat sg & loc
sg -ce; gen pl -ek) f **1** (z papieru)
(paper) bag **2** (damska) handbag,
purse (US)
tor|t (-tu, -ty; loc sg -cie) m cake
(Brit), layer cake (US)
to|st (-stu, -sty; loc sg -ście) m
slice of toast
towa|r (-ru, -ry; loc sg -rze)
m **1** (produkt) commodity
2 (dziewczyna: pot!) babe; **~y
konsumpcyjne** consumer goods
towarowy adj: **pociąg ~** goods
(Brit) lub freight (US) train; **statek
~** cargo vessel; **bon ~** voucher
towarzyski adj **1** (osoba) sociable
2 (impreza, zebranie) social;
rozmowa towarzyska small
talk; **zaczęła pojawiać się w
kronikach ~ch** she began to
feature in the gossip columns
towarzyst|wo (-wa; loc sg -wie;
nom pl -wa) nt **1** (przebywanie)
company **2** (grono przyjaciół)
company **3** (organizacja) society
towarzysz|yć (-ę, -ysz) vi: **~ +dat**
to accompany
tożsamoś|ć (-ci) f
(samoświadomość) identity;
dowód tożsamości ID
tra|cić (-cę, -cisz; imp -ć) vt **1** (pf
s- lub u-) (nie mieć) to lose **2** (pf
s-) (marnować: okazję) to miss
3 (czas, środki finansowe) to waste
▷ vi (pf s-) (znaleźć się w sytuacji
niekorzystnej) to lose (out); **traci
przytomność codziennie** he
loses consciousness on a daily
basis; **dokument traci ważność
we wrześniu** the document
expires in September
tradycj|a (-i, -e; gen pl -i) f

(*obyczaj*) tradition

tradycyjny *adj* (*występujący od dawna*) traditional

tra|fiać (**-fiam, -fiasz**; *pf* **-fić**) *vt* to hit ▷ *vi* **1** (*nie chybiać*) to hit the target **2** (*znajdować właściwą drogę*) to get there; **~ się** *vr* to come up; **nie trafił do celu** he missed his target; **trafił na ostry dyżur** he landed up in casualty; **trafiła w dziesiątkę** she hit the bull's-eye; (*przen*) she was spot-on; **na chybił trafił** (*wybierać*) at random; **trafia się okazja!** opportunity knocks!

tragedi|a (**-i, -e**; *gen pl* **-i**) *f* tragedy

tragiczny *adj* **1** tragic **2** (*pot: wizerunek*) awful

trakt|ować (**-uję, -ujesz**) *vt* (*pf* **po-**) to treat ▷ *vi*: **~ o czymś** (*omawiać*) to discuss sth; **traktuje go źle** he treats him badly; **książka traktuje o miłości** the book deals with love

tramwa|j (**-ju, -je**; *gen pl* **-jów** *lub* **-i**) *m* tram (*Brit*), streetcar (*US*)

transatlantycki *adj* (*lot, rejs*) transatlantic

transpor|t (**-tu, -ty**; *loc sg* **-cie**) *m* **1** (*środek lokomocji*) transport (*Brit*), transportation (*US*) **2** (*towar*) shipment; **~ publiczny** public transport

tra|sa (**-sy, -sy**; *loc sg* **-sie**) *f* **1** (*droga*) route **2** (*wycieczki*) itinerary; **~ maratonu** the marathon route; **jest w trasie od trzech dni** he has been on the road for three days

tra|wa (**-wy, -wy**; *loc sg* **-wie**) *f* **1** (*roślina*) grass **2** (*trawnik*) lawn; **mowa-~** clap-trap

tra|wić (**-wię, -wisz**) *vt* **1** (*pf* **s-**) (*jedzenie*) to digest **2** (*pf* **s-**) (*o bólu*) to consume **3** (*pf* **wy-**) (*Tech, Druk: metal, skło*) to etch

trawie|nie (**-nia**) *nt* **1** (*system*) digestion **2** (*Chem, Druk: płytek drukowanych*) etching

trawni|k (**-ka, -ki**; *inst sg* **-kiem**) *m* lawn

trąb|ka (**-ki, -ki**; *dat sg & loc sg* **-ce**; *gen pl* **-ek**) *f* (*instrument muzyczny*) trumpet

trene|r (**-ra, -rzy**; *loc sg* **-rze**) *m* coach

trenin|g (**-gu, -gi**; *inst sg* **-giem**) *m* (*fizyczny, intelektualny*) training

tren|ować (**-uję, -ujesz**; *pf* **wy-**) *vt, vi* (*sportowców*) to train

tres|ować (**-uję, -ujesz**; *pf* **wy-**) *vt* (*psa*) to train

treś|ć (**-ci, -ci**; *gen pl* **-ci**) *f* **1** (*przemówienia*) content **2** (*powieści*) plot **3** (*życia*) meaning; **spis treści** (table of) contents

trochę *adv* **1** a little, a bit **2** (*przez krótki czas*) (for) a while; **nie rozumiem ani ~** I don't begin to understand; **jedz po trochu** eat a little bit

trolejbu|s (**-su, -sy**; *loc sg* **-sie**) *m* trolley bus

tros|ka (**-ki, -ki**; *dat sg & loc sg* **-ce**) *f* **1** (*zmartwienie*) worry **2** (*opieka*) concern

troskliwie *adv* with care

troskliwoś|ć (**-ci**) *f* (*dbałość*) care

troskliwy *adj* caring

troszczyć się (**-ę, -ysz**) *vr*: **~ się o kogoś/coś** (*zajmować się*) to take care of sb/sth; (*z niepokojem*) to worry about sb/sth

trójkąt (-ta, -ty; *loc sg* -cie) *m* (*figura geometryczna*) triangle; **~ odblaskowy** *lub* **ostrzegawczy** warning triangle; **jeszcze jedna historia ~a małżeńskiego** one more case of the eternal triangle

truci|zna (-zny, -zny; *dat sg & loc sg* -źnie) *f* (*substancja szkodliwa*) poison

tr|uć (-uję, -ujesz; *pf* o-) *vt* to poison

trudno *adv* hard; **~ powiedzieć** it's hard to tell; **~ mu uwierzyć, że...** he finds it hard to believe that...

trudny *adj* (*skomplikowany*) difficult

tru|p (-pa, -py; *loc sg* -pie) *m* (*nieboszczyk*) dead body

truskaw|ka (-ki, -ki; *dat sg & loc sg* -ce; *gen pl* -ek) *f* strawberry

trw|ać (-am, -asz) *vt*: **~ minutę/rok** to last (for) a minute/a year ▷ *vi* **1** to last **2** (*o dyskusji, procesie*) to go on **3** (*pf* wy-) (*nie poddawać się*) to persist; **trwał w bezruchu kilka chwil** he kept still for a moment or two; **~ w milczeniu** to remain silent

trwały *adj* **1** (*wytrzymały*) durable **2** (*nieprzerwany*) lasting; **trwała ondulacja** perm

try|b (-bu, -by; *loc sg* -bie) *m* **1** mode **2** (*w językoznawstwie*) mood; **tryby** *pl* (*w technologii*) gears; **prowadzi siedzący ~ życia** he leads a sedentary life

trzeba *part inv* it is necessary to; **~ mu powiedzieć prawdę** he's got to tell the truth; **~ było go posłuchać** we should have helped him; **~ przyznać, że jest bardzo ładna** admittedly she is very pretty; **jeśli ~ pomożemy mu** if necessary we will help him; **~ wam czegoś?** do you need anything?

trzeci *num* third; **jedna ~a** one third; **po ~e** third(ly); **co ~ miesiąc** every three months

trzeźwie|ć (-ję, -jesz; *pf* wy-) *vi* **1** (*odzyskiwać przytomność*) to come round **2** (*po alkoholu*) to sober up

trzeźwy *adj* (*nie pijany*) sober

trzy *num* three

trzydzieści *num* thirty

trzym|ać (-am, -asz) *vt* **1** (*w ramionach*) to hold **2** (*w lodówce, w więzieniu*) to keep ▷ *vi* (*konstrukcja, materiał*) to hold; **~ się** *vr* +*gen* **1** (*poręczy, gałęzi*) to hold on to **2** (*wytyczonej trasy*) to follow **3** (*prawa*) to adhere to; **nie trzymaj rąk w kieszeniach** don't put your hands in your pockets; **trzymali ją w niecierpliwości** they kept her in suspense; **~ coś (przed kimś) w sekrecie** to keep sth secret (from sb); **on zawsze trzyma jej stronę** he always takes her side; **trzymała to w tajemnicy przed mężem** she kept it a secret from her husband; **trzymajcie się razem!** stick together!; **~ się kogoś/czegoś** to hang on to sb/sth; **trzymaj się prosto!** stand up straight!

trzynasty *num* thirteenth

trzynaście *num* thirteen ·

trzysta *num* three hundred

tu *adv* here; **tu (mówi) Kowalska** this is Kowalska (speaking)

tul|ić (-ę, -isz) *vt* (*w ramionach*) to hug; **~ się** (*pf* przy-) *vr*: **~ się do**

kogoś/czegoś (*obejmować kogoś z czułością*) to snuggle up to sb/sth
tunel (**-u, -e**; *gen pl* **-i** *lub* **-ów**) *m* tunnel
Tunezj|a (**-i**) *f* Tunisia
tuńczy|k (**-ka, -ki**; *inst sg* **-kiem**) *m* tuna (fish)
Turcj|a (**-i**) *f* Turkey
tury|sta (**-sty, -ści**; *dat sg & loc sg* **-ście**) *m decl like f in sg* tourist
turysty|ka (**-ki**; *dat sg & loc sg* **-ce**) *f* (*hobby, sektor gospodarki*) tourism
tutaj *adv* here
tuzi|n (**-na, -ny**; *loc sg* **-nie**) *m* (*dwanaście*) dozen
tuż *adv* **1** (*nieopodal*) close by **2** (*niedługo*) close on; **wakacje ~, ~** the holidays are almost here; **sklep jest ~ za rogiem** the shop is just round the corner
TVP *abbr* (= *Telewizja Polska*) Polish Television
twardy *adj* **1** (*mebel*) hard **2** (*kawałek mięsa*) tough **3** (*zasady moralne*) harsh **4** (*przen: nieprzyjemny*) stern
twarz (**-y, -e**; *gen pl* **-y**) *f* face; **był zwrócony ~ą do mnie** he had his face turned towards me; **jest ci do ~y w tej sukience** this dress suits you; **nie jest ci do ~y w tym stroju** this outfit doesn't flatter you
twarzowy *adj* **1** (*strój*) becoming **2** (*nerw*) facial
twier|dzić (**-dzę, -dzisz**; *impf* **-dź**; *pf* **s-**) *vi* (*stanowczo, jednoznacznie*) to claim
twoja *itd. pron zob.* **twój**
tworz|yć (**-ę, -ysz**; *impf* **twórz**) *vt* **1** (*pf* **s-**) (*dzieło sztuki*) to create **2** (*pf* **u-** *lub* **s-**) (*gabinet polityczny*)

to form **3** (*pf* **s-**) (*muzykę*) to produce **4** (*pf* **u-**) (*stanowić*) to form; **~ się** *vr* **1** (*powstawać*) to be formed **2** (*formować się*) to form; **tworzyły się podziemne organizacje wojskowe** underground military organizations were formed
twój *possessive pron* **1** (*przed rzeczownikiem*) your **2** (*bez rzeczownika*) yours; **czy to są twoje rzeczy?** are these your things?; **czy te rzeczy są twoje?** are these things yours?
twórc|a (**-y, -y**) *m decl like f in sg* **1** (*pisarz*) author **2** (*muzyk, aktor*) artist
ty *pron* you; **jestem z nim na „ty"** I am on first-name terms with him
tych *pron gen, loc od* **ci, te**
tyć (**tyję, tyjesz**; *pf* **u-**) *vi* (*przybierać na wadze*) to put on weight
ty|dzień (**-godnia, -godnie**; *gen pl* **-godni**) *m* week; **pływa co ~** he goes swimming every week; **przyjdzie za ~** come in a week's time; **w przyszłym/zeszłym tygodniu** next/last week; **Wielki T~** Holy Week
tygodni|k (**-ka, -ki**; *inst sg* **-kiem**) *m* weekly
tygodniowo *adv* (*raz na tydzień*) weekly
tygodniowy *adj* **1** (*trwający tydzień*) week's **2** (*pensja*) weekly
tygry|s (**-sa, -sy**; *loc sg* **-sie**) *m* tiger
tyle *pron* **1** (*z rzeczownikiem: rzeczy, danych*) so many **2** (*nienawiści, wody*) so much **3** (*bez rzeczownika*)

this many, this much; **straciłem z tobą ~ czasu** I wasted so much time with you; **tylu uczniów/ zawodników** so many pupils/ contestants; **mam ~ kłopotów co i ty** I've got as many problems as you have; **ona już ~ przeżyła!** she has been through so much already!; **dwa razy ~ wina/ kanapek** twice as much wine/as many sandwiches

tylko part only, just
▷ conj: **gdyby/jeśli ~** if only; **posłuchaj ~ co mam ci do powiedzenia** just listen to what I have got to say to you; **~ nie ona!** anybody lub anyone but her!; **jak ~ zadzwonisz, wyjdę** as soon as you phone, I'll leave; **kiedy ~ miałem możliwość** whenever I had a chance; **kiedy ~ wyszedłem, on zadzwonił** as soon as I came in, he called; **nie ~ ona, ale (również)** jej dzieci not only her, but her children too

ty|ł (**-łu, -ły**; loc sg **-le**) m back; **tyły** pl (Wojsk) rear sg; **stał ~em do ulicy** he stood with his back towards the street; **szedł ~em** he walked backwards; **jechać ~em** (cofać) to reverse; **z ~u sklepu** at the back of the shop; **zrobił krok do ~u i stanął** he took a step backwards and stopped

tym¹ pron instr, loc od **ten, to**
▷ pron dat od **ci, te**

tym² part: **im więcej, ~ lepiej** the more, the better; **~ bardziej, że nie przyszedł** all the more so as he didn't come; **~ lepiej/gorzej dla mnie** so much the better/ worse for me

tymczasowy adj 1 (doryczczy) temporary 2 (rząd) interim 3 (prowizoryczny) provisional

ty|p (loc sg **-pie**; nom pl **-py**) m 1 (gen sg **-pu**) (rodzaj) type 2 (gen sg **-pa**) (pej: osoba) character; **on jest w jej ~ie** he is her type

typowy adj 1 (charakterystyczny) typical 2 (często spotykany) standard; **zachowanie typowe dla nich** typical behaviour (Brit) lub behavior (US) for them

tys. abbr (= tysiące) thousand

tysi|ąc (**-ąca, -ące**; gen pl **-ęcy**) m thousand

tytu|ł (**-łu, -ły**; loc sg **-le**) m (powieści, artykułu) title; **film pod ~em...** a film entitled...; **otrzymał ~ szlachecki** he got a knighthood; **~ profesora** professorship; **~ mistrowski** the championship

tzn. abbr (= to znaczy) i.e.

tzw. abbr (= tak zwany) so-called

u

KEYWORD

u *prep* +gen 1 (*niedaleko*) at; **stać u okna** to stand by the window; **jest u władzy** he's in power; **szuka pomocy u rodziców** he's seeking help from his parents
2 (*część całości*): **palce u rąk/nóg** fingers/toes
3 (*dotyczące osoby, dzieła literackiego*): **zostawiłem klucze u portiera** I left the keys with the concierge; **u Mickiewicza** in Mickiewicz; **co u was słychać?** (*familiar pl*) how are things with you?
4 (*dla określenia miejsca*): **u Jana** at John's (place); **u moich przyjaciół** at my friends' (place);

czy szef jest u siebie (*pot*) is the boss in?

ubezpiecze|nie (**-nia**, **-nia**; *gen pl* **-ń**) *nt* insurance; **~ od ognia/włamania** cover against fire/burglary; **obowiązkowe ~ odpowiedzialności cywilnej** compulsory insurance against civil liability; **~ międzynarodowe** (*samochodowe*) green card; **~ społeczne** national insurance (*Brit*), social security (*US*); **~ maszyn, urządzeń i aparatów technicznych od awarii** insurance of equipment against breakdown; **~ straty spowodowanej przestojem w działalności gospodarczej** loss-of-profits cover
ubiegły *adj* (*rok, miesiąc*) past, last; **w ~m roku/tygodniu** last year/week
ubier|ać (**-am**, **-asz**) *vt* (*pf* **ubrać**) 1 (*człowieka*) to dress 2 (*zakładać ubranie*) to put on 3 (*choinkę, ciasto*) to decorate; **~ się** (*pf* **ubrać**) *vr* (*włożyć na siebie ubranie*) to get dressed; **ubrał się starannie** he dressed with care
ubika|cja (**-cji**, **-cje**; *loc sg & dat sg* **-cji**) *f* toilet, restroom (*US*)
ubi|ór (**-oru**, **-ory**; *loc sg* **-orze**) *m* (*strój*) clothing
ubliż|ać (**-am**, **-asz**; *pf* **-yć**) *vi*: **~ komuś** to insult sb; **~ czemuś** to offend against sth
ubogi *adj* (*biedny*) poor
ubrać (**ubiorę**, **ubierzesz**; *imp* **ubierz**) *vb pf od* **ubierać**
ubra|nie (**-nia**, **-nia**; *gen pl* **-ń**) *nt* 1 (*strój*) clothing 2 (*garnitur*) suit;

~ ochronne protective clothing
ubrany adj dressed; **być ~m w rzeczy codzienne** to be dressed in ordinary clothes
ucho¹ (**ucha**, **uszy**; gen pl **uszu**; dat pl **uszom**; inst pl **uszami**; loc pl **uszach**) nt ear; **mam powyżej uszu tej sytuacji** (pot) I've had it up to here with this
uch|o² (**-a**, **-a**) nt **1** (dzbanka) handle **2** (igły) eye
uciąć (**utnę**, **utniesz**; imp **utnij**; pt **uciął**, **ucięła**, **ucięli**) vb pf od **ucinać**
uciecz|ka (**-ki**, **-ki**; dat sg & loc sg **-ce**; gen pl **-ek**) f escape; **szuka ucieczki w alkoholu/ narkotykach** he's seeking refuge in drink/drugs
uciek|ać (**-am**, **-asz**; pf **uciec**) vi to run away, to escape; **~ się** vr: **~ się do czegoś** to resort to sth; **uciekł mi pociąg** I missed my train; **uciekł się do podstępu** he resorted to deceit
ucin|ać (**-am**, **-asz**; pf **uciąć**) vb (rozmowę, więzi, kontakt) to cut off
uczciwie adv (pracować, zeznawać) honestly
uczciwoś|ć (**-ci**) f (rzetelność, sumienność) honesty
uczciwy adj honest
uczel|nia (**-ni**, **-nie**; dat sg & loc sg **-ni**; gen pl **-ni**) f (szkoła wyższa) university, college
uczennic|a (**-y**, **-e**; dat sg & loc sg **-y**) f (w szkole, liceum) schoolgirl
ucze|ń (**-nia**, **-niowie**; loc sg **-niu**) m (w szkole, liceum) schoolboy
ucze|sać (**-szę**, **-szesz**) vb pf od **czesać**
uczesa|nie (**-nia**, **-nia**; gen pl **-ń**)

nt (fryzura) hairstyle
uczestnicz|yć (**-ę**, **-ysz**) vi (brać udział) to participate
uczestni|k (**-ka**, **-cy**; inst sg **-kiem**) m participant
uczu|cie (**-cia**, **-cia**; gen pl **-ć**) nt **1** (emocja) emotion **2** (lęku) feeling **3** (gorąca, pragnienia) sensation **4** (miłość) affection
uczule|nie (**-nia**) nt: **~ (na coś)** allergy (to sth); **ma ~ na pyłki** he has hayfever; **ma ~ na koty** he is allergic to cats
uczulony adj: **~ na coś** allergic to sth
ucz|yć (**-ę**, **-ysz**; pf **na-**) vt to teach ▷ vi to teach; **~ się** vr to study; **~ (kogoś) fizyki/polskiego** to teach (sb) physics/Polish; **Ewa uczy się dobrze/źle** Ewa is a good/bad student; **~ się do klasówki** to study lub revise (Brit) for a test
udawać (**udaję**, **udajesz**; imp **udawaj**; pf **udać**) vt **1** (chorobę) to fake, to feign **2** (naśladować) to imitate ▷ vi: **udawał, że śpi** he pretended he was sleeping; **~ się** vr (okazać się sukcesem) to be successful; **udawała, że nie wie co on ma na myśli** she pretended not to know what he meant; **udało mi się dopełnić wszystkich formalności** I managed to comply with all the formalities
uderz|ać (**-am**, **-asz**; pf **-yć**) vt: **~ kogoś (w coś)** to hit sb (in lub on sth) ▷ vi **1** (pięścią) to punch **2** (młotkiem) to hit; **~ się** vr **1** (samemu) to hit o.s. **2** (nawzajem) to hit one another; **~ (na kogoś/ coś)** to hit out (at sb/sth), to

attack (sb/sth)

udo (**uda, uda**; *loc sg* **udzie**) *nt* thigh

uf|ać (**-am, -asz**; *pf* **za-**) *vi*: **~ komuś/czemuś** to trust sb/sth; **ufam, że nie narobisz głupstw** I trust that you won't do anything stupid

ufny *adj* trusting

uga|sić (**-szę, -sisz**; *imp* **-ś**) *vb pf od* **gasić** ▷ *vt pf*: **ugasił pragnienie łykiem wina** he quenched his thirst with a gulp of wine; **powstanie zostało ugaszone** the uprising was quelled

ugot|ować (**-uję, -ujesz**) *vb pf od* **gotować**

ugry|źć (**-zę, -ziesz**; *imp* **-ź**) *vb pf od* **gryźć**; **~ się** *vr*: **~ się w język** (*przen*) to hold one's tongue

ujemny *adj* negative; **~ ładunek** negative charge; **mieć na kogoś ~ wpływ** (*przen*) to have a negative influence on sb

ujrz|eć (**-ę, -ysz**; *imp* **-yj**) *vt pf*: **jego dzieło ujrzało światło dzienne** his work saw the light of day

uka|rać (**-rzę, -rzesz**) *vb pf od* **karać**

ukło|nić się (**-nię, -nisz**; *imp* **-ń**) *vb pf od* **kłaniać się**

ukochan|a (**-ej, -e**) *f decl like adj* (*kobieta, którą się kocha*) sweetheart

ukochany *adj* (*mężczyzna, którego się kocha*) beloved ▷ *m decl like adj* sweetheart

ukończ|yć (**-ę, -ysz**) *vt pf* (*pracę, edukację*) to complete, to finish

ukra|ść (**-dnę, -dniesz**; *imp* **-dnij**;

pt **-dł**) *vb pf od* **kraść**

ukry|ć (**-ję, -jesz**) *vb pf od* **ukrywać**

ukr|ywać (**-ywam, -ywasz**) *vb* to hide, to conceal; **nie da się ukryć, że...** there's no hiding that...

ul. *abbr* (= *ulica*) St

ul|egać (**-egam, -egasz**; *pf* **ulec, ulegnąć**) *vb* to surrender; **~ komuś** to surrender to sb

ule|wa (**-wy, -wy**; *loc sg* **-wie**) *f* (*rzęsisty deszcz*) downpour

ul|ga (**-gi**; *dat sg & loc sg* **-dze**) *f* 1 (*wrażenie*) relief 2 (*nom pl* **-gi**) (*zniżka*) concession, allowance; **~ podatkowa** tax relief

ulgowy *adj* 1 (*opłata*) reduced 2 (*traktowanie*) preferential; **opłata ulgowa** reduced fare, concessionary rate

ulic|a (**-y, -e**) *f* street; **na ulicy Mickiewicza** on Mickiewicz Street; **szliśmy/jechaliśmy ulicą** we walked/drove down the street; **przechodzić przez ulicę na światłach** to cross the street at the lights

ulot|ka (**-ki, -ki**; *dat sg & loc sg* **-ce**; *gen pl* **-ek**) *f* (*wyborcza, informacyjna*) leaflet, flyer

ulubienic|a (**-y, -e**) *f* favourite (*Brit*), favorite (*US*); **~ publiczności** the audience's favourite

ulubie|niec (**-ńca, -ńcy**) *m* favourite (*Brit*), favorite (*US*); **~ tłumów** the popular favourite

ulubiony *adj* (*napój, książka*) favourite (*Brit*), favorite (*US*)

ułat|wiać (**-wiam, -wiasz**; *pf* **-wić**) *vt* (*życie, pracę*) to make easier

ułoże|nie (-nia) nt **1** (układ) arrangement **2** (psa: tresura) training

umal|ować (-uję, -ujesz) vt pf **1** (zrobić makijaż) to make up **2** (powieki, usta) to apply (make-up); **~ się** vr to make (o.s.) up

um|awiać (-awiam, -awiasz) vt (pf **umówić**) to arrange; **~ się** vr: **~ się z kimś** to make an appointment with sb; **umówiłam się z chłopakiem** I have a date with a guy; **umówiłem się z nim na szóstą na Rynku** I've arranged to meet him at six on the Market Square; **~ spotkanie** to arrange a meeting; **~ kogoś z kimś** to make an appointment for sb with sb

umiarkowany adj moderate; **~ klimat/entuzjazm** moderate climate/enthusiasm

umieć (umiem, umiesz) vi: **~ coś robić** to know how lub be able to do sth; **nie umiem tańczyć/ śpiewać** I can't dance/sing; **~ po angielsku** (pot) to have some English

umiejętnoś|ć (-ci, -ci; gen pl **-ci)** f **1** (zdolność robienia czegoś) ability **2** (biegłość w czymś) skill

umier|ać (-am, -asz; pf **umrzeć)** vi to die; **~ na gruźlicę** to die of tuberculosis; **~ z głodu** to die of starvation; **umierał z nudów na wykładzie** he was bored to death during the lecture

um|owa (-owy, -owy; loc sg **-owie**; gen pl **-ów)** f (prawna, międzynarodowa) agreement, contract; **zawierać (zawrzeć**

pf) **umowę** to enter into an agreement lub a contract; **związany umową** bound by contract; **wczoraj podpisała umowę o pracę** yesterday she signed an employment contract

umożli|wiać (-wiam, -wiasz; pf **-wić)** vt (czynić możliwym) to make possible; **umożliwi mu kupno domu** it'll enable him to buy a house

um|rzeć (-rę, -rzesz; imp **-rzyj**; pt **-arł)** vb pf od **umierać**

umy|ć (-ję, -jesz) vb pf od **myć**

umy|sł (-słu, -sły; loc sg **-śle)** m (rozum) mind, intellect; **ma bardzo przytomny ~** he has a highly astute mind

uni|a (-i, -e; loc sg **-i)** f union; **U~ Europejska** European Union

uniewin|niać (-niam, -niasz; pf **-nić)** vt (w sądzie) to acquit

uniewinnieni|e (-a) nt acquittal

unijny adj EU; **przepisy unijne** EU regulations

unik|ać (-am, -asz; pf **-nąć)** vt +gen **1** (spotkania, rozmowy) to avoid **2** (uderzenia) to dodge **3** (kary) to escape

uniwersalny adj (ogólny) universal; **klucz ~** master lub skeleton key

uniwersytecki adj university; **miasteczko ~e** campus

uniwersyte|t (-tu, -ty; loc sg **-cie)** m (wyższa uczelnia) university

uno|sić (-szę, -sisz; imp **-ś**; pf **unieść)** vt **1** (podnosić: nogę) to raise **2** (przemieścić) to sweep away; **~ się** vr **1** (wisieć: nad powierzchnią ziemi) to hover **2** (zostać uniesionym: o mgle) to rise

3 (*z krzesła*) to rise **4** (*denerwować się*) to get carried away

unowocześ|niać (**-niam, -niasz;** *pf* **-nić**) *vt* (*firmę, urządzenie*) to modernize

upad|ać (**-am, -asz;** *pf* **upaść**) *vi* (*przewracać się*) to fall (down); **firma chyli się ku upadkowi** the firm is heading for collapse; **upadł ze zmęczenia** he collapsed from exhaustion

upad|ek (**-ku, -ki;** *inst sg* **-kiem**) *m* **1** (*przewrócenie się*) fall **2** (*sztuki, obyczajów*) decay, decline **3** (*klęska*) downfall

upalny *adj* (*dzień, pogoda*) sweltering, (scorching) hot

upał (**-łu, -ły;** *loc sg* **-le**) *m* (*gorąco*) heat

upa|ść (**-dnę, -dniesz;** *imp* **-dnij;** *pt* **-dł**) *vi pf od* **upadać**; (*spaść*) to fall

upew|niać (**-niam, -niasz;** *pf* **-nić**) *vt*: **~ kogoś o czymś** to assure sb of sth; **~ się** *vr* to make sure

upie|c (**-kę, -czesz;** *pt* **-kł**) *vb pf od* **piec**

upier|ać się (**-am, -asz;** *pf* **uprzeć**) *vr* (*nalegać*) to insist; **upiera się przy spotkaniu z nimi** he insists on meeting them

upij|ać (**-am, -asz**) *vt* **1** (*napój*) to take a sip of **2** (*człowieka*) to make drunk; **~ się** *vr* to get drunk

upomin|ek (**-ku, -ki;** *inst sg* **-kiem**) *m* (*prezent*) gift

uporządkowany *adj* (*życie, pokój*) ordered, orderly

upowszech|niać (**-niam, -niasz;** *pf* **-nić**) *vt* (*wiedzę, opinie*) to disseminate; **~ się** *vr* to become widespread

up|ór (**-oru;** *loc sg* **-orze**) *m*

stubbornness; **z uporem obstawał przy swoim** stubbornly he stuck to his guns

uprzejmy *adj* polite; **bądź tak ~ i podaj mi to, proszę** would you be so kind as to pass it to me?

ur. *abbr* (= **urodzony**) b.

Ural (**-u**) *m* the Ural Mountains *pl*

urat|ować (**-uję, -ujesz**) *vb pf od* **ratować**

ura|z (**-zu, -zy;** *loc sg* **-zie**) *m* **1** (*ciała*) injury **2** (*psychiczny*) trauma

uraż|ać (**-am, -asz;** *pf* **-zić**) *vt* to offend

urażony *adj* **1** (*osoba*) offended **2** (*uczucia*) hurt; **czuł się ~ jej zachowaniem** he felt hurt by her behaviour (*Brit*) *lub* behavior (*US*)

urlo|p (**-pu, -py;** *loc sg* **-pie**) *m* **1** (*wychowawczy, zdrowotny*) leave (of absence) **2** (*wakacje*) holiday (*Brit*), vacation (*esp US*); **być na ~ie** to be on holiday; **~ macierzyński** maternity leave; **~ zdrowotny** sick leave; **~ dziekański** sabbatical leave

uroczy *adj* (*człowiek, miejsce*) charming

uroczystoś|ć (**-ci, -ci;** *gen pl* **-ci**) *f* ceremony, celebration(s *pl*)

uroczysty *adj* (*podniosły*) solemn

uroczyście *adv* solemnly

uro|da (**-dy;** *dat sg & loc sg* **-dzie**) *f* (*atrakcyjny wygląd*) beauty, good looks; **ona urodą nie grzeszy** she's not too great in the looks department

uro|dzić (**-dzę, -dzisz;** *imp* **uródź** *lub* **uródź**) *vb pf od* **rodzić**

urodzin|y (**-**) *pl* birthday; **wszystkiego najlepszego w**

dniu urodzin! happy birthday!

urodzony adj **1** born **2** (*rodowity*)
born and bred; **jest ~m aktorem**
he was born to be an actor

urojony adj (*choroba, dolegliwość*)
imaginary

uro|k (-ku, -ki; *inst sg* **-kiem**) *m*
(*wdzięk*) charm

urozmaicony adj (*różnorodny*)
varied, diverse

urz|ąd (-ędu, -ędy; *loc sg* **-ędzie**) *m*
1 (*wojewódzki, pracy*) department
2 (*biuro*) office **3** (*miejsce pracy*)
post; **~ Wojewódzki** ≈ county
council (*Brit*); **~ Pracy** job
centre (*Brit*) *lub* center (*US*); **~
pocztowy** post office; **U~ Miasta
i Gminy** the Municipal Council;
~ Skarbowy ≈ Inland Revenue
(*Brit*), ≈ the IRS (*US*); **U~ Rady
Ministrów** Office of the Council
of Ministers; **~ stanu cywilnego**
registry (*Brit*) *lub* register (*US*)
office

urzą|dzać (-dzam, -dzasz;
pf **-dzić**) *vt* **1** (*dom*) to furnish
2 (*przedstawienie*) to organize;
~ się *vr* (*w nowym domu itp.*) to
settle down

urządze|nie (-nia, -nia; *gen pl* **-ń**)
nt (*maszyna*) device, appliance;
urządzenia *pl* equipment *sg*

urzędnicz|ka (-ki, -ki; *dat sg & loc
sg* **-ce**; *gen pl* **-ek**) *f* (*pracownica
urzędu*) office worker

urzędni|k (-ka, -cy; *inst sg* **-kiem**)
m **1** (*pracownik urzędu*) office
worker **2** (*wysoki rangą*) official

urzędowy adj **1** (*list, tajemnica*)
official **2** (*czas*) standard
3 (*sztywny: styl, relacja*) official

usią|ść (-dę, -dziesz; *imp* **-dź**) *vb*

pf od **siadać**

usłu|ga (-gi, -gi; *dat sg & loc sg*
-dze) *f* (*uprzejmość*) favour (*Brit*),
favor (*US*); **usługi** *pl* (*szewskie,
krawieckie*) services

usłysz|eć (-ę, -ysz) *vb pf od*
słyszeć ▷*vt*: **niedokładnie ~** to
mishear; **~ przez przypadek** to
overhear

usmaż|yć (-ę, -ysz) *vb pf od*
smażyć

usnąć (usnę, uśniesz; *imp* **uśnij**)
vb pf od **usypiać**

uspokaj|ać (-am, -asz; *pf*
uspokoić) *vt* **1** to calm (down)
2 (*uciszyć*) to quieten (*Brit*) *lub*
quiet (*US*) (down) **3** (*przestać się
denerwować*) to calm (down); **~
się** *vr* **1** to calm down **2** (*uciszyć*)
to quieten (*Brit*), to quiet (*US*) **3** (*o
wichurze*) to calm, to subside

**usprawiedli|wiać (-wiam,
-wiasz**; *pf* **-wić**) *vt* **1** (*tłumaczyć*)
to excuse **2** (*uzasadniać*) to
justify; **~ się** (*przed nauczycielem,
pracodawcą*) *vr* to excuse o.s., to
explain o.s.

usprawiedliwie|nie (-nia, -nia;
gen pl **-ń**) *nt* **1** (*wymówka*) excuse
2 (*uzasadnienie*) justification **3** (*w
szkole*) excuse note

**ust|a (-) ** *pl* mouth *sg*; **zrobili mu
oddychanie metodą ~-usta**
they gave him mouth-to-mouth
resuscitation

ustal|ać (-am, -asz; *pf* **-ić**) *vt* **1** to
establish **2** (*datę spotkania*) to fix;
~ się *vr* **1** (*o obyczaju*) to become
established **2** (*stabilizować się*)
to settle

ustale|nie (-nia, -nia; *gen pl* **-ń**)
nt (*decyzja*) decision; **ustalenia**

pl **1** plan *sg*, arrangements **2** (*badanie*) findings
ustalony *adj* **1** (*data spotkania*) fixed **2** (*dane*) established **3** (*reguły*) set, established
ustaw|a (*-y, -y*) *f* law, act of Parliament
usta|wiać (*-wiam, -wiasz; pf -wić*) *vt* **1** (*meble, książki*) to put, to place **2** (*rozmieszczać*) to arrange **3** (*urządzać*) to put up, to set up **4** (*ostrość, wysokość*) to adjust; **~ się** *vr*: **~ się w kolejce** to line up; **ustawił się przodem do wyjścia** he stood facing the exit
uster|ka (*-ki, -ki; dat sg & loc sg -ce; gen pl -ek*) *f* **1** (*w maszynie*) fault **2** (*w danych*) error
ustny *adj* **1** (*egzamin, tradycja*) oral **2** (*zgoda*) verbal; **jama ustna** (*Anat*) the mouth cavity; **harmonijka ustna** harmonica, mouth organ
ustr|ój (*-oju, -oje*) *m* (*Pol*) system
us|ypiać (*-ypiam, -ypiasz*) *vi* to fall asleep ▷ *vt*: **uśpić** (*uśpić pf*) **psa** to put a dog down
uszkodzony *adj* (*popsuty*) damaged
uszy *n zob.* **ucho**
uszy|ć (*-ję, -jesz*) *vb pf od* **szyć**
uścis|k (*-ku, -ki; inst sg -kiem*) *m* hug, embrace; **przywitał go ~iem dłoni** he greeted him with a handshake; **przesyłam wam serdeczne ~i** I send you my love
uści|snąć (*-snę, -śniesz; imp -śnij*) *vt* (*objąć ramionami*) to hug, to embrace; **uścisnął moją dłoń** he shook my hand
uściśl|ać (*-am, -asz; pf -ić*) *vt* **1** (*pojęcie*) to specify **2** (*słowa*) to qualify

uśmiech (*-u, -y*) *m* smile
uśmiech|ać się (*-am, -asz; pf -nąć*) *vr* to smile; **szczęście się do niego ~a** Lady Luck is smiling on him
uśmiechnięty *adj* (*człowiek, twarz*) smiling
uśmierz|ać (*-am, -asz; pf -yć*) *vt* **1** (*koić*) to relieve, to soothe **2** (*tłumić*) to quell
utalentowany *adj* (*uzdolniony*) talented, gifted
uty|ć (*-ję, -jesz*) *vb pf od* **tyć**
uwa|ga (*-gi, -gi; dat sg & loc sg -dze*) *f* **1** (*koncentracja*) attention **2** (*spostrzeżenie*) remark **3** (*upomnienie*) reproof; **~!** (*rozważnie!*) be careful!; (*o nadciągającym niebezpieczeństwie*) look out!; **„U~! Niski strop!"** "Warning! Low ceiling!"; **„U~! Wysokie napięcie!"** "Danger! High voltage!"; **„U~! Gaz palny!"** "Danger! Inflammable gas!"; **„U~! Strefa zagrożona wybuchem"** "Explosion danger"; **brać (wziąć pf) coś pod uwagę** to take sth into consideration; **zwracać (zwrócić pf) uwagę na kogoś/ coś** to pay attention to sb/sth
uważ|ać (*-am, -asz*) *vt*: **~ kogoś za wroga** to consider sb (to be) an enemy ▷ *vi* **1** (*być ostrożnym*) to be careful **2** (*wyrażać opinię*) to think; **~ się** *vr*: **on się uważa za zdolnego pianistę** he considers himself a gifted pianist; **uważaj na nich** keep an eye on them; **rób jak uważasz, ale będziesz żałował** do as you wish, but you'll regret it; **uważaj na siebie** take care (of yourself); **uważaj!** (*strzeż*

się!) be careful!; (*o nadciągającym niebezpieczeństwie*) look out!

uważnie *adv* **1** (*rozglądać się*) attentively **2** (*czytać*) carefully

uważny *adj* **1** (*słuchacz*) attentive **2** (*spojrzenie*) careful

uwielbi|ać (**-am, -asz**) *vt* (*czcić*) to adore

uwierz|yć (**-ę, -ysz**) *vi pf* (*komuś, w coś*) to believe

uzależniać (**-niam, -niasz**; *pf* **-nić**) *vt*: **~ coś od czegoś** (*od okoliczności*) to make sth dependent on sth; **~ się** *vr*: **~ się od** +*gen* (*od osoby*) to become dependent on; **~ się od alkoholu** to become addicted to alcohol

uzależnieni|e (**-a**) *nt* addiction

uzależniony *adj*: **być ~m od kogoś/czegoś** to be dependent on sb/sth

uzasad|niać (**-niam, -niasz**; *pf* **-nić**) *vt* (*tłumaczyć*) to justify

uzasadnie|nie (**-nia, -nia**; *gen pl* **-ń**) *nt* (*podanie powodów*) justification

uzasadniony *adj* justified

uzdrowi|sko (**-ska, -ska**; *inst sg* **-skiem**) *nt* **1** health resort **2** (*z wodami mineralnymi*) spa

uzgad|niać (**-niam, -niasz**; *pf* **uzgodnić**) *vt* (*plan, umowę*) to negotiate, to agree

uzn|awać (**-aję, -ajesz**; *pf* **uznać**) *vb* to acknowledge, to recognize

użytkowni|k (**-ka, -cy**; *inst sg* **-kiem**) *m* user

używ|ać (**-am, -asz**) *vt* (*pf* **użyć**) **1** (*posługiwać się*) to use **2** (*przyjmować lekarstwa*) to take

używany *adj* (*samochód, ubranie*) used, secondhand

video *nt inv* = **wideo**

verte *excl* PTO

versus *conj* versus

w cwartek on Thursday; **w wrześniu** in September
▷ *prep (wskazując na kierunek)* in(to); **spojrzeć w niebo** to gaze at the sky; **skręcać w lewo/prawo** to turn to the left/right; **iść w dół/górę** to go down/up

w *prep* +*loc* **1** *(wskazując na miejsce)* in; **pracuję w domu** I work at home; **w teatrze** at the theatre *(Brit) lub* theater *(US)*; **grać w orkiestrze** to play in an orchestra **2** *(o ubiorze)*: **człowiek z czarną opaską na oku** a man with a black patch over his eye; **pojawiła się starsza kobieta w czerni** an elderly woman in black appeared **3** *(wskazując na postać)*: **sztuka w trzech aktach** a play in three acts; **mleko w proszku** powdered milk; **honorarium w gotówce** a cash fee **4** *(o czasie)*: **w dniu 3 listopada 2005** on the 3rd November 2005;

wa|da (**-dy, -dy**; *dat sg & loc sg* **-dzie**) *f* **1** *(ujemna cecha: towaru)* disadvantage **2** *(Med: nieprawidłowość)* defect **3** *(usterka)* fault
wa|ga (**-gi, -gi**; *dat sg & loc sg* **-dze**) *f* **1** *(przyrząd)* scales *pl* **2** *(znaczenie)* significance **3** *(Astrologia)*: **W~** Libra; **wydarzenie ogromnej wagi** an event of enormous significance
wago|n (**-nu, -ny**; *loc sg* **-nie**) *m (Rail)* **1** *(pasażerski)* carriage *(Brit)*, car *(US)* **2** *(towarowy)* wagon *(Brit)*, freight car *(US)*; **~ dla niepalących** no-smoking carriage
wah|ać się (**-am, -asz**) *vr (pf* **za-**) to hesitate
wakacj|e (**-i**) *pl (letnie, zimowe)* holiday(s *pl) (Brit)*, vacation *(sg) (US)*; **byłem na wakacjach w Polsce** I was on holiday *lub* vacation in Poland; **rodzina jechała na ~** the family used to go on holiday *lub* vacation
walcz|yć (**-ę, -ysz**) *vi* to struggle; **musimy ~ o** *lub* **za prawa człowieka** we have to fight for human rights; **walczyła z chorobą** she struggled against illness
Wali|a (**-i**) *f* Wales
walijski *adj* Welsh
Walijczy|k (**-ka, -cy**; *inst sg* **-kiem**)

m Welshman

Walij|ka (-ki, -ki; *dat sg* **-ce**; *gen pl* **-ek**) *f* Welshwoman

wal|ić (-ę, -isz; *pf* **-nąć**) *vt, vi* (*pot*) to thump; **~ się** *vr* (*mur, dom*) to collapse

waliz|ka (-ki, -ki; *dat sg & loc sg* **-ce**; *gen pl* **-ek**) *f* (*skórzana, podróżna*) (suit)case

wal|ka (-ki, -ki; *dat sg & loc sg* **-ce**; *gen pl* **-k**) *f* fight; **~ na śmierć i życie** battle of life and death

walu|ta (-ty, -ty; *dat sg & loc sg* **-cie**) *f* foreign currency; **silna/ twarda ~** strong/hard currency

wam *pron dat od* **wy**

wampi|r (-ra, -ry; *loc sg* **-rze**) *m* vampire

wandal (-a, -e; *gen pl* **-i** *lub* **-ów**) *m* vandal

wanili|a (-i) *f* vanilla

waniliowy *adj* (*aromat do pieczenia*) vanilla

wan|na (-ny, -ny; *dat sg & loc sg* **-nie**) *f* bath(tub)

waria|t (-ta, -ci; *loc sg* **-cie**) *m* (*pot*) madman; **dom ~ów** (*pot*) madhouse

wari|ować (-uję, -ujesz; *pf* **z-**) *vi* (*pot*) to go crazy

warkocz (-a, -e; *gen pl* **-y**) *m* (*z włosów*) plait (*Brit*), braid (*US*)

Warsza|wa (-wy; *dat sg & loc sg* **-wie**) *f* Warsaw

wart *adj*: **~ pięć tysięcy złotych** worth 5,000 zlotys; **jeden jest ~ drugiego** each is as bad as the other; **~ jest każdej ceny** it's worth any amount of money; **bez miłości świat nic nie jest ~** without love, the world is worth nothing

warto *inv*: **~ zobaczyć** (*pf*)**/ zrobić** (*pf*) it's worth seeing/ doing

wartościowy *adj* (*książka, znajomość, człowiek*) valuable; **papiery wartościowe** (*Fin*) securities

wartoś|ć (-ci) *f* value, worth; **wartości** *pl* (*w filozofie*) values; **towar o wartości 1000 dolarów** 1000 dollars' worth of goods; **fotka nie ma wartości artystycznej** the photo has no artistic value

warun|ek (-ku, -ki; *inst sg* **-kiem**) *m* condition; **warunki** *pl* conditions; **pod warunkiem, że...** on condition (that)...; **pod pewnymi warunkami** under certain conditions

warzywny *adj* vegetable; **bulion ~** vegetable broth; **stragan ~** vegetable stall

warzy|wo (-wa, -wa; *loc sg* **-wie**) *nt* (*smaczne, soczyste, zdrowe*) vegetable

was *pron gen, acc, loc od* **wy**

wasz *possessive pron* **1** (*z rzeczownikiem*) your **2** (*bez rzeczownika*) yours; **~ dom** your house

Watyka|n (-nu; *loc sg* **-nie**) *m* the Vatican

wazo|n (-nu, -ny; *loc sg* **-nie**) *m* (*szklany, kryształowy, ceramiczny*) vase

ważny *adj* **1** (*informacja, osoba*) important **2** (*dokument*) valid **3** (*pot: osoba: zarozumiały*) self-important

waż|yć (-ę, -ysz; *pf* **z-**) *vt* to weigh ▷ *vi*: **on waży 100 kg** he weighs

100 kg; **~ się** vr **1** (Dosl) to weigh o.s. **2** (wynik nieprzewidywalny) to hang in the balance

wą|s (**-sa, -sy**; loc sg **-sie**) m (usu pl) moustache (Brit), mustache (US); **wąsy** pl **1** (u mężczyzny) moustache sg (Brit), mustache sg (US) **2** (u kota) whiskers

wąski adj narrow

wąt|ek (**-ku, -ki**; inst sg **-kiem**) m **1** (powieści) thread **2** (wykładu, filmu, powieści) theme; **chciałbym podjąć ~** I should like to pick up the theme

wąt|pić (**-pię, -pisz**) vi to doubt; **nikt nie wątpił w legalność jego majątku** nobody doubted that his wealth was legally come by; **wątpię o twoich zdolnościach** I am doubtful about your abilities; **wątpię** I doubt it

wątpliwoś|ć (**-ci, -ci**; gen pl **-ci**) f doubt; **istnieją wątpliwości co do jego uczciwości** doubts exist about his honesty; **nie ulega wątpliwości, że jest winny** there's no doubt that he is guilty

wątr|oba (**-oby, -oby**; dat sg & loc sg **-obie**; gen pl **-ób**) f liver

wąż (**węża, węże**; gen pl **węży** lub **węży**) m **1** (Zool) snake **2** (rura) hose

wbrew prep +dat contrary to; **~ naturze** against nature; **~ zakazowi ojca** in defiance of her father

WC, w.c. abbr WC

wcale adv **1** (w ogóle) (not) at all **2** (całkiem: pot) quite; **~ nie!** not at all!; **~ często** quite often

wcho|dzić (**-dzę, -dzisz**; imp **-dź**; pf **wejść**) vi +gen **1** (do budynku)

to enter **2** (do samochodu) to get in; **wejść do firmy** to join the firm; **wszedła do Internetu** she went on (to) the internet; **klucz wchodził do zamka** the key went into the lock; **wyrzucą go drzwiami, a on wchodzi oknem** throw him out the door, he will come in the window

wciąg|ać (**-am, -asz**; pf **-nąć**) vt **1** to pull (in) **2** (powietrze) to draw in **3** (buty, spodnie) to pull on

wciąż adv still

wczas|y (**-ów**) pl holiday sg (Brit), vacation sg (US); **jechał pan na ~** he went on holiday (Brit) lub vacation (US)

wcze|sny adj **1** (ranek, śnieg, godzina) early **2** (przedwczesny) premature

wcześnia|k (**-ka, -ki**; inst sg **-kiem**) m premature baby

wcześnie adv early; **za ~ jeszcze wyrokować** it's still too early to say

wcześniej adv comp od **wcześnie**; (zawczasu) beforehand

wcześniejszy adj comp od **wczesny**; (poprzedzający) previous

wczoraj adv yesterday; **~ rano/ wieczorem** yesterday morning/ evening; **~ w nocy widziałem wilka** last night I saw a wolf

wczorajszy adj yesterday's

wd|owa (**-owy, -owy**; dat sg & loc sg **-owie**; gen pl **-ów**) f widow

wdo|wiec (**-wca, -wcy**) m widower

wdych|ać (**-am, -asz**) vt to breathe in

wdzięczny adj **1** grateful **2** (uroczy: uśmiech, spojrzenie)

graceful **3** (*korzystny*) rewarding
we *prep* = **w**
według *prep* +*gen* according to;
~ mojej matki according to my
mother
weeken|d (**-du, -dy;** *loc sg* **-dzie**)
m weekend
wegetariański *adj* (*danie,
restauracja, dieta*) vegetarian
wejś|cie (**-cia**) *nt* **1** (*wstęp*) access
2 (*zajnomości*) connections *pl*
3 (*nom pl* **-cia**; *gen pl* **-ć**) (*drzwi*)
entrance; „**~**" "entrance"
wej|ść (**-dę, -dziesz;** *imp* **-dź**; *pt*
wszedł, weszła, weszli) *vb pf od*
wchodzić; **(proszę) ~!** come in!
weł|na (**-ny, -ny;** *dat sg* & *loc sg*
-nie; *gen pl* **-en**) *f* wool
Wenezuel|a (**-i**) *f* Venezuela
werdyk|t (**-tu, -ty;** *loc sg* **-cie**) *m*
(*ostateczny, sądowy*) verdict
wersal|ka (**-ki, -ki;** *dat sg* & *loc
sg* **-ce;** *gen pl* **-ek**) *f* (*rozkładana,
wygodna*) sofa bed
wersj|a (**-i, -e;** *gen pl* **-i**) *f* (*językowa,
odmienna*) version
wesel|e (**-a, -a**) *nt* (*huczne,
wystawne*) wedding
wes|oło *adv* happily; **było bardzo
~** it was great fun
wesoły *adj* cheerful; **wesołe
miasteczko** funfair (*Brit*),
amusement park (*US*); **W~ch
Świąt!** (*na Boże Narodzenie*) Merry
Christmas!; (*na Wielkanoc*) Happy
Easter!
weszła *itd. vb zob.* **wejść**
wewnątrz *prep* +*gen* inside ▷ *adv*
inside; **pomieszczenie było
zamknięte od** *lub* **z ~** the flat was
locked from the inside
wewnętrznie *adv* internally

wewnętrzny *adj* **1** internal
2 (*Bud: drzwi, ściany*) interior
3 (*Ekon: handel*) domestic
4 (*Psych: spokój, życie*) inner
▷ *m decl like adj* (*też:* **numer**
lub **telefon ~**) extension;
Ministerstwo Spraw W~ch
Ministry of the Interior, ≈ Home
Office (*Brit*)
wezmę *itd. vb zob.* **wziąć**
weź *itd. vb zob.* **wziąć**
węch (**-u**) *m* **1** (*zmysł: wyostrzony*)
(sense of) smell **2** (*przen*) nose
węd|ka (**-ki, -ki;** *dat sg* & *loc sg* **-ce;**
gen pl **-ek**) *f* fishing rod; **złapać
na wędkę** to catch with rod
and line
wędli|na (**-ny, -ny;** *dat sg* & *loc sg*
-nie) *f* smoked meat(*s pl*)
wędrów|ka (**-ki, -ki;** *dat sg* & *loc sg*
-ce; *gen pl* **-ek**) *f* **1** (*podróż: daleka,
górska*) trek **2** (*piesza*) walking
tour
wę|giel (**-gla**) *m* **1** (*Geol*) coal
2 (*Chem*) carbon; **~ do rysowania**
charcoal; **~ kamienny/brunatny**
bituminous coal/brown coal
węgierski *adj* Hungarian
Wę|gry (**-gier;** *loc pl* **-grzech**) *pl*
Hungary
węższy *adj comp od* **wąski**
WF, wf. *abbr* (= *wychowanie
fizyczne*) PE
wg *abbr* (= *według*) according to
wiadomoś|ć (**-ci, -ci;** *gen pl* **-ci**) *f*
1 (*informacja*) message **2** (*Radio,
TV*) news item; **wiadomości** *pl*
(*wiedza*) **1** information **2** (*Radio,
TV*) the news; **podawać coś
do publicznej wiadomości** to
make sth generally known; **nie
przymuję tego do wiadomości** I

don't accept that

wiad|ro (**-ra**, **-ra**; *loc sg* **-rze**; *gen pl* **-er**) *nt* bucket; **~ wody** bucket of water

wi|ara (**-ary**; *dat sg & loc sg* **-erze**) *f* faith; **~ w Boga** faith in God; **straciła wiarę w siebie** she has lost self-confidence; **wyznanie wiary** (*Rel*) the Creed

wiarogodny, **wiarygodny** *adj* **1** (*wiadomość, człowiek*) credible **2** (*źródło historyczne*) reliable; **~ świadek** a credible witness

wi|atr (**-atru**, **-atry**; *loc sg* **-etrze**) *m* wind; **wiatry** *pl*: **puszczać ~y** to break wind; **pod ~** into the wind; **z ~em** with the wind; **kto sieje ~, zbiera burzę** sow the wind and reap the whirlwind; **biednemu zawsze ~ w oczy** things are always harder if you're poor

widel|ec (**-ca**, **-ce**) *m* fork

wideo *nt inv* video ▷ *adj*: **kaseta ~** video (cassette); **kamera ~** video camera

widny *adj* (*mieszkanie, pokój, pomieszczenie*) light

wido|k (**-ku**, **-ki**; *inst sg* **-kiem**) *m* **1** (*krajobraz: rozległy, zapierający dech w piersiach*) view **2** (*obraz*) sight; **widoki** *pl* (*perspektywy*) prospects

widoków|ka (**-ki**, **-ki**; *dat sg & loc sg* **-ce**; *gen pl* **-ek**) *f* postcard

widowis|ko (**-ka**, **-ka**; *inst sg* **-kiem**) *nt* (*teatralne, cyrkowe*) spectacle

widow|nia (**-ni**, **-nie**; *gen pl* **-ni**) *f* **1** (*widzowie*) audience **2** (*sala dla widzów*) auditorium; **siedzieć na widowni** to sit in the audience

widz (**-a**, **-owie**) *m* **1** (*TV*) viewer **2** (*Sport*) spectator **3** (*świadek: przygodny, przypadkowy*) bystander; **widzowie** *pl* (*publiczność, widownia*) audience

wi|dzieć (**-dzę**, **-dzisz**) *vt*, *vi* to see; **widzę Pałac Prezydencki I** (can) see the Presidential Palace; **widziała już tę sztukę** she has already seen this play; **widzę, że nie ma wszystkich** I can see that they aren't all there; **powinien ~ więcej niż swój nos!** we have to take a broader view here; **sam widzisz, że mamy ograniczone pole manewru** you can see for yourself we have limited room for manoeuvre; **widzimy się z nim jedynie w święta Bożego Narodzenia** we only see him at Christmas

wieczny *adj* eternal; **wieczne miasto Rzym** Rome, the eternal city

wieczorny *adj* **1** (*wczesnym wieczorem: pociąg, seans*) evening **2** (*późnym wieczorem*) night

wiecz|ór (**-oru**, **-ory**; *loc sg* **-orze**) *m* **1** (*część doby*) evening **2** (*impreza: literacki*) soirée; **~ autorski** a meet-the-author event; **dobry ~!** good evening!; **dzisiaj wieczorem** this evening; **wczoraj wieczorem** last night; **co ~** every evening

wiedz|a (**-y**) *f* knowledge; **posiada gruntowną wiedzę z zakresu** she has a sound knowledge of the field; **bez wiedzy matki** without his mother's knowledge

wiedzieć (**wiem**, **wiesz**; *imp*

wiedz) *vt* to know ▷ *vi*: **~ o rolnictwie** to know about agriculture; **wie to od mamy** she knows that from her mum; **wiesz co?** (*pot*) (do) you know what?; **wiem to z własnego doświadczenia** I know from personal experience; **niewiele wiem na ten temat** I don't know much about that

wiejski *adj* 1 (*okolica*) country 2 (*ubranie*) farmer's 3 (*przemysł, życie*) rural

wie|k (**-ku**, **-ki**; *inst sg* **-kiem**) *m* 1 (*liczba lat*) age 2 (*stulecie*) century; **pod koniec XX ~u** the 20th century; **~i średnie** the Middle Ages; **~ szkolny** school age; **~ emerytalny** retirement age; **zespół osób starszego ~u** a group of older people; **jesteśmy w tym samym ~u** we are the same age

wiel|bić (**-bię**, **-bisz**) *vt* to worship

wielbłą|d (**-da**, **-dy**; *loc sg* **-dzie**) *m* (*dwugarbny*) camel

wiele *pron* **~** (+*gen*) a lot (of) ▷ *adv* much, a lot; **na początku ~ kobiet to mówiło** that's what lots of women said, to begin with; **oddał ~ pieniędzy** he spent a lot of money; **podróż samolotem jest o ~ szybsza niż jazda pociągiem** air travel is a lot quicker than the train; **wielu studentów pojechało do Paryża** a lot of students went to Paris; **wyniki końcowe są o ~ lepsze** the final results are a lot better

Wielka Brytania (**Wielkiej Brytanii**) *f* Great Britain

Wielkanoc (**-y**, **-e**) *f* Easter

wielkanocny *adj* (*pisanka, obiad, nabożeństwo*) Easter

wielki *adj* 1 (*ogromny*) large 2 (*znaczny*) great; **W~ Tydzień** (*Rel*) Holy Week; **W~ Piątek** (*Rel*) Good Friday; **W~ Post** (*Rel*) Lent; **Aleksander W~** Alexander the Great; **miała ~e, ciemne oczy** she had big dark eyes; **~ mi ekspert!** what an idiot I am!; **wielka szkoda, że się nie zobaczymy!** too bad we can't see each other!

Wielkopols|ka (**-ki**; *dat sg & loc sg* **-ce**) *f* Greater Poland (*a lowland area in Central Poland containing the ancient capital, Gniezno*)

wielokrotnie *pron* repeatedly

wieloznaczny *adj* (*komentarz, uśmiech*) ambiguous

wielu *pron zob.* **wiele**

wieprzowi|na (**-ny**; *dat sg & loc sg* **-nie**) *f* pork

wieprzowy *adj* (*kotlet*) pork

wiernie *adv* faithfully; **~ naśladować** to copy exactly

wiernoś|ć (**-ci**) *f* 1 faithfulness 2 (*Tech: w odtwarzaniu dźwięków*) fidelity

wierny *adj* faithful; **wierni** *pl* (*Rel*) the faithful; **~ jak pies** (*przen*) faithful as a dog

wiersz (**-a**, **-e**; *gen pl* **-y**) *m* 1 (*utwór*) poem 2 (*linijka wiersza*) line

wierz|yć (**-ę**, **-ysz**) *vi*: **czy wierzysz w niebo i piekło?** do you believe in heaven and hell?; **taka była wersja urzędowa, w którą oczywiście nikt nie wierzył** that was the official version, which obviously nobody

believed; **~ (u~** *pf*) **komuś** to
believe sb; **teraz już mi wierzysz?**
do you believe me now?

wiesz|ać (**-am, -asz**; *pf* **powiesić**)
vt to hang; **~ się** *vr* to hang o.s.;
~ na kimś psy (*przen*) to bad-
mouth sb

wiesza|k (**-ka, -ki**; *inst sg* **-kiem**)
m **1** (*do wieszania ubrań*) stand
2 (*kawalek drut*) loop

wieś (**wsi, wsie**; *gen pl* **wsi**) *f*
1 (*okolica: zapadła, głucha*) country
2 (*miejscowość*) village; **mieszkać
na wsi** to live in the country

wi|eść (**-odę, -edziesz**; *imp*
-edź; *pt* **-ódł, -odła, -edli**) *vt*
1 (*prowadzić: życie*) to lead **2** (*pf*
po-) (*przewodzić*) to lead; **~się** (*pf*
po-) *vr*: **wiodło jej się nieźle** I
was doing OK

Wietna|m (**-mu**; *loc sg* **-mie**) *m*
Vietnam

wietrzny *adj* (*dzień, pogoda,
klimat*) windy; **czy ma właśnie
ospę wietrzną?** has he really got
chickenpox?

wiewiór|ka (**-ki, -ki**; *dat sg & loc sg*
-ce; *gen pl* **-ek**) *f* squirrel

wi|eźć (**-ozę, -eziesz**; *imp* **-eź**;
pt **-ózł, -ozła, -eźli**; *pf* **za-**) *vt*
(*przewozić*) to carry

wież|a (**-y, -e**) *f* **1** (*Archit*) tower
2 (*w szachach*) castle; **~ Babel** the
tower of Babel

więc *conj* so; **tak ~** thus;
zmęczyła się, a ~ usiadła she
was tired, so she sat down;
**wszyscy kraje Europejskie,
a ~ Francja, Niemcy,..** all the
countries of Europe, that is
France, Germany,....

więcej *adv comp od* **dużo,**

wiele more; **nikt ~ nie jest
zainteresowany** nobody else
is interested; **nic ~ nie trzeba
mówić** nothing more *lub* else
need be said; **nigdy ~!** never
again!; **coraz ~** once again;
mniej ~ more or less; **zarabiasz ~
niż ja** you earn more than me

większoś|ć (**-ci**) *f* majority; **~
banków oferuje już usługę
bankowości elektronicznej**
most banks now offer an
electronic banking service; **w
większości przypadków, miała
rację** in most cases she was right

większy *adj comp od* **duży, wielki**

więzie|nie (**-nia**) *nt* (*nom pl* **-nia**;
gen pl **-ń**) prison; **dziesięć lat
siedział w więzieniu** he did ten
years in prison

wię|zień (**-źnia, -źniowie**) *m*
prisoner

wigili|a (**-i, -e**; *gen pl* **-i**) *f*
(*święto*): **W~** Christmas Eve

○ **WIGILIA**
○
○
○ **Wieczór wigilijny** (Christmas
○ Eve) is the most important
○ part of Christmas for Poles.
○ After the first star appears
○ in the sky, the family begins
○ supper by breaking wafers
○ together and exchanging
○ good wishes. The supper
○ should be made up of twelve
○ dishes, such as: **barszcz z
○ uszkami, pierogi z kapustą**,
○ and the obligatory carp.
○ After supper, the family sings
○ Christmas carols and they
○ give each other presents.

wigilijny adj: **wieczór ~** Christmas Eve; **kolacja wigilijna** Christmas Eve supper

wilgo|ć (-ci) f damp

wilgotny adj damp

wi|na (-ny, -ny; dat sg & loc sg **-nie)** f **1** (przyczyna złego) fault **2** (za zły czyn) blame; **nie poczuje się do winy** he doesn't feel guilty; **czyja to ~?** whose fault is it?

win|da (-dy, -dy; dat sg & loc sg **-dzie)** f lift (Brit), elevator (US)

wi|nić (-nię, -nisz; imp **-ń)** vt: **~ kogoś za coś** to blame sb for sth

wi|no (-na, -na; loc sg **-nie)** nt (wytrawne, półsłodkie, musujące) wine

winogro|no (-na, -na; loc sg **-nie)** nt grape

wiosenny adj (poranek, promocja, wyprzedaż) spring

wio|sna (-sny, -sny; dat sg & loc sg **-śnie;** gen pl **-sen)** f spring; **wiosną** lub **na wiosnę** in the springtime

wiozę vb zob. **wieźć**

wiru|s (-sa, -sy; loc sg **-sie)** m virus; **~ grypy** flu virus

wi|sieć (-szę, -sisz; imp **-ś)** vi to hang; **jego życie wisi na włosku** (przen) his life is hanging by a thread

Wi|sła (-sły; dat sg & loc sg **-śle)** f the Vistula

wi|śnia (-śni, -śnie; gen pl **-śni** lub **-sien)** f **1** (owoc: cierpka, dojrzała) cherry **2** (Bot: drzewo) cherry (tree)

wit|ać (-am, -asz; pf **po-** lub **przy-)** vt to welcome; **witamy w Lublinie!** welcome to Lublin!; **~ się** (pf **przy-)** vr: **witała się z każdym** she greeted everyone

witami|na (-ny, -ny; dat sg & loc sg **-nie)** f vitamin; **~ B** vitamin B

wi|za (-zy, -zy; dat sg & loc sg **-zie)** f visa; **pańska ~ wygasła** your visa has expired

wizy|ta (-ty, -ty; dat sg & loc sg **-cie)** f **1** visit **2** (u lekarza, dentysty itp.) appointment; **następnego dnia złożyła mi wizytę** next day she paid me a visit

wizytów|ka (-ki, -ki; dat sg & loc sg **-ce;** gen pl **-ek)** f (business) card

wj|azd (-azdu, -azdy; loc sg **-eździe)** m **1** (czynność) entrance **2** (brama) access; **triumfalny ~ cesarza do miasta** the emperor's triumphal entry into the city; **~ dla wózków inwalidzkich** wheelchair access; **„zakaz ~u"** "no entry"

wj|echać (-adę, -edziesz; imp **-edź)** vb pf od **wjeżdżać**

wjeżdż|ać (-am, -asz; pf **wjechać)** vi **1** (do wewnątrz) to drive in **2** (wyżej) to go up **3** (Rail: na stację) to pull in; **ciężarówka wjechała w dom** the lorry ran into a house

wkład|ać (-am, -asz; pf **włożyć)** vi to put in; **wkładała list w powrotem do szuflady** she put the letter back into the drawer; **włóż płaszcz!** put on your coat!

wkoło prep +gen around

wkrótce adv soon

wlat|ywać (-uję, -ujesz; pf **wlecieć)** vi **1** (o ptakach) to fly in **2** (o dymie, osobach) to rush in

władz|a (-y) f power; **władze** pl (państwowe, lokalne) the authorities; **dojść do władzy** to come to power; **on ma nad nią tajemną władzę** he has

a mysterious hold over her;
**pacjent nie był w pełni władz
umysłowych** the patient was not
in full possession of his faculties
włama|nie (-nia, -nia; gen pl -ń) nt
burglary; **dokonywać** (**dokonać**
pf) **włamania do sejfu** to break in
to a safe; **ślady włamania** signs
of a break-in
włamywacz (-a, -e; gen pl -y) m
burglar
włam|ywać się (-uję, -ujesz; pf
-ać) vr to break in
własnoś|ć (-ci) f 1 (majątek)
property 2 (Jur) ownership; **mieć
coś na ~** to be the owner of sth
własny adj: **mój/jego/jej ~**
my/his/her own; **mówić ~mi
słowami** to talk in one's own
words; **dbać o własną skórę** to
look out for oneself; **każdy ma
własne zdanie** everybody has
their own opinion
właściciel (-a, -e; gen pl -i) m
owner
właściciel|ka (-ki, -ki; dat sg & loc
sg -ce; gen pl -ek) f owner
właściwie adv 1 (należycie)
correctly 2 (tak naprawdę) actually
właśnie adv: **dlatego właśnie
dziś wrócił?** why did he have to
come back today (of all days)?; **to
~ mam zamiar powiedzieć** that's
just what I plan to say; **~ idzie/
przyjechał** he is just coming/has
just arrived; **~ widzę, że pan
jest zajęty** as a matter of fact I
can see that you are busy; **i o to
~ chodzi!** and that's what it's all
about!; **(no) ~!** just so!
Wło|chy (-ch; loc pl -szecg) pl
Italy

wło|s (-sa, -sy; loc sg -sie) m hair;
włosy pl (blond, gęste) hair sg
wł|ożyć (-ożę, -ożysz; imp -óż) vb
pf od **wkładać**
włoski adj Italian
wnętrznośc|i (-i) pl entrails;
wypatroszyć ~ to gut
wni|eść (-osę, -esiesz; imp -eś;
pt -ósł, -osła, -eśli) vb pf od
wnosić
wnikliwy adj 1 (badanie) careful
2 (zapach, dźwięk) penetrating
wnios|ek (-ku, -ki; inst sg -kiem)
m 1 (propozycja) proposal 2 (wynik
rozumowania) conclusion
3 (podanie) application; **musimy
dojść do wniosku, że…** we have
to reach the conclusion that…;
wyciągnęła ~, że… she drew the
conclusion that…
wno|sić (-szę, -sisz; imp -ś; pf
wnieść) vt 1 (umieścić we wnętrzu)
to carry in 2 (przen: radość) to
bring 3 (Fin: opłatę, składkę) to pay
4 (przedstawić: podanie) to put in
WNP abbr (= Wspólnota
Niepodległych Państw) CIS
(= Commonwealth of Independent
States)
wnucz|ek (-ka, -kowie; inst sg
-kiem) m grandson
wnucz|ka (-ki, -ki; dat sg & loc sg
-ce; gen pl -ek) f granddaughter
wnu|k (-ka, -kowie lub -ki; inst sg
-kiem) m grandson; **wnuki** pl
grandchildren
wo|da (-dy, -dy; dat sg & loc sg
-dzie; gen pl wód) f water; **~
miękka/twarda** soft/hard
water; **~ słodka/morska** fresh/
salt water; **~ pitna** drinking
water; **~ święcona** holy water; **~**

powierzchniowa surface water;
spuszczać (spuścić pf**) wodę** to
flush the toilet
Wodni|k (-ka, -ki; inst sg **-kiem)** m
(Astrologia) Aquarius
woj. abbr (= województwo): **~
lublinskie** Lublin Region
województ|wo (-wa, -wa; loc
sg **-wie)** nt region; **~ lublinskie**
Lublin region

- WOJEWÓDZTWO
-
- **Województwo** is an
- administrative unit in
- Poland (the equivalent
- of English "regions"). The
- number of **województwa** has
- changed over the centuries
- and currently there are 16.
- **Województwa** also make
- up part of local government
- – many decisions concerning
- the life of the local community
- are made at this level.

woj|na (-ny, -ny; dat sg & loc
sg **-nie;** gen pl **-en)** f war;
pierwsza/druga ~ światowa
the First/Second World War; **~
partyzancka** guerilla war; **~
domowa** civil war; **~ secesyjna**
the American Civil War
wojs|ko (-ka, -ka; inst sg **-kiem)**
nt army; **pójść do wojsku** to join
the army
wojskowy adj (mundur,
koszary) military ▷ m decl like adj
serviceman
wokali|sta (-sty, -ści; dat sg & loc
sg **-ście)** m decl like f in sg singer
wokalist|ka (-ki, -ki; dat sg & loc sg

-ce; gen pl **-ek)** f singer
wokoło, wokół prep +gen round
▷ adv all around
wol|a (-i) f will; **dobra ~** goodwill;
wolna ~ free will; **brak mu
silnej woli, żeby rzucić palenie**
he hasn't got the willpower to
give up smoking; **ostatnia ~**
(testament) will; **on był tak zły,
że mimo woli musiałem się
roześmiać** he was so angry that I
involuntarily burst out laughing;
jeść do woli to eat one's fill
wol|eć (-ę, -isz) vt, vi to prefer;
wolę herbatę niż kawę I prefer
tea to coffee; **Spartanie woleli
zginąć niż się poddać** the
Spartans would rather die than
surrender; **woli o tym nie mówić**
he'd rather not talk about it;
wolę, jak drzwi są otwarte I'd
prefer the door open
wolno¹ adv **1** (powoli) slowly
2 (swobodnie) freely; **~ stojący
budynek** a free-standing
building
wolno² inv: **tu nie ~ palić** you
can't smoke here; **nie ~ mi palić**
I'm not allowed to smoke; **są
sprawy, o których nie ~ nam
nigdy zapomnieć** there are
things that we have no right ever
to forget; **czy ~ o coś zapytać?**
can I ask you something?
wolnoś|ć (-ci) f freedom
wolny adj **1** (niezależny) free
2 (niezajęty) free **3** (nieżonaty/
niezamężna) single; **3 maja jest
dniem ~m od pracy** the third of
May is a day off work; **czy pan
dyrektor jest ~?** can I have a
moment?

woł|ać (**-am, -asz**; *pf* **za-**) *vt* to call
▷ *vi* to call

wołowi|na (**-ny**; *dat sg & loc sg*
-nie) *f* beef

wołowy *adj*: **mięso wolowe** beef

wo|zić (**-żę, -zisz**; *imp* **woź** *lub*
wóź) *vt* **1** (*towar*) to transport
2 (*samochodem*) to drive

wód|ka (**-ki, -ki**; *dat sg & loc sg* **-ce**;
gen pl **-ek**) *f* vodka

wówczas *adv* then

wóz|ek (**-ka, -ki**; *inst sg*
-kiem) *m* **1** pram (*Brit*), baby
carriage (*US*) **2** (*spacerówka*)
pushchair (*Brit*), stroller (*US*);
~ inwalidzki wheelchair; **~
w supermarkecie/lotnisku**
shopping/baggage trolley

WP *abbr* **1** (= *Wielmożny Pan*) Mr
2 (= *Wielmożna Pani*) Mrs, Ms
3 (= *Wielmożni Państwo*) Mr and
Mrs **4** (= *Wojsko Polskie*) Polish
Army

wpad|ać (**-am, -asz**; *pf* **wpaść**) *vt*
to fall; **~ w panikę** to fall into a
panic; **~ w długi** to run into debt

wpa|ść (**-dnę, -dniesz**; *imp*
-dnij; *pt* **-dł, -dła, -dli**) *vb pf od*
wpadać; **samochód wpadł na
drzewo/wpadł w poślizg** the car
ran into a tree/went into a skid;
mój ojciec wpadł pod pociąg
my father was hit by a train; **na
chwilę wpadła w rozpacz** for a
time she fell victim to despair;
~ w pułapkę to fall into a trap;
może wpadnę dziś wieczorem
maybe I'll drop by tonight; **piłka
wpadła do bramki** the ball went
into the net

wpatr|ywać się (**-uję, -ujesz**; *pf*
wpatrzyć) *vr*: **~ się w** to stare at;

~ się jak sroka w kość (*przen*) to
stare intently

wpi|s (**-su, -sy**; *loc sg* **-sie**) *m* (*w
dokumentach*) entry; **~ do księgi
zwiedzających** an entry in the
visitors' book

wpis|ywać (**-uję, -ujesz**; *pf* **-ać**)
vt **1** to write down **2** (*do rejestru*)
to add

wpła|cać (**-cam, -casz**; *pf*
-cić) *vt* to pay (in); **~ składki
członkowskie** to pay a
membership fee

wpły|w (**-wu, -wy**; *loc sg*
-wie) *m* influence; **wpływy**
pl **1** (*Fin: przychody*) takings
2 (*Teatr: znajomości*) influential
friends; **czy wierzysz we ~
gwiazd na los ludzki?** do you
believe that the stars have an
influence on human affairs?

wpływ|ać (**-am, -asz**; *pf*
wpłynąć) *vi* to come in; **okręt
wpływał do portu** the boat
entered harbour; **pieniądze
wpłynęły na konto parafialne**
money poured into the parish's
account; **to może źle wpłynąć
na pana zdrowie** that can
have an adverse effect on your
health

wpływowy *adj* (*znajomy, polityk*)
influential

wrac|ać (**-am, -asz**; *pf* **wrócić**)
vi to return; **kiedy pan wróci?**
when will you be back?; **wróćmy
do pierwszego pytania** let's
return to the first question

wraz *adv*: **~ z matką zginęło
w wypadku dwoje dzieci** the
accident claimed the lives of two
children along with their mother

wraże|nie (**-nia**, **-nia**; *gen pl* **-ń**) *nt* impression; **ulegam wrażeniu, że...** I have the feeling that...; **ona zrobił złe ~ na mnie** she made a bad impression on me

wrażliwoś|ć (**-ci**) *f* sensitivity

wrażliwy *adj* (*skóra, zmysł węchu*) sensitive; **był bardzo ~m na krzywdę zwierząt** he was very sensitive to animal cruelty; **czy jest pan ~ na ból?** are you sensitive to pain?; **testy są bardzo wrażliwe na zmiany temperatury** the tests are sensitive to changes in temperature

wrób|el (**-la**, **-le**; *gen pl* **-li**) *m* sparrow

wró|cić (**-cę**, **-cisz**; *imp* **-ć**) *vb pf od* **wracać**

wr|óg (**-oga**, **-ogowie**; *inst sg* **-ogiem**) *m* **1** (*nieprzyjaciel*) enemy **2** (*przeciwnik*) opponent

wróż|yć (**-ę**, **-ysz**) *vt* **1** (*pf* **wy-**) (*osoba: przepowiadać*) to predict **2** (*zjawisko, zachowanie: być zapowiedzią*) to foreshadow ▷ *vi*: **~ (po~** *pf*) **komuś z gwiazd** to tell sb's fortune from the stars; **moja matka wróżyła z fusów** my mother used to read fortunes in tea leaves

wrzeć (**wrę, wrzesz**; *3 sg* **wre** *lub* **wrze**; *imp* **wrzyj**) *vi* to boil

wrze|sień (**-śnia**, **-śnie**; *gen pl* **-śniów** *lub* **-śni**) *m* September

wschodni *adj* east; **wiatr ~** an east wind; **Europa W~a** Eastern Europe

wschodnioeuropejski *adj* Eastern European; **czas ~** Eastern European Time

wscho|dzić (**-dzi**; *pf* **wzejść**) *vi* **1** (*o ciałach niebieskich*) to rise **2** (*o roślinach*) to sprout

wsch|ód (**-odu**; *loc sg* **-odzie**) *m* **1** (*nom pl* **-ody**) sunrise **2** (*Geo*) (the) east; **wieje od wschodu** the wind is in the east; **W~** (*kraje wschodnie*) the East

wsi *itd. n zob.* **wieś**

wsiad|ać (**-am**, **-asz**; *pf* **wsiąść**) *vi*: **~ do autobusu/pociągu** to get on a bus/train; **~ do samochodu** to get in a car; **~ na statek** to board a ship

wskazów|ka (**-ki**, **-ki**; *dat sg & loc sg* **-ce**; *gen pl* **-ek**) *f* **1** (*zegara*) hand **2** (*przen*) indicator; **wskazówki dotyczące techniki jazdy** tips on driving technique; **zgodnie z ruchem wskazówek zegara** clockwise; **przeciwnie do ruchu wskazówek zegara** anticlockwise (*Brit*), counterclockwise (*US*)

wskaz|ywać (**-uję**, **-ujesz**; *pf* **-ać**) *vt, vi* to indicate; **czy mógłby pan wskazać powody takiej decyzji?** would you indicate the reasons for this decision?; **dziadek wskazał mnie jako wykonawcę testamentu** grandfather identified me as his executor; **wszystko wskazuje na pogarszanie się sytuacji** all signs point to the fact that the situation is getting worse

wspaniale *adv* magnificently; **to ~!** that's fantastic!

wspaniały *adj* **1** (*efektowny*) wonderful **2** (*strój, uroczystość*) magnificent; **to ~ pomysł!** that's a brilliant idea!

wspier|ać (**-am, -asz**; *pf* **wesprzeć**) *vt* to support; **~ się** *vr* (*podtrzymywać się*) to support one another; **wspierał się na lasce** he leant on his stick; **wspierali się wzajemnie w trudnych sytuacjach** they supported one another through difficult times

wspólnie *adv* together; **~ z kimś** together with sb

współczesność (**-ci**) *f* the present day

współczesny *adj* contemporary; **sztuka współczesna** contemporary art

współczuci|e (**-a**) *nt* sympathy; **proszę przyjąć najszczersze wyrazy współczucia** may I offer my most sincere condolences

współcz|uć (**-uję, -ujesz**) *vi*: **~ komuś** to feel sorry for sb; **~ komuś (z powodu czegoś)** to offer sb one's sympathy (over sth)

współprac|ować (**-uję, -ujesz**) *vi* **1** to co-operate **2** (*o pisarzach*) to collaborate

wst|awać (**-aję, -ajesz**; *imp* **-awaj**; *pf* **-ać**) *vi* to get up; **wstawał bardzo późno** he used to rise late; **odstawiła kubek herbaty i wstała z krzesła** she put down her tea and stood up

wsta|wiać (**-wiam, -wiasz**; *pf* **-wić**) *vt* to set; **~ się** *vr*: **zawsze wstawiała się za synem** she would always put in a good word for her son; **dentysta wstawił ząb** the dentist replaced the tooth; **wstawiłem wodę na herbatę** I put the kettle on for tea

wstecz *adv* (*ruszyć, spojrzeć*) backwards

wstę|p (**-pu, -py**; *loc sg* **-pie**) *m* **1** (*wejście*) entry **2** (*początek: w książce*) introduction; **na ~ie kilka refleksji ogólnych** to begin with, some general reflections

wstępny *adj* **1** (*początkowy*) preliminary **2** (*prowizoryczny*) provisional; **wstępna faza prac** the initial phase; **wstępne oględziny** a preliminary examination

wstrę|t (**-tu**; *loc sg* **-cie**) *m* revulsion; **czuła do niego ~** she found him repulsive

wstrętny *adj* revolting

wsty|d (**-du**; *loc sg* **-dzie**) *m* shame; **czy tu musisz zawsze narobić mi ~u?** must you always make me ashamed of you?; **nie ~ ci, że zapomniałaś o ojcu?** don't you feel shame that you have forgotten your father?

wstydliwy *adj* bashful

wsty|dzić się (**-dzę, -dzisz**; *imp* **-dź**) *vr*: **wstydziłem się za zachowanie mojego ojca** I was embarrassed by my father's behaviour (*Brit*) *lub* behavior (*US*); **nie wstydzisz się, że kłamałaś?** aren't you ashamed that you were crying?; **czy wstydzi się własnej matki?** is he ashamed of his own mother?; **wstydziła się powiedzieć to rodzicom** she was embarrassed to tell her parents

wszedł *itd. vb zob.* **wejść**

wszędzie *adv* everywhere; **~ go pełno!** he gets everywhere!

wszyscy *pron decl like adj* all; **~ ludzie rodzą się równi** everybody is born equal; **~**

wiedzą everybody *lub* everyone knows; **wszystkich nie zadowolisz** you'll never please everybody; **~ razem!** all together!

wszystkie *pron decl like adj* all; **~ drużyny książki** all (the) teams; **na ~ sposoby** in every possible way

wszystko *pron decl like adj* everything; **mimo ~** in spite of everything; **przede wszystkim musisz mu o tym powiedzieć** first and foremost you have got to talk to him about it; **zrobiłbym ~, żeby dostać tę pracę** I'd have done anything to get that job; **gdzie pan chce usiąść? - ~ jedno** where do you wish to sit? - I don't mind; **~ w porządku?** is everything OK?; **wszystkiego najlepszego!** all the best!; **to na dzisiaj ~** that's all for today; **kiedy pan się obudzi, będzie już po wszystkim** when you wake up it will all be over

wściekły *adj* **1** (*o zwierzętach: chory na wściekliznę*) rabid **2** (*o ludzach: zły*) furious

wśród *prep* among

wtedy *pron* then; **~, kiedy...** when...

wtor|ek (**-ku, -ki**; *inst sg* **-kiem**) *m* Tuesday

wuj (**-a, -owie**) *m* uncle

wuj|ek (**-ka, -kowie**; *inst sg* **-kiem**) *m* uncle

ww. *abbr* (= *wyżej wymieniony*) above-mentioned

wy *pron* you

wybacz|ać (**-am, -asz**; *pf* **-yć**) *vt*: **~ (komuś) coś** to forgive (sb) sth

wybier|ać (**-am, -asz**; *pf* **wybrać**) *vt* **1** to choose **2** (*wodę ze studni*) to draw; **~ się** *vr*: **wybieram się do biura/do Warszawy** I'm going to the office/to Warsaw; **wybrała jego numer** she dialled his number; **wybrał sto funtów z konta** he withdrew a hundred pounds; **wybiera się w podróż/na spacer** he's going away/for a walk

wybitny *adj* (*naukowiec, osiągnięcie, dzieło*) outstanding

wyb|ór (**-oru, -ory**; *loc sg* **-orze**) *m* **1** (*zawodu*) choice; **wybory** *pl* election(s *pl*); **nie miałem wyboru** I had no choice

wybrzeż|e (**-a, -a**; *gen pl* **-y**) *nt* coast

wybuch (**-u, -y**) *m* **1** (*eksplozja*) explosion **2** (*gwałtowny początek: paniki*) outbreak; **~ wulkanu** volcanic eruption

wybuch|ać (**-am, -asz**; *pf* **-nąć**) *vi* **1** (*bomba*) to explode **2** (*panika, epidemia*) to break out **3** (*Geol: wulkan*) to erupt; **wybuchał płaczem/gniewem** he burst into tears/flared up angrily; **wybuchała śmiechem** she burst out laughing

wybuchowy *adj* **1** (*substancja*) explosive **2** (*charakter*) quick-tempered; **materiały wybuchowe** explosives

wycho|dzić (**-dzę, -dzisz**; *imp* **-dź**; *pf* **wyjść**) *vi* **1** (*opuścić miejsce*) to leave **2** (*stać się widocznym: słońce, inicjatiwa, pismo*) to come out **3** (*udać się*) to work (out); **wychodził z domu** he went out of the house; **zakładnik wyszedł**

z domu przed chwilą a hostage came out of the house a little while ago; **wychodź na spacer!** go out for a walk!; **bardzo chciałbym ~ z długów** I would love to get out of debt; **musi ~ za mąż** she has to get married; **okno moje wychodzi na zachód** my window looks west; **~ z mody** to go out of fashion

wychowawc|a (**-y, -y**) m decl like f in sg (Szkol) year-group tutor (Brit), home-room teacher (US)

wychowawczy|ni (**-ni, -nie**; gen pl **-ń**) f (Szkol) year-group tutor (Brit), home-room teacher (US)

wychow|ywać (**-uję, -ujesz**; pf **-ać**) vt **1** (uczyć) to bring up **2** (wykształcić) to educate; **~ się** vr to be brought up; **wychowywał się u dziadków** he was brought up by his grandparents

wyciecz|ka (**-ki, -ki**; dat sg & loc sg **-ce**; gen pl **-ek**) f trip, excursion; **~ piesza** a walking trip; **~ po mieście prowadzi za kościół** the city tour takes you behind the church

wycieńczony adj emaciated

wycierać (**-am, -asz**; pf **-trzeć**) vt to wipe up

wycof|ywać (**-uję, -ujesz**; pf **-ać**) vt to withdraw; **~ się** vr to withdraw; **sprawa została wykofana z sądu** the case was withdrawn

wyczerpujący adj **1** (ćwiczenie fizyczne) exhausting **2** (odpowiedź) exhaustive

wydajny adj efficient

wyda|nie (**-nia, -nia**; gen pl **-ń**) nt edition; **~ książki w miękkiej oprawie** paperback edition

wydarze|nie (**-nia, -nia**; gen pl **-ń**) nt event; **ostatnia wydarzenia na Bałkanach budzą niepokój** recent events in the Balkans are worrying

wyd|awać (**-aję, -ajesz**; pf **-ać**) vt **1** (zapłacić) to spend **2** (wystawić) to issue **3** (wydzielić) to serve; **~ się** vr **1** (wyglądać) to seem **2** (o tajemnicach) to come out; **nie mam wydać** I've got no change; **~ kogoś za mąż** to marry sb off (woman to man); **wydał opinię** he expressed an opinion; **stołówka wydaje obiady od 12.00** the canteen serves lunches from 12.00; **wydawał się zmęczony** he seemed exhausted; **wydało się prawdopodobne, że...** it seemed likely that...

wydawc|a (**-y, -y**) m publisher

wydawnict|wo (**-wa, -wa**; loc sg **-wie**) nt **1** (o instytucji) publishing house **2** (o publikacji) publication; **wydawnistwo ciągłe** a periodical

wydech (**-u, -y**) m **1** exhalation **2** (Tech: w samochodzie) exhaust

wydobrz|eć (**-eję, -ejesz**) vi pf to get better

wydorośl|eć (**-eję, -ejesz**) vi pf to grow up

wydzia|ł (**-łu, -ły**; loc sg **-le**) m **1** (w urzędzie) department **2** (w uniwersytecie) faculty

wydźwię|k (**-ku**; inst sg **-kiem**) m overtones pl; **wystawa ma ~ polityczny** the exhibition has political overtones

wyelimin|ować (**-uję, -ujesz**) vb pf od **eliminować**

wyemigr|ować (**-uję, -ujesz**) *vb pf od* **emigrować**

wygani|ać (**-am, -asz**; *pf* **wygonić** *lub* **wygnać**) *vt* to drive (out); **~ na dwór** to chase outside

wygin|ać (**-am, -asz**; *pf* **wygiąć**) *vt* to bend; **~ się** *vr* to bend

wygi|nąć (**-nie**) *vi pf* to become extinct

wyglą|d (**-du**; *loc sg* **-dzie**) *m* appearance

wygląd|ać (**-am, -asz**; *pf* **wyjrzeć**) *vi* to look; **zawsze wygląda przez okno** she is always looking out of the window; **wyglądam na kogoś kto zna cyrylicę** I am on the lookout for somebody who can read Cyrillic script; **czy grubo w tym wyglądam?** does this make me look fat?; **wyglądasz bardzo ładnie w tej sukience** you look really nice in that skirt; **nie wygląda na swoje lata** he doesn't look his age; **jak ona wygląda?** what does she look like?; **wygląda na to, że...** it looks as if...

wygłasz|ać (**-am, -asz**; *pf* **wygłosić**) *vt* (*przemówienie, kwestię*) to deliver (*a speech*)

wygłupi|ać się (**-am, -asz**) *vr* to fool about

wygłu|pić się (**-pię, -pisz**) *vr pf* to make a fool of o.s.

wyg|oda (**-ody, -ody**; *dat sg & loc sg* **-odzie**; *gen pl* **-ód**) *f* convenience; **wygody** *pl* amenities *pl*; **dom z wszelkimi ~mi** a house with all mod cons

wygodnie *adv* comfortably

wygodny *adj* **1** (*fotel*) comfortable

2 (*termin*) convenient **3** (*osoba*) comfort-loving

wygran|a (**-ej, -e**) *f decl like adj* win; **nigdy nie dawała za wygraną** she never gave up; **trafił główną wygraną** he hit the jackpot

wygryw|ać (**-am, -asz**; *pf* **wygrać**) *vt, vi* to win

wyjaś|niać (**-niam, -niasz**; *pf* **-nić**) *vt* to explain; **~ się** *vr* (*o sytuacji, sporze*) to become clear; **tajemnica się wyjaśniła** the mystery is solved

wyjaśnie|nie (**-nia, -nia**; *gen pl* **-ń**) *nt* explanation

wyj|azd (**-azdu, -azdy**; *loc sg* **-eździe**) *m* **1** (*odjazd*) departure **2** (*podróż*) journey **3** (*miejsce*) exit; **rodzinny ~ za miasto** a family trip out of town

wyjąt|ek (**-ku, -ki**; *inst sg* **-kiem**) *m* exception; **zrobiła dla mnie ~** she made an exception for me

wyjątkowo *adv* exceptionally; **~ pozwolę ci oglądać TV do późna** as an exception you can stay up late to watch TV

wyjątkowy *adj*: **uprzejmość, grzeczność** exceptional; **stan ~** (*Pol*) state of emergency

wyj|echać (**-adę, -edziesz**; *imp* **-edź**) *vb pf od* **wyjeżdżać**

wyjeżdż|ać (**-am, -asz**; *pf* **wyjechać**) *vi* **1** (*opuścić miejsce*) to go out **2** (*w podróż*) to go away

wyjm|ować (**-uję, -ujesz**; *pf* **wyjąć**) *vt* to take out; **~ pieniądze z bankomatu** to take money out of a cash machine (*Brit*) *lub* ATM

wyjrz|eć (**-ę, -ysz**; *imp* **-yj**) *vb pf od*

wyglądać

wyj|ście (-cia) *nt* **1** (*czynność*) departure **2** (*nom pl* **-cia**; *gen pl* **-ć**) (*miejsce*) exit **3** (*nom pl* **-cia**; *gen pl* **-ć**) (*z trudną sytuacją: rozwiązanie*) solution; **nie miała wyjścia, jak tylko to zrobić** she had no choice, but to do it

wyj|ść (-dę, -dziesz; *imp* **-dź**; *pt* **wyszedł, wyszła, wyszli)** *vb pf od* **wychodzić**; **~ z siebie ze złości** to fly into a rage

wyka|z (-zu, -zy; *loc sg* **-zie)** *m* (*spis*) register

wyką|pać (-pię, -piesz) *vb pf od* **kąpać**

wyklucz|ać (-am, -asz; *pf* **-yć)** *vt* to rule out; **~ się** *vr* to be mutually exclusive

wykluczony *adj*: **to jest wykluczone** it's out of the question

wykła|d (-du, -dy; *loc sg* **-dzie)** *m* lecture

wykładowc|a (-y, -y) *m decl like f in sg* lecturer

wykonawc|a (-y, -y) *m decl like f in sg* **1** (*wytwórca*) contractor **2** (*realizator: testamentu*) executor **3** (*artysta*) performer

wykon|ywać (-uję, -ujesz; *pf* **-ać)** *vt* to carry out; **wykonać rozkaz** to carry out an order; **~ zawód stolarza** to work as a joiner

wykończony *adj* finished

wykre|s (-su, -sy; *loc sg* **-sie)** *m* (*rysunek*) chart

wykształ|cać (-cam, -casz; *impf* **-cić)** *vt pf* to educate

wykształceni|e (-a) *nt* education; **~ podstawowe**

primary (*Brit*) *lub* elementary (*US*) education; **~ średnie** secondary education; **~ wyższe** higher education; **jest z wykształcenia ekonomistą** he is an economist by training

wykształ|cić (-cę, -cisz; *imp* **-ć)** *vb pf od* **kształcić, wykształcać**

wykształcony *adj* educated

wykwalifikowany *adj* (*położna, pomoc domowa*) qualified; **robotnik ~** skilled worker

wykwintny *adj* (*zapach, potrawa, strój*) (very) fine

wyląd|ować (-uję, -ujesz) *vb pf od* **lądować**

wylecz|yć (-ę, -ysz) *vb pf od* **leczyć**

wyle|w (-wu, -wy; *loc sg* **-wie)** *m*: **~ krwi do mózgu** stroke

wylew|ać (-am, -asz; *pf* **wylać)** *vt* **1** (*płyn*) to pour (out) **2** (*pot: pracownika*) to sack ▷ *vi* (*wstąpić z brzegów*) to overflow; **~ się** *vr* (*rozlewać się*) to spill; **zupa wylewała się na stół** the soup spilled over the table

wylog|ować się (-uję, -ujesz) *vi pf* (*Komput*) to log out

wylo|t (-tu, -ty; *loc sg* **-cie)** *m* exit; **nigdy nie kieruj ~u lufy karabinu w kierunku ludzi** never point the muzzle of a rifle towards people; **przejrzałem go na ~** I saw right through him; **jesteśmy na wylocie** we are just about to leave

wyluz|ować się (-uję, -ujesz) *pf vr* to chill out

wyłącz|ać (-am, -asz; *pf* **-yć)** *vt* (*prąd, telewizor*) to turn off; **~ się** *vr* (*Tel*) to hang up; **~ kogoś/coś**

(**z** +gen) to exclude sb/sth (from); **wyłączając tu obecnych** present company excepted; **czuł się wyłączony z rozmowy** he felt left out of the conversation; **wyłącz żelasko z sieci!** unplug the iron!; **dwa dania sprzeczne wzajemnie się wyłączają** two contradictory statements are mutually incompatible

wyłącznie adv exclusively

wyłączony adj switched off

wymag|ać (**-am, -asz**) vt +gen to require; **wymaga ten projekt czasu** this project requires time

wymagający adj (nauczyciel, rodzic) demanding

wymaga|nia (**-ń**) pl demands

wymagany adj (opłata, strój, dokument) required

wymeldow|ywać się (**-uję, -ujesz**; pf **-ać**) vr to check out; **~ się z hotelu** to check out of a hotel

wymia|na (**-ny, -ny**; dat **-nie**) f 1 exchange 2 (części) replacement; **kantor wymiany** bureau de change

wymie|niać (**-niam, -niasz**; pf **-nić**) vt 1 to exchange 2 (w samochodzie: olej, opony) to change 3 (waluty obce) to change 4 (wyliczać) to list; **wymienił dolary na funty** he changed dollars for pounds; **wymień pięć zwierząt żyjących w Afryce** name five animals living in Africa; **czy mogę to wymienić na rozmiar 12?** could I change this for a 12?

wymienialny adj (waluta, żeton, ubranie) convertible

wymienny adj (element) replaceable; **handel ~** barter

wymiot|ować (**-uję, -ujesz**; pf **z-**) vi to vomit

wymiot|y (**-ów**) pl vomiting sg

wymo|wa (**-wy**; dat sg & loc sg **-wie**) f 1 (Jęz) pronunciation 2 (znaczenie) significance; **to wydarzenie o szczególnej wymowie** it's an event of great significance

wymówie|nie (**-nia, -nia**; gen pl **-ń**) nt (zwolnienie) notice; **dostali miesięczne ~** they got a month's notice; **już złożyła ~** she has already put in her notice

wymusz|ać (**-am, -asz**; pf **wymusić**) vt to extort; **wymuszono na niej przynanie się do winy** they forced her into confessing her guilt

wymyśl|ać (**-am, -asz**) vt (pf **-ić**) to invent ▷ vi: **wymyślał mi** he hurled abuse at me

wynagradz|ać (**-am, -asz**; pf **wynagrodzić**) vt: **~ coś komuś** to make sth up to sb; **wynagrodzono mu straty** they made his losses up to him; **~ kogoś za poniesiony trud** to compensate sb for inconvenience

wynagrodze|nie (**-nia, -nia**; gen pl **-ń**) nt (miesięczne, tygodniowe, sowite) pay

wynajdywać (**-uję, -ujesz**; pf **wynaleźć**) vt to discover

wynaj|em (**-mu**; loc sg **-mie**) m 1 (mieszkania) renting 2 (samochodu) hiring

wynajęci|e (**-a**) nt = **wynajem**; **do wynajęcia** to let (Brit), for rent (US)

wynajm|ować (**-uję, -ujesz**; *pf* **wynająć**) *vt* **1** (*pracownika, samochód*) to hire **2** (*pokój*) to rent

wynalazc|a (**-y, -y**) *m decl like f in sg* inventor

wynalaz|ek (**-ku, -ki**; *inst sg* **-kiem**) *m* (*pożyteczny, pomysłowy, genialny*) invention

wyna|leźć (**-jdę, -jdziesz**; *imp* **-jdź**; *pt* **-lazł, -lazła, -leźli**) *vt pf od* **wynajdywać**

wyni|k (**-ku, -ki**; *inst sg* **-kiem**) *m* **1** (*doskonały, rekordowy, mierny*) result **2** (*rozmów*) outcome; **w ~u śledztwa aresztowano trzy osoby** as a result of the investigation three people have been arrested

wynik|ać (**-a**; *pf* **-nąć**) *vi* arise; **z braku informacji wynikło wiele niepozrumień** many misunderstandings arose from lack of information; **wynika z tego, że...** it follows that...

wynos *inv*: **danie na ~** a take-away (*Brit*), a take-out (*US*)

wyno|sić (**-szę, -sisz**; *imp* **-ś**; *pf* **wynieść**) *vt* **1** to take away **2** (*usunąć*) to take out **3** (*awansować*) to elevate **4** (*Mat, Fin*) to amount to; **~ się** *vr* (*pot: odchodzić*) to clear out; **koszty wynoszą cztery miliony złotych** the costs will amount to four million zlotys; **wynoś się (stąd)!** get out (of here)!

wyobraź|nia (**-ni**) *f* (*chora, bujna*) imagination

wyobraż|ać (**-am, -asz**; *pf* **wyobrazić**) *vt* to represent; **wyobraź sobie, jak nam było wstyd** imagine our embarrassment; **co ty sobie wyobrażasz!** what were you thinking!

wyobraże|nie (**-nia, -nia**; *gen pl* **-ń**) *nt* (*pogląd*) idea

wypad|ać (**-am, -asz**; *pf* **wypaść**) *vi* **1** (*wylecieć: o włosach*) to fall out **2** (*wybiegać*): **wypadł pociąg z torów** the train jumped the track **3** (*wdarzyć się*): **Wielkanoc wypada często w marcu** Easter often falls in March **4** (*wynikać*): **wypada po dwa na każde gospodarstwo** it works out at two for each farm; **wszystko wypadło dobrze** all went well; **kiedy wypada do mnie siedzenie przy dzieckach?** when is it my turn to baby-sit?; **przyjdę, jeżeli nic nie wypadnie** I'll be there, if nothing happens to stop me; **spotkanie wypadło z planu** the meeting had to be put off

wypad|ek (**-ku, -ki**; *inst sg* **-kiem**) *m* **1** (*nieszczęśliwe wydarzenie*) accident **2** (*zdarzenie*) incident; **~ typowy** a typical case; **na ~ wojny/pożaru** in case of war/fire; **w nagłych wypadkach** in cases of emergency; **nie było wypadku** on no occasion; **w tym wypadku miał rację** in that case he was right; **na wszelki ~** just in case

wypakow|ywać (**-uję, -ujesz**; *pf* **-ać**) *vt* (*plecak, walizkę, siatkę*) to unpack

wypełniony *adj* full; **~ po brzegi** full to the brim

wy|pić (**-piję, -pijesz**) *vb pf od* **pić**, **wypijać**

wypijać (-pijam, -pijasz) vb to drain (glass)

wypis|ywać (-uję, -ujesz; pf **-ać)** vt 1 (receptę) to write out 2 (formularz) to fill out 3 (zapisywać) to write down; **~ się** vr (atrament) to run out; **kiedy wypiszą ją ze szpitala?** when are they going to discharge her?; **wypisał się z kościoła ewangelickiego** he left the evangelical church

wypła|cać (-cam, -casz; pf **-cić)** vt: **~ coś (komuś)** (zaliczkę, prowizję) to pay (sb) sth

wypłacalny adj solvent

wypła|ta (-ty, -ty; dat sg & loc sg **-cie)** f (Fin: wypłacanie należności) payment; **należność do wypłaty** amount payable

wypocz|ąć (-nę, -niesz; imp **-nij)** vi pf to get some rest

wypoczęty adj (twarz, cera) well-rested

wypoczyn|ek (-ku; inst sg **-kiem)** m (letni, zimowy, aktywny) rest

wypoczyw|ać (-am, -asz; pf **wypocząć)** vi to rest

wyposażony adj: **dobrze ~** well-equipped; **łódź została wyposażona w motor** the boat was fitted with a motor

wypowie|dź (-dzi, -dzi; gen pl **-dzi)** f statement

wypożycz|ać (-am, -asz; pf **-yć)** vt: **~ coś (komuś)** to lend sth (to sb); **~ coś (od kogoś)** to borrow sth (from sb)

wypożyczal|nia (-ni, -nie; gen pl **-ni)** f hire-shop; **~ strojów karnawałowych** carnival-costume depot; **~ samochodów** car hire (Brit), auto rental (US); **~ video** video shop (Brit), video rental store (US)

wy|prać (-piorę, -pierzesz) vb pf od **prać**

wypras|ować (-uję, -ujesz) vb pf od **prasować**

wypra|wa (-wy, -wy; dat sg & loc sg **-wie)** f (ekspedycja) expedition

wyproduk|ować (-uję, -ujesz) vb pf od **produkować**

wyprze|dzać (-dzam, -dzasz; pf **-dzić)** vt 1 (w drodze) to pass 2 (być bardziej postępowym) to be ahead of

wypyt|ywać (-uję, -ujesz; pf **-ać)** vt: **~ kogoś (o coś)** to question sb (about sth)

wyra|z (-zu, -zy; loc sg **-zie)** m 1 (Ling) word 2 (objaw) expression; **~ obcy** (Ling) a foreign expression; **pisz tę petycję i daj ~ swojej złości!** sign this petition and give expression to your anger!; **~ wdzięczności** an expression of gratitude; **~y współczucia** my sympathies

wyrazisty adj 1 (gest) expressive 2 (nos) distinctive

wyraźnie adv 1 (słyszeć) distinctly 2 (zdenerwowany) evidently

wyraźny adj 1 (pismo) clear 2 (zapach) distinctive 3 (rozkaz) evident

wyraż|ać (-am, -asz; pf **wyrazić)** vt to express; **~ się** vr (wysławiać się) to express o.s.; **rodzice muszą ~ zgodę na adopcję dziecka** the parents must agree to the adoption; **napięcie prądu wyrażamy w woltach** e.m.f. is expressed in volts; **jak ty się**

wyrażasz do nauczyciela! what kind of language is that to use to the teacher!

wyraże|nie (-nia, -nia; *gen pl* -ń) *nt* (*idiomatyczne*) expression

wyro|k (-ku, -ki; *inst sg* -kiem) *m* verdict; **~ już zapadł** the verdict has already been reached; **~ skazujący** guilty verdict

wyrost|ek (-ka, -ki; *inst sg* -kiem) *m* 1 (*też:* **~ robaczkowy**) appendix 2 (*osoba*) youngster

wyrozumiały *adj* understanding

wyrzą|dzać (-dzam, -dzasz; *pf* -dzić) *vt:* **~ komuś krzywdę/ szkodę** to inflict harm/damage on sb

wyrzu|cać (-cam, -casz) *vt* (*pf* -cić) to throw away *lub* out; **~ coś komuś** to reproach sb for sth; **wyrzucić kogoś z pracy/ze szkoły** to sack sb/to exclude sb from school

wysch|nąć (-nę, -niesz; *imp* -nij; *pt* -nął *lub* wysechł, -ła, -li) *vb pf od* schnąć, wysychać

wysiad|ać (-am, -asz; *pf* wysiąść) *vi* 1 (*z pojazdu*) to get off 2 (*z samochodu*) to get out 3 (*pot: psuć się*) to pack up

wysil|ać (-am, -asz; *pf* -ić) *vt:* **~ mózg/pamięć** to rack one's brains/memory; **~ się** *vr* to exert o.s.; **~ słuch** to strain one's ears; **~ się, żeby wstać** to make an effort to get up; **~ się na grzeczność** to try hard to be polite

wysił|ek (-ku, -ki; *inst sg* -kiem) *m* (*fizyczny, umysłowy*) effort; **wysiłki** *pl* efforts; **bez (żadnego) wysiłku** effortlessly

wy|słać¹ (-ślę, -ślesz; *imp* -ślij) *vb*

pf od **wysyłać**

wy|słać² (-ścielę, -ścielisz; *imp* -ściel) *vb pf od* **wyściełać**

wysłuch|ać (-am, -asz) *vt pf* (*koncertu, wykładu*) to listen to; **~ kogoś do końca** to give sb a hearing

wy|soki *adj* 1 (*półka*) high 2 (*budynek, drzewo, człowiek*) tall 3 (*urzędnik*) high(-ranking) 4 (*Fiz: głos*) high-pitched; **~ na 3 metry** 3 metres (*Brit*) *lub* meters (*US*) high

wy|soko *adv* high (up); **~ płatna praca** highly-paid work; **~ postawione osoby** highly placed personages

wys|pa (-py, -py; *dat sg & loc sg* -pie) *f* island; **Wyspy Brytyjskie** the British Isles

wystarcz|ać (-a; *pf* -yć) *vi* to be enough; **godzina wystarczy na przygotowania** an hour will do for preparations; **trzy krzesła wystarczą** three chairs will be enough; **jego nazwisko wystarczyło za reklamę** his name was publicity enough; **czy to wystarczy?** will that do?

wystarczająco *adv:* **~ długi** long enough; **~ dużo** enough

wystarczający *adj* (*kwota, ilość*) sufficient

wystart|ować (-uję, -ujesz) *vb pf od* **startować**

wysta|wa (-wy, -wy; *dat sg & loc sg* -wie) *f* 1 (*malarstwa*) exhibition 2 (*zwierząt*) show 3 (*sklepowa*) window display

wystę|p (-pu, -py; *loc sg* -pie) *m* 1 (*popis*) performance 2 (*udział*) appearance 3 (*wystająca część*)

ledge; **występy** pl show sg
występ|ować (-**uję, -ujesz**;
pf **wystąpić**) vi **1** to occur
2 (w sądzie: zabierać głos) to
speak **3** (Film, Teatr) to appear
4 (Sport) to take part **5** (Med: o
objawach) to appear; **~ w imieniu
kogoś/czegoś** to appear in the
interests of sb/sth; **wystąpiła
z pomysłem** she came forward
with the idea; **on wstępował w
wielu filmach** he has appeared in
many films
wysusz|yć (-**ę, -ysz**) vb pf od
suszyć
wysych|ać (-**a**; pf **wyschnąć**) vi
to dry up
wysył|ka (-**ki, -ki**; dat sg & loc sg
-**ce**; gen pl -**ek**) f (listu, paczki,
towaru) dispatch
wyszczupl|eć (-**eję, -ejesz**) vi pf
to slim down
wyszedł itd. vb zob. **wyjść**
wyszkol|ić (-**ę, -isz**) vb pf od
szkolić
wyszła itd. vb zob. **wyjść**
wyściełać (-**ścielam, -ścielasz**;
imp -**ściel**) vt: **~ pudełko
materiałem** to line the box with
fabric
wyści|g (-**gu, -gi**; inst sg -**giem**)
m race; **~ szczurów** (przen) the
rat race
wyśmienity adj **1** (aktor) splendid
2 (potrawa) delicious
wyświadcz|ać (-**am, -asz**; pf
-**yć**) vt: **~ komuś grzeczność** lub
przysługę to do sb a favour (Brit)
lub favor (US)
wyświetl|ać (-**am, -asz**;
pf -**ić**) vt **1** (film) to project
2 (Komput: informację) to display

wytłumaczeni|e (-**a**) nt (proste,
oczywiste) explanation
wytłumacz|yć (-**ę, -ysz**) vb pf od
tłumaczyć
wytrwały adj persistent
wyt|rzeć (-**rę, -rzesz**; imp -**rzyj**; pt
-**arł**) vb pf od **wycierać**
wytrzeźwi|eć (-**eję, -ejesz**) vb pf
od **trzeźwieć**
wytrzym|ać (-**am, -asz**) vi pf: **nie
~** (o moście, budowli) to give way;
(o człowieku) to lose one's cool
wytrzym|ywać (-**uję, -ujesz**; pf
-**ać**) vt to bear ▷ vi to hold on
wywia|d (-**du, -dy**; loc sg
-**dzie**) m **1** (rozmowa) interview
2 (Pol, Wojsk: instytucja)
intelligence service; **~y można
przeprowadzać również przez
telefon** interviews can also be
done over the phone
wywiąz|ywać się (-**uję, -ujesz** pf
-**ać**) vr **1** (powstawać: dyskusja,
walka) to develop **2** (wypełnić
rolę) to fulfil (expectations);
wywiązywał się z obowiązków
he did his duty; **musisz
wywiązywać się z obietnic** lub
obietnicy you have got to deliver
(the goods)
wyzn|ać (-**am, -asz**) vt pf: **~ coś
(komuś)** (uczucia, tajemnicę) to
confess sth (to sb)
wyzna|nie (-**nia, -nia**; gen pl -**ń**)
nt **1** (sekretu) confession **2** (religia)
religion; **~ wiary** (Rel) the Creed
wyżej adv comp od **wysoko** ▷ adv
(w tekście) above
wyższoś|ć (-**ci**) f superiority;
patrzeć na kogoś z wyższością
to look down on sb
wyższy adj comp od **wysoki**

▷ adj **1** (wykształcenie) higher **2** (urzędnik) higher-ranking; **siła wyższa** force majeure

wyży|wić (-**wię**, -**wisz**) vr pf to feed; **~ się** vr pf to subsist

wyżywieni|e (-**a**) nt food; **pełne/ niepełne ~** full/half board

wzajemnie adv mutually; **pomagajcie sobie ~!** help one another!; **dziękuję, ~!** thank you, the same to you!

wzajemnoś|ć (-**ci**) f mutuality

wzajemny adj (pomoc, opieka, uczucie) mutual

wzdłuż prep +gen along ▷ adv (przeciąć) lengthways; **~ i wszerz** every way

wzgórz|e (-**a**, -**a**) nt hill

wziąć (**wezmę, weźmiesz**; imp **weź**) vb pf od **brać**

wzmacni|ać (-**am**, -**asz**; pf **wzmocnić**) vt **1** (siły) to build up **2** (ścianę) to reinforce **3** (sygnał) to amplify; **~ się** vr (nabierać sił) to get stronger

wzno|sić (-**szę**, -**sisz**; imp -**ś**; pf **wznieść**) vt **1** (podnosić: głowę, szablę) to raise **2** (postawić) to erect; **~ się** vr **1** (pf **wznieść**) (o ptaku) to rise **2** (piąć się w górę: o drodze) to rise **3** (wystawać: o górach) to tower; **~ kielich za kogoś/coś** to propose a toast to sb/sth

wzorowy adj **1** model **2** (uczeń) exemplary; **wzorowe sprawowanie** (Szkol) good conduct

wz|ór (-**oru**, -**ory**; loc sg -**orze**) m **1** (deseń) pattern **2** (konfekcji) model; **~ taktu** a model of tact; **ta książka może służyć za ~**

doskonałej pracy edytorskiej this book can serve as a model of outstanding editorial work

wzro|k (-**ku**; inst sg -**kiem**) m **1** (zmysł: doskonały, przenikliwy, sokoli) (eye)sight **2** (spojrzenie) gaze

wzro|st (-**stu**; loc sg -**ście**) m **1** (człowieka) height **2** (roślin) growth; **być niskiego/ średniego ~u** to be of short/medium height; **nie był wysokiego ~u** he wasn't tall; **miała prawie dwa metry ~u** she was almost two metres (Brit) lub meters (US) tall; **ile masz ~u?** how tall are you?; **~ gospodarczy** (Ekon) economic growth; **~ bezrobocia** (Ekon) a rise in unemployment

wzruszający adj (film, opowieść, książka) moving

wzrusze|nie (-**nia**, -**nia**; gen pl -**ń**) nt emotion

wzwyż adv up(wards); **skok ~** the high jump; **skoczek ~** a high jumper; **od 30 lat ~** 30 years and over

tulipanów a bunch of tulips
7 (*jakiejś dziedziny*): **on jest kiepski z fizyki** he is lousy at physics; **on jest z zawodu piekarzem** he is a baker by profession; **egzamin z historii** a history exam; **ćwiczenie z gramatyki** a grammar exercise

○ KEYWORD

z² *prep +instr* **1** (*razem z kimś*) with; **zatańcz ze mną!** dance with me! **2** (*z jakimś produktem*) with; **herbata z cytryną** tea with lemon; **kanapka z serem** bread and cheese; **z dokładnością** with accuracy
3 (*zawierający coś*) of; **dzbanek z mlekiem** a jug of milk
4 (*określając rzeczownika*) with; **oczy z długimi rzęsami** eyes with long lashes; **sklep z butami** shoe shop

○ KEYWORD

z

○ KEYWORD

z¹, **ze** *prep +gen* **1** (*wyjść lub wracać skądś*) from; **z pracy/wakacji/ kursu** from work/from holiday/ from a course
2 (*pochodzący ze źródła*) from; **z artykułu/filmu/badań** from an article/a film/research
3 (*określając czas*) from; **z wtorku/ wczoraj** from Tuesday/yesterday
4 (*część grupy*) from; **kolega ze studiów** a friend from university; **niektórzy z nas** some of us
5 (*powodu*) out of; **z bólu/ szacunku** out of pain/respect
6 (*surowiec, tworzywo*): **dzbanek z porcelany** a porcelain jug; **zrobiony z plastiku/bawełny** made of plastic/cotton; **bukiet z**

za *prep +inst* **1** (*z tyłu, poza*) behind; **za drzwiami/domem** behind the door/house; **daleko za miastem** far out of town
2 (*w kolejności, następstwie*) after; **jeden za drugim** one after another
3 (*przyczyna czynności*) for; **tęsknić za czymś** to miss sth; **gonić za przygodą** to seek adventure
▷ *prep +acc* **1** (*na tył, poza*) behind; **schować walizkę za szafę** to stow the suitcase behind the

wardrobe; **wyjeżdżać za granicę** to go abroad

2: **chwytać (chwycić** pf**) kogoś za rękę** to grab sb's hand

3 (cel działania) for; **walczyć za równość** to fight for equality; **wznosić (wznieść** pf**) toast za czyjeś powodzenia** to drink (a toast) to sb's success

4 (po jakimś czasie) in; **za dwa tygodnie** in three weeks; **za rok** in a year's time; **jest za dziesięć szósta** it's ten to six

5 (wymieniając na) for; **kupiłem to za sześć złotych** I bought this for six zlotys; **za to, że dałaś mi wykształcenie** in return for giving me my education

6 (zastępując) in place of; **pracować za trzech** to do the work of three

▷ adv **1** (zbytnio) too; **za wcześnie/szybko** too early/quickly; **za dużo** too much/many; **on jest za mało doświadczony na to stanowisko** he's too inexperienced for the job

2 (w formach wykrzyknikowych): **co za film!** what a film!

zaadres|ować (-uję, -ujesz) vb pf od **adresować**

zaakcept|ować (-uję, -ujesz) vb pf od **akceptować**

zaareszt|ować (-uję, -ujesz) vb pf od **aresztować**

zaba|wa (-wy, -wy; dat & loc sg **-wie**) f **1** (dzieci) play **2** (według reguł) game **3** (rozrywka) game **4** (taneczna) party; **plac zabaw** playground; **dobrej zabawy!**

have a good time!; **dla zabawy** for fun

zabaw|ka (-ki, -ki; dat & loc sg **-ce**; gen pl **-ek)** f (dla dzieci) toy

zabawny adj (śmieszny) funny

zabezpiecz|ać (-am, -asz; pf **-yć)** vt **1** (stanowić ochronę) to protect **2** (finansowo) to secure; **~ się** vr (ochronić się): **~ (zabezpieczyć** pf**) się przed czymś** to protect o.s. against sth; **~ (zabezpieczyć** pf**) coś przed czymś** to guard sth against sth

zabezpiecze|nie (-nia, -nia; gen pl **-ń)** nt (ochrona) protection

zabi|ć (-ję, -jesz) vb pf od **zabijać**; **~ się** vr pf **1** (popełnić samobójstwo) to kill o.s. **2** (w wypadku) to be killed

zabierać (-am, -asz; pf **zabrać)** vt to take; **~ kogoś ze sobą w podróż** to take sb along on a journey

zabij|ać (-am, -asz; pf **zabić)** vt **1** (odebrać życie) to kill **2** (godzinę na zegarze) to strike; **~ się** vr (odbierać sobie życie) to kill one another; **~ czas** to kill time

zabity adj (martwy) killed; **spać jak ~** to sleep like a log

zabłą|dzić (-dzę, -dzisz; imp **-dź)** vi pf (zgubić się) to get lost

zabójc|a (-y, -y) m decl like f in sg **1** (przestępca) murderer **2** (zamachowiec) assassin

zabójczy adj **1** (broń) lethal; (strzał) fatal **2** (tempo, pogoda, życie) destructive

zabójst|wo (-wa, -wa; loc sg **-wie)** nt **1** (morderstwo) murder **2** (zamach) assassination

za|brać (-biorę, -bierzesz) vb pf

od **zabierać 1** (odbierać, wziąć ze sobą) to take **2** (czas) to take (up); **~ się** vr pf (pojechać z kimś): **~ się z kimś** (pot) to tag along with sb

zabrak|nąć (3rd pers sg **-nie**; pt **-ło**) vi pf: **zabrakło nam czasu/sił** we ran out of time/energy

zabrani|ać (**-am, -asz**) pf **zabronić**) vt (zakazywać): **~ czegoś** to forbid sth; **~ komuś robić coś** to forbid sb to do sth

zabroniony adj (zakazany) prohibited

zabyt|ek (**-ku, -ki**; inst sg **-kiem**) m (kultury, sztuki) (historic) monument; **zabytki przyrody** sites of scientific interest

zabytkowy adj **1** (budowla) historic **2** (przedmiot) antique

zach. abbr (= zachodni) W.

zachę|cać (**-cam, -casz**; pf **-cić**) vt (motywować): **~ kogoś do czegoś** to encourage sb in sth

zachę|ta (**-ty, -ty**; dat & loc sg **-cie**) f **1** (słowna) encouragement **2** (finansowa) incentive

zachmurzeni|e (**-a**) nt (Meteo) clouds pl

zachmurzony adj (Meteo) cloudy

zachmurz|yć się (**-ę, -ysz**) vr pf **1** (o niebie, czole, oczach) to cloud over **2** (posmutnieć) to become gloomy

zachodni adj **1** (strona świata) west **2** (o wietrze) westerly **3** (kraj, waluta, towar) western; **Europa Z~a** western Europe; **~a Anglia** the west of England

zacho|dzić (**-dzę, -dzisz**; imp **-dź**; pf **zajść**) vt (podchodzić niezauważony): **~ kogoś** to steal up on sb ▷ vi **1** (jak słońce, księżyc)

to set **2** (dojść) to get **3** (składać wizytę) to drop in **4** (o wydarzeniu, błędzie) to occur; **zajść w ciążę** to become pregnant

zachor|ować (**-uję, -ujesz**) vi pf (na grypę, anginę) to be taken ill

zachowani|e (**-a**) nt **1** (o sposobie bycia) behaviour (Brit), behavior (US) **2** (o manierach) manners pl **3** (o ochronie zabytków) preservation

zachow|ywać (**-uję, -ujesz**; pf **-ać**) vt **1** (wspomnienia, przedmioty) to retain **2** (energię, wdzięczność) to retain **3** (zwyczaje) to maintain; **~ się** vr **1** (grzecznie, agresywnie) to behave **2** (o danych, zwyczajach, historiach) to survive

zach|ód (**-odu, -ody**; loc sg **-odzie**) m **1** (zajście): **~ słońca** sunset **2** (o stronie świata) west **3** (o Europie Zachodniej) the West; **na ~ od** +gen west of

zachwycający adj (urzekający) delightful

zachwycony adj (urzeczony) delighted; **jestem ~ widokiem** I am delighted with the view

zacofany adj (zapóźniony) backward

zacz|ąć (**-nę, -niesz**; imp **-nij**) vb pf od **zaczynać**

zaczek|ać (**-am, -asz**) vb pf od **czekać**

zaczyn|ać (**-am, -asz**; pf **zacząć**) vt (nową pracę, projekt, wojnę) to start; **~ się** vr (o filmie, lekcji) to begin; **~ (zacząć** pf) **coś robić** to start doing sth

zada|nie (**-nia, -nia**; gen pl **-ń**) nt **1** (sprawa do wykonania) task **2** (ćwiczenie szkolne) assignment

3 (*Mat, Fiz*) problem; **~ domowe** homework

zad|awać (**-aję, -ajesz**; *pf* **-ać**) *vt* **1** (*zadanie domowe, ćwiczenie*) to set **2** (*ciosy, uderzenia*) to deal; **~ się** *vr* (*pot: utrzymywać znajomość*): **~ się z kimś** to hang around with sb; **zadać** (*pf*) **komuś pytanie** to ask sb a question

zadbany *adj* **1** (*osoba*) well-groomed **2** (*strój, pokój*) neat, tidy

zadecyd|ować (**-uję, -ujesz**) *vb pf od* **decydować**

zademonstr|ować (**-uję, -ujesz**) *vb pf od* **demonstrować**

zadłuż|ać się (**-am, -asz**; *pf* **-yć**) *vr* (*zaciągać dług*) to get into debt

zadłużeni|e (**-a**) *nt* (*zagraniczne, krajowe*) debt

zadłużony *adj* (*szpital, firma*) indebted

zadowal|ać (**-am, -asz**; *pf* **zadowolić**) *vt* **1** (*spełniać potrzeby*) to satisfy **2** (*sprawiać przyjemność*) to please; **~ się** *vr* (*zaakceptować*): **~ się czymś** to settle for sth

zadowalający *adj* (*wynik, stopień*) satisfactory

zadowoleni|e (**-a**) *nt* (*z pracy, z rodziny*) satisfaction

zadowolony *adj* **1** (*uradowany*) pleased **2** (*ze spełnionych oczekiwań*) contented

Zadusz|ki (**-ek**) *pl* (*święto*) All Souls' Day *sg*

○ **ZADUSZKI**
○
○   **Zaduszki** (All Souls' Day), also
○   known as **Święto Zmarłych**,
○   is on 2 November, the day

○   after **Wszystkich Świętych**
○   (All Saints' Day). On this day,
○   people visit the graves of their
○   relatives and friends, where
○   they light small candles to
○   commemorate the dead.

zadział|ać (**-am, -asz**) *vb pf od* **działać**

zadzwon|ić (**-ię, -isz**) *vb pf od* **dzwonić**

zafascynowany *adj* (*bardzo zainteresowany*) fascinated

zagad|ka (**-ki, -ki**; *dat & loc sg* **-ce**; *gen pl* **-ek**) *f* **1** (*problem do rozwiązania*) riddle **2** (*coś tajemniczego*) mystery

zagadkowy *adj* (*tajemniczy*) enigmatic

zagadnie|nie (**-nia, -nia**; *gen pl* **-ń**) *nt* (*kwestia*) problem

zagi|nąć (**-nę, -niesz**; *imp* **-ń**) *vi pf* (*zniknąć*) to go missing; **ślad po niej zaginął** there is no trace of her

zaginiony *adj* (*żołnierz, dziecko*) missing ▷ *m decl like adj* (*człowiek poszukiwany*) missing person

zagląd|ać (**-am, -asz**; *pf* **zajrzeć**) *vi* **1** (*do pokoju*) to look in **2** (*do książki*) to look into

zag|oić (**-oję, -oisz**; *imp* **-ój**) *vb pf od* **goić**

zagorzały *adj* **1** (*wielbiciel*) ardent **2** (*opponent*) fervent **3** (*debata*) heated

zagot|ować (**-uję, -ujesz**) *vb pf od* **gotować**

zagranic|a (**-y**) *f* (*kraje obce*) foreign countries *pl*

zagraniczny *adj* (*obcy*) foreign; **handel ~** foreign trade;

ministerstwo Spraw Z~ch
Ministry of Foreign Affairs,
≈ Foreign Office (*Brit*), ≈ State
Department (*US*)

zagraż|ać (**-am, -asz**; *pf* **zagrozić**)
vi (*grozić*): **~ komuś** to threaten
sb; **to zagraża jego zdrowiu** this
threatens his health

zagroże|nie (**-nia, -nia**; *gen pl* **-ń**)
nt (*pożarem, terroryzmem*) risk

zagu|bić (**-bię, -bisz**) *vt pf* (*utracić*)
to lose; **~ się** *vr* (*zapodziać się*) to
get lost

zainteresowany *adj* (*interesujący
się czymś*): **być czymś ~m** to be
interested in sth

zaj|ąć (**-mę, -miesz**; *imp* **-mij**) *vb
pf od* **zajmować**; **~ się** *vr pf* (*czymś
nowym*) to take up; **zajmiesz się
tym?** will you see to that?; **~ się
malarstwem/architekturą** to
take up painting/architecture

zaję|cie (**-cia, -cia**; *gen pl* **-ć**) *nt* 1 (*o
czynności*) occupation 2 (*o pracy*)
job; **zajęcia** *pl* (*na uniwersytecie*)
classes; **rozkład zajęć** timetable

zajęty *adj* 1 (*osoba*) busy
2 (*siedzenie*) taken 3 (*telefon*) busy;
(*toaleta*) occupied; **jutro jestem ~**
I'm busy tomorrow

zajm|ować (**-uję, -ujesz**; *pf*
zająć) *vt* 1 (*przestrzeń*) to occupy
2 (*pomieszczenie*) to occupy
3 (*miejscowość, państwo*) to
seize 4 (*zaciekawiać*) to engage
5 (*usiąść*) to take 6 (*czas*) to
take; **~ się** *vr* 1 (*ogniem*) to catch
fire 2 (*obowiązkami itp.*): **~ się
czymś/robieniem czegoś** to
busy o.s. with sth/doing sth;
zająć miejsce to take one's seat;
zająć komuś miejsce to save

a seat for sb; **zajęło (nam) to
godzinę** it took (us) an hour;
czym się zajmujesz? (*familiar sg*)
what do you do (for a living)?; **~
się kimś/czymś** (*zaopiekować się*)
to look after sb/sth

zajmujący *adj* 1 (*historia, lektura*)
engrossing 2 (*o pracy*) absorbing
3 (*osoba*) interesting

zajrz|eć (**-ę, -ysz**; *imp* **-yj**) *vb pf od*
zaglądać

zakańcz|ać (**-am, -asz**) *vb* (*imp*
zakończyć) to finish; **~ się** *vr*
(*film, urlop*) to end

zaka|z (**-zu, -zy**; *loc sg* **-zie**) *m*
(*parkowania, palenia*) prohibition;
„**~ skrętu w lewo**" "no left turn";
„**~ wstępu**" "no entry"

zakaz|ywać (**-uję, -ujesz**; *pf* **-ać**)
vt (*zabronić*): **~ komuś czegoś** to
forbid sb to do sth

zakaźny *adj* (*Med*) infectious;
oddział ~ isolation ward

zakaż|ać (**-am, -asz**; *pf* **zakazić**)
vt (*Med*) to infect

zakaże|nie (**-nia, -nia**; *gen pl* **-ń**)
nt (*Med*) infection

zakła|d (**-du, -dy**; *loc sg*
-dzie) *m* 1 (*o jakąś sumę*) bet
2 (*przedsiębiorstwo*) factory
3 (*Uniw*) department 4 (*instytucja
wychowawcza lub lecznicza*)
institution; **~ przemysłowy**
industrial plant; **~ fryzjerski**
(*damski*) hairdresser's; (*męski*)
barber's; **~ badawczy** research
institute; **~ poprawczy** Young
Offender Institution (*Brit*),
Juvenile Detention Center (*US*)

zakłó|cać (**-cam, -casz**; *pf* **-cić**)
vt 1 (*atmosferę, ład, porządek*) to
disturb 2 (*pracę, funcję*) to disrupt

3 (*odbiór, słyszalność*) to interfere
with
zakłóce|nie (**-nia, -nia**; *gen pl* **-ń**)
nt **1** (*w radio*) interference **2** (*w
pracy, funkcji*) disruption
zakoch|ać się (**-am, -asz**) *vb pf
od* **zakochiwać się**
zakochany *adj* (*darzący miłością,
uwielbieniem*): **~ w kimś/czymś** in
love with sb/sth ▷ *m decl like adj*
(*mężczyzna*) lover
zakoch|iwać się (**-uję, -ujesz**; *pf*
zakochać) *vr* (*darzyć miłością*): **~
się (w kimś/czymś)** to fall in love
(with sb/sth)
zakonnic|a (**-y, -e**) *f* (*siostra
zakonna*) nun
zakończe|nie (**-nia, -nia**; *gen pl*
-ń) *nt* **1** (*wykonywania pracy*) end
2 (*filmu, historii*) ending **3** (*artykułu,
dysertacji*) conclusion
zakończ|yć (**-ę, -ysz**) *vb pf od*
kończyć, zakańczać
zakrę|t (**-tu, -ty**; *loc sg* **-cie**) *m*
(*ulicy*) bend; **~ w lewo/prawo**
left/right bend
zaku|p (**-pu, -py**; *loc sg* **-pie**) *m*
(*kupowanie*) purchase; **iść na ~y**
to go shopping; **robić ~y** to shop
zaledwie *adv* (*tylko*) just ▷ *conj*
(*tylko co*): **~ się obudził,...** no
sooner had he woken up than...;
~ godzinę temu just an hour ago
zale|ta (**-ty, -ty**; *dat & loc sg* **-cie**) *f*
(*pozytywna cecha*) virtue
zależ|eć (**-y**) *vi* (*od sytuacji,
kontekstu*): **~ od kogoś/czegoś** to
depend on sb/sth; **bardzo mu na
niej zależy** he cares deeply about
her; **to zależy** it depends; **to
zależy od was** it's up to you
zależnie *adv*: **~ od czegoś**

depending on sth
zależnoś|ć (**-ci, -ci**; *gen pl*
-ci) *f* **1** (*związek*) relationship
2 (*uzależnienie*): **~ od** +*gen*
dependence on; **w zależności od
czegoś** depending on sth
zależny *adj* **1** (*finansowo,
emocjonalnie*) dependent
2 (*Gram*): **mowa zależna** reported
speech
zalicz|ać (**-am, -asz**; *pf* **-yć**) *vt*
1 (*egzamin na uniwersytecie*) to pass
2 (*kurs*) to complete successfully
3 (*zakwalifikować*): **~ kogoś/coś
do** +*gen* to rate sb/sth among; **~
się** *vr* (*przynależeć*): **~ się do** +*gen*
to rank among; **~ komuś coś** to
give sb credit for sth
zalicz|ka (**-ki, -ki**; *dat & loc sg* **-ce**;
gen pl **-ek**) *f* (*część wynagrodzenia*)
advance
zalog|ować się (**-uję, -ujesz**) *pf
vi* (*Komput*) to log in
załam|ywać (**-uję, -ujesz**; *pf* **-ać**)
vt (*giąć*) to bend; **~ się** *vr* **1** (*giąć
się*) to bend **2** (*o dachu, moście,
lodzie*) to collapse **3** (*głos*) to break
4 (*być przygnębionym*) to break
down
załat|wiać (**-wiam, -wiasz**; *pf*
-wić) *vt* **1** (*sprawę*) to take care
of **2** (*pot: obsługiwać*) to serve;
~ się *vr* (*pot: wypróżnić się*) to
relieve o.s.; **on to załatwi** he'll
handle that
załat|wić (**-wię, -wisz**) *vb pf
od* **załatwiać** ▷ *vt*: **~ kogoś**
(*wykiwać*) to fix sb (*pot*);
(*zamordować*) to dispose of sb
załącz|ać (**-am, -asz**; *pf* **-yć**) *vt*
1 (*w liście*) to enclose **2** (*w e-mailu*)
to attach

załączni|k (**-ka, -ki**; *inst sg* **-kiem**) *m* **1** (*w liście*) enclosure **2** (*w e-mailu*) attachment

zał|oga (**-ogi, -ogi**; *dat & loc sg* **-odze**; *gen pl* **-óg**) *f* **1** (*na statku, w samolocie*) crew **2** (*zakładu pracy*) staff

założyciel (**-a, -e**; *gen pl* **-i**) *m* (*instytucji, firmy*) founder

zamach (**-u, -y**) *m* **1** (*o próbie zamordowania*) assassination attempt **2** (*o morderstwie*) assassination **3** (*zbrojny*) attack; **~ stanu** coup d'état

zamacho|wiec (**-wca, -wcy**) *m* **1** (*o zabójcy*) assassin **2** (*o napastniku*) assailant **3** (*osoba podkładająca bombę*) bomber

zamarz|ać (**-am, -asz**; *pf* **-nąć**) *vi* to freeze

zamarz|nąć (**-nę, -niesz**; *imp* **-nij**) *vi pf od* **marznąć, zamarzać**; (*na śmierć*) to freeze to death

zamarznięty *adj* (*pokryty lodem*) frozen

za|mawiać (**-wiam, -wiasz**; *pf* **zamówić**) *vt* **1** (*towar, usługę, posiłek*) to order **2** (*pokój, stolik*) to book

zam|ek (**-ku, -ki**; *inst sg* **-kiem**) *m* **1** (*królewski*) castle **2** (*urządzenie*) lock **3** (*w spodniach*) zip (Brit), zipper (US)

zamężna *adj* (*mężatka*) married

zamia|na (**-ny, -ny**; *dat & loc sg* **-nie**) *f* **1** (*o wymianie*) exchange **2** (*o przekształceniu*) conversion

zamia|r (**-ru, -ry**; *loc sg* **-rze**) *m* intention; **mieć ~ coś zrobić** to intend to do sth

zamiast *prep +gen* instead of; **~ marudzić...** instead of

grumbling...; **~ chleba kupiła bułki** instead of a loaf she bought rolls; **~ tego** instead of this

zamiat|ać (**-am, -asz**; *pf* **zamieść**) *vt* (*podłogę*) to sweep

zamienny *adj*: **części zamienne** spare parts

zamiesz|ać (**-am, -asz**) *vb pf od* **mieszać**

zamieszk|ać (**-am, -asz**) *vi pf* (*zacząć mieszkać*) to settle

zamieszkani|e (**-a**) *nt*: **miejsce zamieszkania** place of residence

zamk|nąć (**-nę, -niesz**; *imp* **-nij**) *vb pf od* **zamykać**

zamknię|cie (**-cia**) *nt* **1** (*na zawsze*) closure **2** (*sklepu itp. na noc*) closing time **3** (*nom pl* **-cia**; *gen pl* **-ć**) (*urządzenie*) lock; **w zamknięciu** under lock and key

zamknięty *adj* **1** (*książka, okno*) closed **2** (*na klucz*) locked **3** (*skryty: osoba*) self-contained; **„zamknięte"** "closed"

zamocow|ywać (**-uję, -ujesz**; *pf* **-ać**) *vt* (*przytwierdzić*) to attach

zamożny *adj* (*bogaty*) wealthy

zamó|wić (**-wię, -wisz**) *vb pf od* **zamawiać**

zamówie|nie (**-nia, -nia**; *gen pl* **-ń**) *nt* (*na towar, usługę*) order; **zrobiony na ~** custom-made

zamraż|ać (**-am, -asz**; *pf* **zamrozić**) *vt* (*żywność, ceny*) to freeze

zamrażalni|k (**-ka, -ki**; *inst sg* **-kiem**) *m* (*w lodówce*) freezer compartment

zamrażar|ka (**-ki, -ki**; *dat & loc sg* **-ce**; *gen pl* **-ek**) *f* (*urządzenie*) freezer

zamy|kać (**-kam, -kasz**; *imp* **-knij**;

pf **zamknąć**) *vt* **1** (*książkę, okno, otwór, oczy*) to close **2** (*na klucz*) to lock **3** (*parasol*) to close **4** (*w sejfie*) to lock up **5** (*likwidować fabrykę itp.*) to close down **6** (*w więzieniu*) to lock up

zaniedbany *adj* **1** (*budynek*) run-down **2** (*wygląd, dziecko, obowiązek*) neglected

za|nieść (**-niosę, -niesiesz** *vb impf od* **zanosić**

zanim *conj* (*przed*) before; **~ wyjdę/wyszłam z domu...** before I leave home/left home...; **nie komentuj, ~ nie przeczytasz** don't comment before you read it through

zano|sić (**-szę, -sisz**; *imp* **-ś**; *pf* **zanieść**) *vt* (*dostarczać*) to take; **~ się** *vr* (*wyglądać na coś*): **zanosi się na deszcz** it looks like rain

zanot|ować (**-uję, -ujesz**) *vb pf od* **notować**

zaoczny *adj* **1** (*proces*) in absentia **2** (*student*) external

zaofer|ować (**-uję, -ujesz**) *vb pf od* **oferować**

zaopiek|ować się (**-uję, -ujesz**) *vb pf od* **opiekować się**

zaoszczę|dzić (**-dzę, -dzisz**; *imp* **-dź**) *vt pf* **1** (*fundusze, siły*) to save **2** (*czegoś przykrego*): **zaoszczędzi ło mu to kłopotów** it saved him some problems; **~ na jedzeniu/ biletach** to save on food/tickets

zapach (**-u, -y**) *m* **1** (*woń*) smell **2** (*kwiatu; perfumy*) fragrance

zapaleni|e (**-a**) *nt* (*stan chorobowy*) inflammation; **~ płuc** pneumonia

zapalnicz|ka (**-ki, -ki**; *dat & loc sg* **-ce**; *gen pl* **-ek**) *f* (*do krzesania ognia*) lighter

zapał|ka (**-ki, -ki**; *dat & loc sg* **-ce**; *gen pl* **-ek**) *f* (*do krzesania ognia*) match

zapar|cie (**-cia, -cia**; *gen pl* **-ć**) *nt* **1** (*zatwardzenie*) constipation **2** (*poświęcenie*) determination; **z ~m** with determination

zapa|s (**-su, -sy**; *loc sg* **-sie**) *m* (*towaru, energii*) (spare) supply; **zapasy** *pl* **1** (*jedzenia*) provisions **2** (*dyscyplina sportowa*) wrestling *sg*; **mieć coś w ~ie** to have sth in reserve; **na ~** (*kupować, jeść*) ahead of time

zapasowy *adj* **1** (*o kole, części*) spare **2** (*o wyjściu, schodach*) emergency

za|piąć (**-pnę, -pniesz**; *imp* **-pnij**) *vb pf od* **zapinać**

zapin|ać (**-am, -asz**; *pf* **zapiąć**) *vt* **1** (*na pasek, rzepy*) to fasten **2** (*na guzik*) to button (up) **3** (*na zamek błyskawiczny*) to zip up **4** (*guzik, zamek błyskawiczny*) to do up; **~ się** (*pf* **zapiąć**) *vr* **1** (*na guzik*) to button up **2** (*na zamek błyskawiczny*) to zip up **3** (*mieć jakieś zapięcie*) to fasten

zapi|s (**-su, -sy**; *loc sg* **-sie**) *m* **1** (*rejestrowanie*) recording **2** (*o tekście, nagraniu, taśmie*) record **3** (*dźwięku*) recording **4** (*sposób zapisania*) notation **5** (*Prawo: testamentowy*) bequest; **zapisy** *pl* **1** (*na kurs*) registration *sg* **2** (*na zakup czegoś*) waiting list *sg*

zapła|ta (**-ty, -ty**; *dat & loc sg* **-cie**) *f* **1** (*za towar, usługę*) payment **2** (*za gościnność, trud*) reward

zapobieg|ać (**-am, -asz**; *pf*

zapobiec) vi (*nie dopuszczać*): **~ czemuś** to prevent sth

zapomin|ać (**-am, -asz**; pf **zapomnieć**) vt +gen to forget ▷ vi (*nie pamiętać*): **~ (o** +loc) to forget (about); **~ się** vr (*źle się zachowywać*) to forget o.s.

zapom|nieć (**-nę, -nisz**; imp **-nij**) vb pf od **zapominać**

zaprasz|ać (**-am, -asz**; pf **zaprosić**) vt (*w odwiedziny, na kolację, spacer*): **~ kogoś na coś** to invite sb to sth; **~ się** vr 1 (*wprosić się*) to invite o.s. 2 (*jeden drugiego*) to exchange invitations

zapro|sić (**-szę, -sisz**; imp **-ś**) vb pf od **zapraszać**

zaprosze|nie (**-nia, -nia**; gen pl **-ń**) nt (*prośba o przyjście*) invitation; **na czyjeś ~** at sb's invitation

zaprzecz|ać (**-am, -asz**; pf **-yć**) vi 1 (*kwestionować*) to disagree 2 (*pogłoskom, pomówieniom*): **~ czemuś** to deny sth 3 (*pozostawać w sprzeczności*) to conflict with; **to zaprzecza faktom historycznym** this conflicts with the historical facts; **~ komuś** to contradict sb

zaprzyjaź|nić się (**-nię, -nisz**; imp **-nij**) vr pf: **~ się z kimś** to make friends with sb

zapuk|ać (**-am, -asz**) vb pf od **pukać**

zapyt|ać (**-am, -asz**) vb pf od **pytać**

zapyta|nie (**-nia, -nia**; gen pl **-ń**) nt (*oficjalne pytanie*) inquiry; **znak zapytania** question mark

zarabi|ać (**-am, -asz**) vt (pf **zarobić**) (*pracować zarobkowo*) to earn ▷ vi (*osiągać zyski*) to make

a profit; **~ na czymś** to make a profit on sth

zaradny adj (*pomysłowy*) resourceful

zaraz adv 1 (*od razu*) right away 2 (*za moment*) soon 3 (*niedaleko*) just; **~ za mostem /parkiem** just over the bridge/just the other side of the park; **~ po wakacjach** immediately after the holidays; **~ wracam** I'll be right back; **zaraz, ~!** wait a minute!

zaraźliwy adj (*choroba, śmiech*) infectious

zaraż|ać (**-am, -asz**; pf **zarazić**) vt (*chorobą, entuzjazmem*) to infect; **~ się** vr (*chorobą*) to get infected; **zarazić się czymś od kogoś** to catch sth from sb

zarezerw|ować (**-uję, -ujesz**) vb pf od **rezerwować**

zaręcz|ać (**-am, -asz**; pf **-yć**) vt (*gwarantować*) to guarantee; **~ za kogoś** to vouch for sb; **zaręczam (wam), że…** I warrant (you) (that)…

zaręczyć się vr pf: **~ się (z kimś)** to get engaged (to sb)

zaręczynowy adj: **pierścionek ~** engagement ring

zaręczyn|y (**-**) pl (*przyrzeczenie małżeństwa*) engagement sg

zarob|ek (**-ku, -ki**; inst sg **-kiem**) m 1 (*o wynagrodzeniu*) wage 2 (*o pracy*) job 3 (*o zysku*) profit; **zarobki** pl (*dochód*) earnings

zarobkowy adj: **praca zarobkowa** paid work

zarzu|t (**-tu, -ty**; loc sg **-cie**) m (*oskarżenie*) accusation; **bez ~u** beyond reproach

zasa|da (**-dy, -dy**; dat & loc sg

-dzie) f **1** (*norma postępowania*) principle **2** (*związek chemiczny*) alkali; **dla zasady** on principle; **w zasadzie** in principle

zaska|kiwać (**-kuję, -kujesz**; *pf* **zaskoczyć**) *vt* (*zdarzyć się nieoczekiwanie*) to surprise ▷ *vi* **1** (*o mechanizmach*) to click **2** (*o silnikach*) to start

zaskakujący *adj* (*niespodziewany*) surprising

zaskoczenie (**-a**) *nt* (*niespodzianka*) surprise

zasłab|nąć (**-nę, -niesz**; *imp* **-nij**; *pt* **-ł** *lub* **-nął, -ła, -li**) *vi pf* (*zemdleć*) to collapse

zasło|na (**-ny, -ny**; *dat & loc sg* **-nie**) f (*w oknach*) curtain (*Brit*), drape (*US*); **zasuwać/rozsuwać zasłony** to draw/open the curtains

zasmu|cać (**-cam, -casz**; *pf* **-cić**) *vt* (*wywoływać smutek*) to sadden; **~ się** *vr* (*posmutnieć*) to be saddened

zasta|wa (**-wy, -wy**; *dat & loc sg* **-wie**) f (*komplet naczyń i sztućców*): **~ stołowa** tableware; **~ do herbaty** tea set

zastęp|ować (**-uję, -ujesz**; *pf* **zastąpić**) *vt* **1** (*wykonywać czyjeś obowiązki*): **~ kogoś** to stand in for sb **2** (*zamieniać*): **~ coś czymś innym** to replace sth with sth else **3** (*zagradzać*): **zastąpić komuś drogę** to bar sb's way

zastosow|ywać (**-uję, -ujesz**; *pf* **-ać**) *vt* (*regułę, technikę*) to apply; **~ się** *vr* (*do reguł, wymagań*): **~ się do czegoś** to comply with sth

zastrzy|k (**-ku, -ki**; *inst sg* **-kiem**) *m* injection; **~ gotówki** a cash injection; **~ energii** a shot in the arm

zaświadcze|nie (**-nia, -nia**; *gen pl* **-ń**) *nt* (*dokument*) certificate; **~ lekarskie** medical certificate

zatelefon|ować (**-uję, -ujesz**) *vb pf od* **telefonować**

zato|ka (**-ki, -ki**; *dat & loc sg* **-ce**) f **1** (*o części morza*) bay **2** (*o części jeziora*) bay **3** (*czołowa, szczękowa*) sinus **4** (*na jezdni*) lay-by

zatrzym|ywać (**-uję, -ujesz**; *pf* **-ać**) *vt* **1** (*człowieka, urządzenie, proces*) to stop **2** (*o policji: aresztować*) to arrest **3** (*pojazd*) to pull over **4** (*zachować*) to keep **5** (*opóźnić*) to detain; **~ się** (*pf* **-ać**) *vr* **1** (*o człowieku, pojeździe*) to stop **2** (*przestać działać*) to (come to a) stop **3** (*w hotelu, schronisku*) to stay

zauf|ać (**-am, -asz**) *vb pf od* **ufać**

zaufani|e (**-a**) *nt* (*wiara, pewność*) confidence; **mieć do kogoś ~** to have confidence in sb; **telefon zaufania** helpline

zauważ|ać (**-am, -asz**; *pf* **-yć**) *vt* (*zobaczyć*) to notice ▷ *vi* (*powiedzieć*) to observe

zawa|ł (**-łu, -ły**; *loc sg* **-le**) *m* (*Med*): **~ serca** heart attack

zawarto|ść (**-ci**) f **1** (*kieszeni, książki*) contents *pl* **2** (*soli, witamin*) content; **produkty o niskiej zawartości tłuszczu** low-fat products

zawier|ać (**-am, -asz**; *pf* **zawrzeć**) *vt* **1** (*zawierać w sobie*) to include **2** (*zgodę*) to reach **3** (*kontrakt*) to enter (into) **4** (*pokój*) to make

zawiły *adj* (*zagmatwany*) complicated

zawodnicz|ka (**-ki, -ki**; *dat &
loc sg* **-ce**; *gen pl* **-ek**) *f* **1** (*Sport*)
competitor **2** (*w konkursie*)
contestant

zawodni|k (**-ka, -cy**; *inst sg* **-kiem**)
m **1** (*Sport*) competitor **2** (*w
konkursie*) contestant

zawodo|wiec (**-wca, -wcy**) *m*
(*profesjonalista*) professional

zawodowy *adj* (*profesjonalny*)
professional; **szkoła zawodowa**
vocational school; **związek ~**
trade union (*Brit*), labor union
(*US*)

zawod|y (**-ów**) *pl* (*sportowe*)
competition; *zob. też* **zawód**

zaw|ód (**-odu, -ody**; *loc sg* **-odzie**)
m **1** (*praca*) profession **2** (*przykre
uczucie*) disappointment

zawsty|dzać (**-dzam, -dzasz**;
pf **-dzić**) *vt* (*wzbudzać wstyd*) to
shame; **~ się** *vr* (*odczuć wstyd*) to
be ashamed

zawstydzony *adj* (*głos, wzrok*)
embarrassed

zawsze *adv* (*ciągle*) always
▷ *part:* **ale ~** but still; **na ~** for
ever; **tyle co ~** as much as usual;
~ gdy whenever

zazdrosny *adj* **1** (*o osobę*): **~ o
kogoś** jealous of sb **2** (*o dom,
samochód*) envious; **~ o coś**
envious of sth

zazdro|ścić (**-szczę, -ścisz**;
imp **-ść**) *vi* (*domu, samochodu*): **~
komuś/czegoś** to envy sb/sth

zazdroś|ć (**-ci**) *f* **1** (*o osobę*)
jealousy **2** (*o dom, samochód*) envy

zazę|biać się (**-bia**; *pf* **-bić**) *vr* **1** (*o
urządzeniu*) to mesh **2** (*przen: o
datach, terminologii*) to be
interconnected

zazię|biać się (**-biam, -biasz**;
pf **-bić**) *vr* (*przeziębić się*) to catch
a cold

zaziębie|nie (**-nia, -nia**; *gen pl* **-ń**)
nt (*przeziębienie*) cold

zaziębiony *adj*: **jestem ~** I have
got a cold

zaznacz|ać (**-am, -asz**; *pf* **-yć**)
vt **1** (*kółkiem, krzyżykiem*) to mark
2 (*w wypowiedzi*) to stress ▷ *vi*
(*podkreślać*): **~, że...** to stress
that...; **~ się** *vr* (*wybijać się*) to be
evident

ząb (**zęba, zęby**; *loc sg* **zębie**) *m*
(*Anat*) tooth; **sztuczne zęby**
false teeth; **boli mnie ~** I have got
toothache

zbier|ać (**-am, -asz**; *pf* **zebrać**)
vt **1** (*znaczki*) to collect **2** (*ludzi*)
to gather **3** (*śmieci*) to gather
4 (*grzyby, poziomki*) to pick
5 (*nabierać wody*) to mop up; **~
się** *vr* **1** (*o ludziach*) to gather
2 (*przygotowywać się*): **~ się (do
czegoś)** to brace o.s. (for sth)

zbieżnoś|ć (**-ci**; *gen pl* **-ci**) *f* **1** (*w
poglądach*) concurrence **2** (*w
działaniu*) coincidence

zbi|ór (**-oru, -ory**; *loc sg* **-orze**)
m **1** (*opowiadań, płyt*) collection
2 (*zbóż, warzyw*) harvest **3** (*zespół
liczb*) set; **zbiory** *pl* (*zebrane zboże,
warzywa*) crop *sg*

zbliż|ać (**-am, -asz**; *pf* **-yć**) *vt*
1 (*przybliżyć*) to bring closer
2 (*przen: upodobaniać*) to bring
together; **~ się** *vr* **1** (*przybliżyć się*)
to approach **2** (*przen: zacieśnić
stosunki*) to become close **3** (*o
dacie, porze roku*) to approach; **nie
zbliżaj się!** keep away!

zbliże|nie (**-nia, -nia**; *gen pl* **-ń**) *nt*

1 (*bliskie kontakty*) close relations
2 (*zdjęcie*) close-up

zbliżony *adj* (*podobny*) similar

zbrod|nia (**-ni, -nie**; *gen pl* **-ni**) *f*
(*przestępstwo*) crime

zbrodniarz (**-a, -e**; *gen pl* **-y**) *m*
(*przestępca*) criminal

zby|t¹ (**-tu**; *loc sg* **-cie**) *m* **1** (*o
popycie*) market **2** (*o sprzedaży*)
sale(s *pl*); **cena ~u** selling price;
rynek ~u market

zbyt² *adv* (*za bardzo*) too

zd|ać (**-am, -asz**) *vb pf od* **zdawać**
▷ *vt*: **~ egzamin** to pass an exam;
~ na uniwersytet to get into
university

zdarz|ać się (**-a**; *pf* **-yć**) *vr* (*stać
się*) to happen, to occur

zda|wać (**-ję, -jesz**; *imp* **-waj**; *pf*
zdać) *vt* **1**: **~ relację** to inform
2 (*butelki, makulaturę*) to return
▷ *vi* (*przystępować do egzaminu*): **~
(na uniwersytet)** to take (one's)
entrance exams (to university);
~ się *vr* **1** (*wywoływać wrażenie*) to
seem **2** (*polegać*): **~ się na kogoś/
coś** to depend on sb/sth; **~ sobie
sprawę z czegoś** to be aware of
sth; **zdaje (mi) się, że...** it seems
(to me) that...

zdecyd|ować (**-uję, -ujesz**) *vb pf
od* **decydować**

zdecydowani|e¹ (**-a**) *nt* (*pewność*)
determination

zdecydowanie² *adv*
1 (*bez wahania*) decidedly
2 (*niewątpliwie*) definitely; **~
najgorszy** by far the worst

zdecydowany *adj* **1** (*osoba*)
determined **2** (*stanowczy*)
decisive **3** (*wyrazisty*)
unquestionable; **~ na coś**

determined about sth

zdejm|ować (**-uję, -ujesz**; *pf*
zdjąć) *vt* **1** (*płaszcz, spodnie*) to
take off **2** (*obraz ze ściany*) to take
down

zdenerw|ować (**-uję, -ujesz**) *vb
pf od* **denerwować**

zdenerwowany *adj* **1** (*przejęty
lękiem*) nervous **2** (*rozdrażniony*): **~
czymś/na kogoś** angry *lub*
annoyed at sth/with sb

zd|jąć (**-ejmę, -ejmiesz**; *imp*
-ejmij) *vb pf od* **zdejmować**

zdję|cie (**-cia, -cia**; *gen pl* **-ć**) *nt*
1 (*Fot*) photograph **2** (*zabranie*)
removal; **robić** (**zrobić** *pf*) **komuś
~** to take a photo of sb

zdobyw|ać (**-am, -asz**; *pf* **zdobyć**)
vt **1** (*kraj, zamek*) to capture
2 (*fortunę*) to gain **3** (*bilet, jedzenie*)
to get **4** (*reputację, przychylność
ludzi, nagrodę*) to win **5** (*Sport: gola*)
to score

zdobywc|a (**-y, -y**) *m decl like f
in sg* **1** (*kraju, zamku*) conqueror
2 (*nagród*) winner **3** (*gola*) scorer

zdolnoś|ć (**-ci, -ci**; *gen pl* **-ci**) *f*
(*umiejętność*) ability; **zdolności** *pl*
(*intelektualne, muzyczne*) gift *sg*

zdolny *adj* **1** (*utalentowany*)
gifted **2** (*mający możliwości*): **~ do
(zrobienia) czegoś** capable of
(doing) sth

zdrowi|e (**-a**) *nt* (*fizyczne,
psychiczne*) health; **ośrodek
zdrowia** health centre (*Brit*) *lub*
center (*US*); **na ~!** (*przy toaście*)
cheers!; (*przy kichnięciu*) bless you!

zdrowo *adv* **1** (*jeść*) healthily
2 (*wyglądać, żyć*) healthy

zdrowotny *adj* (*o warunkach,
klimacie*) healthy; **opieka**

zdrowotna healthcare; **urlop ~**
sick leave
zdrowy adj (nie chory) healthy; **~
rozsądek** common sense
ze prep =**z**
zebra|nie (-nia, -nia; gen pl **-ń)** nt
(spotkanie) meeting
zega|r (-ra, -ry; loc sg **-rze)** m
(wiszący, stojący) clock
zegar|ek (-ka, -ki; inst sg **-kiem)** m
(na rękę) watch; **mój ~ się śpieszy**
my watch is fast
zejś|cie (-cia, -cia; gen pl **-ć)** nt
1 (droga w dół) descent **2** (zgon)
death; **~ na parter** stairs to the
ground floor
zej|ść (-dę, -dziesz; imp **-dź**;
pt **zszedł** lub **zeszedł, zeszła,
zeszli)** vb pf od **schodzić**
zemdl|eć (-eję, -ejesz) vb pf od
mdleć
zem|sta (-sty; dat & loc sg **-ście)** f
(odwet) revenge
zepsu|ć (-ję, -jesz) vb pf od **psuć**
zepsuty adj **1** (telewizor, samochód)
broken **2** (osoba) corrupt
ze|ro (-ra, -ra; loc sg **-rze)** nt
1 (cyfra) zero **2** (przy podawaniu
numerów) zero **3** (zupełny brak)
nought **4** (w meczu piłkarskim)
nil (Brit), nothing (US); (w meczu
tenisowym) love **5** (przen: człowiek
bez wartości) nonentity
zesp|ół (-ołu, -oły; loc pl
-ole) m **1** (muzyczny) group
2 (profesjonalistów, sportowy) team
3 (Bud) complex, set **4** (teatralny)
company **5** (Tech) unit **6** (Med)
syndrome; **~ jazzowy/rockowy**
jazz band/rock group
zesta|w (-wu, -wy; loc sg **-wie)** m
1 (komplet) set **2** (dobór np. barw)

combination **3** (np. wypoczynkowy)
suite **4** (urządzeń, maszyn) kit
zestresowany adj (osoba)
stressed
zewnątrz adv: **na ~** outside; **z** lub
od ~ from the outside
zewnętrzny adj **1** (poza obrębem)
outside, exterior **2** (o wyglądzie)
outward, external; **„do użytku
zewnętrznego"** "for external
use only"
zgadz|ać się (-am, -asz; pf
zgodzić) vr **1** (pozwalać): **~ się na
coś** to agree to sth **2** (podzielać
poglądy): **~ się z kimś** to agree
with sb **3** (okazywać zgodność): **~
się (z czymś)** to tally (with sth)
zgo|da (-dy; dat & loc sg
-dzie) f **1** (harmonia) harmony
2 (zezwolenie) consent **3** (zgodność
zdania) consensus **4** (porozumienie)
reconciliation
zgodnie adv **1** (harmonijnie) in
harmony **2** (według) according
to, in accordance with; **~ z
przepisami** in accordance with
the rules
zgrabny adj **1** (figura) shapely
2 (zwinny) deft **3** (wypowiedź,
utwór) neat
ziar|no (-na, -na; loc sg **-nie**; gen
pl **-en)** nt **1** (zboża, prawdy, piasku)
grain **2** (fasoli, kawy) bean **3** (do
zasiania) seed
zielony adj (kolor) green; **nie
mam zielonego pojęcia** (pot)
I haven't a clue lub the foggiest
(idea)
zie|mia (-mi) f **1** (Astron): **Z~**
Earth **2** (pl **-mie)** (o glebie) soil
3 (o gruncie pod nogami) ground
4 (o podłodze) floor **5** (pl **-mie)**

(*majątek ziemski, terytorium*) land; **do (samej) ziemi** (*firana, płaszcz*) full-length; **trzęsienie ziemi** earthquake

ziemnia|k (**-ka, -ki**; *inst sg* **-kiem**) *m* (*kartofel*) potato

zię|ć (**-cia, -ciowie**) *m* (*mąż córki*) son-in-law

zi|ma (**-my, -my**; *dat & loc sg* **-mie**) *f* (*pora roku*) winter; **zimą** *lub* **w zimie** in winter

zim|no¹ (**-na**; *loc sg* **-nie**) *nt* 1 (*niskie temperatury*) cold 2 (*opryszczka*) cold sore

zimno² *adv* 1 (*o niskiej temperaturze, bez okazywania uczuć*) coldly; **~ mi** I am cold; **~ mi w ręce** my hands are cold

zimny *adj* (*o niskiej temperaturze, bez uczuć*) cold; **zimna wojna** (*historycznie*) the Cold War

zimowy *adj* (*dzień, urlop, pogoda*) winter

zi|oło (**-oła, -oła**; *loc sg* **-ole**; *gen pl* **-ół**) *nt* (*ziele*) herb

ziołowy *adj* (*herbata*) herbal

zj|eść (**-em, -esz**; *pt* **-adł, -adła, -edli**) *vb pf od* **jeść**

zjeżdż|ać (**-am, -asz**; *pf* **zjechać**) *vi* 1 (*dźwigiem*) to go down; (*na snowboardzie, saniach*) to go downhill; (*autem*) to drive downhill; (*rowerem*) to ride downhill; (*zbaczać z trasy*) to turn (off) 3 (*przybyć*) to arrive; **~ się** *vr* (*gromadzić się*) to arrive; **zjeżdżaj stąd!** (*pot*) get out of here!

zle|w (**-wu, -wy**; *loc sg* **-wie**) *m* (*kuchenny*) sink

zlikwid|ować (**-uję, -ujesz**) *vb pf od* **likwidować**

zł *abbr* (= *złoty: waluta*) zloty

zła|mać (**-mię, -miesz**) *vb pf od* **łamać**

złama|nie (**-nia, -nia**; *gen pl* **-ń**) *nt* (*kości*) fracture

złamany *adj* (*ręka, serce*) broken

zła|pać (**-pię, -piesz**) *vb pf od* **łapać**

zł|o (**-a**) *nt* (*odwrotność dobra*) evil

złocisty *adj* (*kolor*) golden

złocony *adj* 1 (*wazon*) gilded 2 (*pierścionek, sztućce*) gold-plated

złoczyńc|a (**-y, -y**) *m decl like f in sg* (*książk: przestępca*) villain

złodziej (**-ja, -je**; *gen pl* **-i**) *m* (*dokonujący kradzieży*) thief; **~ kieszonkowy** pickpocket

zło|m (**-mu**; *loc sg* **-mie**) *m* (*zużyte urządzenie*) scrap (metal)

zło|ścić (**-szczę, -ścisz**; *imp* **-ść**; *pf* **roz-** *lub* **ze-**) *vt* (*wywoływać złość*) to anger; **~ się** *vr* (*odczuwać/ okazywać złość*): **~ się (na kogoś/o coś)** to be angry (with sb/about sth)

złoś|ć (**-ci**) *f* (*gniew*) anger; **na ~ komuś** to spite sb

złośliwy *adj* 1 (*przedmiot, człowiek*) malicious 2 (*nowotwór*) malignant

zło|to (**-ta**; *loc sg* **-cie**) *nt* (*Chem*) gold

złotów|ka (**-ki, -ki**; *dat & loc sg* **-ce**; *gen pl* **-ek**) *f* 1 (*waluta*) one zloty 2 (*o monecie*) one-zloty coin

złot|y¹ (**-ego, -e**) *m decl like adj* (*waluta*) zloty

złoty² *adj* gold; **złota rączka** handyman

zły *adj* 1 (*wynik, ocena, dzień, wiadomość*) bad 2 (*rozgniewany*) angry 3 (*nieetyczny, nieuczciwy*)

evil, wicked **4** (*niepoprawny*)
wrong **5** (*marnej jakości*) poor; **w
~m humorze** in a bad mood; **w
~m guście** in bad taste
zmarł|a (**-ej, -e**) *f decl like adj* the
deceased
zmarły *adj* (*nieżywy*) dead,
deceased ▷ *m decl like adj*
(*nieżyjący mężczyzna*) the deceased;
zmarli *pl* (*nieżyjące osoby*) the
dead; **~ pan Józef Nowak** the late
Mr Nowak
zmarn|ować (**-uję, -ujesz**) *vb pf
od* **marnować**
zmarszcz|ka (**-ki, -ki**; *dat & loc
sg* **-ce**; *gen pl* **-ek**) *f* **1** (*przy oczach*)
wrinkle **2** (*na powierzchni wody*)
ripple **3** (*na tkaninie*) crease
zmarszcz|yć (**-ę, -ysz**) *vb pf od*
marszczyć
zmart|wić (**-wię, -wisz**) *vb pf od*
martwić
zmartwie|nie (**-nia, -nia**; *gen pl*
-ń) *nt* (*problem*) worry
zmartwiony *adj* (*przygnębiony*)
worried
zmądrz|eć (**-eję, -ejesz**) *vb pf od*
mądrzeć
zmęczeni|e (**-a**) *nt* (*znużenie,
wyczerpanie*) tiredness
zmęczony *adj* (*znużony,
wyczerpany*) tired
zmęcz|yć (**-ę, -ysz**) *vb pf od*
męczyć
zmia|na (**-ny, -ny**; *dat & loc sg*
-nie) *f* **1** (*odmiana*) change **2** (*w
pracy*) shift; **~ na lepsze/gorsze**
a change for the better/worse;
dzienna/nocna ~ day/night shift
zmie|niać (**-niam, -niasz**; *pf* **-nić**)
vt (*przeobrażać*) to change; **~ się** *vr*
1 (*ulegać przeobrażeniu*) to change

2 (*między sobą*) to take turns; **~**
(**zmienić** *pf*) **zdanie** to change
one's mind
zmienny *adj* (*niestały*)
changeable; **prąd ~** alternating
current
zmierz|ać (**-am, -asz**) *vi*
(*książk: wybierać się*): **~ do** +*gen*/**w
stronę** +*gen* to head for/towards;
do czego zmierzasz? (*przen*)
what are you driving at?
zmierzch (**-u, -y**) *m* **1** (*pora dnia*)
dusk **2** (*przen: koniec, upadek*)
twilight; **o ~u** at dusk
zmierz|yć (**-ę, -ysz**) *vb pf od*
mierzyć
zmiesz|ać (**-am, -asz**) *vb pf od*
mieszać
zmniejsz|ać (**-am, -asz**; *pf* **-yć**)
vt (*wielkość, odległość*) to reduce;
~ się *vr* (*o wielkości, odległości*) to
reduce
zmocz|yć (**-ę, -ysz**) *vb pf od*
moczyć
zmok|nąć (**-nę, -niesz**; *imp* **-nij**;
pt **-nął** *lub* **zmókł, -ła, -li**) *vb pf od*
moknąć
zmusz|ać (**-am, -asz**; *pf* **zmusić**)
vt (*nakłaniać siłą/groźbami*) to
force; **~ się** *vr* (*robić coś wbrew
sobie*): **~ się do zrobienia czegoś**
to force o.s. to do sth; **~ kogoś
do zrobienia czegoś** to force sb
to do sth
zm|yć (**-yję, -yjesz**) *vb pf od* **myć**;
~ komuś głowę (*przen*) to give sb
a dressing-down
zmy|sł (**-słu, -sły**; *loc sg* **-śle**) *m*
1 sense **2** (*predyspozycja*) aptitude;
~ artystyczny artistic flair
zmyśl|ać (**-am, -asz**; *pf* **-ić**) *vt*
(*mówić nieprawdę*) to make up

zmywar|ka (**-ki, -ki**; *dat & loc sg* **-ce**; *gen pl* **-ek**) *f* (*urządzenie*) dishwasher

znacz|ek (**-ka, -ki**; *inst sg* **-kiem**) *m* **1** *dimin od* **znak** **2** (*naklejka: pocztowy, skarbowy*) stamp **3** (*plakietka*) badge **4** (*graficzny*) mark; **~ pocztowy** (postage) stamp

znacze|nie (**-nia, -nia**; *gen pl* **-ń**) *nt* **1** (*treść*) meaning **2** (*waga*) significance; **to nie ma znaczenia** it doesn't matter; **to jest bez znaczenia** it is of no importance

zn|ać (**-am, -asz**) *vt* (*wiedzieć*) to know; **~ się** *vr* **1** (*samego siebie*) to know o.s. **2** (*z innymi*) to know each other **3** (*być obeznanym*): **~ się na czymś** to be knowledgeable about sth; **dawać** (**dać** *pf*) **komuś ~** (**o czymś**) (*powiadomić*) to let sb know (about sth); **~ kogoś** to know sb

znad *prep* +*gen* **1** (*książki*) from above **2** (*morza*) from

znajd|ować (**-uję, -ujesz**; *pf* **znaleźć**) *vt* **1** (*odszukiwać, natrafiać*) to find **2** (*wsparcie, zrozumienie*) to meet with; **~ się** *vr* **1** (*być położonym*) to be situated **2** (*dać się odszukać*) to be found **3** (*pojawić się*) to turn up

znajomoś|ć (**-ci, -ci**) *f* **1** (*stosunki towarzyskie*) acquaintance **2** (*języka, matematyki*) knowledge; **zawierać** (**zawrzeć** *pf*) **z kimś ~** to make sb's acquaintance

znajomy *adj* (*teren, głos, piosenka*) familiar ▷ *m decl like adj* (*osoba*) acquaintance; **~ prawnik** a lawyer I know

zna|k (**-ku, -ki**; *inst sg* **-kiem**) *m* (*symbol, dowód*) sign; **~ drogowy** road sign; **~ zapytania** question mark; **~ Zodiaku** sign of the Zodiac

znakomitoś|ć (**-ci, -ci**; *gen pl* **-ci**) *f* (*człowiek*) celebrity

znakomity *adj* (*doskonały*) superb

zna|leźć (**-jdę, -jdziesz**; *imp* **-jdź**; *pt* **-lazł, -lazła, -leźli**) *vb pf od* **znajdować**

znany *adj* **1** (*okolica, grupa*) well-known **2** (*artysta, naukowiec*) famous **3** (*kłamca, przestępca*) notorious

znawc|a (**-y, -y**) *m decl like f in sg* (*ekspert, koneser*): **~ (czegoś)** an expert (on sth)

znęc|ać się (**-am, -asz**) *vr* (*pastwić się*): **~ się nad** +*inst* to abuse

znicz (**-a, -e**; *gen pl* **-y** *lub* **-ów**) *m* (*na grobie*) candle; **~ olimpijski** the Olympic torch

zniechę|cać (**-cam, -casz**; *pf* **-cić**) *vt* (*zrazić*): **~ kogoś do czegoś** to discourage sb from sth; **~ się** *vr* (*zrazić się*) to become discouraged

zniechęceni|e (**-a**) *nt* (*brak chęci*) discouragement

zniecierpliwieni|e (**-a**) *nt* (*brak cierpliwości*) impatience

zniecierpliwiony *adj* (*pozbawiony cierpliwości*) impatient

znieczul|ać (**-am, -asz**; *pf* **-ić**) *vt* (*Med*) to anaesthetize (*Brit*), to anesthetize (*US*)

znieczulający *adj*: **środek ~** anaesthetic (*Brit*), anesthetic (*US*)

znieczule|nie (**-nia, -nia**; *gen pl* **-ń**) *nt* (*Med*) anaesthetic (*Brit*), anesthetic (*US*)

znik|ać (**-am, -asz**; *pf* **-nąć**) *vi*
(*ginąć, wychodzić niepostrzeżenie*) to
disappear

znikomy *adj* (*bardzo mały*) slight

zno|sić (**-szę, -sisz**; *imp* **-ś**; *pf*
znieść) *vt* **1** (*na dół*) to carry
down **2** (*zgromadzić*) to gather
3 (*o kurze: jajko*) to lay **4** (*o wodzie,
powietrzu: zmienić kierunek*) to
carry **5** (*bolączki, przykrości,
trudy*) to endure **6** (*przepis, akt*)
to abolish **7** (*zakaz, sankcje*) to
lift **8** (*wytrzymywać, cierpieć*): **nie
znoszę go** I can't stand him; **~
się** *vr* **1** (*wzajemnie usuwać swoje
działanie*) to cancel each other
out **2** (*wytrzymywać ze sobą
wzajemnie*): **oni się nie znoszą**
they hate each other

znowu *adv* (*ponownie*) again
▷ *part* (*konkretnie*) after all; **~ się
spóźnił** he was late again

znużeni|e (**-a**) *nt* (*zmęczenie,
znudzenie*) weariness

znużony *adj* (*zmęczony, znudzony*)
weary

zob. *abbr* (= *zobacz*) see, cf.

zobacz|yć (**-ę, -ysz**) *vt pf* (*widzieć*)
to see; **~ się** *vr* (*spotkać się*): **~ się z
kimś** to see sb

zobowiąza|nie (**-nia, -nia**; *gen pl*
-ń) *nt* (*obowiązek*) commitment

zodia|k (**-ku**; *inst sg* **-kiem**) *m*
(*Astrologia*) zodiac; **znak Z~u** sign
of the Zodiac

zoo *nt inv* (*ogród zoologiczny*) zoo

z o.o. *abbr* (*firma, spółka* Ltd.

zorganizowany *adj* **1** (*drużyna*)
organized **2** (*wyjazd*) guided

zr|obić (**-obię, -obisz**; *imp* **-ób**) *vb
pf od* **robić**

zrozumi|eć (**-em, -esz**; 3 *pl* **-eją**)
vb pf od **rozumieć**

zrównoważony *adj* **1** (*o
człowieku*) even-tempered **2** (*o
charakterze*) level-headed **3** (*o
budżecie*) balanced

zróżnicowany *adj* (*niejednolity*)
diverse

zryw|ać (**-am, -asz**; *pf* **zerwać**)
vt **1** (*jabłka, róże*) to pick
2 (*tapety, ogłoszenia*) to tear off
3 (*węzeł, sznur, pęta*) to break
4 (*kontrakt, zaręczyny*) to break off
5 (*znajomość, kontakty*) to break off
▷ *vi* (*o parze: przestać się spotykać*): **~
(z kimś)** to break up (with sb); **~
się** *vr* **1** (*o sznurze, niciach*) to break
2 (*o osobie: podskoczyć w pośpiechu*)
to jump up **3** (*o wietrze, aplauzie*)
to break out; **~ (zerwać** *pf*) **z
nałogiem** to kick a habit

zszedł *itd. vb zob.* **schodzić**

zu|pa (**-py, -py**; *dat & loc sg* **-pie**) *f*
(*potrawa*) soup; **~ z puszki** tinned
soup

zupełnie *adv* (*całkowicie*)
completely, utterly

zużyty *adj* used, worn out

zwalcz|ać (**-am, -asz**) *vt impf*
(*pf* **-yć**) **1** (*przeciwnikom*) to fight
2 (*słabość, ból*) to overcome
3 (*insekty*) to exterminate; **~ się** *vr*
(*wzajemnie*) to fight each other

zwalcz|yć (**-ę, -ysz**) *vt pf zob.*
zwalczać

zwal|niać (**-niam, -niasz**;
imp **-niaj**) *vt impf* **1** (*tempo*) to
slow down **2** (*z pracy*) to make
redundant **3** (*z obowiązku*) to
exempt, to release

zwany *adj*: **tak ~** so-called

zwari|ować (**-uję, -ujesz**) *vi pf*

(*pot: oszaleć*) to go mad

zwariowany *adj* (*pot: szalony*) mad

zwarz|yć się (**-ę, -ysz**) *vr pf* (*o mleku, śmietanie*) to go sour

zwąt|pić (**-pię, -pisz**) *vb pf od* **wątpić**

zwątpie|nie (**-nia, -nia**; *gen pl* **-ń**) *nt* (*brak pewności/wiary*) pessimism

zwęż|ać (**-am, -asz**; *pf* **zwęzić**) *vt* 1 (*drogę*) to narrow 2 (*ubranie*) to take in; **~ się** *vr* (*o drodze*) to narrow

zwęże|nie (**-nia, -nia**; *gen pl* **-ń**) *nt* (*drogi*) narrowing

związ|ywać (**-uję, -ujesz**; *pf* **-ać**) *vt* (*włosy, paczkę, ręce*) to tie (up)

zwie|dzać (**-dzam, -dzasz**; *pf* **-dzić**) *vt* (*muzeum, kraj*) to visit

zwierz|ę (**-ęcia, -ęta**; *gen pl* **-ąt**) *nt* animal; **~ domowe** pet

zwierzęcy *adj* (*folwark, tłuszcz, nawóz*) animal

zwinny *adj* (*szybki i zgrabny*) agile, nimble

zwłaszcza *adv* (*szczególnie*) especially

zwło|ka (**-ki**; *dat & loc sg* **-ce**) *f* (*opóźnienie*) delay; **grać na zwłokę** to play for time

zwolenni|k (**-ka, -cy**; *inst sg* **-kiem**) *m* 1 (*króla*) follower 2 (*partii, idei*) supporter

zwol|nić (**-nię, -nisz**; *imp* **-nij**) *vb pf od* **zwalniać**

zwolnie|nie (**-nia, -nia**; *gen pl* **-ń**) *nt* 1 (*z pracy*) dismissal 2 (*usprawiedliwienie*) sick note, doctor's note 3 (*ulga*) relief; **~ lekarskie** sick leave; **~ podatkowe** tax exemption

zwro|t (**-tu, -ty**; *loc sg* **-cie**) *m* 1 (*skręt, zmiana*) turn 2 (*długu, książki*) return 3 (*językowy*) expression; **w lewo ~!** left turn!

zwycięst|wo (**-wa, -wa**; *loc sg* **-wie**) *nt* (*wygrana*) victory; **odnieść** (*pf*) **~ (nad kimś/czymś)** to gain a victory (over sb/sth)

zwycięzc|a (**-y, -y**) *m decl like fin sg* (*konkursu, wojny*) winner

zwycięż|ać (**-am, -asz**; *pf* **-yć**) *vt* (*słabości, boleczki, nałóg*) to overcome ▷ *vi* (*w meczu, w walce, w wyborach*) to win

zwyczaj (**-u, -e**) *m* 1 (*tradycja*) custom 2 (*przyzwyczajenie*) habit

zwyczajnie *adv* 1 (*jak zwykle*) as usual 2 (*podkreślając oczywistość*) simply

zwyczajny *adj* 1 (*zwykły, przeciętny*) ordinary 2 (*typowy*) usual 3 (*częsty*) common 4 (*prosty*) common, simple 5 (*kłamca, naiwność*) downright

zwykle *adv* (*zazwyczaj*) usually; **jak ~** as usual

zwykły *adj* 1 (*zwykły, przeciętny*) ordinary 2 (*typowy*) usual 3 (*regularny*) common 4 (*niewyszukany*) common, simple 5 (*naiwność, kłamca*) downright, sheer

zys|k (**-ku, -ki**; *inst sg* **-kiem**) *m* 1 (*dochód*) profit 2 (*pożytek*) gain

Ź ż

źle *adv* **1** (*błędnie odpowiadać*) wrongly **2** (*niestarannie*) poorly, badly; **~ dziś wyglądasz** you don't look well today; **~ się czuję** I don't feel well

źród|ło (**-ła**, **-ła**; *loc sg* **-le**; *gen pl* **-eł**) *nt* **1** (*wiadomości, mocy*) source **2** (*rzeki*) source **3** (*zdrój*) spring **4** (*powód*) source

ża|ba (**-by**, **-by**; *dat sg & loc sg* **-bie**) *f* frog; **będziesz musiał zjeść** *lub* **połknąć tę żabę** you'll just have to live with it

żaden (*f* **żadna**; *nt* **żadne**) *pron* **1** (*przed rzeczownikiem*) no **2** (*zamiast rzeczownika*) none **3** (*ani jeden ani drugi*) neither **4** (*spośród dwóch*) neither (of them); **w ~ sposób tego nie można zrobić** there's no way at all to do this; **w żadnym razie** *lub* **wypadku pójdziemy tam jutro** under no circumstances will we go there tomorrow; **w żadnym wypadku!** no way!; **jego zasługi są żadne** he has no redeeming features; **~ z nich nie przyszedł** none *lub* not one of them came

żaglów|ka (**-ki**, **-ki**; *dat sg & loc*

sg **-ce**; *gen pl* **-ek**) *f* sailing boat (*Brit*), sailboat (*US*)

żakie|t (**-tu**, **-ty**; *loc sg* **-cie**) *m* (*damska marynarka*) jacket

żal (**-u**, **-e**) *m* **1** (*uczucie smutku*) sorrow **2** (*skrucha*) regret **3** (*rozgoryczenie*) bitterness; **żale** *pl* complaints; **było mi jej ~** I felt sorry for her; **mam do ciebie ~ za twój uczynek** I have a grudge against you because of what you did

żal|ić się (**-ę**, **-isz**; *pf* **po-**) *vr* (*narzekać*) to complain

żało|ba (**-by**; *dat sg* & *loc sg* **-bie**) *f* (*smutek po śmierci kogoś, obyczaj*) mourning; **~ narodowa** national mourning

żałobny *adj* (*nabożeństwo*) funeral; **ubiór ~** mourning; **msza żałobna** memorial *lub* funeral service

żał|ować (**-uję**, **-ujesz**; *pf* **po-**) *vt*: **~ czegoś** to regret sth ▷ *vi* to regret; **żałował, że nie przyjechała** he felt sorry that she didn't come; **żałował jej ciastka** he begrudged her a biscuit; **żałuję, że nie wyjechałem** I wish I had left

żarów|ka (**-ki**, **-ki**; *dat sg* & *loc sg* **-ce**; *gen pl* **-ek**) *f* light bulb

żar|t (**-tu**, **-ty**; *loc sg* **-cie**) *m* joke; **zrobił to dla ~u** he did it as a joke; **żarty ~ami** a joke's a joke; **robili sobie z niego ~y** they made fun of him

żart|ować (**-uję**, **-ujesz**; *pf* **za-**) *vi* (*dowcipkować*) to joke; **~ z** +*gen* to make fun of

żąd|ać (**-am**, **-asz**; *pf* **za-**) *vt*: **~ czegoś** (*wymagać*) to demand sth

żąda|nie (**-nia**, **-nia**; *gen pl* **-ń**) *nt* (*wymaganie*) demand; **przystanek autobusowy na ~** request stop (*Brit*), flag stop (*US*)

że *conj* that ▷ *part*: **(po)mimo ~ długo pracowali, nie zdążyli na czas** although they worked long hours they still missed the deadline; **dlatego ~ nie ma racji** because he's wrong; **był tak zmęczony, ~ zasnął w fotelu** he was so tired he fell asleep in his armchair; **jako ~** since; **tyle ~** but, only; **chyba ~ przyjdziecie wszyscy razem** unless you all come together

żebra|k (**-ka**, **-cy**; *inst sg* **-kiem**) *m* beggar

żeb|ro (**-ra**, **-ra**; *loc sg* **-rze**; *gen pl* **-er**) *nt* rib; **porachować komuś żebra** (*pot*) to beat sb up

żeby *conj* (*oznaczenie skutku*) in order to ▷ *part*: **~ tylko nam się udało** if only it all works out for us; **jest zbyt biedny, ~ kupić dom** he's too poor to buy a house; **~ nie przestraszyć kota** so as not to frighten the cat; **~ nie on, zwyciężyłaby** if it weren't for him she would have won; **nie chcę, ~ś tu mieszkał** I don't want you to live here; **~ś mi przestał przeszkadzać!** stop disturbing me!

żeglarz (**-a**, **-e**; *gen pl* **-y**) *m* (*sportowiec*) yachtsman

żegl|ować (**-uję**, **-ujesz**) *vi* to sail

żegn|ać (**-am**, **-asz**; *pf* **po-**) *vt*: **~ kogoś** to say goodbye to sb; **~ się** *vr* **1** (*pf* **po-**) (*na do widzenia*) to say goodbye **2** (*pf* **prze-**) (*w kościele: kreślić znak krzyża*) to cross o.s.; **żegnaj!** farewell!

żelaz|ko (**-ka, -ka**; *inst sg* **-kiem**; *gen pl* **-ek**) *nt* (*urządzenie do prasowania*) iron (*for pressing clothes*)

żelazny *adj* **1** (*zrobiony z żelaza*) iron **2** (*o zdrowiu*) robust; **masz żelazne nerwy** you have nerves of steel

żela|zo (**-za**; *loc sg* **-zie**) *nt* iron

że|nić (**-nię, -nisz**; *imp* **-ń**; *pf* **o-**) *vt* to marry (off); **~ się** *vr*: **~ się z** +*inst* (*o mężczyźnie*) to get married to

żeński *adj* **1** (*dla dziewcząt*) girls' **2** (*płeć*) female; **rodzaj ~** (*w językoznawstwie*) feminine (gender)

żeto|n (**-nu, -ny**; *loc sg* **-nie**) *m* **1** (*do telefonu*) token **2** (*do gier hazardowych*) chip

żłob|ek (**-ka, -ki**; *inst sg* **-kiem**) *m* (*miejsce opieki nad dziećmi*) crèche (*Brit*), day nursery (*US*)

żmij|a (**-i, -je**; *gen pl* **-i**) *f* viper, adder; **hodować (wyhodować** *pf*) **żmiję na własnej piersi** to nurse a viper in one's bosom

żołąd|ek (**-ka, -ki**; *inst sg* **-kiem**) *m* stomach; **przez ~ do serca** the way to a man's heart is through his stomach

żołądkowy *adj* **1** stomach **2** (*soki*) gastric; **krople żołądkowe** ≈ bitters

żołnierz (**-a, -e**; *gen pl* **-y**) *m* (*wojskowy*) soldier

żo|na (**-ny, -ny**; *dat sg & loc sg* **-nie**) *f* (*małżonka*) wife

żonaty *adj* (*mężczyzna*) married

żółt|ko (**-ka, -ka**; *inst sg* **-kiem**; *gen pl* **-ek**) *nt* yolk

żółty *adj* (*barwa*) yellow; **~ ser** hard cheese

żół|w (**-wia, -wie**; *gen pl* **-wi**) *m* **1** (*lądowy*) tortoise, turtle (*US*) **2** (*morski*) turtle

żurawi|na (**-ny, -ny**; *dat sg & loc sg* **-nie**) *f* cranberry

żur|ek (**-ku, -ki**; *inst sg* **-kiem**) *m* (*Kulin*) traditional Polish soup made from fermented rye often with sausage or smoked bacon

życi|e (**-a**) *nt* **1** life **2** (*pot: codzienne*) living (costs); **prowadzić zdrowy tryb życia** to lead a healthy lifestyle; **~ osobiste** private life; **ubezpieczenie na ~** life assurance; **wprowadzać (wprowadzić** *pf*) **coś w ~** to put sth into effect

życiory|s (**-su, -sy**; *loc sg* **-sie**) *m* **1** (*informacja dla pracodawcy*) CV, curriculum vitae (*Brit*), resumé (*US*) **2** (*biografia*) biography

życiowy *adj* **1** (*proces*) vital **2** (*doświadczenie*) practical **3** (*pot: stosunek do rzeczywistości*) realistic

życze|nie (**-nia, -nia**; *gen pl* **-ń**) *nt* (*pragnienie*) wish; **życzenia** *pl* (*świąteczne, imieninowe*) wishes; **usługa na ~** a request service; **składać komuś życzenia z okazji urodzin** to wish sb all the best on their birthday

życzliwoś|ć (**-ci**) *f* kindness

życzliwy *adj* (*człowiek, relacja*) kind

życz|yć (**-ę, -ysz**) *vt*: **~ komuś czegoś** to wish sb sth; **czego państwo sobie życzą?** can I help you?

ży|ć (**-ję, -jesz**) *vi* to live; **niech**

żyje król! long live the king!; **~ z
zapomogi** to live off benefit (*Brit*)
lub social welfare (*US*)
Ży|d (**-da**, **-dzi**; *loc sg* **-dzie**) *m* Jew
Żydów|ka (**-ki**, **-ki**; *dat sg* **-ce**; *gen
pl* **-ek**) *f* Jew
żydowski *adj* (*kultura, teatr*)
Jewish
ży|ła (**-ły**, **-ły**; *loc sg* **-le**) *f* vein;
strach zmroził mu krew w ~ch
he felt a blood-curdling fear
żyra|fa (**-fy**, **-fy**; *loc sg* **-fie**) *f*
giraffe
żytni *adj* (*chleb, mąka*) rye
żywio|ł (**-łu**, **-ły**; *loc sg* **-le**) *m*
(*woda, ziemia, powietrze, ogień*)
element; **być w swoim żywiole**
to be in one's element
żywopło|t (**-tu**, **-ty**; *loc sg* **-cie**)
m hedge
żywy *adj* 1 (*żyjący*) living
2 (*żywiołowy*) lively 3 (*wyrazisty*)
vivid; **to ona, jak żywa** it's her
down to a T; **na żywo** live; **mecz
był transmitowany na żywo** the
match was broadcast live

POLISH
IN ACTION

ANGIELSKI
W AKCJI

CONTENTS   SPIS TREŚCI

KORESPONDENCJA

▶ LIST PRYWATNY

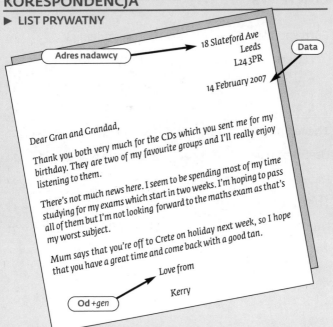

Adres nadawcy →

18 Slateford Ave
Leeds
L24 3PR

Data

14 February 2007

Dear Gran and Grandad,

Thank you both very much for the CDs which you sent me for my birthday. They are two of my favourite groups and I'll really enjoy listening to them.

There's not much news here. I seem to be spending most of my time studying for my exams which start in two weeks. I'm hoping to pass all of them but I'm not looking forward to the maths exam as that's my worst subject.

Mum says that you're off to Crete on holiday next week, so I hope that you have a great time and come back with a good tan.

Love from

Kerry

Od +gen →

POCZĄTEK LISTU PRYWATNEGO

Thank you for your letter.	*Dziękuję za Twój list.* (singular)
	Dziękuję za Wasz list. (plural)
It was lovely to hear from you.	*Miło mi było otrzymać wiadomości od Ciebie.* (singular)
	Miło mi było otrzymać wiadomości od Was. (plural)
I'm sorry I didn't write earlier.	*Przykro mi, że nie napisałem/napisałam wcześniej.*

ZAKOŃCZENIE LISTU PRYWATNEGO

Write soon!	*Napisz wkrótce!* (singular)
	Napiszcie wkrótce! (plural)
Give my love to Vanessa.	*Przekaż serdeczne pozdrowienia dla Vanessy.* (singular)
	Przekażcie serdeczne pozdrowienia dla Vanessy. (plural)
Samuel sends his best wishes.	*Samuel przesyła najlepsze życzenia.*

4

CORRESPONDENCE

▶ PERSONAL LETTER

Katowice, 14 lutego 2007

Place & Date

Droga Babciu, Drogi Dziadku,

Dziękuję Wam obojgu za płyty kompaktowe, które przysłaliście mi z okazji moich urodzin. Są to dwa spośród moich ulubionych zespołów i z przyjemnością będę ich słuchać.

U mnie niewiele nowego. Spędzam większość czasu na przygotowaniach do egzaminów, które zaczynają się za dwa tygodnie. Mam nadzieję, że wszystkie zdam, ale obawiam się o egzamin z matematyki, bo to mój najgorszy przedmiot.

Mama mówi, że w przyszłym tygodniu jedziecie na wakacje na Kretę, mam więc nadzieję, że spędzicie miło czas i wrócicie ładnie opaleni.

Całusy od

Moniki

STARTING A PERSONAL LETTER

Dziękuję za Twój list. *(singular)*	*Thank you for your letter.*
Dziękuję za Wasz list. *(plural)*	
Miło mi było otrzymać wiadomości od Ciebie. *(singular)*	*It was lovely to hear from you.*
Miło mi było otrzymać wiadomości od Was. *(plural)*	
Przykro mi, żnie napisałem/napisałam wcześniej.	*I'm sorry I didn't write earlier.*

ENDING A PERSONAL LETTER

Napisz wkrótce! *(singular)*	*Write soon!*
Napiszcie wkrótce! *(plural)*	
Przekaż serdeczne pozdrowienia dla Vanessy. *(singular)*	*Give my love to Vanessa.*
Przekażcie serdeczne pozdrowienia dla Vanessy. *(plural)*	
Samuel przesyła najlepsze życzenia.	*Samuel sends his best wishes.*

109 Belleview Road
Cumbernauld
CA7 4TX

29th March 2007

Mrs Elaine Harris
Manager
Poppywell Cottage
Devon DV3 8SP

Dear Mrs Harris,

My sister stayed with you last year and has highly recommended your guest house.

I would like to reserve a room for one week from 18th – 24th August of this year. I would be obliged if you would let me know how much this would be for two adults and two children, and whether you have rooms free on those dates.

I hope to hear from you soon,

Yours sincerely,

▶ LETTERS

ul. Conrada 15 m. 109
01-359 Warszawa

29 marca 2007

Sz. P. Maria Nowak
Hotel Chopin
ul. Piekary 7
34-500 Zakopane

Szanowna Pani,

Moja siostra zatrzymała się u Pani w zeszłym roku i gorąco
mi poleciła Pani pensjonat.

Chciałabym zarezerwować pokój na tydzień w terminie
18-24 sierpnia br. Będę wdzięczna za informację, jaki będzie
koszt pobytu dla dwojga dorosłych i dwójki dzieci oraz czy są
wolne pokoje w tym terminie.

Z poważaniem,

Miss K. Urbanowicz
ul. Warszawska 11/67
02-367 Łódź

13th April 2007

Mrs Aileen Fields
Funky Fashions
14 Bracken Lane
Windermere
UK

Dear Mrs Fields,

I am anxious to find a job in Britain during my summer holiday from University and wish to gain experience in the fashion industry. I would be obliged if you could offer me work in any capacity. I can supply references from former employers, if you would like them.

Yours sincerely,

14 Bracken Lane
Windermere
Wielka Brytania

13 kwietnia 2007

Sz. P. Magdalena Batyniak
ul. Radziwiłłowska 55
02-615 Kraków

Szanowna Pani,

Bardzo pragnęłabym znaleźć pracę w Polsce na okres studenckiej przerwy letniej i chciałabym zdobyć doświadczenie w branży mody. Będę wdzięczna, jeśli zechce mi Pani zaproponować zatrudnienie w dowolnym charakterze. Jeśli sobie Pani życzy, prześlę referencje od poprzednich pracodawców.

Z poważaniem,

os. Jagiellońskie 90/4
61-217 Poznań

2nd March 2007

Mr Brian Goodman
Human Resources Manager
DTL Thompson Ltd
30 Brownwood Street
Brighton
BR8 4LJ

Dear Mr Goodman,

I am 19 years old and a student of English at Poznań University. I would like to work in Britain in order to perfect my English. I would be grateful if you would let me know if your agency could offer me work for a period of about ten months from Easter.

Yours in anticipation,

CORRESPONDENCE

▶ **LETTERS**

129 Strathmore Avenue
Edinburgh
EH11 2AD

2 marca 2007

Sz. P. Marek Ptak
Agencja Nowa
ul. Wrocławska 20
Poznań

Szanowny Panie,

Mam 19 lat, jestem studentką polskiego na Uniwersytecie w Edinburgu. Chciałabym pracować w Polsce, by udoskonalić moją znajomość polskiego. Będę wdzięczna za informację, czy Pańska agencja mogłaby zaoferować mi pracę na okres około 10 miesięcy począwszy od Wielkanocy.

Z poważaniem,

Jessica Lister

48 Gill Road
Chesterton
Birmingham
BR6 7NG

28th April 2007

Dear Jack,

Thought I'd write to let you know that we'd arrived safely and are now settled in our lovely new home – all the stress was worth it.

The countryside is beautiful and so peaceful. We are looking forward to taking long walks in summer, when it's a little warmer. The children are already making new friends and Cara is quite happy in her new school.

I hope you are going to be able to come up and spend some time with us soon, George is eager to take you fishing.

Hope Elizabeth and the children are well.

Love
Andrea

CORRESPONDENCE

▶ LETTERS

Jacek Nowak
ul. 3-go Maja 12
00-111 Ciechanów

Warszawa, 28.04.2007

Drogi Jacku!

Pomyślałam, że napiszę do Ciebie, aby dać Ci znać, że dojechaliśmy bezpiecznie i już zadomowiliśmy się w nowym domu. Było to warte tego całego stresu!

Wieś jest taka piękna i spokojna. Czekamy na lato, aby móc pójść na długi spacer, jak tylko trochę się ociepli. Dzieci już mają nowych przyjaciół, zaś Kamila jest zadowolona z nowej szkoły.

Jak będziesz mógł to proszę odwiedź nas wkrótce i spędź z nami trochę czasu. Grzegorz nie może doczekać się wspólnego wędkowania.

Mam nadzieję, że u Ciebie, Elżbiety i dzieci wszystko w porządku.

Pozdrawiam serdecznie
Anna

Rosalind Williamson
11 North Street
Barnton
BN7 2BT

Human Resources Dept
Messrs. J M. Kenyon Ltd.,
Firebrick House
Clifton
MC45 6RB

20th February 2007

Dear Sir or Madam,

With reference to your advertisement in today's Guardian,
I wish to apply for the post of Human Resources Manager.

I enclose my curriculum vitae. Please do not hesitate to
contact me if you require any further details.

Yours faithfully,
Rosalind Williamson

Enc: CV with two references.

ul. Tyniecka 11
04-217 Kraków

20 lutego 2007

Dział Zasobów Ludzkich
Bank Warszawski
ul. Prusa 14
01-612 Warszawa

Szanowni Państwo,

W nawiązaniu do Państwa ogłoszenia w dzisiejszym wydaniu "Gazety Wyborczej" pragnę złożyć kandydaturę na stanowisko Kierownika Zasobów Ludzkich.

Przesyłam w załączeniu mój życiorys. Uprzejmie proszę o kontakt, gdyby potrzebne były dodatkowe informacje.

Z poważaniem,
Dorota Mazowiecka

Zał. : życiorys + dwie referencje

CURRICULUM VITAE

Name:	Rosalind Anna WILLIAMSON
Address:	11 North Street, Barton, BN7 2BT, England
Telephone:	Barton (01294) 476230
Date of Birth:	6.5.1978
Marital Status:	Single
Nationality:	British
Qualifications:	A Levels (1996): Italian (A), French (B), English (D) O-Levels (1994): 9 subjects B.A. 2nd class Honours degree in Italian with French, University of Newby, England (2000)
Present Post:	Assistant Personnel Officer, Metal Company plc. Barton (since February 2002)
Previous Employment:	Nov. 2000 – Jan 2001: Personnel trainee, Metal Company plc Oct. 1996 – June 2000: Student, University of Newby
Skills, Interests and Experience:	Fluent Italian & French; good working knowledge of German; some Russian; car owner and driver (clean licence); riding & sailing.

The following have agreed to provide references:

Ms Alice Bluegown, Personnel Manager, Metal Company plc, Barnton, NB4 3KL

Dr I.O. Sono, Department of Italian, University of Newby, Newby, SR13 2RR

▶ CURRICULUM VITAE

ŻYCIORYS

Imię i nazwisko:	Katarzyna Pietrzyk
Adres:	ul. Kwiatowa 6 m. 18, Warszawa
Numer telefonu:	0022 384 67 82
Data urodzenia:	6 maja 1978 r.
Stan cywilny:	panna
Narodowość:	polska
Kwalifikacje:	Matura w 1996 r., XVI Liceum Ogólnokształcące imienia Adama Mickiewicza, Warszawa Październik 1996 – czerwiec 2000 Studia - Romanistyka, Uniwersytet Warszawski
Obecnie zajmowane stanowisko:	Asystentka w Dziale Zasobów Ludzkich, Przedsiębiorstwo Usługowo- Handlowe ABC (od lutego 2002)
Poprzednio zajmowane stanowisko:	Listopad 2000 – styczeń 2001: Stażystka w Dziale Zasobów Ludzkich, Przedsiębiorstwo Usługowo- Handlowe ABC
Doświadczenie, zainteresowania:	Płynna znajomość francuskiego i włoskiego; dobra znajomość niemieckiego; podstawy rosyjskiego. Posiadam samochód i jestem kierowcą (prawo jazdy bez wykroczeń). Interesuję się jazdą konną i żeglowaniem.

Osoby, które zaproponowały swoje referencje:
Pani Monika Nowak, Kierownik Działu Zasobów Ludzkich,
Przedsiębiorstwo Usługowo- Handlowe ABC, ul. Dobra 18,
01-957 Warszawa
Dr. Jan Nowak, Wydział Romanistyki, Uniwersytet Warszawski, ul.
Obożna 5, 01-719, Warszawa

Abacus Organics

The Old Farm
Wimpley, Nr. Helston
Cornwall CB43 8EZ
Tel: 01783 447 9879
Fax: 01783 447 9878
E-mail: order@abacusorganics.co.uk

Date: 6 November 2006

To: Jane Friel, The Blue Café
From: Adrian Smith
No. of pages to follow: 4

Dear Jane Friel,

Re: Catalogue request

Thank you for your fax. Please find attached a complete list of organic goods available by mail order. Please note that we now offer _free_ delivery for all orders over £50.00, and as a new client you will be eligible for a 15% discount off your first order!

If I can be of any further assistance, please do not hesitate to contact me.

With kindest regards

Adrian Smith

▶ FAX

Abakus Sp. z. oo.

Jan Nowak
Gospodarstwo Ekologiczne
ul. Długa 18
01-123 Mińsk Mazowiecki
tel: 027 56 76 89
faks: 027 57 89 00
e-mail: gospekolg@natura.pl

Warszawa, 6.11.2006

Od: Piotra Kociniaka
Do: Jana Nowaka
Ilość stron: 4

Dotyczy: Zamówienia z katalogu

Szanowny Panie,

Dziękuję za Pański faks. W załączeniu przesyłam pełną listę produktów naturalnych, które możemy przesłać pocztą. Jednocześnie chciałbym Pana zawiadomić, że wszystkie zamówienia powyżej 200 PLN będą dostarczane bezpłatnie. Panu, jako nowemu klientowi, przysługuje także 15% zniże przy pierwszym zamówieniu.

Z chęcią odpowiem na Pana dalsze pytania.

Z wyrazami szacunku,

Piotr Kociniak

KORESPONDENCJA

► E-MAIL

> Aby podać komuś adres emailowy po angielsku należy powiedzieć:
> gemma at n t net dot co dot u k

New message

To:	gemma@ntnet.co.uk
From:	gordon@onemo.net
Subject:	concert next week
cc:	jeremy@bit.com
bcc:	

Attachment **Send**

Hi guys

I've just bought the new album by Rockstar, and it's brilliant! I've got two spare tickets to a concert they're giving in Edinburgh next Wednesday evening, so I hope you can both make it.

See you soon!

New message	Nowa wiadomość
To	Do
From	Od
Subject	Temat
cc	cc
bcc	bcc
Attachment	Załącznik
Send	Wyślij

CORRESPONDENCE

▶ **E-MAIL**

> To give your e-mail address to someone in Polish, say:
> 'anna małpa w p kropka p l'

■ **Nowa wiadomość**

Do:	anna@wp.pl
Od:	kasia@icpnet.pl
Temat:	koncert w przyszłym tygodniu
cc:	przemek@wp.pl
bcc:	

| Załącznik | | Wyślij |

Cześć Wam,

Właśnie kupiłem nowy album Rockstar, jest super! Mam dwa wolne bilety na ich koncert w przyszłą środę wieczór; mam nadzieję, że dacie radę przyjść.

Do zobaczenia!

Nowa wiadomość	New message
Do	To
Od	From
Temat	Subject
cc	cc
bcc	bcc
Załącznik	Attachment
Wyślij	Send

THE TELEPHONE

TELEFON

▶ **WHEN YOUR NUMBER ANSWERS**

- Hello! Could I speak to Susana, please?

- Could you ask him/her to call me back, please?

- I'll call back in half an hour.

▶ **ANSWERING THE TELEPHONE**

- Hello! It's Mark speaking.

- Speaking.

- Who's speaking?

▶ **WHEN THE SWITCHBOARD ANSWERS**

- Who shall I say is calling?

- I'm putting you through.

- Please hold.

- Would you like to leave a message?

▶ **DIFFICULTIES**

- I can't get through.

- I'm sorry, I've got the wrong number.

- This is a very bad line.

- Their phone is out of order.

▶ **GDY DO KOGOŚ TELEFONUJEMY**

- Halo! Czy mogę rozmawiać z Zuzanną?

- Czy może Pan / Pani go / ją poprosić, by do mnie oddzwonił / oddzwoniła?

- Oddzwonię za pół godziny.

▶ **GDY ODBIERAMY TELEFON**

- Halo! Mówi Marek.

- To ja.

- Kto mówi?

▶ **GDY TELEFON ODBIERA CENTRALA**

- Kogo mam zaanonsować?

- Łączę Pana / Panią.

- Proszę czekać.

- Czy chciałby Pan / chciałaby Pani zostawić wiadomość?

▶ **PROBLEMY**

- Nie mogę uzyskać połączenia.

- Przykro mi, mam niewłaściwy numer.

- Jakość połączenia jest bardzo zła.

- Ich telefon nie działa.

USEFUL PHRASES

GREETINGS

Hello!	Cześć!
Goodbye!	Do widzenia!
Bye!	Cześć!
Good morning	Dzień dobry
Good afternoon	Dzień dobry
Good evening	Dobry wieczór
Good night	Dobranoc
What's your name?	Jak Pan/Pani ma na imię?
My name is ...	Mam na imię ...
Where are you from?	Skąd Pan/Pani pochodzi?
I come from ...	Pochodzę z +gen ...
Do you speak English?	Czy mówi Pan/Pani po angielsku?
Sorry, I don't understand.	Przeprasam, nie rozumiem.
Welcome!	Witaj! (greeting a friend)
	Witamy! (formal)
How are you?	Jak się masz? (to one person, familiar)
	Jak się macie? (to more than one person, familiar)
	Jak się Pan / Pani ma? (to a man/ woman, polite)
I'm fine, thank you	Dobrze, dziękuję
Pleased to meet you	Miło mi Cię poznać (singular, familiar)
	Miło mi Was poznać (plural, familiar)
	Miło mi Panią poznać (singular, polite, to a woman)
	Miło mi Pana poznać (singluar, polite, to a man)
How's life?	Co słychać?
See you tomorrow!	Do zobaczenia jutro!
See you later!	Na razie!
Good luck!	Powodzenia!
Congratulations!	Gratulacje!

PRZYDATNE WYRAŻENIA

POZDROWIENIA

USEFUL PHRASES

PRZYDATNE WYRAŻENIA

Have fun!	Baw się dobrze! (*to one person*)
	Bawcie się dobrze! (*to more than one person*)
Cheers!	Na zdrowie!
Bless you!	Na zdrowie!
Take care!	Trzymaj się (*familiar*)
	Wszystkiego dobrego (*polite*)
Enjoy your meal	Smacznego!
Happy Birthday!	Wszystkiego dobrego z okazji urodzin!
Merry Christmas!	Wesołych Świąt Bożego Narodzenia!
Happy New Year!	Szczęśliwego Nowego Roku!

ON THE TELEPHONE

ROZMOWA PRZEZ TELEFON

Hello?	Halo?
Who's speaking?	Kto mówi?
It's Laura speaking	Mówi Laura
Could I speak to... please	Czy mogę mówić z ... +*inst*
My phone number is...	Mój numer telefonu to...
It's engaged.	Numer jest zajęty.
There's no reply.	Nikt nie odbiera.
Do you speak Polish/English?	Czy mówi Pan / Pani po polsku / angielsku?
Please hold the line.	Proszę czekać.
Could you put me through to extension 3395?	Czy mogę prosić o połączenie z numerem 3395?
Would you like to leave a message?	Czy chciałby Pan / chciałaby Pani zostawić wiadomość?
Could you tell him that I called?	Czy może mu Pan / Pani powiedzieć, że zadzwoniłem / zadzwoniłam?
I'll call back later.	Oddzwonię później.
I'm afraid you have the wrong number.	Obawiam się, że to niewłaściwy numer.

USEFUL PHRASES   PRZYDATNE WYRAŻENIA

LETTER WRITING

LISTY

Dear Sir/Madam
  Yours faithfully

Szanowny Panie / Szanowna Pani
  Z poważaniem

Dear Mr. Fontes
  Dear Mrs. Smith

Szanowny Panie
  Szanowna Pani (*surnames are not
  used in formal correspondence*)

  Yours sincerely
  Best wishes
  Kind regards

  Z poważaniem
  Z najlepszymi życzeniami
  Serdeczne pozdrowienia

Dear Katie
  All the best
  With love from ...

Droga Kasiu
  Wszystkiego dobrego
  Serdeczne pozdrowienia od ...
  +gen

Please find enclosed ...
Thank you for your letter.

W załączeniu przesyłam ...
Dziękuję za list.

E-MAIL

Do you have e-mail?

Czy masz adres e-mailowy?
  (*familiar, singular*)
Czy macie adres e-mailowy?
  (*familiar, plural*)
Czy ma Pan / Pani adres e-mailowy?
  (*polite, singular*)

What's your e-mail address?

Jaki jest Twój adres e-mailowy?
  (*familiar, singular*)
Jaki jest Wasz adres e-mailowy?
  (*familiar, plural*)
Jaki jest Pani / Pana adres e-mailowy?
  (*polite, singular*)

My e-mail address is ...
Emma@coolmail.com
(emma at coolmail dot com)
I'll email you the details.

Mój adres e-mailowy to ...

emma małpka coolmail kropka com
Wyślę Ci / Wam / Pani / Panu
  szczegóły e-mailem.

USEFUL PHRASES   PRZYDATNE WYRAŻENIA

FOOD SHOPPING

Where is the nearest
  supermarket?
Where is the nearest baker's?
Where is the nearest butcher's?

ZAKUPY ŻYWNOŚCIOWE

Gdzie jest najbliższy
  supermarket?
Gdzie jest najbliższa piekarnia?
Gdzie jest najbliższy sklep mięsny?

EMERGENCY SERVICES

Help!
Fire!
Please call the emergency
  doctor.
Please call the fire brigade.
Please call the police.
Where is the police station?
Where is the hospital?
There's been an accident.
I've been robbed.

I've been attacked.

SŁUŻYBY RATOWNICZE

Pomocy!
Pożar!
Proszę wezwać lekarza.

Proszę wezwać straż pożarną.
Proszę wezwać policję.
Gdzie jest posterunek policji?
Gdzie jest szpital?
Zdarzył się wypadek.
Zostałem okradziony / Zostałam
  okradziona.
Zostałem zaatakowany / Zostałam
  zaatakowana.

AT THE DOCTOR'S

I need a doctor.
Where is casualty?
I have a pain here.
I feel hot.
I feel cold.
I feel sick.
I feel dizzy.
I am pregnant.

U LEKARZA

Potrzebuję lekarza.
Gdzie jest izba przyjęć?
Boli mnie tutaj.
Jest mi gorąco.
Jest mi zimno.
Niedobrze mi.
Kręci mi się w głowie.
Jestem w ciąży.

DAYS OF THE WEEK

Monday
Tuesday
Wednesday
Thursday
Friday
Saturday
Sunday

DNI TYGODNIA

poniedziałek
wtorek
środa
czwartek
piątek
sobota
niedziela

MONTHS

January
February
March
April
May
June
July
August
September
October
November
December

MIESIĄCE

styczeń
luty
marzec
kwiecień
maj
czerwiec
lipiec
sierpień
wrzesień
październik
listopad
grudzień

USEFUL VOCABULARY

today
tomorrow
the day after tomorrow
yesterday
the day before yesterday
the day before, the previous day
the next or following day
morning
evening
this morning
this evening
this afternoon
yesterday morning
yesterday evening

PRZYDATNE WYRAŻENIA

dziś
jutro
pojutrze
wczoraj
przedwczoraj
w przeddzień, poprzedniego dnia
następnego dnia
rano
wieczór
dziś rano
dziś wieczorem
dziś po południu
wczoraj rano
wczoraj wieczorem

tomorrow morning	jutro rano
tomorrow evening	jutro wieczorem
during Saturday night, during	podczas sobotniej nocy, w nocy
the night of Saturday to Sunday	z soboty na niedzielę
he's coming on Saturday	on przyjdzie w sobotę
on Saturdays	w soboty
every Saturday	w każdą sobotę
last Saturday	w ostatnią sobotę
next Saturday	w następną sobotę
a week on Saturday	od tej soboty za tydzień
a fortnight *or* two weeks on Saturday	od tej soboty za dwa tygodnie
from Monday to Saturday	od poniedziałku do soboty
every day	każdego dnia
once a week	raz w tygodniu
once a month	raz w miesiącu
twice a week	dwa razy w tygodniu
a week ago	tydzień temu
a fortnight *or* two weeks ago	dwa tygodnie temu
last year	zeszłego roku
in two days	za dwa dni, w ciągu dwóch dni
in a week	za tydzień
in a fortnight *or* two weeks	za dwa tygodnie
next month	w przyszłym / następnym miesiącu
next year	w przyszłym / następnym roku
what day is it?	*Jaki dziś mamy dzień?*
the 1ˢᵗ/24ᵗʰ of October 2007,	1/24 października 2007
October the 1ˢᵗ/24ᵗʰ 2007	
in 2012	W 2012
in 1996	w tysiąc dziewięćset dziewięć-
	dziesiątym szóstym roku
44 BC	44 rok przed Chrystusem /
	44 rok przed naszą erą
14 AD	14 rok po Chrystusie /
	14 rok naszej ery
in the nineteenth century	w dziewiętnastym wieku
in the thirties	w latach trzydziestych
once upon a time ...	pewnego razu...

THE TIME

CZAS

WHAT TIME IS IT?

KTÓRA JEST GODZINA?

Jest piętnaście po pierwszej /
jest kwadrans po pierwszej.

It's one fifteen.

Jest południe / północ.

It's midday/midnight.

Jest trzecia trzydzieści /
jest wpół do czwartej.

It's half past three.

Jest za dziesięć druga.

It's ten to two.

Jest dziewiąta rano / wieczorem.

It's nine o'clock in the
morning/at night.

Jest za dwadzieścia ósma.

It's twenty to eight.

THE TIME

CZAS

What time is it?
It's ...

Która godzina?
Jest ...

midnight	północ
one o'clock (in the morning), one (am)	pierwsza (w nocy)
five past one	pięć po pierwszej
ten past one	dziesięć po pierwszej
a quarter past one, one fifteen	kwadrans po pierwszej, pierwsza piętnaście
twenty-five past one, one twenty-five	dwadzieścia pięć po pierwszej, pierwsza dwadzieścia pięć
half past one, one thirty	w pół do drugiej, pierwsza trzydzieści
twenty-five to two, one thirty-five	za dwadzieścia pięć druga, pierwsza trzydzieści pięć
twenty to two, one forty	za dwadzieścia druga, pierwsza czterdzieści
a quarter to two, one forty-five	za kwadrans druga, pierwsza czterdzieści pięć
ten to two, one fifty	za dziesięć druga, pierwsza pięćdziesiąt
twelve o'clock, midday, noon	(godzina) dwunasta, południe
two o'clock (in the afternoon), two (pm)	(godzina) druga po południu, czternasta
seven o'clock (in the evening), seven (pm)	(godzina) siódma (wieczorem), dziewiętnasta

at what time?

o której godzinie?

at midnight	o północy
at seven o'clock	o siódmej
at one o'clock	o pierwszej
in twenty minutes	za dwadzieścia minut
ten minutes ago	dziesięć minut temu

NUMBERS

LICZEBNIKI

CARDINAL NUMBERS

LICZEBNIKI GŁÓWNE

one	1	jeden
two	2	dwa
three	3	trzy
four	4	cztery
five	5	pięć
six	6	sześć
seven	7	siedem
eight	8	osiem
nine	9	dziewięć
ten	10	dziesięć
eleven	11	jedenaście
twelve	12	dwanaście
thirteen	13	trzynaście
fourteen	14	czternaście
fifteen	15	piętnaście
sixteen	16	szesnaście
seventeen	17	siedemnaście
eighteen	18	osiemnaście
nineteen	19	dziewiętnaście
twenty	20	dwadzieścia
twenty-one	21	dwadzieścia jeden
thirty	30	trzydzieści
forty	40	czterdzieści
fifty	50	pięćdziesiąt
sixty	60	sześćdziesiąt
seventy	70	siedemdziesiąt
eighty	80	osiemdziesiąt
ninety	90	dziewięćdziesiąt
a hundred	100	sto
a hundred and one	101	sto jeden
two hundred	200	dwieście
three hundred	300	trzysta
five hundred	500	pięćset
a thousand	1.000/1,000	tysiąc
a million	1.000.000/1,000,000	milion

NUMBERS   LICZEBNIKI

FRACTIONS ETC

zero point five	0,5/0.5
three point four	3,4/3.4
ten per cent	10%
a hundred per cent	100%

UŁAMKI ITP

pół / zero przecinek pięć
trzy przecinek cztery
dziesięć procent
sto procent

ORDINAL NUMBERS

LICZEBNIKI PORZĄDKOWE

(Please note that ordinal numbers decline like adjectives. For example, the masculine is 'pierwszy', the feminine is 'pierwsza' and the neuter is 'pierwsze'.)

first	1./1st	pierwszy
second	2./2nd	drugi
third	3./3rd	trzeci
fourth	4./4th	czwarty
fifth	5./5th	piąty
sixth	6./6th	szósty
seventh	7./7th	siódmy
eighth	8./8th	ósmy
ninth	9./9th	dziewiąty
tenth	10./10th	dziesiąty
eleventh	11./11th	jedenasty
twentieth	20./20th	dwudziesty
thirtieth	30./30th	trzydziesty
fortieth	40./40th	czterdziesty
fiftieth	50./50th	pięćdziesiąty
hundredth	100./100th	setny
hundred-and-first	101./101st	sto pierwszy
thousandth	1000./1000th	tysięczny

Polish-English

Polski-Angielsko

a

○ KEYWORD

a [eɪ, ə] (*before vowel or silent h:* **an**) *indef art* **1** (*article*) *there is no direct equivalent of the indefinite article in Polish*; **a man** mężczyzna; **a human being** człowiek; **a girl** dziewczyna; **an elephant** słoń; **she's a doctor** ona jest lekarzem; **they haven't got a television** oni nie mają telewizora **2** (*one*) *there is no direct equivalent in Polish*; **a year ago** rok temu; **a hundred/thousand/million pounds** sto/tysiąc/milion funtów **3** (*expressing ratios, prices etc*): **five hours a day/week** pięć godzin dziennie/tygodniowo; **100 km an hour** sto km na godzinę

A & E (*Brit*) *n abbr* (= *accident and emergency*) oddział pomocy doraźnej
abandon [əˈbændən] *vt* (*leave: person, family*) porzucać (porzucić *pf*)
abbey [ˈæbɪ] *n* opactwo
abbreviation [əbriːvɪˈeɪʃən] *n* skrót
ability [əˈbɪlɪtɪ] *n* **1** (*capacity*): **~ (to do sth)** umiejętność (zrobienia czegoś) **2** (*talent, skill*) zdolność
able [ˈeɪbl] *adj* **1**: **to be ~ to do sth** (*have skill, ability*) umieć coś zrobić; (*have opportunity*) być w stanie coś zrobić **2** (*clever: pupil, player*) uzdolniony; **you'll be ~ to read in peace here** będziesz tu mógł czytać w spokoju
abolish [əˈbɔlɪʃ] *vt* (*practice*) znosić (znieść *pf*); (*system*) obalać (obalić *pf*)
abortion [əˈbɔːʃən] (*Med*) *n* aborcja; **to have an ~** poddawać (poddać *pf*) się zabiegowi aborcji

○ KEYWORD

about [əˈbaut] *prep* **1** (*relating to*) o; **a book about London** książka o Londynie; **what's it about?** o czym to jest?; **we talked about it** rozmawialiśmy o tym; **I am sorry about that!** przepraszam!; **I am sorry to hear about that** przykro mi to słyszeć; **to be pleased/angry about sth** być zadowolonym/złym z jakiegoś powodu; **what** *or* **how about eating out?** może pójdziemy coś zjeść?

2 (*place*) po; **he was wandering about the garden** błąkał się po ogrodzie
▷ *adv* **1** (*approximately*) mniej więcej; **about a hundred/ thousand people** koło sto/tysiąc osób
2 (*place*) dookoła; **to leave things lying about** zostawiać (zostawić *pf*) wszystko porozrzucane dookoła; **to be about to do sth** właśnie robić (zrobić *pf*) coś

above [əˈbʌv] *prep* **1** (*higher than*) nad; **~ the photograph** nad fotografią **2** (*in rank, authority*) nad (kimś) ▷ *adv* **1** (*in position*) (po)wyżej, u góry **2** (*in amount, number*) powyżej, więcej; **the temperature was ~ 30˚C** temperatura była powyżej trzydziestu stopni Celsjusza
▷ *adj*: **the ~ address** powyższy adres; **~ all** przede wszystkim

abroad [əˈbrɔːd] *adv* **1** (*be*) za granicą **2** (*go*) za granicę

absence [ˈæbsəns] *n* **1** (*of person*) nieobecność **2** (*of thing*) brak

absent [ˈæbsənt] *adj* nieobecny; **to be ~** być nieobecnym

absent-minded [ˈæbsəntˈmaɪndɪd] *adj* roztargniony

absolutely [æbsəˈluːtlɪ] *adv* (*utterly*) całkowicie

absorbent cotton [əbˈzɔːbənt-] (*US*) *n* wata higroskopijna

abuse [*n* əˈbjuːs, *vb* əˈbjuːz] *n* **1** (*insults*) obelgi *f pl* **2** (*ill-treatment: physical*) maltretowanie; (*sexual*) molestowanie **3** (*misuse: of power,* alcohol, drug) nadużywanie ▷ *vt* **1** (*ill-treat: physically*) znęcać się **2** (*sexually: child*) molestować

academic [ækəˈdɛmɪk] *adj* (*books*) naukowy; (*system*) akademicki; (*freedom*) akademicki ▷ *n* pracownik naukowy

academy [əˈkædəmɪ] *n* **1** (*organisation*) akademia **2** (*school, college*) szkoła

accelerate [ækˈsɛləreɪt] *vi* przyspieszać (przyspieszyć *pf*)

accelerator [ækˈsɛləreɪtər] (*Aut*) *n* pedał gazu

accent [ˈæksɛnt] *n* (*pronunciation*) akcent; **to speak with an (Irish/ French) ~** mówić z (irlandzkim/ francuskim) akcentem

accept [əkˈsɛpt] *vt* **1** (*invitation, advice, credit cards etc*) przyjmować (przyjąć *pf*); (*responsibility*) brać (wziąć *pf*) na siebie **2** (*as true, valid: fact, view*) akceptować (zaakceptować *pf*)

acceptable [əkˈsɛptəbl] *adj* **1** (*permissible*) do przyjęcia **2** (*suitable*) właściwy

access [ˈæksɛs] *n* (*to building, room*) dojście; (*to information, papers*) dostęp ▷ *vt* (*Comput*) wchodzić (wejść *pf*); **to have ~ to sb** (*child*) mieć prawo do kontaktu z kimś

accessory [ækˈsɛsərɪ] *n* **1** (*for room, car*) wyposażenie dodatkowe **2** (*Clothing*) dodatek

accident [ˈæksɪdənt] *n* **1** (*involving vehicle*) wypadek **2** (*mishap*) wypadek **3** (*chance event*) przypadek; **to have an ~** mieć wypadek; **by ~** przez przypadek

accidental [æksɪˈdɛntl] adj
przypadkowy
accident and emergency (Brit)
n oddział pomocy doraźnej
accommodation
[əkɔməˈdeɪʃən] n (place to stay)
kwatera; **accommodations** (US)
n pl = **accommodation**
accompany [əˈkʌmpənɪ] vt
1 (formal: escort) towarzyszyć
2 (Mus) akompaniować
according [əˈkɔːdɪŋ]: **~ to** prep
według +gen
account [əˈkaunt] n 1 (with bank,
at shop) konto 2 (report) relacja;
accounts n pl (Comm) rozliczenie;
**to take sth into account, take
~ of sth** brać (wziąć pf) coś pod
uwagę
▶ **account for** vt fus (explain)
wyjaśniać (wyjaśnić pf)
accountant [əˈkauntənt] n
księgowy(-wa) m/f
accuracy [ˈækjurəsɪ] n 1 (of
information, measurements)
dokładność 2 (of person, device)
precyzja
accurate [ˈækjurɪt] adj
1 dokładny 2 (weapon, throw) celny
accurately [ˈækjurɪtlɪ] adv
1 (measure, predict) dokładnie
2 (describe, assess, aim) precyzyjnie;
(report) dokładnie
accuse [əˈkjuːz] vt 1: **to ~ sb of
sth/doing sth** (of dishonesty,
immorality) oskarżać (oskarżyć pf)
kogoś o coś/o zrobienie czegoś
2: **to be ~d of sth** (of crime) być
oskarżonym o coś
ace [eɪs] n as
ache [eɪk] vi 1 (part of body) boleć
2 ▷ n ból; **I've got (a) stomach/**

tooth~ boli mnie brzuch/ząb
achieve [əˈtʃiːv] vt 1 (aim) osiągać
(osiągnąć pf) 2 (victory, success,
result) odnosić (odnieść pf)
achievement [əˈtʃiːvmənt]
n 1 (accomplishment: of person,
organization) osiągnięcie
2 (fulfilment) dokonanie
acid [ˈæsɪd] n (Chem) kwas
▷ adj 1 (Chem: soil) kwaśny
2 (sharp: taste) kwaśny
acne [ˈæknɪ] n trądzik
across [əˈkrɔs] prep 1 (moving
from one side to the other of) przez
2 (situated on the other side of) po
drugiej stronie +gen 3 (extending
from one side to the other of)
przez ▷ adv 1 (from one side to the
other) na drugą stronę 2: **~ from**
(opposite) po drugiej stronie +gen
3 (in width) wszerz
act [ækt] vi 1 (take action)
działać 2 (behave) zachowywać
(zachować pf) się 3 (in play, film)
grać ▷ n 1 (action) akt 2 (Theat: of
play, opera) akt; (of performer)
numer; **~s of sabotage** akty
sabotażu
▶ **act on** vt fus (advice, information)
postępować (postąpić pf) zgodnie
z +inst
action [ˈækʃən] n 1 (steps,
measures) działanie 2 (deed) czyn;
to take ~ podejmować (podjąć
pf) działanie
active [ˈæktɪv] adj 1 (person, life)
aktywny 2 (volcano) czynny
activity [ækˈtɪvɪtɪ] n (pastime)
zajęcie; **activities** n pl (actions)
działania
actor [ˈæktər] n aktor
actress [ˈæktrɪs] n aktorka

actual ['æktjuəl] adj 1 (real, genuine) rzeczywisty 2 (for emphasis) faktyczny

actually ['æktjuəlɪ] adv 1 (indicating or emphasizing truth) w rzeczywistości 2 (in fact) właściwie; **~, we have the same opinion** właściwie mamy takie samo zdanie

AD adv abbr (= Anno Domini) A.D

ad [æd] (inf) n (advertisement) reklama; (classified ad in newspaper, magazine) ogłoszenie

adapt [ə'dæpt] vt (alter, change) adaptować (zaadaptować pf) ▷ vi: **to ~ to sth** przystosowywać (przystosować pf) do czegoś

adaptor [ə'dæptər] (Elec) n rozgałęźnik

add [æd] vt 1 (put in, put on) dodawać (dodać pf) 2: **to ~ (together)** (calculate total of) dodawać (dodać pf) ▷ vi (calculate) dodawać (dodać pf) ▶ **add up** vi (accumulate) powiększać (powiększyć pf) ▷ vt (calculate total of) zgadzać (zgodzić pf) się

addict ['ædɪkt] n osoba uzależniona; **drug ~** narkoman(ka) m/f

addicted [ə'dɪktɪd] adj: **to be ~ to sth** (drugs, drink) być uzależnionym od czegoś

addition [ə'dɪʃən] n (Math) dodawanie; **in ~ to** na dodatek

address [ə'drɛs] n (postal address) adres ▷ vt (letter, parcel) zaadresować; **to be ~ed to sb** (letter, parcel) być zaadresowanym do kogoś

adjective ['ædʒɛktɪv] n przymiotnik

adjust [ə'dʒʌst] vt (device, position) ustawiać (ustawić pf); (setting) regulować pf ▷ vi (adapt: figures) dostosowywać (dostosować pf); (mechanism) przystosowywać (przystosować pf)

adjustable [ə'dʒʌstəbl] adj regulowany

administration [ədmɪnɪs'treɪʃən] n (organizing, supervising) administracja

admiral ['ædmərəl] n admirał

admire [əd'maɪər] vt (like, respect: person) podziwiać

admission [əd'mɪʃən] n 1 (admittance) przyjęcie 2 (also: **~ charge**) opłata za wstęp 3 (confession) przyznanie się; **~ fee** opłata za wstęp

admit [əd'mɪt] vt 1 (confess) przyznawać (przyznać pf) się do +gen 2 (accept: defeat) przyznawać (przyznać pf) się do +gen; (responsibility) przyjmować (przyjąć pf) 3 (to club, organization) przyjmować (przyjąć pf); (to place, area) wpuszczać (wpuścić pf); **he ~s that...** przyznaje, że...; **to be ~ted to hospital** zostać przyjętym do szpitala

adolescent [ædəu'lɛsnt] adj młodzieńczy ▷ n (teenager) nastolatek(-ka) m/f

adopt [ə'dɔpt] vt 1 (approach) przyjmować (przyjąć pf); (attitude) przybierać (przybrać pf); (plan) powziąć 2 (child) adoptować

adopted [ə'dɔptɪd] adj (child) adoptowany

adoption [ə'dɔpʃən] n (of child)

adopcja
adore [ə'dɔːʳ] vt **1** (person)
uwielbiać (uwielbić pf) **2** (inf: film,
activity, food etc) uwielbiać
Adriatic [eɪdrɪ'ætɪk] n Adriatyk;
the ~ Sea Morze Adriatyckie
adult ['ædʌlt] n (person) dorosły
▷ adj (grown-up: life) dorosły
advance [əd'vɑːns] vi **1** (move
forward) posuwać (posunąć pf)
się **2** (make progress) robić (zrobić
pf) postępy ▷ n (development)
postęp ▷ adj (notice, warning)
wcześniejszy; **in ~** (book, prepare,
plan) z wyprzedzeniem
advanced [əd'vɑːnst] adj
1 (highly developed: system,
device) zaawansowany;
(country) rozwinięty **2** (Scol)
zaawansowany
advantage [əd'vɑːntɪdʒ] n
1 (benefit) korzyść **2** (favourable
factor) zaleta; **to take ~
of** (person) wykorzystywać
(wykorzystać pf); (opportunity)
korzystać (skorzystać pf)
adventure [əd'vɛntʃəʳ] n (exciting
event) przygoda
adverb ['ædvəːb] n przysłówek
advert ['ædvəːt] (Brit) n reklama;
(classified ad in newspaper,
magazine) ogłoszenie
advertise ['ædvətaɪz] vi (in
newspaper, on television etc)
reklamować (zareklamować
pf) się ▷ vt **1** (product, event)
promować (wypromować pf)
2 (job) zamieszczać (zamieścić pf)
ofertę +gen
advertisement [əd'vəːtɪsmənt]
(Comm) n (in newspaper, on
television) reklama; (classified ad in

newspaper, magazines) ogłoszenie;
to be an ~ for sth (esp Brit) być
reklamą czegoś
advertising ['ædvətaɪzɪŋ] n
(advertisements) reklama
advice [əd'vaɪs] n rada; **a piece
of ~** porada; **to ask (sb) for ~
(about/on sth)** prosić (poprosić
pf) (kogoś) o radę (na temat
czegoś)
advise [əd'vaɪz] vt (tell): **to ~ sb
to do sth** radzić (poradzić pf)
komuś coś zrobić
aerial ['ɛərɪəl] (Brit) n antena
aerobics [ɛə'rəubɪks] n aerobik
▷ adj: **~ instructor** instruktor
aerobiku
aeroplane ['ɛərəpleɪn] (Brit) n
samolot
aerosol ['ɛərəsɔl] n aerozol
affair [ə'fɛəʳ] n **1** (matter, business)
sprawa **2** (romance) romans;
affairs n pl **1** (matters) sprawy
2 (personal concerns) sprawa; **to
have an ~ (with sb)** mieć romans
(z kimś)
affect [ə'fɛkt] vt (influence: person,
object) wpływać (wpłynąć pf) na
affectionate [ə'fɛkʃənɪt] adj
(person, kiss) serdeczny; (animal)
przywiązany
afford [ə'fɔːd] vt: **to be able to ~
sth** móc sobie pozwolić na coś
afraid [ə'freɪd] adj (frightened)
przestraszony; **to be ~ of sb/sth**
bać się kogoś/czegoś; **to be ~
to do sth/of doing sth** bać się
zrobić coś; **to be ~ that...** (worry,
fear) bać się, że...; (expressing
apology, disagreement) obawiać się,
że...; **I'm ~ so/not** obawiam się,
że tak/nie

Africa [ˈæfrɪkə] *n* Afryka
African [ˈæfrɪkən] *adj* afrykański
▷ *n* (*person*) Afrykanin(-nka) *m/f*
after [ˈɑːftəʳ] *prep* **1** (*in time*)
po **2** (*in place, order*) po ▷ *adv*
(*afterwards*) później ▷ *conj* (*once*)
po; **the day ~ tomorrow**
pojutrze; **it's ten ~ eight** (*US*) jest
dziesięć po ósmej; **day ~ day/
year ~ year** dzień po dniu/rok
po roku; **~ all** mimo wszystko; **~
doing sth** po zrobieniu czegoś
afternoon [ˈɑːftəˈnuːn] *n*
popołudnie; **this ~** dziś po
południu; **tomorrow/yesterday
~** jutro/wczoraj po południu;
(good) ~! (*goodbye*) do widzenia!;
(*hello*) dzień dobry!
after-shave (lotion) [ˈɑːftəʃeɪv-]
n płyn po goleniu
afterwards [ˈɑːftəwədz] (*US*
afterward [ˈɑːftəwəd]) *adv*
później
again [əˈgɛn] *adv* (*a second or
another time*) znów; **~ and ~** or
time and again raz za razem
against [əˈgɛnst] *prep* **1** (*leaning
on, touching*) o **2** (*opposed
to*) przeciwko **3** (*in game or
competition*) przeciwko **4: to
protect ~ sth** chronić przed
czymś; **they'll be playing ~
Australia** oni zagrają przeciwko
Australii; **~ the law/rules** wbrew
prawu/zasadom; **~ one's will**
wbrew czyjejś woli
age [eɪdʒ] *n* **1** (*of person, object*)
wiek **2** (*being old*) starość **3** (*period
in history*) epoka; **what ~ is he?**
ile on ma lat?; **20 years of ~**
dwadzieścia lat; **at the ~ of 20** w
wieku dwudziestu lat; **an ~, ~s**

(*inf*) wieki; **the Stone/Bronze/
Iron A~** era kamienia/brązu/
żelaza
aged¹ [eɪdʒd] *adj*: **~ 10** w wieku
dziesięciu lat
aged² [ˈeɪdʒɪd] *adj* (*elderly*) w
podeszłym wieku ▷ *n pl*: **the ~**
ludzie w podeszłym wieku
agenda [əˈdʒɛndə] *n* **1** (*of meeting*)
porządek dzienny **2** (*political*)
agenda
agent [ˈeɪdʒənt] *n* (*representative*)
przedstawiciel(ka) *m/f*
aggressive [əˈgrɛsɪv] *adj*
(*belligerent*) agresywny
ago [əˈgəu] *adv*: **2 days ~** dwa
dni temu; **long ~/a long time ~**
dawno temu; **how long ~?** jak
dawno temu?
agony [ˈægənɪ] *n* męka
agree [əˈgriː] *vi* **1** (*have same
opinion*) zgadzać (zgodzić *pf*) się
2: to ~ to sth/to do sth zgadzać
(zgodzić *pf*) się na coś/coś zrobić
3: to ~ with sth (*approve of*)
aprobować coś; **to ~ with sb
about sth** (*person*) zgadzać się z
kimś w sprawie czegoś; **to ~ on
sth** (*price, arrangement*) zgadzać
(zgodzić *pf*) się co do czegoś; **to
~ that...** przyznawać (przyznać
pf), że...
agreement [əˈgriːmənt] *n* **1: an
~ (on sth)** (*decision, arrangement*)
porozumienie (w sprawie czegoś)
2 (*consent*) zgoda; **to be in ~ (with
sb/sth)** zgadzać się (z kimś/z
czymś)
agricultural [ægrɪˈkʌltʃərəl] *adj*
(*land, worker*) rolniczy
agriculture [ˈægrɪkʌltʃəʳ] *n*
rolnictwo

ahead [ə'hɛd] *adv* **1** (*in front: of place*) z przodu **2** (*in work, achievements*) do przodu **3** (*in competition*): **to be ~** mieć przewagę **4** (*in the future*) do przodu; **the days/months ~** w następnych dniach/miesiącach; **~ of** (*in front of*) przed; **~ of time** przed czasem; (*in advance of: event*) wcześniej; **to be ~ of one's time** wyprzedzać (wyprzedzić *pf*) swoją epokę; **~ of time/schedule** przed czasem/terminem; **right** *or* **straight ~** (*direction*) prosto przed siebie; (*location*) na wprost; **go ~!** (*giving permission*) proszę bardzo!

aid [eɪd] *n* pomoc

AIDS [eɪdz] *n abbr* (= *acquired immune deficiency syndrome*) AIDS

aim [eɪm] *vt*: **to ~ sth (at sb/sth)** (*camera*) kierować (skierować *pf*) coś (na kogoś/na coś); (*gun*) celować (wycelować *pf*) coś (do kogoś/do czegoś); (*punch, kick*) wymierzać (wymierzyć *pf*) coś (komuś/czemuś) ▷ *vi* (*with weapon*) celować (wycelować *pf*) ▷ *n* cel; **to ~ at sth** (*with weapon*) celować (wycelować *pf*) w coś; **to ~ to do sth** (*inf*) zamierzać (zamierzyć *pf*) coś zrobić

air [ɛəʳ] *n* (*atmosphere*) powietrze ▷ *adj* (*travel, fare*) lotniczy; **in/into/through the ~** w powietrzu; **by ~** (*flying*) drogą lotniczą

air-conditioned ['ɛəkən'dɪʃənd] *adj* klimatyzowany

air conditioning [-kən'dɪʃənɪŋ] *n* klimatyzacja

air force *n* siły powietrzne; **the ~** siły powietrzne

air hostess (*Brit*) *n* stewardesa

airline ['ɛəlaɪn] *n* linia lotnicza

airmail ['ɛəmeɪl] *n*: **by ~** pocztą lotniczą

airplane ['ɛəpleɪn] (*US*) *n* samolot

airport ['ɛəpɔːt] *n* lotnisko

aisle [aɪl] *n* (*in church*) nawa; (*theatre, supermarket, on plane*) przejście; **~ seat** (*on plane*) fotel od strony przejścia

alarm [ə'lɑːm] *n* **1** (*anxiety*) niepokój **2** (*warning device: in house, car etc*) alarm **3** (*on clock*) budzik ▷ *vt* (*person*) niepokoić (zaniepokoić *pf*)

alarm clock *n* budzik

Albania [æl'beɪnɪə] *n* Albania

album ['ælbəm] *n* album

alcohol ['ælkəhɔl] *n* alkohol

alcoholic [ælkə'hɔlɪk] *n* alkoholik(-iczka) *m/f* ▷ *adj* (*drink*) alkoholowy

alert [ə'ləːt] *adj* (*wide awake*) czujny ▷ *n* (*situation*): **a security ~** stan pogotowia ▷ *vt* (*authorities, police*) powiadamiać (powiadomić *pf*)

A level (*Brit*) *n* egzamin kończący szkołę średnią

● **A LEVELS**
●
● Licealiści w wieku 17 lub 18 lat
● podchodzą do egzaminów **A**
● **level** (odpowiednik polskiej
● matury) na koniec szkoły
● średniej. Wyniki egzaminów
● decydują o tym, czy zostaną
● przyjęci na studia.

Algeria [æl'dʒɪərɪə] *n* Algieria

alien ['eɪlɪən] *n* **1** (*foreigner*)
cudzoziemiec(-mka) *m/f* **2** (*extraterrestrial*) istota pozaziemska
▷ *adj* obcy

alike [ə'laɪk] *adj*: **to be/look ~**
być podobnym; **they are all ~** oni
wszyscy są do siebie podobni

alive [ə'laɪv] *adj* (*living*): **to be
~** być żywym; **to keep sb ~**
utrzymywać kogoś przy życiu; **~
and well** cały i zdrowy

○ **KEYWORD**

all [ɔːl] *adj* cały; **all day/night**
cały dzień/całą noc; **all big cities**
wszystkie duże miasta; **all the
time** cały czas; **all his life** całe
swoje życie
▷ *pron* **1** (*of things, everything*)
wszystko; (*of people*) wszyscy *vir
pl*, wszystkie *non-vir pl*; **it's all
settled** wszystko jest załatwione;
all I could do was apologize
wszystko co mogłem zrobić to
przeprosić; **I ate it all, I ate all of
it** wszystko zjadłem; **have you
got it all?** masz wszystko?; **all
of us** wszyscy; **all of the books**
wszystkie książki; **all of the
boys** wszyscy chłopcy; **all of the
women** wszystkie kobiety; **we
all sat down** wszyscy usiedliśmy;
is that all? (*anything else?*) to
wszystko?; (*not more expensive?*)
tylko tyle?
2 (*in expressions*): **after all**
(*considering*) poza tym; (*regardless*)
mimo wszystko; **in all** w sumie;
best of all najlepszy ze wszystkich
▷ *adv* **1** (*emphatic*) zupełnie; **he
was doing it all by himself** robił

to zupełnie samodzielnie; **all
alone** całkiem sam; **all around**
w całym
2 (*in scores*): **the score is 2 all**
remis po dwóch

allergic [ə'lɜːdʒɪk] *adj* (*reaction,
response*) alergiczny; **to be ~
to sth** (*peanuts, cats etc*) być
uczulonym na coś

allergy ['ælədʒɪ] (*Med*) *n* alergia;
to have an ~ to sth mieć alergię
na coś

allow [ə'lau] *vt* **1** (*permit: practice,
behaviour*) pozwalać (pozwolić *pf*)
na **2** (*set aside: sum, time, amount*)
przeznaczać (przeznaczyć *pf*)
3 (*claim, goal*) uznawać (uznać *pf*);
to ~ sb to do sth (*give permission
for sth*) pozwalać (pozwolić *pf*)
komuś coś zrobić; **don't ~ the
soil to dry out** nie pozwól, aby
ziemia wyschła; **smoking is not
~ed** nie wolno palić

all right *adj* (*satisfactory*)
niezły; (*well, safe*) dobrze ▷ *adv*
1 (*well: go, work out*) prawidłowo
2 (*properly: see, hear, work*) dobrze
3 (*as answer: okay*) w porządku;
it's *or* **that's ~ by me** to mi pasuje

almond ['ɑːmənd] *n* **1** (*nut*)
migdał **2** (*tree*) migdałowiec

almost ['ɔːlməust] *adv* prawie;
I spent ~ a month in China
spędziłem prawie miesiąc w
Chinach

alone [ə'ləun] *adj* **1** (*not with
other people*) sam **2** (*having no
family or friends*) samotny **3**: **to
be ~ together** (*with no other
people*) sami ▷ *adv* **1** (*unaided*) w
pojedynkę **2**: **in Florida/France**

~ (*merely: used for emphasis*) tylko na Florydzie/we Francji; **to leave sb/sth ~** (*undisturbed*) zostawiać (zostawić *pf*) kogoś/coś w spokoju; **leave it ~!** zostaw to!

along [ə'lɔŋ] *prep* **1** (*towards one end of*) wzdłuż *+gen* **2** (*on, beside*) wzdłuż *+gen* ▷ *adv* wzdłuż *+gen*; **~ with** (*together with*) razem z *+inst*; **all ~** (*all the time*) przez cały czas

aloud [ə'laud] *adv* (*read*) na głos; (*speak*) głośno

alphabet ['ælfəbɛt] *n*: **the ~** alfabet

Alps [ælps] *n pl*: **the ~** Alpy

already [ɔ:l'rɛdɪ] *adv* już; **I have ~ started making dinner** już zacząłem gotować obiad; **is it five o'clock ~?** (*expressing surprise*) czy już piąta?

also ['ɔ:lsəu] *adv* **1** (*too*) też **2** (*moreover*) poza tym

alter ['ɔltə'] *vt* zmieniać (zmienić *pf*) ▷ *vi* zmieniać (zmienić *pf*) się

alternate [*adj* ɔl'tə:nɪt, *vb* 'ɔltə:neɪt] *adj* **1** (*successive: actions, events*) naprzemienny **2** (*US: alternative*) alternatywny ▷ *vi*: **to ~ (with/between)** zamieniać (zamienić *pf*) się (z *+inst*); **on ~ days/weeks** co drugi dzień/tydzień

alternative [ɔl'tə:nətɪv] *adj* **1** (*Brit: plan, method, solution*) alternatywny **2** (*technology, energy*) alternatywny ▷ *n*: **(an) ~ (to)** alternatywa (dla *+gen*); **to have no ~ (but to)** nie mieć innego wyjścia (niż)

alternatively [ɔl'tə:nətɪvlɪ] *adv* ewentualnie

although [ɔ:l'ðəu] *conj* **1** (*despite the fact that*) mimo że **2** (*but*) chociaż

altogether [ɔ:ltə'gɛðə'] *adv* **1** (*completely*) całkowicie **2** (*in total*) razem; **how much is that ~?** ile to będzie razem?; **~ different/stronger/better** całkiem inny/silniejszy/lepszy

aluminium [ælju'mɪnɪəm] (*US* **aluminum** [ə'lu:mɪnəm]) *n* aluminium

always ['ɔ:lweɪz] *adv* zawsze; **he's ~ late** zawsze się spóźnia

am [æm] *vb see* **be**

a.m. *adv abbr* (= *ante meridiem*): **at 10 ~** o dziesiątej rano

amateur ['æmətə'] *n* (*non-professional*) amator(ka) *m/f* ▷ *adj* amatorski

amaze [ə'meɪz] *vt* zdumiewać (zdumieć *pf*); **to be ~d (at or by sth)** być zdumionym (czymś)

amazing [ə'meɪzɪŋ] *adj* (*surprising, fantastic*) niesamowity

ambassador [æm'bæsədə'] *n* ambasador

ambition [æm'bɪʃən] *n*: **an ~ (to do sth)** ambicja (zrobienia czegoś); **to achieve one's ~** realizować (zrealizować *pf*) czyjeś ambicje

ambitious [æm'bɪʃəs] *adj* ambitny

ambulance ['æmbjuləns] *n* karetka

America [ə'mɛrɪkə] *n* Ameryka

American [ə'mɛrɪkən] *adj* amerykański ▷ *n* (*person*) Amerykanin(-nka) *m/f*

among(st) [ə'mʌŋ(st)] *prep* **1** (*surrounded by, included in: group of people*) wśród *+gen* **2** (*share,*

distribute: between) między +*inst*
amount [ə'maunt] *n* (*quantity*) ilość; (*of money*) suma; (*of work*) ilość
amp ['æmp] *n* amper; **a 13 ~ plug** wtyczka na trzynaście amperów
amphetamine [æm'fɛtəmi:n] *n* amfetamina
amplifier ['æmplɪfaɪə'] *n* wzmacniacz
amuse [ə'mju:z] *vt* **1** (*make laugh*) rozśmieszać (rozśmieszyć *pf*) **2** (*entertain*) rozbawić (bawić *pf*); (*distract*) zabawiać (zabawić *pf*); **to ~ o.s.** zabawiać (zabawić *pf*) się; **to be ~d at/by sth** być rozbawionym czymś
amusement arcade *n* salon gier automatycznych
an [æn, ən] *indef art see* **a**
anaesthetic [ænɪs'θɛtɪk] (*US* **anesthetic**) *n* środek znieczulający; **local ~** znieczulenie miejscowe; **general ~** znieczulenie ogólne; **under ~** pod narkozą
analyse ['ænəlaɪz] (*US* **analyze**) *vt* (*situation, information*) analizować (przeanalizować *pf*)
analysis [ə'næləsɪs] (*pl* **analyses**) *n* (*of situation, statistics*) analiza
analyze ['ænəlaɪz] (*US*) *vt* = **analyse**
ancestor ['ænsɪstə'] *n* przodek
anchor ['æŋkə'] *n* kotwica
ancient ['eɪnʃənt] *adj* **1** (*Greece, Rome, monument*) starożytny **2** (*very old*) pradawny
and [ænd] *conj* i; **men ~ women** kobiety i mężczyźni; **better ~ better** coraz lepiej; **to try ~ do sth** próbować (spróbować *pf*)

coś zrobić
angel ['eɪndʒəl] *n* (*spirit*) anioł
anger ['æŋgə'] *n* gniew
angle ['æŋgl] *n* **1** (*Math*) kąt **2** (*position, direction*) kąt; **at an ~** pod kątem; **an ~ of ninety/ sixty degrees** pod katem dziewięćdziesiąt/sześćdziesiąt stopni
angry ['æŋgrɪ] *adj* (*person*) rozgniewany; (*response*) gniewny; **to be ~ with sb/about sth** złościć się na kogoś/o coś; **to make sb ~** złościć (rozłościć *pf*) kogoś
animal ['ænɪməl] *n* **1** (*creature*) zwierzę **2** (*type of person*) zwierzę **3** (*pej: brute*) bydlę ▷ *adj* zwierzęcy
ankle ['æŋkl] (*Anat*) *n* kostka
anniversary [ænɪ'və:sərɪ] *n* **1**: **~ (of sth)** rocznica (czegoś) **2** (*also:* **wedding ~**) rocznica ślubu
announce [ə'nauns] *vt* ogłaszać (ogłosić *pf*); **the government has ~d that...** rząd ogłosił, że...
announcement [ə'naunsmənt] *n* **1** (*statement*) oświadczenie **2** (*notice: in newspaper*) ogłoszenie **3** (*at airport or station*) ogłoszenie; **to make an ~ (about sth)** obwieścić (coś)
annoy [ə'nɔɪ] *vt* denerwować (zdenerwować *pf*)
annoyed [ə'nɔɪd] *adj* zdenerwowany; **to be ~ at sth/ with sb** być zdenerwowanym czymś/na kogoś
annoying [ə'nɔɪɪŋ] *adj* (*noise, habit, person*) denerwujący
annual ['ænjuəl] *adj* **1** (*once every year*) doroczny **2** (*during a year*) roczny
anorak ['ænəræk] *n* (*jacket*)

anorak

anorexia [ænəˈrɛksɪə] (also: **~ nervosa**: Med) n anoreksja

anorexic [ænəˈrɛksɪk] adj anorektyczny

another [əˈnʌðəʳ] adj 1: **~ book** (one more) następny 2 (a different one) inny 3: **~ 5 years/miles/kilos** kolejne pięć lat/mil/kilo ▷ pron 1 (one more) kolejny 2 (a different one) inny; **one ~** sobie; **they like one ~** lubią się

answer [ˈɑːnsəʳ] n 1 (reply) odpowiedź 2 (solution) rozwiązanie ▷ vi (reply: to question) odpowiadać (odpowiedzieć pf); (to telephone ringing) odbierać (odebrać pf) (telefon); (knock at door) otwierać (otworzyć pf) drzwi ▷ vt (reply to: person) odpowiadać (odpowiedzieć pf) na; (question, letter) odpowiadać (odpowiedzieć pf)

answering machine [ˈɑːnsərɪŋ-] n automatyczna sekretarka

ant [ænt] n mrówka

Antarctic [æntˈɑːktɪk] n: **the ~** Antarktyka

anthem [ˈænθəm] n hymn

antibiotic [ˈæntɪbaɪˈɔtɪk] n antybiotyk

antique [ænˈtiːk] n (valuable old object) antyk ▷ adj (furniture, jewellery) zabytkowy

antiseptic [æntɪˈsɛptɪk] n środek odkażający ▷ adj antyseptyczny

anxious [ˈæŋkʃəs] adj 1 (worried: expression, person) zatroskany 2 (worrying)

niespokojny; **he was ~ for the game to start** pragnął, by gra się już rozpoczęła

○ **KEYWORD**

any [ˈɛnɪ] adj 1 (in negatives) żaden, ani trochę; **I haven't any chocolate/sweets** nie mam żadnej czekolady/żadnych słodyczy; **there was hardly any food** nie było ani trochę jedzenia; **have you got any chocolate/ sweets?** masz jakąś czekoladę/ jakieś słodycze? 2 (in "if" clauses) jakiś; **if there are any tickets left** jeśli są jeszcze jakieś bilety 3 (no matter which) którykolwiek; **take any card you like** wiź którąkolwiek z kart 4 (in expressions): **any day now** niedługo; **(at) any moment** w każdej chwili; **any time** (whenever) zawsze gdy; (also: **at any time**) lada chwila; **at any rate** (more precisely) dokładniej; (whatever the case) w każdym razie ▷ pron 1 (in negatives) ani jednego; **I didn't eat any (of it)** nic nie zjadłem; **I haven't any (of them)** nie mam ani jednego (z nich) 2 (in questions) jakieś; **have you got any?** czy masz jakieś? 3 (in "if" clauses: person) ktokolwiek; (object) cokolwiek; **if any of you would like to take part,...** jeśli ktoś z was będzie chciał wziąć udział,... 4 (no matter which ones) którykolwiek; **help yourself to any of the books** weź

któràkolwiek z książek, proszę
▷ *adv* **1** (*with negative*) już; **I don't
play tennis any more** już nie
gram w tenisa; **don't wait any
longer** nie czekaj już dłużej
2 (*in questions*) trochę; **are you
feeling any better?** czujesz się
trochę lepiej?; **do you want any
more soup/sandwiches?** chcesz
jeszcze trochę zupy/kanapek?
3 (*in "if" clauses*) trochę; **if it had
been any colder we would have
frozen to death** jeśli byłoby
trochę zimniej zamarzlibyśmy
na śmierć

anybody ['ɛnɪbɒdɪ] *pron* =
anyone

anyhow ['ɛnɪhaʊ] *adv* **1** =
anyway 2 (*Brit: inf: haphazardly*)
byle jak

anyone ['ɛnɪwʌn] *pron* **1** (*in
negatives, "if" clauses*) nikt **2** (*in
questions*) ktoś **3** (*no matter who*)
ktokolwiek; **I can't see ~** nikogo
nie wiedzę; **did ~ see you?** czy
ktoś cię widział?; **~ could do it**
każdy mógłby to zrobić

anything ['ɛnɪθɪŋ] *pron* **1** (*in
negatives, questions, "if" clauses*)
nic **2** (*no matter what*) wszystko; **I
will do ~ for you** zrobię dla ciebie
wszystko, cokolwiek; **I can't see
~** nic nie widzę; **hardly ~** prawie
nic; **did you find ~?** znalazłeś
coś?; **if ~ happens to me...** jeśli
coś mi się stanie...; **you can say
~ you like** możesz powiedzieć
co chcesz

anyway ['ɛnɪweɪ] *adv* **1** (*besides*)
w każdym razie **2** (*all the same*)
mimo wszystko **3** (*at least*) w

każdym razie **4** (*in short*) więc
5 (*well*) i tak; **I shall go ~** pójdę
i tak

anywhere ['ɛnɪwɛəʳ] *adv* **1** (*in
negatives*) nigdzie; (*in questions*)
gdzieś **2** (*no matter where*)
gdziekolwiek; **I can't see him ~**
nigdzie go nie widzę; **have you
seen the scissors ~?** widziałeś
gdzieś nożyczki?

apart [ə'pɑːt] *adv* **1** (*move, pull*)
w oddaleniu **2: to sit ~ from the
others** usiąść w oddaleniu od
innych; **to take sth ~** rozkładać
(rozłożyć *pf*) coś na części; **~ from**
(*excepting*) oprócz; (*in addition
to*) poza

apartment [ə'pɑːtmənt] *n* (*US*)
mieszkanie

apologize [ə'pɒlədʒaɪz] *vi*
przepraszać (przeprosić *pf*); **to
~ to sb (for sth)** przepraszać
(przeprosić *pf*) kogoś (za coś)

apology [ə'pɒlədʒɪ] *n*
przeprosiny; **to make (sb) an ~**
przeprosić (kogoś)

apostrophe [ə'pɒstrəfɪ] *n*
apostrof

apparent [ə'pærənt] *adj*
1 (*seeming*) pozorny **2** (*obvious*)
widoczny

apparently [ə'pærəntlɪ] *adv*
najwidoczniej

appeal [ə'piːl] *vi* (*Law*)
odwoływać (odwołać *pf*) się ▷ *vt*
(*US: decision, verdict*) odwoływać
(odwołać *pf*) ▷ *n* **1** (*request*) apel
2 (*for good cause*) apel **3** (*Law*)
apelacja; **he ~ed for calm/
silence** poprosił o spokój/ciszę; **it
doesn't ~ to me** nie przemawia
to do mnie

appear [əˈpɪər] vi 1 (seem)
wydawać (wydać pf) się 2 (come
into view, begin to develop)
pojawiać (pojawić pf) się; **to ~ to
be/have** wydawać (wydać pf) się
być/mieć
appendicitis [əpendɪˈsaɪtɪs]
n zapalenie wyrostka
robaczkowego
appetite [ˈæpɪtaɪt] n 1 (desire to
eat) apetyt 2: **an ~ for sth** (desire)
chętka na coś
applaud [əˈplɔːd] vi (clap) bić
brawo ▷ vt (cheer) oklaskiwać (pf)
applause [əˈplɔːz] n (clapping)
oklaski
apple [ˈæpl] n jabłko
appliance [əˈplaɪəns] n (device)
urządzenie
applicant [ˈæplɪkənt] n (for job,
place at college) kandydat(ka) m/f
application [æplɪˈkeɪʃən] n
1 (for job, grant etc) podanie
2 (use: of knowledge, theory etc)
zastosowanie 3 (Comput: program)
program użytkowy
application form n podanie
apply [əˈplaɪ] vi 1: **to ~ (to sb)** (be
relevant) dotyczyć (kogoś) 2 (make
application) składać (złożyć pf)
podanie; **to ~ for sth** (job, grant,
membership) ubiegać się o coś; **to
~ to sb** (council, governing body)
składać (złożyć pf) podanie do
kogoś; **to ~ to do sth** zgłaszać
(zgłosić pf) się do zrobienia czegoś
appointment [əˈpɔɪntmənt] n
(in business, politics) spotkanie;
(with hairdresser, dentist, doctor)
wizyta; **to make an ~ (with
sb)** (in business, politics) ustalać
(ustalić pf) termin spotkania (z

kimś); **to make an ~ with the
hairdresser/dentist** mieć wizytę
u fryzjera/dentysty
appreciate [əˈpriːʃɪeɪt] vt 1 (like,
value) cenić (docenić pf) 2 (be
grateful for) być wdzięcznym za; **I
(really) ~ your help** (naprawdę)
jestem ci wdzięczny za twoją
pomoc
apprentice [əˈprentɪs] n
praktykant(ka) m/f
approach [əˈprəʊtʃ] vi (draw
near: person) podchodzić
(podejść pf); (car) podjeżdżać
(podjechać pf); (event, time)
zbliżać (zbliżyć pf) się ▷ vt 1 (draw
near to: place, person) zbliżać
(zbliżyć pf) się 2 (consult, speak
to: person) zwracać (zwrócić pf)
się 3 (deal with: situation, problem)
podchodzić (podejść pf) do
+gen ▷ n (to a problem, situation)
podejście
appropriate [əˈprəʊprɪɪt] adj
(suitable: remarks, behaviour,
clothing) stosowny; (person,
authority) właściwy; **it is/seems
~ to...** odpowiedni do...; **it is ~ to
do sth** wypada coś zrobić
approval [əˈpruːvəl] n
1 (permission) zgoda 2 (liking)
aprobata; **to meet with sb's
~** (proposal etc) uzyskać czyjąś
aprobatę
approve [əˈpruːv] vt zatwierdzać
(zatwierdzić pf) ▷ vi zgadzać
(zgodzić pf) się; **to be ~d by sb**
(authorized) uzyskać zgodę od
kogoś
▶ **approve of** vt fus akceptować
(zaakceptować pf)
approximate [əˈprɒksɪmɪt] adj

(*amount, number, age*) przybliżony

apricot ['eɪprɪkɔt] *n* (*fruit*) morela

April ['eɪprəl] *n* kwiecień; *see also* **July**

apron ['eɪprən] *n* (*clothing*) fartuch

Aquarius [ə'kwɛərɪəs] *n* wodnik

Arab ['ærəb] *adj* arabski ▷ *n* Arab(ka) *m/f*

Arabic ['ærəbɪk] *adj* arabski ▷ *n* arabski

arch [ɑːtʃ] *n* (*curved structure*) łuk ▷ *vt* (*one's back*) wyginać (wygiąć *pf*) w łuk

archaeology [ɑːkɪ'ɔlədʒɪ] (*US* **archeology**) *n* archeologia

archbishop [ɑːtʃ'bɪʃəp] *n* arcybiskup

archeology [ɑːkɪ'ɔlədʒɪ] *n* (*US*) = **archaeology**

architect ['ɑːkɪtɛkt] *n* (*of building*) architekt

architecture ['ɑːkɪtɛktʃər] *n* architektura

Arctic ['ɑːktɪk] *n*: **the ~** Arktyka ▷ *adj* (*ice, explorer etc*) arktyczny

are [ɑːr] *vb see* **be**

area ['ɛərɪə] *n* 1 (*region, zone*) obszar 2 (*of room, building etc*) część 3 (*Math, Geom*) pole 4 (*part: of surface*) powierzchnia 5 (*aspect*) zakres; **in the London ~** w rejonie Londynu

area code (*esp US*) *n* numer kierunkowy

Argentina [ɑːdʒən'tiːnə] *n* Argentyna

Argentinian [ɑːdʒən'tɪnɪən] *adj* argentyński ▷ *n* (*person*) Argentyńczyk(-ynka) *m/f*

argue ['ɑːgjuː] *vi* (*quarrel*): **to ~ (with sb) (about sth)** kłócić się

(*z kimś*) (*o coś*) ▷ *vt* (*debate: case, point*) dyskutować

argument ['ɑːgjumənt] *n* 1 (*quarrel*) kłótnia 2 (*reason*) argument; **an ~ for/against sth** argument za czymś/przeciwko czemuś

Aries ['ɛərɪz] *n* Baran

arithmetic [ə'rɪθmətɪk] *n* (*Math*) arytmetyka

arm [ɑːm] *n* 1 (*of person*) ramię 2 (*of jacket, shirt etc*) rękaw 3 (*of chair*) poręcz 4 (*of organization etc*) filia ▷ *vt* (*person, nation*) uzbrajać (uzbroić *pf*); **arms** *n pl* (*weapons*) broń ▷ *adj*: **~s dealer/~s trade** handlarz bronią/handel bronią; **to twist sb's ~** (*inf*) przyprzeć kogoś do muru

armchair ['ɑːmtʃɛər] *n* fotel

armed [ɑːmd] *adj* 1 (*robber, policeman etc*) uzbrojony 2 (*conflict, attack etc*) zbrojny

army ['ɑːmɪ] *n*: **the ~** armia, wojsko

around [ə'raund] *adv* (*about*) dookoła ▷ *prep* 1 (*encircling*) wokół +*gen* 2 (*near*) koło +*gen* 3 (*about, roughly*) około +*gen*

arrange [ə'reɪndʒ] *vt* 1 (*organize*) organizować (zorganizować *pf*) 2 (*put in order*) ustawiać (ustawić *pf*); (*flowers*) układać (ułożyć *pf*) ▷ *vi*: **to ~ to do sth** postanawiać (postanowić *pf*) coś zrobić

arrangement [ə'reɪndʒmənt] *n* 1 (*agreement*) umowa 2 (*grouping, layout*) ustawienie 3 (*display: of flowers*) kompozycja 4 (*of piece of music*) aranżacja; **arrangements** *n pl* (*preparations*) przygotowania; (*plans*) ustalenia

arrest [ə'rɛst] *vt* (*detain*)
aresztować (zaaresztować *pf*); **to
be under ~** być aresztowanym
arrival [ə'raɪvl] *n* **1** (*of person,
vehicle*) przybycie; (*of vehicle*)
przyjazd **2** (*product*) pojawienie
się; (*of invention, idea*) nadejście
arrive [ə'raɪv] *vi* **1** (*person*)
przybywać (przybyć *pf*); (*vehicle*)
przyjeżdżać (przyjechać *pf*)
2 (*letter, meal*) nadchodzić
(nadejść *pf*)
arrow ['ærəʊ] *n* **1** (*weapon*) strzała
2 (*sign*) strzałka
art [ɑːt] *n* sztuka ▷ *adj* (*exhibition,
student*) sztuka; **~ collection**
kolekcja dzieł sztuki; **arts** *n pl*
1: the ~s (*creative activities*)
sztuka **2** (*in education*) nauki
humanistyczne ▷ *adj*: **~s**
(*graduate, student, course*) nauk
humanistycznych; **work of ~**
dzieło sztuki
artery ['ɑːtərɪ] *n* **1** (*blood vessel*)
tętnica **2** (*route*) arteria
art gallery *n* galeria sztuki
article ['ɑːtɪkl] *n* **1** (*formal: object,
item*) przedmiot **2** (*in newspaper*)
artykuł **3** (*Ling*) przedimek
artificial [ɑːtɪ'fɪʃəl] *adj* sztuczny
artist ['ɑːtɪst] *n* artysta(-tka) *m/f*
artistic [ɑː'tɪstɪk] *adj* **1** (*person*)
uzdolniony artystycznie
2 (*tradition, freedom*) artystyczny
3 (*design, arrangement*) artystyczny

○ **KEYWORD**

as [æz, əz] *conj* **1** (*referring to
time*) kiedy; **he came in as I
was leaving** przyszedł kiedy
wychodziłem

2 (*since, because*) ponieważ; **as
you can't come, I'll go on my
own** ponieważ nie możesz przyjść,
pójdę bez ciebie
3 (*referring to manner, way*) jak; **as
you can see** jak widać; **it's on
the left as you go in** jest na lewo
od wejścia
▷ *prep* **1** (*in the capacity of*) jako;
he works as a salesman pracuje
jako sprzedawca; **as a teacher,
I am very aware that...** jako
nauczyciel jestem świadom, że...;
to come as a surprise/shock
okazać się zaskoczeniem/szokiem
2 (*when*) jako; **he was very
energetic as a child** był bardzo
energiczny jako dziecko
▷ *adv* **1** (*in comparisons*): **as big/
good/easy as...** tak duży/dobry/
łatwy jak...; **you're as tall as he is**
or **as him** jesteś tak wysoki jak on;
**as much money/many books
as...** tak dużo pieniędzy/książek
jak...; **as soon as** tak szybko jak
2 (*in expressions*): **as if** or **though**
jakby; **as from** or **of tomorrow**
począwszy od jutra

ash [æʃ] *n* (*from fire, cigarette*)
popiół; **ashes** *n pl* **1** (*of fire*) popiół
2 (*remains*) prochy
ashamed [ə'ʃeɪmd] *adj*: **to
be/feel ~** (*embarrassed, guilty*) być
zawstydzonym; **to be ~ of sb/sth**
wstydzić się kogoś/czegoś
ashtray ['æʃtreɪ] *n* popielniczka
Asia ['eɪʃə] *n* Azja
Asian ['eɪʃən] *adj* azjatycki ▷ *n*
(*person*) Azjata(-tka) *m/f*
ask [ɑːsk] *vt* **1: to ~ (sb) a
question** zadawać (zadać

pf) (komuś) pytanie **2** (*invite*)
zapraszać (zaprosić *pf*) ▷ *vi* pytać;
to ~ (sb) whether/why... pytać
(kogoś) czy...; **to ~ sb to do sth**
prosić (poprosić *pf*) kogoś, żeby
coś zrobił; **to ~ to do sth** prosić
(poprosić *pf*) o pozwolenia na coś;
to ~ sb the time zapytać kogoś o
godzinę; **to ~ sb about sth** pytać
(spytać *pf*) kogoś o coś; **I ~ed him
his name** spytałem go jak ma
na imię; **to ~ sb's opinion** pytać
(zapytać *pf*) kogoś o jego zdanie;
to ~ sb out to dinner zaprosić
kogoś na obiad
▶ **ask after** *vt fus* (*person*)
dopytywać się
▶ **ask for** *vt fus* **1** (*ask to
have: thing*) prosić (poprosić *pf*)
o **2** (*ask to see: person*) prosić o
spotkanie z +*inst*
asleep [əˈsliːp] *adj* pogrążony
we śnie; **to be ~** spać; **to fall ~**
zasypiać (zasnąć *pf*)
asparagus [əsˈpærəɡəs] *n*
szparag
aspirin [ˈæsprɪn] *n* **1** (*drug*)
aspiryna **2** (*tablet*) tabletka
aspiryny
assemble [əˈsɛmbl] *vt* **1** (*people,
group*) gromadzić (zgromadzić
pf) **2** (*machinery, object*)
montować (zmontować *pf*) ▷ *vi*
(*gather: people, crowd*) gromadzić
(zgromadzić *pf*)
assembly [əˈsɛmblɪ] *n* **1** (*meeting*)
zgromadzenie **2** (*construction: of
vehicles etc*) montaż **3** (*in school*)
apel
assignment [əˈsaɪnmənt] *n*
(*task*) zadanie; (*for student*) praca
zadana

assistance [əˈsɪstəns] *n* pomoc
assistant [əˈsɪstənt] *n* **1** (*helper*)
pomocnik(-ica) *m/f*; (*in office*)
zastępca(-czyni) *m/f* **2** (*Brit: in
shop*) ekspedient(ka) *m/f* ▷ *adj*
zastępujący; **~ professor** docent
association [əsəʊsɪˈeɪʃən] *n*
1 (*group*) stowarzyszenie **2: to
have ~s (with sth/for sb)**
(*mental connection*) kojarzyć się
(z czymś/z kimś) **3** (*involvement,
link*): **~ (with sb/sth)** związek (z
kimś/czymś)
assortment [əˈsɔːtmənt] *n* (*of
shapes, colours*) asortyment; (*of
objects, people*) mieszanka
assume [əˈsjuːm] *vt* **1** (*suppose*)
przypuszczać (przypuścić
pf) **2** (*responsibility, power*)
przejmować (przejąć *pf*)
assure [əˈʃʊəʳ] *vt* zapewniać
(zapewnić *pf*)
asterisk [ˈæstərɪsk] *n* gwiazdka
asthma [ˈæsmə] *n* astma
astonishing [əˈstɒnɪʃɪŋ] *adj*
zadziwiający
astrology [əsˈtrɒlədʒɪ] *n*
astrologia
astronaut [ˈæstrənɔːt] *n*
astronauta(-tka) *m/f*
astronomy [əsˈtrɒnəmɪ] *n*
astronomia

○ **KEYWORD**

at [æt] *prep* **1** (*position, time,
age*) w; **we had dinner at a
restaurant** zjedliśmy obiad w
restauracji; **at home** w domu; **at
work** (*not at home*) w pracy; **at
my brother's** u mojego brata;
at the bus stop na przystanku;

to be sitting at a table/desk siedzieć przy stole/biurku; **there's someone at the door** ktoś jest pod drzwiami; (*towards*): **to throw sth at sb** rzucać (rzucić *pf*) czymś w kogoś; **at four o'clock** o czwartej; **at night** w nocy; **at Christmas** na Święta Bożego Narodzenia **2** (*referring to price*) po; (*referring to speed*) z; **apples at £2 a kilo** jabłka po dwa funty za kilo; **at 50 km/h** z prędkością pięćdziesiąt kilometrów na godzinę **3** (*referring to activity*) nad; **he's at work on a novel** pracuje nad powieścią; **to be good at sth/at doing sth** być dobrym w czymś/robieniu czegoś **4** (*in expressions*): **not at all** (*in answer to question*) wcale nie; (*in answer to thanks*) nie ma za co

ate [eɪt] *pt of* **eat**
Athens ['æθɪnz] *n* Ateny
athlete ['æθliːt] *n* sportowiec
athletic [æθ'letɪk] *adj* **1** (*tradition, excellence etc*) sportowy **2** (*sporty: person*) wysportowany **3** (*muscular: build, frame*) atletyczny
athletics [æθ'letɪks] *n* lekka atletyka
Atlantic [ət'læntɪk] *adj* atlantycki ▷ *n*: **the ~ (Ocean)** Atlantyk
atlas ['ætləs] *n* atlas
atmosphere ['ætməsfɪər] *n* **1** (*of planet*) atmosfera **2** (*feel: of place*) nastrój **3** (*air*) powietrze
atom ['ætəm] (*Phys*) *n* atom
atomic [ə'tɔmɪk] *adj* atomowy

attach [ə'tætʃ] *vt* **1** (*fasten, join*) przymocowywać (przymocować *pf*) **2** (*importance, significance etc*) przywiązywać (przywiązać *pf*)
attachment [ə'tætʃmənt] *n* **1** (*affection*): **~ (to sb)** przywiązanie (do kogoś) **2** (*of tool*) nasadka **3** (*Comput*) załącznik
attack [ə'tæk] *vt* **1** (*assault: person*) napadać (napaść *pf*) **2** (*place, troops*) atakować (zaatakować *pf*) **3** (*criticise: person, idea*) atakować (zaatakować *pf*) **4** (*in sport*) atakować (zaatakować *pf*) ▷ *vi* (*Mil, Sport*) atakować (zaatakować *pf*) ▷ *n* **1** (*on person*) napaść **2** (*military assault*) atak **3** (*criticism*) atak **4** (*of illness*) napad **5** (*in sport*) atak; **an ~ on sb** (*assault*) napad na kogoś; (*criticism*) atak krytyki na kogoś
attempt [ə'tempt] *n* (*try*) próba ▷ *vt* (*try*) próbować (spróbować *pf*) ▷ *vi*: **to ~ to do sth** próbować (spróbować *pf*) coś zrobić; **an ~ to do sth** próba zrobienia czegoś
attend [ə'tend] *vt* **1** (*be member of*) uczęszczać do +*gen* **2** (*take part in*) uczęszczać na
▶ **attend to** *vt fus* **1** (*needs, affairs*) zajmować (zająć *pf*) się +*inst* **2** (*patient*) zajmować (zająć *pf*) się +*inst*; (*customer*) obsługiwać (obsłużyć *pf*)
attention [ə'tenʃən] *n* **1** (*concentration*) uwaga **2** (*care*) pomoc ▷ *int* (*Mil*) baczność; **to draw sb's ~ to sth** zwracać (zwrócić *pf*) czyjąś uwagę na coś; **to pay ~ (to sth/sb)** uważać (na coś/kogoś)
attic ['ætɪk] *n* strych

attitude ['ætɪtjuːd] n 1 (*mental view*) pogląd 2 (*behaviour*) postawa

attorney [əˈtəːnɪ] (*US*) n (*lawyer*) adwokat

attract [əˈtrækt] vt 1 (*people, animals, metal*) przyciągać (przyciągnąć pf) 2 (*gain: support, publicity*) zyskiwać (zyskać pf); (*sb's attention*) przyciągać (przyciągnąć pf); (*sb's interest*) wzbudzać (wzbudzić pf)

attraction [əˈtrækʃən] n (*of person*) urok; **attractions** n pl (*also:* **tourist ~s**: *amusements*) atrakcja

attractive [əˈtræktɪv] adj 1 (*man, woman, place*) atrakcyjny; (*thing*) ładny 2 (*interesting: price, idea, offer*) atrakcyjny; **he was very ~ to women** był bardzo atrakcyjny dla kobiet

aubergine [ˈəubəʒiːn] (*Brit*) n (*vegetable*) bakłażan

auburn [ˈɔːbən] adj (*hair*) kasztanowy

auction [ˈɔːkʃən] n aukcja ▷ vt sprzedawać (sprzedać pf) na aukcji
▶ **auction off** vt sprzedawać (sprzedać pf) na aukcji

audience [ˈɔːdɪəns] n 1 (*in theatre etc*) widownia 2 (*Rad, TV*) widownia 3 (*public*) publiczność

August [ˈɔːgəst] n sierpień; *see also* **July**

aunt [ɑːnt] n (*father's sister*) ciotka; (*father's brother's wife*) stryjenka; (*mother's sister*) ciotka; (*mother's brother's wife*) wujenka

auntie, aunty [ˈɑːntɪ] (*inf*) n = **aunt**

au pair [ˈəuˈpɛəʳ] n au pair

Australia [ɔsˈtreɪlɪə] n Australia

Australian [ɔsˈtreɪlɪən] adj australijski ▷ n (*person*) Australijczyk(-jka) m/f

Austria [ˈɔstrɪə] n Austria

Austrian [ˈɔstrɪən] adj austriacki ▷ n (*person*) Austriak(-aczka) m/f

author [ˈɔːθəʳ] n autor(ka) m/f

autobiography [ɔːtəbaɪˈɔgrəfɪ] n autobiografia

autograph [ˈɔːtəgrɑːf] n autograf

automatic [ɔːtəˈmætɪk] adj automatyczny ▷ n (*car*) automatyczny

automatically [ɔːtəˈmætɪklɪ] adv 1 (*by itself*) automatycznie 2 (*without thinking*) odruchowo 3 (*as a matter of course*) automatycznie

automobile [ˈɔːtəməbiːl] (*US*) n samochód

autumn [ˈɔːtəm] (*Brit*) n jesień; **in (the) ~** jesienią

availability [əveɪləˈbɪlɪtɪ] n (*of goods*) dostępność; (*staff*) osiągalność

available [əˈveɪləbl] adj 1 (*obtainable: article, service*) dostępny 2 (*person: unoccupied*) wolny; **is the manager ~?** czy dyrektor jest wolny?; **to make sth ~ to sb** udostępniać (udostępnić pf) komuś coś

avalanche [ˈævəlɑːnʃ] n lawina

avenue [ˈævənjuː] n aleja

average [ˈævərɪdʒ] n 1 (*Math: mean*) średnia 2: **the ~ (for sth/sb)** rednia (dla czegoś/kogoś) ▷ adj 1 (*Math*) średni 2 (*ordinary*) zwyczajny 3 (*mediocre*)

przeciętny; **on ~** przeciętnie; **above/below (the) ~** powyżej/poniżej średniej
▶ **average out** *vi*: **to ~ out at/to sth** wynosić (wynieść *pf*) przeciętnie średnio coś
avocado [ævəˈkɑːdəʊ] (*Brit*) *n* (*also*: **~ pear**) awokado
avoid [əˈvɔɪd] *vt* **1** (*person*) omijać (ominąć *pf*); (*obstacles*) unikać (uniknąć *pf*) +*gen* **2** (*prevent: trouble, danger*) unikać (uniknąć *pf*) +*gen* **3** (*evade, shun*) uchylać (uchylić *pf*) się od +*gen*; **to ~ doing sth** unikać (uniknąć *pf*) zrobienia czegoś
awake [əˈweɪk] (*pt* **awoke**, *pp* **awoken** *or* **awakened**) *adj*: **to be ~** nie spać
award [əˈwɔːd] *n* (*prize*) nagroda ▷ *vt* **1** (*prize*) przyznawać (przyznać *pf*) **2** (*penalty, free kick*) przyznawać (przyznać *pf*)
aware [əˈwɛər] *adj*: **politically/socially ~** świadomy politycznie/społecznie; **to be ~ of sth** (*know about*) być zorientowanym w czymś; (*be conscious of*) zdawać sobie sprawę z czegoś; **to be ~ that...** zdawać sobie sprawę, że...
away [əˈweɪ] *adv* **1** (*move, walk*) od **2** (*not present*) nieobecny **3**: **to put sth ~** odłożyć coś **4**: **to fade ~** zacierać (zatrzeć *pf*) się ▷ *adj* (*match, game*) wyjazdowy; **a week/month ~** za tydzień/miesiąc; **the exam is three weeks ~** egzamin będzie za trzy tygodnie; **two kilometres ~** dwa kilometry stąd; **it's two hours ~ by car** dwie godziny jazdy samochodem stąd; **~ from** z dala

awful [ˈɔːfəl] *adj* **1** (*frightful*) okropny **2** (*dreadful: shock, crime etc*) straszny **3**: **to look/feel ~** (*ill*) wyglądać/czuć się strasznie ▷ *adv* (*US: inf: very*) strasznie; **an ~ lot** strasznie dużo
awkward [ˈɔːkwəd] *adj* **1** (*clumsy*) niezgrabny **2** (*inconvenient*) niedogodny **3** (*difficult to use, do, or carry*) niewygodny **4** (*deliberately difficult: person*) trudny
axe [æks] (*US* **ax**) *n* siekiera

b

baby ['beɪbɪ] *n* **1** (*infant*) niemowlę **2** (*esp US: inf: darling*) dzidziuś ▷ *adj* (*seal, elephant*) młody; **to have a ~** mieć dziecko

baby carriage (*US*) *n* wózek dziecięcy

babysit ['beɪbɪsɪt] (*pt, pp* **babysat**) *vi* opiekować się

babysitter ['beɪbɪsɪtə^r] *n* opiekun(ka) *m/f* do dziecka

bachelor ['bætʃələ^r] *n* **1** (*unmarried man*) kawaler **2: ~ of Arts/Science** (*degree*) licencjat; (*Brit: person*) osoba z tytułem licencjata

back [bæk] *n* **1** (*of person*) plecy; (*of animal*) grzbiet **2** (*not front: of hand*) wierzch; (*of neck, legs*) tył; (*of house, door, book, car, train*) tył; (*of chair*) oparcie **3** (*Football: defender*) obrońca ▷ *vt* **1** (*support: candidate, plan*) popierać (poprzeć *pf*); (*financially*) wspierać (wesprzeć *pf*) **2** (*bet on: horse, team*) stawiać (postawić *pf*) na **3** (*reverse: car*) cofać (cofnąć *pf*) ▷ *vi* (*reverse: person, car etc*) cofać (cofnąć *pf*) się ▷ *adj* tylny ▷ *adv* **1** (*not forward*) do tyłu **2** (*returned*): **to be ~** z powrotem; **to do sth behind sb's ~** robić (zrobić *pf*) coś za plecami kogoś; **can I have it ~?** czy mogę prosić o zwrot?; **at the ~ (of)** (*of crowd, building*) na tyłach +*gen*; **~ to front** (*esp Brit*) tył na przód

▶ **back down** *vi* ustępować (ustąpić *pf*)

▶ **back out** *vi* (*withdraw*) cofać (wycofać *pf*) się

▶ **back up** *vt* **1** (*support: statement, theory etc*) popierać (poprzeć *pf*) **2** (*Comput: disk*) robić (zrobić *pf*) kopia zapasowa +*gen*

backache ['bækeɪk] *n* ból pleców

backbone ['bækbəʊn] *n* kręgosłup

backfire [bæk'faɪə^r] *vi* (*plan*) przynosić (przynieść *pf*) odwrotny skutek

background ['bækgraʊnd] *n* **1** (*of picture, scene, events*) tło **2** (*of person: origins*) pochodzenie; (*experience*) tło ▷ *adj* (*noise, music*) w tle; (*information*) wprowadzający; **in the ~** w tle

backing ['bækɪŋ] *n* (*support*) poparcie; (*financial*) wsparcie

backpack ['bækpæk] *n* plecak

backpacker ['bækpækə^r] *n* turysta(-tka) *m/f* podróżujący(-ca) z plecakiem

backstroke [ˈbækstrəuk] n
(also: **the ~**) styl grzbietowy

backup [ˈbækʌp] adj 1 (staff,
services) rezerwowy 2 (Comput)
zapasowy ▷ n 1 (support) poparcie
2 (reserve) rezerwa

backward [ˈbækwəd] adj (glance,
movement) do tyłu ▷ adv (esp US) =
backwards

backwards [ˈbækwədz]
adv 1 (move, look) w tył 2 (in
reverse: count, work) wstecz 3 (in
time) wstecz

bacon [ˈbeɪkən] n bekon

bad [bæd] adj 1 (not good) zły
2 (naughty) niegrzeczny 3 (serious)
poważny 4 (injured: back, arm)
uszkodzony 5 (rotten: fruit, meat
etc) zepsuty; **to be ~ for sth/sb**
być niedobrym dla czegoś/kogoś;
to be ~ at sth/at doing sth nie
być dobrym w czymś/robieniu
czegoś; **not ~** nieźle

badge [bædʒ] n (Brit) guzik

badger [ˈbædʒər] n borsuk

badly [ˈbædlɪ] adv 1 (poorly) źle
2 (seriously) ciężko; **to want sth ~**
bardzo czegoś chcieć

badminton [ˈbædmɪntən] n
badminton

bad-tempered [ˈbædˈtempəd]
adj (by nature) wybuchowy; (on
one occasion) zirytowany

bag [bæg] n 1 (made of paper,
plastic) torebka 2 (suitcase) torba
3 (handbag) torebka; **to pack
one's ~s** pakować (spakować pf)
manatki

baggage [ˈbægɪdʒ] n bagaż

baggage (re)claim n odbiór
bagażu

bagpipes [ˈbægpaɪps] n pl dudy

bake [beɪk] vt piec (upiec pf)

baker [ˈbeɪkər] n (shop: also: **~'s**)
piekarnia

bakery [ˈbeɪkərɪ] n piekarnia

balance [ˈbæləns] n 1 (equilibrium)
równowaga 2 (in bank account)
saldo 3 (remainder to be paid)
różnica ▷ vt (object) utrzymywać
(utrzymać pf) w równowadze ▷ vi
(person, object) balansować; **to
keep/lose one's ~** utrzymywać
(utrzymać pf)/tracić (stracić pf)
równowagę

balanced [ˈbælənst] adj
zrównoważony

balcony [ˈbælkənɪ] n (of
building: open) balkon; (covered)
loggia

bald [bɔːld] adj (head, person) łysy;
to go ~ łysieć (wyłysieć pf)

ball [bɔːl] n 1 (football, golf ball
etc) piłka 2 (of wool, string) kłębek
3 (sphere) kula

ballet [ˈbæleɪ, US bæˈleɪ] n balet

ballet dancer n tancerz(-rka) m/f
baletowy(-a)

balloon [bəˈluːn] n 1 (child's)
balonik 2 (also: **hot-air ~**) balon

ballpoint (pen) [ˈbɔːlpɔɪnt(-)]
n długopis

ban [bæn] n (prohibition) zakaz
▷ vt (prohibit) zakazywać
(zakazać pf) +gen

banana [bəˈnɑːnə] n banan

band [bænd] n 1 (group) grupa
2 (Mus: jazz, rock etc) zespół
▶ **band together** vi skrzykiwać
(skrzyknąć pf) się

bandage [ˈbændɪdʒ] n bandaż
▷ vt (wound, leg) bandażować
(zabandażować pf)

Band-Aid® [ˈbændeɪd] (US) n

plaster z opatrunkiem
bang [bæŋ] n 1 (noise: of door)
trzask; (of gun, exhaust) huk
2 (blow) huk ▷ int bum! ▷ vt
1 (door) trzaskać (trzasnąć pf)
2 (also: ~ on: wall, drum etc) walić
(walnąć pf) 3 (one's head, elbow
etc) walić (walnąć pf) ▷ vi 1 (door)
trzaskać (trzasnąć pf) 2 (firework,
engine) huknąć; **bangs** n pl
(US: fringe) grzywka sg; **to ~ into
sth/sb** wpadać (wpaść pf) na
coś/kogoś
bank [bæŋk] n 1 (Fin: building,
institution) bank 2 (of river, lake)
brzeg 3 (of earth) wał
▶ **bank on** vt fus (rely on) liczyć na
bank account n konto bankowe
bank card n 1 (Brit: for cash
machine) karta bankowa
2 (US: credit card) karta kredytowa
banker ['bæŋkə'] n bankier
bank holiday (Brit) n dzień wolny
od pracy

banknote ['bæŋknəut] n
banknot
bar [bɑ:'] n 1 (place for drinking)
bar 2 (counter: in pub) bar 3 (rod: of
metal etc) pręt 4 (on window, in
prison) krata 5 (tablet: of soap)
kostka; (of chocolate) tabliczka

▷ vt 1 (way, road) blokować
(zablokować pf) 2 (door, window)
ryglować (zaryglować pf)
barbecue ['bɑ:bɪkju:] n 1 (cooking
device) grill 2 (meal, party)
barbecue
bare [bɛə'] adj 1 (naked: body, feet)
nagi 2 (not covered: rock, floor) goły
barefoot(ed) ['bɛəfut(ɪd)] adv
na bosaka
barely ['bɛəlɪ] adv (scarcely)
ledwie
bargain ['bɑ:gɪn] n 1 (good buy)
okazja 2 (deal, agreement) umowa
▷ vi 1 (negotiate): **to ~ (with sb)**
pertraktować (z kimś) 2 (haggle)
targować się
▶ **bargain for, bargain on** vt fus
spodziewać się +gen
barge [bɑ:dʒ] n (boat) barka
▶ **barge in** (inf) vi (enter)
wtargnąć
bark [bɑ:k] n 1 (of tree) kora
2 (of dog) szczeknięcie ▷ vi (dog)
szczekać (zaszczekać pf)
barmaid ['bɑ:meɪd] (esp Brit) n
barmanka
barman ['bɑ:mən] (irreg) n (esp
Brit) barman
barn [bɑ:n] n stodoła
barrel ['bærəl] n 1 (of wine, beer)
beczka; (of oil) baryłka 2 (of gun)
lufa
barrier ['bærɪə'] n bariera
bartender ['bɑ:tɛndə'] (US) n
barman(ka) m/f
base [beɪs] n 1 (of post, tree)
podstawa 2 (basis) podstawa
3 (centre: military) baza; (for
individual, organization) siedziba
▷ vt: **to ~ sth on** or **upon sth**
opierać (oprzeć pf) coś na czymś;

to be ~d on sth być opartym na czymś; **I'm ~d in London** mam siedzibę w Londynie

baseball ['beɪsbɔːl] n (Sport) baseball

basement ['beɪsmənt] n piwnica ▷ adj (flat, apartment, kitchen etc) w suterenie

bash [bæʃ] (inf) vt (hit) walić (walnąć pf) ▷ vi (crash): **to ~ into/ against sth/sb** walić (walnąć pf) w coś/kogoś

basic ['beɪsɪk] adj 1 (principle, rule, right) podstawowy 2 (facilities) prymitywny; see also **basics**

basically ['beɪsɪklɪ] adv 1 (fundamentally) zasadniczo 2 (in fact, put simply) właściwie

basics ['beɪsɪks] n pl: **the ~** podstawy

basin ['beɪsn] n 1 (bowl) miska 2 (also: **wash ~**) umywalka 3 (of river, lake) dorzecze

basis ['beɪsɪs] (pl **bases**) n 1 (starting point) punkt wyjściowy 2 (foundation) podstawa; **on a regular ~** regularnie

basket ['bɑːskɪt] n kosz

basketball ['bɑːskɪtbɔːl] n (Sport) koszykówka

bass [beɪs] (Mus) n 1 (singer) bas 2 (also: **~ guitar**) gitara basowa 3 (on radio, music system etc) basy

bat [bæt] n 1 (animal) nietoperz 2 (for cricket, baseball) kij 3 (Brit: for table tennis) rakietka

bath [bɑːθ] n 1 (Brit: bathtub) wanna 2 (act of bathing) kąpiel ▷ vt (Brit: baby, patient) kąpać (wykąpać pf); **baths** n pl (swimming pool) basen sg; **to have** or **take a ~** kąpać (wykąpać pf) się

bathe [beɪð] vi kąpać (wykąpać pf) się ▷ vt 1 (wound) przemywać (przemyć pf) 2 (US: baby, patient) kąpać (wykąpać pf)

bathroom ['bɑːθrum] n 1 (in house) łazienka 2 (US: toilet) toaleta; **to go to the ~** (US) iść (pójść pf) do toalety

bath towel n ręcznik kąpielowy

bathtub ['bɑːθtʌb] (US) n wanna

batter ['bætər] vt (child, wife) maltretować ▷ n (Culin) rzadkie ciasto

battery ['bætərɪ] n 1 (for torch, radio etc) bateria 2 (in car) akumulator

battle ['bætl] n 1 (Mil) bitwa 2 (fig: struggle) walka ▷ vi 1 (fight) walczyć 2 (struggle): **to ~ for sth/to do sth** walczyć o coś/o zrobienie czegoś

bay [beɪ] n (Geo) zatoka

BC adv abbr (= before Christ) p.n.e.

○ **KEYWORD**

be [biː] (pt **was, were**, pp **been**) vi 1 (with complement) być; **I'm English** jestem Anglikiem; **she's tall/pretty** jest wysoka/ładna; **I'm tired/hot** jestem zmęczony/ jest mi gorąco; **he's a doctor** jest lekarzem; **this is my mother** to jest moja matka; **who is it?** kto to jest?; **be careful/quiet!** bądź ostrożny/cicho!
2 (referring to time, date) być; **it's 5 o'clock** jest piąta; **it's the 28th of April, it's April 28th** jest dwudziestego ósmego kwietnia
3 (describing weather): **it's hot/ cold** jest gorąco/zimno

4 (*talking about health*): **how are you?** jak się masz?
5 (*talking about age*) mieć; **how old are you?** ile masz lat?; **I'll be 18 on Friday** skończę osiemnaście lat w piątek
6 (*talking about place*) jest; **Madrid is in Spain** Madryt jest w Hiszpanii; **the supermarket isn't far from here** supermarket jest niedaleko stąd; **I won't be here tomorrow** nie będzie mnie tu jutro; **have you been to Warsaw?** byłeś w Warszawie?; **we've been here for ages** jesteśmy tu od wieków; **where have you been?** gdzie byłeś?; **the meeting will be in the canteen** spotkanie będzie w stołówce
7 (*referring to distance*) być; **it's 10 km to the village** jest dziesięć kilometrów do wioski
8 (*cost*) być; **how much was the meal?** ile kosztował posiłek?; **that'll be £5, please** to będzie pięć funtów, proszę
9 (*linking clauses*) być; **the problem is that...** problem jest w tym, że...
10 (*exist, occur etc*) być; **is there a God?** czy Bóg istnieje?
11 (*assessing a situation*): **it is likely that he'll resign** możliwe, że zrezygnuje; **it is difficult for me to complain** trudno jest mi narzekać
▷ *aux vb* **1** (*forming continuous tenses*): **what are you doing?** co robisz?; **they're coming tomorrow** przyjdą jutro
2 (*forming passives*): **to be murdered** zostać

zamordowanym; **he was killed in a car crash** został zabity w wypadku samochodowym; **the box had been opened** pudełko zostało otwarte
3 (*with "to" infinitive*): **the house is to be sold** dom zostanie sprzedany; **these flowers are to be found all over the country** te kwiaty można znaleźć w całym kraju
4 (*in tag questions*): **it was fun, wasn't it?** było fajnie, prawda?; **he's good-looking, isn't he?** jest przystojny, prawda?
5 (*in short answers*): **"was the vase where I said?" – "yes, it was/no, it wasn't"** "czy wazon był tam gdzie mówiłem?" – "tak był/nie, nie było"

beach [biːtʃ] *n* plaża
bead [biːd] *n* (*glass, plastic etc*) koralik; **beads** *n pl* (*necklace*) korale
beak [biːk] *n* dziób
beam [biːm] *n* **1** (*of wood, metal*) belka **2** (*of light*) promień **3** (*Rad, Phys*) wiązka; **to drive on full** or **main** or (*US*) **high ~** jechać na długich światłach
bean [biːn] *n* fasola; **coffee/cocoa ~s** ziarno kawy/kakao
bear [bɛə^r] (*pt* **bore**, *pp* **borne**) *n* (*animal*) niedźwiedź(-dzica) *m/f*
▷ *vt* **1** (*support: weight*) dźwigać (dźwignąć *pf*) **2** (*responsibility*) ponosić (ponieść *pf*) **3** (*tolerate*) znosić (znieść *pf*)
beard [bɪəd] *n* broda
bearded ['bɪədɪd] *adj* brodaty
beat [biːt] (*pt* **beat**, *pp* **beaten**)

n **1** (*of heart*) bicie **2** (*Mus: rhythm*)
rytm ▷ *vt* **1** (*strike: wife,
child*) uderzać (uderzyć *pf*)
2 (*eggs, cream*) ubijać (ubić
pf) **3** (*defeat: opponent, record*)
pobić ▷ *vi* (*heart*) bić; **to ~ time**
(*Mus: drum, percussion*) uderzać
(uderzyć *pf*); (*rhythm*) wybijać
(wybić *pf*)
▶ **beat up** *vt* (*person*) bić (pobić *pf*)
beautiful ['bjuːtɪful] *adj*
1 (*woman, day, place, weather*)
piękny **2** (*shot, performance*)
wspaniały
beautifully ['bjuːtɪflɪ] *adv* **1** (*play,
sing etc*) świetnie **2** (*quiet, written
etc*) idealnie
beauty ['bjuːtɪ] *n* (*quality*) piękno
became [bɪ'keɪm] *pt of* **become**
because [bɪ'kɔz] *conj* ponieważ,
bo; **~ of** z powodu +*gen*
become [bɪ'kʌm] (*pt* **became**,
pp **become**) *vi* stawać (stać *pf*)
się; **what has ~ of him?** co się z
nim stało?
bed [bɛd] *n* **1** (*piece of furniture*)
łóżko **2** (*bottom: of river, sea*) dno
3 (*of flowers*) grządka; **to go to ~**
iść do łóżka; **to go to ~ with sb**
pójść z kimś do łóżka
bed and breakfast *n* **1** (*service*)
zakwaterowanie ze śniadaniem
2 (*guest house*) pensjonat

● **BED AND BREAKFAST**
●
● **Bed and breakfast**
● – mały pensjonat z pokojami
● gościnnymi oraz śniadaniem
● wliczonym w cenę noclegu.
● Popularnie zwane **B&B** (skrót
● od **bed and breakfast**),

● oferują swoim gościom
● przystępne ceny.

bedclothes ['bɛdkləuðz] *n pl*
przykrycie
bedding ['bɛdɪŋ] *n* pościel
bedroom ['bɛdrum] *n* sypialnia
bedspread ['bɛdsprɛd] *n* narzuta
bedtime ['bɛdtaɪm] *n* pora na
sen; **at ~** przed snem
bee [biː] *n* pszczoła
beech [biːtʃ] *n* **1** (*tree*) buk **2** (*wood*)
drewno bukowe
beef [biːf] *n* wołowina; **roast ~**
pieczeń wołowa
beefburger ['biːfbəːgəʳ] (*Brit*) *n*
hamburger z wołowiny
been [biːn] *pp of* **be**
beer [bɪəʳ] *n* (*substance*) piwo;
would you like a ~? napijesz
się piwa?
beet [biːt] *n* burak
beetle ['biːtl] *n* żuk
beetroot ['biːtruːt] (*Brit*) *n* burak
before [bɪ'fɔːʳ] *prep* (*in time*)
przed +*inst* ▷ *conj* (*in time*) zanim
▷ *adv* (*time*) przedtem, wcześniej;
~ doing sth przed zrobieniem
czegoś; **I've never seen it ~** nigdy
tego nie widziałem przedtem
beforehand [bɪ'fɔːhænd] *adv*
zawczasu
beg [bɛg] *vi* (*beggar*) żebrać;
to ~ for sth błagać o coś; **to
~ sb to do sth** błagać kogoś o
zrobienie czegoś; **I ~ your pardon**
(*apologizing*) przepraszam; (*not
hearing*) słucham?
began [bɪ'gæn] *pt of* **begin**
beggar ['bɛgəʳ] *n* żebrak(-aczka)
m/f
begin [bɪ'gɪn] (*pt* **began**, *pp*

begun) *vt* zaczynać (zacząć *pf*)
▷ *vi* zaczynać (zacząć *pf*) się; **to
~ doing** *or* **to do sth** zaczynać
(zacząć *pf*) coś robić; **to ~ with...**
zaczynać (zacząć *pf*) się od *+gen*...
beginner [bɪˈɡɪnəʳ] *n*
początkujący
beginning [bɪˈɡɪnɪŋ] *n* (*of event,
period, book*) początek; **at the ~**
na początku
begun [bɪˈɡʌn] *pp of* **begin**
behalf [bɪˈhɑːf] *n*: **on ~ of**, (*US*) **in
~ of** (*as representative of*) w imieniu
+gen; (*for benefit of*) na rzecz
+gen; **on my/his ~** w moim/jego
imieniu
behave [bɪˈheɪv] *vi* 1 (*person*)
zachowywać (zachować *pf*)
się 2 (*behave well*) zachowywać
(zachować *pf*) się dobrze; **to ~
oneself** dobrze się zachowywać
(zachować *pf*)
behaviour [bɪˈheɪvjəʳ] (*US*
behavior) *n* zachowanie
behind [bɪˈhaɪnd] *prep* 1 (*at the
back of*) za *+inst* 2 (*supporting*) za
+inst 3 (*in race, career etc*) w tyle za
+inst ▷ *adv* (*at/towards the back*)
z tyłu 2: **Jane asked me to stay
~** Jane poprosiła, żebym został
▷ *n* (*inf: buttocks*) siedzenie; **to
be ~ (schedule)** pozostawać
(pozostać *pf*) w tyle; **to leave
sth ~** (*forget*) pozostawiać
(pozostawić *pf*) coś za sobą
beige [beɪʒ] *adj* beżowy
Belgian [ˈbɛldʒən] *adj* belgijski
▷ *n* (*person*) Belg(ijka) *m/f*
Belgium [ˈbɛldʒəm] *n* Belgia
believe [bɪˈliːv] *vt* (*person,
story*) wierzyć (uwierzyć *pf*) *+dat*
▷ *vi*: **to ~ in** (*God, ghosts*) wierzyć

(uwierzyć *pf*) w; **to ~ that...**
wierzyć (uwierzyć *pf*), że...; **I
don't ~ in corporal punishment**
nie wierzę w kary cielesne
bell [bɛl] *n* 1 (*of church*) dzwon
2 (*also:* **hand~**) dzwonek 3 (*on
door*) dzwonek
belong [bɪˈlɔŋ] *vi*: **to ~ to** (*person*)
należeć do *+gen*; (*club, society etc*)
należeć do *+gen*; **this book ~s
here** ta książka powinna być tu
belongings [bɪˈlɔŋɪŋz] *n pl*
dobytek *sg*
below [bɪˈləu] *prep* 1 (*beneath*)
pod *+inst* 2 (*less than: level, rate*)
poniżej *+gen* ▷ *adv* 1 (*beneath*) niżej
2 (*less*) poniżej; **~ zero** poniżej
zera; **temperatures ~ normal**
or **average** temperatura poniżej
normalnej
belt [bɛlt] *n* 1 (*clothing*) pasek 2 (*of
land, sea, air*) pas 3 (*Tech*) taśma
bench [bɛntʃ] *n* 1 (*seat*) ławka
2 (*table: in factory, laboratory
etc*) stół
bend [bɛnd] (*pt, pp* **bent**) *vt* (*leg,
arm, bar, wire*) zginać (zgiąć *pf*) ▷ *vi*
1 (*person*) pochylać (pochylić *pf*) się
2 (*leg, arm, bar, wire*) zginać (zgiąć
pf) się 3 (*road, river*) zakręcać
(zakręcić *pf*) się ▷ *n* (*in road, river*)
zakręt
▶ **bend down** *vi* pochylać
(pochylić *pf*) się
beneath [bɪˈniːθ] *prep* 1 (*in
position*) pod *+inst* 2 (*in status*): **~
him/her** poniżej jego/jej ▷ *adv*
poniżej
benefit [ˈbɛnɪfɪt] *n* 1 (*advantage*)
korzyść 2 (*money*) zysk ▷ *vt*
przynosić (przynieść *pf*) korzyści
+dat ▷ *vi*: **to ~ from sth** korzystać

(skorzystać pf) z czegoś
bent [bɛnt] pt, pp of **bend** ▷ adj (wire, pipe) zgięty
beret ['bɛreɪ] n beret
berth [bə:θ] n (bed: on boat) koja; (on train) kuszetka
beside [bɪ'saɪd] prep (next to) obok +gen; see also **besides**
besides [bɪ'saɪdz] adv **1** (also: **beside**: in addition) ponadto **2** (in any case) poza tym ▷ prep (also: **beside**: in addition to, as well as) poza +inst
best [bɛst] adj najlepszy ▷ adv najlepiej ▷ n najlepszy; **the ~ thing to do is...** najlepsze co można zrobić, to...; **to do** or **try one's ~** starać się ze wszystkich sił
best man n drużba
bet [bɛt] (pt, pp **bet** or **betted**) n (wager) zakład ▷ vt **1** (wager): **to ~ sb £100 that...** zakładać (założyć pf) się o sto funtów, że... **2** (expect, guess): **to ~ (that)** założyć się (że) ▷ vi (wager): **to ~ on** (horse, result) robić (zrobić pf) zakłady na
better ['bɛtə'] adj **1** lepszy **2** (after an illness or injury): **to feel ~** czuć (poczuć pf) się lepiej ▷ adv lepiej; **to get ~** polepszyć; **I'd ~ go** or **I had ~ go** lepiej już pójdę
between [bɪ'twi:n] prep między +inst ▷ adv: **in ~** pośrodku; **to choose ~** (two things) wybierać (wybrać pf) pomiędzy +inst; **to be shared/divided ~ people** być podzielonym między ludźmi; **~ you and me, ~ ourselves** między tobą a mną, między nami
beyond [bɪ'jɔnd] prep **1** (on the other side of) po drugiej stronie +gen **2** (fig) poza +inst **3** (after: time,

date, age) po +loc ▷ adv dalej; **~ doubt** poza wszelką wątpliwością
Bible ['baɪbl] (Rel) n: **the ~** Biblia
bicycle ['baɪsɪkl] n rower; **to ride a ~** jeździć na rowerze
big [bɪg] adj **1** (in size: man, country, object) duży **2** (inf: person: important) ważny **3** (major: change, increase, problem) duży; **~ brother/sister** starszy brat/starsza siostra; **in a ~ way** (inf) na wielką skalę
bigheaded ['bɪg'hɛdɪd] (inf) adj zarozumiały
bike [baɪk] n **1** (bicycle) rower **2** (motorcycle) motor
bikini [bɪ'ki:nɪ] n bikini
bilingual [baɪ'lɪŋgwəl] adj dwujęzyczny; **to be ~** być dwujęzycznym
bill [bɪl] n **1** (requesting payment) rachunek **2** (Brit: in restaurant) rachunek **3** (US: banknote) banknot
billfold ['bɪlfəuld] (US) n portfel
billiards ['bɪljədz] n bilard
billion ['bɪljən] n miliard
bin [bɪn] n **1** (Brit: for rubbish) kosz na śmieci **2** (container) pojemnik
binoculars [bɪ'nɔkjuləz] n pl lornetka sg
biochemistry [baɪə'kɛmɪstrɪ] n biochemia
biography [baɪ'ɔgrəfɪ] n biografia; **a ~ of Dylan Thomas** biografia Dylana Thomasa
biology [baɪ'ɔlədʒɪ] n biologia
bird [bə:d] n (Zool) ptak
bird-watching ['bə:dwɔtʃɪŋ] n ptasiarstwo
Biro® ['baɪərəu] (Brit) n długopis
birth [bə:θ] n (of baby, animal)

narodziny; **to give ~ (to)** (*child, animal*) rodzić (urodzić *pf*)

birth certificate *n* metryka urodzenia

birth control *n* regulacja urodzeń

birthday ['bə:θdeɪ] *n* urodziny ▷ *adj* urodzinowy

biscuit ['bɪskɪt] *n* **1** (*Brit: cookie*) ciastko **2** (*US: cake*) ciasto

bisexual ['baɪ'sɛksjuəl] *adj* biseksualny ▷ *n* biseksualista(-tka) *m/f*

bishop ['bɪʃəp] *n* (*Rel*) biskup

bit [bɪt] *pt of* **bite** ▷ *n* **1** (*esp Brit: piece*) kawałek **2** (*esp Brit: part*) fragment **3** (*Comput*) bit **4** (*US: coin*) moneta; **a ~ of** trochę +*gen*; **a ~ mad/dangerous** trochę szalony/niebezpieczny; **~ by bit** stopniowo; **every ~ as good/interesting as** równie dobry/interesujący jak; **for a ~** (*inf*) na trochę; **quite a ~** sporo

bite [baɪt] (*pt* **bit**, *pp* **bitten** ['bɪtn]) *vt* (*person, dog, snake, mosquito*) gryźć (pogryźć *pf*) ▷ *vi* (*dog etc*) gryźć (pogryźć *pf*) ▷ *n* **1** (*mouthful*) kęs **2** (*from dog*) ugryzienie **3** (*from snake, mosquito*) ukąszenie; **to ~ one's nails** obgryzać paznokcie

bitter ['bɪtər] *adj* gorzki

black [blæk] *adj* **1** (*in colour: paint, jacket, cat*) czarny **2** (*person*) czarnoskóry **3** (*tea, coffee*) czarny ▷ *n* **1** (*colour*) czerń **2** (*person*) czarnoskóry; **~ and blue** (*bruised*) posiniaczony

▶ **black out** *vi* (*faint*) tracić (stracić *pf*) przyjemność

blackberry ['blækbərɪ] *n* jeżyna

blackbird ['blækbə:d] *n* kos

blackboard ['blækbɔ:d] *n* tablica

blackcurrant ['blæk'kʌrənt] (*Brit*) *n* czarna porzeczka

blackmail ['blækmeɪl] *n* szantaż ▷ *vt* szantażować (zaszantażować *pf*)

black pudding (*Brit*) *n* kaszanka

blade [bleɪd] *n* (*of knife, sword*) ostrze

blame [bleɪm] *n* wina ▷ *vt*: **to ~ sb for sth** winić kogoś za coś; **to be to ~ (for sth)** być winnym (czegoś); **to ~ sth on sb** obwiniać (obwinić *pf*) kogoś za coś; **you can't ~ him for trying** nie możesz winić go za to, że próbował

blank [blæŋk] *adj* (*paper, cassette*) czysty ▷ *n* (*on form*) puste miejsce; **my mind went ~** *or* **was a blank** miałem pustkę w głowie

blanket ['blæŋkɪt] *n* (*for bed*) koc ▷ *adj* (*comprehensive: ban, coverage*) całkowity

blast [blɑ:st] *n* (*explosion*) wybuch ▷ *vt* **1** (*blow up*) wysadzać (wysadzić *pf*) **2** (*shoot*) strzelać (strzelić *pf*)

▶ **blast off** *vi* (*Space*) odpalać (odpalić *pf*)

blaze [bleɪz] *n* (*fire*) pożar ▷ *vi* (*fire*) płonąć (zapłonąć *pf*) ▷ *vt*: **to ~ a trail** przecierać (przetrzeć *pf*) szlaki; **in a ~ of publicity** w błysku reflektorów

blazer ['bleɪzər] *n* marynarka

bleach [bli:tʃ] *n* (*chemical*) wybielacz ▷ *vt* **1** (*fabric, foodstuff etc*) wybielać (wybielić *pf*) **2** (*hair*) utleniać (utlenić *pf*)

bleed [bli:d] (*pt, pp* **bled** [blɛd]) *vi* (*Med*) krwawić; **my nose is ~ing**

leci mi krew z nosa
blender ['blɛndə^r] n mikser
bless [blɛs] vt (Rel) błogosławić
(pobłogosławić pf); **~ you!** (after
sneeze) na zdrowie!; (inf: expressing
affection) Bóg zapłać!
blew [blu:] pt of **blow**
blind [blaɪnd] adj (Med)
niewidomy ▷ n (for window)
roleta ▷ vt oślepiać (oślepić
pf); **the blind** n pl (blind people)
niewidomi; **to go ~** oślepnąć; **to
turn a ~ eye (to sth)** przymykać
(przymknąć pf) oczy (na coś)
blink [blɪŋk] vi (person, animal)
mrugać (mrugnąć pf) ▷ vt: **to ~
one's eyes** mrugać (mrugnąć pf)
powiekami
blister ['blɪstə^r] n (on skin)
pęcherz ▷ vi (skin) pokrywać
(pokryć pf) się pęcherzami
blizzard ['blɪzəd] n śnieżyca
block [blɔk] n 1 (group of buildings)
blok 2 (of stone, wood, ice) blok
▷ vt 1 (entrance, road) blokować
(zablokować pf) 2 (view) zasłaniać
(zasłonić pf); **~ of flats** or (US)
apartment ~ blok mieszkalny;
3 ~s from here trzy ulice stąd
▶ **block up** vt (sink, pipe etc)
zatykać (zatkać pf) ▷ vi (sink, pipe)
zatykać (zatkać pf) się
blog [blɔg] (Comput) n blog
blond(e) [blɔnd] adj 1 (hair) blond
2 (person) jasnowłosy ▷ n: **blonde**
(woman) blondynka
blood [blʌd] n (Bio) krew; **in cold
~** z zimną krwią
blood pressure n ciśnienie
krwi; **to have high/low ~** mieć
wysokie/niskie ciśnienie krwi; **to
take sb's ~** mierzyć (zmierzyć pf)

komuś ciśnienie krwi
blood test n badanie krwi
blouse [blauz, US blaus]) n
(woman's garment) bluzka
blow [bləu] (pt **blew**, pp **blown**) n
1 (punch) uderzenie 2 (fig: setback)
cios ▷ vi 1 (wind, sand, dust
etc) wiać 2 (person) dmuchać
(dmuchnąć pf) 3 (whistle,
horn) dmuchać (dmuchnąć pf)
▷ vt 1 (wind) wiać 2 (whistle,
horn) dmuchać (dmuchnąć
pf); **to ~ one's nose** dmuchać
(wydmuchać pf) nos
▶ **blow away** vt odfruwać
(odfrunąć pf) ▷ vi odfruwać
(odfrunąć pf)
▶ **blow down** vt (tree, house)
przewracać (przewrócić pf)
▶ **blow out** vt (flame, candle) gasić
(zgasić pf)
▶ **blow up** vi (explode)
wybuchać (wybuchnąć pf) ▷ vt
1 (destroy: bridge etc) wysadzać
(wysadzić pf) 2 (inflate: balloon,
tyre) dmuchać (nadmuchać pf)
blow-dry ['bləudraɪ] vt (hair)
suszyć (wysuszyć pf)
blown [bləun] pp of **blow**
blue [blu:] adj 1 (in colour)
niebieski 2 (inf: depressed) smutny
▷ n błękit; **blues** n pl (Mus): **the
~s** blues; **out of the ~** ni z tego
ni z owego
blunder ['blʌndə^r] n gafa ▷ vi
popełniać (popełnić pf) gafę
blunt [blʌnt] adj 1 (pencil, knife)
tępy 2 (person, remark) szczery,
bez ogródek; **to be ~...** mówiąc
szczerze...
blush [blʌʃ] vi rumienić
(zarumienić pf) się ▷ n rumieniec

board [bɔːd] n **1** (*piece of wood*)
deska **2** (*also*: **notice~**) tablica
3 (*also*: **black~**) tablica **4** (*for
chess etc*) plansza **5** (*committee*)
rada **6** (*at hotel*) wyżywienie ▷ vt
(*formal: ship, train, plane*) wchodzić
(wejść pf) na pokład +gen ▷ vi
(*formal: on ship, train, plane*)
wchodzić (wejść pf) na pokład;
~ and lodging mieszkanie z
wyżywieniem; **on ~** na pokładzie
▶ **board up** vt (*door, window*)
zabijać (zabić pf) deskami
board game n gra planszowa
boarding card ['bɔːdɪŋ-] n karta
pokładowa
boarding school n szkoła z
internatem
boast [bəust] vi: **to ~ (about** or **of
sth)** przechwalać się (czymś) ▷ n
przechwałka
boat [bəut] n **1** (*small vessel*) łódka
2 (*ship*) łódź; **to go by ~** pływać
(płynąć pf) łódką
body ['bɔdɪ] n ciało
bodybuilding ['bɔdɪ'bɪldɪŋ] n
kulturystyka
bodyguard ['bɔdɪgɑːd] n
ochroniarz
boil [bɔɪl] vt **1** (*water*) gotować
(zagotować pf) **2** (*eggs, potatoes
etc*) gotować (ugotować pf) ▷ vi
(*liquid*) gotować (zagotować pf)
się ▷ n (*Med*) czyrak; **to ~ a kettle**
gotować (zagotować pf) wodę
w czajniku
boiled egg ['bɔɪld-] n jajko
gotowane
boiler ['bɔɪləʳ] n (*device*) bojler
boiling (hot) ['bɔɪlɪŋ-] (*inf*)
adj: **I'm ~** jest mi tak gorąco, że
można się ugotować

bolt [bəult] n **1** (*to lock door*) rygiel
2 (*used with nut*) śruba ▷ vt (*door*)
ryglować (zaryglować pf)
bomb [bɔm] n bomba ▷ vt
bombardować (zbombardować
pf)
bomber ['bɔməʳ] n **1** (*Aviat*)
bombowiec **2** (*terrorist*)
zamachowiec podkładający
bomby
bombing ['bɔmɪŋ] n
bombardowanie
bone [bəun] n **1** (*in human, animal*)
kość **2** (*in fish*) ość
bonfire ['bɔnfaɪəʳ] n ognisko

● **BONFIRE NIGHT**
●
● **Bonfire Night** przypada na 5
● listopada, kiedy to w Wielkiej
● Brytanii rozpalane są ogniska
● i puszczane sztuczne ognie w
● celu upamiętnienia spisku Guy
● Fawkesa, który w 1605 roku
● usiłował zabić króla poprzez
● wysadzenie w powietrze
● budynków parlamentu.

bonnet ['bɔnɪt] n (*Brit: of car*)
maska
bonus ['bəunəs] n **1** (*extra
payment*) premia **2** (*additional
benefit*) dodatek
book [buk] n **1** (*novel etc*) książka
2 (*of stamps, tickets*) bloczek
▷ vt (*ticket, table, seat, room*)
rezerwować (zarezerwować
pf); **fully ~ed** wszystkie miejsca
zarezerwowane
▶ **book in** (*Brit*) vi (*at hotel*)
meldować (zameldować pf) się
▶ **book into** (*Brit*) vt fus (*hotel*)

meldować (zameldować *pf*) się w +*loc*

bookcase ['bʊkkeɪs] *n* biblioteczka

booklet ['bʊklɪt] *n* broszurka

bookmark ['bʊkmɑːk] *n* zakładka

bookshelf ['bʊkʃɛlf] *n* pólka na książki

bookshop ['bʊkʃɔp] (*Brit*) *n* księgarnia

bookstore ['bʊkstɔːʳ] (*esp US*) *n* = **bookshop**

boot [buːt] *n* **1** (*footwear: for winter*) kozak; (*for football, walking etc*) but **2** (*Brit: of car*) bagażnik
▶ **boot up** (*Comput*) *vt* ładować (załadować *pf*) ▷ *vi* ładować (załadować *pf*) się

border ['bɔːdəʳ] *n* (*of country*) granica

bore [bɔːʳ] *pt of* **bear** ▷ *vt* **1** (*hole*) drążyć *pf* **2** (*oil well, tunnel*) wywiercać (wywiercić *pf*) **3** (*person*) zanudzać (zanudzić *pf*) ▷ *n*: **to be a ~** (*person*) być nudziarzem; (*situation*) być nudnym; **to be ~d (with sth)** być znudzonym (czymś)

boring ['bɔːrɪŋ] *adj* (*person, job, film*) nudny

born [bɔːn] *adj*: **to be ~** (*baby*) rodzić (urodzić *pf*) się

borrow ['bɔrəu] *vt* (*from sb, from library*) pożyczać (pożyczyć *pf*); **can I ~ a pen, please?** mogę pożyczyć długopis?

boss [bɔs] *n* szef

bossy ['bɔsɪ] *adj* apodyktyczny

both [bəuθ] *adj* obaj ▷ *pron* **1** (*things*) oba *m*, *nt*, obie *f* **2** (*people*) obaj ▷ *conj*: **~ A and B** zarówno A

jak i B; **~ of us went** *or* **we ~ went** obaj poszliśmy

bother ['bɔðəʳ] *vt* **1** (*worry*) martwić (zmartwić *pf*) **2** (*disturb*) niepokoić (zaniepokoić *pf*) ▷ *vi* robić (zrobić *pf*) sobie kłopot ▷ *n* (*trouble*) kłopot; **to ~ doing sth** *or* **to do sth** zadawać (zadać *pf*) sobie trud, aby coś zrobić; **I can't be ~ed to go** nie chce mi się iść; **don't ~** nie kłopocz się

bottle ['bɔtl] *n* butelka ▷ *vt* (*beer, wine*) butelkować; **a ~ of wine/milk** butelka wina/mleka; **a wine/milk ~** butelka na wino/mleko

bottle bank (*Brit*) *n* pojemnik na szkło

bottle opener *n* otwieracz do butelek

bottom ['bɔtəm] *n* **1** (*of container, sea*) dno **2** (*of page, list*) dół **3** (*of class, league*) ostatnie miejsca **4** (*of hill, tree, stairs*) dół **5** (*buttocks*) pośladki **6** (*also*: **~s**: *of bikini, tracksuit*) dół ▷ *adj* (*lowest*) najniższy; **at the ~ of** na dole +*gen*

bought [bɔːt] *pt, pp of* **buy**

bounce [bauns] *vi* (*ball*) odbijać (odbić *pf*) się ▷ *vt* (*ball*) odbijać (odbić *pf*) ▷ *n* (*of ball*) odbicie

bouncer ['baunsəʳ] (*inf*) *n* (*at dance, club*) bramkarz

bound [baund] *pt, pp of* **bind** ▷ *vi* (*leap*) przeskakiwać (przeskoczyć *pf*) ▷ *adj*: **to be ~ to do sth** (*certain*) na pewno coś zrobić

boundary ['baundrɪ] *n* (*border, limit*) granica

bow¹ [bau] *n* **1** (*knot*) kokarda **2** (*weapon*) łuk **3** (*Mus*) smyczek

bow² [bau] *vt* (*head*) skinąć +*inst*

bowl [bəul] n miska
bowling ['bəulɪŋ] n (game)
kręgle; **to go ~** iść na kręgle
bow tie [bəu-] n muszka
box [bɔks] n **1** (container)
pudło **2** (contents) pudło
3 (also: **cardboard ~**) pudło
tekturowe **4** (crate) skrzynia ▷ vi
(Sport) boksować
boxer ['bɔksə'] n (person) bokser
boxer shorts, **boxers** n pl
bokserki
boxing ['bɔksɪŋ] (Sport) n boks
Boxing Day (Brit) n drugi dzień
Świąt Bożego Narodzenia

- **BOXING DAY**
-
- **Boxing Day** – tak w kręgu
- kultury brytyjskiej nazywany
- jest drugi dzień świąt
- Bożego Narodzenia, który
- także jest dniem wolnym
- od pracy. Jego nazwa
- wywodzi się od dawnego
- zwyczaju obdarowywania
- prezentami (**Christmas
- boxes**) pracowników przez
- pracodawców.

boy [bɔɪ] n **1** (male child) chłopiec
2 (young man) chłopak
boyfriend ['bɔɪfrɛnd] n chłopak
bra [brɑː] n stanik
brace [breɪs] n (on teeth) aparat
na zęby
bracelet ['breɪslɪt] n bransoletka
bracket ['brækɪt] n (group, range)
przedział ▷ vt (word, phrase) brać
(wziąć pf) w nawias; **in ~s** w
nawiasie
braid [breɪd] n (US: plait) warkocz

brain [breɪn] n mózg; **brains** n pl
(intelligence) mózg; **he's got ~s**
ma głowę
brainy ['breɪnɪ] adj (inf) bystry
brake [breɪk] n (Aut) hamulec
▷ vi (driver, vehicle) hamować
(zahamować pf)
branch [brɑːntʃ] n **1** (of tree) gałąź
2 (of shop, bank etc) oddział
brand [brænd] n (make) marka
brand-new ['brænd'njuː] adj
nowiutki
brandy ['brændɪ] n brandy
brass [brɑːs] n (metal)
mosiądz; **the ~ (section)** (Mus)
instrumenty dęte blaszane
brass band n orkiestra dęta
blaszana
brave [breɪv] adj **1** (person) dzielny
2 (attempt, smile, action) śmiały
Brazil [brə'zɪl] n Brazylia
bread [brɛd] n chleb
break [breɪk] (pt **broke**, pp
broken) vt **1** (cup, window etc)
tłuc (stłuc pf) **2** (leg, arm) łamać
(złamać pf) **3** (contract) zrywać
(zerwać pf); (promise) łamać
(złamać pf) **4** (law, rule) łamać
(złamać pf) **5** (record) bić (pobić
pf) **6** (habit, pattern etc) zrywać
(zerwać pf) ▷ vi (cup, window
etc) tłuc (stłuc pf) się ▷ n **1** (rest)
przerwa **2** (pause, interval) przerwa
3 (fracture) pęknięcie **4** (holiday)
przerwa; **to ~ the news to sb**
przekazywać (przekazać pf)
komuś wiadomości; **to take a
~** (for a few minutes) robić (zrobić
pf) sobie przerwę; (have a holiday)
mieć przerwę; **without a ~** bez
przerwy
▶ **break down** vi (machine, car)

psuć (zepsuć pf) się ▷ vt (door etc)
wyważać (wyważyć pf)
▶ **break in** vi (burglar) włamywać
(włamać pf) się
▶ **break into** vt fus (house)
włamywać (włamać pf) się do +gen
▶ **break off** vi 1 (branch)
odłamywać (odłamać pf) się
2 (speaker) przerywać (przerwać
pf) ▷ vt 1 (branch, piece of chocolate)
odłamywać (odłamać pf)
2 (engagement, relationship) zrywać
(zerwać pf)
▶ **break out** vi 1 (begin) wybuchać
(wybuchnąć pf) 2 (escape) uciekać
(uciec pf); **to ~ out in spots/a
rash** pokrywać (pokryć pf) się
plamami/wysypką; **to ~ out in
a sweat** zalewać (zalać pf) się
potem
▶ **break up** vi 1 (couple, marriage)
zrywać (zerwać pf) ze sobą
2 (meeting, party) kończyć
(skończyć pf) się 3 (Brit: Scol)
kończyć (skończyć pf) się ▷ vt
1 (fight etc) przerywać (przerwać
pf) 2 (meeting, demonstration)
przerywać (przerwać pf); **to ~
up with sb** zrywać (zerwać pf) z
kimś; **you're ~ing up** (on mobile
phone) coś mi przerywa, nie słyszę
pana
breakdown ['breɪkdaun]
n 1 (Aut) awaria 2 (of system,
talks) zerwanie 3 (of marriage)
rozpad 4 (Med: also: **nervous ~**)
załamanie nerwowe; **to have
a ~** załamywać (załamać pf) się
psychicznie
breakfast ['brɛkfəst] n śniadanie
break-in ['breɪkɪn] n włamanie
breast [brɛst] n pierś

breaststroke ['brɛststrəʊk] n
(also: **the ~**) żabka
breath [brɛθ] n 1 (intake of air)
wdech 2 (air from mouth) wydech;
out of ~ bez tchu; **bad ~** nieświeży
oddech; **to get one's ~ back**
(Brit) łapać (złapać pf) oddech;
to hold one's ~ wstrzymywać
(wstrzymać pf) oddech
breathe [briːð] vt (air) oddychać
(odetchnąć pf) +inst ▷ vi oddychać
(odetchnąć pf)
▶ **breathe in** vi robić (zrobić pf)
wdech
▶ **breathe out** vi robić (zrobić
pf) wydech
breed [briːd] (pt, pp **bred**
[brɛd]) vt (animals) hodować
(wyhodować pf) ▷ vi (Zool)
rozmnażać (rozmnożyć pf) się ▷ n
(Zool) rasa
breeze [briːz] n wiaterek
brewery ['bruːərɪ] n browar
bribe [braɪb] n łapówka ▷ vt
(person, witness) przekupywać
(przekupić pf); **to ~ sb to do sth**
proponować (zaproponować
pf) komuś łapówkę za zrobienie
czegoś
brick [brɪk] n (for building) cegła
bride [braɪd] n panna młoda
bridegroom ['braɪdgruːm] n
pan młody
bridesmaid ['braɪdzmeɪd] n
druhna
bridge [brɪdʒ] n 1 (Archit) most
2 (Cards) brydż
brief [briːf] adj 1 (period, visit,
appearance) krótki 2 (description,
speech) zwięzły; **briefs** n pl 1 (for
men) slipy 2 (for women) figi
briefcase ['briːfkeɪs] n teczka

briefly ['bri:flɪ] adv (smile)
przelotnie; (talk, explain, say)
zwięźle

bright [braɪt] adj 1 (light) jasny
2 (clever: person) bystry; (idea)
genialny 3 (colour) jasny

brilliant ['brɪljənt] adj 1 (person,
mind) błyskotliwy 2 (idea,
performance) znakomity 3 (esp
Brit: inf: wonderful) fantastyczny

bring [brɪŋ] (pt, pp **brought**) vt
1 (thing, person: with you) przenosić
(przenieść pf); (to sb) przynosić
(przynieść pf)
► **bring about** vt (cause)
powodować (spowodować pf)
► **bring along** vt przyprowadzać
(przyprowadzić pf) ze sobą
► **bring back** vt (return) przywozić
(przywieźć pf)
► **bring forward** vt (meeting)
przyspieszać (przyspieszyć pf)
► **bring round** vt (unconscious
person) cucić (ocucić pf)
► **bring up** vt 1 (rear: child)
wychowywać (wychować pf)
2 (question, subject) podnosić
(podnieść pf); (food) wymiotować
(zwymiotować pf)

Britain ['brɪtən] n (also: **Great ~**)
Wielka Brytania; **in ~** w Wielkiej
Brytanii

British ['brɪtɪʃ] adj brytyjski
▷ n pl: **the ~** Brytyjczycy

broad [brɔ:d] adj (street, shoulders)
szeroki; **in ~ daylight** w biały
dzień

broadband ['brɔ:dbænd]
(Comput) n sztywne łącze

broad bean (esp Brit) n bób

broadcast ['brɔ:dkɑ:st] (pt,
pp **broadcast**) n audycja
▷ vt nadawać (nadać pf) ▷ vi
prowadzić program

broccoli ['brɔkəlɪ] n brokuły

brochure ['brəʊʃjʊə', US brəʊ'ʃʌr]
n (booklet) broszura

broil [brɔɪl] (US) vt opiekać
(opiec pf)

broke [brəʊk] pt of **break** ▷ adj
(inf: penniless) spłukany

broken ['brəʊkn] pp of **break**
▷ adj 1 (window, cup etc) rozbity
2 (machine) zepsuty; **a ~ leg**
złamana noga; **a ~ marriage**
rozbite małżeństwo

bronchitis [brɔŋ'kaɪtɪs] n
zapalenie oskrzeli

bronze [brɔnz] n 1 (metal) brąz
2 (Sport: also: **~ medal**) brąz ▷ adj
(in colour) brąz

brooch [brəʊtʃ] n broszka

broom [bru:m] n (for cleaning)
miotła

brother ['brʌðə'] n brat

brother-in-law ['brʌðərɪnlɔ:] n
szwagier

brought [brɔ:t] pt, pp of **bring**

brown [braun] adj 1 (in
colour: object) brązowy; (hair, eyes)
brązowy 2 (tanned: skin, person)
opalony ▷ n (colour) brąz

browse [brauz] vi 1 (Comput)
przeglądać (przejrzeć pf) 2 (in
shop) szperać (wyszperać pf)

browser ['brauzə'] (Comput) n
przeglądarka

bruise [bru:z] n (on face etc) siniak
▷ vt posiniaczyć (posiniaczyć pf)

brush [brʌʃ] n (for cleaning, for
decorating) miotła; (for hair)
szczotka; (artist's) pędzel ▷ vt
1 (carpet etc) zmiatać (zmieść
pf) 2 (hair) szczotkować

(wyszczotkować pf); **to ~ one's
teeth** myć (umyć pf) zęby
Brussels sprout ['brʌslz-] n
brukselka
bubble ['bʌbl] n **1** (in liquid)
pęcherzyk **2** (also: **soap ~**) bańka
▷ vi (liquid) bulgotać (zabulgotać
pf)
bubble bath n (liquid) płyn do
kąpieli
bubble gum n guma balonowa
bucket ['bʌkɪt] n wiadro
buckle ['bʌkl] n (on shoe, belt)
klamra ▷ vt (shoe, belt) zapinać
(zapiąć pf) na klamrę
Buddhism ['budɪzəm] n
buddyzm
Buddhist ['budɪst] adj buddyjski
▷ n buddysta(-yjka) m/f
buffet ['bufeɪ, US bu'feɪ] n bufet
bug [bʌg] n **1** (esp US: insect) robak
2 (Comput) błąd **3** (inf: virus) wirus
build [bɪld] (pt, pp **built**) n (of
person) budowa ciała ▷ vt (house,
machine) budować (zbudować pf)
▶ **build up** vi (accumulate)
narastać
builder ['bɪldə'] n (worker)
robotnik budowlany
building ['bɪldɪŋ] n (house, office
etc) budynek

● **BUILDING SOCIETY**
●
● **Building societies**
● – oszczędnościowe kasy
● mieszkaniowe, pierwotnie
● zakładane po to, aby udzielać
● kredytów na zakup mieszkań,
● obecnie zaś oferujące większy
● zakres usług finansowych.

built [bɪlt] pt, pp of **build**
▷ adj: **well-/heavily-~** (person)
dobrze zbudowany
bulb [bʌlb] n **1** (Elec) żarówka
2 (Bot) cebulka
Bulgaria [bʌl'gɛərɪə] n Bułgaria
bull [bul] n (Zool) byk
bullet ['bulɪt] n pocisk
bulletin ['bulɪtɪn] n (TV etc: news
update) biuletyn
bulletin board n **1** (Comput)
tablica ogłoszeniowa
2 (US: noticeboard) tablica
informacyjna
bullfighting ['bulfaɪtɪŋ] n walki
pl byków
bully ['bulɪ] n łobuz ▷ vt
zastraszać (zastraszyć pf)
bum [bʌm] (inf) n **1** (Brit: backside)
tyłek **2** (esp US: tramp) menel
bump [bʌmp] n **1** (swelling: on
head) guz **2** (jolt) wstrząs **3** (on
road) wyboje ▷ vt (strike) uderzać
(uderzyć pf)
▶ **bump into** vt fus **1** (strike:
obstacle, person) uderzać (uderzyć
pf) **2** (inf: meet: person) wpadać
(wpaść pf) na
bumper ['bʌmpə'] n (Aut) zderzak
bumpy ['bʌmpɪ] adj (road)
wyboisty
bun [bʌn] n (Culin) bułka
bunch [bʌntʃ] n **1** (of flowers)
bukiet **2** (of keys) pęk; (of bananas,
grapes) kiść; **bunches** n pl (Brit: in
hair) kucyki
bungalow ['bʌŋgələu] n dom
parterowy
bunk [bʌŋk] n (bed) łóżko
piętrowe
burger ['bə:gə'] n hamburger
burglar ['bə:glə'] n

włamywacz(ka) m/f
burglar alarm n alarm
antywłamaniowy
burglary ['bə:glərɪ] n włamanie
burn [bə:n] (pt, pp **burned** or
burnt) (Brit) vt **1** (papers etc) palić
(spalić pf) **2** (fuel) spalać (spalić pf)
3 (toast, rice) przypalać (przypalić
pf) ▷ vi **1** (fire, flame) palić się
2 (house, car) palić (spalić pf) się
▷ n oparzenie; **I've ~t myself!**
oparzyłem się!
▶ **burn down** vi (house etc) palić
(spalić pf) się
burst [bə:st] (pt, pp **burst**) vt (bag,
balloon etc) przekłuwać (przekłuć
pf) ▷ vi (pipe, tyre) pękać (pęknąć
pf); **to ~ into flames** wybuchać
(wybuchnąć pf) płomieniem; **to ~
into tears** wybuchać (wybuchnąć
pf) płaczem; **to ~ out laughing**
wybuchać (wybuchnąć pf)
śmiechem
bury ['bɛrɪ] vt **1** (in ground)
zakopywać (zakopać pf) **2** (dead
person) chować (pochować pf)
bus [bʌs] n autobus
bus driver n kierowca autobusu
bush [buʃ] n (plant) krzak
business ['bɪznɪs] n biznes; **to
be away on ~** być w podróży
służbowej; **to do ~ with sb** robić
(zrobić pf) z kimś interesy; **it's
none of your ~** to nie twoja
sprawa
businessman ['bɪznɪsmən]
(irreg) n przedsiębiorca
businesswoman
['bɪznɪswumən] (irreg) n kobieta
interesu
bus station n dworzec
autobusowy

bus stop n przystanek
autobusowy
bust [bʌst] vt ▷ n (breasts) biust
busy ['bɪzɪ] adj **1** (person)
zajęty **2** (shop, street) ruchliwy
3 (schedule, time, day) pracowity
4 (esp US: Tel: line) zajęty ▷ vt: **to
~ oneself (with sth)** zajmować
(zająć pf) się (czymś); **I'm ~** jestem
zajęty

○ **KEYWORD**

but [bʌt] conj **1** (yet, however) ale;
I'd love to come, but I'm busy
bardzo chciałbym przyjść, ale
jestem zajęty; **not only... but
also** nie tylko... ale także
2 (showing disagreement,
surprise etc): **but that's far too
expensive!** ale to jest za drogie!
▷ prep (apart from, except) poza
+inst; **nothing but** nic poza +inst;
anything but wszystko poza
+inst; **they've got no-one but
themselves to blame** nikogo nie
mogą winić poza sobą
▷ adv **1** (just, only) tylko
2: but for (without) gdyby nie;
(except for) gdyby nie; **but for his
help/him, we wouldn't have
finished the job** gdyby nie jego
pomoc/on, nie skończylibyśmy
pracy

butcher ['butʃər] n **1** (person)
rzeźnik(-iczka) m/f **2** (shop: also:
~'s) sklep mięsny
butter ['bʌtər] n masło
butterfly ['bʌtəflaɪ] n **1** (insect)
motyl **2** (also: **the ~**: in swimming)
motylek

button [ˈbʌtn] n 1 (on clothes)
guzik 2 (on machine) przycisk
3 (US: badge) znaczek ▷ vt (also: ~
up) zapinać (zapiąć pf)

buy [baɪ] (pt, pp **bought**) vt
kupować (kupić pf) ▷ n (purchase)
zakup; **to ~ sb sth** kupować
(kupić pf) coś komuś; **to ~ sth off**
or **from sb** kupować (kupić pf) coś
od kogoś

buzz [bʌz] vi (insect) bzyczeć
(bzyknąć pf); (machine) brzęczeć
(zabrzęczeć pf)

○ **KEYWORD**

by [baɪ] prep 1 (referring to cause,
agent): **a painting by Picasso**
obraz Picassa; **surrounded by a
fence** otoczony ogrodzeniem
2 (referring to method, manner,
means): **by bus/car/train**
autobusem/samochodem/
pociągiem; **to pay by cheque**
płacić (zapłacić pf) czekiem;
**she grabbed him by the
arm** chwyciła go za rękę; **by
moonlight/candlelight** przy
świetle księżyca/świecach
3 (via, through) przez; **he came in
by the back door** wszedł przez
tylne drzwi
4 (close to, beside) przy +loc; **he
was standing by the door** stał
przy drzwiach; **the house by the
river** dom przy rzece
5 (past) obok +gen
6 (with times, dates, years) do +gen;
by 4 o'clock do czwartej godziny;
by this time tomorrow o tej
porze jutro; **by the time I got
here** zanim tu przyszedłem; **by**

now/then już
7 (during): **by day/night** w ciągu
dnia/nocy
8 (specifying number, quantity, rate)
na +acc; **sold by the kilo/metre**
sprzedawane na kilogramy/metry
9 (specifying degree of change) o;
**crime has increased by 10 per
cent** przestępczość wzrosła o
dziesięć procent
10 (in measurements): **a room 3
metres by 4** pokój trzy metry
na cztery
11 (Math): **to divide/multiply by
3** dzielić/mnożyć przez trzy
12 (according to): **by law** według
prawa; **it's all right by me** nie
mam nic przeciwko temu; **by
profession/birth/nature** z
zawodu/urodzenia/natury
13: **by myself/himself** etc
(unaided) samemu; (alone) sam

bye(-bye) [ˈbaɪ(ˈbaɪ)] (inf) int
pa, pa
bypass [ˈbaɪpɑːs] n (Aut)
obwodnica ▷ vt (town) omijać
(ominąć pf)

C

cab [kæb] n (taxi) taksówka
cabbage ['kæbɪdʒ] n kapusta
cabin ['kæbɪn] n kabina
cable ['keɪbl] n 1 (rope) lina 2 (Elec) kabel 3 (also: ~ **television**) kablówka
cable car n wagonik kolejki linowej
cable television n telewizja kablowa
cactus ['kæk] (pl **cactuses** or **cacti** ['kæktaɪ]) n kaktus
cafeteria [kæfɪ'tɪərɪə] n bufet
cage [keɪdʒ] n klatka
cagoule [kə'guːl] n sztormiak
cake [keɪk] n (large) ciasto; (small) ciastko
calculate ['kælkjuleɪt] vt (work out) obliczać (obliczyć pf); **to ~ (that)...** (using maths) obliczać

(obliczyć pf), (że)...
calculation [kælkju'leɪʃən] n (Math) obliczenie
calculator ['kælkjuleɪtəʳ] n kalkulator
calendar ['kæləndəʳ] n (showing date) kalendarz
calf [kɑːf] (pl **calves**) n 1 (Zool: of cow) cielę 2 (Anat) łydka
call [kɔːl] vt 1 (name) nazywać (nazwać pf) 2 (address as) zwracać (zwrócić pf) się 3 (describe as) nazywać (nazwać pf) 4 (Tel) dzwonić (zadzwonić pf) 5 (summon: person) wołać (zawołać pf) ▷ vi (telephone) dzwonić (zadzwonić pf) ▷ n 1 (Tel) telefon 2 (demand): **~ for sth** żądanie czegoś 3 (visit) wizyta; **to be ~ed** (person) nazywać się; (object) nazywać się; **who's ~ing?** (Tel) kto mówi?; **to make a phone ~** dzwonić (zadzwonić pf); **to give sb a ~** zadzwonić do kogoś
▶ **call back** vi 1 (return) wracać (wrócić pf) 2 (Tel) oddzwonić ▷ vt (Tel) dzwonić (zadzwonić pf)
▶ **call for** vt fus (fetch: person) wstępować (wstąpić pf) po; (parcel) odbierać (odebrać pf)
▶ **call off** vt (deal, event) odwoływać (odwołać pf)
▶ **call out** vi wołać
callbox ['kɔːlbɒks] (Brit: Tel) n budka telefoniczna
call centre (US **call center**) n (Tel) call centre
calm [kɑːm] adj 1 (person) opanowany; (voice) cichy; (place) spokojny 2 (not stormy: sea) spokojny
▶ **calm down** vt (person, animal)

uspokajać (uspokoić *pf*) ▷ *vi*
(*person*) uspokajać (uspokoić
pf) się
calorie ['kælərɪ] *n* kaloria
calves [kɑːvz] *n pl* of **calf**
camcorder ['kæmkɔːdəʳ] *n*
kamera wideo
came [keɪm] *pt of* **come**
camel ['kæməl] *n* wielbłąd(zica)
m/f
camera ['kæmərə] *n* **1** (*Phot*)
aparat fotograficzny **2** (*Cine, TV*)
kamera
cameraman ['kæmərəmæn]
(*irreg*) *n* operator
camp [kæmp] *n* **1** (*for refugees,
prisoners, soldiers*) obóz
2 (*encampment*) obozowisko ▷ *vi*
biwakować (*pf*)
campaign [kæm'peɪn] *n* (*for
change*) kampania
camper ['kæmpəʳ] *n* **1** (*person*)
obozowicz(ka) *m/f* **2** (*also*: **~ van**)
samochód kempingowy
camping ['kæmpɪŋ] *n*
biwakowanie; **to go ~** jechać
(pojechać *pf*) pod namiot *lub* na
kemping
campsite ['kæmpsaɪt] *n*
kemping
campus ['kæmpəs] *n* miasteczko
uniwersyteckie
can¹ [kæn] *n* **1** (*for food, drinks*)
puszka; (*for petrol, oil*) kanister
2 (*contents*) puszka

○ **KEYWORD**

can² [kæn] (*negative* **cannot,
can't**, *conditional, pt* **could**) *aux vb*
1 (*be able to*) móc; **can I help you?**
(*in shop*) w czym mogę panu/pani

pomóc?; (*in general*) mogę jakoś
pomóc?; **you can do it if you try**
możesz to zrobić, jeśli spróbujesz;
I can't hear/see anything nic nie
słyszę/widzę; **she can't sleep** nie
może spać; **I can't understand
why...** nie mogę zrozumieć
dlaczego...
2 (*know how to*) umieć; **I can
swim/drive** umiem pływać/
kierować (pojazdem)
3 (*permission, requests*) móc;
can I use your phone? mogę
skorzystać z twojego telefonu?;
can you help me? możesz mi
pomóc?
4 (*disbelief, puzzlement*): **it can't
be true!** to nie może być prawda!;
you can't be serious! nie mówisz
poważnie!
5 (*possibility*) móc, potrafić; **he
can be very unpleasant** potrafi
być bardzo niemiły; **can she have
finished already?** czy mogła już
skończyć?

Canada ['kænədə] *n* Kanada
Canadian [kə'neɪdɪən]
adj kanadyjski ▷ *n* (*person*)
Kanadyjczyk(-jka) *m/f*
canal [kə'næl] *n* (*for ships, barges*)
kanał
Canaries [kə'nɛərɪz] *n pl*: **the ~**
Wyspy Kanaryjskie
canary [kə'nɛərɪ] *n* kanarek
cancel ['kænsəl] *vt* odwoływać
(odwołać *pf*)
cancer ['kænsəʳ] *n* **1** (*Med*)
nowotwór **2** (*Astrol*): **C~** Rak
candidate ['kændɪdeɪt] *n* **1** (*for
job*) kandydat(ka) *m/f* **2** (*in exam*)
zdający(-ca) *m/f*

candle ['kændl] n świeca
candy ['kændɪ] (US) n słodycze;
piece of ~ cukierek
candyfloss ['kændɪflɒs] (Brit) n
wata cukrowa
canned [kænd] adj (fruit,
vegetables) w puszce
cannot ['kænɒt] = **can not**
canoe [kə'nuː] n kajak
canoeing [kə'nuːɪŋ] n
kajakarstwo; **to go ~** pływać
(płynąć pf) kajakiem
can opener [-'əupnəʳ] n
otwieracz do puszek
can't [kɑːnt] = **can not**
canteen [kæn'tiːn] n (in
workplace, school) stołówka
canter ['kæntəʳ] vi (horse) biec
krótkim galopem
canvas ['kænvəs] n (fabric)
płótno
cap [kæp] n 1 (hat) czapka
2 (top: of bottle) nakrętka
capable ['keɪpəbl] adj
(able: person) sprawny; **to be ~ of
sth** (speed, output) potrafić coś;
to be ~ of doing sth być w stanie
coś zrobić
capacity [kə'pæsɪtɪ] n
pojemność; **filled to ~** zapchany;
a ~ crowd wypełniony do
ostatniego miejsca; **~ for sth/to
do sth** zdolność do czegoś/do
zrobienia czegoś
capital ['kæpɪtl] n 1 (city) stolica
2 (money) fundusze, kapitał
3 (also: **~ letter**) wielka litera;
in ~s dużymi literami; **~ R/L**
duże R/L
capitalism ['kæpɪtəlɪzəm] n
kapitalizm
Capricorn ['kæprɪkɔːn] n (Astrol)
Koziorożec
captain ['kæptɪn] n kapitan
capture ['kæptʃəʳ] vt
(catch: animal) chwytać (schwytać
pf); (person) pojmać (pf)
car [kɑːʳ] n 1 (Aut) samochód
2 (US: Rail) wagon; **by ~**
samochodem
caramel ['kærəməl] (Culin) n
karmel
caravan ['kærəvæn] n
(Brit: vehicle) przyczepa
kempingowa

   CAR BOOT SALE

   Car boot sale to brytyjska
   odmiana pchlego targu,
   gdzie sprzedaje się rzeczy
   używane. Wyprzedaże takie
   odbywają się na terenach
   otwartych, często np.
   parkingach. Sprzedawane
   dobra prezentowane są na
   rozkładanych stołach lub
   w otwartych bagażnikach
   samochodów.

card [kɑːd] n 1 (record card, index
card etc) kartka 2 (also:
playing ~) karta 3 (greetings card) kartka
z życzeniami 4 (also: **business ~**)
wizytówka 5 (bank card, credit card
etc) karta; **to play ~s** grać w karty
cardboard ['kɑːdbɔːd] n karton
cardigan ['kɑːdɪgən] n sweter
rozpinany
care [kɛəʳ] n (attention)
ostrożność ▷ vi przejmować
(przejąć pf) się; **with ~** ostrożnie;
take ~! (saying goodbye) trzymaj
się!; **to take ~ to do sth** starać

(postarać *pf*) się coś zrobić; **to take ~ of sb** opiekować się kimś; **to take ~ of sth** (*possession, clothes*) dbać (zadbać *pf*) o coś; (*problem, situation*) zajmować (zająć *pf*) się czymś; **I don't ~** nie obchodzi mnie to
▶ **care about** *vt fus* (*person, thing, idea*) interesować się +*inst*
▶ **care for** *vt fus* (*look after*) opiekować (zaopiekować *pf*) się +*inst*

career [kə'rɪə^r] *n* **1** (*job, profession*) zawód **2** (*working life*) kariera

careful ['kɛəful] *adj* **1** (*cautious*) ostrożny **2** (*thorough: work, thought, analysis*) staranny; **(be) ~!** uważaj!; **to be ~ with sth** (*money*) ostrożnie się z czymś obchodzić; (*fragile object*) ostrożnie się z czymś obchodzić; **to be ~ to do sth/not to do sth** uważać, żeby coś zrobić/czegoś nie zrobić

carefully ['kɛəfəlɪ] *adv*
1 (*cautiously*) ostrożnie
2 (*methodically*) skrupulatnie

careless ['kɛəlɪs] *adj* (*negligent: person, worker*) nieuważny; (*driving*) nieostrożny; (*mistake*) wynikający z nieuwagi; **to be ~ with sth** (*money, resources*) trwonić coś

caretaker ['kɛəteɪkə^r] *n* (*Brit: of building*) dozorca(-czyni) *m/f*

car ferry *n* prom samochodowy

cargo ['kɑːgəʊ] (*pl* **cargoes**) *n* ładunek

car hire (*Brit*) *n* wynajem samochodów

Caribbean [kærɪ'biːən] *n*: **the ~ (Sea)** Morze Karaibskie ▷ *adj* karaibski

carnation [kɑː'neɪʃən] *n* goździk

carnival ['kɑːnɪvl] *n* **1** (*festival*) karnawał **2** (*US*) parada

carol ['kærəl] *n*: **(Christmas) ~** kolęda

car park (*Brit*) *n* parking

carpenter ['kɑːpɪntə^r] *n* stolarz

carpentry ['kɑːpɪntrɪ] *n* stolarstwo

carpet ['kɑːpɪt] *n* (*fitted*) wykładzina; (*rug*) dywan

car rental *n* wynajem samochodów

carriage ['kærɪdʒ] *n* (*Brit: Rail*) wagon

carrier bag ['kærɪə^r-] (*Brit*) *n* reklamówka

carrot ['kærət] *n* marchewka

carry ['kærɪ] *vt* **1** (*person*) nieść (zanieść *pf*); (*by hand with the arm down*) przenosić (przenieść *pf*); (*on one's back*) przenosić (przenieść *pf*); (*by hand*) nosić (nieść *pf*) **2** (*transport: ship, plane*) przewozić (przewieźć *pf*)
▶ **carry on** *vi* (*continue*) kontynuować ▷ *vt* (*continue: work, tradition*): **to ~ on with sth** kontynuować coś; **to ~ on doing sth** kontynuować coś robić
▶ **carry out** *vt* (*order, instruction*) realizować (zrealizować *pf*)

cart [kɑːt] *n* **1** (*for people, goods*) wóz **2** (*US: also:* **shopping ~**) wózek

carton ['kɑːtən] *n* karton

cartoon [kɑː'tuːn] *n* **1** (*drawing*) dowcip rysunkowy **2** (*Brit: comic strip*) komiks **3** (*animated*) kreskówka

cartridge ['kɑːtrɪdʒ] *n* **1** (*for gun*) nabój **2** (*of ink: for printer*)

wkład drukujący **3** (*for camera*)
rolka filmu
carve [kɑːv] *vt* **1** (*Culin: meat*) kroić
(pokroić *pf*) **2** (*wood, stone, figure*)
rzeźbić (wyrzeźbić *pf*)
case [keɪs] *n* **1** (*instance*)
przypadek **2** (*container*)
opakowanie **3** (*Brit: also:* **suit~**)
walizka; **lower/upper ~**
małe/duże litery; **in ~ of** (*fire,
emergency*) w razie; **in ~ he comes**
jeśli przyjdzie; **in any ~** w każdym
przypadku; **just in ~** na wszelki
wypadek; **in that ~** w takim razie
cash [kæʃ] *n* **1** (*notes and coins*)
gotówka **2** (*money*) pieniądze ▷ *vt*
(*cheque, money order*) realizować
(zrealizować *pf*); **to pay (in) ~**
płacić (zapłacić *pf*) gotówką
cash dispenser [kæʃ dɪsˈpɛnsəʳ]
(*Brit*) *n* bankomat
cashew [kæˈʃuː] *n* (*also:* **~ nut**)
nerkowiec
cashier [kæˈʃɪəʳ] *n* (*in bank*)
kasjer(ka) *m/f*
cashmere [ˈkæʃmɪəʳ] *n* kaszmir
▷ *adj* kaszmirowy
casino [kəˈsiːnəu] *n* kasyno
cassette [kæˈsɛt] *n* kaseta
cast [kɑːst] (*pt, pp* **cast**) *n* (*Theat*)
obsada; **to ~ one's vote** oddawać
(oddać *pf*) głos
castle [ˈkɑːsl] *n* zamek
casual [ˈkæʒjul] *adj*
1 (*chance: remark*) przypadkowy
2 (*unconcerned*) swobodny
3 (*informal: clothes*) swobodny
casualty [ˈkæʒjultɪ] *n* **1** (*of war,
accident: injured*) ofiara; (*dead*)
ofiara śmiertelna **2** (*Brit: in
hospital*) ostry dyżur
cat [kæt] *n* kot

catalogue [ˈkætəlɔg] (*US*
catalog) *n* katalog
catastrophe [kəˈtæstrəfɪ] *n*
katastrofa
catch [kætʃ] (*pt, pp* **caught**)
vt **1** łapać (złapać *pf*)
2 (*discover: person*) przyłapać;
3 (*flu, illness*) łapać (złapać *pf*)
▷ *n*: **to ~ sb doing sth** łapać
(złapać *pf*) kogoś na robieniu
czegoś; **to be** *or* **get caught in
sth** (*storm*) być złapanym przez
coś; (*traffic jam*) utkwić w czymś
▶ **catch up** *vi* (*walking, driving*)
nadganiać (nadgonić *pf*)
▶ **catch up with** *vt fus* doganiać
(dogonić *pf*)
category [ˈkætɪgərɪ] *n* kategoria
catering [ˈkeɪtərɪŋ] *n* **1** (*industry*)
gastronomia **2** (*for specific
occasion*) catering
cathedral [kəˈθiːdrəl] *n* katedra
Catholic [ˈkæθəlɪk] *adj* katolicki
▷ *n* katolik(-iczka) *m/f*
cattle [ˈkætl] *n pl* bydło
caught [kɔːt] *pt, pp of* **catch**
cauliflower [ˈkɔlɪflauəʳ] *n*
kalafior
cause [kɔːz] *n* **1** (*of event*)
przyczyna **2** (*reason*) powód ▷ *vt*
(*produce, lead to*) powodować
(spowodować *pf*); **to ~ sb to do
sth** skłonić kogoś do czegoś; **to ~
sth to happen** spowodować coś
cautious [ˈkɔːʃəs] *adj* ostrożny;
to be ~ about doing sth robić
(zrobić *pf*) coś ostrożnie
cave [keɪv] *n* jaskinia
CCTV *n abbr* (= *closed-circuit
television*) telewizja przemysłowa
CD *n abbr* (= *compact disc*) płyta
kompaktowa

CD player n odtwarzacz płyt kompaktowych

CD-ROM [si:di:'rɔm] n abbr (= compact disc read-only memory) CD-ROM; **on ~** na CD-ROMie

ceiling ['si:lɪŋ] n (in room) sufit

celebrate ['sɛlɪbreɪt] vt 1 (success, birthday) świętować 2 (Rel: mass) celebrować ▷ vi świętować

celebrity [sɪ'lɛbrɪtɪ] n (person) znana osobistość

celery ['sɛlərɪ] n seler naciowy; **a stick of ~** łodyga selera naciowego

cell [sɛl] n 1 (Bio) komórka 2 (in prison) cela

cellar ['sɛlər] n piwnica

cello ['tʃɛləu] n wiolonczela

cellphone ['sɛlfəun] n (US) telefon komórkowy

cellular phone ['sɛljulə-] n (US) = **cellphone**

cement [sə'mɛnt] n 1 (powder) cement 2 (concrete) beton ▷ vt (stick, glue) cementować

cemetery ['sɛmɪtrɪ] n cmentarz

cent [sɛnt] n cent

centenary [sɛn'ti:nərɪ] (Brit) n stulecie

centennial [sɛn'tɛnɪəl] (US) n stulecie

center ['sɛntər] (US) n = **centre**

centigrade ['sɛntɪgreɪd] adj w skali Celsjusza

centimetre ['sɛntɪmi:tər] (US **centimeter**) n centymetr

central ['sɛntrəl] adj 1 (in the centre) centralny 2 (most important: idea, figure) główny

central heating n centralne ogrzewanie

centre ['sɛntər] (US **center**) n

1 (of circle, line) środek; (of town, activity) centrum 2 (building) ośrodek; **to be at the ~ of sth** być w centrum czegoś; **to be the ~ of attention/interest** być w centrum uwagi/zainteresowania; **to ~** or **be centred on sth** (focus on) skupiać (skupić pf) się na czymś

century ['sɛntjurɪ] n (period) wiek; **in the twenty-first ~** w dwudziestym pierwszym wieku

cereal ['si:rɪəl] n 1 (plant, crop) zboże 2 (also: **breakfast ~**) płatki śniadaniowe

ceremony ['sɛrɪmənɪ] n (event) uroczystość; (ritual) ceremonia

certain ['sə:tən] adj pewny; **to be ~ that...** (person) być pewnym, że...; **it is ~ that...** jest pewne, że...; **to make ~ that...** upewnić się, że...; **to be ~ of** być pewnym +gen; **a ~ amount of sth** pewna ilość czegoś; **to know sth for ~** wiedzieć coś na pewno

certainly ['sə:tənlɪ] adv 1 (undoubtedly) z pewnością 2 (of course) oczywiście; **~ not** zdecydowanie nie

certificate [sə'tɪfɪkɪt] n 1 (of birth, marriage etc) świadectwo 2 (diploma) dyplom, certyfikat

chain [tʃeɪn] n 1 łańcuch 2 (piece of jewellery) łańcuszek ▷ vt: **to ~ sb/sth to sth** przykuć kogoś/coś łańcuchami do czegoś

chair [tʃɛər] n krzesło; (armchair) fotel

chair lift n wyciąg krzesełkowy

chairman ['tʃɛəmən] (irreg) n przewodniczący

chairwoman ['tʃɛəwumən]

(*irreg*) *n* przewodnicząca
chalet ['ʃæleɪ] *n* drewniana chata
chalk [tʃɔːk] *n* **1** kreda **2** (*for writing*) kreda; **a piece of ~** (*for blackboard*) kawałek kredy
challenge ['tʃælɪndʒ] *n* **1** (*hard task*) wyzwanie **2** (*to authority, ideas*) podważenie; (*to rival, competitor*) wyzwanie ▷ *vt* (*authority, right, idea*) kwestionować (zakwestionować *pf*); (*rival, competitor*) rzucać (rzucić *pf*) wyzwanie +*dat*; **to ~ sb to do sth** rzucać (rzucić *pf*) komuś wyzwanie do zrobienia czegoś; **to ~ sb to a fight** wyzwać kogoś na pojedynek
champagne [ʃæm'peɪn] *n* szampan
champion ['tʃæmpɪən] *n* (*of league, contest*) mistrz(yni) *m/f*
championship ['tʃæmpɪənʃɪp] *n* (*contest*) mistrzostwa
chance [tʃɑːns] *n* **1** (*likelihood, possibility*) szansa **2** (*opportunity*) okazja **3** (*luck*) traf ▷ *adj* (*meeting, discovery*) przypadkowy; **he hasn't much ~ of winning** nie ma wielu szans na wygraną; **to stand a ~ of (doing) sth** mieć szansę na zrobienie czegoś; **the ~s are that...** są szanse, że...; **the ~ to do sth** okazja do zrobienia czegoś; **by ~** przypadkiem
change [tʃeɪndʒ] *vt* **1** (*alter*) zmieniać (zmienić *pf*) **2** (*replace: wheel, battery etc*) wymieniać (wymienić *pf*) **3** (*trains, buses etc*) przesiadać (przesiąść *pf*) się **4** (*clothes*) przebierać (przebrać *pf*) się **5** (*job, address*) zmieniać (zmienić *pf*) **6** (*put fresh nappy*

on: baby) przewijać (przewinąć *pf*) **7** (*replace: nappy*) zmieniać (zmienić *pf*) **8** (*exchange: money*) wymieniać (wymienić *pf*) **9** (*transform*): **to ~ sb/sth into sth** zamieniać (zamienić *pf*) kogoś/coś w coś ▷ *vi* **1** (*alter*) zmieniać (zmienić *pf*) **2** (*change clothes*) zmieniać (zmienić *pf*) **3** (*traffic lights*) zmieniać (zmienić *pf*) **4** (*on bus, train etc*) przesiadać (przesiąść *pf*) się **5** (*be transformed*): **to ~ into sth** zmieniać (zmienić *pf*) w coś ▷ *n* **1** (*alteration*) zmiana **2** (*novelty*) odmiana **3** (*referring to money: coins*) drobne; (*money returned*) reszta; **to ~ sth for sth** zamieniać (zamienić *pf*) coś na coś; **to ~ one's mind** zmienić zdanie; **to ~ gear** (*Brit: Aut*) zmieniać (zmienić *pf*) bieg; **she ~d into an old skirt** przebrała się w starą spódnicę; **for a ~** dla odmiany; **a ~ of clothes/ underwear** zmiana ubrania/ bielizny; **small ~** drobne; **to give sb ~ for** *or* **of £10** rozmieniać (rozmienić *pf*) komuś dziesięć funtów; **keep the ~** reszty nie trzeba
changing room ['tʃeɪndʒɪŋ ruːm] (*Brit*) *n* **1** (*in shop*) przymierzalnia **2** (*Sport*) szatnia
channel ['tʃænl] *n* **1** (*TV*) kanał **2** (*for water*) kanał; **the (English) C~** Kanał La Manche
chaos ['keɪɔs] *n* chaos
chapel ['tʃæpl] *n* **1** (*in church*) kaplica **2** (*in hospital, prison, school*) kaplica **3** (*non-conformist chapel*) kościół
chapter ['tʃæptər] *n* (*of book*)

rozdział
character ['kærɪktər] *n*
1 (*nature: of person, place*) charakter
2 (*in novel, film*) postać **3** (*letter, symbol etc*) znak; **a strange/sad ~**
(*inf*) dziwna/żałosna osoba
characteristic [kærɪktə'rɪstɪk]
adj charakterystyczny ▷ *n* cecha
charakterystyczna; **to be ~ of
sb/sth** być charakterystycznym
dla kogoś/czegoś
charcoal ['tʃɑːkəul] *n* (*for fuel*)
węgiel drzewny; **a piece of ~**
kawałek węgla
charge [tʃɑːdʒ] *n* **1** (*fee*) opłata
2 (*accusation*) oskarżenie ▷ *vt*
1 (*sum of money*) liczyć (policzyć
pf); (*customer, client*) pobierać
(pobrać *pf*) **2** (*also: ~ up: battery*)
ładować (naładować *pf*); **charges**
n pl (*bank charges, telephone
charges etc*) opłata; **there's no ~**
nie ma opłat; **free of ~** bezpłatnie;
to take ~ of sth obejmować
(objąć *pf*) kierownictwo czegoś;
to be in ~ of sth/sb (*of person,
machine*) kierować czymś/kimś;
how much do you ~? ile to
będzie kosztować?; **to ~ sb £20
for sth** liczyć (policzyć *pf*) komuś
dwadzieścia funtów za coś
charity ['tʃærɪtɪ] *n* (*organization*)
organizacja dobroczynna; **to
give money to ~** dawać (dać *pf*)
pieniądze na cele dobroczynne

CHARITY SHOP

Charity shop – sklep
prowadzony przez
wolontariuszy, w którym
sprzedawane są używane

ubrania, książki oraz
artykuły gospodarstwa
domowego. Zyski ze sprzedaży
przekazywane są organizacji
dobroczynnej, którą wspiera
sklep.

charm [tʃɑːm] *n* (*of place, thing*)
czar; (*of person*) urok ▷ *vt*
oczarowywać (oczarować *pf*)
charming ['tʃɑːmɪŋ] *adj* (*person*)
czarujący; (*place, custom*) uroczy
chart [tʃɑːt] *n* (*graph, diagram*)
wykres; **the charts** *n pl* (*Mus*)
lista przebojów; **to be in the
~s** (*song, pop group*) być na liście
przebojów
charter flight ['tʃɑːtər-] *n* lot
czarterowy
chase [tʃeɪs] *vt* (*pursue*) gonić ▷ *n*
(*pursuit*) pościg
chat [tʃæt] *vi* (*also:* **have a ~**)
ucinać (uciąć *pf*) sobie pogawędkę
▷ *n* (*conversation*) pogawędka;
(*Comput*) czat
▶ **chat up** (*Brit: inf*) *vt* przygadać
(*pf*) sobie
chat room (*Comput*) *n* pokój
czata
chat show (*Brit*) *n* talk show
chauvinist ['ʃəuvɪnɪst] *n*
(*also:* **male ~**) męski szowinista
cheap [tʃiːp] *adj* **1** (*inexpensive*)
tani **2** (*reduced*) zniżkowy
cheat [tʃiːt] *vi* (*in game, exam*)
oszukiwać (oszukać *pf*) ▷ *vt*
oszukiwać (oszukać *pf*) ▷ *n* (*in
games, exams*) oszust(ka) *m/f*
▶ **cheat on** (*inf*) *vt fus* (*husband,
girlfriend, etc*) zdradzać (zdradzić
pf)
check [tʃɛk] *vt* (*examine, verify*)

sprawdzać (sprawdzić pf);
(passport, ticket) kontrolować
(skontrolować pf) ▷ vi (investigate)
sprawdzać (sprawdzić pf) ▷ n
1 (inspection) kontrola **2** (US: in
restaurant etc) rachunek **3** (US: Fin)
= **cheque 4** (pattern: gen pl)
kratka **5** (US: mark) ptaszek ▷ adj
(also: **~ed**: pattern, cloth) w kratę;
to ~ that... sprawdzać (sprawdzić
pf), czy...; **to ~ sth against sth**
sprawdzać (sprawdzić pf) coś z
czymś; **to ~ on sb/sth** sprawdzać
(sprawdzić pf) kogoś/coś; **to ~
with sb** pytać (zapytać pf) kogoś;
to keep a ~ on sb/sth (watch)
obserwować kogoś/coś
▶ **check in** vi (at hotel) meldować
(zameldować pf) się; (to clinic)
zgłaszać (zgłosić pf) się; (at
airport) zgłaszać (zgłosić pf) się
do odprawy ▷ vt sprawdzać
(sprawdzić pf)
▶ **check into** vt (hotel) meldować
(zameldować pf) się w; (clinic)
zgłaszać (zgłosić pf) się do +gen
▶ **check out** vi (of hotel)
wymeldowywać (wymeldować
pf) się
▶ **check up** vi sprawdzać
(sprawdzić pf)
checkbook ['tʃɛkbuk] (US) n =
cheque book
checked [tʃɛkt] adj see **check**
checkers ['tʃɛkəz] (US) n pl
warcaby
check-in ['tʃɛkɪn] (also: **~ desk**) n
(at airport) stanowisko odprawy
checkout ['tʃɛkaut] n (in shop)
kasa
check-up ['tʃɛkʌp] n (by doctor)
badanie; (by dentist) kontrola; **to**

have a ~ (by doctor) mieć badanie
lekarskie; (by dentist) mieć
kontrolę u dentysty
cheek [tʃiːk] n **1** (on face) policzek
2 (inf: impudence) tupet; **to have
the ~ to do sth** mieć czelność
coś zrobić
cheeky ['tʃiːkɪ] (esp Brit) adj
bezczelny
cheer [tʃɪər] vt (team, speaker)
wiwatować ▷ vi wiwatować ▷ n
wiwat; **~s!** (esp Brit: toast) na
zdrowie!; (Brit: inf: thanks) dzięki!
▶ **cheer up** vt (person) rozweselać
(rozweselić pf) ▷ vi (person)
rozchmurzać (rozchmurzyć pf)
się
cheerful ['tʃɪəful] adj **1** (wave,
smile, person) pogodny **2** (place,
object) wesoły
cheese [tʃiːz] n ser
chef [ʃɛf] n szef kuchni
chemical ['kɛmɪkl] adj (reaction,
composition) chemiczny ▷ n
substancja chemiczna
chemist ['kɛmɪst] n **1** (Brit: also:
~'s) aptekarz(-rka) m/f **2** (Brit: in
shop) aptekarz(-rka) m/f
3 (scientist) chemik
chemistry ['kɛmɪstrɪ] n chemia
cheque [tʃɛk] (US **check**) n czek;
to pay by ~ płacić (zapłacić pf)
czekiem
cheque book ['tʃɛkbuk] (US
checkbook) n książeczka
czekowa
cherry ['tʃɛrɪ] n **1** (fruit) czereśnia
2 (also: **~ tree**) czereśnia
chess [tʃɛs] n szachy
chest [tʃɛst] n **1** (part of body)
klatka piersiowa **2** (box) skrzynia
chestnut ['tʃɛsnʌt] n **1** (nut)

kasztan **2** (*also:* **~ tree**) kasztan
chew [tʃuː] *vt* (*food, gum*) żuć;
(*pen, fingernails*) obgryzać (obgryźć
pf) ▷ *vi* żuć
chewing gum ['tʃuːɪŋ] *n* guma
do żucia
chick [tʃɪk] *n* (*young bird*) pisklę
chicken ['tʃɪkɪn] *n* **1** (*bird: young*)
kurczak; (*grown*) kura **2** (*meat*)
kurczak
chickenpox ['tʃɪkɪnpɒks] *n* ospa
wietrzna
chickpea ['tʃɪkpiː] *n* ciecierzyca
chief [tʃiːf] *n* (*of organization,
department*) szef ▷ *adj* główny
child [tʃaɪld] (*pl* **children**) *n*
dziecko; **she's just had her
second ~** właśnie urodziła drugie
dziecko
childish ['tʃaɪldɪʃ] *adj* (*pej: person,
behaviour*) dziecinny
child minder [tʃaɪld 'maɪndər]
(*Brit*) *n* opiekun(ka) *m/f* do
dziecka
children ['tʃɪldrən] *n pl of* **child**
Chile ['tʃɪlɪ] *n* Chile
chill [tʃɪl] *vt* (*cool: food, drinks*)
studzić (ostudzić *pf*); **to catch
a ~** ziębiać (zaziębić *pf*) się; **to
serve ~ed** podawać schłodzone
chilli ['tʃɪlɪ] (*US* **chili**) *n* chili
chilly ['tʃɪlɪ] *adj* (*weather, day*)
chłodny; **it's a bit ~ today** dzisiaj
jest trochę chłodno
chimney ['tʃɪmnɪ] *n* komin
chin [tʃɪn] *n* broda
China ['tʃaɪnə] *n* Chiny
china ['tʃaɪnə] *n* (*crockery*)
zastawa ▷ *adj* (*cup, plate*)
porcelanowy
Chinese [tʃaɪ'niːz] (*pl* **Chinese**)
adj chiński ▷ *n* (*language*) chiński

chip [tʃɪp] *n* **1** (*Brit*) frytka **2** (*US*
chips **3** (*Comput: also:* **micro~**)
mikroprocesor

- **CHIP SHOP**
-
- **Chip shops** – zwane także **fish
- and chip shops** to popularne
- brytyjskie fast foody,
- sprzedające ryby z frytkami,
- jak również inne smażone
- potrawy kuchni angielskiej.
- Jedzenie zamawia się tam
- na miejscu, lub, zwyczajowo
- zawinięte w gazetę, zabiera
- na wynos.

chiropodist [kɪ'rɒpədɪst] (*Brit*)
n podiatra
chives [tʃaɪvz] *n pl* szczypiorek
sg
chocolate ['tʃɒklɪt] *n* czekoladka
▷ *adj* (*cake, pudding, mousse*)
czekoladowy; **bar of ~** tabliczka
czekolady; **piece of ~** kostka
czekolady
choice [tʃɔɪs] *n* wybór; **a wide
~** szeroki wybór; **to make a ~**
dokonywać (dokonać *pf*) wyboru;
to have no/little ~ nie mieć
wyboru
choir ['kwaɪər] *n* chór
choke [tʃəʊk] *vi* krztusić
(zakrztusić *pf*) się; **to ~ on sth**
dławić (zadławić *pf*) się czymś
choose [tʃuːz] (*pt* **chose**, *pp*
chosen) *vt* (*clothes, profession,
candidate etc*) wybierać (wybrać
pf) ▷ *vi:* **to ~ between** wybierać
(wybrać *pf*) pomiędzy +*inst*;
to ~ to do sth postanawiać
(postanowić *pf*) coś zrobić

chop [tʃɔp] vt **1** (wood)
rąbać (porąbać pf) **2** (also: ~
up: vegetables, fruit, meat) kroić
(pokroić pf) ▷ n (Culin) kotlet
▶ **chop down** vt (tree) ciąć
(ściąć pf)
▶ **chop up** vt kroić (pokroić
pf)
chopsticks ['tʃɔpstɪks] n pl
pałeczki
chore [tʃɔːʳ] n (unpleasant task)
obowiązek; **the chores** n pl
obowiązki; **household ~s**
obowiązki domowe
chose [tʃəuz] pt of **choose**
chosen ['tʃəuzn] pp of **choose**
Christ [kraɪst] n Chrystus
christening ['krɪsnɪŋ] n chrzest
Christian ['krɪstɪən]
adj chrześcijański ▷ n
chrześcijanin(-nka) m/f
Christian name n imię
Christmas ['krɪsməs] n
1 (Rel: festival) Boże Narodzenie
2 (period) Święta Bożego
Narodzenia; **Happy** or **Merry ~!**
Wesołych Świąt!; **at ~** na Boże
Narodzenie; **for ~** na Święta
Bożego Narodzenia
Christmas Eve n Wigilia Bożego
Narodzenia

CHRISTMAS PUDDING

Christmas Pudding
– świąteczny pudding – to
gotowana na parze odmiana
deseru, zawierająca dużą
ilość suszonych owoców,
tradycyjnie podawana w Boże
Narodzenie.

Christmas tree n choinka
chunk [tʃʌŋk] n (of ice, food etc)
kawał
church [tʃəːtʃ] n **1** (building)
kościół **2** (denomination) wyznanie
cider ['saɪdəʳ] n **1** (Brit: alcoholic)
cydr **2** (US: non-alcoholic)
jabłecznik
cigar [sɪ'gɑːʳ] n cygaro
cigarette [sɪgə'rɛt] n papieros
cinema ['sɪnəmə] n (Brit: place)
kino
cinnamon ['sɪnəmən] n
cynamon
circle ['səːkl] n koło
circular ['səːkjuləʳ] adj **1** (shape)
okrągły; (movement, motion)
okrężny ▷ n (letter) okólnik
circumstances ['səːkəmstənsɪz]
n pl **1** (conditions, state of affairs)
położenie **2** (of accident, death)
okoliczności; **in** or **under the ~** w
tych okolicznościach
circus ['səːkəs] n (show) cyrk
citizen ['sɪtɪzn] n (of country)
obywatel(ka) m/f; (of town, area)
mieszkaniec(-nka) m/f
citizenship ['sɪtɪznʃɪp] n
obywatelstwo
city ['sɪtɪ] n miasto; **the C~**
(Brit: Fin) Londyńskie City
city centre (esp Brit) n centrum
miasta
civilization [sɪvɪlaɪ'zeɪʃən] n
(society) cywilizacja
civilized ['sɪvɪlaɪzd] adj **1** (socially
advanced: society, people)
cywilizowany **2** (polite: person,
behaviour) kulturalny
civil partnership ['sɪvɪl
'pɑːtnəʃɪp] n zawarty zgodnie z
prawem związek pary jednopłciowej

(homoseksualnej) dający takie same prawa jak małżeństwo

civil servant ['sɪvɪl 'səːvənt] *n* urzędnik(-iczka) *m/f* służby cywilnej

civil war ['sɪvɪl wɔːʳ] *n* wojna domowa

claim [kleɪm] *vt* **1** *(demand: expenses)* występować (wystąpić *pf*) o; *(rights, inheritance)* domagać się +*gen* **2** *(compensation, damages, benefit)* występować (wystąpić *pf*) o ▷ *vi (for insurance)* występować (wystąpić *pf*) o odszkodowanie ▷ *n (application)* podanie; **to ~** *or* **make a ~ on one's insurance** składać (złożyć *pf*) wniosek o odszkodowanie; **insurance ~** roszczenie ubezpieczeniowe

clap [klæp] *vi (audience)* klaskać ▷ *n*: **to give sb a ~** bić komuś brawo

clarinet [klærɪ'nɛt] *(Mus) n* klarnet

clash [klæʃ] *vi* **1** konfrontować (skonfrontować *pf*) **2** *(colours, styles)* gryźć się **3** *(events, dates, appointments)* kolidować

clasp [klɑːsp] *vt (hold, embrace)* ściskać (ścisnąć *pf*)

class [klɑːs] *n* **1** *(Scol: group of pupils)* klasa; *(lesson)* lekcja **2** *(social)* klasa ▷ *adj (structure, conflict, struggle)* klasa ▷ *vt (categorize)*: **to ~ sb/sth as** klasyfikować (zaklasyfikować *pf*) kogoś/coś jako; **in ~** *(Scol)* na lekcji

classic ['klæsɪk] *adj* **1** *(example)* typowy **2** *(film, work etc)* klasyczny ▷ *n (film, novel etc)* klasyka

classical ['klæsɪkl] *adj* klasyczny

classmate ['klɑːsmeɪt] *n* kolega(-eżanka) *m/f* z klasy

classroom ['klɑːsrum] *n* sala lekcyjna

claw [klɔː] *n (of cat, tiger)* pazur; *(of bird)* szpon

clay [kleɪ] *n* glina

clean [kliːn] *adj* czysty ▷ *vt (car, cooker etc)* myć (umyć *pf*); *(room)* czyścić (wyczyścić *pf*) ▷ *n*: **to give sth a ~** czyścić (wyczyścić *pf*) coś; **a ~ driving licence** *or (US)* **record** czysta kartoteka; **to ~ one's teeth** *(Brit)* myć (umyć *pf*) zęby ▶ **clean up** *vt (room, place)* sprzątać (posprzątać *pf*); *(mess)* porządkować (uporządkować *pf*) ▷ *vi* sprzątać (sprzątnąć *pf*)

cleaner ['kliːnəʳ] *n* **1** *(person)* sprzątacz(ka) *m/f* **2** *(substance)* środek czyszczący

cleanser ['klɛnzəʳ] *n (for face)* środek do czyszczenia twarzy

clear [klɪəʳ] *adj* **1** *(explanation, account)* klarowny **2** *(footprint, photograph)* wyraźny **3** *(voice, echo)* wyraźny **4** *(obvious)* oczywisty **5** *(glass, plastic, water)* przezroczysty **6** *(road, way, floor etc)* wolny **7** *(day, sky)* jasny ▷ *vt (place, room)* opróżniać (opróżnić *pf*) ▷ *vi (weather, sky)* przejaśniać (przejaśnić *pf*) się; *(fog, smoke)* rozchodzić (rozejść *pf*) się ▷ *adv*: **~ of sth** *(place, ground)* z dala od czegoś; **to be ~ about sth** rozumieć (zrozumieć *pf*) coś; **to make o.s. ~** wyrażać (wyrazić *pf*) się jasno; **to make sth ~ to sb** wyjaśniać (wyjaśnić *pf*) coś komuś; **to ~ the table**

sprzątać (sprzątnąć pf) ze stołu;
to ~ one's throat odchrząkiwać
(odchrząknąć pf)
▶ **clear away** vt (*plates etc*)
sprzątać (posprzątać pf) ▷ vi
(*remove plates etc*) sprzątać
(posprzątać pf)
▶ **clear off** (*inf*) vi (*leave*) zmywać
(zmyć pf) się
▶ **clear up** vt 1 (*room, mess*)
sprzątać (posprzątać pf)
2 (*mystery, problem*) wyjaśniać
(wyjaśnić pf) ▷ vi (*tidy up*)
sprzątać (posprzątać pf)
clearly ['klɪəlɪ] adv 1 wyraźnie;
(*think*) jasno 2 (*visible, audible*)
dobrze 3 (*obviously*) najwyraźniej
clever ['klɛvə^r] adj 1 (*intelligent*)
zdolny 2 (*sly, crafty*) sprytny
3 (*ingenious: device, arrangement*)
zmyślny
click [klɪk] vi 1 (*device, switch,
camera*) pstrykać (pstryknąć pf)
2: to ~ (on sth) (*Comput*) klikać
(kliknąć pf) (na coś) ▷ n 1 (*sound*)
pstryknięcie 2 (*Comput*): **with a
~ of one's mouse** po kliknięciu
myszą
client ['klaɪənt] n klient(ka) m/f
cliff [klɪf] n klif
climate ['klaɪmɪt] n (*weather*)
klimat
climb [klaɪm] vt (*also: ~ up: tree,
hill etc*) wspinać (wspiąć pf) się
na; (*stairs, steps*) wdrapywać
(wdrapać pf) się po +loc ▷ vi 1 (*on
frame, up mountain etc*) wspinać
(wpiąć pf) się 2 (*move with
effort*): **to ~ into a car** wsiadać
(wsiąść pf) do samochodu ▷ n (*of
mountain, hill*) wspinaczka; **to ~
into bed** kłaść (położyć pf) się do

łóżka; **to ~ onto sth** (*roof, table*)
wchodzić (wejść pf) na coś; **to ~
over sth** (*wall, fence*) przechodzić
(przejść pf) przez coś
climber ['klaɪmə^r] n (*mountaineer*)
alpinista(-tka) m/f
climbing ['klaɪmɪŋ] n
wspinaczka; **to go ~** wspinać
(wspiąć pf) się
clingfilm ['klɪŋfɪlm] (*Brit*) n folia
clinic ['klɪnɪk] (*Med*) n (*place*)
przychodnia; (*session*) wykład
kliniczny
clip [klɪp] n (*for papers etc*)
spinacz; (*for hair*) spinka ▷ vt
1 (*fasten*) przypinać (przypiąć
pf) 2 (*cut: hedge, nails*) obcinać
(obciąć pf)
cloakroom ['kləukrum] n 1 (*for
coats*) szatnia 2 (*Brit: bathroom*)
toaleta publiczna
clock [klɔk] n zegar; **around the
~** (*work, guard*) dwadzieścia cztery
godziny na dobę; **to turn** or **put
the ~ back** (*fig*) cofać (cofnąć
pf) czas
▶ **clock in** vi (*for work*) odbijać
(odbić pf) kartę przychodząc do
pracy
▶ **clock off** vi (*from work*) odbijać
(odbić pf) kartę wychodząc z pracy
▶ **clock on** vi = **clock in**
▶ **clock out** vi = **clock off**
close¹ [kləus] adj 1 (*near*) bliski
2 (*relative*) bliski 3 (*contest*)
wyrównany ▷ adv (*near*) blisko;
~ to (*near*) w pobliżu; **a ~ friend**
bliski przyjaciel; **to see sth ~ up**
or **to** widzieć (zobaczyć pf) coś
w zbliżeniu; **~ by, ~ at hand** w
zasięgu ręki; **she was ~ to tears**
była bliska łez

close² [kləuz] vt zamykać
(zamknąć pf) ▷ vi zamykać
(zamknąć pf) się
▶ **close down** vi (factory, business)
zostać zamkniętym
closed [kləuzd] adj zamknięty
closely ['kləuslı] adv blisko
closet ['klɔzɪt] n (US) szafa
cloth [klɔθ] n 1 (fabric) tkanina
2 (for cleaning, dusting) ścierka
3 (tablecloth) obrus; **piece of ~**
materiał
clothes [kləuðz] n pl ubranie;
to take one's ~ off rozbierać
(rozebrać pf) się
clothing ['kləuðɪŋ] n odzież;
an item or **a piece of ~** sztuka
odzieży
cloud [klaud] n chmura
▶ **cloud over** vi (sky) chmurzyć
(zachmurzyć pf) się
cloudy ['klaudı] adj (day, sky,
weather) pochmurny; **it's ~** jest
pochmurno
clove [kləuv] n 1 (spice) goździk
2 (of garlic) ząbek
clown [klaun] n (in circus) klaun
club [klʌb] n 1 (society, place)
klub 2 (Sport) klub 3 (nightclub)
klub nocny 4 (stick: also: **golf ~**)
kij golfowy ▷ vi: **to ~ together**
(Brit: for gift, card) składać (złożyć
pf) się; **clubs** n pl (Cards) trefl
clue [kluː] n wskazówka; **I
haven't a ~** (inf) nie mam pojęcia
clumsy ['klʌmzı] adj (person)
niezdarny
clutch [klʌtʃ] vt ściskać (ścisnąć
pf) ▷ n (Aut) sprzęgło
clutter ['klʌtər] vt (also: **~ up**)
zagracać (zagracić pf) ▷ n rupiecie
coach [kəutʃ] n 1 (Brit)

autokar 2 (Brit: of train) wagon
3 (Sport: trainer) trener(ka) m/f ▷ vt
(Sport) trenować
coal [kəul] n (substance) węgiel
coarse [kɔːs] adj 1 (cloth, salt,
sand) szorstki 2 (vulgar: person,
remark) ordynarny
coast [kəust] n wybrzeże
coastguard ['kəustgaːd] (esp
Brit) n 1 (person) strażnik straży
przybrzeżnej 2: **the ~** (service)
straż przybrzeżna
coat [kəut] n 1 (overcoat) płaszcz
2 (of animal) sierść 3 (of paint,
varnish) warstwa
coat hanger n wieszak
cobweb ['kɔbwɛb] n pajęczyna
cocaine [kə'keɪn] n kokaina
cock [kɔk] n (Brit) kogut
cockerel ['kɔkərəl] (esp Brit) n
kogucik
cocoa ['kəukəu] n kakao
coconut ['kəukənʌt] n kokos
cod [kɔd] (pl **cod** or **cods**) n 1 (fish)
dorsz 2 (as food) dorsz
code [kəud] n 1 (cipher) szyfr
2 (Tel) numer kierunkowy
3 (Comput, Sci) kod
coffee ['kɔfı] n 1 kawa 2 (cup of
coffee) filiżanka kawy; **black ~**
czarna kawa; **white ~** kawa z
mlekiem
coffee table n ława
coffin ['kɔfɪn] n trumna
coin [kɔɪn] n moneta
coincidence [kəu'ɪnsɪdəns] n
zbieg okoliczności
Coke® [kəuk] n (drink) Coca Cola
colander ['kɔləndər] n durszlak
cold [kəuld] adj zimny ▷ n
1 (weather): **the ~** zimno 2 (illness)
przeziębienie; **it's ~** jest zimno; **I**

am/feel ~ (*person*) jest mi zimno;
to catch (a) ~ zaziębić się
coleslaw ['kəulslɔː] (*Culin*) n
surówka z białej kapusty
collapse [kə'læps] vi (*building,
table*) walić (zawalić pf) się;
(*person*) padać (paść pf)
collar ['kɔlər] n (*of coat, shirt*)
kołnierz
collarbone ['kɔləbəun] n
obojczyk
colleague ['kɔliːg] n
kolega(-eżanka) m/f
collect [kə'lɛkt] vt 1 (*wood, litter
etc*) zbierać (zebrać pf) 2 (*as hobby*)
zbierać (zebrać pf) 3 (*Brit: fetch*)
odbierać (odebrać pf) 4 (*money,
donations*) zbierać (zebrać pf) ▷ vi
(*for charity, gift*) kwestować; **to
call ~, make a ~ call** (*US: Tel*)
rozmowa na koszt rozmówcy
collection [kə'lɛkʃən] n 1 (*of art,
stamps etc*) kolekcja 2 (*of poems,
stories etc*) antologia 3 (*for charity,
gift*) zebrane pieniądze
collector [kə'lɛktər] n (*of art,
stamps etc*) kolekcjoner(ka) m/f
college ['kɔlidʒ] n 1 (*for further
education*) szkoła wyższa 2 (*of
university*) wydział; **to go to ~**
studiować
collide [kə'laɪd] vi (*cars, people*)
zderzać (zderzyć pf) się; **to ~ with
sth/sb** zderzać (zderzyć pf) się z
czymś/kimś
collision [kə'lɪʒən] n (*of vehicles*)
kolizja
colon ['kəulən] n 1 (*punctuation
mark*) dwukropek 2 (*Anat*)
okrężnica
colonel ['kəːnl] n pułkownik
color etc ['kʌlər] (*US*) = **colour** etc

colour ['kʌlər] (*US* **color**) n kolor
▷ vt (*with paint, crayons, dye*)
kolorować (pokolorować pf)
▷ adj (*film, photograph, television*)
kolorowy; **in ~** (*film, illustrations*)
barwny
colourful ['kʌləful] (*US* **colorful**)
adj (*brightly coloured*) barwny
colour television (*US* **color
television**) n telewizja kolorowa
column ['kɔləm] n 1 (*Archit*)
kolumna 2 (*in newspaper etc*)
rubryka
comb [kəum] n grzebień ▷ vt
(*hair*) czesać (uczesać pf)
combination [kɔmbɪ'neɪʃən] n
(*mixture*) połączenie
combine [kəm'baɪn] vt: **to ~ sth
with sth** łączyć (połączyć pf) coś
z czymś ▷ vi (*qualities, situations*)
łączyć (połączyć pf); (*people,
groups*) jednoczyć (zjednoczyć pf);
a ~d effort wspólny wysiłek

○ **KEYWORD**

come [kʌm] (*pt* **came**, *pp*
come) vi 1 (*move towards, arrive*)
przychodzić (przyjść pf); **come
here!** chodź tutaj!; **can I come
too?** czy też mogę przyjść?; **come
with me** chodź ze mną; **a girl
came into the room** dziewczyna
weszła do pokoju; **why don't you
come to lunch on Saturday?**
może przyjdziesz na obiad w
sobotę?; **he's come here to work**
przyszedł tu pracować
2: to come to (*reach*) sięgać
(sięgnąć pf) do +gen; (*amount to*)
wynosić (wynieść pf); **to come to
a decision** podejmować (podjąć

pf) decyzję; **the bill came to £40** rachunek wyniósł czterdzieści funtów

3 (*be, become*): **to come first/ second/last** być pierwszym/ drugim/ostatnim

4 (*be available*): **it comes in blue or green** dostępne jest w kolorach niebieskim i zielonym

▶ **come across** *vt fus* (*find*) spotykać (spotkać *pf*)

▶ **come apart** *vi* rozpadać (rozpaść *pf*) się

▶ **come back** *vi* (*return*) wracać (wrócić *pf*) do +*gen*; **I'm coming back to that** (*in discussion etc*) wrócę do tego

▶ **come down** *vi* **1** (*price*) spadać (spaść *pf*) **2** (*fall to ground: plane*) spadać (spaść *pf*) **3** (*descend*) schodzić (zejść *pf*)

▶ **come down with** *vt fus*: **to come down with sth** (*illness*) zachorować na coś

▶ **come forward** *vi* (*volunteer*) zgłaszać (zgłosić *pf*) się

▶ **come from** *vt fus* (*place, source*) pochodzić z +*gen*; **I come from London** pochodzę z Londynu; **where do you come from?** skąd pochodzisz?

▶ **come in** *vi* (*to room, house etc*) wchodzić (wejść *pf*); **come in!** wejdź!

▶ **come off** *vi* **1** (*button, handle*) urywać (urwać *pf*) się **2** (*succeed: event, attempt, plan*) dojść do skutku

▶ **come on** *vi* (*progress*) robić (zrobić *pf*) postępy; **come on!** (*giving encouragement*) no, spróbuj!; (*hurry up*) pospiesz się!

▶ **come out** *vi* **1** (*person: out of house, for evening etc*) wychodzić (wyjść *pf*) **2** (*appear: sun*) wyglądać (wyjrzeć *pf*) **3** (*become available: book*) pojawiać (pojawić *pf*) się; (*film*) wchodzić (wejść *pf*) na ekrany

▶ **come over** (*visit*) wpadać (wpaść *pf*); **I'll come over later** wpadnę później

▶ **come through** *vt fus* (*survive*) przechodzić (przejść *pf*)

▶ **come to** *vi* (*regain consciousness*) ocknąć się

▶ **come up** *vi* **1** (*approach*) podchodzić (podejść *pf*) **2** (*arise: problem, opportunity*) pojawiać (pojawić *pf*) się

▶ **come upon** *vt fus* (*find*) natknąć (*pf*) się na

▶ **come up to** *vt fus* **1** (*get on for*): **it's coming up to 11 o'clock** zbliża się jedenasta **2** (*approach*) zbliżać (zbliżyć *pf*) się do +*gen* **3** (*meet*): **the film didn't come up to our expectations** film nie spełnił naszych oczekiwań

comedian [kə'miːdɪən] (*Theat, TV*) *n* komik

comedy ['kɔmɪdɪ] *n* komedia

comfortable ['kʌmfətəbl] *adj* **1** (*person*): **to be ~** (*physically*) być odprężonym **2** (*furniture, room, clothes*) wygodny; **to make o.s. ~** siadać (usiąść *pf*) wygodnie

comic ['kɔmɪk] *adj* **1** (*also*: **~al**) komiczny **2** (*actor, opera*) komediowy ▷ *n* **1** (*comedian*) komik **2** (*Brit: magazine*) komiks

comic book (*US*) *n* komiks

comma ['kɔmə] *n* przecinek

command [kəˈmɑːnd] n 1 (order)
rozkaz 2 (Comput) polecenie
comment [ˈkɔmɛnt] n (written,
spoken) komentarz ▷ vi: **to
~ (on sth)** komentować
(skomentować pf) (coś); **"no ~"**
"bez komentarza"; **to ~ that...**
zauważać (zauważyć pf), że...
commentary [ˈkɔməntərɪ] n (on
match, proceedings) komentarz
commentator [ˈkɔmənteɪtəʳ]
n (describing match, proceedings)
komentator(ka) m/f
commercial [kəˈmɜːʃəl] adj
(organization, activity) handlowy;
(success, failure) komercyjny;
(television, radio) komercyjny ▷ n
(advertisement) reklama
commit [kəˈmɪt] vt (crime,
offence) popełniać (popełnić pf); **to
~ suicide** popełnić samobójstwo
committee [kəˈmɪtɪ] n komitet
common [ˈkɔmən] adj (usual)
pospolity; **~ to** wspólny; **to have
sth in ~** mieć coś wspólnego; **to
have sth in ~ with sb/sth** mieć
coś wspólnego z kimś/czymś
Commons [ˈkɔmənz] (Brit)
n: **the (House of) ~** Izba Gmin

● COMMONS
●
● **Commons** – w Wielkiej
● Brytanii, Izba Gmin (**House of
● Commons**) jest jedną z dwóch
● izb parlamentu. Zasiada w niej
● 650 wybranych w wyborach
● powszechnych posłów
● (**Members of Parliament**),
● popularnie zwanych **MPs**.

common sense n zdrowy

rozsądek
communicate [kəˈmjuːnɪkeɪt]
vi 1 (by writing, speaking etc)
komunikować (skomunikować
pf) się 2 (talk openly) porozumieć
(porozumiewać pf) się ▷ vt (idea,
decision, feeling) przekazywać
(przekazać pf)
communication
[kəmjuːnɪˈkeɪʃən] n
komunikacja; **communications**
n pl łączność
communion [kəˈmjuːnɪən] n
(also: **Holy C~**) Komunia Święta
communism [ˈkɔmjunɪzəm] n
komunizm
community [kəˈmjuːnɪtɪ] n
1 (neighbourhood) społeczność
2: the business ~ świat biznesu;
the black/Jewish ~ czarna/
żydowska społeczność
commute [kəˈmjuːt] vi
dojeżdżać do pracy; **to ~ to/from
London/Brighton** dojeżdżać
do/z Londynu/Brighton
compact disc [ˈkɔmpækt dɪsk] n
płyta kompaktowa
company [ˈkʌmpənɪ] n
1 (firm) firma 2 (companionship)
towarzystwo; **Smith and C~**
Smith i wspólnicy; **to keep sb
~** dotrzymać (dotrzymywać pf)
komuś towarzystwa
comparatively [kəmˈpærətɪvlɪ]
adv (relatively) stosunkowo
compare [kəmˈpɛəʳ] vt
porównywać (porównać
pf) ▷ vi: **to ~ favourably/
unfavourably (with sth/sb)**
prezentować (zaprezentować pf)
się korzystnie/niekorzystnie (w
porównaniu z czymś/kimś); **to ~**

sb/sth to (liken to) porównywać (porównać pf) kogoś/coś do +gen; **~d with** or **to** w porównaniu z +inst

comparison [kəm'pærɪsn] n porównanie; **in** or **by ~ (with)** w porównaniu (z +inst); **(there's) no ~** nie ma porównania

compartment [kəm'pɑːtmənt] n (Rail) przedział

compass ['kʌmpəs] n **1** (for finding direction) kompas **2** (also: **pair of ~es**: for drawing circles) cyrkiel

compatible [kəm'pætɪbl] adj (people) zgodny; (Comput) kompatybilny; **to be ~ with sth** (activity, idea) być zgodnym z czymś; (Comput) być kompatybilnym z czymś

compensation [kɔmpən'seɪʃən] n (money) rekompensata; **~ for sth** (money) rekompensata za coś

compete [kəm'piːt] vi (companies, rivals) konkurować; (in contest, game) rywalizować; **to ~ for sth** (companies, rivals) konkurować o coś; (in contest, game) rywalizować o coś; **to ~ with sb/sth (for sth)** (companies, rivals) konkurować z kimś/czymś (o coś); (in contest, game) rywalizować z kimś/czymś (o coś)

competent ['kɔmpɪtənt] adj (person) kompetentny; (piece of work) zadowalający

competition [kɔmpɪ'tɪʃən] n **1** (rivalry) konkurencja **2** (contest) rywalizacja; **in ~ with** rywalizować z +inst

competitive [kəm'pɛtɪtɪv] adj **1** (industry, society) konkurencyjny

2 (person) ambitny

competitor [kəm'pɛtɪtəʳ] n **1** (in business) konkurent(ka) m/f **2** (participant) uczestnik(-iczka) m/f

complain [kəm'pleɪn] vi: **to ~ (about sth)** (to relevant person) składać (złożyć pf) skargę (na coś); (grumble) skarżyć (poskarżyć pf) się (na coś); **to ~ to sb (about sth)** skarżyć (poskarżyć pf) się komuś (na coś)

complaint [kəm'pleɪnt] n (criticism) skarga; **to make a ~ (to sb)** wnosić (wnieść pf) skargę (na ręce kogoś)

complete [kəm'pliːt] adj **1** (total) zupełny **2** (whole) całkowity **3** (finished) ukończony ▷ vt **1** (finish) kończyć (ukończyć pf) **2** (fill in) wypełniać (wypełnić pf); **~ with** wraz z +inst

completely [kəm'pliːtlɪ] adv (different, satisfied, untrue etc) całkowicie; (forget, destroy etc) zupełnie

complexion [kəm'plɛkʃən] n (colouring) karnacja

complicate ['kɔmplɪkeɪt] vt komplikować (skomplikować pf)

complicated ['kɔmplɪkeɪtɪd] adj skomplikowany

compliment [n 'kɔmplɪmənt, vb 'kɔmplɪmɛnt] n (remark) komplement ▷ vt chwalić (pochwalić pf); **to pay sb a ~** chwalić (pochwalić pf) kogoś; **to ~ sb on sth** gratulować (pogratulować pf) komuś czegoś

composer [kəm'pəuzəʳ] n kompozytor(ka) m/f

comprehension
[kɔmprɪ'henʃən] *n*
1 (*understanding*) zrozumienie
2 (*Scol*) ćwiczenia sprawdzające
rozumienie

comprehensive
[kɔmprɪ'hensɪv] *adj* **1** (*review,
list*) wyczerpujący **2** (*of insurance*)
pełny ▷ *n* (Brit: *also:* **~ school**)
szkoła średnia ogólna

● **COMPREHENSIVE SCHOOL**
●
● **Comprehensive school** to w
● Wielkiej Brytanii państwowa
● szkoła średnia dla uczniów w
● wieku 11 – 18 lat.

compulsory [kəm'pʌlsərɪ] *adj*
obowiązkowy
computer [kəm'pjuːtər] *n*
komputer ▷ *adj* komputerowy
computer game *n* gra
komputerowa
computer programmer *n*
programista (-tka) *m/f*
computer science *n*
informatyka
computing [kəm'pjuːtɪŋ] *n*
(*also:* **~ studies**) informatyka
concentrate ['kɔnsəntreɪt] *vi*
koncentrować (skoncentrować
pf) się; **to ~ on sth** (*keep
attention on*) koncentrować
(skoncentrować *pf*) się na czymś;
(*focus on*) skupiać (skupić *pf*) się
na czymś
concentration [kɔnsən'treɪʃən]
n **1** (*ability to concentrate*)
koncentracja **2** (*focus*): **~ on
sth/on doing sth** koncentracja
na czymś/na robieniu czegoś

concern [kən'səːn] *n* **1** (*anxiety*)
niepokój **2** (*affair*) sprawa ▷ *vt*
(*worry*) martwić (zmartwić *pf*); **~
for sb** obawa o kogoś; **as far as
I'm ~ed** o ile mi wiadomo; **the
people ~ed** zainteresowani
concerned [kən'səːnd] *adj*
(*worried*) zaniepokojony;
to be ~ about sb/sth być
zaniepokojonym o kogoś/coś;
we're ~ for her niepokoimy się
o nią
concerning [kən'səːnɪŋ] *prep*
odnośnie +*gen*
concert ['kɔnsət] *n* koncert
concert hall *n* sala koncertowa
conclusion [kən'kluːʒən]
n **1** (*end: of speech, chapter*)
zakończenie **2** (*deduction*)
wniosek; **to come to the ~
that…** dochodzić (dojść *pf*) do
wniosku, że…
concrete ['kɔnkriːt] *n* beton
▷ *adj* **1** (*lit: block, floor*) betonowy
2 (*fig: proposal, evidence*) konkretny
condemn [kən'dem] *vt*
(*denounce*) potępiać (potępić *pf*)
condition [kən'dɪʃən] *n* **1** (*state*)
stan **2** (*stipulation*) warunek;
conditions *n pl* warunki; **in
good/poor ~** w dobrych/złych
warunkach; **on ~ that…** pod
warunkiem, że…; **weather ~s**
warunki pogodowe
conditional [kən'dɪʃənl] *adj*
warunkowy ▷ *n* (*Ling*): **the ~** tryb
warunkowy
conditioner [kən'dɪʃənər] *n* (*for
hair*) odżywka
condom ['kɔndəm] *n*
prezerwatywa
conduct [kən'dʌkt] *vt* (*orchestra,*

choir etc) dyrygować
conductor [kən'dʌktər] n **1** (*of orchestra*) dyrygent(ka) *m/f* **2** (*US: on train*) konduktor(ka) *m/f* **3** (*on bus*) konduktor(ka) *m/f*
cone [kəun] n **1** (*shape*) stożek **2** (*also:* **traffic ~**) pachołek **3** (*on tree*) szyszka **4** (*also:* **ice cream ~**) rożek
conference ['kɔnfərəns] n (*meeting*) konferencja
confess [kən'fɛs] vi (*to sin, crime*) przyznawać (przyznać *pf*) się; **to ~ to sth/to doing sth** przyznawać (przyznać *pf*) się do czegoś/ zrobienia czegoś; **I must ~ that...** muszę przyznać, że...
confession [kən'fɛʃən] n **1** (*admission*) przyznanie się **2** (*written*) zeznanie **3** (*Rel*) spowiedź; **to make a ~** przyznawać (przyznać *pf*) się
confidence ['kɔnfɪdns] n **1** (*faith*) zaufanie **2** (*self-assurance*) pewność siebie; **in ~** (*speak, say, write etc*) w tajemnicy
confident ['kɔnfɪdənt] adj (*self-assured*) pewny siebie; **to be ~ that...** być pewnym, że...
confidential [kɔnfɪ'dɛnʃəl] adj (*report, information*) poufny
confirm [kən'fə:m] vt potwierdzać (potwierdzić *pf*); **to ~ that...** (*person, data*) potwierdzać (potwierdzić *pf*), że...
confiscate ['kɔnfɪskeɪt] vt konfiskować (skonfiskować *pf*); **to ~ sth from sb** konfiskować (skonfiskować *pf*) coś komuś
confuse [kən'fju:z] vt **1** (*perplex*) gmatwać (zagmatwać *pf*) **2** (*mix up*) mylić (pomylić *pf*)

confused [kən'fju:zd] adj (*bewildered*) zdezorientowany
confusing [kən'fju:zɪŋ] adj zagmatwany
confusion [kən'fju:ʒən] n **1** (*uncertainty*) zamieszanie **2** (*mix-up*) nieporozumienie
congratulate [kən'grætjuleɪt] vt gratulować (pogratulować *pf*); **to ~ sb on sth/on doing sth** gratulować (pogratulować *pf*) komuś z okazji czegoś/zrobienia czegoś
congratulations [kəngrætju'leɪʃənz] n pl gratulacje; **~ on your engagement!** gratulacje z okazji zaręczyn!
Congress ['kɔngrɛs] n (*US*) Kongres
congressman ['kɔngrɛsmən] (*irreg*) n (*US*) kongresman
congresswoman ['kɔngrɛswumən] (*irreg*) n (*US*) członkini Kongresu
conjunction [kən'dʒʌŋkʃən] (*Ling*) n spójnik
connection [kə'nɛkʃən] n **1** (*link*) związek **2** (*Elec*) podłączenie **3** (*train, plane etc*) połączenie; **what is the ~ between them?** jaki jest między nimi związek?
conscience ['kɔnʃəns] n (*sense of morality*) sumienie; **to have a guilty ~** mieć wyrzuty sumienia; **to have clear ~** mieć czyste sumienie
conscientious [kɔnʃɪ'ɛnʃəs] adj sumienny
conscious ['kɔnʃəs] adj **1** (*awake*) świadomy **2** (*deliberate: decision, effort*) świadomy; **to be ~ of sth**

być świadomym czegoś; **to be ~ that...** być świadomym tego, że...

consciousness ['kɔnʃəsnɪs] n (Med) przytomność; **to lose ~** (black out) tracić (stracić pf) przytomność

consequence ['kɔnsɪkwəns] n (result) konsekwencja

consequently ['kɔnsɪkwəntlɪ] adv w konsekwencji

conservation [kɔnsə'veɪʃən] n (of environment) ochrona; (of energy etc) oszczędzanie

conservative [kən'sə:vətɪv] adj **1** (traditional) konserwatywny **2** (Brit: Pol): **C~** konserwatywny ▷ n (Brit: Pol): **C~** konserwatysta(-tka) m/f

conservatory [kən'sə:vətrɪ] n (on house) oszklona weranda

consider [kən'sɪdə[r]] vt **1** (think about) rozważać (rozważyć pf) **2** (take into account) rozpatrywać (rozpatrzyć pf) **3** (believe): **to ~ sb (to be) an idiot/a coward** uważać kogoś za idiotę/tchórza; **to ~ doing sth** zastanawiać (zastanowić pf) się nad zrobieniem czegoś; **all things ~ed** w sumie

considerate [kən'sɪdərɪt] adj taktowny

considering [kən'sɪdərɪŋ] prep zważywszy ▷ conj: **~ (that)...** zważywszy (że)...

consist [kən'sɪst] vi: **to ~ of** składać się z

consonant ['kɔnsənənt] n spółgłoska

constant ['kɔnstənt] adj **1** (ever-present) stały **2** (repeated) ciągły **3** (fixed) stały

constantly ['kɔnstəntlɪ] adv **1** (repeatedly) ciągle **2** (uninterruptedly) nieustannie

constipated ['kɔnstɪpeɪtɪd] adj cierpiący na zaparcie

construct [kən'strʌkt] vt budować (zbudować pf)

construction [kən'strʌkʃən] n **1** (of building, road, machine) budowa **2** (structure) konstrukcja

consult [kən'sʌlt] vt (doctor, lawyer, friend) radzić (poradzić pf) się +gen; (book, map) sprawdzać (sprawdzić pf)

consumer [kən'sju:mə[r]] n (of goods, services) konsument(ka) m/f; (of resources) odbiorca

contact ['kɔntækt] n kontakt ▷ vt kontaktować (kontaktować pf) się z +inst; **to be in ~ with sb** kontaktować (skontaktować pf) się z kimś

contact lenses n pl szkła kontaktowe

contain [kən'teɪn] vt zawierać (zawrzeć pf)

container [kən'teɪnə[r]] n **1** (box, jar etc) pojemnik **2** (for transport) kontener

content¹ ['kɔntɛnt] n (of speech, book, film) treść; **contents** n pl (of bottle, packet) zawartość

content² [kən'tɛnt] adj (satisfied) zadowolony

contest [n 'kɔntɛst n (competition) konkurs

contestant [kən'tɛstənt] n zawodnik(-iczka) m/f

context ['kɔntɛkst] n kontekst

continent ['kɔntɪnənt] n kontynent; **on the C~** (Brit) na kontynencie europejskim

continental breakfast
[kɒntɪ'nɛntl 'brɛkfəst] *n*
śniadanie kontynentalne

continue [kən'tɪnjuː] *vi* **1** (*carry on uninterrupted*) kontynuować **2** (*after interruption: event*) wznawiać (wznowić *pf*); (*speaker*) mówić dalej ▷ *vt* **1** (*carry on uninterrupted*) trwać **2** (*after interruption*) wznawiać (wznowić *pf*); **to ~ to do sth** *or* **doing sth** robić coś dalej; **to ~ with sth** kontynuować coś

continuous [kən'tɪnjuəs] *adj* **1** (*process, growth etc*) stały **2** (*Ling: tense*) ciągły

contraception [kɒntrə'sɛpʃən] *n* antykoncepcja

contraceptive [kɒntrə'sɛptɪv] *n* (*drug*) tabletka antykoncepcyjna; (*device*) środek antykoncepcyjny

contract [*n* 'kɒntrækt *n* umowa

contradict [kɒntrə'dɪkt] *vt* (*person, statement etc*) zaprzeczać (zaprzeczyć *pf*)

contradiction [kɒntrə'dɪkʃən] *n* sprzeczność

contrary ['kɒntrərɪ] *adj* (*opposite, different*) sprzeczny ▷ *n*: **the ~** przeciwieństwo; **on the ~** wręcz przeciwnie

contrast [*n* 'kɒntrɑːst, *vb* kən'trɑːst] *n* **1** kontrast **2: to be a ~ to sth** stanowić kontrast względem czegoś ▷ *vt* porównywać (porównać *pf*) ▷ *vi*: **to ~ with sth** zestawiać (zestawić *pf*) z czymś; **to ~ sth with sth** zestawiać (zestawić *pf*) coś z czymś

contribute [kən'trɪbjuːt] *vi* (*with money*) ofiarowywać

(ofiarować *pf*) ▷ *vt*: **to ~ £10 (to sth)** przekazywać (przekazać *pf*) dziesięć funtów (na coś)

contribution [kɒntrɪ'bjuːʃən] *n* (*donation*) datek

control [kən'trəul] *vt* (*country, organization*) kierować; (*person, emotion, disease, fire*) kontrolować (skontrolować *pf*) ▷ *n* (*of country, organization*) władza; (*of people*) panowanie; (*of vehicle, machine*) kierowanie; **controls** *n pl* (*of vehicle, machine*) stery; (*of TV*) regulacja; **to ~ o.s.** panować nad sobą; **to lose ~ (of sth)** (*emotionally*) tracić (stracić *pf*) panowanie (nad czymś); (*in vehicle, on machine*) tracić (stracić *pf*) panowanie (nad czymś); **to be in ~ (of sth)** (*of situation, car etc*) kontrolować (skontrolować *pf*) (coś); **to have sth under ~** (*fire, situation*) panować nad czymś; **to be out of ~** (*fire, situation*) tracić (stracić *pf*) panowanie; **circumstances beyond our ~** okoliczności niezależne od nas

controversial [kɒntrə'vəːʃl] *adj* kontrowersyjny

convenient [kən'viːnɪənt] *adj* (*method, system, time*) praktyczny; (*place*) dogodny

conventional [kən'vɛnʃənl] *adj* konwencjonalny

conversation [kɒnvə'seɪʃən] *n* rozmowa; **to have a ~ (about sth/with sb)** rozmawiać (porozmawiać *pf*) (o czymś/z kimś)

convert [kən'vəːt] *vt* (*transform: substance*) przetwarzać (przetworzyć *pf*); (*building*) przerabiać (przerobić pf); **to ~ sth into sth** (substance) zmieniać (zmienić pf) coś w coś; (building) przerabiać (przerobić pf) coś na coś

convince [kən'vɪns] vt 1 (cause to believe) przekonywać (przekonać pf) 2 (esp US: persuade) namawiać (namówić pf); **to ~ sb that...** przekonywać (przekonać pf) kogoś, że...; **to ~ sb to do sth** (esp US) namawiać (namówić pf) kogoś do zrobienia czegoś

cook [kuk] vt (food, meat, vegetables) gotować (ugotować pf); (meal) przyrządzać (przyrządzić pf) ⊳ vi 1 (person) gotować (ugotować pf) 2 (food) gotować (ugotować pf) się ⊳ n kucharz(-rka) m/f; **he is a good ~** on dobrze gotuje

cooker ['kukər] (Brit) n kuchenka

cookery ['kukərɪ] n sztuka kulinarna

cookie ['kukɪ] n 1 (US: for eating) ciastko 2 (Comput) cookies

cooking ['kukɪŋ] n 1 (activity) gotowanie 2 (food) kuchnia ⊳ adj (apples, chocolate) jadalny; (utensils) kuchenny

cool [ku:l] adj 1 (water, breeze, evening, place) chłodny 2 (calm, unemotional) spokojny 3 (inf: good) na luzie; (fashionable) cool, odjazdowy ⊳ vt studzić (ostudzić pf) ⊳ vi stygnąć (ostygnąć pf) ⊳ n: **to keep one's ~** (inf) zachowywać (zachować pf) spokój; **to lose one's ~** (inf) tracić (stracić pf) głowę; **to keep sth ~** przechowywać (przechować pf) coś w chłodnym miejscu

▶ **cool down** vi (become colder) stygnąć (ostygnąć pf)

co-operate [kəʊ'ɔpəreɪt] vi 1 (collaborate) współpracować 2 (be helpful) współdziałać

cop [kɔp] (inf) n gliniarz

cope [kəʊp] vi radzić (poradzić pf) sobie; **to ~ with sth** (problem, situation, task) radzić (poradzić pf) sobie z czymś

copper ['kɔpər] n (metal) miedź

copy ['kɔpɪ] n 1 (duplicate) kopia 2 (issue) egzemplarz ⊳ vt 1 (imitate: person, idea etc) naśladować 2 (also: ~ out) przepisywać (przepisać pf); **to make a ~ of sth** robić (zrobić pf) kopię czegoś

▶ **copy down** vt przepisywać (przepisać pf)

core [kɔːr] n (of fruit) gniazdo; (of nuclear reactor) rdzeń

cork [kɔːk] n korek

corkscrew ['kɔːkskruː] n korkociąg

corn [kɔːn] n 1 (Brit: cereal crop) zboże 2 (US: maize) kukurydza; **~ on the cob** kolba kukurydzy

corner ['kɔːnər] n 1 kąt 2 (of road) róg; **to be (just) round** or **around the ~** (fig) być za rogiem

cornflakes ['kɔːnfleɪks] n pl płatki kukurydziane

corpse [kɔːps] n zwłoki

correct [kə'rɛkt] adj (answer, details, amount, spelling) poprawny; (decision, means, procedure) właściwy ⊳ vt poprawiać (poprawić pf); **you are ~** masz rację

correction [kə'rɛkʃən] n korekta

corridor ['kɔrɪdɔːr] n korytarz

corruption [kə'rʌpʃən] *n* korupcja

cosmetics [kɒz'mɛtɪks] *n pl* (*beauty products*) kosmetyki

cosmetic surgery [kɒz'mɛtɪk 'səːdʒərɪ] *n* chirurgia plastyczna

cost [kɒst] (*pt, pp* **cost**) *n* koszt ▷ *vt* (*be priced at*) kosztować; **how much does it ~?** ile to kosztuje?; **it ~s 5 pounds/too much** kosztuje pięć funtów/zbyt dużo; **the ~ of living** koszty utrzymania

costume ['kɒstjuːm] *n* (*of actor, artist*) kostium

cosy ['kəuzɪ] (*US* **cozy**) *adj* (*room, house*) przytulny

cot [kɒt] *n* **1** (*Brit: child's*) łóżeczko dziecięce **2** (*US: bed*) łóżko polowe

cottage ['kɒtɪdʒ] *n* chata

cotton ['kɒtn] *n* **1** (*fabric*) bawełna **2** (*thread*) bawełna ▷ *adj* (*dress, sheets etc*) bawełniany

cotton candy (*US*) *n* wata cukrowa

cotton wool (*Brit*) *n* wata

couch [kautʃ] *n* kanapa

cough [kɒf] *vi* (*person*) kasłać (kaszlnąć *pf*) ▷ *n* (*noise, illness*) kaszel; **to have a ~** mieć kaszel

○ **KEYWORD**

could [kud] *aux vb* **1** (*referring to past*) **we couldn't go to the party** nie mogliśmy iść na przyjęcie; **he couldn't read or write** nie umiał ani czytać ani pisać; **we could hear him whistling** słyszeliśmy jak gwizdał; **she said she couldn't hear me** powiedziała, że mnie nie słyszy **2** (*possibility*): **he could be in the**

library może jest w bibliotece; **he could be released next year** może być zwolniony w przyszłym roku; **you could have been killed!** mogłeś zostać zabity! **3** (*in conditionals with "if"*): **if we had more time, I could finish this** jeśli mielibyśmy więcej czasu, mógłbym to skończyć; **we'd have a holiday, if we could afford it** pojechalibyśmy na wakacje, jeśli moglibyśmy sobie na to pozwolić **4** (*in offers, suggestions, requests*) móc; **I could call a doctor** mógłbym zadzwonić po lekarza; **couldn't she give him a call?** mogłaby do niego zadzwonić?; **could I borrow the car?** mógłbym pożyczyć samochód?; **if I could just interrupt you for a minute** mogę przerwać Ci na chwilę; **he asked if he could make a phone call** zapytał, czy może zadzwonić **5** (*emphatic*): **he could at least be polite!** mógłby chociaż być miły!; **he could have told me!** mógłby mi powiedzieć!

council ['kaunsl] *n* (*of city, county*) rada

councillor ['kaunslər] *n* radny(-na) *m/f*

count [kaunt] *vt* **1** (*also:* **~ up**) liczyć (policzyć *pf*) **2** (*include*) zaliczać (zaliczyć *pf*) ▷ *vi* **1** (*add*) liczyć (policzyć *pf*) **2** (*matter*) liczyć się; **to ~ (up) to 10** liczyć (policzyć *pf*) do dziesięciu; **to keep/lose ~ of sth** tracić (stracić *pf*) rachubę czegoś

▶ **count on**, **count upon** *vt fus*

liczyć na

counter ['kauntə^r] *n* **1** (*desk: in shop, café*) lada; (*bank, post office*) okienko **2** (*in game*) pionek

country ['kʌntri] *n* **1** (*nation*) kraj **2** (*population*) naród **3** (*native land*) ojczyzna **4** (*countryside*): **the ~** wieś

countryside ['kʌntrisaid] *n* wieś

county ['kaunti] *n* hrabstwo

couple ['kʌpl] *n* para; **a ~ of** (*two*) para +*gen*; (*a few*) parę +*gen*

courage ['kʌridʒ] *n* odwaga

courageous [kə'reidʒəs] *adj* odważny

courgette [kuə'ʒet] (*Brit*) *n* cukinia

courier ['kuriə^r] *n* **1** (*messenger*) kurier **2** (*rep*) posłaniec

course [kɔːs] *n* **1** (*educational*) kurs **2** (*of meal*) danie **3** (*for golf*) pole; (*horse-racing*) tor; **of ~** (*naturally*) oczywiście; (*certainly*) naturalnie; **of ~!** oczywiście!; **of ~ not!** oczywiście, że nie!

court [kɔːt] *n* **1** (*Law: place*) sąd **2** (*for tennis, badminton etc*) kort **3** (*royal*) dwór; **to take sb to ~** pozywać (pozwać *pf*) kogoś do sądu

courthouse ['kɔːthaus] (*US*) *n* gmach sądu

courtyard ['kɔːtjɑːd] *n* dziedziniec

cousin ['kʌzn] *n* kuzyn(ka) *m/f*

cover ['kʌvə^r] *vt* **1**: **to ~ sth (with sth)** przykrywać (przykryć *pf*) coś (czymś) **2** (*in insurance*): **to ~ sb (against sth)** ubezpieczać (ubezpieczyć *pf*) kogoś (na wypadek czegoś) **3** (*be sufficient money for*) pokrywać (pokryć *pf*) ▷ *n* **1** (*for furniture, machinery etc*) nakrycie **2** (*jacket: of book, magazine*) okładka **3** (*insurance*) ochrona; **covers** *n pl* (*on bed*) nakrycie; **to be ~ed in sth** (*mud, blood, dust etc*) być pokrytym czymś

▶ **cover up** *vt* (*facts, feelings, mistakes*) ukrywać (ukryć *pf*) ▷ *vi*: **to ~ up for sb** kryć kogoś

cow [kau] *n* (*farm animal*) krowa

coward ['kauəd] *n* tchórz

cowboy ['kaubɔi] *n* (*in US*) kowboj

cozy ['kəuzi] (*US*) *adj* = **cosy**

crab [kræb] *n* krab

crack [kræk] *n* **1** (*in bone, dish, glass, wall*) pęknięcie **2** (*gap*) szpara **3** (*inf: drug*) crack ▷ *vt* **1** (*dish, glass, mirror*) zarysowywać (zarysować *pf*); (*nut, egg*) rozbijać (rozbić *pf*) ▷ *vi* (*dish, mirror, pipe*) pękać (pęknąć *pf*)

▶ **crack down on** *vt fus* (*drug dealers, crime etc*) rozprawiać (rozprawić *pf*) się z +*inst*

▶ **crack up** *vi* (*inf: mentally*) wariować (zwariować *pf*)

cracked [krækt] *adj* (*dish, glass, mirror*) popękany

cracker ['krækə^r] *n* **1** (*biscuit*) krakers **2** (*also*: **Christmas ~**) zabawka bożonarodzeniowa z niespodzianką, wydająca dźwięk podobny do trzaśnięcia podczas otwierania

cradle ['kreidl] *n* (*baby's*) kołyska

craft [krɑːft] *n* **1** (*pl* **craft**) (*boat*) statek; (*plane*) samolot **2** (*weaving, pottery etc*) rzemiosło

cramp [kræmp] *n* skurcz

crane [krein] *n* (*machine*) dźwig

crash [kræʃ] n 1 (of car) wypadek; (of plane) katastrofa 2 (noise) trzask ▷ vt (car, plane etc) rozbijać (rozbić pf) ▷ vi 1 rozbijać (rozbić pf) się 2 (Comput) zawieszać (zawiesić pf) się; **a car/plane ~** katastrofa samochodowa/lotnicza; **to ~ into sth** wpadać (wpaść pf) na coś

crawl [krɔ:l] vi (adult, child) czołgać się; (insect) pełzać; (vehicle) wlec się ▷ n (also: **the ~**: in swimming) kraul; **to do the ~** pływać (płynąć pf) kraulem

crayon ['kreɪən] n kredka

crazy ['kreɪzɪ] (inf) adj (mad) szalony; **to be ~ about sth** szaleć za czymś; **to go ~** oszaleć

cream [kri:m] n 1 (dairy cream) śmietanka 2 (for skin) krem ▷ adj (in colour) kremowy

crease [kri:s] n (in cloth, paper: fold) zagięcie; (wrinkle) zmarszczka; (in trousers) kant ▷ vt (wrinkle) marszczyć (zmarszczyć pf)

create [kri:'eɪt] vt (job, situation, wealth, problem etc) stwarzać (stworzyć pf); (feeling) wywoływać (wywołać pf)

creative [kri:'eɪtɪv] adj (person) twórczy

creature ['kri:tʃər] n (animal) stworzenie

crèche [krɛʃ] (Brit) n żłobek

credit ['krɛdɪt] n 1 (financial) kredyt 2 (recognition) uznanie 3 (Scol, Univ) punkty ▷ vt: **the money will be ~ed to your account** pieniądze zostaną zaksięgowane na pana/pani koncie; **credits** n pl napisy; **to**

be in ~ (esp Brit: person, bank account) mieć dodatnie saldo; **on ~** na kredyt

credit card n karta kredytowa

crew [kru:] n 1 (of ship, aircraft, spacecraft) załoga 2 (TV) ekipa

crib [krɪb] n (US: for baby) łóżeczko dziecięce

cricket ['krɪkɪt] n 1 (Sport) krykiet 2 (insect) świerszcz

crime [kraɪm] n 1 (illegal act) przestępstwo 2 (illegal activities) przestępczość 3 (fig) zbrodnia

criminal ['krɪmɪnl] n przestępca(-czyni) m/f ▷ adj (Law) przestępczy

crisis ['kraɪsɪs] (pl **crises** ['kraɪsi:z]) n kryzys

crisp [krɪsp] adj (bacon, biscuit) chrupiący; (lettuce, apple) kruchy ▷ n (Brit) chips

critical ['krɪtɪkl] adj 1 (crucial) decydujący 2 (serious) krytyczny 3 (seriously ill) krytyczny

criticism ['krɪtɪsɪzəm] n krytyka

criticize ['krɪtɪsaɪz] vt krytykować (skrytykować pf)

Croatia [krəu'eɪʃə] n Chorwacja

crochet ['krəuʃeɪ] n szydełkowanie ▷ vi, vt szydełkować

crocodile ['krɔkədaɪl] n krokodyl

crook [kruk] n (inf: criminal) oszust(ka) m/f

crooked ['krukɪd] adj 1 (twisted: nose, teeth) krzywy; (line) zakrzywiony 2 (off-centre: picture, tie) przekrzywiony

crop [krɔp] n 1 (plants) uprawa 2 (amount produced) plon

cross [krɔs] n 1 (x shape) krzyżyk 2 (crucifix shape) krzyż 3 (Rel)

krzyż **4** (*mixture*): **a ~ between sth and sth** krzyżówka czegoś z czymś ▷ *vt* przechodzić (przejść *pf*) ▷ *vi* (*roads, lines*) krzyżować (skrzyżować *pf*) się ▷ *adj* (*angry*) rozgniewany; **to be/get ~ about sth** być złym z powodu czegoś
▶ **cross off** *vt* (*delete*) skreślać (skreślić *pf*)
▶ **cross out** *vt* (*delete*) skreślać (skreślić *pf*)
▶ **cross over** *vi* (*cross the street*) przechodzić (przejść *pf*) na drugą stronę

cross-country [krɔsˈkʌntrɪ] *n* (*running*) bieg przełajowy ▷ *adj* (*running, race, skier, journey etc*) przełajowy ▷ *adv*: **to go ~** biegać na przełaj

crossing [ˈkrɔsɪŋ] *n* **1** (*voyage*) przeprawa **2** (*Brit: also:* **pedestrian ~**) przejście dla pieszych

crossroads [ˈkrɔsrəudz] (*pl* **crossroads**) *n* skrzyżowanie

crosswalk [ˈkrɔswɔːk] (*US*) *n* przejście dla pieszych

crossword [ˈkrɔswəːd] *n* (*also:* **~ puzzle**) krzyżówka

crouch [krautʃ] *vi* (*also:* **~ down**) robić (zrobić *pf*) przysiad

crow [krəu] *n* (*bird*) wrona

crowd [kraud] *n* (*of people, fans etc*) tłum ▷ *vi* (*gather*): **to ~ around sb/sth** gromadzić (zgromadzić *pf*) się wokół kogoś/czegoś; **~s of people** tłumy ludzi

crowded [ˈkraudɪd] *adj* **1** (*full: room, ship, train*) zatłoczony **2** (*densely populated: area*) przeludniony

crown [kraun] *n* (*of monarch*)

korona

crude [kruːd] *adj* **1** (*simple*) prymitywny **2** (*not processed*) surowy

cruel [ˈkruəl] *adj* okrutny; **to be ~ to sb** być okrutnym w stosunku do kogoś

cruelty [ˈkruəltɪ] *n* (*of person*) okrucieństwo

cruise [kruːz] *n* rejs ▷ *vi* (*go on cruise*) odbywać (odbyć *pf*) rejs; **to be/go on a ~** odbywać (odbyć *pf*) rejs

crumb [krʌm] *n* (*of bread, cake*) okruch

crunchy [ˈkrʌntʃɪ] *adj* chrupiący

crush [krʌʃ] *vt* **1** (*tin, box*) zgniatać (zgnieść *pf*) **2** (*break up: garlic*) wyciskać (wycisnąć *pf*); (*ice*) kruszyć (rozkruszyć *pf*) **3** (*squeeze: person*) miażdżyć (zmiażdżyć *pf*)

crutch [krʌtʃ] *n* (*stick*) kula inwalidzka

cry [kraɪ] *vi* (*weep*) płakać ▷ *vt* (*also:* **~ out**) krzyczeć (krzyknąć *pf*) ▷ *n* krzyk; **what are you ~ing about?** dlaczego płaczesz?

crystal [ˈkrɪstl] *n* kryształ

cub [kʌb] *n* **1** (*young lion, wolf, fox, bear*) młode **2** (*also:* **~ scout**) zuch; **the Cubs** *n pl* (*also:* **the C~ Scouts**) Zuchy

cube [kjuːb] *n* **1** (*shape*) sześcian **2** (*Math: of number*) trzecia potęga

cuckoo [ˈkukuː] *n* kukułka

cucumber [ˈkjuːkʌmbəʳ] *n* ogórek

cuddle [ˈkʌdl] *vt* przytulać (przytulić *pf*) ▷ *vi* przytulać (przytulić *pf*) się ▷ *n*: **to give sb a ~** przytulać (przytulić *pf*) kogoś

cue [kju:] n (fig): **a ~ for sth** znak do rozpoczęcia czegoś

cultural ['kʌltʃərəl] adj (heritage, tradition, exchange) kulturowy

culture ['kʌltʃəʳ] n kultura

cunning ['kʌnɪŋ] adj (person, plan, idea) przebiegły

cup [kʌp] n 1 (for drinking) filiżanka 2 (trophy) puchar 3 (quantity) szklanka; **a ~ of tea** filiżanka herbaty

cupboard ['kʌbəd] n szafka

curb [kə:b] n (US) = **kerb**

cure [kjuəʳ] vt leczyć (wyleczyć pf) ▷ n (Med) kuracja

curious ['kjuərɪəs] adj 1 (inquisitive) ciekawy 2 (strange): **to be ~ about sth** być ciekawym czegoś; **I'm ~ about her** ona mnie interesuje

curl [kə:l] n (of hair) lok ▷ vi (hair) kręcić (zakręcić pf) się

curly ['kə:lɪ] adj (hair, tail) kręcony; (leaves) poskręcany

currant ['kʌrnt] n (dried grape) koryntka

currency ['kʌrnsɪ] n waluta

current ['kʌrnt] n prąd ▷ adj (present) obecny

current affairs n pl aktualne wydarzenia; **a ~ programme** aktualności f pl

curriculum [kə'rɪkjuləm] (pl **curriculums** or **curricula** [kə'rɪkjulə]) n program nauczania

curriculum vitae [-'vi:taɪ] (esp Brit) n CV

curry ['kʌrɪ] n (dish) curry

cursor ['kə:səʳ] n (Comput) n kursor

curtain ['kə:tn] n (esp Brit: at window) zasłona; **to draw the**

~s (together) zasuwać (zasunąć pf) zasłony; (apart) rozsuwać (rozsunąć pf) zasłony

cushion ['kuʃən] n (on sofa, chair) poduszka

custard ['kʌstəd] n budyń

custody ['kʌstədɪ] n 1 (of child) opieka 2 (for offenders) areszt

custom ['kʌstəm] n 1 (tradition) obyczaj 2 (convention) zwyczaj; **customs** n pl odprawa celna; **to go through ~s** przechodzić (przejść pf) przez odprawę celną

customer ['kʌstəməʳ] n (in shop) klient(ka) m/f

customs officer ['kʌstəmz 'ɔfɪsəʳ] n celnik(-iczka) m/f

cut [kʌt] (pt, pp **cut**) vt 1 (bread, meat) kroić (pokroić pf) 2 (injure): **to ~ one's hand/knee** kaleczyć (skaleczyć pf) się w rękę/kolano 3 (shorten: grass, hair, nails) przycinać (przyciąć pf) 4 (remove: scene, episode, paragraph) wycinać (wyciąć pf) 5 (reduce: prices, spending) obniżać (obniżyć pf) ▷ n 1 (injury) skaleczenie 2 (reduction) cięcie; **to ~ sth in half** (food, object) przecinać (przeciąć pf) coś na pół; **to ~ o.s.** zaciąć się; **to get** or **have one's hair ~** ostrzyc się; **to make a ~ in sth** nacinać (naciąć pf) coś; **a ~ and blow-dry** strzyżenie i modelowanie

▶ **cut down** vt 1 (tree) ścinać (ściąć pf) 2 (reduce: consumption etc) obniżać (obniżyć pf)

▶ **cut down on** vt fus (alcohol, coffee, cigarettes etc) ograniczać (ograniczyć pf)

▶ **cut off** vt odcinać (odciąć pf)

▶ **cut out** *vt* (*coupon, newspaper article*) wycinać (wyciąć *pf*)
▶ **cut up** *vt* (*paper, food*) kroić (pokroić *pf*)
cute [kjuːt] *adj* **1** (*inf: sweet*) słodki **2** (*esp US: inf: attractive*) fajny
cutlery ['kʌtlərı] (*Brit*) *n* sztućce
CV *n abbr* (= *curriculum vitae*) CV
cybercafé ['saɪbəkæfeɪ] *n* kawiarnia internetowa
cyberspace ['saɪbəspeɪs] *n* cyberprzestrzeń
cycle ['saɪkl] *n* (*bicycle*) rower ▷ *vi* jeździć na rowerze ▷ *adj* (*shop, helmet, ride*) rowerowy
cycle lane ['saɪkl leɪn] *n* ścieżka rowerowa
cycle path *n* ścieżka rowerowa
cycling ['saɪklıŋ] *n*: **to go ~** jeździć na rowerze
cyclist ['saɪklıst] *n* kolarz, rowerzysta(-tka) *m/f*
cylinder ['sılındə^r] *n* **1** (*shape*) walec **2** (*of gas*) butla
cynical ['sınıkl] *adj* (*person, attitude*) cyniczny
Cyprus ['saɪprəs] *n* Cypr
Czech [tʃɛk] *adj* czeski ▷ *n* **1** (*person*) Czech(-eszka) *m/f* **2** (*language*) czeski
Czech Republic *n*: **the ~** Republika Czeska

d

dad [dæd] (*inf*) *n* tata
daffodil ['dæfədıl] *n* żonkil
daft [dɑːft] (*Brit: inf*) *adj* głupi
daily ['deɪlı] *adj* codzienny ▷ *n* (*newspaper*) dziennik ▷ *adv* codziennie; **twice ~** dwa razy dziennie; **~ life** życie codzienne
daisy ['deɪzı] *n* stokrotka
dam [dæm] *n* (*on river*) tama ▷ *vt* (*river*) budować (wybudować *pf*) tamę na +*loc*
damage ['dæmıdʒ] *n* **1** (*harm*) szkoda **2** (*dents, scratches etc*) uszkodzenie **3** (*to sb's reputation etc*) szkoda ▷ *vt* **1** (*object, building*) uszkadzać (uszkodzić *pf*) **2** (*reputation, economy*) szkodzić (zaszkodzić *pf*); **damages** *n pl* (*Law*) odszkodowanie *n sg*; **to pay £5,000 in ~s** płacić

(zapłacić pf) pięć tysięcy funtów
odszkodowania; **to cause/inflict
~ on** (physically) uszkadzać
(uszkodzić pf); (fig) narażać
(narazić pf) na szwank
damp [dæmp] adj wilgotny
▷ n (in air, in walls) wilgoć ▷ vt
(also: **~en**: cloth) zwilżać (zwilżyć
pf); (enthusiasm, spirits etc) studzić
(ostudzić pf)
dance [dɑ:ns] n 1 (waltz, tango)
taniec 2 (social event) tańce
3 (dancing) dancing ▷ vi tańczyć
(zatańczyć pf); **to ~ the tango**
tańczyć (zatańczyć pf) tango;
to ~ with sb tańczyć (zatańczyć
pf) z kimś
dancer ['dɑ:nsə^r] n tancerz(-rka)
m/f; **to be a good/bad ~** być
dobrym/złym tancerzem
dandruff ['dændrəf] n łupież
Dane [deɪn] n Duńczyk (Dunka)
m/f
danger ['deɪndʒə^r] n
niebezpieczeństwo; **there
is a ~ of/that...** istnieje
niebezpieczeństwo, że...;
"~!" (on sign) "uwaga!"; **your
life is in ~** pana/pani życie
jest w niebezpieczeństwie;
out of ~ (patient) nie zagraża
niebezpieczeństwo
dangerous ['deɪndʒrəs] adj
niebezpieczny; **it's ~ to...**
niebezpiecznie jest...
Danish ['deɪnɪʃ] adj duński ▷ n
(language) duński
dare [dɛə^r] vt: **to ~ sb to do
sth** rzucać (rzucić pf) komuś
wyzwanie, żeby coś zrobił ▷ vi: **to
~ (to) do sth** ośmielać (ośmielić
pf) się coś zrobić ▷ n wyzwanie; **I**

~n't tell him (Brit) nie odważę się
mu powiedzieć; **I ~ say** (I suppose)
zapewne; **don't you ~** nie waż
się; **how ~ you!** jak śmiesz!; **to do
sth for a ~** robić (zrobić pf) coś w
odpowiedzi na wyzwanie
daring ['dɛərɪŋ] adj
1 (audacious: escape, rescue, person)
odważny 2 (bold: film, question,
artist) śmiały
dark [dɑ:k] adj 1 ciemny
2 (time, look) ponury; (remark)
mroczny; (rumour) czarny
▷ n: **the ~** ciemno; **~ blue/green**
ciemnoniebieski/ciemnozielony;
~ chocolate gorzka czekolada;
it is ~ jest ciemno; **it is getting ~**
ściemnia się; **after ~** po zmroku;
to be in the ~ about sth nic nie
wiedzieć o czymś
darkness ['dɑ:knɪs] n ciemność
darling ['dɑ:lɪŋ] n (as
address: dear) kochanie ▷ adj
kochany
dart [dɑ:t] vi rzucać (rzucić pf)
▷ n 1 (in game) strzałka 2 (weapon)
strzała; **darts** n pl gra w strzałki
data ['deɪtə] n pl dane
database ['deɪtəbeɪs] n baza
danych
date [deɪt] n 1 (particular day)
data 2 (meeting with friend)
spotkanie 3 (friend) randka
4 (fruit) daktyl ▷ vt 1 (establish
date of: event) ustalać (ustalić pf)
datę +gen; (object) ustalać (ustalić
pf) wiek +gen 2 (letter, cheque)
pisać (napisać pf) datę na 3 (go
out with: person) iść (pójść pf)
na randkę z + inst ▷ vi (become
old-fashioned) wychodzić (wyjść
pf) z mody; **what's the ~ today?,**

what's today's date? którego dzisiaj mamy?; **~ of birth** data urodzenia; **to ~** (*until now*) do dzisiaj; **to be out of ~** (*old-fashioned*) być przestarzałym; (*expired*) być przeterminowanym; **to be up to ~** (*modern*) być nowoczesnym; **to bring sb up to ~** zapoznawać (zapoznać *pf*) kogoś z najnowszymi informacjami; **to keep up to ~** uaktualniać (uaktualnić *pf*) na bieżąco; **it was ~d 5th July** (*letter*) to było z datą piątego lipca
▶ **date from** *vi* datować się od *+gen*

daughter ['dɔːtəʳ] *n* córka

daughter-in-law ['dɔːtərɪnlɔː] (*pl* **daughters-in-law**) *n* synowa

dawn [dɔːn] *n* **1** (*of day*) świt **2**: **the ~ of sth** początek czegoś
▷ *vi* (*day*) świtać (zaświtać *pf*); **from ~ to dusk** od świtu do zmierzchu
▶ **dawn on, dawn upon** *vt fus*: **it ~ed on me/him that...** zaświtało mi/mu w głowie, że...

day [deɪ] *n* **1** (*period of 24 hours*) doba **2** (*daylight hours*) dzień **3** (*working day*) dzień **4** (*heyday*) okres rozkwitu; **the ~ after tomorrow** pojutrze; **the ~ before yesterday** przedwczoraj; **these ~s** (*nowadays*) dziś; **~ in, ~ out** dzień w dzień; **the following ~** następnego dnia; **the ~ that I... w dniu, w którym ja...; ~ by ~/from ~ to ~** z dnia na dzień; **one ~ a week** jeden dzień w tygodniu; **one ~/some ~/one of these ~s** któregoś dnia; **the other ~** tamtego dnia; **by ~** w ciągu dnia;

all ~ (long) przez cały dzień; **~ and night** dzień i noc; **to work an 8-hour ~** pracować osiem godzin dziennie

dead [dɛd] *adj* **1** (*person*) martwy; (*animal*) zdechły; (*plant*) zwiędły **2** (*phone, line*) nieczynny; (*battery*) wyładowany **3** (*total, absolute*): **~ centre** w samym środku; (*silence*) zupełny ▷ *adv* **1** (*inf*: *very*) zupełnie **2**: **~ against** (*completely*) zdecydowanie przeciw ▷ *n pl*: **the ~** zmarli; **to drop (down) ~** paść martwym; **to stop ~** stawać (stanąć *pf*) jak wryty; **~ tired** śmiertelnie zmęczony; **~ on time** punktualny; **~ centre/in the middle** sam środek; **over my ~ body!** (*inf*) po moim trupie!; **at/ in the ~ of night** w środku nocy

dead end *n* (*street*) ślepa uliczka

deadline ['dɛdlaɪn] *n* nieprzekraczalny termin; **to work to a ~** pracować do deadline'u; **to meet a ~** zdążać (zdążyć *pf*) przed deadline'm

deaf [dɛf] *adj* (*totally*) głuchy; (*partially*) niedosłyszący
▷ *n pl*: **the ~** głusi

deafening ['dɛfnɪŋ] *adj* (*noise*) ogłuszający

deal [diːl] (*pt, pp* **dealt**) *n* (*agreement*) umowa ▷ *vt* **1**: **to ~ (out)** (*cards*) rozdawać (rozdać *pf*) **2** (*sell*: *drugs*) handlować; **to do/ make/strike a ~ with sb** robić (zrobić *pf*)/ubijać (ubić *pf*) z kimś interes; **it's a ~!** (*inf*) zgoda!; **a good/fair/bad ~** dobry/uczciwy/ zły interes; **a good** *or* **great ~ (of)** duża ilość (+*gen*)
▶ **deal in** (*Comm*) *vt fus*

handlować
▶ **deal with** vt fus **1** (criminal etc)
uporać (pf) się z + inst **2** (company)
robić interesy z +inst **3** (problem)
radzić (poradzić pf) sobie z +inst
4 (book, film: subject) zajmować
(zająć pf) się +inst

dealer ['di:lə^r] n **1** (in goods,
services) handlowiec **2** (in drugs)
diler **3** (in card game) rozdający

dealt [dɛlt] pt, pp of **deal**

dear [dɪə^r] adj **1** (friend, house, car)
drogi **2: to be ~ to sb** by drogim
dla kogoś **3** (esp Brit: expensive)
drogi ▷ n: **(my) ~** (mój) drogi
▷ int: **oh ~/~ ~/~ me!** o jejku!; **~
Sir/Madam** (in letter) szanowny
Panie/Szanowna Pani; **~ Mr
Smith/Mrs Dmowska** szanowny
Pan John Smith/Szanowna Pani
Agnieszka Dmowska; **~ Peter/
Jane** drogi Piotrze/Droga Jane

death [dɛθ] n śmierć; **(a matter
of) life and ~** (sprawa) życia
i śmierci; **to stab/beat to ~**
zadźgać/pobić na śmierć; **to
scare/bore sb to ~** przestraszyć/
zanudzić (zanudzić pf) na śmierć

debate [dɪ'beɪt] n debata ▷ vt
1 (topic, issue, motion) debatować
nad +inst **2** (course of action)
zastanawiać (zastanowić pf) się
nad +inst

debt [dɛt] n dług; **to be in ~** mieć
długi; **to get into ~** popadać
(popaść pf) w długi; **to get out
of ~** wydobywać (wydobyć pf)
się z długów; **bad ~** nieściągalne
długi n pl

decade ['dɛkeɪd] n dekada

decaffeinated [di'kæfɪneɪtɪd]
adj (coffee) bezkofeinowy

deceive [dɪ'si:v] vt (fool)
oszukiwać (oszukać pf)

December [dɪ'sɛmbə^r] n
grudzień; see also **July**

decent ['di:sənt] adj przyzwoity;
that was very ~ of him to było
bardzo miło z jego strony; **are
you ~?** (inf: dressed) jesteś ubrany?

decide [dɪ'saɪd] vt
1 (question, argument)
rozstrzygać (rozstrzygnąć pf)
2 (persuade: person) przekonywać
(przekonać pf) ▷ vi decydować
(zdecydować pf); **to ~ to do sth**
decydować (zdecydować pf) się
coś zrobić; **to ~ on** or **upon sth**
(choose) decydować (zdecydować
pf) się na coś; **to ~ that...**
decydować (zdecydować pf), że...;
I can't ~ whether... nie mogę
zdecydować, czy...

decimal ['dɛsɪməl] adj (system,
currency) dziesiętny ▷ n ułamek
dziesiętny; **to three ~ places** do
trzech miejsc po przecinku

decision [dɪ'sɪʒən] n **1** (choice)
decyzja **2** (act of choosing)
decydowanie; **to make a ~**
podejmować (podjąć pf) decyzję

deck [dɛk] n **1** (on ship: floor)
pokład; (top deck) górny pokład
2 (of bus) piętro **3** (also: **tape ~,
cassette ~**) magnetofon **4** (esp
US: of cards) talia; **(to go up) on ~**
(wyjść) na pokład; **below ~(s)** pod
pokładem

deckchair ['dɛktʃeə^r] n leżak

declare [dɪ'kleə^r] vt **1** (intention,
attitude) oznajmiać (oznajmić
pf); (support) deklarować
(zadeklarować pf) **2** (at customs)
zgłaszać (zgłosić pf) ▷ vi

opowiadać (opowiedzieć *pf*) się; **to ~ sb innocent/insane** uznawać (uznać *pf*) kogoś winnym/szalonym; **to ~ war** wypowiadać (wypowiedzieć *pf*) wojnę

decorate ['dɛkəreɪt] *vt* **1** (*adorn*): **to ~ (with sth)** dekorować (udekorować *pf*) (czymś) **2** (*paint etc: room, house*) dekorować (udekorować *pf*)

decrease [*n* 'diːkriːs, *vb* diːˈkriːs] *n*: **~ (in sth)** spadek (czegoś) ▷ *vt, vi* spadać (spaść *pf*); **to be on the ~** obniżać (obniżyć *pf*) się

dedication [dɛdɪˈkeɪʃən] *n* **1** (*devotion*) oddanie **2** (*in book*) dedykacja; (*on radio*) dedykacja

deduct [dɪˈdʌkt] *vt*: **to ~ sth (from sth)** dedukować (wydedukować *pf*) coś (z czegoś)

deep [diːp] *adj* **1** (*water, hole, cut, breath*) głęboki **2** (*voice, sound*) głęboki **3** (*sleep*) mocny **4** (*profound: person*) poważny; (*thoughts, ideas*) głęboki; (*love, sympathy etc*) głęboki **5** (*serious: trouble, concern*) poważny **6** (*colour*) ciemny ▷ *adv* głęboko; **it is 1 m ~** to ma jeden metr głębokości; **to take a ~ breath** brać (wziąć *pf*) głęboki oddech; **ankle-/knee-~ (in water)** po kostki/kolana (w wodzie)

deeply ['diːplɪ] *adv* **1** głęboko **2** (*sleep*) mocno

deer [dɪəʳ] (*pl* **deer**) *n* jeleń; **red ~** jeleń szlachetny; **roe ~** sarna

defeat [dɪˈfiːt] *n* **1** (*of army*) klęska **2** (*of team*) porażka **3** (*failure*) porażka ▷ *vt* **1** (*enemy, opposition*) pokonywać (pokonać *pf*) **2** (*team*) zwyciężać (zwyciężyć *pf*) **3** (*plan, proposal etc*) odrzucić (odrzucić *pf*)

defect [*n* 'diːfɛkt, *vb* dɪˈfɛkt] *n* (*flaw*) wada ▷ *vi*: **to ~ (to/from)** uciekać (uciec *pf*) (do/z +*gen*); **hearing ~** wada słuchu

defence [dɪˈfɛns] (*US* **defense**) *n* obrona ▷ *adj* (*spending, cuts, minister*) obrony; **defences** *n pl* obrona *n sg*; **to come to sb's ~** stawać (stanąć *pf*) w czyjejś obronie; **in ~ of sth/sb** w obronie czegoś/kogoś; **the Ministry of D~**, (*US*) **the Department of Defense** Ministerstwo Obrony Narodowej; **witness for the ~** świadek obrony

defend [dɪˈfɛnd] *vt* bronić (obronić *pf*); **to ~ o.s.** bronić (obronić *pf*) się

defender [dɪˈfɛndəʳ] *n* obrońca(-czyni) *m/f*

defense [dɪˈfɛns] (*US*) *n* = **defence**

define [dɪˈfaɪn] *vt* **1** (*limits, boundaries, role*) określać (określić *pf*) **2** (*expression, word*) definiować (zdefiniować *pf*)

definite ['dɛfɪnɪt] *adj* **1** (*plan, answer, views*) wyraźny **2** (*improvement, possibility, advantage*) wyraźny **3** (*certain: proof, evidence, information*) pewny; **is that ~?** czy to pewne?

definitely ['dɛfɪnɪtlɪ] *adv* z pewnością

definition [dɛfɪˈnɪʃən] *n* **1** (*of word*) definicja **2** (*clarity: of thought, expression*) sprecyzowanie **3** (*of photograph, features*) rozdzielczość; **by ~** z definicji

degree [dɪ'griː] n stopień; **to some ~/a certain ~** do pewnego stopnia; **10 ~s below (zero)** dziesięć stopni poniżej zera; **a ~ in maths** dyplom z matematyki; **by ~s** (gradually) stopniowo

delay [dɪ'leɪ] vt 1 (postpone: decision, ceremony) opóźniać (opóźnić pf) 2 (make late: person) zatrzymywać (zatrzymać pf) ▷ n opóźnienie; **to be ~ed** (person, flight, departure etc) spóźniać (spóźnić pf) się; **without ~** bez opóźnień

delete [dɪ'liːt] vt 1 (cross out) wykreślać (wykreślić pf) 2 (Comput) kasować (skasować pf)

deliberate [dɪ'lɪbərɪt] adj 1 (intentional) zamierzony 2 (careful) uważny; **it wasn't ~** to nie było naumyślnie

deliberately [dɪ'lɪbərɪtlɪ] adv 1 (intentionally) umyślnie 2 (carefully) rozważnie

delicate ['dɛlɪkɪt] adj delikatny

delicatessen [dɛlɪkə'tɛsn] n delikatesy

delicious [dɪ'lɪʃəs] adj (food, smell) pyszny

delight [dɪ'laɪt] n (feeling) zachwyt ▷ vt (please) zachwycać (zachwycić pf) ▷ vi: **to ~ in sth** czerpać radość z czegoś; **to my ~...** ku memu zadowoleniu...

delighted [dɪ'laɪtɪd] adj: **~ (at or with sth)** zachwycony (czymś); **to be ~ to do sth** zrobić coś z przyjemnością; **I'd be ~** z przyjemnością

deliver [dɪ'lɪvəʳ] vt 1 (bring: letter, parcel etc) dostarczać (dostarczyć pf) 2 (baby) odbierać (odebrać pf) 3 (speech, lecture etc) wygłaszać (wygłosić pf) 4 (formal: verdict, judgement) ogłaszać (ogłosić pf)

delivery [dɪ'lɪvərɪ] n 1 (distribution: of goods, mail) dostawa 2 (consignment) dostawa 3 (Med) poród; **~ man** dostawca; **to take ~ of sth** dostawać (dostać pf) coś; **allow 3 days for ~** dostawa w ciągu trzech dni

demand [dɪ'mɑːnd] vt domagać się +gen ▷ n 1 (request) żądanie 2 (for product) popyt; **demands** n pl (requirements) wymogi; **to ~ to do sth** dać zrobienia czegoś; **to be in ~** mieć wzięcie; **on ~** na żądanie

democracy [dɪ'mɔkrəsɪ] n 1 (system) demokracja 2 (country) państwo demokratyczne

democratic [dɛmə'krætɪk] adj demokratyczny

demolish [dɪ'mɔlɪʃ] vt 1 (building) burzyć (zburzyć pf) 2 (argument) obalać (obalić pf)

demonstrate ['dɛmənstreɪt] vt 1 (make clear: theory) demonstrować (zademonstrować pf) 2 (show: skill, appliance) wykazywać (wykazać pf) 3 (prove) dowodzić (dowieść pf) ▷ vi: **to ~ (for/against sth)** demonstrować (na rzecz czegoś/ przeciw czemuś); **to ~ that...** dowodzić (dowieść pf), że...; **to ~ how to do sth** demonstrować (zademonstrować pf) jak coś zrobić

demonstration
[dɛmən'streɪʃən] n 1 (protest
march) demonstracja 2 (proof)
dowód 3 (of appliance, cooking
etc) pokaz; **to hold/stage a ~**
przeprowadzać (przeprowadzić
pf) demonstrację

demonstrator ['dɛmənstreɪtə^r]
n 1 (protester) demonstrant(ka)
m/f 2 (sales person)
demonstrator(ka) m/f

denim ['dɛnɪm] n (fabric) dżins;
denims n pl (jeans) dżinsy

Denmark ['dɛnmɑːk] n Dania

dense [dɛns] adj 1 (crowd,
forest) gęsty 2 (smoke, fog) gęsty
3 (inf: stupid) tępy

dent [dɛnt] n (in metal, box)
wgniecenie ▷ vt 1 (metal, box)
wgniatać (wgnieść pf) 2 (pride,
ego, confidence) zadawać (zadać
pf) cios +dat

dental ['dɛntl] adj (treatment,
hygiene etc) dentystyczny

dentist ['dɛntɪst] n 1 (person)
dentysta(-tka) m/f 2: **the ~('s)**
gabinet dentystyczny

deny [dɪ'naɪ] vt 1 (charge,
allegation, accusation) zaprzeczać
(zaprzeczyć pf) 2: **to ~ sb sth**
odmawiać (odmówić pf) komuś
czegoś; **he denies having said it**
wypiera się, że to powiedział; **to
~ that...** zaprzeczać (zaprzeczyć
pf), że...

deodorant [diː'əudərənt] n
dezodorant

depart [dɪ'pɑːt] vi 1: **to ~ (from/
for)** (traveller, visitor) wyruszać
(wyruszyć pf) (z/do +gen); (bus,
train) odjeżdżać (odjechać pf)
(z/do +gen); (plane) odlatywać

(odlecieć pf) (z/do +gen) 2: **to ~
from sth** (stray from) odchodzić
(odejść pf) od czegoś

department [dɪ'pɑːtmənt] n
1 (in shop) stoisko 2 (in school or
college) wydział 3 (in government)
ministerstwo; **that's not my ~**
to nie moja działka; **D~ of State**
(US) Departament Stanu; **D~ of
Health/the Environment** (Brit)
Ministerstwo Zdrowia/Ochrony
Środowiska

department store n dom
towarowy

departure [dɪ'pɑːtʃə^r] n 1 (of
visitor, traveller) wyjazd; (plane)
odlot 2 (scheduled journey)
odjazd 3 (formal: of employee,
colleague) odejście 4: **a ~ from sth**
odstępstwo od czegoś; **a new ~**
nowy kierunek

departure lounge n hala
odlotów

depend [dɪ'pɛnd] vi 1: **to ~ on sth**
(be decided by) polegać na czymś
2: **you can ~ on me/him** (rely on,
trust) może pan/pani na mnie/
nim polegać 3: **to ~ on sb/sth** (for
survival) być zależnym od kogoś/
czegoś; **it (all) ~s** (wszystko)
zależy; **~ing on the result...** w
zależności od wyniku...

deposit [dɪ'pɔzɪt] n 1 (money: in
account) wpłata; (on goods)
kaucja; (on house, bottle, when
hiring) zaliczka 2 (residue) osad
▷ vt 1 (money) wpłacać (wpłacić
pf) 2 (put, leave) zdeponować (pf);
to put down a ~ of £50 dawać
(dać pf) zaliczkę w wysokości
pięćdziesięciu funtów

depressed [dɪ'prɛst] adj (person)

przygnębiony; **to feel ~** być przygnębionym; **to get ~** wpadać (wpaść pf) w depresję

depressing [dɪ'prɛsɪŋ] adj (place, situation etc) przygnębiający

depth [dɛpθ] n **1** (from top to bottom) głębokość **2** (from front to back) głębokość **3** (of emotion, feeling) głębia **4** (of knowledge) głębia; (of understanding etc) głębia **5: the depths** (liter: of ocean, earth) czeluść; **at/to/from a ~ of 3 metres** na/do/od głębokości trzech metrów; **18 metres in ~** osiemnaście metrów głębokości; **to be/go out of one's ~** (in water) nie sięgać (sięgnąć pf) gruntu; **to be/feel out of one's ~** (fig) czuć (poczuć pf) się zagubionym; **to study/analyse sth in ~** studiować (przestudiować pf)/analizować (przeanalizować pf) coś dogłębnie; **in the ~s of despair/recession/winter** w otchłani rozpaczy/recesji/zimy

descend [dɪ'sɛnd] vt (formal: stairs, hill) schodzić (zejść pf) ▷ vi **1** (formal: go down) zejść (schodzić pf) **2: to ~ (on/upon)** (visitors, tourists) zwalać (zwalić pf) się (do +gen) (inf); **in ~ing order** w kolejności od największego

describe [dɪs'kraɪb] vt opisywać (opisać pf); **to ~ sb/sth to sb** opisywać (opisać pf) kogoś/coś komuś

description [dɪs'krɪpʃən] n opis

desert [n 'dɛzət, vb dɪ'zə:t] n pustynia ▷ vt (leave: place) opuszczać (opuścić pf); (person) opuszczać (opuścić pf) ▷ vi (Mil)

dezerterować (zdezerterować pf)

deserve [dɪ'zə:v] vt zasługiwać (zasłużyć pf) na; **to ~ to do sth** zasługiwać (zasłużyć pf) na zrobienie czegoś

design [dɪ'zaɪn] n **1** (art, process, layout, shape) projekt **2** (drawing) projekt **3** (pattern) wzór ▷ vt projektować (zaprojektować pf); **to be ~ed for sb/to do sth** być zaprojektowanym dla kogoś/do zrobienia czegoś; **by ~** (on purpose) celowo

designer [dɪ'zaɪnər] n projektant(ka) m/f ▷ adj (clothes, label, jeans etc) markowy

desire [dɪ'zaɪər] n (formal: urge) ochota ▷ vt (formal: want) pragnąć (zapragnąć pf) +gen; **the ~d effect/result** pożądany efekt/wynik

desk [dɛsk] n **1** (in office) biurko **2** (for pupil) ławka **3** (in hotel, at airport, hospital etc) recepcja **4: news/fashion ~** (department) dział

desk clerk (US) n recepcjonista(-tka) m/f

despair [dɪs'pɛər] n rozpacz ▷ vi rozpaczać; **in ~** w rozpaczy; **to ~ of doing sth** tracić (stracić pf) nadzieję na zrobienie czegoś

desperate ['dɛspərɪt] adj **1** (person) zdesperowany **2** (attempt, effort) rozpaczliwy **3** (situation) rozpaczliwy **4** (criminal) zdesperowany; **to be ~ for sth/to do sth** rozpaczliwie wyczekiwać czegoś/zrobienia czegoś

desperately ['dɛspərɪtlɪ] adv **1** (struggle, shout etc) rozpaczliwie

2 (*ill, unhappy etc*) strasznie;
he ~ needs help rozpaczliwie
potrzebuje pomocy
despise [dɪs'paɪz] *vt* gardzić
(wzgardzić *pf*) +*loc*
despite [dɪs'paɪt] *prep* pomimo
+*gen*
dessert [dɪ'zəːt] *n* deser
destination [dɛstɪ'neɪʃən] *n* (*of
traveller*) cel
destroy [dɪs'trɔɪ] *vt* **1** (*building,
object*) niszczyć (zniszczyć
pf) **2** (*faith*) obalać (obalić *pf*);
(*confidence*) niszczyć (zniszczyć *pf*)
3 (*animal*) uśmiercać (uśmiercić *pf*)
destruction [dɪs'trʌkʃən] *n* **1** (*act
of destroying*) niszczenie **2** (*state of
being destroyed*) zniszczenie
detail ['diːteɪl] *n* szczegół ▷ *vt*
(*formal: list*) wyszczególniać
(wyszczególnić *pf*); **details** *n pl*
szczegóły; **in ~** w szczegółach; **to
(not) go into ~s** (*usually negative*)
(nie) wdawać (wdać *pf*) się w
szczegóły
detailed ['diːteɪld] *adj* (*account,
description*) szczegółowy
detective [dɪ'tɛktɪv] *n* (*in police*)
oficer prowadzący dochodzenie;
~ inspector komisarz;
(*Brit*): **(private) ~** (prywatny)
detektyw
detention [dɪ'tɛnʃən] *n* **1** (*arrest*)
zatrzymanie **2** (*at school*) zostać
po lekcjach; **to be in ~** zostawać
(zostać *pf*) po lekcjach za karę
detergent [dɪ'təːdʒənt] *n* środek
czyszczący
determined [dɪ'təːmɪnd] *adj*
1 (*person*) zdecydowany **2** (*effort,
attempt*) stanowczy
detour ['diːtuə^r] *n* **1: to make**

a ~ jechać (pojechać *pf*) okrężną
drogą **2** (*US: on road*) objazd
develop [dɪ'vɛləp] *vt* **1** (*change
and improve*) rozwijać (rozwinąć
pf); (*land*) zagospodarowywać
(zagospodarować *pf*); (*resource*)
wykorzystywać (wykorzystać
pf) **2** (*produce: product, weapon*)
pracować nad powstaniem +*gen*
3 (*Phot*) wywoływać (wywołać *pf*)
4 (*fault, engine trouble*) pojawiać
(pojawić *pf*); (*disease*) złapać (*pf*)
▷ *vi* **1** (*evolve: person*) rozwijać
(rozwinąć *pf*) się; (*country,
situation, friendship, skill*) rozwijać
(rozwinąć *pf*) się **2** (*appear*) pojawiać
(pojawić *pf*) się; **to ~ a taste for
sth** polubić (*pf*) coś; **to ~ into sth**
rozwijać (rozwinąć *pf*) się w coś
development [dɪ'vɛləpmənt]
n **1** rozwój **2** (*building complex*)
osiedle; **an unexpected ~**
niespodziewane wydarzenie
devil ['dɛvl] *n* **1** (*evil spirit*) diabeł
2: poor ~ biedaczysko; **lucky ~**
szczęściarz **3: the D~** szatan; **talk
of the ~!** o wilku mowa!
devoted [dɪ'vəutɪd] *adj* oddany;
~ to sth (*specialising in*) oddany
czemuś; **to be ~ to sb** być
oddanym komuś
diabetes [daɪə'biːtiːz] *n* cukrzyca
diabetic [daɪə'bɛtɪk] *adj* **1** (*person,
patient*) chory na cukrzycę
2 (*coma*) cukrzycowy **3** (*chocolate,
jam*) dla diabetyków ▷ *n* cukrzyk
diagonal [daɪ'ægənl] *adj* (*line*)
ukośny ▷ *n* **1** (*in geometry*)
przekątna **2** (*in pattern or design*)
linia ukośna
diagram ['daɪəgræm] *n* schemat
dial ['daɪəl] *n* **1** (*on clock or meter*)

tarcza **2** (on radio) pokrętło **3** (on telephone) tarcza ▷ vt (number) wykręcać (wykręcić pf) ▷ vi wykręcać (wykręcić pf); **can I ~ London direct?** czy mogę zadzwonić bezpośrednio do Londynu?

dialling tone (Brit) n sygnał

dialogue ['daɪəlɔg] (US **dialog**) n dialog

dial tone (US) n = **dialling tone**

diamond ['daɪəmənd] n **1** (gem) diament **2** (shape) romb; **diamonds** n pl (on playing cards) kara; **the six/king of ~s** szóstka/król karo

diaper ['daɪəpər] (US) n pieluszka

diarrhoea [daɪə'riːə] (US **diarrhea**) n biegunka; **to have ~** mieć biegunkę

diary ['daɪərɪ] n **1** (engagements book) terminarz **2** (daily account) dziennik; **to keep a ~** prowadzić dziennik; **video ~** pamiętnik video

dice [daɪs] (pl **dice**) n **1** (in game) kostka **2** (game) kości ▷ vt (in cooking) kroić (pokroić pf) w kostkę

dictation [dɪk'teɪʃən] n **1** (of letter) dyktowanie **2** (at school, college) dyktando

dictionary ['dɪkʃənrɪ] n słownik

did [dɪd] pt of **do**

die [daɪ] vi **1** (person) umierać (umrzeć pf); (animal) zdychać (zdechnąć pf); (plant) usychać (uschnąć pf) pf **2** (love, hope) umierać (umrzeć pf) ▷ n (pl **dice**) (for games) kostka n sg; **to ~ of** or **from sth** umierać (umrzeć pf) od czegoś; **to be dying** (person) być umierającym; (plant) usychać

(uschnąć pf); (animal) zdychać (zdechnąć pf); **old habits ~ hard** przyzwyczajenie drugą naturą człowieka; **I'm dying of thirst/boredom** umieram z pragnienia/nudów; **to be dying for sth/to do sth** marzyć o czymś/o zrobieniu czegoś

▶ **die down** vi **1** (wind) uspokajać (uspokoić pf) się **2** (fire) gasić (zgasić pf) **3** (excitement, controversy, laughter) gasić (zgasić pf)

▶ **die out** vi **1** (custom, way of life) zanikać (zaniknąć pf) **2** (species) wymierać (wymrzeć pf)

diesel ['diːzl] n **1** (also: **~ oil**) olej napędowy **2** (vehicle) diesel

diet ['daɪət] n **1** (food intake) odżywianie **2** (restricted food) dieta ▷ vi być na diecie ▷ adj dietetyczny; **to be on a ~** być na diecie; **to go on a ~** przechodzić (przejść pf) na dietę; **to live on a ~ of fish and rice** żywić się rybami i ryżem

difference ['dɪfrəns] n różnica; **the ~ in size/colour** różnica w rozmiarze/kolorze; **to make a ~ (to sb/sth)** mieć znaczenie (dla kogoś/czegoś); **to make no ~ (to sb/sth)** nie mieć znaczenia (dla kogoś/czegoś); **I can't tell the ~ between them** nie widzę różnicy między nimi; **to settle/resolve one's ~s** zgadzać (zgodzić pf) się

different ['dɪfrənt] adj **1** (not the same) różny **2** (unusual) inny; **~ from** inny niż; **~ to** or (US) **than** inny niż

difficult ['dɪfɪkəlt] adj trudny; **I found it ~ to…** było mi trudno…;

it is ~ being a parent trudno jest być rodzicem
difficulty ['dɪfɪkəltɪ] *n* trudność; **to have ~/difficulties** mieć trudności; **to be in ~** mieć kłopot; **he stood up with ~** stał z trudnością
dig [dɪg] (*pt, pp* **dug**) *vt* **1** (*hole*) kopać **2** (*garden*) skopywać (skopać *pf*) ▷ *vi* (*with spade*) skopywać (skopać *pf*) ▷ *n* **1** (*prod*): **to give sb a ~ in the ribs** szturchać (szturchnąć *pf*) kogoś w żebra **2** (*also*: **archaeological ~**: *excavation*) wykopalisko **3** (*inf*): **to have/take a ~ at sb** (*criticism*) robić (zrobić *pf*) przytyk pod adresem kogoś
▶ **dig out** *vt* **1** (*survivors, car*) odkopywać (odkopać *pf*) **2** (*inf: find*) odgrzebywać (odgrzebać *pf*)
▶ **dig up** *vt* **1** (*plant, body*) wykopywać (wykopać *pf*) **2** (*land, area*) przekopywać (przekopać *pf*) **3** (*discover: information, evidence*) wydobywać (wydobyć *pf*) na jaw
digestion [dɪ'dʒestʃən] *n* trawienie
digital ['dɪdʒɪtl] *adj* cyfrowy
digital camera *n* aparat cyfrowy
digital radio *n* radio cyfrowe
digital television *n* telewizja cyfrowa
dim [dɪm] *adj* **1** (*not bright: light*) przyciemniony; (*room, place*) ciemny **2** (*unclear: outline, figure*) niewyraźny **3** (*faint: memory, sight*) mglisty **4** (*future, prospects*) ponury **5** (*inf: stupid*) tępy ▷ *vt* **1** (*light*) przyciemniać (przyciemnić *pf*) **2** (*US: Aut*): **to ~ one's lights**

wyłączać (wyłączyć *pf*) światła mijania ▷ *vi* (*light*) ściemniać (ściemnić *pf*) się
dime [daɪm] (*US*) *n* dziesięciocentówka
dimension [daɪ'menʃən] *n* wymiar; **dimensions** *n pl* wymiar
din [dɪn] *n* (*row, racket*) gwar
diner ['daɪnər] *n* **1** (*person*) gość **2** (*US: restaurant*) niedroga restauracja
dinghy ['dɪŋgɪ] *n* **1** (*inflatable: also*: **rubber ~**) jolka **2** (*also*: **sailing ~**) mała łódka
dining room *n* **1** (*in house*) jadalnia **2** (*in hotel*) sala restauracyjna
dinner ['dɪnər] *n* **1** (*evening meal: small*) kolacja; (*: large*) obiad **2** (*lunch: large*) obiad **3** (*formal meal*) przyjęcie
dinner party *n* przyjęcie
dinner time *n* **1** (*in evening*) pora kolacji **2** (*at midday*) pora obiadowa
dinosaur ['daɪnəsɔːr] *n* dinozaur
diploma [dɪ'pləumə] *n* dyplom
direct [daɪ'rekt] *adj* bezpośredni ▷ *vt* **1** (*show*) zaprowadzać (zaprowadzić *pf*) **2** (*send: letter*) kierować (skierować *pf*) **3** (*focus: attention, remark*) kierować (skierować *pf*) **4** (*manage: company, project etc*) kierować (pokierować *pf*) **5** (*play, film, programme*) reżyserować (wyreżyserować *pf*) ▷ *adv* (*go, write, fly*) bezpośrednio; **to ~ one's attention to sth** kierować (skierować *pf*) czyjąś uwagę na coś
direction [dɪ'rekʃən] *n* **1** (*way*)

kierunek **2** (*of film, play etc*)
reżyseria; **directions** *n pl*
wskazówki; **sense of ~** orientacja
(w terenie); **in the ~ of** (*towards*)
w kierunku +*gen*; **in all ~s**
(*everywhere*) ze wszystkich stron;
to ask for ~s pytać (zapytać *pf*)
o drogę; **~s for use** instrukcja
obsługi

director [dɪˈrɛktəʳ] *n* **1** (*of
company*) dyrektor(ka) *m/f* **2** (*of
organization, public authority*)
kierownik(-iczka) *m/f* **3** (*of play,
film etc*) reżyser(ka) *m/f*

directory [dɪˈrɛktərɪ] *n*
1 (*also*: **telephone ~**) książka
telefoniczna **2** (*list of names,
addresses etc*) spis **3** (*Comput*)
katalog

dirt [dəːt] *n* **1** brud **2** (*earth*)
ziemia; **to treat sb like ~**
traktować (potraktować *pf*)
kogoś jak szmatę

dirty [ˈdəːtɪ] *adj* **1** (*clothes, face
etc*) brudny **2** (*joke, magazine*)
nieprzyzwoity ▷ *vt* (*clothes, face
etc*) brudzić (ubrudzić *pf*)

disabled [dɪsˈeɪbld] *adj*
1 (*physically*) niepełnosprawny
2 (*mentally*) upośledzony
▷ *n pl*: **the ~** niepełnosprawni

disadvantage [dɪsədˈvɑːntɪdʒ]
n (*drawback*) wada; **to be** or
work to sb's ~ działać na czyjąś
niekorzyść; **to be at a ~** być w
niekorzystnej sytuacji

disagree [dɪsəˈgriː] *vi*: **to ~ (with
sb)** nie zgadzać (zgodzić *pf*) się (z
kimś); **to ~ (with sth)** nie zgadzać
(zgodzić *pf*) się (z czymś): **to ~
with sth** (*oppose*) sprzeciwiać
(sprzeciwić *pf*) się czemuś; **I ~**

with you nie zgadzam się z tobą;
garlic ~s with me czosnek mi
nie służy

disagreement [dɪsəˈgriːmənt]
n niezgoda; **to have a ~ (with
sb)** nie zgadzać (zgodzić *pf*) się
(z kimś)

disappear [dɪsəˈpɪəʳ] *vi* znikać
(zniknąć *pf*); **to ~ from view**
znikać (zniknąć *pf*) z oczu

disappearance [dɪsəˈpɪərəns] *n*
1 (*of person*) zniknięcie **2** (*of vehicle,
object*) zaginięcie **3** (*of custom,
species*) zanik

disappointed [dɪsəˈpɔɪntɪd] *adj*
rozczarowany; **to be ~ in sb** być
rozczarowanym kimś; **to be ~
that...** być rozczarowanym, że...

disappointment
[dɪsəˈpɔɪntmənt] *n* **1** (*emotion*)
rozczarowanie **2** (*cause*) zawód;
to my ~ ku memu rozczarowaniu

disaster [dɪˈzɑːstəʳ] *n*
1 (*earthquake, flood etc*) klęska
żywiołowa **2** (*accident, crash
etc*) katastrofa **3** (*fiasco*) klęska
4 (*serious situation*) nieszczęście

disastrous [dɪˈzɑːstrəs] *adj*
1 (*catastrophic*) katastrofalny
2 (*unsuccessful*) nieudany

disc [dɪsk] *n* dysk; *see also* **disk**

discipline [ˈdɪsɪplɪn] *n*
dyscyplina ▷ *vt* **1** (*train*): **to ~ o.s.
(to do sth)** narzucić (narzucić
pf) sobie dyscyplinę (żeby coś
zrobić) **2** (*punish*) dyscyplinować
(zdyscyplinować *pf*)

disc jockey *n* dysk dżokej

disco [ˈdɪskəʊ] *n* dyskoteka

disconnect [dɪskəˈnɛkt] *vt*
1 (*pipe, tap, hose etc*) odłączać
(odłączyć *pf*) **2** (*computer, cooker,*

TV etc) wyłączać (wyłączyć *pf*)

discount [*n* 'dıskaunt, *vb* dıs'kaunt] *n* rabat, zniżka ▷ *vt* **1** (*goods*) obniżać (obniżyć *pf*) cenę +*gen* **2** (*ignore, reject*) pomijać (pominąć *pf*); **to give sb a ~ on sth** dawać (dać *pf*) komuś zniżkę na coś; **at a ~** (*cheaply*) ze zniżką

discourage [dıs'kʌrıdʒ] *vt* **1** (*dishearten: person*) zniechęcać (zniechęcić *pf*) **2** (*dissuade*): **to ~ sb from doing sth** odwodzić (odwieść *pf*) kogoś od zrobienia czegoś **3** (*activity*) zniechęcać (zniechęcić *pf*); **to be ~d** być zniechęconym

discover [dıs'kʌvəʳ] *vt* odkrywać (odkryć *pf*); **to ~ that...** (*find out*) dowiadywać (dowiedzieć *pf*) się, że...; **to ~ how to do sth** dowiadywać (dowiedzieć *pf*) się, jak coś zrobić

discrimination [dıskrımı'neıʃən] *n* dyskryminacja; **racial/sexual ~** dyskryminacja rasowa/płci

discuss [dıs'kʌs] *vt* **1** (*talk over*) dyskutować (przedyskutować *pf*) **2** (*analyse*) omawiać (omówić *pf*)

discussion [dıs'kʌʃən] *n* **1** (*talk*) rozmowa **2** (*debate: in article, lecture etc*) dyskusja; **the matter under ~** sprawa będąca przedmiotem dyskusji

disease [dı'ziːz] *n* choroba

disgraceful [dıs'greısful] *adj* haniebny

disguise [dıs'gaız] *n* (*make-up, costume*) przebranie ▷ *vt* **1**: **to be ~d (as sth/sb)** (*person*) przebierać (przebrać *pf*) się (za coś/kogoś) **2** (*fact, emotions*) ukrywać (ukryć

pf) **3** (*voice*) zmieniać (zmienić *pf*); **in ~** w przebraniu; **to ~ o.s. (as sb)** przebierać (przebrać *pf*) się (za kogoś)

disgusted [dıs'gʌstıd] *adj* pełen obrzydzenia

disgusting [dıs'gʌstıŋ] *adj* **1** (*food, habit*) wstrętny **2** (*behaviour, situation*) odrażający

dish [dıʃ] *n* **1** (*piece of crockery: for serving*) naczynie; (*for eating*) talerz **2** (*contents*) potrawa **3** (*recipe, food*) potrawa **4** (*also:* **satellite ~**) antena satelitarna; **dishes** *n pl* naczynia; **to do** *or* **wash the ~es** myć (umyć *pf*) naczynia

dishonest [dıs'ɔnıst] *adj* nieuczciwy

dishwasher ['dıʃwɔʃəʳ] *n* zmywarka do naczyń

dishwashing liquid ['dıʃwɔʃıŋ-] (*US*) *n* płyn do mycia naczyń

disinfectant [dısın'fektənt] *n* środek dezynfekujący

disk [dısk] *n* (*Comput: hard*) dysk; (*floppy*) dyskietka

dismal ['dızml] *adj* **1** (*weather, place, mood*) ponury **2** (*prospects, record, failure*) czarny

dismiss [dıs'mıs] *vt* **1** (*worker*) zwalniać (zwolnić *pf*) **2** (*send away*) odprawiać (odprawić *pf*) **3** (*case, charge*) oddalać (oddalić *pf*) **4** (*possibility, problem, idea*) odrzucać (odrzucić *pf*)

disobedient [dısə'biːdıənt] *adj* nieposłuszny

display [dıs'pleı] *n* **1** (*in shop, at exhibition*) wystawa **2** (*exhibition*) wystawa **3** (*show: of feeling*) przejaw **4** (*screen*) monitor ▷ *vt* **1** (*show: exhibits*) wystawiać (wystawić pf); (feelings, courage) okazywać (okazać pf) **2** (results, information) pokazać (pokazywać pf) **3** (information on screen) wyświetlać (wyświetlić pf); **on ~** (exhibits, goods, work) na wystawie

disposable [dɪs'pəuzəbl] adj jednorazowy; **~ income** dochód netto

disqualify [dɪs'kwɔlɪfaɪ] vt (team, competitor) dyskwalifikować (zdyskwalifikować pf); **to ~ sb from (doing) sth** pozbawiać (pozbawić pf) kogoś prawa robienia czegoś

disrupt [dɪs'rʌpt] vt **1** (conversation, meeting) przerywać (przerwać pf) **2** (disturb: plan) krzyżować (pokrzyżować pf); (process) przerywać (przerwać pf)

dissolve [dɪ'zɔlv] vt **1** (in liquid) rozpuszczać (rozpuścić pf) **2: to be ~d** (organization, parliament) rozwiązywać (rozwiązać pf) się; (marriage) unieważniać (unieważnić pf) ▷ vi (material) rozwiewać (rozwiać pf) się; **to ~ in(to) tears** zalewać (zalać pf) się łzami

distance ['dɪstns] n **1** (between two places) odległość **2** (remoteness) odległość **3** (formal: reserve) dystans ▷ vt: **to ~ o.s. (from sb/sth)** dystansować (zdystansować pf) się (od kogoś/czegoś); **in the ~** w dali; **from a ~** z daleka; **what's the ~ to London?** jak daleko jest do Londynu?; **to be some distance/quite a distance/a fair ~ from sth** (far) być w jakiejś

odległości/w sporej odległości/w dużej odległości od czegoś; **within walking ~** można tam dojść na piechotę; **(at) a ~ of 2 metres** w odległości dwóch metrów; **keep your ~!** trzymaj się z daleka!

distant ['dɪstnt] adj **1** (place) odległy **2** (future) daleki; (past) odległy **3** (relative, cousin) daleki **4** (aloof: person, manner) chłodny **5** (absent: person, look) nieobecny

distract [dɪs'trækt] vt (person) rozpraszać (rozproszyć pf); **to ~ sb's attention** odwracać (odwrócić pf) czyjąś uwagę

distribute [dɪs'trɪbjuːt] vt **1** (food, leaflets) rozdawać (rozdać pf) **2** (resources, profits, work etc) rozdzielać (rozdzielić pf) **3** (goods: to shops) rozprowadzać (rozprowadzić pf)

district ['dɪstrɪkt] n **1** (of country) region; (town) dzielnica **2** (official area) okręg **3** (in titles) dystrykt

disturb [dɪs'təːb] vt **1** (interrupt) zakłócać (zakłócić pf) **2** (upset) niepokoić (zaniepokoić pf); **sorry to ~ you** przepraszam, że przeszkadzam

ditch [dɪtʃ] n **1** (at roadside, in field) rów **2** (also: **irrigation ~**) rów

dive [daɪv] vi **1** (swimmer: into water) skakać (skoczyć pf) do wody; (under water) nurkować (zanurkować pf) **2** (bird) spadać (spaść pf) lotem nurkowym ▷ n **1** (into water) skok do wody **2** (underwater) nurkowanie **3** (inf, pej: place) spelunka

diver ['daɪvəʳ] n (deep sea) nurek;

(*from board*) skoczek

diversion [daɪˈvəːʃən] n **1** (*Brit: for traffic*) objazd **2** (*distraction*) rozrywka **3** (*of profits, funds*) przekazanie; **to create a ~** odwracać (odwrócić *pf*) uwagę

divide [dɪˈvaɪd] vt **1: to ~ (up)** (*separate*) dzielić (podzielić *pf*) **2** (*in maths*) dzielić (podzielić *pf*) **3: to ~ sth between/among sb/sth** (*share*) dzielić (podzielić *pf*) coś między kogoś/coś **4: to ~ sth (from sth)** (*keep separate*) oddzielać (oddzielić *pf*) coś (od czegoś) **5** (*split*) dzielić (podzielić *pf*) ▷ vi dzielić (podzielić *pf*) się ▷ n (*gulf, rift*) przepaść; **to ~ sth in half** dzielić (podzielić *pf*) coś na pół; **40 ~d by 5** czterdzieści podzielić przez pięć; **~ 7 into 35** podzielić siedem na trzydzieści pięć

diving [ˈdaɪvɪŋ] n **1** (*underwater*) nurkowanie **2** (*from board*) skoki do wody

division [dɪˈvɪʒən] n **1** (*splitting up*) podział **2** (*Math*) dzielenie **3** (*of labour, resources*) podział **4** (*gulf*) przepaść **5** (*department*) wydział **6** (*military unit*) dywizja

divorce [dɪˈvɔːs] n rozwód ▷ vt (*spouse*) rozwodzić (rozwieść *pf*) ▷ vi rozwodzić (rozwieść *pf*) się

divorced [dɪˈvɔːst] adj rozwiedziony; **to get ~** brać (wziąć *pf*) rozwód

DIY (*Brit*) n abbr (= *do-it-yourself*) majsterkowanie; **to do ~** majsterkować

dizzy [ˈdɪzɪ] adj **1: to feel ~** kręcić się w głowie **2** (*woman, blonde*) zakręcony; **I had a ~**

spell zakręciło mi się w głowie; **to make sb ~** przyprawiać (przyprawić *pf*) kogoś o zawrót głowy

DJ n abbr **1** (= *disc jockey*) didżej **2** (*Brit: = dinner jacket*) smoking

○ **KEYWORD**

do [duː] (*pt* **did**, *pp* **done**) vt **1** (*be engaged in, achieve*) robić (zrobić *pf*); **what are you doing?** co pan/pani robi?; **what is he doing here?** co on tu robi?; **are you doing anything tomorrow evening?** robi pan/pani coś jutro wieczorem?; **what you should do is...** to, co powinien pan/powinna pani zrobić, to...; **we must do everything possible to help them** musimy zrobić wszystko, aby mu pomóc; **what did you do with the money?** (*how did you spend it?*) co pan zrobił/pani zrobiła z pieniędzmi?; (*where did you put it?*) gdzie to pan położył/pani położyła?; **what are you going to do about this?** co z tym pan/pani zrobi?

2 (*for a living*): **what do you do?** gdzie pan/pani pracuje?

3 (*with noun*): **to do the cooking** gotować (ugotować *pf*); **to do one's teeth** myć (umyć *pf*) zęby; **to do one's hair** układać (ułożyć *pf*) sobie włosy; **we're doing "Othello" at school** (*studying it*) czytamy "Othella" w szkole; (*performing it*) gramy w "Othellu" w szkole

4 (*referring to speed, distance*): **the car was doing 100** samochód jechał setką; **we've done 200 km already** zrobiliśmy już dwieście kilometrów

5 (*cause*): **the explosion did a lot of damage** eksplozja spowodowała wiele szkód; **a holiday will do you good** wakacje się panu/pani przydadzą ▷ *vi* **1** (*act, behave*) robić (zrobić *pf*); **do as I do** rób, co ja robię; **do as I tell you** rób, co ci mówię **2** (*get on*) radzić (poradzić *pf*) sobie; **he's doing well/badly at school** radzi sobie w szkole dobrze/źle; **the firm is doing well** firma prosperuje dobrze; **"how do you do?" — "how do you do?"** "miło mi" — "miło mi" **3** (*suit*) nadawać się (*pf*); **will it do?** czy to się nada? **4** (*be sufficient*) wystarczać (wystarczyć *pf*); **will £15 do?** piętnaście funtów wystarczy?; **that'll do** to wystarczy; **that'll do!** (*in annoyance*) dosyć! ▷ *aux vb* **1** (*in negative constructions*): **I don't understand** nie rozumiem; **she doesn't want it** ona nie chce tego; **he didn't seem to care** wydaje się, że go to nie obchodzi; **don't be silly!** nie wygłupiaj się! **2** (*to form questions*): **do you like jazz?** lubisz jazz?; **what do you think?** co myślisz?; **where does she live?** gdzie ona mieszka?; **didn't you know?** nie wiedziałeś?; **why didn't you come?** dlaczego nie przyszedłeś? **3** (*for emphasis, in polite expressions*): **people do make mistakes sometimes** ludzie

istotnie czasami robią błędy; **she does seem rather late** ona się istotnie trochę spóźnia; **do sit down/help yourself** proszę, niech pan/pani usiądzie/ poczęstuje się; **do take care!** uważaj na siebie!; **oh do shut up!** och, zamknij się!

4 (*used to avoid repeating vb*) używany, by uniknąć powtarzania czasownika; **I make more money than he does** zarabiam więcej pieniędzy niż on; **they say they don't care, but they do** mówią, że ich to nie obchodzi, a jednak tak jest; **he asked me to help him and I did** poprosił mnie o pomoc i mu pomogłem; **(and) so do I** (i) ja też; **and neither did we** i my nie; **better than I do** lepiej niż ja; **"who made this mess?" — "I did"** "kto zrobił bałagan?" — "Ja"; **"do you have a metal detector?" — "no, I don't"** "czy pan/pani ma wykrywacz metali?" — "nie, nie mam"

5 (*in question tags*): **I don't know him, do I?** nie znam go, prawda?; **you like him, don't you?** (*familiar*) lubisz go, prawda?; **she lives in London, doesn't she?** mieszka w Londynie, prawda? ▷ *n* (*Brit: inf: party etc*) przyjęcie; **we're having a little do on Saturday** robimy małe przyjęcie w sobotę; **it was quite a do** to było niezłe przyjęcie
▶ **do away with** *vt fus* (*get rid of*) likwidować (zlikwidować *pf*)
▶ **do in** (*inf*) *vt* (*kill*) ukatrupiać (ukatrupić *pf*)
▶ **do out of** (*inf*) *vt* (*deprive of*)

pozbawiać (pozbawić *pf*); **he did me out of my share** pozbawił mnie mojej doli
▶ **do up** *vt fus* **1** (*fasten*) zapinać (zapiąć *pf*) **2** (*esp Brit: renovate: room, house*) odnawiać (odnowić *pf*)
▶ **do with** *vt fus* **1** (*need*): **I could do with a drink** napiłbym się czegoś; **I could do with some help** przydałaby mi się pomoc **2** (*be connected*): **to have to do with** mieć związek z +*inst*; **what has it got to do with you?** jaki to ma związek z tobą?; **I won't have anything to do with it** nie będę mieć z tym nic wspólnego; **it has to do with money** ma to związek z pieniędzmi; **it was something to do with football** to ma jakiś związek z futbolem
▶ **do without** *vt fus* obywać (obyć *pf*) się bez +*gen* ▷ *vi* robić (zrobić *pf*)

doctor ['dɔktə'] *n* **1** (*medic*) lekarz(-rka) *m/f* **2**: **the ~'s** gabinet lekarski **3** (*PhD etc*) doktor ▷ *vt* (*food, drink*) zatruwać (zatruć *pf*); (*figures, photograph*) fałszować (sfałszować *pf*); **~'s office** (*US*) przychodnia
document ['dɔkjumənt] *n* dokument
documentary [dɔkju'mɛntərɪ] *n* film dokumentalny ▷ *adj* (*evidence*) dokumentalny
dodge [dɔdʒ] *vt* **1** (*blow, ball, car*) uchylać (uchylić *pf*) się od +*gen* **2** (*tax, military service*) unikać (uniknąć *pf*) +*gen* **3** (*question, issue etc*) unikać (uniknąć *pf*) +*gen*

does [dʌz] *vb see* **do**
doesn't ['dʌznt] = **does not**
dog [dɔg] *n* **1** pies **2** (*male*) samiec ▷ *vt* (*problems, injuries*) utrudniać (utrudnić *pf*); **to go to the ~s** schodzić (zejść *pf*) na psy
do-it-yourself ['du:ɪtjɔ:'sɛlf] *n* majsterkowanie ▷ *adj* (*store*) dla majsterkowiczów
dole [dəul] (*inf*) *n* (*Brit*): **(the) ~** (*payment*) zasiłek; **(to be) on the ~** (*Brit*) (być) na zasiłku
▶ **dole out** *vt* rozdzielać (rozdzielić *pf*)
doll [dɔl] *n* (*toy*) lalka
dollar ['dɔlə'] *n* dolar
dolphin ['dɔlfɪn] *n* delfin
dominoes ['dɔmɪnəuz] *n* domino
donate [də'neɪt] *vt* **1**: **to ~ (to sb)** (*money, clothes*) ofiarowywać (ofiarować *pf*) (komuś) **2** (*blood, organs*) oddawać (oddać *pf*)
done [dʌn] *pp of* **do**
donkey ['dɔŋkɪ] *n* osioł
don't [dəunt] = **do not**
donut ['dəunʌt] (*US*) *n* = **doughnut**
door [dɔ:'] *n* **1** (*of house, room, etc*) drzwi *n pl* **2** (*doorway*) wejście; **to answer the ~** otwierać (otworzyć *pf*) drzwi; **out of ~s** na dworze; **to go from ~ to door** chodzić od domu do domu
doorbell ['dɔ:bɛl] *n* dzwonek do drzwi
doorstep ['dɔ:stɛp] *n* próg; **on one's ~** za progiem
dormitory ['dɔ:mɪtrɪ] *n* **1** (*room*) sala **2** (*US: building*) akademik
dot [dɔt] *n* **1** (*small round mark*)

kropka **2** (*in the distance*) punkt
▷ *vt*: **~ted with** usiany kropkami;
on the ~ (*punctually*) co do
minuty
dot-com [dɔt'kɔm] *n* firma
internetowa
double ['dʌbl] *adj* **1** podwójny
2 (*for two: room, sheet*)
dwuosobowy ▷ *n* **1: to be sb's ~**
być czyimś sobowtórem **2** (*drink*)
setka ▷ *vt* (*offer, size*) podwajać
(podwoić *pf*) ▷ *vi* (*population, size*)
podwajać (podwoić *pf*) się; **~ five
two six** (*Brit:* 5526) pięćdziesiąt
pięć, dwadzieścia sześć; **it's spelt
with a ~ "M"** piszę się przez dwa
"M"; **~ the size/number (of sth)**
podwójny rozmiar/podwójna
liczba (czegoś); **~ in size/
weight** podwójny rozmiar/
waga; **to ~ as sth** służyć również
jako coś
▶ **double back** *vi* (*person*)
zawracać (zawrócić *pf*)
▶ **double up** *vi* (*bend over*) skręcać
(skręcić *pf*) się we dwoje ▷ *vt*
podwajać (podwoić *pf*); **to be
~d up with pain** skręcać się z
bólu; **to be ~d up with laughter**
pokładać się ze śmiechu
double bass *n* kontrabas
double-click ['dʌbl'klɪk] *vi*: **to
~ on sth** klikać (kliknąć *pf*) dwa
razy na coś
double glazing [-'gleɪzɪŋ] (*Brit*)
n podwójne szyby
doubles ['dʌblz] *n* (*Tennis*)
debel
doubt [daut] *n* (*uncertainty*)
wątpliwość ▷ *vt* **1** (*disbelieve*)
wątpić (zwątpić *pf*) w **2** (*mistrust, suspect*) wątpić (zwątpić *pf*) w;

without (a) ~ bez wątpienia; **to
be in ~** mieć wątpliwości; **beyond
~** poza wątpliwością; **no ~** bez
wątpienia; **to ~ if** *or* **whether...**
wątpić (zwątpić *pf*) czy...; **I ~
it (very much)** (bardzo) w to
wątpię; **I don't ~ that...** nie mam
wątpliwości, że...
doubtful ['dautful] *adj*
1 (*questionable*): **it is ~ that/
whether...** nie jest pewne, czy...
2 (*unconvinced: person*): **to be ~
about sth** mieć wątpliwości co do
czegoś; **I'm a bit ~** mam pewne
wątpliwości
dough [dəu] *n* **1** (*Culin*) ciasto
2 (*inf: money*) szmal
doughnut ['dəunʌt] (*US* donut)
n pączek
down [daun] *n* (*soft feathers*) puch
▷ *adv* **1** (*downwards*) w dół **2** (*in a
lower place*) na dole **3** (*in the south*)
na południu; (*towards the south*)
na południe ▷ *prep* **1** (*towards lower
level*) w dół **2** (*at lower part of*) dalej
3 (*along*) wzdłuż ▷ *vt* (*inf: drink*)
wypić (*pf*) jednym haustem; **~
there** tam na/w dole; **~ here** tu
na/w dole; **the price of meat is
~** (*lower*) cena mięsa spadła; **I've
got it ~ in my diary** (*written*)
zapisałem to w kalendarzu; **to
pay 5 pounds ~** (*esp US*) płacić
(wpłacić *pf*) pięć funtów zaliczki;
England are two goals ~ (*behind*)
Anglia przegrywa dwoma golami;
I'm ~ to my last five pounds
zostało mi ostatnie pięć funtów;
five ~, two to go mamy już pięć,
dwa zostały; **to be ~ for sth**
zapisywać (zapisać *pf*) się na
coś; **it's all ~ to hard work**

wszystko jest wynikiem ciężkiej pracy

download ['daunləud] *vt*
ściągać (ściągnąć *pf*) ▷ *n* dane *pl*
ściągnięte z serwera

downstairs ['daun'stɛəz] *adv*
1 (*to floor below*) na dół; (*on floor below*) na dole 2 (*to ground floor*)
na dół; (*on ground floor*) na dole
▷ *adj* na dole

downtown ['daun'taun] (*US*)
adv centrum ▷ *adj*: ~ **Chicago**
centrum Chicago

doze [dəuz] *vi* drzemać
(zdrzemnąć *pf*) się ▷ *n*: **to have a**
~ robić (zrobić *pf*) sobie drzemkę
▶ **doze off** *vi* drzemać
(zdrzemnąć *pf*) się

dozen ['dʌzn] *n* tuzin; **a ~ books**
tuzin książek; **two ~ eggs** dwa
tuziny jajek; **~s of** tuzin +*gen*

draft [drɑːft] *n* 1 (*first version*)
szkic 2 (*of bill*) projekt
3 (*also*: **bank ~**) przekaz 4: **the ~**
(*US: Mil*) pobór ▷ *vt* 1 (*letter, book, speech*) pisać (napisać *pf*) roboczą
wersję +*gen* 2 (*Mil*): **to be ~ed**
powoływać (powołać *pf*); *see also*
draught

drag [dræg] *vt* 1 (*pull: large object, body*) ciągnąć 2 (*force*): **to ~ sb out
of a car** wyciągać (wyciągnąć *pf*)
kogoś z samochodu 3 (*fig*): **it's
impossible to ~ him out of bed**
nie można go wyciągnąć z łóżka
4 (*search: river, lake*) przeszukiwać
(przeszukać *pf*) ▷ *vi* (*time, film*)
dłużyć się ▷ *n* 1 (*inf*): **a ~** (*person*)
nudziarz(-ra) *m/f*; (*situation*)
nuda 2 (*women's clothing*): **in ~**
w damskim przebraniu 3 (*Naut, Aviat*) opór; **to ~ sth out of sb**
wyciągać (wciągnąć *pf*) coś z kogoś
▶ **drag away** *vt*: **to ~ sb away
(from sth)** odciągać (odciągnąć
pf) kogoś (od czegoś); **to ~ o.s.
away (from sth)** wyrywać
(wyrwać *pf*) się (z czegoś)
▶ **drag on** *vi* (*meeting, concert*)
dłużyć się; (*war*) ciągnąć się
▶ **drag out** *vt* (*prolong*) przeciągać
(przeciągnąć *pf*)

dragon ['drægn] *n* smok

drain [dreın] *n* 1 (*in street*)
studzienka ściekowa 2: **to be
a ~ on sth** (*resources, funds*)
pochłaniać coś ▷ *vt* 1 (*land,
marsh, pond*) osuszać (osuszyć
pf) 2 (*vegetables*) odsączać
(odsączyć *pf*) 3 (*liquid*) spuszczać
(spuścić *pf*) 4 (*glass, cup*) wypić
do dna *pf* 5 (*exhaust: person*)
wyczerpywać (wyczerpać *pf*) ▷ *vi*
(*liquid*) wyciekać (wyciec *pf*); **to
go down the ~** (*inf*) marnować
(zmarnować *pf*) się

drama ['drɑːmə] *n* 1 (*theatre*)
dramat 2 (*play*) sztuka
3 (*excitement*) dramat

dramatic [drə'mætɪk] *adj*
dramatyczny ▷ *adj* (*society, group*)

dramatyczny

drank [dræŋk] *pt of* **drink**

drapes [dreɪps] *(US) n pl* zasłony

draught [drɑːft] *(US* **draft**) *n (of air)* przeciąg ▷ *adj (beer, bitter etc)* beczkowy; **on ~** *(beer)* z beczki

draughts [drɑːfts] *(Brit) n* warcaby

draw [drɔː] *(pt* **drew**, *pp* **drawn**) *vt* **1** *(picture, map)* rysować (narysować *pf*) **2** *(pull: cart)* ciągnąć (pociągnąć *pf*) **3** *(curtains, blinds: close)* zasuwać (zasunąć *pf*); *(open)* odsuwać (odsunąć *pf*) **4** *(take out: gun, knife, sword)* wyciągać (wyciągnąć *pf*) **5** *(breath)* wciągać (wciągnąć *pf*) **6: to ~ (out) money from a bank/an account** wypłacać (wypłacić *pf*) pieniądze z banku/z konta **7: to ~ a conclusion (from sth)** wyciągać (wyciągnąć *pf*) wnioski (z czegoś) **8: to ~ a comparison/distinction (between two things)** pokazywać (pokazać *pf*) podobieństwa/różnice (pomiędzy dwoma rzeczami) ▷ *vi* **1** *(with pen, pencil etc)* rysować (narysować *pf*) **2: to ~ near** *(move)* zbliżać (zbliżyć *pf*) się; **to ~ away** oddalać (oddalić *pf*) się **3** *(esp Brit: Sport)* remisować (zremisować *pf*) ▷ *n* **1** *(esp Brit: Sport)* remis **2** *(lottery)* los; **to ~ (sb's) attention (to sth)** kierować (skierować *pf*) (czyjąś) uwagę (na coś); **to ~ near** *or* **close** *(approach)* zbliżać (zbliżyć *pf*) się; **to ~ to a close** dobiegać (dobiec *pf*) końca

▶ **draw in** *vi (Brit: nights)* stawać (stać *pf*) się krótszym ▷ *vt (also: ~*

into: *involve)* wciągać (wciągnąć *pf*)

▶ **draw on** *vt fus (also: ~ upon)* wykorzystywać (wykorzystać *pf*)

▶ **draw up** *vi (stop: car, bus etc)* ruszać (ruszyć *pf*) ze stacji ▷ *vt* **1** *(document, plan)* sporządzać (sporządzić *pf*) **2** *(chair etc)* przysuwać (przysunąć *pf*)

drawback ['drɔːbæk] *n* cecha ujemna

drawer [drɔːʳ] *n (of desk etc)* szuflada; **drawers** *n pl (o.f.: knickers)* kalesony

drawing ['drɔːɪŋ] *n* rysunek

drawing pin *(Brit) n* pinezka

drawn [drɔːn] *pp of* **draw** ▷ *adj (haggard)* mizerny

dreadful ['drɛdful] *adj* okropny; **I feel ~!** *(ill)* okropnie się czuję!; *(ashamed)* czuję się głupio!

dream [driːm] *(pt, pp* **dreamed** *or* **dreamt**) *n* **1** *(when asleep)* sen **2** *(ambition)* marzenie ▷ *vi*: **to ~ about** *(when asleep)* śnić o; **I ~t that...** śniło mi się, że...; **to have a ~ about sb/sth** *(when asleep)* śnić o kimś/czymś; **sweet ~s!** *(sleep well!)* miłych snów!; **to ~ that...** *(when asleep)* śniić, że...; *(when wishing for sth)* marzyć, że...; **I wouldn't ~ of...** nie śmiałbym myśleć o +loc...

▶ **dream up** *vt (plan, idea etc)* wymyślać (wymyślić *pf*)

drench [drɛntʃ] *vt (soak)* zamakać (zamoknąć *pf*); **~ed to the skin** przemoczony do suchej nitki

dress [drɛs] *n* **1** *(frock)* sukienka **2** *(clothing)* ubranie ▷ *vt* **1** *(child)* ubierać (ubrać *pf*) **2** *(wound)* opatrywać (opatrzyć *pf*) **3** *(salad)*

przyprawiać (przyprawić *pf*) ▷ *vi*
ubierać (ubrać *pf*) się; **to ~ o.s.,
get dressed** ubierać (ubrać *pf*)
się; **she ~es in jeans** ubiera się
w dżinsy
▶ **dress down** *vi* ubierać (ubrać
pf) się na luzie
▶ **dress up** *vi* **1** (*wear best clothes*)
stroić (wystroić *pf*) **2: to ~ up
as** (*in fancy dress*) przebierać
(przebrać *pf*) za
dresser ['drɛsər] *n* **1** (*Brit:
cupboard*) kredens **2** (*US: chest of
drawers*) szafka
dressing gown *n* szlafrok
dressing table *n* toaletka
drew [dru:] *pt of* **draw**
dried [draɪd] *adj* (*fruit, herbs*)
suszony; **~ milk/eggs** mleko/
jajka w proszku
drier ['draɪər] *n* = **dryer**
drift [drɪft] *vi* **1** (*boat*) dryfować
(podryfować *pf*) **2** (*sand, snow*)
tworzyć (utworzyć *pf*) zaspy ▷ *n*
(*snow*) zaspa; **to ~ away** (*crowd,
people*) rozchodzić (rozejść *pf*) się; **to
~ apart** (*friends, couple*) oddalać
(oddalić *pf*) się; **to get** *or* **follow
sb's ~** rozumieć (zrozumieć *pf*) o
co komuś chodzi
▶ **drift off** *vi*: **to ~ off (to sleep)**
zapadać (zapaść *pf*) w sen
drill [drɪl] *n* **1** (*for DIY etc*)
wiertarka; (*of dentist*) wiertło;
(*for mining etc*) świder **2** (*for fire,
air raid*) próbny alarm ▷ *vt* (*hole*)
wiercić (wywiercić *pf*) ▷ *vi* **1: to
~ (into sth)** (*wall, floor etc*)
wiercić (w czymś) **2: to ~ (for
sth)** (*oil, water, gas*) wiercić (w
poszukiwaniu czegoś)
drink [drɪŋk] (*pt* **drank**, *pp*

drunk) *n* **1** (*tea, water etc*) napój
2 (*alcohol*) drink ▷ *vt* pić (wypić
pf) ▷ *vi* (*drink alcohol*) pić (wypić
pf); **to have a ~** napić (*pf*) się; **a
~ of water** łyk wody; **would you
like something to ~?** czy chciałby
pan/chciałaby pani się czegoś
napić?
▶ **drink to** *vt fus* pić (wypić *pf*) za
▶ **drink up** *vt, vi* pić (wypić *pf*)
do dna
drive [draɪv] (*pt* **drove**, *pp* **driven**)
n **1** (*journey*) jazda **2** (*also: ~way*)
droga dojazdowa **3** (*energy*) zapał
4 (*campaign*) działania **5** (*also:* **CD-
ROM/disk ~**) stacja dysków ▷ *vt*
1 (*vehicle*) kierować +*inst* **2: to
~ sb to the station/airport**
podwozić (podwieźć *pf*) kogoś na
stację/lotnisko **3** (*run: machine,
motor, wheel*) kierować +*inst*
4 (*nail, stake etc*): **to ~ sth into sth**
wbijać (wbić *pf*) coś w coś **5** (*incite,
encourage*) kierować +*inst* ▷ *vi*
1 (*at controls of vehicle*) prowadzić
2 (*travel*) jechać (pojechać *pf*); **to
go for a ~** jechać na przejażdżkę;
it's a 3-hour ~ from London to
jest trzy godziny jazdy z Londynu;
left-/right-hand ~ car samochód
z kierownicą po lewej/prawej
stronie; **front-/rear-wheel ~**
samochód z napędem przednim/
tylnim; **he ~s a taxi/lorry** jest
kierowcą taksówki/ciężarówki;
to ~ sb mad/to desperation
doprowadzać (doprowadzić *pf*)
kogoś do szaleństwa/rozpaczy;
to ~ sb to (do) sth doprowadzać
(doprowadzić *pf*) kogoś do
(zrobienia) czegoś; **to ~ at 50
km an hour** jechać z prędkością

pięćdziesiąt kilometrów na
godzinę
▶ **drive away** vt zniechęcać
(zniechęcić pf)
▶ **drive off** vi (car, driver)
odjeżdżać (odjechać pf)
▶ **drive out** vt (force to leave)
wypędzać (wypędzić pf)
driver ['draɪvəʳ] n **1** kierowca
2 (chauffeur) szofer
driver's license ['draɪvəz-] (US)
n prawo jazdy
driving instructor n
instruktor(ka) m/f jazdy
driving lesson n lekcja jazdy
driving licence (Brit) n prawo
jazdy
driving test n egzamin na prawo
jazdy
drop [drɔp] n **1** (of liquid)
kropla **2** (reduction): **a ~ in
sth** spadek czegoś **3** (vertical
distance): **a 300m drop, a ~ of
300m** trzysta metrowy spadek
▷ vt **1** (accidentally) upuszczać
(upuścić pf); (deliberately) zrzucać
(zrzucić pf) **2** (lower: arm, leg,
hand etc) opuścić (opuszczać
pf) **3** (reduce: price) zniżać (zniżyć
pf) **4** (abandon: idea, case etc)
porzucać (porzucić pf) **5** (from
team) odpadać (odpaść pf)
▷ vi **1** (fall) spadać (spaść pf)
2 (die down: wind) przycichać
(przycichnąć pf) **3** (fall: voice)
zniżać (zniżyć pf); **drops** n pl
(medicine) krople; **a ~ of ten
percent** spadek o dziesięć
procent; **chocolate/fruit ~s**
drops czekoladowy/owocowy; **to
~ sb a line** skrobnąć do kogoś parę
słów; **to ~ a hint** robić (zrobić

pf) aluzję
▶ **drop by** vi (inf: visit) wpadać
(wpaść pf)
▶ **drop in** (inf) vi (visit): **to ~ in
(on sb)** wpadać (wpaść pf) (do
kogoś)
▶ **drop off** vi (fall asleep) zasypiać
(zasnąć pf) ▷ vt (passenger)
podrzucać (podrzucić pf)
▶ **drop out** vi **1** (withdraw)
wycofywać (wycofać pf) się **2** (of
college, university etc) porzucać
(porzucić pf)
drought [draut] n susza
drove [drəuv] pt of **drive**
drown [draun] vt **1** (person,
animal) topić (utopić pf) **2** (also: ~
out: sound, voice) zagłuszać
(zagłuszyć pf) ▷ vi (person, animal)
tonąć (utonąć pf)
drug [drʌg] n **1** (prescribed)
lekarstwo **2** (recreational)
narkotyk ▷ vt (sedate: person,
animal) podawać (podać pf)
środki nasenne +dat; **to be on ~s**
zażywać (zażyć pf) leki; **to take ~s**
brać leki; **hard/soft ~s** twarde/
miękkie narkotyki
druggist ['drʌgɪst] (US) n
1 (person) aptekarz(-rka) m/f
2: ~('s) (shop) apteka
drugstore ['drʌgstɔːʳ] (US) n
apteka

● **DRUGSTORE**
●
●
● W USA **drugstore** to drogeria
● pełniąca także funkcje
● kawiarenki. Poza lekarstwami
● i kosmetykami można tam
● również zamówić napoje i
● drobne przekąski.

drum [drʌm] *n* **1** (*instrument*)
bęben **2** (*container*) beczka ▷ *vi*
1 (*rain*) dudnić **2** (*with fingers*)
bębnić ▷ *vt* (*fingers*) bębnić;
drums *n pl* (*kit*) perkusja
▶ **drum up** *vt* (*enthusiasm,*
support) pozyskiwać (pozyskać *pf*)
drummer ['drʌmə^r] *n* perkusista
drunk [drʌŋk] *pp of* **drink** ▷ *adj*
pijany ▷ *n* (*drunkard*) pijak; **to get**
~ upijać (upić *pf*) się
dry [draɪ] *adj* **1** suchy
2 (*empty: lake, riverbed, well*)
wyschnięty **3** (*wine, sherry*)
wytrawny **4** (*humour, account*)
ironiczny **5** (*uninteresting: lecture,*
style) nudny ▷ *vt* (*clothes, hair*)
wysuszać (wysuszyć *pf*) ▷ *vi*
(*paint, washing*) wysychać
(wyschnąć *pf*); **on ~ land** na
suchym lądzie; **to ~ (up) the**
dishes wycierać (wytrzeć *pf*)
naczynia; **to ~ one's hands/hair**
suszyć (wysuszyć *pf*) ręce/włosy;
to ~ one's eyes ocierać (otrzeć
pf) łzy
▶ **dry off** *vi* wysychać (wyschnąć
pf) ▷ *vt* wychychać (wyschnąć *pf*)
▶ **dry out** *vi* wysychać (wyschnąć
pf)
▶ **dry up** *vi* **1** (*river, well*) wysychać
(wyschnąć *pf*) **2** (*supply, flow etc*)
wyczerpywać (wyczerpać *pf*) się
dry-cleaner ['draɪ'kliːnə^r] *n*
(*also*: **dry cleaner's**) pralnia
chemiczna
dryer ['draɪə^r] *n* suszarka
dub [dʌb] *vt* **1** (*film, TV programme*)
dubbingować (zdubbingować
pf) **2** (*nickname*): **a man ~bed**
"the terminator" człowiek
zwany "terminator"; **~bed into**

Spanish/French z hiszpańskim/
francuskim dubbingiem
duck [dʌk] *n* kaczka ▷ *vi* (*also:* **~**
down) schylać (schylić *pf*) się
▷ *vt* (*blow*) uchylać (uchylić *pf*) się
przed +*inst*
due [djuː] *adj* **1** (*person, train,*
bus) planowy przyjazd **2**: **to be ~**
(*baby*) mieć termin porodu **3** (*rent,*
payment) należny **4**: **to be ~ to**
sb (*owed: money, holidays*) należeć
się komuś **5** (*proper: consideration*)
stosowny ▷ *n*: **to give sb his/her**
~ oddawać (oddać *pf*) mu/jej
sprawiedliwość ▷ *adv*: **~ north/**
south dokładnie na północ/
południe; **dues** *n pl* (*for club,*
union) składki; **~ to...** (*because of*) z
powodu +*gen*...; **to be ~ to sth/sb**
przysługiwać czemuś/komuś;
in ~ course (*eventually*) we
właściwym czasie
dug [dʌg] *pt, pp of* **dig**
dull [dʌl] *adj* **1** (*weather, day*)
pochmurny; (*light, colour*)
mroczny **2** (*boring*) nudny
3 (*sound, pain*) tępy ▷ *vt* **1** (*pain,*
grief) uśmierzać (uśmierzyć
pf) **2** (*mind, senses*) przytępiać
(przytępić *pf*)
dumb [dʌm] *adj* **1** (*mute, silent*)
niemy **2** (*pej: stupid, foolish*) tępy
3 (*US: inf: silly, annoying*) głupi; **to**
be struck ~ oniemieć (*pf*)
dummy ['dʌmɪ] *n* **1** (*Brit: for baby*)
smoczek **2** (*mannequin*) manekin
dump [dʌmp] *n* **1** (*tip: for rubbish*)
wysypisko **2** (*inf: pigsty, tip*) nora
3 (*store: for ammunition, arms*)
skład ▷ *vt* **1** (*put down*) rzucać
(rzucić *pf*) **2** (*get rid of*) wyrzucać
(wyrzucić *pf*) **3** (*computer data*)

zrzucać (zrzucić *pf*); **to be down in the ~s** (*inf*) być w dołku; **"no ~ing"** "zakaz wysypywania śmieci"
Dumpster® ['dʌmpstər] (*US*) *n* kontener
dungarees [dʌŋgə'ri:z] *n pl* (*for work*) kombinezon *sg*; (*for child, woman*) ogrodniczki
dungeon ['dʌndʒən] *n* loch
during ['djʊərɪŋ] *prep* **1** (*throughout*) podczas +*gen* **2** (*at some point in*) w trakcie +*gen*
dusk [dʌsk] *n* zmierzch; **at ~** o zmierzchu
dust [dʌst] *n* (*dirt: outdoors*) pył; (*indoors*) kurz ▷ *vt* **1** (*furniture*) odkurzać (odkurzyć *pf*) **2: to ~ sth with sth** (*cake: with flour, sugar*) posypywać (posypać *pf*) coś czymś
dustbin ['dʌstbɪn] (*Brit*) *n* kosz na śmieci
dustman ['dʌstmən] (*irreg*) *n* (*Brit*) śmieciarz
dusty ['dʌstɪ] *adj* zakurzony
Dutch [dʌtʃ] *adj* holenderski ▷ *n* (*language*) holenderski; **the Dutch** *n pl* (*people*) Holendrzy
duty ['dju:tɪ] *n* **1** (*responsibility*) obowiązek **2** (*tax*) cło; **duties** *n pl* (*tasks*) obowiązki; **it is my ~ to...** to mój obowiązek, aby...; **to pay ~ on sth** płacić (zapłacić *pf*) cło za coś; **to report for ~** meldować (zameldować *pf*) się na stanowisku pracy; **to be on/off ~** (*policeman, nurse*) być na/po służbie; **~ chemist/officer/doctor** dyżurny aptekarz/policjant/lekarz
duty-free ['dju:tɪ'fri:] *adj* (*drink, cigarettes*) wolnocłowy; **~ shop**

sklep wolnocłowy
duvet ['du:veɪ] (*Brit*) *n* kołdra
DVD *n* DVD
DVD player *n* odtwarzacz DVD
dwarf [dwɔ:f] [dwɔ:vz]) (*pl* **dwarves**) *n* (*in stories*) krasnoludek ▷ *adj* (*shrub, plant etc*) karłowaty
dying ['daɪɪŋ] *adj* **1** (*person, animal*) umierający **2** (*final*) ostatni ▷ *n pl*: **the ~** umierający
dynamic [daɪ'næmɪk] *adj* dynamiczny
dyslexia [dɪs'lɛksɪə] *n* dysleksja
dyslexic [dɪs'lɛksɪk] *n* dyslektyk(-yczka) *m/f* ▷ *adj*: **a ~ child** dziecko z dysleksją

e

each [i:tʃ] *adj* (*thing, person, idea*) każdy ▷ *pron* (*each one*) każdy; **~ one of them** każdy z nich; **~ other** nawzajem; **they have 2 books ~** mają po dwie książki każdy; **they cost 5 pounds ~** kosztują (po) pięć funtów za sztukę; **~ of us** każdy z nas

eagle ['i:gl] *n* orzeł

ear [ɪə^r] *n* (*Anat*) ucho

earlier ['ə:lɪə^r] *adj* wcześniejszy ▷ *adv* (*leave, go etc*) wcześniej; **~ this year** wcześniej w tym roku; **she left ~ than us** wyszła wcześniej niż my; **I can't come any ~** nie mogę przyjść wcześniej

early ['ə:lɪ] *adv* wcześnie ▷ *adj* 1 (*near the beginning: stage, career*) wczesny 2 (*in history*) pierwszy 3 (*premature: death,*

departure) przedwczesny 4 (*quick: reply*) szybki; **~ in the morning** wcześnie rano; **~ in the spring** wczesną wiosną; **the ~ 80s** we wczesnych latach osiemdziesiątych; **in the ~ 19th century** na początku dziewiętnastego wieku; **she's in her ~ forties** jest po czterdziestce; **you're ~!** jesteś wcześnie!

earn [ə:n] *vt* 1 (*salary, money*) zarabiać (zarobić *pf*) 2 (*Comm: interest*) przynosić (przynieść *pf*) 3 (*praise, reputation*) zyskiwać (zyskać *pf*); **to ~ one's** or **a living** zarabiać (zarobić *pf*) na życie

earnings ['ə:nɪŋz] *n pl* zarobki

earring ['ɪərɪŋ] *n* kolczyk

earth [ə:θ] *n* 1 (*also:* **the E~**: *planet*) Ziemia 2 (*land surface*) ziemia 3 (*soil*) ziemia

earthquake ['ə:θkweɪk] *n* trzęsienie ziemi

easily ['i:zɪlɪ] *adv* 1 (*without difficulty*) łatwo 2 (*for emphasis*) bez wątpienia 3 (*quickly*) łatwo 4 (*in a relaxed way*) swobodnie

east [i:st] *n* 1 wschód 2: **the E~** (*the Orient*) wschód ▷ *adj* wschodni ▷ *adv* na wschód; **the ~ of Spain** wschodnia część Hiszpanii; **to the ~** na wschód; **the ~ wind** wschodni wiatr; **~ of** na wschód od +*gen*

Easter ['i:stə^r] *n* Wielkanoc; **the ~ holidays** Święta Wielkanocne; **happy ~!** wesołych Świąt Wielkanocnych!

Easter egg *n* pisanka

eastern ['i:stən] *adj* 1 (*Geo*) wschodni 2: **~** (*oriental*)

dalekowschodni; **~ Europe**
Europa Wschodnia
easy ['iːzɪ] *adj* **1** (*simple*)
łatwy **2** (*relaxed*) spokojny
3 (*comfortable: life, time*)
łatwy **4** (*target, prey*) łatwy
▷ *adv*: **to take it** *or* **things ~** nie
przejmować się; **it's ~ for sb to
do sth** łatwo komuś coś zrobić;
to make life easier ułatwiać
(ułatwić *pf*) życie
eat [iːt] (*pt* **ate**, *pp* **eaten** ['iːtn])
vt (*food, breakfast, lunch, etc*) jeść
(zjeść *pf*) ▷ *vi* **1** (*consume food*) jeść
(zjeść *pf*) **2** (*have a meal*) jeść (zjeść
pf) posiłek
echo ['ɛkəu] (*pl* **echoes**) *n* **1** (*of
sound*) echo **2** (*of opinion, attitude*)
odbicie echem ▷ *vt* (*fig: repeat*)
powtarzać (powtórzyć *pf*)
▷ *vi* **1** (*sound*) odbijać (odbić
pf) się echem **2** (*cave, room*)
rozbrzmiewać (rozbrzmieć *pf*)
eco-friendly ['iːkəu'frendlɪ] *adj*
przyjazny dla środowiska
ecological [iːkə'lɒdʒɪkəl] *adj*
ekologiczny
ecology [ɪ'kɒlədʒɪ] *n*
1 (*environment*) ekosystem
2 (*subject*) ekologia
economic [iːkə'nɒmɪk]
adj **1** (*system, history, reform*)
gospodarczy **2** (*profitable: business
etc*) rentowny
economical [iːkə'nɒmɪkl]
adj **1** (*system, car, machine*)
ekonomiczny **2** (*person*) oszczędny
economics [iːkə'nɒmɪks] *n*
1 (*Scol, Univ*) ekonomia *f sg* **2** (*of
project, situation*) ekonomika *f sg*
economy [ɪ'kɒnəmɪ] *n* **1** (*of
country*) gospodarka **2** (*thrift*)

oszczędność
edge [ɛdʒ] *n* **1** (*border: of road,
town*) granica; (*of lake*) brzeg
2 (*of table, chair etc*) krawędź **3** (*of
knife, sword etc*) ostrze ▷ *vi*: **to
~ forward** posuwać (posunąć
pf) się do przodu; **to be on ~** być
spiętym
editor ['ɛdɪtər] *n* **1** (*of newspaper,
magazine, book*) redaktor(ka) *m/f*
2 (*of text, report*) redaktor(ka) *m/f*
3 (*Rad, TV*) montażysta(-tka) *m/f*
education [ɛdju'keɪʃən] *n*
(*schooling, teaching*) edukacja
educational [ɛdju'keɪʃənl]
adj **1** (*institution, policy,
needs*) oświatowy
2 (*instructive: experience*)
pouczający
educator ['ɛdjukeɪtər] (*esp US*) *n*
wychowawca(-czyni) *m/f*
effect [ɪ'fɛkt] *n* **1** (*result,
consequence*) skutek **2** (*impression*)
wrażenie; **effects** *n pl*
1 (*formal: belongings*) rzeczy
osobiste **2** (*Cine*) efekty specjalne;
to come into *or* **take ~** (*law*)
wchodzić (wejść *pf*) w życie; **to
take ~** (*drug*) zaczynać (zacząć
pf) działać; **to put** *or* **bring** *or*
carry sth into ~ wprowadzać
(wprowadzić *pf*) coś w życie; **to
have an ~ on sb/sth** mieć wpływ
na kogoś/coś; **in ~** w praktyce
effective [ɪ'fɛktɪv] *adj*
1 (*successful*) skuteczny
2 (*actual: leader, command*)
faktyczny; **to become ~** (*Law*)
wchodzić (wejść *pf*) w życie
effectively [ɪ'fɛktɪvlɪ] *adv*
1 (*successfully*) skutecznie **2** (*in
reality*) faktycznie

efficient [ɪ'fɪʃənt] adj (person)
sprawny; (organization, system)
wydajny

effort ['ɛfət] n 1 (energy) wysiłek
2 (attempt) próba 3 (physical/
mental exertion) trud; **to make an
~ to do sth** dokładać (dołożyć pf)
starań, aby coś zrobić

e.g. adv abbr (= exempli gratia) np.

egg [ɛg] n 1 (of bird, turtle etc) jajo
2 (for eating) jajko 3 (Bio) jajo

eggplant ['ɛgplɑːnt] (US) n
bakłażan

Egypt ['iːdʒɪpt] n Egipt

eight [eɪt] num osiem; see also
five

eighteen [eɪ'tiːn] num
osiemnaście; see also **fifteen**

eighteenth [eɪ'tiːnθ] num
osiemnasty; see also **fifth**

eighth [eɪtθ] num 1 ósmy
2 (fraction) ósma część; see also
fifth

eighty ['eɪtɪ] num osiemdziesiąt;
see also **fifty**

Eire ['ɛərə] n Irlandia

either ['aɪðər] adj 1 (one or other)
obojętnie który 2 (both, each)
i jeden i drugi ▷ pron 1 (after
negative) ani jeden ani drugi
2 (after interrogative) którykolwiek
▷ adv (in negative statements) też
(nie) ▷ conj: **~... or...** albo...albo;
on ~ side po obu stronach; **I
don't like ~ of them** nie lubię ani
jednego ani drugiego; **no, I don't
~** nie, ja też nie; **I haven't seen ~
one or the other** nie widziałem
ani jednego ani drugiego

elastic [ɪ'læstɪk] n (material)
elastik ▷ adj (stretchy) rozciągliwy

elastic band (Brit) n gumka

elbow ['ɛlbəu] n (Anat) łokieć
▷ vt: **to ~ one's way through the
crowd** przepychać (przepchnąć
pf) się przez tłum

elder ['ɛldər] adj (brother, sister etc)
starszy ▷ n (formal: older person)
osoba w podeszłym wieku; (in
tribe etc) starszyzna

elderly ['ɛldəlɪ] adj (old) starszy
▷ n pl: **the ~** ludzie starsi

eldest ['ɛldɪst] adj (child, daughter)
najstarszy ▷ n najstarszy

elect [ɪ'lɛkt] vt (government,
councillor, spokesman etc) wybierać
(wybrać pf); **to ~ to do sth**
(formal: choose) postanawiać
(postanowić pf) coś zrobić

election [ɪ'lɛkʃən] n wybory
m pl; **to hold an ~** przeprowadzać
(przeprowadzić pf) wybory

electric [ɪ'lɛktrɪk] adj
1 elektryczny 2 (fig: mood,
atmosphere) naelektryzowany

electrical [ɪ'lɛktrɪkl] adj
elektryczny

electrician [ɪlɛk'trɪʃən] n
elektryk

electricity [ɪlɛk'trɪsɪtɪ] n
1 (energy) elektryczność 2 (supply)
prąd ▷ adj (bill, meter) rachunek
za prąd

electronic [ɪlɛk'trɔnɪk] adj
elektroniczny

electronics [ɪlɛk'trɔnɪks] n
(technology) elektronika f sg

elegant ['ɛlɪgənt] adj 1 (person,
building) elegancki 2 (idea, prose)
zgrabny

elementary school (US) n
szkoła podstawowa

elephant ['ɛlɪfənt] n słoń

elevator ['ɛlɪveɪtər] (US) n winda

eleven [ɪ'lɛvn] *num* jedenaście; *see also* **five**

eleventh [ɪ'lɛvnθ] *num* jedenasty; *see also* **fifth**

else [ɛls] *adv*: **or ~** (*otherwise*) bo inaczej; (*threatening*) bo jak nie; **something ~, anything ~** coś innego; **where ~?** gdzie jeszcze?; **what ~?** co jeszcze?; **somewhere ~** gdzie indziej; **everywhere ~** wszędzie indziej; **everyone ~** wszyscy inni; **nobody ~** nikt inny; **if nothing ~** przynajmniej

email ['iːmeɪl] *n* email ▷ *vt* **1** (*person*) wysyłać (wysłać *pf*) emaila +*dat* **2** (*file, document*) wysyłać (wysłać *pf*)

email address *n* adres emailowy

embarrassed [ɪm'bærəst] *adj* (*laugh, silence*) pełen zażenowania; **to be ~** być zażenowanym

embarrassing [ɪm'bærəsɪŋ] *adj* **1** (*statement, situation*) żenujący **2** (*to politician, government*) kłopotliwy

embassy ['ɛmbəsɪ] *n* ambasada

emergency [ɪ'məːdʒənsɪ] *n* (*crisis*) nagły wypadek ▷ *adj* (*repair, talks, supplies, aid*) nadzwyczajny; **in an ~** w razie potrzeby

emigrate ['ɛmɪgreɪt] *vi* emigrować (wyemigrować *pf*)

emotion [ɪ'məʊʃən] *n* (*feeling*) uczucie

emotional [ɪ'məʊʃənl] *adj* **1** (*support, problems*) emocjonalny **2** (*person*) uczuciowy **3** (*speech, plea*) wzruszający; **to get ~** wzruszać (wzruszyć *pf*) się

emperor ['ɛmpərər] *n* cesarz

emphasize ['ɛmfəsaɪz] *vt* **1** (*word, point*) podkreślać (podkreślić *pf*) **2** (*make conspicuous*) uwydatniać (uwydatnić *pf*); **I must ~ that...** muszę podkreślić, że...

empire ['ɛmpaɪər] *n* imperium; **a business/publishing ~** imperium biznesowe/wydawnicze

employ [ɪm'plɔɪ] *vt* **1** (*person, workforce*) zatrudniać (zatrudnić *pf*) **2** (*use: methods, materials*) stosować (zastosować *pf*); **he was ~ed as a technician** był zatrudniony jako technik

employee [ɪmplɔɪ'iː] *n* pracownik(-ica) *m/f*

employer [ɪm'plɔɪər] *n* pracodawca(-czyni) *m/f*

employment [ɪm'plɔɪmənt] *n* (*work*) praca; **to find ~** znajdować (znaleźć *pf*) pracę; **to be in ~** mieć pracę

empty ['ɛmptɪ] *adj* **1** (*glass, container*) pusty **2** (*place, street*) wyludniony **3** (*house, room*) niezamieszkany **4** (*threat, gesture*) pusty ▷ *vt* **1** (*bin, ashtray*) opróżniać (opróżnić *pf*) **2** (*room, house etc*) opróżniać (opróżnić *pf*) ▷ *vi* (*room, building*) opróżniać (opróżnić *pf*) się; **to ~ sth into sth** (*pour out*) wylewać (wylać *pf*) coś z czegoś

enclose [ɪn'kləʊz] *vt* **1** (*garden, space*) otaczać (otoczyć *pf*) **2** (*object in wrapping etc*) zamykać (zamknąć *pf*) **3** (*in letter: cheque*) załączać (załączyć *pf*); **please find ~d** w załączeniu przesyłam

encourage [ɪn'kʌrɪdʒ] *vt* **1** (*person*) zachęcać (zachęcić *pf*) **2** (*activity, attitude*) sprzyjać **3** (*growth, industry*) zachęcać (zachęcić *pf*); **to ~ sb to do sth** zachęcać (zachęcić *pf*) kogoś do zrobienia czegoś; **to be ~d by sth** być zachęconym przez coś

encouragement [ɪn'kʌrɪdʒmənt] *n* (*support*) zachęta

end [ɛnd] *n* **1** (*of period, event*) koniec **2** (*of film, book*) zakończenie **3** (*of street, queue, rope, table*) koniec **4** (*of town*) kraniec **5** (*of pencil, finger etc*) końcówka **6** (*purpose*) cel ▷ *vt* (*fighting, strike*) kończyć (skończyć *pf*) ▷ *vi* kończyć (skończyć *pf*) się; **at the ~ of the day** (*fig*) koniec końców; **to come to an ~** kończyć (skończyć *pf*) się; **to be at an ~** kończyć się; **in the ~** w końcu; **for hours on ~** całymi godzinami; **to bring sth to an ~, put an ~ to sth** zakończyć (*pf*) coś; **to make ~s meet** wiązać koniec z końcem; **to ~ (up) in tragedy/disaster** skończyć (*pf*) się tragedią/katastrofą ▶ **end up** *vi*: **to ~ up in** (*place*) znaleźć (*pf*) się w +*loc*; **he ~ed up buying it himself** skończyło się tak, że sam to kupił

ending ['ɛndɪŋ] *n* (*of book, film, play etc*) zakończenie; **a happy ~** szczęśliwe zakończenie

endless ['ɛndlɪs] *adj* **1** (*drought, war, speech*) niekończący się **2** (*arguments, meetings*) niekończący się **3** (*forest, beach*) bezkresny **4** (*possibilities*) nieskończony

enemy ['ɛnəmɪ] *n* **1** (*opponent*) przeciwnik(-iczka) *m/f* **2**: **the ~** (*Mil*) wróg ▷ *adj* (*forces, strategy, aircraft*) nieprzyjacielski

energetic [ɛnə'dʒɛtɪk] *adj* **1** (*person*) energiczny **2** (*activity*) dynamiczny

energy ['ɛnədʒɪ] *n* **1** (*strength*) siła **2** (*power*) energia

engaged [ɪn'geɪdʒd] *adj* **1** (*to be married*) zaręczony **2** (*Brit: Tel*) zajęty **3** (*Brit: toilet*) zajęty; **to get ~ (to sb)** zaręczać (zaręczyć *pf*) się (z kimś)

engagement [ɪn'geɪdʒmənt] *n* **1** (*formal: appointment*) spotkanie **2** (*to marry*) zaręczyny *f pl*

engine ['ɛndʒɪn] *n* **1** (*Aut*) silnik **2** (*Rail*) lokomotywa

engineer [ɛndʒɪ'nɪər] *n* **1** (*who designs machines, bridges etc*) inżynier **2** (*who repairs machines, phones etc*) mechanik **3** (*US: train driver*) maszynista(-tka) *m/f*

engineering [ɛndʒɪ'nɪərɪŋ] *n* **1** (*of roads, bridges, machinery*) konstrukcja **2** (*science*) inżynieria

England ['ɪŋglənd] *n* Anglia

English ['ɪŋglɪʃ] *adj* angielski ▷ *n* (*language*) angielski; **the English** *n pl* (*people*) Anglicy; **an ~ speaker** osoba mówiąca po angielsku

Englishman ['ɪŋglɪʃmən] (*irreg*) *n* Anglik

Englishwoman ['ɪŋglɪʃwumən] (*irreg*) *n* Angielka

enjoy [ɪn'dʒɔɪ] *vt* **1** (*take pleasure in*) lubić **2** (*formal: have benefit of*) cieszyć się +*inst*; **to ~ doing sth** (*like doing*) lubić coś robić; **to ~ o.s.** dobrze się bawić; **~ your meal!** smacznego!

enjoyable [ɪn'dʒɔɪəbl] *adj*

przyjemny

enormous [ɪˈnɔːməs] *adj* **1** (*in size or amount*) olbrzymi **2** (*in degree or extent*) ogromny

enough [ɪˈnʌf] *adj* (*time, books, people*) dość +*gen* ▷ *pron* wystarczająco dużo ▷ *adv* **1: big/old/tall ~** wystarczająco duży/stary/wysoki **2** (*reasonably*): **it's nice/interesting ~** to dość miły/ciekawy; **~ time/money to do sth** dość czasu/pieniędzy, aby coś zrobić; **he has not worked ~** nie pracował wystarczająco dużo; **have you got ~?** wystarczy?; **~ to eat** dość do jedzenia; **will 5 be ~?** czy pięć wystarczy?; **I've had ~!** mam dość!; **he was kind ~ to lend me the money** był tak miły i pożyczył mi pieniądze; **(that's) ~!** wystarczy!; **I've had ~ of him** mam go dość; **that's ~, thanks** wystarczy, dziękuję

enquiry [ɪnˈkwaɪərɪ] *n* = **inquiry**

enter [ˈɛntəʳ] *vt* **1** (*formal: room, building*) wchodzić (wejść *pf*) do +*gen* **2** (*army, profession*) wstępować (wstąpić *pf*) do +*gen* **3** (*race, competition*) zgłaszać (zgłosić *pf*) się do +*gen* **4** (*new phase, period*) zaczynać (zacząć *pf*) **5** (*Comput: data*) wprowadzać (wprowadzić *pf*) do +*gen* ▷ *vi* (*formal: come or go in*) wchodzić (wejść *pf*); **to ~ sb for sth** (*for competition, race*) zgłaszać (zgłosić *pf*) kogoś do czegoś

▶ **enter into** (*formal*) *vt fus* (*agreement, talks*) podejmować (podjąć *pf*)

entertain [ɛntəˈteɪn] *vt* **1** (*amuse*) zabawiać (zabawić

pf) **2** (*invite: guest*) podejmować (podjąć *pf*) **3** (*formal: consider idea, suggestion*) rozważać (rozważyć *pf*) ▷ *vi* zabawiać (zabawić *pf*) się

enthusiasm [ɪnˈθuːzɪæzəm] *n* (*eagerness*) entuzjazm; **~ for sth** zapał do czegoś

enthusiastic [ɪnθuːzɪˈæstɪk] *adj* (*excited, eager: person*) zapalony; (*response, reception*) entuzjastyczny; **to be ~ about sth** odnosić (odnieść *pf*) się do czegoś z entuzjazmem

entire [ɪnˈtaɪəʳ] *adj* cały

entirely [ɪnˈtaɪəlɪ] *adv* (*wholly*) całkowicie

entrance [ˈɛntrns] *n* wejście; **the ~ to sth** wejście do czegoś; **to gain ~ to** zostać przyjętym do +*gen*

entry [ˈɛntrɪ] *n* **1** (*way in*) wejście **2** (*in competition*) przystąpienie **3** (*item: in diary*) notatka; (*in reference book*) hasło; (*Comput*) wprowadzenie; **"no ~"** wstęp wzbroniony; (*Aut*) wjazd

envelope [ˈɛnvələup] *n* koperta

environment [ɪnˈvaɪərnmənt] *n* (*surroundings*) otoczenie; **the ~** (*natural world*) środowisko naturalne

environmental [ɪnvaɪərnˈmɛntl] *adj* **1** (*of the natural world*) ekologiczny **2** (*of surroundings*) środowiskowy

envy [ˈɛnvɪ] *n* (*jealousy*) zazdrość ▷ *vt* (*be jealous of*) być zazdrosnym o; **to ~ sb sth** zazdrościć komuś czegoś

episode [ˈɛpɪsəud] *n* **1** (*period, event*) wydarzenie **2** (*Rad, TV: instalment*) odcinek

equal ['iːkwl] *adj* **1** (*size, number, amount*) równy **2** (*intensity, importance*) jednakowy ▷ *n* (*peer*) równy ▷ *vt* **1** (*number, amount*) równać się **2** (*match, rival*) dorównywać (dorównać *pf*) +*dat*; **they are roughly ~ in size** są mniej więcej tego samego rozmiaru; **to be ~ to** (*the same*) być równym +*dat*; **79 minus 14 ~s 65** siedemdziesiąt dziewięć odjąć czternaście równa się sześćdziesiąt pięć

equality [iːˈkwɔlɪtɪ] *n* równość

equipment [ɪˈkwɪpmənt] *n* sprzęt

error ['ɛrər] *n* błąd; **to make an ~** robić (zrobić *pf*) błąd; **typing ~** literówka; **mathematical ~** błąd rachunkowy

escalator ['ɛskəleɪtər] *n* schody ruchome

escape [ɪsˈkeɪp] *n* **1** ucieczka **2** (*from accident*): **to have a narrow** *or* **lucky ~** o włos uniknąć (*pf*) nieszczęścia ▷ *vi* **1** (*get away*) uciekać (uciec *pf*) **2** (*from jail*) uciekać (uciec *pf*) **3** (*from accident*): **to ~ unhurt** wyjść (*pf*) cało **4** (*leak: liquid*) wyciekać (wyciec *pf*); (*gas*) ulatniać (ulotnić *pf*) się; (*heat*) uciekać (uciec *pf*) ▷ *vt* (*injury*) unikać (uniknąć *pf*) +*gen*; **to ~ from** (*place*) uciekać (uciec *pf*) do +*gen*

escort [*n* 'ɛskɔːt, *vb* ɪsˈkɔːt] *n* **1** (*Mil*) eskorta **2** (*companion*) osoba towarzysząca ▷ *vt* (*person*) towarzyszyć +*dat*; **to ~ sb to the door** odprowadzać (odprowadzić *pf*) kogoś do drzwi

especially [ɪsˈpɛʃlɪ] *adv* **1** (*particularly*) zwłaszcza **2** (*happy, gifted, fond of sb*) szczególnie

essay ['ɛseɪ] *n* **1** (*Scol*) wypracowanie **2** (*paper, discussion*) praca

essential [ɪˈsɛnʃl] *adj* **1** (*necessary, vital*) niezbędny **2** (*basic*) podstawowy; **essentials** *n pl* (*necessities*) rzeczy niezbędne; **it is ~ that...** musimy...; **it is ~ to...** należy koniecznie...

estate [ɪsˈteɪt] *n* **1** (*land*) posiadłość **2** (*Brit: also:* **housing ~**) osiedle mieszkaniowe **3** (*Law*) majątek

estate agent (*Brit*) *n* pośrednik(-iczka) *m/f* w handlu nieruchomościami

estimate [*n* 'ɛstɪmət, *vb* 'ɛstɪmeɪt] *n* **1** (*calculation*) obliczenie **2** (*assessment*) ocena **3** (*Comm: of price*) wycena ▷ *vt* (*reckon, calculate*) szacować (oszacować *pf*); **the damage was ~d at 300 million pounds** szkody oszacowano na trzysta milionów funtów; **I ~ that...** oceniam, że...

etc (*esp US* **etc.**) *abbr* (= *et cetera*) itd., itp.

ethnic [ˈɛθnɪk] *adj* etniczny

EU *n abbr* (= *European Union*): **the EU** UE

euro ['juərəu] *n* euro

Europe ['juərəp] *n* Europa

European [juərəˈpiːən] *adj* europejski ▷ *n* (*person*) Europejczyk(-jka) *m/f*

European Union *n*: **the ~** Unia Europejska

eve [iːv] *n*: **on the ~ of** w przeddzień +*gen*

even ['iːvn] *adv* nawet ▷ *adj* **1** (*flat*) równy **2** (*constant: temperature, rate*) stały **3** (*equal*) równy **4** (*number*) parzysty; **~ more** nawet więcej; **~ better/faster** jeszcze lepiej/szybciej; **~ if** nawet jeśli; **~ though** mimo że; **~ so** mimo wszystko; **not ~** nawet nie; **~ he was there** nawet on tam był; **~ on Sundays** nawet w niedziele; **to break ~** wychodzić (wyjść *pf*) na zero; **to get ~ with sb** (*inf*) policzyć (*pf*) się z kimś

evening ['iːvnɪŋ] *n* wieczór; **in the ~** wieczorem; **this ~** dziś wieczorem; **tomorrow/ yesterday ~** jutro/wczoraj wieczorem

evening class *n* kurs wieczorowy

event [ɪ'vɛnt] *n* **1** (*occurrence*) zdarzenie **2** (*Sport*) konkurencja; **in the ~ of...** w razie +*gen*...

eventual [ɪ'vɛntʃuəl] *adj* (*outcome, aim*) ostateczny

eventually [ɪ'vɛntʃuəlɪ] *adv* **1** (*finally*) ostatecznie **2** (*ultimately*) w końcu

ever ['ɛvəʳ] *adv* **1** (*at any time*) kiedykolwiek **2** (*always*) zawsze; **have you ~ seen it/been there?** czy kiedykolwiek widziałeś to/ byłeś tam?; **~ since** (*adv*) od tego czasu; (*conj*) od kiedy; **why ~ not?** ależ dlaczego nie?; **who ~ would do such a thing?** kto zrobił by coś takiego?; **the best ~** najlepszy; **hardly ~** prawie nigdy; **better than ~** lepszy niż kiedykolwiek;

as ~ jak zawsze

○ **KEYWORD**

every ['ɛvrɪ] *adj* **1** (*each*) każdy; **every village should have a post office** każda wioska powinna mieć pocztę; **every one of them** (*people*) każdy z nich; (*objects*) każdy z nich **2** (*all possible*) każdy; **there is every chance that...** są wszelkie szanse, że...; **recipes for every occasion** przepisy na każdą okazję **3** (*with time words*) każdy; **every day/week** każdego dnia/każdego tygodnia; **every Sunday** w każdą niedzielę; **every other week** co drugi tydzień; **every other/third day** co drugi/trzeci dzień; **every few days/minutes** co kilka dni/minut; **every now and then** *or* **again** od czasu do czasu **4** (*statistics*): **one in every five people** co piąta osoba

everybody ['ɛvrɪbɔdɪ] *pron* wszyscy; **~ knows about it** wszyscy o tym wiedzą; **~ else** wszyscy inni

everyone ['ɛvrɪwʌn] *pron* = **everybody**

everything ['ɛvrɪθɪŋ] *pron* wszystko; **is ~ OK?** czy wszystko w porządku?; **he did ~ possible** zrobił wszystko co było można

everywhere ['ɛvrɪwɛəʳ] *adv* wszędzie ▷ *pron* wszędzie; **there's rubbish ~** wszędzie są śmieci; **~ you go** gdziekolwiek pójdziesz

evil ['iːvl] *adj (person, system)* zły
▷ *n (wickedness)* zło
exact [ɪɡ'zækt] *adj* **1** *(time, number, word etc)* dokładny
2 *(person, worker)* dokładny **3** *(used for emphasis)* dokładnie
exactly [ɪɡ'zæktlɪ] *adv*
1 *(precisely)* dokładnie **2** *(indicating emphasis)* właśnie **3** *(indicating agreement)* właśnie tak; **at 5 o'clock ~** punktualnie o piątej;
not ~ *(indicating disagreement)* niezupełnie; **he's not ~ rich/poor** właściwie nie jest bogaty/biedny
exaggerate [ɪɡ'zædʒəreɪt] *vi* przesadzać (przesadzić *pf*) ▷ *vt*
1 *(situation, effects)* wyolbrzymiać (wyolbrzymić *pf*) **2** *(feature, quality)* popadać (popaść *pf*) w przesadę
exam [ɪɡ'zæm] *n* egzamin
examination [ɪɡzæmɪ'neɪʃən] *n* **1** *(inspection)* kontrola
2 *(formal: Scol, Univ)* egzamin
3 *(Med)* badanie
examine [ɪɡ'zæmɪn] *vt*
1 *(inspect)* sprawdzać (sprawdzić *pf*) **2** *(Scol, Univ)* egzaminować (przeegzaminować *pf*) **3** *(Med)* badać (zbadać *pf*)
example [ɪɡ'zɑːmpl] *n* przykład;
for ~ na przykład; **an ~ of sth** przykład czegoś; **to set an ~** dawać (dać *pf*) przykład; **to follow sb's ~** iść za przykładem kogoś
excellent ['ɛksələnt] *adj* doskonały ▷ *int*: **~!** doskonale!
except [ɪk'sɛpt] *prep (apart from)* poza +*inst*; **~ for** poza +*inst*; **~ that...** tyle tylko, że...; **~ if/when** chyba że

exception [ɪk'sɛpʃən] *n (special case)* wyjątek; **to make an ~** robić (zrobić *pf*) wyjątek; **with the ~ of** z wyjątkiem +*gen*; **to take ~ (to sth)** czuć (poczuć *pf*) się dotkniętym (czymś)
exchange [ɪks'tʃeɪndʒ] *vt*
1 wymieniać (wymienić *pf*) **2**: **to ~ sth (for sth)** *(goods)* zamieniać (zamienić *pf*) coś (na coś) ▷ *n* wymiana; **in ~ (for)** w zamian (za)
exchange rate *n* kurs wymiany walut
excited [ɪk'saɪtɪd] *adj* podekscytowany; **to be ~ about sth/about doing sth** być podekscytowanym czymś/z powodu robienia czegoś; **to get ~** zachwycać (zachwycić *pf*) się
excitement [ɪk'saɪtmənt] *n (exhilaration)* rozemocjonowanie
exciting [ɪk'saɪtɪŋ] *adj (time, event, place)* ekscytujący
exclamation mark *(US* **exclamation point)** *n* wykrzyknik
excuse [*n* ɪks'kjuːs, *vb* ɪks'kjuːz] *n (justification)* usprawiedliwienie ▷ *vt* **1** *(justify: person, behaviour)* usprawiedliwiać (usprawiedliwić *pf*) **2** *(forgive: person, behaviour)* wybaczać (wybaczyć *pf*); **an ~ to do/not to do sth** wymówka do robienia/do nie robienia czegoś; **to make an ~** znajdować (znaleźć *pf*) wymówkę; **to make ~s for sb** tłumaczyć (wytłumaczyć *pf*) się za kogoś; **there's no ~ for such behaviour** nie ma usprawiedliwienia dla takiego zachowania; **to be ~d from (doing) sth** zostawać (zostać

pf) zwolnionym z (robienia) czegoś; **to ~ sb for sth/for doing sth** przepraszać (przeprosić *pf*) kogoś za coś/za zrobienie czegoś; **~ me!** (*attracting attention*) przepraszam!; (*as apology*) przepraszam; **~ me, please** przepraszam; **~ me?** (*US*) słucham?

exercise ['ɛksəsaɪz] *n* **1** (*physical exertion*) ćwiczenie **2** (*series of movements*) gimnastyka **3** (*Scol, Mus*) ćwiczenie **4** (*Mil*) musztra ▷ *vt* **1** (*use*) wykazywać (wykazać *pf*) się **2** (*muscles*) ćwiczyć; (*mind*) ćwiczyć ▷ *vi* (*person*) ćwiczyć; **to take** *or* **get ~** ćwiczyć; **to do ~s** (*Sport*) gimnastykować się; **to ~ one's right to do sth** korzystać (wykorzystać *pf*) prawo do zrobienia czegoś

exhausted [ɪg'zɔːstɪd] *adj* (*tired*) wyczerpany

exhibition [ɛksɪ'bɪʃən] *n* **1** (*of paintings etc*) wystawa **2** (*display: of skill, talent etc*) pokaz

exist [ɪg'zɪst] *vi* **1** (*be present*) istnieć **2** (*live, subsist*) egzystować; **to ~ on sth** żywić się czymś

exit ['ɛksɪt] *n* **1** (*from room, building, motorway etc*) wyjście **2** (*departure*): **to make a hasty** *or* **quick ~** ulatniać (ulotnić *pf*) się ▷ *vt* **1** (*formal: room, building*) wychodzić (wyjść *pf*) z +*gen* **2** (*Comput*) wychodzić (wyjść *pf*) z +*gen*

expect [ɪks'pɛkt] *vt* **1** (*anticipate*) oczekiwać +*gen* **2** (*await*) spodziewać się +*gen* **3** (*baby*) spodziewać się +*gen* **4** (*require*) oczekiwać +*gen* **5** (*suppose*)

przypuszczać ▷ *vi*: **to be ~ing** (*be pregnant*) spodziewać się dziecka; **to ~ sth to happen** spodziewać się czegoś; **to ~ sb to do sth** (*anticipate*) spodziewać się, że ktoś coś zrobi; **to ~ to do sth** planować coś; **I ~ so** sądzę, że tak; **as ~ed** jak się spodziewano

expedition [ɛkspə'dɪʃən] *n* wyprawa

expel [ɪks'pɛl] *vt* **1** (*child: from school*) wydalać (wydalić *pf*) z +*gen* **2** (*person: from place*) usuwać (usunąć *pf*) z +*gen*

expensive [ɪks'pɛnsɪv] *adj* **1** (*article*) drogi **2** (*mistake*) kosztowny; (*tastes*) drogi

experience [ɪks'pɪərɪəns] *n* doświadczenie ▷ *vt* (*feeling, problem*) doświadczać (doświadczyć *pf*) +*gen*

experienced [ɪks'pɪərɪənst] *adj* doświadczony

experiment [*n* ɪks'pɛrɪmənt, *vb* ɪks'pɛrɪmɛnt] *n* **1** (*Sci*) eksperyment **2** (*trial*) doświadczenie ▷ *vi* **1: to ~ (with/on)** (*Sci*) przeprowadzać (przeprowadzić *pf*) eksperyment (z +*inst*/na +*loc*) **2** (*fig*) próbować (spróbować *pf*) **2**; **to perform** *or* **conduct** *or* **carry out an ~** przeprowadzać (przeprowadzić *pf*) eksperyment

expert ['ɛkspəːt] *n* (*specialist*) specjalista(-tka) *m/f* ▷ *adj* (*help, advice*) fachowy; **an ~ on sth** specjalista od czegoś; **to be ~ in** *or* **at doing sth** radzić sobie doskonale z robieniem czegoś

expire [ɪks'paɪəʳ] *vi* (*passport, licence etc*) tracić (stracić *pf*)

ważność
explain [ɪks'pleɪn] *vt* **1** (*clarify*)
tłumaczyć (wytłumaczyć *pf*)
2 (*give reasons for*) wyjaśniać
(wyjaśnić *pf*); **to ~ why/how**
wyjaśniać (wyjaśnić *pf*) dlaczego/
jak; **to ~ sth to sb** wyjaśniać
(wyjaśnić *pf*) coś komuś; **to ~
that...** wyjaśniać (wyjaśnić *pf*), że...
explanation [ɛksplə'neɪʃən] *n*
1 (*reason*): **~ (for sth)** wyjaśnienie
(czegoś) **2** (*description*): **~ (of sth)**
wytłumaczenie (czegoś)
explode [ɪks'pləud] *vi* **1** (*bomb*)
wybuchać (wybuchnąć *pf*)
2 (*population*) gwałtownie
wzrastać (wzrosnąć *pf*)
3 (*person: with rage etc*) wybuchać
(wybuchnąć *pf*) ▷ *vt* **1** (*bomb, tank*)
eksplodować **2** (*myth, theory*)
obalać (obalić *pf*)
explore [ɪks'plɔːʳ] *vt* **1** (*place,
space*) penetrować (spenetrować
pf) **2** (*with hands*) badać (zbadać
pf) **3** (*idea, suggestion*) zgłębiać
(zgłębić *pf*) ▷ *vi* (*look around*)
prowadzić (przeprowadzić *pf*)
poszukiwania
explosion [ɪks'pləuʒən] *n* **1** (*of
bomb*) wybuch **2** (*increase: of
population*) gwałtowny wzrost
3 (*outburst: of rage, laughter etc*)
wybuch
export [*vb* ɛks'pɔːt, *n, adj* 'ɛkspɔːt]
vt eksportować (wyeksportować
pf) ▷ *n* **1** (*process*) eksport
2 (*product*) towar eksportowy
▷ *adj* (*duty, permit, licence*)
eksportowy
express [ɪks'prɛs] *vt* **1** (*idea,
view, concern*) wyrażać
(wyrazić *pf*) **2** (*formal: quantity,*

number): **~ed as a percentage/
fraction** wyrażone w
procentach/ułamkach ▷ *adj*
1 (*formal: command, wishes etc*)
wyraźny **2** (*purpose, intention*)
wyraźny **3** (*service, mail*)
ekspresowy ▷ *n* (*train, coach*)
ekspres ▷ *adv* (*send*) ekspresowo;
to ~ o.s. wyrażać (wyrazić *pf*) się
expression [ɪks'prɛʃən] *n*
1 (*word, phrase*) wyrażenie **2** (*on
face*) wyraz **3** (*of idea, emotion*)
wyraz **4** (*feeling: of actor, singer etc*)
ekspresja
extension [ɪks'tɛnʃən] *n* **1** (*of
building*) przybudówka **2** (*of
contract, visa*) przedłużenie **3** (*of
rights, campaign, idea*) rozszerzenie
4 (*Elec*) przedłużacz **5** (*of road,
railway*) przedłużenie **6** (*Tel*)
numer wewnętrzny; **~ 3718** (*Tel*)
numer wewnętrzny trzydzieści
siedem osiemnaście
extent [ɪks'tɛnt] *n* **1** (*of area, land
etc*) rozmiar **2** (*of problem, damage
etc*) zakres; **to a certain ~** w
pewnym stopniu; **to a large ~** w
znacznym stopniu; **to some ~** do
pewnego stopnia; **to what ~?** do
jakiego stopnia?
extinct [ɪks'tɪŋkt] *adj* (*animal,
plant*) wymarły
extra ['ɛkstrə] *adj* (*thing,
person, amount*) dodatkowy
▷ *adv* **1** (*in addition*) dodatkowo
2 (*inf: particularly*) szczególnie ▷ *n*
1 (*luxury*) dodatek **2** (*surcharge*)
dodatek **3** (*Cine, Theat*)
statysta(-tka) *m/f*; **wine will cost
~** za wino trzeba zapłacić osobno
extraordinary [ɪks'trɔːdnrɪ]
adj **1** (*exceptional*) niezwykły

2 (formal: meeting) nadzwyczajny
extreme [ɪks'triːm] adj 1 (poverty, caution) skrajny 2 (opinions, methods etc) ekstremalny 3 (point, edge) skrajny
extremely [ɪks'triːmlɪ] adv wyjątkowo
extremist [ɪks'triːmɪst] n ekstremista(-tka) m/f ▷ adj (views, group) ekstremistyczny
eye [aɪ] n (Anat) oko; **to keep an ~ on sb/sth** pilnować kogoś/ czegoś; **to catch sb's ~** (action, movement) zwracać (zwrócić pf) czyjąś uwagę; (person: deliberately) ściągać (ściągnąć pf) kogoś wzrokiem; **to have one's ~ on sth** (inf: want) mieć na coś oko; **to keep an ~ out for sb/sth** rozglądać (rozejrzeć pf) się za kimś/czymś; **to look sb in the ~** or **to meet sb's ~s** patrzeć (popatrzeć pf) komuś w oczy
eyebrow ['aɪbrau] n brew
eyelash ['aɪlæʃ] n rzęsa
eyelid ['aɪlɪd] n powieka
eyesight ['aɪsaɪt] n wzrok

f

fabric ['fæbrɪk] n (cloth) tkanina
fabulous ['fæbjuləs] adj 1 (inf: fantastic) wspaniały 2 (extraordinary) bajeczny
face [feɪs] n 1 (Anat) twarz 2 (expression) mina 3 (of clock) tarcza ▷ vt 1 (direction: person) patrzeć (popatrzeć pf) na 2 (confront: unpleasant situation) stawać (stanąć pf) w obliczu +gen 3 ▷ vi: **to stand facing sth** (person) stać (stanąć pf) przodem do czegoś; **to ~ towards sth** (building, seat, car) wychodzić (wejść pf) na coś; **I can't** or **couldn't ~ it** nie mogę stawić temu czoła; **to come ~ to ~ with sb** stawać (stanąć pf) oko w oko z kimś; **to come ~ to ~ with sth** stawać (stanąć pf) oko w oko z

czymś
▶ **face up to** vt fus **1** (truth, facts)
godzić (pogodzić pf) się z +inst
2 (responsibilities, duties) sprostać
(pf) +dat
face cloth (Brit) n myjka do
twarzy
facility [fə'sɪlɪtɪ] n (service)
udogodnienie
fact [fækt] n fakt; **in (actual) ~**
or **as a matter of ~** (for emphasis)
faktycznie; (when disagreeing)
tak naprawdę; (when qualifying
statement) rzeczywiście; **~s and
figures** fakty i cyfry
factory ['fæktərɪ] n fabryka
fail [feɪl] vt (exam, test) nie zdać
(pf) +gen ▷ vi **1** (candidate) nie zdać
(pf) **2** (attempt, plan, remedy) nie
powieść (pf) się; **to ~ to do sth**
(not succeed) nie zdołać (pf) czegoś
zrobić; **without ~** (definitely)
z całą pewnością; (without
exception) niezawodnie
failure ['feɪljər] n **1** (lack of
success) niepowodzenie **2** (person)
nieudacznik(-ica) m/f; **~ in sth**
niezrobienie czegoś
faint [feɪnt] adj **1** (sound, light,
smell, hope) słaby **2** (mark, trace)
niewyraźny ▷ vi (Med) zasłabnąć
(pf); **to feel ~** czuć (poczuć pf)
się słabo
fair [feər] adj **1** (person, decision,
trial) sprawiedliwy **2** (size, number,
distance) spory **3** (chance, guess,
idea) niezły **4** (skin, complexion)
jasny; (hair) blond ▷ n **1** (trade
fair) targi m pl **2** (Brit: also: **fun~**)
wesołe miasteczko; **it's not ~!** to
niesprawiedliwe!
fairground ['fɛəgraund] n

wesołe miasteczko
fairly ['fɛəlɪ] adv **1** (justly: share,
distribute) sprawiedliwie
2 (quite: heavy, fast, good) dość
fairy ['fɛərɪ] n wróżka
fairy tale n bajka
faith [feɪθ] n wiara; **to have
~ in sb/sth** ufać (zaufać pf)
komuś/czemuś
faithful ['feɪθful] adj wierny
faithfully ['feɪθfəlɪ] adv wiernie;
yours ~ (Brit) z wyrazami
szacunku
fake [feɪk] n (painting, antique,
document) imitacja ▷ adj (painting,
document) fałszywy
fall [fɔːl] (pt **fell**, pp **fallen**) vi
1 (person, object) spadać (spaść pf)
2 (fall over: person, building) upadać
(upaść pf) **3** (snow, rain) padać
(spaść pf) **4** (price, temperature,
currency) spadać (spaść pf) ▷ n
1 (of person) upadek **2** (in price,
temperature) spadek **3** (US: autumn)
jesień; **to ~ in love (with sb/sth)**
zakochiwać (zakochać pf) się (w
kimś/czymś)
▶ **fall down** vi **1** (person) upadać
(upaść pf) **2** (building) spadać
(spaść pf)
▶ **fall for** vt fus **1** (trick, story, lie)
dawać (dać pf) się nabrać na
2 (person) zakochiwać (zakochać
pf) się w +loc
▶ **fall off** vi (person, object)
odpadać (odpaść pf)
▶ **fall out** vi (friends) kłócić
(pokłócić pf) się; **to ~ out
with sb** kłócić (pokłócić pf) się
z kimś
▶ **fall over** vi (person, object)
przewracać (przewrócić pf) się

▶ **fall through** vi (plan) nie udać (pf) się

fallen ['fɔːlən] pp of **fall**

false [fɔːls] adj 1 (artificial) sztuczny 2 (untrue) fałszywy

fame [feɪm] n sława

familiar [fəˈmɪlɪəʳ] adj (well-known) znajomy; **to be ~ with** (subject) znać

family ['fæmɪlɪ] n rodzina

famine ['fæmɪn] n głód

famous ['feɪməs] adj znany

fan [fæn] n 1 (admirer) fan(ka) m/f 2 (Elec) wentylator 3 (folding) wachlarz

fanatic [fəˈnætɪk] n fanatyk(-yczka) m/f

fancy ['fænsɪ] vt 1 (esp Brit: inf: feel like, want) mieć ochotę na 2 (inf: person): **she really fancies him** on bardzo jej się podoba; **~ seeing you here!** ty tutaj?

fancy dress n kostium

fancy-dress party ['fænsɪdrɛs-] n bal przebierańców

fantastic [fænˈtæstɪk] adj 1 (wonderful) fantastyczny 2 (enormous) niesamowity

FAQ n abbr (= frequently asked question) FAQ (często zadawane pytania)

far [fɑːʳ] adj 1 (distant) daleki 2 (extreme): **the ~ end/side** drugi koniec ▷ adv 1 (a long way) daleko 2 (much, greatly) o wiele; **as ~ as I know** o ile wiem; **by ~** zdecydowanie; **so ~** jak do tej pory; **is it ~ to London?** czy daleko jest stąd do Londynu?; **it's not ~ from here** to niedaleko stąd; **how ~?** (in distance) jak daleko?; (in degree) jak bardzo?; (in progress) jak daleko?; **~ away** daleko; **~ better** znacznie lepszy

fare [fɛəʳ] n (price) opłata za przejazd; **half ~/full ~** opłata ze zniżką/pełna opłata

Far East n: **the ~** Daleki Wschód

farm [fɑːm] n gospodarstwo rolne

farmer ['fɑːməʳ] n rolnik

farmhouse ['fɑːmhaus] n dom wiejski

farming ['fɑːmɪŋ] n rolnictwo

fascinating ['fæsɪneɪtɪŋ] adj fascynujący

fashion ['fæʃən] n moda; **in ~** w modzie

fashionable ['fæʃnəbl] adj modny

fast [fɑːst] adj szybki ▷ adv (run, act, think) szybko; **my watch is 5 minutes ~** mój zegarek spieszy się o pięć minut; **~ asleep** pogrążony w głębokim śnie; **as ~ as I can** tak jak mogę najszybciej

fast food n (burger etc) fast food

fat [fæt] adj gruby ▷ n tłuszcz

fatal ['feɪtl] adj 1 (accident, injury, illness) śmiertelny 2 (fig: mistake) fatalny

father ['fɑːðəʳ] n 1 (parent) ojciec 2 (Rel) ksiądz

Father Christmas (Brit) n Święty Mikołaj

father-in-law ['fɑːðərɪnlɔː] (pl **fathers-in-law**) n teść

faucet ['fɔːsɪt] (US) n kran

fault [fɔːlt] n 1 (mistake) błąd 2 (defect: in person) wada; (in machine) usterka; **it's my ~** to moja wina

fava bean ['fɑːvə-] (US) n bób

favour ['feɪvəʳ] (US **favor**) n

(*approval*) przychylność (*act
of kindness*) przysługa; **to ask
a ~ of sb** prosić (poprosić *pf*)
kogoś o przysługę; **to do sb a ~**
wyświadczać (wyświadczyć *pf*)
komuś przysługę; **to be in ~ of
sth/doing sth** być za czymś/
zrobieniem czegoś
favourite ['feɪvrɪt] (*US* **favorite**)
adj ulubiony ▷ *n* **1** (*person*)
ulubieniec(-ica) *m/f* **2** (*in race*)
faworyt(ka) *m/f*
fax [fæks] *n* **1** (*document*)
faks **2** (*also:* **~ machine**) faks
▷ *vt* (*document*) faksować
(przefaksować *pf*)
fear [fɪəʳ] *n* **1** (*terror*) strach
2 (*anxiety*) lęk ▷ *vt* (*be scared of*) bać
się +*gen*; **to ~ that...** bać się, że...
feather ['fɛðəʳ] *n* (*of bird*) pióro
feature ['fiːtʃəʳ] *n* (*characteristic*)
cecha
February ['fɛbruərɪ] *n* luty; *see
also* **July**
fed [fɛd] *pt, pp of* **feed**
fed up (*inf*) *adj*: **to be ~ with sth**
mieć czegoś dosyć
fee [fiː] *n* opłata
feeble ['fiːbl] *adj* **1** (*person, animal,
voice*) słaby **2** (*attempt, excuse,
argument*) nieprzekonujący
feed [fiːd] (*pt, pp* **fed**) *vt* **1** (*baby,
invalid, dog*) karmić (nakarmić *pf*)
2 (*family*) żywić (wyżywić *pf*)
feel [fiːl] (*pt, pp* **felt**) *vt*
1 (*touch: object, face*) dotykać
(dotknąć *pf*) +*gen* **2** (*experience*)
czuć (poczuć *pf*) **3** (*think, believe*)
sądzić; **to ~ that...** czuć (poczuć
pf), że...; **to ~ hungry** być
głodnym; **to ~ cold** odczuwać
(odcuć *pf*) zimno; **to ~ lonely/**

better czuć się samotnym/
lepszym; **I don't ~ well** nie czuję
się dobrze; **to ~ sorry for sb**
współczuć komuś; **it ~s colder
here** tu jest zimniej; **to ~ like**
(*want*) mieć ochotę na; **it ~s like** *or*
it ~s as if... wygląda na to, że...
feeling ['fiːlɪŋ] *n* **1** (*emotion*)
uczucie **2** (*physical sensation*)
uczucie **3** (*impression*) wrażenie;
feelings *n pl* **1** (*attitude*) opinia *f
sg* **2** (*emotions*) uczucia; **what are
your ~s about the matter?** jaka
jest twoja opinia o tej sprawie?; **I
have a ~ that...** mam wrażenie,
że...; **to hurt sb's ~s** ranić (zranić
pf) czyjeś uczucia
feet [fiːt] *n pl of* **foot**
fell [fɛl] *pt of* **fall**
felt [fɛlt] *pt, pp of* **feel** ▷ *n* (*fabric*)
filc
felt-tip pen, **felt-tip** ['fɛlttɪp-] *n*
flamaster
female ['fiːmeɪl] *n* **1** (*Zool*)
samica **2** (*woman*) kobieta ▷ *adj*
1 (*Zool*) żeński **2** (*sex, character,
child*) żeński **3** (*relating to women*)
kobiecy; **male and ~ students**
studenci i studentki
feminine ['fɛmɪnɪn] *adj*
1 (*clothing, behaviour*) kobiecy
2 (*Ling*) w rodzaju żeńskim
feminist ['fɛmɪnɪst] *n*
feminista(-tka) *m/f*
fence [fɛns] *n* (*barrier*) ogrodzenie
fencing ['fɛnsɪŋ] *n* (*Sport*)
szermierka
fern [fəːn] *n* paproć
ferry ['fɛrɪ] *n* (*also:* **~boat**) prom
festival ['fɛstɪvəl] *n* **1** (*Rel*) święto
2 (*Theat, Mus*) festiwal
fetch [fɛtʃ] *vt* (*bring*) przynosić

(przynieść *pf*); **to ~ sth for sb, ~
sb sth** przynosić (przynieść *pf*)
coś komuś

fever ['fiːvə^r] *n* (*Med*) gorączka

few [fjuː] *adj* **1** (*not many: vir*)
niewielu +*gen*; (*non-vir*) niewiele
+*gen* **2**: **a ~** (*some: vir*) kilku +*gen*;
(*non-vir*) kilka +*gen* ▷ *pron* **1**: **a
~ Poles/Americans** (*some*)
kilku Polaków/Amerykanów;
(*not many*) mało Polaków/
Amerykanów **2**: **in the next ~
days** przez kilka następnych dni;
in the past ~ days przez kilka
ostatnich dni; **a ~ of us/them**
kilku z nas/z nich; **a ~ more times**
jescze kilka razy; **very ~ survive**
niewielu przeżywa

fewer ['fjuːə^r] *adj* mniej; **no ~
than** nie mniej niż

fiancé [fɪ'ɔnseɪ] *n* narzeczony

fiancée [fɪ'ɔnseɪ] *n* narzeczona

fiction ['fɪkʃən] *n* (*novels, stories*)
literatura piękna

field [fiːld] *n* **1** (*grassland*) łąka
2 (*cultivated*) pole **3** (*Sport: pitch*)
boisko **4** (*subject, area of interest*)
dziedzina **5** (*Comput*) pole

fierce [fɪəs] *adj* **1** (*animal*)
groźny; (*battle*) zażarty
2 (*loyalty, resistance, competition*)
bezwzględny

fifteen [fɪf'tiːn] *num* piętnaście;
that will be ~ pounds, please
piętnaście funtów, proszę; **she's
~ (years old)** ma piętnaście
lat; **there are ~ of us** jest nas
piętnaście osób

fifteenth [fɪf'tiːnθ] *num*
piętnasty; *see also* **fifth**

fifth [fɪfθ] *num* **1** (*in series*) piąty
2 (*fraction*) piąta część ▷ *adv*: **to**

come ~ (*in race, competition*) zająć
piąte miejsce; **on July ~, on the ~
of July** piątego lipca

fifty ['fɪftɪ] *num* pięćdziesiąt;
he's in his fifties ma pięćdziesiąt
kilka lat

fight [faɪt] (*pt, pp* **fought**) *n*
walka ▷ *vt* walczyć z +*inst* ▷ *vi*
walczyć; **to ~ with sb** walczyć
z kimś; **to ~ for/against sth**
walczyć za czymś/przeciwko
czemuś

figure ['fɪgə^r] *n* **1** (*number, statistic*)
liczba **2** (*digit*) cyfra **3** (*body, shape*)
figura ▷ *vt* (*esp US: inf: reckon*)
myśleć (pomyśleć *pf*); **that ~s**
(*inf*) to jasne
▶ **figure out** (*inf*) *vt* (*work out*)
rozgryźć (*pf*)

file [faɪl] *n* **1** (*dossier*) akta *nt pl*
2 (*folder*) teczka **3** (*Comput*)
plik **4** (*tool*) pilnik ▷ *vt* **1** (*also: ~
away*: *papers, document*)
katalogować (skatalogować *pf*)
2 (*wood, metal, fingernails*) piłować
(opiłować *pf*)

fill [fɪl] *vt* **1** (*container*) napełniać
(napełnić *pf*) **2** (*space, area*)
wypełniać (wypełnić *pf*) **3** (*tooth*)
plombować (zaplombować *pf*);
to ~ sth with sth wypełniać
(wypełnić *pf*) coś czymś
▶ **fill in** *vt* (*esp Brit: form*)
wypełniać (wypełnić *pf*); (*name*)
wpisywać (wpisać *pf*)
▶ **fill out** *vt* (*form*) wypełniać
(wypełnić *pf*)
▶ **fill up** *vt* (*cup, saucepan*)
napełniać (napełnić *pf*); **~ it** *or* **her
up, please** (*Aut*) do pełna, proszę!
▷ *vi* (*room, stadium*) wypełniać
(wypełnić *pf*) się

filling ['fɪlɪŋ] n 1 (*in tooth*)
wypełnienie 2 (*of cake, pie,
sandwich*) nadzienie
film [fɪlm] n 1 (*esp Brit*: TV) film
2 (*Phot*) film ▷ vt (*scene, person,
book*) filmować (sfilmować *pf*)
film star n (*esp Brit*) gwiazda
filmowa
filthy ['fɪlθɪ] adj (*dirty*) brudny
final ['faɪnl] adj 1 (*last*) ostatni
2 (*definitive*) ostateczny ▷ n
(*Sport*) finał; **finals** n pl (*Sport*)
finał m sg
finally ['faɪnəlɪ] adv 1 (*eventually*)
w końcu 2 (*lastly*) na koniec
3 (*definitively*) ostatecznie
find [faɪnd] (*pt, pp* **found**)
vt 1 (*locate: person, object,
exit*) znajdować (znaleźć *pf*)
2 (*discover: answer, solution*)
odkrywać (odkryć *pf*) 3 (*get: work,
money, time*) znajdować (znaleźć
pf) ▷ n (*discovery*) odkrycie; **to ~
sb guilty/not guilty** uznawać
(uznać *pf*) kogoś za winnego/
niewinnego; **to ~ one's way (to)**
trafiać (trafić *pf*) (do +*gen*); **to ~
sth easy/difficult** uważać, że coś
jest łatwe/trudne
▶ **find out** vt (*fact, truth*)
dowiadywać (dowiedzieć *pf*) się
o czymś ▷ vi: **to ~ out about sth**
dowiadywać (dowiedzieć *pf*) się
o czymś
fine [faɪn] adj 1 (*satisfactory*)
dobry 2 (*excellent: object, person*)
świetny 3 (*in texture*) cienki
4 (*pleasant: weather, day*) piękny
▷ adv (*well*) świetnie ▷ n (*Law*)
grzywna ▷ vt (*Law*) karać (ukarać
pf) grzywną; **(I'm) ~** czuję się
dobrze; **(that's) ~** dobrze; **you're**

doing ~ idzie ci dobrze
finger ['fɪŋgəʳ] n (*Anat*) palec;
to keep one's ~s crossed (*fig*)
trzymać kciuki
fingernail ['fɪŋgəneɪl] n
paznokieć u ręki
finish ['fɪnɪʃ] n 1 (*end*) koniec
2 (*Sport*) finisz ▷ vt kończyć
(skończyć *pf*) ▷ vi kończyć
(skończyć *pf*); **to ~ doing sth**
kończyć (skończyć *pf*) coś robić
Finland ['fɪnlənd] n Finlandia
Finnish ['fɪnɪʃ] adj fiński ▷ n
(*language*) fiński
fir [fə:ʳ] n (*also*: **~ tree**) jodła
fire ['faɪəʳ] n ogień ▷ vt 1 (*shoot:
gun, bullet, shot, arrow*) strzelać
(strzelić *pf*) 2 (*inf: dismiss*)
zwalniać (zwolnić *pf*) ▷ vi (*shoot*)
wystrzeliwać (wystrzelić *pf*); **on ~**
w ogniu; **electric/gas ~** (*esp Brit*)
grzejnik elektryczny/gazowy; **to
catch ~** zapalić (*pf*) się
fire alarm n alarm pożarowy
fire brigade [-brɪgeɪd] n straż
pożarna
fire engine (*Brit*) n wóz strażacki
firefighter ['faɪəfaɪtəʳ] n strażak
fireman ['faɪəmən] (*irreg*) n
strażak
fireplace ['faɪəpleɪs] n kominek
fire station n remiza strażacka
fire truck (*US*) n wóz strażacki
firework ['faɪəwə:k] n (*explosive*)
fajerwerk; **fireworks** n pl (*display*)
pokaz m sg sztucznych ogni
firm [fə:m] adj 1 (*mattress, ground*)
twardy 2 (*person*) stanowczy ▷ n
(*company*) firma; **to be ~ with sb**
być stanowczym wobec kogoś
first [fə:st] adj pierwszy ▷ adv
1 (*before anyone else*) jako pierwszy

2 (*before other things*) najpierw
3 (*when listing reasons*) najpierw
4 (*for the first time*) po raz pierwszy
5 (*in race, competition*): **to come
~** zajmować (zająć *pf*) pierwsze
miejsce ▷ *n* (*Aut: also:* **~ gear**)
pierwszy bieg; **at ~** na początku;
the ~ of January pierwszy
stycznia; **to put sb/sth ~** stawiać
(postawić *pf*) kogoś/coś na
pierwszym miejscu

first aid *n* pierwsza pomoc
first-class [fəːstˈklɑːs] *adj*
1 (*excellent*) pierwszorzędny
2 (*carriage, ticket*) pierwszej klasy;
(*letter, stamp*) priorytetowy ▷ *adv*
(*travel*) pierwszą klasą; (*send*)
ekspresem
firstly [ˈfəːstlɪ] *adv* po pierwsze
first name *n* imię
fish [fɪʃ] *n* ryba ▷ *vi* (*commercially*)
łowić (złowić *pf*); (*as sport, hobby*)
łowić; **to go ~ing** iść na ryby
fisherman [ˈfɪʃəmən] (*irreg*) *n*
rybak; (*angler*) wędkarz
fishing [ˈfɪʃɪŋ] *n* rybołówstwo
fishing boat *n* kuter rybacki
fishing rod *n* wędka
fist [fɪst] *n* pięść
fit [fɪt] *adj* (*healthy*) w dobrej
formie ▷ *vt* (*clothes, shoes*)
pasować na ▷ *vi* **1** (*clothes,
shoes*) pasować **2** (*in space, gap*)
mieścić (zmieścić *pf*) się; **to keep
~** utrzymywać (utrzymać *pf*)
kondycję; **a ~ of giggles** atak
śmiechu; **to have a ~** (*Med*) mieć
atak; (*inf: fig*) dostać (*pf*) szału; **to
be a good ~** dobrze leżeć
▶ **fit in** *vi* **1** (*lit: person, object*)
mieścić (zmieścić *pf*) się
2 (*fig: person*) pasować ▷ *vt*

(*fig: appointment*) znajdować
(znaleźć *pf*) czas na; (*visitor*)
znajdować (znaleźć *pf*) czas
dla +*gen*
fitness [ˈfɪtnɪs] *n* (*Med*)
sprawność fizyczna
five [faɪv] *num* pięć; **that will be
~ pounds, please** pięć funtów,
proszę; **she's ~ (years old)** ma
pięć lat; **it's ~ o'clock** jest piąta;
there are ~ of us jest nas pięć
osób
fix [fɪks] *vt* **1** (*date, price, meeting*)
ustalać (ustalić *pf*) **2** (*machine,
leak, fault*) naprawiać (naprawić
pf) **3** (*problem*) rozwiązywać
(rozwiązać *pf*); **to ~ sth to/on
sth** (*attach*) przymocowywać
(przymocować *pf*) coś do czegoś
▶ **fix up** *vt* (*arrange*) organizować
(zorganizować *pf*)
fizzy [ˈfɪzɪ] (*Brit*) *adj* (*drink*)
gazowany
flag [flæg] *n* flaga
flame [fleɪm] *n* (*of fire*) płomień;
to burst into ~s stanąć w
płomieniach; **in ~s** w płomieniach
flan [flæn] *n* tarta
flap [flæp] *vt* (*arms, wings*)
machać (machnąć *pf*) +*inst*
flash [flæʃ] *vi* (*lightning, light*)
błyskać (błysnąć *pf*) ▷ *n* **1** (*of light,
lightning*) błysk **2** (*Phot*) flesz
3 (*US: inf: also:* **~light**) latarka;
in a ~ w okamgnieniu; **quick as
a ~** w okamgnieniu; **to ~ one's
headlights** dawać (dać *pf*)
sygnał światłami; **to ~ by** or **past**
przemykać (przemknąć *pf*)
flashlight [ˈflæʃlaɪt] (*esp US*) *n*
latarka
flask [flɑːsk] *n* (*also:* **vacuum**

~) termos

flat [flæt] adj **1** (level: ground, surface) płaski **2** (tyre, ball) flakowaty **3** (Brit: battery) rozładowany ▷ n (Brit: in building) mieszkanie ▷ adv (lie) płasko; **in 10 minutes ~** równo w dziesięć minut

flatter ['flætə^r] vt **1** (praise) pochlebiać **2: this hairstyle doesn't ~ her** nie do twarzy jej w tej fryzurze

flavour ['fleɪvə^r] (US **flavor**) n (of food, drink) smak ▷ vt (food, drink) przyprawiać (przyprawić pf); **strawberry-~ed** o smaku truskawkowym

flea [fliː] n pchła

flew [fluː] pt of **fly**

flexible ['flɛksəbl] adj elastyczny

flick [flɪk] vt (with fingers) pstrykać (pstryknąć pf) +inst; (switch) pstrykać (pstryknąć pf) +inst

▶ **flick through** vt fus (book, pages) przeglądać (przejrzeć pf)

flight [flaɪt] n **1** (Aviat) lot **2** (also: **~ of stairs, ~ of steps**) schody m pl

flight attendant [-ətɛndənt] n steward(esa) m/f

fling [flɪŋ] (pt, pp **flung**) vt (ball, stone, hat) ciskać (cisnąć pf); (one's arms) zarzucić (pf)

flipper ['flɪpə^r] n płetwa

float [fləʊt] vi **1** (on water: object) płynąć **2** (stay afloat: swimmer, object) unosić się na wodzie

flock [flɔk] n (of sheep, birds) stado

flood [flʌd] n **1** (of water) powódź **2** (of letters, requests, imports) zalew ▷ vt zalewać (zalać pf)

floor [flɔː^r] n **1** (of room) podłoga **2** (storey) piętro; **on the ~** na podłodze; **ground ~** (Brit) parter; **first ~** (Brit) pierwsze piętro; (US) parter

floppy ['flɔpɪ] n (also: **~ disk**) dyskietka

florist ['flɔrɪst] n **1** (shopkeeper) kwiaciarz(-rka) m/f **2** (also: **~'s**) kwiaciarnia

flour ['flaʊə^r] n mąka

flow [fləʊ] vi **1** (liquid, gas, electricity) płynąć **2** (traffic, people) napływać (napłynąć pf) ▷ n **1** (of liquid, gas) przepływ; (of electricity) prąd **2** (of traffic) przepływ

flower ['flaʊə^r] n kwiat ▷ vi (plant, tree) zakwitać (zakwitnąć pf); **in ~** w rozkwicie

flown [fləʊn] pp of **fly**

flu [fluː] n grypa

fluent ['fluːənt] adj biegły; **to speak ~ French, be ~ in French** mówić biegle po francusku

flung [flʌŋ] pt, pp of **fling**

flush [flʌʃ] n (of toilet) spłuczka ▷ vt: **to ~ the toilet** spuszczać (spuścić pf) wodę

flute [fluːt] n flet

fly [flaɪ] (pt **flew**, pp **flown**) vt **1** (plane) latać +inst **2** (distance) lecieć (przelecieć pf) **3** (kite) puszczać (puścić pf) ▷ vi latać ▷ n (insect) mucha; **to ~ into a rage** wpaść we wściekłość

▶ **fly away** vi (bird, insect) odlatywać (odlecieć pf)

focus ['fəʊkəs] (pl **focuses**) n **1** (Phot) ostrość **2** (fig: subject) nacisk ▷ vi: **to ~ (on)** (with camera) ustawiać (ustawić pf) ostrość (na); (fig: concentrate on) skupiać (skupić pf) się (na +loc); **in ~/out of ~** ostry/nieostry; **to be the ~ of attention** być w centrum zainteresowania; **to ~ (one's) attention on sb/sth** skupiać (skupić pf) (swoją) uwagę na kimś/czymś

fog [fɔg] n mgła

foggy ['fɔgɪ] adj (day, climate) mglisty; **it's ~** jest mgła

foil [fɔɪl] n (also: **kitchen ~**) folia aluminiowa

fold [fəʊld] n (in paper) zagięcie; (in cloth) fałda ▷ vt **1** (also: **~ up**: cloth, clothes, paper) składać (złożyć pf) **2** (one's arms, hands) splatać (spleść pf)

folder ['fəʊldəʳ] n (for papers) teczka

follow ['fɔləʊ] vt **1** (person: go behind) chodzić/iść (pójść pf) za +inst; (car) jechać (pojechać pf) za +inst **2** (take heed of) postępować (postąpić pf) zgodnie z +inst **3** (trace: route, path) biec wzdłuż +gen **4** (understand: event, story) nadążać (nadążyć pf) za +inst; **I don't quite ~ you** nie bardzo rozumiem pana/pani; **as ~s** (when listing) następujący; (in this way) następująco

following ['fɔləʊɪŋ] prep (after) po +loc ▷ adj **1** (next: day, week) następny **2** (next-mentioned: way, list etc) następny

fond [fɔnd] adj: **to be ~ of sb** lubić kogoś; **to be ~ of doing sth** (eating, walking) lubić coś robić

food [fuːd] n jedzenie

food poisoning [-pɔɪzənɪŋ] n zatrucie pokarmowe

fool [fuːl] n (idiot) głupiec ▷ vt (deceive) oszukiwać (oszukać pf); **you can't ~ me** nie oszukasz mnie ▶ **fool about, fool around** (pej) vi (behave foolishly) wygłupiać się

foot [fut] (pl **feet**) n **1** (measure) stopa **2** (of person) stopa **3** (of animal) łapa; **on ~** pieszo; **to put one's ~ down** (in car: accelerate) wciskać (wcisnąć pf) gaz; (say no) postawić (pf) się; **to put one's feet up** (relax) kłaść (położyć pf) się wygodnie

football ['futbɔːl] n **1** (ball) piłka nożna **2** (sport: Brit) piłka nożna; (US) futbol amerykański

footballer ['futbɔːləʳ] (Brit) n piłkarz(-rka) m/f

footpath ['futpɑːθ] n ścieżka

footprint ['futprɪnt] n (of person, animal) ślad

footstep ['futstɛp] n (sound) krok

○ **KEYWORD**

for [fɔːʳ] prep **1** (recipient) dla +gen; **is this for me?** czy to dla mnie?; **a table for two** stolik dla dwóch osób

2 (purpose) do +gen; **what's it for?** do czego to służy?; **it's time for lunch** czas na lunch; **what for?** po co?; **a knife for chopping vegetables** nóż do krojenia warzyw

3 (time): **he was away for two years** nie było go przez dwa lata; **she will be away for a month** nie będzie jej przez miesiąc; **it hasn't rained for three weeks** nie padało przez trzy tygodnie; **the trip is scheduled for June** **5** podróż jest zaplanowana na

piątego czerwca
4 (*in exchange for*): **I sold it for
£50** sprzedałem to za pięćdziesiąt
funtów; **to pay 50 pence for
a ticket** zapłacić pięćdziesiąt
pensów za bilet
5 (*reason*) z powodu +*gen*; **for
this reason** z tego powodu; **our
reasons for doing this** nasze
powody dla zrobienia czegoś
6 (*on behalf of, representing*) dla
+*gen*; **he works for a local firm**
pracuje dla miejscowej firmy; **g
for George** g jak George
7 (*destination*) do +*gen*; **he left for
Rome** wyjechał do Rzymu
8 (*with infinitive clause*): **it is not
for me to decide** nie ode mnie to
zależy; **there is still time for you
to do it** nadal ma pan/pani czas
na zrobienie tego
9 (*to get*) po; **for further
information, see...** po więcej
informacji niech pan/pani patrzy...
10 (*with regard to*) jak na; **it's
cold for July** jest zimno jak na
lipiec; **for scientists, this is less
important** dla naukowców to jest
mniej ważne; **another word for
this is...** inne słowo na określenie
tego to...
11 (*in favour of*) za +*inst*
12 (*referring to distance*) na
przestrzeni; **there are
roadworks for 50 km** roboty
są na przestrzeni pięćdziesięciu
kilometrów
13 (*with "if"*): **I wouldn't be alive
today, if it weren't for him** nie
byłbym dziś żywy, gdyby nie on

forbid [fə'bɪd] (*pt* **forbade**,

pp **forbidden**) *vt* zakazywać
(zakazać *pf*) +*gen*; **to ~ sb to
do sth** zakazywać (zakazać *pf*)
komuś robienia czegoś
forbidden [fə'bɪdn] *pp of* **forbid**
force [fɔːs] *n* **1** (*violence*) siła
2 (*strength*) siła **3** (*Phys*) siła ▷ *vt*
(*drive, compel*) zmuszać (zmusić
pf); **forces** *n pl* (*Mil*): **the F~s**
(*Brit*) siły zbrojne; **to be in ~** (*law,
system*) obowiązywać; **a ~ 5 gale**
sztorm o sile pięciu stopni w
skali Beauforta; **to ~ o.s. to do
sth** zmuszać (zmusić *pf*) się do
zrobienia czegoś; **to ~ sb to do
sth** zmuszać (zmusić *pf*) kogoś do
zrobienia czegoś
forecast ['fɔːkɑːst] (*pt, pp*
forecast *or* **forecasted**) *n* (*of
weather*) prognoza ▷ *vt* (*predict*)
przepowiadać (przepowiedzieć
pf)
forehead ['fɔrɪd] *n* czoło
foreign ['fɔrɪn] *adj* (*country,
language*) obcy; (*holiday*)
zagraniczny
foreigner ['fɔrɪnəʳ] *n*
cudzoziemiec(-mka) *m/f*
forest ['fɔrɪst] *n* las
forever [fə'rɛvəʳ] *adv*
1 (*permanently*) wiecznie **2** (*always*)
zawsze; **it has gone ~** odszedł
na zawsze
forgave [fə'geɪv] *pt of* **forgive**
forge [fɔːdʒ] *vt* (*signature,
banknote*) podrabiać (podrobić *pf*)
forget [fə'gɛt] (*pt* **forgot**, *pp*
forgotten) *vt* **1** (*not remember*)
zapominać (zapomnieć *pf*) o +*loc*
2 (*leave behind: object*) zapominać
(zapomnieć *pf*) +*gen* **3** (*put out of
mind: quarrel, person*) zapominać

(zapomnieć pf) o +loc ▷ vi (fail to remember) zapominać (zapomnieć pf); **to ~ to do sth** zapominać (zapomnieć pf) coś zrobić; **to ~ how to do sth** zapominać (zapomnieć pf), jak coś się robi; **to ~ that...** zapominać (zapomnieć pf), że...

forgive [fə'gɪv] (pt **forgave**, pp **forgiven** [fə'gɪvn]) vt (pardon) wybaczać (wybaczyć pf) +dat; **to ~ sb for sth** wybaczać (wybaczyć pf) komuś coś

forgot [fə'gɔt] pt of **forget**

forgotten [fə'gɔtn] pp of **forget**

fork [fɔːk] n 1 (for eating) widelec 2 (for gardening) widły 3 (in road, river, railway) rozwidlenie

form [fɔːm] n 1 (type) forma 2 (manner) sposób 3 (Brit: Scol: class) klasa 4 (document) formularz 5 (Sport) forma ▷ vt 1 (make: shape, queue, object) tworzyć (stworzyć pf) 2 (create: group, organization, company) stwarzać (stworzyć pf); **in the ~ of** w postaci +gen; **to be in good** or **top ~** (Brit) być w dobrej formie

formal ['fɔːməl] adj oficjalny

former ['fɔːmə'] adj 1 (no longer: husband, president) były 2 (earlier: power, authority) dawny ▷ pron: **the ~** pierwszy; **in ~ times/years** w poprzednich latach

fortnight ['fɔːtnaɪt] (Brit) n dwa tygodnie; **it's a ~ since...** minęły dwa tygodnie, odkąd...

fortunate ['fɔːtʃənɪt] adj szczęśliwy; **he was ~ to survive** miał szczęście, że przeżył

fortunately ['fɔːtʃənɪtlɪ] adv na szczęście

fortune ['fɔːtʃən] n (wealth) fortuna; **to make a ~** zbijać (zbić pf) fortunę; **to tell sb's ~** wróżyć (powróżyć pf) komuś

forty ['fɔːtɪ] num czterdzieści

forward ['fɔːwəd] adj 1 (in position) z przodu 2 (in movement) do przodu ▷ n (Sport) napastnik ▷ adv = **forwards**

forwards ['fɔːwədz] adv (in space, time) do przodu

foster ['fɔstə'] vt (child) wychowywać (wychować pf) ▷ adj (parent, mother, child) przybrany

fought [fɔːt] pt, pp of **fight**

foul [faul] adj 1 (filthy) obrzydliwy 2 (dreadful: temper, mood) paskudny; (day, time, luck) ohydny; (weather) paskudny ▷ n (Sport) faul

found [faund] pt, pp of **find** ▷ vt (organization, company) zakładać (założyć pf)

fountain ['fauntɪn] n (lit) fontanna

fountain pen n wieczne pióro

four [fɔː'] num cztery; see also **five**

fourteen ['fɔː'tiːn] num czternaście; see also **fifteen**

fourteenth ['fɔː'tiːnθ] num czternasty; see also **fifth**

fourth ['fɔːθ] num 1 czwarty 2 (US: quarter) czwarta część ▷ n (Aut: also: ~ **gear**) czwarty bieg; see also **fifth**

fox [fɔks] n lis

fragile ['frædʒaɪl] adj 1 (object, structure) kruchy 2 (delicate) delikatny

frame [freɪm] n 1 (of picture, mirror, door, window) rama 2 (also: ~s: of spectacles) ramka f sg

France [frɑːns] n Francja

frantic ['fræntɪk] adj 1 (person) oszalały 2 (rush, pace, search) gorączkowy

fraud [frɔːd] n 1 (crime) oszustwo 2 (person) oszust(ka) m/f

freckle ['frɛkl] n pieg

free [friː] adj 1 (costing nothing) darmowy 2 (available) wolny ▷ vt (release: prisoner, slave) uwalniać (uwolnić pf); ~ (of charge) or for ~ za darmo; **admission ~** wstęp wolny; **to be ~ of** or **from sth** być wolnym od czegoś; **to be ~ to do sth** mieć możliwość zrobienia czegoś

freedom ['friːdəm] n (liberty) wolność

freeway ['friːweɪ] (US) n autostrada

freeze [friːz] (pt **froze**, pp **frozen**) vi 1 (liquid, weather) zamarzać (zamarznąć pf) 2 (pipe) zamarzać (zamarznąć pf) 3 (person: with cold) przemarzać (przemarznąć pf) ▷ vt 1 (water, lake) skuwać (skuć pf) lodem 2 (food) zamrażać (zamrozić pf); **it may ~ tonight** wieczorem może być mróz

freezer ['friːzər] n zamrażarka

freezing ['friːzɪŋ] adj (also: ~ **cold**: day, weather) mroźny; (person, hands) przemarznięty; **I'm ~** jestem przemarznięty; **3 degrees below ~** trzy stopnie poniżej zera

French [frɛntʃ] adj francuski ▷ n (language) francuski; **the French**

n pl (people) Francuzi

French bean (Brit) n fasolka

French fries [-fraɪz] (esp US) n pl frytki

frequent ['friːkwənt] adj (occurrence, visitor) częsty

fresh [frɛʃ] adj świeży; ~ **air** świeże powietrze; **to make a ~ start** zaczynać (zacząć pf) od nowa

Friday ['fraɪdɪ] n piątek; see also **Tuesday**

fridge [frɪdʒ] (Brit) n lodówka

fried [fraɪd] pt, pp of **fry** ▷ adj (food) smażony

friend [frɛnd] n przyjaciel(-iółka) m/f; **to be ~s with sb** przyjaźnić się z kimś; **to make ~s with sb** zaprzyjaźniać (zaprzyjaźnić pf) się z kimś

friendly ['frɛndlɪ] adj 1 (amicable) przyjazny 2 (Brit: Sport) towarzyski; **to be ~ with** przyjaźnić się z +inst

friendship ['frɛndʃɪp] n (relationship) przyjaźń

fright [fraɪt] n 1 (terror) przerażenie 2 (shock) szok; **to give sb a ~** przestraszyć (pf) kogoś

frighten ['fraɪtn] vt przerażać (przerazić pf)

frightened ['fraɪtnd] adj (person, animal): **to be ~** bać się; **to be ~ of sth/of doing sth** or **to do sth** bać się czegoś/zrobić coś

frightening ['fraɪtnɪŋ] adj (experience, prospect) przerażający

fringe [frɪndʒ] n (Brit: hair) grzywka

frog [frɔg] (Zool) n żaba

○ KEYWORD

from [frɔm] prep **1** (indicating starting place) z +gen; **where are you from?** skąd pan/pani pochodzi?; **from London to Glasgow** z Londynu do Glasgow **2** (indicating origin) z +gen; **a present/letter from sb** prezent/list od kogoś **3** (with time, distance, price, numbers) od +gen; **from one o'clock to** or **until two** od pierwszej do drugiej; **it's 1 km from the beach** jest jeden kilometr od plaży; **unemployment has fallen from 7.5% to 7.2%** bezrobocie spadło z siedem i pół procent do siedem i dwie dziesiąte procent **4** (because of, on the basis of) z +gen; **from what he says** z tego, co mówi **5** (out of): **made from** z +gen

front [frʌnt] n **1** (of house) front; (of dress) przód; (of coach, train, car) przód ▷ adj (garden, entrance etc) frontowy; (seat) przedni; **in ~** z przodu; **in ~ of** (facing) przed +inst; (in the presence of) przy +loc
front door n drzwi frontowe
frontier ['frʌntɪəʳ] n (Brit) granica
frost [frɔst] n **1** (weather) mróz **2** (icy covering) szron
frosty ['frɔstɪ] adj (day, night, weather) mroźny; (grass, window) oszroniony
frown [fraun] n zmarszczenie brwi ▷ vi marszczyć (zmarszczyć pf) brwi
froze [frəuz] pt of **freeze**

frozen ['frəuzn] pp of **freeze** ▷ adj **1** (food) mrożony; (ground, lake) zamarznięty **2** (person, fingers) przemarznięty
fruit [fruːt] (pl **fruit** or **fruits**) n owoc
fruit machine (Brit) n automat do gry
frustrated [frʌs'treɪtɪd] adj sfrustrowany
fry [fraɪ] (pt, pp **fried**) vt (Culin) smażyć (usmażyć pf); **fries** n pl (Culin) frytki
frying pan ['fraɪɪŋ-] n patelnia
fuel ['fjuəl] n (for heating etc) paliwo
full [ful] adj pełny; **I'm ~ (up)** najadłem się; **~ marks** (Brit: Scol) maksymalny wynik; **at ~ speed** pełnym gazem; **~ of** pełny +gen; **to write one's name in ~** pisać (napisać pf) pełne imię i nazwisko
full stop (Brit) n kropka; **to come to a ~** (fig) utknąć w martwym punkcie
full-time ['ful'taɪm] adj (work) na pełnym etacie; (study) w pełnym wymiarze godzin; (student) dzienny; (staff) pełnoetatowy ▷ adv (work, study) na pełnym etacie
fully ['fulɪ] adv **1** (completely) w pełni **2** (in full) dokładnie
fumes [fjuːmz] n pl (of fire, fuel, car) opary
fun [fʌn] n zabawa; **to have ~** bawić się; **he's good ~** jest fajnym gościem; **it's not much ~** to nie jest zabawne; **to do sth for ~** zrobić coś dla przyjemności; **to make ~ of sb/sth** nabijać się z kogoś/czegoś

fund [fʌnd] *n* (*of money*) fundusz;
  funds *n pl* (*money*) fundusze
funeral ['fju:nərəl] *n* pogrzeb
funfair ['fʌnfɛəʳ] (*Brit*) *n* wesołe
  miasteczko
funny ['fʌnɪ] *adj* **1** (*amusing*)
  śmieszny **2** (*strange*) dziwny
fur [fəːʳ] *n* (*of animal*) futro
furious ['fjuərɪəs] *adj* **1** (*person*)
  wściekły **2** (*row, argument*)
  zażarty; **to be ~ with sb** być
  wściekłym na kogoś
furniture ['fəːnɪtʃəʳ] *n* meble *m
  pl*; **a piece of ~** mebel
further ['fəːðəʳ] *adv* (*farther: in
  distance, time*) dalej; **how much
  ~ is it?** o ile to jest dalej?; **full of**
  pełny +*gen*
further education *n*
  doskonalnie zawodowe
fuse [fju:z] (*US* **fuze**) *n* **1** (*Elec: in
  plug, circuit*) bezpiecznik **2** (*for
  bomb, firework*) zapalnik; **a ~ has
  blown** bezpiecznik się przepalił
fuss [fʌs] *n* **1** (*bother*) kłopot
  2 (*disturbance*) awantura; **to
  make** *or* **kick up a ~ (about sth)**
  (*inf*) robić (zrobić *pf*) zamieszanie
  (wokół czegoś)
fussy ['fʌsɪ] *adj* (*person*) grymaśny
future ['fju:tʃəʳ] *adj* przyszły
  ▷ *n* **1** (*time to come*): **the ~**
  przyszłość **2** (*prospects*) przyszłość
  3 (*Ling: also*: **~ tense**): **the ~** czas
  przyszły; **in (the) ~** (*from now on*)
  w przyszłości; **in the near ~** w
  najbliższej przyszłości
fuze [fju:z] (*US*) *n* = **fuse**

g

gadget ['gædʒɪt] *n* gadżet
gain [geɪn] *vt* **1** (*speed, weight,
  confidence*) nabierać (nabrać *pf*)
  +*gen* **2** (*obtain*) zyskiwać (zyskać
  pf) ▷ *n* (*increase, improvement*)
  zysk; **to ~ in value/popularity**
  zyskiwać (zyskać *pf*) wartość/
  popularność; **to ~ from sth**
  (*money*) zyskiwać (zyskać *pf*) na
  czymś
gallery ['gælərɪ] *n* (*also*: **art ~**)
  galeria
gamble ['gæmbl] *vi* **1** (*bet*)
  uprawiać hazard **2** (*take a risk*)
  ryzykować (zaryzykować *pf*) ▷ *n*
  (*risk*) ryzyko; **to ~ on sth** stawiać
  (postawić *pf*) na coś; (*success,
  outcome*) postawić (*pf*) na coś
gambling ['gæmblɪŋ] *n* hazard
game [geɪm] *n* **1** (*sport*) gra

2 (*activity: children's*) zabawa
3 (*also:* **board ~**) gra planszowa;
(*also:* **computer ~**) gra
komputerowa **4** (*match*) mecz
5: a ~ of football/tennis mecz
piłki nożnej/tenisa
gang [gæŋ] *n* (*of criminals,
hooligans*) banda
gangster ['gæŋstər] *n* gangster
gap [gæp] *n* (*space*) odstęp
gap year (*Brit*) *n* rok przerwy
między ukończeniem szkoły średniej a
podjęciem studiów, podczas którego
młodzi ludzie pracują zawodowo, jako
wolontariusze lub podróżują
garage ['gærɑːʒ] *n* **1** (*of private
house*) garaż **2** (*for car repairs*)
warsztat samochodowy
3 (*Brit: petrol station*) stacja
benzynowa
garbage ['gɑːbɪdʒ] *n* **1** (*esp
US: rubbish*) śmieci *m pl*
2 (*nonsense*) bzdury *f pl*
garbage can (*US*) *n* pojemnik
na śmieci
garbage man (*irreg*) *n* (*US*)
śmieciarz
garden ['gɑːdn] *n* ogród ▷ *vi*
pracować w ogrodzie
gardener ['gɑːdnər] *n*
ogrodnik(-iczka) *m/f*
gardening ['gɑːdnɪŋ] *n* (*non-
professional*) uprawianie ogródka
garlic ['gɑːlɪk] *n* czosnek
garment ['gɑːmənt] *n* część
garderoby
gas [gæs] *n* **1** (*Chem*) gaz
2 (*for cooking, heating*) gaz
3 (*US: inf: also:* **~oline**) benzyna
gasoline ['gæsəliːn] (*US*) *n*
benzyna
gas station (*US*) *n* stacja

benzynowa
gate [geɪt] *n* **1** (*of garden, field*)
furtka; (*of building*) brama **2** (*at
airport*) wyjście
gather ['gæðər] *vt* (*understand*): **to
~ (that)...** rozumieć (zrozumieć
pf), (że)... ▷ *vi:* **to ~ speed**
nabierać (nabrać *pf*) prędkości
gave [geɪv] *pt of* **give**
gay [geɪ] *adj* (*homosexual*)
homoseksualny ▷ *n* (*homosexual*)
gay
GCSE (*Brit*) *n abbr* (= *General
Certificate of Secondary Education*)

- **G C S E**
-
- **GCSE** to egzaminy do których
- przystępują piętnastoletni
- i szesnastoletni uczniowie
- na zakończenie szkoły
- średniej w Anglii, Walii i
- Irlandii Północnej. Niektóre
- przedmioty są obowiązkowe,
- inne do wyboru przez ucznia.

gear [gɪər] *n* **1** (*Tech: of car,
bicycle*) bieg **2** (*equipment*) sprzęt
3 (*clothing*) strój; **to change** *or*
(*US*) **shift ~** zmieniać (zmienić
pf) bieg
gear lever, **gear stick** (*Brit*) *n*
dźwignia zmiany biegów
gearshift ['gɪəʃɪft] (*US*) *n*
dźwignia zmiany biegów
geese [giːs] *n pl of* **goose**
gel [dʒɛl] *n* (*for hair, washing,
shaving*) żel; **bath/shower ~** żel
do kąpieli/pod prysznic
Gemini ['dʒɛmɪnaɪ] *n* (*Astrol*)
Bliźnięta
gender ['dʒɛndər] *n* **1** (*sex*) płeć

2 (*Ling*) rodzaj
general ['dʒɛnərl] *adj*
1 (*overall: situation*) ogólny;
(*decline, standard*) powszechny
2 (*non-specific: terms, outline, idea*)
ogólny ▷ *n* (*Mil*) generał; **in ~** (*as a whole*) ogólnie; (*on the whole*)
generalnie
general election *n* (*in Britain, United States*) wybory powszechne *m pl*
generally ['dʒɛnrəlɪ] *adv* **1** (*on the whole*) ogólnie **2** (*usually*) na ogół
generation [dʒɛnə'reɪʃən] *n* (*of people, family*) pokolenie
generous ['dʒɛnərəs]
adj **1** (*person*) hojny
2 (*sizeable: measure, gift*) pokaźny
genetically modified
[dʒɪ'nɛtɪklɪ'mɔdɪfaɪd] *adj*
modyfikowany genetycznie
genetics [dʒɪ'nɛtɪks] *n* (*science*)
genetyka *f sg*
genius ['dʒiːnɪəs] *n* (*person*)
geniusz
gentle ['dʒɛntl] *adj* **1** (*person, nature*) łagodny **2** (*light: movement, breeze, shake*) delikatny
3 (*Culin: heat*) mały
gentleman ['dʒɛntlmən] (*irreg*) *n*
1 (*man*) pan **2** (*well-mannered man*)
dżentelmen
gently ['dʒɛntlɪ] *adv* **1** (*touch, move*) delikatnie **2** (*Culin: cook, heat*) na małym ogniu
gents [dʒɛnts] *n*: **the ~** (*Brit: inf*)
toaleta męska
genuine ['dʒɛnjuɪn] *adj* **1** (*real*)
prawdziwy **2** (*sincere: person*)
szczery; (*emotion, interest*)
autentyczny
geography [dʒɪ'ɔgrəfɪ] *n*

geografia
geometry [dʒɪ'ɔmətrɪ] *n* (*science*)
geometria
germ [dʒɜːm] (*Bio*) *n* zarazek
German ['dʒɜːmən] *adj* niemiecki
▷ *n* **1** (*person*) Niemiec(-mka) *m/f*
2 (*language*) niemiecki
Germany ['dʒɜːmənɪ] *n* Niemcy

○ **KEYWORD**

get [gɛt] (*pt, pp, pp* **got**, (*US*) *pp*
gotten) *vt* **1**: **to have got**; *see also*
have, got
2 (*money, permission, information*)
otrzymywać (otrzymać *pf*); (*job, flat, room*) dostawać (dostać *pf*);
he got a job in London dostał
pracę w Londynie; **we can get
something to eat on the train**
możemy dostać coś do jedzenia
w pociągu
3 (*fetch*) sprowadzać (sprowadzić
pf); **to get sth for sb** przynosić
(przynieść *pf*) coś komuś; **can I
get you a coffee?** czy przynieść
panu/pani kawę?; **I'll come and
get you** przyjdę i panu/pani
przyniosę
4 (*receive*) otrzymywać (otrzymać
pf); **what did she get for
her birthday?** co dostała na
urodziny?; **he gets a lot of
pleasure from music** czerpie z
muzyki wiele przyjemności
5 (*board*): **to get a plane/bus**
wchodzić (wejść *pf*) na pokład
samolotu/autobusu; **I'll get the
bus** pojadę autobusem
6 (*cause to be/become*): **to get
sth/sb ready** przygotowywać
(przygotować *pf*) coś/kogoś; **did**

you get the answer right? czy otrzymałeś właściwą odpowiedź? **7** (*seize, catch*) łapać (złapać *pf*); **the police will get him eventually** policja w końcu go złapie
8 (*hit: target etc*) trafiać (trafić *pf*) do +*gen*
9 (*take, move*) zawozić (zawieźć *pf*) do +*gen*; **we must get him to hospital** musimy zwieźć go do szpitala
10 (*buy*) dostawać (dostać *pf*); (*regularly*) kupować (kupić *pf*); **I'll get some milk from the supermarket** kupię mleko w supermarkecie; **let me get you a drink** pozwól mi postawić ci drinka
11 (*be infected by*) chorować (zachorować *pf*); **you'll get a cold** przeziębisz się
12 (*understand: joke, point*) rozumieć (zrozumieć *pf*)
13 (*hear*) słyszeć (usłyszeć *pf*)
14 (*have: time, opportunity*) mieć; **I got a shock when I saw him** doznałem szoku, kiedy go zobaczyłem
15: to get sth done (*do oneself*) zrobić (*pf*) coś; (*have done*) oddawać (oddać *pf*) do zrobienia czegoś; **to get one's hair cut** obcinać (obciąć *pf*) włosy; **to get sb to do sth** nakłaniać (nakłonić *pf*) kogoś, by coś zrobił
16 (*inf: annoy*) złościć (zezłościć *pf*); **what gets me is his attitude** to, co mnie złości, to jego postawa
▷ *vi* **1** (*become, be: adj*) stawać (stać *pf*) się +*inst*; **to get old/tired/ cold/dirty** stawać (stać *pf*) się

starym/zmęczonym/zimnym/ brudnym; **to get drunk** upijać (upić *pf*) się
2 (*go*): **to get to work/the airport** dostawać (dostać *pf*) się do pracy/na lotnisko; **how did he get here?** jak się tu dostał?; **he didn't get home till 10pm** nie wrócił do domu przed 22; **the talks are getting nowhere** te rozmowy prowadzą do nikąd
3 (*begin*): **to get to know sb** poznawać (poznać *pf*) kogoś; **let's get going/started!** chodźmy/zaczynajmy!
4 (*manage*): **how often do you get to see him?** jak często udaje się panu/pani z nim widzieć?
▷ *aux vb* **1: to have got to**; *see also* **have, got**
2 (*passive use*): **to get killed** zostać (*pf*) zabitym
▶ **get around to** *vt fus*: **to get around to sth/to doing sth** zabierać (zabrać *pf*) się za coś/za robienie czegoś
▶ **get away** *vi* (*leave*) odjeżdżać (odjechać *pf*); (*on holiday*) wyjeżdżać (wyjechać *pf*); (*escape*) uciekać (uciec *pf*)
▶ **get away with** *vt fus* unikać (uniknąć *pf*) +*gen*; **he'll never get away with it!** nie ujdzie mu to na sucho!
▶ **get back** *vi* (*return*) wracać (wrócić *pf*)
▷ *vt* (*reclaim*) odzyskiwać (odzyskać *pf*)
▶ **get back to** *vt fus* (*return to*) powracać (powrócić *pf*) do +*gen*; **to get back to sleep** zasypiać (zasnąć *pf*) ponownie

▶ **get in** vi **1** (arrive: train, bus) przyjeżdżać (przyjechać pf); (plane) przylatywać (przylecieć pf) **2** (arrive home) wchodzić (wejść pf)
▶ **get into** vt fus **1: to get into university** dostać (pf) się na uniwersytet **2** (vehicle) wsiadać (wsiąść pf) do +gen **3** (in expressions): **to get into bed** chodzić/iść (pójść pf) do łóżka
▶ **get off** vi (from train, bus) wysiadać (wysiąść pf)
▷ vt (as holiday): **we get three days off at Christmas** na Boże Narodzenie mamy trzy dni wolnego
▷ vt fus (leave: train, bus) wysiadać (wysiąść pf) do +gen
▶ **get on** vi (be friends): **to get on well with sb** być z kimś w dobrych stosunkach **2** (progress): **how are you getting on?** jak ci idzie?
▷ vt fus (bus, train) wsiadać (wsiąść pf) do +gen
▶ **get on with** vt fus **1** (be friends with: person) być w dobrych stosunkach z +inst **2** (continue, start) kontynuować
▶ **get out** vi: **to get out (of)** (person: of place) wychodzić (wyjść pf) (z +gen); (of vehicle) wysiadać (wysiąść pf) (z +gen)
▷ vt **1** (take out: book, object etc) wyciągać (wyciągnąć pf) z +gen
▶ **get out of** vt fus (vehicle) wysiadać (wysiąść pf) z +gen
▶ **get over** vt fus (illness, shock) wychodzić (wyjść pf) z +gen
▶ **get through** vi (Tel) dodzwonić (pf) się
▷ vt fus (finish) kończyć (skończyć pf)

▶ **get together** vi (people) gromadzić (zgromadzić pf) się
▶ **get up** vi (rise: from chair, sofa) podnosić (podnieść pf) się; (out of bed) wstawać (wstać pf)

ghost [gəʊst] n (spirit) duch
giant ['dʒaɪənt] n (in stories) olbrzym ▷ adj (huge) olbrzymi
gift [gɪft] n **1** (present) prezent **2** talent; **to have a ~ for sth** (talent) mieć do czegoś talent
gin [dʒɪn] n (alcohol) dżin
ginger ['dʒɪndʒəʳ] n (spice) imbir ▷ adj (colour) rudy
giraffe [dʒɪ'rɑːf] n żyrafa
girl [gəːl] n (child) dziewczynka; (young woman) dziewczyna
girlfriend ['gəːlfrɛnd] n **1** (of girl) przyjaciółka **2** (of boy) dziewczyna
Girl Scout (US) n **1: the ~s** (organization) harcerstwo dziewcząt **2** (person) harcerka

○ **KEYWORD**

give [gɪv] (pt **gave**, pp **given**) vt **1** (hand over): **to give sb sth, give sth to sb** dawać (dać pf) komuś coś; (as gift) darować (podarować pf) komuś coś; **I gave David the book, I gave the book to David** podarowałem Dawidowi książkę; **give it to him** daj mu to **2** (provide) dawać (dać pf); **to give sb sth** (opportunity, surprise, job) dawać (dać pf) coś komuś; **I gave him the chance to deny it** dałem mu szansę zaprzeczenia temu **3** (deliver): **to give a speech/a lecture** wygłaszać (wygłosić pf)

przemówienie/wykład
4 (*organize*): **to give a party/ dinner party** organizować (zorganizować *pf*) przyjęcie/ proszony obiad
▶ **give back** *vt* (*money, book etc*) oddawać (oddać *pf*); **to give sth back to sb** oddawać (oddać *pf*) coś komuś
▶ **give in** *vi* (*yield*) ustępować (ustąpić *pf*)
▷ *vt* (*essay etc*) składać (złożyć *pf*)
▶ **give out** *vt* (*distribute*) rozdawać (rozdać *pf*)
▶ **give up** *vi* (*stop trying*) poddawać (poddać *pf*) się; **to give up smoking** rzucać (rzucić *pf*) palenie

glad [glæd] *adj* (*happy, pleased*) zadowolony; **to be ~ that...** być zadowolonym, że...; **I'd be ~ to help you** z przyjemnością panu/ pani pomogę
glamorous ['glæmərəs] *adj* olśniewający
glass [glɑːs] *n* **1** (*substance*) szkło **2** (*container*) szklanka **3** (*glassful*) kieliszek; **glasses** *n pl* (*spectacles*) okulary; **a pair of ~es** para okularów
glider ['glaɪdəʳ] *n* szybowiec
global ['gləubl] *adj* globalny
global warming [-'wɔːmɪŋ] *n* globalne ocieplenie
globe [gləub] *n* **1: the ~** (*the world*) kula ziemska **2** (*model*) globus; **around the ~** dookoła świata
gloomy ['gluːmɪ] *adj* **1** (*dark*) posępny **2** (*sad*) ponury
glorious ['glɔːrɪəs] *adj* **1** (*sunshine,* *day, weather*) cudowny **2** (*victory, occasion, career*) wspaniały
glove [glʌv] *n* rękawiczka; **a pair of ~s** para rękawiczek
glow [gləu] *vi* (*face, skin, cheeks*) czerwienić (zaczerwienić *pf*) się
glue [gluː] *n* klej ▷ *vt* kleić (skleić *pf*)
GM *adj abbr* (= *genetically modified*) modyfikowany genetycznie

○ **KEYWORD**

go [gəu] (*pt* **went**, *pp* **gone**, *pl* **goes**) *vi* **1** (*travel, move: on foot*) iść (pójść *pf*); (*on foot, attend habitually*) chodzić; (*by transport*) jechać (pojechać *pf*); (*habitually*) jeździć; (*by plane*) lecieć (polecieć *pf*); (*habitually*) latać; (*by boat*) płynąć (popłynąć *pf*); (*habitually*) pływać; **he's going to New York** on jedzie do Nowego Jorku; **where's he gone?** gdzie on poszedł?; (*by car, bike, bus, train etc*) gdzie on pojechał?; **shall we go by car or train?** pojedziemy samochodem czy pociągiem?; **to go to do sth, go and do sth** (*Brit*) chodzić/iść (pójść *pf*) coś zrobić **2** (*depart: on foot*) chodzić/iść (pójść *pf*); (*by transport*) wyjeżdżać (wyjechać *pf*); **let's go** chodźmy; **I must be going** muszę iść; **our plane goes at 11pm** nasz samolot odlatuje o 23
3 (*disappear*) znikać (zniknąć *pf*); **all her jewellery had gone** zniknęła jej cała biżuteria
4 (*attend*): **to go to school/ university** (*habitually*) chodzić do szkoły/na uniwersytet

5 (*with activity*): **to go for a walk** iść (pójść *pf*) na spacer; (*habitually*) chodzić na spacer; **to go on a trip** chodzić/iść (pójść *pf*) na wycieczkę; (*by transport*) jechać (pojechać *pf*) na wycieczkę
6 (*work: clock, video etc*) działać
7 (*become*): **to go pale/mouldy/bald** blednąć (zblednąć *pf*)/pleśnieć (spleśnieć *pf*)/łysieć (wyłysieć *pf*)
8 (*be about to, intend to*): **are you going to come?** zamierzasz przyjść?; (*formal*) czy zamierza pan/pani przyjść?; **I think it's going to rain** myślę, że będzie padać
9 (*progress*) mijać (minąć *pf*); **time went very slowly/quickly** czas mijał bardzo powoli/szybko; **how did it go?** jak było?
10 (*be placed*): **where does this cup go?** gdzie ma stać ta filiżanka?
11 (*lead*) prowadzić (poprowadzić *pf*)
12 (*US: to take away*): **a hamburger and fries to go** hamburger i frytki na wynos
13 (*in other expressions*): **there's still a week to go before the exams** jest jeszcze tydzień do egzaminów; **to keep going** iść (pójść *pf*) dalej; (*by transport*) jechać (pojechać *pf*) dalej
▷ *n* **1** (*try*) próba; **to have a go (at doing sth)** próbować (spróbować *pf*) (coś robić)
2 (*turn*) kolej; **whose go is it?** czyja teraz kolej?
▶ **go after** *vt fus* **1** (*pursue: person*) ruszać (ruszyć *pf*) w pogoń za +*inst*
2 (*try to get: job*) szukać (*pf*) +*gen*

▶ **go ahead** *vi* **1** (*take place: event*) odbywać (odbyć *pf*) się **2** (*press on*): **to go ahead with sth** przystępować (przystąpić *pf*) do czegoś; **go ahead!** (*encouraging*) proszę bardzo!
▶ **go around** *vi* (*circulate: news, rumour*) krążyć
▶ **go away** *vi* **1** (*leave*) odchodzić (odejść *pf*) **2** (*on holiday*) wyjeżdżać (wyjechać *pf*)
▶ **go back** *vi* (*return*) wracać (wrócić *pf*)
▶ **go back to** *vt fus* (*activity, work, school*) wracać (wrócić *pf*) do +*gen*
▶ **go by** *vi* (*vehicle, years, time*) mijać (minąć *pf*)
▶ **go down** *vi* **1** (*fall: price, level, amount*) obniżać (obniżyć *pf*) **2** (*set: sun*) zachodzić (zajść *pf*) **3** (*crash: computer*) psuć (zepsuć *pf*) się
▷ *vt fus* (*stairs, ladder*) schodzić (zejść *pf*)
▶ **go for** *vt fus* (*fetch*) chodzić/iść (pójść *pf*) po +*loc*
▶ **go in** *vi* (*enter*) wchodzić (wejść *pf*)
▶ **go in for** *vt fus* (*competition*) startować (wystartować *pf*) w +*loc*
▶ **go into** *vt fus* (*enter: building, room*) wchodzić (wejść *pf*) do +*gen*
▶ **go off** *vi* **1** (*leave*) wychodzić (wyjść *pf*); **he's gone off to work** wyszedł do pracy **2** (*explode*) eksplodować **3** (*sound: alarm*) włączać (włączyć *pf*) się **4** (*switch off*) wyłączać (wyłączyć *pf*) się
▶ **go on** *vi* (*continue*) iść (pójść *pf*) dalej; **to go on with one's work** pracować dalej; **to go on doing**

sth robić coś dalej **2** (*happen*) dziać się; **what's going on here?** co się tu dzieje? **3** (*lights etc*) zapalać (zapalić *pf*) się
▶ **go on about** *vt fus*: **to go on about sth** ciągle o czymś mówić
▶ **go out** *vi* **1** (*person*) wychodzić (wyjść *pf*); **we are going out for a drink tonight** wychodzimy dziś wieczorem na drinka **2** (*couple*) chodzić ze sobą; **they've been going out for 3 years** chodzą ze sobą od trzech lat; **to go out with sb** chodzić z kimś **3** (*be extinguished*) gasnąć (zgasnąć *pf*)
▶ **go over** *vt* (*check*) sprawdzać (sprawdzić *pf*)
▶ **go round** *vi* = **go around**
▶ **go through** *vt fus* **1** (*place, town*) przechodzić (przejść *pf*) przez **2** (*undergo*) przechodzić (przejść *pf*) przez; **he's going through a difficult time** przechodzi teraz trudny okres
▶ **go together** *vi* (*colours, clothes, foods*) pasować do siebie
▶ **go up** *vi* **1** (*rise: price, level, value*) wzrastać (wzrosnąć *pf*) **2** (*go upstairs*) chodzić/iść (pójść *pf*) na górę
▶ **go up to** *vt fus* chodzić/iść (pójść *pf*) do +*gen*
▶ **go with** *vt fus* **1** (*combine well with*) pasować do +*gen* **2** (*accompany*) towarzyszyć
▶ **go without** *vt fus* (*food, treats*) nie mieć

goal [gəul] *n* **1** (*Sport*) gol; (*on pitch*) bramka **2** (*aim*) cel; **to score a ~** strzelać (strzelić *pf*) gola
goalie [ˈgəuli] *n* (*inf*)
bramkarz(-arka) *m/f*
goalkeeper [ˈgəulkiːpəʳ] *n* bramkarz(-arka) *m/f*
goat [gəut] *n* kozioł
God [gɔd] *n* Bóg, Boże
god [gɔd] *n* Bóg
goddaughter [ˈgɔddɔːtəʳ] *n* chrześniaczka
godfather [ˈgɔdfɑːðəʳ] *n* ojciec chrzestny
godmother [ˈgɔdmʌðəʳ] *n* matka chrzestna
godson [ˈgɔdsʌn] *n* chrześniak
goggles [ˈgɔglz] *n pl* gogle
gold [gəuld] *n* **1** (*metal*) złoto **2** (*Sport: inf: also*: **~ medal**) złoty medal ▷ *adj* (*ring, watch, tooth*) złoty
goldfish [ˈgəuldfɪʃ] (*pl* **goldfish**) *n* złota rybka
golf [gɔlf] *n* golf; **to play ~** grać w golfa
golf course *n* pole golfowe
gone [gɔn] *pp of* **go** ▷ *adj* miniony; **the food's all ~** nie ma już jedzenia
good [gud] *adj* **1** dobry **2** (*well-behaved*) grzeczny ▷ *n* (*right*) dobro; **~!** dobrze!; **to be ~ at sth** być dobrym w czymś; **to be no ~ at sth** być kiepskim w czymś; **it didn't do any ~** to było do niczego; **it's ~ for him** to jest dla niego dobre; **to be ~ with people/with figures** dobrze sobie radzić z ludźmi/z liczbami; **it's ~ to see you** miło pana/panią widzieć; **it's a ~ thing he was there** (*Brit*) dobrze, że tam był; **that's very ~ of you** to bardzo miło z pana/pani strony; **~ morning/afternoon!**

dzień dobry!; **~ evening!** dobry
wieczór!; **~ night!** (*before going
home*) dobrej nocy!; (*before going to
bed*) dobranoc!; **to take a ~ look**
dobrze się przyglądać (przyjrzeć
pf); **for ~** (*forever*) na zawsze; **to
do sb ~** robić (zrobić *pf*) komuś
dobrze; *see also* **goods**
goodbye [gud'baɪ] *int* do
widzenia; **to say ~** żegnać
(pożegnać *pf*) się
Good Friday *n* Wielki Piątek
good-looking ['gud'lukɪŋ] *adj*
atrakcyjny
goods ['gudz] *n pl* **1** (*Comm*)
towary **2** (*possessions*) dobytek
m sg
goose [gu:s] (*pl* **geese**) *n* gęś
gorgeous ['gɔ:dʒəs] *adj*
1 (*necklace, dress*) cudowny;
(*weather, day*) wspaniały **2** (*person*)
cudowny
gorilla [gə'rɪlə] *n* (*animal*) goryl
gossip ['gɔsɪp] *n* **1** (*rumours*)
plotka **2** (*chat*) plotkowanie ▷ *vi*
(*chat*) plotkować (poplotkować
pf); **to ~ with sb** plotkować
(poplotkować *pf*) z kimś
got [gɔt] *pt, pp of* **get**; **have you
~ an umbrella?** czy ma pan/pani
parasol?; **he has ~ to accept the
situation** musi zaakceptować
tę sytuację
gotten ['gɔtn] (*US*) *pp of* **get**
government ['gʌvnmənt] *n*
(*institution*) rząd
GP *n abbr* (= general practitioner)
lekarz(-rka) *m/f*
grab [græb] *vt* **1** (*seize*) chwytać
(chwycić *pf*) **2** (*chance, opportunity*)
korzystać (skorzystać *pf*) z +*gen*
graceful ['greɪsful] *adj* pełen

wdzięku
grade [greɪd] *n* **1** (*school mark*)
ocena **2** (*US: school class*) klasa
grade crossing (*US*) *n* przejazd
kolejowy
grade school (*US*) *n* szkoła
podstawowa
gradual ['grædjuəl] *adj* (*change,
process, improvement*) stopniowy
gradually ['grædjuəlɪ] *adv*
stopniowo
graffiti [grə'fi:tɪ] *n* graffiti
grain [greɪn] *n* **1** (*of wheat, rice*)
ziarno **2** (*cereals*) zboże **3** (*US: corn*)
zboże **4** (*of sand, salt, sugar*)
ziarenko **5: the ~** (*of wood*) słój;
it goes against the ~ to kłóci się
z zasadami; **a ~ of truth** ziarno
prawdy
gram [græm] *n* gram
grammar ['græmə'] *n*
gramatyka
grammar school (*Brit*) *n* liceum
ogólnokształcące

gramme [græm] (*Brit*) *n* = **gram**
grand [grænd] *adj* (*impressive*)
okazały

grandad, granddad ['grændæd])
n dziadek
grandchild ['grænt∫aɪld] (pl
grandchildren) n (male) wnuk;
(female) wnuczka
granddaughter ['grændɔ:tə^r]
n wnuczka
grandfather ['grændfɑ:ðə^r] n
dziadek
grandma ['grænmɑ:] n babcia
grandmother ['grænmʌðə^r]
n babcia
grandpa ['grænpɑ:] n dziadziuś
grandparents ['grændpɛərənts]
n pl dziadkowie
grandson ['grænsʌn] n wnuk
granny, grannie ['grænɪ]) n (inf)
babunia
grape [greɪp] n winogrono; **a
bunch of ~s** kiść winogron
grapefruit ['greɪpfru:t] (pl
grapefruit) n grejpfrut
graph [grɑ:f] n wykres
graphics ['græfɪks] n (design)
grafika f sg ▷ n pl (images) grafiki
grass [grɑ:s] n (Bot) trawa; **the ~**
(the lawn) trawnik
grasshopper ['grɑ:shɔpə^r] n
konik polny
grate [greɪt] vt (food) ucierać
(utrzeć pf)
grateful ['greɪtful] adj (person)
wdzięczny; **to be ~ for** (help,
opportunity) być wdzięcznym
za; **to be ~ to sb for sth** być
wdzięcznym komuś za coś
grave [greɪv] n (tomb) grób
gravel ['grævl] n żwir
graveyard ['greɪvjɑ:d] n
cmentarz
gravy ['greɪvɪ] n (sauce) sos
gray [greɪ] (US) adj = **grey**

grease [gri:s] n (lubricant)
smar ▷ vt 1 (lubricate) smarować
(nasmarować pf) 2 (cooking dish)
smarować (posmarować pf)
tłuszczem
greasy ['gri:sɪ] adj 1 (tools, hands)
natłuszczony 2 (food) tłusty
3 (skin, hair) przetłuszczający się
great [greɪt] adj 1 (large) wielki
2 (success, achievement) wspaniały;
(pleasure, difficulty, value) wielki;
(risk) ogromny 3 (important,
famous) znaczący 4 (terrific: person,
place) wspaniały; (idea) świetny
▷ int: **~!** (enthusiastically)
świetnie!; **we had a ~ time**
świetnie się bawiliśmy
Great Britain n Wielka Brytania

● **GREAT BRITAIN**
●
● **Great Britain** – wyspa
● Wielka Brytania składa
● się z Anglii, Szkocji i Walii.
● Kraje te, wspólnie z Irlandią
● Północną (częścią wyspy
● Irlandia), tworzą Zjednoczone
● Królestwo Wielkiej Brytanii i
● Irlandii Północnej (po polsku
● najczęściej nazywane po
● prostu Wielką Brytanią).

great-grandfather
[greɪt'grænfɑ:ðə^r] n pradziadek
great-grandmother
[greɪt'grænmʌðə^r] n prababcia
Greece [gri:s] n Grecja
greedy ['gri:dɪ] adj chciwy
Greek [gri:k] adj grecki ▷ n
1 (person) Grek(-eczynka) m/f
2 (modern language) współczesna
greka 3 (also: **ancient ~**)

starożytna greka

green [gri:n] *adj* **1** (*colour*) zielony
2 (*environmental*) proekologiczny
▷ *n* **1** (*colour*) zieleń **2** (*Pol*): **the**
G~s zieloni

greengrocer ['gri:ngrəusə'] (*esp*
Brit) *n* (*shop: also:* **~'s**) warzywniak

greenhouse ['gri:nhaus] *n*
szklarnia ▷ *adj* (*gas, emissions*)
cieplarniany

Greenland ['gri:nlənd] *n*
Grenlandia

greetings card ['gri:tıŋz-] *n*
kartka z życzeniami

grew [gru:] *pt of* **grow**

grey [greı] (*US* **gray**) *adj* **1** (*colour*)
szary; (*hair*) siwy **2** (*dull: weather,*
day) szary ▷ *n* (*colour*) szarość

grey-haired [greı'hɛəd] *adj*
siwowłosy

grid [grıd] *n* **1** (*pattern*) krata
2 (*cover for drain*) kratka ściekowa

grief [gri:f] *n* zmartwienie

grill [grıl] *n* (*Brit: on cooker*) ruszt
▷ *vt* (*Brit: food*) piec (upiec *pf*) na
ruszcie

grin [grın] *n* (*smile*) szeroki
uśmiech ▷ *vi* uśmiechać ·
(uśmiechnąć *pf*) się szeroko

grip [grıp] *vt* (*object*) chwytać
(chwycić *pf*)

grit [grıt] *n* (*sand, gravel*) grys

groan [grəun] *n* (*of pain*) jęk; (*of*
unhappiness) pomruk ▷ *vi* (*in pain*)
jęczeć (jęknąć *pf*)

grocer ['grəusə'] *n* (*shop: also:* **~'s**)
sklep spożywczy

grocery ['grəusərı] *n* sklep
spożywczy; **groceries** *n pl*
(*provisions*) artykuły spożywcze

groom [gru:m] *n* (*also:* **bride~**)
pan młody

gross [grəus] *adj* **1** (*misconduct,*
indecency, negligence) rażący
2 (*horrible*) obrzydliwy

ground [graund] *pt, pp of*
grind ▷ *n* **1** (*floor*): **the ~** podłoga
2 (*earth, soil, land*): **the ~** ziemia
3 (*Sport*) boisko ▷ *adj* mielony; **on**
the ~ na ziemi; **below/above ~**
pod/nad ziemią; **~s for** (*optimism,*
hope, concern) podstawy do
+*gen*; (*divorce, appeal, complaint*)
przyczyny +*gen*; **on the ~s that...**
z powodu tego, że...; **on medical/**
humanitarian ~s z przyczyn
medycznych/humanitarnych

ground floor *n* parter

group [gru:p] *n* **1** (*of people,*
buildings etc) grupa **2** (*also:* **pop**
~, rock ~) zespół ▷ *vt* (*organize,*
arrange) grupować (zgrupować
pf); **in ~s** w grupach; **age/**
income ~ grupa wiekowa/
zarobkowa

grow [grəu] (*pt, pp* **grew**) *vi*
1 (*plant, tree*) rosnąć (wyrosnąć *pf*);
(*person, animal*) rosnąć (urosnąć
pf) **2** (*increase: amount, feeling,*
problem) rosnąć (wzrosnąć *pf*)
▷ *vt* (*flowers, vegetables*) hodować
(wyhodować *pf*); (*beard, hair*)
zapuszczać (zapuścić *pf*); **to ~**
by 10% wzrastać (wzrosnąć *pf*)
o dziesięć procent; **to ~ rich/old**
bogacić (wzbogacić *pf*)/starzeć
(zestarzeć *pf*) się
  ▶ **grow out of** *vt fus* (*clothes*)
wyrastać (wyrosnąć *pf*) z +*gen*
  ▶ **grow up** *vi* (*be brought up*)
wychowywać (wychować *pf*) się;
(*be mature*) dojrzewać (dojrzeć *pf*)

growl [graul] *vi* (*dog, bear, lion*)
warczeć (warknąć *pf*) ▷ *n* (*of dog,*

bear, lion) warknięcie

grown [grəun] *pp of* **grow**

grown-up [grəun'ʌp] *n (adult)* dorosły

growth [grəuθ] *n* wzrost; **a ~ in sth** przyrost czegoś

grudge [grʌdʒ] *n (grievance)* uraza; **to have** or **bear a ~ (against sb)** żywić (do kogoś) urazę

gruesome ['gru:səm] *adj (murder, discovery, details)* makabryczny

grumble ['grʌmbl] *vi (complain)* zrzędzić

guarantee [gærən'ti:] *n* **1** *(assurance)* zapewnienie **2** *(Comm)* gwarancja ▷ *vt* **1** *(promise)* gwarantować (zagwarantować *pf)* **2** *(ensure)* zapewniać (zapewnić *pf);* **a/no ~ that...** pewność/nie ma pewności, że...; **to ~ (that)...** gwarantować (zagwarantować *pf),* (że)...

guard [gɑ:d] *n* **1** *(sentry)* strażnik(-iczka) *m/f* **2** *(Brit: Rail)* konduktor(ka) *m/f* ▷ *vt (building, entrance, door)* strzec +*gen; (person)* ochraniać (ochronić *pf);* **to be on one's ~ (against)** mieć się na baczności (przed +*inst);* **to be on ~** stać na warcie

▷ **guard against** *vt fus (disease, damage)* chronić (uchronić *pf)* się przed +*inst*

guess [gɛs] *vt, vi* **1** *(conjecture)* zgadywać (zgadnąć *pf)* **2** *(work out)* odgadywać (odgadnąć *pf)* ▷ *n* przypuszczenie; **I ~ so** myślę, że tak; **to ~ (that)...** *(conjecture)* zgadywać (zgadnąć *pf),* (że)...; *(work out)*

zastanawiać (zastanowić *pf)* się, (że)...; *(suppose)* zastanawiać (zastanowić *pf)* się, (że)...; **~ what I did last night** zgadnij co zrobiłem wczoraj w nocy; **you're right, I ~** chyba masz rację; **my ~ is that...** przypuszczam, że...; **to take** or **have a ~** próbować (spróbować *pf)* zgadnąć

guest [gɛst] *n* gość ▷ *adj (speaker, appearance)* gościnny

guesthouse ['gɛsthaus] *(Brit) n* pensjonat

guide [gaɪd] *n* **1** *(tour guide)* przewodnik(-iczka) *m/f* **2** *(local guide)* miejscowy(-owa) przewodnik(-iczka) *m/f* **3** *(also: ~ book)* przewodnik **4: G~** *(Brit: group member)* harcerka *f;* **Guides** *n pl (Brit: youth group)* harcerki *f* ▷ *vt* **1** *(round city, museum etc)* oprowadzać (oprowadzić *pf)* **2** *(lead)* prowadzić (poprowadzić *pf)*

guidebook ['gaɪdbuk] *n* przewodnik

guide dog *(Brit) n* pies przewodnik

guided tour ['gaɪdɪd-] *n* zwiedzanie z przewodnikiem

guilty ['gɪltɪ] *adj* **1** *(remorseful)* winny **2** *(secret, conscience)* nieczysty **3** *(responsible)* odpowiedzialny **4** *(Law)* winny; **~ of murder/manslaughter** winny morderstwa/zabójstwa

guinea pig ['gɪnɪ-] *n (animal)* świnka morska

guitar [gɪ'tɑ:ʳ] *n* gitara

gum [gʌm] *n* **1** *(Anat)* dziąsło **2** *(also: **chewing ~**)* guma do żucia

gun [gʌn] *n (small, medium-sized)*

pistolet; (*large*) strzelba
gunpoint ['gʌnpɔɪnt] *n*: **at ~** na
muszce
guy [gaɪ] *n* (*man*) facet; **(you) ~s** wy
gym [dʒɪm] *n* (*also*: **~nasium**)
sala gimnastyczna
gymnast ['dʒɪmnæst] *n*
gimnastyk(-yczka) *m/f*
gymnastics [dʒɪm'næstɪks] *n*
gimnastyka *f sg*
gypsy ['dʒɪpsɪ] *n* Cygan(ka) *m/f*

habit ['hæbɪt] *n* (*custom, practice*)
zwyczaj; **to be in the ~ of doing
sth** mieć w zwyczaju robić coś;
to get out of the ~ of doing sth
odzwyczajać (odzwyczaić *pf*) się
od robienia czegoś; **to get into
the ~ of doing sth** przyzwyczajać
(przyzwyczaić *pf*) się do robienia
czegoś; **a bad ~** zły nawyk
had [hæd] *pt, pp of* **have**
hadn't ['hædnt] = **had not**
hail [heɪl] *n* grad
hair [heəʳ] *n* (*human: on head*)
włosy *m pl*; (*single strand*) włos;
to do one's ~ układać (ułożyć
pf) sobie fryzurę; **to have** *or* **get
one's ~ cut** strzyc (ostrzyc *pf*) się
hairbrush ['heəbrʌʃ] *n* szczotka
do włosów
haircut ['heəkʌt] *n* **1** (*at*

hairdresser's etc) strzyżenie
2 (*hairstyle*) fryzura; **to have** or
get a ~ strzyc (ostrzyc *pf*) się
hairdresser ['hɛədresəʳ]
n **1** (*person*) fryzjer(ka) *m/f*
2 (*also:* **~'s**) salon fryzjerski
hairdryer ['hɛədraɪəʳ] *n* suszarka
do włosów
hair gel *n* żel do włosów
hairspray ['hɛəspreɪ] *n* lakier
do włosów
hairstyle ['hɛəstaɪl] *n* fryzura
half [hɑːf] (*pl* **halves**) *n, pron*
1 (*of amount, object*) połowa
2 (*Brit: child's ticket*) bilet ze zniżką
pięćdziesięciu procent ▷ *adj* (*bottle*)
pół +*gen* ▷ *adv* (*inf: empty, closed,
open, asleep*) do połowy; **the first/
second ~** (*Sport*) pierwsza/druga
połowa; **to cut sth in ~** przecinać
(przeciąć *pf*) coś na pół; **two/
three and a ~** dwa/trzy i pół; **~ a
pound/kilo/mile** pół funta/kilo/
mili; **a day/week/pound and a
~** półtora dnia/tygodnia/funta;
~ an hour pół godziny; **~ past
four/five** wpół do piątej/szóstej;
to be ~ German/Irish być w
połowie Niemcem/Irlandczykiem;
to go halves (with sb) dzielić
(podzielić się *pf*) (z kimś) po
połowie; **she's ~ his age** ona jest
od niego o połowę młodsza
half-brother ['hɑːfbrʌðəʳ] *n* brat
przyrodni
half-hour [hɑːfauəʳ] *n* pół
godziny
half price *adj* o połowę tańszy
▷ *adv* za pół ceny
half-sister ['hɑːfsɪstəʳ] *n* siostra
przyrodnia
half-term [hɑːftəːm] (*Brit: Scol*)

n przerwa semestralna; **at ~** w
czasie przerwy semestralnej

half-time [hɑːftaɪm] (*Sport*) *n*
przerwa; **at ~** w przerwie
halfway ['hɑːfweɪ] *adv* (*between
two points*) w połowie drogi; **~
through sth** w połowie czegoś
hall [hɔːl] *n* **1** (*esp Brit: entrance*)
hol **2** (*room*) przedpokój
Halloween ['hæləʊ'iːn] *n* wigilia
Wszystkich Świętych

hallway ['hɔːlweɪ] (*Brit*) *n*
(*vestibule*) przedpokój
ham [hæm] *n* (*meat, joint*) szynka
▷ *adj* (*sandwich, roll, salad*) z
szynką
hamburger ['hæmbəːgəʳ] *n*

hamburger

hammer ['hæmə^r] n (tool) młotek pf

hamster ['hæmstə^r] n chomik

hand [hænd] n **1** (Anat) ręka **2** (of clock) wskazówka **3** (of cards) karty f pl ▷ vt (pass, give) podawać (podać pf) +dat; **to do sth by ~** robić (zrobić pf) coś ręcznie; **~ in ~** (holding hands) trzymając się za ręce; **to give** or **lend sb a ~ (with sth)** pomagać (pomóc pf) komuś (w czymś); **on the one ~..., on the other ~...** z jednej strony..., z drugiej strony...
  ▶ **hand in** vt (submit) składać (złożyć pf); (homework) oddawać (oddać pf)
  ▶ **hand out** vt rozdawać (rozdać pf)
  ▶ **hand over** vt (object, present, letter) przekazywać (przekazać pf)

handbag ['hændbæg] (Brit) n torebka

handcuffs ['hændkʌfs] n pl kajdanki; **in ~** w kajdankach

handkerchief ['hæŋkətʃɪf] n chusteczka

handle ['hændl] n (of bag) rączka; (of knife, paintbrush, broom, spade) trzonek; (of cup) ucho; (of door, window) klamka ▷ vt (deal with: problem, job, responsibility) zajmować (zająć pf) się +inst; (people) radzić (poradzić pf) sobie z +inst; **"~ with care"** "ostrożnie"

handlebars ['hændlbɑː(z)] n pl kierownica roweru

handmade ['hænd'meɪd] adj wykonany ręcznie

handset [hændsɛt] n (Tel) słuchawka

hands-free kit ['hændz'friː-] n samochodowy zestaw słuchawkowy

handsome ['hænsəm] adj przystojny

handwriting ['hændraɪtɪŋ] n charakter pisma

handy ['hændɪ] adj **1** (useful) przydatny **2** (close at hand) pod ręką

hang [hæŋ] (pt, pp **hung**) vt **1** (clothes, light, picture) wieszać (powiesić pf) ▷ vi (be suspended) wisieć (zawisnąć pf) ▷ n: **to get the ~ of sth** (inf) chwytać (chwycić pf) o co w czymś chodzi; **I've got the ~ of it now** teraz juz chwyciłem o co w tym chodzi
  ▶ **hang about** vi = **hang around**
  ▶ **hang around** (inf) vi pałętać się
  ▶ **hang on** vi (wait) czekać (poczekać pf)
  ▶ **hang onto, hang on to** vt fus **1** (grasp) kurczowo trzymać się +gen **2** (inf: fig: keep) trzymać się +gen
  ▶ **hang round** (Brit) vi = **hang around**
  ▶ **hang up** vi (Tel) odkładać (odłożyć pf) słuchawkę ▷ vt (coat, hat, clothes) wieszać (powiesić pf)

hanger ['hæŋə^r] n (also: **coat ~**) wieszak

hangover ['hæŋəuvə^r] n (after drinking) kac

happen ['hæpən] vi (occur, result: incident, accident) wydarzać (wydarzyć pf) się; **what will ~ if...?** co się stanie jeśli...?; **tell me what ~ed** powiedz mi co się stało; **to ~ to do sth** przypadkowo coś robić (zrobić pf)

happily ['hæpɪlɪ] adv (cheerfully) radośnie; **~ married** szczęśliwie zaślubiony

happiness ['hæpɪnɪs] n szczęście

happy ['hæpɪ] adj szczęśliwy; **to be ~ with sth** (satisfied) być z czegoś zadowolonym; **to be ~ to do sth** (willing) robić (zrobić pf) coś chętnie; **~ birthday!** wszystkiego najlepszego z okazji urodzin!; **~ Christmas!** Wesołych Świąt!

harassment ['hærəsmənt] n nękanie

harbour ['hɑːbəʳ] (US harbor) n (Naut) przystań

hard [hɑːd] adj 1 (not soft: surface, object) twardy 2 (not easy: question, problem) trudny; (work) ciężki 3 (violent: push, punch, kick) silny ▷ adv 1 (work) ciężko; (try) bardzo; (think) usilnie 2 (laugh) głośno; (rain, snow) mocno 3 (violently: hit, punch, kick) mocno; **it's ~ to tell** or **say** trudno powiedzieć; **such events are ~ to understand** trudno jest zrozumieć takie rzeczy; **it's ~ work serving in a shop** obsługiwanie w sklepie to ciężka praca; **to try ~** bardzo się starać (postarać pf)

hard disk (Comput) n twardy dysk

hardly ['hɑːdlɪ] adv 1 (scarcely) ledwo 2 (no sooner): **he had ~ sat down when the door burst open** ledwie usiadł, drzwi otwarły się z hukiem; **~ ever/any/anyone** prawie nigdy/żaden/nikt; **I can ~ believe it** prawie nie mogę w to uwierzyć

hard up (inf) adj spłukany

hardware ['hɑːdwɛəʳ] n (Comput) sprzęt komputerowy

hardworking [hɑːd'wəːkɪŋ] adj pracowity

hare [hɛəʳ] n (animal) zając

harm [hɑːm] vt vt 1 (damage) krzywdzić (skrzywdzić pf) 2 (injure) uszkadzać (uszkodzić pf)

harmful ['hɑːmful] adj szkodliwy

harmless ['hɑːmlɪs] adj (safe) niegroźny

harp [hɑːp] n (Mus) harfa

harvest ['hɑːvɪst] n 1 (harvest time) żniwa 2 (crop) zbiory

has [hæz] vb see **have**

hasn't ['hæznt] = **has not**

hat [hæt] n kapelusz

hate [heɪt] vt (person) nienawidzić (znienawidzić pf); (food, activity, sensation) nie znosić (pf); **to ~ doing sth** nie znosić (pf) robienia czegoś

hatred ['heɪtrɪd] n nienawiść

haunted ['hɔːntɪd] adj (house, building) nawiedzony

○ KEYWORD

have [hæv] (pt, pp had) vt 1 (possess) mieć; **he has** or **he has got blue eyes/dark hair** on ma niebieskie oczy/ciemne włosy; **do you have** or **have you got a car/phone?** masz samochód/ telefon?; **to have** or **have got sth to do** mieć coś do zrobienia; **she had her eyes closed** miała zamknięte oczy 2 (with meals, drinks): **to have breakfast** zjeść śniadanie; **to have a drink/a cigarette** napić się/zapalić papierosa 3 (with activity): **to have a swim/**

bath popływać/wykąpać się; **to have a meeting/party** mieć spotkanie/przyjęcie
4 (*receive, obtain*) dostawać (dostać *pf*); **can I have your address?** czy może mi pan/pani podać swój adres?; **you can have it for £5** możesz to dostać za pięć funtów
5 (*give birth to*): **to have a baby** rodzić (urodzić *pf*) dziecko
6: **to have one's hair cut** obciąć (*pf*) sobie włosy (u fryzjera)
7 (*experience, suffer*): **to have a headache** mieć ból głowy; **to have an operation** mieć operację; **she had her bag stolen** ukradziono jej torbę; **she had her arm broken** złamała sobie rękę
▷ *aux vb* **1**: **she has arrived** przyjechała; **has he told you?** powiedział panu/pani?; **when she had dressed, she went downstairs** kiedy się ubrała, zeszła na dół; **I haven't seen him for ages/since July** nie widziałem go od dawna/od stycznia
2 (*in tag questions*): **he's done it, hasn't he?** zrobił to, prawda?
3 (*in short answers and questions*): **yes, I have** tak, zrobiłem (to); **no I haven't** nie, nie zrobiłem (tego); **so have I!** ja też!; **neither have I** ja też nie; **I've finished, have you?** ja już skończyłem, a ty?
4 (*be obliged*): **to have (got) to do sth** mieć coś do zrobienia; **she has (got) to do it** ona musi to zrobić; **this has (got) to be a mistake** to musi być jakaś pomyłka

▶ **have on** *vt* (*clothes*) mieć na sobie; **he didn't have anything on** nie miał nic na sobie; **I don't have any money on me** nie mam przy sobie żadnych pieniędzy

haven't ['hævnt] = **have not**
hay [heɪ] *n* siano
hay fever *n* katar sienny
hazel ['heɪzl] *adj* (*eyes*) orzechowy
hazelnut ['heɪzlnʌt] *n* orzech laskowy
he [hiː] *pron* (*man, boy*) on
head [hɛd] *n* **1** (*Anat*) głowa **2** (*mind*) głowa **3** (*of company, organization, department*) dyrektor(ka) *m/f* **4** (*Brit: head teacher*) dyrektor(ka) *m/f* ▷ *vt* **1** (*list, group*) być na początku +*gen* **2** (*Football: ball*) grać (zagrać *pf*) główką; **10 pounds a** *or* **per ~** dziesięć funtów na głowę; **it went to his ~** (*alcohol*) poszło mu do głowy; (*success, power*) uderzył mu do głowy; **to lose one's ~** tracić (stracić *pf*) głowę; **I can't make ~ or** *or* **nor tail of this** (*inf*) nic z tego nie rozumiem; **from ~ to foot** *or* **toe** od stóp do głów; **~s or tails?** orzeł czy reszka?
▶ **head for** *vt fus* (*place*) zmierzać do +*gen*; **to be ~ing** *or* **~ed for Glasgow** zmierzać w stronę Glasgow
▶ **head off** *vi* (*leave*) wyjeżdżać (wyjechać *pf*)
headache ['hɛdeɪk] *n* **1** (*pain*) ból głowy **2** (*problem*) utrapienie; **to have a ~** cierpieć na ból głowy
headlamp ['hɛdlæmp] (*Brit*) *n* = **headlight**

headlight ['hɛdlaɪt] n reflektor

headline ['hɛdlaɪn] n nagłówek; **the ~s** (*Publishing*) nagłówki; (*TV, Rad*) skrót najważniejszych wiadomości

headmaster [hɛd'mɑːstə^r] (*Brit*) n dyrektor szkoły

headmistress [hɛd'mɪstrɪs] (*Brit*) n dyrektorka szkoły

headphones ['hɛdfəunz] n pl słuchawki

headquarters ['hɛdkwɔːtəz] n pl (*of company, organization*) siedziba główna

head teacher (*Brit*) n dyrektor(ka) m/f szkoły

heal [hiːl] vi (*physically*) goić (zagoić pf) się

health [hɛlθ] n zdrowie; **to be good for one's ~** służyć czyjemuś zdrowiu; **to be bad for one's ~** szkodzić (zaszkodzić pf) czyjemuś zdrowiu; **to drink (to) sb's ~** pić (wypić pf) czyjeś zdrowie

healthy ['hɛlθɪ] adj zdrowy

heap [hiːp] n (*pile: of clothes, papers*) sterta; **heaps** or **a ~ of** (*inf*) kupa +gen

hear [hɪə^r] (*pt, pp* **heard** [həːd]) vt 1 (*sound, voice, music*) słyszeć (usłyszeć pf) 2 (*news, lecture, concert*) słuchać (posłuchać pf) +gen; **to ~ sb doing sth** słyszeć (usłyszeć pf) jak ktoś coś robi; **to ~ that...** słyszeć (usłyszeć pf), że...; **to ~ about sth/sb** słyszeć (usłyszeć pf) o czymś/kimś; **to ~ from sb** dostawać (dostać pf) wiadomość od kogoś; **I've never ~d of him** nigdy o nim nie słyszałem

heart [hɑːt] n serce; **hearts** n pl (*Cards*) kier sg; **to learn sth (off) by ~** uczyć (nauczyć pf) się czegoś na pamięć; **to know sth (off) by ~** znać coś na pamięć; **the ~ of London** serce Londynu; **to lose ~** tracić (stracić pf) ducha; **to break sb's ~** łamać (złamać pf) komuś serce; **my ~ sank** straciłem zapał; **to one's ~'s content** ile dusza zapragnie

heart attack n atak serca; **to have a ~** mieć atak serca

heartbroken ['hɑːtbrəukən] adj zrozpaczony

heat [hiːt] n 1 (*warmth*) ciepło 2 (*temperature*) ciepło 3 (*hob, flame etc*) temperatura 4 (*Sport: also:* **qualifying ~**) zawody eliminacyjne pl ▷ vt (*water, food*) podgrzewać (podgrzać pf); (*room, house*) ogrzewać (ogrzać pf); **I find the ~ unbearable** ten upał jest nie do wytrzymania
▶ **heat up** vt (*food*) podgrzewać (podgrzać pf)

heater ['hiːtə^r] n (*electric heater, gas heater*) grzejnik; (*in car*) ogrzewanie

heather ['hɛðə^r] n wrzos

heating ['hiːtɪŋ] n (*system*) ogrzewanie

heatwave ['hiːtweɪv] n fala upałów

heaven ['hɛvn] n niebo

heavy ['hɛvɪ] adj 1 (*in weight*) ciężki 2 (*well-built: person*) dobrze zbudowany 3 (*thick: material, door etc*) gruby 4 (*traffic*) duży; (*fine, penalty, sentence*) ciężki; (*drinking, smoking, gambling*) nałogowy; (*rain, snow*) obfity; **how ~ are you/is it?** ile pan/pani/to waży?;

a ~ drinker/smoker osoba która
dużo pije/pali
he'd [hi:d] = **he would, he had**
hedge [hɛdʒ] *n* żywopłot
hedgehog ['hɛdʒhɒg] *n* jeż
heel [hi:l] *n* **1** (*of foot*) pięta **2** (*of
shoe*) obcas; **heels** *n pl* (*also:* **high
~s**) wysokie obcasy
height [haɪt] *n* **1** (*of person, tree,
building*) wysokość **2** (*altitude*)
wysokość; **of average** or
medium ~ średniego wzrostu;
what ~ are you? ile ma pan/pani
wzrostu?; **to gain ~** nabierać
(nabrać *pf*) wysokości; **to lose
~** tracić (stracić *pf*) wysokość;
at knee/waist/shoulder ~ na
wysokości kolana/talii/ramion; **it
is the ~ of fashion/good taste** to
jest szczyt mody/dobrego gustu
held [hɛld] *pt, pp of* **hold**
helicopter ['hɛlɪkɒptər] *n*
helikopter
hell [hɛl] *n* (*Rel*) piekło ▷ *int* (*inf!*)
piekło; **a** or **one ~ of a lot of** (*inf*)
piekielnie dużo +*gen*; **to go to ~**
(*Rel*) iść (pójść *pf*) do piekła; **go to
~!** (*fig: inf!*) idź do diabła!; **it was ~**
(*inf*) to był koszmar; **oh, to ~ with
it!** (*inf*) ech, mam to gdzieś!
he'll [hi:l] = **he will, he shall**
hello [hə'ləu] *int* (*as greeting*)
cześć; (*Tel*) halo; (*to attract
attention*) halo
helmet ['hɛlmɪt] *n* (*of
motorcyclist, cyclist, astronaut*)
kask; (*of soldier, policeman,
fireman*) hełm
help [hɛlp] *n* pomoc; (*when in
danger*) ratunek ▷ *vt* (*person*)
pomagać (pomóc *pf*) +*dat* ▷ *vi*
1 (*assist*) pomagać (pomóc *pf*)

2 (*be useful*) przydawać (przydać
pf) się; **she needs ~ to get up the
stairs** ona potrzebuje pomocy
żeby dostać się na górę; **he's been
a great ~** bardzo mi pomógł;
with the ~ of sb/sth z pomocą
kogoś/czegoś; **I ~ed him (to) fix
his car** pomogłem mu naprawić
jego samochód; **~!** ratunku!; **can
I ~ you?** (*in shop*) czym mogę
panu/pani służyć?; **to ~ o.s. to
sth** (*serve oneself*) częstować
(poczęstować *pf*) się czymś;
(*inf: steal*) podkradać (podkraść
pf) coś; **he can't ~ it** nie może nic
na to poradzić; **I can't ~ feeling
sorry for him** jakoś mi go szkoda;
it can't be ~ed nic się na to nie
poradzi
helpful ['hɛlpful] *adj* (*person*)
pomocny; (*advice, suggestion*)
przydatny
helping ['hɛlpɪŋ] *n* (*of food*)
porcja
helpless ['hɛlplɪs] *adj*
(*defenceless*) bezbronny
hen [hɛn] *n* kura
her [həːr] *pron* (*acc*) ją; (*gen, dat*)
jej; (*inst*) nią; (*loc*) niej ▷ *adj* jej;
(*referring to subject of sentence*)
swój; **~ face was very red** jej
twarz była bardzo zaczerwieniona
herb [həːb, *US* əːrb] *n* ziele
herd [həːd] *n* stado
here [hɪər] *adv* **1** (*in/to this place*)
tutaj **2** (*near me*) tutaj; **"~!"**
(*present*) "jestem!"; **~'s my phone
number** to mój numer telefonu;
~ he is (*he's just arrived*) oto i on; **~
you are** (*take this*) proszę; **~ we
are!** (*found it!*) jest!; (*we've arrived!*)
jesteśmy na miejscu!; **~ and there**

tu i tam; **I'm ~ to help you** jestem
tutaj żeby panu/pani pomóc
hero ['hɪərəu] (pl **heroes**) n
bohater
heroin ['hɛrəuɪn] n heroina
heroine ['hɛrəuɪn] n bohaterka
hers [hɜːz] pron **1** (of woman,girl)
jej **2** (of female animal) jej; **this
is ~** to jest jej; **a friend of ~** jej
znajomy
herself [hə'sɛlf] pron **1** (gen, acc)
siebie; (dat, loc) sobie; (inst) sobą;
(reflexive pronoun) się **2** (emphatic)
sama; **she hurt ~** zrobiła sobie
krzywdę; **she lives by ~** mieszka
sama
he's [hiːz] = **he is, he has**
hesitate ['hɛzɪteɪt] vi wahać
(zawahać pf) się; **he did not ~
to take action** nie zawahał się
przed podjęciem działań; **don't ~
to contact me** proszę się ze mną
kontaktować bez wahania
heterosexual
['hɛtərəu'sɛksjuəl] adj
heteroseksualny ▷ n osoba
heteroseksualna
hi [haɪ] int cześć
hiccup ['hɪkʌp] n: **to have/get
(the) ~s** mieć czkawkę/dostawać
(dostać pf) czkawki
hide [haɪd] (pt **hid**, pp **hidden**) vt
ukrywać (ukryć pf) ▷ vi chować
(schować pf) się; **to ~ from sb**
chować (schować pf) się przed
kimś; **to ~ sth from sb** (lit)
chować (schować pf) coś przed
kimś; (fig) ukrywać (ukryć pf) coś
przed kimś
hi-fi ['haɪfaɪ] n zestaw hi-fi
high [haɪ] adj wysoki ▷ adv
wysoko; **it is 20m ~** to jest

wysokie na dwadzieścia metrów;
foods that are ~ in fat produkty
spożywcze zawierające duże
ilości tłuszczu; **the temperature
was in the ~ eighties**
temperatura sięgnęła blisko
dziewięćdziesięciu stopni; **safety
has always been our ~est
priority** zawsze stawialiśmy
bezpieczeństwo na pierwszym
miejscu; **~ up** (above the ground)
wysoko w górze; **to search** or
look ~ and low for sth szukać
czegoś wszędzie
higher education ['haɪə^r-] n
wyższe wykształcenie
high heels n pl wysokie obcasy
high jump n (Sport): **the ~** skok
wzwyż
high-rise ['haɪraɪz] adj w
wieżowcu ▷ n wieżowiec
high school n **1** (Brit: for students
aged 11-18) szkoła ogólnokształcąca
2 (US: for students aged 14-18)
liceum

- **HIGH SCHOOL**
-
- **High school** – W Wielkiej
- Brytanii uczniowie
- uczęszczają do szkoły średniej
- (**high school**) pomiędzy 11
- a 18 rokiem życia. W USA
- wcześniej jeszcze jest **junior
- high school**, do **high school**
- uczęszcza się pomiędzy 14 a 18
- rokiem życia.

hijack ['haɪdʒæk] vt (plane)
porywać (porwać pf); (idea, event)
przejmować (przejąć pf) ▷ n
porwanie

hijacker ['haɪdʒækə^r] n porywacz(ka) m/f

hike [haɪk] vi (go walking) wędrować (powędrować pf) ▷ n (walk) wędrówka

hiking ['haɪkɪŋ] n piesze wycieczki pl; **to go ~** iść/chodzić (pójść pf) na pieszą wędrówkę

hilarious [hɪ'lɛərɪəs] adj (account, adventure) komiczny

hill [hɪl] n (hillock) wzgórze; (slope) wzniesienie

hill-walking ['hɪlwɔːkɪŋ] n turystyka górska

him [hɪm] pron (acc, gen) jego, go; (dat) jemu, mu; (inst, loc) nim; **I haven't seen ~** nie widziałem go; **they gave ~ the job** dali mu tą pracę

himself [hɪm'sɛlf] pron 1 (gen, acc) siebie; (dat, loc) sobie; (inst) sobą; (reflexive pronoun) się 2 (emphatic) sam; **he hurt ~** skaleczył się; **he prepared the supper ~** sam przygotował kolację; **he lives by ~** mieszka sam

Hindu ['hɪnduː] n Hindus ▷ adj hinduski

hip [hɪp] n (Anat) biodro

hippie ['hɪpɪ] n hipis(ka) m/f

hippopotamus [hɪpə'pɔtəməs] (pl **hippopotamuses** or **hippopotami** [hɪpə'pɔtəmaɪ]) n hipopotam

hire ['haɪə^r] vt (esp Brit: car, equipment, hall) wynajmować (wynająć pf); (worker) zatrudniać (zatrudnić pf) ▷ n (Brit: of car, hall etc) wynajem; **for ~** (esp Brit: car, boat, building) do wynajęcia; (taxi) wolny

his [hɪz] adj 1 (of man, boy) jego 2 (of animal) jego; (referring to subject of sentence) swój ▷ pron jego; **~ face was very red** jego twarz była bardzo czerwona; **these are ~** te są jego; **a friend of ~** jego przyjaciel

history ['hɪstərɪ] n historia; **to make ~** przechodzić (przejść pf) do historii

hit [hɪt] (pt, pp **hit**) vt 1 (strike) uderzać (uderzyć pf) 2 (collide with) uderzać (uderzyć pf) 3 (target: bomb, bullet) trafiać (trafić pf) ▷ n 1 uderzenie 2 (on website) trafienie 3 (hit song) przebój; **to be/become a ~** (song, film, play) być/stawać (stać pf) się przebojem

▶ **hit off** vt: **to ~ it off (with sb)** (inf) zaprzyjaźniać (zaprzyjaźnić pf) się (z kimś)

hitch [hɪtʃ] n (difficulty) szkopuł; **technical ~** drobny problem techniczny

hitchhike ['hɪtʃhaɪk] vi jeździć (pojechać pf) autostopem

hitchhiker ['hɪtʃhaɪkə^r] n autostopowicz(ka) m/f

hitchhiking ['hɪtʃhaɪkɪŋ] n autostop

HIV n abbr (= human immunodeficiency virus) wirus HIV; **to be ~ positive/negative** być seropozytywnym/seronegatywnym

hoarse [hɔːs] adj (voice etc) zachrypnięty

hobby ['hɔbɪ] n hobby

hockey ['hɔkɪ] n 1 (Brit: on grass)

hokej na trawie **2** (*US: on ice*)
hokej

Hogmanay – tak w Szkocji
nazywana jest wigilia
Nowego Roku (31 grudnia).
Według tradycji tuż po
północy odwiedza się rodzinę
i przyjaciół obnosząc ze
sobą whisky oraz kawałek
węgla, co ma przynieść
szczęście w nowym roku.
Zwyczaj ten nazywany jest
first footing – pierwsza
osoba przekraczająca próg
domu ma ponoć wpływ na
powodzenie jego gospodarzy
w nadchodzącym roku.

hold [həuld] (*pt, pp* **held**) *vt*
1 (*grip*) trzymać **2** (*contain*)
zawierać (zawrzeć *pf*) ▷ *vi*
(*Tel*) czekać (poczekać *pf*) ▷ *n*
1 (*grasp*) uścisk **2** (*of ship, plane*)
ładownia; **to ~ sb responsible**
obarczać (obarczyć *pf*) kogoś
odpowiedzialnością; **~ the
line!** (*Tel*) proszę czekać!;
to ~ sb prisoner/hostage
przetrzymywać (przetrzymać *pf*)
kogoś jako więźnia/zakładnika;
~ it! chwileczkę!; **to get** *or* **grab
~ of sb/sth** chwytać (chwycić *pf*)
kogoś/coś; **I need to get ~ of Bob**
muszę złapać Boba
▶ **hold against** *vt*: **to ~ sth
against sb** mieć coś komuś za złe
▶ **hold on** *vi* **1** (*keep hold*) nie
puszczać (puścić *pf*) **2** (*inf: wait*)
czekać (poczekać *pf*)

▶ **hold on to** *vt fus* (*grasp*) łapać
(złapać *pf*) się +*gen*
▶ **hold up** *vt* **1** (*lift up*) unosić
(unieść *pf*) **2** (*delay*) zatrzymywać
(zatrzymać *pf*) **3** (*rob: person, bank*)
napadać (napaść *pf*) na
hold-up ['həuldʌp] *n* **1** (*robbery*)
napad z bronią w ręku **2** (*delay*)
opóźnienie; (*in traffic*) korek
hole [həul] *n* dziura
holiday ['hɔlɪdeɪ] (*Brit*) *n*
wakacje *f pl*; **public ~** dzień wolny
od pracy; **the school/summer ~s**
(*Brit: Scol*) wakacje szkolne/
letnie; **the Christmas ~s** ferie
świąteczne; **to be on ~** być na
wakacjach
Holland ['hɔlənd] *n* Holandia
hollow ['hɔləu] *adj* pusty
holly ['hɔlɪ] *n* ostrokrzew
holy ['həulɪ] *adj* święty
home [həum] *n* **1** (*house*)
dom **2** (*country, area*) ojczyzna
3 (*institution*) dom ▷ *adj*
(*Sport: team*) miejscowy; (*game*)
na własnym boisku ▷ *adv* (*be*)
w domu; (*go*) do domu; **at ~** (*in
house*) w domu; (*comfortable*) jak
w domu; **make yourself at ~** czuj
się jak u siebie w domu
homeland ['həumlænd] *n* kraj
rodzinny
homeless ['həumlɪs] *adj* (*family,
refugee*) bezdomny ▷ *n pl*: **the ~**
bezdomni
homepage ['həumpeɪdʒ]
(*Comput*) *n* strona główna
homesick ['həumsɪk] *adj*
tęskniący za domem; **to be ~**
tęsknić (zatęsknić *pf*) za domem
homework ['həumwəːk] *n*
zadanie domowe; **to do one's ~**

(*lit*) odrabiać (odrobić *pf*) zadanie domowe

homophobia [həuməfəubɪə] *n* homofobia

homosexual [hɔməu'sɛksjuəl] *adj* homoseksualny ▷ *n* homoseksualista(-tka) *m/f*

honest ['ɔnɪst] *adj* **1** (*truthful*) uczciwy **2** (*trustworthy*) godny zaufania; **to be ~,...** mówiąc szczerze,...

honestly ['ɔnɪstlɪ] *adv* **1** (*with integrity*) uczciwie **2** (*bluntly*) szczerze **3** (*emphasizing sth*) serio

honesty ['ɔnɪstɪ] *n* uczciwość

honey ['hʌnɪ] *n* **1** (*food*) miód **2** (*esp US: inf: darling*) kochanie

honeymoon ['hʌnɪmuːn] *n* (*lit, fig*) miesiąc miodowy; **to be on (one's) ~** być w podróży poślubnej

Hong Kong ['hɔŋ'kɔŋ] *n* Hong Kong

honour ['ɔnəʳ] (*US* **honor**) *n* **1** (*pride, self-respect*) honor **2** (*tribute*) zaszczyt; **the ~ of hosting the Olympic Games** zaszczyt bycia gospodarzem Igrzysk Olimpijskich

hood [hud] *n* **1** (*of coat etc*) kaptur **2** (*US: Aut*) maska

hoof [huːf] (*pl* **hooves**) *n* kopyto

hook [huk] *n* hak; **to take the phone off the ~** zdejmować (zdjąć *pf*) słuchawkę z widełek

hooligan ['huːlɪɡən] *n* chuligan

hooray [huː'reɪ] *int* hura

Hoover® ['huːvəʳ] (*Brit*) *n* odkurzacz ▷ *vt* (*carpet*) odkurzać (odkurzyć *pf*)

hooves [huːvz] *n pl of* **hoof**

hop [hɔp] *vi* (*jump: person*) skakać (skoczyć *pf*); (*bird*) podskakiwać

(podskoczyć *pf*)

hope [həup] *vt* mieć nadzieję ▷ *vi* mieć nadzieję ▷ *n* nadzieja; **I ~ so/not** mam nadzieję/ma nadzieję, że nie; **to ~ to do sth** mieć nadzieję, że coś się zrobi; **to have no ~ of sth/doing sth** nie mieć szans na coś/na zrobienie czegoś; **in the ~ of/that...** w nadziei na/że...

hopefully ['həupfulɪ] *adv* (*expectantly*) z nadzieją; **~,...** przy odrobinie szczęścia,...

hopeless ['həuplɪs] *adj* beznadziejny; **I'm ~ at cooking** jestem beznadziejny w gotowaniu

horizon [hə'raɪzn] *n* (*skyline*): **the ~** horyzont; **on the ~** (*fig*) na horyzoncie

horizontal [hɔrɪ'zɔntl] *adj* poziomy

horn [hɔːn] *n* **1** (*of animal*) róg **2** (*Mus*) róg **3** (*Aut*) klakson

horoscope ['hɔrəskəup] *n* horoskop

horrible ['hɔrɪbl] *adj* (*colour, food, mess*) okropny; (*accident, crime*) straszny; (*experience, situation, dream*) straszny

horrifying ['hɔrɪfaɪɪŋ] *adj* przerażający

horror ['hɔrəʳ] *n* (*alarm*) przerażenie

horror film *n* horror

horse [hɔːs] *n* koń

horse racing *n* wyścigi konne *pl*

horse riding *n* jazda konna

hose [həuz] *n* (*also:* **~pipe**) wąż

hospital ['hɔspɪtl] *n* szpital; **to be in ~** or (*US*) **in the ~** być w szpitalu

hospitality [hɔspɪ'tælɪtɪ] *n*

gościnność
host [həust] *n* gospodarz
hostage ['hɒstɪdʒ] *n* (*prisoner*)
zakładnik(-iczka) *m/f*; **to be
taken/held ~** być wziętym/
przetrzymywanym jako zakładnik
hostel ['hɒstl] (*esp Brit*) *n* (*for
homeless etc*) schronisko
hostess ['həustɪs] *n* gospodyni
hot [hɒt] *adj* **1** (*very warm*) gorący
2 (*spicy: food*) ostry
hot dog *n* hot dog
hotel [həu'tɛl] *n* hotel; **to stay at
a ~** zatrzymywać (zatrzymać *pf*)
się w hotelu
hour ['auə^r] *n* godzina; **hours**
n pl (*ages*) całe godziny; **the
buses leave on the ~** autobusy
odjeżdżają o równych godzinach;
for three/four ~s przez
trzy/cztery godziny; **(at) 60
kilometres/miles an** *or* **per
~** z prędkością sześćdziesięciu
kilometrów/mil na godzinę; **to
pay sb by the ~** płacić (zapłacić
pf) komuś od godziny; **lunch ~**
pora lunchu
hourly ['auəlɪ] *adv* (*once each
hour*) co godzinę ▷ *adj* **1** (*once each
hour*) cogodzinny **2** (*per hour: rate,
income*) od godziny
house [haus] *n* (*home*) dom; **at
my ~/to my ~** w moim domu/do
mojego domu

○ **HOUSES OF PARLIAMENT**

Houses of Parliment – w
Wielkiej Brytanii parlament
składa się z dwóch Izb: Izby
Gmin i Izby Lordów.

housewife ['hauswaɪf] (*pl*
housewives) *n* gospodyni
domowa
housework ['hauswəːk] *n* prace
domowe *pl*
housing estate ['hauzɪŋ-] (*Brit*)
n osiedle mieszkaniowe
hovercraft ['hɒvəkrɑːft] (*pl*
hovercraft) *n* poduszkowiec

○ **KEYWORD**

how [hau] *adv* **1** (*in questions*) jak;
how did you do it? jak to pan
zrobił/pani zrobiła?; **how are
you?** jak się pan/pani miewa?;
**"how do you do?" — "how
do you do?"** "miło mi!" — "miło
mi!"; **how long have you lived
here?** jak długo pan/pani tutaj
mieszka?; **how much milk/how
many people?** ile mleka/ilu
ludzi?; **how old are you?** ile ma
pan/pani lat?; **how tall is he?**
jakiego on jest wzrostu?
2 (*in exclamations*): **how lovely/
awful!** to wspaniale/okropne!
3 (*in suggestions*): **how about a
cup of tea/a walk?** co powie
pan/pani na filiżankę herbaty/
spacer?; **how about going to
the cinema?** co powie pan/pani
na kino?
4 (*avoiding repetition*): **how about
you?** a pan/pani?
▷ *conj* jak; **I know how she did
it** wiem jak pani to zrobiła; **to
know how to do sth** wiedzieć jak
coś zrobić

however [hau'ɛvə^r] *adv* **1** (*but*)
jednak **2** (*with adj, adv*) bez

względu na to jak **3** (*in questions*)
jakim cudem
hug [hʌg] *vt* (*person*) przytulać
(przytulić *pf*) ▷ *n* uścisk; **to give
sb a ~** przytulać (przytulić *pf*)
kogoś
huge [hju:dʒ] *adj* ogromny
hum [hʌm] *vt* (*tune, song*) nucić
(zanucić *pf*) ▷ *vi* (*person*) nucić;
(*machine*) buczeć (zabuczeć *pf*);
(*insect*) brzęczeć (zabrzęczeć *pf*)
human [ˈhju:mən] *adj* ludzki ▷ *n*
(*also*: **~ being**) człowiek; **the ~
race** rasa ludzka; **~ nature** natura
ludzka
humour [ˈhju:məʳ] (*US* **humor**)
n humor; **sense of ~** poczucie
humoru
hundred [ˈhʌndrəd] *num* sto;
hundreds *n pl* setki; **a** *or* **one ~
books/dollars** sto książek/
dolarów; **a** *or* **one ~ people** stu
ludzi
hung [hʌŋ] *pt, pp of* **hang**
Hungarian [hʌŋˈgɛərɪən]
adj węgierski ▷ *n* **1** (*person*)
Węgier(ka) *m/f* **2** (*language*)
węgierski
Hungary [ˈhʌŋgərɪ] *n* Węgry *f pl*
hunger [ˈhʌŋgəʳ] *n* głód
hungry [ˈhʌŋgrɪ] *adj* głodny; **to
be ~** być głodnym
hunt [hʌnt] *vt* **1** (*for food, sport*)
polować (zapolować *pf*) na
2 (*criminal, fugitive*) poszukiwać
+*gen* ▷ *vi* polować (zapolować *pf*)
▷ *n* **1** (*for food, sport*) polowanie
2 (*for missing person*) poszukiwania
nt pl; **detectives are ~ing for
clues** policja poszukuje tropów
hunting [ˈhʌntɪŋ] *n* polowanie;
job/house ~ polowanie na

pracę/dom
hurdle [ˈhə:dl] *n* (*difficulty*)
przeszkoda; **hurdles** *n pl* (*Sport*)
płotki
hurricane [ˈhʌrɪkən] *n* huragan;
~ Charley/Tessa huragan
Charley/Tessa
hurry [ˈhʌrɪ] *vi* śpieszyć
(pośpieszyć *pf*) się ▷ *n*: **to be in
a ~ (to do sth)** śpieszyć się (żeby
coś zrobić); **to ~ home** śpieszyć
(pośpieszyć *pf*) się do domu; **to do
sth in a ~** robić (zrobić *pf*) coś w
pośpiechu; **there's** *or* **I'm in no ~**
nie ma pośpiechu; **what's the ~?**
po co ten pośpiech?
▷ **hurry up** *vi* śpieszyć
(pośpieszyć *pf*) się ▷ *vt* popędzać
(popędzić *pf*)
hurt [hə:t] (*pt, pp* **hurt**) *vt* **1** (*cause
pain to*) sprawiać (sprawić *pf*)
+*dat* ból **2** (*injure*) ranić (zranić *pf*)
3 (*emotionally*) ranić (zranić *pf*) ▷ *vi*
(*be painful*) boleć (zaboleć *pf*) ▷ *adj*
1 (*injured*) zraniony **2** (*emotionally*)
urażony; **to ~ o.s.** ranić (zranić
pf) się; **I didn't want to ~ your
feelings** nie chciałem zranić
twoich uczuć; **where does it ~?**
gdzie boli?
husband [ˈhʌzbənd] *n* mąż
hut [hʌt] *n* **1** (*house*) chata **2** (*shed*)
szopa
hymn [hɪm] *n* hymn
hyperlink [ˈhaɪpəlɪŋk] *n* link
hyphen [ˈhaɪfn] *n* łącznik

oblodzony

ID n abbr (= identification) dowód
osobisty

I'd [aɪd] = **I would, I had**

idea [aɪ'dɪə] n **1** (scheme) pomysł
2 (opinion, theory) opinia **3** (notion)
wyobrażenie; **(what a) good ~!**
(cóż za) dobry pomysł!; **I haven't
the slightest** or **faintest ~** nie
mam zielonego pojęcia

ideal [aɪ'dɪəl] adj (person, world)
idealny

identical [aɪ'dɛntɪkl] adj
identyczny; **~ to** dokładnie taki
sam jak

identification [aɪdɛntɪfɪ'keɪʃən]
n identyfikacja

identify [aɪ'dɛntɪfaɪ] vt
(recognize) rozpoznawać
(rozpoznać pf)

identity card n dowód osobisty

idiot ['ɪdɪət] n idiota(-tka) m/f

i.e. abbr (= id est) tj.

I [aɪ] pron ja

ice [aɪs] n lód

iceberg ['aɪsbə:g] n góra lodowa;
the tip of the ~ (fig) wierzchołek
góry lodowej

ice cream n lody m pl

ice cube n kostka lodu

ice hockey (esp Brit) n hokej

Iceland ['aɪslənd] n Islandia

ice rink [-rɪŋk] n lodowisko

ice-skating ['aɪsskeɪtɪŋ] n
łyżwiarstwo; (figure skating)
łyżwiarstwo figurowe

icing ['aɪsɪŋ] (Culin) n lukier

icon ['aɪkɔn] n ikona

ICT (Brit) n abbr (= Information and
Communication Technology) ICT

icy ['aɪsɪ] adj (air, water,
temperature) lodowaty; (road)

○ **KEYWORD**

if [ɪf] conj **1** (conditional use) jeśli;
I'll go if you come with me pójdę
jeśli pójdzie pan/pani ze mną; **if
anyone comes in...** jeśli ktoś
przyjdzie...; **if I were you** gdybym
był tobą; **if necessary** jeśli to
konieczne; **if so** jeśli tak; **if not**
jeśli nie

2 (whenever) kiedy; **if we are in
Hong Kong, we always go to
see her** kiedy jesteśmy w Hong
Kongu, zawsze jedziemy ją
odwiedzić

3 (whether) czy; **I don't know if
he's in** nie wiem, czy jest w domu;

ask him if he can come zapytaj, czy może przyjść
4 (*in expressions*): **if ever** jeśli; **if only we had more time!** gdybyśmy mieli więcej czasu!

ignore [ɪg'nɔːʳ] *vt* ignorować (zignorować *pf*)
I'll [aɪl] = **I will**, **I shall**
ill [ɪl] *adj* (*sick*) chory; **the ill** *n pl*: **the mentally/terminally ~** umysłowo/śmiertelnie chorzy; **to fall** *or* **be taken ~** zachorować (*pf*)
illegal [ɪ'liːgl] *adj* nielegalny
illness ['ɪlnɪs] *n* choroba
illusion [ɪ'luːʒən] *n* **1** (*false idea*) iluzja **2** (*false appearance*) złudzenie
illustration [ɪlə'streɪʃən] *n* (*picture*) ilustracja
image ['ɪmɪdʒ] *n* **1** (*mental picture*) wyobrażenie **2** (*public face*) wizerunek
imagination [ɪmædʒɪ'neɪʃən] *n* wyobraźnia
imagine [ɪ'mædʒɪn] *vt* **1** (*envisage*) wyobrażać (wyobrazić *pf*) sobie **2** (*dream*) wyobrażać (wyobrazić *pf*) sobie **3** (*suppose*) przypuszczać
imitate ['ɪmɪteɪt] *vt* **1** (*copy*) imitować **2** (*mimic*) naśladować
imitation [ɪmɪ'teɪʃən] *n* (*copy*) imitacja ▷ *adj* sztuczny
immediate [ɪ'miːdɪət] *adj* natychmiastowy
immediately [ɪ'miːdɪətlɪ] *adv* **1** (*at once*) natychmiast **2** (*apparent, obvious*) bezpośrednio ▷ *conj*: **~ he had said it, he regretted it** jak tylko to powiedział, pożałował; **~ before/**

after zaraz przed +*inst*/po +*loc*
immigrant ['ɪmɪgrənt] *n* imigrant(ka) *m/f*
immigration [ɪmɪ'greɪʃən] *n* **1** (*process*) imigracja **2** (*also*: **~ control**: *at airport, port, border*) kontrola paszportowa ▷ *adj* (*policy, controls, officer*) imigracyjny
impatience [ɪm'peɪʃəns] *n* niecierpliwość
impatient [ɪm'peɪʃənt] *adj* (*at waiting*) niecierpliwy; **to get ~ (at** *or* **with sth)** niecierpliwić (zniecierpliwić *pf*) się (czymś)
impolite [ɪmpə'laɪt] *adj* niegrzeczny
import [ɪm'pɔːt] *vt* (*goods*) importować (zaimportować *pf*)
importance [ɪm'pɔːtns] *n* **1** (*significance*) znaczenie **2** (*influence*) waga
important [ɪm'pɔːtənt] *adj* ważny; **it is ~ to eat sensibly** ważne, żeby jeść rozsądnie; **it is ~ for them to understand that...** ważne, żeby zrozumieli, że...; **it's not ~** to nie ważne
impossible [ɪm'pɔsɪbl] *adj* **1** (*task, demand*) niewykonalny **2** (*situation, position*) niemożliwy; **it is ~ to understand what's going on** nie można zrozumieć o co chodzi; **it's ~ for me to leave now** nie mogę teraz wyjść
impress [ɪm'prɛs] *vt* (*person*) robić (zrobić *pf*) wrażenie na +*loc*; **to be ~ed by** *or* **with sb/sth** być pod wrażeniem kogoś/czegoś
impression [ɪm'prɛʃən] *n* **1** (*of place, situation, person*) wrażenie **2** (*imitation*) udawanie; **to be under the ~ that...** mieć

wrażenie, że…; **to make** or **create a good/bad ~** robić (zrobić pf) dobre/złe wrażenie

impressive [ɪmˈprɛsɪv] adj imponujący

improve [ɪmˈpruːv] vt poprawiać (poprawić pf) ▷ vi poprawiać (poprawić pf) się

improvement [ɪmˈpruːvmənt] n poprawa; **~ in** postęp w +loc

○ **KEYWORD**

in [ɪn] prep **1** (indicating place, position) w +loc; **it's in the house/garden/box** to jest w domu/ogrodzie/pudełku; **put it in the house/garden/box** połóż to w domu/ogrodzie/pudełku; **in here/there** tu/tam
2 (with place names) w +loc; **in London/England** w Londynie/ Anglii
3 (time: during) w ciągu +gen; (within: referring to future) w +loc; (referring to past) w +loc; **in 1988/ in May** w roku tysiąc dziewięćset osiemdziesiątym ósmym/w maju; **in spring/summer** wiosną/latem; **in the morning/ afternoon** rano/popołudniu; **I'll see you in two weeks' time** or **in two weeks** zobaczymy się za dwa tygodnie; **I did it in three hours/days** zrobiłem to w ciągu trzech godzin/dni
4 (indicating manner, style etc) w +loc; **in pencil/ink** ołówkiem/ atramentem; **the boy in the blue shirt** chłopiec w niebieskiej bluzce; **in the sun/rain** w słońcu/deszczu

5 (with languages) po +loc; **in English/French** po angielsku/ francusku
6 (with ratios, numbers) na; **one in ten people** jedna na dziesięć osób; **they lined up in twos** ustawili się po dwóch
7 (in book, film, activity) w +loc; **I read it in a newspaper** czytałem o tym w gazecie
8 (amongst) w +loc; **the best athlete in the team** najlepszy sportowiec w drużynie
▷ adv **1**: **to be in** (at home) być w domu; (at work) być obecnym; **is Harry in?** czy jest Harry?; **to ask sb in** zapraszać (zaprosić pf) kogoś do środka
2 (shock, surprise): **he is in for a shock** czeka go wstrząs

inch [ɪntʃ] n cal

include [ɪnˈkluːd] vt zawierać (zawrzeć pf)

including [ɪnˈkluːdɪŋ] prep w tym; **it costs £15, ~ postage and packing** kosztuje piętnaście funtów, w tym wysyłka i pakowanie; **nine people were injured, ~ two Britons** dziewięć osób zostało rannych, w tym dwoje Brytyjczyków

income [ˈɪnkʌm] n dochód

income tax n podatek dochodowy

inconsistent [ɪnkənˈsɪstnt] adj nierówny

inconvenient [ɪnkənˈviːnjənt] adj (time, moment) niewygodny; **that's very ~ for me** to dla mnie bardzo kłopotliwe

incorrect [ɪnkəˈrɛkt] adj

(*information, answer*) błędny
increase [*n* 'ɪnkriːs, *vb* ɪn'kriːs]
n wzrost ▷ *vi* (*price, level,
productivity*) rosnąć (urosnąć *pf*)
▷ *vt* (*price, number, level*) podnosić
(podnieść *pf*); **a 5% ~, an ~ of 5%**
pięcioprocentowy wzrost; **to be
on the ~** wzrastać (wzrosnąć *pf*)
incredible [ɪn'krɛdɪbl]
adj **1** (*amazing, wonderful*)
niesamowity **2** (*unbelievable*)
niewiarygodny
indeed [ɪn'diːd] *adv* (*certainly*)
rzeczywiście; **yes ~!** tak,
oczywiście!
independence [ɪndɪ'pɛndns]
n niepodległość; **to declare
~** ogłaszać (ogłosić *pf*)
niepodległość; **~ of mind/spirit**
niezależność myśli/ducha

○ **INDEPENDENCE DAY**
○
○ **Independence Day** – Dzień
○ Niepodległości przypada 4
○ lipca. W USA jest to święto
○ narodowe, upamiętniające
○ podpisanie w 1776 roku
○ Deklaracji Niepodległości
○ głoszącej niezależność 13
○ kolonii amerykańskich od
○ Wielkiej Brytanii.

independent [ɪndɪ'pɛndnt]
adj (*person, inquiry, organization*)
niezależny; (*country*) niepodległy;
financially ~ niezależny
finansowo
index [ˈɪndɛks] (*pl* **indexes**) *n* (*in
book*) indeks; (*library etc*)
katalog
India [ˈɪndɪə] *n* Indie *f pl*

Indian [ˈɪndɪən] *adj* indyjski ▷ *n*
(*person from India*) Hindus(ka) *m/f*
indicate [ˈɪndɪkeɪt] *vt* **1** (*show*)
pokazywać (pokazać *pf*) **2** (*point
to*) wskazywać (wskazać *pf*)
indicator [ˈɪndɪkeɪtər] *n* (*Brit: on
car*) kierunkowskaz
indifferent [ɪn'dɪfrənt]
adj **1** (*uninterested*) obojętny
2 (*mediocre*) przeciętny
indigestion [ɪndɪ'dʒɛstʃən] *n*
niestrawność
individual [ɪndɪ'vɪdjuəl] *n*
(*single person*) jednostka ▷ *adj*
1 (*personal*) osobisty **2** (*particular*)
indywidualny
indoor [ˈɪndɔːʳ] *adj* we wnętrzach
indoors [ɪn'dɔːz] *adv* wewnątrz
industrial [ɪn'dʌstrɪəl] *adj*
(*equipment, production, waste*)
przemysłowy; (*accident*) w
miejscu pracy
industrial estate (*Brit*) *n* strefa
przemysłowa
industrial park (*US*) *n* strefa
przemysłowa
industry [ˈɪndəstrɪ] *n* przemysł
inevitable [ɪn'ɛvɪtəbl] *adj*
nieunikniony ▷ *n*: **the ~** to, co
nieuniknione
inexperienced [ɪnɪk'spɪərɪənst]
adj niedoświadczony

○ **INFANT SCHOOL**
○
○ Brytyjskie **infant schools**
○ (szkoły dla najmłodszych)
○ to odpowiedniki
○ przedszkoli. Chodzą do nich,
○ obowiązkowo, dzieci w wieku
○ od lat pięciu (czasem czterech)
○ do lat siedmiu.

infection [ɪnˈfɛkʃən] n 1 (disease)
infekcja 2 (contagion) zakażenie;
to have an ear/throat ~ mieć
zapalenie ucha/gardła

infectious [ɪnˈfɛkʃəs] adj (disease)
zakaźny

inflation [ɪnˈfleɪʃən] n inflacja

influence [ˈɪnfluəns] n wpływ
▷ vt (person, situation, choice)
wpływać (wpłynąć pf) na; **to be a
good/bad ~ on sb** mieć dobry/zły
wpływ na kogoś

inform [ɪnˈfɔːm] vt (tell)
powiadamiać (powiadomić
pf); **to ~ sb that...** informować
(poinformować pf) kogoś, że...

informal [ɪnˈfɔːml] adj 1 (person,
speech, behaviour) bezpośredni
2 (clothes, party) swobodny
3 (unofficial) nieformalny

information [ɪnfəˈmeɪʃən]
n informacja; **a piece of ~**
informacja; **for your ~** do twojej
wiadomości

information technology n
technika informacyjna

infuriating [ɪnˈfjuərieɪtɪŋ] adj
irytujący

ingredient [ɪnˈgriːdiənt] n (in
food) składnik

inhabitant [ɪnˈhæbɪtnt] n
mieszkaniec(-nka) m/f

inherit [ɪnˈhɛrɪt] vt (property,
money) dziedziczyć (odziedziczyć
pf)

initial [ɪˈnɪʃl] n (letter) pierwsza
litera; **initials** n pl (of name)
inicjały

injection [ɪnˈdʒɛkʃən] n (Med)
zastrzyk; **to give sb an ~** robić
(zrobić pf) komuś zastrzyk

injure [ˈɪndʒəʳ] vt (person) ranić

(zranić pf); **he was badly ~d in
the attack** został poważnie ranny
podczas ataku

injured [ˈɪndʒəd] adj (person, part
of body) ranny ▷ n pl: **the ~** ofiary

injury [ˈɪndʒərɪ] n (wound) rana;
to escape without ~ uciec bez
szwanku

ink [ɪŋk] n (in pen) atrament

in-laws [ˈɪnlɔːz] n pl teściowie

innocent [ˈɪnəsnt] adj (not guilty)
niewinny; **to be ~ of a crime** nie
być winnym zbrodni

insane [ɪnˈseɪn] adj
1 (clinically: person) obłąkany
2 (foolish: idea, scheme) szalony

insect [ˈɪnsɛkt] n owad

insect repellent [-rɪˈpɛlənt] n
środek odstraszający owady

insert [ɪnˈsəːt] vt (object: into sth)
wstawiać (wstawić pf)

inside [ˈɪnsaɪd] n wnętrze ▷ adj
(wall, surface) wewnętrzny ▷ adv
1 (go) do środka; (be) wewnątrz
2 (indoors) wewnątrz ▷ prep (place,
container) wewnątrz +gen

inside out adv na lewą stronę

insist [ɪnˈsɪst] vi, vt nalegać; **to
~ on sth/doing sth** nalegać na
coś/na zrobienie czegoś

inspector [ɪnˈspɛktəʳ] n 1 (official)
inspektor(ka) m/f 2 (Brit: Police)
inspektor(ka) m/f 3 (Brit: also:
ticket ~) kontroler(ka) m/f

install, instal [ɪnˈstɔːl] vt
instalować (zainstalować pf)

instalment [ɪnˈstɔːlmənt] (US
installment) n 1 (payment) rata
2 (of story, TV serial) odcinek

instance [ˈɪnstəns] n (example)
przykład; **for ~** na przykład

instant [ˈɪnstənt] n (moment)

chwila ▷ adj 1 (reaction, success)
natychmiastowy 2 (coffee)
rozpuszczalny; (soup, noodles)
błyskawiczny; **for an ~** przez
chwilę

instantly ['ɪnstəntlɪ] adv od razu

instead [ɪn'stɛd] adv natomiast;
~ of zamiast +gen

instinct ['ɪnstɪŋkt] n instynkt

instruct [ɪn'strʌkt] vt (tell): **to
~ sb to do sth** instruować
(poinstruować pf) kogoś, aby
coś zrobił

instruction [ɪn'strʌkʃən] adj
instrukcyjny; **~ manual** or **leaflet**
instrukcja; **instructions** n pl
instrukcja f sg

instructor [ɪn'strʌktə^r] n
instruktor(ka) m/f

instrument ['ɪnstrumənt] n
1 (tool, device) przyrząd 2 (Mus)
instrument

insulin ['ɪnsjulɪn] n insulina

insult [n 'ɪnsʌlt, vb ɪn'sʌlt] n
obelga ▷ vt obrażać (obrazić pf)

insurance [ɪn'ʃuərəns]
n ubezpieczenie; **life ~**
ubezpieczenie na życie; **health ~**
ubezpieczenie zdrowotne

insure [ɪn'ʃuə^r] vt (house, car)
ubezpieczać (ubezpieczyć pf)

intelligent [ɪn'tɛlɪdʒənt] adj
(person) inteligentny

intend [ɪn'tɛnd] vt: **to ~ to do
sth** zamierzać coś zrobić; **to be
~ed for sb/sth** (gift, money) być
przeznaczonym dla kogoś/czegoś

intense [ɪn'tɛns] adj 1 (great: heat,
pain) intensywny; (competition)
zacięty 2 (person) zasadniczy

intensive [ɪn'tɛnsɪv] adj
intensywny

intensive care n: **to be in ~** być
leczony na oddziale intensywnej
opieki medycznej

intention [ɪn'tɛnʃən] n zamiar;
to have no/every ~ of doing sth
nie mieć zamiaru/mieć zamiar
coś zrobić

interest ['ɪntrɪst] n 1 (in subject,
idea, person) zainteresowanie
2 (pastime, hobby) zainteresowanie
3 (on loan, savings) odsetki m pl ▷ vt
(work, subject, idea) interesować
(zainteresować pf); **to take
an ~ in sth/sb** interesować
(zainteresować pf) się czymś/
kimś; **to lose ~ (in sth/sb)** tracić
(stracić pf) zainteresowanie
(czymś/kimś); **to be in sb's ~s** być
w kogoś interesie

interested ['ɪntrɪstɪd] adj: **to be
~ (in sth/doing sth)** interesować
(zainteresować pf) się (czymś/
robieniem czegoś)

interesting ['ɪntrɪstɪŋ] adj (idea,
place, person) interesujący; **it
will be ~ to see how he reacts**
ciekawie będzie zobaczyć jak on
zareaguje

interfere [ɪntə'fɪə^r] vi (meddle)
ingerować; **to ~ with sth** (plans,
career, duty) kolidować z czymś

interior [ɪn'tɪərɪə^r] n (of building,
car, box) wnętrze ▷ adj (door,
window, room) wewnętrzny

international [ɪntə'næʃənl] adj
międzynarodowy

internet ['ɪntənɛt] n: **the ~**
internet

internet café [-'kæfeɪ] n
kawiarenka internetowa

interpreter [ɪn'tə:prɪtə^r] n
tłumacz(ka) m/f

interrupt [ɪntə'rʌpt] *vt* **1** (*speaker, conversation*) przerywać (przerwać *pf*) **2** (*activity*) przerywać (przerwać *pf*) ▷ *vi* (*in conversation*) przerywać (przerwać *pf*)

interruption [ɪntə'rʌpʃən] *n* przerwa

interval ['ɪntəvl] *n* **1** (*break, pause*) przerwa **2** (*Brit: Theat*) antrakt; (*Mus*) interwał; (*Sport*) przerwa

interview ['ɪntəvjuː] *n* **1** (*for job*) rozmowa kwalifikacyjna **2** (*Publishing, Rad, TV*) wywiad ▷ *vt* **1** (*for job*) przeprowadzać (przeprowadzić *pf*) rozmowę kwalifikacyjną z +*inst* **2** (*Publishing, Rad, TV*) przeprowadzać (przeprowadzić *pf*) wywiad z +*inst*; **to go for/have an ~** iść na/mieć rozmowę kwalifikacyjną

interviewer ['ɪntəvjuər] *n* (*Rad, TV*) dziennikarz(-rka) *m/f* przeprowadzający(-ca) wywiad

intimidate [ɪn'tɪmɪdeɪt] *vt* zastraszać (zastraszyć *pf*)

into ['ɪntu] *prep* (*indicating motion, direction*) do +*gen*; **to come ~ the house/garden** wchodzić (wejść *pf*) do domu/ogrodu; **to get ~ the car** wchodzić (wejść *pf*) do samochodu; **he threw some socks ~ his case** wrzucił skarpetki do walizki; **let's go ~ town** chodźmy do miasta; **to translate sth from English ~ French** tłumaczyć (przetłumaczyć *pf*) coś z angielskiego na francuski; **research ~ cancer** badania nad rakiem; **he worked late ~ the night** pracował do późnej nocy; **they got ~ trouble** wpakowali się w kłopoty; **I'd like to change**

some zlotys ~ pounds chciałbym wymienić trochę złotych na funty

introduce [ɪntrə'djuːs] *vt* **1** (*new idea, measure, technology*) przedstawiać (przedstawić *pf*) **2** (*speaker, TV show, radio programme*) poprzedzać (poprzedzić *pf*) słowem wstępnym **3: to ~ sb (to sb)** przedstawiać (przedstawić *pf*) kogoś (komuś) **4: to ~ sb to sth** (*pastime, technique*) prezentować (zaprezentować *pf*) komuś coś

introduction [ɪntrə'dʌkʃən] *n* **1** (*of new idea, measure, technology*) prezentacja **2** (*of person*) przedstawienie **3** (*beginning: of book, talk*) wstęp

invade [ɪn'veɪd] *vt* (*Mil*) atakować (zaatakować *pf*)

invalid ['ɪnvəlɪd] *n* inwalida(-dka) *m/f*

invent [ɪn'vɛnt] *vt* wynaleźć (*pf*)

invention [ɪn'vɛnʃən] *n* wynalazek

investigate [ɪn'vɛstɪgeɪt] *vi* przeprowadzać (przeprowadzić *pf*) dochodzenie

investigation [ɪnvɛstɪ'geɪʃən] *n* dochodzenie

invisible [ɪn'vɪzɪbl] *adj* niewidoczny

invitation [ɪnvɪ'teɪʃən] *n* zaproszenie

invite [ɪn'vaɪt] *vt* zapraszać (zaprosić *pf*); **to ~ sb to do sth** zapraszać (zaprosić *pf*) kogoś do zrobienia czegoś; **to ~ sb to dinner** zapraszać (zaprosić *pf*) kogoś na obiad

involve [ɪn'vɒlv] *vt* **1** (*entail*) wymagać +*gen* **2** (*concern, affect*) dotyczyć (pf) +gen; **to ~ sb (in sth)** włączać (włączyć pf) kogoś (w coś)

iPod® ['aɪpɒd] n iPod ®

Iran [ɪ'rɑːn] n Iran

Iraq [ɪ'rɑːk] n Irak

Ireland ['aɪələnd] n Irlandia; **the Republic of ~** republika Irlandii

Irish ['aɪrɪʃ] adj irlandzki ▷ n (language) irlandzki; **the Irish** n pl Irlandczycy

Irishman ['aɪrɪʃmən] (irreg) n Irlandczyk

Irishwoman ['aɪrɪʃwumən] (irreg) n Irlandka

iron ['aɪən] n 1 (metal) żelazo 2 (for clothes) żelazko ▷ adj (bar, railings) żelazny ▷ vt (clothes) prasować (wyprasować pf)

ironing ['aɪənɪŋ] n prasowanie; **to do the ~** prasować (wyprasować pf)

ironing board n deska do prasowania

irresponsible [ɪrɪ'spɒnsɪbl] adj nieodpowiedzialny; **it is ~ to drive when tired** prowadzenie pojazdu jak się jest zmęczonym to przejaw nieodpowiedzialności

irritating ['ɪrɪteɪtɪŋ] adj irytujący

is [ɪz] vb of **be**

Islam ['ɪzlɑːm] n islam

Islamic [ɪz'læmɪk] adj (law, faith) islamski; (country) islamski

island ['aɪlənd] n (Geo) wyspa

isle [aɪl] n wyspa

isolated ['aɪsəleɪtɪd] adj 1 (place) odosobniony 2 (person) samotny 3 (incident, case, example) pojedynczy

Israel ['ɪzreɪl] n Izrael

issue ['ɪʃjuː] n (problem, subject)

kwestia; **to ~ sb with sth** wydawać (wydać pf) komuś coś

IT n abbr (= information technology) IT

it [ɪt] pron 1 (object or animal) to; (referring to baby) ono 2 (impersonal): **I can't find it** nie mogę tego znaleźć; **it's raining** pada; **it doesn't matter** to nie ma znaczenia; **what is it?** (thing) co to jest?; (what's the matter?) o co chodzi?; **"who is it?" — "it's me"** "kto tam?" — "to ja"

Italian [ɪ'tæljən] adj włoski ▷ n 1 (person) Włoch(-oszka) m/f 2 (language) włoski

Italy ['ɪtəlɪ] n Włochy

itch [ɪtʃ] vi (person, part of body) swędzić (zaswędzić pf)

itchy ['ɪtʃɪ] adj (skin, nose, eyes, scalp etc) swędzący; (piece of clothing) drapiący

it'd ['ɪtd] = **it would, it had**

item ['aɪtəm] n 1 (on list, agenda) rzecz; (on bill) pozycja; (in collection) przedmiot 2 (in newspaper, on TV) artykuł; **~s of clothing** odzież f sg

it'll ['ɪtl] = **it will**

its [ɪts] adj 1 (m, nt) jego; (f) jej; (referring to subject of sentence) swój 2 (of baby) swój

it's [ɪts] = **it is, it has**

itself [ɪt'sɛlf] pron 1 (reflexive) się 2 (after preposition: gen, acc) siebie; (dat, loc) sobie; (inst) sobą 3 (emphatic) sam; **it switches ~ on automatically** to włącza się automatycznie

I've [aɪv] = **I have**

j

jack [dʒæk] *n* **1** (*Aut*) lewarek **2** (*Cards*) walet
jacket ['dʒækɪt] *n* **1** (*garment*) marynarka **2** (*esp US: also:* **dust ~**) obwoluta; **~ potatoes** (*Brit*) ziemniaki w mundurkach
jail [dʒeɪl] *n* więzienie ▷ *vt* więzić (uwięzić *pf*); **in ~** w więzieniu
jam [dʒæm] *n* **1** (*Brit: preserve*) dżem **2** (*also:* **traffic ~**) korek
jammed [dʒæmd] *adj* **1** (*roads*) zapchany **2** (*mechanism, machine*) unieruchomiony
janitor ['dʒænɪtə'] *n* dozorca(-czyni) *m/f*
January ['dʒænjuərɪ] *n* styczeń; *see also* **July**
Japan [dʒə'pæn] *n* Japonia
Japanese [dʒæpə'niːz] (*pl* **Japanese**) *adj* japoński ▷ *n*

(*language*) japoński
jar [dʒɑː'] *n* słoik
javelin ['dʒævlɪn] *n*: **the ~** rzut oszczepem
jaw [dʒɔː] (*Anat*) *n* szczęka; **jaws** *n pl* szczęki
jazz [dʒæz] *n* (*Mus*) jazz
jealous ['dʒɛləs] *adj* zazdrosny; **to be ~ of sb/sth** być zazdrosnym o kogoś/coś
jeans [dʒiːnz] *n pl* dżins; **a pair of ~** dżinsy
Jell-O® ['dʒɛləu] (*US*) *n* galaretka
jelly ['dʒɛlɪ] *n* **1** (*Brit: dessert*) galaretka **2** (*US: preserve*) dżem
jellyfish ['dʒɛlɪfɪʃ] (*pl* **jellyfish**) *n* meduza
jersey ['dʒəːzɪ] *n* (*pullover*) sweter
Jesus ['dʒiːzəs] *n* (*Rel*) Jezus; **~ Christ** Jezus Chrystus
jet [dʒɛt] *n* (*aeroplane*) odrzutowiec
jet lag [-læg] *n* zmęczenie po długiej podróży samolotem związane ze zmianą stref czasowych
Jew [dʒuː] *n* Żyd(ówka) *m/f*
jewel ['dʒuːəl] *n* (*gem*) klejnot
jeweller ['dʒuːələ'] (*US* **jeweler**) *n* **1** (*person*) jubiler **2** (*also:* **~'s**) sklep jubilerski
jewellery ['dʒuːəlrɪ] (*US* **jewelry**) *n* biżuteria
Jewish ['dʒuːɪʃ] *adj* żydowski
jigsaw ['dʒɪgsɔː] *n* (*also:* **~ puzzle**) układanka
job [dʒɔb] *n* **1** (*position*) praca **2** (*task*) zadanie **3** (*function*) zadanie; **Anne got a ~ as a secretary** Anne dostała pracę sekretarki; **it's a good ~ that...** dobrze, że...; **I had a ~ finding it** nie było łatwo to znaleźć; **a part-**

time/full-time ~ praca na pół etatu/na cały etat

jobless ['dʒɔblɪs] *adj* bezrobotny ▷ *n pl*: **the ~** bezrobotni

jockey ['dʒɔkɪ] *n* (*Sport*) dżokej(ka) *m/f*

jog [dʒɔg] *vi* biegać ▷ *n*: **to go for a ~** iść pobiegać

jogging ['dʒɔgɪŋ] *n* jogging; **to go ~** biegać

join [dʒɔɪn] *vt* **1** (*become member of*) wstępować (wstąpić *pf*) do +*gen* **2** (*meet: person*) dołączać (dołączyć *pf*) do +*gen*; **will you ~ us for dinner?** zjesz z nami obiad?; **I'll ~ you later** dołączę do was później
▶ **join in** *vi* przyłączać (przyłączyć *pf*) się ▷ *vt fus* (*work, discussion etc*) przyłączać (przyłączyć *pf*) się do +*gen*

joiner ['dʒɔɪnəʳ] (*Brit*) *n* stolarz

joint [dʒɔɪnt] *n* (*Anat*) staw; (*Brit: Culin*) mięso na pieczeń

joke [dʒəuk] *n* (*funny story*) żart ▷ *vi* żartować (zażartować *pf*); **it's no ~** (*inf*) to nie jest zabawne; **you must be joking!** (*inf*) chyba kpisz!

journalism ['dʒəːnəlɪzəm] *n* (*profession*) dziennikarstwo

journalist ['dʒəːnəlɪst] *n* dziennikarz(-rka) *m/f*

journey ['dʒəːnɪ] *n* podróż; **a 5-hour ~** 5 godzinna podróż; **to go on a ~** udawać (udać *pf*) się w podróż

joy [dʒɔɪ] *n* **1** (*happiness*) radość **2** (*delight*) zadowolenie

joystick ['dʒɔɪstɪk] *n* (*Comput*) joystick

judge [dʒʌdʒ] *n* **1** (*Law*) sędzia(-ina) *m/f* **2** (*in competition*) juror(ka) *m/f* ▷ *vt* **1** (*exhibits, competition etc*) sędziować **2** (*estimate: age, weight, size*) oceniać (ocenić *pf*)

judo ['dʒuːdəu] *n* judo

jug [dʒʌg] *n* dzbanek

juggler ['dʒʌgləʳ] *n* żongler(ka) *m/f*

juice [dʒuːs] *n* (*from fruit*) sok

July [dʒuː'laɪ] *n* lipiec; **the first of ~** pierwszy lipca; **at the beginning/end of ~** na początku/końcu lipca; **during ~** w lipcu; **each** *or* **every ~** zawsze w lipcu

jumble sale (*Brit*) *n* wyprzedaż rzeczy używanych

○ **JUMBLE SALE**
○
○ **Jumble sale** to wyprzedaż
○ różnego rodzaju używanych
○ artykułów i ubrań,
○ odbywająca się zazwyczaj
○ w miejscach takich jak
○ kościoły bądź szkolne hole.
○ Często urządzana w celu
○ zgromadzenia pieniędzy na
○ cele dobroczynne.

jump [dʒʌmp] *vi* (*into air*) skakać (skoczyć *pf*) ▷ *vt* (*fence, stream*) przeskakiwać (przeskoczyć *pf*) ▷ *n* (*leap*) skok; **to ~ over sth** przeskakiwać (przeskoczyć *pf*) przez coś; **to ~ out of a window** wyskakiwać (wyskoczyć *pf*) przez okno; **to ~ on sth** wskakiwać (wskoczyć *pf*) na coś; **to ~ off sth** zeskakiwać (zeskoczyć *pf*) z czegoś; **to ~ the queue** (*Brit*)

wpychać (wepchnąć *pf*) się poza
kolejnością
jumper ['dʒʌmpə^r] *n*
(*Brit: sweater*) pulower
junction ['dʒʌŋkʃən] (*Brit*) *n* **1** (*of
roads*) skrzyżowanie **2** (*Rail*) węzeł
kolejowy
June [dʒu:n] *n* czerwiec; *see
also* **July**
jungle ['dʒʌŋgl] *n* dżungla
junior ['dʒu:nɪə^r] *adj* młody
▷ *n* (*Brit: Scol*) uczeń(-ennica)
m/f szkoły podstawowej; **George
Bush J~** (*US*) George Bush Junior
junior high (*US: also: ~ school*) *n*
gimnazjum
junior school (*Brit*) *n* szkoła
podstawowa
junk [dʒʌŋk] *n* (*inf: rubbish*) grat
jury ['dʒuərɪ] *n* **1** (*Law*) sąd **2** (*in
competition*) jury
just [dʒʌst] *adj* (*decision,
punishment, reward*) sprawiedliwy;
(*society, cause*) słuszny ▷ *adv*
1 (*exactly*) dokładnie **2** (*merely*)
zaledwie **3** (*for emphasis*) po prostu
4 (*in instructions, requests: only*)
tylko; **it's ~ right** właśnie tak;
I'm ~ finishing this już kończę;
we were ~ going właśnie
wychodziliśmy; **I was ~ about to
phone** *or* **I was ~ going to phone**
właśnie miałem dzwonić; **~ now**
(*a moment ago*) przed chwilą; (*at
the present time*) właśnie teraz; **~
about everything/everyone**
to już wszystko/wszyscy; **~ as
he was leaving** właśnie jak
wychodził; **~ before/after...** tuż
przed/po +*inst*...; **~ enough time/
money** dokładnie tyle czasu/
pieniędzy; **he ~ missed** (*failed

to hit target) ledwo spudłował;
~ a minute, ~ one moment
(*asking someone to wait*) chwilę;
(*interrupting*) chwilkę!
justice ['dʒʌstɪs] *n* **1** (*Law*)
sprawiedliwość **2** (*legitimacy: of
cause, complaint*) zasadność

K

K abbr **1** (*inf: = thousands*) tys
2 (*Comput: = kilobytes*) kB
kabob [kə'bɔb] (*US*) n = **kebab**
kangaroo [kæŋgə'ruː] n
kangur(zyca) m/f
karaoke [kɑːrə'əukɪ] n karaoke
karate [kə'rɑːtɪ] n karate
kebab [kə'bæb] n kebab
keen [kiːn] adj **1** (*enthusiastic*)
chętny **2** (*competition*) zagorzały;
to be ~ to do sth być chętnym do
zrobienia czegoś; **to be ~ on sth**
uwielbiać coś; **to be ~ on doing
sth** (*eager to do*) chcieć coś zrobić
keep [kiːp] (*pt, pp* **kept**) vt
1 (*retain*) zachowywać (zachować
pf) **2** (*store*) trzymać **3** (*detain*)
zatrzymywać (zatrzymać pf)
4 (*support: family*) utrzymywać
(utrzymać pf) ▷ vi (*stay*)
utrzymywać (utrzymać pf); **to
~ doing sth** (*repeatedly*) robić
(zrobić pf) coś raz za razem;
(*continuously*) robić coś ciągle;
to ~ sb waiting kazać komuś
czekać; **to ~ the room tidy**
utrzymywać (utrzymać pf) pokój
w czystości; **to ~ a promise**
dotrzymywać (dotrzymać pf)
obietnicy; **can you ~ a secret?**
możesz dotrzymać tajemnicy?;
to ~ a record (of sth) notować
(zanotować pf) (coś); **what kept
you?** co cię zatrzymało?; **how are
you ~ing?** (*inf*) jak się trzymasz?
▶ **keep away** vi: **to ~ away (from
sth)** trzymać się z dala (od czegoś)
▶ **keep back** vt (*information*)
zatajać (zataić pf)
▶ **keep off** vt fus: **~ off the grass!**
nie deptać trawników!
▶ **keep on** vi: **to ~ on doing sth**
nie przestawać (przestać pf)
coś robić
▶ **keep up** vi: **to ~ up**
kontynuować; **to ~ up with sb**
(*walking, moving*) dotrzymywać
(dotrzymać pf) kroku komuś;
(*in work*) nadążać (nadążyć pf)
za kimś
keep-fit [kiːp'fɪt] adj (*class,
session, course*) gimnastyczny
kept [kɛpt] pt, pp of **keep**
kerb [kəːb] (*US* **curb**) n krawężnik
ketchup ['kɛtʃəp] n keczup
kettle ['kɛtl] n czajnik; **the ~'s
boiling** woda się gotuje
key [kiː] n **1** (*for lock*) klucz **2** (*of
computer, piano*) klawisz
keyboard ['kiːbɔːd] n klawiatura;
keyboards n pl syntezator n sg
keyhole ['kiːhəul] n dziurka od

klucza

kick [kɪk] vt (person, ball) kopać (kopnąć pf) ▷ n **1** (blow from person, animal) kopniak **2** (Sport) kopnięcie; **to give sb a ~** kopać (kopnąć pf) kogoś
▶ **kick off** vi (Sport) rozpoczynać (rozpocząć pf) mecz

kick-off ['kɪkɔf] (Sport) n rozpoczęcie meczu

kid [kɪd] n **1** (inf: child) dziecko; (teenager) dzieciak **2** (goat) koźlę ▷ vi (inf: joke) stroić sobie żarty; **you're ~ding!** żartujesz!

kidnap ['kɪdnæp] vt porywać (porwać pf)

kidney ['kɪdnɪ] n **1** (Anat) nerka **2** (Culin) cynaderka

kill [kɪl] vt zabijać (zabić pf); **my back's ~ing me** (inf) okropnie bolą mnie plecy

killer ['kɪlər] n **1** (murderer) zabójca(-yni) m/f **2** (disease, activity) zabójczy

kilo ['ki:ləu] n kilo

kilometre ['kɪləmi:tər] (US **kilometer**) n kilometr

kilt [kɪlt] n kilt

kind [kaɪnd] adj życzliwy ▷ n (type, sort) rodzaj; **an opportunity to meet all ~s of people** możliwość spotkania bardzo różnych ludzi; **it was ~ of them to help** miło z ich strony, że pomogli

kindness ['kaɪndnɪs] n (quality) życzliwość

king [kɪŋ] n król

kingdom ['kɪŋdəm] n królestwo; **the animal/plant ~** królestwo zwierząt/roślin

kiosk ['ki:ɔsk] n (shop) kiosk

kiss [kɪs] n pocałunek ▷ vt całować (pocałować pf) ▷ vi całować (pocałować pf) się; **to give sb a ~** całować (pocałować pf) kogoś; **to ~ sb goodbye/ goodnight** całować (pocałować pf) kogoś na do widzenia/ dobranoc

kit [kɪt] n (esp Brit: equipment) zestaw; (clothing) strój

kitchen ['kɪtʃɪn] n kuchnia

kite [kaɪt] n (toy) latawiec

kitten ['kɪtn] n kociak

kiwi fruit ['ki:wi:-] n kiwi

knee [ni:] n kolano; **to be on one's ~s** klęczeć

kneel [ni:l] (pt, pp **knelt**) vi (also: **~ down**) klękać (klęknąć pf); **to be ~ing** klęczący

knew [nju:] pt of **know**

knickers ['nɪkəz] (Brit) n pl majtki; **a pair of ~** para majtek

knife [naɪf] (pl **knives**) n nóż; **~ and fork** nóż i widelec

knit [nɪt] vt (garment) robić (zrobić pf) na drutach ▷ vi (with wool) robić (zrobić pf) na drutach

knitting ['nɪtɪŋ] n (activity) robienie na drutach

knives [naɪvz] n pl of **knife**

knob [nɔb] n (on door) gałka

knock [nɔk] vt (strike) stukać (stuknąć pf) ▷ vi (on door, window) pukać (zapukać pf) ▷ n **1** (blow, bump) uderzenie **2** (on door) pukanie; **to ~ sb unconscious** ogłuszać (ogłuszyć pf) kogoś; **he ~ed on or at the door** zapukał do drzwi
▶ **knock down** vt **1** (run over) przewracać (przewrócić pf) **2** (demolish) rozbierać (rozebrać pf)

▶ **knock out** *vt* **1** (*make unconscious*) ogłuszać (ogłuszyć *pf*) **2** (*eliminate*) eliminować (wyeliminować *pf*)
▶ **knock over** *vt* przewracać (przewrócić *pf*)
knot [nɔt] *n* (*in rope, string*) węzeł; **to tie a ~** wiązać (zawiązać *pf*) węzeł
know [nəu] (*pt* **knew**, *pp* **known**) *vt* **1** (*facts, dates etc*) wiedzieć **2** (*language*) znać **3** (*person, place, subject*) znać; **to ~ that...** wiedzieć, że...; **to ~ where/when** wiedzieć gdzie/kiedy; **do you ~ how to swim?** umiesz pływać?; **to get to ~ sb** poznawać (poznać *pf*) kogoś; **to ~ sth about sb/sth** wiedzieć coś o kimś/czymś; **to ~ about sth** wiedzieć o czymś; **I don't ~ about that** nic o tym nie wiem; **yes, I ~** tak, wiem; **you never ~** tego nigdy się nie wie; **you ~** (*used for emphasis*) wiesz
knowledge ['nɔlɪdʒ] *n* wiedza; **to (the best of) my ~** o ile wiem
known [nəun] *pp of* **know**
Koran [kɔ'rɑːn] *n*: **the ~** Koran
Korea [kə'rɪə] *n see* **North Korea, South Korea**
kosher ['kəuʃər] *adj* (*meat, restaurant*) koszerny

lab [læb] (*inf*) *n* (*laboratory*) laboratorium
label ['leɪbl] *n* **1** (*on clothing*) metka; (*on bottle, tin*) nalepka; (*on suitcase*) przywieszka ▷ *vt* (*object*) oznakowywać (oznakować *pf*)
labor ['leɪbər] (*US*) *n* = **labour**

LABOR DAY

Labor Day – Święto Pracy jest obchodzone w USA oraz w Kanadzie w pierwszy poniedziałek września. Pierwotnie jego obchody miały charakter polityczny, obecnie święto traktowane jest po prostu jako okazja do odpoczynku w długi weekend.

laboratory [lə'bɒrətərɪ] *n*
laboratorium

labor union (*US*) *n* związek
zawodowy

labour ['leɪbəʳ] (*US* **labor**) *n*
1 (*manpower*) siła robocza **2** (*Med*)
poród **3: L~** (*also:* **L~ Party**) Partia
Pracy ▷ *vt:* **to be in ~** (*Med*) rodzić;
to vote L~ głosować (zagłosować
pf) na Partię Pracy

lace [leɪs] *n* **1** (*fabric*) koronka
2 (*of shoe etc*) sznurowadło ▷ *vt*
(*also:* **~ up:** *shoe etc*) sznurowywać
(zasznurować *pf*)

lack [læk] *n* (*absence*) brak ▷ *vt*
brakować; **to be ~ing in sth**
prezentować (zaprezentować *pf*)
brak czegoś

lad [læd] (*inf*) *n* (*boy*) chłopiec;
(*young man*) chłopak

ladder ['lædəʳ] *n* drabina

lady ['leɪdɪ] *n* (*woman*) pani;
ladies and gentlemen... panie
i panowie...; **young ~** młoda
kobieta; **the ladies'** (*Brit*) or **the
ladies' room** (*US*) toaleta damska

ladybird ['leɪdɪbəːd] (*Brit*) *n*
biedronka

ladybug ['leɪdɪbʌg] (*US*) *n*
biedronka

lager ['lɑːgəʳ] (*Brit*) *n* piwo pełne
jasne

laid [leɪd] *pt, pp of* **lay**

laid-back [leɪd'bæk] (*inf*) *adj*
wyluzowany

lain [leɪn] *pp of* **lie**

lake [leɪk] *n* jezioro

lamb [læm] *n* **1** (*animal*) jagnię
2 (*meat*) jagnięcina

lamp [læmp] *n* lampa

lamp-post ['læmppəust] (*Brit*)
n latarnia

lampshade ['læmpʃeɪd] *n* abażur

land [lænd] *n* **1** (*area of open
ground*) teren **2** (*not sea*) ląd ▷ *vi*
lądować (wylądować *pf*); **to go/
travel by ~** podróżować drogą
lądową; **on dry ~** na stałym lądzie

landing ['lændɪŋ] *n* **1** (*on stairs*)
podest **2** (*Aviat*) lądowanie

landlady ['lændleɪdɪ] *n*
właścicielka

landlord ['lændlɔːd] *n* właściciel

landscape ['lændskeɪp] *n*
krajobraz

lane [leɪn] *n* **1** (*in country*) wąska
droga **2** (*Aut: of road*) pas

language ['læŋgwɪdʒ] *n*
1 (*English, Polish etc*) język
2 (*speech*) mowa

language laboratory *n*
laboratorium językowe

lap [læp] *n* **1** (*of person*) kolana
2 (*in race*) okrążenie

laptop ['læptɒp] *n* (*also:* **~
computer**) laptop

large [lɑːdʒ] *adj* duży

laser ['leɪzəʳ] *n* laser

last [lɑːst] *adj* **1** (*most recent*)
ostatni; (*Monday, July, weekend
etc*) zeszły **2** (*final*) ostatni ▷ *pron*
ostatni ▷ *adv* **1** (*most recently*)
ostatnio **2** (*at the end*) na końcu
3 (*in final position*) na końcu ▷ *vi*
(*continue*) trwać; **~ week** zeszły
tydzień; **~ night** (*yesterday
evening*) wczorajsza noc; (*during
the night*) zeszłej nocy; **the ~ time**
(*the previous time*) ostatni raz; **at
(long) ~** (*finally*) wreszcie; **our
house is the ~ but one** nasz dom
jest przedostatni; **it ~s (for) two
hours** to trwa 2 godziny

lastly ['lɑːstlɪ] *adv* wreszcie

late [leɪt] *adj* późny ▷ *adv* późno;
  we're ~ spóźniliśmy się; **sorry**
  I'm ~ przepraszam za spóźnienie;
  to be ten minutes ~ spóźniać
  (spóźnić *pf*) się dziesięć minut;
  it's ~ jest późno; **to be in one's**
  ~ thirties/forties zbliżać
  (zbliżyć *pf*) się do czterdziestki/
  pięćdziesiątki; **to work ~**
  pracować do późna; **in ~ May** pod
  koniec maja

lately ['leɪtlɪ] *adv* (*recently*)
  ostatnio

later ['leɪtər] *adv* później; **some**
  time jakiś czas później; **some**
  weeks/years ~ kilka tygodni/lat
  później; **~ on** później

latest ['leɪtɪst] *adj* **1** (*book, film,*
  news etc) ostatni **2** (*fashion*)
  najnowszy; **at the ~** najpóźniej

Latin ['lætɪn] *n* (*language*) łacina

Latin America *n* Ameryka
  Łacińska

latter ['lætər] *n*: **the ~** ostatni z
  wymienionych

laugh [lɑːf] *n* śmiech ▷ *vi* śmiać
  się
  ▶ **laugh at** *vt fus* **1** (*lit*) śmiać się
  z +*gen* **2** (*fig: mock*) wyśmiewać
  się z +*gen*

launch [lɔːntʃ] *vt* **1** (*Space*)
  wystrzeliwać (wystrzelić
  pf) **2** (*fig: product, publication*)
  wprowadzać (wprowadzić *pf*)
  na rynek

Launderette® [lɔːn'drɛt] (*Brit*) *n*
  pralnia samoobsługowa

Laundromat® ['lɔːndrəmæt]
  (*US*) *n* pralnia samoobsługowa

laundry ['lɔːndrɪ] *n* pranie; **to do**
  the ~ robić (zrobić *pf*) pranie

laundry detergent [dɪ'tɜːdʒənt]
  (*US*) *n* proszek do prania

lavatory ['lævətərɪ] (*Brit: o.f.*)
  n toaleta

lavender ['lævəndər] *n* (*plant*)
  lawenda

law [lɔː] *n* prawo; **against the ~**
  niezgodnie z prawem; **to break**
  the ~ łamać (złamać *pf*) prawo;
  by ~ zgodnie z prawem; **to study**
  ~ studiować prawo; **~ and order**
  prawo i porządek

lawn [lɔːn] *n* trawnik

lawnmower ['lɔːnməuər] *n*
  kosiarka do trawy

lawyer ['lɔːjər] *n* prawnik(-iczka)
  m/f

lay [leɪ] (*pt, pp* **laid**) *pt of* **lie** ▷ *vt*
  1 (*put*) kłaść (położyć *pf*) **2** (*egg*)
  znosić (znieść *pf*); **to ~ the table**
  nakrywać (nakryć *pf*) do stołu
  ▶ **lay down** *vt* (*put down*) kłaść
  (położyć *pf*); **to ~ down the law**
  ustanawiać (ustanowić *pf*) prawo

lay-by ['leɪbaɪ] (*Brit*) *n* zatoczka

layer ['leɪər] *n* (*of substance,*
  material) warstwa

layout ['leɪaut] *n* rozkład

lazy ['leɪzɪ] *adj* (*person*) leniwy

lead¹ [liːd] (*pt, pp* **led**) *n* **1** (*esp*
  Brit: for dog) smycz **2** (*Elec*)
  kabel ▷ *vt* **1** (*guide*) prowadzić
  (zaprowadzić *pf*) **2** (*be at the*
  head of) prowadzić (poprowadzić
  pf) ▷ *vi* (*in race, competition*)
  prowadzić; **to be in the ~** (*in race,*
  competition, poll) prowadzić; **to ~**
  an active life prowadzić aktywne
  życie; **to ~ the way** wskazywać
  (wskazać *pf*) drogę
  ▶ **lead away** *vt* (*prisoner etc*)
  odprowadzać (odprowadzić *pf*)
  ▶ **lead to** *vt fus* (*result in*)

prowadzić do +gen

lead² [lɛd] n (metal) ołów

leader ['li:dəʳ] n (of group, organization) lider(ka) m/f

lead-free ['lɛdfri:] adj (petrol, paint) bezołowiowy

lead singer [li:d-] n solista(-tka) m/f

leaf [li:f] (pl **leaves**) n (of tree, plant) liść

leaflet ['li:flɪt] n ulotka

league [li:g] n (Sport) liga

leak [li:k] n **1** (of liquid, gas) wyciek **2** (hole: in roof, pipe etc) pęknięcie ▷ vi przeciekać

lean [li:n] (pt, pp **leaned** or **leant**) vt: **to ~ sth on/against sth** opierać (oprzeć pf) coś o coś ▷ adj (meat) chudy; **to ~ against sth** (person) opierać (oprzeć pf) się o coś; **to ~ forward/back** pochylać (pochylić pf) się do przodu/tyłu ▶ **lean on** vt fus (rest against) wspierać (wesprzeć pf) się na +inst

leap [li:p] (pt, pp **leaped** or **leapt**) vi **1** (jump) skakać (skoczyć pf) **2**: **to ~ into/onto sth** wskakiwać (wskoczyć pf) do czegoś

leap year n rok przestępny

learn [lə:n] (pt, pp **learned** or **learnt**) vt uczyć (nauczyć pf) się +gen ▷ vi uczyć (nauczyć pf) się; **to ~ about sth** (study) uczyć (nauczyć pf) się czegoś; **to ~ how to do sth** uczyć (nauczyć pf) się jak coś robić

learner ['lə:nəʳ] n **1** (student) uczący się **2** (Brit: also: **~ driver**) zdający na prawo jazdy

learnt [lə:nt] pt, pp of **learn**

least [li:st] adj najmniejszy ▷ adv **1** (with adjective): **the**

~ expensive/attractive/ interesting najmniej drogi/ atrakcyjny/interesujący **2** (with verb) najmniej ▷ pron: **the ~** najmniej; **at ~** (in comparisons) najmniej; (still) przynajmniej

leather ['lɛðəʳ] n skóra ▷ adj (jacket, shoes, chair) skórzany

leave [li:v] (pt, pp **left**) vt **1** (depart from) opuszczać (opuścić pf) **2** (give up: school, job) porzucać (porzucić pf) **3** (leave behind) zostawiać (zostawić pf) **4** (message) zostawiać (zostawić pf) ▷ vi **1** (depart: person) odchodzić (odejść pf); (bus, train) odjeżdżać (odjechać pf) **2** (give up school) rzucać (rzucić pf); (give up job) odchodzić (odejść pf) ▷ n (time off) urlop; (Mil) przepustka; **to ~ sth to sb** (money, property etc) zostawiać (zostawić pf) coś dla kogoś; **to ~ sb/sth alone** zostawiać (zostawić pf) kogoś/coś w spokoju; **to ~ for** (destination) jechać (pojechać pf) do +gen ▶ **leave behind** vt (forget) zostawiać (zostawić pf) ▶ **leave on** vt (light, heating) zostawiać (zostawić pf) włączone ▶ **leave out** vt pomijać (pominąć pf); **to ~ sb/sth out of sth** pomijać (pominąć pf) kogoś podczas czegoś

leaves [li:vz] n pl of **leaf**

lecture ['lɛktʃəʳ] n (talk) wykład; **to give a ~ (on sth)** wygłaszać (wygłosić pf) wykład (na jakiś temat)

lecturer ['lɛktʃərəʳ] n wykładowca

led [lɛd] pt, pp of **lead¹**

leek [liːk] n por

left¹ [lɛft] adj (not right) lewy
▷ n: **the ~** lewica ▷ adv (turn, go, look) w lewo; **on the ~** na lewo; **to the ~** na lewo

left² [lɛft] pt, pp of **leave** ▷ adj: **to be ~ over** (food, money etc) zostawiać (zostawić pf)

left-hand ['lɛfthænd] adj (side, corner) lewy

left-handed [lɛft'hændɪd] adj leworęczny

left-luggage [lɛft'lʌgɪdʒ] (Brit) n: **~ locker** przechowalnia bagażu

leg [lɛg] n 1 (of person, table, chair) noga; (of bird) udko 2 (Culin) noga

legal ['liːgl] adj 1 (relating to law: system, requirement) prawny 2 (allowed by law: action, situation) legalny

legal holiday (US) n dzień ustawowo wolny od pracy

leggings ['lɛgɪŋz] n pl (woman's) legginsy

leisure ['lɛʒəʳ, US 'liːʒəʳ] n (free time) wypoczynek

leisure centre (Brit) n centrum rekreacji

lemon ['lɛmən] n cytryna

lemonade [lɛmə'neɪd] n lemoniada

lend [lɛnd] (pt, pp **lent**) vt 1: **to ~ sth to sb** pożyczać (pożyczyć pf) coś komuś 2 (loan: bank etc) pożyczać (pożyczyć pf)

length [lɛŋθ] n długość; **it is 10 metres in ~** to ma 10 metrów długości

lens [lɛnz] n (of spectacles) soczewka; (of telescope, camera) obiektyw

Lent [lɛnt] n Wielki Post

lent [lɛnt] pt, pp of **lend**

lentil ['lɛntɪl] n soczewica

Leo ['liːəu] n (Astrol) Lew

leopard ['lɛpəd] n lampart

leotard ['liːətɑːd] n (for dancing etc) trykot

lesbian ['lɛzbɪən] adj lesbijski
▷ n lesbijka

less [lɛs] adj mniej ▷ adv 1 (with adjective/adverb) mniej 2 (with verb) rzadziej ▷ pron mniej
▷ prep: **~ tax/10% discount** minus podatek/10% zniżki; **~ of the money/time** mniej pieniędzy/czasu; **~ than half** mniej niż połowa; **~ and ~** (as adj) coraz mniej; (as adv) coraz mniej

lesson ['lɛsn] n (class) lekcja

let [lɛt] (pt, pp **let**) vt 1: **to ~ sb do sth** (give permission) pozwalać (pozwolić pf) komuś coś robić (zrobić pf) 2: **to ~ sth happen** pozwalać (pozwolić pf) na coś; **to ~ sb know that...** powiedzieć komuś, że...; **to ~ sb in/out** wpuszczać (wpuścić pf)/wypuszczać (wypuścić pf) kogoś; **~'s go/eat** chodźmy/zjedzmy; **"to ~"** "do wynajęcia"; **to ~ go** (release one's grip) puszczać (puścić pf); **to ~ sb/sth go** (release) wypuszczać (wypuścić pf) kogoś/coś
▶ **let down** vt (fail: person) zawodzić (zawieść pf)
▶ **let in** vt wpuszczać (wpuścić pf)
▶ **let out** vt (scream, cry) wydawać (wydać pf)

letter ['lɛtəʳ] n 1 (piece of writing) list 2 (of alphabet) litera

letterbox ['lɛtəbɔks] (*Brit*) *n* (*in door*) skrzynka pocztowa

LETTERBOX

Letterbox, czyli skrzynka na listy ma bardzo często w Wielkiej Brytanii formę podłużnego prostokątnego wycięcia w drzwiach domu, przez które listonosz dostarcza listy na podany adres.

lettuce ['lɛtɪs] *n* sałata
leukaemia [luːˈkiːmɪə] (*US* **leukemia**) *n* białaczka
level ['lɛvl] *adj* równy ▷ *adv*: **to draw ~ with** (*esp Brit* zrównywać (zrównać *pf*) się z +*inst* ▷ *n* poziom; **to ~ the score** (*Sport*) wyrównywać (wyrównać *pf*) wynik
level crossing (*Brit*) *n* przejazd kolejowy
lever ['liːvəʳ, *US* 'lɛvəʳ] *n* (*to operate machine*) dźwignia
liar ['laɪəʳ] *n* kłamca
liberal ['lɪbərl] *adj* (*tolerant*) liberalny ▷ *n* (*Pol*): **L~** liberał
Libra ['liːbrə] *n* (*Astrol*) Waga
librarian [laɪˈbrɛərɪən] *n* bibliotekarz(-rka) *m/f*
library ['laɪbrərɪ] *n* biblioteka
licence ['laɪsns] (*US* **license**) *n* **1** (*permit*) zezwolenie **2** (*also*: **driving ~**) prawo jazdy
license plate (*US*) *n* tablica rejestracyjna
lick [lɪk] *vt* lizać (polizać *pf*)
lid [lɪd] *n* **1** (*of box, case*) wieko; (*of pan*) pokrywka **2** (*eyelid*) powieka
lie¹ [laɪ] (*pt* **lay**, *pp* **lain**) *vi* leżeć

▶ **lie about** (*Brit*) *vi* = **lie around**
▶ **lie around** *vi* (*things*) poniewierać się
▶ **lie down** *vi* (*person*) kłaść się
lie² [laɪ] *vi* kłamać (skłamać *pf*) ▷ *n* kłamstwo; **to tell ~s** kłamać (skłamać *pf*)
lie-in ['laɪɪn] (*Brit: inf*) *n*: **to have a ~** poleżeć sobie
lieutenant [lɛfˈtɛnənt, *US* luːˈtɛnənt] *n* porucznik
life [laɪf] (*pl* **lives**) *n* życie; **his personal/working ~** jego życie osobiste/zawodowe
lifebelt ['laɪfbɛlt] *n* pas ratunkowy
lifeboat ['laɪfbəut] *n* łódź ratunkowa
lifeguard ['laɪfgɑːd] *n* ratownik(-iczka) *m/f*
life jacket *n* kamizelka ratunkowa
life preserver [-prɪˈzəːvəʳ] (*US*) *n* (*lifebelt*) pas ratunkowy; (*life jacket*) kamizelka ratunkowa
lifestyle ['laɪfstaɪl] *n* styl życia
lift [lɪft] *vt* podnosić (podnieść *pf*) ▷ *n* (*Brit*) winda; **to give sb a ~** (*esp Brit: Aut*) podwozić (podwieźć *pf*) kogoś
▶ **lift up** *vt* (*person, thing*) podnosić (podnieść *pf*)
light [laɪt] (*pt, pp* **lit**) *n* **1** (*from sun, moon, lamp, fire*) światło **2** (*for cigarette etc*) ogień ▷ *vt* (*candle, fire, cigarette*) zapalać (zapalić *pf*) ▷ *adj* **1** (*pale: colour*) jasny **2** (*not heavy: object*) lekki; **lights** *n pl* (*Aut: also*: **traffic ~s**) światła uliczne; **to turn** *or* **switch the ~ on/off** włączać (włączyć *pf*)/ wyłączać (wyłączyć *pf*) światło

light bulb n żarówka
lighter ['laɪtə'] n (also: **cigarette ~**) zapalniczka
lighthouse ['laɪthaus] n latarnia morska
lightning ['laɪtnɪŋ] n piorun
like¹ [laɪk] prep **1** (similar to) taki jak **2** (in comparisons) jak **3** (such as) taki jak; **a house ~ ours** dom taki jak nasz; **to be ~ sth/sb** być jak coś/ktoś; **what's he ~?** jaki on jest?; **what's the weather ~?** jaka jest pogoda?; **to look ~** wyglądać jak; **what does it look/sound/taste ~?** jak to wygląda/brzmi/smakuje?; **~ this** jak to
like² [laɪk] vt lubić ▷ n: **his ~s and dislikes** to co lubi i czego nie lubi; **to ~ doing sth** lubić coś robić; **I would** or **I'd ~ an ice cream/to go for a walk** chciałbym loda/iść na spacer; **would you ~ a coffee?** chciałby pan kawy?; **if you ~** (in offers, suggestions) jak wolisz
likely ['laɪklɪ] adj **1** (probable) prawdopodobny **2** (person, place, thing) odpowiedni; **it is ~ that...** jest prawdopodobne, że...; **to be ~ to do sth** prawdopodobnie coś zrobić
lime [laɪm] n (fruit) limonka
limit ['lɪmɪt] n **1** (maximum point) kres **2** (restriction) ograniczenie
limp [lɪmp] n: **he walks with a ~** kuleje ▷ vi (person, animal) kuleć
line [laɪn] n **1** (long thin mark) linia **2** (of people, things) rząd **3** (of words) linijka **4** (also: **washing ~**) sznur **5** (Tel) linia **6** (railway track) linia; **hold the ~ please!** (Tel) proszę nie odkładać słuchawki; **to stand/wait in ~** (esp US) stać/

czekać w kolejce; **on the right ~s** w dobrym kierunku; **to draw the ~ at doing sth** odmawiać (odmówić pf) robienia (zrobienia pf) czegoś
linen ['lɪnɪn] n **1** (cloth) płótno **2** (tablecloths) bielizna stołowa; (sheets) bielizna pościelowa ▷ adj (jacket, sheets, etc) lniany
lining ['laɪnɪŋ] n (of garment) podszewka
link [lɪŋk] n **1** (connection) związek **2** (Comput: also: **hyper~**) link ▷ vt łączyć (połączyć pf)
lion ['laɪən] n lew
lip [lɪp] n (Anat) warga
lip-read ['lɪpriːd] vi czytać z ruchu warg
lipstick ['lɪpstɪk] n szminka
liquid ['lɪkwɪd] n płyn
liquidizer ['lɪkwɪdaɪzə'] (esp Brit: Culin) n mikser
liquor ['lɪkə'] (US) n alkohol wysokoprocentowy
list [lɪst] n lista ▷ vt (record: person) spisywać (spisać pf)
listen ['lɪsn] vi słuchać; **to ~ to sb** słuchać kogoś; **to ~ to sth** słuchać czegoś; **~!** słuchaj!
lit [lɪt] pt, pp of **light**
liter ['liːtə'] (US) n = **litre**
literature ['lɪtrɪtʃə'] n literatura
litre ['liːtə'] (US **liter**) n litr
litter ['lɪtə'] n (rubbish) śmieć
litter bin (Brit) n kosz na śmieci
little ['lɪtl] adj **1** (small: thing, person) mały **2** (young: child) mały **3** (younger): **~ brother/sister** młodszy brat/młodsza siostra **4** (quantifier): **to have ~ time/money** mieć mało czasu/

pieniędzy ▷ *adv* mało; **a ~** mało
+*gen*; **a ~ boy of eight** chłopiec lat
osiem; **a ~ bit of** trochę +*gen*; **~ by
~** po trochu
live¹ [lɪv] *vi* **1** (*reside*) mieszkać
2 (*lead one's life*) żyć ▷ *vt* (*life*) żyć
▶ **live on** *vt fus* (*money*) przeżyć
▶ **live together** *vi* mieszkać
razem
▶ **live with** *vt fus* (*partner*)
mieszkać z +*inst*
live² [laɪv] *adj* **1** (*animal, plant*)
żywy ▷ *adv* (*broadcast*) na żywo
lively [ˈlaɪvlɪ] *adj* (*person*) żwawy;
(*place, event*) wesoły; (*discussion*)
ożywiony
liver [ˈlɪvəʳ] *n* **1** (*Anat*) wątroba
2 (*Culin*) wątróbka
lives [laɪvz] *n pl of* **life**
living [ˈlɪvɪŋ] *n* (*life*) życie; **for a
~** na życie; **to earn** or **make a ~**
zarabiać (zarobić *pf*) na życie
living room *n* pokój dzienny
lizard [ˈlɪzəd] *n* jaszczurka
load [ləud] *n* ładunek ▷ *vt*
1 (*also*: **~ up**: *vehicle, ship etc*)
ładować (załadować *pf*)
2 (*Comput*) wgrywać (wgrać *pf*);
loads of or a **~ of money/people**
(*inf*) wiele pieniędzy/ludzi
loaf [ləuf] (*pl* **loaves**) *n*: **a ~ (of
bread)** bochenek (chleba)
loan [ləun] *n* (*sum of money*)
pożyczka ▷ *vt*: **to ~ sth (out)
to sb** (*money, thing*) pożyczać
(pożyczyć *pf*) coś komuś
loaves [ləuvz] *n pl of* **loaf**
lobster [ˈlɔbstəʳ] *n* homar
local [ˈləukl] *adj* **1** (*council,
newspaper, library*) lokalny;
(*residents*) miejscowy **2** (*Tel*: *call*)
miejscowy

location [ləuˈkeɪʃən] *n* (*place*)
położenie
loch [lɔx] *n* jezioro
lock [lɔk] *n* (*of door, drawer
etc*) zamek ▷ *vt* **1** (*door, drawer
etc*) zamykać (zamknąć *pf*)
2 (*Comput: screen*) blokować
(zablokować *pf*)
▶ **lock in** *vt* (*person, object*)
zamykać (zamknąć *pf*) w +*loc*
▶ **lock out** *vt*: **to ~ o.s. out**
zatrzaskiwać (zatrzasnąć *pf*) się
▶ **lock up** *vt* zamykać (zamknąć
pf)
locker [ˈlɔkəʳ] *n* szafka
lodger [ˈlɔdʒəʳ] *n* lokator(ka) *m/f*
loft [lɔft] *n* (*attic*) strych
log [lɔg] *n* (*from tree*: *trunk*) kłoda;
(*for fuel etc*) bierwiono
▶ **log in**, **log on** (*Comput*) *vi*
logować (zalogować *pf*) się
▶ **log into** (*Comput*) *vt fus*
logować (zalogować *pf*) się do +*gen*
▶ **log out**, **log off** (*Comput*) *vi*
wylogować się
logical [ˈlɔdʒɪkl] *adj* logiczny
login [ˈlɔgɪn] *n* (*Comput*)
logowanie (się)
lollipop [ˈlɔlɪpɔp] *n* lizak
London [ˈlʌndən] *n* Londyn
Londoner [ˈlʌndənəʳ] *n*
londyńczyk(-ynka) *m/f*
loneliness [ˈləunlɪnɪs] *n*
samotność
lonely [ˈləunlɪ] *adj* **1** (*sad*: *person*)
samotny **2** (*unfrequented*: *place*)
odludny
long [lɔŋ] *adj* długi ▷ *adv* (*time*)
długo ▷ *vi*: **to ~ for sth/to do sth**
tęsknić (zatęsknić *pf*) za czymś/za
robieniem (zrobieniem *pf*) czegoś;
how ~ is the lesson? jak długa

jest lekcja?; **six metres ~** sześć metrów długości; **so** or **as ~ as** tak długo jak; **~ ago** dawno temu; **it won't take ~** to nie potrwa długo; **a ~ way** daleko

long jump (Sport) n: **the ~** skok w dal

loo [lu:] (Brit: inf) n ubikacja

look [luk] vi **1** (glance, gaze) spoglądać (spojrzeć pf) **2** (seem, appear) wyglądać ▷ n (expression) wyraz; **to ~ out of the window** wyglądać (wyjrzeć pf) z okna; **~ out!** uważaj!; **to ~ like sb/sth** wyglądać jak ktoś/coś; **it ~s as if...** wygląda na to, że...; **to have** or **take a ~ at** (examine) przyglądać (przyjrzeć pf) się +dat
▶ **look after** vt fus (care for) opiekować (zaopiekować pf) się +inst
▶ **look at** vt fus (gaze at) spoglądać (spojrzeć pf)
▶ **look for** vt fus szukać +gen
▶ **look forward to** vt fus cieszyć się na; **to ~ forward to doing sth** cieszyć się na robienie czegoś; **we ~ forward to hearing from you** czekamy na twoją odpowiedź
▶ **look into** vt fus (investigate) badać (zbadać pf)
▶ **look round**, **look around** vi rozglądać (rozejrzeć pf) się ▷ vt fus (place, building) rozglądać (rozejrzeć pf) się za +inst
▶ **look through** vt fus (book, magazine, papers) przeglądać (przejrzeć pf)
▶ **look up** vt (information, meaning etc) sprawdzać (sprawdzić pf)

loose [lu:s] adj **1** (screw, connection, tooth) luźny **2** (hair)

rozpuszczony **3** (clothes, trousers etc) luźny

lord [lɔːd] (Brit) n (peer) lord

> ● **LORDS**
> ●
> ● Izba Lordów (**House of**
> ● **Lords**) jest jedną z dwóch izb
> ● parlamentu brytyjskiego.

lorry ['lɔrɪ] (Brit) n ciężarówka

lorry driver (Brit) n kierowca ciężarówki

lose [lu:z] (pt, pp **lost**) vt **1** (mislay: keys, pen etc) gubić (zgubić pf) **2** (contest, fight, argument) przegrywać (przegrać pf) **3** (relative, wife etc) tracić (stracić pf) ▷ vi (in competition, argument) przegrywać (przegrać pf); **to ~ weight** tracić (stracić pf) na wadze

loser ['lu:zəʳ] n **1** (in game, contest) przegrywający **2** (inf: failure) nieudacznik(-ica) m/f; **to be a good/bad ~** umieć/nie umieć przegrywać

loss [lɔs] n strata

lost [lɔst] pt, pp of **lose** ▷ adj (object) zagubiony; (person, animal) zaginiony; **to get ~** (lose one's way) gubić (zgubić pf) się

lost and found (US) n = **lost property**

lost property n **1** (things) rzeczy znalezione **2** (Brit: office) biuro rzeczy znalezionych

lot [lɔt] n: **a ~** dużo; **a ~ of** dużo +gen; **~s of** (things, people) dużo +gen; **he reads/smokes a ~** on dużo czyta/pali

lottery ['lɔtərɪ] n (game) loteria

loud [laud] *adj* głośny ▷ *adv*
(*speak etc*) głośno
loudly ['laudlɪ] *adv* głośno
loudspeaker [laud'spiːkə^r] *n*
głośnik
lounge [laundʒ] *n* **1** (*in hotel*) hol
2 (*at airport, station*) poczekalnia
3 (*esp Brit: in house*) salon
love [lʌv] *n* miłość ▷ *vt* (*partner,
child, pet*) kochać; (*thing, food,
activity*) uwielbiać; **to be in ~
(with sb)** być zakochanym (w
kimś); **to fall in ~ (with sb)**
zakochiwać (zakochać *pf*) się
(w kimś); **to make ~** kochać
się; **~ (from) Anne** (*on letter*)
pozdrowienia (od) Anne; **to ~
doing/to do sth** uwielbiać coś
robić; **I'd ~ to come** przyjdę z
chęcią
lovely ['lʌvlɪ] (*esp Brit*)
adj **1** (*beautiful*) uroczy
2 (*delightful: holiday, meal, present*)
cudowny; (*person*) śliczny; **how ~
to see you!** miło cię widzieć!
lover ['lʌvə^r] *n* (*sexual partner*)
kochanek(-nka) *m/f*; **an art ~**
miłośnik sztuki
low [ləu] *adj* niski ▷ *adv* (*fly*)
nisko; **~ in calories/salt/fat**
mało kalorii/soli/tłuszczu
lower ['ləuə^r] *vt* obniżać (obniżyć
pf)

loyal ['lɔɪəl] *adj* lojalny
loyalty ['lɔɪəltɪ] *n* lojalność

luck [lʌk] *n* szczęście; **good ~**
szczęście; **good ~!** *or* **best of ~!**
powodzenia!; **bad ~** pech; **bad**
or **hard** *or* **tough ~!** (*showing
sympathy*) pech!
luckily ['lʌkɪlɪ] *adv* na szczęście;
~ for me/us szczęśliwie dla
mnie/nas
lucky ['lʌkɪ] *adj* (*person*)
szczęśliwy; **to be ~** (*person*) mieć
szczęście; **I'm ~ to be alive** mam
szczęście, że żyję; **it is ~ that...**
szczęście, że...; **to have a ~
escape** cudem ujść cało; **you'll be
~!** (*inf*) ale byś miał szczęście!
luggage ['lʌgɪdʒ] *n* bagaż; **piece
of ~** bagaż
lump [lʌmp] *n* **1** (*piece: of clay*)
bryła; (*of butter*) kawałek; (*of
wood, sugar*) kostka **2** (*on body*) guz
lunch [lʌntʃ] *n* **1** (*meal*) lunch;
(*large*) obiad **2** (*lunchtime*) pora
lunchu; **to have ~ (with sb)**
jeść (zjeść *pf*) (z kimś) lunch; **to
have sth for ~** jeść (zjeść *pf*) coś
na lunch
lung [lʌŋ] *n* płuco
Luxembourg ['lʌksəmbəːg] *n*
Luksemburg

luxurious [lʌg'zjuərɪəs] *adj*
luksusowy
luxury ['lʌkʃərɪ] *n* **1** (*comfort*)
luksus **2** (*extra*) zbytek ▷ *adj* (*hotel,
car, goods etc*) luksusowy
lying ['laɪɪŋ] *vb see* **lie¹**, **lie²** ▷ *n*
kłamstwo
lyrics ['lɪrɪks] *n pl* (*of song*) tekst *sg*

mac [mæk] (*Brit: inf*) *n* płaszcz
przeciwdeszczowy
macaroni [mækə'rəunɪ] *n*
makaron rurki
machine [mə'ʃi:n] *n* maszyna
machine gun *n* karabin
maszynowy
machinery [mə'ʃi:nərɪ] *n*
mechanizm
mad [mæd] *adj* **1** (*insane*) szalony
2 (*inf: angry*) zły; **to go ~** (*inf: go
insane*) oszaleć (*pf*); (*get angry*)
złościć (zezłościć *pf*) się; **to be ~
about sth** (*inf*) szaleć (oszaleć *pf*)
na punkcie czegoś; **to be ~ about
sb** (*inf*) szaleć na punkcie kogoś
madam ['mædəm] *n* (*form of
address*) pani; **Dear M~** Szanowna
Pani
made [meɪd] *pt, pp of* **make**

madness ['mædnɪs] n **1** (*insanity*) szaleństwo **2** (*foolishness*) głupota

magazine [mægə'ziːn] n czasopismo

maggot ['mægət] n robak

magic ['mædʒɪk] n **1** (*supernatural power*) magia **2** (*conjuring*) sztuczki magiczne ▷ *adj* magiczny

magician [mə'dʒɪʃən] n (*wizard*) czarownik; (*conjurer*) magik

magnet ['mægnɪt] n magnes

magnifying glass ['mægnɪfaɪɪŋ-] n szkło powiększające

maid [meɪd] n (*servant*) pokojówka

maiden name ['meɪdn-] n nazwisko panieńskie

mail [meɪl] n poczta ▷ vt (*lettter etc*) wysyłać (wysłać pf); **by ~** (*email*) emailem; (*post*) pocztą

mailbox ['meɪlbɒks] n **1** (*US*) skrzynka na listy **2** (*Comput*) skrzynka odbiorcza

mailman ['meɪlmæn] (*irreg*) n (*US*) listonosz

mailwoman ['meɪlwumən] (*irreg*) n (*US*) listonoszka

main [meɪn] *adj* główny

main course n danie główne

mainly ['meɪnlɪ] *adv* głównie

main road n główna droga

majesty ['mædʒɪstɪ] n (*title*): **Your/His/Her M~** Wasza/ Jego/Jej Królewska Mość

major ['meɪdʒər] *adj* ważny ▷ n **1** (*Mil*) major **2** (*US: Scol*) specjalizacja

majority [mə'dʒɔrɪtɪ] n (*of people, things*) większość

make [meɪk] (*pt, pp* **made**) vt **1** (*object, clothes, cake*) robić (zrobić pf); (*noise*) robić (narobić pf); (*mistake*) popełniać (popełnić pf) **2** (*manufacture: goods*) produkować (wyprodukować pf) **3** (*cause to be*): **to ~ sb sad** zmuszać (zasmucić pf) kogoś **4** (*force*): **to ~ sb do sth** zmuszać (zmusić pf) kogoś do zrobienia czegoś **5** (*earn: money*) zarabiać (zarobić pf) **6** (*equal*): **two and two ~ four** dwa plus dwa równa się cztery ▷ n (*brand*) marka; **to ~ a profit** zarabiać (zarobić pf); **to ~ a loss** tracić (stracić pf); **what time do you ~ it?** która jest godzina?; **to ~ do with sth** zadowalać (zadowolić pf) się czymś; **it's made (out) of glass** jest zrobiony ze szkła

▶ **make out** vt (*write: cheque*) wypisywać (wypisać pf)

▶ **make up** vt (*invent: story, excuse*) wymyślać (wymyślić pf) ▷ vi (*after quarrel*) godzić (pogodzić pf) się; **to ~ up one's mind** podejmować (podjąć pf) decyzję; **to ~ o.s. up** malować (umalować pf) się

make-up ['meɪkʌp] n (*cosmetics*) kosmetyki n pl

male [meɪl] *adj* (*employee, child, friend etc*) płci męskiej; (*animal, insect, plant, tree etc*) męski

malicious [mə'lɪʃəs] *adj* (*person, gossip*) złośliwy

mall [mɔːl] n (*also:* **shopping ~**) centrum handlowe

mammal ['mæml] n ssak

man [mæn] (*pl* **men**) n **1** (*person*) mężczyzna **2** (*mankind*) człowiek

manage ['mænɪdʒ] vt zarządzać ▷ vi (*cope*) radzić (poradzić pf)

sobie; **to ~ to do sth** radzić
(poradzić *pf*) sobie ze zrobieniem
czegoś
management ['mænɪdʒmənt]
n **1** (*managing*) zarządzanie
2 (*managers*) kierownictwo
manager ['mænɪdʒə^r] *n*
1 (*of business, department etc*)
kierownik(-iczka) *m/f* **2** (*Sport*)
manager
manageress [mænɪdʒə'rɛs] *n*
kierowniczka
mandarin ['mændərɪn] *n* **1**: **M~
(Chinese)** dialekt mandaryński
2 (*also*: **~ orange**) mandarynka
mango ['mæŋɡəʊ] (*pl* **mangoes**)
n (*fruit*) mango
mania ['meɪnɪə] *n* (*craze*) mania
maniac ['meɪnɪæk] *n* **1** (*lunatic*)
maniak(-aczka) *m/f* **2** (*idiot*)
wariat(ka) *m/f*
mankind [mæn'kaɪnd] *n* (*human
beings*) ludzkość
manner ['mænə^r] *n* (*way*) sposób;
manners *n pl* (*polite behaviour*)
maniery; **bad ~s** złych manier
mansion ['mænʃən] *n* rezydencja
mantelpiece ['mæntlpi:s] *n*
gzyms kominka
manual ['mænjuəl] *n* (*handbook*)
podręcznik
manufacture [mænju'fæktʃə^r]
vt (*goods*) produkować
(wyprodukować *pf*)
manufacturer
[mænju'fæktʃərə^r] *n*
producent(ka) *m/f*
many ['mɛnɪ] *adj* (*a lot of*) wiele
+*gen* ▷ *pron* wiele; **how ~** (*direct
question*) ile +*gen*; **twice as ~ as**
(*comparison*) dwa razy tyle +*gen*
map [mæp] *n* mapa

marathon ['mærəθən] *n* (*race*)
maraton
marble ['mɑ:bl] *n* (*stone*)
marmur; **marbles** *n pl* (*game*)
kulki
March [mɑ:tʃ] *n* marzec; *see
also* **July**
march [mɑ:tʃ] *vi* maszerować
▷ *n* marsz
mare [mɛə^r] *n* klacz
margarine [mɑ:dʒə'ri:n] *n*
margaryna
margin ['mɑ:dʒɪn] *n* (*on page*)
margines
marijuana [mærɪ'wɑ:nə] *n*
marihuana
mark [mɑ:k] *n* **1** (*cross, tick etc*)
znak **2** (*stain*) plama **3** (*Brit: grade,
score*) ocena ▷ *vt* **1** (*indicate: place*)
oznaczać (oznaczyć *pf*)
2 (*Brit: Scol*) oceniać (ocenić *pf*)
marker ['mɑ:kə^r] *n* (*also*: **~ pen**)
flamaster
market ['mɑ:kɪt] *n* (*in town,
village etc: place*) rynek; (*event*) targ
marketing ['mɑ:kɪtɪŋ] *n*
marketing
marmalade ['mɑ:məleɪd] *n*
marmolada
marriage ['mærɪdʒ] *n*
1 (*relationship, institution*)
małżeństwo **2** (*wedding*) ślub
married ['mærɪd] *adj* (*man*)
żonaty; (*woman*) zamężna; **to
be ~ to sb** (*to a woman*) żonaty
z kimś; **to be ~ to sb** (*to a man*)
zamężna z kimś; **to get ~** pobierać
(pobrać *pf*) się
marry ['mærɪ] *vt* (*man, woman*)
poślubiać (poślubić *pf*)
marsh [mɑ:ʃ] *n* (*bog*) bagno
marvellous ['mɑ:vləs] (*US*

marvelous) *adj* cudowny
marzipan ['mɑːzɪpæn] *n*
marcepan
mascara [mæsˈkɑːrə] *n* tusz
do rzęs
masculine ['mæskjulɪn] *adj*
męski (*Ling*) rodzaj męski
mashed potato [mæʃt-] *n* puree
ziemniaczane
mask [mɑːsk] *n* maska
mass [mæs] *n* (*large amount,
number*) masa; **~es of** (*inf*) masy
+*gen*
massage ['mæsɑːʒ] *n* masaż
massive ['mæsɪv] *adj* ogromny
master ['mɑːstər] *vt* (*learn: skill,
language*) doskonalić
masterpiece ['mɑːstəpiːs] *n*
(*great work*) arcydzieło
mat [mæt] *n* **1** (*on floor*) dywanik
2 (*also*: **door~**) wycieraczka
3 (*also*: **table ~**) podstawka
match [mætʃ] *n* **1** (*game*) mecz
2 (*for lighting fire etc*) zapałka ▷ *vt*
(*go well with*) pasować do +*gen* ▷ *vi*
(*go together*) pasować
mate [meɪt] *n* **1** (*Brit: inf: friend*)
kumpel(ka) *m/f* **2** (*animal*) samiec
material [məˈtɪərɪəl] *n* materiał;
materials *n pl* (*equipment*)
materiały
math [mæθ] (*US*) *n* = **maths**
mathematics [mæθəˈmætɪks]
(*formal*) *n* matematyka
maths [mæθs] (*Brit*) *n*
matematyka
matter ['mætər] *n* (*affair,
situation, problem*) sprawa ▷ *vi*
(*be important*) mieć znaczenie;
what's the ~ (with…)? co się
dzieje (*z* +*inst*…)?; **as a ~ of fact**
w istocie; **it doesn't ~** to nie ma

znaczenia
mattress ['mætrɪs] *n* materac
mature [məˈtjuər] *adj* (*not
childlike*) dojrzały
maximum ['mæksɪməm] *adj*
maksymalny ▷ *n* maksimum
May [meɪ] *n* maj; *see also* **July**

○ **KEYWORD**

may [meɪ] *aux vb* **1** (*possibility*): **it
may rain later** może później
będzie padać; **we may not be
able to come** może nie uda nam
się przyjść; **he may have hurt
himself** może się zranił
2 (*permission*): **may I come in?**
mogę wejść?; **you may go now**
może teraz iść

maybe ['meɪbiː] *adv* może; **~
so/not** może tak/ nie
mayonnaise [meɪəˈneɪz] *n*
majonez
mayor [mɛər] *n* burmistrz
me [miː] *pron* (*nom*) ja; (*gen, acc,
loc*) mnie; (*dat*) mi; (*inst*) mną; **it's
me** to ja
meal [miːl] *n* posiłek; **to go out
for a ~** pójść (*pf*) do restauracji
mean [miːn] (*pt, pp* **meant**)
vt **1** (*signify*) znaczyć **2** (*refer
to*) mieć na myśli **3** (*involve*)
oznaczać **4** (*intend*): **to ~ to do
sth** mieć zamiar coś robić (zrobić
pf) ▷ *adj* **1** (*not generous*) skąpy
2 (*unkind: person*) niemiły; **what
does "imperialism" ~?** co znaczy
"imperialism"?; **what do you
~?** co masz na myśli?; **to be ~ to
sb** (*unkind*) być niemiłym wobec
kogoś; *see also* **means**

meaning ['miːnɪŋ] n znaczenie
means [miːnz] (pl **means**) n
(method) sposób sg
meant [mɛnt] pt, pp of **mean**
meanwhile ['miːnwaɪl] adv
tymczasem
measles ['miːzlz] n odra
measure ['mɛʒəʳ] vt mierzyć
(zmierzyć pf) ▷ vi (room, person,
object) mierzyć (zmierzyć pf)
measurement ['mɛʒəmənt]
n: **~s** (of person) wymiary
meat [miːt] n mięso
Mecca ['mɛkə] n Mekka
mechanic [mɪ'kænɪk] n
mechanik
medal ['mɛdl] n (award) medal
media ['miːdɪə] pl of **medium**
▷ n pl: **the ~** media
medical ['mɛdɪkl] adj (treatment,
care) medyczny ▷ n (examination)
badania
medicine ['mɛdsɪn] n 1 (science)
medycyna 2 (medication) lek
Mediterranean
[mɛdɪtə'reɪnɪən] n: **the ~** (sea)
Morze Śródziemne; (region) region
Morza Śródziemnego
medium ['miːdɪəm] adj średni
medium-sized ['miːdɪəm'saɪzd]
adj w średnim rozmiarze
meet [miːt] (pt, pp **met**) vt
1 (friend: accidentally) spotykać
(spotkać pf); (by arrangement)
spotykać (spotkać pf) się z
+inst 2 (stranger: for the first
time) spotykać (spotkać pf);
(be introduced to) poznawać
(poznać pf) 3 (go and fetch) witać
(przywitać pf) ▷ vi spotykać
(spotkać pf) się; **pleased to ~ you**
miło pana/panią poznać

▶ **meet up** vi spotykać (spotkać
pf) się
meeting ['miːtɪŋ] n spotkanie
megabyte ['mɛgəbaɪt] n
megabyte
melon ['mɛlən] n melon
melt [mɛlt] vi topić (stopić pf) się
▷ vt topić (stopić pf)
member ['mɛmbəʳ] n
członek(-nkini) m/f
memorial [mɪ'mɔːrɪəl] n pomnik
memorize ['mɛməraɪz] vt: **to ~
sth** uczyć (nauczyć pf) się czegoś
na pamięć
memory ['mɛmərɪ] n 1 (ability
to remember) pamięć 2 (thing
remembered) wspomnienie
3 (Comput) pamięć; **to have
a good/bad ~ (for sth)** mieć
dobrą/złą pamięć (do czegoś)
men [mɛn] n pl of **man**
mend [mɛnd] vt (repair: object)
naprawiać (naprawić pf)
mental ['mɛntl] adj 1 (ability,
effort, development) umysłowy
2 (illness) umysłowy; (health)
psychiczny
mention ['mɛnʃən] vt
wspominać (wspomnieć pf) o +loc;
don't ~ it! nie ma za co!
menu ['mɛnjuː] n menu
meringue [mə'ræŋ] n beza
merry ['mɛrɪ] adj: **M~
Christmas!** Wesołych Świąt!
merry-go-round
['mɛrɪgəʊraʊnd] n karuzela
mess [mɛs] n bałagan; **to be in a
~ (room)** mieć bałagan
▶ **mess about, mess around**
(inf) vi tracić (stracić pf) czas
▶ **mess up** (inf) vt (make untidy)
robić (zrobić pf) bałagan w +loc

message ['mɛsɪdʒ] n (to sb)
wiadomość; **to leave (sb) a ~**
zostawiać (zostawić pf) (komuś)
wiadomość

messenger ['mɛsɪndʒəʳ] n
posłaniec

messy ['mɛsɪ] adj (untidy: person,
activity) niechlujny; (thing, place)
nieuporządkowany

met [mɛt] pt, pp of **meet**

metal ['mɛtl] n metal

meter ['mi:təʳ] n **1** (for gas, water,
electricity) licznik; (also: **parking
~**) parkomat **2** (US: unit) = **metre**

method ['mɛθəd] n (way)
metoda, sposób

metre ['mi:təʳ] (US **meter**) n
(unit) metr

metric ['mɛtrɪk] adj metryczny

Mexico ['mɛksɪkəu] n Meksyk

mice [maɪs] n pl of **mouse**

microchip ['maɪkrəutʃɪp] n
mikrochip

microphone ['maɪkrəfəun] n
mikrofon

microscope ['maɪkrəskəup] n
mikroskop

microwave ['maɪkrəuweɪv] n
(also: **~ oven**) mikrofalówka

midday [mɪd'deɪ] n (noon)
południe; **at ~** w południe

middle ['mɪdl] n **1** (centre) środek
2 (half-way point): **in the ~ of
the night** w środku nocy ▷ adj
(position, event, period) środkowy

middle-aged [mɪdl'eɪdʒd] adj w
średnim wieku

middle class adj: **~ values**
zasady typowe dla klasy średniej

Middle East n: **the ~** Bliski
Wschód

middle name n drugie imię

midge [mɪdʒ] n muszka

midnight ['mɪdnaɪt] n północ;
at ~ o północy

midwife ['mɪdwaɪf] (pl
midwives) n położna

might [maɪt] aux vb
1 (possibility): **I ~ get home
late** może będę w domu późno
2 (suggestions): **you ~ try the
bookshop** może spróbuje pan
w księgarni; **it ~ have been an
accident** to mógł być wypadek

migraine ['mi:greɪn] n migrena

mike [maɪk] (inf) n (microphone)
mikrofon

mild [maɪld] adj lekki

mile [maɪl] n mila; **miles** n pl
(inf: a long way) bardzo daleko; **70
~s per** or **an hour** siedemdziesiąt
mil na godzinę

military ['mɪlɪtərɪ] adj (leader,
action) wojskowy

milk [mɪlk] n mleko

milk chocolate n czekolada
mleczna

milkman ['mɪlkmən] (irreg) n
mleczarz

milkshake ['mɪlkʃeɪk] n koktajl
mleczny

millennium [mɪ'lɛnɪəm] (pl
millenniums or **millennia**
[mɪ'lɛnɪə]) n (1000 years)
tysiąclecie

millimetre ['mɪlɪmi:təʳ] (US
millimeter) n milimetr

million ['mɪljən] num milion;
millions n pl miliony; **a** or **one ~
books/people/dollars** milion
książek/ludzi/dolarów

millionaire [mɪljə'nɛəʳ] n
milioner(ka) m/f

mince [mɪns] n (Brit: Culin) mięso

mielone

mind [maɪnd] n (intellect) umysł
▷ vt **1** (Brit: look after) zajmować
(zająć pf) się +inst **2** (be careful of)
uważać na **3** (object to): **would
you ~ (if...)?** ma pan/pani coś
przeciwko temu, (żeby...)?
4 (have a preference): **I don't ~
(what/who...)** jest mi wszystko
jedno (co/kto...) **5: to make
up one's ~** or **make one's ~ up**
podejmować (podjąć pf) decyzję;
to change one's ~ zmieniać
(zmienić pf) zdanie; **never ~**
nieważne; **I wouldn't ~ a coffee** z
chęcią napiję się kawy; **~ the step**
uwaga na stopień

mine¹ [maɪn] pron (m sg) mój; (f
sg) moja; (nt sg) moje; (pl) moje;
(pl vir) moi; **a friend of ~** mój
przyjaciel; **this is ~** to jest moje;
these are ~ te są moje

mine² [maɪn] n (for coal, gold etc)
kopalnia

miner ['maɪnə^r] n górnik

mineral water n woda
mineralna

miniature ['mɪnətʃə^r] adj
miniaturowy ▷ n miniatura

minibus ['mɪnɪbʌs] n mikrobus

Minidisc® ['mɪnɪdɪsk] n minidisc

minimum ['mɪnɪməm] adj
(lowest, smallest) minimalny ▷ n
minimum

miniskirt ['mɪnɪskə:t] n
spódnica mini

minister ['mɪnɪstə^r] n **1** (Brit: Pol)
minister **2** (Rel) pastor

minor ['maɪnə^r] adj drobny

minority [maɪ'nɔrɪtɪ] n
mniejszość

mint [mɪnt] n **1** (plant) mięta

2 (sweet) miętówka

minus ['maɪnəs] prep
(inf: without) minus; **12 ~ 3 (is
or equals 9)** dwanaście minus
trzy (równa się dziewięć); **~ 24
(degrees)** (temperature) minus
dwadzieścia cztery (stopnie)

minute¹ [maɪ'nju:t] adj (amount)
drobny

minute² ['mɪnɪt] n **1** (unit) minuta
2 (fig: short time) chwila; **wait** or
just a ~! chwilę!

miracle ['mɪrəkl] n cud

mirror ['mɪrə^r] n lustro; (in car)
lusterko

misbehave [mɪsbɪ'heɪv] vi źle się
zachowywać (zachować pf)

miscellaneous [mɪsɪ'leɪnɪəs] adj
(people, objects) różny

mischief ['mɪstʃɪf] n (playfulness,
fun) psoty

mischievous ['mɪstʃɪvəs] adj
(playful, fun-loving) figlarny

miser ['maɪzə^r] n (pej) n skąpiec

miserable ['mɪzərəbl] adj
1 (unhappy: person) nieszczęsny
2 (unpleasant: weather, day)
ponury; **to feel ~** czuć (poczuć pf)
się okropnie

misery ['mɪzərɪ] n nieszczęście

Miss [mɪs] n **1** (before surname)
panna **2** (esp Brit: as form of
address) panno; **Dear ~ Lily Smith**
Droga Pani Lily Smith

miss [mɪs] vt **1** (fail to hit) chybiać
(chybić pf) **2** (Sport: shot, penalty)
nie trafiać (trafić pf) **3** (train,
bus, plane) nie zdążać (zdążyć
pf) **4** (feel the absence of): **I ~ my
mum** tęsknię za mamą **5** (chance,
opportunity) tracić (stracić pf) ▷ vi
(fail to hit: person) chybiać (chybić

pf); **you can't ~ it** nie może pan
tego przeoczyć
missing ['mɪsɪŋ] *adj* (*absent,
lost: person*) zaginiony; (*object*)
brakujący
mist [mɪst] *n* mgła
mistake [mɪs'teɪk] (*pt* **mistook**,
pp **mistaken**) *n* błąd; **to make a
~** popełniać (popełnić *pf*) błąd; **to
do sth by ~** robić (zrobić *pf*) coś
przez pomyłkę
mistaken [mɪs'teɪkən] *pp of*
mistake ▷ *adj*: **if I'm not** *or*
unless I'm ~ jeśli się nie mylę
mistletoe ['mɪsltəu] *n* jemioła
mistook [mɪs'tuk] *pt of* **mistake**
misty ['mɪstɪ] *adj* (*day, weather*)
mglisty; **it's ~** jest mgliście
misunderstand
[mɪsʌndə'stænd] (*pt, pp*
misunderstood) *vt, vi* źle
rozumieć (zrozumieć *pf*)
misunderstanding
['mɪsʌndə'stændɪŋ] *n*
nieporozumienie
misunderstood [mɪsʌndə'stud]
pt, pp of **misunderstand**
mix [mɪks] *vt* (*liquids, ingredients,
colours*) mieszać (zmieszać *pf*)
▷ *vi* (*socially*): **to ~ (with sb)**
zadawać (zadać *pf*) się (z kimś)
▷ *n* (*combination*) mieszanina; **to
~ sth with sth** (*activities*) mieszać
(zmieszać *pf*) coś z czymś
▸ **mix up** *vt* mylić (pomylić *pf*)
mixed [mɪkst] *adj* **1** (*salad,
herbs*) mieszany **2** (*diverse: group,
community*) zróżnicowany
3 (*school, education*) koedukacyjny
mixer ['mɪksər] *n* **1** (*also:* **food ~**)
mikser **2** (*person*): **to be a good ~**
łatwo nawiązywać (nawiązać *pf*)

kontakty
mixture ['mɪkstʃər] *n* mieszanina
mix-up ['mɪksʌp] (*inf*) *n*
nieporozumienie
moan [məun] *vi* (*inf: complain*): **to
~ (about sth)** narzekać (na coś)
mobile ['məubaɪl] *n* (*Brit: also:* **~
phone**) telefon komórkowy
mobile home *n* mieszkalna
przyczepa kampingowa
mobile phone (*Brit*) *n* telefon
komórkowy
mock [mɔk] *vt* (*ridicule*)
wyśmiewać się z +*gen*
model ['mɔdl] *n* **1** (*of boat, building
etc*) model **2** (*fashion model*)
model(ka) *m/f* ▷ *adj* **1** (*exemplary*)
modelowy **2** (*miniature*): **~
aircraft/train** model
samolotu/pociągu ▷ *vt* (*clothes*)
prezentować (zaprezentować *pf*)
modem ['məudɛm] *n* modem
moderate ['mɔdərət] *adj* (*views,
people*) umiarkowany
modern ['mɔdən] *adj* **1** (*present-
day*) współczesny **2** (*up-to-date*)
nowoczesny
modernize ['mɔdənaɪz] *vt*
modernizować (zmodernizować
pf)
modern languages *n pl* języki
nowożytne
modest ['mɔdɪst] *adj* (*not
boastful: person*) skromny
moisturizer ['mɔɪstʃəraɪzər] *n*
krem nawilżający
moldy ['məuldɪ] (*US*) *adj* =
mouldy
mole [məul] *n* **1** (*on skin*) pieprzyk
2 (*animal*) kret
moment ['məumənt] *n* chwila;
at the/this (present) ~ w tej

chwili; **(at) any ~ (now)** w każdej chwili; **at the last ~** w ostatniej chwili

monarchy ['mɔnəkɪ] *n* monarchia

Monday ['mʌndɪ] *n* poniedziałek; *see also* **Tuesday**

money ['mʌnɪ] *n* pieniądze; **to make ~** (*person, business*) zarabiać (zarobić *pf*)

mongrel ['mʌŋgrəl] *n* kundel

monitor ['mɔnɪtər] *n* monitor

monkey ['mʌŋkɪ] *n* (*Zool*) małpa

monotonous [mə'nɔtənəs] *adj* monotonny

monster ['mɔnstər] *n* (*imaginary creature*) potwór

month [mʌnθ] *n* (*calendar month*) miesiąc; **every ~** co miesiąc

monthly ['mʌnθlɪ] *adj* miesięczny ▷ *adv* miesięcznie

monument ['mɔnjumənt] *n* (*memorial*) pomnik

mood [muːd] *n* (*of person*) nastrój; **to be in a good/bad/awkward ~** być w dobrym/złym/dziwnym nastroju

moody ['muːdɪ] *adj* humorzasty

moon [muːn] *n*: **the ~** księżyc

moonlight ['muːnlaɪt] *n* światło księżyca

moped ['məupɛd] *n* motorower

moral ['mɔrl] *adj* moralny ▷ *n* (*of story*) morał

○ KEYWORD

more [mɔːr] *adj* **1** (*in comparisons with uncount noun, plural noun*) więcej +*gen*; **I get more money/holidays than you do** mam więcej pieniędzy/wakacji niż ty

2 (*additional: with uncount noun, plural noun*) jeszcze; **would you like some more tea/peanuts?** chce pan/pani jeszcze kawy/orzeszków?; **is there any more wine?** czy jest jeszcze wino?; **a few more weeks** kilka tygodniu dłużej

▷ *pron* **1** (*in comparisons: more in quantity, number*) więcej; **there's/there are more than I thought** jest więcej niż myślałem; **more than 20** więcej niż dwadzieścia; **she's got more than me** ma więcej niż ja

2 (*further, additional: in quantity*) jeszcze; **is there/are there any more?** czy jest jeszcze?; **have you got any more of it?** czy pan ma to jeszcze?; **a little/a few more** trochę więcej; **much/many more** wiele więcej

▷ *adv* **1** (*to form comparative*) bardziej; **more dangerous/difficult (than)** bardziej niebezpieczny/trudny (niż); **more easily/quickly (than)** łatwiej/szybciej (niż)

2 (*in expressions*): **more and more** coraz więcej; **more or less** (*adj, adv*) mniej więcej; **more than ever** więcej niż kiedykolwiek; **once more** raz jeszcze

morning ['mɔːnɪŋ] *n* (*early in the morning*) wcześnie rano; (*later in the morning*) późnym rankiem; **good ~!** dzień dobry!; **at three o'clock/seven o'clock in the ~** o trzeciej/siódmej nad ranem; **this ~** tego ranka; **on Monday ~** w poniedziałek rano

mortgage ['mɔːgɪdʒ] n hipoteka
▷ vt (house, property) obciążać
(obciążyć pf) hipotekę **to take
out a ~** zaciągać (zaciągnąć pf)
kredyty hipoteczny
Moslem ['mɔzləm] adj, n =
Muslim
mosque [mɔsk] n meczet
mosquito [mɔsˈkiːtəu] (pl
mosquitoes) n komar

○ **KEYWORD**

most [məust] adj **1** (almost
all: with uncount noun, plural noun)
większość +gen; **most people**
większość ludzi
2 (in comparisons): **(the) most**
(with uncount noun, plural noun)
najwięcej +gen; **who won the
most money/prizes?** kto wygrał
najwięcej pieniędzy/nagród?
▷ pron większość; **most of
it/them** większość z tego/nich;
I paid the most zapłaciłem
większość; **to make the most of
sth** wykorzystywać (wykorzystać
pf) maksymalnie coś; **at the
(very) most** co najwyżej
▷ adv (superlative) **1** (with
verb): **(the) most** najbardziej;
what I miss (the) most is...
to, czego mi brakuje najbardziej
to...
2 (with adj): **the most
comfortable/expensive sofa in
the shop** najbardziej wygodna/
najdroższa sofa w sklepie
3 (with adv): **most efficiently/
effectively** najwydajniej/
najefektywniej; **most of all**
przede wszystkim

moth [mɔθ] n ćma
mother ['mʌðəʳ] n (parent) matka
mother-in-law ['mʌðərɪnlɔː] (pl
mothers-in-law) n teściowa
Mother's Day (Brit) n Dzień
Matki
motivated ['məutɪveɪtɪd] adj
zmotywowany
motivation [məutɪˈveɪʃən] n
(motive) motywacja
motor ['məutəʳ] n (of machine,
vehicle) silnik
motorbike ['məutəbaɪk] n
motocykl
motorboat ['məutəbəut] n
motorówka
motorcycle ['məutəsaɪkl] n
motocykl
motorcyclist ['məutəsaɪklɪst] n
motocyklista(-tka) m/f
motorist ['məutərɪst] (esp Brit)
n kierowca
motor racing (Brit) n wyścigi
samochodowe
motorway ['məutəweɪ] (Brit) n
autostrada
mouldy ['məuldɪ] (US **moldy**) adj
(bread, cheese) spleśniały
mount [maunt] vt (organize)
organizować (zorganizować
pf) ▷ vi (increase) gromadzić
(zgromadzić pf) się
mountain ['mauntɪn] n góra
mountain bike n rower górski
mountaineer [mauntɪˈnɪəʳ] n
alpinista(-tka) m/f
mountaineering
[mauntɪˈnɪərɪŋ] n wspinaczka
wysokogórska; **to go ~** wspinać
się
mountainous ['mauntɪnəs] adj
(country, area) górzysty

mouse [maus] (*pl* **mice**) *n* **1** (*Zool*) mysz **2** (*Comput*) myszka

mouse mat ['mausmæt] *n* podkładka pod myszkę

mousse [muːs] *n* mus

moustache [məs'tɑːʃ] (*US* **mustache**) *n* wąsy *pl*

mouth [mauθ] *n* **1** (*of person, animal*) usta **2** (*of river*) ujście

mouthful ['mauθful] *n* (*of food*) kęs

mouth organ (*esp Brit*) *n* harmonijka ustna

move [muːv] *vi* **1** (*change position*) ruszać (ruszyć *pf*) się **2** (*relocate*) przeprowadzać (przeprowadzić *pf*) się; (*from activity*) przenosić (przenieść *pf*) się ▷ *vt* **1** (*change position of*) przestawiać (przestawić *pf*) **2** (*affect emotionally*) wzruszać (wzruszyć *pf*) ▷ *n* **1** (*change: of house*) przeprowadzka **2** (*in game: go, turn*) ruch; **to ~ house** przeprowadzać (przeprowadzić *pf*) się; **to ~ jobs/offices** zmieniać (zmienić *pf*) pracę/biuro; **to get a ~ on** (*inf*) pospieszyć (*pf*) się

▶ **move away** *vi* (*from town, area*) wyprowadzać (wyprowadzić *pf*) się; (*from window, door*) odsuwać (odsunąć *pf*) się

▶ **move back** *vi* **1** (*return: to town, area*) wracać (wrócić *pf*) **2** (*backwards: person, troops, vehicle*) cofać (cofnąć *pf*)

▶ **move forward** *vi* (*person, troops, vehicle*) posuwać (posunąć *pf*) się do przodu

▶ **move in** *vi* (*into house*) wprowadzać (wprowadzić *pf*) się

▶ **move into** *vt fus* (*house, area*) wprowadzać (wprowadzić *pf*) się w

▶ **move out** *vi* (*of house*) wyprowadzać (wyprowadzić *pf*) się

▶ **move over** *vi* (*to make room*) przesuwać (przesunąć *pf*) się

movement ['muːvmənt] *n* ruch

movie ['muːvɪ] (*US*) *n* film; **the movies** *n pl* kino

movie theater (*US*) *n* kino

moving ['muːvɪŋ] *adj* **1** (*emotionally*) poruszający **2** (*not static*) ruchomy

MP *n abbr* (*Brit*: = *Member of Parliament*) poseł (posłanka) *m/f*

MP3 [empiː'θriː] *n* MP3; **~ player** odtwarzacz MP3

mph *abbr* (= *miles per hour*) mil na godzinę

Mr ['mɪstə^r] (*US* **Mr.**) *n*: **Mr Edward Smith** pan Edward Smith

Mrs ['mɪsɪz] (*US* **Mrs.**) *n*: **~ Anna Smith** pani Anna Smith

Ms [mɪz] (*US* **Ms.**) *n* (*Miss or Mrs*): **Ms Tracey Smith** pani Tracey Smith

● **MR/MRS/MISS/MS**

● Grzecznościowe formy w języku angielskim to **Mr/Mrs/Miss/Ms**, co odpowiada polskim zwrotom: pan/pani/panna/pani. W języku angielskim nazwisko poprzedzone jest właśnie jedną z tych form, na przykład: Mr. Smith. Tych form grzecznościowych używa się w oficjalnych sytuacjach,

- zwracając się do osób, których
- się dobrze nie zna lub osób
- starszych. Inaczej niż w języku
- polskim, formy **Mr/Mrs/**
- **Miss/Ms** nie mogą być
- używane bez nazwiska.

○ KEYWORD

much [mʌtʃ] adj dużo +gen; **we haven't got much time/money** nie mamy dużo czasu/pieniędzy ▷ pron dużo; **there isn't much left** dużo nie zostało; **he doesn't do much at the weekends** nie robi zbyt dużo podczas weekendu ▷ adv **1** (a great deal) bardzo; **he hasn't changed much** bardzo się nie zmienił; **"did you like her?" — "not much"** "lubiłeś ją?" — "nie bardzo"
2 (far) wiele; **I'm much better now** teraz czuję się o wiele lepiej; **those trousers are much too big for you** te spodnie są wiele za duże na ciebie
3 (often) często; **do you go out much?** często gdzieś wychodzisz?

mud [mʌd] n błoto
muddle ['mʌdl] n bałagan ▷ vt (also: ~ up) mieszać (wymieszać pf); **to be in a ~** mieć mętlik w głowie
muddy ['mʌdɪ] adj zabłocony
muesli ['mjuːzlɪ] n muesli
mug [mʌg] n **1** (large cup: for drinks) kubek; (for beer) kufel
2 (contents) kubek ▷ vt (rob) okradać (okraść pf)
mugging ['mʌgɪŋ] n (assault)

kradzież (na ulicy)
multiplication [mʌltɪplɪ'keɪʃən] n (Math) mnożenie
multiply ['mʌltɪplaɪ] vt (Math): **to ~ sth (by sth)** mnożyć (pomnożyć pf) coś (przez coś) ▷ vi (increase) mnożyć (pomnożyć pf) się
mum [mʌm] n (Brit: inf) mama
mummy ['mʌmɪ] n (Brit: inf) mamusia
mumps [mʌmps] n świnka
murder ['məːdəʳ] n (killing) morderstwo ▷ vt (kill) mordować (zamordować pf)
murderer ['məːdərəʳ] n morderca(-rczyni) m/f
muscle ['mʌsl] n (Anat) mięsień
museum [mjuː'zɪəm] n muzeum
mushroom ['mʌʃrum] n grzyb
music ['mjuːzɪk] n muzyka
musical ['mjuːzɪkl] adj **1** (career, skills) muzyczny **2** (musically gifted: person) muzykalny
musical instrument n instrument muzyczny
musician [mjuː'zɪʃən] n muzyk
Muslim, Moslem ['muzlɪm]) n muzułmanin(-nka) m/f ▷ adj muzułmański
mussel ['mʌsl] n małż
must [mʌst] aux vb musieć; **you ~ be joking** chyba żartujesz; **the doctor ~ allow the patient to decide** lekarz musi pozwolić pacjentowi podjąć decyzję; **I really ~ be getting back** naprawdę muszę wracać
mustard ['mʌstəd] n musztarda
mustn't ['mʌsnt] = **must not**
mutton ['mʌtn] n baranina
my [maɪ] adj (m sg) mój; (f sg)

moja; (*nt sg*) moje; (*pl*) moje; (*pl vir*) moi; (*referring to subject of sentence*) swój

myself [maɪˈsɛlf] *pron* **1** (*gen, acc*) siebie; (*dat, loc*) sobie; (*inst*) sobą; (*reflexive pronoun*) się **2** (*emphatic: m sg*) sam; (*f sg*) sama **3** (*me*) ja; **I hurt ~** skaleczyłem się; **by ~** (*unaided, alone*) sam

mysterious [mɪsˈtɪərɪəs] *adj* (*strange*) tajemniczy

mystery [ˈmɪstərɪ] *n* tajemnica

myth [mɪθ] *n* mit

nag [næg] *vt* naprzykrzać się +*dat*

nail [neɪl] *n* **1** (*of finger, toe*) paznokieć **2** (*for hammering*) gwóźdź ▷ *vt* (*attach*): **to ~ sth to/on sth** przybijać (przybić *pf*) coś do czegoś

nail file [ˈneɪlfaɪl] *n* pilnik do paznokci

nail polish *n* lakier do paznokci

nail varnish (*Brit*) *n* = **nail polish**

naked [ˈneɪkɪd] *adj* (*person, body*) nagi

name [neɪm] *n* (*of person: forename*) imię; (*surname*) nazwisko; (*of thing*) nazwa ▷ *vt* **1** (*give name to: child*) dawać (dać *pf*) na imię +*dat*; (*ship, street*) nazywać (nazwać *pf*) **2** (*identify*) wymieniać (wymienić *pf*) z nazwiska; **what's your**

~? (*surname*) jak się pan/pani nazywa?; (*forename*) jak pan/pani ma na imię?; **my ~ is Peter** mam na imię Peter; **to give one's ~ and address** podawać (podać *pf*) swoje nazwisko i adres

nanny ['nænı] *n* opiekunka do dziecka

napkin ['næpkın] *n* serwetka

nappy ['næpı] (*Brit*) *n* pielucha

narrow ['nærəu] *adj* (*road, ledge, feet*) wąski ▷ *vi* (*road, river*) zwężać (zwężić *pf*) się

nasty ['nɑːstı] *adj* 1 (*bad, obnoxious*) wstrętny 2 (*serious*) poważny; **to be ~ to sb** być złośliwym dla kogoś

nation ['neıʃən] *n* (*country*) państwo; (*people*) naród

national ['næʃənl] *adj* (*election*) powszechny; (*newspaper*) ogólnokrajowy; (*interest*) krajowy ▷ *n* (*citizen*) obywatel(ka) *m/f*

national anthem *n* hymn państwowy

national holiday (*US*) *n* święto państwowe

nationality [næʃə'nælıtı] *n* narodowość

national park *n* park narodowy

- **NATIONAL TRUST**
-
- **National Trust** to
- organizacja, która została
- powołana aby chronić
- budowle, monumenty
- oraz wszelkie miejsca
- upamiętniające historię i
- kulturę, jak również pominki
- przyrody.

native ['neıtıv] *adj* ojczysty

natural ['nætʃrəl] *adj* 1 (*normal*) naturalny 2 (*innate: flair, aptitude*) wrodzony 3 (*not man-made*) naturalny

naturally ['nætʃrəlı] *adv* 1 (*unsurprisingly*) oczywiście 2 (*occur, happen*) w sposób naturalny

nature ['neıtʃər] *n* 1 (*also:* **N~**) natura 2 (*of person*) charakter

naughty ['nɔːtı] *adj* (*disobedient: child*) niegrzeczny

navy ['neıvı] *n*: **the ~** marynarka wojenna ▷ *adj* (*also:* **~-blue**) granatowy

near [nıər] *adj* (*physically, in time*) bliski ▷ *adv* (*close*) blisko ▷ *prep* (*also:* **~ to**) 1 (*physically*) blisko +*gen* 2: **~ the end of the year** niedługo przed końcem roku; **~ the beginning of the game** niedługo po rozpoczęciu meczu; **the ~est shops are 5 km away** najbliższe sklepy są pięć kilometrów stąd; **my office is quite ~** moje biuro jest dosyć blisko; **in the ~ future** w niedalekiej przyszłości

nearby [nıə'baı] *adj* pobliski ▷ *adv* w pobliżu

nearly ['nıəlı] *adv* prawie; **he's ~ as tall as I am** jest prawie tak samo wysoki jak ja; **I (very) ~ fell over** prawie się przewróciłem; **~ always** prawie zawsze

near-sighted [nıə'saıtıd] (*US*) *adj* (*short-sighted: person*) krótkowzroczny

neat [niːt] *adj* 1 (*tidy: house, desk*) uporządkowany; (*pile*) równy; (*clothes*) porządny; (*handwriting*) staranny 2 (*US: inf: great*) świetny

neatly ['ni:tlɪ] *adv* (*tidily*) starannie

necessarily ['nɛsɪsrɪlɪ] *adv* (*inevitably*) koniecznie

necessary ['nɛsɪsrɪ] *adj* konieczny; **if/when/where ~** jeśli/kiedy/gdzie to konieczne; **it may be ~ (for us) to buy a new cooker** kupno nowej kuchenki może się okazać (dla nas) konieczne

neck [nɛk] *n* **1** (*Anat*) szyja **2** (*of shirt, dress, jumper*) kołnierz

necklace ['nɛklɪs] *n* naszyjnik

necktie ['nɛktaɪ] (*US*) *n* krawat

nectarine ['nɛktərɪn] *n* (*fruit*) nektarynka

need [ni:d] *vt* **1** (*require*) potrzebować +*gen* **2** (*want*): **I ~ a cigarette** muszę zapalić ▷ *n* (*necessity*) potrzeba; **I ~ a haircut/bath/wash** muszę obciąć włosy/wziąć kąpiel/umyć się; **I ~ a holiday** przydałby mi się urlop; **to ~ to do sth** musieć coś zrobić; **the car ~s servicing** samochód wymaga przeglądu; **there's no ~ to shout** (*please don't*) nie ma powodu do krzyku

needle ['ni:dl] *n* **1** (*for sewing*) igła **2** (*for knitting*) drut **3** (*for injections*) igła do zastrzyków

negative ['nɛgətɪv] *adj* **1** negatywny **2** (*Math*) ujemny ▷ *n* (*Ling*) przeczenie

neglected [nɪ'glɛktɪd] *adj* zaniedbany

negotiate [nɪ'gəʊʃɪeɪt] *vi* negocjować (wynegocjować *pf*) ▷ *vt* (*treaty, contract*) negocjować (wynegocjować *pf*)

neighbour ['neɪbər] (*US*

neighbor) *n* sąsiad(ka) *m/f*

neighbourhood ['neɪbəhʊd] (*US* **neighborhood**) *n* (*place*) okolica

neither ['naɪðər] *pron* (*person, thing*) żaden ▷ *conj*: **I didn't move and ~ did John** ani ja się nie ruszyłem, ani John; **~ do I** ja też nie; **~ of us went** żaden z nas nie poszedł; **~...nor...** ani...ani...

nephew ['nɛvju:] *n* (*brother's son*) bratanek; (*sister's son*) siostrzeniec

nerve [nə:v] *n* **1** (*Anat*) nerw **2** (*courage*) odwaga; **nerves** *n pl* (*anxiety*) nerwy; **to lose one's ~** tracić (stracić *pf*) zimną krew; **to get on sb's ~s** działać (podziałać *pf*) komuś na nerwy

nervous ['nə:vəs] *adj* **1** (*worried*) zdenerwowany **2** (*by nature*) nerwowy; **to be ~ about sth/about doing sth** obawiać się czegoś/zrobienia czegoś

nest [nɛst] *n* (*of bird*) gniazdo

net [nɛt] *n* **1** (*for fishing, trapping, in games*) sieć **2** (*Comput*): **the N~** internet ▷ *adj* **1** (*also*: **~t**: *assets, income, profit*) netto **2** (*final: result, effect*) końcowy; **an income/ profit of 10,000 pounds ~** dochód/zysk dziesięciu tysięcy funtów netto

netball ['nɛtbɔ:l] *n* netball

Netherlands ['nɛðələndz] *n pl*: **the ~** Holandia

network ['nɛtwə:k] *n* sieć

neutral ['nju:trəl] *adj* (*Elec: wire*) zerowy

never ['nɛvər] *adv* nigdy; **I ~ met him** nigdy go nie poznałem; **we ~ saw him again** nigdy więcej go nie widzieliśmy

new [njuː] *adj* **1** nowy
2 (*inexperienced: mother, member*)
młody; **I'm ~ here** jestem tutaj
nowy

news [njuːz] *n* wiadomości *f pl*;
a piece of ~ wiadomość; **good/
bad ~** dobre/złe wiadomości; **the
~** (*TV, Rad*) wiadomości

newsagent ['njuːzeɪdʒənt] (*Brit*)
n (*also: ~'s*) kiosk

newscaster ['njuːzkɑːstə'] (*US*)
n prezenter(ka) *m/f*

newspaper ['njuːzpeɪpə'] *n*
gazeta

newsreader ['njuːzriːdə'] (*Brit*) *n*
prezenter(ka) *m/f*

New Year *n*: **(the) ~** nowy Rok;
in the ~ w Nowym Roku; **Happy
~!** Szczęśliwego Nowego Roku!;
to wish sb a Happy ~ yczy komuś
Szczęśliwego Nowego Roku

New Year's Day (*US* **New
Year's**) *n* Nowy Rok

New Year's Eve (*US* **New Year's**)
n sylwester

New Zealand [-'ziːlənd] *n* Nowa
Zelandia

next [nɛkst] *adj* **1** (*next in time*)
następny; (*next week, month*)
przyszły **2** (*adjacent: house,
street, room*) przyległy **3** (*in
queue, series, list*) następny ▷ *adv*
następnie ▷ *pron* następny; **the ~
day/morning** następnego dnia/
poranka; **the ~ five years/weeks
will be very important** następne
pięć lat/tygodni będzie bardzo
ważne; **the ~ flight/prime
minister** następny lot/premier;
~ time, be a bit more careful
następnym razem bądź trochę
bardziej ostrożny; **who's ~?** kto

następny?; **the week after ~**
za dwa tygodnie; **~ to** (*beside*)
obok +*gen*

next door *adv* w sąsiedztwie
▷ *adj* (*building, house, flat, room*)
sąsiedni; **my mother lives ~ to
her** moja matka mieszka w jej
sąsiedztwie; **my ~ neighbour**
mój sąsiad obok

NHS (*Brit*) *n abbr* (= *National Health
Service*): **the ~** państwowa służba
zdrowia

nice [naɪs] *adj* **1** (*good: time,
holiday*) przyjemny; (*meal*)
smaczny; (*weather*) ładny
2 (*person: likeable, friendly*) miły
3 (*lovely*) miły; **to look ~** (*person,
place*) wyglądać ładnie; **it's ~ to
see you** miło pana/panią widzieć

nickname ['nɪkneɪm] *n*
przezwisko

niece [niːs] *n* (*brother's daughter*)
bratanica; (*sister's daughter*)
siostrzenica

night [naɪt] *n* **1** (*period of darkness*)
noc **2** (*evening*) wieczór; **at ~** w
nocy; (*in the evening*) wieczorem;
**from nine o'clock at ~ until nine
in the morning** od dziewiątej
wieczorem do dziewiątej rano;
by ~ nocą; **in the middle of the
~** w środku nocy; **the ~ before
sth** wieczór przed czymś; **the ~
before** poprzedniego wieczoru

nightclub ['naɪtklʌb] *n* klub
nocny

nightie ['naɪtɪ] *n* koszula nocna

nightmare ['naɪtmɛə'] *n*
koszmar; **to have a ~** mieć
zły sen; **the bus journey was
a ~** podróż autobusem była
koszmarem

nil [nɪl] n (Brit: Sport) zero; **they lost two ~ to Italy** przegrali dwa do zera z Włochami; **their chances of survival are ~** mają zerowe szanse na przetrwanie

nine [naɪn] num dziewięć; see also **five**

nineteen ['naɪn'tiːn] num dziewiętnaście; see also **fifteen**

nineteenth [naɪn'tiːnθ] num dziewiętnasty; see also **fifth**

ninety ['naɪntɪ] num dziewięćdziesiąt; see also **fifty**

ninth [naɪnθ] num **1** (in series) dziewiąty **2** (fraction) dziewiąta; see also **fifth**

○ **KEYWORD**

no [nəʊ] adv (opposite of "yes") nie; **"did she see it?" — "no (she didn't)"** "widziała to?" — "nie (nie widziała tego)"; **no thank you, no thanks** nie, dziękuję
▷ adj (not any): **I have no milk/ books** nie mam mleka/książek; **there's no other solution** nie ma innego rozwiązania; **"no smoking"** "zakaz palenia"; **no way!** nie ma mowy!

nobody ['nəʊbədɪ] pron nikt

nod [nɒd] vi (to show agreement) kiwać (kiwnąć pf) głową; **to ~ agreement to** przytakiwać (przytaknąć pf) +dat
▶ **nod off** (inf) vi przysypiać (przysnąć pf)

noise [nɔɪz] n **1** (sound) dźwięk **2** (din) hałas; **to make a ~** hałasować

noisy ['nɔɪzɪ] adj (people, machine) głośny; (place) hałaśliwy

nominate ['nɒmɪneɪt] vt (propose: for job, award) nominować; **to ~ sb/sth for sth** (award, prize) nominować kogoś/ coś do czegoś

none [nʌn] pron: **~ of us/them** nikt z nas/nich; **I've ~ left** (not any) nic mi nie zostało; **there's ~ left** nic nie zostało; **~ at all** (not any) żaden

nonsense ['nɒnsəns] n (rubbish) nonsens

non-smoking ['nɒn'sməʊkɪŋ] adj (area, carriage) dla niepalących

non-stop ['nɒn'stɒp] adj (activity, music) bez przerwy; (flight) bez międzylądowania ▷ adv **1** (ceaselessly) nieustannie **2** (fly, drive) bez przerwy

noodles ['nuːdlz] n pl kluski

noon [nuːn] n południe ▷ adj południowy; **at ~** w południe

no-one ['nəʊwʌn] pron = **nobody**

nor [nɔːʳ] conj ani; **~ me!** ani ja!; see also **neither**

normal ['nɔːməl] adj normalny; **to get back** or **return to ~** wracać (wrócić pf) do normy; **higher/worse than ~** powyżej normy/gorzej niż zwykle

normally ['nɔːməlɪ] adv **1** (usually) zwykle **2** (conventionally: act, behave) normalnie; **to be working ~** pracować normalnie

north [nɔːθ] n północ ▷ adj północny ▷ adv (movement) na północ; (location) na północy; **the ~ of France** północ Francji; **to the ~ of** na północ od +gen; **it's 15 miles or so ~ of Oxford** jest około piętnaście mil na północ od Oksfordu

North America n Ameryka Północna

north-east [nɔ:θ'i:st] n północny wschód ▷ adj północno-wschodni ▷ adv (movement) na północny wschód; (location) na północnym wschodzie

northern ['nɔ:ðən] adj północny; **the ~ hemisphere** północna półkula

Northern Ireland n Irlandia Północna

North Korea n Korea Północna

North Pole n: **the ~** biegun północny

North Sea n: **the ~** Morze Północne

north-west [nɔ:θ'wɛst] n północny zachód ▷ adj północno-zachodni ▷ adv (movement) na północny zachód; (location) na północnym zachodzie

Norway ['nɔ:weɪ] n Norwegia

Norwegian [nɔ:'wi:dʒən] adj norweski ▷ n 1 (person) Norweg(-eżka) m/f 2 (language) norweski

nose [nəuz] n (on face) nos; **to poke** or **stick one's ~ into sth** (inf) wtrącać (wtrącić pf) się do czegoś

nosebleed ['nəuzbli:d] n krwawienie z nosa; **I often have ~s** często leci mi krew z nosa

nosy ['nəuzɪ] (inf) adj wścibski

not [nɔt] adv nie; **he is ~** or **isn't here** jego tu nie ma; **I do ~** or **don't want to go out tonight** nie chcę nigdzie wychodzić dziś wieczorem; **it's too late, isn't it?**

jest za późno, prawda?; **he asked me ~ to do it** poprosił mnie, żebym tego nie robił; **are you coming or ~?** idzie pan/pani, czy nie?; **~ at all** (in answer to question) wcale nie; (in answer to thanks) nie ma za co; **~ yet** jeszcze nie; **~ now** nie teraz; **~ really** raczej nie

note [nəut] n 1 (message, reminder) notatka 2 (Brit: banknote) banknot 3 (Mus: sound) nuta ▷ vt (observe) zauważać (zauważyć pf); **notes** n pl (from lecture) notatki; **to make a ~ of sth** notować (zanotować pf) coś; **to take ~s** robić (zrobić pf) notatki; **to take ~ (of sth)** zauważać (zauważyć pf) (coś); **please ~ that...** proszę zauważyć, że...

notebook ['nəutbuk] n 1 notes 2 (Comput) notatnik

notepad ['nəutpæd] n notes

nothing ['nʌθɪŋ] pron (not anything) nic; **~ new/serious** nic nowego/poważnego; **there's ~ to worry about** nie ma się czym martwić; **~ much** nic takiego; **~ else** nic innego; **for ~** (free) za nic; (in vain) na próżno; **~ at all** absolutnie nic; **~ but** nic oprócz +gen

notice ['nəutɪs] vt (observe) zauważać (zauważyć pf) ▷ n 1 (sign) ogłoszenie 2 (warning) zawiadomienie; **to ~ that...** zauważać (zauważyć pf), że...; **to bring sth to sb's ~** zwracać (zwrócić pf) czyjąś uwagę na coś; **to take no ~ of sb/sth** nie zwracać (zwrócić pf) na kogoś/coś uwagi; **to give sb ~ of sth** zawiadamiać (zawiadomić

pf) kogoś o czymś; **without ~**
bez uprzedzenia; **at short ~** w
krótkim czasie; **to hand in** or
give in one's ~ składać (złożyć pf)
wymówienie
noticeboard ['nəutɪsbɔːd] (Brit)
n tablica ogłoszeniowa; **on the ~**
na tablicy ogłoszeniowej
nought [nɔːt] (esp Brit) num zero
noun [naun] n rzeczownik
novel ['nɔvl] n powieść
novelist ['nɔvəlɪst] n
powieściopisarz(-rka) m/f
November [nəu'vɛmbə^r] n
listopad; see also **July**
now [nau] adv **1** (at the present
time) teraz **2** (these days) obecnie
3 (under the circumstances) teraz
4 (specifying length of time): **it has
been five weeks ~ since I saw
him** minęło już pięć tygodni,
od kiedy go ostatnio widziałem
▷ conj: **~ (that)** skoro już; **right
~** w tej chwili; **by ~** do tej pory;
just ~ (at the moment) w tej chwili;
from ~ on od tej chwili; **in 3 days
from ~** za trzy dni; **between
~ and Monday** do przyszłego
poniedziałku; **that's all for ~** to
by było na tyle; **any day/time ~**
lada dzień/chwila
nowhere ['nəuwɛə^r] adv (no
place: emphatic) nigdzie; **~ else**
(no place else: emphatic) nigdzie
indziej; **this is getting us ~** to
nigdzie nas nie zaprowadzi
nuclear ['njuːklɪə^r] adj nuklearny
nuisance ['njuːsns] n (person)
uciążliwa osoba; **to be a ~** (thing)
być uciążliwym
numb [nʌm] adj zdrętwiały
number ['nʌmbə^r] n **1** (Math)

liczba **2** (telephone number)
numer telefonu **3** (of house, bank
account, bus) numer **4** (quantity: of
things, people) ilość ▷ vt (pages)
numerować (ponumerować pf); **a
~ of** (several) kilka +gen; **a large/
small ~ of** duża/mała ilość +gen
number plate (Brit) n tablica
rejestracyjna
Number Ten (Brit) n (10 Downing
Street) Downing Street numer 10
(siedziba premiera Wielkiej Brytanii)
nun [nʌn] n zakonnica
nurse [nəːs] n (in hospital)
pielęgniarz(-ka) m/f ▷ vt (patient)
opiekować (zaopiekować pf)
się +inst
nursery ['nəːsərɪ] n
1 (kindergarten) przedszkole
2 (garden centre) szkółka
nursery school n przedszkole
nut [nʌt] n **1** (Bot, Culin) orzech
2 (Tech) nakrętka
nylon ['naɪlɔn] n nylon ▷ adj
(shirt, sheets) nylonowy

oak [əuk] *n* dąb
oar [ɔːʳ] *n* wiosło
oats [əuts] *n pl* owies *m sg*
obedient [ə'biːdɪənt] *adj* (*child, dog*) posłuszny
obese [ə'biːs] *adj* otyły
obey [ə'beɪ] *vt* (*person*) być posłusznym +*dat*; (*orders*) wykonywać (wykonać *pf*); (*law, regulations*) przestrzegać +*gen* ▷ *vi* podporządkowywać (podporządkować *pf*) się
object [*n* 'ɔbdʒɛkt, *vb* əb'dʒɛkt] *n* **1** (*thing*) przedmiot **2** (*aim, purpose*) cel **3** (*Ling*) dopełnienie ▷ *vi* sprzeciwiać (sprzeciwić *pf*) się +*dat*
objection [əb'dʒɛkʃən] *n* sprzeciw
oblige [ə'blaɪdʒ] *vt* (*compel*): **to**

~ sb to do sth zobowiązywać (zobowiązać *pf*) kogoś do zrobienia czegoś
oboe ['əubəu] *n* obój
obsess [əb'sɛs] *vt*: **to be ~ed by** *or* **with sb/sth** mieć obsesję na punkcie kogoś/czegoś
obsession [əb'sɛʃən] *n* obsesja
obtain [əb'teɪn] (*formal*) *vt* (*information, degree etc*) uzyskiwać (uzyskać *pf*); (*book*) otrzymywać (otrzymać *pf*)
obvious ['ɔbvɪəs] *adj* oczywisty
obviously ['ɔbvɪəslɪ] *adv* **1** (*of course*) oczywiście **2** (*noticeably*) wyraźnie
occasion [ə'keɪʒən] *n* **1** (*point in time*) okazja **2** (*event, celebration*) wydarzenie **3** (*opportunity*): **an ~ for sth/for doing sth** okazja do czegoś/do zrobienia czegoś
occasionally [ə'keɪʒənəlɪ] *adv* czasami
occupation [ɔkju'peɪʃən] *n* (*job*) zawód
occupy ['ɔkjupaɪ] *vt* **1** (*inhabit*) zajmować (zająć *pf*) **2**: **to be occupied** (*seat, place etc*) być zajętym **3** (*take possession of*) okupować (zająć *pf*) **4** (*take up*) zajmować (zająć *pf*) **5** (*fill: time*) zajmować (zająć *pf*)
occur [ə'kəːʳ] *vi* (*happen*) zdarzać (zdarzyć *pf*) się; **to ~ to sb** wydarzać (wydarzyć *pf*) się komuś
ocean ['əuʃən] *n* ocean
o'clock [ə'klɔk] *adv*: **six ~** o godzinie szóstej; **it is nine ~** jest (godzina) dziewiąta
October [ɔk'təubəʳ] *n* październik; *see also* **July**

octopus ['ɔktəpəs] n ośmiornica
odd [ɔd] adj 1 (strange) dziwny
2 (not paired): **he was wearing
~ socks** miał skarpetki nie do
pary 3 (number) nieparzysty; see
also **odds**
odour ['əudəʳ] (US **odor**) n zapach

○ KEYWORD

of [ɔv, əv] prep 1 od +gen, ode +gen,
z +gen, ze +gen; **that was nice of
him!** to było miłe z jego strony!;
the history of China historia
Chin; **at the end of the street**
na końcu ulicy; **the city of New
York** miasto Nowy Jork
2 (expressing quantity, amount): **a
kilo of flour** kilogram mąki; **a cup
of tea/vase of flowers** filiżanka
herbaty/wazon kwiatów; **there
were three of them** było ich
trzech; **can one of you help?** ktoś
z was może pomóc?; **an annual
income of less than 30,000
pounds** roczny dochód poniżej
30.000 funtów
3 (made of) z +gen, ze +gen; **made
of wood** zrobiony z drewna
4 (in dates): **the 5th of July** piąty
lipca
5 (US: in times): **at five of three** za
pięć trzecia

○ KEYWORD

off [ɔf] adj 1 (not turned on)
wyłączony
2 (cancelled) odwołany
▷ adv 1 (away): **I must be off**
muszę iść; **where are you off to?**

dokąd pan/pani idzie?; **it's a long
way off** (in distance) to daleko
stąd; **my holiday is a long way
off** do moich wakacji jest jeszcze
daleko
2 (not at work): **to be off** (on
holiday) mieć wolne; (due to illness)
być na zwolnieniu; **to have a
day off** (as holiday) mieć dzień
wolnego; (because ill) być na
zwolnieniu jeden dzień
3 (Comm): **10% off** zniżka dziesięć
procent
▷ prep 1 (indicating motion, removal
etc): **to take a picture off the
wall** zdejmować (zdjąć pf) obraz
ze ściany
2 (distant from): **it's just off the
motorway** tuż przy autostradzie

offence [ə'fɛns] (US **offense**) n
(crime) przestępstwo
offend [ə'fɛnd] vt (upset) obrażać
(obrazić pf)
offense [ə'fɛns] (US) n = **offence**
offer ['ɔfəʳ] vt 1 (product,
making invitation) oferować
(zaoferować pf); (seat, cigarette
etc) proponować (zaproponować
pf) 2 (bid: money) oferować
(zaoferować pf) ▷ n 1 (proposal)
oferta 2 (special deal) promocja
office ['ɔfɪs] n 1 (room) biuro
2 (department): **the Foreign
O~** Ministerstwo Spraw
Zagranicznych 3 (US: of doctor,
dentist) gabinet
office block n biurowiec
officer ['ɔfɪsəʳ] n 1 (Mil) oficer
2 (also: **police ~**) policjant(ka) m/f
office worker n urzędnik(-iczka)
m/f

official [ə'fɪʃl] *adj* oficjalny
off-licence ['ɒflaɪsns] (*Brit*) *n*
(*shop*) monopolowy
offside ['ɒf'saɪd] *adj*: **to be ~**
(*Sport*) być na spalonym
often ['ɒfn] *adv* (*frequently*)
często; **how ~ do you wash the
car?** jak często pan/pani myje
samochód?; **I wash up twice as
~ as them** *or* **as they do** zmywam
dwa razy częściej niż oni *lub* od
nich
oil [ɔɪl] *n* (*in cooking*) olej;
(*petroleum*) ropa ▷ *vt* (*engine,
machine*) oliwić (naoliwić *pf*)
oil rig *n* (*on land*) szyb naftowy; (*at
sea*) platforma wiertnicza
ointment ['ɔɪntmənt] *n* maść
okay [əu'keɪ] (*inf*) *adj*
1 (*acceptable*) do przyjęcia **2** (*safe
and well*) w porządku ▷ *adv*
(*acceptably*) w porządku ▷ *int*
zgoda; **are you ~?** (*familiar*)
wszystko u ciebie w porządku?;
(*polite*) wszystko u pana/pani w
porządku?; **it's ~ with** *or* **by me**
pasuje mi
old [əuld] *adj* **1** stary **2** (*long-
standing*) dawny; **how ~ are you?**
ile masz lat?; **he's 8 years ~** on ma
osiem lat; **~er brother/~er sister**
starszy brat/starsza siostra
old age pensioner (*Brit*) *n* (*senior
citizen*) emeryt(ka) *m/f*
old-fashioned ['əuld'fæʃnd] *adj*
(*object*) staromodny; (*custom,
idea*) staroświecki; (*person*) starej
daty
olive ['ɒlɪv] *n* (*fruit*) oliwka ▷ *adj*
(*also:* **~-green**) oliwkowy
olive oil *n* oliwa z oliwek
Olympic [əu'lɪmpɪk] *adj*

olimpijski; **the Olympics** *n pl*
igrzyska olimpijskie
omelette ['ɒmlɪt] (*US* **omelet**)
n omlet

○ **KEYWORD**

on [ɒn] *prep* **1** (*indicating position*)
na +*loc*; **it's on the table/wall**
jest na stole/na ścianie; **the
house is on the main road** dom
stoi przy głównej ulicy; **on the
left/right** na lewo/prawo; **on
the top floor** na najwyższym
piętrze
2 (*indicating means, method,
condition etc*): **on foot** pieszo;
I'm on the train/bus jestem
w pociągu/autobusie; **on the
television/radio** w telewizji/
radio; **on the internet** w
Internecie; **to be on antibiotics**
brać antybiotyki
3 (*referring to time*) w; **on Friday**
w piątek; **on Fridays** w piątki;
on Friday, June 20th w piątek
20 czerwca
4 (*about, concerning*) o +*loc*,
na temat +*gen*; **information
on train services** informacje
na temat połączeń
kolejowych
▷ *adv* **1** (*clothes*): **to have one's
coat on** mieć na sobie płaszcz;
what's she got on? co ona ma
na sobie?
2 (*covering, lid etc*): **screw the
lid on tightly** dokręcić mocno
wieczko
▷ *adj* **1** (*turned on*) włączony
2 (*happening*): **is the meeting
still on?** czy spotkanie się

odbędzie?; **there's a good film on at the cinema** w kinie grają dobry film

once [wʌns] *adv* **1** (*one time only*) raz **2** (*at one time*) kiedyś **3** (*on one occasion*) jeden raz ▷ *conj* (*as soon as*) zaraz po tym jak; **at ~** (*immediately*) natychmiast; **~ a** or **every month** raz na miesiąc; **~ upon a time** (*in stories*) dawno dawno temu; (*in the past*) pewnego razu; **~ in a while** raz na jakiś czas; **~ or twice** (*a few times*) raz czy dwa

○ **KEYWORD**

one [wʌn] *adj* **1** (*number*) jeden; **he's one year old** on ma rok; **it's one o'clock** jest pierwsza godzina; **one hundred/thousand children** sto/tysiąc dzieci; **there will be one or two changes** będzie jedna lub dwie zmiany
2 (*same*) jeden; **shall I put it all on the one plate?** czy mam to wszystko położyć na jeden talerz? ▷ *pron* **1** (*number*) jeden; **I've already got one** już mam jeden; **one of them** jeden z nich; **one of the chairs** jedno z krzeseł; **one by one** pojedynczo
2 (*with adj*): **I've already got a red one** mam już czerwony
3 (*in generalizations*): **what can one do?** co można zrobić?; **to cut one's finger** kaleczyć (skaleczyć *pf*) się w palec; **to cut one's hair** obcinać (obciąć *pf*) sobie włosy; **this one** ten; **that one** tamten;

one another nawzajem; **they love one another** kochają się; **one never knows** nigdy nie wiadomo
▷ *n* (*numeral*) jeden

oneself *pron* (*gen, acc*) siebie; (*dat, loc*) sobie; (*inst*) sobą; (*reflexive pronoun*) się; **to talk to ~** mówić do siebie; **to hurt ~** kaleczyć (skaleczyć *pf*) się; **by ~** (*alone*) sam

one-way ['wʌnweɪ] *adj* **1** (*street, traffic*) jednokierunkowy **2** (*ticket, trip*) w jedną stronę

onion ['ʌnjən] *n* cebula

only ['əunlɪ] *adv* tylko ▷ *adj* (*sole*) jedyny ▷ *conj* (*but*) tylko; **I was ~ joking** tylko żartowałem; **I saw her ~ last week** widziałem ją zaledwie w zeszłym tygodniu.; **not ~... but (also)...** nie tylko... ale również...; **an ~ child** jedynak(-aczka) *m/f*

onto, on to ['ɔntu]) *prep* na +*loc*, do +*gen*; **he put the book on the shelf** położył książkę na półce; **to get ~ a bus/train/plane** wsiadać (wsiąść *pf*) do autobusu/pociągu/samolotu

onwards ['ɔnwədz] *adv* dalej; **from that time ~** od tamtego czasu

open ['əupn] *adj* otwarty ▷ *vt* (*door, book, eyes*) otwierać (otworzyć *pf*) ▷ *vi* (*door, lid*) otwierać (otworzyć *pf*) się; **in the ~ air** na świeżym powietrzu

opener ['əupnə'] *n* (*also*: **bottle ~**) otwieracz

opening hours *n pl* godziny otwarcia

open-minded [əupn'maɪndɪd]
adj bez uprzedzeń

● **OPEN UNIVERSITY**
●
● **Open University**
● – Uniwersytet Otwarty
● został założony w 1969
● roku. Jego specyfika polega
● na studiowaniu drogą
● korespondencyjną. Wykłady
● transmitowane są przez radio
● i telewizję, organizowane są
● również szkoły letnie.

opera ['ɔpərə] *n* opera
operate ['ɔpəreɪt] *vt* (*machine,
vehicle, system*) obsługiwać;
(*company, organization*) prowadzić
(poprowadzić *pf*) ▷ *vi* **1** (*machine,
vehicle, system*) działać; (*company,
organization*) prowadzić
(poprowadzić *pf*) działalność
2 (*Med*) operować (zoperować
pf); **to ~ on sb** (*Med*) operować
(zoperować *pf*) kogoś
operation [ɔpə'reɪʃən] *n*
operacja; **to have an ~** (*Med*)
mieć operację
operator ['ɔpəreɪtə'] *n* (*Tel*)
telefonista(-ka) *m/f*
opinion [ə'pɪnjən] *n* opinia; **in
my/her ~** moim/jej zdaniem
opinion poll *n* badanie opinii
publicznej
opponent [ə'pəunənt] *n*
przeciwnik(-iczka) *m/f*
opportunity [ɔpə'tju:nɪtɪ] *n*
okazja; **to take the ~ of doing
sth** *or* **to do sth** korzystać
(skorzystać *pf*) z okazji, żeby coś
zrobić

oppose [ə'pəuz] *vt* (*person, idea*)
sprzeciwiać (sprzeciwić *pf*) się
+*dat*; **to be ~d to sth** mieć coś
przeciwko czemuś
opposite ['ɔpəzɪt] *adj*
1 (*facing: side, house*) przeciwny
2 (*farthest: end, corner*)
przeciwległy **3** (*contrary: meaning,
direction*) przeciwny ▷ *adv* (*live,
work, sit*) naprzeciwko ▷ *prep*
(*across from*) naprzeciw +*gen*
▷ *n*: **the ~** przeciwieństwo; **the ~
sex** płeć przeciwna
opposition [ɔpə'zɪʃən] *n*
(*resistance: military*) opór;
(*objection, lack of agreement*)
sprzeciw
optician [ɔp'tɪʃən] *n* **1** (*person*)
optyk(-yczka) *m/f* **2** (*also:* **~'s**)
zakład optyczny
optimistic [ɔptɪ'mɪstɪk] *adj*
optymistyczny
option ['ɔpʃən] *n* **1** (*choice*) opcja;
(*possibility*) możliwość **2** (*Scol,
Univ*) przedmiot nadobowiązkowy
or [ɔ:'] *conj* **1** (*linking alternatives*)
albo **2** (*also:* **or else**) bo inaczej
oral ['ɔ:rəl] *adj* (*test, report*) ustny
▷ *n* (*spoken examination*) egzamin
ustny
orange ['ɔrɪndʒ] *n* (*fruit*)
pomarańcza ▷ *adj* (*in colour*)
pomarańczowy
orange juice ['ɔrɪndʒdʒu:s] *n*
sok pomarańczowy
orchard ['ɔ:tʃəd] *n* sad
orchestra ['ɔ:kɪstrə] *n* orkiestra
order ['ɔ:də'] *n* **1** (*command*)
rozkaz **2** (*in restaurant*)
zamówienie **3** (*sequence*) porządek
▷ *vt* **1** (*command*) kazać (rozkazać
pf) +*dat* **2** (*in restaurant, shop*)

zamawiać (zamówić pf) ▷ vi (in restaurant) składać (złożyć pf) zamówienie; **in alphabetical ~** w kolejności alfabetycznej; **out of ~** (not working) awaria; **in ~ to do sth** żeby coś robić (zrobić pf); **to ~ sb to do sth** rozkazywać (rozkazać pf) komuś, żeby coś zrobił

▶ **order around, order about** vt dyrygować +inst

ordinary ['ɔːdnrɪ] adj (everyday) zwykły

organ ['ɔːgən] n 1 (Anat) organ 2 (Mus) organy m pl

organic [ɔːˈgænɪk] adj 1 (food, farming) naturalny 2 (substance) organiczny

organization [ɔːgənaɪˈzeɪʃən] n organizacja

organize ['ɔːgənaɪz] vt organizować (zorganizować pf)

original [əˈrɪdʒɪnl] adj 1 (first, earliest) pierwotny 2 (authentic) oryginalny 3 (imaginative) oryginalny

originally [əˈrɪdʒɪnəlɪ] adv (at first) początkowo

ornament ['ɔːnəmənt] n ozdoba

orphan ['ɔːfn] n sierota

other ['ʌðər] adj 1 (additional) jeszcze jeden 2 (not this one) inny 3: **the ~...** (of two things or people) ten drugi... 4 (apart from oneself) inny ▷ pron 1 (additional one, different one) drugi 2 (of two things or people): **the ~** ten drugi; **the ~ day** (inf: recently) wczoraj; **the ~ week** tydzień temu

otherwise ['ʌðəwaɪz] adv 1 (if not) w przeciwnym razie 2 (apart from that) poza tym

otter ['ɔtər] n wydra

ought [ɔːt] (pt ought) aux vb 1 (indicating advisability): **she ~ to see a doctor** powinna pójść do lekarza 2 (indicating likelihood): **he ~ to be there now** powinien tam teraz być

our ['auər] adj (m sg) nasz; (f sg) nasza; (nt sg) nasze; (pl vir) nasi; (pl non-vir) nasze; (referring to subject of sentence) swój

ours [auəz] pron: **a friend of ~** nasz przyjaciel; **that book is ~** ta książka jest nasza; **this is ~** to jest nasze

ourselves [auəˈsɛlvz] pl pron (gen, acc) siebie; (dat, loc) sobie; (inst) sobą; (reflexive pronoun) się; **we didn't hurt ~** nie skaleczyliśmy się; **by ~** (unaided, alone: vir) sami; (non-vir) same

○ KEYWORD

out [aut] adv 1 (outside) na zewnątrz; **out here/there** tutaj/tam 2 (absent, not in) nie ma +gen; **Mr Green is out at the moment** Pana Greena nie ma w tej chwili; **to have a day/night out** spędzać (spędzić pf) dzień/wieczór poza domem; **the ball was out** piłka była na aucie ▷ adj 1: **to be out** (out of game) być wyeliminowanym; (extinguished) być zgaszonym ▷ prep: **out of** 1 (outside: with movement) z +gen, ze +gen; (beyond) poza; **to go/come out of the house** wychodzić (wyjść pf) z domu

2 (*from among: ratio*) na; **one out of every three smokers** jeden na trzech palaczy
3 (*without*): **we are out of milk/petrol** nie mamy mleka/benzyny

outdoor [aut'dɔːʳ] *adj* na powietrzu
outdoors [aut'dɔːz] *adv* na dworze
outer space *n* przestrzeń kosmiczna
outfit ['autfɪt] *n* strój
outing ['autɪŋ] *n* (*excursion*) wycieczka
outlet ['autlɛt] *n* **1** (*hole, pipe*) odpływ **2** (*US: Elec*) gniazdko
outline ['autlaɪn] *n* zarys
outside [aut'saɪd] *n* (*exterior*) na zewnątrz ▷ *adj* (*exterior*) zewnętrzny ▷ *adv* na zewnątrz ▷ *prep* **1** (*on the outside of*) na zewnątrz +*gen*; (*from outside of*) z zewnątrz +*gen* **2** (*near to: larger place*) koło +*gen*
outskirts ['autskəːts] *n pl*: **the ~** peryferie; **on the ~ of...** na peryferiach +*gen*...
outstanding [aut'stændɪŋ] *adj* **1** (*excellent*) wybitny **2** (*obvious: example*) znakomity
oval ['əuvl] *adj* owalny
oven ['ʌvn] *n* piekarnik

○ **KEYWORD**

over ['əuvəʳ] *adj* (*finished*) zakończony
▷ *prep* **1** (*more than*) ponad +*inst*; **over 200 people came** przyszło ponad dwieście osób
2 (*indicating position: above, on top of*) nad +*inst*; (*spanning*) ponad +*inst*; (*across*) ponad +*inst*; (*on the other side of*) po drugiej stronie +*gen*; **a bridge over the river** most nad rzeką
3 (*during*) podczas +*gen*; **we talked about it over dinner** rozmawialiśmy o tym podczas obiadu
4 (*recovered from: illness, shock, trauma*) po +*loc*; **he's returned to work and is over his illness** wrócił do pracy i jest już po chorobie
5: **all over the town/house** po całym mieście/mieszkaniu
▷ *adv* **1** (*across*) przez; **over here/there** tutaj/tam
2 (*more, above*): **people aged 65 and over** osoby w wieku lat sześćdziesięciu pięciu i starsze
3 (*in expressions*): **all over** (*everywhere*) wszędzie

overcast ['əuvəkɑːst] *adj* zachmurzony
overdose ['əuvədəus] *n* nadmierna dawka
overdraft ['əuvədrɑːft] *n* debet
overseas [əuvə'siːz] *adv* za granicą ▷ *adj* (*foreign*) zagraniczny
overtake [əuvə'teɪk] (*pt* **overtook**, *pp* **overtaken**) *vt* (*esp Brit: Aut*) wyprzedzać (wyprzedzić *pf*)
overtime ['əuvətaɪm] *n* nadgodziny *f pl*
overtook [əuvə'tuk] *pt of* **overtake**
overweight [əuvə'weɪt] *adj* (*person*) z nadwagą
owe [əu] *vt*: **to ~ sb sth** być

winnym komuś coś
owing to ['əuɪŋ-] *prep* (*because of*)
z powodu +*gen*
owl [aul] *n* sowa
own [əun] *adj* własny ▷ *vt*
(*possess*) posiadać; **a room of
my ~** mój własny pokój; **on
one's ~** sam; **she lived on her ~**
mieszkała sama
▶ **own up** *vi* (*confess*) przyznawać
(przyznać *pf*) się
owner ['əunə'] *n* właściciel(ka)
m/f
ox [ɔks] (*pl* **oxen**) *n* wół
oxygen ['ɔksɪdʒən] *n* tlen
oyster ['ɔɪstə'] *n* ostryga
ozone layer *n* warstwa ozonowa

Pacific [pə'sɪfɪk] *n*: **the ~
(Ocean)** Pacyfik
pacifier ['pæsɪfaɪə'] (*US*) *n* (*for
sucking*) smoczek
pack [pæk] *vt* pakować
(spakować *pf*) ▷ *vi* pakować
(spakować *pf*) się ▷ *n* (*of cards*)
talia; **~ it in!** (*stop it!*) przestań!
▶ **pack up** *vi* (*Brit: put things away*)
pakować (spakować *pf*) się
package ['pækɪdʒ] *n* **1** (*parcel*)
paczka **2** (*Comput*) pakiet
packed [pækt] *adj* (*crowded*)
zatłoczony
packed lunch (*Brit*) *n* drugie
śniadanie
packet ['pækɪt] *n* paczka
pad [pæd] *n* (*of paper*) blok
paddle ['pædl] *n* **1** (*for canoe*)
wiosło **2** (*US: for table tennis*)

rakietka ▷ *vt* (*boat, canoe*) wiosłować +*inst*

padlock ['pædlɔk] *n* kłódka

paedophile ['pi:dəufaɪl] (*US* **pedophile**) *n* pedofil(ka) *m/f*

page [peɪdʒ] *n* (*of book etc*) strona

pain [peɪn] *n* 1 (*physical*) ból 2 (*inf: nuisance*): **to be a ~ (in the neck)** sprawiać (sprawić *pf*) kłopot; **to have a ~ in one's chest/arm** odczuwać ból w klatce piersiowej/w ręce; **to be in ~** odczuwać ból; **what a ~!** (*inf*) co za cholerstwo!

painful ['peɪnful] *adj* bolesny

painkiller ['peɪnkɪlə'] *n* środek przeciwbólowy

paint [peɪnt] *n* farba ▷ *vt* 1 (*decorate*) malować (pomalować *pf*) 2 (*portray*) malować (namalować *pf*) 3 (*create: picture, portrait*) malować (namalować *pf*) ▷ *vi* (*creatively*) malować (namalować *pf*); **a tin of ~** puszka farby; **to ~ sth blue/white** malować (pomalować *pf*) coś na niebiesko/na biało

paintbrush ['peɪntbrʌʃ] *n* pędzel

painter ['peɪntə'] *n* malarz(-rka) *m/f*

painting ['peɪntɪŋ] *n* 1 (*activity: artistic*) malarstwo; (*decorating walls, doors*) malowanie 2 (*picture*) obraz

pair [pɛə'] *n* para; **a ~ of scissors** nożyczki *m pl*; **a ~ of trousers** para spodni; **in ~s** w parach

pajamas [pə'dʒɑ:məz] (*US*) *n pl* = **pyjamas**

Pakistan [pɑ:kɪ'stɑ:n] *n* Pakistan

Pakistani [pɑ:kɪ'stɑ:nɪ] *adj* pakistański ▷ *n*

Pakistańczyk(-anka) *m/f*

palace ['pæləs] *n* pałac

pale [peɪl] *adj* 1 (*colour*) jasny 2 (*fair: skin, complexion*) jasny 3 (*from sickness, fear*) blady; **~ blue/pink** jasnoniebieski/jasnoróżowy

Palestine ['pælɪstaɪn] *n* Palestyna

palm [pɑ:m] *n* 1 (*also: ~ tree*) palma 2 (*of hand*) dłoń

pan [pæn] *n* 1 (*also: sauce~*) garnek 2 (*US: for baking*) forma

pancake ['pænkeɪk] *n* naleśnik

panda ['pændə] *n* panda

panic ['pænɪk] *n* 1 (*anxiety*) lęk 2 (*scare*) panika ▷ *vi* (*person, crowd*) wpadać (wpaść *pf*) w panikę

panther ['pænθə'] *n* pantera

PANTOMIME

Pantomime – W Wielkiej Brytanii mianem pantomimy (**pantomime**) określa się komedie teatralne z muzyką, oparte na popularnych bajkach, takich jak Kopciuszek albo Kot w butach. Adresowane głównie do dzieci, pantomimy wystawiane są w teatrach w okresie świąt Bożego Narodzenia.

pants [pænts] *n pl* 1 (*Brit: underwear*) majtki 2 (*US: trousers*) spodnie

pantyhose ['pæntɪhəuz] (*US*) *n pl* rajstopy; **a pair of ~** para rajstop

paper ['peɪpə'] *n* 1 papier 2 (*also: **news~***) gazeta

3 (*wallpaper*) tapeta; **a piece of ~** (*odd bit*) kawałek papieru; (*sheet*) kartka papieru
paperback ['peɪpəbæk] *n* książka w miękkich okładkach
paper clip *n* spinacz
parachute ['pærəʃuːt] *n* spadochron
parade [pə'reɪd] *n* parada
paradise ['pærədaɪs] *n* raj
paragraph ['pærəɡrɑːf] *n* akapit
parallel ['pærəlɛl] *adj* równoległy
paralysed ['pærəlaɪzd] (*US* **paralyzed**) *adj* (*Med*) sparaliżowany
paramedic [pærə'mɛdɪk] *n* ratownik(-iczka) *m/f* medyczny(-na)
parcel ['pɑːsl] *n* (*package*) paczka
pardon ['pɑːdn] *n*: **(I beg your) ~?** or **~ me?** (*US: what did you say?*) przepraszam, niedosłyszałem?
parent ['pɛərənt] *n* rodzic; **parents** *n pl* rodzice
park [pɑːk] *n* (*public garden*) park ▷ *vt* parkować (zaparkować *pf*) ▷ *vi* parkować (zaparkować *pf*)
parking ['pɑːkɪŋ] *n* parkowanie; **"no ~"** "zakaz parkowania"
parking lot (*US*) *n* parking
parking meter *n* parkomat
parking ticket *n* mandat za nieprawidłowe parkowanie
parliament ['pɑːləmənt] (*Brit*) *n* parlament
parole [pə'rəul] *n* zwolnienie warunkowe
parrot ['pærət] *n* papuga
parsley ['pɑːslɪ] *n* natka pietruszki
part [pɑːt] *n* **1** (*section, division*) część **2** (*of machine, vehicle*)

część **3** (*role*) rola; **to take ~ in** (*participate in*) brać (wziąć *pf*) udział w +*loc*
▶ **part with** *vt fus* oddawać (oddać *pf*)
participate [pɑː'tɪsɪpeɪt] *vi* brać (wziąć *pf*) udział; **to ~ in sth** (*activity, discussion*) brać (wziąć *pf*) udział w czymś
particular [pə'tɪkjulə*r*] *adj* **1** (*specific*) konkretny **2** (*great*) szczególny; **particulars** *n pl* (*details*) szczegóły; (*name, address etc*) szczegółowe dane
particularly [pə'tɪkjul+lɪ] *adv* (*difficult, good, badly*) szczególnie; (*like, dislike, want*) wyjątkowo
partly ['pɑːtlɪ] *adv* (*to some extent*) częściowo
partner ['pɑːtnə*r*] *n* partner(ka) *m/f* ▷ *vt* (*person: at dance*) partnerować +*dat*
part-time ['pɑːt'taɪm] *adj* (*work, course*) w niepełnym wymiarze godzin; (*staff*) zatrudniony w niepełnym wymiarze godzin ▷ *adv* (*work, study*) na pół etatu; **~ student** student(ka) *m/f* zaoczny(-na)
party ['pɑːtɪ] *n* **1** (*Pol*) partia **2** (*social event*) przyjęcie; **birthday ~** przyjęcie urodzinowe
pass [pɑːs] *vt* **1** (*hand*): **to ~ sb sth** podawać (podać *pf*) coś komuś **2** (*go past: place, person*) mijać (minąć *pf*) **3** (*exam, test*) zdać (*pf*) **4** (*Sport*): **to ~ sb the ball** podawać (podać *pf*) komuś piłkę ▷ *vi* **1** (*go past: vehicles, people*) mijać (minąć *pf*) się **2** (*in exam*) zdać (*pf*); **to get a ~ (in sth)** (*Scol, Univ*) zdać (*pf*) egzamin z (*czegoś*)

▶ **pass away** vi (die) umrzeć (pf)

▶ **pass on** vt: **to ~ sth on (to sb)** (news, information, message) przekazywać (przekazać pf) coś (komuś)

▶ **pass out** vi (faint) mdleć (zemdleć pf)

passage ['pæsɪdʒ] n **1** (corridor) korytarz **2** (in book, speech, piece of music) ustęp

passenger ['pæsɪndʒəʳ] n pasażer(ka) m/f

passion ['pæʃən] n namiętność

passive ['pæsɪv] adj (person, attitude) bierny ▷ n: **the ~** (Ling) strona bierna

passport ['pɑːspɔːt] n **1** paszport **2** (fig): **a** or **the ~ to** klucz do +gen

password ['pɑːswəːd] n hasło

past [pɑːst] prep (in front of) obok +gen; (beyond) za +inst; (later than) po +loc ▷ adv (by): **to go/walk ~** przechodzić (przejść pf) ▷ adj (previous) poprzedni; (week, month, year) zeszły ▷ n: **the ~** przeszłość; (tense) czas przeszły; **it's ~ midnight** jest po północy; **ten/(a) quarter ~ eight** dziesięć/kwadrans po ósmej; **for the ~ few/3 days** przez ostatnie kilka/trzy dni; **the ~ tense** czas przeszły; **in the ~** (before now) w przeszłości; (in the past tense) w czasie przeszłym

pasta ['pæstə] n makaron

pasteurized ['pæstʃəraɪzd] adj pasteryzowany

pastry ['peɪstrɪ] n **1** (dough) ciasto **2** (cake) ciastko

patch [pætʃ] n **1** (piece of material) łata **2** (area) płat

path [pɑːθ] n (track) droga; (in garden) ścieżka

pathetic [pə'θɛtɪk] adj (excuse, effort, attempt) żałosny

patience ['peɪʃns] n cierpliwość

patient ['peɪʃnt] n (Med) pacjent(ka) m/f ▷ adj (person) cierpliwy

patio ['pætɪəu] n patio

patrol [pə'trəul] vt (city, streets, area) patrolować (spatrolować pf); **to be on ~** pójść na patrol

pattern ['pætən] n wzór

pause [pɔːz] n (temporary halt) przerwa ▷ vi robić (zrobić pf) przerwę

pavement ['peɪvmənt] n (Brit) chodnik

paw [pɔː] n łapa

pay [peɪ] (pt, pp **paid**) n (wage, salary) pensja ▷ vt **1** (debt, bill, tax) płacić (zapłacić pf) **2** (person: as wage, salary) płacić (zapłacić pf) +dat **3**: **to ~ sb sth** płacić (zapłacić pf) komuś coś; **to get paid** otrzymywać (otrzymać pf) wynagrodzenie; **how much did you ~ for it?** ile za to zapłacił pan/zapłaciła pani?

▶ **pay back** vt spłacać (spłacić pf)

▶ **pay for** vt fus (purchases) płacić (zapłacić pf) za

payment ['peɪmənt] n (sum of money) opłata

payphone ['peɪfəun] n automat telefoniczny

PC n abbr (= personal computer) komputer osobisty

PDA n abbr (= personal digital assistant) palmtop

PE (Scol) n abbr (= physical education) WF

pea [piː] n groszek

peace [piːs] n 1 (not war) pokój
2 (calm) spokój; (inner, personal)
wyciszenie
peaceful ['piːsful] adj spokojny
peach [piːtʃ] n brzoskwinia
peacock ['piːkɔk] n paw
peak [piːk] n (of mountain)
szczyt ▷ adj (level) górny; **at ~
times** w okresach szczytowego
zapotrzebowania
peanut ['piːnʌt] n orzeszek
ziemny
peanut butter n masło
orzechowe
pear [pɛəʳ] n gruszka
pearl [pɜːl] n perła
pebble ['pɛbl] n kamyk
peculiar [pɪ'kjuːlɪəʳ] adj (strange)
dziwny
pedal ['pɛdl] n pedał ▷ vi
pedałować
pedestrian [pɪ'dɛstrɪən] n
pieszy(-za) m/f
pedestrian crossing (Brit) n
przejście dla pieszych
pedophile ['piːdəufaɪl] (US) n =
paedophile
pee [piː] (inf) vi siusiać (wysiusiać
pf) się ▷ n: **to have a ~** robić
(zrobić pf) siusiu
peel [piːl] n (of orange, potato)
skórka ▷ vt (vegetables, fruit)
obierać (obrać pf)
peg [pɛg] n 1 (for coat, hat, bag)
wieszak 2 (Brit: also: **clothes ~**)
klamerka
pelvis ['pɛlvɪs] n miednica
pen [pɛn] n (for writing) pióro;
(also: **fountain ~**) pióro wieczne;
(also: **ballpoint ~**) długopis
penalty ['pɛnltɪ] n 1 (punishment,
fine) grzywna 2 (Football, Rugby)

rzut karny
pence [pɛns] (Brit) n pl of **penny**
pencil ['pɛnsl] n ołówek
pencil case n piórnik
pencil sharpener n temperówka
pendant ['pɛndnt] n wisiorek
penfriend ['pɛnfrɛnd] (Brit)
n korespondencyjny(-na)
przyjaciel(-iółka) m/f
penguin ['pɛŋgwɪn] n pingwin
penicillin [pɛnɪ'sɪlɪn] n
penicylina
penis ['piːnɪs] n penis
penknife ['pɛnnaɪf] (pl
penknives) n scyzoryk
penny ['pɛnɪ] (pl **pennies** or
pence) n 1 (Brit) pens 2 (US: inf)
cent
pen pal [-pæl] n
korespondencyjny(-na)
przyjaciel(-iółka) m/f
pension ['pɛnʃən] n emerytura
pensioner ['pɛnʃənəʳ] (Brit) n
emeryt(ka) m/f
Pentagon ['pɛntəgən] (US)
n: **the ~** Pentagon

● **PENTAGON**
●
●
● **Pentagon** to budynek w
● Arlington w stanie Virginia,
● siedziba Departamentu
● Obrony USA.

people ['piːpl] n pl ludzie; **old ~**
starzy ludzie; **many ~** wielu ludzi;
~ say that... mówi się, że...
pepper ['pɛpəʳ] n 1 (spice) pieprz
2 (vegetable) papryka
peppermint ['pɛpəmɪnt] n
(sweet, candy) miętówka
per [pəːʳ] prep na; **~ day** na dzień;

~ **person** na osobę; ~ **hour** na
godzinę; ~ **annum** na rok
per cent, percent [pə'sɛnt]) (*pl*
per cent) *n* procent; **by 15 ~** o
piętnaście procent
percentage [pə'sɛntɪdʒ] *n*
(*amount*) procent
percussion [pə'kʌʃən] *n* perkusja
perfect ['pə:fɪkt] *adj* doskonały
▷ *n*: **the ~ (tense)** (*czas*) przeszły
dokonany
perfectly ['pə:fɪktlɪ] *adv*
1 (*perform, work, do, speak*)
doskonale **2** (*emphatic*) całkowicie
perform [pə'fɔ:m] *vt* **1** (*piece
of music, dance*) wykonywać
(wykonać *pf*); (*play*) wystawiać
(wystawić *pf*) ▷ *vi* (*actor, singer,
dancer*) występować (wystąpić *pf*)
performance [pə'fɔ:məns] *n*
1 (*Theat*) przedstawienie **2** (*of
employee, athlete, team*) wynik
perfume ['pə:fju:m] *n* **1** perfumy
f pl **2** (*of flowers, spices*) zapach
perhaps [pə'hæps] *adv* może; ~
not może nie
period ['pɪərɪəd] *n* **1** (*interval,
stretch*) okres **2** (*time*) okres **3** (*era*)
epoka **4** (*Scol*) godzina lekcyjna
5 (*esp US: punctuation mark*) kropka
6 (*also:* **menstrual ~**) okres; **to
have one's ~** mieć okres
perm [pə:m] *n* (*Brit*) trwała
permanent ['pə:mənənt] *adj*
trwały ▷ *n* (*US*) = **perm**
permission [pə'mɪʃən] *n*
1 (*consent*) pozwolenie **2** (*official
authorization*) zezwolenie
permit ['pə:mɪt] *n* (*authorization*)
zezwolenie; **fishing ~** karta
wędkarska
persecute ['pə:sɪkju:t] *vt*

prześladować (*pf*)
person ['pə:sn] (*pl* **people**) *n*
osoba; **in ~** osobiście; **first/
second/third ~** pierwsza/druga/
trzecia osoba
personal ['pə:snl] *adj* **1** (*opinion,
habits*) własny; (*care, contact,
appearance, appeal*) osobisty **2** (*life,
matter, relationship*) prywatny;
nothing ~! bez urazy!
personality [pə:sə'nælɪtɪ] *n*
1 (*character*) osobowość **2** (*famous
person*) osobistość
personally ['pə:snəlɪ] *adv* (*for my
part*) osobiście
personal stereo *n* odtwarzacz
osobisty
perspiration [pə:spɪ'reɪʃən]
n pot
persuade [pə'sweɪd] *vt*: **to
~ sb to do sth** przekonywać
(przekonać *pf*) kogoś do zrobienia
czegoś
pessimistic [pɛsɪ'mɪstɪk] *adj*
pesymistyczny
pest [pɛst] *n* **1** (*insect*) szkodnik
2 (*fig: inf: person*) utrapieniec
pester ['pɛstə] *vt* dokuczać
(dokuczyć *pf*) +*dat*
pet [pɛt] *n* zwierzę
petrol ['pɛtrəl] (*Brit*) *n* benzyna
petrol station (*Brit*) *n* stacja
benzynowa
pharmacy ['fɑ:məsɪ] *n* **1** (*shop*)
apteka **2** (*science*) farmacja
pheasant ['fɛznt] *n* bażant
philosophy [fɪ'lɔsəfɪ] *n* filozofia
phobia ['fəubjə] *n* fobia
phone [fəun] *n* telefon ▷ *vt*
(*person, organization*) dzwonić
(zadzwonić *pf*) do +*gen* ▷ *vi*
dzwonić (zadzwonić *pf*); **to be on**

the ~ rozmawiać (porozmawiać
pf) przez telefon; **by ~** przez
telefon
▶ **phone back** vt **1** (return call
of) oddzwaniać (oddzwonić pf)
do +gen **2** (call again): **to ~ sb
back** dzwonić (zadzwonić pf) do
kogoś później ▷ vi **1** (return call)
oddzwaniać (oddzwonić pf) **2** (call
again) dzwonić (zadzwonić pf)
później
phone bill n rachunek
telefoniczny
phone book n książka
telefoniczna
phone booth [-buːð] (US) n
budka telefoniczna
phone box (Brit) n budka
telefoniczna
phone call n rozmowa
telefoniczna; **to make a ~**
dzwonić (zadzwonić pf)
phonecard ['fəʊnkɑːd] n karta
telefoniczna
phone number n numer
telefonu
photo ['fəʊtəʊ] (inf) n zdjęcie; **to
take a ~ (of sb/sth)** robić (zrobić
pf) zdjęcie (komuś/czemuś)
photocopier ['fəʊtəʊkɒpiəʳ] n
kserokopiarka
photocopy ['fəʊtəʊkɒpi] n
kserokopia ▷ vt (document, picture)
robić (zrobić pf) kserokopię +gen
photograph ['fəʊtəgræf] n
zdjęcie ▷ vt (person, object, place)
robić (zrobić pf) zdjęcie +dat; **to
take a ~ of sb/sth** robić (zrobić
pf) zdjęcie komuś/czemuś
photographer [fə'tɒgrəfəʳ] n
fotograf(ka) m/f
photography [fə'tɒgrəfi] n

fotografia
phrase [freɪz] n wyrażenie
phrase book n rozmówki
physical ['fɪzɪkl] adj (not mental)
fizyczny
physical education n
wychowanie fizyczne
physician [fɪ'zɪʃən] (US) n
lekarz(-rka) m/f
physicist ['fɪzɪsɪst] n fizyk
physics ['fɪzɪks] n fizyka
physiotherapist
[fɪzɪəʊ'θerəpɪst] n
fizjoterapeuta(-tka) m/f
physiotherapy [fɪzɪəʊ'θerəpɪ] n
fizjoterapia
pianist ['piːənɪst] n pianista(-tka)
m/f
piano [pɪ'ænəʊ] n fortepian
pick [pɪk] vt **1** (choose) wybierać
(wybrać pf) **2** (gather: fruit, flowers)
zbierać (zebrać pf) **3** (remove,
take): **to ~ sth out of or from sth**
wybierać (wybrać pf) coś spośród
czegoś; **take your ~** proszę
wybrać
▶ **pick on** (inf) vt fus (person)
czepiać (czepić pf) się +gen
▶ **pick out** vt **1** (recognise,
identify: person, thing)
rozpoznawać (rozpoznać pf)
2 (select: person, thing) wybierać
(wybrać pf)
▶ **pick up** vt **1** (object) podnosić
(podnieść pf) **2** (collect: person,
parcel) zbierać (zebrać pf)
3 (inf: learn) uczyć (nauczyć pf)
się +gen
pickpocket ['pɪkpɒkɪt] n
kieszonkowiec
picnic ['pɪknɪk] n (meal) piknik
▷ vi urządzać (urządzić pf) piknik

picture ['pɪktʃə'] n 1 (painting, drawing, print) obraz 2 (photograph) zdjęcie 3 (film, movie) film ▷ vt (imagine) wyobrażać (wyobrazić pf) sobie; **the pictures** n pl (Brit: inf) kino sg

picture message [-'mɛsɪdʒ] n wiadomość graficzna

pie [paɪ] n pasztecik

piece [piːs] n kawałek; **a ~ of paper** kartka papieru; **a 10p ~** (Brit) moneta dziesięciopensowa

pier [pɪə'] n molo

pierce [pɪəs] vt (surface, material, skin) przekłuwać (przekłuć pf); **to have one's ears ~d** przekłuwać (przekłuć pf) sobie uszy

pierced [pɪəst] adj (ears, nose, lip) przekłuty

piercing ['pɪəsɪŋ] n przekłucie

pig [pɪg] n 1 świnia 2 (inf: person: unkind) świnia; (greedy) żarłok

pigeon ['pɪdʒən] n gołąb

piggy bank ['pɪgɪ-] n skarbonka

pigtail ['pɪgteɪl] n warkocz

pile [paɪl] n sterta ▷ vt (objects) układać (ułożyć pf) na kupę; **piles** n pl (haemorrhoids) hemoroidy; **piles of** or **a ~ of sth** (inf) sterta f sg czegoś

pill [pɪl] n pigułka; **the ~** (contraceptive pill) pigułka antykoncepcyjna; **to be on the ~** brać (wziąć pf) pigułki antykoncepcyjne

pillow ['pɪləu] n poduszka

pilot ['paɪlət] n (Aviat) pilot ▷ vt (aircraft) pilotować

pimple ['pɪmpl] n pryszcz

PIN [pɪn] n abbr (= personal identification number) (also: ~ number) numer PIN

pin [pɪn] n (used in sewing) szpilka ▷ vt (on wall, door, board) przypinać (przypiąć pf); **~s and needles** mrowienie nt sg

pinch [pɪntʃ] vt 1 (person) szczypać (szczypnąć pf) 2 (inf: steal) kraść (ukraść pf)

pine [paɪn] n 1 (also: ~ **tree**) sosna 2 (wood) drewno sosnowe

pineapple ['paɪnæpl] n ananas

pink [pɪŋk] adj różowy ▷ n róż

pint [paɪnt] n (measure: Brit) jednostka miary objętości, ok. pół litra (568 ml); (US) jednostka miary objętości, ok. pół litra (473 ml)

pipe [paɪp] n 1 (for water, gas) rura 2 (for smoking) fajka

pirate ['paɪərət] n pirat

pirated ['paɪərətɪd] adj (video, CD, software etc) piracki

Pisces ['paɪsiːz] n (Astrol) Ryba

pistol ['pɪstl] n pistolet

pitch [pɪtʃ] n (Brit: Sport: field) boisko ▷ vt (tent) rozbijać (rozbić pf)

pity ['pɪtɪ] n 1 (compassion) litość 2 (misfortune): **it is a ~ that...** szkoda, że... ▷ vt (person) litować (zlitować pf) się nad +inst; **what a ~!** szkoda!

pizza ['piːtsə] n pizza

place [pleɪs] n miejsce ▷ vt (put: object) kłaść (położyć pf); **in ~s** w niektórych miejscach; **to change ~s with sb** (fig) zamieniać (zamienić pf) się miejscami z kimś; **at sb's ~** (home) u kogoś w domu; **to sb's ~** do kogoś do domu; **to take sb's/sth's ~** zajmować (zająć pf)

czyjeś/czegoś miejsce; **to take ~**
(*happen*) wydarzyć (*pf*) się; **some
~** (*US: inf*) gdzieś; **any ~** (*US: inf*)
gdziekolwiek
placement ['pleɪsmənt] *n* (*job*)
staż
plain [pleɪn] *adj* **1** (*not patterned*)
gładki **2** (*simple*) prosty **3** (*clear,
easily understood*) jasny ▷ *n* (*area of
land*) równina
plain chocolate (*Brit*) *n* gorzka
czekolada
plait [plæt] *n* (*of hair*) warkocz
▷ *vt* (*hair, rope, leather*) pleść
(zapleść *pf*)
plan [plæn] *n* **1** (*scheme, project*)
plan **2** (*drawing*) plan ▷ *vt* (*crime,
holiday, future etc*) planować
(zaplanować *pf*) ▷ *vi* (*think ahead*)
snuć plany; **plans** *n pl* (*intentions*)
plany; **to ~ to do sth** planować
(zaplanować *pf*) zrobienie czegoś
plane [pleɪn] *n* samolot
planet ['plænɪt] *n* planeta
plant [plɑːnt] *n* **1** roślina
2 (*factory, power station*) zakład
▷ *vt* (*flower, tree, crop etc*) sadzić
(zasadzić *pf*)
plaster ['plɑːstə**ʳ**] *n* **1** (*for walls,
ceilings*) tynk; (*Brit: also: **sticking
~***) plaster; **in ~** (*Brit*) w gipsie
plastic ['plæstɪk] *n* plastik ▷ *adj*
plastikowy
plastic wrap (*US*) *n* folia
plate [pleɪt] *n* (*dish*) talerz; (*for
serving*) talerz
platform ['plætfɔːm] *n* **1** (*stage*)
estrada **2** (*Rail*) peron; **the train
leaves from ~ 7** pociąg odjeżdża z
peronu siódmego
play [pleɪ] *n* (*Theat, TV, Rad*)
sztuka ▷ *vt* **1** (*game, chess*)

grać (zagrać *pf*) w **2** (*compete
against: team, opponent*)
grać (zagrać *pf*) z +*inst* **3** (*in
play, film*) grać (zagrać *pf*)
4 (*Mus: instrument*) grać (zagrać
pf) na +*loc*; (*piece of music*) grać
(zagrać *pf*) **5** (*listen to: CD, tape*)
słuchać (wysłuchać *pf*) ▷ *vi*
1 (*children*) bawić (pobawić *pf*) się
2 (*orchestra, band*) grać (zagrać *pf*)
3 (*CD, tape, radio*) grać; **to ~ cards**
grać (zagrać *pf*) w karty; **to ~ a
part** or **role in sth** (*fig*) odgrywać
(odegrać *pf*) jakąś rolę w czymś
▶ **play back** *vt* (*message, video*)
puszczać (puścić *pf*)
▶ **play down** *vt* pomniejszać
(pomniejszyć *pf*)
player ['pleɪə**ʳ**] *n* **1** (*Sport*) gracz
2 (*Mus*): **a piano ~** pianista(-tka)
m/f
playground ['pleɪɡraund] *n* (*at
school*) boisko do zabaw; (*in park*)
plac zabaw
playing card ['pleɪɪŋ-] *n* karta
do gry
playing field ['pleɪɪŋ-] *n* boisko
sportowe; **a level ~** (*fig*) równe
szanse
playtime ['pleɪtaɪm] *n* przerwa
w szkole
pleasant ['plɛznt] *adj*
1 (*agreeable*) miły **2** (*friendly*)
sympatyczny
please [pliːz] *int* **1** (*in polite
requests, written instructions*)
proszę **2** (*accepting sth*) poproszę
▷ *vt* (*satisfy*) zadowalać
(zadowolić *pf*); **yes, ~** tak,
poproszę; **~ don't cry!** proszę,
nie płacz!
pleased [pliːzd] *adj* (*happy,*

satisfied) zadowolony; **to be ~ that...** byc zadowolonym, że...; **~ to meet you** miło mi pana/panią poznać; **~ with sth** zadowolony z czegoś

pleasure ['plɛʒəʳ] n 1 (*happiness, satisfaction*) zadowolenie 2 (*fun*) przyjemność 3 (*enjoyable experience*) przyjemność; **"it's a ~", "my ~"** "cała przyjmeność po mojej stronie"

plenty ['plɛntɪ] pron 1 (*lots*) dużo 2 (*sufficient*) wiele; **~ of** (*food, money, time*) dużo +gen; (*jobs, people, houses*) wiele +gen; **we've got ~ of time to get there** mamy dużo czasu, żeby tam dotrzeć

pliers ['plaɪəz] n pl szczypce

plot [plɒt] n 1 (*secret plan*): **a ~ (to do sth)** intryga (w celu zrobienia czegoś) 2 (*of story, play, film*) fabuła ▷ vi (*conspire*) spiskować; **to ~ to do sth** knuć plany zrobienia czegoś

plough [plaʊ] (*US* **plow**) n pług

plug [plʌg] n 1 (*Elec: on appliance*) wtyczka; (*inf: socket*) gniazdko 2 (*in sink, bath*) korek
▷ **plug in** (*Elec*) vt włączać (włączyć pf)

plum [plʌm] n (*fruit*) śliwka

plumber ['plʌməʳ] n hydraulik

plump [plʌmp] adj pulchny

plural ['pluərl] adj zróżnicowany ▷ n liczba mnoga

plus [plʌs] conj plus ▷ adv (*additionally*) dodatkowo ▷ n (*inf*): **it's a ~** to jest na plus

p.m. adv abbr (= *post meridiem*) po południu

pneumonia [njuːˈməʊnɪə] n zapalenie płuc

poached [pəʊtʃt] adj (*egg*) gotowany w koszulce

pocket ['pɒkɪt] n kieszeń

pocketbook ['pɒkɪtbuk] n 1 (*US: wallet*) portfel 2 (*US: handbag*) torebka

pocket money (*esp Brit*) n kieszonkowe

poem ['pəʊɪm] n wiersz

poet ['pəʊɪt] n poeta(-tka) m/f

poetry ['pəʊɪtrɪ] n poezja

point [pɔɪnt] n 1 (*in report, lecture, interview*) punkt 2 (*of argument, discussion*) sedno 3 (*purpose: of action*) cel 4 (*place*) miejsce 5 (*moment*) moment 6 (*of needle, knife, instrument*) czubek 7 (*in score, competition, game*) punkt 8 (*also:* **decimal ~**) przecinek ▷ vi: **to ~ at sth/sb** (*with finger, stick*) wskazywać (wskazać pf) na coś/kogoś ▷ vt: **to ~ sth at sb** (*gun, finger, stick*) wskazywać (wskazać pf) czymś na kogoś; **the research made some valid ~s** badania naukowe wskazały na kilka ważnych punktów; **there's no ~ (in doing that)** nie ma sensu (tego robić); **at that ~** w tym momencie; **two ~ five** (2.5) dwa przecinek pięć; **the ~s of the compass** kierunki na kompasie
▷ **point out** vt (*person, place, mistake, fact*) wskazywać (wskazać pf) na; **to ~ out that...** wskazywać (wskazać pf) na to, że...

pointless ['pɔɪntlɪs] adj bezcelowy; **it is ~ to complain** nie ma sensu narzekać

poison ['pɔɪzn] n trucizna ▷ vt
(*person, animal*) truć (otruć *pf*)
poisonous ['pɔɪzənəs] *adj* trujący
poke [pəuk] vt (*jab: with finger,
stick*) szturchać (szturchnąć
pf); **to ~ one's head out of the
window** wystawiać (wystawić *pf*)
głowę za okno
poker ['pəukər] n (*Cards*) poker
Poland ['pəulənd] n Polska
polar bear ['pəulər-] n
niedźwiedź polarny
Pole [pəul] n Polak(-lka) *m/f*
pole [pəul] n 1 (*stick*) kij 2 (*Geo*)
biegun
police [pə'li:s] n pl (*organization*)
policja *sg*
policeman [pə'li:smən] (*irreg*) n
policjant
police station n posterunek
policji
policewoman [pə'li:swumən]
(*irreg*) n policjantka
Polish ['pəulɪʃ] *adj* polski ▷ n
(*language*) polski
polish ['pɔlɪʃ] n 1 (*substance: for
shoes, furniture, floor*) pasta
2 (*shine: on shoes, furniture, floor*)
połysk ▷ vt (*shoes*) pastować
(wypastować *pf*); (*furniture, floor*)
polerować (wypolerować *pf*)
polite [pə'laɪt] *adj* grzeczny
political [pə'lɪtɪkl] *adj* polityczny
politician [pɔlɪ'tɪʃən] n polityk
politics ['pɔlɪtɪks] n 1 (*activity*)
polityka 2 (*subject*) nauki *pl*
polityczne
pollute [pə'lu:t] vt
zanieczyszczać (zanieczyścić *pf*)
polluted [pə'lu:tɪd] *adj*
zanieczyszczony
pollution [pə'lu:ʃən] n

zanieczyszczenie
polythene bag ['pɔlɪθi:n-] n
torebka plastikowa
pond [pɔnd] n staw
pony ['pəunɪ] n kucyk
ponytail ['pəunɪteɪl] n koński
ogon
pony trekking [-trekɪŋ] (*Brit*)
n jazda konna; **to go ~** jeździć
konno
pool [pu:l] n 1 (*pond*) staw
2 (*also:* **swimming ~**) basen
3 (*game*) pul ▷ vt (*money, resources,
ideas*) gromadzić (zgromadzić *pf*);
pools n pl (*Brit: also:* **football ~s**)
totalizator piłkarski *m sg*; **to do
the (football) ~s** grać (zagrać *pf*)
w totalizatora piłkarskiego
poor [puər] *adj* 1 (*not rich*) biedny
2 (*bad: quality, performance*) słaby;
(*wages, conditions, results*) marny
▷ n pl: **the ~** biedni
pop [pɔp] n 1 (*Mus*) muzyka pop
2 (*US: inf: father*) tata ▷ vi (*balloon,
cork*) pękać (pęknąć *pf*) z hukiem
▶ **pop in** (*inf*) vi wpadać (wpaść
pf)
▶ **pop out** (*inf*) vi wyskakiwać
(wyskoczyć *pf*)
popcorn ['pɔpkɔ:n] n popcorn
pope [pəup] n papież
poppy ['pɔpɪ] n mak
popular ['pɔpjulər] *adj*
popularny; **to be ~ with sb**
(*food, activity etc*) cieszyć (*pf*) się
popularnością wśród kogoś
population [pɔpju'leɪʃən] n
1 (*inhabitants*) ludność 2: **the
male/civilian/elephant ~**
populacja osobników męskich/
cywilna/słoni
porch [pɔ:tʃ] n 1 (*entrance*) ganek

2 (*US: veranda*) weranda

pork [pɔːk] *n* wieprzowina

porridge ['pɔrɪdʒ] *n* owsianka

port [pɔːt] *n* **1** (*harbour*) port
2 (*town*) miasto portowe

portable ['pɔːtəbl] *adj* przenośny

porter ['pɔːtəʳ] *n* **1** (*Brit: doorkeeper*) portier **2** (*US: on train*) tragarz

portion ['pɔːʃən] *n* (*helping of food*) porcja

portrait ['pɔːtreɪt] *n* (*picture*) portret

Portugal ['pɔːtjugəl] *n* Portugalia

Portuguese [pɔːtju'giːz] (*pl* **Portuguese**) *adj* portugalski ▷ *n* (*language*) portugalski

posh [pɔʃ] (*inf*) *adj* **1** (*smart*) ekskluzywny **2** (*upper-class: person*) elegancki; (*voice*) podniosły

position [pə'zɪʃən] *n* **1** (*place*) pozycja **2** (*posture*) postawa **3** (*in race, competition*) pozycja

positive ['pɔzɪtɪv] *adj*
1 (*good: situation, experience*) pozytywny **2** (*affirmative: test, result*) twierdzący **3** (*sure*): **to be ~ (about sth)** być pewnym (czegoś); **to be ~ that...** (*sure*) być pewnym, że...

possession [pə'zɛʃən] *n* (*act, state*) posiadanie; **possessions** *n pl* własność *f sg*

possibility [pɔsɪ'bɪlɪtɪ] *n*
1 (*chance: that sth is true*) możliwość; (*of sth happening*) szansa **2** (*option*) możliwość

possible ['pɔsɪbl] *adj* (*conceivable*) możliwy; **it's ~ (that...)** możliwe (że...); **if ~** jeśli to możliwe; **as soon as ~** jak najszybciej; **as**

much as ~ jak najwięcej

possibly ['pɔsɪblɪ] *adv* być może; **if you ~ can** jeśli tylko pan/pani może

post [pəust] *n* **1** (*Brit*): **the ~** (*service, system*) poczta; (*letters, delivery*) poczta **2** (*pole*) słup **3** (*job*) posada ▷ *vt* (*Brit: letter*) wysyłać (wysłać *pf*); **by ~** (*Brit*) pocztą

postbox ['pəustbɔks] (*Brit*) *n* (*in street*) skrzynka na listy

postcard ['pəustkɑːd] *n* pocztówka

postcode ['pəustkəud] (*Brit*) *n* kod pocztowy

poster ['pəustəʳ] *n* plakat

postman ['pəustmən] (*irreg*) *n* (*Brit*) listonosz

post office *n* (*building*) poczta

postpone [pəus'pəun] *vt* odkładać (odłożyć *pf*)

postwoman ['pəustwumən] (*irreg*) *n* (*Brit*) listonoszka

pot [pɔt] *n* **1** (*for cooking*) garnek **2** (*also*: **tea~**) dzbanek **3** (*also*: **coffee~**) dzbanek na kawę **4** (*for paint, jam etc*) słoik **5** (*also*: **flower~**) doniczka

potato [pə'teɪtəu] (*pl* **potatoes**) *n* ziemniak

potato chips (*US*) *n pl* czipsy

pottery ['pɔtərɪ] *n* **1** (*work, hobby*) garncarstwo **2** (*factory, workshop*) garncarnia

pound [paund] *n* **1** (*unit of money*) funt **2** (*unit of weight*) funt; **a ~ coin** moneta jednofuntowa; **a five-~ note** pięciofuntowy banknot; **half a ~ (of sth)** pół funta (czegoś)

pour [pɔːʳ] *vt*: **to ~ sth (into/ onto sth)** (*liquid*) wlewać (wlać

pf) coś (do czegoś); **it is ~ing (with rain)** leje (deszcz)
▶ **pour out** *vt* (*tea, wine etc*) wylewać (wylać *pf*)
poverty ['pɒvətɪ] *n* bieda
powder ['paudər] *n* puder
power ['pauər] *n* 1 (*control*) władza 2 (*electricity*) energia
powerful ['pauəful] *adj* 1 (*influential*) potężny 2 (*physically strong*) silny
practical ['præktɪkl] *adj* praktyczny
practically ['præktɪklɪ] *adv* (*almost*) niemal
practice ['præktɪs] *n* praktyka ▷ *vt, vi* (*US*) = **practise**; **it's normal** *or* **standard ~** taka jest praktyka; **in ~** (*in reality*) w praktyce; **2 hours' piano ~** dwie godziny ćwiczeń na pianinie
practise ['præktɪs] (*US* **practice**) *vt* 1 (*sport, technique, piece of music*) ćwiczyć (przećwiczyć *pf*); (*musical instrument*) ćwiczyć na +*loc* ▷ *vi* (*in music, theatre, sport*) ćwiczyć
praise [preɪz] *vt* chwalić (pochwalić *pf*); **to ~ sb for doing sth** chwalić (pochwalić *pf*) kogoś za zrobienie czegoś
pram [præm] (*Brit*) *n* wózek dziecięcy
prawn [prɔːn] (*Brit*) *n* krewetka
pray [preɪ] *vi* modlić (pomodlić *pf*) się; **to ~ for/that** (*Rel*) modlić (pomodlić *pf*) się o/żeby
prayer [prɛər] (*Rel*) *n* modlitwa
precaution [prɪ'kɔːʃən] *n* zabezpieczenie
precious ['prɛʃəs] *adj* cenny
precise [prɪ'saɪs] *adj* 1 dokładny 2 (*detailed*) precyzyjny; **to be ~** (*in*

fact) dokładnie mówiąc
precisely [prɪ'saɪslɪ] *adv* dokładnie; **~!** dokładnie!
predict [prɪ'dɪkt] *vt* (*event, death etc*) przewidywać (przewidzieć *pf*); **to ~ that...** przewidywać (przewidzieć *pf*), że...
prediction [prɪ'dɪkʃən] *n* przewidywanie
prefect ['priːfɛkt] (*Brit*) *n* (*in school*) starszy uczeń w szkole odpowiedzialny za innych uczniów
prefer [prɪ'fəːr] *vt* woleć; **to ~ coffee to tea** woleć kawę od herbaty; **to ~ doing sth** woleć coś robić; **I'd ~ to go by train** wolałbym jechać pociągiem
pregnant ['prɛgnənt] *adj* (*woman, animal*) w ciąży; **3 months ~** w trzecim miesiącu ciąży; **to get ~** zajść (*pf*) w ciążę
prejudice ['prɛdʒudɪs] *n* (*bias*) uprzedzenie
prejudiced ['prɛdʒudɪst] *adj* (*biased: person*) uprzedzony
premature ['prɛmətʃuər] *adj* przedwczesny; **~ baby** wcześniak
Premier League (*Brit: Football*) *n*: **the ~** angielska ekstraklasa piłkarska
prep [prɛp] *n* (*Brit: homework*) zadanie domowe
preparation [prɛpə'reɪʃən] *n* (*activity*) przygotowanie; **preparations** *n pl* (*arrangements*): **~s (for sth)** przygotowania (do czegoś); **in ~ for sth** w przygotowaniu na coś
prepare [prɪ'pɛər] *vt* przygotowywać (przygotować *pf*) ▷ *vi*: **to ~ (for sth)** przygotowywać (przygotować

pf) się (do czegoś); **to ~ to do sth** (*get ready*) przygotowywać (przygotować *pf*) się do czegoś

prepared [prɪ'pɛəd] *adj*: **to be ~ to do sth** (*willing*) być gotowym coś zrobić; **~ (for sth)** (*ready*) przygotowany (do czegoś)

prep school *n* **1** (*Brit*) prywatna szkoła podstawowa dla dzieci w wieku 6-13 lat przygotowująca do nauki w szkole prywatnej **2** (*US*) prywatna szkoła ponadpodstawowa przygotowująca młodzież do nauki w szkole wyższej

prescribe [prɪ'skraɪb] *vt* (*Med*) przepisywać (przepisać *pf*); **to ~ sth for sb/sth** zapisywać (zapisać *pf*) coś komuś/na coś

prescription [prɪ'skrɪpʃən] *n* (*Med: slip of paper*) recepta; (*medicine*) przepisane lekarstwo; **to give sb a ~ for sth** zapisywać (zapisać *pf*) komuś lekarstwo na coś

present [*adj, n* 'prɛznt, *vb* prɪ'zɛnt] *adj* **1** (*current*) teraźniejszy **2** (*in attendance*) obecny ▷ *n* **1** (*not past*): **the ~** teraźniejszość **2** (*gift*) prezent **3**: **the ~** (*also*: **~ tense**) czas teraźniejszy ▷ *vt* **1** (*give*): **to ~ sth (to sb)** (*prize, award*) wręczać (wręczyć *pf*) coś (komuś) **2** (*difficulty, problem, threat*) stanowić **3** (*Rad, TV: programme*) prowadzić (poprowadzić *pf*); **to be ~ at sth** być obecnym na czymś; **at ~** obecnie; **to give sb a ~** dawać (dać *pf*) komuś prezent; **to ~ sb with sth** (*prize, award*) wręczać (wręczyć *pf*) coś komuś

presenter [prɪ'zɛntər] *n* (*on radio,*

TV) prezenter

president ['prɛzɪdənt] *n* (*Pol*) prezydent

press [prɛs] *n* (*newspapers, journalists*): **the ~** prasa ▷ *vt* **1** (*button, switch, bell*) naciskać (nacisnąć *pf*); (*accelerator*) przyciskać (przycisnąć *pf*) **2** (*iron*) prasować (wyprasować *pf*); **to be ~ed for time/money** mieć mało czasu/pieniędzy; **to ~ (down) on sth** naciskać (nacisnąć *pf*) coś

press-up ['prɛsʌp] (*Brit*) *n* (*exercise*) pompka; **to do ~s** robić (zrobić *pf*) pompki

pressure ['prɛʃər] *n* **1** (*physical force*) nacisk **2** (*fig: coercion*): **~ (to do sth)** przymus (zrobienia czegoś) **3** (*stress*) napięcie; **high/ low ~** wysokie/niskie ciśnienie; **to put ~ on sb (to do sth)** wywierać (wywrzeć *pf*) presję na kogoś (by coś zrobił); **to be under ~ to do sth** być pod presją zrobienia czegoś; **to ~ sb into doing sth** zmuszać (zmusić *pf*) kogoś do zrobienia czegoś

presume [prɪ'zjuːm] *vt* (*assume*): **to ~ (that...)** przypuszczać (przypuścić *pf*), (że...); **I ~ so** przypuszczam, że tak

pretend [prɪ'tɛnd] *vt*: **to ~ that...** (*make believe*) udawać (udać *pf*), że...

pretty ['prɪtɪ] *adj* ładny ▷ *adv* (*inf: quite*) całkiem; **~ much** or **well** (*inf: more or less*) prawie

prevent [prɪ'vɛnt] *vt* (*war, disease, situation*) zapobiegać (zapobiec *pf*) +*dat*; **to ~ sb (from) doing sth** przeszkadzać (przeszkodzić *pf*) komuś w

zrobieniu czegoś; **to ~ sth (from) happening** zapobiegać (zapobiec pf) czemuś
previous ['pri:vɪəs] *adj* poprzedni
previously ['pri:vɪəslɪ] *adv* wcześniej; **10 days ~** dziesięć dni wcześniej
price [praɪs] *n* cena
price list *n* cennik
prick [prɪk] *n* (*sting*) ukłucie ▷ *vt* (*scratch*) kłuć (ukłuć *pf*)
pride [praɪd] *n* **1** (*satisfaction, dignity, self-respect*) duma **2** (*arrogance*) arogancja; **to take (a) ~ in sb/sth** być dumnym z kogoś/czegoś
priest [pri:st] *n* ksiądz
primarily ['praɪmərɪlɪ] *adv* głównie
primary ['praɪmərɪ] *adj* **1** (*reason, aim, cause*) główny **2** (*Brit: education, teacher*) podstawowy
primary school (*Brit*) *n* szkoła podstawowa
Prime Minister [praɪm-] *n* (*of Poland*) Prezes Rady Ministrów; (*of other countries*) premier
prince [prɪns] *n* książę
princess [prɪn'ses] *n* księżniczka
principal ['prɪnsɪpl] *adj* (*main*) główny ▷ *n* (*head teacher: of school, college*) dyrektor(ka) *m/f*
principle ['prɪnsɪpl] *n* (*moral belief*) zasada; **in ~** (*in theory*) w zasadzie; **on ~** dla zasady
print [prɪnt] *n* **1** (*type*) druk **2** (*picture*) rycina **3** (*photograph*) odbitka ▷ *vt* **1** (*publish: story, article*) drukować (wydrukować *pf*) **2** (*stamp: word, number, pattern*) wytłaczać (wytłoczyć *pf*) **3** (*write*)

pisać (napisać *pf*) drukowanymi literami **4** (*Comput*) drukować (wydrukować *pf*); **prints** *n pl* (*fingerprints*) odciski (palców)
  ▶ **print out** *vt* (*Comput: document, file*) drukować (wydrukować *pf*)
printer ['prɪntə⟨r⟩] *n* **1** (*machine*) drukarka **2** (*firm: also: ~'s*) drukarnia
printout ['prɪntaut] *n* wydruk
priority [praɪ'ɔrɪtɪ] *n* (*concern*) sprawa nadrzędna; **priorities** *n pl* priorytety; **to give ~ to sth/sb** dawać (dać *pf*) pierwszeństwo czemuś/komuś
prison ['prɪzn] *n* **1** (*institution*) więzienie **2** (*imprisonment*) kara więzienia; **in ~** w więzieniu
prisoner ['prɪznə⟨r⟩] *n* więzień; (*during war*) jeniec
private ['praɪvɪt] *adj* **1** (*property, land, plane*) prywatny; (*performance, ceremony*) niedostępny dla osób postronnych **2** (*not state-owned*) prywatny **3** (*confidential*) poufny **4** (*personal*) osobisty; **in ~** na osobności
prize [praɪz] *n* nagroda
prize-giving ['praɪzgɪvɪŋ] *n* rozdanie nagród
prizewinner ['praɪzwɪnə⟨r⟩] *n* **1** (*in competition*) zdobywca(-czyni) *m/f* nagrody **2** (*Scol, Univ*) laureat(ka) *m/f*
pro [prəu] *n* (*professional*) zawodowiec: **the ~s and cons (of doing sth)** zalety i wady (robienia czegoś) ▷ *prep* (*in favour of*) za +*inst*
probability [prɔbə'bɪlɪtɪ] *n*: **~ (of sth/that...)** prawdopodobieństwo (czegoś/

że...); **the ~ of sth happening**
prawdopodobieństwo, że coś
się zdarzy

probable ['prɔbəbl] *adj*
prawdopodobny; **it is/seems
~ that...** jest/wydaje się
prawdopodobne, że...

probably ['prɔbəblɪ] *adv*
prawdopodobnie; **~!/~ not!**
prawdopodobnie!/
prawdopodobnie nie!

problem ['prɔbləm] *n* **1** (*difficulty*)
problem **2** (*puzzle*) zagadka;
what's the ~? w czym problem?;
I had no ~ finding her znalazłem
ją bez problemu; **no ~!** (*inf*) nie
ma sprawy!

process ['prəʊsɛs] *n* (*procedure*)
proces ▷ *vt* (*Comput: data*)
przetwarzać (przetworzyć *pf*); **to
be in the ~ of doing sth** być w
trakcie robienia czegoś

procession [prə'sɛʃən] *n* pochód

produce [prə'djuːs] *vt* **1** (*effect,
result etc*) przynosić (przynieść *pf*)
2 (*goods, commodity*) produkować
(wyprodukować *pf*) **3** (*play,
film, programme*) produkować
(wyprodukować *pf*)

producer [prə'djuːsə^r] *n* **1** (*Theat,
Cine, Mus*) producent(ka) *m/f* **2** (*of
food, material: country*) producent;
(*company*) producent

product ['prɔdʌkt] *n* produkt

production [prə'dʌkʃən] *n*
1 (*process*) produkcja; (*amount
produced, amount grown*)
produkcja **2** (*play, show*)
wystawienie

profession [prə'fɛʃən] *n* (*job*)
zawód

professional [prə'fɛʃənl] *adj*

1 (*work-related: activity, context,
capacity*) zawodowy **2** (*not
amateur*) zawodowy; (*advice, help*)
fachowy **3** (*skilful*) profesjonalny
▷ *n* (*Sport*) zawodowiec

professor [prə'fɛsə^r] *n* **1** (*Brit*)
profesor **2** (*US*) nauczyciel
akademicki

profit ['prɔfɪt] *n* zysk; **to
make a ~** osiągać (osiągnąć
pf) zysk

profitable ['prɔfɪtəbl] *adj*
korzystny

program ['prəʊgræm] *n*
1 (*also:* **computer ~**) program
2 (*US*) = **programme** ▷ *vt*
1 (*Comput*): **to ~ sth (to do sth)**
programować (zaprogramować
pf) coś (do zrobienia czegoś)
2 (*US*) = **programme**

programme ['prəʊgræm] (*US*
program) *n* program ▷ *vt*: **to ~
sth (to do sth)** (*machine, system*)
programować (zaprogramować
pf) coś (do zrobienia czegoś); *see
also* **program**

programmer ['prəʊgræmə^r]
(*Comput*) *n* programista(-tka)
m/f

progress ['prəʊgrɛs] *n* postęp;
to make ~ (with sth) robić
(zrobić *pf*) postępy (w
czymś)

prohibit [prə'hɪbɪt] (*formal*)
vt zakazywać (zakazać *pf*);
"smoking ~ed" "palenie
zabronione"

project ['prɔdʒɛkt] *n* **1** (*plan,
scheme*) projekt **2** (*Scol, Univ*)
referat

projector [prə'dʒɛktə^r] *n*
rzutnik

prom [prɔm] n (Brit: by sea)
promenada.

promise ['prɔmɪs] n obietnica
▷ vi obiecywać (obiecać pf)
▷ vt: **to ~ sb sth, ~ sth to
sb** obiecywać (obiecać pf)
coś komuś; **to make a ~ (to
do sth)** składać (złożyć pf)
obietnicę (zrobienia czegoś);
to break a ~ (to do sth) łamać
(złamać pf) obietnicę (zrobienia
czegoś); **to keep a ~ (to do sth)**
dotrzymywać (dotrzymać pf)
obietnicy (zrobienia czegoś); **to
~ (sb) that...** obiecywać (obiecać
pf) (komuś), że...; **to ~ to do sth**
obiecywać (obiecać pf) coś zrobić
promote [prə'məut] vt
(employee) awansować; **the team
was ~d to the first division**
(Brit: Sport) drużyna awansowała
do pierwszej ligi
promotion [prə'məuʃən] n **1** (at
work) awans **2** (Brit: Sport) awans
prompt [prɔmpt] adj **1** (on
time) punktualny **2** (rapid)
natychmiastowy ▷ n (Comput)
znak zachęty systemu; **at 8
o'clock ~** punktualnie o godzinie

ósmej
pronoun ['prəunaun] n zaimek
pronounce [prə'nauns] vt (word,
name) wymawiać (wymówić pf)
pronunciation [prənʌnsɪ'eɪʃən]
n wymowa
proof [pru:f] n dowód
proper ['prɔpər] adj **1** (genuine:
job, meal etc) porządny
2 (correct: procedure, place, word)
właściwy **3** (socially acceptable)
stosowny
properly ['prɔpəlɪ] adv
1 (adequately) odpowiednio
2 (decently) stosownie
property ['prɔpətɪ] n
1 (possessions) mienie **2** (buildings
and land) nieruchomość
propose [prə'pəuz] vt (plan, idea)
proponować (zaproponować pf)
▷ vi (offer marriage) oświadczać
(oświadczyć pf) się; **to ~ to do
or doing sth** (intend) zamierzać
coś robić; **to ~ a toast** wznosić
(wznieść pf) toast
prosecute ['prɔsɪkju:t] vt: **to
~ sb (for sth/for doing sth)**
oskarżać (oskarżyć pf) kogoś (o
coś/o zrobienie czegoś)
prostitute ['prɔstɪtju:t] n
(female) prostytutka; **a male ~**
męska prostytutka
protect [prə'tɛkt] vt (person, floor,
rights, freedom) chronić; **to ~ sb/
sth from or against sth** chronić
kogoś/coś przed czymś
protection [prə'tɛkʃən] n: **~
(from or against sth)** ochrona
(przed czymś)
protein ['prəuti:n] n białko
protest [n 'prəutɛst, vb prə'tɛst]
n protest ▷ vi: **to ~ about**

or **against** *or* **at sth** (*Brit*)
protestować (zaprotestować *pf*)
przeciwko czemuś ▷ *vt* (*US: voice*
opposition to) zgłaszać (zgłosić *pf*)
sprzeciw wobec +*gen*

Protestant ['prɒtɪstənt]
n protestant(ka) *m/f* ▷ *adj*
protestancki

protester [prə'tɛstə^r] *n*
protestujący(-ca) *m/f*

proud [praud] *adj* 1 (*parents,*
owner) dumny 2 (*arrogant*)
pyszny 3 (*dignified*) dostojny; **to**
be ~ of sb/sth być dumnym z
kogoś/czegoś

prove [pruːv] *vt* (*idea, theory*)
udowadniać (udowodnić *pf*)
▷ *vi*: **to ~ that...** udowadniać
(udowodnić *pf*), że...; **to ~ sb**
right/wrong udowadniać
(udowodnić *pf*), że ktoś ma rację/
nie ma racji

proverb ['prɒvɜːb] *n* przysłowie

provide [prə'vaɪd] *vt* 1 (*food,*
money, shelter) zapewniać
(zapewnić *pf*); (*answer,*
opportunity, details) dostarczać
(dostarczyć *pf*); **to ~ sb with sth**
(*food, job, resources*) zaopatrywać
(zaopatrzyć *pf*) kogoś w coś
▸ **provide for** *vt fus* (*person*)
zapewniać (zapewnić *pf*) +*dat*

provided (that) [prə'vaɪdɪd-]
conj pod warunkiem, że

prune [pruːn] *n* suszona śliwka

PS *abbr* (= *postscript*) postscriptum

psychiatrist [saɪ'kaɪətrɪst] *n*
psychiatra

psychological [saɪkə'lɒdʒɪkl]
adj (*effect, problem, disorder*)
psychiczny

psychologist [saɪ'kɒlədʒɪst] *n*

psycholog

psychology [saɪ'kɒlədʒɪ] *n*
(*science*) psychologia

PTO *abbr* (= *please turn over*) verte,
proszę odwrócić

pub [pʌb] (*Brit*) *n* piwiarnia

public ['pʌblɪk] *adj* 1 (*from*
people: support, opinion, interest)
społeczny 2 (*for people: building,*
service, library) publiczny 3 (*not*
private) publiczny ▷ *n*: **the**
(general) ~ społeczeństwo; **in ~**
(*speak, smoke, drink*) publicznie

public holiday *n* święto
państwowe

publicity [pʌb'lɪsɪtɪ] *n*
1 (*information, advertising*) reklama
2 (*attention*) rozgłos

public school *n* 1 (*Brit*)
szkoła prywatna 2 (*US*) szkoła
państwowa

public transport *n* komunikacja
publiczna

publish ['pʌblɪʃ] *vt* 1 (*book,*
magazine) wydawać (wydać
pf) 2 (*letter, article*) publikować
(opublikować *pf*)

publisher ['pʌblɪʃə^r] *n* wydawca

pudding ['pudɪŋ] *n* (*Brit: dessert*
in general) deser; **rice ~** deser
ryżowy; **black ~,** (*US*) **blood ~**
kaszanka

puddle ['pʌdl] *n* (*of rain*) kałuża

puff pastry ['pʌf-] *n* ciasto
francuskie

pull [pul] *vt* 1 (*rope, hair*) ciągnąć
(pociągnąć *pf*) za; (*handle, door,*
cart, carriage) pociągać (pociągnąć
pf) 2 (*curtain, blind*) zaciągać
(zaciągnąć *pf*) 3 (*trigger*) naciskać
(nacisnąć *pf*) ▷ *n* (*tug*): **to give**
sth a ~ pociągnąć (*pf*) za coś; **to ~**

a muscle naciągnąć (pf) mięsień;
to ~ a face robić (zrobić pf) minę;
to ~ sb's leg (fig) nabierać (nabrać pf) kogoś
▶ **pull down** vt (building) rozbierać (rozebrać pf)
▶ **pull in** vi (at the kerb) zatrzymywać (zatrzymać pf) się
▶ **pull out** vi **1** (Aut: from kerb) odjeżdżać (odjechać pf); (when overtaking) zmieniać (zmienić pf) pas ruchu **2** (withdraw: from agreement, contest) wycofywać (wycofać pf) się
▶ **pull through** vi (from illness) wyzdrowieć; (from difficulties) wydobywać (wydobyć pf) się (z kłopotów)
▶ **pull up** vi (stop: driver, vehicle) zatrzymywać (zatrzymać pf) się ▷ vt **1** (raise: socks, trousers) podciągać (podciągnąć pf) **2** (uproot: plant, weed) wyrywać (wyrwać pf)
pullover ['puləuvə^r] n pulower
pulse [pʌls] n (Anat) tętno; **pulses** n pl (Culin) jadalne nasiona roślin strączkowych; **to take** or **feel sb's ~** mierzyć (zmierzyć pf) komuś tętno
pump [pʌmp] n pompa
▶ **pump up** vt (inflate) pompować (napompować pf)
pumpkin ['pʌmpkɪn] n dynia
punch [pʌntʃ] n (blow) uderzenie pięścią ▷ vt **1** (hit) uderzać (uderzyć pf) pięścią **2** (button, keyboard) naciskać **3** (make a hole in: ticket, paper) dziurkować (przedziurkować pf); **to ~ sb on the nose/in the eye** uderzać (uderzyć pf) kogoś pięścią w

nos/oko
punctual ['pʌŋktjuəl] adj punktualny
punctuation [pʌŋktju'eɪʃən] n interpunkcja
puncture ['pʌŋktʃə^r] n przebicie dętki ▷ vt (tyre, lung) przebijać (przebić pf); **to have a ~** złapać (pf) gumę
punish ['pʌnɪʃ] vt (person) karać (ukarać pf); **to ~ sb for sth/for doing sth** karać (ukarać pf) kogoś za coś/za zrobienie czegoś
punishment ['pʌnɪʃmənt] n kara
punk [pʌŋk] n **1** (also: ~ **rocker**) punk **2** (also: ~ **rock**) punk rock **3** (US: inf) chuligan
pupil ['pju:pl] n (student) uczeń(-ennica) m/f
puppet ['pʌpɪt] n **1** (on strings) marionetka **2** (also: **glove ~**) pacynka
puppy ['pʌpɪ] n szczeniak
purchase ['pə:tʃɪs] vt nabywać (nabyć pf) ▷ n **1** (act of buying) kupno **2** (item bought) nabytek
pure [pjuə^r] adj **1** (silk, gold, wool) czysty **2** (clean: water, air) czysty **3** (theoretical) teoretyczny; **a ~ wool jumper** bluza z czystej wełny
purple ['pə:pl] adj fioletowy ▷ n fiolet
purpose ['pə:pəs] n cel; **on ~** celowo
purr [pə:^r] vi mruczeć (zamruczeć pf)
purse [pə:s] n **1** (Brit) portmonetka **2** (US) torebka
pursue [pə'sju:] (formal) vt ścigać
push [puʃ] n naciśnięcie ▷ vt

1 (press: button) naciskać (nacisnąć pf) **2** (shove: car, door, person) popychać (popchnąć pf) ▷ vi **1** (press) naciskać (nacisnąć pf) **2** (shove) popychać (popchnąć pf); **to give sth/sb a ~** (with hand) popychać (popchnąć pf) coś/kogoś; **to ~ one's way through the crowd** torować (utorować pf) sobie drogę w tłumie przepychając się; **to ~ sth/sb out of the way** spychać (zepchnąć pf) coś/kogoś z drogi; **to ~ a door open/shut** otwierać (otworzyć pf)/zamykać (zamknąć pf) drzwi; **"~"** (on door) "pchać"; **to ~ sb to do sth** nakłaniać (nakłonić pf) kogoś do zrobienia czegoś; **to be ~ed for time/money** (inf) mieć mało czasu/pieniędzy; **to ~ forward** posuwać (posunąć pf) się na przód; **to ~ through the crowd** przepychać (przepchnąć pf) się przez tłum

▶ **push around** (inf) vt (bully) pomiatać +inst
▶ **push in** vi (in queue) wpychać (wepchnąć pf) się
▶ **push over** vt (person, object) przewracać (przewrócić pf)
▶ **push through** vt (measure, scheme) przeprowadzać (przeprowadzić pf)
▶ **push up** vt (total, prices) podnosić (podnieść pf)
pushchair ['pʊʃtʃɛəʳ] (Brit) n spacerówka
pusher ['pʊʃəʳ] (inf) n (drug dealer) handlarz narkotykami
push-up ['pʊʃʌp] (US) n pompka; **to do ~s** robić (zrobić pf) pompki
put [pʊt] (pt, pp **put**) vt

1 (place: thing) kłaść (położyć pf); (person: in institution) umieszczać (umieścić pf) **2** (confidence, trust, faith: in person, thing) pokładać **3** (write, type: word, information) zapisywać (zapisać pf); **to ~ a lot of time/energy into doing sth** włożyć dużo czasu/energii w zrobienie czegoś; **how shall I ~ it?** jak by to powiedzieć?

▶ **put across**, **put over** vt (ideas, argument) wyjaśniać (wyjaśnić pf)
▶ **put aside** vt odkładać (odłożyć pf)
▶ **put away** vt (store, unpack) chować (pochować pf)
▶ **put back** vt **1** (replace) odkładać (odłożyć pf) **2** (watch, clock) cofać (cofnąć pf)
▶ **put down** vt **1** (on floor, table) odstawiać (odstawić pf) **2** (in writing) zapisywać (zapisać pf) **3** (put to sleep: animal) usypiać (uśpić pf)
▶ **put forward** vt **1** (ideas, proposal, name) wysuwać (wysunąć pf) **2** (watch, clock) przesuwać (przesunąć pf) do przodu
▶ **put in** vt **1** (request, complaint, application) składać (złożyć pf) **2** (gas, electricity, sink) instalować (zainstalować pf)
▶ **put off** vt **1** (delay) odkładać (odłożyć pf) **2** (Brit: distract) rozpraszać (rozproszyć pf) **3** (discourage) zniechęcać (zniechęcić pf); **to ~ off doing sth** (postpone) odkładać (odłożyć pf) robienie (zrobienie pf) czegoś; **to ~ sb off doing sth** odwodzić (odwieść pf) kogoś od zrobienia

czegoś

▶ **put on** vt **1** (*clothes, make-up, glasses*) zakładać (założyć *pf*) **2** (*switch on*) włączać (włączyć *pf*); (*kettle*) wstawiać (wstawić *pf*) **3** (*organize: play, exhibition*) wystawiać (wystawić *pf*); **to ~ on weight/three kilos** przybierać (przybrać *pf*) na wadze/trzy kilo

▶ **put out** vt **1** (*candle, cigarette*) gasić (zgasić *pf*); (*fire, blaze*) gasić (ugasić *pf*) **2** (*electric light*) wyłączać (wyłączyć *pf*) **3** (*inf: inconvenience: person*) fatygować (pofatygować *pf*); **to ~ out one's tongue** wystawiać (wystawić *pf*) język

▶ **put through** vt (*Tel: person, phone call*) łączyć (połączyć *pf*),

▶ **put up** vt **1** (*fence, building, tent*) stawiać (postawić *pf*); (*poster, sign*) wywieszać (wywiesić *pf*) **2** (*umbrella, hood*) rozkładać (rozłożyć *pf*) **3** (*increase: price, cost*) podnosić (podnieść *pf*) **4** (*accommodate*) przenocowywać (przenocować *pf*); **to ~ up one's hand** podnosić (podnieść *pf*) rękę

▶ **put up with** vt *fus* godzić (pogodzić *pf*) się z +*inst*

puzzle ['pʌzl] *n* zagadka; (*jigsaw*) układanka (*mystery*) zagadka

puzzled ['pʌzld] *adj* zaintrygowany; **to be ~ by** or **about sth** głowić się nad czymś

pyjamas [pə'dʒɑːməz] (*US* **pajamas**) *n pl* piżama *f sg*; **a pair of ~** piżama

pylon ['paɪlən] *n* słup sieci wysokiego napięcia

pyramid ['pɪrəmɪd] *n* piramida

q

qualification [kwɔlɪfɪ'keɪʃən] *n* kwalifikacje *n pl*

qualified ['kwɔlɪfaɪd] *adj* (*trained*) dyplomowany; **fully ~** wykwalifikowany

qualify ['kwɔlɪfaɪ] *vi* **1** (*pass examinations*) zdobywać (zdobyć *pf*) kwalifikacje **2** (*in competition*) zakwalifikować się; **to ~ as an engineer/a nurse** zdobywać (zdobyć *pf*) dyplom inżyniera/pielęgniarki

quality ['kwɔlɪtɪ] *n* **1** (*standard*) jakość **2** (*characteristic: of person*) cecha; **~ of life** jakość życia

quantity ['kwɔntɪtɪ] *n* ilość; **in large/small quantities** w dużych/małych ilościach

quarantine ['kwɔrəntiːn] *n* kwarantanna; **in ~** w

kwarantannie

quarrel ['kwɔrəl] n kłótnia ▷ vi kłócić (pokłócić pf) się

quarry ['kwɔrɪ] n (for stone, minerals) kopalnia

quarter ['kwɔːtəʳ] n 1 (fourth part) ćwierć 2 (three months) kwartał 3 (US: coin) dwadzieścia pięć centów; **to cut/divide sth into ~s** ciąć (pociąć pf)/dzielić (podzielić pf) coś na ćwiartki; **a ~ of an hour** kwadrans; **it's a ~ to three** or (US) **of three** jest za kwadrans trzecia; **it's a ~ past three** or (US) **after three** jest kwadrans po trzeciej

quarter-final ['kwɔːtə'faɪnl] n ćwierćfinał

quartet [kwɔː'tɛt] n kwartet

quay [kiː] n nabrzeże

queen [kwiːn] n królowa

query ['kwɪərɪ] n (question) pytanie ▷ vt (check) sprawdzać (sprawdzić pf)

question ['kwɛstʃən] n 1 (query) pytanie 2 (issue) zagadnienie 3 (in written exam) pytanie ▷ vt (interrogate) pytać (zapytać pf); **to ask sb a ~, to put a ~ to sb** zadawać (zadać pf) komuś pytanie; **to be out of the ~** nie podlegać dyskusji

question mark n znak zapytania

questionnaire [kwɛstʃə'nɛəʳ] n kwestionariusz

queue [kjuː] (esp Brit) n kolejka ▷ vi (also: **~ up**) ustawiać (ustawić pf) się w kolejce; **to ~ for sth** stawać (stać pf) w kolejce po coś

quick [kwɪk] adj 1 (fast) szybki 2 (brief) krótki ▷ adv (inf: quickly) szybko; **be ~!** szybko!

quickly ['kwɪklɪ] adv szybko

quiet ['kwaɪət] cichy; **be ~!** ucisz się!

quietly ['kwaɪətlɪ] adv cicho

quilt [kwɪlt] n 1 (covering) narzuta 2 (Brit: duvet) kołdra

quit [kwɪt] (pt, pp vt 1 (esp US: give up) przestawać (przestać pf) 2 (inf: leave: job) rzucać (rzucić pf) ▷ vi 1 (give up) przestawać (przestać pf) 2 (resign) rezygnować (zrezygnować pf)

quite [kwaɪt] adv 1 (rather) dość 2 (completely) całkiem; **I see them ~ a lot** widuję ich dość często; **it costs ~ a lot to go to the States** wyjazd do Stanów sporo kosztuje; **~ a lot of money** całkiem sporo pieniędzy; **~ a few** całkiem sporo; **it's not ~ finished** to jest nie całkiem skończone; **there aren't ~ enough glasses** nie ma wystarczającej ilości szklanek; **I can't ~ remember** nie całkiem pamiętam; **~ (so)!** właśnie!; **it was ~ a sight** to był niezły widok

quiz [kwɪz] n (game) quiz

quotation [kwəu'teɪʃən] n 1 (from book, play etc) cytat 2 (estimate) wycena

quote [kwəut] vt cytować (zacytować pf) ▷ n (from book, play, person) cytat; **quotes** n pl (inf: quotation marks) cudzysłów; **in ~s** w cudzysłowie

r

rabbi ['ræbaɪ] n rabin
rabbit ['ræbɪt] n królik
rabies ['reɪbiːz] n wścieklizna
race [reɪs] n **1** (speed contest)
wyścig **2** (ethnic group) rasa ▷ vi
1 (compete in races) ścigać się
2 (hurry) śpieszyć (pf) się ▷ vt
(person) ścigać się z +inst; **a ~
against time** wyścig z czasem
race car (US) n = **racing car**
racecourse ['reɪskɔːs] (Brit) n tor
wyścigowy
racehorse ['reɪshɔːs] n koń
wyścigowy
racetrack ['reɪstræk] n (for cars)
tor wyścigowy; (US: for horses) tor
wyścigów konnych
racial ['reɪʃl] adj rasowy
racing car ['reɪsɪŋ-] (Brit) n
samochód wyścigowy

racing driver ['reɪsɪŋ-] (Brit) n
kierowca wyścigowy
racism ['reɪsɪzəm] n rasizm
racist ['reɪsɪst] adj rasistowski
▷ n rasista(-tka) m/f
rack [ræk] n **1** (also: **luggage
~**) półka na bagaż **2** (for hanging
clothes, dishes) wieszak
racket ['rækɪt] n **1** (for tennis,
squash etc) rakieta **2** (noise: inf)
hałas
racquet ['rækɪt] n rakieta
radar ['reɪdɑːr] n radar
radiation [reɪdɪ'eɪʃən] n
(radioactivity) promieniowanie
radiator ['reɪdɪeɪtər] n (on wall)
kaloryfer
radio ['reɪdɪəu] n radio; **on the
~** w radiu
radioactive ['reɪdɪəu'æktɪv] adj
radioaktywny
radio station n stacja radiowa
radish ['rædɪʃ] n rzodkiew
RAF (Brit) n abbr (= Royal Air
Force): **the ~** królewskie Siły
Powietrzne
raffle ['ræfl] n loteria
raft [rɑːft] n (also: **life ~**) tratwa
rag [ræg] n szmata
rage [reɪdʒ] n wściekłość
raid [reɪd] vt (soldiers, police)
atakować (zaatakować pf);
(criminal) napaść (napadać pf) na
rail [reɪl] n **1** (for safety on stairs)
poręcz; (on bridge, balcony)
barierka **2** (for hanging clothes)
drążek **3** (for trains) szyny f pl; **by ~**
(by train) koleją
railcard ['reɪlkɑːd] (Brit) n
zniżkowa karta kolejowa
railroad ['reɪlrəud] (US) n =
railway

railway ['reɪlweɪ] (*Brit*) *n* (*system*) kolej

railway line (*Brit*) *n* linia kolejowa

railway station (*Brit*) *n* (*large*) dworzec kolejowy; (*small*) stacja kolejowa

rain [reɪn] *n* deszcz ▷ *vi* padać; **in the ~** w deszczu; (*stand*) na deszczu; (*walk*) po deszczu; **it's ~ing** pada (deszcz)

rainbow ['reɪnbəu] *n* tęcza

raincoat ['reɪnkəut] *n* płaszcz przeciwdeszczowy

rainforest ['reɪnfɔrɪst] *n* las deszczowy

rainy ['reɪnɪ] *adj* deszczowy

raise [reɪz] *vt* **1** (*lift: hand, glass*) podnosić (podnieść *pf*) **2** (*salary, rate, morale, standards*) podnosić (podnieść *pf*); (*speed limit*) zwiększyć (zwiększać *pf*) **3** (*child, family*) wychowywać (wychować *pf*) ▷ *n* (*US: pay rise*) podwyżka

raisin ['reɪzn] *n* rodzynek

rake [reɪk] *n* (*tool*) grabie

rally ['rælɪ] *n* **1** (*public meeting*) wiec **2** (*Aut*) rajd **3** (*Tennis*) wymiana

rambler ['ræmblə^r] *n* (*Brit: walker*) wędrowiec(-wczyni) *m/f*

ramp [ræmp] *n* podjazd

ran [ræn] *pt of* **run**

random ['rændəm] *adj* **1** (*arrangement, selection*) losowy **2** (*haphazard*) przypadkowy ▷ *n*: **at ~** na chybił trafił

rang [ræŋ] *pt of* **ring**

range [reɪndʒ] *n* **1** (*of ages, prices*) rozpiętość; (*of subjects, possibilities, responsibilities*) zakres; (*products in a shop*) asortyment **2** (*also*: **mountain ~**) pasmo górskie ▷ *vt* (*place in a line*) ustawiać (ustawić *pf*); **to ~ from... to...** wahać się od +*gen*... do +*gen*...

rap [ræp] *n* (*also*: **~ music**) rap

rape [reɪp] *n* (*crime*) gwałt ▷ *vt* gwałcić (zgwałcić *pf*)

rapids ['ræpɪdz] *n pl* bystrza

rare [rɛə^r] *adj* **1** (*uncommon*) rzadki **2** (*lightly cooked*) krwisty

rarely ['rɛəlɪ] *adv* rzadko

rasher ['ræʃə^r] (*Brit*) *n* plasterek

raspberry ['rɑːzbərɪ] *n* (*fruit*) malina

rat [ræt] *n* (*Zool*) szczur

rate [reɪt] *n* (*speed*): **at a ~ of 60 kph** z prędkością sześćdziesiąt kilometrów na godzinę ▷ *vt* (*estimate*) oceniać (ocenić *pf*); **at this/that ~** w tym tempie; **at any ~** (*at least*) w każdym razie

rather ['rɑːðə^r] *adv* (*somewhat*) raczej; **~ a lot** dość dużo; **I would ~ go than stay** wolałbym iść niż zostać; **I'd ~ not say** wolałbym nie mówić; **~ than** (*instead of*) zamiast +*gen*

rave [reɪv] *n* (*Brit: inf: dance*) rave ▷ **rave about** *vt fus* (*inf*) zachwycać (zachwycić *pf*) się +*inst*

raw [rɔː] *adj* surowy

raw materials *n pl* surowce

razor ['reɪzə^r] *n* **1** (*also*: **safety ~**) maszynka do golenia **2** (*also*: **electric ~**) golarka

razor blade *n* żyletka

RE (*Brit: Scol*) *n abbr* (= *religious education*) religia

reach [riːtʃ] *vt* **1** (*arrive at: place, destination*) docierać (dotrzeć *pf*)

do +gen; (*conclusion*) dochodzić
(dojść *pf*) do +gen; (*agreement*)
osiągać (osiągnąć *pf*); (*decision*)
podejmować (podjąć *pf*); (*stage,
level, age*) osiągać (osiągnąć *pf*)
2 (*be able to touch*) sięgać (sięgnąć
pf) +gen; **within ~ of** w zasięgu
+gen; **out of ~ of** poza zasięgiem
+gen; **within easy ~ of...** w
pobliżu +gen...

react [riːˈækt] *vi* (*respond*)
reagować (zareagować *pf*)

reaction [riːˈækʃən] *n* (*response*)
reakcja

reactor [riːˈæktər] *n* reaktor

read [riːd] (*pt, pp* **read** [rɛd])
vi (*person*) czytać (przeczytać
pf) ▷ *vt* **1** (*book, newspaper etc*)
czytać (przeczytać *pf*) **2** (*study at
university: Brit*) studiować
▶ **read out** *vt* odczytywać
(odczytać *pf*)
▶ **read through** *vt* czytać
(przeczytać *pf*)

reading [ˈriːdɪŋ] *n* (*activity*)
czytanie

ready [ˈrɛdɪ] *adj* (*prepared,
available*) gotowy; **to get ~**
(*prepare o.s.*) przygotowywać
(przygotować *pf*) się; **to get
sb/sth ~** przygotowywać
(przygotować *pf*) kogoś/coś;
to be ~ to do sth (*prepared*) być
gotowym do zrobienia czegoś;
(*willing*) być chętnym do zrobienia
czegoś

real [rɪəl] *adj* prawdziwy; **in ~ life**
w rzeczywistości

realistic [rɪəˈlɪstɪk] *adj*
realistyczny

reality [riːˈælɪtɪ] *n* (*real
things*) rzeczywistość; **in ~** w

rzeczywistości

realize [ˈrɪəlaɪz] *vt* (*understand*)
zdawać (zdać *pf*) sobie sprawę z
+gen; **to ~ that...** zdawać (zdać *pf*)
sobie sprawę, że...

really [ˈrɪəlɪ] *adv* **1** (*very*): **~
good/delighted** naprawdę
dobry/zadowolony **2** (*genuinely*)
naprawdę **3** (*after negative*)
naprawdę; **~?** (*indicating surprise,
interest*) naprawdę?

realtor [ˈrɪəltɔːr] (*US*) *n* pośrednik
w handlu nieruchomościami

rear [rɪər] *n* (*back*) tył ▷ *vt*
(*raise: cattle, chickens: esp Brit*)
hodować (wyhodować *pf*);
(*family, children*) wychowywać
(wychować *pf*)

reason [ˈriːzn] *n* (*cause*) powód;
the ~ for sth powód dla czegoś;
the ~ why powód, dla którego

reasonable [ˈriːznəbl] *adj*
1 (*person, decision*) rozsądny **2** (*not
bad*) znośny; **be ~!** bądź rozsądny!

reasonably [ˈriːznəblɪ] *adv*
rozsądnie

reassure [riːəˈʃuər] *vt* uspokajać
(uspokoić *pf*)

rebellious [rɪˈbɛljəs] *adj*
buntowniczy

receipt [rɪˈsiːt] *n* (*for purchases*)
paragon

receive [rɪˈsiːv] *vt* otrzymywać
(otrzymać *pf*)

receiver [rɪˈsiːvər] *n* (*of telephone*)
słuchawka

recent [ˈriːsnt] *adj* niedawny

recently [ˈriːsntlɪ] *adv* ostatnio;
until ~ do niedawna

reception [rɪˈsɛpʃən] *n* **1** (*in
public building*) recepcja **2** (*party*)
przyjęcie **3** (*welcome*) przyjęcie

receptionist [rɪ'sɛpʃənɪst] (*esp Brit*) *n* recepcjonista(-tka) *m/f*

recipe ['rɛsɪpɪ] (*Culin*) *n* przepis

reckon ['rɛkən] *vt* **1** (*consider*) uważać **2** (*calculate*) szacować (oszacować *pf*); **I ~ that...** (*think: inf*) myślę, że...

recognize ['rɛkəgnaɪz] *vt* rozpoznawać (rozpoznać *pf*)

recommend [rɛkə'mɛnd] *vt*: **to ~ sth to sb** polecać (polecić *pf*) coś komuś

reconsider [ri:kən'sɪdər] *vt* rozważać (rozważyć *pf*) ponownie ▷ *vi* zastanawiać (zastanowić *pf*) się jeszcze raz

record [*n, adj* 'rɛkɔːd, *vb* rɪ'kɔːd] *n* **1** (*sound-recording*) płyta **2** (*unbeaten statistic*) rekord ▷ *vt* (*make recording of*) nagrywać (nagrać *pf*) ▷ *adj* (*sales, profits, levels*) rekordowy; **records** *n pl* akta *m pl*; **in ~ time** w rekordowym czasie; **to keep a ~ of sth** zapisywać (zapisać *pf*) coś

recorded delivery [rɪ'kɔːdɪd-] (*Brit*) *n* poczta polecona

recorder [rɪ'kɔːdər] *n* (*Mus*) flet

recording [rɪ'kɔːdɪŋ] *n* nagranie

record player *n* adapter

recover [rɪ'kʌvər] *vi* zdrowieć (wyzdrowieć *pf*)

recovery [rɪ'kʌvərɪ] *n* (*from illness, operation*) wyzdrowienie

rectangle ['rɛktæŋgl] *n* prostokąt

rectangular [rɛk'tæŋgjulər] *adj* prostokątny

recycle [riː'saɪkl] *vt* przetwarzać (przetworzyć *pf*)

recycling [riː'saɪklɪŋ] *n* recykling

red [rɛd] *adj* **1** czerwony **2** (*hair*) rudy ▷ *n* czerwień

Red Cross *n*: **the ~** czerwony Krzyż

redcurrant ['rɛdkʌrənt] (*Brit*) *n* czerwona porzeczka

red-haired [rɛd'hɛəd] *adj* rudowłosy

redo [riː'duː] *vt* (*pt* **redid**, *pp* **redone**) przerabiać (przerobić *pf*)

reduce [rɪ'djuːs] *vt* zmniejszać (zmniejszyć *pf*); **to ~ sth by** zmniejszać (zmniejszyć *pf*) coś o; **"~ speed now"** (*Aut*) "zwolnij"

reduction [rɪ'dʌkʃən] *n* **1** (*decrease*) obniżenie **2** (*discount*) obniżka

redundant [rɪ'dʌndnt] (*Brit*) *adj* (*unemployed*) bezrobotny; **to be made ~** (*worker*) zostać (*pf*) zwolnionym z pracy

refer [rɪ'fəːr]
  ▶ **refer to** *vt fus* **1** (*mention*) wspominać (wspomnieć *pf*) o +*loc* **2** (*relate to*) nawiązywać (nawiązać *pf*) do +*gen* **3** (*mean*) oznaczać

referee [rɛfə'riː] *n* (*Sport*) sędzia(-ina) *m/f*

reference ['rɛfrəns] *n* **1** (*mention*) wzmianka **2** (*for job application: letter*) referencje *f pl*

refill [riː'fɪl] *vt* napełniać (napełnić *pf*) ponownie

reflect [rɪ'flɛkt] *vt* (*image, light, heat*) odbijać (odbić *pf*)

reflection [rɪ'flɛkʃən] *n* **1** (*image*) odbicie **2** (*thought*) refleksja

reflex ['riːflɛks] *n* (*Physiol*) odruch

refreshing [rɪ'frɛʃɪŋ] *adj* orzeźwiający

refreshments [rɪ'frɛʃmənts] *n pl* napoje

refrigerator [rɪˈfrɪdʒəreɪtəʳ] n
lodówka
refuge [ˈrɛfjuːdʒ] n (safe house)
schronienie
refugee [rɛfjuˈdʒiː] n
uchodźca(-źczyni) m/f
refund [n ˈriːfʌnd, vb rɪˈfʌnd]
n zwrot pieniędzy ▷ vt (money)
refundować (zrefundować pf)
refuse¹ [rɪˈfjuːz] vt odmawiać
(odmówić pf) +gen; **to ~ to do sth**
odmawiać (odmówić pf) zrobienia
czegoś; **to ~ sb permission**
odmawiać (odmówić pf) komuś
pozwolenia
refuse² [ˈrɛfjuːs] n śmieci m pl
regain [rɪˈgeɪn] vt odzyskiwać
(odzyskać pf)
regard [rɪˈgɑːd] vt (consider, view)
uważać ▷ n (esteem) szacunek; **to
give one's ~s to sb** pozdrawiać
(pozdrowić pf) kogoś
regime [reɪˈʒiːm] n (system of
government) reżim
regiment [ˈrɛdʒɪmənt] n (Mil)
pułk
region [ˈriːdʒən] n (area) region
regional [ˈriːdʒənl] adj
regionalny
register [ˈrɛdʒɪstəʳ] n (in school)
lista obecności
registered [ˈrɛdʒɪstəd] adj (letter,
mail) polecony
registration [rɛdʒɪsˈtreɪʃən]
n (of birth, death, students etc)
rejestracja
regret [rɪˈgrɛt] n żal ▷ vt (one's
action) żałować (pożałować pf)
+gen; **to have no ~s** w ogóle nie
żałować; **to ~ that...** żałować
(pożałować pf), że...
regular [ˈrɛgjuləʳ] adj 1 (even)

regularny 2 (frequent) regularny;
(visitor) stały 3 (normal) normalny
regularly [ˈrɛgjulːəlɪ] adv
regularnie
regulation [rɛgjuˈleɪʃən] n (rule)
przepis
rehab [riːˈhæb] (inf) n odwyk
rehearsal [rɪˈhəːsəl] n próba
rehearse [rɪˈhəːs] vt robić (zrobić
pf) próbę +gen ▷ vi robić (zrobić
pf) próbę
reins [reɪnz] n pl (for horse) lejce
reindeer [ˈreɪndɪəʳ] (pl **reindeer**)
n renifer
reject [rɪˈdʒɛkt] vt odrzucać
(odrzucić pf)
related [rɪˈleɪtɪd] adj (people)
spokrewniony; **to be ~ to sb** być z
kimś spokrewniony
relation [rɪˈleɪʃən] n 1 (relative)
krewny(-na) m/f 2 (connection)
relacja; **in ~ to** w odniesieniu
do +gen
relationship [rɪˈleɪʃənʃɪp] n
1 (connection) związek 2 (between
two people, countries) stosunki m pl
3 (affair) związek; **to have a good
~** mieć dobre stosunki
relative [ˈrɛlətɪv] n (member of
family) krewny(-na) m/f
relatively [ˈrɛlətɪvlɪ] adv
stosunkowo
relax [rɪˈlæks] vi (person: unwind)
odprężać (odprężyć pf) się
relaxation [riːlækˈseɪʃən] n
(rest) relaks
relaxed [rɪˈlækst] adj (person)
odprężony; (discussion,
atmosphere) spokojny
relaxing [rɪˈlæksɪn] adj
odprężający
relay [ˈriːleɪ] n (also: **~ race**)

sztafeta
release [rɪ'liːs] n (of prisoner)
zwolnienie ▷ vt 1 (person) zwalniać
(zwolnić pf) 2 (record) wydawać
(wydać pf); (film) wypuszczać
(wypuścić pf)
relevant ['rɛləvənt] adj 1 (fact,
information, question) istotny
2 (chapter, area) odnośny; ~ **to**
mający związek z +inst
reliable [rɪ'laɪəbl] adj (person,
news, information) pewny; (method,
machine) niezawodny
relief [rɪ'liːf] n (gladness) ulga
relieved [rɪ'liːvd] adj
odczuwający ulgę; **to be ~ that...**
odczuwać (odczuć pf) ulgę, że...
religion [rɪ'lɪdʒən] n 1 (belief)
wyznanie 2 (set of beliefs) religia
religious [rɪ'lɪdʒəs] adj religijny
religious education n
wychowanie religijne
reluctant [rɪ'lʌktənt] adj
niechętny; **to be ~ to do sth** nie
mieć ochoty zrobić czegoś
reluctantly [rɪ'lʌktəntlɪ] adv
niechętnie
rely on [rɪ'laɪ-] vt fus 1 (be
dependent on) zależeć od +gen
2 (trust) polegać na +loc
remain [rɪ'meɪn] vi 1 (continue
to be) pozostawać (pozostać pf)
2 (stay) zostawać (zostać pf); **to
~ silent** zachowywać (zachować
pf) milczenie
remaining [rɪ'meɪnɪŋ] adj
pozostały
remark [rɪ'mɑːk] n uwaga
remarkable [rɪ'mɑːkəbl] adj
nadzwyczajny
remarkably [rɪ'mɑːkəblɪ] adv
nadzwyczajnie

remember [rɪ'mɛmbər] vt 1 (still
have in mind) pamiętać 2 (bring
back to mind) przypominać
(przypomnieć pf) sobie 3 (bear in
mind) pamiętać (zapamiętać pf);
she ~ed to do it pamiętała, żeby
to zrobić

REMEMBRANCE DAY

Remembrance Day – Dzień
Pamięci obchodzony jest
w Wielkiej Brytanii co roku
w niedzielę najbliższą
11 Listopada. Święto to
upamiętnia poległych w
obu wojnach światowych.
W powszechnym zwyczaju
jest noszenie w ten dzień w
klapach marynarek i płaszczy
sztucznych kwiatów maku.

remind [rɪ'maɪnd] vt
przypominać (przypomnieć
pf) +dat; **to ~ sb to do sth**
przypominać (przypomnieć
pf) komuś, by coś zrobił; **to ~
sb of sb/sth** (be reminiscent of)
przypominać (przypomnieć pf)
komuś kogoś/coś
remote [rɪ'məut] adj (place)
odległy
remote control n (device: for TV
etc) pilot
remotely [rɪ'məutlɪ] adv (at all)
w ogóle
remove [rɪ'muːv] vt 1 (object,
organ) usuwać (usunąć
pf) 2 (clothing, bandage etc)
zdejmować (zdjąć pf) 3 (stain)
usuwać (usunąć pf)
renew [rɪ'njuː] vt (loan, contract)

odnawiać (odnowić pf)

renovate ['rɛnəveɪt] vt odnawiać (odnowić pf)

rent [rɛnt] n (for building, room, land) czynsz ▷ vt **1** (hire) dzierżawić (wydzierżawić pf) **2** (also: **~ out**: house, room) wynajmować (wynająć pf)

reorganize [riːˈɔːɡənaɪz] vt reorganizować (zreorganizować pf)

rep [rɛp] n (representative: for group) przedstawiciel(ka) m/f; (also: **sales ~**) przedstawiciel(ka) m/f handlowy(-wa)

repair [rɪˈpɛəʳ] n naprawa ▷ vt **1** (object, building) remontować (wyremontować pf) **2** (damage) naprawiać (naprawić pf)

repay [riːˈpeɪ] (pt, pp **repaid**) vt (loan, debt, person) spłacać (spłacić pf)

repeat [rɪˈpiːt] vt **1** (statement, question) powtarzać (powtórzyć pf) **2** (action, mistake) ponawiać (ponowić pf) ▷ vi: **I ~** powtarzam ▷ n (Rad, TV) powtórka

repeatedly [rɪˈpiːtɪdlɪ] adv wielokrotnie

repetitive [rɪˈpɛtɪtɪv] adj powtarzający się

replace [rɪˈpleɪs] vt **1** (put back) odkładać (odłożyć pf) **2** (take the place of) zastępować (zastąpić pf)

replay [n ˈriːpleɪ, vb riːˈpleɪ] n **1** (TV: repeat showing) powtórka **2** (of match) powtórnie rozegrany mecz ▷ vt (on CD) odtwarzać (odtworzyć pf) ponownie; **to ~ a match** ponownie rozgrywać (rozegrać pf) mecz

reply [rɪˈplaɪ] n (answer)

odpowiedź ▷ vi (to question, letter) odpowiadać (odpowiedzieć pf); **there's no ~** (Tel) nikt nie odpowiada

report [rɪˈpɔːt] n **1** (account) sprawozdanie **2** (bulletin) relacja **3** (Brit: also: **school ~**) świadectwo szkolne ▷ vt (theft, accident, death) zgłaszać (zgłosić pf); (person) donosić (donieść pf) na

report card n świadectwo szkolne

reporter [rɪˈpɔːtəʳ] n reporter(ka) m/f

represent [rɛprɪˈzɛnt] vt (act on behalf of) reprezentować

representative [rɛprɪˈzɛntətɪv] n przedstawiciel(ka) m/f

reptile [ˈrɛptaɪl] n gad

republic [rɪˈpʌblɪk] n republika

reputation [rɛpjuˈteɪʃən] n reputacja

request [rɪˈkwɛst] n (polite demand) prośba ▷ vt prosić (poprosić pf) o

require [rɪˈkwaɪəʳ] vt **1** (need) potrzebować +gen **2** (demand) wymagać +gen; **to be ~d** (approval, permission) być wymaganym

rescue [ˈrɛskjuː] n ratunek ▷ vt ratować (uratować pf); **to go/ come to sb's ~** iść/przychodzić (przyjść pf) komuś na ratunek

research [rɪˈsəːtʃ] n badanie; **to do ~** prowadzić badania

resemblance [rɪˈzɛmbləns] n podobieństwo

resemble [rɪˈzɛmbl] vt być podobnym do +gen

resent [rɪˈzɛnt] vt (attitude, treatment) czuć (poczuć pf)

się urażonym +*inst*; (*person*)
odczuwać (odczuć *pf*) urazę
do +*gen*

resentful [rɪ'zɛntful] *adj* urażony

reservation [rɛzə'veɪʃən] *n*
(*booking*) rezerwacja; **to make a ~**
robić (zrobić *pf*) rezerwację

reservation desk (*US*) *n* (*in
hotel*) recepcja

reserve [rɪ'zə:v] *vt* (*seat,
table, ticket etc*) rezerwować
(zarezerwować *pf*) ▷ *n* (*Brit: Sport*)
rezerwowy(-wa) *m/f*

reserved [rɪ'zə:vd]
adj 1 (*unavailable: seat*)
zarezerwowany 2 (*restrained*)
powściągliwy

residence permit (*Brit*) *n*
pozwolenie na pobyt

resident ['rɛzɪdənt] *n*
mieszkaniec(-nka) *m/f*

residential [rɛzɪ'dɛnʃəl] *adj*
(*area*) mieszkaniowy

resign [rɪ'zaɪn] *vi* ustępować
(ustąpić *pf*)

resist [rɪ'zɪst] *vt* (*temptation, urge*)
opierać (oprzeć *pf*) się +*dat*

resit [ri:'sɪt] (*Brit*) *vt* (*exam*)
przystępować (przystąpić *pf*)
ponownie do +*gen* ▷ *n* powtórka
egzaminu pisemnego

resolution [rɛzə'lu:ʃən] *n*
zdecydowanie; **to make a
~** zrobić (*pf*) postanowienie;
New Year's ~ noworoczne
postanowienie

resort [rɪ'zɔ:t] *n* 1 (*also*: **holiday
~**) miejscowość wypoczynkowa
2 (*recourse*): **without ~ to** bez
uciekania się do +*gen* ▷ *vi*: **to
~ to sth** uciekać (uciec *pf*) się
do czegoś; **a seaside ~** kurort

nadmorski; **winter sports ~**
ośrodek sportów zimowych; **as a
last ~** w ostateczności

resource [rɪ'zɔ:s]: **resources** *n pl*
1 (*coal, iron, oil*) zasoby 2 (*money*)
środki pieniężne; **natural ~s**
bogactwa naturalne

respect [rɪs'pɛkt] *n* szacunek ▷ *vt*
(*person*) szanować (uszanować
pf); **to have ~ for sb/sth** mieć
szacunek dla kogoś/czegoś

respectable [rɪs'pɛktəbl] *adj*
1 (*area, background*) przyzwoity
2 (*person*) porządny 3 (*standard,
mark*) przyzwoity

responsibility [rɪspɔnsɪ'bɪlɪtɪ] *n*
obowiązek; **responsibilities** *n pl*
obowiązki

responsible [rɪs'pɔnsɪbl] *adj*
odpowiedzialny

rest [rɛst] *n* 1 (*relaxation*) relaks
2 (*break*) odpoczynek 3 (*remainder*)
reszta ▷ *vi* 1 (*relax*) odpoczywać
(odpocząć *pf*) 2 (*be supported*): **to
~ on/against sth** opierać (oprzeć
pf) się na czymś/o coś ▷ *vt*
(*relax: eyes, legs, muscles*) dawać
(dać *pf*) odpocząć +*dat*; **to ~ sth
on sth** (*lean*) opierać (oprzeć *pf*)
coś na czymś; **the ~ (of them)**
reszta

rest area (*US*) *n* miejsce
odpoczynku przy drodze

restaurant ['rɛstərɔn] *n*
restauracja

restless ['rɛstlɪs] *adj*
1 (*dissatisfied*) niezadowolony
2 (*fidgety*) niespokojny

restore [rɪ'stɔ:ʳ] *vt* (*painting,
building etc*) odrestaurowywać
(odrestaurować *pf*)

restrict [rɪs'trɪkt] *vt* ograniczać

(ograniczyć pf)
rest room (US) n toaleta
result [rɪˈzʌlt] n (of event, action)
skutek; (of match, election,
exam, competition) rezultat; (of
calculation) wynik ▷ vi: **to ~ in**
prowadzić (doprowadzić pf) do
+gen; **as a ~ of** w wyniku +gen; **to
~ from** wynikać (wyniknąć pf) z
+gen; **as a ~ it is...** w rezultacie
to jest...
resume [rɪˈzjuːm] vt (work,
journey) podejmować (podjąć pf)
na nowo
résumé [ˈreɪzjuːmeɪ] n (US: CV)
życiorys
retire [rɪˈtaɪəʳ] vi (give up work)
przechodzić (przejść pf) na
emeryturę
retired [rɪˈtaɪəd] adj
emerytowany
retiree [rɪtaɪəˈriː] (US) n
emeryt(ka) m/f
retirement [rɪˈtaɪəmənt] n
emerytura
return [rɪˈtəːn] vi (person)
wracać (wrócić pf); (situation,
symptom) powracać (powrócić
pf) ▷ vt (something borrowed
or stolen) zwracać (zwrócić pf)
▷ n **1** (of person) powrót **2** (of
something borrowed or stolen)
zwrot **3** (Comput: key) klawisz
powrotu ▷ adj **1** (Brit: journey,
ticket) powrotny **2** (Brit: match)
rewanżowy; **in ~ for** w zamian
za; **many happy ~s (of the day)!**
wszystkiego najlepszego (z okazji
urodzin)!
reunion [riːˈjuːnɪən] n zjazd
reveal [rɪˈviːl] vt (make known)
ujawniać (ujawnić pf)

revenge [rɪˈvɛndʒ] n zemsta;
to take (one's) ~ (on sb)
dokonywać (dokonać pf) (na
kimś) zemsty
reverse [rɪˈvəːs] adj (process,
effect) przeciwny ▷ vt (car: esp Brit)
cofać (cofnąć pf) ▷ vi (esp Brit: Aut)
cofać (cofnąć pf) się; **in ~ order** w
odwrotnej kolejności
reverse-charge call
[rɪˈvəːstʃɑːdʒ-] (Brit) n rozmowa
na koszt rozmówcy
review [rɪˈvjuː] n (of book, film etc)
recenzja
revise [rɪˈvaɪz] vt (Brit: study)
powtarzać (powtórzyć pf) ▷ vi
(Brit) powtarzać (powtórzyć pf)
revision [rɪˈvɪʒən] n
(Brit: studying) powtórka
revolting [rɪˈvəultɪŋ] adj
odrażający
revolution [rɛvəˈluːʃən] n
rewolucja
reward [rɪˈwɔːd] n (for service,
merit, work) nagroda ▷ vt (person)
nagradzać (nagrodzić pf)
rewarding [rɪˈwɔːdɪŋ] adj cenny
rewind [riːˈwaɪnd] (pt, pp
rewound) vt (wool, tape)
przewijać (przewinąć pf)
rhinoceros [raɪˈnɔsərəs] n
nosorożec
rhubarb [ˈruːbɑːb] n rabarbar
rhythm [ˈrɪðm] n rytm
rib [rɪb] n (Anat) żebro
ribbon [ˈrɪbən] n wstążka
rice [raɪs] n ryż
rich [rɪtʃ] adj (person, country)
bogaty ▷ n pl: **the ~** bogaci
rid [rɪd] (pt, pp **rid**) vt: **to ~ sb/sth
of sth** uwalniać (uwolnić pf)
kogoś/coś od czegoś; **to get ~ of**

sth/sb pozbywać (pozbyć pf) się czegoś/kogoś

ride [raid] (pt **rode**, pp **ridden** ['rɪdn]) vi **1** (travel: on bicycle, on horse) jechać (pojechać pf) **2** (in car, on bus, on train: US) jechać (pojechać pf) ▷ vt **1** (horse, bicycle, motorcycle: habitually) jeździć na +loc **2** (traverse: distance: on horseback) przemierzać (przemierzyć pf) konno; **to go for a ~** jechać (pojechać pf) na przejażdżkę; **to give sb a ~** (US) podwozić (podwieźć pf) kogoś

rider ['raidəʳ] n (on horse) jeździec(ka) m/f; (on bicycle) rowerzysta(-tka) m/f; (on motorcycle) motocyklista(-tka) m/f

ridiculous [rɪ'dɪkjuləs] adj śmieszny

riding ['raidɪŋ] n jazda konna; **to go ~** jeździć konno

rifle ['raifl] n karabin

right [rait] adj **1** (not left) prawy **2** (correct: answer, size, person) właściwy; (appropriate: person, place, clothes) odpowiedni; (decision, direction, time) właściwy ▷ n **1** (not left) prawa strona **2** (entitlement) prawo ▷ adv **1** (correctly) poprawnie **2** (properly, fairly) słusznie **3** (not to/on the left) po prawo ▷ int dobra jest!; **do you have the ~ time?** masz dokładną godzinę?; **to be ~** (person) mieć rację; (answer, fact) zgadzać (zgodzić pf) się; (clock) dobrze chodzić; **you did the ~ thing** postąpił pan/postąpiła pani słusznie; **~ ahead** prosto; **to** or **on the ~** (position) po prawo; **to the ~** (movement) na prawo

right-hand drive ['raithænd-] adj (vehicle) z kierownicą po prawej stronie

right-handed [rait'hændɪd] adj praworęczny

rightly ['raitlɪ] adv (with reason) słusznie; **if I remember ~** (Brit) jeśli dobrze pamiętam

ring [rɪŋ] (pt **rang**, pp **rung**) n (on finger) pierścionek ▷ vi dzwonić (zadzwonić pf) ▷ vt **1** (bell, doorbell) dzwonić (zadzwonić pf) +inst **2** (Brit: Tel) dzwonić (zadzwonić pf) do +gen; **there was a ~ at the door, the doorbell rang** zadzwonił ktoś do drzwi; **to give sb a ~** (Brit: Tel) dzwonić (zadzwonić pf) do kogoś
▶ **ring back** (Brit: Tel) vt oddzwaniać (oddzwonić pf) do +gen ▷ vi oddzwaniać (oddzwonić pf)
▶ **ring up** (Brit: Tel) vt dzwonić (zadzwonić pf) do +gen

rinse [rɪns] vt płukać (spłukać pf); (also: **~ out**: mouth) płukać (wypłukać pf)

riot ['raiət] n (disturbance) zamieszki m pl ▷ vi buntować (zbuntować pf) się

rip [rip] vt rozedrzeć (rozdzierać pf) ▷ vi drzeć (podrzeć pf) się
▶ **rip off** vt (inf: swindle) zdzierać (zedrzeć pf) z +gen

ripe [raip] adj (fruit, corn) dojrzały

rip-off ['ripɔf] (inf) n zdzierstwo

rise [raiz] (pt **rose**, pp **risen** ['rizn]) n **1** (Brit: salary increase) podwyżka **2** (in prices, temperature, crime rate) podwyżka ▷ vi **1** (move upwards) podnosić (podnieść pf) się **2** (prices, numbers) wzrastać

(wzrosnąć pf) **3** (sun, moon)
wschodzić (wzejść pf) **4** (from
chair) wstawać (wstać pf)
risk [rɪsk] n (danger, possibility,
chance) ryzyko ▷ vt (take the chance
of) ryzykować (zaryzykować
pf); **to take a ~** ryzykować
(zaryzykować pf); **at one's own
~** na własne ryzyko; **to ~ it** (inf)
ryzykować (zaryzykować pf)
rival ['raɪvl] n rywal(ka) m/f ▷ adj
przeciwny
river ['rɪvər] n rzeka
river bank n brzeg rzeki
road [rəud] n **1** (in country) droga
2 (in town) ulica **3** (fig) droga; **it
takes four hours by ~** podróż
samochodem trwa cztery godziny
road map n mapa samochodowa
road rage n agresja na drodze
road sign n znak drogowy
roadworks ['rəudwəːks] n pl
roboty drogowe
roast [rəust] vt (food) piec
(upiec pf)
rob [rɔb] vt okradać (okraść pf);
to ~ sb of sth okradać (okraść pf)
kogoś z czegoś
robber ['rɔbər] n złodziej
robbery ['rɔbərɪ] n rabunek
robin ['rɔbɪn] n rudzik
robot ['rəubɔt] n robot
rock [rɔk] n **1** (boulder) skała
2 (esp US: small stone) kamień
3 (Mus: also: **~ music**) rock ▷ vt
1 (swing gently: child) kołysać
(ukołysać pf) **2** (shake: explosion)
trząść (zatrząść pf) +inst
rock climbing n wspinaczka
rocket ['rɔkɪt] n **1** (Space) rakieta
2 (firework) raca
rocking horse ['rɔkɪŋ-] n koń na

biegunach
rod [rɔd] n **1** (pole) pręt
2 (also: **fishing ~**) wędka
rode [rəud] pt of **ride**
role [rəul] n rola
roll [rəul] n **1** (of paper, cloth, film)
rolka **2** (also: **bread ~**) bułka
▷ vt **1** (ball, stone, dice etc) toczyć
(potoczyć pf) **2** (also: **~ out**: pastry)
wałkować (rozwałkować pf) ▷ vi
(ball, stone etc) toczyć (potoczyć
pf) się; **cheese/ham ~** bułka z
serem/szynką
▸ **roll about, roll around** vi (inf)
turlać (poturlać pf) się
Rollerblades® ['rəuləbleɪdz] n pl
łyżworolki ®
roller coaster [-'kəustər] n
kolejka górska
roller skates n pl wrotki
roller skating n jazda na
wrotkach
Roman ['rəumən] adj rzymski
Roman Catholic adj
rzymskokatolicki ▷ n
katolik(-iczka $) m/f
romance [rə'mæns] n **1** (affair)
romans **2** (charm, excitement)
romantyczność
Romania [rə'meɪnɪə] n Rumunia
romantic [rə'mæntɪk] adj
romantyczny
roof [ruːf] n dach
roof rack (Brit: Aut) n bagażnik
dachowy
room [ruːm] n **1** (in house) pokój
2 (also: **bed~**) sypialnia **3** (space)
miejsce; **single/double ~** pokój
jednoosobowy/dwuosobowy
root [ruːt] n (Bot) korzeń
rope [rəup] n lina
▸ **rope in** vt (inf: person) ściągać

(ściągnąć *pf*) do pomocy
rose [rəuz] *pt of* **rise** ▷ *n* (*flower*)
róża
rosy ['rəuzɪ] *adj* (*complexion*)
różowy
rot [rɔt] *vt* (*cause to decay*) niszczyć
(zniszczyć *pf*) ▷ *vi* (*decay: teeth*)
psuć (popsuć *pf*) się; (*wood, fruit
etc*) gnić (zgnić *pf*)
rotten ['rɔtn] *adj* **1** (*decayed: food*)
zepsuty **2** (*inf: awful*) okropny; **to
feel ~** (*ill: inf*) czuć się okropnie
rough [rʌf] *adj* **1** (*skin, surface,
cloth*) szorstki **2** (*terrain*) nierówny
3 (*sea*) wzburzony; (*crossing*)
ciężki **4** (*violent: person*) brutalny;
(*town, area*) niebezpieczny
5 (*hard: life, conditions, journey*)
ciężki **6** (*approximate: outline, plan,
idea*) roboczy; **to feel ~** (*Brit: inf*)
czuć się źle
roughly ['rʌflɪ] *adv* **1** (*violently*)
brutalnie **2** (*approximately*) mniej
więcej; **~ speaking** mniej więcej
round [raund] *adj* **1** (*circular*)
okrągły **2** (*spherical*) okrągły
3 (*approximate: figure, sum*)
przybliżony ▷ *n* **1** (*in competition*)
runda (*of drinks*) kolejka
3 (*Golf*) partia **4** (*Boxing*) runda
▷ *prep* **1** (*surrounding*) naokoło
+*gen* **2** (*near*) blisko +*gen* **3: ~ the
corner** za rogiem **4** (*indicating
circular movement*): **to move ~ the
room/sail ~ the world** chodzić
wokół pokoju/żeglować dookoła
świata; **all ~** generalnie; **to go ~
sth** kręcić (skręcić *pf*) się wokół
czegoś; **to go ~ to sb's house**
chodzić wokół czyjegoś domu; **all
(the) year ~** cały rok; **to ask sb
~** zapraszać (zaprosić *pf*) kogoś

do siebie; **I'll be ~ at 6 o'clock**
przyjdę na szóstą; **~ about** (*esp
Brit: approximately*) w przybliżeniu;
~ the clock (*inf*) całą dobę; **a ~
of applause** burza oklasków; **a
~ of toast/sandwiches** (*Brit*)
grzanka/kanapka
▶ **round off** *vt* (*meal, evening etc*)
kończyć (zakończyć *pf*)
▶ **round up** *vt* **1** (*cattle, sheep*)
spędzać (spędzić *pf*) **2** (*people*)
zgromadzać (zgromadzić
pf) **3** (*price, figure*) zaokrąglać
(zaokrąglić *pf*) w górę
roundabout ['raundəbaut] *n*
(*Brit*) (*Aut*) rondo **2** (*at funfair*)
karuzela
round trip *n* podróż w obie strony
▷ *adj* (*also:* **round-trip:** *US*) w
obie strony
route [ruːt] *n* **1** (*path, journey*)
droga **2** (*of bus, train*) trasa
routine [ruː'tiːn] *n* (*procedure*)
ustalony porządek
row¹ [rəu] *n* rząd ▷ *vi* (*in boat*)
wiosłować (powiosłować *pf*) ▷ *vt*
(*boat*) płynąć (popłynąć *pf*) +*inst*;
in a ~ w rzędzie
row² [rau] *n* **1** (*noise: Brit: inf*)
hałas **2** (*noisy quarrel*) kłótnia
rowboat ['rəubəut] (*US*) *n* łódź
wiosłowa
rowing ['rəuɪŋ] (*Sport*) *n*
wioślarstwo
rowing boat (*Brit*) *n* łódź
wiosłowa
royal ['rɔɪəl] *adj* królewski; **the ~
family** rodzina królewska
RSI (*Med*) *n abbr* (= *repetitive strain
injury*) zespół RSI
rub [rʌb] *vt* (*with hand, fingers*)
trzeć (potrzeć *pf*); (*with cloth,*

substance) przecierać (przetrzeć pf)

▶ **rub out** vt (erase) wymazywać (wymazać pf)

rubber ['rʌbəʳ] n 1 (substance) guma 2 (Brit) gumka do wycierania

rubber boot (US) n kalosz

rubbish ['rʌbɪʃ] (Brit) n 1 (refuse) śmieci m pl 2 (inferior material) tandeta 3 (nonsense) bzdury f pl ▷ adj (Brit: inf): **I'm ~ at golf** jestem słaby w grze w golfa

rubbish bin (Brit) n kosz na śmieci

rucksack ['rʌksæk] n plecak

rude [ruːd] adj 1 (person, behaviour, remark) niegrzeczny 2 (vulgar: word, joke) wulgarny; (noise) nieprzywoity; **to be ~ to sb** być niegrzecznym wobec kogoś

rug [rʌg] n 1 (carpet) chodnik 2 (Brit: blanket) koc

rugby ['rʌgbɪ] n (also: ~ **football**) rugby

ruin ['ruːɪn] n (destruction: of building) ruina ▷ vt (spoil: clothes, carpet etc) niszczyć (zniszczyć pf); (plans, prospects etc) rujnować (zrujnować pf); **ruins** n pl (of building, castle etc) ruiny; **to be in ~s** (building, town) lec w gruzach

rule [ruːl] n 1 (regulation) reguła 2 (of language) zasada; **it's against the ~s** to niezgodne z przepisami; **as a ~** z reguły ▶ **rule out** vt (idea, possibility etc) wykluczać (wykluczyć pf)

ruler ['ruːləʳ] n (for measuring) linijka

rum [rʌm] n rum

rumour ['ruːməʳ] (US **rumor**) n plotka

run [rʌn] (pt **ran**, pp **run**) n 1 (as exercise, sport) bieg 2 (Cricket, Baseball) punkt ▷ vt 1 (race, distance) przebiegać (przebiec pf) 2 (operate: business, shop, country) prowadzić (poprowadzić pf) 3 (water, bath) puszczać (puścić pf) 4 (perform: program, test) przeprowadzać (przeprowadzić pf) ▷ vi 1 (person, animal) biec (pobiec pf) 2 (flee) uciekać (uciec pf) 3 (bus, train: operate) jeździć; **to go for a ~** (as exercise) biegać (pobiegać pf); **in the long ~** na dłuższą metę; **I'll ~ you to the station** podwiozę pana/panią na dworzec; **to ~ on** or **off petrol/batteries** działać na benzynę/baterie

▶ **run after** vt fus (chase) ganiać (gonić pf)

▶ **run away** vi (from home, situation) uciekać (uciec pf)

▶ **run into** vt fus 1 (meet: person) wpadać (wpaść pf) na; (trouble, problems) popadać (popaść pf) w

▶ **run off** vi (person, animal) uciekać (uciec pf); **to ~ off with sb** uciekać (uciec pf) z kimś

▶ **run out** vi 1 (time, money, luck) kończyć (skończyć pf) się 2 (lease, passport) wygasać (wygasnąć pf)

▶ **run out of** vt fus nie mieć już +gen

▶ **run over** vt (Aut: person) potrącać (potrącić pf)

rung [rʌŋ] pp of **ring**

runner ['rʌnəʳ] n (in race) biegacz(ka) m/f

runner-up [rʌnər'ʌp] n zdobywca(-czyni) m/f drugiego

miejsca

running ['rʌnɪŋ] n (sport) biegi m pl; **6 days ~** sześć dni z rzędu

run-up ['rʌnʌp] n: **the ~ to...** (election) okres poprzedzający...

runway ['rʌnweɪ] n (Aviat) pas startowy

rush [rʌʃ] n (hurry) pośpiech ▷ vi (person) śpieszyć (pośpieszyć pf) się; **to be in a ~ (to do sth)** śpieszyć (pośpieszyć pf) się (ze zrobieniem czegoś)
▶ **rush through** vt (order, application) wykonywać (wykonać pf) w pośpiechu

rush hour n godziny szczytu

Russia ['rʌʃə] n Rosja

Russian ['rʌʃən] adj rosyjski ▷ n 1 (person) Rosjanin(ka) m/f 2 (language) rosyjski

rust [rʌst] n rdza

rusty ['rʌstɪ] adj 1 (surface, object) zardzewiały 2 (skill) przykurzony

RV (US) n abbr (= recreational vehicle) pojazd rekreacyjny

rye [raɪ] n (cereal) żyto

S

Sabbath ['sæbəθ] n szabat

sack [sæk] n worek ▷ vt wyrzucać (wyrzucić pf) z pracy; **to get the ~** zostać (pf) wyrzuconym z pracy

sacred ['seɪkrɪd] adj (holy) święty

sacrifice ['sækrɪfaɪs] n (fig) poświęcenie

sad [sæd] adj 1 (unhappy) smutny 2 (distressing) przykry 3 (regrettable) godny ubolewania; **he was ~ to see her go** było mu smutno, że odeszła

saddle ['sædl] n (for horse) siodło; (on bike, motorbike) siodełko

safe [seɪf] adj bezpieczny ▷ n sejf

safety ['seɪftɪ] n bezpieczeństwo

Sagittarius [sædʒɪ'tɛərɪəs] n (Astrol) Strzelec

said [sɛd] pt, pp of **say**

sail [seɪl] n (of boat, yacht) żagiel
▷ vi płynąć (popłynąć pf)
sailing ['seɪlɪŋ] n żeglarstwo;
to go ~ wybierać (wybrać pf) się
na żagle
sailor ['seɪlər] n (for pleasure)
żeglarz(-rka) m/f; (seaman)
marynarz
saint [seɪnt] n święty(-ta) m/f
sake [seɪk] n: **for the ~ of** (health,
career, person) ze względu na
salad ['sæləd] n sałatka
salami [sə'lɑːmɪ] n salami
salary ['sælərɪ] n pensja
sale [seɪl] n 1 (selling) sprzedaż
2 (with reductions) wyprzedaż;
sales n pl (quantity sold) sprzedaż
f sg; **to be (up) for ~** być
wystawiony na sprzedaż; **to be
on ~** (Brit) być w sprzedaży
sales assistant ['seɪlz-] (Brit) n
sprzedawca(-czyni) m/f
sales clerk ['seɪlz-] (US) n
sprzedawca(-czyni) m/f
salesman ['seɪlzmən] (irreg) n
akwizytor
saleswoman ['seɪlzwumən]
(irreg) n (representative)
akwizytorka
salmon ['sæmən] (pl **salmon**)
n łosoś
salon ['sælɔn] n (hairdresser's
shop) salon fryzjerski
salt [sɔːlt] n sól
salty ['sɔːltɪ] adj (food) słony
same [seɪm] adj 1 (similar) taki
sam 2 (also: **very ~**: identical)
ten sam ▷ pron: **the ~** (similar)
to samo; **the ~ as** taki sam jak;
the ~ book/place as taka sama
książka/takie samo miejsce jak;
at the ~ time (simultaneously) w

tym samym czasie; **all** or **just the
~** mimo to
sample ['sɑːmpl] n próbka
sand [sænd] n piasek
sandal ['sændl] n sandał
sand castle n zamek z piasku
sandwich ['sændwɪtʃ] n
kanapka; **a cheese/ham/jam
~** kanapka z serem/szynką/
dżemem
sang [sæŋ] pt of **sing**
sanitary napkin ['sænɪtərɪ-]
(US) n podpaska
sanitary towel (Brit) n podpaska
sank [sæŋk] pt of **sink**
Santa (Claus) ['sæntə('klɔːz)] n
Święty Mikołaj
sarcastic [sɑː'kæstɪk] adj
sarkastyczny
sardine [sɑː'diːn] n sardynka
SAT n abbr (US) = Scholastic
Aptitude Test) egzamin sprawdzający
zdolności naukowe kandydata na
studia wyższe
sat [sæt] pt, pp of **sit**
satchel ['sætʃl] n torba na ramię
satellite ['sætəlaɪt] n satelita
satellite television n telewizja
satelitarna
satisfactory [sætɪs'fæktərɪ] adj
zadowalający
satisfied ['sætɪsfaɪd] adj
zadowolony; **to be ~ with sth** być
zadowolonym z czegoś
Saturday ['sætədɪ] n sobota; see
also **Tuesday**
sauce [sɔːs] n (savoury) sos;
(sweet) polewa
saucepan ['sɔːspən] n rondel
saucer ['sɔːsər] n spodek
sausage ['sɔsɪdʒ] n kiełbasa
save [seɪv] vt 1 (person) ratować

(uratować *pf*) **2** (*also:* **~ up**)
oszczędzać (oszczędzić *pf*)
3 (*economize on: money, time*)
oszczędzać (oszczędzić *pf*)
4 (*Comput*) zapisywać (zapisać
pf) ▷ *vi* (*also:* **~ up**) oszczędzać
(oszczędzić *pf*); **to ~ sb's life**
ratować (uratować *pf*) komuś
życie
▶ **save up** *vi* oszczędzać
(zaoszczędzić *pf*)
saving ['seɪvɪŋ] *n* (*of time, money*)
oszczędność; **savings** *n pl*
(*money*) oszczędności
savoury ['seɪvərɪ] (*US* **savory**) *adj*
nie słodki
saw¹ [sɔ:] *pt of* **see**
saw² [sɔ:] (*pt* **sawed**, *pp* **sawed**
or **sawn**) *vt* piłować (spiłować
pf) ▷ *n* piła
saxophone ['sæksəfəun] *n*
saksofon
say [seɪ] (*pt, pp* **said**) *vt* **1** (*utter*)
mówić (powiedzieć *pf*) **2** (*indicate*)
wskazywać (wskazać *pf*); **to
~ that...** (*verbally*) mówić
(powiedzieć *pf*), że...; (*in writing*)
twierdzić (stwierdzić *pf*), że...; **to
~ sth to sb** mówić (powiedzieć *pf*)
coś komuś; **to ~ yes/no** zgadzać
(zgodzić *pf*) się/nie zgadzać
(zgodzić *pf*) się; **to ~ goodbye
(to sb)** żegnać (pożegnać *pf*)
się (z kimś); **to ~ sorry to sb**
przepraszać (przeprosić *pf*)
kogoś; **I must ~ that...** muszę
powiedzieć, że...
saying ['seɪɪŋ] *n* powiedzenie
scale [skeɪl] *n* **1** (*size, extent*) skala
2 (*of map, model*) skala **3** (*Mus*)
gama; **scales** *n pl* (*for weighing*)
waga; **on a large/small ~** na

dużą/na małą skalę
scampi ['skæmpɪ] (*Brit*) *n pl*
panierowane krewetki
scandal ['skændl] *n* **1** (*shocking
event*) skandal **2** (*gossip*) plotki *f pl*
Scandinavia [skændɪ'neɪvɪə] *n*
Skandynawia
scanner ['skænə^r] *n* (*Comput*)
skaner
scar [skɑ:] *n* blizna
scarce [skɛəs] *adj* rzadki
scarcely ['skɛəslɪ] *adv* ledwo; **~
anybody** prawie nikt
scare [skɛə^r] *vt* przestraszać
(przestraszyć *pf*) ▷ *n* (*public panic*)
panika; **a security ~** zagrożenie
bezpieczeństwa
scarecrow ['skɛəkrəu] *n* strach
na wróble
scared ['skɛəd] *adj*: **to be ~ of sb/
sth** bać się kogoś/czegoś; **to be
~ stiff** *or* **~ to death** śmiertelnie
bać się
scarf [skɑ:f] (*pl* **scarfs** *or* **scarves**)
n (*long*) szalik; (*square*) chusta
scary ['skɛərɪ] (*inf*) *adj* straszny
scene [si:n] *n* (*of crime, accident*)
miejsce; **to make a ~** robić (zrobić
pf) scenę
scenery ['si:nərɪ] *n* krajobraz
schedule ['ʃɛdju:l, *US* 'skɛdju:l] *n*
1 (*agenda*) harmonogram **2** (*US: of
trains, buses*) rozkład jazdy; **on ~**
według planu; **to be ahead of ~**
być przed czasem; **to be behind ~**
mieć opóźnienie
scheduled flight ['ʃɛdju:ld-, *US*
'skɛdju:ld-] *n* lot rejsowy
scheme [ski:m] *n* **1** (*esp Brit*)
program **2** (*plan*) plan
scholarship ['skɔləʃɪp] *n*
stypendium

school [sku:l] n 1 szkoła
2 (US: university) uniwersytet ▷ adj
(uniform, shoes, year) szkolny;
to go to ~ (child) iść/chodzić
(pójść pf) do szkoły; (US: adult)
uczęszczać do szkoły; **to go
to law/medical ~** iść/chodzić
(pójść pf) do szkoły prawniczej/
medycznej
schoolboy ['sku:lbɔɪ] n uczeń
schoolchildren ['sku:ltʃɪldrən]
n pl uczniowie
schoolgirl ['sku:lgə:l] n
uczennica
science ['saɪəns] n 1 (scientific
study) nauka 2 (school subject)
przedmioty m pl ścisłe; (branch
of science) nauki f pl ścisłe; **the ~s**
nauki ścisłe
science fiction n fantastyka
naukowa
scientific [saɪən'tɪfɪk] adj
naukowy
scientist ['saɪəntɪst] n
naukowiec
scissors ['sɪzəz] n pl nożyce; **a
pair of ~** nożyczki
scooter ['sku:tər] n 1 (also: **motor
~**) skuter 2 (child's) hulajnoga
score [skɔ:r] n wynik ▷ vt (goal,
point) zdobywać (zdobyć pf) ▷ vi
(in game, sport) zdobywać (zdobyć
pf) punkt
Scorpio ['skɔ:pɪəu] n (Astrol)
Skorpion
Scot [skɔt] n Szkot(ka) m/f
Scotch tape® ['skɔtʃ-] (US) n
taśma klejąca
Scotland ['skɔtlənd] n Szkocja
Scots [skɔts] adj szkocki
Scotsman ['skɔtsmən] (irreg)
n Szkot

Scotswoman ['skɔtswumən]
(irreg) n Szkotka
Scottish ['skɔtɪʃ] adj szkocki
scout [skaut] n (also: **boy ~**)
harcerz
scrambled egg ['skræmbld-] n
jajecznica
scrap [skræp] n 1 (of paper,
cloth) skrawek 2 (inf: fight) bójka
▷ vt 1 (car, ship) przeznaczać
(przeznaczyć pf) na złom
2 (project, system, tax) rezygnować
(zrezygnować pf) z +gen
scrapbook ['skræpbuk] n album
z wycinkami
scratch [skrætʃ] n 1 (on car,
furniture) rysa 2 (on body)
zadrapanie ▷ vt 1 (damage)
rysować (porysować pf) 2 (because
of itch) drapać (podrapać pf) 3 (cat
etc) drapać (zadrapać pf) ▷ vi
drapać (podrapać pf) się; **to do
sth from ~** robić (zrobić pf) coś
od zera
scream [skri:m] n krzyk ▷ vi
krzyczeć (krzyknąć pf) ▷ vt: **to ~
sth** krzyczeć (krzyknąć pf) coś;
to ~ at sb krzyczeć (krzyknąć pf)
na kogoś
screen [skri:n] n ekran
screw [skru:] n śruba
screwdriver ['skru:draɪvər] n
śrubokręt
scribble ['skrɪbl] vt (note)
gryzmolić (nagryzmolić pf) ▷ vi
(write quickly) pisać (napisać pf)
pośpiesznie
scrub [skrʌb] vt szorować
(wyszorować pf)
sculpture ['skʌlptʃər] n 1 (art)
rzeźbiarstwo 2 (object) rzeźba
sea [si:] n 1: **the ~** morze 2 (in

names): **the North/Irish/Dead Sea** Morze Północne/Irlandzkie/Martwe; **beside** *or* **by the ~** nad morzem; **by ~** morzem

seafood ['si:fu:d] *n* owoce morza *m pl*

seagull ['si:gʌl] *n* mewa

seal [si:l] *n* **1** *(animal)* foka **2** *(official stamp)* pieczęć ▷ *vt* *(envelope)* zaklejać (zakleić *pf)*

search [sə:tʃ] *n* **1** *(for missing person)* poszukiwania *nt pl* **2** *(of place)* przeszukanie **3** *(Comput)* szukanie ▷ *vt* *(place, person)* przeszukiwać (przeszukać *pf)* ▷ *vi*: **to ~ for sb/sth** poszukiwać kogoś/czegoś; **a ~ for** *(object, person)* poszukiwanie +*gen*
▶ **search for** poszukiwać (poszukać *pf)* +*gen*

search engine *(Comput)* *n* wyszukiwarka

search party *n* ekipa poszukiwawcza

seashore ['si:ʃɔ:ʳ] *n* brzeg morza; **on the ~** nad brzegiem morza

seasick ['si:sɪk] *adj*: **to be** *or* **feel ~** cierpieć na chorobę morską

seaside ['si:saɪd] *(Brit)* *n*: **the ~** wybrzeże; **at the ~** nad morzem

season ['si:zn] *n* **1** *(of year)* pora roku **2** *(for activity)* sezon; **the football ~** sezon piłkarski; **raspberries are in ~/out of ~** jest sezon/nie ma sezonu na maliny

seat [si:t] *n* **1** *(chair)* siedzenie; *(in car, theatre, cinema)* miejsce **2** *(place: in theatre, bus, train)* miejsce; **are there any ~s left?** czy są jakieś wolne miejsca?; **to take a** *or* **one's ~** zajmować (zająć *pf)* (swoje) miejsce; **to be ~ed** *(be*

sitting) siedzieć

seat belt *n* pas bezpieczeństwa

seaweed ['si:wi:d] *n* wodorosty *m pl*

second ['sɛkənd] *adj* drugi ▷ *adv* **1** *(come, finish)* jako drugi **2** *(secondly)* po drugie ▷ *n* *(unit of time)* sekunda; **~ floor** *(Brit)* drugie piętro; *(US)* pierwsze piętro; **just a ~!** chwileczkę!

secondary school *n* szkoła średnia

second-class ['sɛkənd'klɑ:s] *adj* **1** *(letter, stamp)* zwykły **2** *(ticket, carriage)* drugiej klasy ▷ *adv* **1** *(travel)* drugą klasą **2** *(send, post)*: **to send sth ~** wysyłać (wysłać *pf)* coś jako zwykły list

second-hand ['sɛkənd'hænd] *adj* używany; **to buy sth ~** kupować (kupić *pf)* coś używanego

secondly ['sɛkəndlɪ] *adv* po drugie

secret ['si:krɪt] *adj* tajny ▷ *n* sekret; **to keep sth ~ (from sb)** trzymać coś (przed kimś) w tajemnicy; **can he keep a ~?** czy potrafi dochować tajemnicy?; **in ~** potajemnie

secretary ['sɛkrətərɪ] *n* *(in office)* sekretarz(-rka) *m/f*

secretly ['si:krɪtlɪ] *adv* potajemnie

section ['sɛkʃən] *n* **1** *(part)* część **2** *(department)* dział

security [sɪ'kjuərɪtɪ] *n* **1** *(precautions)* środki bezpieczeństwa **2** *(of country, building, person)* bezpieczeństwo **3** *(of job)* bezpieczeństwo; **to increase** *or* **tighten ~**

wzmacniać (wzmocnić *pf*) środki bezpieczeństwa

security guard n (*at building*) strażnik(-iczka) *m/f*; (*transporting money*) konwojent(ka) *m/f*

see [siː] (*pt* **saw**, *pp* **seen**) *vt*
1 widzieć (zobaczyć *pf*) **2** (*meet*) widywać (widzieć *pf*) się z +*inst* **3** (*film, play etc*) oglądać (obejrzeć *pf*) **4** (*understand*) rozumieć (zrozumieć *pf*) **5** (*notice*) zauważać (zauważyć *pf*) ▷ *vi* widzieć; **I can ~ something** widzę coś; **to ~ sb doing** or **do sth** widzieć, że ktoś coś robi; **have you ~n my glasses?** (*familiar*) czy widziałeś moje okulary?; **to go and ~ sb** odwiedzać (odwiedzić *pf*) kogoś; **to ~ that...** (*realize, notice*) zauważać (zauważyć *pf*), że...; **to ~ if** (*find out if*) zobaczyć czy; **~ you (soon)!** (*inf*) do zobaczenia (wkrótce)!; **~ you later!** do zobaczenia!; **I'll ~ what I can do** zobaczę, co mogę zrobić; **let me ~, let's ~** (*let me think*) niech pomyślę; **I ~** rozumiem; **you ~** (*in explanations*) otóż; **as far as I can ~** o ile się orientuję
▶ **see to** *vt fus* zajmować (zająć *pf*) się +*inst*

seed [siːd] n nasienie

seeing-eye dog [siːɪŋˈaɪ-] (*US*) n pies przewodnik

seek [siːk] (*pt, pp* **sought**) *vt* szukać +*gen*; **to ~ advice/help from sb** szukać rady/pomocy u kogoś

seem [siːm] *vi* wydawać (wydać *pf*) się; **it ~s like...** wydaje się, że...; **to ~ (to be) happy/interested** wydawać

(wydać *pf*) się szczęśliwym/zainteresowanym; **there ~s to be...** zdaje się, że jest...

seen [siːn] *pp* of **see**

seesaw [ˈsiːsɔː] n huśtawka

seldom [ˈsɛldəm] *adv* rzadko

select [sɪˈlɛkt] *vt* wybierać (wybrać *pf*)

selection [sɪˈlɛkʃən] n wybór

self-catering [sɛlfˈkeɪtərɪŋ] (*Brit*) *adj* z wyżywieniem we własnym zakresie

self-confidence [sɛlfˈkɔnfɪdns] n wiara w siebie

self-conscious [sɛlfˈkɔnʃəs] *adj* skrępowany; **to ~ about sth** być czymś skrępowanym

self-defence [sɛlfdɪˈfɛns] (*US* **self-defense**) n samoobrona; **in ~** w samoobronie

self-employed [sɛlfɪmˈplɔɪd] *adj* pracujący na własny rachunek

selfish [ˈsɛlfɪʃ] *adj* samolubny

self-service [sɛlfˈsəːvɪs] *adj* samoobsługowy

sell [sɛl] (*pt, pp* **sold**) *vt* sprzedawać (sprzedać *pf*); **to ~ sb sth, ~ sth to sb** sprzedawać (sprzedać *pf*) coś komuś
▶ **sell off** *vt* wyprzedawać (wyprzedać *pf*)
▶ **sell out** *vi* (*shop*) zostać (*pf*) wyprzedany

sell-by date [ˈsɛlbaɪ-] (*Brit*) n data ważności

Sellotape® [ˈsɛləuteɪp] (*Brit*) n taśma klejąca

semicircle [ˈsɛmɪsəːkl] n półkole

semi-colon [sɛmɪˈkəulən] n średnik

semi-final [sɛmɪˈfaɪnl] n półfinał

semi-skimmed (milk)
[sɛmɪ'skɪmd(-)] (Brit) n półtłusty
send [sɛnd] (pt, pp **sent**) vt: **to ~
sth (to sb)** (letter, money) wysyłać
(wysłać pf) coś (komuś); **to ~
sth by post** or (US) **mail** wysyłać
(wysłać pf) coś pocztą
▶ **send away for** vt fus zamawiać
(zamówić pf) pocztą
▶ **send back** vt (goods) odsyłać
(odesłać pf)
▶ **send off** vt: **to ~ sth off (to sb)**
(goods, parcel) wysyłać (wysłać pf)
coś (komuś)
▶ **send out** vt (invitation, leaflet)
wysyłać (wysłać pf)
senior ['siːnɪəʳ] adj (staff,
manager, officer) wyższy rangą;
(job, position) wysoki
senior citizen n emeryt(ka) m/f
senior high (US) n (also: ~
school) wyższe klasy szkoły średniej
sensational [sɛn'seɪʃənl] adj
1 (wonderful) wspaniały **2** (event)
sensacyjny
sense [sɛns] n **1** (of smell, taste)
zmysł **2** (good sense) rozsądek
3 (meaning) sens; **a keen ~ of
smell** dobry węch; **it makes ~**
(can be understood) to ma sens; (is
sensible) to jest rozsądne
sensible ['sɛnsɪbl] adj rozsądny;
(shoes, clothes) praktyczny
sensitive ['sɛnsɪtɪv] adj
wrażliwy; **to be ~ to sth** (sb's
feelings) być wyczulonym na coś
sent [sɛnt] pt, pp of **send**
sentence ['sɛntns] n **1** (Ling)
zdanie **2** (Law) wyrok ▷ vt: **to ~
sb to death/to 5 years in prison**
skazywać (skazać pf) kogoś na
śmierć/na pięć lat więzienia

sentimental [sɛntɪ'mɛntl] adj
(person) sentymentalny
separate [adj 'sɛprɪt, vb
'sɛpəreɪt] adj osobny ▷ vt (split
up) rozdzielać (rozdzielić pf)
▷ vi **1** (objects, groups) rozdzielać
(rozdzielić pf) się **2** (parents,
couple) rozchodzić (rozejść pf)
się; **to keep sth ~ from** trzymać
coś oddzielnie od +gen; **to ~ from**
(husband, wife) odchodzić (odejść
pf) od +gen; **to be ~d** (couple) być
w separacji
separated ['sɛpəreɪtɪd] adj (not
divorced) w separacji
separately ['sɛprɪtlɪ] adv osobno
separation [sɛpə'reɪʃən] n **1** (of
things, groups) oddzielenie **2** (from
loved ones) rozłąka **3** (of couple)
rozejście się
September [sɛp'tɛmbəʳ] n
wrzesień; see also **July**
sequel ['siːkwl] n dalszy ciąg
sergeant ['sɑːdʒənt] n sierżant
serial ['sɪərɪəl] n (on TV, radio)
serial; (in magazine) powieść w
odcinkach
series ['sɪərɪz] (pl **series**) n seria
serious ['sɪərɪəs] adj poważny;
are you ~? czy pan/pani mówi
poważnie?
seriously ['sɪərɪəslɪ] adv
poważnie; **to take sb/sth ~** brać
(wziąć pf) kogoś/coś na poważnie
servant ['səːvənt] n służący(-ca)
m/f
serve [səːv] vt **1** (in shop, bar)
obsługiwać (obsłużyć pf) **2** (food,
drink, meal) podawać (podać pf)
3 (prison term) odbywać (odbyć pf)
▷ vi **1** (at table) podawać (podać pf)
2 (Tennis) serwować (zaserwować

pf); **it ~s you right** dobrze tak panu/pani

service ['sə:vɪs] *n* **1** (*facility*) usługa **2** (*in hotel, restaurant*) obsługa **3** (*train/bus service*) połączenie **4** (*Rel*) nabożeństwo **5** (*Aut*) przegląd ▷ *vt* (*vehicle, machine*) dokonywać (dokonać *pf*) przeglądu +*gen*; **military** or (*esp Brit*) **national ~** służba wojskowa; **~ included/not included** (*on menu*) obsługa wliczona/nie wliczona w cenę; **to have one's car ~d** oddawać (oddać *pf*) samochód do przeglądu

service charge *n* (*restaurant*) opłata za obsługę; (*bank*) ≈ prowizja

service station *n* stacja obsługi

serviette [sə:vɪ'ɛt] (*Brit*) *n* serwetka

session ['sɛʃən] *n* sesja

set [sɛt] (*pt, pp* **set**) *n* **1** (*of cutlery, saucepans etc*) komplet; (*of golf clubs, spanners*) zestaw **2** (*TV, Rad*) telewizor **3** (*Tennis*) set ▷ *adj* (*routine, time, price*) ustalony ▷ *vt* **1** (*put*) umieszczać (umieścić *pf*) **2** (*table*) przygotowywać (przygotować *pf*) **3** (*time, price, rules etc*) ustalać (ustalić *pf*) **4** (*record*) ustanawiać (ustanowić *pf*) **5** (*adjust*) nastawiać (nastawić *pf*) ▷ *vi* (*sun*) zachodzić (zajść *pf*); **a ~ of dining-room furniture** komplet mebli stołowych; **a chess ~** szachy; **all ~ to do sth** (*ready*) w pełni gotowy coś zrobić; **a novel ~ in Rome** powieść, której akcja rozgrywa się w Rzymie; **to ~ sb free** uwalniać (uwolnić *pf*) kogoś

▶ **set off** *vi* (*depart*): **to ~ off (for)** wyruszać (wyruszyć *pf*) (do +*gen*) ▷ *vt* (*alarm*) uruchamiać (uruchomić *pf*)

▶ **set out** *vi* (*depart*) wyruszać (wyruszyć *pf*)

▶ **set up** *vt* **1** (*organization, service*) zakładać (założyć *pf*) **2** (*roadblock*) wznosić (wznieść *pf*) ▷ *vi*: **to ~ up in business** zakładać (założyć *pf*) interes

settee [sɛ'ti:] *n* sofa

settle ['sɛtl] *vt* **1** (*argument, question*) rozstrzygać (rozstrzygnąć *pf*) **2** (*bill, account, debt*) regulować (uregulować *pf*); **that's ~d then!** no to załatwione!

▶ **settle down** *vi* **1** (*live stable life*) osiedlać (osiedlić *pf*) się **2** (*become calm*) uspokajać (uspokoić *pf*) się

▶ **settle in** *vi* przyzwyczajać (przyzwyczaić *pf*) się

▶ **settle on** *vt fus* decydować (zdecydować *pf*) się na

seven ['sɛvn] *num* siedem; *see also* **five**

seventeen [sɛvn'ti:n] *num* siedemnaście; *see also* **fifteen**

seventeenth [sɛvn'ti:nθ] *num* siedemnasty; *see also* **fifth**

seventh ['sɛvnθ] *num* siódmy; *see also* **fifth**

seventy ['sɛvntɪ] *num* siedemdziesiąt; *see also* **fifty**

several ['sɛvrəl] *adj, pron* kilka; **~ times** kilka razy

severe [sɪ'vɪəʳ] *adj* **1** (*pain*) ostry; (*damage, shortage*) poważny **2** (*punishment, criticism*) srogi; (*winter, climate*) surowy **3** (*person, expression*) surowy

sew [səu] (*pt* **sewed**, *pp* **sewn**)

vi, vt szyć (uszyć *pf*); **to ~ sth
together** zszywać (zszyć *pf*) coś
▶ **sew up** *vt* zszywać (zszyć *pf*)
sewing ['səʊɪŋ] *n* szycie
sewing machine *n* maszyna
do szycia
sewn [səʊn] *pp of* **sew**
sex [sɛks] *n* **1** (*gender*) płeć
2 (*lovemaking*) seks; **to have ~
with sb** uprawiać z kimś seks
sexism ['sɛksɪzəm] *n* seksizm
sexist ['sɛksɪst] *adj* seksistowski
sexual ['sɛksjʊəl] *adj* (*attraction,
relationship, health*) seksualny;
(*differences, discrimination*) płciowy
sexuality [sɛksjuˈælɪtɪ] *n*
seksualność
sexy ['sɛksɪ] *adj* seksowny
shabby ['ʃæbɪ] *adj* (*clothes, place*)
zaniedbany; (*person*) obdarty
shade [ʃeɪd] *n* **1** (*shelter*) cień **2** (*of
colour*) odcień **3** (*also:* **lamp~**)
abażur **4** (*US: on window*) roleta;
in the ~ w cieniu
shadow ['ʃædəʊ] *n* cień; **in the ~
of sth** w cieniu czegoś
shake [ʃeɪk] (*pt* **shook**, *pp*
shaken ['ʃeɪkn]) *vt* (*dice, rug,
person*) potrząsać (potrząsnąć *pf*)
+*inst*; (*bottle, cocktail, medicine*)
wstrząsać (wstrząsnąć *pf*) +*inst*;
(*buildings, ground*) trząść (zatrząść
pf) +*inst* ▷ *vi* (*person, part of the
body*) drżeć (zadrżeć *pf*); (*building,
table, ground*) trząść (zatrząść
pf) się; **to ~ one's head** kręcić
(pokręcić *pf*) głową; **to ~ one's
fist (at sb)** wygrażać (komuś)
pięścią; **to ~ hands (with sb)**
uścisnąć (*pf*) (komuś) dłoń
shall [ʃæl] *aux vb* **1** (*indicating
future in 1st person*): **I ~ go** pójdę

2 (*in 1st person questions*): **~ I/we
open the door?** czy mam/mamy
otworzyć drzwi? **3** (*in 1st person
tag questions*): **I'll get some, ~ I?**
przyniosę trochę, dobrze?
shallow ['ʃæləʊ] *adj* płytki
shambles ['ʃæmblz] *n* bałagan
shame [ʃeɪm] *n* wstyd; **it is a ~
that...** szkoda, że...; **it would be
a ~ to waste this** szkoda byłoby
to zmarnować; **what a ~!** jaka
szkoda!
shampoo [ʃæmˈpuː] *n* szampon
shandy ['ʃændɪ] (*Brit*) *n* piwo z
lemoniadą
shape [ʃeɪp] *n* kształt ▷ *vt*
kształtować (ukształtować *pf*); **in
the ~ of a heart** w kształcie serca
share [ʃɛəʳ] *n* **1** (*part*) część
2 (*Comm, Fin*) udział ▷ *vt* **1** (*room,
bed, taxi*) dzielić **2** (*job, cooking,
task*) dzielić (podzielić *pf*)
3 (*divide*): **to ~ sth among/
between** dzielić (podzielić *pf*) coś
pomiędzy +*inst*; **to ~ sth with sb**
(*room, bed, taxi*) dzielić coś z kimś;
to ~ in (*success, profits, benefits*)
mieć swój udział w +*loc*
▶ **share out** *vt* rozdzielać
(rozdzielić *pf*)
shareholder ['ʃɛəhəʊldəʳ] *n*
akcjonariusz(ka) *m/f*
shark [ʃɑːk] *n* rekin
sharp [ʃɑːp] *adj* **1** (*not blunt*)
ostry **2** (*abrupt: increase, change*)
nagły; (*curve, bend*) ostry
▷ *adv* (*precisely*): **at 2 o'clock ~**
punktualnie o godzinie drugiej;
C ~/F ~ cis/fis
sharpener ['ʃɑːpnəʳ] *n*
(*also:* **pencil ~**) temperówka
shave [ʃeɪv] *vt* golić (ogolić *pf*)

▷ vi golić (ogolić pf) się
▶ **shave off** vt (beard) golić (zgolić pf)
shaver ['ʃeɪvəʳ] n (also: **electric ~**) golarka
shaving cream ['ʃeɪvɪŋ-] n krem do golenia
shaving foam ['ʃeɪvɪŋ-] n pianka do golenia
she [ʃiː] pron (woman, girl) ona
shed [ʃed] n szopa
she'd [ʃiːd] = **she had, she would**
sheep [ʃiːp] (pl **sheep**) n owca
sheepdog ['ʃiːpdɔg] n owczarek
sheer [ʃɪəʳ] adj czysty; **it was ~ luck** to było zupełne szczęście
sheet [ʃiːt] n 1 (on bed) prześcieradło 2 (of paper) kartka; (of glass, metal, ice) tafla
shelf [ʃelf] (pl **shelves**) n półka
shell [ʃel] n 1 (on beach) muszla 2 (of tortoise, snail, crab) skorupa 3 (explosive) pocisk
she'll [ʃiːl] = **she will**
shellfish ['ʃelfɪʃ] n pl małże
shelter ['ʃeltəʳ] n 1 (building) schronienie 2 (protection) osłona ▷ vi chronić (schronić pf) się; **to take ~ (from sth)** znajdować (znaleźć pf) schronienie (przed czymś)
shelves [ʃelvz] n pl of **shelf**
shepherd ['ʃepəd] n pasterz(-rka) m/f
sheriff ['ʃerɪf] (US) n szeryf
sherry ['ʃerɪ] n sherry
she's [ʃiːz] = **she is, she has**
shift [ʃɪft] n zmiana ▷ vt przesuwać (przesunąć pf)
shin [ʃɪn] n goleń
shine [ʃaɪn] (pt, pp **shone**) vi świecić (zaświecić pf) ▷ vt (torch,

light) świecić (zaświecić pf) +inst
shiny ['ʃaɪnɪ] adj błyszczący
ship [ʃɪp] n statek
shirt [ʃəːt] n koszula
shiver ['ʃɪvəʳ] n drżenie ▷ vi drżeć (zadrżeć pf)
shock [ʃɔk] n 1 szok 2 (also: **electric ~**) porażenie ▷ vt (offend, scandalize) szokować (zszokować pf); **to be in ~** (Med) być w szoku
shocked [ʃɔkt] adj zszokowany; **I was ~ to learn that...** byłem zszokowany, gdy dowiedziałem się, że...
shocking ['ʃɔkɪŋ] adj (outrageous) szokujący
shoe [ʃuː] n but; **a pair of ~s** buty
shoelace ['ʃuːleɪs] n sznurowadło
shoe polish n pasta do butów
shoe shop n sklep obuwniczy
shone [ʃɔn] pt, pp of **shine**
shook [ʃuk] pt of **shake**
shoot [ʃuːt] (pt, pp **shot**) vt 1 (kill: person, animal) zastrzelić (pf) 2 (Brit: hunt) polować na 3 (film) kręcić (nakręcić pf) ▷ vi 1 (with gun, bow): **to ~ at sb/sth** strzelać (strzelić pf) do kogoś/czegoś 2 (Football etc) strzelać (strzelić pf); **to ~ sb in the back/leg** strzelać (strzelić pf) kogoś w plecy/w nogę
shooting ['ʃuːtɪŋ] n 1 (attack, murder, shots) strzelanina 2 (Brit: hunting) polowanie
shop [ʃɔp] n (esp Brit) sklep ▷ vi robić (zrobić pf) zakupy
shop assistant (Brit) n sprzedawca(-czyni) m/f
shopkeeper ['ʃɔpkiːpəʳ] (Brit) n sklepikarz(-rka) m/f
shoplifting ['ʃɔplɪftɪŋ] n kradzież

sklepowa

shopping ['ʃɒpɪŋ] n zakupy m pl; **to do the ~** robić (zrobić pf) zakupy; **to go ~** iść/chodzić (pójść pf) na zakupy

shopping cart (US) n wózek sklepowy

shopping centre (US **shopping center**) n centrum handlowe

shopping mall n centrum handlowe

shopping trolley (Brit) n wózek sklepowy

shop window n wystawa sklepowa

shore [ʃɔːʳ] n brzeg; **on ~** na lądzie

short [ʃɔːt] adj **1** (in time) krótki **2** (in length) krótki **3** (not tall) niski; **shorts** n pl **1** (short trousers) szorty **2** (esp US: underpants) bokserki; **at ~ notice** w krótkim czasie; **to be ~ of sth** nie mieć czegoś; **a pair of ~s** para szortów

shortage ['ʃɔːtɪdʒ] n niedobór

short cut n skrót

shortly ['ʃɔːtlɪ] adv wkrótce; **~ after/before** krótko po +loc/ krótko przed +inst

short-sighted [ʃɔːt'saɪtɪd] adj (Brit) krótkowzroczny

shot [ʃɒt] pt, pp of **shoot** ▷ n **1** (from gun) wystrzał **2** (Football) strzał **3** (injection) zastrzyk **4** (Cine, Phot) ujęcie; **to fire a ~ at sb/sth** strzelać (strzelić pf) do kogoś/czegoś

shotgun ['ʃɒtɡʌn] n śrutówka

should [ʃʊd] aux vb **1** (indicating advisability): **I ~ go now** powinienem już iść **2** (indicating obligation): **he ~ listen to me** powinien mnie posłuchać

3 (indicating likelihood): **she ~ be there by now** powinna tam teraz być **4** (after "that"): **it's not right that we ~ be fined** nie powinniśmy być ukarani mandatem; **she ~ have been more careful** powinna była być bardziej ostrożna; **he ~ have arrived by now** już powinien przyjechać; **I ~ go if I were you** na pana/pani miejscu poszedłbym

shoulder ['ʃəʊldəʳ] n bark

shouldn't ['ʃʊdnt] = **should not**

shout [ʃaut] n krzyk ▷ vt (also: ~ out) krzyczeć (krzyknąć pf) ▷ vi (also: ~ out) krzyczeć (krzyknąć pf)

shovel ['ʃʌvl] n łopata

show [ʃəʊ] (pt **showed**, pp **shown**) n **1** (exhibition) pokaz **2** (Theat) przedstawienie **3** (TV, Rad) program ▷ vt **1** pokazywać (pokazać pf) **2** (illustrate, depict) przedstawiać (przedstawić pf) ▷ vi (be visible) być widocznym; **on ~** (exhibits) wystawiany; **to ~ sb sth** or **to ~ sth to sb** pokazywać (pokazać pf) coś komuś; **to ~ that...** pokazywać (pokazać pf), że...; **to ~ sb how to do sth** pokazywać (pokazać pf) komuś jak coś zrobić

▶ **show around** vt oprowadzać (oprowadzić pf)

▶ **show off** vi popisywać (popisać pf) się ▷ vt popisywać (popisać pf) się +inst

▶ **show up** vi **1** (be visible, noticeable) ukazywać (ukazać pf) się **2** (arrive, appear) pojawiać (pojawić pf) się

shower ['ʃauəʳ] n **1** (rain) przelotny deszcz **2** (for washing)

prysznic ▷ *vi* brać (wziąć *pf*)
prysznic; **to have** *or* **take a ~** brać
(wziąć *pf*) prysznic
show jumping [-dʒʌmpɪŋ] *n*
konkurs hipiczny
shown [ʃəʊn] *pp of* **show**
show-off ['ʃəʊɔf] *n* pozer(ka) *m/f*
shrank [ʃræŋk] *pt of* **shrink**
shriek [ʃriːk] *vi* wrzeszczeć
(wrzasnąć *pf*) ▷ *n* wrzask
shrimp [ʃrɪmp] *n* krewetka
shrink [ʃrɪŋk] (*pt* **shrank**, *pp*
shrunk) *vi* kurczyć (skurczyć
pf) się

- **SHROVE TUESDAY**
-
- **Shrove Tuesday**
- (polskie Ostatki) to dzień
- poprzedzający Środę
- Popielcową i początek
- Wielkiego Postu. Ponieważ
- tradycyjnie w Wielkiej
- Brytanii je się wtedy naleśniki
- (**pancakes**), dzień ten również
- nazywany jest **Pancake Day**
- (Dzień naleśników).

shrug [ʃrʌg] *vi* wzruszać
(wzruszyć *pf*) ramionami ▷ *vt*: **to
~ one's shoulders** wzruszać
(wzruszyć *pf*) ramionami
shrunk [ʃrʌŋk] *pp of* **shrink**
shuffle ['ʃʌfl] *vi*: **to ~ along**
przechodzić (przejść *pf*)
powłócząc nogami ▷ *vt* (*cards*)
tasować (potasować *pf*)
shut [ʃʌt] (*pt, pp* **shut**) *vt* zamykać
(zamknąć *pf*) ▷ *vi* zamykać
(zamknąć *pf*) się ▷ *adj* zamknięty
▶ **shut down** *vt* (*factory*) zamykać
(zamknąć *pf*) ▷ *vi* (*factory*)

zamykać (zamknąć *pf*) się
▶ **shut out** *vt* nie wpuszczać
(wpuścić *pf*) +*gen* do środka
▶ **shut up** *vi* (*inf*) zamykać
(zamknąć *pf*) się ▷ *vt* (*inf: person*)
uciszać (uciszyć *pf*); **~ up!** (*inf*)
zamknij się!
shuttle ['ʃʌtl] *n* (*plane, bus etc*)
transport wahadłowy
shuttlecock ['ʃʌtlkɔk] *n* lotka
shy [ʃaɪ] *adj* (*person*) nieśmiały;
(*animal*) płochliwy
sick [sɪk] *adj* **1** chory **2** (*vomit*): **to
be ~** wymiotować (zwymiotować
pf); **to feel ~** leż się czuć (poczuć
pf); **to be ~ of sth/of doing sth**
(*inf*) mieć dość czegoś/robienia
czegoś
sickness ['sɪknɪs] *n* **1** (*illness*)
choroba **2** (*vomiting*) wymioty *m pl*
side [saɪd] *n* **1** strona **2** (*of building,
vehicle*) bok; (*of body*) bok **3** (*of
paper, face*) strona; (*of tape*)
strona **4** (*of road, bed*) strona
5 (*of hill, valley*) zbocze **6** (*aspect*)
strona **7** (*Brit: team*) drużyna
8 (*in conflict, contest*) strona ▷ *adj*
(*door, entrance*) boczny; **on the
other ~ of sth** po drugiej stronie
czegoś; **the right/wrong ~ of
sth** właściwa/niewłaściwa strona
czegoś; **by the ~ of** przy +*loc*; **~ by
~** tuż obok siebie; **they are on our
~** oni są po naszej stronie; **to take
sb's ~** opowiadać (opowiedzieć
pf) się po czyjejś stronie
sideboard ['saɪdbɔːd] *n* kredens
side-effect ['saɪdɪfɛkt] *n* skutek
uboczny
sidewalk ['saɪdwɔːk] (*US*) *n*
chodnik
sideways ['saɪdweɪz] *adv* w bok

sieve [sɪv] n sito ▷ vt przesiewać (przesiać pf)

sigh [saɪ] n westchnienie ▷ vi wzdychać (westchnąć pf)

sight [saɪt] n 1 (faculty) wzrok 2 (spectacle) widok; **sights** n pl: **the ~s** atrakcje turystyczne; **out of ~** niewidoczny; **I know her by ~** znam ją z widzenia

sightseeing ['saɪtsiːɪŋ] n zwiedzanie; **to go ~** zwiedzać (zwiedzić pf)

sign [saɪn] n znak ▷ vt (document) podpisywać (podpisać pf); **a plus/minus ~** znak plus/ minus; **he was showing ~s of improvement** wykazywał oznaki poprawy; **it's a good/bad ~** to dobry/zły znak

▶ **sign on** vi (Brit) (as unemployed) zgłaszać (zgłosić pf) się jako bezrobotny; **to ~ on for sth** (course) zapisywać (zapisać pf) się na coś

▶ **sign up** vi: **to ~ up for** (course, trip) zapisywać (zapisać pf) się na

signal ['sɪɡnl] n 1 (to do sth) sygnał 2 (indication) znak 3 (Rail) sygnał 4 (Elec, Tel) sygnał ▷ vi 1 (with gesture, sound): **to ~ (to sb)** dawać (dać pf) (komuś) znak 2 (Aut: with indicator) sygnalizować (zasygnalizować pf)

signature ['sɪɡnətʃər] n podpis

significance [sɪɡ'nɪfɪkəns] n znaczenie

significant [sɪɡ'nɪfɪkənt] adj 1 (important) ważny 2 (considerable) znaczny

sign language n język migowy

signpost ['saɪnpəust] n znak drogowy

silence ['saɪləns] n cisza; **in ~** w ciszy

silent ['saɪlənt] adj (person) cichy

silk [sɪlk] n jedwab ▷ adj (scarf, shirt) jedwabny

silky ['sɪlkɪ] adj jedwabisty

silly ['sɪlɪ] adj głupi

silver ['sɪlvər] n srebro ▷ adj 1 (hair) siwy 2 (spoon, necklace) srebrny

SIM card ['sɪm-] n karta SIM

similar ['sɪmɪlər] adj podobny; **to be ~ to sth** być podobnym do czegoś

simple ['sɪmpl] adj 1 (easy) prosty 2 (basic) zwyczajny 3 (mere) prosty 4 (Ling: tense) prosty; **it would be ~r to move house** łatwiej byłoby przeprowadzić się

simply ['sɪmplɪ] adv po prostu

sin [sɪn] n grzech

since [sɪns] adv (from then onwards) od tego czasu ▷ prep 1 (from) od +gen 2 (after) po +loc ▷ conj 1 (from when) odkąd 2 (after) od kiedy 3 (as) ponieważ; **~ then** or **ever ~** od tej pory; **I've been here ~ the end of June** jestem tu od końca czerwca; **~ it was Saturday, he stayed in bed** ponieważ to była sobota, leżał w łóżku

sincere [sɪn'sɪər] adj szczery

sincerely [sɪn'sɪəlɪ] adv szczerze; **yours ~** or (US) **Sincerely yours** z wyrazami szacunku

sing [sɪŋ] (pt **sang**, pp **sung**) vi śpiewać (zaśpiewać pf) ▷ vt (song) śpiewać (zaśpiewać pf)

singer ['sɪŋər] n śpiewak(-aczka) m/f

singing ['sɪŋɪŋ] n (activity)

śpiewanie; (*sounds*) śpiew

single ['sɪŋgl] *adj* **1** (*solitary*) jeden **2** (*unmarried*) stanu wolnego ▷ *n* (*Brit*) (*also:* **~ ticket**) bilet w jedną stronę; **every ~ day** codziennie

single bed *n* łóżko jednoosobowe

single parent *n* rodzic samotnie wychowujący dziecko

singular ['sɪŋgjuləʳ] *adj* pojedynczy ▷ *n*: **the ~** liczba pojedyncza; **in the ~** w liczbie pojedynczej

sink [sɪŋk] (*pt* **sank**, *pp* **sunk**) *n* zlew ▷ *vi* (*ship*) tonąć (zatonąć *pf*); **my heart sank** podupadłem na duchu

sir [səʳ] *n* pan; **yes, ~** tak, proszę pana; **dear S~** szanowany Panie; **dear S~ or Madam** szanowni Państwo; **~ John Smith** sir John Smith (*tytuł szlachecki*)

siren ['saɪərn] *n* syrena

sister ['sɪstəʳ] *n* siostra; **my brothers and ~s** moi bracia i siostry

sister-in-law ['sɪstərɪnlɔ:] (*pl* **sisters-in-law**) *n* (*husband or wife's sister*) szwagierka; (*brother's wife*) bratowa

sit [sɪt] (*pt*, *pp* **sat**) *vi* **1** (*also:* **~ down**) siadać (usiąść *pf*) **2** (*be sitting*) siedzieć ▷ *vt* (*Brit*: *exam*) podchodzić (podejść *pf*) do +*gen* ▶ **sit down** *vi* siadać (usiąść *pf*); **to be ~ting down** siedzieć ▶ **sit up** *vi* siadać (usiąść *pf*) z pozycji leżącej

site [saɪt] *n* **1** (*of event*) miejsce **2** (*building site*) plac budowy **3** (*also:* **web~**) witryna internetowa

sitting room ['sɪtɪŋ-] (*Brit*) *n* salon

situated ['sɪtjueɪtɪd] *adj*: **to be ~ in/on/near sth** być usytuowanym w/na czymś/obok czegoś

situation [sɪtju'eɪʃən] *n* sytuacja

six [sɪks] *num* sześć; *see also* **five**

sixteen [sɪks'ti:n] *num* szesnaście; *see also* **fifteen**

sixteenth [sɪks'ti:nθ] *num* szesnasty; *see also* **fifth**

sixth [sɪksθ] *num* **1** (*in series*) szósty **2** (*fraction*) szósta część; **the upper/lower ~** (*Brit*: *Scol*) ostatnia/przedostatnia klasa w szkole brytyjskiej; *see also* **fifth**

⊙ SIXTH FORM
⊙
⊙ **Sixth form** – w szkołach
⊙ brytyjskich są to dwa
⊙ lata nauki po ukończeniu
⊙ obowiązkowej edukacji
⊙ w wieku 16 lat. Uczniowie
⊙ przygotowują się wtedy do
⊙ egzaminów **A-levels**.

sixty ['sɪkstɪ] *num* sześćdziesiąt; *see also* **fifty**

size [saɪz] *n* wielkość; (*of clothing, shoes*) rozmiar; **what ~ shoes do you take?** jaki pan/pani nosi rozmiar butów?

skate [skeɪt] *n* **1** (*ice skate*) łyżwa **2** (*roller skate*) wrotka ▷ *vi* **1** (*ice skate*) jeździć na łyżwach **2** (*roller skate*) jeździć na wrotkach

skateboard ['skeɪtbɔ:d] *n* deskorolka

skateboarding ['skeɪtbɔ:dɪŋ] *n* jazda na deskorolce

skating ['skeɪtɪŋ] *n* (*ice-skating*)

łyżwiarstwo; **to go ~** (on ice skates) jeździć na łyżwach; (on roller skates) jeździć na wrotkach
skating rink n lodowisko
skeleton ['skɛlɪtn] n szkielet
sketch [skɛtʃ] n **1** (drawing) szkic **2** (outline) zarys ▷ vt szkicować (naszkicować pf)
ski [skiː] n narta ▷ vi jeździć na nartach
skid [skɪd] vi (car, driver) wpadać (wpaść pf) w poślizg
skier ['skiːəʳ] n narciarz(-rka) m/f
skiing ['skiːɪŋ] n narciarstwo; **to go ~** jeździć na nartach
skilful ['skɪlful] (US **skillful**) adj (person, player) zręczny; (use, choice, management) sprawny
skill [skɪl] n umiejętność
skilled [skɪld] adj (person) wykwalifikowany; (work) wymagający kwalifikacji
skillful ['skɪlful] (US) adj = **skilful**
skimmed milk [skɪmd-] (Brit) n mleko odtłuszczone
skim milk [skɪm-] (US) n mleko odtłuszczone
skin [skɪn] n **1** (of person) skóra; (of animal) skóra; (complexion) cera **2** (of fruit, vegetable) skórka
skinhead ['skɪnhɛd] (Brit) n skin
skinny ['skɪnɪ] (inf) adj chudy
skip [skɪp] vi (hop) podskakiwać (podskoczyć pf) ▷ vt (miss) opuszczać (opuścić pf) ▷ n (Brit: container) kontener
skirt [skəːt] n spódnica
skive [skaɪv] (Brit: inf) vi wymigiwać (wymigać pf) się
▶ **skive off** (Brit: inf) vt fus (school, work) urywać (urwać pf) się z +gen ▷ vi wymigiwać (wymigać pf) się

skull [skʌl] n czaszka
sky [skaɪ] n niebo
skyscraper ['skaɪskreɪpəʳ] n drapacz chmur
slam [slæm] vt trzaskać (trzasnąć pf) +inst ▷ vi zatrzaskiwać (zatrzasnąć pf) się
slang [slæŋ] n slang
slap [slæp] n klepnięcie ▷ vt uderzać (uderzyć pf); **to give sb a ~** uderzyć (pf) kogoś
slate [sleɪt] n (on roof) dachówka łupkowa
slave [sleɪv] n niewolnik(-ica) m/f
sled [slɛd] (US) n sanie ▷ vi: **to go ~ding** jeździć na saniach
sledge [slɛdʒ] (Brit) n sanie ▷ vi: **to go sledging** jeździć na saniach
sleep [sliːp] (pt, pp **slept**) n **1** sen **2** (nap) drzemka ▷ vi (be asleep) spać; (spend the night) zatrzymywać (zatrzymać pf) się na noc; **to go to ~** zasypiać (zasnąć pf); **to have a good night's ~** dobrze się wyspać; **to put a cat/dog to ~** usypiać (uśpić pf) kota/psa
▶ **sleep around** (inf) vi puszczać się
▶ **sleep in** (Brit) vi zasypiać (zaspać pf)
▶ **sleep with** vt fus sypiać (spać pf) z +inst
sleeping bag ['sliːpɪŋ-] n śpiwór
sleeping pill n tabletka nasenna
sleepy ['sliːpɪ] adj śpiący
sleet [sliːt] n deszcz ze śniegiem
sleeve [sliːv] n rękaw; **with long/short ~s** z długim/krótkim rękawem
slept [slɛpt] pt, pp of **sleep**

slice [slaɪs] n (of meat, lemon) plasterek; (of bread) kromka ▷ vt kroić (pokroić pf); **~d bread** pokrojony chleb

slide [slaɪd] (pt, pp **slid**) n **1** (in playground) zjeżdżalnia **2** (Phot) slajd **3** (Brit: also: **hair ~**) wsuwka do włosów ▷ vi: **to ~ down sth** zjeżdżać (zjechać pf) w dół po czymś; **to ~ off sth** zsuwać (zsunąć pf) się z czegoś

slight [slaɪt] adj niewielki; **the ~est noise/problem** najmniejszy hałas/problem

slightly ['slaɪtlɪ] adv nieco

slim [slɪm] adj szczupły ▷ vi (lose weight) chudnąć (schudnąć pf)

sling [slɪŋ] n temblak; **to have one's arm in a ~** mieć rękę na temblaku

slip [slɪp] vi (person) poślizgnąć (pf) się; (object) zsuwać (zsunąć pf) się ▷ n (mistake) pomyłka; **to ~ sth on/off** wkładać (włożyć pf)/zdejmować (zdjąć pf) coś; **a ~ of the tongue** przejęzyczenie
▶ **slip up** vi (make mistake) mylić (pomylić pf) się

slipper ['slɪpəʳ] n kapeć

slippery ['slɪpərɪ] adj śliski

slope [sləup] n **1** (gentle hill) zbocze **2** (ski slope) stok narciarski ▷ vi: **to ~ down** opadać (opaść pf)

slot [slɔt] n **1** (in machine) otwór **2** (fig: in timetable) okienko

slot machine n (for drinks etc) automat z napojami; (for gambling) automat do gier

slow [sləu] adj powolny ▷ adv (inf) wolno; **my watch is 20 minutes ~** mój zegarek spóźnia się o dwadzieścia minut

▶ **slow down** vi (become less active) zwalniać (zwolnić pf) tempo życia

slowly ['sləulɪ] adv powoli

slug [slʌg] n ślimak

slum [slʌm] n (area) slums

sly [slaɪ] adj (smile) chytry; (expression, remark) fałszywy; (person) przebiegły

smack [smæk] n uderzenie ▷ vt (as punishment) dawać (dać pf) klapsa +dat

small [smɔːl] adj mały; **to get** or **grow ~er** (thing) maleć (zmaleć pf)

smart [smɑːt] adj **1** (esp Brit: neat, tidy) elegancki **2** (fashionable) elegancki **3** (clever) bystry

smart card n karta chipowa

smash [smæʃ] vt tłuc (stłuc pf) ▷ vi (break) tłuc (stłuc pf) się
▶ **smash up** vt demolować (zdemolować pf)

smashing ['smæʃɪŋ] (Brit: inf) adj fantastyczny

smell [smɛl] (pt, pp **smelled** or **smelt**) n zapach ▷ vt czuć (poczuć pf) ▷ vi (have unpleasant odour) śmierdzieć; **to ~ nice/delicious/spicy** pachnieć ładnie/cudownie/pikantnymi przyprawami; **sense of ~** węch; **to ~ of** pachnieć +inst

smelly ['smɛlɪ] (pej) adj śmierdzący

smelt [smɛlt] pt, pp of **smell**

smile [smaɪl] n uśmiech ▷ vi: **to ~ (at sb)** uśmiechać (uśmiechnąć pf) się (do kogoś)

smoke [sməuk] n dym ▷ vi **1** (use tobacco) palić (wypalić pf) **2** (chimney) dymić się ▷ vt

1 (*cigarette, cigar, pipe*) palić (zapalić *pf*) **2** (*fish, meat*) wędzić (uwędzić *pf*); **do you ~?** pan/pani pali?

smoke alarm *n* czujnik dymu

smoker ['sməukə^r] *n* (*person*) palacz(ka) *m/f*

smoking ['sməukɪŋ] *n* palenie; **"no ~"** "zakaz palenia"

smooth [smu:ð] *adj* **1** (*not rough*) gładki **2** (*successful*) płynny

smother ['smʌðə^r] *vt* dusić (udusić *pf*)

SMS *n abbr* (= *short message service*) sms

smudge [smʌdʒ] *n* plama ▷ *vt* rozmazywać (rozmazać *pf*)

smuggle ['smʌgl] *vt* przemycać (przemycić *pf*); **to ~ sth in/out** przemycać (przemycić *pf*) coś do środka/na zewnątrz

smuggler ['smʌglə^r] *n* przemytnik(-iczka) *m/f*

smuggling ['smʌglɪŋ] *n* przemyt

snack [snæk] *n* przekąska; **to have a ~** przekąsić (*pf*) coś

snack bar *n* bar szybkiej obsługi

snail [sneɪl] *n* ślimak

snake [sneɪk] *n* wąż

snap [snæp] *vt* łamać (złamać *pf*) ▷ *vi* (*rope, stick*) pękać (pęknąć *pf*); **to ~ one's fingers** (*lit*) pstrykać (pstryknąć *pf*) palcami

snapshot ['snæpʃɔt] *n* zdjęcie

snatch [snætʃ] *vt* **1** (*grab*) chwytać (chwycić *pf*) **2** (*steal: handbag*) wyrywać (wyrwać *pf*)

sneak [sni:k] (*pt, pp* **sneaked** or (*US*) **snuck**) *vi:* **to ~ out/in** wymykać (wymknąć *pf*) się/ wślizgać (wślizgnąć *pf*) się ▷ *vt:* **to ~ a look at sth** zerkać (zerknąć

pf) na coś

sneakers ['sni:kəz] (*US*) *n pl* tenisówki

sneeze [sni:z] *vi* kichać (kichnąć *pf*)

sniff [snɪf] *vi* pociągać (pociągnąć *pf*) nosem ▷ *vt* wąchać (powąchać *pf*)

snob [snɔb] (*pej*) *n* snob(ka) *m/f*

snooker ['snu:kə^r] *n* (*Sport*) snooker

snooze [snu:z] (*inf*) *n* drzemka ▷ *vi* drzemać; **to have a ~** zdrzemnąć (*pf*) się

snore [snɔ:^r] *vi* chrapać (chrapnąć *pf*)

snow [snəu] *n* śnieg; **it's ~ing** pada śnieg

snowball ['snəubɔ:l] *n* śnieżka

snuck [snʌk] (*US*) *pt, pp of* **sneak**

○ **KEYWORD**

so [səu] *adv* **1** (*thus, likewise*) tak; **they do so because...** robią tak, ponieważ...; **if you don't want to go, say so** jeśli pan/pani nie chce iść, proszę powiedzieć; **if so** jeśli tak; **"it's five o'clock" — "so it is!"** "jest piąta" — "rzeczywiście!"; **I hope/think so** mam nadzieję/ myślę, że tak; **so far** do tej pory; **and so on** i tak dalej
2 (*also*): **so do I/so am I** ja też
3 (*to such a degree*) do takiego stopnia; **so quickly/big (that)** tak szybko/duży (że); **not so clever (as)** nie tak mądry (jak)
4 (*very*) tak; **we were so worried** tak się martwiliśmy; **so much** tak bardzo; **there's so much work to do** jest tak dużo pracy do zrobienia; **I love you so much**

tak bardzo cię kocham; **so many** tak wiele; **I've got so many things to do** mam tyle rzeczy do zrobienia
5 (*linking events*) tak więc; **so I was right after all** tak więc miałem rację; **so how was your day?** więc jak minął panu/pani dzień?
6 (*in approximations*) **ten or so** dziesięć lub coś koło tego
▷ *conj* **1** (*expressing purpose*): **so (that)** aby; **I brought it so (that) she could see it** przyniosłem to, żeby mogła zobaczyć; **so as to** aby
2 (*expressing result*) więc; **he didn't come so I left** nie przyszedł, więc wyszedłem

soak [səuk] *vt* **1** (*drench*) moczyć (zmoczyć *pf*) **2** (*leave in water*) namaczać (namoczyć *pf*)
soaking ['səukɪŋ] *adj* (*also:* **~ wet**) przemoczony
soap [səup] *n* **1** mydło **2** (*also:* **~ opera**) opera mydlana
soap opera *n* opera mydlana
soap powder *n* proszek do prania
sob [sɔb] *vi* szlochać (zaszlochać *pf*)
sober ['səubə'] *adj* trzeźwy
▶ **sober up** *vi* trzeźwieć (wytrzeźwieć *pf*)
soccer ['sɔkə'] *n* piłka nożna
social ['səuʃl] *adj* **1** (*problems, change etc*) społeczny **2** (*event, function*) towarzyski
socialism ['səuʃəlɪzəm] *n* socjalizm
socialist ['səuʃəlɪst] *adj* socjalistyczny ▷ *n* socjalista(-tka)

m/f
social security (*Brit*) *n* zasiłek; **to be on ~** być na zasiłku
social worker *n* pracownik(-ica) *m/f* opieki społecznej
society [sə'saɪətɪ] *n* **1** (*people in general*) społeczeństwo **2** (*community*) towarzystwo
sociology [səusɪ'ɔlədʒɪ] *n* socjologia
sock [sɔk] *n* skarpeta
socket ['sɔkɪt] *n* (*Brit*) gniazdko elektryczne
sofa ['səufə] *n* sofa
soft [sɔft] *adj* (*towel, bed*) miękki; (*skin*) delikatny
soft drink *n* napój bezalkoholowy
software ['sɔftweə'] *n* oprogramowanie
soil [sɔɪl] *n* gleba
solar ['səulə'] *adj* słoneczny
solar power *n* energia słoneczna
sold [səuld] *pt, pp of* **sell**
soldier ['səuldʒə'] *n* żołnierz
sole [səul] *n* podeszwa
solicitor [sə'lɪsɪtə'] (*Brit*) *n* adwokat
solid ['sɔlɪd] *adj* **1** (*not soft*) twardy **2** (*without gaps*) jednolity **3** (*not liquid*) stały **4** (*pure: gold, oak*) lity
solo ['səuləu] *n* solo
solution [sə'luːʃən] *n* rozwiązanie
solve [sɔlv] *vt* **1** (*mystery, case*) wyjaśniać (wyjaśnić *pf*) **2** (*problem*) rozwiązywać (rozwiązać *pf*)

○ **KEYWORD**

some [sʌm] *adj* **1** (*a little, a few*) trochę +*gen*; **some milk/books**

troch mleka/ksiek; **would you like some wine?** moe troch wina?
2 (*certain, in contrasts*: vir) niektórzy; (*non-vir*) niektóre;
some people say that... niektórzy ludzie mówi, e...
3 (*unspecified*): **some (or other)** jaki; **we'll meet again some day** pewnego dnia spotkamy si jeszcze
▷ pron (*a certain amount, certain number*) kilka; **I've got some (books)** mam kilka (ksiek); **I've got some (milk)** mam troch (mleka); **there was/were some left** troch zostao; **some of them** (*vir*) niektórzy z nich; (*non-vir*) niektóre z nich; **could I have some of that cheese?** czy mog prosi troch tego sera?

somebody ['sʌmbədɪ] *pron* = **someone**
somehow ['sʌmhaʊ] *adv* jako
someone ['sʌmwʌn] *pron* kto; **there's ~ coming** kto idzie; **I saw ~ in the garden** widziaem kogo w ogrodzie; **~ else** kto inny
someplace ['sʌmpleɪs] (*US*) *adv* = **somewhere**
something ['sʌmθɪŋ] *pron* co; **there was obviously ~ wrong** najwidoczniej co byo nie tak; **~ else** co innego; **would you like a sandwich or ~?** chciaby pan/chciaaby pani kanapk albo co takiego?
sometime ['sʌmtaɪm] *adv* kiedy
sometimes ['sʌmtaɪmz] *adv* czasami

somewhere ['sʌmwɛəʳ] *adv* gdzie; **I need ~ to live** musz gdzie mieszka; **I must have lost it ~** musiaem to gdzie zgubi; **let's go ~ quiet** chodmy w jakie ciche miejsce; **~ else** gdzie indziej
son [sʌn] *n* syn
song [sɒŋ] *n* **1** piosenka **2** (*of bird*) piew
son-in-law ['sʌnɪnlɔ:] (*pl* **sons-in-law**) *n* zi
soon [su:n] *adv* **1** (*in a short time*) wkrótce **2** (*a short time later*) niedugo potem **3** (*early*) wczenie; **~ afterwards** wkrótce potem; **as ~ as** jak tylko; **quite ~** za niedugo; **how ~?** kiedy?; **see you ~!** do zobaczenia wkrótce!
sooner ['su:nəʳ] *adv*: **I would ~...** wolabym raczej...; **~ or later** prdzej czy póniej; **the ~ the better** im szybciej tym lepiej
sophomore ['sɒfəmɔ:ʳ] (*US*) *n* student(ka) *m/f* drugiego roku
soprano [sə'prɑ:nəʊ] *n* (*woman, girl*) sopranistka; (*boy*) sopran
sore [sɔ:ʳ] *adj* **1** (*painful*) oboly **2** (*US: inf: angry*) uraony ▷ *n* rana; **to be ~ about sth** (*US: inf*) by uraonym czym
sorry ['sɒrɪ] *adj*: **(I'm) ~!** (*apology*) przepraszam!; **~?** (*pardon?*) sucham?; **to feel ~ for sb** wspóczu komu; **to be ~ about sth** aowa czego; **I'm ~ to hear that** przykro mi to sysze
sort [sɔ:t] *n* rodzaj ▷ *vt* sortowa (posortowa *pf*); **~ of** (*inf*) w pewnym sensie; **all ~s of books/ devices** wszelkiego rodzaju ksiki/urzdzenia

▶ **sort out** vt **1** (separate)
porządkować (uporządkować pf)
2 (solve) rozwiązywać (rozwiązać
pf)
sought [sɔːt] pt, pp of **seek**
soul [səʊl] n dusza
sound [saʊnd] adj **1** (advice)
rozsądny **2** (reliable, thorough)
solidny ▷ adv: **he is ~ asleep** pi
mocno ▷ n dźwięk ▷ vt (alarm)
włączać (włączyć pf); (bell)
dzwonić (zadzwonić pf) +inst ▷ vi
1 (alarm, bell) dzwonić (zadzwonić
pf) **2** (seem) brzmieć (zabrzmieć
pf); **to make a ~** brzmieć
(zabrzmieć pf); **that ~s like an
explosion** brzmi to jak wybuch;
that ~s like a great idea to
świetny pomysł; **it ~s as if...** (fig)
wygląda na to, że...
soundtrack ['saʊndtræk] n
ścieżka dźwiękowa
soup [suːp] n zupa
sour ['saʊər] adj kwaśny; **to go**
or **turn ~** (milk, wine) kwaśnieć
(skwaśnieć pf)
south [saʊθ] n południe ▷ adj
południowy ▷ adv na południe;
in the ~ na południu; **to the ~**
na południe; **the ~ of France**
południe Francji; **~ of...** na
południe od +gen...
South Africa n Afryka
Południowa
South America n Ameryka
Południowa
south-east [saʊθ'iːst] n
południowy wschód ▷ adj
południowo-wschodni ▷ adv na
południowy wschód; **in the ~** na
południowym wschodzie
southern ['sʌðən] adj

południowy; **the ~ hemisphere**
południowa półkula
South Korea n Korea
Południowa
South Pole n: **the ~** biegun
południowy
south-west [saʊθ'wɛst]
n południowy zachód ▷ adj
południowo-zachodni ▷ adv na
południowy zachód; **in the ~** na
południowym zachodzie
souvenir [suːvə'nɪər] n pamiątka
soy [sɔɪ] (US) n soja
soya ['sɔɪə] (Brit) n soja
soy sauce n sos sojowy
space [speɪs] n **1** (gap, place)
miejsce **2** (beyond Earth) kosmos;
to clear a ~ for sth robić (zrobić
pf) miejsce dla czegoś
spacecraft ['speɪskrɑːft] (pl
spacecraft) n statek kosmiczny
spade [speɪd] n **1** (tool) łopata
2 (child's) łopatka; **spades** n pl
(Cards) piki
spaghetti [spə'gɛtɪ] n spaghetti
Spain [speɪn] n Hiszpania
spam [spæm] (Comput) n spam
Spanish ['spænɪʃ] adj hiszpański
▷ n (language) hiszpański; **the
Spanish** n pl Hiszpanie
spanner ['spænər] (Brit) n klucz
do nakrętek
spare [spɛər] adj **1** (free) wolny
2 (extra) dodatkowy ▷ n (also: ~
part) część zamienna ▷ vt (afford
to give) mieć na zbyciu
spare part n część zamienna
spare time n wolny czas
sparrow ['spærəʊ] n wróbel
spat [spæt] pt, pp of **spit**
speak [spiːk] (pt **spoke**, pp
spoken) vt (language) mówić po

+*dat* ▷ vi mówić; **to ~ to sb about sth** rozmawiać (porozmawiać *pf*) z kimś o czymś; **generally ~ing** ogólnie mówiąc; **technically ~ing** z technicznego punktu widzenia

▶ **speak up** vi: **~ up!** niech mówi pan/pani głośniej!

speaker ['spiːkə'] n 1 (*in debate*) mówca(-czyni) *m/f* 2 (*also*: **loud~**) głośnik; **a French/Russian ~** osoba znająca francuski/rosyjski

special ['spɛʃl] adj 1 (*important*) specjalny 2 (*particular*) szczególny; **we only use these plates on ~ occasions** używamy tych talerzy tylko przy specjalnych okazjach; **to take ~ care** zachowywać (zachować *pf*) szczególne środki ostrożności; **it's nothing ~** to nic szczególnego

specialist ['spɛʃəlɪst] n (*Med*) lekarz specjalista

speciality [spɛʃɪˈælɪtɪ] (*US* **specialty** ['spɛʃəltɪ]) n 1 (*food*) specjalność 2 (*subject area*) specjalizacja

specialize ['spɛʃəlaɪz] vi: **to ~ in** specjalizować (wyspecjalizować *pf*) się w *+loc*

specially ['spɛʃlɪ] adv 1 (*specifically*) specjalnie 2 (*inf: particularly*) szczególnie

special needs n pl: **children with ~** (*Brit*) dzieci specjalnej troski

specialty ['spɛʃəltɪ] (*US*) n = **speciality**

species ['spiːʃiːz] n gatunek

specific [spəˈsɪfɪk] adj 1 (*fixed*) określony 2 (*exact*) dokładny

spectacle ['spɛktəkl] n

widowisko; **spectacles** n pl (*glasses*) okulary

spectacular [spɛkˈtækjulə'] adj spektakularny

spectator [spɛkˈteɪtə'] n widz

speech [spiːtʃ] n (*talk, lecture*) przemówienie

speechless ['spiːtʃlɪs] adj oniemiały

speed [spiːd] n 1 (*rate, promptness*) prędkość 2 (*fast movement*) szybkość 3 (*rapidity*) szybkość ▷ vi (*drive too fast*) przekraczać (przekroczyć *pf*) dozwoloną prędkość; **at full** *or* **top ~** z maksymalną prędkością; **at a ~ of 70km/h** z prędkością siedemdziesiąt kilometrów na godzinę

▶ **speed up** (*pt, pp* **speeded up**) vi 1 (*car, runner etc*) przyśpieszać (przyśpieszyć *pf*) 2 (*process*) nabierać (nabrać *pf*) tempa

speedboat ['spiːdbəut] n wyścigowa łódź motorowa

speeding ['spiːdɪŋ] (*Law*) n przekroczenie dozwolonej prędkości

speed limit (*Law*) n ograniczenie prędkości

spell [spɛl] (*pt, pp* **spelled** *or* **spelt**) n 1 (*period*) okres 2 (*also*: **magic ~**) zaklęcie ▷ vt literować (przeliterować *pf*); **to cast a ~ on sb** rzucać (rzucić *pf*) na kogoś urok; **he can't ~** on robi błędy ortograficzne

spelling ['spɛlɪŋ] n (*of word*) pisownia; **~ mistake** błąd ortograficzny

spelt [spɛlt] pt, pp of **spell**

spend [spɛnd] (*pt, pp* **spent**) vt

1 (*money*) wydawać (wydać *pf*)
2 (*time, life*) spędzać (spędzić *pf*);
to ~ time/energy doing sth
spędzać (spędzić *pf*) czas/
zużywać (zużyć *pf*) siły na robienie
czegoś; **to ~ the night in a hotel**
spędzić (*pf*) noc w hotelu
spent [spɛnt] *pt, pp of* **spend**
spice [spaɪs] *n* przyprawa
spicy ['spaɪsɪ] *adj* pikantny
spider ['spaɪdə^r] *n* pająk; **~'s web**
pajęczyna
spill [spɪl] (*pt, pp* **spilt** *or* **spilled**)
vt rozlewać (rozlać *pf*) ▷ *vi*
rozlewać (rozlać *pf*) się; **to ~ sth
on/over sth** rozlewać (rozlać *pf*)
coś na coś
spinach ['spɪnɪtʃ] *n* szpinak
spine [spaɪn] *n* kręgosłup
spire ['spaɪə^r] *n* iglica
spirit ['spɪrɪt] *n* **1** (*soul*) duch
2 (*ghost*) duch **3** (*energy,
courage*) odwaga; **spirits** *n pl*
1 (*Brit: whisky etc*) alkohol *m sg*
wysokoprocentowy **2** (*frame
of mind*): **in good ~s** w dobrym
nastroju
spiritual ['spɪrɪtjuəl] *adj* **1** (*of
the spirit*) duchowy **2** (*religious*)
religijny
spit [spɪt] (*pt, pp* **spat**) *vi* spluwać
(splunąć *pf*)
▶ **spit out** *vt* wypluwać (wypluć
pf)
spite [spaɪt] *n* złośliwość; **in ~ of**
pomimo +*gen*
spiteful ['spaɪtful] *adj* złośliwy
splash [splæʃ] *n* **1** (*sound*) plusk
2 (*of liquid*) plama **3** (*of colour*)
plama ▷ *vt* ochlapywać (ochlapać
pf)
splendid ['splɛndɪd] *adj*

wspaniały
splinter ['splɪntə^r] *n* drzazga
split [splɪt] (*pt, pp* **split**) *vt*
1 (*divide*) dzielić (podzielić *pf*)
2 (*share equally*) dzielić (podzielić
pf) się +*inst* ▷ *vi* (*party, group*)
dzielić (podzielić *pf*) się
▶ **split up** *vi* rozchodzić (rozejść
pf) się
spoil [spɔɪl] (*pt, pp* **spoiled**
or **spoilt**) *vt* **1** (*damage*) psuć
(popsuć *pf*) **2** (*child*) rozpieszczać
(rozpieścić *pf*)
spoilt [spɔɪlt] *pt, pp of* **spoil** ▷ *adj*
rozpieszczony
spoke [spəuk] *pt of* **speak**
spoken ['spəukn] *pp of* **speak**
spokesman ['spəuksmən] (*irreg*)
n rzecznik
spokeswoman
['spəukswumən] (*irreg*) *n*
rzeczniczka
sponge [spʌndʒ] *n* **1** (*material*)
gąbka **2** (*for washing*) gąbka
3 (*also:* **~ cake**) biszkopt
sponsor ['spɔnsə^r] *n* sponsor
▷ *vt* **1** (*player, event*) sponsorować
2 (*Brit: for charity*) wspomagać
(wspomóc *pf*)
spontaneous [spɔn'teɪnɪəs] *adj*
spontaniczny
spooky ['spu:kɪ] (*inf*) *adj* straszny
spoon [spu:n] *n* łyżka
sport [spɔ:t] *n* sport
sportsman ['spɔ:tsmən] (*irreg*) *n*
sportowiec
sportswear ['spɔ:tswɛə^r] *n*
ubranie sportowe
sportswoman ['spɔ:tswumən]
(*irreg*) *n* sportsmenka
sporty ['spɔ:tɪ] *adj*
wysportowany

spot [spɔt] n **1** (mark) plama **2** (dot) kropka **3** (pimple) pryszcz **4** (place) miejsce ▷ vt (notice) zauważać (zauważyć pf); **on the ~** (in that place) na miejscu; (immediately) w tej samej chwili

spotless ['spɔtlɪs] adj bez skazy

spotlight ['spɔtlaɪt] n **1** (on stage) reflektor **2** (in room) światło punktowe

sprain [spreɪn] vt: **to ~ one's ankle/wrist** skręcać (skręcić pf) sobie kostkę/nadgarstek

spray [spreɪ] n (in can) spray ▷ vt **1** (liquid) rozpryskiwać (rozpryskać pf) **2** (crops) opryskiwać (opryskać pf) **3** (with paint) pryskać (prysnąć pf)

spread [sprɛd] (pt, pp **spread**) n (on bread) pasta ▷ vt **1: to ~ sth on/over** rozprowadzać (rozprowadzić pf) coś na +loc **2** (butter, jam) smarować (posmarować pf) +inst **3** (disease) roznosić (roznieść pf) ▷ vi (news) rozchodzić (rozejść pf) się; (disease) rozprzestrzeniać (rozprzestrzenić pf) się
▸ **spread out** vi rozpraszać (rozproszyć pf) się

spreadsheet ['sprɛdʃiːt] n arkusz kalkulacyjny

spring [sprɪŋ] n **1** (season) wiosna **2** (wire coil) sprężyna **3** (of water) źródło; **in (the) ~** wiosną

sprinkle ['sprɪŋkl] vt **1** (with liquid) kropić (pokropić pf) **2** (with powder) posypywać (posypać pf)

sprint [sprɪnt] n sprint ▷ vi biegać (pobiec pf) sprintem

spy [spaɪ] n szpieg ▷ vi: **to ~ on sb**

(watch) szpiegować kogoś

spying ['spaɪɪŋ] n szpiegostwo

square [skwɛər] n **1** kwadrat **2** (in town) plac ▷ adj (in shape) kwadratowy; **2 metres ~** w kształcie kwadratu o bokach o długości dwóch metrów; **2 ~ metres** dwa metry kwadratowe

squash [skwɔʃ] n **1** (Brit): **orange ~** sok pomarańczowy **2** (US: vegetable) kabaczek **3** (Sport) squash ▷ vt zgniatać (znieść pf)

squeak [skwiːk] vi **1** (door) skrzypieć (skrzypnąć pf) **2** (mouse) piszczeć (zapiszczeć pf)

squeeze [skwiːz] vt ściskać (ścisnąć pf)
▸ **squeeze out** vt wyciskać (wycisnąć pf)

squirrel ['skwɪrəl] n wiewiórka

stab [stæb] vt (person) pchnąć (pf) nożem

stable ['steɪbl] adj stały ▷ n (for horse) stajnia

stack [stæk] n sterta

stadium ['steɪdɪəm] (pl **stadia** ['steɪdɪə] or **stadiums**) n stadion

staff [stɑːf] n personel

stage [steɪdʒ] n **1** (in theatre) scena **2** (platform) estrada; **to do sth in ~s** robić coś stopniowo; **in the early/final ~s** we wczesnym/końcowym stadium

stain [steɪn] n plama ▷ vt plamić (zaplamić pf)

stainless steel ['steɪnlɪs-] n stal nierdzewna

stair [stɛər] n (step) stopień; **stairs** n pl (flight of steps) schody

staircase ['stɛəkeɪs] n klatka schodowa

stale [steɪl] adj czerstwy; (cheese)

wyschnięty

stall [stɔːl] n stragan ▷ vi (engine, car) gasnąć (zgasnąć pf); **the stalls** n pl (Brit) parter m sg

stammer ['stæmər] vi jąkać się

stamp [stæmp] n 1 (for letter) znaczek 2 (in passport etc) pieczątka ▷ vi (with foot) tupać (tupnąć pf) ▷ vt (passport, visa) stemplować (podstemplować pf); **to ~ one's foot** tupać (tupnąć pf) nogą

stand [stænd] (pt, pp **stood**) n (Brit: podium) trybuna ▷ vi 1 (be upright) stać 2 (rise) wstawać (wstać pf) 3: **to ~ aside** schodzić (zejść pf) na bok ▷ vt (bear): **I can't ~ him/it** nie znoszę go/tego; **to ~ back** odsuwać (odsunąć pf) się do tyłu
▶ **stand for** vt fus 1 (abbreviation) oznaczać 2 (tolerate): **I will not ~ for it** nie pozwolę na to
▶ **stand in for** vt fus (teacher) zastępować (zastąpić pf)
▶ **stand out** vi wyróżniać (wyróżnić pf) się
▶ **stand up** vi 1 (rise) wstawać (wstać pf) 2 (be on one's feet) wstawać (wstać pf)
▶ **stand up for** vt fus stawać (stanąć pf) w obronie +gen

standard ['stændəd] n 1 (level, quality) poziom 2 (norm, criterion) standard ▷ adj 1 (size) standardowy 2 (procedure, practice) normalny 3 (model, feature) standardowy

stank [stæŋk] pt of **stink**

staple ['steɪpl] n (for paper) zszywka ▷ vt (fasten) zszywać (zszyć pf)

star [stɑːr] n gwiazda ▷ vi: **to ~ (in)** (play, film) grać (zagrać pf) główną rolę (w +loc); **the stars** n pl (horoscope) horoskop m sg; **a 4-~ hotel** hotel czterogwiazdkowy

stare [stɛər] vi: **to ~ (at sb/sth)** wpatrywać się (w kogoś/coś)

star sign n znak zodiaku

start [stɑːt] n początek ▷ vt 1 (begin) zaczynać (zacząć pf) 2 (cause: fire, panic) powodować (spowodować pf) 3 (business) zakładać (założyć pf) 4 (engine, car) uruchamiać (uruchomić pf) ▷ vi 1 (begin) zaczynać (zacząć pf) się 2 (engine, car) zapalać (zapalić pf); **to ~ doing** or **to do sth** zaczynać (zacząć pf) coś robić
▶ **start off** vi (begin moving) ruszać (ruszyć pf) się
▶ **start out** vi (begin) zaczynać (zacząć pf) się
▶ **start up** vt zakładać (założyć pf)

starter ['stɑːtər] n (Brit) przystawka

starve [stɑːv] vi 1 (be very hungry) głodować 2 (die from hunger) umierać (umrzeć pf) z głodu; **I'm starving!** (inf) umieram z głodu!

state [steɪt] n 1 (condition) stan 2 (country) państwo 3 (part of country) stan ▷ vt (say, declare) oświadczać (oświadczyć pf); **the States** n pl (inf) Stany Zjednoczone; **~ of affairs** stan rzeczy

statement ['steɪtmənt] n oświadczenie

station ['steɪʃən] n 1 (railway station) dworzec 2 (on radio) stacja

stationary ['steɪʃnərɪ] adj

nieruchomy

stationery ['steɪʃnərɪ] n
materiały biurowe m pl

statue ['stætjuː] n posąg

stay [steɪ] n pobyt ▷ vi **1** (in
place, position) zostawać
(zostać pf) **2** (in town, hotel etc)
zatrzymywać (zatrzymać pf) się
3 (in state, situation) pozostawać
(pozostać pf) ▷ vt: **to ~ the night**
zatrzymywać (zatrzymać pf) się
na noc; **to ~ with sb** zatrzymywać
(zatrzymać pf) się u kogoś
▶ **stay in** vi zostawać (zostać pf)
w domu
▶ **stay up** vi nie kłaść (położyć pf)
się do łóżka

steady ['stedɪ] adj **1** (progress,
increase, fall) ciągły **2** (job, income)
stały **3** (reliable) solidny **4** (object,
hand) pewny **5** (look, voice)
spokojny

steak [steɪk] n stek

steal [stiːl] (pt **stole**, pp **stolen**)
vt kraść (ukraść pf) ▷ vi (be a thief)
kraść (ukraść pf); **he stole it from
me** on to mi ukradł

steam [stiːm] n para ▷ vt
gotować (ugotować pf) na parze

steel [stiːl] n stal ▷ adj stalowy

steep [stiːp] adj **1** (hill, staircase)
stromy **2** (increase, rise)
gwałtowny

steeple ['stiːpl] n wieża strzelista

steering wheel ['stɪərɪŋ-] n
kierownica

step [stɛp] n **1** (footstep) krok
2 (stage) krok **3** (of stairs) stopień
▷ vi: **to ~ forward/backward**
robić (zrobić pf) krok do przodu/
do tyłu
▶ **step aside** vi = **step down**

▶ **step back** vi: **to ~ back (from
sth)** (fig) nabierać (nabrać pf)
dystansu (do czegoś)
▶ **step down**, **step aside** vi
odsuwać (odsunąć pf) się na bok

stepbrother ['stɛpbrʌðər] n
przyrodni brat

stepdaughter ['stɛpdɔːtər] n
pasierbica

stepfather ['stɛpfɑːðər] n ojczym

stepladder ['stɛplædər] n
drabina

stepmother ['stɛpmʌðər] n
macocha

stepsister ['stɛpsɪstər] n
przyrodnia siostra

stepson ['stɛpsʌn] n pasierb

stereo ['stɛrɪəu] n zestaw stereo

sterling ['stəːlɪŋ] n funt szterling;
one pound ~ jeden funt szterling

stew [stjuː] n potrawka

steward ['stjuːəd] n steward

stewardess ['stjuːədɛs] n
stewardesa

stick [stɪk] (pt, pp **stuck**) n **1** (of
wood) kij **2** (walking stick) laska
▷ vt **1**: **to ~ sth on/to sth** (with
glue etc) przyklejać (przykleić pf)
coś na coś/do czegoś ▷ vi: **to ~
(to sth)** (stamp, sticker) przyklejać
(przykleić pf) się (do czegoś)
▶ **stick out** vi wystawać ▷ vt
(tongue, hand) wystawiać
(wystawić pf)
▶ **stick up for** vt fus bronić
(obronić pf) +gen
▶ **stick with** vt fus trzymać się
+gen

sticker ['stɪkər] n naklejka

sticky ['stɪkɪ] adj **1** (substance)
lepki **2** (tape, paper)
samoprzylepny

stiff [stɪf] *adj* **1** (*with aching muscles*) zesztywniały **2** (*competition*) ostry ▷ *adv*: **to be bored ~** nudzić się śmiertelnie; **to be scared ~** być śmiertelnie przerażonym

still [stɪl] *adj* **1** (*person, hands*) nieruchomy **2** (*Brit: not fizzy*) niegazowany ▷ *adv* **1** (*up to the present*) ciągle **2** (*possibly*) jeszcze **3** (*even*) jeszcze **4** (*yet*) jeszcze **5** (*nonetheless*) mimo to; **to stand ~** stać nieruchomo; **to keep ~** być nieruchomym; **he ~ hasn't arrived** on jeszcze nie przyjechał; **better ~** jeszcze lepiej

sting [stɪŋ] (*pt, pp* **stung**) *n* użądlenie ▷ *vt* (*insect*) żądlić (użądlić *pf*); (*nettle*) parzyć (oparzyć *pf*) ▷ *vi* (*ointment, eye, cut*) szczypać (zaszczypać *pf*)

stink [stɪŋk] (*pt* **stank**, *pp* **stunk**) *n* smród ▷ *vi* śmierdzieć

stir [stəːʳ] *vt* mieszać (zamieszać *pf*)

stitch [stɪtʃ] *n* **1** (*in sewing*) ścieg **2** (*Med*) szew ▷ *vt*: **to ~ sth to sth** przyszywać (przyszyć *pf*) coś do czegoś

stock [stɔk] *n* **1** (*supply*) zapas **2** (*in shop*) towar **3** (*gravy*) wywar ▷ *vt* (*goods*) prowadzić sprzedaż +*gen*; **in ~** w sprzedaży; **out of ~** wyprzedany
▶ **stock up** *vi*: **to ~ up (on** or **with sth)** zaopatrywać (zaopatrzyć *pf*) się (w coś)

stockbroker [ˈstɔkbrəukəʳ] *n* makler giełdowy

stock exchange *n* giełda papierów wartościowych

stockholder [ˈstɔkhəuldəʳ] (*US*)
n akcjonariusz(ka) *m/f*

stocking [ˈstɔkɪŋ] *n* pończocha

stole [stəul] *pt of* **steal**

stolen [ˈstəuln] *pp of* **steal**

stomach [ˈstʌmək] *n* **1** (*organ*) żołądek **2** (*abdomen*) brzuch

stomach ache *n* ból brzucha; **I've got ~** boli mnie brzuch

stone [stəun] *n* **1** kamień **2** (*pebble*) kamyk **3** (*Brit: in fruit*) pestka **4** (*Brit: weight*) jednostka wagi, równa sześć i trzydzieści pięć setnych kilograma

stood [stud] *pt, pp of* **stand**

stool [stuːl] *n* stołek

stop [stɔp] *vt* **1** zatrzymywać (zatrzymać *pf*) **2** (*prevent*) powstrzymywać (powstrzymać *pf*) ▷ *vi* **1** (*person, vehicle*) zatrzymywać (zatrzymać *pf*) się **2** (*rain, noise, activity*) ustawać (ustać *pf*) ▷ *n* (*for bus*) przystanek; (*for train*) stacja; **to ~ doing sth** przestawać (przestać *pf*) coś robić; **to ~ sb (from) doing sth** powstrzymywać (powstrzymać *pf*) kogoś przed zrobieniem czegoś; **~ it!** przestań!

stoplight [ˈstɔplaɪt] (*US*) *n* **1** (*in road*) czerwone światło **2** (*on vehicle*) światło stopu

store [stɔːʳ] *n* **1** (*of food*) zapas **2** (*Brit: large shop*) sklep **3** (*US: shop*) sklep ▷ *vt* (*information*) przechowywać (przechować *pf*)

storekeeper [ˈstɔːkiːpəʳ] (*US*) *n* właściciel(ka) *m/f* sklepu

storey [ˈstɔːrɪ] (*US* **story**) *n* piętro

storm [stɔːm] *n* burza

stormy [ˈstɔːmɪ] *adj* burzowy

story [ˈstɔːrɪ] *n* **1** (*account*) opowieść **2** (*tale*) historia **3** (*in*

news) artykuł **4** (*US: of building*)
= **storey**

stove [stəʊv] n **1** (*for cooking*)
kuchnia **2** (*for heating*) piecyk

straight [streɪt] adj **1** (*not
curving*) prosty **2** (*hair*)
prosty **3** (*inf: heterosexual*)
heteroseksualny ▷ adv **1** (*walk,
stand, look*) prosto **2** (*immediately*)
zaraz; **~ away, ~ off** natychmiast

straightforward [streɪt'fɔ:wəd]
adj prosty

strain [streɪn] n **1** (*pressure*)
obciążenie **2: back/muscle ~**
nadwyrężenie pleców/mięśnia
▷ vt (*back, muscle*) naprężać
(naprężyć pf)

strange [streɪndʒ] adj **1** (*odd*)
dziwny **2** (*unfamiliar*) obcy

stranger ['streɪndʒər] n obcy(-ca)
m/f

strangle ['stræŋgl] vt dusić
(udusić pf)

strap [stræp] n pasek

straw [strɔ:] n **1** słoma **2** (*drinking
straw*) słomka

strawberry ['strɔ:bərɪ] n
truskawka

stray [streɪ] adj bezpański

stream [stri:m] n strumień

street [stri:t] n ulica

streetcar ['stri:tkɑ:r] (*US*) n
tramwaj

strength [streŋθ] n **1** siła **2** (*of
object, material*) wytrzymałość

stress [strɛs] n stres ▷ vt
podkreślać (podkreślić pf)

stressful ['strɛsful] adj (*job,
situation*) stresujący

stretch [strɛtʃ] vi **1** (*person,
animal*) przeciągać (przeciągnąć
pf) się **2** (*elastic, garment*)

rozciągać (rozciągnąć pf) się ▷ vt
1 (*arm, leg*) wyciągać (wyciągnąć
pf) **2** (*elastic, garment*) naciągać
(naciągnąć pf)
▶ **stretch out** vt (*arm, leg*)
wyciągać (wyciągnąć pf)

stretcher ['strɛtʃər] n nosze m pl

strict [strɪkt] adj **1** (*rule,
instruction*) ścisły **2** (*person*) surowy

strike [straɪk] (*pt, pp* **struck**) n
strajk ▷ vt **1** (*hit: person, thing*)
uderzać (uderzyć pf) **2** (*match*)
zapalać (zapalić pf) ▷ vi **1** (*workers*)
strajkować (zastrajkować pf)
2 (*clock*) bić (wybić pf); **to be/go
on ~** strajkować (zastrajkować
pf); **the clock struck nine** zegar
wybił dziewiątą

striker ['straɪkər] n **1** (*person
on strike*) strajkujący(-ca) m/f
2 (*Football*) napastnik(-iczka) m/f

string [strɪŋ] n **1** sznurek **2** (*Mus*)
struna

string bean (*US*) n fasolka
szparagowa

strip [strɪp] n (*of paper, cloth*)
pasek ▷ vi (*undress*) rozbierać
(rozebrać pf) się

stripe [straɪp] n pas

striped [straɪpt] adj w pasy

stroke [strəʊk] n (*Med*) udar ▷ vt
(*person, animal*) głaskać (pogłaskać
pf); **a ~ of luck** łut szczęścia

stroll [strəʊl] n spacer; **to go
for a ~** chodzić/iść (pójść pf) na
spacer

stroller ['strəʊlər] (*US*) n wózek
spacerowy

strong [strɔŋ] adj **1** (*person, arms,
grip*) silny **2** (*object, material*)
mocny **3** (*wind, current*) silny

strongly ['strɔŋlɪ] adv **1** (*made,*

built) porządnie **2** (*defend, advise, argue*) mocno; **I feel ~ about it** jest to dla mnie bardzo ważne

struck [strʌk] *pt, pp of* **strike**

struggle ['strʌgl] *n* walka ▷ *vi* **1** (*try hard*) walczyć **2** (*fight*) bić (pobić *pf*) się

stubborn ['stʌbən] *adj* uparty

stuck [stʌk] *pt, pp of* **stick**
▷ *adj*: **to be ~** (*object*) być zablokowanym; (*person*) nie móc się ruszyć (poruszyć *pf*)

stud [stʌd] *n* **1** (*on clothing*) ćwiek **2** (*earring*) kolczyk **3** (*Brit: on soles of boots*) kołek

student ['stju:dənt] *n* **1** (*at university*) student(ka) *m/f* **2** (*at school*) uczeń(-ennica) *m/f*; **a law/medical ~** student(ka) *m/f* prawa/medycyny

student driver (*US*) *n* uczestnik(-iczka) *m/f* kursu prawa jazdy

studio ['stju:dɪəu] *n* **1** (*TV, Rad, Mus*) studio **2** (*of artist*) pracownia; (*of photographer*) studio

study ['stʌdɪ] *n* (*room*) gabinet
▷ *vt* studiować ▷ *vi* uczyć się

stuff [stʌf] *n* **1** (*things*) rzeczy *f pl* **2** (*substance*) coś ▷ *vt* (*Culin*) nadziewać (nadziać *pf*)

stuffing ['stʌfɪŋ] *n* (*in sofa*) materiał wypełniający; (*in chicken*) nadzienie

stuffy ['stʌfɪ] *adj* duszny

stumble ['stʌmbl] *vi* potykać (potknąć *pf*) się

stung [stʌŋ] *pt, pp of* **sting**

stunk [stʌŋk] *pp of* **stink**

stunned [stʌnd] *adj* (*shocked*) zaszokowany; **a ~ silence** grobowa cisza

stunning ['stʌnɪŋ] *adj* **1** (*impressive*) imponujący **2** (*beautiful*) olśniewający

stunt [stʌnt] *n* wyczyn kaskaderski

stupid ['stju:pɪd] *adj* głupi

stutter ['stʌtər] *vi* jąkać się

style [staɪl] *n* **1** (*type*) styl **2** (*elegance*) styl **3** (*design*) fason

stylish ['staɪlɪʃ] *adj* elegancki

subject [*n* 'sʌbdʒɪkt *n* **1** (*matter*) temat **2** (*Scol*) przedmiot **3** (*Gram*) podmiot

submarine [sʌbmə'ri:n] *n* łódź podwodna

subscription [səb'skrɪpʃən] *n* prenumerata

subsidy ['sʌbsɪdɪ] *n* dotacja

substance ['sʌbstəns] *n* substancja

substitute ['sʌbstɪtju:t] *n* **1** (*person*) osoba w zastępstwie **2** (*thing*) substytut **3** (*Football*) zawodnik rezerwowy ▷ *vt*: **to ~ sth (for sth)** zastępować (zastąpić *pf*) coś (czymś)

subtitles ['sʌbtaɪtlz] *n pl* napisy

subtle ['sʌtl] *adj* subtelny

subtract [səb'trækt] *vt*: **to ~ sth (from sth)** odejmować (odjąć *pf*) coś (od czegoś)

suburb ['sʌbə:b] *n* przedmieście; **the suburbs** *n pl* przedmieścia

subway ['sʌbweɪ] *n* **1** (*US: underground railway*) metro **2** (*Brit: underpass*) przejście podziemne

succeed [sək'si:d] *vi* (*plan*) powieść (*pf*) się; (*person*) odnosić (odnieść *pf*) sukces; **to ~ in doing sth** odnosić (odnieść *pf*) sukces w

robieniu czegoś
success [sək'sɛs] n sukces;
without ~ bez powodzenia
successful [sək'sɛsful] adj
1 (attempt) pomyślny; (film,
product) odnoszący sukcesy
2 (writer) słynny
successfully [sək'sɛsfəlɪ] adv z
powodzeniem
such [sʌtʃ] adj **1** (of this kind) taki
2 (so much) tak; **~ was his anger,
that...** był tak zły, że...; **~ a(n)**
taki; **~ a lot of** tak dużo +gen; **~ as**
(like) taki jak; **as ~** (on its own) sam
such-and-such ['sʌtʃənsʌtʃ] adj
taki a taki
suck [sʌk] vt ssać
sudden ['sʌdn] adj nagły; **all of
a ~** nagle
suddenly ['sʌdnlɪ] adv nagle
suede [sweɪd] n zamsz ▷ adj
(shoes, handbag) zamszowy
suffer ['sʌfər] vi **1** (be in pain)
cierpieć (wycierpieć pf) **2** (be badly
affected) cierpieć (ucierpieć pf)
suffocate ['sʌfəkeɪt] vi (die) dusić
(udusić pf) się
sugar ['ʃugər] n cukier
suggest [sə'dʒɛst] vt sugerować
(zasugerować pf); **to ~ that...**
sugerować (zasugerować pf), że...
suggestion [sə'dʒɛstʃən] n
sugestia; **to make a ~** sugerować
(zasugerować pf)
suicide ['suɪsaɪd] n
samobójstwo; **a ~ bomber**
zamachowiec samobójca;
to commit ~ popełnić (pf)
samobójstwo
suit [suːt] n (man's) garnitur;
(woman's) kostium ▷ vt pasować
+dat

suitable ['suːtəbl] adj **1** (time,
place) dogodny **2** (person, clothes)
odpowiedni
suitcase ['suːtkeɪs] n walizka
suite [swiːt] n apartament
sulk [sʌlk] vi dąsać się
sultana [sʌl'tɑːnə] (Brit) n
sułtanka
sum [sʌm] n suma; **to do a ~**
robić (zrobić pf) rachunki
▶ **sum up** vt sumować
(podsumować pf) ▷ vi
reasumować (zreasumować pf)
summarize ['sʌməraɪz] vt
streszczać (streścić pf)
summary ['sʌmərɪ] n
streszczenie
summer ['sʌmər] n lato ▷ adj
letni; **in (the) ~** latem
summertime ['sʌmətaɪm] n lato
summit ['sʌmɪt] n szczyt
sun [sʌn] n słońce
sunbathe ['sʌnbeɪð] vi opalać
(opalić pf) się
sunburn ['sʌnbəːn] n oparzenie
słoneczne
sunburned ['sʌnbəːnd],
sunburnt adj poparzony przez
słońce
sun cream n krem z filtrem
przeciwsłonecznym
Sunday ['sʌndɪ] n niedziela; see
also **Tuesday**
sunflower ['sʌnflauər] n
słonecznik
sung [sʌŋ] pp of **sing**
sunglasses ['sʌnglɑːsɪz] n pl
okulary przeciwsłoneczne
sunk [sʌŋk] pp of **sink**
sunlight ['sʌnlaɪt] n światło
słoneczne
sunny ['sʌnɪ] adj słoneczny; **it is**

~ jest słoneczna pogoda
sunrise ['sʌnraɪz] *n* wschód
słońca; **at ~** o wschodzie słońca
sun roof *n* (*on car*) szyberdach
sunset ['sʌnsɛt] *n* zachód słońca;
at ~ o zachodzie słońca
sunshine ['sʌnʃaɪn] *n* słońce
suntan ['sʌntæn] *n* opalenizna
▷ *adj* (*lotion, cream*) do opalania;
to get a ~ opalić (*pf*) się
super ['su:pər] (*Brit: inf*) *adj*
świetny
supermarket ['su:pɑ̄mɑːkɪt] *n*
supermarket
supernatural [su:pə'nætʃərəl]
adj nadprzyrodzony
superstitious [su:pə'stɪʃəs] *adj*
przesądny
supervise ['su:pəvaɪz] *vt*
nadzorować (*pf*)
supervisor ['su:pəvaɪzər] *n* **1** (*of
workers*) nadzorca(-czyni) *m/f* **2** (*of
student*) promotor(ka) *m/f*
supper ['sʌpər] *n* kolacja; **to
have ~** jeść (zjeść *pf*) kolację
supplement ['sʌplɪmənt] *n*
(*additional amount*) suplement
supply [sə'plaɪ] *vt* dostarczać
(dostarczyć *pf*) ▷ *n* zapas;
supplies *n pl* zapasy; **to ~
sb/sth with sth** zaopatrywać
(zaopatrzyć *pf*) kogoś/coś w coś
support [sə'pɔ:t] *n* **1** (*moral*)
wsparcie **2** (*for object, structure*)
podpora ▷ *vt* **1** (*morally*) popierać
(poprzeć *pf*) **2** (*financially*)
utrzymywać (utrzymać *pf*)
3 (*football team*) kibicować +*dat*
supporter [sə'pɔ:tər] *n* **1** (*of
politician, policy*) zwolennik(-iczka)
m/f **2** (*of team*) kibic
suppose [sə'pəuz] *vt*

przypuszczać; **I ~** przypuszczam;
he's about sixty, I ~
przypuszczam, że on ma około
sześćdziesiątki; **I ~ so/not**
przypuszczam, że tak/nie; **he's
~d to be an expert** on ma być
ekspertem
supposing [sə'pəuzɪŋ] *conj*
przypuśćmy, że
sure [ʃuər] *adj* **1** pewny
2 (*certain*): **she's ~ to do it** ona
na pewno to zrobi; **to make ~
that...** (*take action*) upewniać
(upewnić *pf*) się, że...; **~!** (*inf: of
course*) jasne!; **I'm ~ of it** jestem
tego pewien; **I'm not ~ how/
why/when** nie jestem pewien
jak/dlaczego/kiedy
surely ['ʃuəlɪ] *adv* na pewno; **~
you don't mean that!** nie chodzi
ci chyba o coś takiego!
surf [sə:f] *vi* surfować ▷ *vt*: **to
~ the internet** surfować po
Internecie
surface ['sə:fɪs] *n* powierzchnia;
on the ~ na powierzchni
surfboard ['sə:fbɔ:d] *n* deska
surfingowa
surfing ['sə:fɪŋ] *n* surfing; **to go
~** surfować
surgeon ['sə:dʒən] *n* chirurg
surgery ['sə:dʒərɪ] *n* **1** (*treatment*)
operacja **2** (*Brit: of doctor, dentist*)
przychodnia
surname ['sə:neɪm] *n* nazwisko
surprise [sə'praɪz] *n* **1** (*unexpected
event*) niespodzianka
2 (*astonishment*) zaskoczenie
▷ *vt* dziwić (zdziwić *pf*); **to my
(great) ~** ku memu (wielkiemu)
zdziwieniu
surprised [sə'praɪzd] *adj*

zdziwiony; **to be ~ to find/see
sth** ze zdziwieniem znajdować
(znaleźć pf)/zobaczyć coś
surprising [sə'praɪzɪŋ] adj
zaskakujący
surrender [sə'rɛndə^r] vi
poddawać (poddać pf) się
surround [sə'raund] vt otaczać
(otoczyć pf)
surroundings [sə'raundɪŋz] n pl
otoczenie nt sg
survey ['sə:veɪ] n sondaż
survive [sə'vaɪv] vi przeżyć pf ▷ vt
(accident, illness) przeżyć (pf)
survivor [sə'vaɪvə^r] n ocalały
suspect [n 'sʌspɛkt, vb
səs'pɛkt] n podejrzany ▷ vt
1 (person) podejrzewać 2 (sb's
motives) wątpić w; **to ~ that...**
podejrzewać, że...
suspend [səs'pɛnd] vt zawieszać
(zawiesić pf)
suspense [səs'pɛns] n
1 (uncertainty) stan niepewności
2 (in novel, film) napięcie
suspicious [səs'pɪʃəs] adj
1 (showing suspicion) podejrzliwy
2 (arousing suspicion) podejrzany
swallow ['swɔləu] vt połykać
(połknąć pf) ▷ vi przełykać
(przełknąć pf)
swam [swæm] pt of **swim**
swan [swɔn] n łabędź
swap [swɔp] vt: **to ~ sth (for)**
(exchange for) zamieniać (zamienić
pf) coś (na); (replace with)
wymieniać (wymienić pf) coś (na);
to ~ places (with sb) zamieniać
(zamienić pf) się miejscami (z
kimś)
swear [swɛə^r] (pt **swore**, pp
sworn) vi (curse) przeklinać

(przekląć pf) ▷ vt (promise)
przysięgać (przysiąc pf); **to ~
that...** (promise) przysięgać
(przysiąc pf), że...
swear word n przekleństwo
sweat [swɛt] n pot ▷ vi pocić
(spocić pf) się
sweater ['swɛtə^r] n sweter
sweatshirt ['swɛtʃə:t] n bluza
sportowa
Sweden ['swi:dn] n Szwecja
Swedish ['swi:dɪʃ] adj szwedzki
▷ n (language) szwedzki
sweep [swi:p] (pt, pp **swept**) vt
zamiatać (zamieść pf)
sweet [swi:t] n (Brit) 1 (chocolate,
mint) cukierek 2 (pudding) deser
▷ adj 1 słodki 2 (cute) uroczy; **~
and sour** słodko-kwaśny
sweetcorn ['swi:tkɔ:n] n
kukurydza
swept [swɛpt] pt, pp of **sweep**
swerve [swə:v] vi gwałtownie
skręcać (skręcić pf)
swim [swɪm] (pt **swam**, pp
swum) vi płynąć (popłynąć
pf) ▷ vt (distance) przepływać
(przepłynąć pf) ▷ n: **to go for a ~**
chodzić/iść (pójść pf) popływać
swimmer ['swɪmə^r] n
pływak(-aczka) m/f; **he's a good
~** jest dobrym pływakiem
swimming ['swɪmɪŋ] n
pływanie; **to go ~** pływać
swimming pool n basen
swimsuit ['swɪmsu:t] n kostium
kąpielowy
swing [swɪŋ] (pt, pp **swung**) n
(in playground) huśtawka ▷ vt
machać (machnąć pf) +inst ▷ vi
1 (pendulum) wahać się 2 (door)
chwiać (zachwiać pf) się

Swiss [swɪs] *adj* szwajcarski
switch [swɪtʃ] *n* ("*on*" *switch*)
włącznik; ("*off*" *switch*) wyłącznik
▷ *vt* (*change*) zmieniać (zmienić *pf*)
▶ **switch off** *vt* wyłączać
(wyłączyć *pf*)
▶ **switch on** *vt* włączać (włączyć
pf)
Switzerland ['swɪtsələnd] *n*
Szwajcaria
swollen ['swəʊlən] *adj*
spuchnięty
swop [swɔp] *n*, *vt* = **swap**
sword [sɔːd] *n* szpada
swore [swɔːʳ] *pt of* **swear**
sworn [swɔːn] *pp of* **swear**
swum [swʌm] *pp of* **swim**
swung [swʌŋ] *pt*, *pp of* **swing**
syllabus ['sɪləbəs] (*esp Brit*) *n*
program nauczania; **on the ~** w
programie nauczania
symbol ['sɪmbl] *n* symbol
sympathetic [sɪmpə'θɛtɪk] *adj*
1 (*understanding*) współczujący
2 (*supportive*) przychylny
sympathize ['sɪmpəθaɪz] *vi*: **to ~
with sb** współczuć komuś
sympathy ['sɪmpəθɪ] *n*
współczucie; **"with deepest
~"** "z wyrazami najgłębszego
współczucia"
symptom ['sɪmptəm] *n* objaw
synagogue ['sɪnəgɔg] *n*
synagoga
syringe [sɪ'rɪndʒ] *n* strzykawka
system ['sɪstəm] *n* system

t

table ['teɪbl] *n* (*piece of furniture*)
stół; **to lay** *or* **set the ~** nakrywać
(nakryć *pf*) do stołu; **to clear the
~** sprzątać (sprzątnąć *pf*) ze stołu
tablecloth ['teɪblklɔθ] *n* obrus
tablespoon ['teɪblspuːn] *n* łyżka
stołowa
tablet ['tæblɪt] *n* (*Med*) tabletka
table tennis (*Sport*) *n* ping-pong

● **TABLOID**
●
● **Tabloids** – Tabloidy to
● popularne dzienniki
● z dużą ilością zdjęć.
● Inaczej po polsku zwane
● brukowcami, szczególnym
● zainteresowaniem gazety
● te darzą sensację, sport oraz
● życie gwiazd show biznesu.

Angielskie słowo **tabloid** oznacza przede wszystkim mniejszy, poręczniejszy format, w jakim ukazują się tego typu gazety.

tact [tækt] n takt
tactful ['tæktful] adj taktowny
tactics ['tæktɪks] n pl taktyka f sg
tadpole ['tædpəul] n kijanka
taffy ['tæfɪ] (US) n toffi
tag [tæg] n (label) metka
tail [teɪl] n (of animal) ogon; **"heads or ~s?" — "~s"** "orzeł czy reszka?" — "reszka"
tailor ['teɪlə⁺] n (person) krawiec
take [teɪk] (pt **took**, pp **taken**) vt **1** (holiday, vacation) robić (zrobić pf) sobie; (shower, bath) brać (wziąć pf); (decision) podejmować (podjąć pf) **2** (take hold of: sb's arm) brać (wziąć pf) za **3** (steal) zabierać (zabrać pf) **4** (accompany: person) zabierać (zabrać pf) **5** (carry, bring: handbag, camera) zabierać (zabrać pf) **6** (travel along: road) jechać (pojechać pf) +inst **7** (car, train etc) jechać (pojechać pf) +inst **8** (size) mieć **9** (time) zabrać (zabierać pf) **10** (exam, test) zdawać **11** (drug, pill etc) brać (wziąć pf); **don't forget to ~ your umbrella** nie zapomnij zabrać parasolki; **she's not yet ~n her driving test** jeszcze nie zdawała egzaminu na prawo jazdy
▶ **take after** vt fus (resemble) przypominać (przypomnieć pf)
▶ **take apart** vt (dismantle) rozbierać (rozebrać pf)
▶ **take away** vt zabierać (zabrać pf)
▶ **take back** vt (return: goods) zwracać (zwrócić pf)
▶ **take down** vt (write down) notować (zanotować pf)
▶ **take in** vt **1** (deceive: person) omamiać (omamić pf) **2** (understand) pojmować (pojąć pf)
▶ **take off** vi (aircraft) startować (wystartować pf) ▷ vt **1** (time from work): **to ~ two days off work** brać (wziąć pf) dwa dni wolnego **2** (clothes, glasses, make-up) zdejmować (zdjąć pf)
▶ **take out** vt **1** (invite: person) zabierać (zabrać pf) **2** (remove: tooth) wyrywać (wyrwać pf)
▶ **take over** vi: **to ~ over from sb** przejmować (przejąć pf) coś od kogoś
▶ **take up** vt **1** (start: hobby, sport) zaczynać (zacząć pf) **2** (occupy: time, space) zajmować (zająć pf)
takeaway ['teɪkəweɪ] (Brit) n **1** (shop, restaurant) restauracja z jedzeniem na wynos **2** (food) jedzenie na wynos
taken ['teɪkən] pp of **take**
takeoff ['teɪkɔf] n (of plane) start
takeout ['teɪkaut] (US) n **1** (shop, restaurant) restauracja z jedzeniem na wynos **2** (food) jedzenie na wynos
tale [teɪl] n (story) opowieść
talent ['tælnt] n talent; **to have a ~ for sth** mieć talent do czegoś
talented ['tæləntɪd] adj (person, actor etc) utalentowany
talk [tɔːk] n **1** (prepared speech) wystąpienie **2** (conversation)

rozmowa **3** (*gossip*) pogłoska
4 (*discussion*) rozmowa
▷ vi **1** (*speak*) rozmawiać
(porozmawiać *pf*) **2** (*chat*)
rozmawiać (porozmawiać
pf) **3** (*gossip*) gadać; **to give
a ~** przemawiać (przemówić
pf); (*politician*) przemawiać
(przemówić *pf*); **to ~ to** or **with
sb** rozmawiać (porozmawiać *pf*) z
kimś; **to ~ about sth** rozmawiać
(porozmawiać *pf*) o czymś
▶ **talk over**, **talk through** vt
(*problem*) przedyskutowywać
(przedyskutować *pf*)
talkative ['tɔːkətɪv] *adj*
gadatliwy
talk show (*TV*, *Rad*) *n* talk show
tall [tɔːl] *adj* wysoki; **how ~ are
you?** ile ma pan/pani wzrostu?;
he's two metres ~ ma dwa metry
wzrostu
tame [teɪm] *adj* (*animal*, *bird*)
oswojony
tampon ['tæmpɔn] *n* tampon
tan [tæn] *n* (*also*: **sun~**)
opalenizna ▷ vi (*person*) opalać
(opalić *pf*) się; **to get a ~** opalić
(*pf*) się
tangerine [tændʒə'riːn] *n* (*fruit*)
mandarynka
tangle ['tæŋgl] *n* (*of branches*,
knots, *wire*) plątanina
tank [tæŋk] *n* **1** (*Mil*) czołg **2** (*for
petrol*, *water*) zbiornik **3** (*also*: **fish
~**) akwarium
tanker ['tæŋkəʳ] *n* **1** (*ship*)
tankowiec **2** (*truck*) cysterna
tanned [tænd] *adj* (*skin*, *person*)
opalony
tap [tæp] *n* **1** (*esp Brit*: *on sink*, *pipe
etc*) kran **2** (*gentle blow*) stuknięcie

tap-dancing ['tæpdɑːnsɪŋ] *n*
stepowanie
tape [teɪp] *n* **1** (*cassette*) taśma
2 (*adhesive*) taśma ▷ vt **1** (*record*)
nagrywać (nagrać *pf*) **2** (*attach*)
przyklejać (przykleić *pf*)
tape measure *n* centymetr
tape recorder *n* magnetofon
tar [tɑː] *n* (*on road etc*) smoła
target ['tɑːgɪt] *n* cel
tart [tɑːt] *n* (*cake*) tarta
tartan ['tɑːtn] *n* szkocka krata
▷ *adj* (*rug*, *scarf etc*) w szkocką
kratę
task [tɑːsk] *n* zadanie
taste [teɪst] *n* **1** smak **2** (*choice*,
liking) gust ▷ vt **1** (*get flavour of*)
smakować (posmakować *pf*) +gen
2 (*test*, *detect*) czuć (poczuć *pf*)
smak +gen ▷ vi: **to ~ of** or **like sth**
smakować jak coś
tasty ['teɪstɪ] *adj* (*food*) smaczny
tattoo [tə'tuː] *n* (*on skin*) tatuaż
taught [tɔːt] *pt*, *pp* of **teach**
Taurus ['tɔːrəs] *n* (*Astrol*) Byk
tax [tæks] *n* (*Comm*) podatek
taxi ['tæksɪ] *n* taksówka
taxi rank [-ræŋk] (*Brit*) *n* postój
taksówek
taxi stand (*US*) *n* postój
taksówek
TB *n abbr* (= *tuberculosis*) gruźlica
tea [tiː] *n* **1** (*drink*) herbata
2 (*Brit*: *evening meal*) kolacja
teach [tiːtʃ] (*pt*, *pp* **taught**)
vt: **to ~ sb sth**, **~ sth to sb** uczyć
(nauczyć *pf*) kogoś czegoś ▷ vi (*be
a teacher*) uczyć (nauczyć *pf*); **to ~
sb how to do sth** uczyć (nauczyć
pf) kogoś jak coś się robi
teacher ['tiːtʃəʳ] *n* nauczyciel(ka)
m/f

teaching ['ti:tʃɪŋ] *n* (*job*) nauczanie

team [ti:m] *n* **1** (*of people, experts*) grupa **2** (*Sport*) drużyna

teapot ['ti:pɔt] *n* imbryczek do herbaty

tear¹ [tɛə^r] (*pt* **tore**, *pp* **torn**) *n* (*rip, hole*) dziura ▷ *vt* (*rip*) drzeć (podrzeć *pf*)

▶ **tear up** *vt* (*sheet of paper, cheque*) drzeć (podrzeć *pf*)

tear² [tɪə^r] *n* (*when crying*) łza; **to burst into ~s** zalewać (zalać *pf*) się łzami

tease [ti:z] *vt* drażnić

teaspoon ['ti:spu:n] *n* (*spoon, amount*) łyżeczka

teatime ['ti:taɪm] (*Brit*) *n* pora podwieczorku

tea towel (*Brit*) *n* ścierka do naczyń

technical ['tɛknɪkl] *adj* techniczny

technician [tɛk'nɪʃən] *n* technik

technological [tɛknə'lɔdʒɪkl] *adj* technologiczny

technology [tɛk'nɔlədʒɪ] *n* technologia

teddy (bear) ['tɛdɪ(-)] *n* miś pluszowy

teenage ['ti:neɪdʒ] *adj* (*children, fashions etc*) młodzieżowy

teenager ['ti:neɪdʒə^r] *n* nastolatek(-tka) *m/f*

teens [ti:nz] *n pl*: **to be in one's ~** mieć naście lat

tee-shirt ['ti:ʃə:t] *n* = **T-shirt**

teeth [ti:θ] *n pl* of **tooth**

telephone ['tɛlɪfəun] *n* telefon

telephone book, **telephone directory** *n* książka telefoniczna

telescope ['tɛlɪskəup] *n* teleskop

television ['tɛlɪvɪʒən] *n* **1** (*also*: **~ set**) telewizor **2** (*system*) telewizja **3** (*business*) telewizja

tell [tɛl] (*pt, pp* **told**) *vt* **1** (*inform*): **to ~ sb sth** powiedzieć *pf* komuś coś **2** (*relate: story, joke*) opowiadać (opowiedzieć *pf*) **3** (*distinguish*): **to ~ sth from sth** odróżniać (odróżnić *pf*) coś od czegoś; **to ~ sb to do sth** powiedzieć komuś, żeby coś zrobił; **to ~ sb that...** powiedzieć komuś, że...

▶ **tell off** *vt*: **to ~ sb off** karcić (skarcić *pf*) kogoś

teller ['tɛlə^r] (*US*) *n* (*in bank*) kasjer(ka) *m/f*

telly ['tɛlɪ] (*Brit: inf*) *n* telewizja; **on ~** w telewizji

temper ['tɛmpə^r] *n* charakter; **to lose one's ~** tracić (stracić *pf*) panowanie nad sobą

temperature ['tɛmprətʃə^r] *n* temperatura; **to have** *or* **be running a ~** mieć temperaturę

temple ['tɛmpl] *n* (*building*) świątynia

temporary ['tɛmpərərɪ] *adj* chwilowy

temptation [tɛmp'teɪʃən] *n* pokusa

tempting ['tɛmptɪŋ] *adj* kuszący

ten [tɛn] *num* dziesięć

tend [tɛnd] *vi*: **to ~ to do sth** zwykle coś robić

tennis ['tɛnɪs] *n* tenis

tennis court *n* kort tenisowy

tennis player *n* tenisista(-tka) *m/f*

tenor ['tɛnə^r] *n* (*Mus*) tenor

tenpin bowling ['tɛnpɪn-] (*esp Brit*) *n* kręgle *pl*

tense [tɛns] adj spięty ▷ n (Ling) czas
tension ['tɛnʃən] n napięcie
tent [tɛnt] n namiot
tenth [tɛnθ] num 1 (in series) dziesiąty 2 (fraction) dziesiąta część; see also **fifth**
term [təːm] n (at school, university) trymestr; (at university) semestr; **in the short/long ~** w krótkim/długim czasie; **to be on good ~s with sb** być z kimś w dobrych relacjach; **to come to ~s with sth** godzić (pogodzić pf) się z czymś
terminal ['təːmɪnl] adj (disease, patient) śmiertelny ▷ n 1 (Comput) terminal 2 (at airport) terminal
terminally ['təːmɪnlɪ] adv: **~ ill** śmiertelnie chory
terrace ['tɛrəs] n 1 (Brit: row of houses) szeregowiec 2 (patio) taras
terraced ['tɛrəst] adj (house) szeregowy
terrible ['tɛrɪbl] adj 1 (accident, winter) okropny 2 (very poor) nędzny 3 (awful) straszny
terribly ['tɛrɪblɪ] adv 1 (very) okropnie 2 (very badly) strasznie
terrific [tə'rɪfɪk] adj świetny
terrified ['tɛrɪfaɪd] adj przerażony
terror ['tɛrə'] n przerażenie
terrorism ['tɛrərɪzəm] n terroryzm
terrorist ['tɛrərɪst] n terrorysta(-tka) m/f ▷ adj terrorystyczny
test [tɛst] n 1 (trial, check) test 2 (Med) badanie 3 (Scol) test 4 (also: **driving ~**) egzamin (na prawo jazdy) ▷ vt 1 (try out) testować (przetestować pf) 2 (Med) badać (zbadać pf) 3 (Scol) sprawdzać (sprawdzić pf)

test tube n probówka
text [tɛkst] n 1 (written material) tekst 2 (book) tekst 3 (also: **~ message**) sms ▷ vt: **to ~ sb** (on mobile phone) wysyłać (wysłać pf) komuś smsa
textbook ['tɛkstbʊk] n podręcznik
text message n sms
than [ðæn, ðən] prep (in comparisons) od +gen ▷ conj niż; **it's smaller ~ a matchbox** jest mniejszy niż pudełko od zapałek; **more/less ~ Paul** więcej/mniej niż Paul; **more ~ 20** więcej niż dwadzieścia; **she's older ~ you think** jest starsza niż się panu/pani wydaje
thank [θæŋk] vt (person) dziękować (podziękować pf) +dat; **~ you (very much)** dziękuję (bardzo); **no, ~ you** nie, dziękuję; **to ~ sb for sth/for doing sth** dziękować (podziękować pf) komuś za coś/zrobienie czegoś
thanks [θæŋks] n pl podziękowania ▷ int (inf) dzięki; **many ~, ~ a lot** dziękuję bardzo; **no, ~** nie, dziękuję; **~ to sb/sth** dzięki komuś/czemuś
Thanksgiving (Day) ['θæŋksgɪvɪŋ(-)] (US) n Święto Dziękczynienia

● **THANKSGIVING DAY**
●
● **Thanksgiving Day**
● – Święto Dziękczynienia
● przypada w USA na czwarty
● czwartek listopada, a
● w Kanadzie na drugi

- poniedziałek października.
- Według tradycji w ten
- dzień ludzie składają Bogu
- podziękowania za wszystko
- co mają. Tradycyjnym daniem
- podczas obchodów Święta
- Dziękczynienia jest indyk.

○ **KEYWORD**

that [ðæt] (pl **those**) adj (m) ten; (f) ta; (nt) to; **that man/woman/ book** ten człowiek/ta kobieta/ta książka; **that one** ten
▷ pron **1** (demonstrative) to; **who's/ what's that?** kto/co to?; **is that you?** czy to ty?; **will he eat all that?** czy zje to wszystko?; **that's my house** to mój dom; **that's it** (finished) to tyle; (exactly) właśnie **2** (relative: m) który; (f) która; (nt) które; **the girl that came in** dziewczyna, która weszła; **the man that I saw** mężczyzna, którego widziałem; **the woman that he spoke to** kobieta, z którą rozmawiał
▷ conj że; **he thought that I was ill** myślał, że jestem chory
▷ adv (so) tak; **that much/bad/ high** tak dużo/źle/wysoko

○ **KEYWORD**

the [ði:, ðə] def art **1: the man/ girl/house/book** mężczyzna/ dziewczyna/dom/książka; **the men/women/houses/books** mężczyźni/kobiety/domy/ książki; **the best solution** najlepsze rozwiązanie; **I'm going to the butcher's/the cinema** idę do rzeźnika/kina
2 (in dates, decades): **the fifth of March** piąty marca; **the nineties** lata dziewięćdziesiąte
3 (in titles): **Peter the Great** Piotr Wielki
4 (in comparisons): **the faster he works, the more mistakes he makes** im szybciej pracuje, tym więcej robi błędów

theatre ['θɪətəʳ] (US **theater**) n **1** (building) teatr **2** (entertainment) teatr **3** (Med: also: **operating ~**) sala operacyjna **4** (US: also: **movie theater**) kino
theft [θeft] n kradzież
their [ðɛəʳ] adj ich; (after prepositions) nich; (referring to subject of sentence) swój
theirs [ðɛəz] pron ich; (referring to subject of sentence) swój; **a friend of ~** ich przyjaciel
them [ðɛm, ðəm] pron **1** (direct object: vir) ich; (non-vir) je; (after preposition: vir) nich **2** (indirect object) im; (after preposition) nim
theme park ['θi:m-] n park rozrywki
themselves [ðəm'sɛlvz] pl pron **1** (gen, acc) siebie; (dat, loc) sobie; (inst) sobą; (reflexive pronoun) się **2** (emphatic: vir) sami; (non-vir) same; **they enjoyed ~** dobrze się bawili; **by ~** (unaided) sami; (alone) sami
then [ðɛn] adv **1** (at that time: past) wtedy; (future) wtedy **2** (after that) później **3** (therefore) toteż; **by ~** wtedy; **before ~** wcześniej; **until ~** do tego czasu; **since ~** od tego

czasu; **well, OK ~** no to dobrze
there [ðɛəʳ] *adv (referring to place, pointing, indicating)* tam; **they've lived ~ for 30 years** mieszkają tam od trzydziestu lat; **is Shirley ~ please?** *(on telephone)* czy jest Shirley?; **it's over ~** jest tam; **~ he is!** tam jest!; **~ you are** *(offering something)* proszę; **~ is/~ are** jest/są; **~ has been an accident** był wypadek; **~ are 3 of them** jest ich troje

therefore ['ðɛəfɔ:ʳ] *adv* dlatego

there's ['ðɛəz] = **there is, there has**

thermometer [θə'mɔmɪtəʳ] *n* termometr

these [ði:z] *pl adj (demonstrative: vir)* ci; *(non-vir)* te ▷ *pl pron (vir)* ci; *(non-vir)* te; **~ days** te dni

they [ðeɪ] *pl pron* 1 *(vir)* oni; *(non-vir)* one 2 *(in generalizations)* oni

they'd [ðeɪd] = **they had, they would**

they'll [ðeɪl] = **they shall, they will**

they're [ðɛəʳ] = **they are**

they've [ðeɪv] = **they have**

thick [θɪk] *adj* 1 *(slice, line, book, clothes etc)* gruby 2 *(sauce, mud, fog)* gęsty; **it's 20 cm ~** ma dwadzieścia centymetrów grubości

thief [θi:f] *(pl* **thieves** [θi:vz]*) n* złodziej(ka) *m/f*

thigh [θaɪ] *n* udo

thin [θɪn] *adj* 1 *(slice, line, book, material etc)* cienki 2 *(person, animal)* chudy

thing [θɪŋ] *n* 1 rzecz 2 *(matter, subject)* sprawa; **things** *n pl*

(belongings) rzeczy; **a strange ~ happened** dziwna rzecz miała miejsce; **how are ~s going?** jak sprawy?; **the ~ is...** chodzi o to, że...; **for one ~** po pierwsze; **the best ~ would be to...** najlepiej byłoby...; **first ~ (in the morning)** zaraz (rano); **last ~ (at night)** tuż przed położeniem się spać

think [θɪŋk] *(pt, pp* **thought**) *vi* myśleć (pomyśleć *pf*) ▷ *vt* myśleć (pomyśleć *pf*); **what do you ~ of...?** co pan/pani myśli o *+loc*...?; **to ~ about sth/sb** myśleć (pomyśleć *pf*) o czymś/kimś; **to ~ of doing sth** zastanawiać (zastanowić *pf*) się nad zrobieniem czegoś; **I ~ so/not** myślę, że tak/nie
▶ **think over** *vt* przemyśleć *(pf)*

third [θə:d] *num* 1 *(in series)* trzeci 2 *(fraction)* trzecia część; **a ~ of sth** jedna trzecia czegoś; *see also* **fifth**

thirdly ['θə:dlɪ] *adv* po trzecie

Third World *n*: **the ~** trzeci Świat ▷ *adj* trzeciego świata

thirst [θə:st] *n* pragnienie

thirsty ['θə:stɪ] *adj* spragniony; **I'm ~** pić mi się chce

thirteen [θə:'ti:n] *num* trzynaście; *see also* **fifteen**

thirteenth [θə:'ti:nθ] *num* trzynasty; *see also* **fifth**

thirty ['θə:tɪ] *num* trzydzieści; *see also* **fifty**

○ **KEYWORD**

this [ðɪs] *(pl* **these**) *adj* 1 *(demonstrative: m)* ten; *(f)* ta; *(nt)* to; **this man** ten człowiek;

this house ten dom; **this one is better than that one** ten jest lepszy niż tamten
2 (with days, months, years): **this Sunday/month/year** ta niedziela/ten miesiąc/ten rok ▷ pron to; **who's/what's this?** kto/co to?; **this is Janet** (in introduction) to jest Janet; (on telephone) tu Janet; **like this** jak to ▷ adv (demonstrative): **this much/high/long** tak dużo/wysoko/długo

thistle ['θɪsl] n oset
thorn [θɔːn] n cierń
thorough ['θʌrə] adj **1** (search, investigation etc) wnikliwy
2 (methodical: person) dokładny
3 (complete) całościowy
those [ðəuz] pl adj (vir) ci; (non-vir) te ▷ pl pron (vir) ci; (non-vir) te; **~ people/books** ci ludzie/te książki; **THOSE boots!** TE buty!; **are ~ yours?** czy tamte należą do pana/pani?
though [ðəu] conj (although) chociaż ▷ adv (however) jednak; **even ~** mimo że
thought [θɔːt] pt, pp of **think** ▷ n (idea) myśl
thoughtful ['θɔːtful] adj **1** (deep in thought) zamyślony **2** (considerate) troskliwy
thoughtless ['θɔːtlɪs] adj bezmyślny
thousand ['θauzənd] num: **a or one ~** tysiąc; **~s of sth** tysiące czegoś
thousandth ['θauzəntθ] num (in series) tysięczny
thread [θrɛd] n (yarn) nić

threat [θrɛt] n groźba
threaten ['θrɛtn] vi (storm, danger) grozić (zagrozić pf) ▷ vt grozić (zagrozić pf) +dat; **to ~ to do sth** grozić (zagrozić pf), że coś się zrobi
three [θriː] num trzy; see also **five**
three-quarters [θriːˈkwɔːtəz] n pl trzy czwarte ▷ adv: **~ full/empty** w trzech czwartych pełny/pusty ▷ pron trzy czwarte; **~ of an hour** trzy kwadranse
threw [θruː] pt of **throw**
thriller ['θrɪlər] n dreszczowiec
thrilling ['θrɪlɪŋ] adj (performance, news etc) pasjonujący
throat [θrəut] n gardło; **to have a sore ~** mieć ból gardła
through [θruː] prep przez ▷ adj (ticket, train) bezpośredni; **(from) Monday ~ Friday** (US) (od) poniedziałku do piątku
throughout [θruːˈaut] prep przez ▷ adv **1** (everywhere) wszędzie
2 (the whole time) przez cały czas
throw [θrəu] (pt, pp **thrown** [θrəun]) vt **1** rzucać (rzucić pf) **2** (fig: confuse) zaskakiwać (zaskoczyć pf)
▶ **throw away** vt **1** (rubbish) wyrzucać (wyrzucić pf)
2 (opportunity) marnować (zmarnować pf)
▶ **throw out** vt wyrzucać (wyrzucić pf)
▶ **throw up** (inf) vi (vomit) wymiotować (zwymiotować pf)
thru [θruː] (US) = **through**
thumb [θʌm] n (on hand) kciuk
thumbtack ['θʌmtæk] (US) n

pinezka

thump [θʌmp] *vt (hit)* walić (walnąć *pf*)

thunder ['θʌndə^r] *n (in sky)* grzmot

thunderstorm ['θʌndəstɔːm] *n* burza

Thursday ['θəːzdɪ] *n* czwartek; *see also* **Tuesday**

tick [tɪk] *n* **1** *(esp Brit: mark)* ptaszek **2** *(Brit: inf: moment)* sekunda ▷ *vi (clock, watch)* tykać ▷ *vt (esp Brit: item on list)* odhaczać (odhaczyć *pf*)
▶ **tick off** *vt (esp Brit: item on list)* odhaczać (odhaczyć *pf*)

ticket ['tɪkɪt] *n* **1** bilet **2** *(Aut: also:* **parking ~**) mandat za złe parkowanie

ticket inspector *n (on train, bus)* konduktor(ka) *m/f*

ticket office *n* kasa biletowa

tickle ['tɪkl] *vt (person)* łaskotać (połaskotać *pf*)

tide [taɪd] *n (incoming tide)* przypływ; *(outgoing tide)* odpływ; **high/low ~** przypływ/odpływ

tidy ['taɪdɪ] *adj* uporządkowany ▷ *vt (also:* **~ up**) sprzątać (posprzątać *pf*)
▶ **tidy up** *vt, vi* sprzątać (posprzątać *pf*)

tie [taɪ] *n* **1** *(clothing)* krawat **2** *(esp Brit: Sport: match)* spotkanie **3** *(draw: in competition)* remis ▷ *vt (also:* **~ up**: *shoelaces etc)* wiązać (zawiązać *pf*)
▶ **tie up** *vt* **1** *(parcel etc)* wiązać (zawiązać *pf*) **2** *(dog)* uwiązywać (uwiązać *pf*) **3** *(person)* przywiązywać (przywiązać *pf*)

tiger ['taɪgə^r] *n* tygrys

tight [taɪt] *adj* **1** *(shoes, clothes)* ciasny **2** *(budget, schedule)* napięty; *(security, controls)* surowy ▷ *adv (hold, squeeze, shut)* mocno

tighten ['taɪtn] *vt* **1** *(rope, strap)* dociskać (docisnąć *pf*) **2** *(screw, bolt)* dokręcać (dokręcić *pf*)

tightly ['taɪtlɪ] *adv (firmly)* mocno

tights [taɪts] *(Brit) n pl* rajstopy

tile [taɪl] *n* **1** *(on roof)* dachówka **2** *(on floor, wall)* płytka

till [tɪl] *n (Brit: in shop etc)* kasa ▷ *prep, conj* = **until**

timber ['tɪmbə^r] *(Brit) n* drewno

time [taɪm] *n* **1** czas **2** *(period)* czas **3** *(by clock)* pora **4** *(occasion)* raz; **to have a good/bad ~** dobrze/źle się bawić; **to spend one's ~ doing sth** spędzać (spędzić *pf*) czas coś robiąc; **three ~s a day** trzy razy dziennie; **three ~s the size of sth** trzy razy większy niż coś; **all the ~** przez cały czas; **from ~ to ~** od czasu do czasu; **at the same ~** *(nevertheless)* o tej samej porze; *(simultaneously)* równolegle; **at ~s** *(sometimes)* czasami; **she arrived in ~ for the start** zdążyła w sam raz na początek; **in a week's/month's ~** za tydzień/miesiąc; **any ~** kiedykolwiek; **on ~** na czas; **5 ~s 5 is 25** pięć razy pięć jest dwadzieścia pięć; **what ~ is it?, what's the ~?** która godzina?; **~ off** *(from work)* czas wolny; **to take ~** zabierać (zabrać *pf*) sporo czasu

timetable ['taɪmteɪbl] *n* **1** *(Brit: Rail etc)* rozkład jazdy **2** *(Brit: Scol)* plan lekcji **3** *(programme of events)*

harmonogram
tin [tɪn] n **1** (metal) cyna
2 (Brit: can) puszka **3** (for biscuits, tobacco etc) pudełko
tin opener [-əupnəʳ] (Brit) n otwieracz do puszek
tiny ['taɪnɪ] adj mały
tip [tɪp] n **1** (of branch, paintbrush etc) czubek **2** (to waiter) napiwek
3 (Brit: for rubbish) wysypisko
4 (advice) porada ▷ vt **1** (waiter) dawać (dać pf) napiwek +dat
2 (pour) wylewać (wylać pf)
tiptoe ['tɪptəu] vi chodzić na palcach; **on ~** na paluszkach
tire ['taɪəʳ] n (US) = **tyre**
tired ['taɪəd] adj zmęczony; **to be ~ of doing sth** być zmęczonym robieniem czegoś
tiring ['taɪərɪŋ] adj męczący
tissue ['tɪʃuː] n chusteczka
title ['taɪtl] n tytuł

○ **KEYWORD**

to [tuː, tə] prep **1** (direction) do +gen; **to France/London/school** do Francji/Londynu/szkoły; **to the station** na stację
2 (as far as): **from here to London** stąd do Londynu
3 (position, direction) na; **to the left/right** na lewo/prawo
4 (in time expressions): **it's five/ten/a quarter to five** jest za pięć/dziesięć/kwadrans piąta
5 (for, of) do +gen; **a letter to his wife** list do jego żony
6 (indirect object): **to give sth to sb** dawać (dać pf) coś komuś; **to talk to sb** mówić do kogoś; **it was clear to me that...** było dla

mnie jasne, że...; **damage to sth** zniszczenie czegoś; **a danger to sb** niebezpieczeństwo dla kogoś
7 (towards): **to be friendly/kind/loyal to sb** być przyjacielskim/miłym/lojalnym wobec kogoś
8 (in relation to): **30 miles to the gallon** trzydzieści mil na galon; **three goals to two** trzy gole do dwóch
9 (purpose, result): **to come to sb's aid** pomagać (pomóc pf) komuś
10 (indicating range, extent): **from... to...** od +gen... do +gen...; **from May to September** od maja do września
▷ with verb **1** (simple infinitive) forma bezokolicznikowa; **to go/eat** iść/jeść
2 (with vb omitted): **I don't want to** nie chcę
3 (in order to) aby; **I did it to help you** zrobiłem to, aby panu/pani pomóc
4 (equivalent to relative clause): **I have things to do** mam coś do roboty
5 (after adjective): **to be ready to go** być gotowym do wyjścia; **too old/young to do sth** zbyt stary/młody aby coś zrobić
6 (and): **he awoke/arrived to find that everyone had gone** obudził się/przyjechał i dowiedział się, że wszyscy już poszli; **to and fro** tam i z powrotem

toad [təud] n ropucha
toast [təust] n **1** (Culin) tost
2 (drink) toast; **a piece** or **slice of ~** kromka chleba tostowego; **to**

drink a ~ to sb pić (wypić pf) toast za kogoś

toaster ['təustə'] n toster

tobacco [tə'bækəu] n tytoń

tobacconist's (shop) [tə'bækənɪsts-] n sklep tytoniowy

today [tə'deɪ] adv dzisiaj ▷ n dziś; **what day is it ~?** który jest dzisiaj?; **~ is the 4th of March** dziś jest czwarty marca

toddler ['tɒdlə'] n dziecko raczkujące

toe [təu] n 1 (of foot) palec 2 (of shoe) nosek; (of sock) palec; **big/little ~** duży/mały palec

toffee ['tɒfɪ] n toffi

together [tə'gɛðə'] adv razem; **~ with** razem z +inst

toilet ['tɔɪlət] n toaleta; **to go to the ~** (esp Brit) iść (pójść pf) do toalety

toilet paper n papier toaletowy

toiletries ['tɔɪlətrɪz] n pl przybory toaletowe

toilet roll n rolka papieru toaletowego

told [təuld] pt, pp of **tell**

toll [təul] n 1 (of casualties, accidents) liczba 2 (on road, bridge) opłata

tomato [tə'mɑːtəu] (pl **tomatoes**) n pomidor

tomorrow [tə'mɔrəu] adv jutro ▷ n jutro; **the day after ~** pojutrze; **~ morning** jutro rano

ton [tʌn] n 1 (Brit) tona 2 (US: also: **short ~**) tona

tongue [tʌn] n (Anat) język

tonic ['tɒnɪk] n (also: **~ water**) tonik

tonight [tə'naɪt] adv dziś wieczorem

tonsil ['tɒnsl] n migdałek

tonsillitis [tɒnsɪ'laɪtɪs] n zapalenie migdałków

too [tuː] adv 1 (excessively) za 2 (also) też; **you're from Brooklyn? Me ~!** pan/pani jest z Brooklynu? Ja też!; **~ bad!** bardzo niedobrze!

took [tuk] pt of **take**

tool [tuːl] n (implement) narzędzie

tooth [tuːθ] (pl **teeth**) n (Anat) ząb

toothache ['tuːθeɪk] n ból zęba; **to have ~** mieć ból zęba

toothbrush ['tuːθbrʌʃ] n szczoteczka do zębów

toothpaste ['tuːθpeɪst] n pasta do zębów

top [tɒp] n 1 (of mountain) szczyt; (of building, tree, stairs) góra 2 (of page) góra 3 (of surface, table) góra 4 (lid: of box, jar, bottle) przykrywka 5 (blouse) bluzka ▷ adj 1 (shelf, step, storey, marks) wysoki 2 (executive, golfer) najlepszy; **~ speed** największa prędkość; **at the ~ of the stairs/page** na górze schodów/strony; **at the ~ of the street** na końcu ulicy; **on ~ of** (in addition to) w dodatku +gen; **from ~ to bottom** z dołu do góry; **to be ~** or **come ~** być najlepszym

topic ['tɒpɪk] n temat

torch [tɔːtʃ] n (Brit) latarka

tore [tɔː'] pt of **tear**[1]

torn [tɔːn] pp of **tear**[1]

tortoise ['tɔːtəs] n żółw

torture ['tɔːtʃə'] n tortura ▷ vt torturować

total ['təutl] adj całkowity ▷ n suma; **in ~** w sumie

totally ['təutəlɪ] adv całkowicie

touch [tʌtʃ] n (contact) dotyk
▷ vt 1 (with hand, foot) dotykać
(dotknąć pf) +gen 2 (tamper
with) majstrować przy +loc
3 (move: emotionally) poruszać
(poruszyć pf) ▷ vi (be in contact)
dotykać (dotknąć pf); **to be/keep
in ~ (with sb)** pozostawać
(pozostać pf) w kontakcie (z
kimś); **to get in ~ with sb**
kontaktować (skontaktować pf)
się z kimś; **to lose ~ (with sb)**
tracić (stracić pf) kontakt (z kimś)
▶ **touch down** vi (aircraft)
lądować (wylądować pf)
tough [tʌf] adj 1 (material) mocny
2 (meat) twardy 3 (person, animal)
mocny 4 (difficult) ciężki 5 (rough)
niebezpieczny
tour ['tuə'] n 1 (journey) wycieczka
2 (of town, factory, museum)
wycieczka 3 (by pop group, sports
team etc) trasa ▷ vt (country, city
etc) zwiedzać (zwiedzić pf); **to
go on a ~ of** (region) zwiedzać
(wiedzieć pf)
tourism ['tuərɪzm] n turystyka
tourist ['tuərɪst] n turysta(-tka)
m/f ▷ adj (season, attraction)
turystyczny
tow [təu] vt (vehicle, trailer)
holować (odholować pf)
▶ **tow away** vt (vehicle)
odholować (pf)
toward(s) [tə'wɔːd(z)] prep 1 (in
direction of: lit) do +gen 2 (near) w
pobliżu +gen 3 (as contribution to)
na rzecz +gen
towel ['tauəl] n ręcznik
tower ['tauə'] n wieża
tower block (Brit) n wieżowiec
town [taun] n miasto

town hall (Brit) n ratusz
tow truck (US) n (breakdown lorry)
samochód pomocy drogowej
toy [tɔɪ] n zabawka ▷ adj (train,
car etc) zabawkowy
trace [treɪs] n ślad ▷ vt
(draw: picture) kalkować
(przekalkować pf)
track [træk] n 1 (path) ścieżka
2 (Rail) tor 3 (Mus) ścieżka
4 (Sport) tor
▶ **track down** vt (prey, criminal)
śledzić (wyśledzić pf)
tracksuit ['træksuːt] (Brit) n dres
tractor ['træktə'] n traktor
trade [treɪd] n 1 (buying and
selling) handel 2 (skill, job) branża
▷ vt (exchange): **to ~ sth (for sth)**
(esp US) wymieniać (wymienić pf)
coś (na coś)
trademark ['treɪdmɑːk] n znak
firmowy
trade union (esp Brit) n związek
zawodowy
tradition [trə'dɪʃən] n tradycja
traditional [trə'dɪʃənl] adj
tradycyjny
traffic ['træfɪk] n (vehicles) ruch
traffic circle (US) n rondo
traffic jam n korek
traffic lights n pl światła uliczne
traffic warden [-wɔːdn] (esp
Brit) n funkcjonariusz(ka) m/f
kontrolujący(-ca) prawidłowość
parkowania
tragedy ['trædʒədɪ] n tragedia
tragic ['trædʒɪk] adj tragiczny
trailer ['treɪlə'] n 1 (Aut)
przyczepa 2 (US: caravan)
przyczepa kempingowa 3 (Cine,
TV) zwiastun
train [treɪn] n (Rail) pociąg ▷ vt

1 (*teach skills to*) uczyć (nauczyć *pf*) **2** (*athlete*) trenować (wytrenować *pf*) ▷ vi **1** (*learn a skill*) uczyć (nauczyć *pf*) się **2** (*Sport*) trenować (wytrenować *pf*)

trained [treɪnd] *adj* (*worker, teacher*) wykwalifikowany

trainee [treɪ'niː] *n* praktykant(ka) *m/f*

trainer ['treɪnə'] *n* **1** (*Sport*) trener(ka) *m/f* **2** (*Brit: shoe*) tenisówka

training ['treɪnɪŋ] *n* **1** (*for occupation*) szkolenie **2** (*Sport*) trening

training course *n* kurs szkoleniowy

tram [træm] (*Brit*) *n* (*also:* **~car**) tramwaj

tramp [træmp] *n* kloszard

trampoline ['træmpəliːn] *n* trampolina

transfer ['trænsfə'] *n* **1** (*flow: of information*) przepływ; (*of money*) przelew **2** (*Sport*) transfer **3** (*Brit: picture, design*) nadruk

transit ['trænzɪt] *n* **1: in ~** (*people*) w drodze **2** (*US*) transport

translate [trænz'leɪt] *vt* (*word, book etc*) tłumaczyć (przetłumaczyć *pf*)

translation [trænz'leɪʃən] *n* tłumaczenie

translator [trænz'leɪtə'] *n* tłumacz(ka) *m/f*

transparent [træns'pærnt] *adj* prześwitujący

transplant [*vb* træns'plɑːnt, *n* 'trænsplɑːnt] *vt* (*Med: organ*) przeszczepiać (przeszczepić *pf*) ▷ *n* (*Med: operation*) przeszczep

transport [*n* 'trænspɔːt,

vb træns'pɔːt] *n* (*transportation*) transport ▷ *vt* (*move*) transportować (przetransportować *pf*); **public ~** (*esp Brit*) transport publiczny

transportation ['trænspɔː'teɪʃən] *n* (*US: transport*) transport

trap [træp] *n* (*for animals*) pułapka ▷ *vt* **1** (*animal*) łapać (złapać *pf*) **2** (*in building*) zatrzymywać (zatrzymać *pf*)

trash [træʃ] *n* **1** (*US*) śmieć **2** (*pej: tasteless stuff*) szmira

trash can (*US*) *n* kosz na śmieci

travel ['trævl] *n* (*travelling*) podróż ▷ *vi* (*person*) podróżować ▷ *vt* (*distance*) przemierzać (przemierzyć *pf*)

travel agency [-eɪdʒənsɪ] *n* biuro podróży

travel agent *n* **1** (*shop, office*) biuro podróży **2** (*person*) pracownik(-ica) *m/f* biura podróży

traveller ['trævlə'] (*US* **traveler**) *n* podróżnik(-iczka) *m/f*

traveller's cheque (*US* **traveler's check**) *n* czek podróżny

travelling ['trævlɪŋ] (*US* **traveling**) *n* podróżowanie

travel sickness *n* choroba lokomocyjna

tray [treɪ] *n* taca

tread [trɛd] (*pt* **trod**, *pp* **trodden**) *vi* stąpać (stąpnąć *pf*)
  ▸ **tread on** *vt fus* stąpać (stąpnąć *pf*) po +*loc*

treasure ['trɛʒə'] *n* (*gold, jewels etc*) skarb

treat [triːt] *n* przyjemność ▷ *vt* **1** (*behave towards: person, object*)

traktować (potraktować *pf*)
2 (*Med: patient, illness*) leczyć
(wyleczyć *pf*); **to ~ sb to sth**
fundować (zafundować *pf*)
komuś coś

treatment ['tri:tmənt] *n* (*Med*)
leczenie

treble ['trɛbl] *vi* potrajać (potroić
pf) się

tree [tri:] *n* drzewo

tremble ['trɛmbl] *vi* drżeć
(zadrżeć *pf*)

tremendous [trɪ'mɛndəs] *adj*
1 (*enormous*) ogromny **2** (*excellent*)
wspaniały

trend [trɛnd] *n* **1** (*tendency*)
tendencja **2** (*fashion*) trend

trendy ['trɛndɪ] (*inf*) *adj* modny

trial ['traɪəl] *n* (*Law*) proces; **on
~** (*Law*) sądzony; (*on approval*)
testowany

triangle ['traɪæŋgl] *n* (*Math*)
trójkąt

tribe [traɪb] *n* plemię

trick [trɪk] *n* **1** (*by conjuror*)
sztuczka **2** (*deception*) podstęp
3 (*skill, knack*) trik ▷ *vt* (*deceive*)
oszukiwać (oszukać *pf*); **to play
a ~ on sb** oszukiwać (oszukać
pf) kogoś

tricky ['trɪkɪ] *adj* (*job, problem*)
trudny

tricycle ['traɪsɪkl] *n* rower na
trzech kółkach

trim [trɪm] *vt* (*cut: hair, beard*)
przycinać (przyciąć *pf*)

trip [trɪp] *n* **1** (*journey*) podróż
2 (*outing*) wycieczka ▷ *vi* (*also: ~
up: stumble*) potykać (potknąć
pf) się; **to go on a ~** wybierać
(wybrać *pf*) się na wycieczkę

triple ['trɪpl] *adj* potrójny ▷ *vi*

potrajać (potroić *pf*) się

triplets ['trɪplɪts] *n pl* trojaczki

triumph ['traɪʌmf] *n* triumf

trivial ['trɪvɪəl] *adj* trywialny

trod [trɒd] *pt of* **tread**

trodden ['trɒdn] *pp of* **tread**

trolley ['trɒlɪ] *n* **1** (*Brit: for
luggage, in supermarket*) wózek
2 (*US: vehicle*) tramwaj

trombone [trɒm'bəʊn] *n* puzon

troop [tru:p] *n* (*of people, animals*)
grupa; **troops** *n pl* (*Mil*) wojska

trophy ['trəʊfɪ] *n* trofeum

tropical ['trɒpɪkl] *adj* tropikalny

trouble ['trʌbl] *n* kłopot; **to be
in ~** (*with police, authorities*) mieć
kłopoty; (*ship, climber etc*) mieć
problemy; **the ~ is...** problem
w tym, że...; **stomach/back ~**
kłopoty z żołądkiem/kręgosłupem

troublemaker ['trʌblmeɪkə^r] *n*
osoba siejąca zamęt

trousers ['traʊzəz] (*Brit*) *n pl*
spodnie; **a pair of ~** para spodni

trout [traʊt] *n* pstrąg

truant ['truənt] *n:* **to play ~**
chodzić (pójść *pf*) na wagary

truck [trʌk] *n* (*esp US*) ciężarówka

truck driver (*esp US*) *n* kierowca
ciężarówki

true [tru:] *adj* (*story, motive,
feelings*) prawdziwy; **to come ~**
stawać (stać *pf*) się prawdą

truly ['tru:lɪ] *adv* **1** (*genuinely*)
prawdziwie **2** (*for emphasis*)
naprawdę **3** (*truthfully*) naprawdę;
yours ~ (*in letter*) z poważaniem

trumpet ['trʌmpɪt] *n* trąbka

trunk [trʌŋk] *n* **1** (*of tree*) pień
2 (*of elephant*) trąba **3** (*case*) kufer
4 (*US: of car*) bagażnik; **trunks** *n pl*
(*also:* **swimming ~s**) kąpielówki

trust [trʌst] *vt* ufać (zaufać *pf*)
+*dat*
truth [truːθ] (*pl* **truths** [truːðz])
n prawda
try [traɪ] *n* próba ▷ *vt* próbować
(spróbować *pf*) +*gen* ▷ *vi* (*make
effort*) próbować (spróbować
pf); **to have a ~ at sth, give sth
a ~** próbować (spróbować *pf*)
czegoś; **to ~ to do sth, ~ doing
sth** próbować (spróbować *pf*)
coś zrobić
▶ **try on** *vt* (*dress, hat, shoes*)
mierzyć (zmierzyć *pf*)
▶ **try out** *vt* (*test*) wypróbowywać
(wypróbować *pf*)
T-shirt [ˈtiːʃəːt] *n* T-shirt
tub [tʌb] *n* **1** (*container*) kubek
2 (*US*) wanna
tube [tjuːb] *n* **1** (*pipe*) rura
2 (*container*) tubka **3** (*Brit*): **the ~**
(*underground*) metro
tuberculosis [tjubəːkjuˈləusɪs]
n gruźlica
Tuesday [ˈtjuːzdɪ] *n* wtorek;
it is ~ 23rd March jest wtorek
dwudziesty trzeci marca; **on ~**
we wtorek; **on ~s** we wtorki;
every ~ co wtorek; **last/next ~**
w zeszły/następny wtorek; **on ~
morning/afternoon/evening**
we wtorek rano/po południu/
wieczorem
tuition [tjuːˈɪʃən] *n* **1** nauka
2 (*fees*) czesne
tulip [ˈtjuːlɪp] *n* tulipan
tumble dryer [ˈtʌmbl-] (*Brit*) *n*
suszarka do ubrań
tummy [ˈtʌmɪ] (*inf*) *n* brzuszek
tuna [ˈtjuːnə] *n* (*also*: **~ fish**)
tuńczyk
tune [tjuːn] *n* (*melody*) melodia;

to be in ~ (*instrument*) być
nastrojonym; (*singer*) śpiewać
(zaśpiewać *pf*) czysto; **to be
out of ~** (*instrument*) nie być
nastrojonym; (*singer*) fałszować
(sfałszować *pf*)
Tunisia [tjuːˈnɪzɪə] *n* Tunezja
tunnel [ˈtʌnl] *n* tunel
Turkey [ˈtəːkɪ] *n* Turcja
turkey [ˈtəːkɪ] *n* indyk
Turkish [ˈtəːkɪʃ] *adj* turecki ▷ *n*
(*language*) turecki
turn [təːn] *n* **1** (*in road*) zakręt
2 (*in game, queue, series*) kolej
▷ *vt* **1** (*part of body*) przekręcać
(przekręcić *pf*) **2** (*object*) obracać
(obrócić *pf*) **3** (*handle, key*)
przekręcać (przekręcić *pf*) **4** (*page*)
przewracać (przewrócić *pf*) ▷ *vi*
1 (*rotate: object, wheel*) obracać
(obrócić *pf*) się **2** (*change direction*)
skręcać (skręcić *pf*); **it's my ~ to...**
moja kolej, aby...; **to take it in
~s to do sth** robić (zrobić *pf*) coś
po kolei
▶ **turn around** *vi* = **turn round**
▶ **turn back** *vi* zawracać
(zawrócić *pf*)
▶ **turn down** *vt* **1** (*request, offer*)
odrzucać (odrzucić *pf*) **2** (*heat,
sound*) przykręcać (przykręcić *pf*)
▶ **turn into** *vt fus* zmieniać
(zmienić *pf*) się w
▶ **turn off** *vt* **1** (*light, radio*)
gasić (zgasić *pf*); (*tap*) zakręcać
(zakręcić *pf*) **2** (*engine*) gasić
(zgasić *pf*)
▶ **turn on** *vt* **1** (*light, radio*)
włączać (włączyć *pf*); (*tap*)
odkręcać (odkręcić *pf*) **2** (*engine*)
zapalać (zapalić *pf*)
▶ **turn out** *vt* (*light, gas*) wyłączać

(wyłączyć *pf*); **to ~ out to be**
(*prove to be*) okazywać (okazać
pf) się
▶**turn round, turn around**
vi **1** (*person, vehicle*) zawracać
(zawrócić *pf*) **2** (*rotate*) obracać
(obrócić *pf*) się ▷ *vt* (*person,
vehicle*) zawracać (zawrócić *pf*)
▶**turn up** *vi* **1** (*arrive: person*)
przychodzić (przyjść *pf*) **2** (*be
found: lost object*) znajdować
(znaleźć *pf*) się ▷ *vt* (*radio, heater
etc*) podkręcać (podkręcić *pf*)
turning ['tə:nɪŋ] *n* (*in road*) zakręt
turnip ['tə:nɪp] *n* rzepa
turn signal (*US*) *n*
kierunkowskaz
turquoise ['tə:kwɔɪz] *n* (*stone*)
turkus ▷ *adj* (*colour*) turkusowy
turtle ['tə:tl] (*Brit*) *n* żółw
tutor ['tju:təʳ] *n* **1** (*Brit: Scol*)
nauczyciel(ka) *m/f* **2** (*private tutor*)
korepetytor(ka) *m/f* ▷ *vt* (*teach*)
uczyć (nauczyć *pf*); **she ~s adults
in arithmetic** uczy dorosłych
arytmetyki
tuxedo [tʌk'si:dəu] (*US*) *n*
smoking
TV *n abbr* (= *television*) TV
tweezers ['twi:zəz] *n pl* pęseta
f sg; **a pair of ~** pęseta
twelfth [twɛlfθ] *num* **1** (*in series*)
dwunasty **2** (*fraction*) dwunasta
część; *see also* **fifth**
twelve [twɛlv] *num* dwanaście;
at ~ (o'clock) (*midday*) o
dwunastej w południe; (*midnight*)
o dwunastej w nocy; *see also* **five**
twentieth ['twɛntɪɪθ] *num*
dwudziesty
twenty ['twɛntɪ] *num*
dwadzieścia; **~-one** dwadzieścia

jeden; *see also* **fifty**
twice [twaɪs] *adv* dwa razy; **~
as much/long as** dwa razy
więcej/dłużej niż
twin [twɪn] *adj* (*sister, brother*)
bliźniaczy ▷ *n* **1** (*person*)
bliźnię **2** (*also:* **~ room**) pokój
dwuosobowy z dwoma łóżkami
twist [twɪst] *vt* **1** (*turn*) przekręcać
(przekręcić *pf*) **2** (*injure: ankle etc*)
skręcać (skręcić *pf*) **3** (*fig: meaning,
words*) przekręcać (przekręcić *pf*)
two [tu:] *num* dwa; *see also* **five**
two-percent milk [tu:pə'sɛnt-]
(*US*) *n* mleko o dwóch procentach
zawartości tłuszczu
type [taɪp] *n* **1** (*category, example*)
typ **2** (*sort, kind*) typ **3** (*Typ*)
czcionka ▷ *vt, vi* (*on computer*)
pisać (napisać *pf*) na komputerze
typewriter ['taɪpraɪtəʳ] *n*
maszyna do pisania
typical ['tɪpɪkl] *adj* (*behaviour,
weather etc*) typowy
typist ['taɪpɪst] *n* maszynistka
tyre ['taɪəʳ] (*US* **tire**) *n* opona
tyre pressure (*US* **tire pressure**)
n ciśnienie w oponach

u

UFO *n abbr* (= *unidentified flying object*) UFO

ugly ['Aglı] *adj* **1** (*person, dress, building*) brzydki **2** (*situation, incident*) paskudny

UK *n abbr* (= *United Kingdom*): **the UK** Zjednoczone Królestwo Wielkiej Brytanii i Irlandii Północnej

ulcer ['Alsər] *n* wrzód

umbrella [Am'brelə] *n* parasol

umpire ['Ampaıər] *n* arbiter

UN *n abbr* (= *United Nations*): **the UN** ONZ

unable [An'eıbl] *adj*: **to be ~ to do sth** nie być w stanie czegoś zrobić

unanimous [juː'nænıməs] *adj* (*decision*) jednomyślny

unavoidable [Anə'vɔıdəbl] *adj* (*delay, job losses etc*) nieunikniony

unbearable [An'bɛərəbl] *adj* (*heat, pain*) nie do wytrzymania

unbelievable [Anbı'liːvəbl] *adj* **1** (*implausible*) niewiarygodny **2** (*amazing*) niesamowity

unbreakable [An'breıkəbl] *adj* niezniszczalny

uncertain [An'səːtn] *adj* (*future, outcome*) niepewny; **to be ~ about sth** być niepewnym czegoś

uncle ['Aŋkl] *n* wujek

uncomfortable [An'kAmfətəbl] *adj* niewygodny

unconscious [An'kɔnʃəs] *adj* (*not awake*) nieprzytomny

uncontrollable [Ankən'trəuləbl] *adj* **1** (*person*) nieokiełznany **2** (*temper, laughter*) niepohamowany

under ['Andər] *prep* **1** (*beneath*) pod +*inst* **2** (*less than: age, price*) poniżej +*gen* ▷ *adv*: **children aged 12 and ~** dzieci w wieku lat dwunastu i młodsze

under-age [Andər'eıdʒ] *adj* (*person*) niepełnoletni

underground ['Andəgraund] *n*: **the ~** (*Brit: railway*) metro ▷ *adj* podziemny

underline [Andə'laın] (*Brit*) *vt* podkreślać (podkreślić *pf*)

underneath [Andə'niːθ] *adv* (*below*) pod spodem ▷ *prep* pod +*inst*

underpants ['Andəpænts] *n pl* slipy

underpass ['Andəpɑːs] *n* (*for pedestrians*) przejście podziemne

undershirt ['Andəʃəːt] (*US*) *n* podkoszulek

understand [Andə'stænd]

(*pt, pp* **understood**) *vt* rozumieć (zrozumieć *pf*)

understanding [ʌndə'stændɪŋ] *adj* wyrozumiały

understood [ʌndə'stud] *pt, pp of* **understand**

undertaker ['ʌndəteɪkə^r] (*Brit*) *n* przedsiębiorca pogrzebowy

underwater ['ʌndə'wɔːtə^r] *adv* (*swim etc*) pod wodą

underwear ['ʌndəwɛə^r] *n* bielizna

undo [ʌn'duː] (*pt* **undid**, *pp* **undone**) *vt* (*shoelaces, knot*) rozwiązywać (rozwiązać *pf*); (*buttons, trousers*) rozpinać (rozpiąć *pf*)

undress [ʌn'drɛs] *vi* rozbierać (rozebrać *pf*) się ▷ *vt* rozbierać (rozebrać *pf*)

uneasy [ʌn'iːzɪ] *adj* (*worried*) niepewny; **to be ~ about sth** być niepewnym czegoś

unemployed [ʌnɪm'plɔɪd] *adj* (*person*) bezrobotny ▷ *n pl*: **the ~** bezrobotni

unemployment [ʌnɪm'plɔɪmənt] *n* bezrobocie

unexpected [ʌnɪks'pɛktɪd] *adj* nieoczekiwany

unexpectedly [ʌnɪks'pɛktɪdlɪ] *adv* nieoczekiwanie

unfair [ʌn'fɛə^r] *adj* niesprawiedliwy; **to be ~ to sb** być niesprawiedliwym dla kogoś

unfamiliar [ʌnfə'mɪlɪə^r] *adj* (*place, person, subject*) nieznany

unfashionable [ʌn'fæʃnəbl] *adj* (*clothes, ideas, place*) niemodny

unfit [ʌn'fɪt] *adj* (*physically*) nie w formie; **to be ~ for sth/to do sth** być niezdolnym do czegoś/do

zrobienia czegoś; **~ for work** niezdolny do pracy; **~ for human consumption** nienadający się do spożycia przez ludzi

unfold [ʌn'fəuld] *vt* (*sheet, map*) rozkładać (rozłożyć *pf*)

unforgettable [ʌnfə'gɛtəbl] *adj* niezapomniany

unfortunately [ʌn'fɔːtʃənətlɪ] *adv* niestety

unfriendly [ʌn'frɛndlɪ] *adj* (*person*) nieprzyjazny

ungrateful [ʌn'greɪtful] *adj* niewdzięczny

unhappy [ʌn'hæpɪ] *adj* nieszczęśliwy

unhealthy [ʌn'hɛlθɪ] *adj* niezdrowy

uniform ['juːnɪfɔːm] *n* mundur; **in ~** w mundurze

uninhabited [ʌnɪn'hæbɪtɪd] *adj* niezamieszkany

union ['juːnjən] *n* (*also:* **trade ~**) związek zawodowy

Union Jack *n* flaga brytyjska

unique [juː'niːk] *adj* **1** (*individual: number, pattern etc*) jedyny w swoim rodzaju **2** (*distinctive: ability, skill, performance*) wyjątkowy

unit ['juːnɪt] *n* **1** (*single whole*) jedność **2** (*group, centre*) sekcja **3** (*measurement*) jednostka **4** (*in course book*) część

United Kingdom *n*: **the ~** Zjednoczone Królestwo Wielkiej Brytanii i Irlandii Północnej

United Nations *n*: **the ~** Organizacja Narodów Zjednoczonych

United States (of America) *n*: **the ~** Stany Zjednoczone

(Ameryki Północnej)
universe ['juːnɪvəːs] n
wszechświat
university [juːnɪ'vəːsɪtɪ] n
uniwersytet ▷ adj uniwersytecki;
to go to ~ chodzić na studia
unkind [ʌn'kaɪnd] adj niemiły; **to
be ~ to sb** być niemiłym dla kogoś
unknown [ʌn'nəʊn] adj
nieznany
unleaded [ʌn'lɛdɪd] adj
bezołowiowy ▷ n paliwo
bezołowiowe
unless [ʌn'lɛs] conj chyba, że
unlikely [ʌn'laɪklɪ] adj mało
prawdopodobny: **he is ~ to win**
jest mało prawdopodobne, że
on wygra
unload [ʌn'ləʊd] vt
rozładowywać (rozładować pf)
unlock [ʌn'lɔk] vt (door, car,
suitcase) otwierać (otworzyć pf)
unlucky [ʌn'lʌkɪ] adj 1 (person)
mający pecha 2 (object, number)
pechowy
unmarried [ʌn'mærɪd] adj
(woman) niezamężna; (man)
nieżonaty
unnatural [ʌn'nætʃrəl] adj (not
normal) nienaturalny
unnecessary [ʌn'nɛsəsərɪ] adj
niekonieczny
unpack [ʌn'pæk] vi
rozpakowywać (rozpakować
pf) się ▷ vt (suitcase, bag)
rozpakowywać (rozpakować pf)
unpleasant [ʌn'plɛznt] adj
(experience, task, situation)
nieprzyjemny; (person, manner)
niemiły
unplug [ʌn'plʌg] vt wyłączać
(wyłączyć pf) z sieci

unpopular [ʌn'pɔpjʊləʳ] adj
(person, decision) niepopularny
unrealistic ['ʌnrɪə'lɪstɪk] adj
nierealny; **it is ~ to expect that...**
nie można oczekiwać, że...
unreasonable [ʌn'riːznəbl] adj
1 (person, attitude) niedorzeczny
2 (decision) nierozsądny 3 (price,
amount) wygórowany
unreliable [ʌnrɪ'laɪəbl] adj
1 (person, firm) niesolidny
2 (machine, method) zawodny
unroll [ʌn'rəʊl] vt rozwijać
(rozwinąć pf)
unscrew [ʌn'skruː] vt (lid, cap)
odkręcać (odkręcić pf)
unsuccessful [ʌnsək'sɛsful] adj
1 (attempt) nieudany; (application)
odrzucony 2 (person, applicant)
odrzucony
unsuitable [ʌn'suːtəbl]
adj 1 (place, time, clothes)
nieodpowiedni 2 (candidate,
applicant) niewłaściwy; **to be ~
for sth** nie nadawać (nadać pf) się
do czegoś
untidy [ʌn'taɪdɪ] adj 1 (room)
nieporządny 2 (person, appearance)
niechlujny
untie [ʌn'taɪ] vt rozwiązywać
(rozwiązać pf)
until [ən'tɪl] prep do +gen ▷ conj
aż; **~ now** aż do teraz; **~ then** aż
do tego czasu
unusual [ʌn'juːʒʊəl] adj
1 (strange) niezwykły 2 (distinctive)
nadzwyczajny
unwilling [ʌn'wɪlɪŋ] adj: **to be
~ to do sth** być niechętnym do
zrobienia czegoś
unwrap [ʌn'ræp] vt
rozpakowywać (rozpakować pf)

○ KEYWORD

up [ʌp] prep 1 (to higher point on) na; **he went up the stairs/the hill/the ladder** wszedł na schody/górę/drabinę

2 (along: road, river) wzdłuż +gen

3 (at higher point on) na górze; **up the road** trochę dalej; **they live further up the street** mieszkali trochę dalej przy tej ulicy

▷ adv 1 (towards higher point) na/w górę; **the lift only goes up to the 12th floor** winda dochodzi tylko do dwunastego piętra

2 (at higher point) na górze; **up here/there** tutaj/tam

3: **to be up** (be out of bed) wstawać (wstać pf)

4 (to/in the north) do +gen, na +acc; **he often comes up to Scotland** on często przyjeżdża do Szkocji

5 (approaching): **to go/come up (to sb)** podchodzić (podejść pf) (do kogoś); **to run up (to sb)** podbiegać (podbiec pf) (do kogoś)

6: **up to** do +gen; **I can spend up to £100** mogę wydać do stu funtów; **up to 100 people** aż do stu osób

7: **up to** or **until** aż do +gen; **I'll be here up to** or **until 5.30 pm** będę tu do siedemnastej trzydzieści; **up to now** do chwili obecnej

8: **it is up to you** to zależy od pana/pani

9: **to feel up to doing sth** czuć się na siłach coś zrobić

10 (in other expressions): **to be up against sth/sb** napotykać (napotkać pf) coś/kogoś

update [vb ʌp'deɪt, n 'ʌpdeɪt] vt aktualizować (zaktualizować pf)

▷ n aktualizacja

uphill ['ʌp'hɪl] adv w górę

upper ['ʌpəʳ] adj górny

● **UPPER SIXTH**
●
●
● **Upper sixth** to drugi z dwóch
● ostatnich lat szkoły średniej
● (**secondary school**), kiedy to
● uczniowie przygotowują się
● do egzaminów **A-levels**.

upright ['ʌpraɪt] adv prosto

upset [vb ʌp'sɛt, n 'ʌpsɛt] (pt, pp **upset**) vt (make unhappy: person) zasmucać (zasmucić pf)

▷ adj 1 (unhappy) zasmucony

2 (stomach) chory ▷ n: **to have a stomach ~** (Brit) mieć rozstrój żołądka; **to be ~ about sth** martwić (zmartwić pf) się czymś

upside down [ʌpsaɪd-] adv (hang, hold, turn) do góry nogami

upstairs [ʌp'stɛəz] adv 1 (be) na górze 2 (go) na górę

up-to-date ['ʌptə'deɪt] adj (modern) aktualny

upwards ['ʌpwədz] adv w górę

urgent ['ɜːdʒənt] adj (letter, message etc) pilny

US n abbr (= United States): **the US** USA

us [ʌs] pron (gen, acc, loc) nas; (dat) nam; (inst) nami

USA n abbr (= United States of America): **the ~** USA

use [n juːs, vb juːz] n (purpose) zastosowanie ▷ vt 1 (object, tool) używać (użyć pf) +gen 2 (word, *phrase*) używać (użyć *pf*) +*gen*; **to make ~ of sth** używać (użyć *pf*) czegoś; **it's no ~** to na nic; **it's no ~ crying/arguing** nie ma co płakać/się kłócić; **to be no ~ (to sb)** być nieprzydatnym (dla kogoś); **to have a ~ for sth** mieć dla czegoś zastosowanie; **she ~d to do it** dawniej to robiła; **I didn't ~ to** *or* **I ~d not to worry so much** dawniej nie martwiłem się tak; **to be ~d to sth/to doing sth** być przyzwyczajonym do czegoś/do robienia czegoś; **to get ~d to sth/to doing sth** przyzwyczajać (przyzwyczaić *pf*) się do czegoś/ do robienia czegoś

▶ **use up** *vt* zużywać (zużyć *pf*)

used [juːzd] *adj* (*car*) używany

useful ['juːsful] *adj* przydatny; **to be ~ for sth/doing sth** być przydatnym do czegoś/do zrobienia czegoś; **it's ~ to keep a diary** warto prowadzić dziennik; **to come in ~** przydawać (przydać *pf*) się

useless ['juːslɪs] *adj* **1** (*unusable*) bezużyteczny **2** (*pointless*) bezcelowy **3** (*inf: hopeless*) beznadziejny; **to be ~ at sth/at doing sth** (*inf*) być beznadziejnym w czymś/w robieniu czegoś

user ['juːzəʳ] *n* (*of product, service*) użytkownik(-iczka) *m/f*

user-friendly ['juːzə'frɛndlɪ] *adj* przyjazny dla użytkownika

usual ['juːʒʊəl] *adj* (*time, place etc*) zwykły; **as ~** jak zwykle; **warmer/colder than ~** cieplej/ zimniej niż zwykle

usually ['juːʒʊəlɪ] *adv* zazwyczaj

V

vacancy ['veɪkənsɪ] *n* (*job*) wakat; (*hotel room*) wolny pokój; **"no vacancies"** "nie ma wolnych miejsc"

vacant ['veɪkənt] *adj* (*seat, bathroom*) wolny

vacation [vəˈkeɪʃən] *n* **1** (*esp US*) urlop **2** (*at university etc*) wakacje *pl*; **to take a ~** brać (wziąć *pf*) urlop; **to be on ~** być na wakacjach; **to go on ~** jechać (pojechać *pf*) na wakacje

vaccinate ['væksɪneɪt] *vt*: **~ sb (against sth)** szczepić (zaszczepić *pf*) kogoś (przeciwko czemuś)

vacuum ['vækjum] *vt* (*room, carpet etc*) odkurzać (odkurzyć *pf*)

vacuum cleaner *n* (*also*: **vacuum**) odkurzacz

vagina [və'dʒaɪnə] n pochwa
vague [veɪg] adj niejasny
vain [veɪn] adj (conceited: person) próżny; **in ~** na próżno
Valentine's Day ['væləntaɪnz-] n dzień Świętego Walentego
valid ['vælɪd] adj 1 (ticket, document) ważny 2 (argument, reason) uzasadniony
valley ['vælɪ] n dolina
valuable ['væljuəbl] adj cenny
value ['vælju:] n 1 (financial worth) wartość 2 (importance) waga
van [væn] n (Aut) furgonetka
vandal ['vændl] n wandal
vandalism ['vændəlɪzəm] n wandalizm
vandalize ['vændəlaɪz] vt dewastować (zdewastować pf)
vanilla [və'nɪlə] n wanilia
vanish ['vænɪʃ] vi znikać (zniknąć pf)
variety [və'raɪətɪ] n 1 (diversity) różnorodność 2 (range) wybór
various ['vɛərɪəs] adj (several) różny
vary ['vɛərɪ] vt (make changes to) urozmaicać (urozmaicić pf) ▷ vi (be different) różnić się +inst
vase [vɑ:z, US veɪs] n wazon
VAT [vi:eɪ'ti:, væt] (Brit) n abbr (= value added tax) VAT
VCR n abbr (= video cassette recorder) magnetowid
VDT (US) n abbr (= visual display terminal) monitor
VDU (Brit) n abbr (= visual display unit) monitor
veal [vi:l] n cielęcina
vegan ['vi:gən] n weganin(ka) m/f
vegetable ['vɛdʒtəbl] n warzywo

vegetarian [vɛdʒɪ'tɛərɪən] n wegetarianin(-anka) m/f ▷ adj wegetariański
vehicle ['vi:ɪkl] n pojazd
vein [veɪn] n (in body) żyła
velvet ['vɛlvɪt] n aksamit
vending machine ['vɛndɪŋ-] n automat (z napojami, słodyczami itd)
verb [və:b] n czasownik
verdict ['və:dɪkt] n 1 (Law) orzeczenie 2 (opinion) opinia
versus ['və:səs] prep przeciwko +dat
vertical ['və:tɪkl] adj pionowy
very ['vɛrɪ] adv bardzo; **at the ~ end/beginning** na samym końcu/początku; **~ much so** zdecydowanie tak; **~ little** bardzo mało; **there isn't ~ much (of...)** jest niezbyt dużo (+gen...); **I like him ~ much** bardzo go lubię
vest [vɛst] n 1 (Brit: underwear) podkoszulek 2 (US: waistcoat) kamizelka
vet [vɛt] n 1 (esp Brit: veterinary surgeon) weterynarz 2 (US: inf: veteran) kombatant(ka) m/f
veterinarian [vɛtrɪ'nɛərɪən] (US) n weterynarz
veterinary surgeon ['vɛtrɪnərɪ-] (formal: Brit) n weterynarz
via ['vaɪə] prep przez
vicar ['vɪkəʳ] n pastor
vicious ['vɪʃəs] adj 1 (attack, blow) wściekły 2 (person, dog) zły
victim ['vɪktɪm] n ofiara; **to be the ~ of** być ofiarą +gen
victory ['vɪktərɪ] n zwycięstwo
video ['vɪdɪəu] n 1 (film) wideo

2 (*system*) wideo **3** (*cassette*)
kaseta wideo **4** (*esp Brit: machine*)
magnetowid ▷ *vt* (*esp Brit*)
nagrywać (nagrać *pf*) na wideo
video camera *n* kamera wideo
video game *n* gra wideo
video recorder *n* magnetowid
Vietnam ['vjɛt'næm] *n* Wietnam
view [vju:] *n* **1** (*from window,
hilltop etc*) widok **2** (*opinion*)
pogląd
viewer ['vju:əʳ] *n* (*of TV*) widz
viewpoint ['vju:pɔɪnt] *n*
1 (*attitude*) punkt widzenia
2 (*place*) punkt obserwacyjny
vile [vaɪl] *adj* okropny
villa ['vɪlə] *n* **1** (*in countryside*)
rezydencja **2** (*in town*) willa
village ['vɪlɪdʒ] *n* wioska
vine [vaɪn] *n* winorośl
vinegar ['vɪnɪgəʳ] *n* ocet
vineyard ['vɪnjɑːd] *n* winnica
viola [vɪ'əʊlə] *n* altówka
violence ['vaɪələns] *n* przemoc
violent ['vaɪələnt] *adj* (*person*)
agresywny; (*crime*) brutalny
violin [vaɪə'lɪn] *n* skrzypce
violinist [vaɪə'lɪnɪst] *n*
skrzypek(-paczka) *m/f*
virgin ['vɜːdʒɪn] *n* dziewica
Virgo ['vɜːgəʊ] *n* (*Astrol*) Panna
virtual reality *n* rzeczywistość
wirtualna
virus ['vaɪərəs] (*Med, Comput*)
n wirus
visa ['viːzə] *n* wiza
visible ['vɪzəbl] *adj* **1** (*able to be
seen*) widoczny **2** (*fig: noticeable*)
wyraźny
visit ['vɪzɪt] *n* **1** (*to person*) wizyta
2 (*to place*) pobyt ▷ *vt* **1** (*person*)
odwiedzać (odwiedzić *pf*) **2** (*place*)

odwiedzać (odwiedzić *pf*)
▶ **visit with** (*US*) *vt fus* odwiedzać
(odwiedzić *pf*)
visitor ['vɪzɪtəʳ] *n* **1** (*to city,
country*) osoba przyjezdna **2** (*to
person, house*) gość
visual ['vɪzjuəl] *adj* wizualny
vital ['vaɪtl] *adj* (*essential*)
niezbędny
vitamin ['vɪtəmɪn, *US* vaɪtəmɪn]
n witamina
vivid ['vɪvɪd] *adj* **1** (*description,
memory*) żywy **2** (*colour, light*)
jaskrawy
vocabulary [vəʊ'kæbjʊlərɪ]
n **1** (*of person*) zasób słów **2** (*of
language*) słownictwo
vocational [vəʊ'keɪʃənl] *adj*
zawodowy
vodka ['vɔdkə] *n* wódka
voice [vɔɪs] *n* głos
voice mail *n* poczta głosowa
volcano [vɔl'keɪnəʊ] (*pl*
volcanoes) *n* wulkan
volleyball ['vɔlɪbɔːl] *n* siatkówka
volume ['vɔljuːm] *n* (*sound level*)
głośność; **~ one/two** (*of book*)
tom pierwszy/drugi
voluntary ['vɔləntərɪ] *adj* **1** (*not
compulsory*) dobrowolny **2** (*work,
worker*) ochotniczy **3** (*organization*)
społeczny
volunteer [vɔlən'tɪəʳ] *n*
ochotnik(-iczka) *m/f* ▷ *vt* **to ~ to
do sth** zgłaszać (zgłosić *pf*) się na
ochotnika do robienia (zrobienia
pf) czegoś
vomit ['vɔmɪt] *n* wymiociny
pl ▷ *vt* (*blood etc*) wymiotować
(zwymiotować *pf*) +*inst* ▷ *vi*
wymiotować (zwymiotować *pf*)
vote [vəʊt] *n* głos ▷ *vt*: **to**

~ Labour/Green głosować (zagłosować *pf*) na Partię Pracy/Zielonych ▷ *vi* głosować (zagłosować *pf*); **to ~ to do sth** głosować (zagłosować *pf*) za zrobieniem czegoś; **to ~ for sb** głosować (zagłosować *pf*) na kogoś; **to ~ for sth** głosować (zagłosować *pf*) za czymś; **to ~ against sth** głosować (zagłosować *pf*) przeciwko czemuś

voucher ['vautʃəʳ] *n* kupon

vowel ['vauəl] *n* samogłoska

vulgar ['vʌlgəʳ] *adj* (*rude: person, joke, gesture*) wulgarny

wage [weɪdʒ] *n* (*also:* **~s**) zarobki *m pl*

waist [weɪst] *n* **1** pas **2** (*of clothing*) talia

waistcoat ['weɪskəut] (*Brit*) *n* kamizelka

wait [weɪt] *vi* czekać (poczekać *pf*) ▷ *n* (*interval*) okres oczekiwania; **to ~ for sb/sth** czekać (poczekać *pf*) na kogoś/coś; **I can't ~** *or* **I can hardly ~ to tell her** nie mogę się doczekać jak jej powiem; **~ a minute!** poczekaj chwilę!; **to keep sb ~ing** kazać komuś czekać
  ▸ **wait up** *vi* nie kłaść (położyć *pf*) się spać

waiter ['weɪtəʳ] *n* kelner

waiting list ['weɪtɪŋ-] *n* lista oczekujących

waiting room ['weɪtɪŋ-] n poczekalnia

waitress ['weɪtrɪs] n kelnerka

wake [weɪk] (pt, pp **woke**)
▶ **wake up** vt budzić (obudzić pf)
▷ vi budzić (obudzić pf) się

Wales [weɪlz] n Walia; **the Prince of ~** książę Walii

walk [wɔːk] n spacer ▷ vi chodzić/iść (pójść pf) ▷ vt (distance) przechodzić (przejść pf); **to go for a ~** chodzić/iść (pójść pf) na spacer; **to take the dog for a ~** wyprowadzać (wyprowadzić pf) psa na spacer; **it's 10 minutes' ~ from here** stąd idzie się dziesięć minut

walking ['wɔːkɪŋ] n spacerowanie

walking stick n laska

Walkman® ['wɔːkmən] n walkman

wall [wɔːl] n 1 (of building, room) ściana 2 (around garden, field) mur

wallet ['wɔlɪt] n portfel

wallpaper ['wɔːlpeɪpəʳ] n tapeta ▷ vt tapetować (wytapetować pf)

walnut ['wɔːlnʌt] n orzech włoski

wander ['wɔndəʳ] vi (roam) przechadzać się

want [wɔnt] vt 1 (wish for) chcieć +gen 2 (inf: need) potrzebować +gen; **to ~ to do sth** chcieć coś robić (zrobić pf); **to ~ sb to do sth** chcieć, aby ktoś coś zrobił

war [wɔːʳ] n wojna

ward [wɔːd] n (in hospital) oddział

wardrobe ['wɔːdrəub] n szafa

warehouse ['wɛəhaus] n magazyn

warm [wɔːm] adj ciepły; **it's ~** jest ciepło; **are you ~ enough?** czy jest panu/pani wystarczająco ciepło?
▶ **warm up** vi (athlete, pianist etc) rozgrzewać (rozgrzać pf) się ▷ vt 1 (food) podgrzewać (podgrzać pf) 2 (person) ogrzewać (ogrzać pf)

warn [wɔːn] vt: **to ~ sb that** ostrzegać (ostrzec pf) kogoś, że; **to ~ sb not to do sth** ostrzegać (ostrzec pf) kogoś przed zrobieniem czegoś

warning ['wɔːnɪŋ] n 1 (action, words, sign) ostrzeżenie 2 (notice) zapowiedź

wart [wɔːt] n brodawka

was [wɔz] pt of **be**

wash [wɔʃ] vt 1 (clothes) prać (uprać pf) 2 (dishes, paintbrush) myć (umyć pf) ▷ vi (person) myć (umyć pf) się ▷ n (clean) mycie; **to ~ one's face/hands/hair** myć (umyć pf) twarz/ręce/włosy; **to have a ~** myć (umyć pf) się
▶ **wash up** vi 1 (Brit: wash dishes) zmywać (pozmywać pf) 2 (US: have a wash) myć (umyć pf) się

washbasin ['wɔʃbeɪsn] n umywalka

washcloth ['wɔʃklɔθ] (US) n myjka (do twarzy)

washing ['wɔʃɪŋ] n 1 (dirty) rzeczy do prania 2 (clean) pranie; **to do the ~** robić (zrobić pf) pranie

washing machine n pralka

washing powder (Brit) n proszek do prania

washing-up [wɔʃɪŋ'ʌp] (Brit) n brudne naczynia pl; **to do the ~** zmywać (pozmywać pf) naczynia

washing-up liquid (Brit) n płyn

do zmywania naczyń

wasn't ['wɔznt] = **was not**

wasp [wɔsp] n osa

waste [weɪst] n **1** (of resources, food, money) marnowanie **2** (rubbish) śmieci m pl ▷ vt (money, energy, time, opportunity) marnować (zmarnować pf); **it's a ~ of time** to strata czasu

wastepaper basket ['weɪstpeɪpə-] (Brit) n kosz na śmieci

watch [wɔtʃ] n (wristwatch) zegarek ▷ vt **1** (look at: people, objects) patrzeć (popatrzeć pf) na **2** (match, programme, TV) oglądać (obejrzeć pf) **3** (pay attention to) uważać na ▷ vi patrzeć (popatrzeć pf); **to ~ sb do/doing sth** patrzeć (popatrzeć pf) jak ktoś coś robi ▶ **watch out** vi uważać; **~ out!** (inf) uważaj!

water ['wɔːtə^r] n woda ▷ vt (plant) podlewać (podlać pf); **a drink of ~** szklanka wody

waterfall ['wɔːtəfɔːl] n wodospad

watering can ['wɔːtərɪŋ-] n konewka

watermelon ['wɔːtəmɛlən] n arbuz

waterproof ['wɔːtəpruːf] adj wodoodporny

water-skiing ['wɔːtəskiːɪŋ] n: **to go ~** jeździć na nartach wodnych

wave [weɪv] n **1** (of hand) machnięcie **2** (on water) fala ▷ vi (gesture) machać (pomachać pf) ▷ vt (motion with: hand) machać (pomachać pf) +inst; **to give sb a ~** machać (pomachać pf) do kogoś; **to ~ goodbye to sb, ~ sb**

goodbye machać (pomachać pf) komuś na pożegnanie

wax [wæks] n wosk

way [weɪ] n **1** (route) droga **2** (path, access) ścieżka **3** (distance) odległość **4** (direction) kierunek **5** (manner, method) sposób ▷ adv (far, a lot) dużo; **ways** n pl (habits) nawyki; **"which ~?"** — **"this ~"** "którędy?" — "tędy"; **on the ~** w drodze; **it's a long ~ away** to daleko stąd; **to lose one's ~** gubić (zgubić pf) drogę; **the ~ back** droga powrotna; **to give ~** (break, collapse) upadać (upaść pf); (stop resisting) poddawać (poddać pf) się; **the wrong ~ round** tyłem na przód; **in a ~** w pewnym sensie; **by the ~** a propos; **"~ in"** (Brit) "wejście"; **"~ out"** (Brit) "wyjście"; **~ of life** sposób życia; **do it this ~** zrób to w ten sposób

we [wiː] pl pron my

weak [wiːk] adj słaby

wealthy ['wɛlθɪ] adj bogaty

weapon ['wɛpən] n (lit) broń

wear [wɛə^r] (pt **wore**, pp **worn**) vt nosić; **I can't decide what to ~** nie mogę się zdecydować, w co się ubrać ▶ **wear out** vi przecierać (przetrzeć pf) się

weather ['wɛðə^r] n pogoda; **what's the ~ like?** jaka jest pogoda?

weather forecast n prognoza pogody

web [wɛb] n **1** (spider's) pajęczyna **2**: **the W~** internet; **on the W~** w internecie

web page n strona internetowa

website ['wɛbsaɪt] *n* witryna internetowa

we'd [wiːd] = **we had, we would**

wedding ['wɛdɪŋ] *n* (*ceremony*) ślub; (*reception*) wesele

Wednesday ['wɛdnzdɪ] *n* środa; *see also* **Tuesday**

weed [wiːd] *n* chwast

week [wiːk] *n* tydzień; **this/ next/last ~** w tym/przyszłym/ zeszłym tygodniu; **once/twice a ~** raz/dwa razy w tygodniu; **in two ~s' time** za dwa tygodnie

weekday ['wiːkdeɪ] *n* dzień powszedni; **on ~s** w dni powszednie

weekend [wiːk'ɛnd] *n* weekend; **at the ~** w weekend; **this/next/ last ~** w ten/następny/poprzedni weekend

weigh [weɪ] *vt* ważyć (zważyć *pf*) ▷ *vi*: **she ~s 50kg** ona waży pięćdziesiąt kg

weight [weɪt] *n* 1 waga 2 (*heavy object*) ciężarek; **weights** *n pl* (*in gym*) ciężarki; **to lose ~** tracić (stracić *pf*) na wadze; **to put on ~** przybierać (przybrać *pf*) na wadze

weightlifting ['weɪtlɪftɪŋ] *n* podnoszenie ciężarów

weird [wɪəd] *adj* dziwny

welcome ['wɛlkəm] *n* powitanie ▷ *vt* 1 (*visitor, speaker etc*) witać (powitać *pf*) 2 (*news, change etc*) witać (powitać *pf*) z entuzjazmem; **~ to Beijing!** witamy w Pekinie!; **"thank you" — "you're ~!"** "dziękuję" — "proszę bardzo!" **to give sb a warm ~** witać (przywitać *pf*) kogoś ciepło

welfare ['wɛlfɛəʳ] *n* (*US: social aid*) opieka społeczna

well [wɛl] *n* (*for water*) studnia ▷ *adv* 1 (*to a high standard*) dobrze 2 (*completely*) dobrze 3 (*emphatic with adv, adj, phrase*) naprawdę ▷ *adj* (*healthy*) zdrowy ▷ *int* no cóż; **to do ~** (*person*) dobrze radzić (poradzić *pf*) sobie; (*business*) dobrze wypadać (wypaść *pf*) finansowo; **~ done!** brawo!; **as ~** (*in addition*) również; **I don't feel ~** nie czuję się dobrze; **get ~ soon!** szybkiego powrotu do zdrowia!; **~, as I was saying...** a więc, jak mówiłem...

we'll [wiːl] = **we will, we shall**

well-behaved ['wɛlbɪ'heɪvd] *adj* grzeczny

wellington ['wɛlɪŋtən] (*esp Brit*) *n* (*also: ~ boot*) kalosz

well-known ['wɛl'nəun] *adj* (*person*) słynny; (*fact, brand*) znany

well-off ['wɛl'ɔf] *adj* zamożny

Welsh [wɛlʃ] *adj* walijski ▷ *n* (*language*) język walijski ▷ *n pl*: **the ~** walijczycy

Welshman ['wɛlʃmən] (*irreg*) *n* Walijczyk

Welshwoman ['wɛlʃwumən] (*irreg*) *n* Walijka

went [wɛnt] *pt of* **go**

were [wəːʳ] *pt of* **be**

we're [wɪəʳ] = **we are**

weren't [wəːnt] = **were not**

west [wɛst] *n* 1 (*direction*) zachód 2: **the W~** (*Pol*) Zachód ▷ *adj* zachodni ▷ *adv* na zachód; **in the ~ (of Ireland)** na zachodzie (Irlandii); **to the ~** na zachód; **~ of** na zachód od +*gen*

western ['wɛstən] *adj* zachodni ▷ *n* (*film*) western

wet [wɛt] *adj* **1** (*person, clothes, paint, cement*) mokry **2** (*rainy: weather, day*) deszczowy; **to get ~** moknąć (zmoknąć *pf*)
wet suit *n* strój do nurkowania
we've [wi:v] = **we have**
whale [weɪl] *n* wieloryb

○ **KEYWORD**

what [wɔt] *pron* **1** (*interrogative subject, object, object of prep*) co; **what is happening?** co się dzieje?; **what is this?** co to jest?; **what are you doing?** co robisz?; **what?, what did you say?** co?, co powiedziałeś?
2 (*in indirect questions*) co; **do you know what's happening?** czy pan/pani wie, co się dzieje?
3 (*relative*) co; **I saw what was on the table** widziałem co było na stole
▷ *adj* **1** (*in direct/indirect questions*) który; **what time is it?** która godzina?; **tell me, what size is this shirt?** proszę mi powiedzieć, jaki rozmiar ma ta koszula
2 (*in exclamations*) cóż za; **what a mess!** co za bałagan; **what a lovely day!** jaki ładny dzień!
▷ *int* (*disbelieving*) co!; **what, no coffee!** co, nie ma kawy?

whatever [wɔt'ɛvəʳ] *conj* (*no matter what*) cokolwiek ▷ *adv* (*whatsoever*) cokolwiek ▷ *pron*: **do ~ is necessary/you want** zrób co tylko jest konieczne/co chcesz
wheat [wi:t] *n* pszenica
wheel [wi:l] *n* **1** koło **2** (*also:* **steering ~**) kierownica

wheelbarrow ['wi:lbærəu] *n* taczka
wheelchair ['wi:ltʃɛəʳ] *n* wózek inwalidzki

○ **KEYWORD**

when [wɛn] *adv* (*interrogative*) kiedy; **when did it happen?** kiedy to się stało?
▷ *pron* (*relative*): **the day when** w dniu, kiedy
▷ *conj* (*in time clauses*) kiedy; **be careful when you cross the road** uważaj, kiedy przechodzisz przez jezdnię; **she was reading when I came in** czytała, kiedy wszedłem; **I know when it happened** wiem, kiedy to się wydarzyło

where [wɛəʳ] *adv* (*in or to what place*) gdzie; (*to what place*) dokąd ▷ *conj* (*the place in which*) tam, gdzie; **~ are you from?** skąd pan/pani pochodzi?
whether ['wɛðəʳ] *conj* czy; **I don't know ~ to accept or not** nie wiem, czy mam przyjąć, czy nie

○ **KEYWORD**

which [wɪtʃ] *adj* **1** (*interrogative: m sg*) który; (*f sg*) która; (*nt sg*) które; (*vir pl*) którzy; (*non-vir pl*) które; **which picture do you want?** który chcesz obraz?
2 (*in indirect questions: m sg*) który; (*f sg*) która; (*nt sg*) które; (*vir pl*) którzy; (*non-vir pl*) które; **he asked which book I wanted**

zapytał, którą chcę książkę
▷ pron 1 (*interrogative subject,
object: m sg*) który; (*f sg*) która;
(*nt sg*) które; (*vir pl*) którzy;
(*non-vir pl*) które; **which of
these is yours?** który z nich jest
pana/pani?
2 (*in indirect questions subject,
object*) który; **ask him which of
the models is the best** zapytaj
go, który z modeli jest najlepszy
3 (*relative subject, object, referring
to noun: m sg*) który; (*f sg*) która;
(*nt sg*) które; (*vir pl*) którzy; (*non-
vir pl*) które; **the book which
he read/which is very good**
książka, którą czytał/która jest
bardzo dobra
4 (*referring to clause*) co; **she
said it was an accident, which
was true** powiedziała, że to był
wypadek, co było prawdą

while [waɪl] *n* chwila ▷ *conj*
1 (*at the same time as*) podczas
2 (*during the time that*) podczas
gdy 3 (*although*) chociaż; **for a ~**
na jakiś czas
whip [wɪp] *n* bat ▷ *vt*
1 (*hit: person, animal*) chłostać
(wychłostać *pf*) 2 (*beat: cream,
eggs*) ubijać (ubić *pf*)
whipped cream [wɪpt-] *n* bita
śmietana
whiskers ['wɪskəz] *n pl* (*of
animal*) wąsy; (*of man*) zarost *sg*
whisky ['wɪskɪ] (*US* **whiskey**) *n*
whisky
whisper ['wɪspəʳ] *n* szept ▷ *vi*
szeptać (szepnąć *pf*) ▷ *vt* szeptać
(szepnąć *pf*)
whistle [wɪsl] *vi* (*person:*

melodiously) gwizdać (gwizdnąć
pf) ▷ *vt* (*tune*) gwizdać (zagwizdać
pf) ▷ *n* 1 (*device*) gwizdek 2 (*sound*)
gwizd
white [waɪt] *adj* 1 biały 2 (*with
milk: coffee*) z mlekiem 3 (*person*)
biały ▷ *n* (*colour*) biel

○ **KEYWORD**

who [huː] *pron* 1 (*interrogative
subject, object, object of prep*) kto;
who is it? kto to jest?; **who did
you discuss it with?** (*polite m sg*)
z kim pan o tym rozmawiał?
2 (*in indirect questions subject,
object, after preposition*) kogo; **I
told her who I was** powiedziałem
jej kim jestem; **I don't know who
he gave it to** nie wiem, komu
on to dał
3 (*relative subject, object*) który; **the
girl who came in** dziewczyna,
która weszła; **the man who
we met in Sydney** mężczyzna,
którego poznaliśmy w Sydney

whole [həʊl] *adj* cały ▷ *n* całość;
the ~ of sth całość czegoś; **the ~
(of the) time** cały czas; **on the
~** ogólnie
wholemeal ['həʊlmiːl] (*Brit*) *adj*
pełnoziarnisty
wholewheat ['həʊlwiːt] *adj* =
wholemeal

○ **KEYWORD**

whom [huːm] (*formal*) *pron*
1 (*interrogative*) kogo; (*to whom?*)
komu; **whom did you see?** kogo
widziałeś?; **to whom did she**

give it? komu to dała?
2 (*relative*): **the man whom
I saw** mężczyzna, którego
widziałem; **the man to whom
I spoke** mężczyzna, z którym
rozmawiałem

whose [hu:z] *adj* **1** (*interrogative*)
czyj **2** (*relative*) którego ▷ *pron* (*m
sg*) czyj; (*f sg*) czyja; (*nt sg*) czyje;
(*vir pl*) czyi; (*non-vir pl*) czyje; **~
is this?** czyje to jest?; **~ book is
this?** czyja to książka?; **~ coats
are these?** czyje są te płaszcze?;
the woman ~ car was stolen
kobieta, której samochód został
skradziony

○ KEYWORD

why [waɪ] *adv* dlaczego; **why
is he always late?** dlaczego on
zawsze się spóźnia?; **why not?**
dlaczego nie?; **I don't know why**
nie wiem dlaczego
▷ *conj* dlaczego; **I wonder why
he said that** zastanawiam się,
dlaczego on to powiedział; **the
reason why he did it** zrobił to
dlatego

wicked ['wɪkɪd] *adj* (*evil: person*)
podły; (*act, crime*) ohydny
wide [waɪd] *adj* szeroki ▷ *adv*
szeroko
widow ['wɪdəu] *n* wdowa
widower ['wɪdəuəʳ] *n* wdowiec
width [wɪdθ] *n* szerokość; **to
swim a ~** przepływać (przepłynąć
pf) szerokość basenu
wife [waɪf] (*pl* **wives**) *n* żona
wig [wɪg] *n* peruka

wild [waɪld] *adj* **1** (*animal,
plant*) dziki **2** (*person, behaviour*)
szalony
wildlife ['waɪldlaɪf] *n*
natura

○ KEYWORD

will [wɪl] *aux vb* **1** (*forming future
tense*): **I will call you tonight**
zadzwonię do ciebie dziś
wieczorem; **what will you do
next?** co potem zrobisz?
2 (*in conjectures, predictions*): **he'll
be there by now** pewnie jest już
na miejscu
3 (*in commands, requests,
offers*): **will you be quiet!** bądź
cicho!
4 (*be prepared to*): **I won't put up
with it!** nie będę tego znosił!
▷ *n* **1** (*volition*) wola; **against his
will** wbrew jego woli
2 (*testament*) testament; **to
make a will** spisywać (spisać *pf*)
testament

willing ['wɪlɪŋ] *adj*: **to be ~ to
do sth** być chętnym do robienia
(zrobienia *pf*) czegoś
win [wɪn] (*pt, pp* **won**) *n*
zwycięstwo ▷ *vt* wygrywać
(wygrać *pf*) ▷ *vi* odnosić (odnieść
pf) zwycięstwo
wind [wɪnd] *n* wiatr
window ['wɪndəu] *n* **1** (*in house,
building*) okno; (*in shop*) witryna;
(*in car, train*) okno **2** (*pane*) szyba
3 (*Comput*) okno
windscreen ['wɪndskri:n] (*Brit*)
n szyba przednia
windscreen wiper [-waɪpəʳ]

(Brit) n wycieraczka
windshield ['wɪndʃiːld] (US) n
szyba przednia
windshield wiper [-waɪpəʳ] (US)
n wycieraczka
windsurfing ['wɪndsəːfɪŋ] n
windsurfing
windy ['wɪndɪ] adj wietrzny; **it's
~** wieje wiatr
wine [waɪn] n wino
wing [wɪŋ] n skrzydło
wink [wɪŋk] vi mrugać (mrugnąć
pf); **to ~ at sb** mrugać (mrugnąć
pf) do kogoś
winner ['wɪnəʳ] n
zwycięzca(-czyni) m/f
winning ['wɪnɪŋ] adj zwycięski
winter ['wɪntəʳ] n zima; **in (the)
~** zimą
wipe [waɪp] vt wycierać (wytrzeć
pf); **to ~ one's nose** wycierać
(wytrzeć pf) nos
▶ **wipe up** vt wycierać (wytrzeć
pf)
wire ['waɪəʳ] n 1 (metal) drut
2 (Elec: uninsulated) przewód;
(insulated) kabel
wisdom ['wɪzdəm] n (of person)
mądrość; (of action, remark)
trafność
wisdom tooth (pl **wisdom
teeth**) n ząb mądrości
wise [waɪz] adj (person) mądry
wish [wɪʃ] n życzenie ▷ vt życzyć
sobie +gen; **best ~es** najlepsze
życzenia; **with best ~es** (in letter)
z najlepszymi życzeniami; **give
her my best ~es** przekaż jej
moje najserdeczniejsze życzenia;
to ~ to do sth chcieć coś robić
(zrobić pf)
wit [wɪt] n (wittiness) dowcip

witch [wɪtʃ] n wiedźma

○ **KEYWORD**

with [wɪð, wɪθ] prep 1 (together
with, at the house of) z +inst; **I was
with him** byłam z nim; **I'll be
with you in a minute** przyjdę
do ciebie za chwilę; **we stayed
with friends** zatrzymaliśmy się u
znajomych
2 (indicating feature, possession) z
+inst; **the man with the grey hat**
mężczyzna w szarym kapeluszu;
the man with blue eyes
mężczyzna z niebieskimi oczami
3 (indicating manner) z +inst; **with
a sigh/laugh** z westchnieniem/
ze śmiechem
4 (indicating means, substance)
instrumental case; **to walk with
a stick** chodzić/iść (pójść pf)
o lasce; **to fill sth with water**
napełniać (napełnić pf) coś wodą
5 (indicating cause) z +gen; **red
with anger** czerwony ze złości

without [wɪð'aut] prep bez +gen;
~ a coat bez płaszcza; **~ speaking**
bez słów
witness ['wɪtnɪs] n świadek
witty ['wɪtɪ] adj dowcipny
wives [waɪvz] n pl of **wife**
wizard ['wɪzəd] n czarodziej
woke [wəuk] pt of **wake**
woken ['wəukn] pp of **wake**
wolf [wulf] (pl **wolves** [wulvz])
n wilk
woman ['wumən] (pl **women**)
n kobieta
won [wʌn] pt, pp of **win**
wonder ['wʌndəʳ] vt: **to ~**

whether/why zastanawiać (zastanowić *pf*) się, czy/dlaczego itd. ▷ *vi* zastanawiać (zastanowić *pf*) się

wonderful ['wʌndəful] *adj* cudowny

won't [wəunt] = **will not**

wood [wud] *n* **1** drewno **2** (*forest*) las

wooden ['wudn] *adj* (*object*) drewniany

woodwork ['wudwə:k] *n* (*craft*) stolarka

wool [wul] *n* wełna

word [wə:d] *n* słowo; **what's the ~ for "pen" in French?** jak jest "długopis" po francusku?; **in other ~s** innymi słowy

word processing [-'prəusɛsɪŋ] *n* przetwarzanie tekstów

word processor [-prəusɛsəʳ] *n* (*machine*) procesor tekstów

wore [wɔ:ʳ] *pt of* **wear**

work [wə:k] *n* praca ▷ *vi* **1** (*have job, do tasks*) pracować **2** (*function: mechanism, machine*) działać (zadziałać *pf*) **3** (*be successful: idea, method*) sprawdzać (sprawdzić *pf*) się; **to go to ~** chodzić/iść (pójść *pf*) do pracy; **to be out of ~** być bez pracy; **to ~ hard** pracować ciężko

▶ **work on** *vt fus* (*busy o.s. with*) pracować nad +*inst*

▶ **work out** *vi* (*Sport*) ćwiczyć ▷ *vt* (*answer, solution*) rozwiązywać (rozwiązać *pf*); (*plan, details*) rozpracowywać (rozpracować *pf*); **it ~s out at 100 pounds** wychodzi sto funtów; **I can't ~ out why...** nie mogę pojąć dlaczego...

worker ['wə:kəʳ] *n* (*employed person*) pracownik(-ica) *m/f*; **a hard/good ~** dobry(-ra) pracownik(-ica) *m/f*

work experience *n* doświadczenie zawodowe

working-class *adj* robotniczy

workman ['wə:kmən] (*irreg*) *n* robotnik

worksheet ['wə:kʃi:t] *n* spis zadań na kartce na lekcji szkolnej

workshop ['wə:kʃɔp] *n* warsztat

workstation ['wə:ksteɪʃən] *n* **1** (*desk*) stanowisko pracy **2** (*computer*) stacja robocza

world [wə:ld] *n* (*earth*): **the ~** świat ▷ *adj* światowy; **all over the ~** na całym świecie

World Cup (*Football*) *n*: **the ~** mistrzostwa świata w piłce nożnej *n pl*

world-wide web [wə:ld'waɪd-] *n*: **the ~** internet

worm [wə:m] *n* (*also:* **earth~**) robak

worn [wɔ:n] *pp of* **wear** ▷ *adj* wytarty

worried ['wʌrɪd] *adj* zmartwiony; **to be ~ about sth/sb** martwić (zmartwić *pf*) się o coś/z powodu kogoś

worry ['wʌrɪ] *n* **1** (*feeling of anxiety*) niepokój **2** (*cause of anxiety*) zmartwienie ▷ *vt* martwić (zmartwić *pf*) ▷ *vi* martwić (zmartwić *pf*) się

worse [wə:s] *adj* gorszy ▷ *adv* gorzej; **to get ~** pogarszać (pogorszyć *pf*) się

worst [wə:st] *adj* najgorszy ▷ *adv* najgorzej ▷ *n* najgorszy; **at ~** w najgorszym przypadku

worth [wə:θ] n wartość ▷ adj: **to be ~ £50** być wartym pięćdziesiąt funtów; **it's ~ it** warto (to) zrobić; **400 dollars' ~ of damage** wartość szkody wynosi czterysta dolarów; **it would be (well) ~ doing...** (naprawdę) warto by było zrobić...

○ **KEYWORD**

would [wud] aux vb 1 (conditional mood): **I would love to go to Italy** chciałbym bardzo pojechać do Włoch; **I'm sure he wouldn't do that** jestem pewien, że on tego by nie zrobił; **if she asked him he would do it** jeśliby go poprosiła, zrobiłby to
2 (in offers, invitations, requests): **would you like a biscuit?** może ciastko?; **would you ask him to come in?** poprosiłby go pan, żeby wszedł?
3 (be willing to): **she wouldn't help me** ona nie chciała mi pomóc; **the door wouldn't open** drzwi nie chciały się otworzyć
4 (in indirect speech): **he said he would be at home later** powiedział, że będzie w domu później
5 (used to): **he would spend every day on the beach** spędzał każdy dzień na plaży

wouldn't ['wudnt] = **would not**
wrap [ræp] vt zawijać (zawinąć pf); **to ~ sth around sth/sb** zawijać (zawinąć pf) coś wokół czegoś/kogoś
▶ **wrap up** vt (pack) owijać

(owinąć pf)
wrapping paper ['ræpɪŋ-] n (gift wrap) papier do pakowania
wreck [rɛk] n 1 (wreckage) wrak 2 (US: accident) wypadek 3 (inf: person) wrak człowieka ▷ vt (equipment, room etc) niszczyć (zniszczyć pf); (life, chances, marriage) rujnować (zrujnować pf)
wrestler ['rɛslə^r] n zapaśnik(-iczka) m/f
wrestling ['rɛslɪŋ] n zapasy pl
wrinkled ['rɪŋkld] adj (skin, face) pomarszczony
wrist [rɪst] n nadgarstek
write [raɪt] (pt **wrote**, pp **written**) vt 1 (note down) pisać (zapisać pf) 2 (compose: letter, note) pisać (napisać pf) 3 (create: novel, music etc) pisać (napisać pf) 4 (also: ~ **out**: cheque, receipt, prescription) wypisywać (wypisać pf) ▷ vi pisać (napisać pf); **to ~ to sb** pisać (napisać pf) do kogoś
▶ **write down** vt zapisywać (zapisać pf)
writer ['raɪtə^r] n (author) pisarz(-rka) m/f
writing ['raɪtɪŋ] n 1 (sth written) pismo 2 (handwriting) charakter pisma; **in ~** na piśmie
written ['rɪtn] pp of **write**
wrong [rɔŋ] adj 1 (inappropriate) nieodpowiedni 2 (incorrect) błędny 3 (morally bad) zły ▷ adv (incorrectly) źle; **to be ~** być w błędzie; **to be ~ (about sth)** (person) mylić (pomylić pf) się (w stosunku do czegoś); **what's ~?** co jest nie w porządku?; **what's ~ with you?** co ci dolega?; **there's nothing ~** nic złego się nie dzieje;

to go ~ (*plan*) nie udawać (udać
pf) się; (*machine*) psuć (popsuć
pf) się
wrote [rəut] *pt of* **write**
www (*Comput*) *n abbr* (= world-
wide web) www

xenophobia [zɛnə'fəubɪə] *n*
ksenofobia
Xmas ['ɛksməs] *n abbr*
(= *Christmas*) Boże Narodzenie
X-ray ['ɛksreɪ] *n* (*photo*)
prześwietlenie ▷ *vt* robić (zrobić
pf) prześwietlenie +*gen*; **to
have an ~** robić (zrobić *pf*) sobie
prześwietlenie
xylophone ['zaɪləfəun] *n*
ksylofon

nie; (*in questions*) już **2** (*now: in negatives*) jeszcze ▷ *conj* mimo to; **they haven't finished ~** jeszcze nie skończyli; **~ again** znów

yog(h)urt ['jəugət] *n* jogurt

yolk [jəuk] *n* żółtko

○ KEYWORD

you [juː] *pron* **1** (*familiar sg*) ty; (*familiar pl*) wy; (*m sg polite*) pan; (*f sg polite*) pani; (*polite vir m pl*) panowie; (*polite non-vir f pl*) panie; (*polite vir m/f pl*) państwo; **do you know her?** (*polite m/f sg*) czy zna ją pan/pani?; **I like you** (*familiar sg*) lubię cię; **I'll send you the photos when I've got them** (*familiar sg*) wyślę ci zdjęcia, jak je dostanę; **I gave it to you** (*familiar sg*) dałem ci to; **it's for you** (*familiar sg*) to dla ciebie **2** (*in generalizations: one*); **you can't put metal dishes in a microwave** nie wkłada się metalowych naczyń do kuchenki mikrofalowej; **you never know** nigdy nie wiadomo

young [jʌŋ] *adj* młody; **my ~er brother** mój młodszy brat; **my ~er sister** moja młodsza siostra

your [jɔːʳ] *adj* (*familiar m sg*) twój; (*familiar f sg*) twoja; (*familiar nt sg*) twoje; (*familiar pl*) wasz; (*polite m sg*) pana; (*polite f sg*) pani; (*polite vir m pl*) panów; (*polite non-vir f pl*) pań; (*polite vir m/f pl*) państwa; (*referring to subject of sentence*) swój; **~ house** (*polite m/f sg*) pana/pani dom; **have you cleaned ~ teeth?** (*familiar sg*)

y

yacht [jɔt] *n* **1** (*sailing boat*) żaglówka **2** (*luxury craft*) jacht

yard [jɑːd] *n* (*US: garden*) ogród

yawn [jɔːn] *vi* ziewać (ziewnąć *pf*) ▷ *n* ziewanie

year [jɪəʳ] *n* rok; (*m pl*) lat, lata; **he's 8 ~s old** on ma osiem lat; **we lived there for 2 ~s** mieszkaliśmy tam przez dwa lata; **every ~** co roku; **this ~** tego roku; **last ~** zeszłego roku; **a** *or* **per ~** rocznie

yell [jɛl] *vi* krzyczeć (krzyknąć *pf*)

yellow ['jɛləu] *adj* żółty ▷ *n* żółty

yes [jɛs] *adv* (*replying to question*) tak ▷ *n* (*answer*) tak

yesterday ['jɛstədɪ] *adv* wczoraj ▷ *n* wczoraj; **the day before ~** przedwczoraj

yet [jɛt] *adv* **1** (*up to now*) jak dotąd; (*with negative*) jeszcze

umyłeś zęby?

yours [jɔːz] *pron (familiar sg)*
twój; *(familiar pl)* wasz; *(polite m
sg)* pana; *(polite f sg)* pani; *(polite
vir pl)* panów; *(polite non-vir f pl)*
pań; *(polite vir m/f pl)* państwa; **is
this ~?** *(familiar sg)* czy to twoje?;
(polite m/f sg) czy to jest pana/
pani?; **~ sincerely/faithfully** z
wyrazami szacunku

○ KEYWORD

yourself [jɔːˈsɛlf] *pron* **1** *(gen,
acc)* siebie; *(dat, loc)* sobie; *(inst)*
sobą; *(reflexive pronoun)* się; **have
you hurt yourself?** *(familiar)*
skaleczyłeś się?
2 *(emphatic: m)* sam; *(f)* sama; **did
you paint the room yourself?**
(polite m) czy sam pomalował pan
ten pokój?; *(polite f)* czy sama pani
pomalowała ten pokój?
3 *(you: familiar)* ty; *(polite m)* pan;
(polite f) pani; **an intelligent
person like yourself** *(polite
m/f)* taka inteliegntna osoba jak
pan/pani; **by yourself** *(unaided,
alone)* sam

○ KEYWORD

yourselves [jɔːˈsɛlvz] *pl pron*
1 *(gen, acc)* siebie; *(dat, loc)* sobie;
(inst) sobą; *(reflexive pronoun)* się;
buy yourselves something nice
(familiar) kupcie sobie coś ładnego
2 *(emphatic: vir)* sami; *(non-vir)*
same; **did you paint the house
yourselves?** *(polite non-vir)* czy
panie same pomalowały dom?

3 *(you: familiar)* wy; *(polite
m vir)* panowie; *(polite f
non-vir)* panie; *(polite vir m/f)*
państwo; **intelligent people
like yourselves** *(polite vir)*
inteligentni ludzie jak panowie;
by yourselves *(unaided, alone: vir)*
sami; *(non-vir)* same

youth [juːθ] *n* młodość; *(young
person)* młodzieniec; **in my ~** w
czasach mojej młodości
youth club *n* klub młodzieżowy
youth hostel *n* schronisko
młodzieżowe

Z

zebra ['ziːbrə] *n* zebra
zebra crossing (*Brit*) *n* przejście dla pieszych
zero ['zɪərəu] (*pl* **zero** *or* **zeroes**) *n* zero; **5 degrees below ~** pięć stopni poniżej zera
zigzag ['zɪgzæg] *vi* iść zygzakiem
zip [zɪp] *n* (*Brit: fastener*) suwak ▷ *vt* (*also*: **~ up**) zapinać (zapiąć *pf*)
zip code (*US*) *n* kod pocztowy
zipper ['zɪpəʳ] (*US*) *n* suwak
zodiac ['zəudɪæk] *n*: **the ~** zodiak
zone [zəun] *n* (*area*) strefa
zoo [zuː] (*pl* **zoos**) *n* zoo
zucchini [zuːˈkiːnɪ] (*pl* **zucchini** *or* **zucchinis**) (*US*) *n* cukinia